RODRIQUEZ CANTIERE NAVALE S.p.A.

MESSINA – ITALY

SHOWN HERE ONE OF THE FOUR TYPES OF HYDROFOILS
BUILT TO FULFIL MODERN REQUIREMENTS FOR HIGH SPEED
WATERBORNE TRANSPORTATION:

— COMFORT
— LOW FUEL CONSUMPTION
— ECONOMICAL OPERATING COSTS

For further information, please contact:
Rodriquez Cantiere Navale S.p.A.
22, Via S. Raineri – 98100 Messina
Phone (090) 7765 – Cable Rodriquez
Telex 980030 RODRIK I

High performance diesel engines and propulsion systems

Years in the forefront of technology and constant involvement with specific requirements of our international customers have given us the leading edge and the widest experience in the field.

The MTU package

Diesel Engines
ranging from 400–10,000 HP with an optimum balance of power concentration, operational reliability and service life

Application Engineering
Fully engineered engine systems for all operational and environmental requirements

Systems Engineering
with single source responsibility for complete and specific propulsion systems

Product Support
with a worldwide parts and service network and a high degree of individual maintenance, training and technical assistance programs

Motoren- und Turbinen-Union Friedrichshafen GmbH
P.O. Box 2040 · D-7990 Friedrichshafen/W. Germany

JANE'S
SURFACE SKIMMERS
1985

Jane's Publishing Company Limited, 238 City Road, London EC1V 2PU, England
Jane's Publishing Inc, 13th Floor, 135 West 50th Street, New York, NY 10020, USA

Alphabetical list of advertisers

Move Anything, Anywhere, Anytime

Lightweight, easily portable, simple to use and virtually maintenance free.
Hoversystems modular hover platform kits can be configured to carry a wide variety of payloads over virtually any terrain — without the need for expensive groundworks.

Maintenance Staging — for use within hangars. These structures are frequently custom made to suit user requirements. In addition, Aero-Docks have developed a wide range of standard stagings, many of which feature universal facilities.

Saudia Airlines' maintenance facility at Jeddah uses the first of an advanced and sophisticated new generation of Universal Tail Docks. B747, L-1011, B707 and A310 are among the aircraft to be accommodated for both major and minor maintenance work.

Special Projects — Total environmental enclosures are the modern replacement for the traditional hangar. Not only is the capital cost lower, costs for heating/air conditioning and lighting are reduced by the more economical shape.
Aero-Docks can also provide a design and build team or full turnkey capability for specific projects.

For information and literature contact Aero-Docks, pioneers of modern solutions to the needs of the aviation industry.
Aero-Docks Ltd (incorporating **Hoversystems**), Brooklands, Landford, Wiltshire SP5 2AA, U.K. Telephone: 0794 390213/390693. Telex: 47106

Classified list of advertisers

The companies advertising in this publication have informed us that they are involved in the fields of manufacture indicated below

ACV manufacturers
Aero-Docks

ACV research and design
Aero-Docks

Catamaran displacement craft
Marinteknik

Diesel engines
Mitsui Engineering
Motoren-und Turbinen-Union

Elastomeric components
Northern Rubber

Electronic equipment
Consorzio Selenia/Elsag

Gas turbine engines
FIAT Aviazione

Hovercraft consultants
Aero-Docks

Hovercraft manufacturers
Aero-Docks
Mitsui Engineering

Hoverpallet manufacturers
Aero-Docks

Hydrofoil boats and ships
Rodriquez Cantiere Navale

Hydrofoil interior design
Rodriquez Cantiere Navale

Hydrofoil interior furnishing
Rodriquez Cantiere Navale

Hydrofoil missile / gun boat combat systems
Consorzio Selenia/Elsag

Hydrofoil missile / gun boats
Fincantieri-Cantieri Navali Italiani
Rodriquez Cantiere Navale

Hydrofoil research and design
Fincantieri-Cantieri Navali Italiani
Rodriquez Cantiere Navale

Instruments, electronic
Consorzio Selenia/Elsag

Marine propulsion systems
FIAT Aviazione

Patrol boats
Mitsui Engineering

Skirt components
Aero-Docks
Northern Rubber

Skirt consultants
Northern Rubber

Skirt design
Aero-Docks
Northern Rubber

Skirt materials
Northern Rubber

Surveillance systems
Consorzio Selenia/Elsag

SEN COMBAT SYSTEMS

During last years, many Navies have shown a growing interest in ships of medium/low tonnage, such as Corvettes, FPBs, FACs etc, where operational and space restrictions are impending. At the same time, the requirement for systems suited to the operational tasks of modern warfare asks for sophisticated equipment based on the most updated technologies.

The Selenia-Elsag Naval Systems Consortium has designed and developed a family of Combat Systems — the SEN Series — with the aim of meeting the above requirements. The Sen Series is a modular, fully integrated Combat System, conceived for ships, such as:

- **OPVs**
- **HYDROFOILS**
- **FPBs**

The SEN Combat Systems take into account not only the self-defence capability required against attacks from the air and from surface ships, but also cover the carrying out of a wide range of peace-time jobs, for instance:

- **Surveillance and Control for Coastal Waters**
- **Protection of the Trade Lanes**
- **Guarding of EEZ**
- **Intruders Prevention**

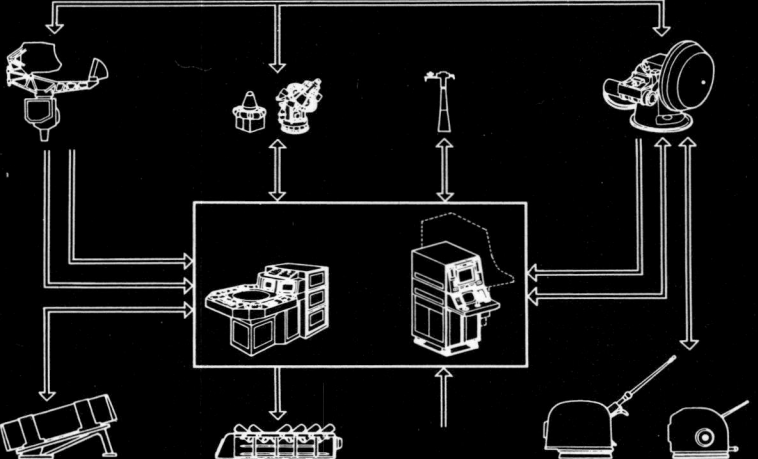

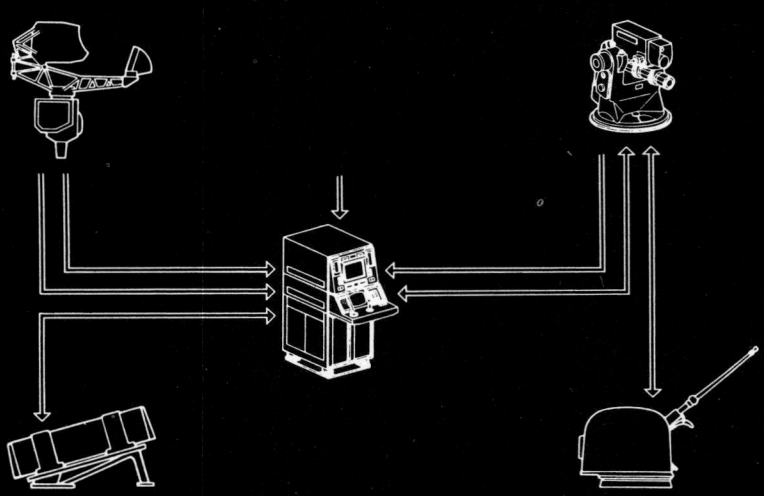

RAGGRUPPAMENTO
SELENIA ELSAG

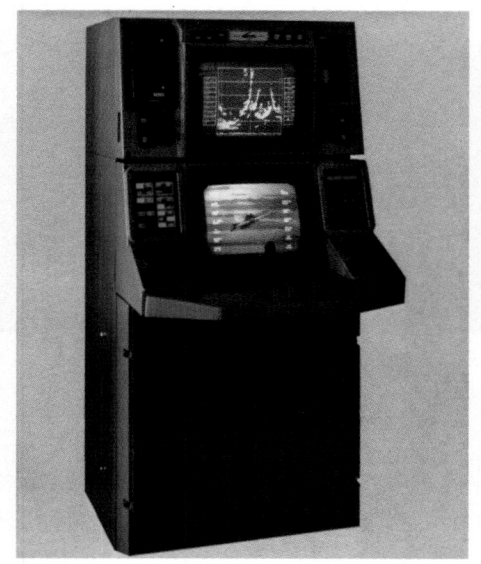

First Bell Landing Craft, Air Cushion (LCAC)

JANE'S
SURFACE SKIMMERS

EIGHTEENTH EDITION

EDITED BY
ROY McLEAVY

1985

ISBN 0 7106-0809-8

JANE'S YEARBOOKS

"Jane's" is a registered trade mark

In the USA and its dependencies
Jane's Publishing Inc, 13th Floor, 135 West 50th Street, New York, NY 10020, USA

LM 2500. Gas turbine

DERIVED FROM G.E. TF39/C-

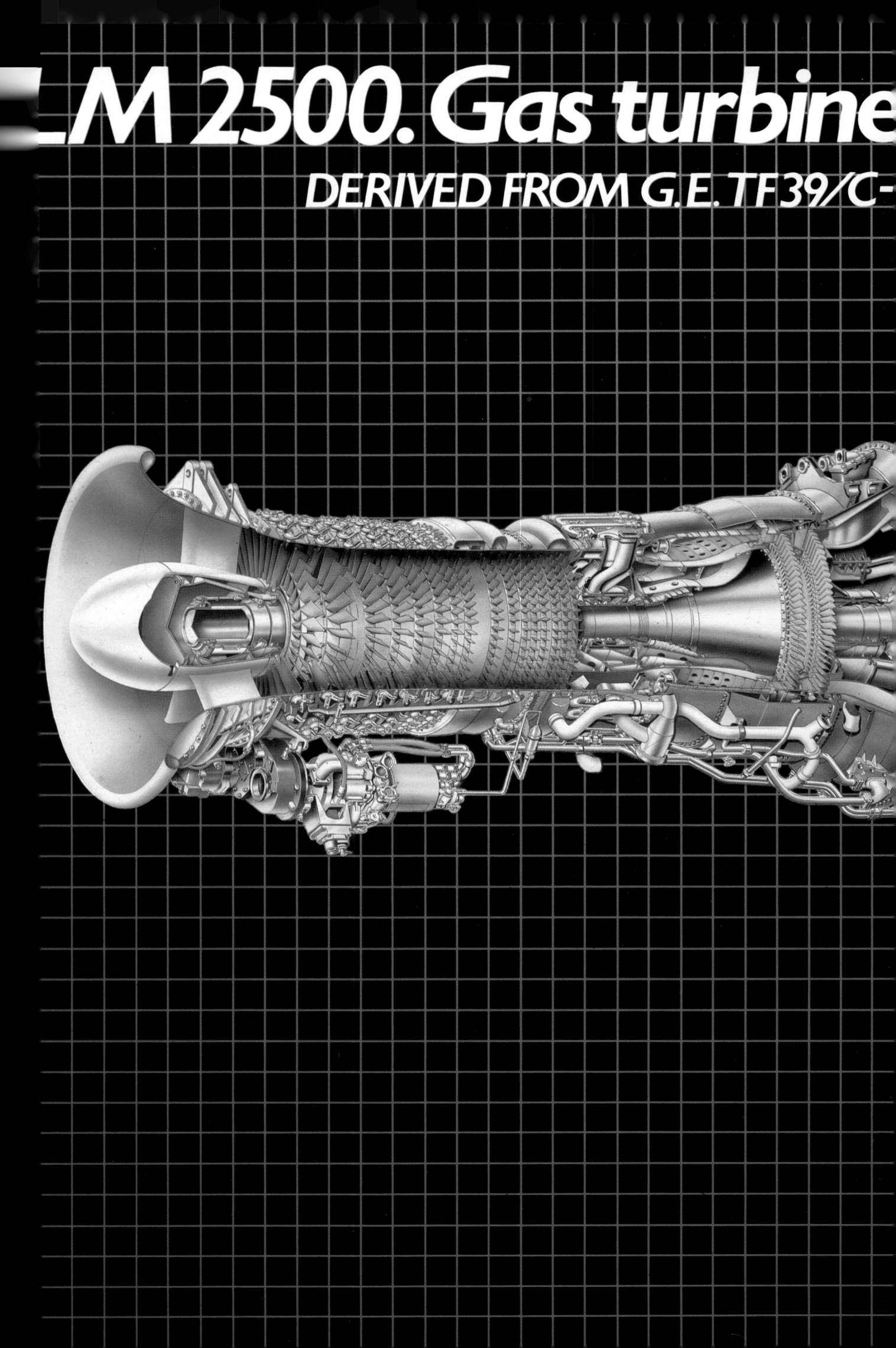

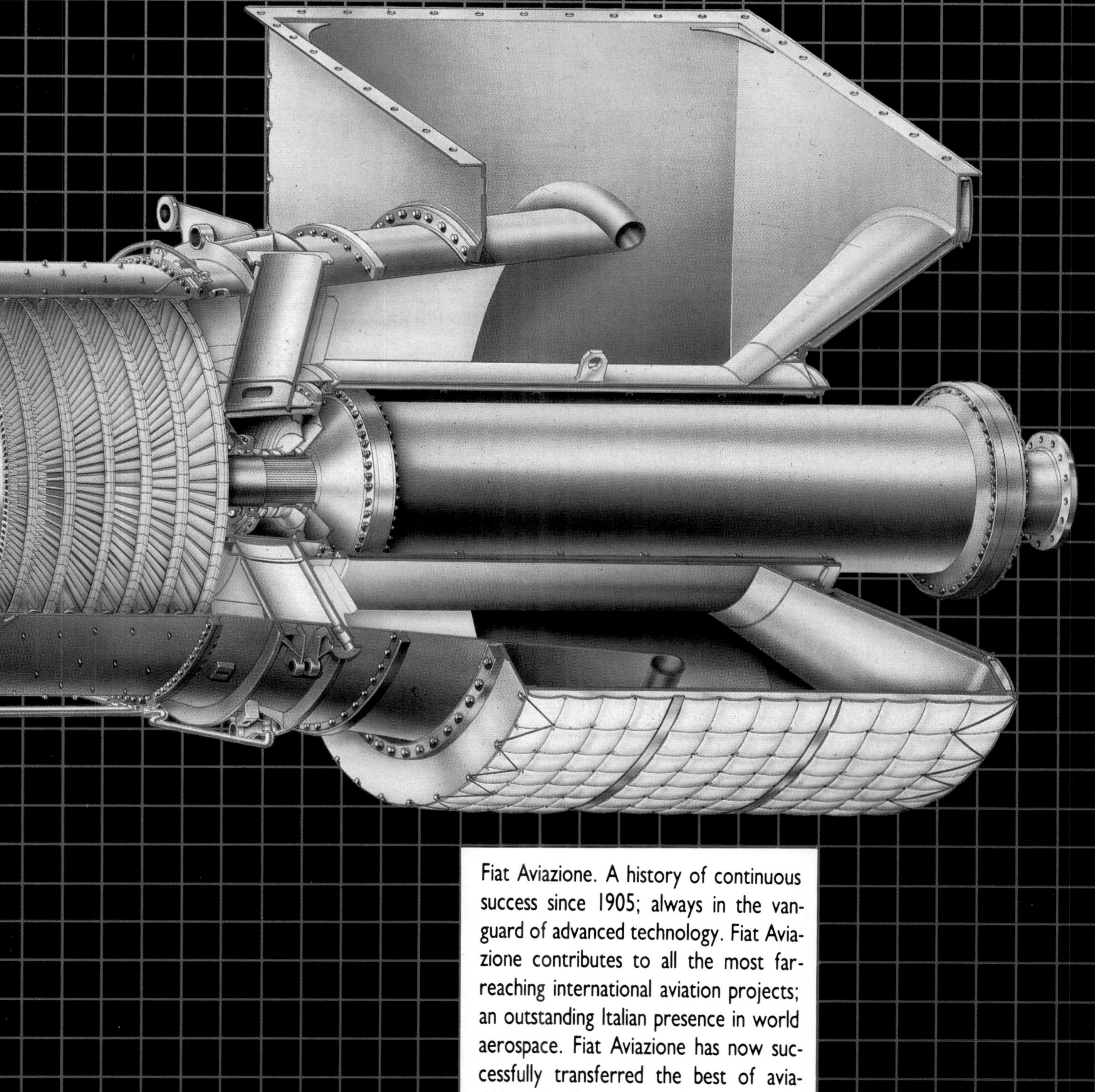

Contents

Stronger, Faster, Better

with speeds up to 40 knots

The 33M Marinteknik
MARINJET CATAMARAN

The fastest and the only diesel powered waterjet propelled catamaran in production in the world today designed and built by **Marinteknik**, for use as:—

- Passenger ferries
- Crewboats for the Offshore oil & gas industry
- Fast Patrol boats for Navy, Marine Police & Custom
- Fire-fighting and Pollution control

The **MARINJET** offers the following features:—
- Simplicity of operation
- Service speeds up to 40 knots
- Flat unobstructed payload area
- Very good operating economy
- A high degree of manoeuvrability
- A very shallow draught, fully laden
- Very comfortable and stable ride
- Environmental acceptability
- A high level of reliability and safety

Over 65 million passenger miles of operation, with no repairs or replacement impellers required in the waterjet propulsion system

Marinteknik International Ltd
33/F New World Tower
16-18 Queen's Road Central
Hongkong
Telephone: 5-218302
Telex: 74493 HMHCO HX

Marinteknik Verkstads AB
P O Box 7 Varvsvägen
S-740 71 Oregrund
Sweden
Telephone: (0) 173 30460
Telex: 76182 MARTAB S

Marinteknik Shipbuilders (S) Pte Ltd
Lot A 6961 Pioneer Sector 1
Jurong
Singapore 2262
Telephone: 8611707 9811706
Telex: RS 53419 MARJET
Cable: GREENTECH

FOREWORD

SES: Shape of Warship 2000

For the first time in history, monohull warships are to give way to vessels of a different configuration. Warship 2000 will be a cross between a catamaran and a hovercraft, with rigid side hulls and flexible bow and stern skirts. Known as surface effect ships (SESs), vessels of this type will ride on an air cushion for high speed operation between 50 to 60 knots in calm seas and at 40 knots or more in five-metre high waves. Their exceptional stability in heavy seas makes then ideal platforms for helicopters and VTOL aircraft. The first generation of SES warships will begin to enter service during the 1990s and will probably displace between one to 1500 tons.

In future naval conflicts surface ships will be under constant threat of attack by continuously submerged nuclear submarines, some of which can attain speeds well in excess of 30 knots. Operating under the cover of moderate to heavy seas, they have far greater tactical flexibility than either conventionally-hulled escort vessels or ASW aircraft flying from carriers. Countering the problem calls for a new generation warship capable of speed bursts of at least 50 knots. The minimum size of a monohull warship which could attain anything like this performance would be 6,000 tons. Not only would its speed be limited to about 30 knots in high sea states, but its cost would be prohibitive to nations which need to purchase it in any quantity. Detailed assessment of the new naval vehicle concepts which have reached a sufficiently advanced stage of development and are capable of the required performance led planners to the large surface effect ship.

Like the hydrofoil, but without the speed limits imposed by foil cavitation, the SES maintains its speed and manoeuvrability in heavy seas and, with the aid of a ride control system (RCS) which reduces heave motion caused by waves pumping into the cushion, a comfortable working environment is provided for the crew and a stable operating platform for helicopters. Interest in the SES as a potential weapons platform has been growing in the USA since the US Navy's XR-1 first demonstrated the concept there in 1963. Its success led to the construction of two 100-ton test craft, the 75-knot SES-100A and the 80-knot SES-100B.

In 1976 RMI won a $350 million contract to build the first 3,000-ton ocean-going SES. In 1979, less than a month from the start of construction, President Carter withdrew all funds, which were then diverted to existing conventional ship programmes. At that stage no other navy in the world was in a comparable position in the development of SES technology. However, despite this major setback, the following year a new US Navy programme began. This was a low cost programme based on proven technology and aided by the diesel-powered SES-200, a modified Bell Halter BH-110 Mk 1. After evaluation the craft was lengthened by a 50-foot hull extension amidship to demonstrate the benefits of a high length-to-beam SES.

An important objective in SES design is to achieve efficient operation at task force speeds, without losing the ability to detach from the force when necessary and operate at high speeds to intercept approaching targets. A method of achieving this flexibility is to increase the cushion length-to-beam (L/B) ratio, which decreases the wave drag in the secondary and primary hump regions at the expense of increasing it at speeds above the primary hump. Increasing the L/B ratio also moves the peak of the primary drag hump to a higher speed. Tests with the SES-200 have validated the concept, which will make the selection of the correct length-to-beam ratio an important factor in the design of multi-thousand-ton vessels of this type in future.

Within the USA, the advantages of the SES are widely recognised and its future is becoming assured. Under the Naval Sea Systems Command (NAVSEA) Surface Ship Continuing Concept Formulation (CONFORM) Program which analyses the relative merits of the alternative options, studies of new ship requirements automatically include SES vessels provided they are suitable for the mission areas defined. A typical SES project under examination for availability in the year 2005 has a displacement of 8,000 to 9,000 tons, the speed and range of a typical destroyer but with burst speed capability. It would be employed for ASW surveillance, ASW attack and minelaying and would carry two VSTOL aircraft.

Confirmation of the US Navy's increasing confidence in smaller size SESs was evident when it issued instructions last November to begin the production of the first-of-line of the world's first warship of this type intended for series production, the diesel-powered 110-ton Special Warfare Craft, Medium (SWCM). It will be carried in the well decks of US amphibious transport ships and operate with task forces and US Rapid Deployment Forces. It will provide a high speed platform for multi-mission roles including missile strike craft, radar picket, troop transport, coastal defence, diver support and search and rescue. Technical and operational evaluation of the first craft will be undertaken in early 1986. Follow-on-orders for up to 18 craft are anticipated. Late in November 1984 Bell Aerospace Textron was awarded a $27·3 million contract for the detail design and construction of the first Minesweeper Hunter (MSH) for the US Navy. The MSH, a 450-ton SES in which the air cushion is used to make it less susceptible to underwater shock from mine explosions, is a new class of minesweeper designed to ensure that access to US ports and coastal waterways is maintained in the event of mine attack. The contract also provided the US Navy with two additional options to acquire eight more MSHs at a cost of $126·6 million. The first MSH is due to be delivered in 1987.

Since Soviet nuclear attack submarines are seen as a potential threat to the security of shipping lanes and sea defences the world over, a number of other maritime nations are also examining methods of countering the problem. Many navies have reached the same conclusion as the USA and feel the only practical response lies in the augmentation of existing vessels by SESs. Other nations planning to follow suit include Canada, China, France, West Germany, Israel, Japan, South Korea, Norway, the Netherlands, Spain, Sweden and the United Kingdom. In a move to keep NATO navies abreast of SES developments in the USA, plans are being made for the SES-200 to be demonstrated in Western Europe in early 1986.

Among the European nations best qualified to start the development and construction of the SESs are the United Kingdom, France, the Netherlands, Norway and Sweden. In the UK, Vosper Hovermarine Limited's past experience is ideal since the company has already built and sold more than 100 SESs for fast ferry or public service duties to 30 nations. Fast patrol and fast strike variants of the HM 527 were added to the range in 1982 and VHL is now offering a 600-ton offshore patrol SES which employs its Deep Cushion concept. The vessel, the HM 700, will have a cushion depth in excess of six metres (26 feet). Gas turbines will provide the craft with an 'on-cushion' speed of over 50 knots. Another likely UK contender in the SES field is British Hovercraft Corporation (BHC). Under its licensing agreement with Bell Aerospace Textron, provision is made for a reciprocal arrangement under which BHC has access to Bell's SES technology. Under pressure of market demand it is highly probable that BHC would undertake the manufacture of SESs as well as hovercraft. Unlike the French Navy, which has already analysed and defined its first, second and third stages in the development of a 1,000-ton SES to meet its needs from 1995 onwards, the UK Ministry of Defence has not announced its requirements. It must therefore be assumed that whatever work is undertaken on naval SESs by UK companies in the immediate future will be for overseas navies.

The basis of the French programme is a high length-to-beam ratio vessel capable of an on-cushion speed of about 50 knots and a hullborne speed of about 18 knots. An ocean-going ASW vessel, it will also carry weapons to protect the craft against surface and air attack. One of the stages in the prototype development programme will be the design and construction of an operational vessel of 200 tons to serve as a dynamic model. Building is due to start in 1986. DCN, the co-ordinating body, is also studying the feasibility of building a number of smaller craft of about five tonnes' displacement in order to apply the *Navir à Effet de Surface* (NES) concept to as wide a range of tonnage as possible.

In the Netherlands, Le Comte-Holland BV is continuing its development of a 26-metre SES prototype which, on completion, will be used as a full scale test bed for the Le Comte air cushion seal system.

One of the big surprises of 1984 was the unexpected appearance of the 264-seat SES Norcat, the first of its type to be built in northern Europe. Designed by Cirrus A/S in Bergen and built by Brodrene Aa, the vessel was partly funded by a 50 per cent loan from the Norwegian government. Powered by two 1,600 hp GM

[16]

Detroit Diesel Allison diesels, SES Norcat has a service speed of 36 knots and a top speed of 42 knots. Future craft of this type with more powerful engines could, according to Brodrene, reach 55 knots. Warship variants are under consideration.

Sweden's link with SESs is via Karlskronavarvet, the ship design and construction company. Bell's new 450-ton MSH coastal mine countermeasures craft is built in grp, employing a technique devised by the company which is also a specialist in small warships. It is understood that a technology exchange agreement gives Karlskronavarvet access to Bell SES technology, making the company a leading candidate as an SES builder for the Swedish Navy.

As the technology develops, alternative forms of SES are being studied. These include the Surface Effect Catamaran (SECAT), the Air Ride system and the Deep Cushion SES. The SECAT has a low length-to-beam platform supported by twin high length-to-beam cushions. Its resistance and head sea motions are similar to that of a higher length-to-beam SES but it must operate at a much higher cushion pressure than comparable sidewall craft because of the reduced area. Model tests of an 800-ton vessel show that the twin, widely-spaced cushions and high cross-structure height minimise slamming and virtually eliminate green water appearing over the deck in sea state 6.

Outwardly, Air Ride craft have the appearance of conventional vessels. Beneath the hull, however, there is a long shallow plenum for pressurised air. Mixed-flow fans feed air into the chamber where it is retained by two shallow sidewalls, transverse frames fore and aft and the water surface below. The designer claims that the efficiency is comparable to that of an SES or sidewall craft. The ride is stated to be better than on conventional boats as there is less wetted hull impact area. The bow, similar to that of a normal boat, shapes the waves permitting the use of a shallow air cushion. Since vehicles of this type do not have a high centre of gravity they do not need wide sidewall spacing for stability. There is virtually no size limitation on vessels employing the concept. Swiftships Inc, Morgan City, Louisana and Lantana Boatyard, Lantana, Florida, are both working on military and commercial boats, several over 200 feet in length, employing the Air Ride concept.

On Vosper Hovermarine's Deep Cushion SES concept, the payload is carried within the sidewalls together with the propulsion system and fuel. As a result it is possible to raise the bracing structure above the cushion, providing a much greater overwave clearance with negligible effect on the craft. Since the area above the bracing structure will not carry any considerable load apart from the lift fans and the powerplant, it will be little more than a flexible surface to carry the lift cushion load over the sidewalls. The company's 700 series SES displaces only 600 tons but it is capable of 40 knots in four-metre seas and has a calm water speed in excess of 50 knots. The maximum range at high speed is 1,500 nautical miles, the patrol range at 15 to 20 knots is 5,000 nautical miles.

It is stated that the concept will provide a cushion depth of six metres or more on a 60-metre vessel with an overall beam of 25 metres.

Amphibious hovercraft

Although no major orders for medium or large hovercraft were announced in 1984, news of several substantial contracts is expected in 1985.

In December 1984 it was announced that the first Bell Aerospace Textron 150-ton Landing Craft, Air Cushion (LCAC) had successfully passed its US Navy "At Sea" trials and has been accepted and delivered to Navy Assault Craft Unit Five at Panama City, Florida. It was stated that ruggedness of the craft was fully demonstrated during the trials in high sea states and that the performance was in excess of that required by the contract specifications in terms of speed, range and payload. The LCAC is designed to spearhead amphibious assault landings by the US Marine Corps and carry ashore medium battle tanks and other heavy items of marine equipment which cannot be airlifted ashore by helicopter. The LCAC would normally carry a 60-ton plus load at 50 to 60 knots. It will replace Second World War type landing craft which are due for retirement by the mid-1990s. Training is now beginning with the LCAC and next year the first six craft will be moved to an LCAC base being constructed at Camp Pendleton, California. An East Coast LCAC base will be established at the Naval Amphibious Base, Little Creek, Virginia in 1987.

Twelve LCACs are currently under construction by Bell Aerospace Textron in New Orleans for Naval Sea Systems Command's Amphibious Warfare and Strategic Sealift Program (PMS 377). An option has also been placed for a second batch of twelve. LCAC-002 was due for delivery in late 1984, three are to be delivered in 1985 and seven are scheduled for completion in 1986. The US Navy hopes to have 66 in service by 1991. It anticipates ordering a minimum of 90 craft to support the ship-to-shore requirements of the amphibious fleet.

Basic instruction in hovercraft operation for trainee LCAC commanders is being undertaken with the aid of Hover-travel/BHC's AP.1-88-002 *Resolution*. Hovertravel has leased the craft to Bell Aerospace for twelve months. It was delivered to Navy Assault Craft Unit Five at Panama City, Florida in December 1984. Although slightly smaller than the LCAC, it is expected to prove ideal for the purpose. Like the LCAC, the AP.1-88 has twin ducted propellers for thrust, a BHC peripheral bag and finger skirt of the latest pattern and a bow thruster for low speed manoeuvrability. Before the training programme began, it is understood that minor modifications were made to the control system and the bow thruster so that they more closely resemble those on LCAC. A further modification proposed is the substitution of the AP.1-88's fixed-pitch propellers by variable-pitch propellers. Consideration is being given to the purchase of a number of specially built AP.1-88s which will not only have a similar control system but will also bear a closer physical resemblance to the LCAC.

The growth of activity associated with the LCAC has led Avon Industrial Polymers, part of the Avon Rubber Group and one of the industry's best known suppliers, to open a new factory at Picayune, Mississippi. A joint venture between Avon and Bell Aerospace Textron, it will trade as Bell Avon Inc. Initially the new company will manufacture and maintain hovercraft skirt components for existing US Navy and commercial craft. Avon has been supplying materials and components to British Hovercraft Corporation, the skirt supplier for the first twelve LCACs, and has also made skirts for Bell Halter's three Model 522A SESs operated by the US Coast Guard in the Gulf of Mexico and the Caribbean Sea.

Among the new craft to be launched during the coming months is the Chaconsa VCA-36, the first large hovercraft to be built in Spain. Designed to improve the rapid-lift capability of the Spanish armed forces, the craft will carry a 14-tonne payload, equivalent to three Land-Rovers and 70 fully armed marines or infantry, to a beach landing zone at a speed of 60 knots. Its dimensions (25·17 × 11·04 × 9·5 metres) will allow it to operate from the the docking wells of a number of LSDs and from ro/ro vessels with sufficient headroom and suitable ramps.

A clear indication that the Soviet Navy plans to extend its hovercraft activities is the doubling of Aist production facilities at Dekabristov, Leningrad. About 16 Aists are in service at present; if output is expanded to take full advantage of both old and new production facilities a new Aist could be launched every 12 weeks. Another new development in the Soviet Union is the introduction of a combat mission simulator representing the operation of the 270-ton Aist.

The simulator is described as having three basic uses: to enhance the skill of commanders in operating Aists across sea or beach interfaces; to assist the commander in co-ordinating crew activities during an operation; and to help in assessing the psychological and physiological fitness of officers taking command of the craft. At present Aist is the only Soviet Navy hovercraft for which a simulator has been designed. A Soviet press report suggests that they should be built for each of the hovercraft in service and should be available to all operational units.

Work on Soviet power-augmented ram-wing-in-ground-effect machines (PAR-WIGS) continues, the latest development being a new version of the turboprop-powered craft known by the NATO codename Casp B. Unlike the earlier model, which has a nose that hinges sideways to permit the loading and off-loading of troops, weapons, equipment and vehicles, the new variant mounts two or more SS-N-22 sea-skimming anti-ship missiles. In a future conflict one of the major aims of the Soviet Navy will be the disruption of enemy sea communications using submarines, surface ships and long-range aircraft. Casp B is destined to join them as a fast surface raider, designed to make surprise attacks on enemy merchant shipping.

Arctic activity

During 1983-84, Jeff(A), one of the two 160-ton amphibious landing craft (AALC) prototypes from which the US Marine

Corps' LCAC was developed, completed nearly seven months of operation in Arctic conditions in the Beaufort Sea. Leased from the US Navy by RMI Inc, it was chartered to the Sohio Alaska Petroleum Company to support drilling operations. Extensive testing was also undertaken to obtain data for use in the design, construction and operation of large, heavy lift, self-propelled ACVs for use in the Arctic. Between January and February 1984, Jeff(A) operated between Prudhoe Bay and Mukluk Island, a man-made, gravel-based oil exploration site in Harrison Bay. In winter this 56km stretch of water is frozen to a depth of several feet. After establishing operating routes to the island through the ice rubble, Jeff(A) took part in the demobilisation of a drilling rig at Mukluk, achieved in February by a combination of Jeff(A), Catco all-terrain units and the Global Marine/Veco ACT-100 hoverbarge, towed by Catco units. Jeff(A) hauled approximately 20 per cent of the rig equipment from the island, including a 102-ton crane.

The operation is believed to be the first major use of ACVs in an oilfield application. Sohio Oil's drilling manager points out that the Jeff(A) programme was a success for two reasons: it resulted in the acquisition of technical data, and it proved the concept that ACVs are a viable tool in support of oilfield operations in the near shore ice regions of the Beaufort Sea. The data gathered will assist in the design of much larger self-propelled hover-platforms for Arctic use, one of which is the projected Sohio/RMI ACV 300. This is a 1,000-ton vehicle needed to lift 300 to 350 tons of cargo and equipment on each run during oil drilling operations in northern Alaska. In typical conditions of solid ice with scattered ridges and a 12-knot wind, the vehicle will be able to maintain an average speed of over 15 knots.

RMI is under contract as design manager for the project, BHC is providing the propeller pylons and British Aerospace Corporation the propellers. The skirt system has been designed by Hovercraft Consultants Limited and is being made by Avon.

Another hover-platform kept busy in Alaska during 1984 was Hover Systems' 50·8-tonne amphibious transporter, popularly known as the D-PAAC (Demonstration Program Alaskan Air Cushion). The craft continued to deliver fuel, oil, lumber and construction material to Eskimo villages. On each voyage 12,000 gallons of fuel are pumped from internal tanks and metered to village storage tanks. The average summer and winter voyages each cover 200 miles, servicing four different villages on three different routes every three weeks. Average continuous hover time per trip has been 28 hours, with no shutdowns or overnight stops. A paddle-wheel adaptation involving steel caged, moulded paddle wheels bolted onto the wheelhubs, gives the craft a speed equivalent to shallow draught Alaskan tug-barges. Two grounded barges and one tug were pulled to safety by D-PAAC during the August low river water period.

A new range of hoverbarges is under development by British Hovercraft Corporation. Two of the design studies undertaken have been for logistics-over-the-shore (LOTS) applications by the US Army, and more recently the company has examined the possibility of adapting and using SR.N4 and BH.7 components on a craft built to the LAMP(H) requirement. BHC is currently designing a number of hoverbarges, with payloads ranging from 50 to 200 tons, based on the use of standard modules. This form of hoverbarge is seen as being the cheapest and quickest to erect and

has the advantage that it can be built to meet specific requirements. It can also be increased in size or be dismantled and carried elsewhere. At the end of 1984 BHC received a contract from the UK's Central Electricity Generating Board worth approximately £390,000 for a design feasibility study of a hoverbarge capable of carrying a payload of 700 tons. The programme will last nine months, including one month of mould testing.

A newcomer from Bell Aerospace is the company's Arctic Supply ACV 52-metre craft with a maximum load of 372 tons. It employs marine diesels for lift and propulsion and can carry payloads of up to 100 tons across 2·28- to 2·43-metre high ice ridges while cruising at speeds of up to 20 knots. It can also operate over water, snow and tundra. Power is supplied by four Caterpillar 3516 diesels each driving a 5·02-metre controllable pitch air propeller. Two 2·43-metre retractable wheels, each driven by a 150 hp hydraulic motor, are installed near the midship position to improve low-speed control in winds as well as grade climbing ability.

SWATHs

To demonstrate the exceptional seakeeping qualities of the SWATH, RMI Inc recently built the world's first SWATH demonstrator, the 57-ton SD-60 *Halycon*, a vessel designed for a variety of commercial and military uses, from crewboat to patrol craft. A SWATH is defined as a vessel comprising two parallel, torpedo-like underwater hulls, supporting two or more streamlined struts which pierce the water surface and carry an above-water platform. Stabiliser fins are attached to the aft end of each hull and a pair of smaller fins are attached near their forward ends.

The first full-size example, the 190-ton *Kaimalino*, was built by the Semi-Submerged Ship Corporation, as a range support vessel for the US Navy in 1975. In 1977 Mitsui of Japan built the experimental 18-ton *Marine Ace* to test the configuration. In 1979 this was followed by the 22-knot *Seagull* passenger ferry. Mitsui has since built the 254-ton *Kotozaki*, the world's first SWATH hydrographic survey vessel, and in May 1985 is due to launch the world's biggest SWATH, the 2,800-ton *Kaiyo* for the Japanese Science and Technology Centre. Although the two main centres of SWATH technology are Japan and the USA, other nations are keen on developing the technology including Canada and the Soviet Union which is planning a SWATH luxury liner.

Halycon's stabilisation system is computer controlled and uses four hydraulically-operated control surfaces, two forward and two aft, on the inner faces of the two subsea hulls. These are employed collectively or differentially and control roll, pitch and heave motions.

Power is supplied by twin deck-mounted Caterpillar 3408-TA marine diesels each of which drives controllable and reversible-pitch propellers at the end of each subsea hull. A 15-foot middle body extension can be fitted to the basic SD-60 hull providing sufficient room for a landing platform for a light observation helicopter. *Halycon's* appearance confirms that, as far as small craft are concerned, the technology has reached the production stage. With a hull depth of 14 feet, it is one of the few small craft available capable of operating in both shallow waters and in sea state 4. Looking ahead, Mitsui's 2,800-ton *Kaiyo* points the way to the multi-thousand-ton SWATH which could join the SES as another new silhouette on the high seas.

Acknowledgements

Due to illness, the Editor was unable to mention individually the many people who, by providing information and suggestions, helped in the compilation of this edition. The publishers would like, therefore, to thank on his behalf all who assisted in any way.

No illustrations from this book may be reproduced without the publishers' permission but the Press, in reviewing the work, may reproduce information provided JANE'S SURFACE SKIMMERS is acknowledged as the source. Photographs must not be reproduced without permission from the originator.

Self-propelled Amphibious ACVs Designed by the A M Gorki Memorial Marine Institute of Technology

by S F Kirkin, Chief Manager

Since 1970 the Marine Institute of Technology has been working on the design of self-propelled air cushion vehicles. Technical specifications of some of these appear in the following text.

In 1978 the Institute built the SAVR-1M, an amphibious ACV. This can carry three people and a 500kg load over snow, slush, ice and open water. It has two powerplants, one for propulsion and one for lift. Cushion air is produced by an axial fan in the nose. Horizontal thrust is provided by a two-blade, engine-driven airscrew. Directional control is by means of an air rudder behind the airscrew.

The hull of the SAVR-1M rests on four skids. In order to reduce the volume of air escaping from the cushion, the gap between the hull and skids is covered with rubberised fabric. Beneath the bow section of the craft is a flexible skirt with open segments; the rear skirt has closed segments.

Specifications, SAVR-1M
Total weight: 1·8 tonnes
Load capacity: 0·8 tonnes
Propulsion engine: 72kW
Lift engine: 30kW
Max speed over snow: 70km/h

Performance tests were carried out during winter and spring over snow, slush, ice and open water. The tests produced a great deal of experimental data which was used by the Institute in subsequent work on similar craft.

In 1980 the Institute's workers designed and built their second experimental, self-propelled amphibious ACV, the SAVR-1. This is intended for high-speed transport of personnel and urgent cargoes of up to 1·3 tonnes over roadless areas, during the construction and maintenance of pipelines. It may be used all the year round in the search for and development of oil and gas fields in flat, marshy areas.

Specifications, SAVR-1
DIMENSIONS
Length: 7,500mm
Width: 3,800mm
Height with airscrew vertical: 3,300mm
WEIGHTS
Total weight: 2·9 tonnes
Max useful load: 1·3 tonnes
PERFORMANCE
Operating speed, on snow: 50km/h
    on water: 40km/h
POWERPLANT
Propulsion engine: 118kW
Lift engine: 72kW

The SAVR-1 comprises the following main components: hull, lift unit, propulsion unit, air rudder and skirt. The hull is built in sheet duralumin and includes a central plenum chamber of honeycomb construction. The chamber is hermetically sealed and ensures the unsinkability of the craft when the lift unit is not in operation. There is a cabin for the pilot and passenger, as well as a cargo area covered with a canvas hood. The aft part of the hull contains the propulsion unit, a 160hp aero engine driving a two-metre diameter, two-blade airscrew. A steel grid, made of thin-wall pipes, prevents accidental contact with the airscrew. The engine is mounted on the hull by four vertical struts, using rubber shock absorbers, and is covered by a cowling.

Cushion air is produced by two standard centrifugal fans driven via an angled transmission by a 98hp car engine. The fans are located on both sides, in the mid section of the hull. A clutch is fitted between the engine and the fans, allowing for disconnection during engine startup and idling. Fuel to supply the lift and propulsion engines is contained in a single, 180-litre fuel tank in the mid-section of the central chamber. Steering is accomplished by the movement of two air rudders in the airstream, behind the airscrew. The air cushion is produced using a plenum system. The skirt of the air cushion consists of forward, open type segments, and aft closed segments together with special side skirts which allow the craft to operate either in full or partial lift mode.

Operational tests on the SAVR-1 were undertaken in the first half of 1980, on snow, slush, ice, open water, muddy and dry land. The tests showed that the most economic mode of operation is on snow and slush using 30 to 40 per cent lift. When operating over wet ground and mud the lift must be increased to 90 to 100 per cent, so that the craft is operated like an ordinary amphibious ACV. The tests also showed that the craft confidently handles obstacles such as snow or earth banks, up to 0·6 metre in height and 10 degrees gradient. It also crossed ditches up to seven metres wide and two metres deep. Over ice or compact snow the craft can move with the fans turned off using the airscrew thrust only, like an ordinary aerosledge.

In 1982 the Institute began tests on a new amphibious ACV, the SAVR-2. This is capable of travelling over low weight-bearing surfaces – deep and soft snow, slush, cracked ice with water, mud, and open water. Here it must be said that the construction of a ground air cushion craft presents many interconnected problems, the solution of which requires extensive theoretical and experimental research work. One of these problems is the design of a suitable air cushion skirt which would reduce to a minimum the amount of air escaping from the high pressure zone underneath the craft and, at the same time, would not present any great resistance when travelling. The existing flexible skirts of a modern ACV are of no great use in rough ground operations as they do not adequately follow the ground contours. They present considerable resistance when travelling, have a short life-span due to intensive abrasion and do not allow the craft to operate in a partial lift mode. Very often, for example when travelling over excavations, canals, ice crevasses, trenches and other similar obstacles, the flexible skirts appear totally inadequate as they do not prevent the air escaping from the air cushion. As a result, the pressure quickly drops and the craft hangs over the obstacle with no means of overcoming it on its own.

The experimental model of the SAVR-2 used two 'flexible' skids as the side skirts for the air cushion, placed on each side, underneath the craft. The 'flexible' skid consists of hinged right-angle plates, with removable soles made of sheet stainless steel or low-pressure polyethylene. The plates are fixed to the hull by a special lever suspension and spring shock absorbers. The space between the skid and hull is covered with rubberised fabric. Such a skirt, unlike standard types, can adequately and faithfully follow ground contours including depressions, resulting in a reduced rate of air escaping from the pressure zone, which in turn results in a reduction in the power required from the lift engine. Due to the presence of spring shock absorbers between the 'flexible' skids and the hull it is possible, when travelling over ice or snow, to operate the craft in the reduced lift mode using minimum energy for lift. In certain circumstances it is often convenient to skid over the snow maintaining a low residual pressure, rather than travel fully on the air cushion. The durability of the skirt with a 'flexible' skid is higher than that of an ordinary, rubberised fabric skirt.

One should, however, mention the fact that along with their many advantages, 'flexible' skids also have several shortcomings. their construction is complicated and they are heavy. The suspension elements and shock absorbers are difficult to protect against clogging by snow and mud. At present, work at the Institute continues aimed at removing these shortcomings and improving the design of the skirts. The hull of the SAVR-2 has three main parts: the central platform and two side sections, made of sheet duralumin. The central platform is of honeycomb construction, with cavities filled with foam plastic to ensure unsinkability in an emergency.

The forward section of the hull contains a cabin for the operator and two passengers. It has thermal insulation and soundproofing made of foam plastic and polyurethane foam coating. Inside the cabin are the controls and an instrument panel. Behind the cabin is the lift engine compartment, the angled transmission from the engine to the fans, the clutch and the engine cooling system. The engine compartment is separated from the cabin by a thermo-insulating and soundproof partition. Behind the engine compartment is the cargo hold, designed to take various loads up to two tonnes in weight. When necessary, the hold may be converted to take 14 to 16 passengers.

The aft part of the hull contains the propulsion unit, consisting of an aero-engine and a three-blade, variable pitch airscrew. Engine startup is by means of bottled, compressed air. The fuel used is motor-car petrol, also used to drive the fan engine. The fuel for both engines is carried in two tanks of 400-litre total capacity, inside the central platform and is pumped to the engine carburettors.

Operational tests on the SAVR-2 experimental craft were performed in spring thaw conditions. First of all the performance capabilities of the empty craft were established. Then the tests were repeated for a craft with loads of 0·5 tonne, one tonne, 1·5 tonnes and two tonnes respectively. The craft travelled over flat, muddy ground; over a meadow covered with a thin layer of water; over a dry, grass-covered meadow; ploughland; damp ground; and open water. The tests included checking the starting and stopping performance of the craft (take-off and landing), its manoeuvrability and directional control, the optimum operational performance of the lift and propulsion units in various route conditions, stability and buoyancy, and convenience of handling and operation.

Specifications, SAVR-2
DIMENSIONS
Length: 9,800mm
Width: 4,500mm
Height to top of pylon of airscrew propulsion unit: 3,700mm
WEIGHTS
Max load capacity: 2 tonnes
Total weight, inc load: 5,900kg
PERFORMANCE
Operational speed: 50km/h
Max pressure in air cushion: 1,400Pa
Powerplant: 294kW

The tests showed that to cross damp, muddy ground or areas covered with a thin layer of water requires only a minimum of energy. When crossing open water the energy consumption increases, in this case the pressure in the air cushion must be increased to 1,000 to 1,200Pa. The least favourable surfaces are dry soil and ploughland. The air cushion pressure must then be increased to 1,400Pa, its maximum value.

AIR CUSHION VEHICLES

AUSTRALIA

HOVERMAC HOVERCRAFT AUSTRALIA

Greenglades, Old Gympie Road, Narangba, Queensland 4504, Australia
Telephone: 07 204 1210
Officials:
Vernon W McKay, *Manager*
Geoffrey R Abbott, *Manager*
Jeffrey R Morris, *Manager*

Hovermac Hovercraft was founded by Vernon W McKay in 1977. It designs and constructs light recreational hovercraft and is developing a grp-hulled hovercraft powered by a V8 engine for commercial applications. The company also supplies engines, fans, grp ducts, skirt materials and other components for homebuilt hovercraft.

Descriptions of the company's Hovermac I and II can be found in *Jane's Surface Skimmers 1984* and earlier editions.

HOVERMAC III

This is a lengthened version of Hovermac II seating a driver forward and two passengers side-by-side aft of the driving seat.
LIFT AND PROPULSION: Lift is supplied by a vertically mounted 8bhp Solo two-stroke driving a five-blade Multiwing fan with blades set at 30 degrees. Thrust is provided by a 28bhp Kawasaki KT-300 two-stroke driving, via twin-toothed belt transmission, two five-bladed 630mm (2ft 1in) ducted Breeza fans.
HULL: Lightweight grp construction. Sheeted polyurethane foam for buoyancy.
SKIRT: Simple loop type fabricated in 430g/m² polyurethane-coated nylon.
DIMENSIONS
Length: 3·6m (11ft 9·5in)
Beam: 1·78m (5ft 10·5in)
Height on landing pads: 1·1m (3ft 7·25in)
WEIGHTS
Normal payload: 210kg (463lb)
PERFORMANCE
Max speed across land and calm water (dependent on installed power): 60-80km/h (37-49mph)
Vertical obstacle clearance: 200mm (7·87in)

HOVERMAC IV

Intended primarily for home construction, this two- to three-seater is of simple layout and is easily built from readily available materials. Three prototypes were built to test various power arrangements.
LIFT AND PROPULSION: Lift is supplied by a single 8hp two- or four-stroke driving either a five- or ten-blade axial fan with blades set at 30 degrees. Thrust is provided by one 40bhp engine driving, via a toothed belt transmission, twin five-bladed 600mm (2ft) ducted Multiwing or Breeza fans or one 730mm (2ft 4·75in) diameter six-bladed Z-type ducted Multiwing fan.
HULL: Exterior grade ply structure with 20 × 20mm wooden stringers. Built-in sealed buoyancy chambers can be filled with polyurethane foam. Joints and skids on underside reinforced with grp.
SKIRT: Simple loop type in 430g/m² polyurethane-coated nylon.
DIMENSIONS
Length: 3·6m (11ft 9·75in)
Beam: 1·8m (5ft 11in)
Height on landing skids: 1·2m (3ft 11·25in)

Hovermac III

Hovermac IV

WEIGHTS
Normal payload: 150kg (330lb)
PERFORMANCE
Max speed across land and calm water (dependent on installed power): 60-80km/h (37-49mph)
Vertical obstacle clearance: 175mm (7in)
Fuel consumption (dependent on installed power): approx 10 litres/h (2·2 gallons/h)

HOVERMAC V

Intended for light utility applications, Hovermac V is a grp-hulled eight-seater powered by a 4·2-litre aluminium V8 engine. It will be suitable for search and rescue operations in sheltered areas, fisheries support, harbour work and light transport duties across shallow and marginal terrain.

LIFT AND PROPULSION: Integrated system powered by a 4·2-litre aluminium V8 engine driving, via a heavy toothed belt, multiple Z-type ducted Multiwing fans.
HULL: Built in grp and pvc foam sandwich. Available with removable folding hood or hard-top cabin.
SKIRT: Loop and segment type in 430g/m² polyurethane-coated nylon.
DIMENSIONS
Length: 7m (22ft 11·62in)
Beam: 3·4m (11ft 2in)
Height on landing skids: 1·6m (5ft 3in)
WEIGHTS
Normal payload: 450kg (992lb)
PERFORMANCE
Cruising speed: 35 knots
Vertical obstacle clearance: 450mm (1ft 7in)

LIGHT HOVERCRAFT COMPANY

11 Hayward Street, Stafford, Queensland 4053, Australia
Telephone: 59 7006
Officials:
H B Standen, *Manager*

Light Hovercraft Company was founded in Brisbane, Australia, in 1971. Its first product was a small transportable ACV but series production of this particular craft ended in 1973.

Currently, Light Hovercraft is concentrating on the sale of plans to homebuilders and producing light hovercraft tailor-made to the needs of individual purchasers. The company offers plans for 12 different craft ranging in seating capacity from one to sixteen.

The majority of the company's clients reside in Australia, New Zealand, the Pacific Islands and South America.

MURRAY PARTNERS AUSTRALIA PTY LIMITED, HOVERJET TRANSPORT DIVISION

Head Office: 401 Collins Street, Melbourne, Victoria 3000, Australia
Telephone: 61 3374
Telex: AA34436
Works: Corner Wells and Boundary Road, Mordralloc 3195, Australia
Telephone: 580 7084/8396

Murray Partners Australia Pty Ltd has acquired all marketing and manufacturing rights to the Hoverjet range of air cushion vehicles. In addition to building leisure variants of the Hoverjet in Australia, the company exports light military patrol models to neighbouring countries.

HOVERJET

This lightweight, amphibious two-seater is designed for use on sheltered waterways, in tidal estuaries and across reasonably flat land. Built in fibreglass reinforced plastics, it is 3·4m (11ft) long and has a maximum payload capacity of about 160kg (360lb). It can be driven straight off a trailer onto land or water. The craft is built to standards specified by the Marine Board of Victoria.

LIFT AND PROPULSION: Cushion air is supplied by a 9·3kW (12·5hp) Solo 210cc engine driving a 3·48m (11ft 7in) diameter lift fan mounted ahead of the open cockpit. On the standard model thrust is supplied by an identical Solo 210cc engine driving a 760mm (2ft 6in) diameter ducted fan. The Solo thrust engine can also be fitted with a tuned exhaust which provides an extra 3·5hp to improve performance.

HULL: Moulded fibreglass reinforced plastic. Buoyancy is 270kg (600lb).

SKIRT: Bag type in neoprene-impregnated nylon.

ACCOMMODATION: Open cockpit with seat for driver and one passenger.

DIMENSIONS
Length: 3·4m (11ft)
Width: 1·8m (5ft 10in)
Height: 1·2m (3ft 6in)
Clearance, hard structure: 210mm (8in)

Hoverjet two-seat sports craft

WEIGHTS
Empty: 114kg (250lb)
Max payload: 160kg (360lb)
PERFORMANCE
Solo 210cc

Thrust engine rated at 6000rpm	With standard exhaust	With tuned exhaust (optional extra)
	9·3kW (12·5hp)	12kW (16hp)
Static thrust:	30kg	38kg
Max speed:		
1 man	40km/h (25mph)	50km/h (30mph)
2 man	35km/h (20mph)	40km/h (25mph)
Max continuous slope:		
1 man	1 : 7·6	1 : 6
2 man	1 : 9·5	1 : 7·8
Fuel consumption	5 litres/h (1·1gal/h)	5·7 litres/h (1·25 gal/h)

NEOTERIC ENGINEERING AFFILIATES PTY LIMITED

Box 2438, GPO Melbourne, Victoria 3001, Australia
Telephone: (03) 391 3639
Officials:
Christopher J Fitzgerald, *Managing Director*

Robert K Wilson, *General Manager*
Alan Fitzgerald, *Company Accountant*

Neoteric Engineering Affiliates Pty Limited specialises in the development of the Neova II and Lémere light hovercraft and the company concentrates on marketing two-seat models

which are available in kit or ready-built form.

In 1975 Neoteric USA Incorporated was established at the Fort Harrison Industrial Park, Terre Haute, Indiana 47804. Details of the Neova range of light hovercraft will be found in this edition under the entry for Neoteric-USA Inc.

STOLKRAFT PRODUCTION PTY LIMITED

Head Office: Level 23, ANZ Tower, 55 Collins Street, Melbourne, Victoria 3000, Australia
Telephone: 03 654 1055
Officials:
Robert E Rees, *Chairman*
Rhoda G Stolk, *Director*
Paul Van Epenhuysen, *Director*
Ben Lexcen, *Director*
John A Leckey, *Director*

Consultant and Naval Architect:
Ship Technology Unit (A Division of Vickers Cockatoo Dockyard Pty Ltd), 5 Northcliff Street, Milsons Point, New South Wales 2061, Australia

Leo D Stolk's Stolkraft concept of optimising the benefits of air lubrication on a planing hull can be summarised as follows:

At speed an appreciable amount of aerodynamic lift is built up by a ram-air cushion at the bow, and this, combined with air fed through twin bow intakes, creates a second ram-air cushion and lifts the craft so as to reduce frictional resistance.

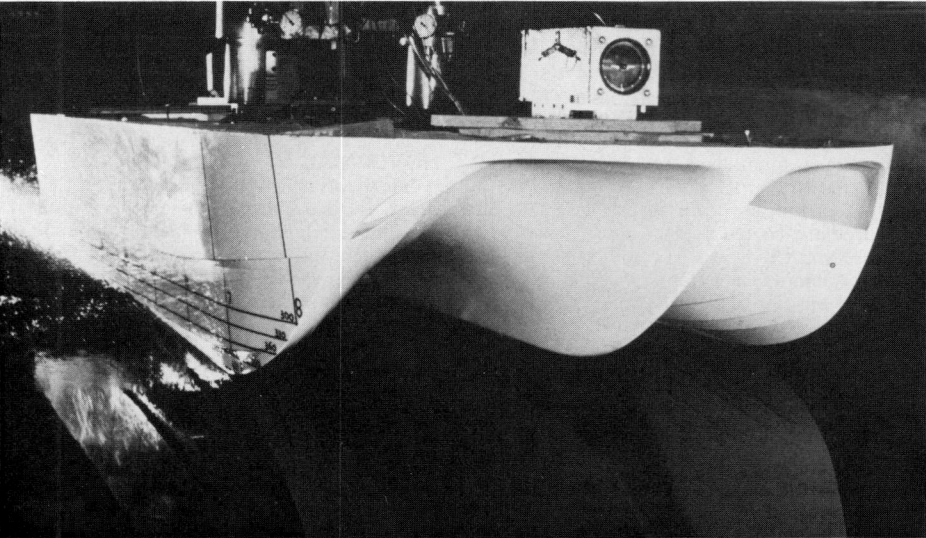

2·4m (7ft 11in) Stolkraft test model

A feature of the concept is the absence of trim variation. The craft rises bodily, parallel to the surface, and has no tendency to porpoise. At speed it creates neither bow-wash nor hull spray outward. The aerodynamic lift reduces fuel consumption.

Tests have been undertaken with a 2·4m (7ft 11in) model at the Netherlands Ship Model Basin, Wageningen, the Netherlands. The performance of this model was monitored in the high-speed tank and actual sea tests with 4·95m (16ft) and 8·45m (28ft) vessels provided additional data. During the tank tests speeds of up to 80 knots were simulated with no performance problems.

These tests fully supported Leo Stolk's earlier theoretical predictions as to the applicability of this design concept to larger vessels such as passenger ferries, naval craft, cargo offshore services and work boats.

INCEPTOR II SK.16 Mk 1

The prototype of the company's first production runabout is the fibreglass-hulled seven-seater Inceptor II SK.16 Mk 1.

PROPULSION: A Volvo Aquamatic stern-drive single 170hp drives a water screw for propulsion. Alternatively, single or twin outboards can be fitted. Twin bow intakes feed pressurised air to a ventilated transverse step and thence to a second air cushion created beneath the hull aft. Fuel is carried in two 90·9-litre (20-gallon) tanks located amidships, port and starboard.

HULL: Stepped trimaran configuration. Moulded fibreglass construction with bulkheads in fibreglass-covered seaply. Craft has eight foam-filled airtight compartments for positive buoyancy.

ACCOMMODATION: Open cockpit for driver, six adults and up to two children.

DIMENSIONS
Length overall: 4·95m (16ft 3in)
Beam: 2·13m (7ft)
Width overall: 2·44m (8ft)
WEIGHTS
Normal load: 550kg (1,200lb)
Max load: 680kg (1,500lb)
PERFORMANCE
PROTOTYPE, INCEPTOR II
Max speed/load 600lb/170hp: 80km/h (50mph)

STOLKRAFT Mk III

This 8·53m (28ft) 14-seater was built for a series of tests at the Netherlands Ship Model Basin. These tests fully supported earlier theoretical predictions regarding stability and performance.

The large cockpit space makes the craft suitable for a variety of applications, including rescue, diving platform, naval, police and fisheries patrol.

The prototype is powered by three 200hp outboard engines.

DIMENSIONS
Length: 8·53m (28ft)
Beam: 4·26m (14ft)
PERFORMANCE
Max speed: in excess of 40 knots

22-METRE FAST PATROL BOAT

This patrol boat incorporates the features of generous deck space, high speed and sea keeping capability. The design can be easily adapted for use as a weapons platform.

PROPULSION: Motive power is supplied by twin high-speed marine diesels or twin marinised gas turbines driving waterjets or surface-piercing water propellers. Where a maximum speed of 45 knots is required, twin diesels, each with ratings of about 2,000shp, would be installed. Gas turbines would be employed when a maximum speed over 45 knots is specified. Two gas-turbines, each developing 3,500shp, would give the vessel a maximum speed of more than 60 knots. A third, low-power propulsion unit can be installed on the centre line for economic loiter performance. All machinery is located aft. Access panels in the aft deck facilitate the installation and removal of machinery.

HULL: All-welded structure in marine grade aluminium alloy, using conventional patrol boat

Inceptor II SK.16 Mk I

SK.16 Mk II at speed showing absence of wave formation, bow wash and outward hull spray

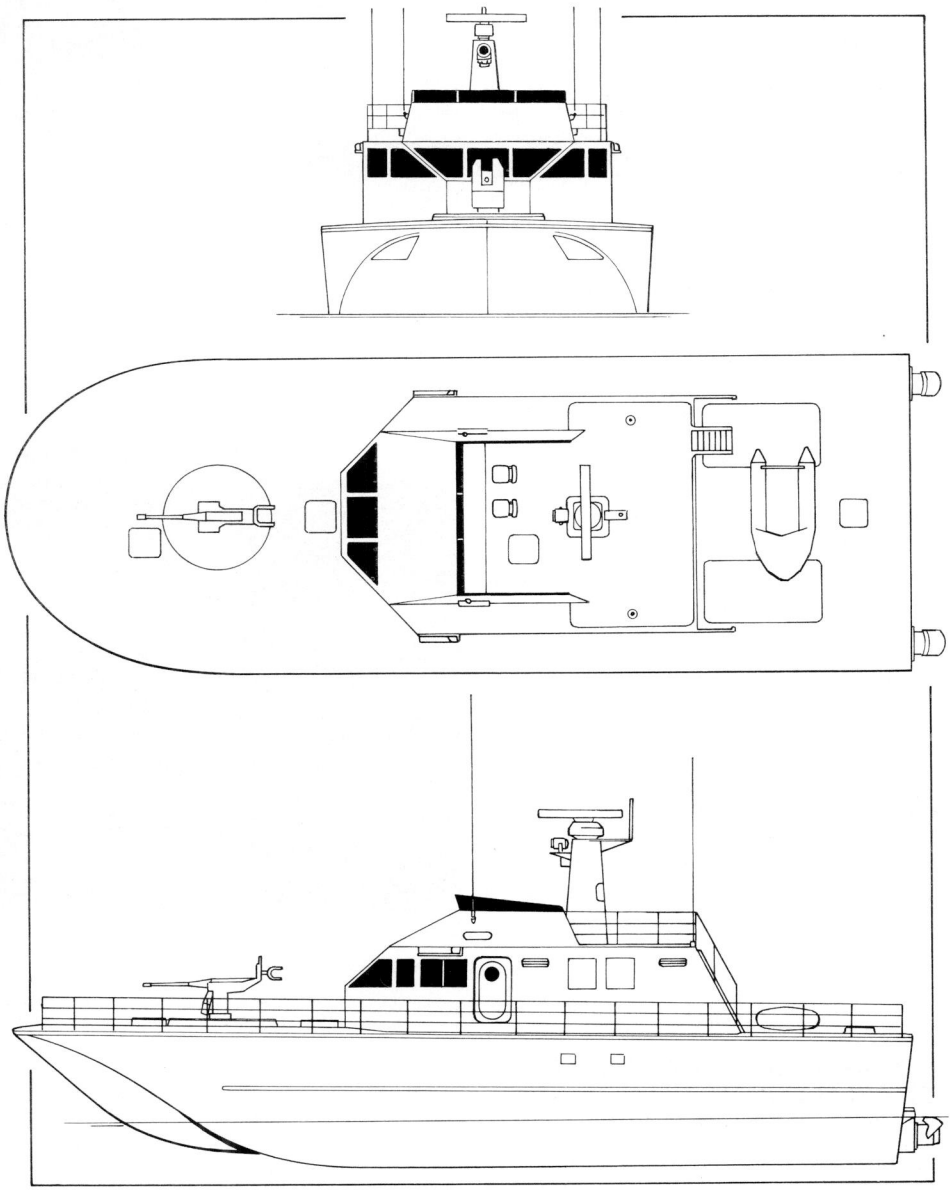
22-metre fast patrol boat

construction techniques. The lower hull is divided into watertight compartments by four transverse bulkheads. The craft will remain afloat if any one compartment floods.
ACCOMMODATION: Living and work spaces for eleven amidship. Wheelhouse, galley and diving facilities are within the superstructure. Four sleeping cabins, one single-berth, one double and two four-berth, are below the main deck.
DIMENSIONS
Length, overall: 22m (72·2ft)
Beam, moulded: 8m (26·2ft)
Drift to DWL, waterjet powered version: 1·1m (3·6ft)
WEIGHTS
Fuel capacity, typical: 5 tonnes
Fresh water capacity, typical: 1 tonne

Stolkraft Mk III

CANADA

ACV SALES INC
Box 11107, Royal Centre, 1400-1055 West Georgia Street, Vancouver, British Columbia V6E 3P3, Canada
Telephone: (604) 685 9824
Officials:
A Robertson, *President*

ACV Sales Inc builds the Amphibian hovercraft, designed to meet all-year-round climatic conditions in the Canadian north and other locations. It is suitable for a variety of commercial and military applications.

AMPHIBIAN
TYPE: Light amphibious multi-duty ACV capable of carrying an operator and up to four passengers or 453·6kg (1,000lb) of freight.
LIFT AND PROPULSION: Integrated system powered by a single 340hp Ford Type 429 CID water-cooled petrol engine. Mounted inboard the engine drives two axial-flow fans mounted at the opposite ends of a split-transverse shaft. Air flow is ducted beneath the craft for lift and via port and starboard outlets aft for thrust. Recommended fuel is premium gasoline.
CONTROLS: Craft heading is controlled by multiple rudders in the thrust duct apertures or by the manipulation of port and starboard thrust duct gates. Driving controls comprise a steering wheel, thrust gate control switches, an electric starter switch and a throttle control for lift and thrust. Reverse thrust gates provide braking, stopping and manoeuvring capabilities.
HULL: Moulded fibreglass and corrosion resistant aluminium construction. Buoyancy: 150 per cent.
ACCOMMODATION: Access to the enclosed cabin is via twin sliding doors, one port, one starboard.
DIMENSIONS
Length on cushion: 7·44m (24ft 4in)
Beam on cushion: 3·4m (11ft 2in)
Height on cushion: 2·67m (8ft 9in)
WEIGHTS
Net weight: 1,905kg (4,200lb)
Payload: 453·6kg (1,000lb)
PERFORMANCE
Max speed (land, water, ice and snow): 48km/h (30mph)
Range: 277km (172 miles)
Max gradient: 15°

Amphibian showing thrust duct apertures

Amphibian light multi-duty ACV

ADVANTECH DEVELOPMENT CORPORATION
PO Box 24, Downsview, Ontario M3M 3A6, Canada
Telephone: (416) 298 3199
Officials:
Norbert C Fan, *President*

Advantech Development Corporation is developing a new amphibious ACV based on the company's 'active controlled fully responsive' skirt concept. The skirt employs the newly developed bag-shoe technology.

Construction of the prototype Fan Ko Mk I, which will have a payload capacity of 5 tons, was expected to be completed by early 1985. A joint venture with the Fan Keung Motor Company of Hong Kong will exploit the potential of the craft.

Fan Ko Mk I is expected to precede much larger craft of the same type.

AIR TREK SYSTEMS LTD

PO 1224, Chatham, Ontario N7M 5L8, Canada
Telephone: (519) 352 7040
Officials:
John R De Koning, P.Eng, *President*
John Curtin, P.Eng, *General Manager*

Air Trek Systems Ltd is developing a range of multi-duty vehicles employing proven ACV technology. Rugged industrial components and modern manufacturing techniques are incorporated into the company's designs to produce low cost machines requiring limited maintenance. The company's latest design is the Air Trek 149, a 60-passenger craft.

AIR TREK 140

Designed for use in arctic conditions, this utility hovercraft carries up to 16 passengers or freight weighing up to 1,360kg (2,998lb). The main structure is built in marine-grade aluminium and is stressed to operate at 61km/h (38mph) in 0·9m (3ft) high seas. The craft has received full certification from the Canadian Coast Guard.

LIFT AND PROPULSION: Integrated system powered by a single Caterpillar 3208 turbocharged, after-cooled diesel rated at 360hp for 5 minutes and 350hp continuous. Thrust is supplied by a ducted, four-bladed wooden propeller. Power is transmitted to two centrifugal lift fans behind the driver's and crewman's seats via an Eaton Hydrostatic drive system. The operator can select the fan speed to suit the terrain or wave conditions; the fans will then remain at that speed constantly irrespective of the main engine rpms.

CONTROLS: Multiple rudders operating in the propeller slipstream provide directional control and act as shut-off doors to modulate thrust. Louvres in the duct wall between the propeller and the rudders give reverse thrust.

SKIRT: HDL 'kneed' segments in 16oz neoprene.

HULL: Marine-grade aluminium.

ACCOMMODATION: Cabin with independent diesel heater and heavily insulated for arctic conditions. Dual operating position.

DIMENSIONS
Length: 11·2m (36ft 9in)
Width: 5·73m (18ft 10in)
Passenger cabin length: 3·55m (140in)
  width: 3·52m (132in)
WEIGHTS
Max load: 1,360kg (2,998lb)
Fuel capacity: 363kg (800lb)
Crew of two: 145kg (319·6lb)
Craft weight: 3,574kg (7,879lb)
Max all-up weight: 5,442kg (11,997·5lb)
PERFORMANCE
Cruising speed, ice and water: 61km/h (38mph)
Cruising speed, ice: 72km/h (45mph)
Fuel duration at max cruising speed: 8 hours
Fuel consumption at max cruising speed: 45kg/h (100lb/h)

AIR TREK 149

At the design stage is a 60-seat amphibious fast ferry, designated the Air Trek 149. The craft will be powered by two modified Caterpillar 3208 diesels, each driving a centrifugal lift fan and a ducted propeller.

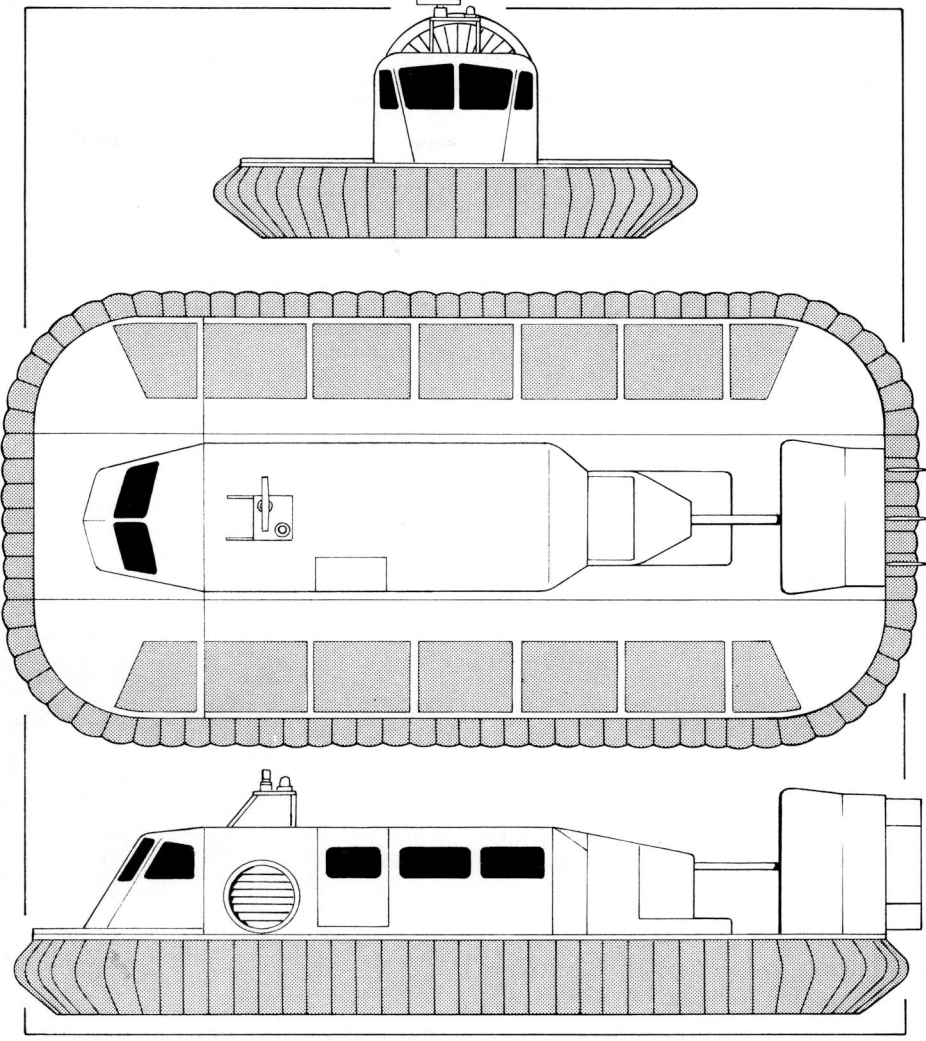

Air Trek 140

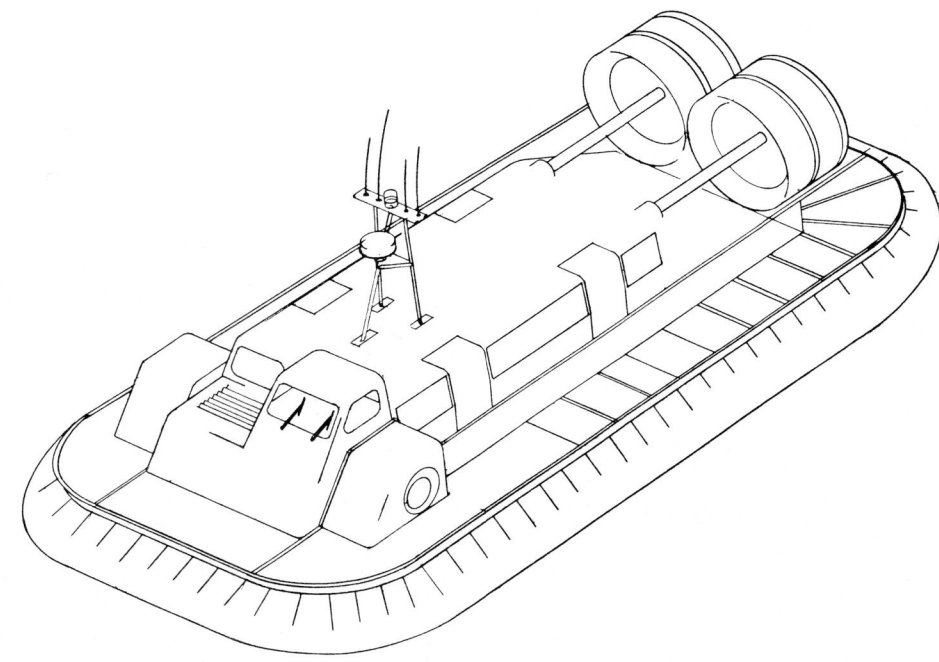

Air Trek 149

BELL AEROSPACE CANADA TEXTRON
(A division of Textron Canada Ltd)

PO Box 160, Grand Bend, Ontario N0M 1T0, Canada
Telephone: (519) 238 2333
Telex: 064 7268
Officials:
Norton C Willcox, *President*
Joseph R Piselli, *Vice President*
John W McKinney, *Vice President*
John B Timbrell, *Managing Director*
Derek Angus, *Marketing Director*

In January 1971 Bell Aerospace Canada Textron acquired facilities at Grand Bend, Ontario, for the development and production of its Model 7380 Voyageur heavy haul ACV and the smaller 17-ton Viking multi-duty craft.

The facilities at Grand Bend Airport include two buildings with a total of 3,350m² (30,000ft²) of floor space on a 21-hectare (52-acre) site.

The company worked closely with the Cana-dian Department of Industry, Trade and Commerce in planning a programme which has led to the establishment in Canada of a commercially viable air cushion industry to meet the growing requirements for Coast Guard, remote area cargo hauling, high speed passenger ferry services and other specialised applications.

The first two 40-ton Voyageurs were built under a joint agreement between the company and the Canadian Department of Industry, Trade and Commerce. The prototype, Voyageur 001, differed from later craft insofar as it was fitted with two GE LM100 engines, as opposed to the ST6T-75 Twin-Pac gas turbines which are now standard.

The Voyageur features a basic flatbed hull of all-welded extruded marine aluminium that can be adapted to a variety of operational needs by adding the required equipment and superstructure.

Construction of Voyageur 001 started in March 1971 and operational trials and certification testing began in November 1971. Voyageurs have operated in the Canadian and American Arctic regions on oil industry exploration logistics support. Voyageur 002 is owned and operated by the Canadian Coast Guard and since March 1975 has worked as an ACV icebreaker. Ice in excess of 1·01m (3ft 4in) thick has been successfully broken.

Voyageur 003 is at Grand Bend pending upgrading to AL-30 standards and Voyageur 004 is at Panama City, Florida, where it is employed to train US Navy personnel in the operation of air cushion craft.

A stretched version of the Voyageur, the Model 7467 LACV-30, has been built to meet US Army requirements for a high-speed amphibious vehicle for LOTS (Logistics-over-the-shore) operations. The LACV-30 is intended to replace conventional vessels of the LARC-5 and LARC-15 types. Details will be found in the entry for Bell Aerospace Textron, USA.

Bell Aerospace Canada Textron provides the major components of the LACV-30. The Model 7380 has been succeeded in production by the Bell AL-30, the commercial variant of the US Army's LACV-30. Details of the Model 7380 Voyageur may be found in *Jane's Surface Skimmers 1980* and earlier editions.

BELL AL-30

A commercial derivative of the US Army's LACV-30, the Bell AL-30 amphibious lighter is intended for use in port cargo handling systems and is particularly suited to the rapid transfer of containers from ships to shore. Fully amphibious, it can carry a 30 short ton (60,000lb) payload, ranging from vehicles to break-bulk type cargo. In an integrated lighterage cargo transfer system, the AL-30 can offload ships independently of existing berth and dock facilities and will permit the direct transfer of cargo from the ship into the transport system of the country, hence speeding its arrival at its final destination.

LIFT AND PROPULSION: Integrated system powered by two Pratt & Whitney ST6T Twin-Pac gas turbines mounted aft, one at each side of the raised control cabin. Each engine is rated at 1,800shp maximum and 1,400shp at normal output. The output of each is absorbed by a three-bladed Hamilton Standard 43D50-363 reversible-pitch propeller and a 2·13m (7ft) diameter, twelve-bladed, fixed pitch light aluminium alloy, centrifugal lift fan. Cushion pressure at maximum gross weight is 267kg/m² (54·7lb/ft²).

FUEL SYSTEM: Recommended fuel is standard aviation kerosene, Jet A1, JP4, JP5 or JP8 or light diesel fuel oil. Main fuel usable capacity is 9,419 litres (2,272 US gallons). Fuel ballast/

emergency fuel capacity is 6,960 litres (1,531 US gallons). Estimated fuel consumption during lighterage missions is 454kg/h (1,000lb/h) (147 US gallons/h).

SYSTEMS, ELECTRICAL: Starter generators: four gearbox driven brushless, 28V dc, 200A each. Batteries: two nickel cadmium, 28V dc, 40A each.

DIMENSIONS
Length overall, on cushion, without optional swing crane: 23·3m (76ft 6in)
Beam overall, skirt inflated: 11·2m (36ft 8in)
Height overall, on landing pads: 7·86m (25ft 9in)
 on cushion: 8·83m (29ft)
Length, cargo deck: 15·7m (51ft 6in)
Width, cargo deck: 9·9m (32ft 6in)
Height, cargo deck, off cushion: 1·2m (3ft 11·5in)
Cushion height: 1·22m (4ft)
WEIGHTS
Gross: 52,163kg (115,000lb)
PERFORMANCE
Max speed (calm water, zero wind, at 52,163kg (115,000lb) gross weight)
 normal rating: 74km/h (46mph)
 max rating: 90km/h (56mph)

Bell AL-30

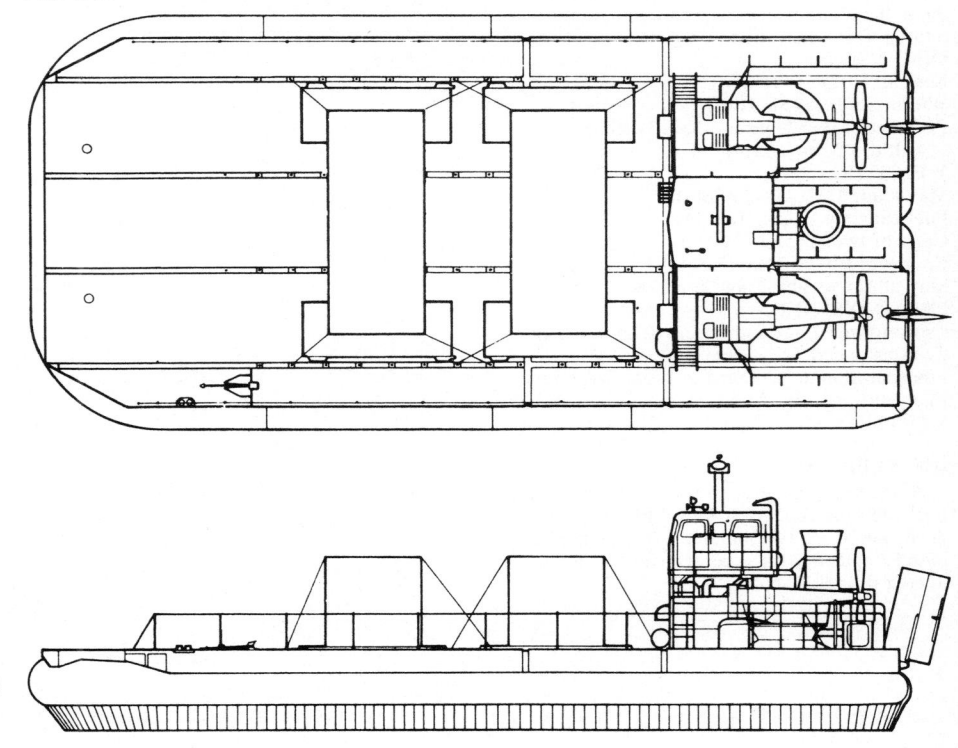

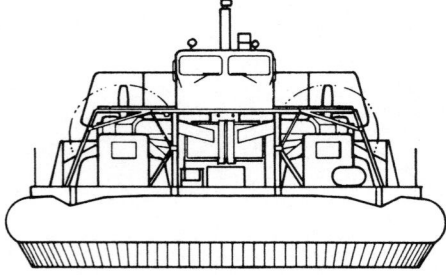

Bell AL-30

COLUMBIA HOVERCRAFT LIMITED

12311, Road One, Richmond, British Columbia V7E 1T6, Canada
Telephone: (604) 271 0084
Officials:
Colin Shew, *President*
Gregory Nicholson, *Director*
Dennis Nairn, *Director*

Columbia Hovercraft Limited was incorporated in 1982 to develop, manufacture, operate and lease commercial, utility and recreational ACVs. The company builds and markets several designs. The latest craft is a commercial variant of the UH-26 designed in the USA by Bob Windt. Columbia Hovercraft's intention is to build simple designs that are easy to maintain and repair. Power is supplied by internationally available engines, and standard belt drives are used for

power transmission. The company also designs and builds air cushion modules to assist standard wheeled and tracked vehicles to cross marginal terrain. Current production craft are the Columbia 13, derived from the UH-13, and the Columbia 18, derived from the Windt-designed UH-18.

COLUMBIA 13

An amphibious three-seat recreational craft, Columbia 13 has a load capacity of 90·7-181·4kg

(400-800lb) depending on installed horsepower.
LIFT AND PROPULSION: Lift is supplied by
an 8hp four-cycle vertical shaft mower engine, or
equivalent, driving a 0·6m (2ft 2in) diameter
four-bladed fan. Thrust is provided by a two-
cycle 20-66hp engine driving, via a V-belt, a
1·2m (4ft) diameter two-bladed propeller. Fuel
capacity provides the craft with an endurance of
between 2 and 6 hours.
HULL: Welded aluminium frame with riveted
skin. Plastic foam packed into the hull provides
150 per cent buoyancy.
SKIRT: Bag type in neoprene nylon.
DIMENSIONS
Length: 4·4m (4ft 6in)
Beam: 1·9m (6ft 6in)
WEIGHTS
Payload: 90·7-181·4kg (400-800lb)
PERFORMANCE
Max speed, depending on installed power: 48·2-
 96·5km/h (30-60mph)

COLUMBIA 18

The standard version of the Columbia 18 seats
6 to 8, but with modification the cabin will
accommodate light freight, fuel drums or stretchers.
LIFT AND PROPULSION: Integrated system.
Power is supplied by a single four-cylinder,
liquid-cooled 2,300cc Ford automotive engine
which drives, via an automatic lift system, a
0·85m (2ft 10in) diameter 4-bladed axial fan for
lift and a 1·87m (6ft 2in) diameter two-bladed
propeller.
CONTROLS: Directional control is by triple
aerodynamic rudders behind the propeller.
HULL: All-metal structure. Welded aluminium
frame with riveted skin. Two interior watertight
bulkheads. Plastic foam packed into the hull pro-
vides 150 per cent buoyancy. Self-draining hull.
Bilge pumps supplied as standard.
SKIRT: Simple bag type.
ACCOMMODATION: Enclosed cabin for
driver and up to seven passengers.
DIMENSIONS
Length: 6·4m (21ft)
Beam: 2·4m (8ft)
WEIGHTS
Loaded weight: 1,360·1kg (2,999lb)
Normal payload: 544·2kg (1,200lb)
Max payload: 680·2kg (1,500lb)
PERFORMANCE
Max speed: 80·4km/h (50mph)
PRICE: C$22,500, FOB Richmond BC (1983).

COLUMBIA 26

This commercial variant of the UH-26S is
under development, but production craft were
due to be available in late 1984. It will carry a
driver and up to 14 passengers and will have a
normal payload capacity of 1,360·5kg (3,000lb).

AIR CUSHION MODULES

Columbia Hovercraft Ltd designs and builds
air cushion modules to enable standard vehicles
to cross marginal terrain. The accompanying
photograph shows a module developed to allow
the use of golf carts in Canada during the three
wet months when they would otherwise be ex-
cluded from courses. No modification was made
to the golf cart. Use of the module does not affect
the capability of the cart and there is very little
loss of traction.

Columbia 13

Columbia 18

Columbia air cushion-assisted golf cart

JONES KIRWAN & ASSOCIATES

Box 4406, Station 'D', Hamilton, Ontario,
Canada

Officials:
D Jones, *President*

Jones Kirwan & Associates was responsible for
the design of the Air Trek 140, as well as a
number of other Canadian hovercraft. The company also designs agricultural spray booms.

TRANSPORT CANADA
Air Cushion Vehicle Division

Tower A, Place de Ville, Ottawa, Ontario K1A
0N7, Canada

Officials:
T F Melhuish, *Chief ACV Division*

The Air Cushion Vehicle Division, Transport
Canada, was established in 1968 as part of the
Marine Administration. The Division is respon-
sible to the Director, Canadian Coast Guard Ship
Safety Branch for all aspects of air cushion vehi-
cle certification and regulation.

On the operations side, the Division has direct
responsibility to the Director, Canadian Coast
Guard Fleet Systems Branch to advise and assist
Coast Guard in its air cushion vehicle activities.
This includes the use of air cushion technology
for icebreaking and the Division has been
responsible for the development of this new
technology within the Canadian Coast Guard.

There is also close collaboration with Trans-
port Canada's Policy and Planning Branch,
Surface Administration and Research and
Development Centre.

The Division works with the National
Research Council's Research Group on Air
Cushion Technology, and participates as Canada's representative on the US SNAME Panel
MSI on High Speed Craft. Close liaison is maintained with industry, government and military
organisations in Canada and abroad.

TRANSPORTATION DEVELOPMENT CENTRE (TDC)

Complex Guy Favreau, 200 Dorchester West, Suite 601, Montreal, Québec H2Z 1X4, Canada
Officials:
J E Laframboise, *Senior Development Officer*

Founded in Montreal in 1970, the Transportation Development Centre (TDC) is the research and development arm of Transport Canada. TDC studies, promotes and directs the application of science and technology towards a more efficient and effective national transport system. Working in co-operation with the Canadian transport community, TDC conducts and commissions research projects covering all modes of transport.

AEROBAC AB-7

This is a concept developed by the Transportation Development Centre, Transport Canada, following trials in the Canadian hinterland with air cushion trailers. The Aerobac combines the air cushion platform with muskeg tractor tracks. In the varied environment of the Canadian north, Aerobac can carry its weight on its tracks, on its air cushion, or in any combination as local conditions dictate.

Its current definition is the result of a feasibility study for TDC by the SNC Group, in collaboration with Bombardier Limited and SEDAM, and based on a requirement of Hydro-Québec for power line construction. Aerobac is under evaluation as an airport rescue vehicle at airports where local terrain makes off-runway movements impracticable for wheeled vehicles.

VRV Inc, 330 Sauvé Street West, Montreal, Quebec H3L 1Z7, Canada is marketing the concept through a technology transfer agreement with the Canadian government.
LIFT AND PROPULSION: Integrated system powered by a single Detroit Diesel 8V92TAV8 developing 415bhp at 2,100rpm. Power is transmitted to two double-inlet lift fans, with a total flow of 20m³/second, and the track system which is used for propulsion. Left- and right-hand tracks are 1m wide and are made with rubber belting and steel struts. Each track is mounted on four solid rubber wheels. Fuel capacity is 810 litres.
SKIRT: SEDAM multicell system comprising peripheral and inner skirts. Bi-conical front skirt. Off-road bi-conical skirt at rear.
CONSTRUCTION: Welded aluminium alloy.
ACCOMMODATION: Enclosed cabin seating three.
DIMENSIONS
Length overall: 11·5m

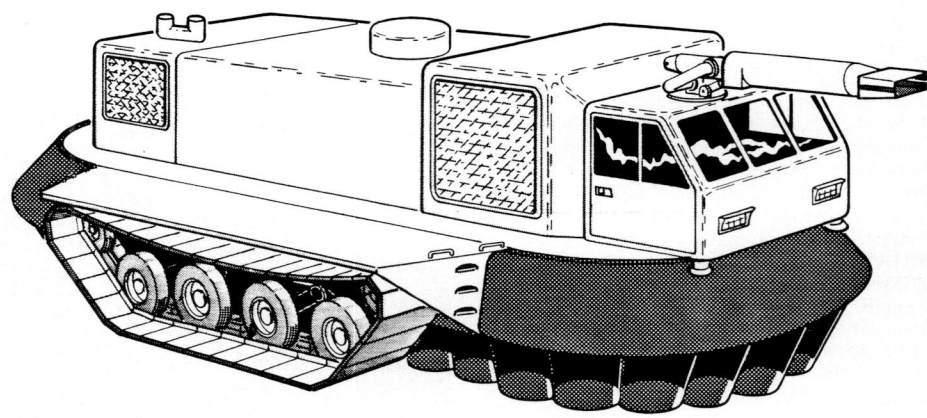

Airport rescue version of Aerobac with foam capacity of 4,500 litres

Aerobac AB-7

Width overall: 6·2m
Height overall: 3·37m
Skirt height: 0·6m
Cargo deck: 12m²
WEIGHTS
Empty: 14 tonnes
Max: 21 tonnes
Payload: 7 tonnes
PERFORMANCE
Max speed: 30km/h
Endurance: 13 hours
Ground pressure,
   air cushion only: 6·3k Pa
   tracks only: 35·6k Pa
Max performance on slopes,
   tracks only: 40%
   approach angle: 17 degrees

Aerobac AB-7

CHINA, PEOPLE'S REPUBLIC

MARINE DESIGN AND RESEARCH INSTITUTE OF CHINA (MARIC)

Shanghai, China

An ACV research and development programme has been under way in China since 1970. Much of the experimental work has been undertaken at a shipyard in the Shanghai area which has constructed a small number of test craft, one of which is being operated from Chungking on a passenger ferry service. It is understood that this craft is fully amphibious, is powered by one aircraft piston-engine and operates at between 25 and 30 knots. The craft is constructed in aluminium and steel and the skirt is of simple bag type. Although the skirt has proved adequate for this craft it is clear that a great deal of development work has to be undertaken in this area of ACV technology before Chinese-designed amphibious ACVs can operate satisfactorily across open waters.

At present, Chinese interest in amphibious craft is focused on vehicles in the SR.N6 to SR.N4 range (approximately 10 to 300 tons). These are required for a variety of military and civil applications, including the operation of fast passenger ferry services over river networks with route distances of up to 240 to 320km (150 to 200 miles).

Initially, interest was limited to craft of approximately 10 to 60 tons but this is because the smaller craft present fewer problems when selecting power plants, in addition to which they can be built more easily by smaller shipyards.

The largest hovercraft to be built in China is a 65-ton assault landing craft prototype which was launched at Tieangin in August 1979. The craft, which resembles a scaled-down SR.N4, is undergoing evaluation trials.

Considerable interest is centred on sidewall-type ACVs with moulded grp hulls, and wing-in-ground-effect machines for high-speed, long-distance river services.

Type 722 65-ton multi-duty hovercraft

TYPE 722 65-TON MULTI-DUTY AMPHIBIOUS HOVERCRAFT

The largest ACV to be built in China, this 65-ton vehicle has been designed specifically for a range of naval and military applications. The prototype is under evaluation in the amphibious initial assault role, although a passenger/vehicle ferry version has been exhibited in model form. In overall appearance the craft resembles a scaled-down BHC SR.N4.

Design was undertaken by the Shanghai Shipbuilding Research Institute and the craft was built at the Dagu Shipyard with the assistance of some 52 other specialist engineering, technical and military groups. Construction began in December 1977 and the craft was launched in August 1979. The initial trials programme began in September 1979.

The vehicle is described as being capable of operating over water, land, grasslands, marshlands, lakes, shallows and beaches. It can clear vertical obstacles 1m (3ft 3in) high and ditches up to 5m (16ft 4in) wide.

LIFT AND PROPULSION: Two 1,850hp and two 1,530hp engines drive four air propellers and six Type 4-73 centrifugal fans. Air for the engines appears to be drawn in through filtered roof intakes. Fan air, which is taken through three large filtered ducts each side of the superstructure, is discharged into the cushion via a continuous peripheral loop skirt with segmented fringes.

CONTROLS: It is believed that craft heading is controlled by swivelling the forward propeller pylons, operating them in conjunction with the twin aerodynamic rudders aft. Reverse thrust is applied for braking and reversing. Elevator provides pitch trim at cruising speed.

HULL: Riveted skin and stringer structure employing alloy sheet. Main hull is formed by a buoyancy raft based on a grid of longitudinal and transverse frames which form a number of flotation compartments. Two main longitudinal vertically stiffened bulkheads run the length of the craft separating the control load deck from the outer sidestructures which contain the lift fan engines, lift fans, transmissions and auxiliary power systems. The freight deck is reinforced to permit the carriage of armoured troop carriers and heavy vehicles. A stern door and bow loading door/ramp provide a drive-on, drive-off through-loading facility. Separate side doors, port and starboard, give access to the two cabins which flank the load deck forward.

SKIRT: Loop and segment type tapered skirt, similar to that of the SR.N6, in coated nylon fabric.

ARMAMENT: Machine gun turret on bow port quarter on the amphibious assault landing craft version.

DIMENSIONS
Length: 27·2m (89ft 3in)
Beam: 13·8m (45ft 3in)
Height: 9·6m (31ft 6in)
Cushion depth: 1·5m-1·8m (4ft 11in-5ft 11in)
WEIGHTS
All-up weight: 65 tonnes
Useful load: 15 tonnes

Bow-on view of Type 722 65-ton multi-duty hovercraft in amphibious assault configuration

Model of experimental three-engined amphibious passenger ferry

PERFORMANCE
Speed, calm water: 55 knots

THREE-ENGINED AMPHIBIOUS PASSENGER FERRY

One of a number of development craft designed and built by the Shanghai Shipbuilding Research Institute, this machine is powered by three radial aircraft engines. Two of the engines drive two-bladed propellers for thrust while the third, mounted centrally aft, drives a lift fan at the rear end of the cabin superstructure via a shaft extending forward externally to a right-angle drive above a horizontally-mounted centrifugal lift fan.

The skirt is of fingered bag configuration similar to that of the BHC SR.N5.

The hull is of the light alloy buoyancy type. Twin aerodynamic rudders provide directional control and an elevator set high on the twin fins aft provides pitch trim at cruising speed.

Type 722 65-ton multi-duty amphibious hovercraft

JING-SAH RIVER TEST CRAFT

Before constructing the ACV passenger ferry prototype described above, the Shanghai Shipbuilding Research Institute built a small-scale version powered by two 270bhp Type 604-1 air-cooled radial engines.

In elevation the craft is not unlike a scaled-down SR.N5 with a radial engine mounted on each of its twin fins, each radial driving a two-bladed propeller. However, the power sharing arrangement is unique: a shaft with a universal joint extends from each of the propeller hubs and both meet in a mixing gearbox and right-angle drive above a horizontally-mounted centrifugal lift fan located behind the cabin. The skirt is of the continuous peripheral loop type with segmented fringes.

DIMENSIONS
Length overall: 11·74m (38ft 6·25in)
Beam overall: 5·1m (18ft 8·75in)
Height overall: 3·76m (12ft 4in)
WEIGHTS
Empty: 2·96 tonnes
Payload: 0·84 tonnes
PERFORMANCE
Max speed: 54 knots
Range: 300km (162n miles)

JING-SAH RIVER PASSENGER FERRY

One of the largest air cushion vehicles under development in China is this 70-seat rigid sidewall passenger ferry which is similar to the Vosper Hovermarine HM 218 but has a higher length-to-beam ratio. Like the HM 218, the craft is diesel-powered and propelled by waterscrews. It was built during 1979 and began trials in 1980.
LIFT AND PROPULSION: Motive power for the lift fan is provided by a 380bhp 12V135CZ marine diesel. Propulsive thrust is supplied by two identical 12V135CZ high-speed marine diesels driving waterscrews.
SKIRT: Finger seal at bow and rigid balanced seal aft.
DIMENSIONS
Length overall: 22·3m (73ft 2·25in)
Beam overall: 6·4m (21ft)
Height overall: 4·27m (14ft 0·25in)
WEIGHTS
Empty: 21 tonnes
Loaded: 30 tonnes
PERFORMANCE
Max speed: 31 knots
Range: 269km (145n miles)

SHALLOW-DRAUGHT SIDEWALL HOVERCRAFT

China's first sidewall hovercraft for shallow inland waterways has been built in Anhui province. The craft accommodates 40 passengers, each with up to 20 kg of luggage. It has an endurance of 11 hours at 40 km/h; twice as fast as the country's conventional inland river ferries.

Its limited draught requirements and low wave-making characteristics also make it suitable for search and rescue and river patrol.

During tests in 1981, the craft successfully covered a distance of 2,000km. The design was developed jointly by the Shanghai Shipbuilding Research Institute, the Anhui Communications Science Research Institute, the Ministry of Communications and the Chaohu Shipyard.
HULL: Glass fibre construction.
DIMENSIONS
Length: 19·45m (63ft 10in)
Beam: 3·9m (12ft 10in)
Height: 3·75m (12ft 4in)

JINXIANG

An 80-seat sidewall passenger ferry, Jinxiang is a joint project of the Chinese Marine Design and Research Institute and the Dagu Shipyard, Tieangin. In July 1983 it successfully completed a 128km maiden voyage along the Yangtse river from Shanghai to Vantong in under three hours. The craft is diesel-powered and has a maximum speed of 55km/h.
HULL: High strength, corrosion-resistant aluminium alloy.

Jing-Sah river test craft in role of fast-patrol boat. Note weapons hatch in cabin roof

Jing-Sah river passenger ferry

Jing-Sah river test craft

Water-jet propelled SES on Lake Tai

40-passenger SES

DIMENSIONS
Length: 22·2m
Beam: 6·9m
Height: 5·2m

TAI HU PASSENGER FERRY

A 42-seat waterjet-propelled passenger ferry, this craft has been built for operation across Lake Tai. It was delivered during early 1983. Unconfirmed reports credit the craft with a speed of 40km/h and a range of 450km.

TYPE 7203 SIDEWALL HOVERCRAFT

Derived from Types 713 and 717 (built in the 1970s), Type 7203 is a high-speed passenger ferry for use on coastal and sheltered waters. Alternative applications include coastguard patrol and port/harbour firefighting duties.

Built at the Dagu Shipyard, Tieangin, the prototype was launched in September 1982 and underwent trials on the Hai river and in Tang-Gu in late 1982.

LIFT AND PROPULSION: A multi-fan system improves seakeeping performance. Three centrifugal fans of different diameters are separately fitted in the bow, amidship and stern. Each feeds air to the bow and stern skirts and the air cushion at different volumes and pressures. Diameters of the bow, amidship and stern fans are 800mm, 1,200mm and 450mm respectively. The lift system is powered by a single 12150C high-speed diesel rated at 300hp at 1,500rpm. The lift engine directly drives the amidship and stern fans. The bow fan is driven via a hydraulic pump and motor. Total lift power is about 250hp. Disengaging the bow fan reduces lift power consumption to about 100hp in calm waters. When operating in waves the bow fan is required since it affects the craft's trim. Propulsive power is supplied by two 12150CZ water-cooled, turbocharged, high-speed marine diesels, each rated at 450hp at 1,450rpm. Each drives a three-bladed propeller via a V-type transmission.

CONTROLS: Craft direction controlled by twin rudders and by differential use of water propellers.

ACCOMMODATION: In standard configuration passenger cabin seats 81 passengers. If required, seating capacity can be increased to 100. Two corridors between seats are 800mm wide.

SKIRT: Loop and segment type in bonded raw rubber.

DIMENSIONS
Length overall: 22·2m
Beam overall: 6·9m
Height overall: 5·2m
Height sidewalls: 1·1m
Draught, hullborne: 2·06m
Draught, on cushion: 1·22m
WEIGHTS
Gross: 35 tonnes
PERFORMANCE
Max speed: 30 knots
Cruising speed: 26 knots
Range: 180n miles

NAVAL INLAND WATER CRAFT

Rigid sidewall hovercraft are being developed as river patrol craft for the Chinese Navy. One of the first to be built has an all-up weight of 15·2 tonnes and is being used to test the viability of waterjet propulsion on China's main inland waterways.

Built during 1977, the craft is smaller than the 70-seat sidewall passenger ferry illustrated, but appears to employ the same basic hull design.

LIFT AND PROPULSION: Motive power for the lift system is supplied by two 350bhp 12V150Z high-speed diesels. A third engine, of identical design, powers the waterjet system. Cushion pressure is reported to be 230kg/m².

SKIRT: Loop and segment type at bow; planing rigid type seal aft.

DIMENSIONS
Length overall: 17·3m (56ft 9·5in)
Beam overall: 4·1m (13ft 6in)
Height overall: 4·27m (14ft)

Type 7203 fast ferry

Naval inland water craft

2·8-tonne utility hovercraft

WEIGHTS
Empty: 12 tonnes
Payload: 3 tonnes
All-up: 15·2 tonnes
PERFORMANCE
Max speed: 26·5 knots
Range: 500km (270n miles)

2·8-TONNE UTILITY HOVERCRAFT

A fully amphibious utility hovercraft was completed in 1980 by the Shipbuilding and Marine Engineering Establishment, Shanghai. Although intended primarily for seismic prospecting in offshore areas and marshes, it is suitable for a variety of other utility roles. Sturdily built in riveted aluminium alloy, it carries a driver and up to seven passengers at a speed of 23-33km/h.

Two craft of this type are reported to be in service with the Chinese onshore oil industry.

LIFT AND PROPULSION: Lift is provided by a 85hp BJ492Q-1 four-stroke automobile petrol-engine driving, via a universal coupling and gearbox, a centrifugal aluminium fan. Thrust is supplied by a second engine of identical type driving, via a transmission shaft, elastic coupling,

2·8-tonne utility hovercraft

transmission gear and thrust bearing, a 1·4m, four-bladed, variable-pitch aircraft propeller built in grp. Range of pitch variation is from +15 to −15 degrees. When the vehicle is operating with the propeller at constant pitch, the rotational speed is charged through the adjustment of the engine throttle. Cushion pressure is 94·5kg/m².

CONTROLS: Craft direction is controlled by twin aerodynamic rudders at the rear of the propeller duct.

HULL: Built in 919 medium strength seawater resistant aluminium alloy. Riveted construction.

SKIRT: Segmented bag-type fabricated in rubberised fabric. Height of fingers, 250mm, representing 50 per cent of the total skirt height. Tensile strength is 500 to 450kg/5cm.

DIMENSIONS
Length: 9·19m
Width: 4·76m
Height: 3·32m
Deck area: 9m²
Cabin, internal height: 1·47m
Average draught: 0·219m

WEIGHTS
Fully loaded: 2,769kg
Useful load (8 personnel × 75kg = 600kg, fuel and water, 118kg): 718kg

PERFORMANCE
Max speed during tests, still water: 42km/h
Speed at wind scale 3: 23-33km/h
Vertical obstacle clearance: 0·5m

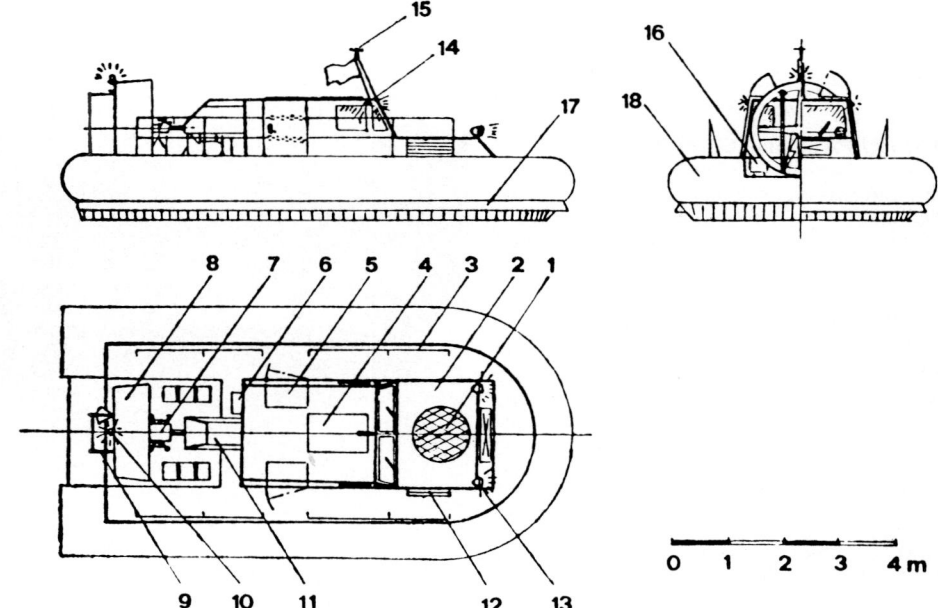

2·8-tonne utility hovercraft (**1**) lift fan(**2**) fan platform (**3**) handrail (**4**) cabin access panel (**5**) cabin door (**6**) battery (**7**) transmission gear (**8**) propeller duct (**9**) twin rudders (**10**) flashing light (**11**) 85hp petrol engine (**12**) air intake (**13**) navigation light (**14**) side light (**15**) speed indicator (**16**) fuel tank (**17**) spray skirt (**18**) skirt

COLOMBIA

EMPRESA METALURGICA COLOMBIANA SA (EMC)

Carrera 19 No 16/75, Apartado Aereo 978, Bucaramanga, Colombia

Telephone: 31142
Telex: 77835 EM C BUCO

Official:
Hermes Nunez Martinez, *General Manager*

EMC experimental ACV design

Empresa Metalurgica Colombiana SA (EMC) chiefly specialises in designing and producing grain- and grass-drying equipment. Since the movement of heavy loads is sometimes restricted in Colombia, due to soft ground or damaged roadways, EMC has begun to investigate the potential for using air-supported platforms.

The most recent development within the company is a multi-cell platform in which each cell can articulate into any position, thus keeping the platform parallel to the ground. Cells can be added or removed according to requirements. Each cell has a load capacity of about 10 tonnes and can be powered either by its own motor or by one feeding a group of cells.

A prototype of a single lifting cell for a multi-cell platform has been built and fitted with a propulsion system to assess its behaviour when moving over a variety of surfaces. The manned craft has been constructed in grp from 16 similar sectors locked together by three tensioned bands around the periphery of the craft. Three centrifugal fans on a common vertical shaft provide air for lift and propulsion. The upper pair work in series to eject air from four ports around the edge of the craft while the third fan supplies air to the cushion and the bag skirt.

DIMENSIONS
Diameter: 4·72m
Height: 2·84m (9·3ft)
Cushion area: 14·4m² (155ft²)

WEIGHTS
All-up: 1·5 tons

POWER
Porsche 40hp petrol engine (to be replaced by a Jacobs Radial Engine at a later date)

CZECHOSLOVAKIA

AERO VODOCHODY

V-66 AERO

The V-66, an amphibious three-seat hovercraft, was displayed in public for the first time in September 1978 at an 'air day' held at the Bino Svazaim airfield and sponsored by the magazine *Science and Technology for the Younger Generation*. The craft has since attracted widespread interest and was lent to the Czechoslovak Army for trials.

Design and construction was undertaken by a group of young workers employed by the state aircraft manufacturer, Aero Vodochody. The engineer in charge was V Leiniveter.

LIFT AND PROPULSION: Integrated system. Motive power is supplied by a single 115hp four-cylinder air-cooled M-1104 helicopter engine

V-66 Aero

with a horizontal shaft. Power is transmitted to a 1·5m diameter variable-pitch two-bladed propeller via a belt drive and to two counter-rotating lift fans via a gearbox. Air is fed into the cushion via a series of 46 deflector vanes. Movement of the deflector blades permits the craft to move sideways.

CONTROLS: Craft heading is controlled by an aerodynamic rudder attached to the rear of the propeller duct. Propeller pitch can be varied by ±20 degrees, giving forward and rearward propulsion and braking.

DIMENSIONS
Length: 4·5m (14ft 9in)
Beam: 2·5m (8ft 2in)
Height: 2·1m (6ft 10in)

WEIGHTS
Max weight, with three persons: 820kg (1,808lb)
Normal operating weight: 580kg (1,235lb)

PERFORMANCE
Max speed: 60km/h (37·28mph)
Vertical obstacle clearance: 250mm (9·8in)

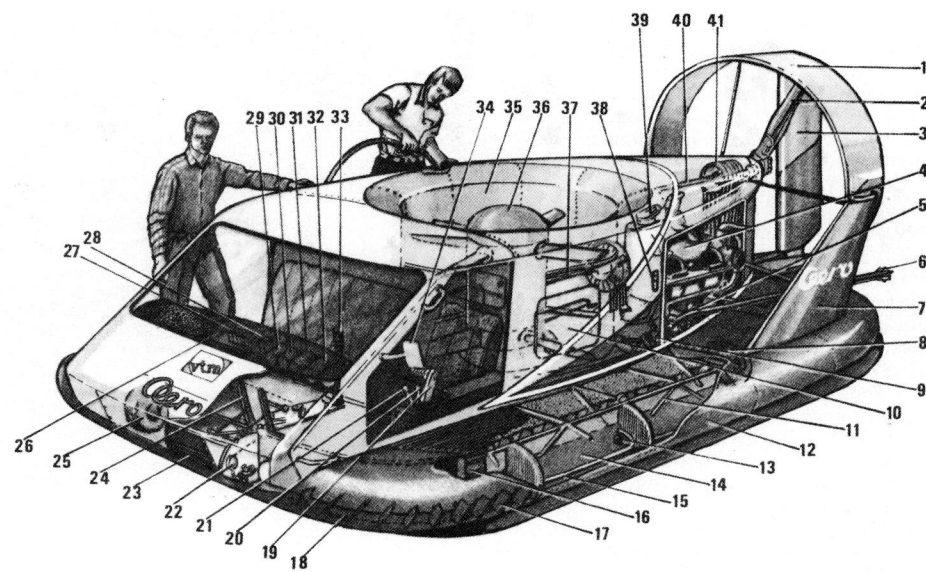

Cutaway of V-66 Aero: **(1)** propeller duct **(2)** propeller blade **(3)** rudder **(4)** engine **(5)** fuel and oil pipes **(6)** exhaust **(7)** fin **(8)** rear wheels for ground movement **(9)** lever **(10)** luggage door **(11)** tubular framework **(12)** outer structure **(13)** mechanism for side deflector vane rotation **(14)** stationary deflector **(15)** side rotating deflector **(16)** inner rotors **(17)** outer rotors **(18)** blade rotation cable **(19)** lever for adjusting propeller pitch **(20)** brake **(21)** throttle **(22)** pulleys **(23)** front rotating plate **(24)** pedals for control of rotors and deflectors **(25)** front wheels for ground movement **(26)** engine correction control rod **(27)** panel for electric instruments **(28)** magneto control **(29)** volt meter **(30)** shaft head temperature indicator **(31)** fuel, oil pressure and oil temperature indicators **(32)** tachometer **(33)** control lever **(34)** rear view mirror **(35)** supercharger **(36)** power take-off shaft **(37)** left fuel tank with level indicator **(38)** fuel inlet cover **(39)** fuel cap **(40)** control cable for propeller blades **(41)** belt transmission

FINLAND

OY WÄRTSILÄ AB

Wärtsilä Helsinki Shipyard, PO Box 132, SF-00151 Helsinki 15, Finland
Telephone: 358 0 1941
Telex: 121246 WHT SF

Founded in 1834, Wärtsilä has grown to be one of the largest industrial companies in Finland. The company operates production plants in 11 localities in Finland and has subsidiaries and offices in Finland, Norway, Singapore, Sweden, USSR, USA and Venezuela. Shipbuilding accounts for two thirds of Wärtsilä's income, but the company also produces diesel engines, wood-processing machinery, foundry products, hydraulic machinery, steel structures, glass and porcelain. The Wärtsilä Shipbuilding Division comprises the Helsinki, Turku and Perno Shipyards, the Ylivieska Factory and a repair yard in Kotka.

Traditional products of the Helsinki Shipyard are icebreakers, car and passenger ferries, cruise liners, naval craft and cable layers. The yard, which employs about 2,700 people, has captured the greater part of the world market for icebreakers. By July 1981 it had delivered 45 diesel-electric icebreakers, ranging from smaller harbour and lake icebreakers up to arctic icebreakers of 26·5mW (36,000shp).

The yard's arctic design and marketing department (WADAM) is continuously engaged in feasibility studies and research on the development of ice-going tonnage and future transport needs in the Arctic and Antarctic areas.

Wärtsilä has an icebreaking model basin which performs research for Wärtsilä and also accepts orders from outside interests. The basin is the largest in the world for testing ships and other structures in ice.

Since 1976 Wärtsilä's Helsinki Shipyard has been applying the experience gained in its construction of icebreakers to the development of air cushion craft capable of negotiating the physical conditions encountered in cold regions. The prototype of the PUC 22, a fully amphibious ACV mixed-traffic ferry with a 30-tonne capacity, is in service and a 70-tonne capacity ferry, the *Arctic Express*, is projected.

The company has also designed and built a number of TAV 40, 40-tonne capacity hover lighters to solve cargo transfer problems in the

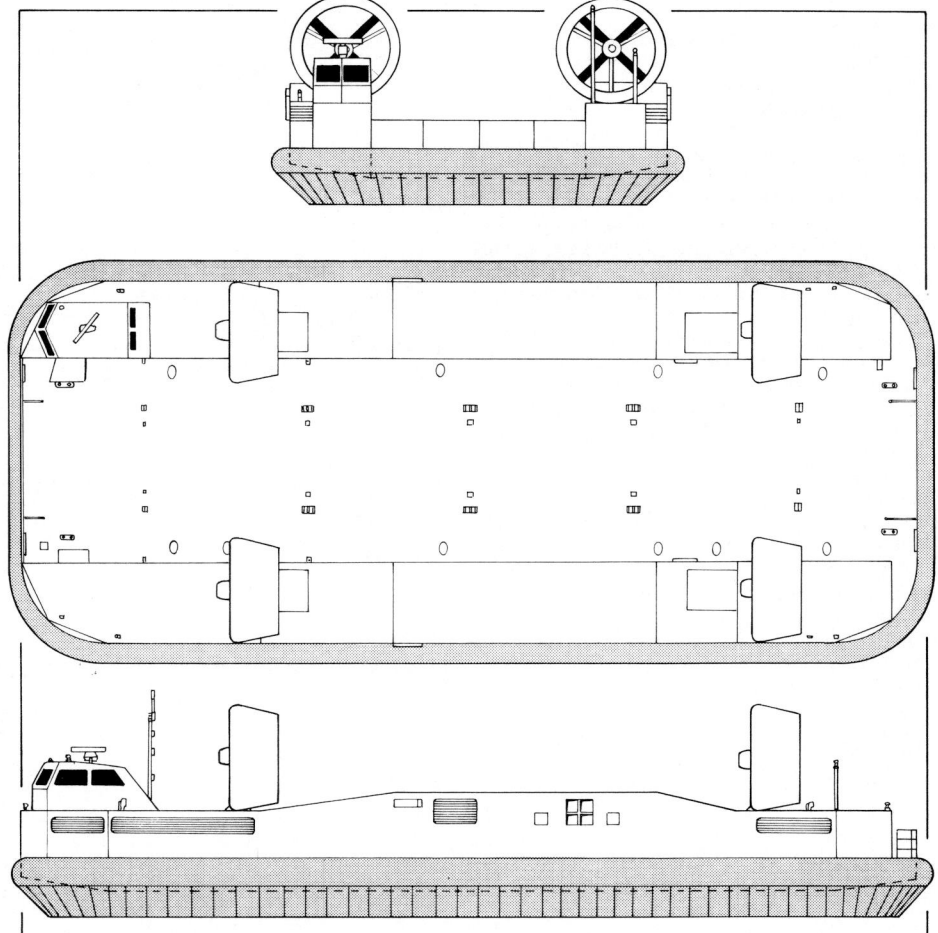

General arrangement of PUC 22

Arctic. A derivative of this design is the Vector 4, which is self-propelled and fitted with steerable outrigged crawler tractor units fore and aft. Two recent additions to this range of self-propelled, year-round, heavy cargo transporters, are the Vector 75 and Vector 200.

Details of the TAV 40, Vector 4, Vector 75 and Vector 200 will be found in the ACV Trailers and Heavy Lift Systems section.

PUC 22

Larus, the prototype of this 30-tonne capacity amphibious mixed-traffic ferry, was ordered by the Finnish Board of Roads and Waterways from the Wärtsilä Helsinki Shipyard in January 1980 and was delivered in December 1981.

The craft is designed to carry winter traffic in the south west area of the Finnish archipelago where ice precludes the use of conventional ferries. It will carry up to 16 light motor vehicles or two buses or one heavy lorry and 50 passengers.

Although *Larus* has been developed for use as a ro-ro ferry, a variety of other offshore applications are under consideration.

LIFT AND PROPULSION: Integrated system powered by four high-speed marine diesels, each rated at 650kW. The engines are mounted one forward and one aft in each of the two sidestructures. Each diesel drives, via a main gearbox, either one or two centrifugal fans and, via a bevel gear and vertical shaft, a four-bladed pylon-mounted ducted controllable-pitch propeller.

CONTROLS: Each propeller pylon rotates to provide both propulsion and directional control.

HULL: Built in marine grade aluminium. Buoyancy raft type structure with port and starboard longitudinal sidestructures. Each sidestructure contains two diesels, one forward, one aft, together with their associated fans, ducted propellers, transmission and auxiliary power systems. Hydraulically operated bow and stern loading ramps provide roll-on, roll-off through loading facilities.

SKIRT: 1m (3ft 3in) deep bag and segment type.

ACCOMMODATION: All controls are in a raised bridge well forward on the starboard superstructure. Passengers are seated amidships in two 25-seat cabins, one in each sidestructure.

DIMENSIONS
Length overall: 33m (108ft 3in)
  hull: 32m (105ft)
Beam overall: 14·7m (48ft 3in)
  hull: 13·5m (44ft 3·5in)
Height overall: 8·2m (26ft 11in)
  hull side: 1m (3ft 3in)
Main deck: 25m × 7m (82ft × 23ft)
WEIGHTS
Useful load: 25 tonnes
PERFORMANCE
Speed over water: 25 knots
Clearance height: 1m (3ft 3in)

ARCTIC EXPRESS

Larger craft are under development employing a similar design configuration to the PUC 22 but capable of carrying much heavier loads. Arctic Express is a diesel-powered, mixed-traffic ferry with a payload capacity of 70 tonnes.

The hull is based on a buoyancy raft structure with port and starboard side structures. Each longitudinal structure contains two diesels, one forward driving the lift fan system, and one aft which drives a four-bladed, ducted controllable-pitch propeller.

All controls are in a raised bridge amidships above the starboard superstructure. Passengers are seated amidships in two cabins, one in each sidestructure.

The skirt is of bag and segment type, surrounded by an anti-spray apron.

DIMENSIONS
Length: 35m
Beam: 17m
Width across deck: 8·9m
WEIGHTS
Payload: 70 tonnes
PERFORMANCE
Cruising speed: 34 knots, approx

Larus, first of PUC 22 series

PUC 22

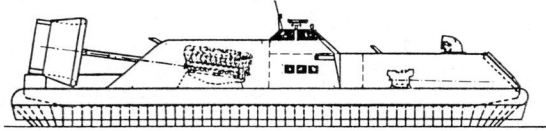
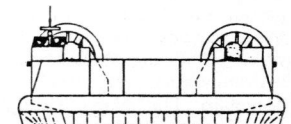

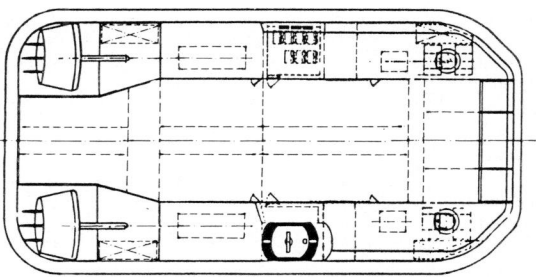

Arctic Express

FIJI

A Fijian company has been licensed to build 9- and 15-seat versions of the Jorg TAF VIII-3 Skimmerfoil. The first craft are under construction and it is understood that they will provide high-speed passenger ferry services between the islands.

FRANCE

SOCIÉTÉ BERTIN & CIE

BP 3, 78370 Plaisir, France
Telephone: (3) 056 25 00
Telex: 696231
Officials:
Eric Barsalou, *President, Director General*
Michel Perineau, *Director General*
Georges Mordchelles-Regnier, *Director General*

Société Bertin & Cie has been engaged in developing the Bertin principle of separately fed multiple plenum chambers surrounded by flexible skirts since 1956. A research and design organisation, the company employs a staff of more than 500, mainly scientists and design engineers who are involved in many areas of industrial research, including air cushion techniques and applications.

SEDAM was originally responsible for developing the Naviplane and Terraplane vehicles but this responsibility has now passed to IFREMER (see later entry in this section). The Bertin principle of multiple air cushions has also led to the development of the Aérotrain high-speed tracked transport system (see entry in the Tracked Skimmers section) and to numerous applications in the area of industrial handling and aeronautics. These applications, developed by Bertin, are described in the sections devoted to Air Cushion Applicators, Conveyors and Pallets in this edition, and Air Cushion Landing Systems in *Jane's Surface Skimmers 1980* and earlier editions.

GEORGES HENNEBUTTE

Société d'Exploitation et de Développement des Brevets Georges Hennebutte

Head Office: 43 avenue Foch, 64200 Biarritz, France

Works: 23 impasse Labordotte, 64200 Biarritz, France

Telephone: 23 03 70
Telex: 22128

Official:
G Hennebutte, *Managing Director*

Etablissements G Hennebutte was founded in 1955 to design and build inflatable dinghies. Its Espadon series of sports craft is used extensively by French lifeguard patrols and the French Navy.

The Espadon 422 is the only inflatable craft to have crossed the Etal Barrier.

Development of the Espadon to meet a range of special requirements led to the construction of a number of experimental craft, including one equipped with foils, one with hydroskis and a third with an inflatable parasol delta wing for aerodynamic lift. Several of these have been described and illustrated in earlier editions of *Jane's Surface Skimmers*.

Georges Hennebutte's latest released craft is a further variant of the Espadon 422 inflatable sports craft equipped with hydroskis, wings and an air-propeller for thrust. A preliminary description of this project, designated the Etel 422 Swordfish, will be found in the Hydrofoils section of this edition.

L'INSTITUT FRANÇAIS DE RECHERCHE POUR L'EXPLOITATION DES MERS (IFREMER)

66 avenue d Iéna, 75116 Paris, France
Telephone: 723 55 28
Telex: 610775F

IFREMER has been given the responsibility of handling the patents previously held by SEDAM and all future business activity and development of Naviplane and Terraplane vehicles.

Z O ORLEY

1 allée du Capitaine Dupont, 94260 Fresnes, France

GLIDERCRAFT

Z O Orley and Ivan Labat have designed a range of lightweight recreational craft employing the glidercraft air cushion system invented by M Orley. The object of the system is to reduce the loss of cushion air by fully skirted vehicles when crossing uneven surfaces.

Beneath the hard structure of the glidercraft is an air cushion chamber in rubberised fabric, the base of which is divided into a number of small cell compartments. Each cell is equipped at the lower end with a perforated shutter.

A short surface sensor protruding beneath each shutter is designed to open up, to deliver cushion air fully, whenever the cell encounters an obstacle rising above the general plane of the reaction surface, and reduce cushion air delivery when crossing a hollow.

A design study is being undertaken for a small commercial craft for operations in South America to carry twelve passengers and freight.

M Orley and his partner will build to order commercial and military prototypes employing his system for use over arctic and tropical terrain. Illustrations of a dynamic model incorporating the glidercraft air cushion system appeared in *Jane's Surface Skimmers 1973-74* and earlier editions.

DCN (DIRECTION DES CONSTRUCTIONS NAVALES)

2 rue Royale, 75008 Paris, France

Telephone: 260 33 30

Officials:
J Favier, *Le Chef de Bureau des Relations Extérieures*

The Délégation Générale pour l'Armament has been engaged in full-scale research into SES (known in France as Navir à Effet de Surface à quilles latéral (NES/AQL)) technology. As part of an overall plan to meet the needs of the French Navy from 1995 onwards, DCN has been studying a project for an SES of approximately 1,000 tons for use as an ocean-going ASW vessel.

The vessel is being developed in conjunction with Service Technique des Constructions et Armes Navales (STCAN), and the French Navy has designated the project, Escorteur Océanique Léger à Effet de Surface (EOLES). The specification requires an on cushion speed of more than 40 knots and a hullborne speed of about 18 knots. The weapons fit will give the craft protection against surface and air attacks.

There will be several intermediate stages before the craft can be built and it is envisaged that the prototype development programme will

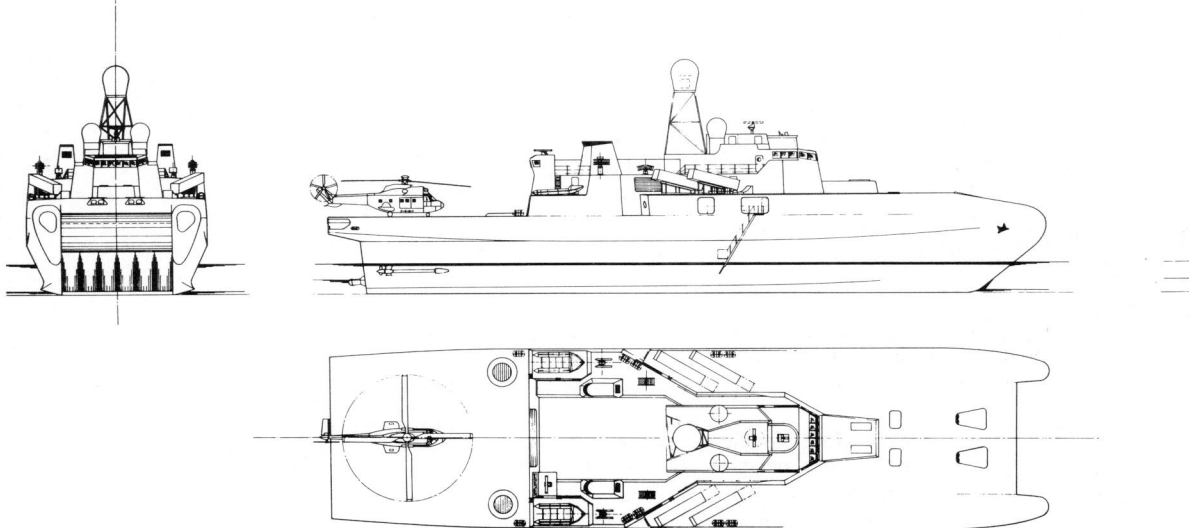
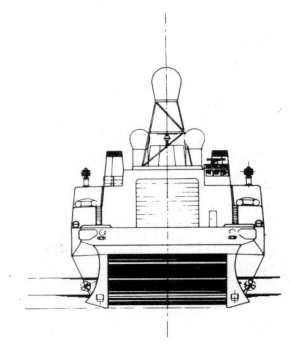

EOLES

include building a large experimental craft and designing and constructing an operational vessel of 200 tons to serve as a dynamic model of the 1,000-ton craft.

The basis of the programme is a vessel with a high length-to-beam ratio. The requirements of the craft are high speeds over choppy water, operation at speed without variable-geometry waterjet inlets and the provision of an effective ride control system to reduce heave motions.

MOLENES (Modèle Libre Experimental de Naviane à Effet de Surface)

In 1980 DCN constructed a platform of about 5 tons which began sea trials at Toulon at the end of 1981. A dynamic model, the craft is providing data for the development of multi-thousand ton SESs of high length-to-beam ratio. The purpose of MOLENES is to confirm the results obtained from tank test models, to assess manoeuvrability and to measure craft accelerations and their effects upon the structure, equipment and crew.

LIFT AND PROPULSION: Propulsion is by two 55hp waterjets. Two centrifugal flow lift fans give a cushion pressure of 1,800pa for an average flow of 4m³/s.

HULL: Two wooden sidewalls are linked by a central tubular buoyancy structure in light aluminium alloy 7020.

DIMENSIONS
Length overall: 12·1m
Beam overall: 3·43m
WEIGHT
Displacement: 5·5 tonnes

NESSIE

NES 200

Prepared by STCAN, this design study for a 200-tonne SES has two primary objectives: to confirm the feasibility and performance of the NES/AQL concept in the chosen configuration at a significant tonnage, and to use this experience for possible operational military or civil applications. The size was limited to 200 tons, obviating the need to develop the special systems and components required for larger craft. Suitable propulsion systems, lift fans and flexible skirts are readily available.

Diesel engines will be used for economic reasons. The selected tonnage provides a vessel with dimensions, performance and load capacity suitable for a number of applications. Four versions have been studied for the following duties: coast guard, fast passenger/light vehicle ferry, fast patrol boat, and crew/supply boat for servicing offshore oil rigs.

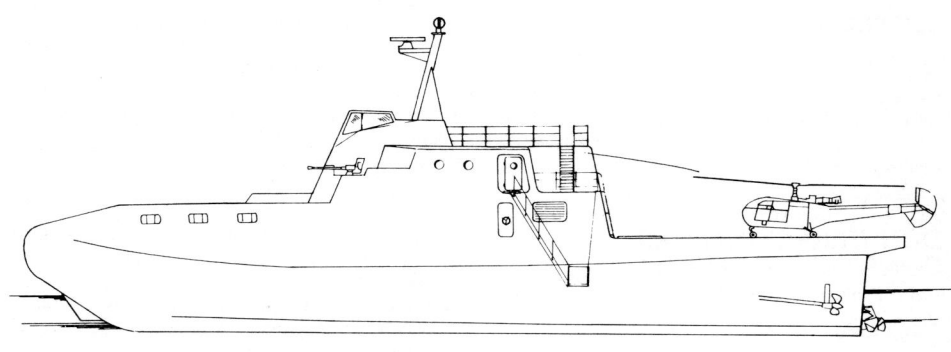

NESSIE (Navine à Effet de Surface de Surveillance des Intérêts Economiques)

A variant of NES 200, NESSIE is intended for coastguard duties and EEZ patrol. It has a length-to-beam ratio of 4·75 metres and its partially buoyant sidewalls provide 15 per cent of the lift when on cushion and fully loaded.

LIFT AND PROPULSION: Motive power for the lift system is provided by two 590kW diesels, each driving a centrifugal fan. Off cushion, the lift system diesels drive two reversible-pitch propellers for hullborne propulsion. Cushionborne propulsion is by two diesels of between 2,200 and 3,000kW, each driving a Rocketdyne Powerjet 24 single-stage, axial-flow waterjet.

HULL: Corrosion-resistant, light alloy structure. Lift and propulsion machinery, steering gear, auxiliary units, fuel and storage spaces are in the sidewalls, each of which is divided into seven watertight compartments.

ACCOMMODATION: Living, sleeping and working quarters for crew of 23. Temporary passenger accommodation can be arranged in sick bay and storerooms. Crew space and technical installations are grouped in three-deck superstructure on main upper and bridge deck. Catwalks and platforms provide crew access at each level of the superstructure.

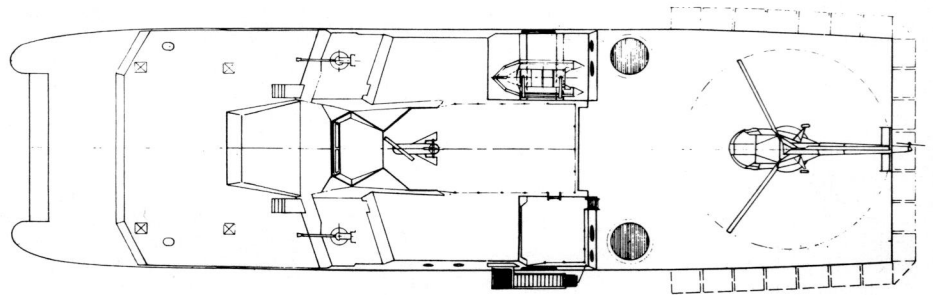

General arrangement of NESSIE

Ecureuil helicopter is housed in telescopic hangar retracting into rear of superstructure.

EQUIPMENT: Two 150hp inflatable rubber dinghies.

ARMAMENT: Manually-operated 20mm cannon, one port, one starboard, at sides of bridge.

DIMENSIONS
Length overall: 46m
Beam overall: 13m
Draught, on cushion: 0·9m
        off cushion: 2·4m

WEIGHTS
Total all-up weight: 201 tonnes
Fuel: 35 tonnes
Helicopter fuel: 10 tonnes
PERFORMANCE
According to installed power, on cushion:
Speed, sea/wind force 0: 40 knots plus
        sea/wind force 4: 30 knots
Range, sea/wind force 2: 960n miles
Hullborne
    Speed: 15 knots
    Endurance: 7 days at 12 knots

NES 200 CREW/SUPPLY BOAT

Main characteristics of this variant are as for NESSIE.

ACCOMMODATION: Main deck: Accommodation for 120 passengers with luggage; helicopter platform; deck space for rig supplies.
Upper deck: Seats for 30 to 40 passengers; accommodation for captain and second-in-command; kitchen and dining area.

FIREFIGHTING EQUIPMENT: Equipment for delivering seawater, aspirated protein foam, high pressure fog and dry powder. Two monitors, one seawater, one foam.

PAYLOAD
40 tonnes, comprising passengers, supplies, fuel and drinking water.

PERFORMANCE
Speed: as for NESSIE
Range, on cushion, calm sea: 240 miles at 40 knots
    300 miles at 35 knots
Range, off cushion, calm sea: 750n miles at 12 knots

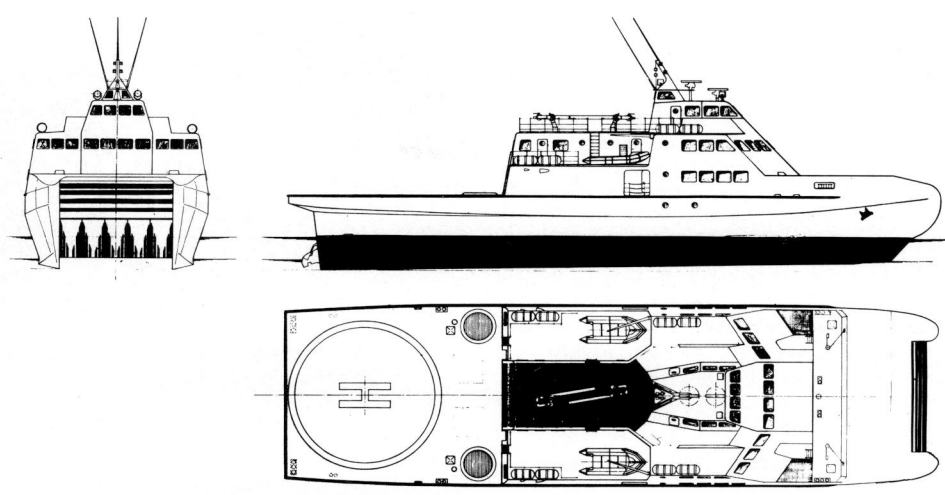
NES 200 crew/supply boat configuration

NES 200 PASSENGER/LIGHT VEHICLE FERRY

Main characteristics are as for NESSIE.

ACCOMMODATION: Main deck: Space for 20 light vehicles. Car deck in central area of craft. Ramps fore and aft for through-deck roll-on/roll-off loading. Four passenger cabins accommodate 140 passengers including luggage.
Upper deck: Cabin seating 102 plus luggage. Dining saloon seating 92. Vessel can be fitted with snack bar, two cabins for 80 passengers and self-service counter.

PERFORMANCE
Speed: as for coastguard version
Range, on cushion with 300 passengers and 20 cars: over 300 miles (40 knots at sea state 2)

NES 200 passenger/light vehicle ferry

NES 200 FAST PATROL SES

Main characteristics are as for NESSIE.

ARMAMENT: Four NM40 surface-to-surface missiles; two 40mm cannon; one twin 30mm cannon; Triton radar with CSEE Naja fire control director; two Dagaie countermeasures launches.

ACCOMMODATION: Provision for crew of 23.

FUEL: 23 tonnes

PERFORMANCE
Speed: as for NESSIE
Endurance on cushion: 900 miles (sea state 2) at 40 knots
    off cushion: 2,400n miles at 12 knots

NES 200 fast patrol SES

DUBIGEON-NORMANDIE SHIPYARDS

15 boulevard de l'Amiral Bruix, 75116 Paris, France
Telephone: 502 1220
Telex: 612921 F DUBINOR

The SEDAM division of Dubigeon-Normandie was closed down in spring 1983. The future of the N 500-02 cross-Channel passenger/car ferry was being decided at the time of going to press. A description of the N 300 and other SEDAM designs appeared in *Jane's Surface Skimmers 1983* and earlier editions.

JACQUES M THILLOY

25 rue Neuve, Ostwald, 67400 Illkirch Graffenstaden, France
Telephone: 88 66 72 83

This company offers a range of three light amphibious hovercraft in kit form for home construction. Lestes 03 is designed for cruising on inland waterways; Rov' Air for use in junior competitive events and Rov' Air Mk 2 for Formula 3 racing or waterway explorations.

LESTES 03

This craft was completed in July 1979 and is now operational. It has performed well over land and water and is on sale commercially in kit form for home assembly.

LIFT AND PROPULSION: A single JLO 198cc engine, rated at 7·3bhp at 4,500rpm, drives a 600mm diameter, five-bladed Multiwing axial lift fan. Blades have 30-degree pitch. A single Hirth

Lestes 03

twin-cylinder 438cc engine rated at 32bhp at 5,600rpm is employed for propulsion and drives, via a notched belt, a 1·1m diameter two-bladed ducted propeller. Cushion pressure of the loaded craft is estimated at 45kg/m² (10lb/ft²). The craft can carry 30 litres of fuel for cruising.

CONTROLS: A throttle lever controls the lift engine and a twist-grip throttle controls the propulsion engine. Twin aerodynamic rudders, operated by handlebar, provide directional control.

HULL: All-wooden hull built in 4mm marine plywood with wooden stringers. The fuel tank and battery are under the seat. Closed compartments along each side of craft packed with polyurethane foam provide 150 per cent buoyancy.

SKIRT: Pressurised bag skirt with separate segments.

ACCOMMODATION: Although designed as a single-seater, the craft is capable of carrying two persons in tandem.

DIMENSIONS
Length overall: 3·6m (11ft 9in)
Width overall: 1·9m (5ft 11in)
Height overall, hovering: 1·75m (5ft 9in)
    at rest: 1·5m (4ft 11in)
WEIGHTS
Empty: 160kg (353lb)
All-up weight, one person: 245kg (540lb)
PERFORMANCE
Max speed estimated: 85-90km/h (53-56mph)
Endurance: 2 hours
Obstacle clearance: 0·25m (10in)

ROV' AIR

This 2·4m single-seater is suitable for a range of leisure applications, including river cruising, touring inland waterways, fishing and exploring marginal terrain. A low-cost craft of simple design, it is easy to operate and maintain.

Rov' air is available in kit form for home building and can also be supplied as a partially- or fully-assembled structure. A wide range of completed components is offered from the engine mounting to the skirt system.

LIFT AND PROPULSION: Integrated system. A 225cc KEC two-stroke engine, rated at 12·5bhp at 5,500rpm, drives direct a 600mm (23in) diameter ducted axial fan. Air from this unit is used for lift and thrust. Engine frame is rubber-mounted to reduce vibration and entry to the fan duct is covered by a heavy mesh safety guard.

CONTROLS: Control column, which incorporates engine throttle, operates single aerodynamic rudder.

HULL: 4mm marine grade plywood construction. Polystyrene foam within the hull floor and sidebodies provides buoyancy. Highly stressed areas are strengthened with fibre glass.

SKIRT: Either a simple bag skirt made from polyurethane-coated nylon fabric or a pressure-fed segmented skirt in neoprene-coated nylon can be fitted. Each option gives about 0·15m (6in) obstacle clearance.

ACCOMMODATION: Open cockpit with single seat for driver.

DIMENSIONS
Length overall: 2·4m (8ft)
Width: 1·4m (4ft 8in)
Height on landing pads: 0·85m (2ft 10in)
WEIGHTS
Empty: 60kg (133lb)
Payload: 75kg (165lb)
PERFORMANCE
Max speed, over calm water: 30km/h (20mph)
Hard structure clearance: 0·17m (6·5in)
Endurance: 1 hour

ROV' AIR Mk 2

This new compact single-seat hovercraft is designed for a variety of leisure applications including racing, fishing and cruising. It can be lifted by two people and can be carried on the roof of a car.

LIFT AND PROPULSION: Integrated system powered by a single 249cc Robin two-stroke

Lestes 03

Rov' Air single-seater

Rov' Air single-seater

Rov' Air Mk 2 during Formula 3 event

running at 5,500rpm. Power is transmitted via a toothed belt to a 600mm (24in) diameter axial fan. The pressurised air is then used for lift and propulsion.
CONTROLS: A handlebar, incorporating the engine throttle, operates a single aerodynamic rudder.
HULL: Built in 3mm marine grade plywood. Bottom of hull and stressed areas reinforced with fibre glass. Polystyrene foam within hull floor provides buoyancy.
SKIRT: Pressure-fed segmented type in neoprene-coated nylon fabric.
ACCOMMODATION: Open cockpit with single seat for driver. 10-litre petrol tank beneath driver's seat.
DIMENSIONS
Length overall: 2·6m (8ft 8in)
Beam overall: 1·6m (5ft 4in)
Height, off-cushion: 0·7m (2ft 4in)
WEIGHTS
Empty: 65kg (144lb)
Payload: 85kg (188lb)
PERFORMANCE
Speed over calm water: 35-40km/h (23 mph)
Vertical clearance: 0·2m (8in)
Endurance: 1h

GERMANY, DEMOCRATIC REPUBLIC

JOACHIM BERTOLDT

A model of the *Atlant*, a nuclear-powered ACV ferry, featured in the New Marine Transport Technology Exhibition held in Rostock in 1983. Designed by Joachim Bertoldt, an East German engineer, the vessel would have a displacement of 15,000 tonnes and would accommodate 4,000 passengers and 2,000 vehicles. With a speed of 130 knots, it could cross the Atlantic in less than two days. Thermal power of the nuclear reactor would be 1,300mW. It was stated that the ferry's size and air cushion would virtually eliminate rolling even in heavy seas.

GERMANY, FEDERAL REPUBLIC

HORST FALKE

Dasnochel 46, 5600 Wuppertal-1, Federal Republic of Germany
RACING HOVERCRAFT
This two-seat amphibious sports hovercraft was completed in 1979. It has competed in several West German hovercraft rallies, including meetings held in Munich and Bainberg.
LIFT AND PROPULSION: Power for the lift system is provided by a 9hp two-stroke ahead of the open cockpit and directly coupled to an axial lift fan. Thrust is supplied by a 40hp Hirth engine driving two ducted fans via toothed belts.
CONTROLS: Craft heading is controlled by twin rudders, one hinged to the rear of each thrust duct. Handlebars control rudder movement.
HULL: Laminated polyester.
SKIRT: Segmented skirt in neoprene and pvc coated nylon.
DIMENSIONS
Length overall: 3·4m (11ft 2in)
Beam overall: 1·8m (5ft 11in)

Horst Falke in his amphibious sports hovercraft

GÜNTHER W JÖRG

Odenwaldring 24, 6101 Gross-Bieberau, Federal Republic of Germany
Telephone: 061 62 3624

Günther W Jörg was for a number of years a constructor, works manager and development engineer for various West German vertical take-off and landing (VTOL) projects. He sees his Tandem Aerofoil Boat (TAB) concept as a means of providing fast, economical and comfortable long-distance travel. His experiments began in the 1960s with a series of radio-controlled models. Wind-tunnel tests were also undertaken and the results were checked by a computer. The first Günther Jörg ram wing, a two-seater powered by a modified Volkswagen engine, was designed in 1973, and first flew in 1974. After an extensive test programme, Jorg II was designed, performing its first flight in 1976. This incorporated more than 25 design improvements and has travelled more than 10,000km. During 1978 and 1979, Jörg designed a glass-fibre-hulled four- to six-seater, Jörg III, which would have been put into series production in Poland had it not been for political tension. The first prototype was completed in 1980. Designs are being prepared for larger and faster craft capable of carrying heavier loads over greater distances.

Stabilisation of the pitch and roll axes and maintaining the flying height of the TAB can be regulated independently by the ground/water surface reaction and therefore requires only a simple steering control for movement around the vertical axis. This basic requirement led to the development of a tandem wing configuration, the

Jörg IV Skimmerfoil

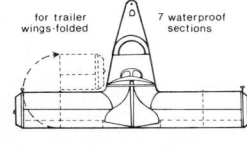
for trailer wings-folded
7 waterproof sections

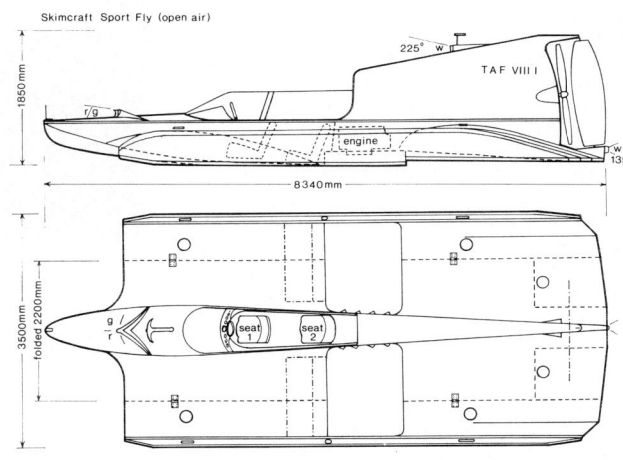
Skimcraft Sport Fly (open air)
Jörg Sportfly

handling characteristics of which were first tested on models and then on two-seat research craft. Tests showed that the tandem wings had good aerodynamic qualities, even above turbulent water, with or without water contact.

TABs have ample buoyancy and are seaworthy, even while operating at low speed (cruising in displacement condition). After increasing speed the craft lifts to the surface of the water and the resulting air cushion reduces the effects of the waves. After losing water contact the boat starts its ram wing flight at a height of 4 to 8 per cent of the profile depth. A two-seater with a wingspan of 3·2m (10ft 6in) and a profile length of 3·05m (10ft), it will have a flying height above the water surface of 102 to 203mm (4 to 8in) at a speed of 96·6km/h (60mph). The low power requirement of this type of craft is achieved through the improved lift/drag ratio of a wing in ground effect as compared to free flight.

The exceptionally high lift/drag ratio of these craft keep the thrust requirements per kilogram of weight low, thus transport efficiency is high. The ratio of deadweight to payload for the test craft is 2:1, but calculations already show that it will be 1:1 with more advanced designs; large transport craft might be 1:2. A craft of more than 300 tons would have a wing chord of 36m and fly under ground effect conditions at between 3·5 and 7m. It would have a wing span of 40m and a length of 100m, requiring engine thrust of 55,000hp (40,000kW). Cruising speed would be 250km/h from 10,000hp (7,350kW) and craft of this size could travel all-year-round over 90 per cent of the world's sea areas.

The main components of a Tandem Aerofoil Boat are: forward main wing; aft wing; vertical stabiliser and rudder; longitudinal tip fence/float; fuselage for passengers and/or cargo and the power plant. The latter comprises an engine with propeller or ducted propeller, which can be mounted as a pod on the rear wing or as a unit integrated with the rear fuselage.

Additional equipment might include a retractable undercarriage, which would enable the craft, under its own power, to run on to dry land or move from land to water for take-off. Towing connections can be provided for water-skiing and an electrically operated anchor winch can be fitted.

The following operational possibilities are foreseen:

INLAND WATERWAYS AND OFFSHORE AREAS: Suitable for rescue boats, customs, police, coast guard units, patrol boats, high speed ferries, leisure craft.
COASTAL TRAFFIC: Large craft would be operated as fast passenger and passenger/car ferries and mixed-traffic freighters.
OVERLAND: Suitable for crossing swamps, flat sandy areas, snow and ice regions. Another possible application is as a high speed tracked skimmer operating in conjunction with a guide carriage above a monorail.

TAB SIZES

Small craft, displacing 1 ton or more, can travel over the supporting surface at a height of 304mm (12in) or more at a speed of 96·6 to 144·8km/h (60 to 90mph).

Larger craft, weighing 10 to 50 tons will be able to fly at a height of 914mm to 1·98m (3ft to 6ft 6in) at a speed of 129 to 177km/h (80 to 110mph).

Coastal craft displacing more than 100 tons will fly at a height of 3·04m (10ft) or even higher.

The basic advantage of the TAB is its ability to transport passengers and freight far quicker than conventional ship, rail or road transport. The ratio between empty weight and service load is about 2:1 but can certainly be improved. Fuel consumption is 80 to 85 per cent lower than that of a boat of similar construction.

Jörg I
Total wingspan: 4·1m (13ft 6in)
Length overall: 6·2m (20ft 4in)
Wing profile length: 2·5m (8ft 2in)
Max take-off weight: 700kg (1,543lb)

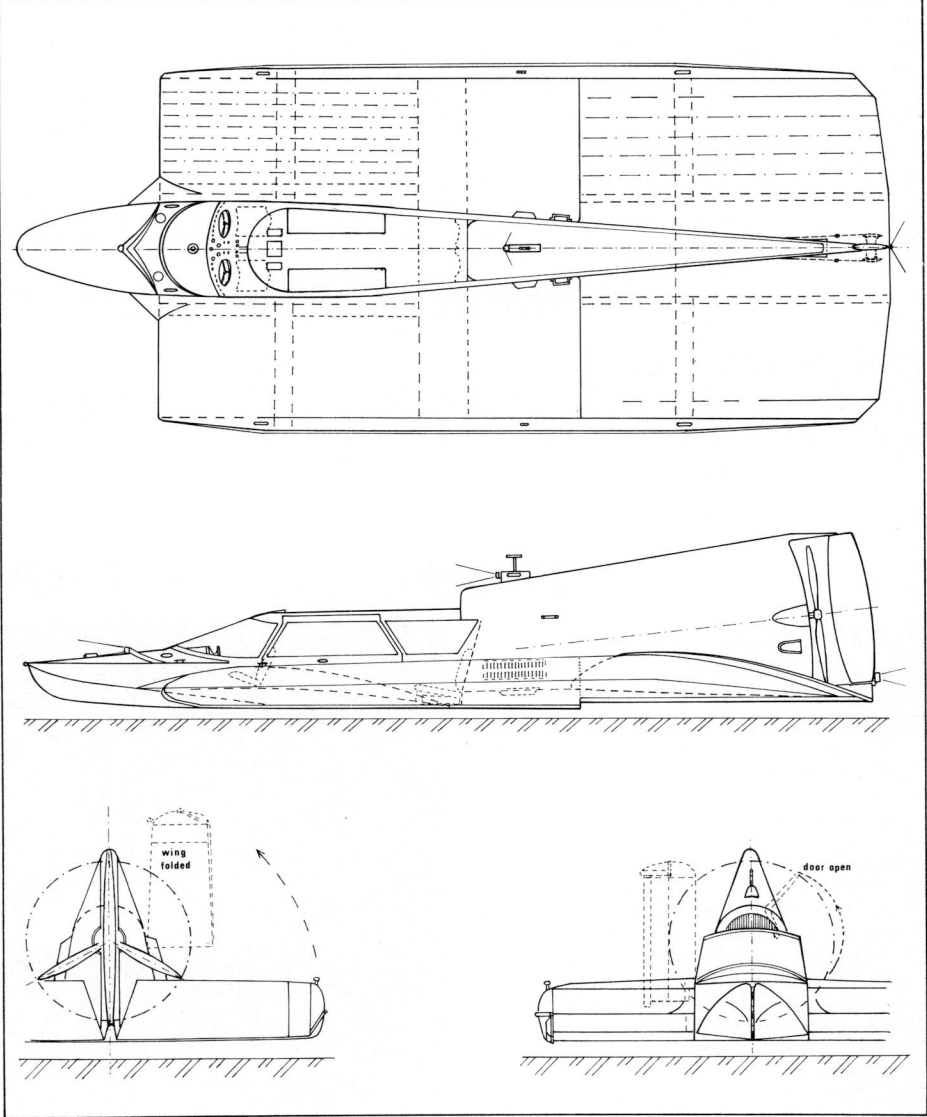
Jörg IV Skimmerfoil

Jörg IV Skimmerfoil

Passengers: 2
Cruising speed: 100km/h (62·1mph)
Installed power: 70hp
Average cruising height: 0·1m (4in)
Max flying height: 0·5m (20in)
Year of construction:.1973-74
Construction: grp/wood
Range: 300km (186 miles)

Jörg II Sportfly
(Series production model)
Total wingspan: 3·28m (10ft 9in)
Length overall: 8·3m (27ft 3in)
Wing profile length: 3m (9ft 10in)
Max take-off weight: 770kg (1,700lb)
Passengers: 2
Cruising speed: 135km/h (84mph)

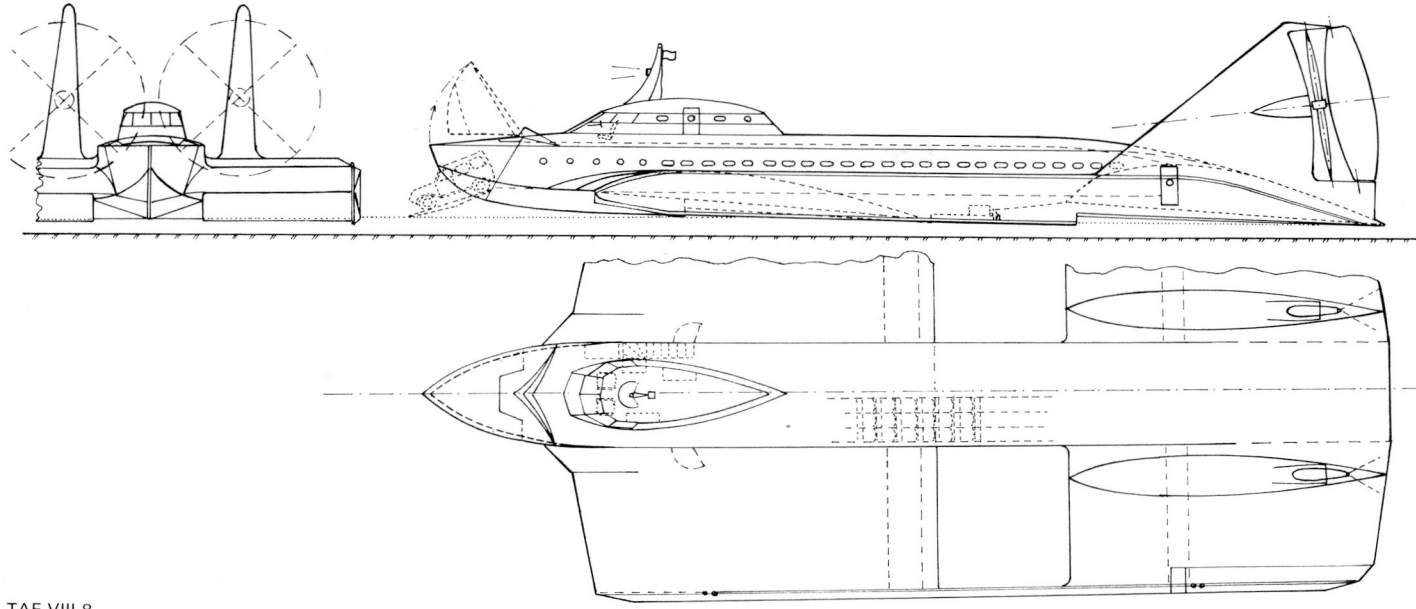

TAF VIII-8

Installed power: 105hp
Average cruising height: 0·12m (4·75in)
Max flying height: 1m (3ft 3in)
Year of construction: 1983
Construction: aluminium and fibreglass
Range: 500km (310 miles)
(with long-range tanks, more than 1,000km (620 miles))

Jörg IV

Total wingspan: 5m (16ft 5in)
Length overall: 11m (36ft 1in)
Wing profile length: 3·9m (12ft 10in)
Max take-off weight: 1,500-1,700kg (3,307-3,748lb)
Passengers: 4
Cruising speed: 127km/h (79mph)
Installed power: 220hp (3·5-litre BMW car engine)
Average cruising height (calm water): 0·17m (7in)
Max flying height: 1·2m (4ft) waves
Year of construction: 1981
Construction: Aluminium
Range: 500-600km (310-370 miles), 4-4·75 hours

TAF VIII-3
(9- or 15-seater)
Total wingspan, 9-seater: 5·8m (19ft)
Total wingspan, 15-seater: 6·6m (27ft 8in)
Length overall: 14m (45ft 11in)
Max take-off weight: 2·6 or 4·1 tonnes
Passengers: 8 or 14 plus 1 crew
Cruising speed: 115-135km/h (72-84mph)
Installed power (take-off with 2 engines, flight with 1 engine): 2 × 220hp or 2 × 320hp
Average cruising height: 0·51m (20in)
Max flying height: 1·02m (40in)
Year of construction: 1981-82
Construction: Aluminium
Range (according to installed power, speed, weight and operating height): 400-1,500km (248-932 miles)

TAF VIII-8
Inter-island passenger or passenger/vehicle ferry
Total wingspan: 16·6m
Length overall: 39·6m
Height: 9m
Max take-off weight: 60 tonnes
Passengers: 135
Crew: 3
Cruising speed: 200-250km/h
Engines: Two 2,800kW turboprops plus two 100kW high-speed diesels for harbour manoeuvring

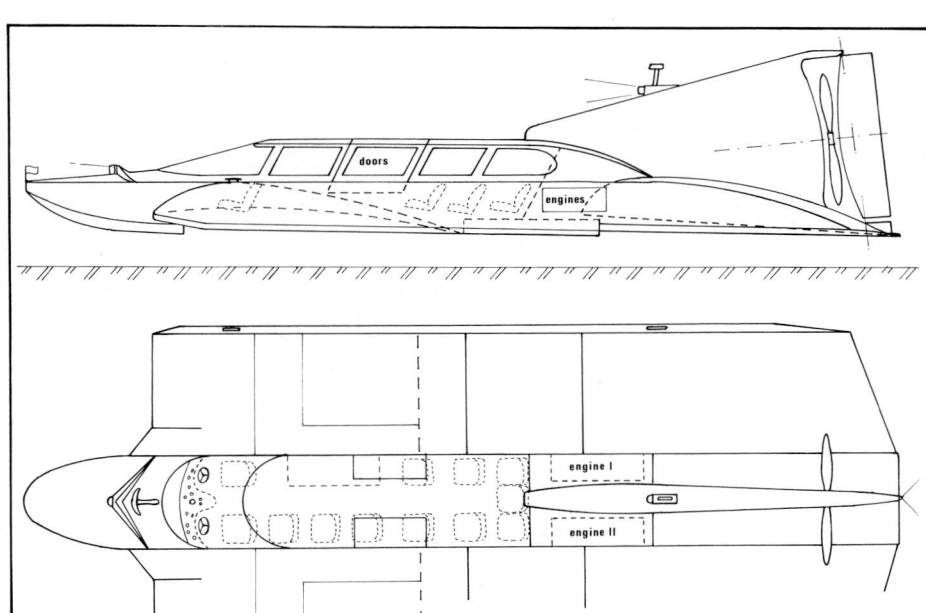

TAF VIII-3

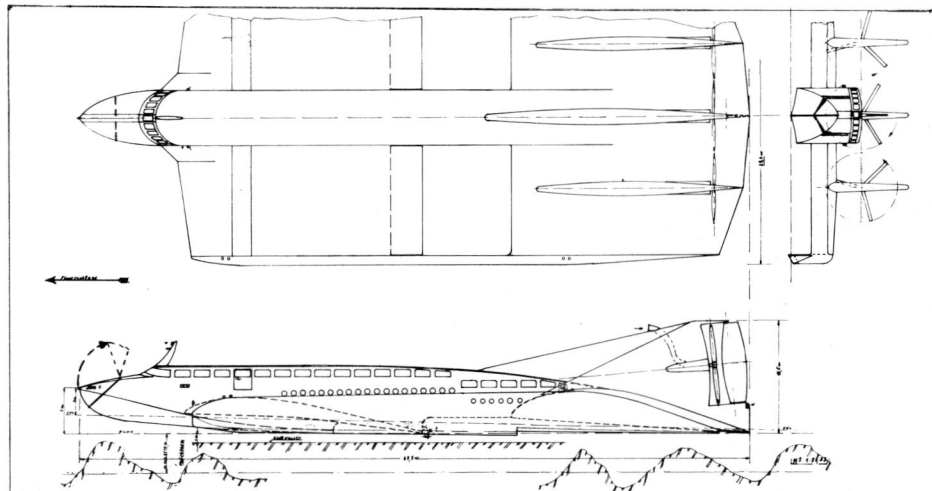

TAF VIII-10 showing how craft seeks its own stability height above rough water

TAF VIII-10
Total wingspan: 29·6m (97ft)
Length overall: 68m (223ft)
Height: 15·8m (51ft)
Max take-off weight: 120 tonnes
Passengers: 400 passengers or 40-tonne payload
Cruising speed: 175km/h (108·7mph)
Max speed: 200km/h (124·2mph)

Average cruising height: 1m (3ft 4in)
Max flying height: 3·5-4m (11ft 6in-13ft 2in) (sufficient to fly over the Mediterranean all-year-round)
Construction: Welded and riveted aluminium
Crew: Three operating crew, seven cabin crew
Range: 2,000km (1,242 miles)

RHEIN-FLUGZEUGBAU GmbH (RFB)

(Subsidiary of Messerschmitt-Bölkow-Blohm

Head Office and Main Works: Flugplatz, Postfach 408, D-4050 Mönchengladbach, Federal Republic of Germany
Telephone: (02161) 6820
Telex: 08/52506
Other Works: Flughafen Köln-Bonn, Halle 6, D-5050 Porz-Wahn, Federal Republic of Germany
Flugplatz, D-2401 Lübeck-Blankensee, Federal Republic of Germany
Officials:
Dipl-Volkswirt Wolfgang Kutscher, *President*
Dipl-Ing Alfred Schneider, *President*

RFB is engaged in the development and construction of airframe structural components, with particular emphasis on wings and fuselages made entirely of glassfibre-reinforced resins. Research and design activities include studies for the Federal German Ministry of Defence.

Current manufacturing programmes include series and individual production of aircraft components and assemblies made of light alloy, steel and glassfibre-reinforced resin for aircraft in quantity production, as well as spare parts and ground equipment. The company is also active in the areas of shelter and container construction.

Under contract to the West German Government, RFB services certain types of military aircraft and provides target-towing flights and other services with special aircraft.

The X-113 Am Aerofoil Boat was built and tested under the scientific direction of the late Dr A M Lippisch. Flight tests of the six- to seven-seat RFB X-114 have been successfully completed and after some hydrodynamic modifications, including the fitting of hydrofoils beneath the sponsons, it is undergoing a new series of tests.

In 1982, the company began an extensive weather survey to determine the potential sales for a production craft with dimensions similar to those of the X-114 and designed for operation in coastal regions.

RFB (LIPPISCH) X-113 Am AEROFOIL BOAT

The Aerofoil Boat was conceived in the United States by Dr A M Lippisch. The first wing-in-ground-effect machine built to Lippisch designs was the Collins X-112, which was employed by Lippisch to examine the stability problems likely to be encountered in the design of larger machines of this type.

Since 1967 further development of the concept has been undertaken by RFB with government backing. The single-seat X-113 has been built as a test craft to provide data for the design of larger craft of the same type.

The X-113 Am underwent its first airworthiness test from Lake Constance in October 1970.

During the first series of tests, the craft demonstrated its operating ability on water as well as flight capability at very low altitudes. These tests were followed, in autumn 1971, by a second series of trials during which performance measurements were taken. A cine camera built into the cockpit recorded instrument readings and a camera built into the lateral stabilisers took pictures of small threads on the upper wing surface for current flow analysis.

In November/December 1972 a third series of tests were conducted in the North Sea in the Weser estuary area.

Apart from various performance measurements, the aim of these trials was to investigate the machine's capabilities in roughish weather conditions. Although the machine was originally designed for only a brief general demonstration on calm water, it proved capable of take-offs and landings in a moderate sea

Remarkably good sea behaviour was shown from the outset. Take-offs and landings in wave heights of about 0·75m (2ft 6in) presented no problem. Flights were made in the coastal region,

and sometimes on the Wattenmeer, in wind forces of up to 25 knots, without any uncontrollable flying tendencies being observed in low-level flight.

The flight performance measurements gave a gliding angle of 1 : 30, which cannot be greatly improved by enlarging the machine. The relatively thin outer laminate of the gfr wing sandwich, with a thickness of 0·4mm, stood up to the loads involved in taking off in a roughish sea and also remained watertight throughout the whole period of trials.

Towards the end of the trials, in order to reduce noise and give the airscrew better protection from spray, the machine was converted to pusher propulsion.

The company envisages a range of Aerofoil craft for a variety of civil and military purposes, from single-seat runabouts to cargo transporters with payloads of up to 10 tons. As transports they could be employed on coastal, inter-island and river services. Military variants could be used as assault craft, FPBs and ASW vessels.

Flight tests, including a series performed over rough water in the North Sea near Bremerhaven, have established that 50 per cent less power is required in ground effect, enabling operations in excess of 50-ton-miles per gallon of fuel at speeds in the 90- to 180-knot range.

RFB X-114 AEROFOIL BOAT

Evolved from the X-113, this six- to seven-seater has a maximum take-off weight of 1,500kg and is fitted with a retractable wheel undercarriage, enabling it to operate from land or water.

Power is provided by a 200hp Lycoming IO-360 four-cylinder horizontally-opposed air-cooled engine driving a specially-designed Rhein-Flugzeugbau ducted fan. Range, with 100kg (220lb) of fuel, is more than 1,000km (621 miles). Operational speed is 75 to 200km/h (46 to 124mph).

An initial trials programme was successfully completed in 1977. A new series of trials is now being undertaken after hydrodynamic

RFB X-113 Am during flight demonstration over Wattenmeer

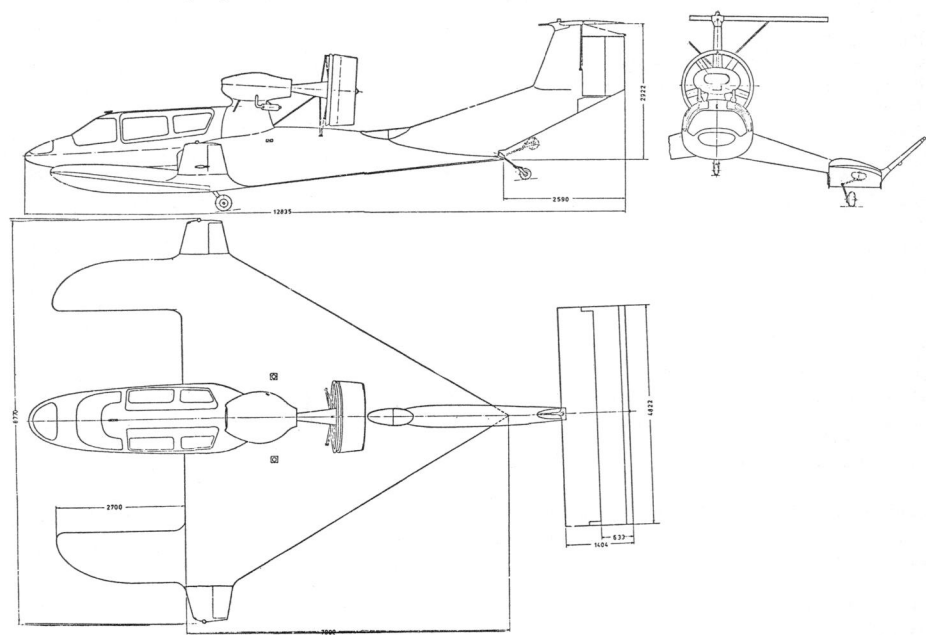

General arrangement of RFB X-114

X-114H with hydrofoils extended

modifications that included the fitting of hydrofoils beneath the sponsons, raising maximum take-off weight to 1,750kg. In this configuration it is known as the X-114H.

The vehicle is designed to operate over waves up to 1·5m (4ft 11in) in ground effect and can therefore be used without restriction during 80 per cent of the year in the Baltic Sea area and 60 per cent of the year in the North Sea. In high seas

of more than 1·5m (4ft 11in), take-off and landing takes place in waters near the coast. Flying is virtually unrestricted, providing due allowance is made for the loss in economy.

Fuel consumption costs, while flying in ground effect, are lower than those for cars. RFB states that its economics cannot be matched by any other form of transport aircraft.

Although built primarily as a research craft to

extend the experience gained with the X-113 Am single-seater, Aerofoil boats of the size of the X-114 are suitable for air-taxi work along coastlines, the supervision of restricted areas, patrol, customs and coastguard purposes, and search and rescue missions.

Without any significant new research the construction of a vehicle with a take-off weight of approximately 18,000kg is possible. On a vehicle of this size, the ratio of empty weight to take-off weight is less than 50 per cent.

DIMENSIONS
Length overall: 12·8m (42ft)
Wing span: 7m (22ft 11·62in)
Height overall: 2·9m (9ft 6·12in)
WEIGHTS
Max take-off
X-114: 1,500kg (3,307lb)
X-114H: 1,750kg (3,858lb)
Payload: 500kg (1,102lb)
PERFORMANCE
Max cruising speed: 200km/h (124mph)
Cruising speed in ground effect: 150km/h (93mph)
Max flight range: 2,150km (1,336 miles)

RFB X-114 Aerofoil boat

HONG KONG

CHEOY LEE SHIPYARDS LTD
Hong Kong

Cheoy Lee Shipyards Ltd is to construct

22·86m (75ft) fibreglass craft based on the designs of Air Ride Marine Inc, Miami, Florida. Hong Kong is also showing considerable interest in Air Ride Marine's passenger ferries which

employ a structural bow and a long, shallow plenum chamber for pressurised air in the underside. Details of these designs will be found on page 122 of this edition.

INDONESIA

LAPAN
LEMBAGA PENERBANGAN
DAN ANTARIKSA NASIONAL
(The National Institute of Aeronautics and Space)

Head Office: Jalan Pemuda Persil No 1, Jakarta Timur, Indonesia

Mailing Address: PO Box 3048, Jakarta, Indonesia

Telephone: (021) 48 28 02; (021) 48 51 25
Telex: 45675 LAPAN IA
Cable: LAPAN JAKARTA

Officials:
Air Vice Marshal J Salatum, *Chairman*
Prof Wiranto Arismunandar, *Vice Chairman*

PUSAT TEKNOLOGI DIRGANTARA
(Aerospace Technology Centre)
Rumpin Airfield, Bogor, West Java
Officials:
Dr Haryono Djojodohardjo, *Head, Aerospace Technology Centre*
Ir Jaidun Kromodihardjo, *Manager, Aerospace Technology Development*

Lapan was established in 1963 to pioneer indigenous capabilities in aeronautics and space in support of the National Five Year Plan. At the beginning of 1978, Lapan had 527 personnel, divided among the Space Applications Centre (Jakarta), the Aerospace Technology Centre (Rumpin Airfield, near Bogor), the Atmospheric and Space Research Centre (Bandung) and the Aerospace Study Centre (Jakarta).

In 1977 Lapan undertook the design and construction of an experimental hovercraft designated XH-01.

LAPAN XH-01
Lapan's first research craft is a two-seater with a moulded fibreglass hull.

LIFT AND PROPULSION: A McCullough 6hp engine drives a 70mm (2ft 3·5in) fan at 6,000rpm for cushion lift. Propulsion is supplied by two 6hp McCullough engines aft, each driving a 60cm (1ft 11·5in) ducted fan for propulsion.
CONTROLS: A single rudder in each thrust duct provides the craft with directional control.
HULL: Moulded grp with integral buoyancy.
ACCOMMODATION: Open cockpit with side-by-side seating for two persons.
DIMENSIONS
Length overall: 3m (9ft 10in)
Beam overall: 1·5m (4ft 11in)
WEIGHTS
Empty: 250kg (550·66lb)
Max all-up: 370kg (815lb)
PERFORMANCE: Not available.

JAPAN

HOVERMARINE PACIFIC
COMPANY LIMITED
Head Office: Maritime and Shipping Department, Taiyo Fishery Co Ltd, 1-2, 1-chome, Ohtemachi, Chiyoda-ku, Tokyo 100, Japan
Telephone: (03) 214 3943
Telex: J22278 (OCEANFIS)
Works: c/o Sasebo Heavy Industries Co Ltd, Tategami-cho, Sasebo 857, Japan
Telephone: (0956) 32 9125
Officials:
K Hishiya, *President*
A Okiyoshi, *Customer Service Manager*
T Nakamae, *Marketing Manager*
K Hayashi, *Sales Manager*
Hovermarine Pacific is a joint venture by Vosper Hovermarine Ltd, Taiyo Fishery Co Ltd, Sasebo Heavy Industries Ltd, and Fairfield

First two HM.2 Mk 4s built by Hovermarine Pacific

International Limited. Taiyo is a fish processing company, and Sasebo is one of the world's largest shipbuilders. Fairfield International is a private company with extensive interests in shipping. The company was established in 1976 with a capital of Y100,000,000.

Hovermarine is licensed by Hovercraft Development Ltd, an agency of the National Research Development Corporation, under various world-wide patents relating to air cushion technology.

The company imported a 65-seat HM.2 Mk III from Vosper Hovermarine Ltd in 1976. Named *Hovstar* it was in service as a passenger ferry on Lake Biwa during 1979-80.

In July 1981 *Hovstar* was sold to Fuke Kaiun Co Ltd which put the craft into service between Sumoto and Fuke, near Osaka. This is the first all-year-round service to be provided in Japan with a sidewall hovercraft.

The company's first craft, a 93-seat HM.2 Mk 4, was completed in 1978 at Hovermarine Pacific's factory at Sasebo, on the Japanese island of Kyushu. Five craft have been built and one is being operated by Saihi Kanko Kisen on a lake in a national park in the Kyushu area.

The company is also undertaking the marketing of HM.5 and HM.2 Mk 4 based fireboats, crewboats and patrol boats. Future plans include the building of the 100-ton payload Hoverfreighter, a joint technical development with Vosper Hovermarine Ltd. The Hoverfreighter, designated HM.100F, will have all the characteristics of the basic Vosper Hovermarine designs and is intended to meet the need for heavy cargo transport where limited harbour facilities exist and speed of movement is a primary requirement.

Hovermarine Pacific is currently working on the preliminary design of the HM.100F Car Ferry. Dimensions will be approximately 70 to 75m (230 to 246ft) long and 14·5m (47ft) wide. It will have a maximum speed of 40 knots, a cruising speed of 32 knots and range of 320n miles. The craft will be able to carry 350 passengers, 30 cars and 4 buses or trucks.

KANAZAWA INSTITUTE OF TECHNOLOGY

Hydrodynamic Laboratory, Department of Mechanical Engineering, Kanazawa Institute of Technology, Kanazawa South, Ishikawa 921, Japan
Telephone: (0762) 48-1100
Officials:
Mutsushige Kyoto, *President*
Shoichi Fukumitsu, *Programme Manager*
Dr Yoshio Fujimura, *Chairman, Dept of Mechanical Engineering*

WATER SPIDER II

The Department of Mechanical Engineering, Kanazawa Institute of Technology, is conducting a research programme to determine the performance potential of ACVs operating across snow-covered terrain. The programme is being conducted in conjunction with the Japanese National Ship Research Institute and Nihon University at Narashino.

In Japan the specific gravity of snow is between 0·1 and 0·5 and Kanazawa is an area which generally experiences heavy annual snowfalls. The Department of Mechanical Engineering built its first hovercraft, the Water Spider I, in 1976. An improved model, the Water Spider II, was completed the following year.

LIFT AND PROPULSION: Lift is provided by a 30hp Fuji Subaru EK-33 two-cycle, twin-cylinder air-cooled automobile engine located ahead of the cockpit and driving a five-bladed axial fan. Thrust is supplied by an identical engine driving a ducted Yashima Kogyo seven-bladed axial fan aft. Two fuel tanks are fitted, one for each engine. Total fuel capacity is 20 litres (2·64 gallons).
CONTROLS: Craft direction is controlled by a single aerodynamic rudder hinged to the rear of the thrust fan duct and operated by a handle bar.
HULL: Aircraft-grade plywood construction.
SKIRT: Bag type, 20cm (8in) deep, fabricated in nylon satin material.
DIMENSIONS
Length overall, power off: 3·9m (12ft 9·5in)
    skirt inflated: 4·12m (13ft 6·25in)
Beam overall, power off: 2m (6ft 6·75in)

Water Spider I

Water Spider II operating across 457mm (1ft 6in) deep snow in Kanazawa

    skirt inflated: 2·44m (8ft)
Height overall on landing pads, power off: 1·1m (3ft 7·25in)
    skirt inflated: 1·3m (4ft 3·12in)
Draught afloat: 24cm (9·5in)
Skirt depth: 20cm (7·87in)
WEIGHTS
Normal empty: 242kg (534lb)

Normal all-up: 250kg (551lb)
Normal gross: 320kg (706lb)
Normal payload: 70kg (154lb)
Max payload: 100kg (220lb)
PERFORMANCE
Max speed, over calm water: 30km/h (18mph)
    over snow: 25km/h (15mph)
Vertical obstacle clearance: 20cm (7·87in)

MITSUI ENGINEERING & SHIPBUILDING CO LTD

6-4, Tsukiji 5-chome, Chuo-ku, Tokyo 104, Japan
Telephone: 544-3451
Telex: JSS821, J22924
Officials:
Isamu Yamashita, *Chairman*
Kazuo Maeda, *President*
Isshi Suenaga, *Senior Managing Director*
Takashi Furuno, *Managing Director*
Taku Kono, *Managing Director, Ship Sales Department*
Yoshio Yamashita, *Manager, Naval and Special Craft Sales Department*

Mitsui's Hovercraft Department was formed in May 1964, following the signing of a licensing agreement in 1963 with Hovercraft Development Ltd and Vickers Ltd, whose ACV interests were later merged with those of British Hover-

craft Corporation. In addition, the company was licensed by Westland SA in 1967, following the formation of BHC.

The company has built two 11-seat MV-PP1s, one of which has been supplied to the Thai Customs Department; 19 MV-PP5s; four MV-PP15s and two prototype MV-PP05As.

The MV-PP5 was put into production at the initial rate of four craft a year. In the summer of 1969 the craft was put into service by Meitetsu Kaijo Kankosen Co Ltd, between Gamagoori and Toba, Ise Bay.

Since October 1971 three MV-PP5s, designated Hobby 1, 2 and 3, have been operated by Oita Hoverferry Co Ltd on a coastal route linking Oita airport with the cities of Oita and Beppu.

The company has also developed the MV-PP05A, a 2·8-tonne utility craft and the MV-PP5 Mk II, a 76-seat stretched variant of MV-PP5. Four existing PP5s have been converted to Mk IIs and one new Mk II is in service with Japanese National Railways.

MV-PP15

Developed from the earlier PP5, the Mitsui MV-PP15 is designed for high-speed passenger-ferry services on coastal and inland waterways. Accommodation is provided for 155 passengers and a crew of five. Four craft of this type have been completed.

LIFT AND PROPULSION: Two Avco Lycoming TF25 gas turbines, each with a maximum continuous output of 2,200hp at 15°C, drive the integrated lift/propulsion system. Each turbine drives a 2·3m (7ft 6in) diameter, 13-bladed centrifugal fan and a 3·2m (10ft 6in) diameter, four-bladed variable-pitch propeller. Power is transmitted via a main gearbox, propeller gearbox, fan gearbox and an auxiliary gearbox, all connected by shafting and flexible couplings. Auxiliary systems, such as hydraulic pumps for propeller pitch and lubricating oil pumps, are driven directly by auxiliary gears. Fuel is carried in two flexible tanks immediately ahead of the lift fan assemblies. Total volume of the fuel tanks is 6m³ (21·2ft³).

CONTROLS: Twin aerodynamic rudders in the propeller slipstream and differential propeller pitch provide directional control. The rudders are operated hydraulically by a wheel from the commander's position.

A thrust port air bleed system provides lateral control at slow speeds. Four ports are located beneath the passenger doors, port and starboard. A water ballast system is provided for longitudinal and transverse centre of gravity adjustment.

HULL: Construction is primarily in corrosion resistant aluminium alloy. The basic structure is the main buoyancy chamber which is divided into watertight sub-divisions for safety, and includes the fore and aft ballast tanks. Overall dimensions of the main buoyancy raft structure are 19·8m (64ft 10·5in) long by 7·1m (23ft 3·5in) wide by 0·7m (2ft 4in) high. Sidebodies of riveted construction are attached to the sides of the main buoyancy structure. The outer shell of the main buoyancy chamber, machinery deck space, the forward deck and passageways around the cabin interior, are all constructed in honeycomb panels with aluminium cores. The lift fan air intake, inner window frames and hood for the electric motor that rotates the radar scanner are in glass fibre reinforced plastics.

Six rubber-soled landing pads are fitted to the hull base, together with jacking pads. Four lifting eyes for hoisting the craft are provided in the buoyancy chamber.

SKIRT: Tapered skirt of Mitsui design, fabricated in nylon-based sheet and coated both sides with synthetic rubber. Two transverse and one longitudinal stability bags are included in the skirt system to minimise pitch and roll.

ACCOMMODATION: The passenger cabin, containing 155 seats, is located above the forward part of the main buoyancy chamber. The seats are arranged in three groups and divided by two longitudinal aisles. Seats in the two outer sections are arranged in rows of three abreast, and in the centre section, six abreast.

The four cabin entrance doors, two port, two starboard, are divided horizontally, the top section opening upwards and the lower section opening sideways. A lavatory, toilet unit, pantry and luggage room are provided aft, and a second luggage room is located forward. Lockers are sited close to the forward entrance doors. The control cabin is located above the passenger cabin superstructure and provides a 360-degree view. It is reached from the passenger saloon by a companion ladder. An emergency exit is provided on the starboard side.

The cabin has a total of four seats, one each for the commander and navigator, plus two spare ones of the flip-up type. The wheel for the air rudders, the two propeller pitch-control levers, instrument panel and switches are arranged on a console ahead of the commander; and the radio, fuel tank gauge, water ballast gauge and fire warning system are arranged ahead of the navigator.

On the cabin roof are the radar-scanner, mast for navigation lights, a siren and a searchlight.

SYSTEMS, ELECTRICAL: 28·5V dc. Two 9kW generators are driven directly by the main engines. One 24V 175Ah battery is employed for starting, and another for control. Both are located in the engine room and are charged by the generators when the main engines are operating. A shore-based power source is used for battery charging when the main engines are not in use.

RADIO/NAVIGATION: Equipment includes one 25·4cm (10in) radar, compass, radio and one 22cm (9in), 250W searchlight.

MV-PP15 showing raised control cabin, pylon-mounted propellers, lift fan air intakes and thrust ports beneath passenger doors, port and starboard

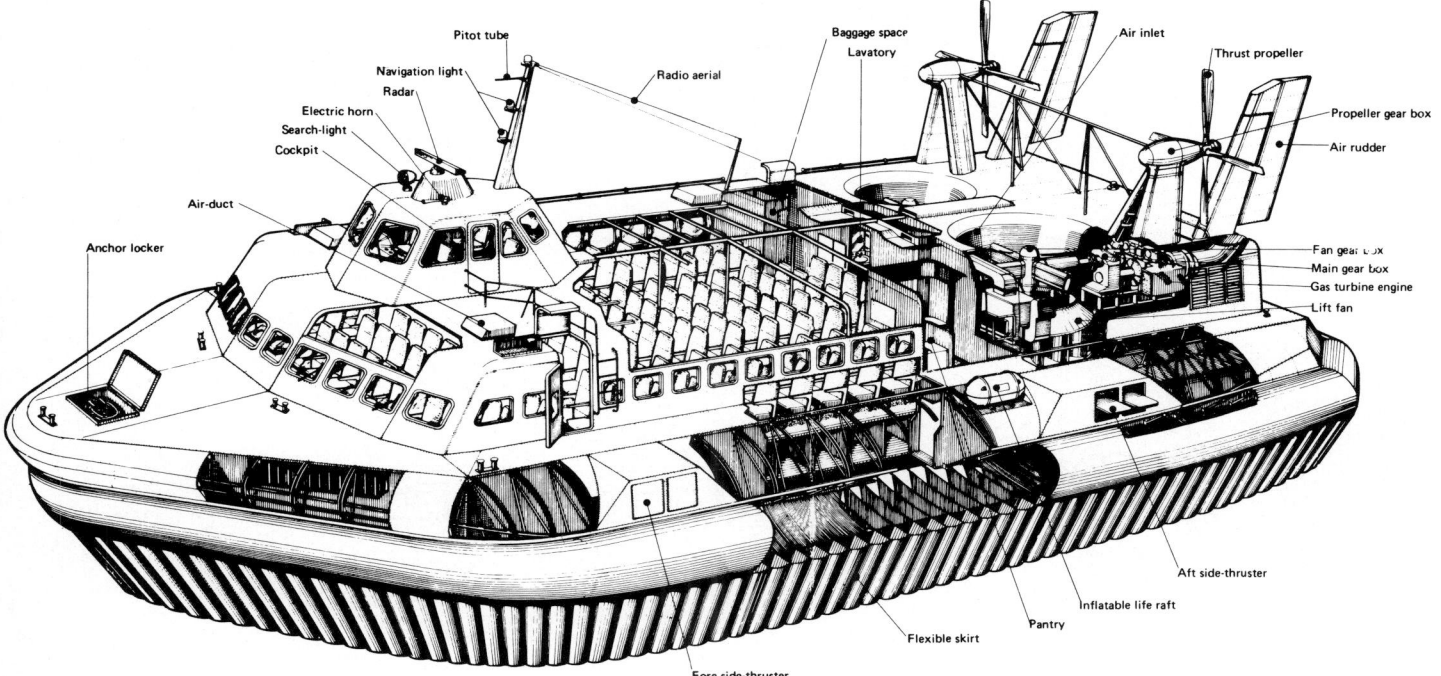

MV-PP15 cutaway

AIR CONDITIONING: Two air coolers, each with a capacity of 20,000 Kcal/h. Compressors are driven by belts from the auxiliary gearboxes and cooled air is supplied via air-conditioning ducts. Four ceiling ventilators are provided, each equipped with a 40W fan.

SAFETY: Remotely-controlled BCF or BTM fire extinguishers provided in the engine room. Portable extinguishers provided in the passenger cabin. Inflatable life boats, life jackets, automatic SOS signal transmitter and other equipment carried according to Japanese Ministry of Transport regulations.

DIMENSIONS

EXTERNAL

Length overall, on cushion: 26·4m (86ft 8in)
  on landing pads: 25·09m (82ft 4in)
Beam overall, on cushion: 13·9m (45ft 7in)
  on landing pads: 11·1m (36ft 5in)
Height, on cushion: 8·6m (28ft 3in)
  on landing pads to tip of propeller blade: 6·9m (22ft 8in)
Skirt depth, at bow: 2m (6ft 7in)
  at stern: 1·6m (5ft 3in)

INTERNAL

Passenger cabin including toilet, pantry and locker rooms
Length: 14·14m (46ft 5in)
Max breadth: 7·06m (23ft 2in)
Max height: 2·1m (6ft 11in)
Floor area: 93m² (1,001ft²)

WEIGHTS

All-up: about 56 tons

PERFORMANCE

Max speed: about 60 knots
Cruising speed: about 50 knots
Fuel consumption: about 280g/shp/h at 15°C
Endurance: about 4 hours

MV-PP5

Mitsui's first large hovercraft, the 50-seat MV-PP5, is a gas-turbine powered craft intended primarily for fast ferry services on Japanese coastal and inland waters.

LIFT AND PROPULSION: All machinery is aft to minimise noise in the passenger cabin. A single IHI IM-100 gas turbine (licence-built General Electric LM100) with a maximum continuous rating of 1,050hp at 19,500rpm drives the integrated lift/propulsion system. Its output shaft pas-

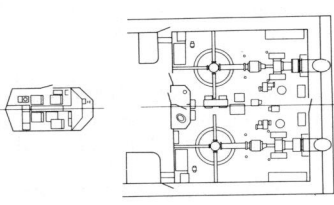
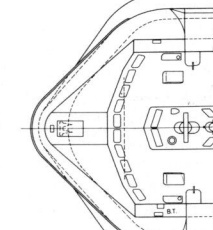
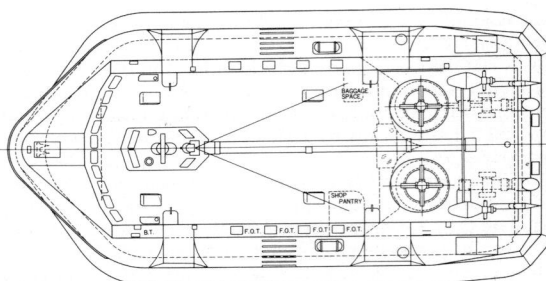
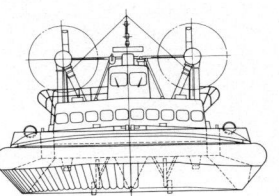
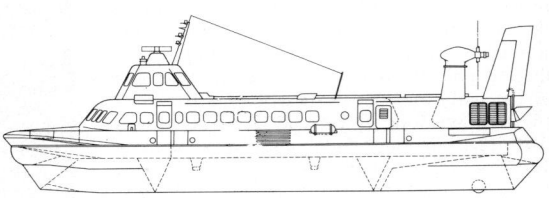

MV-PP15

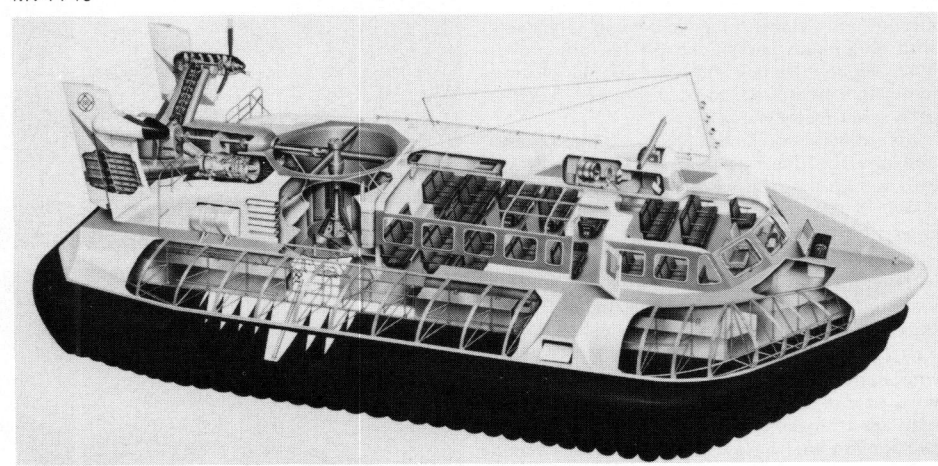

MV-PP5 showing integrated lift/propulsion system

ses first to the main gearbox from which shafts extend sideways and upwards to two three-bladed Hamilton/Sumitomo variable-pitch propulsion propellers of 2·59m (8ft 6in) diame-

ter. A further shaft runs forward to the fan gearbox from which a drive shaft runs vertically downwards to a 2·27m (7ft 7in) 13-bladed lift fan mounted beneath the air intake immediately aft

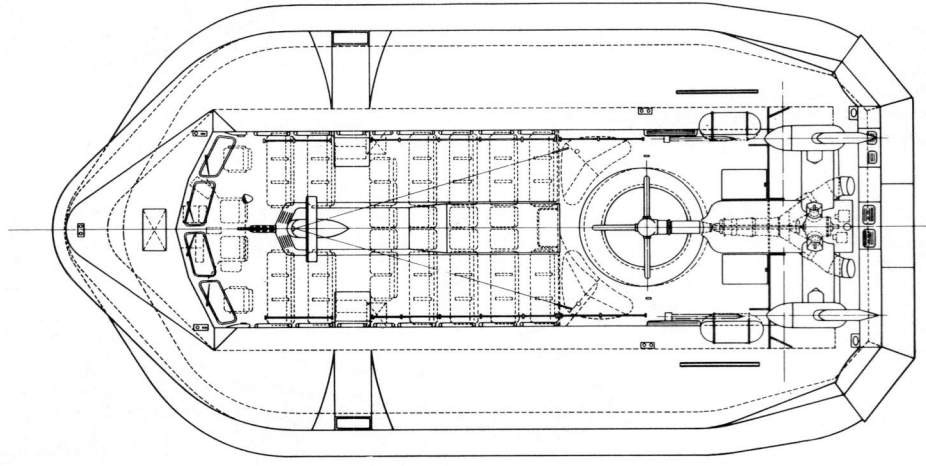

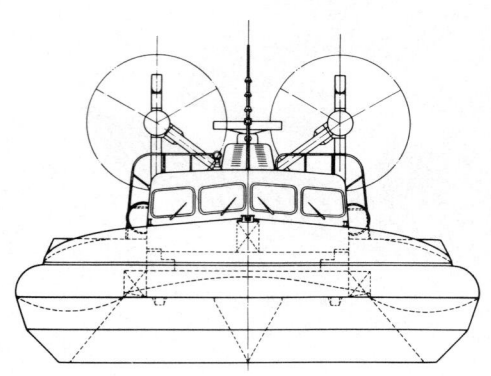

MV-PP5

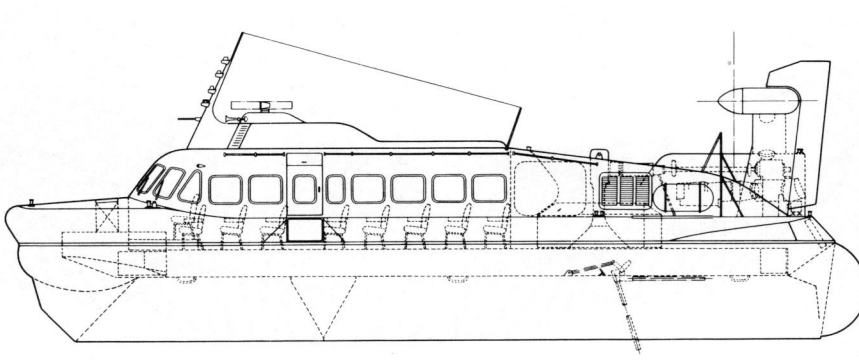

of the passenger saloon roof. The fan is constructed in aluminium alloy and the disc plate is a 40mm (1·5in) thick honeycomb structure.

To prevent erosion from water spray the propeller blades are nickel plated.

Fuel is carried in two metal tanks, with a total capacity of 1,900 litres (416 gallons), located immediately ahead of the lift fan assembly.

CONTROLS: Twin aerodynamic rudders in the propeller slipstream and differential thrust from the propellers provide directional control. The rudders are controlled hydraulically from the commander's position.

A thrust-port air bleed system provides lateral control at slow speeds. The thrust ports are actuated by air extracted from the engine compressor and are located beneath the passenger doors, port and starboard.

HULL: Construction is primarily of high strength AA502 aluminium alloy suitably protected against the corrosive effects of sea water. The basic structure is the main buoyancy chamber which is divided into eight watertight subdivisions for safety, and includes fore and aft trimming tanks. Two further side body tanks, each divided into three watertight compartments, are attached to the sides of the main buoyancy chamber. To facilitate shipment the side body tanks can be removed, reducing the width to 3·75m (12ft 4in).

The outer shell of the main buoyancy chamber, the machinery deck space, the forward deck and the passage decks around the cabin exterior are all constructed in honeycomb panels with aluminium cores.

The lift fan air intake, radar cover, part of the air conditioning duct, and inside window frames are grp.

Design loads are as required by the Provisional British ACV Safety Regulations.

SKIRT: The flexible skirt was designed by Mitsui following research conducted with aid of the RH-4 (MV-PP1 prototype). It is made of 0·8mm (1/32in) thick chloroprene-coated nylon sheet. A fringe of finger type nozzles is attached to the skirt base at the bow and on both sides. At the stern a D-section bag skirt is used to avoid scooping up water.

Two transverse and one longitudinal stability bags are fitted.

ACCOMMODATION: The passenger cabin is sited above the forward end of the main buoyancy chamber. Seats for the two crew members are on a raised platform at the front of the cabin. All controls, navigation and radio equipment are concentrated around the seats. The windows ahead are of reinforced tempered glass and have electric wipers.

The two cabin entrance doors are divided horizontally, the lower part opening sideways, the top part upwards. The standard seating arrangement is for 42 passengers but ten additional seats can be placed in the centre aisle.

In accordance with Japanese Ministry of Transport regulations a full range of safety equipment is carried, including two inflatable life rafts, 54 life jackets, one automatic manually activated fire extinguisher for the engine casing and two portable fire extinguishers in the cabin. Other standard equipment includes ship's navigation lights, marine horn, searchlight and mooring equipment, including an anchor. The 12 side windows can be used as emergency exits and are made of acrylic resin.

SYSTEMS, ELECTRICAL: Two 2kW, 28·5V ac/dc generators driven by belts from the main gearbox. One 24V, 100Ah battery for engine starting.

PNEUMATIC SYSTEMS: A 4·7-7kg/cm² (56·8-99·5lb/in²) pneumatic system for thrust port operation.

COMMUNICATIONS AND NAVIGATION: Equipment includes a radio and radar.

DIMENSIONS
EXTERNAL
Length overall: 16m (52ft 6in)
Beam overall: 8·6m (28ft 2in)
Height overall on landing pad: 4·81m (15ft 9in)
Skirt depth: 1·2m (3ft 11in)

Draught afloat: 0·2m (8in)
Cushion area: 88m² (741ft²)
INTERNAL
Cabin
Length: 7·1m (23ft 4in)
Max width: 3·8m (12ft 6in)
Max height: 1·9m (6ft 3in)
Floor area: 26m² (280ft²)
Doors:
Two 0·65 × 1·4m (2ft 1·5in × 4ft 6in), one each side of cabin
Baggage-hold volume: 0·6m³ (24ft³)
WEIGHTS
Normal all-up: 16·3 tons
Normal payload: 4·3 tons
PERFORMANCE
Max speed, calm water: 102km/h (55 knots)
Cruising speed, calm water: 83km/h (45 knots)
Still air range and endurance at cruising speed: about 160n miles, 4 hours approx
Vertical obstacle clearance: 0·6m (2ft) approx

MV-PP5 Mk II

This is a stretched version of the MV-PP5 fast passenger ferry. Lift and propulsion systems and power arrangements are identical to those of the standard MV-PP5, but the hull has been lengthened by 2·18m (7ft 2in) raising the maximum passenger seating capacity from 52 to 76. Maximum speed in calm water is 52 knots. Endurance and cruising speeds are unaffected.

Four PP5s have been converted to Mk II configuration and one newly built Mk II is in service with Japanese National Railways.

DIMENSIONS
Length overall: 18·18m (59ft 7in)
Beam overall: 8·6m (28ft 2in)
Height overall on landing pad to top of mast: 4·81m (15ft 9in)
Skirt depth: 1·2m (3ft 11in)
Draught afloat: 0·2m (8in)
Cushion area: 104m² (1,120ft²)
WEIGHTS
Normal all-up: 19·3 tons
Normal payload: 7·2 tons
PERFORMANCE
Max speed, calm water: approx 52 knots
Cruising speed, calm water: approx 45 knots
Endurance at cruising speed: approx 4 hours
Passenger capacity, max: 76

MV-PP5 Mk II

MV-PP5 02 *Hakucho No 2* in service with Meitetsu Kaijo Kankosen KK

MV-PP5 02 *Hakucho No 2*

MV-PP1

The MV-PP1 is a small peripheral jet ACV built for river and coastal services and fitted with a flexible skirt. It seats a pilot and ten passengers and cruises at 40 knots.

Two craft of this type have been built to date: the prototype, which was completed in July 1964 and has been designated RH-4, and the first production model, the PP1-01.

The latter was sold to the Thai Customs Department for service in the estuary of the Menam Chao Phya and adjacent waters and has been named *Customs Hovercraft 1*. It has been in service with the Thai Customs Department since September 1967.

Details of construction, weights, performance, etc will be found in *Jane's Surface Skimmers 1970-71* and earlier editions.

MV-PP05A

Two prototypes of this 2·8-tonne amphibious utility craft were delivered to the Japanese National Polar Research Institute expedition in Antarctica early in 1981. The expansion of expeditions in Antarctica has led to a greater need for a safe and rapid means of surface transport, for personnel and supplies, over floating ice and crevassed areas. One consideration was that ACVs would be less expensive to operate than helicopters and also less affected by adverse weather conditions. A unique feature of the MV-PP05A is the provision of an auxiliary propulsion system thought to be used for climbing slopes and attaining high speeds.

The two prototypes are considered as research craft only, but they are expected to lead to the design of a larger machine which will combine the duties of cargo and personnel carrier.

LIFT AND PROPULSION: Integrated system powered by a single 1,990cc Nissan GA 135 petrol engine rated at 90kW at 5,000rpm. Power is transmitted to two transverse shafts at the opposite ends of which are two 13-blade centrifugal lift fans. Air is fed downwards into the cushion and backwards through airjet ducts for propulsion. Auxiliary propulsion is supplied by two pylon-mounted, fixed-pitch free-air propellers at the rear of the fan volutes. These are powered by two 1,584cc Volkswagen VW 126A automotive engines, each rated at 33kW at 3,600rpm.
CONTROLS: Craft heading is controlled by interconnected rudder vanes set in the airjet ducts aft. The airflow is deflected forwards for braking and reversing by reversible vanes.
SKIRT: Peripheral loop segment type, 0·6m (2ft) deep. Cushion pressure is 1·3k Pa.
DIMENSIONS
SKIRT INFLATED
Length: 8·1m (26ft 7in)
Beam: 4·8m (15ft 9in)
Height: 3·5m (11ft 6in)
WEIGHTS
All-up, with payload: 2·8 tonnes
Payload: 0·6 tonne
PERFORMANCE
Max speed, across ice: 55km/h (34mph)

MV-PP05A polar terrain test craft

NIHON UNIVERSITY, NARASHINO

Aerodynamics Section, Nihon University at Narashino, 7-1591 Narashinodai, Funabashi, Chiba-Ken, Japan
Telephone: 0474 66 1111 4
Officials:
Masahiro Mino, *Senior Director*
Toyoaki Enda, *Director*

The Aerodynamics Section of the Physical Science Laboratory, Nihon University, is conducting an extensive ACV research programme, which includes the construction and test of four small experimental craft: the Pastoral light amphibious single-seater; the Mistral, propelled by either waterscrew or waterjet; the Floral, a two-seat sidewall craft; and the N 73.

An air boat, the Ripple, is employed as a chase craft to record on film the behaviour of these light ACVs over water.

Nihon University's ACV design group works in close co-operation with similar groups at the Institute of Technology, Ashikaga, and the University of Aoyama Gakuin. Pastoral, in modified form, is now being employed in a research programme conducted by the Institute of Technology, Ashikaga.

The LJ-10 Jimny, a combined ground effect machine and wheeled vehicle, has been completed by Nihon in conjunction with Aoyama Gakuin University.

FLORAL 1

This experimental two-seater was completed in February 1971 and was the first sidewall craft to be built in Japan. In calm water the performance has proved to be superior to that of standard displacement runabouts of similar size and output. The craft was reconstructed in 1972 when the twin outboard propulsion units were replaced by a single unit and a new stern skirt and trim flaps were introduced. Instrumentation includes trim, roll angle and speed indicators and gauges for measuring pressure in the plenum chamber.
LIFT AND PROPULSION: Lift is provided by a single 8hp ZD-305 two-cycle single-cylinder air-cooled engine, located aft of the open cockpit and driving an F S Anderson 710-20-3L plastic

fan. Propulsion is provided by a single Penta 550 outboard engine driving a waterscrew.
CONTROL: Engine/propeller unit turns for steering.
DIMENSIONS
Length overall: 5·2m (17ft 1in)
Beam overall: 1·8m (5ft 11in)
Height overall: 0·8m (2ft 7·5in)
WEIGHTS
Normal gross: 540kg (1,191lb)
PERFORMANCE
Max speed, over calm water: 62·7km/h (39mph)
 0·4m (16in) waves: 52·1km/h (32mph)

Floral 1 two-seater sidewall ACV

Mistral 2

MISTRAL 2

Developed jointly by Nihon University, Masahiro Mino and the Institute of Technology, Ashikaga, the Mistral 2 is an experimental waterscrew-propelled single-seater derived from the SEA-NAC.
LIFT AND PROPULSION: A single 8hp Fuji ES-162DS two-cycle single-cylinder air-cooled engine, mounted immediately aft of the cockpit, drives a 580mm (22·87in) S11-03-FS03 five-bladed aluminium alloy fan for lift. Propulsion is supplied by either a 22hp Fuji KB-2 or 50hp Mercury 500 driving a waterscrew.

HULL: Moulded glass fibre, with inflated fabric-reinforced neoprene sidebody/skirt.
CONTROLS: Engine/propeller unit turns for steering.
DIMENSIONS
Length overall: 4·1m (13ft 5in)
Beam overall: 1·8m (5ft 11in)
Height overall: 1·09m (3ft 7in)
WEIGHTS
Normal gross: 310kg (664lb)
PERFORMANCE
Max speed, over calm water: 67·5 km/h (42mph)
0·6m (2ft) waves: 45·5km/h (28mph)

N 73

This experimental single-seater has attained 90km/h (55mph) over water and 60km/h (37mph) during trials over land.
LIFT AND PROPULSION: A single 13hp Daihatsu two-cycle, single-cylinder, air-cooled engine immediately ahead of the cockpit drives a 560mm (22in) diameter Multiwing fan for lift. Propulsion is supplied by a 40hp Xenoah G44B two-cycle, twin-cylinder engine driving a 1·2m (3ft 11·25in) diameter two-bladed propeller.
CONTROLS: Craft heading is controlled by twin aerodynamic rudders hinged to the rear of the

propeller shroud and operated by a handlebar.
HULL: Moulded glass fibre with inflated fabric-reinforced neoprene sidebody/skirt.
DIMENSIONS
Length overall: 4·5m (14ft 9in)
Beam overall: 1·8m (5ft 10·87in)
Height: 1·55m (5ft 1in)

N 73 during trials

WEIGHTS
Normal empty: 340kg (750lb)
Normal payload: 215kg (474lb)
PERFORMANCE
Max speed, over water: 90km/h (55mph)
over land: 60km/h (37mph)
Range: 150km (93·2 miles)

YAHIYU AIRCRAFT CORPORATION

2-15-3 Chofugaoka Chofu, Tokyo 182, Japan
Telephone: 0424 87 1162
Officials:
Yasuhito Kaneko, *Director, Hovercraft Division*

Yahiyo Aircraft Corporation supplies amateur hovercraft builders with plans and components. It has introduced and is marketing in kit form a single-seat craft, the K-1.

K-1

An amphibious single-seat runabout, the K-1 has an empty weight of 88kg and a maximum speed of 56·3km.
LIFT AND PROPULSION: Integrated system powered by a 250cc, 2-cycle, single-cylinder air-cooled petrol engine. Power is transmitted to a 580cm diameter, 5-bladed ducted fan which supplies air to the lift and propulsion systems. Cushion area is 3·7m² and cushion pressure is 40kg/m².
CONTROLS: Craft direction is controlled by a column operating twin rudders in the propulsion duct and incorporating a twist-grip engine throttle.
SKIRT: Bag type, 20cm deep.
ACCOMMODATION: Open cockpit with single seat.
DIMENSIONS
Length: 2·9m
Beam: 1·6m
Height, off cushion: 0·84m
on cushion: 1·04m
WEIGHTS
Empty: 88kg
Max load: 90kg
PERFORMANCE
Max speed, over water: 40·2km/h
over sand: 56·3km/h
Max gradient: 18%

Yahiyu K-1

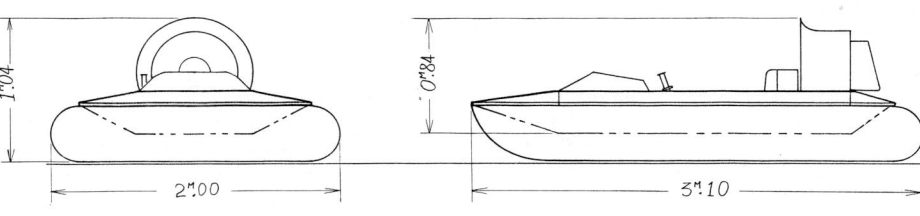

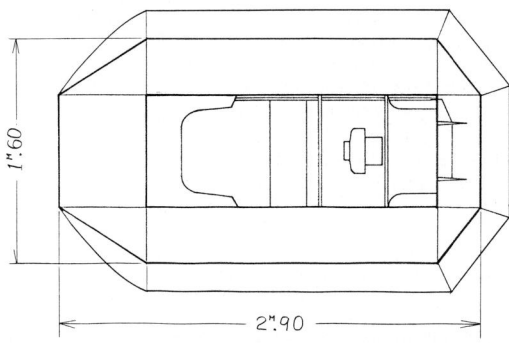

General arangement of Yahiyu K-1

KOREA, REPUBLIC

DAEWOO SHIPBUILDING & HEAVY MACHINERY LTD

Ayangri, Changsung Po, Koje-Kun, Kyungnam, Republic of Korea
Telephone: 558-4 2151-9
Telex: Dwokpo K29131-3

Daewoo specialises in the design and construction of high technology vessels, including tankers, and LNG and LPG carriers. One of its most recent designs is a 490-ton SES troop/vehicle transport.

LIFT AND PROPULSION: Four 1,080shp marine diesels power the lift fans. The propulsion system comprises two 6,000shp gas turbines driving waterjets. Two 150kW ac diesel generators are fitted for auxiliary power and lighting.
ACCOMMODATION: Facilities for carrying 250 troops and 90 tons of vehicles and cargo. A helipad is provided on the aft deck.
ARMAMENT AND SENSORS: Fire control console; optical fire director; one 30mm cannon.
DIMENSIONS
Length overall: 54·9m

Beam: 19·5m
Draught, off-cushion: 2·4m
on-cushion: 0·6m

WEIGHTS
Displacement, loaded: 490 tons
light: 290 tons

PERFORMANCE
Max speed, calm conditions: 52 knots
Endurance, calm conditions, 40 knots and 80 tons fuel: 1,000 n miles

KOREA TACOMA MARINE INDUSTRIES LIMITED

Korea Tacoma Marine Industries Limited has built a variety of fast patrol boats for the South Korean Navy since 1976. These include three 250-ton PSMM multi-mission patrol ships and four 71-ton CPIC coastal patrol interdiction craft.

In 1979 the company began marketing three metal-hulled surface effect ships for a variety of commercial applications. Lengths of the three craft are 8, 15 and 18 metres and each can be fitted with a range of alternative power plants according to performance requirements.

The company's latest designs are two SES passenger ferries: an 11-metre craft for inland waterways and a 23-metre craft for coastal waters.

TURTLE III HOVERCRAFT

This fully-amphibious five-seater has an overall length of 7·65 metres and a maximum speed of 50 knots.

LIFT AND PROPULSION: Motive power for the lift system is a single 140hp engine. Thrust is supplied by a single 175hp engine driving a 1·35m diameter free-air propeller.

CONTROLS: Craft direction is controlled by twin aerodynamic rudders operating in the propeller slipstream.

HULL: Welded marine-grade aluminium.

SKIRT: Bag and segment type.

ACCOMMODATION: Enclosed cabin with seats for driver and four passengers.

DIMENSIONS
Length overall: 7·65m
Beam: 4m
Height to tip of thrust propeller: 2·87m
   to top of cabin: 1·3m
WEIGHTS
Loaded: 2·27 tonnes
PERFORMANCE
Max speed: 50 knots

KOREA TACOMA 8m SES

This was the first of a projected series of multi-purpose surface effect craft. Passenger ferry, freight and crewboat versions are planned.

LIFT AND PROPULSION: Motive power for the lift system is provided by a single 80hp automotive engine. Thrust is supplied by two water propellers powered by twin outboards or diesel outdrive units of 80, 100 or 150hp.

CONTROLS: Craft direction is controlled by twin water rudders aft or rotation of the engine/propeller units.

HULL: Primary structure in welded marine aluminium alloy.

SKIRT: Segmented skirt at the bow and stern.

ACCOMMODATION: Choice of seating arrangements for five, ten or fifteen passengers.

DIMENSIONS
Length overall: 8·2m (26ft 11in)
Beam overall: 4·4m (14ft 5in)
Draught, hullborne: 0·6m (2ft)
   on cushion: 0·1m (4in)
WEIGHTS
Normal all-up (according to power arrangements
   and passenger load): 3·5-4·5 tons

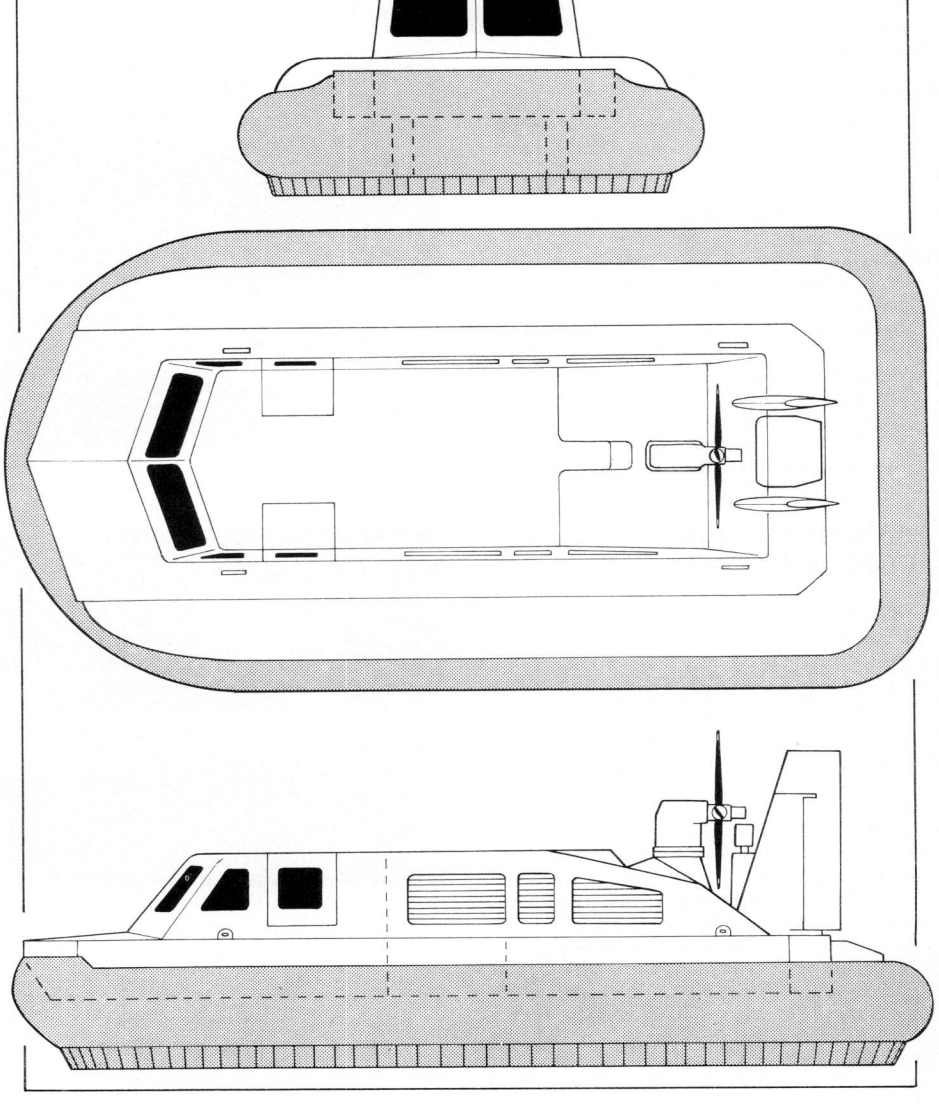

Turtle III Hovercraft

Turtle III Hovercraft

KTMI 8m SES

KTMI 11m SES

PERFORMANCE
Max speed, twin 80hp engines: 30 knots
  twin 100hp engines: 40 knots
  twin 150hp engines: 45 knots
Range: 120n miles

KOREA TACOMA 11m SES

This 48- to 60-seat high-speed passenger ferry operates at speeds up to 30 knots. It is designed for services on inland waters, in waves up to a metre high with a payload of 5·5 tons.
LIFT AND PROPULSION: Power for the lift system is provided by a single Volvo Penta MD40A marine diesel rated at 72hp at 3,000rpm. Propulsion engines are two marine diesel Volvo Penta AQAD 40/280Bs, rated at 155hp at 3,600rpm, and each incorporates stern drive units.
CONTROLS: Propeller units rotate for steering. Additional control is by differential use of the propellers.
HULL: Main structure in welded marine aluminium alloy.
SKIRT: Loops and fingers at bow and stern.
ACCOMMODATION: Standard seating accommodates 48 passengers. This can be varied from 40 to 60 passengers according to route requirements.
DIMENSIONS
Length overall: 11m
Beam overall: 4·6m
Draught off cushion: 0·96m
  on cushion: 0·65m
All-up weight: 12 tons
PERFORMANCE
Service speed, fully loaded: 25 knots

KOREA TACOMA 15m SES

This high-speed passenger ferry/freighter is capable of operating at speeds of up to 50 knots. In passenger/crewboat configuration accommodation is provided for up to 50 seated passengers.
LIFT AND PROPULSION: Motive power for the lift system is provided by a single marinised diesel engine of 200 to 300hp. Power for the propulsion system is provided by twin diesels of 350, 500 or 800hp, according to the performance required, each driving a water propeller via a reversing gearbox and an inclined shaft.
CONTROLS: Twin water rudders aft, one on each sidehull. Differential propeller thrust for slow-speed manoeuvring.
HULL: Main structure in welded marine-grade aluminium alloy.
SKIRT: Flexible segmented skirt at the bow and stern.
ACCOMMODATION: Configurations for 35, 40 and 50 passengers according to route requirements.
DIMENSIONS
Length overall: 15m (49ft 2·5in)
WEIGHTS
Normal all-up (according to power arrangements and passenger load): 17-20 tons
PERFORMANCE
Max speed, twin 350hp diesels: 35 knots
  500hp diesels: 40 knots
  800hp diesels: 50 knots

KOREA TACOMA 18m SES

The 18m (59ft) design has buoyant catamaran-type sidewalls almost identical in shape to those of the two smaller craft.
LIFT AND PROPULSION: Power for the lift system is provided by a single marine diesel in the 400 to 500hp range. Power for the propulsion system is provided by twin diesels of 650, 800 or 1,300hp, each driving a water propeller via a reversing gearbox and an inclined shaft.
CONTROLS: Twin water rudders aft, one on each sidehull. Differential propeller thrust for slow-speed manoeuvring.
HULL: Main structure built in welded marine aluminium alloy.
SKIRT: Segmented skirt at the bow and stern.
ACCOMMODATION: Seating arrangements for 60, 80 and 90 passengers according to route requirements.

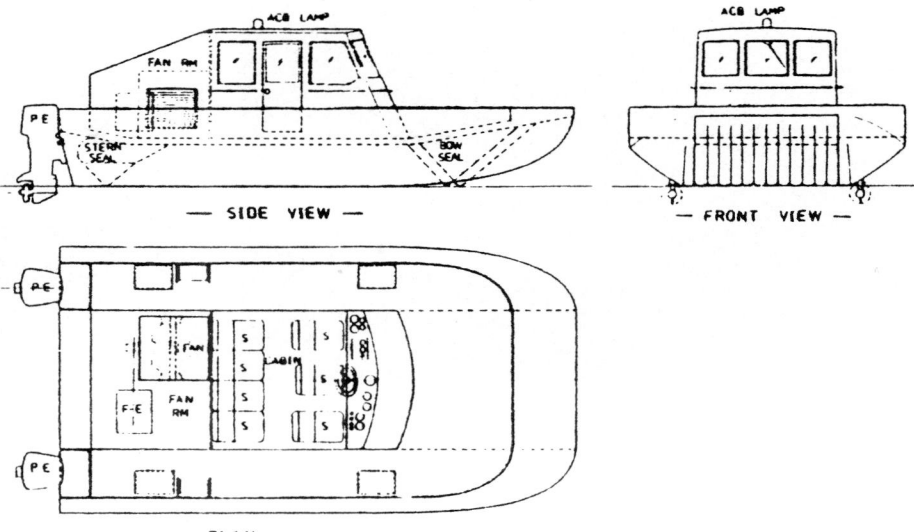

— SIDE VIEW — — FRONT VIEW —

— PLAN —

KTMI 8m SES

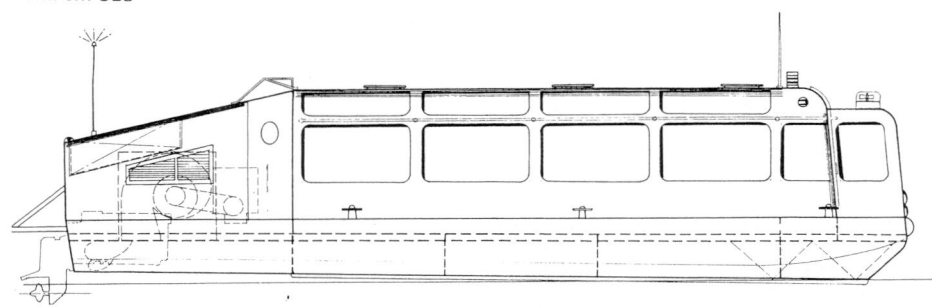

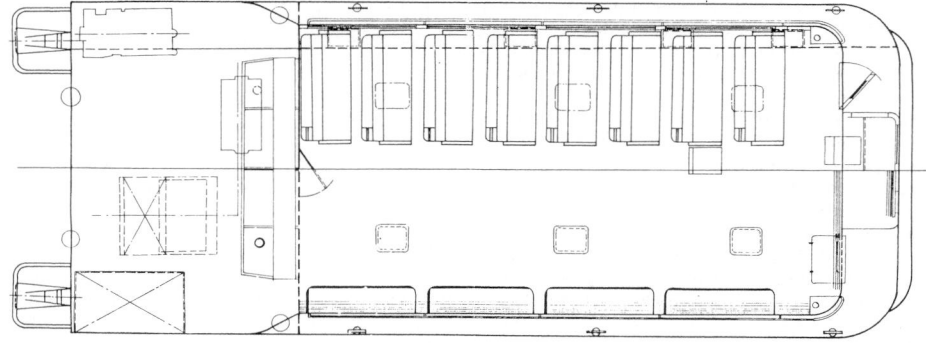

KTMI 11m SES

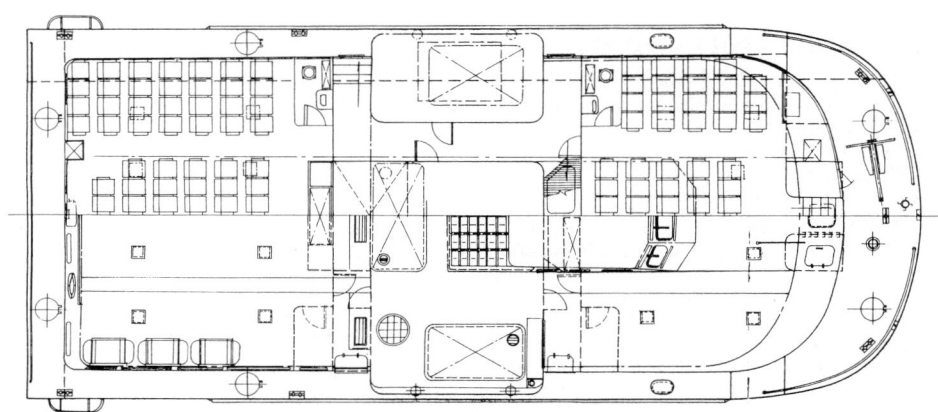

KTMI 18m SES

KTMI 18m SES

KTMI 23m SES

DIMENSIONS
Length overall: 18·1m (59ft 5in)
Beam overall: 9m (29ft 7in)
Draught, hullborne: 1·74m (5ft 8·5in)
  on cushion: 1·08m (3ft 6·5in)
WEIGHTS
Normal all-up weight: 36 tons
PERFORMANCE
Max speed, twin 650hp diesels: 35 knots
  twin 800hp diesels: 40 knots
  twin 1,300hp diesels: 50 knots

KOREA TACOMA 23m SES

The largest of Korea Tacoma's range of high-speed SES passenger ferries, this 23·5-metre design has buoyant catamaran-type sidewalls. It operates on coastal and inland waters in waves up to 2·5 metres high and has a payload of 16·5 tons.
LIFT AND PROPULSION: Motive power for the lift system is a General Motors Detroit Diesel Allison GM 12V 71TI (W/N70 injector) rated at 510shp at 2,100rpm. This drives a dual 1·06m lift fan directly to provide plenum air and, via a hydraulic pump and hydraulic motors, two secondary 0·6m diameter fans for skirt inflation. The propulsion engines are two MTU 8V 396 TB 83 diesels rated at 1,025 ps at 1,940rpm. Each incorporates a ZF BW 255 reverse reduction gearbox and drives a single three-bladed propeller via transmission shafting inclined at 12 degrees. The propellers rotate outwards and operate at up to 1,320rpm. One GM2-71N diesel generator, rated at 30kW, 60Hz, 220V, is provided. Fuel is carried in a single 3·5-tonne capacity tank.
CONTROLS: Craft direction is controlled by twin balanced HY-80 high tensile steel rudders operated hydraulically. Additional control is by differential use of the water propellers.
HULL: Main hull structure is welded marine aluminium alloy. Superstructure is in riveted marine aluminium alloy.
ACCOMMODATION: Air-conditioned accommodation for 10 crew members and 158

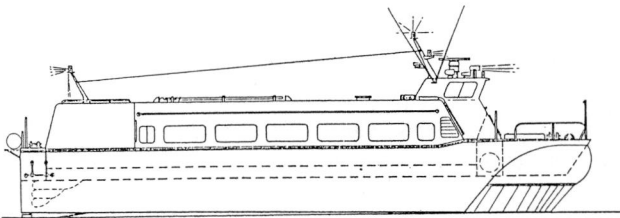

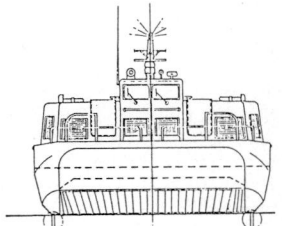

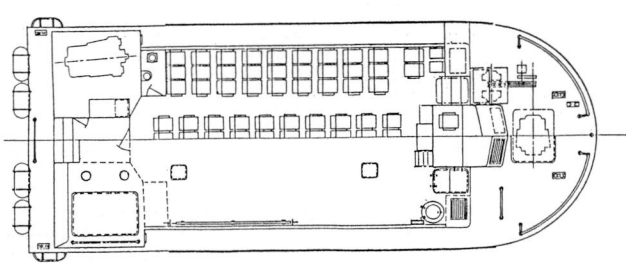

KTMI 23m SES

passengers in airline-type seating. The bridge usually accommodates the commander, navigator and engineer. Passenger access is via doors port and starboard in the forward and aft saloons. There are emergency exits in both saloons. Two toilet/washbasin units are provided plus two bars. Safety equipment includes life rafts, inflatable life jackets, lifebuoys and line-throwing equipment.
SKIRTS: The main plenum chamber receives air from dual 1·06m diameter fans located amidships. Bow and stern seals receive air from 0·6m fans, located amidships port and starboard, via ducts forming part of the superstructure. The bow skirt is made of two tailored loops joined at their edges to form a regularly-shaped inflatable compartment.

DIMENSIONS
Length overall: 23·5m
Beam overall: 10·2m
Height, overall (up to P/H top): 6·1m
Draught, off cushion, navigational: 2·46m
  on cushion, navigational: 1·45m
All-up weight: 65 tons
Standard passenger capacity, forward saloon: 68
  aft saloon: 90
Crew: 10
PERFORMANCE
Max continuous speed (fully loaded, calm water): 35 knots
Standard range (max continuous power, fully loaded): 250n miles
Standard endurance at max continuous power: 7 hours

NETHERLANDS

LE COMTE-HOLLAND BV

Stuartweg 4, 4131 NJ Vianen, Netherlands
Postbus 24, 4130 EA Vianen, Netherlands
Telephone: 03473 7 19 04
Telex: 40475 lecom
Officials:
A le Comte, *General Manager*

Mr A le Comte of Le Comte-Holland BV Shipyard has developed a sidewall hovercraft with a new seal system based on a fringe of floating, hydrodynamically-shaped planing elements hinged on the wet deck of the craft. Each element operates independently and has restricted vertical movement. Tank tests have successfully demonstrated the hydrodynamic drag and sealing characteristics of this system, even in higher sea states.

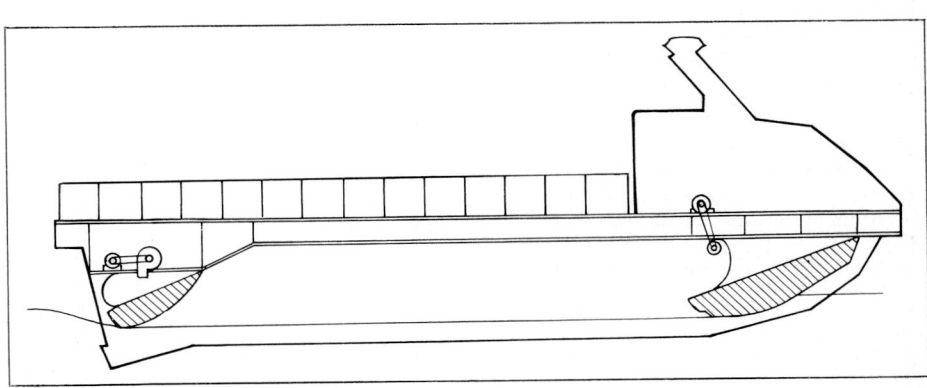

Le Comte-Holland SES air cushion sealing system

The initial cost of the system is higher than that of a flexible skirt, but its long life expectancy will reduce maintenance costs.

The segments are made from polyaramide reinforced polyester, which combines high impact strength with low weight. Low friction polyethylene plates the segments' sides, and assists vertical movement.

It is said that the immersion depth of the vessel does not affect the system, which rotates around the hinges until the lift forces are balanced by the internal restraining forces. The system is claimed to give a more accurate following of irregular incoming wave patterns and to be resistant to damage by floating objects. If the front seal elements are damaged, replacement can be undertaken without dry-docking the craft.

The project, which is backed by the Netherlands government, has undergone extensive model tests. Designs have been prepared for passenger ferries and patrol craft of 26, 34 and 40 metres, and a 40-metre missile craft is also available. A 26-metre craft has been ordered by a Middle Eastern country.

26m SES

As a fast passenger ferry, this variant will seat 160 in two saloons. In patrol boat configuration the craft has a deck area of 75m² aft of the deckhouse superstructure.

LIFT AND PROPULSION: The vessel will accommodate marine diesels, marine gas turbines or a combination of both, driving conventional propellers or waterjets. Lift is supplied by 251kW Mercedes-Benz OM 404 marine diesels, one in each of the two main engine rooms in the sidehulls. Power is transmitted hydraulically to five centrifugal lift fans, one of which supplies the stern seal. The four main fans are driven partly by the main engines and partly by the lift engines. The propulsion system comprises two 1,150kW (1,560hp) MTU 12V 396 TB83 marine diesels driving two 28in diameter fixed-pitch propellers. Fuel capacity is 6,000 litres for the patrol boat and 2,000 litres for the fast passenger ferry.
CONTROLS: NACA profiled rudders control craft direction at high speed. Differential propeller thrust controls heading at low speed. An automatic roll stabilisation system is fitted.
HULL: Built in grp, light alloy or steel. Deck/wheelhouse would normally be built in grp sandwich, including the bulkheads, for weight reduction and insulation against temperature differences. The deck combines hard grade alloy I-beams with stiffened deck planking.
SYSTEMS, ELECTRICAL: Auxiliary generating units and electrical systems available for 24V dc, 110V ac and/or 220V ac. Two Mercedes-Benz OM 314, rated at 42hp at 1,500rpm (50 cycles) or 51hp at 1,800rpm (60 cycles).
DIMENSIONS
Length: 26m
Beam: 7·5m
Draught keel, on cushion: 0·7m
  propeller, on cushion: 1·45m
  propeller, off cushion: 2·05m
WEIGHTS
Max: 61·5 tons
Light ship: 46 tons
Max deck load (patrol boat): 8·5 tons
PERFORMANCE

Cruising speed	Sea State 0	Sea State 3
on cushion	40 knots	36 knots
off cushion	16 knots	13 knots
Range:	430n miles	360n miles

34m SES

In passenger ferry configuration this design will accommodate 240. As a fast patrol boat, the craft has a deck area of 109m² for weapons and other equipment.
LIFT AND PROPULSION: On the standard version lift is supplied by two 336kW Mercedes-Benz OM 404A marine diesels mounted aft of the main engines in the two sidehulls. Power is transmitted hydraulically to five centrifugal lift fans, one of which supplies the stern seal. The four main fans are driven partly by the main engines and partly by the lift engines.

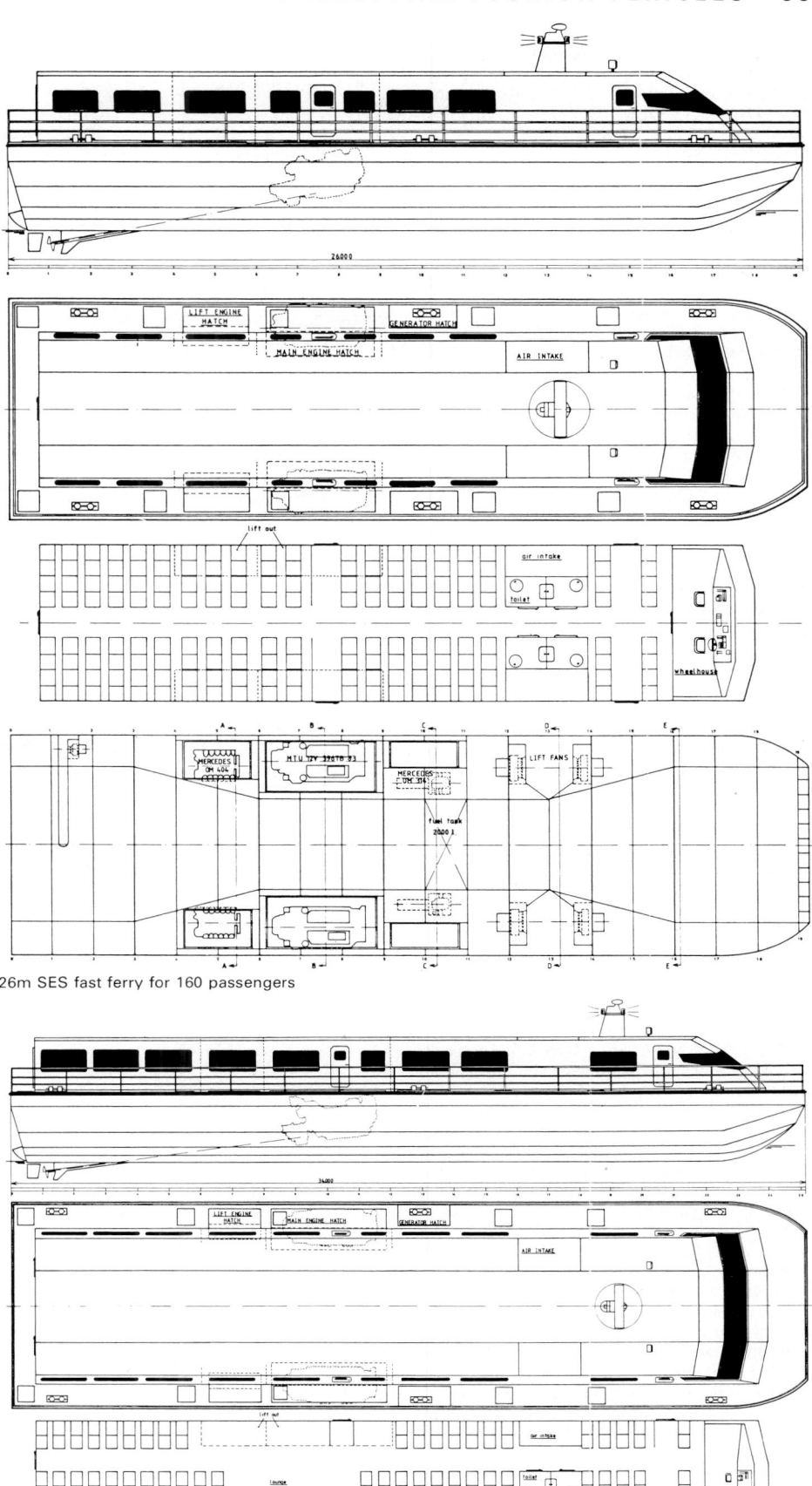

26m SES fast ferry for 160 passengers

34m SES fast ferry for 184 passengers

Two 1,540kW (2,095hp) MTU 16V 396 TB83s drive two 32in diameter fixed-pitch propellers. Fuel capacity is 8,000 litres for the fast patrol boat and 4,000 litres for the passenger version.

CONTROLS, HULL, ELECTRICAL SYSTEMS: As for 26m SES.

DIMENSIONS
Length: 34·9m
Beam: 9m
Draught keel, on cushion: 0·7m
  propeller, on cushion: 1·55m
  propeller, off cushion: 2·15m

WEIGHTS
Max: 103·5 tons
Light ship: 77·5 tons
Max deckload (patrol boat): 17·5 tons
Water: 500 litres
Fuel, patrol boat: 8,000 litres
  passenger version: 4,000 litres

PERFORMANCE

Cruising speed	Sea State 0	Sea State 3
on cushion:	40 knots	36 knots
off cushion:	16 knots	13 knots
Range:	430n miles	360n miles

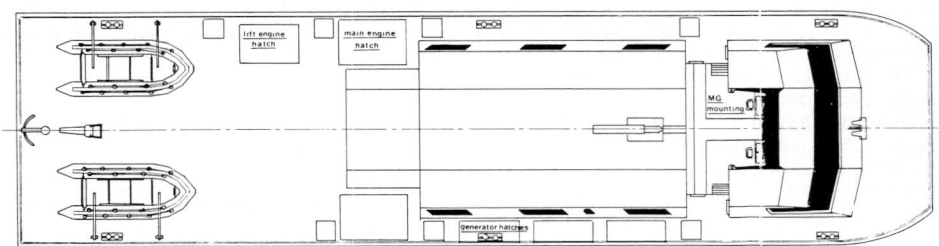

34m SES fast patrol boat

40m SES

A double-deck derivative of the le Comte-Holland SES, the 40m commercial version seats 500 passengers and cruises at 39 knots. Its naval counterpart is a patrol fast attack craft with a twin barrel 40mm cannon and eight surface-to-surface missiles. A reconnaissance helicopter can be housed in a lightweight concertina-type folding hangar on the aft deck.

LIFT AND PROPULSION: Power for the lift system is supplied by three diesels: two MAN D 2542 MLEs, each driving two centrifugal lift fans, and one MAN D 2530ME, mounted in the auxiliary engine room aft, and driving a single fan aft which supplies air to the stern seal. The standard propulsion system comprises two MTU 12V 538 TB 92 marine diesels, each rated at 2,555hp at 1,790rpm and driving, via ZF BW1200 gearboxes, two fixed-pitch propellers. Alternative arrangements include the installation of two 2,500shp Avco Lycoming gas turbines. Fuel capacity is 20 tons.

CONTROLS, HULL: As for 26 and 34m SES designs.

PATROL/FAST ATTACK VERSION

WEAPONS AND ELECTRONICS: The vessel can carry a naval helicopter on the aft deck for reconnaissance, search and rescue. The shipborne helicopter can be used for ASW and MCM warfare using a towing sonar and for over-the-horizon targeting of missiles if so equipped. A Vesta helicopter transponder system can receive and display defined echo signals from objects with a small radar cross-section, even in an environment with clutter, thereby extending radar range. A landing grid on the aft deck gives additional safety for landings in rough seas. Any naval helicopter with a total weight not exceeding five tons can be operated from the vessel. The total weight of the vessel and the required speed dictate the quantity of helicopter fuel that can be carried on board.

The craft can carry a full range of weapons, sensors, control systems and navigation equipment. Le Comte-Holland BV recommends a modular system for ease of installation and maintenance, such as the Gemini system of Hollandse Signaalapparaten BV. The tested modular control system, with antennae, is bolted on to the superstructure at the shipyard. Once the connections from the power supplier and weapons have been plugged in the system is fully operational.

DIMENSIONS
Length overall: 40m
Beam overall: 15m
Draught, on cushion: 2·1m
  off cushion: 3·55m

WEIGHTS
Registered tonnage: 145 tons
Max: 185 tons
Normal: 155 tons
Light ship: 136 tons
Max deckload: 34 tons
Fuel: 20 tons

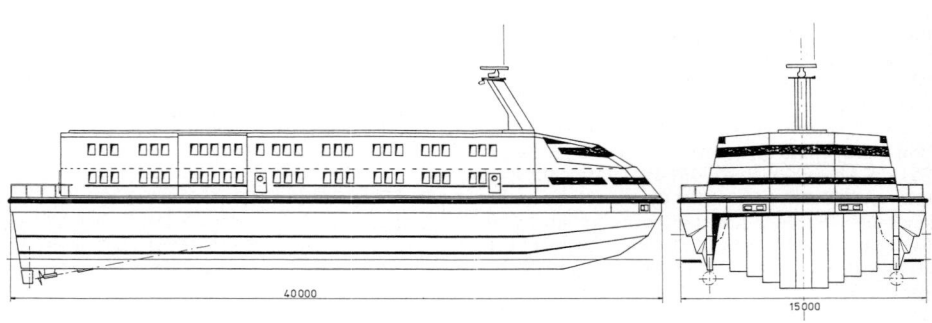

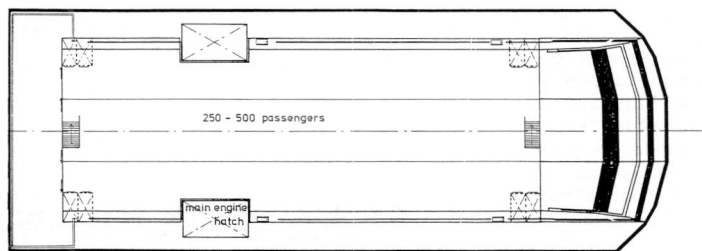

40m SES seating 250-500 passengers

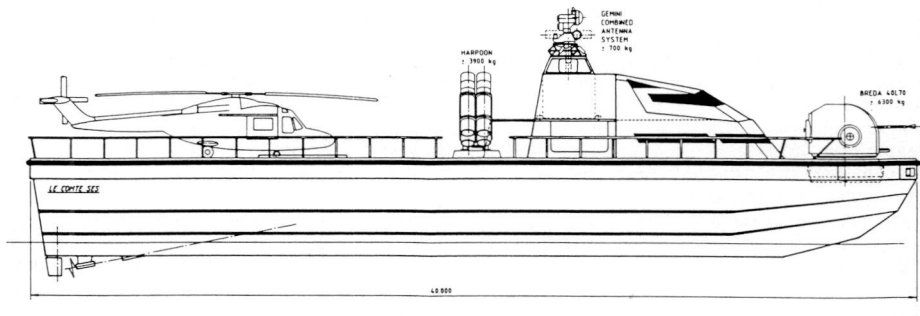

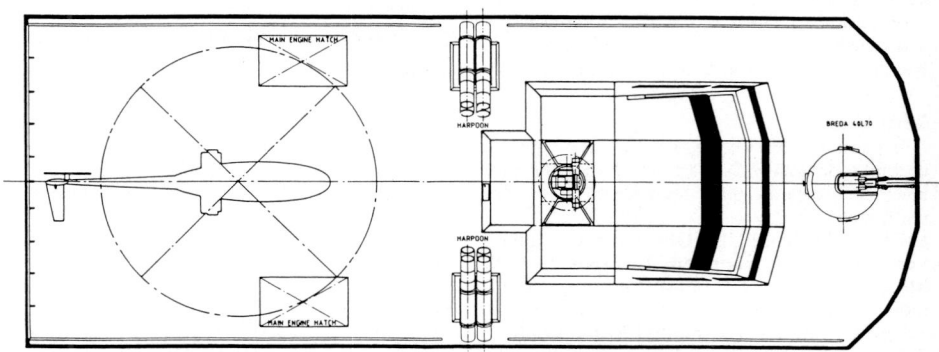

40m patrol/fast attack SES with dual purpose rapid-fire cannon, eight Harpoon anti-ship missiles and helicopter

PERFORMANCE

Cruising speed	Sea State 0	Sea State 3
on cushion:	39 knots	31 knots
off cushion:	15 knots	13 knots
Range:	780n miles	700n miles
	(approx)	(approx)

Tank test model of Le Comte-Holland SES

NEW ZEALAND

HOVERCRAFT MANUFACTURERS NEW ZEALAND LIMITED

PO Box 11095, 23 Watts Road, Christchurch, New Zealand
Telephone: 03 486 821
03 487 021
Telex: 74 5237 LAB DUN
Works: 13 Harden Street, Leith Valley, Dunedin, New Zealand
Telephone: 024 775351
Officials:

Morgan W Wallace, *Director, Operations and Marketing*
James H M Sutherland, *Director, Operations and Marketing*
L Ross McLeod, *Director, Design and Works Manager*
Selwyn Paynter, *Director, Works and Marketing*

Hovercraft Manufacturers (NZ) began the design and construction of commercial and sports hovercraft in New Zealand in mid-1982.

The company operates a Riverland Surveyor 8, on Lake Rotorua, in the North Island. The craft, which seats eight passengers, carries tourists and acts as a rescue craft for the airport adjoining the lake. A second craft of this type is operating at Queenstown in the South Island and a third on Lake Wanaka.

Interest in the eight- and twelve-passenger craft has been shown in Australia, New Guinea, New Caledonia and other Pacific islands. At least four will be built within the next two years.

A new five-seater craft, the Ranger 5, was introduced into the range in 1984.

AIRDASH

TYPE: Fully-amphibious two-seater for sports and light-utility applications, including surveying, weed spraying and rescue missions.
LIFT AND PROPULSION: Integrated system powered by 34kW (46hp) air-cooled, twin-cylinder two-stroke. Power is transmitted via a toothed drive belt to a 780mm (2ft 7in) diameter ducted polypropylene fan with replaceable blades. Fuji Robin electric start motor. Fuel capacity is 33 litres (7·28 gallons) and recommended fuel is 96 octane oil pre-mix. Fuel consumption is 8 to 11·3 litres/h (1·75 to 2·75 gallons/h).
HULL: Monocoque construction in fibreglass. Deck, cockpit, seat and duct system moulded in one-piece grp. Hull base is moulded separately in one piece using core-mat/grp laminate. This is bonded to the top moulding to form a one-piece, lightweight, impact-resistant structure.

SKIRT: Fully-segmented type in pvc or neoprene-coated nylon. Segments individually replaceable using quick-release clips and nylon ties.
DIMENSIONS
Length: 3·45m (11ft 6in)
Width: 1·78m (5ft 9in)
WEIGHTS
Empty: 148kg (326lb)
Payload: 165kg (364lb)

PERFORMANCE
Max recorded speed, over land: 90km/h (56mph)
Max speed, still air, over water: 77·2km/h (48mph)
Normal cruising speed over water with full load: 48·2km/h (30mph)
Max wave height: 0·5-0·6m (20-24in)
PRICE: NZ $4,800, plus sales tax and freight (1983). Ten per cent spare skirt components included. Basic colour optional with order.

Airdash

Airdash

RIVERLAND SURVEYOR 8 & 12

Eight- and twelve-passenger versions of this multi-duty hovercraft are available. At least four machines of the 8 and 12 series are to be built over the next four years.

LIFT AND PROPULSION: Integrated system powered by a single 4·1-litre Buick V6 automotive engine on the Surveyor 8 and one 5·7-litre Chevrolet V8 on the Surveyor 12. The engine room is pressurised to exclude dust and water when operating over dirty terrain or in salt water conditions. Power is transmitted to the lift fan hydrostatically and to two four-bladed ducted fans by HTD belts and drive shafts. Fuel capacity is 120 litres. Larger tanks are optional.

CONTROLS: Craft heading is controlled by twin aerodynamic rudders attached to the rear of the twin thrust ducts. Elevators behind each thrust fan provide craft pitch and roll control.

HULL: Built in foam sandwich grp.

SKIRT: HDL bag and segment type in neoprene-coated nylon. Segments attached to the bag by quick-release nylon fasteners to facilitate servicing.

ACCOMMODATION: Bucket seats for driver and front passenger and normally two removable bench-type seats for passengers.

RIVERLAND SURVEYOR 8
DIMENSIONS
EXTERNAL
Length: 6·7m
Beam: 3·44m
Height: 2m
INTERNAL
Cabin
Length: 2·45m
Width: 1·74m
Height: 1·25m
Door width: 0·87-1·09m
Door height: 1·28m
WEIGHTS
Empty: 1,030kg
Max normal all-up weight: 1,800kg
Max overload all-up weight: 2,100kg
PERFORMANCE
Cruising speed: 35-60km/h
Max recommended speed: 80km/h
Max normal wave height: 1m
(Can be operated in surf up to 1·5m high)
Hard structure clearance: 0·5m
Fuel consumption: 18-32 litres/h
Noise level: 76d B-A scale. Peak reading craft passing at 8m from instrument while cruising on water

RIVERLAND SURVEYOR 12
DIMENSIONS
EXTERNAL
Length, off cushion: 7·52m
  on cushion: 6·8m
Width, off cushion: 3·44m
  on cushion: 4·19m
Height, off cushion: 2m
  on cushion: 2·5m
INTERNAL
Cabin
Height: 1·25m
Width: 1·74m
Length: 3·07m
Door width: 0·87-1·09m
Door height: 1·28m
Cushion depth: 0·5m
WEIGHTS
Empty: 1,200kg
Max normal all-up weight: 2,200kg
Max overload all-up weight: 2,450kg
PERFORMANCE
Cruising speed: 35-60 km/h
Max recommended speed: 80km/h
Fuel capacity: 120 litres (optional larger tanks)
Fuel consumption: 20-35 litres/h
27 litres/h at 3,300rpm cruise
Noise level: 76d B-A scale peak reading craft passing at 8 metres from instrument while cruising on water
Normal wave height: 1m
(Can be operated in surf up to 1·5m)

RANGER 5

For road transport, the sidebodies of this projected five-seater fold upwards and the twin

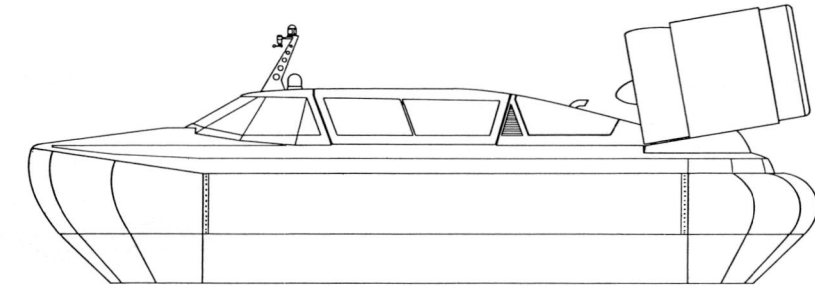

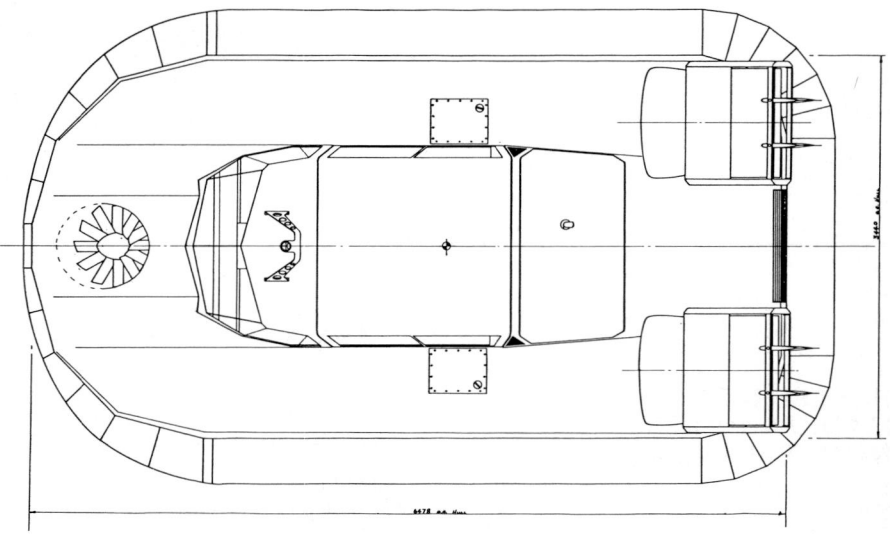

RiverLand Surveyor

Surveyor 8

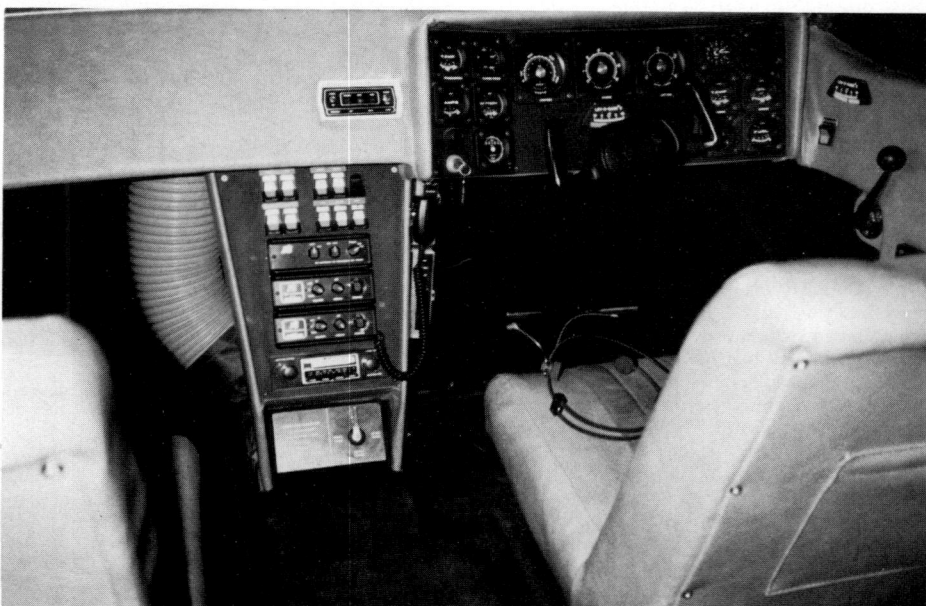

Driving position, Surveyor 8

thrust units fold inwards to reduce the width to two metres.

LIFT AND PROPULSION: Integrated system powered by a single 54kW (72hp), 4-cylinder, 4-cycle water-cooled automotive engine. Power is transmitted by vee belts to two 840mm diameter, 4-blade, reversible-pitch duct-mounted thrust fans, and, via a hydraulic motor, to one 630mm diameter multiwing lift fan.

CONTROLS: Craft heading is controlled by pitch control of the thrust fans, operated by a joystick. Engine speed is controlled by a governor.

HULL: Vacuum formed, cold moulded grp and pvc foam sandwich construction.

SKIRT: Tapered loop and segment type in neoprene coated nylon.

ACCOMMODATION: Driver and one passenger sit forward in bucket seats. Up to three additional passengers sit on contoured bench seat to rear. Rear seat is removable to carry freight. Open cabin. Optional soft top.

DIMENSIONS
Length, static: 5m
  on cushion: 5·4m
Width, static: 2·7m
  on cushion: 3·5m
  sidebodies folded: 2m
WEIGHTS
Empty: 350kg approx
Max normal all-up weight: 750kg

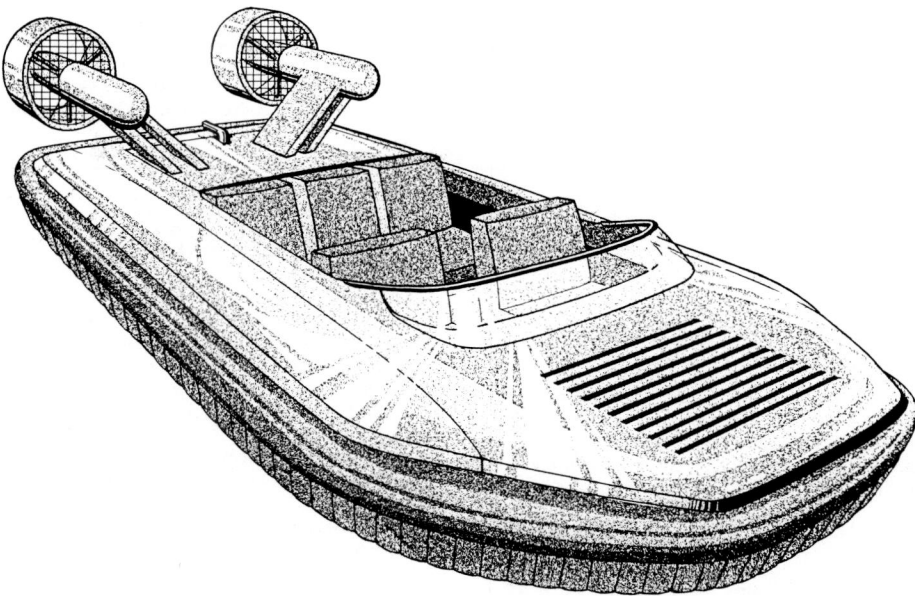

Ranger 5

PERFORMANCE
Cruising speed: 40-50km/h

Max recommended speed: 70km/h
Obstacle clearance height: 380mm

NORWAY

BRØDRENE AA BÄTBYGGERI A/S

N-6780 Hyen, Norway
Telephone: 47 57 69 800
Telex: 42162 BRAA

CIRR 105P NORCAT

Brødrene AA, with Cirrus A/S, has designed and built the new Norcat SES to meet increasing demand for fast ferries based on this principle.

The Norcat, which is diesel-powered and of fibre reinforced plastic sandwich construction, seats 264 passengers and cruises at 36 knots. It was designed originally for inter-city services within Norway, but is suitable for services in many other parts of the world.

The vessel is classified by all major classification societies as a catamaran and the lift fans are regarded as an auxiliary system.

LIFT AND PROPULSION: The lift system comprises two Detroit Diesel 8V 92Ts, each rated at 260/305bhp, and each driving a stainless steel centrifugal fan. Propulsive power is provided by two 1,600bhp Detroit Diesel 16V 149 TIB marine diesels each driving a semi-cavitating controllable-pitch propeller.

CONTROLS: Craft direction is by twin rudders operated electro-hydraulically. Additional control by differential use of water propellers.

HULL: FRP/sandwich construction. Structure to Det Noorske Veritas requirements.

ACCOMMODATION: Norcat seats 264 passengers in two saloons, a forward compartment seating 112 and an aft compartment seating 152. For short routes seating arrangements for up to 300 passengers are offered. Among alternative designs is the CIRR 105 UT with a capacity for 100 passengers and 20 tons of freight.

SYSTEMS
NAVIGATION AND ELECTRONICS: Radar, coloured, two sets; one compass, magnetic; one gyrocompass; one log; one LLTV; two VHF; two trim indicators; one Intercom system; two TV/video systems; one NMT phonebox.

DIMENSIONS
Length overall: 32·2m
Beam: 11m
Draught off-cushion: 2·6m (propeller tips)
  on-cushion: 1·7m (propeller tips)
WEIGHTS
Gross tonnage: 290 tons
PERFORMANCE
Service speed: 36 knots
Max speed: 42 knots
Fuel consumption: 560 litres/h; 15·5 litres/n mile

SES Norcat

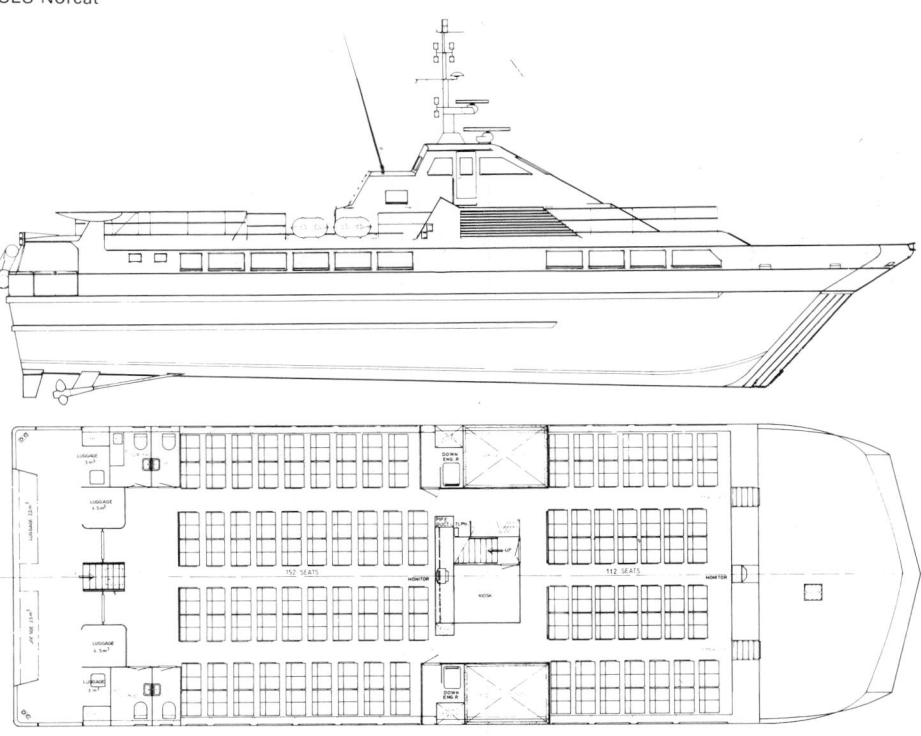

Outboard profile and passenger deck, SES Norcat

CIRRUS A/S

PO Box 223, N-5032 Minde, Bergen, Norway

Telephone: 47 5 29 79 01
Telex: 40422 CIRR

Cirrus A/S was responsible for the design of the CIRR 105P Norcat SES, for operation on inter-city passenger ferry services in Norway. It is also undertaking the marketing and sales of the vessel. A description of the Norcat, which was built by Brødrene AA Batbyggeri A/S, precedes this entry.

POLAND

WARSAW YOUNG TECHNICIANS CENTRE

Warsaw, Poland

Authorities in the Soviet Union and Eastern Europe are encouraging the construction and operation of light recreational hovercraft by schools, colleges, universities and other youth groups.

Above: SMT-1 amphibious single-seater
Below: impression of Horizonty Technicki two-seater

Although no official association has yet been formed, encouragement is also being given to the staging of national and international race meetings. Reviewing the light hovercraft situation in 1980, one aviation magazine stated, 'Given that successful prototype mini-ACVs have been successfully built in the Soviet Union, Czechoslovakia, Bulgaria, Romania and Poland, competitions between socialist countries are highly likely'.

The Polish press has reported the existence of a number of nationally-designed and constructed ACVs, from large-scale prototypes for agricultural, industrial and maritime uses, to small sports and leisure craft.

Brief descriptions of two light hovercraft have been published, the SMT-1 and the Horizonty Technicki.

SMT-1

This amphibious single-seater was designed and built by students at the Warsaw Young Technician's Centre. It has operated successfully over land, ice and water. The prototype, built in 1964, was underpowered. A more powerful version, fitted with a modified modern wood-saw, motorcycle or PF 126P car engine, is under consideration as a production model.

LIFT AND PROPULSION: Lift is supplied by a single S-1 125cc motorcycle two-stroke driving a six-bladed duct-mounted axial fan. Power for the propulsion system is provided by a second S-1 125cc two-stroke.

CONTROLS: Craft direction is controlled by an aerodynamic rudder operated by a rudder bar.

DIMENSIONS
Length: 2·2m (7ft 2in)
Beam: 1·4m (4ft 7in)
Height: 1·2m (3ft 11in)

PERFORMANCE
Speed (prototype with 125cc S-1 motorcycle engine powering thrust system): 25km/h (15mph)

HORIZONTY TECHNICKI

This is either a single- or two-seater, the prototype of which was built in 1971. A sketch of the craft appears alongside.

LIFT AND PROPULSION: Integrated system. Motive power is supplied by a single motorcycle two-stroke rated at 10kW.

CONTROLS: Directional control is supplied by an aerodynamic rudder.

DIMENSIONS
Length: 3·5m (11ft 6in)
Beam: 1·9m (6ft 2in)
Height: 1·7m (5ft 7in)

WEIGHTS
Empty: 200kg (441lb)
Loaded: 300kg (661lb)

PERFORMANCE
Max speed: 60km/h (37mph)

ROMANIA

NAVIMPEX CENTRALA NAVALA

Galatz, Romania

Navimpex Centrala Navala, Romania's central marine import/export organisation, is promoting a new range of high-speed catamaran ferries with seats for up to 150 passengers and also a new sidewall hovercraft. Powered by two 215bhp MAN diesels driving waterjets, the hovercraft is 15 metres long, has a beam of 5 metres and a height above water of 2·7 metres. It is built in aluminium and is said to be capable of high speeds.

SINGAPORE

SEACONSTRUCT

RMI Inc, of Chula Vista, California, and the Singapore-based shipbuilder, Seaconstruct, are jointly investigating the possibility of building the RMI-designed Light Multi-purpose Surface Effect Ship (LMSES) in Singapore. The craft, which would be built in aluminium, would be 46·3m (152ft) long and have a beam of 14·6m (48ft). Its range would be 750 nautical miles at a speed of about 60 knots.

In passenger ferry configuration the LMSES would accommodate up to 360 persons, but alternative versions would be available for a range of duties including offshore servicing, in which it would carry a mixed payload of passengers and freight of up to 100 tons.

Initial marketing studies have suggested that suitable routes include Singapore-Jakarta, Singapore-Kuching, Surabaya-Balikpapan and Port Kelang-Penang.

Further details and an illustration of the LMSES will be found in the entry for RMI Inc, USA, in the ACV section.

SPAIN

CHACONSA

Compañia Hispano Americana de Construcciones Conserveras, SA, Mayor, 17 Puente Tocinos, Apart 419 Marcia, Spain
Telephone: 230200; 238512; 230604
Telex: 67248 ABRO E

A contract to develop military hovercraft has been awarded to the Aeronavals Division of Chaconsa by the Spanish Ministry of Defence. The aim of the programme is the design, development, construction and testing of a 60-knot amphibious assault landing craft for the Spanish navy.

Chaconsa launched its air cushion vehicle research programme in 1973. In 1976 it received a contract for the development of the VCA-36 from the Spanish Ministry of Defence. Design of the lift and propulsion system was aided by experiments with laboratory models. Two manned research models, the 750kg VCA-2 and the 5-tonne VCA-3, were later built to evaluate and refine the system.

In addition to its military programme, Chaconsa plans to build commercial hovercraft and is also examining industrial and agricultural applications of air cushion technology.

VCA-2

The first manned air cushion vehicle to be designed and built by Chaconsa, the VCA-2 has an all-up weight of 750kg. Like the VCA-3, described and illustrated below, it was employed as a test craft during the development of the lift system for the VCA-36 amphibious assault craft.

VCA-3

A 2·5 scale model of the VCA-36, the VCA-3, was built in 1978. Powered by two Porsche engines, it seats seven and has a maximum speed of 50 knots. At least one variant is likely to enter production.

LIFT AND PROPULSION: Integrated system powered by two 300hp Porsche 928-5 automotive engines. Each engine drives a centrifugal lift fan and a 2m diameter variable-pitch, two-bladed propeller for thrust.

CONTROLS: Craft heading is controlled by twin aerodynamic rudders operating in the propeller slipstream. At low speed direction control is by differential propeller pitch. A ballast system adjusts longitudinal and transverse trim.

HULL: Corrosion-resistant aluminium alloy. Buoyancy chamber includes compartments filled with plastic foam for reserve buoyancy. Six rubber landing pads are fitted to the hull base. Four lifting eyes are provided in the hull.

SKIRT: 0·53m deep, fingered-bag type of Chaconsa design, fabricated in nylon coated with synthetic rubber.

DIMENSIONS
EXTERNAL
Length overall, on cushion: 10·36m
Beam overall, on cushion: 4·45m
Height, on cushion: 4m
Skirt depth: 0·53m
INTERNAL
Cabin, max dimensions
Length: 4·1m
Width: 3·2m
WEIGHTS
All-up: 5,000kg
Payload: 1,000kg
PERFORMANCE
Max speed: 50 knots
Cruising speed: 40 knots
Max gradient, continuous: 12%
Endurance: 3 hours

VCA-36

Designed to improve the rapid-lift capability of the Spanish armed forces, the VCA-36 will carry a 14-tonne payload, equivalent to three Land-Rovers and 70 fully-armed marines or infantrymen, to a beach landing zone at a speed of 60 knots. It could also be used for lighter-over-the-shore applications. Its dimensions will allow it to operate from the docking wells of a number of LSDs, and from ro/ro vessels with sufficient headroom and suitable ramps. Lifting eyes in the hull will enable it to be hoisted on and off the decks of cargo ships. A removable roof above the cargo deck will permit the craft to be loaded alongside supply ships.

LIFT AND PROPULSION: Integrated system powered by two Avco Lycoming TF25 gas turbines, each with a maximum output of 2,500hp. Each drives two centrifugal fans and a 4m diameter, five-bladed, variable-pitch propeller. Power is transmitted via two gearboxes with auxiliary outputs for lubrication, hydraulic pumps and generators.

CONTROLS: All controls are in a raised cabin, well forward on the forward starboard quarter and providing a 360-degree view. Directional control is by twin aerodynamic rudders and differential propeller pitch. A ballast system adjusts longitudinal and transverse trim.

HULL: Riveted aluminium structure based on a grid of longitudinal and transverse frames which form a number of watertight buoyancy compartments. Fuel, ballast tanks and bilge systems are contained within these compartments. Access to the cargo deck is via hydraulically-operated bow and stern ramps or the removable cargo deck roof. The central cargo deck is 18·65m long by 2·6m wide by 2·25m high. Two main longitudinal vertically stiffened bulkheads run the length of the hull. These separate the central vehicle/cargo deck from the sidestructures which contain the gas turbines, lift fans, transmissions, auxiliary power systems and cabins. Marines or assault troops are accommodated in two 35-seat cabins, 7·4m long by 2·35m wide, one in the forward section of each sidestructure. Four landing pads

VCA-2

VCA-3

VCA-36

Hull structure of VCA-36, seen from stern

are fitted to the hull base. Four lifting eyes are provided for hoisting the craft.

SKIRT: 1·4m deep, fingered-bag type of Chaconsa design in nylon coated with synthetic rubber.

SYSTEMS, ELECTRICAL: Two 15kVA generators driven by the main engines provide three-phase 50Hz at 380V for ac and dc supplies.

DIMENSIONS
Length overall, on cushion: 25·5m
Beam overall, on cushion: 11·04m
Height on cushion: 9·5m
Skirt depth: 1·4m
WEIGHTS
All-up: 36 tonnes
Payload: 14 tonnes
PERFORMANCE
Max speed: 60 knots
Cruising speed: 50 knots
Endurance: 3 hours

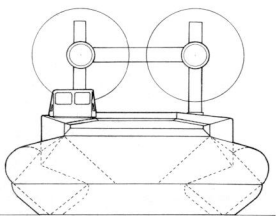
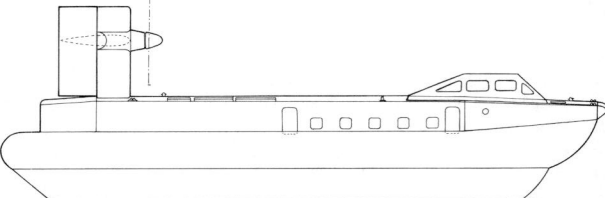
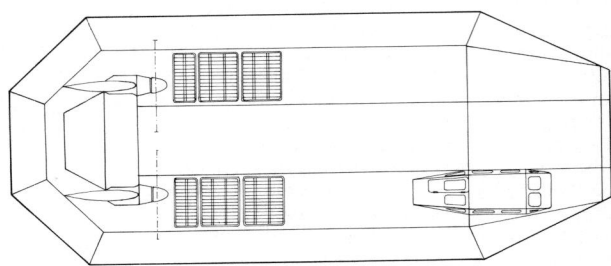

General arrangement of VCA-36

FM-AERODESLIZADORES

R Parque Iviasa, Bloque 32 5°C, Alcalá de Henares, Madrid, Spain
Officials:
Julián Martin Sanz, *Mechanical Engineer*
Joaquin Heras Muriel, *Electrical Engineer*

VAM-F1B

Trials of this interesting Spanish craft began in the summer of 1979 and proved the craft's ability to carry three persons. It is being employed as a research craft. It has an open cockpit and is fitted with a loop and segment skirt.

LIFT AND PROPULSION: A single Volkswagen engine provides power for both the lift and propulsion systems, with a centrifugal clutch for the centrifugal lift fan. Thrust is supplied by a five-bladed axial fan driven by toothed belt.

CONTROLS: Craft direction is controlled by twin rudder vanes in the thrust fan slipstream and operated by a wheel.

HULL: Glass fibre structure, reinforced where necessary with aluminium tube.

SKIRT: Loop and segment type, fabricated in neoprene/nylon.

ACCOMMODATION: Open cockpit for driver and two passengers.

SYSTEMS, ELECTRICAL: 6V battery for starting and services.

DIMENSIONS
Length overall: 3·1m (10ft 2in)
Width, sidebodies: 2·48m (8ft 1in)
  sides folded for transport: 1·04m (3ft 5in)
Height, skirt inflated: 1·26m (4ft 1·5in)
PERFORMANCE
Max speed, estimated: 60km/h (37·3mph)

FM-AXZ-001

This is a design study for a high-speed amphibious two-seater powered by a 385hp gas turbine.

LIFT AND PROPULSION: Motive power is supplied by a single 385hp Allison 250B17 gas turbine. This drives two centrifugal lift fans and two ducted variable-pitch fans for thrust.

HULL: Mixed fibreglass reinforced plastics and aluminium construction.

CONTROLS: Craft direction is controlled by twin rudders aft of the propeller ducts. Pitch stability is provided by a horizontal stabiliser.

ACCOMMODATION: Enclosed cabin with two side-by-side seats.

SKIRT: Fingered-bag type.

DIMENSIONS
Length overall: 5·5m (18ft 2in)
Width: 2·85m (9ft 4in)
Max height: 2m (6ft 7in)
Skirt height: 0·53m (1ft 9in)
WEIGHTS
Total payload: 1,150kg (2,535lb)
Empty furnished: 590kg (1,300lb)
Payload: 220kg (485lb)

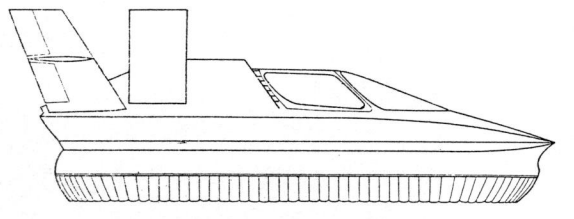
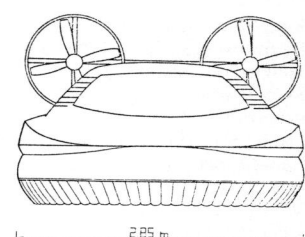
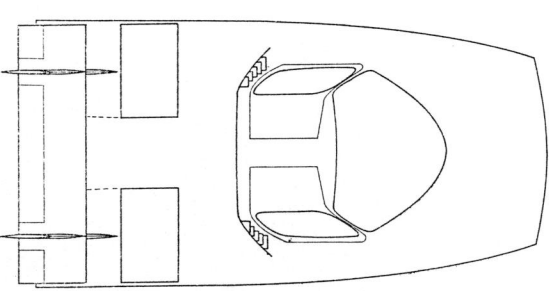

General arrangement of FM-AXZ-001

Model of Interceptor 1

INTERCEPTOR 1

This fully amphibious four-seater is intended for coast guard, military patrol and ambulance applications on estuaries and navigable rivers.

LIFT AND PROPULSION: Integrated system. A single air-cooled engine drives a centrifugal lift fan and two multi-bladed fixed-pitch thrust fans.

CONTROLS: Two rudders placed in the thrust fan slipstreams provide directional control. Pitch stability is provided by a horizontal stabiliser.

HULL: Aluminium structure. Sealed tanks provide reserve buoyancy.

SKIRT: Open loop type with segments in the stern. Will be provided with conical ducts for avoiding water collection. Skirt material is nylon covered neoprene.

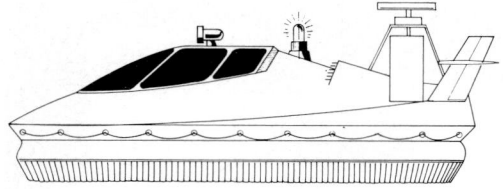

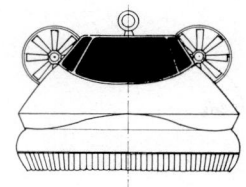

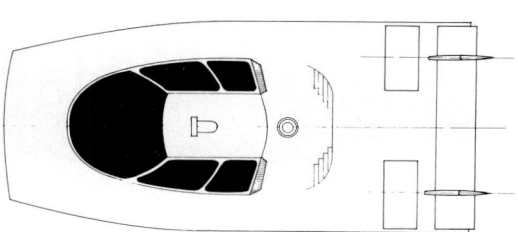

Interceptor 1

ACCOMMODATION: Enclosed cabin seats four. As an ambulance or rescue craft, the cabin could accommodate a stretcher beside the driver.
DIMENSIONS
Length overall: 5·15m
Beam overall: 2·6m
Height without inflated skin: 1·9m
WEIGHTS
Empty: 455kg
Max payload: 360kg

All-up: 1,000kg
PERFORMANCE
Max speed over water: 55km/h (34mph)
 over land: 70km/h (43mph)
Endurance: 5 hours
Max vertical obstacle clearance: 0·4m (15·75in)

INTERCEPTOR 2
This craft is similar to Interceptor 1 but is diesel-powered.

LIFT AND PROPULSION: Integrated system powered by either one or two diesel engines. Power is transmitted to two sets of two, or three, centrifugal fans for lift, and via toothed belts to two multi-blade, fixed-pitch fans for thrust.
CONTROLS: Craft direction is controlled by twin rudder vanes operating in the thrust fan slipstream. For pitch and roll control, the craft has controllable vanes at the bow and stern, and port and starboard, which cut off the air flow to the cushion.
HULL: Glassfibre structure, reinforced with aluminium tubing.
SKIRT: Loop and segment type, in neoprene/nylon.
SYSTEMS, ELECTRICAL: A 24V, 45Ah battery, in conjunction with an engine-driven generator, supplies its power for engine-starting lights, instruments and emergency systems.
DIMENSIONS
Length overall: 5·15m (16ft 11in)
Beam overall: 2·6m (8ft 6in)
Height, without inflated skirt: 1·9m (6ft 3in)
WEIGHTS
Empty: 455kg
Max payload: 360kg
All-up weight: 1,000kg
PERFORMANCE
Max speed, over water: 55km/h (34mph)
Max speed, over land: 70km/h (43mph)
Endurance: 5 hours
Vertical obstacle clearance: 0·4m

Projected Interceptor variants:

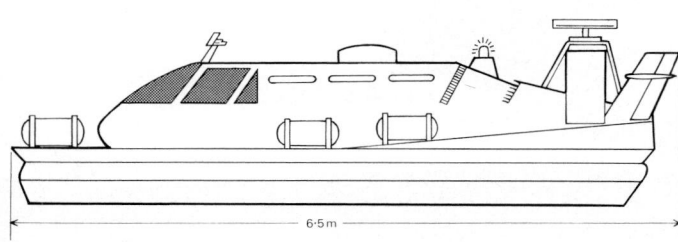

Command centre

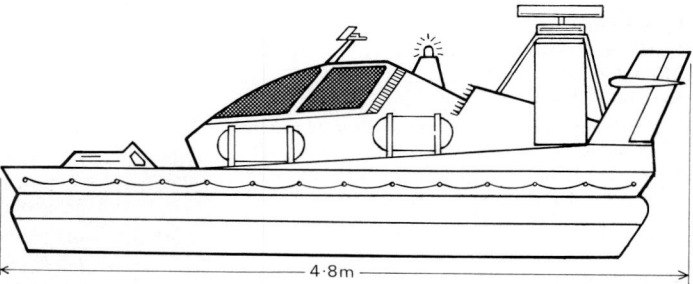

Coast guard and patrol

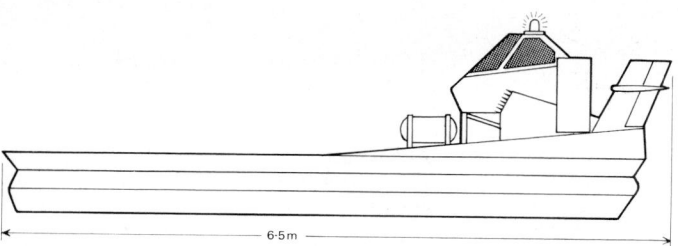

Search and rescue

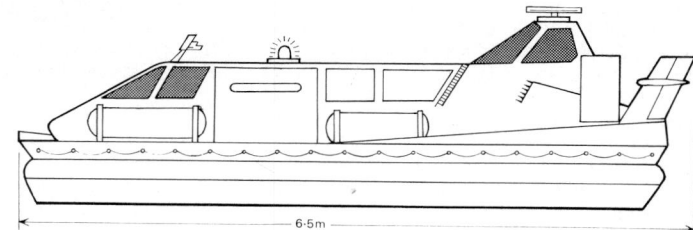

Light cargo craft

ALBERTO GIMENEZ DE LOS GALANES

Reyes 7, Madrid 8, Spain
Telephone: (341) 231 5289
Officials:
Jorge Gomez Gomez
Eduardo Sanchiz Garrote

After several years of studying the theoretical aspects of hovercraft at the Escuela Tecnica Superior de Ingenieros Aeronauticos in Madrid, a group of aeronautical engineers decided, in September 1979, to verify their technical predictions by constructing a small craft. The craft, named Furtivo I, is being used to provide confirmation of earlier theoretical studies, but a design is being developed which is likely to incorporate certain improvements such as the HDL Skirt Shift system. Furtivo I performed its first flight in February 1980.

Furtivo II, which will be based on Furtivo I, is in the final stages of design. It was expected to fly during 1983.

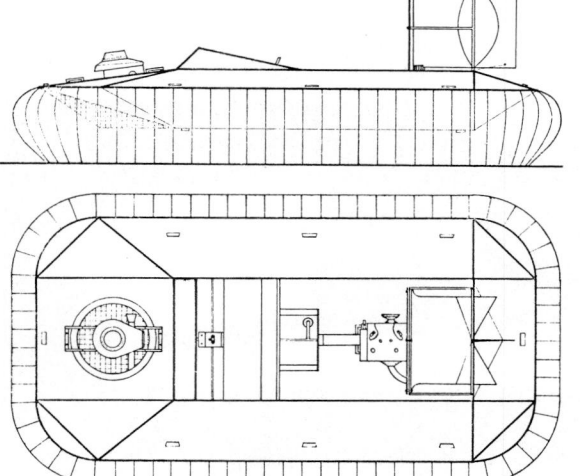

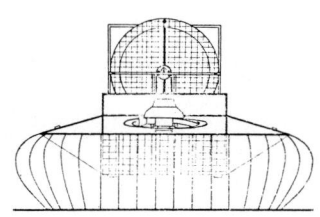

General arrangement of Furtivo I

FURTIVO I

LIFT AND PROPULSION: Lift is provided by a single Kyoritsu KEC 225cc two-stroke driving a 550mm (1ft 10in) diameter Multiwing axial fan. Cushion pressure is 10lb/ft^2. Thrust is provided by a single 38·5hp Rotax 640 two-stroke, air-cooled engine driving a 710mm (2ft 4in) diameter ducted axial fan filled with Multiwing blades. The fan provides forward or reverse thrust.
CONTROLS: Craft heading is controlled by a centrally-located column which operates a single aerodynamic rudder. The throttle control for the thrust engine is mounted on the stick. Another small column in the cockpit operates the thrust reversal mechanism.
HULL: Plywood structure with grp skin.
SKIRT: Fully-segmented type in neoprene-coated nylon.
ACCOMMODATION: Side-by-side seating for two in an open cockpit.
DIMENSIONS
Length overall, power off: 4m (13ft 1·5in)
Beam overall, power off: 2m (6ft 6·75in)
Height overall, skirt inflated: 1·58m (5ft 2·25in)
Draught afloat: 8·5cm (3·25in)
Cushion area: 7·78m^2 (84ft^2)

Furtivo I

Skirt depth: 0·3m (12in)
WEIGHTS
Normal empty: 203kg (448lb)
Normal payload: 183kg (403lb)
Max payload: 197kg (434lb)

PERFORMANCE
CALM CONDITIONS
Max speed: 78km/h (48·5mph)
Gradient capability: 1 : 7
Vertical obstacle clearance: 0·3m (12in)

SWITZERLAND

ULM AIRCRAFT SA

PO Box 492, CH-1470 Estavayer-le-Lac, Switzerland
Telephone: 41-37 77 26 20
Telex: 942 404 ULM CH
Officials:
Jean René Ramuz

This company is marketing several new light amphibious hovercraft: the Mini-Adoc, the three-seat Adoc M.60H and the 14-seat Adoc 14, designed in France by Aeroplast of Lunel, and the Transfutur TH6.

MINI-ADOC

A compact, single-seat sports craft, the Mini-Adoc employs a single ducted fan for the integrated lift and propulsion system.
LIFT AND PROPULSION: Integrated system powered by 25hp Rotax twin-cylinder two-stroke. Power is transmitted by a toothed belt to an 800mm, six-bladed ducted fan. A 20-litre fuel tank gives a cruising endurance of over two hours.
CONTROLS: Twin-aerodynamic rudders operated by a handlebar. Twist grip throttle mounted on handlebar.
HULL: Laminated glass reinforced plastics.
SKIRT: Segmented type.
DIMENSIONS
Length overall: 3m
Beam: 1·8m
Height off cushion: 1·15m
WEIGHTS
Empty: 130kg
Max payload: 120kg
PERFORMANCE
Max speed: 70km/h
Cruising speed: 40km/h

Mini-Adoc

Max continuous gradient from static hover: 5
　degrees, 1:10
Max short gradient at speed: 45 degrees
Vertical hard obstacle clearance: 200mm
Max wave height capability: 0·4m
Max wind force: Beaufort 3-4
Buoyancy: 150%

MINI-ADOC S

Identical to the Mini-Adoc apart from the installation of a 50hp Rotax engine.

ADOC 3

This variant is lengthened to seat two to three passengers. Payload is 220kg. The engine is a 25hp Rotax. Length 3·6m.

ADOC 35

This is similar to the Adoc 3, but fitted with a 50hp Rotax engine.

ADOC M.60H

An amphibious three-seater for sheltered water operation; the ADOC M.60H is intended for a range of commercial and public service applications.
LIFT AND PROPULSION: Integrated system powered by a 67hp BMW R90S flat twin automotive engine. Hydraulic transmission supplies power to twin ducted fans aft for thrust and a single lift fan ahead of the open cockpit. Fuel capacity is 30 litres. Recommended fuel is super grade petrol.
CONTROLS: Twin rudders hinged to rear of twin thrust ducts give directional control.
HULL: Reinforced polyester.
SKIRT: Bag or segmented tyres.
ACCOMMODATION: Open cockpit with single-bench seat for three side-by-side; central seat for driver.
SYSTEMS, ELECTRICAL: 12V for starting and services.
DIMENSIONS
Length overall: 4·2m
Beam overall: 2·5m
Height on cushion: 1·45m
WEIGHTS
Empty: 360kg
Loaded: 600kg
Max load: 240kg
PERFORMANCE
Max speed: 60km/h

Mini-Adoc

Cruising speed: 40km/h
Endurance: 6 hours
Fuel consumption: 5 litres/h
Radius of action: 200km
Obstacle clearance height, with segmented skirt:
40cm

TH6

Developed from the Transfutur TH4 four-seater, the TH6 six-seater has the same basic hull, lift, propulsion and control systems as the TH4, but has a more powerful engine.

LIFT AND PROPULSION: Integrated system powered by a 110bhp two-litre four-cylinder automotive engine. Recommended engines are the Renault 20, Peugeot 505 and Citroën CX Reflex. Power is transmitted via a toothed belt and flexible coupling to a single eight-bladed 1·25m (4ft 1·25in) diameter ducted fan. The primary airflow is ducted aft for propulsion while the secondary airflow is ducted into the plenum below for cushion lift. Fuel capacity is 48 litres (10·6 imperial gallons). Fuel consumption is 12 litres/hour.

CONTROLS: Craft direction is controlled by two rudders hinged to the rear of the propeller duct and operated by a control column. A hand lever is provided for engine throttle control.

HULL: Glass-reinforced polyester plastic structure built in two halves, upper and lower, and bonded together around craft periphery. Spaces between the two hull shells are fitted with polystyrene foam. Reinforced areas are provided for four lifting points, three landing pads, one towing point and one for the engine mounting. The fan duct is also manufactured in grp.

SKIRT: HDL loop and segment type fabricated in polyurethane coated nylon fabric.

DIMENSIONS
Length: 4·78m (15ft 8in)
Beam: 2·48m (8ft 1·5in)
Height off cushion: 1·7m (5ft 7in)
Cushion inflated: 2m (6ft 7·5in)

WEIGHTS
Empty: 550kg (1,200lb)
Fuel: 48 litres (10·6 imperial gallons), 40kg (84lb)

PERFORMANCE
AT NORMAL GROSS WEIGHT, CALM WATER
Cruising speed: 50km/h (30 knots)
Max speed: 70km/h (37 knots)
Range: 200km (124 miles)
Endurance: 4 hours
Max gradient: 1 : 10
Vertical obstacle clearance: 25cm (10in)
Max wave capability: 0·6-1m (2ft-3ft 3in), sea state 2 to 3
Max wind for acceptable operation: Beaufort 5
Sound level: Max 75dBA at 25m (75ft) from fan centre

Adoc M.60H

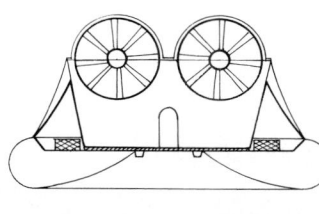
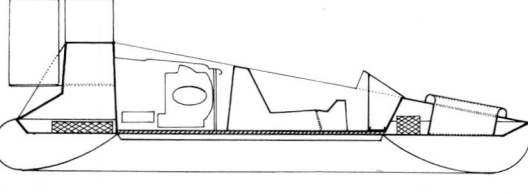
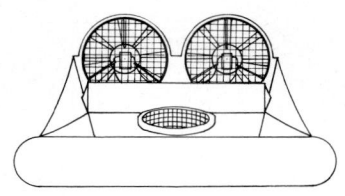
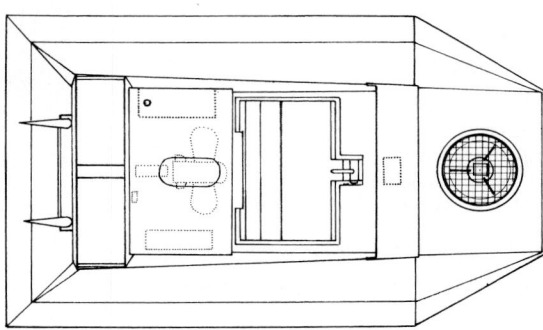
General arrangement of Adoc M.60H

ADOC 14

This new 14-seat light transport is powered by four 52hp Rotax engines and has a maximum speed of 72km/h.

LIFT AND PROPULSION: Cushion air is provided by two 52hp, two-cylinder Rotax 462 engines, each of which drives, via a lay-shaft, two polypropylene-type TLZ, double-entry, 450mm diameter, centrifugal fans. Propulsive thrust is supplied by two eight-bladed, 0·94m diameter, duct-mounted fans, each powered by a separate 52hp Rotax 462 engine. Transmission is via notched pulley and rubber belts. Fuel capacity is 270kg.

CONTROLS: Four rudder vanes hinged at the aft end of each fan duct provide directional control at cruising speed. Differential thrust is employed at low speeds. Elevators provide trim and assist braking by reducing thrust.

HULL: Built in composite material with some sections of hull and deck in 6·35mm balsa sandwich. A floor, built in plastified CTBX, is set into central section to support loads, also anchor points for lifting jacks and for hoisting. Buoyancy provided by waterproof tanks incorporated into the 30cm deep floor, giving a total volume of 6 cubic metres. There are four manually operated hydraulic jacks under the base plate for raising the hull. Four anchor points are provided for hoisting.

SKIRT: 1mm thick Sedam-type bi-conical skirt fabricated in reinforced-nylon, coated in butyl. Overall height of outer skirt, 1·3m; inner skirt, 0·95m. Width of skirt, 0·5m.

ACCOMMODATION: Access to crew cabin via two gull-wing doors, one port and one starboard. The sound-insulated and air-conditioned cabin is built in reinforced polyester. The 12 passengers carried aft of the cabin sit on two bench-type seats. A removable cabin top is provided, made in soft plastic.

SYSTEMS
NAVIGATION AND COMMUNICATIONS: High-resolution radar; gyro-compass; prismatic compass; VHF radio with marine wavelength reception; foghorn; anemometer; navigation lights, mobile spotlight.

SAFETY EQUIPMENT: Equipment corresponding to that decreed by the French navigation laws for craft remaining within 20 miles of a port. Act dated March 27, 1980.

DIMENSIONS
Length on cushion: 9m

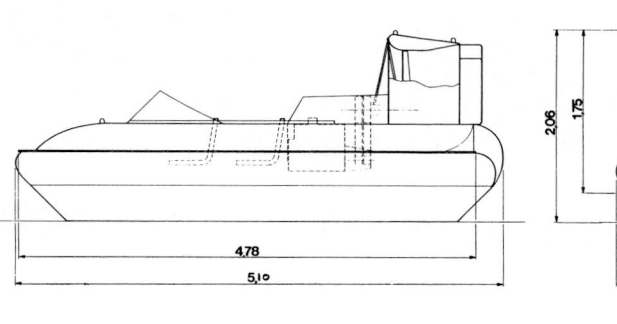
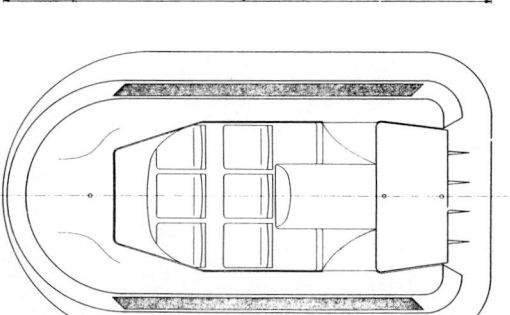
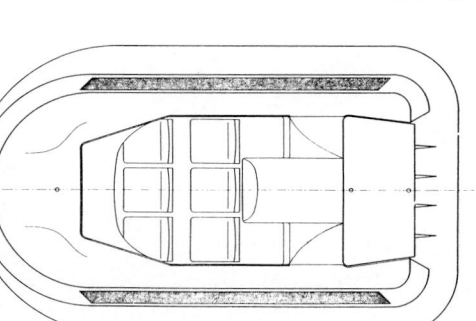

TH6

Beam on cushion: 5m
Height overall on cushion: 2·7m
WEIGHTS
Empty weight: 1,330kg
Loaded capacity: 1,400kg
Max loaded weight: 3,000kg
PERFORMANCE
Cruising speed: 54km/h
Max speed: 72km/h
Endurance: 7 hours at cruising speed
Max operating conditions: wind, force 3-4; waves 0·8m max
Fuel consumption: 40 litres/h at 54km/h

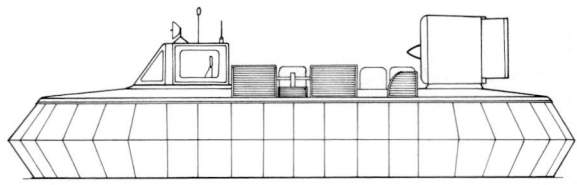
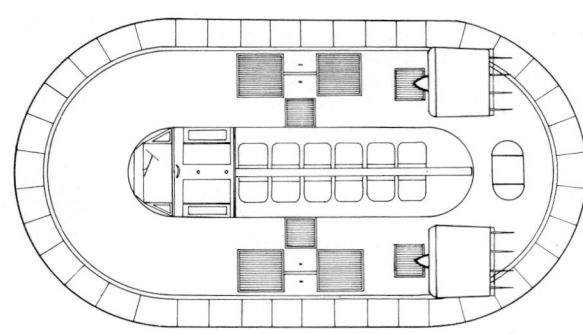

Adoc 14

TAIWAN

CHIVALRY UNIVERSAL COMPANY LIMITED

PO Box 36-48 Taipei, Taiwan

Telephone: 02 7637101/7626110/7692511

Telex: 19113 Finfong

Cables: CUCL Taipei

Officials:
C S Lee, *President*
H J Tsai, *Vice President, Research and Development*
T P Doo, *Vice President, Engineering*

Overseas Office: Chivalry Universal Company Ltd, PO Box 967, Kerrville, Texas 78028, USA

Officials:
J T P Dodd *Vice President, Engineering*

The Siren CY-10 is Chivalry Universal's first commercial hovercraft, although its design was preceded by more than eleven years' research and development. The six-seater CY-6 Mk III is an improved version of the CY-6 Mk II experimental vehicle and was due to be in production by the end of 1984. Chivalry, in conjunction with the International Vehicle Research Inc in the United States, is developing the CY-6 series hovercraft and the new CY-12 8-ton utility hovercraft.

SIREN CY-10

A highly manoeuvrable light ACV, the CY-10 is intended for recreational use. The design combines an FRP hull with an integrated lift/propulsion system and a fully segmented skirt.
LIFT AND PROPULSION: Integrated system powered by a single 40hp Hirth 276R 3E two-stroke. This drives, via a toothed belt, a 12-blade ducted fan which provides air for lift and propulsion.
CONTROLS: Twin aerodynamic rudders at rear of thrust duct, in conjunction with cg movement, control craft heading.
HULL: Fibreglass reinforced plastic structure filled with polyurethane and PVC foam.
SKIRT: Nylon-coated segmented skirt.
ACCOMMODATION: Open tandem seat for driver and passenger.
SYSTEMS, ELECTRICAL: 12V dc with engine-driven 123W magneto generator and 40Ah battery for engine starting and navigation lights.
DIMENSIONS
Length overall: 3·7m
Beam: 1·9m
Height: 1·3m
WEIGHTS
Empty: 190kg
Payload: 150kg
PERFORMANCE
Max speed: 35 knots

CY-10

Siren CY-10

CY-6

CY-6 MK III

This is the latest version of the CY-6 series. The main design changes from the earlier experimental CY-6 Mk II are a single 120hp engine, with integrated transmission system; a single ducted fan for propulsion; a stronger and lighter composite sandwich structure and an enlarged six-seat cabin.

LIFT AND PROPULSION: A single 120hp L20E engine with integrated transmission system drives the lift and propulsion fans via toothed belts. Cushion air is supplied by two 530mm diameter centrifugal fans. Thrust is provided by a 1,070mm diameter axial flow ducted fan.

HULL: Fibreglass reinforced plastic with close-cell form sandwich structure.

CONTROLS: Deflection of three rudder vanes at aft end of thrust fan duct provides heading control.

SKIRT: Bag-finger type

ACCOMMODATION: Enclosed cabin for pilot and five passengers.

SYSTEMS, ELECTRICAL: 12V dc system.

DIMENSIONS
Length, off cushion: 5·8m
  on cushion: 6·15m
Beam, off cushion: 2·8m
  on cushion: 3·25m
  sidebodies folded: 2·05m
Height, off cushion: 1·36m
  on cushion: 1·7m
WEIGHTS
Normal empty: 750kg
  gross: 1,250kg
  payload: 500kg
PERFORMANCE
Max speed: 70km/h
Cruising speed: 50km/h
Endurance: 3 hours

CY-12

This 8-ton utility hovercraft, currently in the preliminary design phase, will be employed as a testbed for a family of hovercraft. Modular system and structural assemblies will facilitate modification and stretching for various applications.

The craft can be easily stretched from 13 to 18 metres.

LIFT AND PROPULSION: Two 500hp engines drive two centrifugal fans for lift and two ducted fans for propulsion.

Lift and propulsion systems are interconnected for single engine operation.

CONTROLS: Aerodynamic rudders behind the ducted fans provide heading control. Bow thrusters are mounted forward on the fuselage side structure.

HULL: Welded aluminium structure with fibreglass reinforced plastic sub-structure.

SKIRT: Bag-finger type, with independent cell for additional cushion stability.

ACCOMMODATION: Open deck has a 9·5 by 4 metre cargo area. Wide bow and stern ramps simplify loading and unloading. Cabin can be added for 40 passengers.

DIMENSIONS
Length overall: 13·2m
Width overall: 9·4m
Height, on landing pad: 3·7m
  on cushion: 4·9m
WEIGHTS
Max gross: 8 tons
Payload: 3 tons
PERFORMANCE
Max speed, calm water: 50 knots
Cruising speed: 40 knots
Endurance: 5 hours

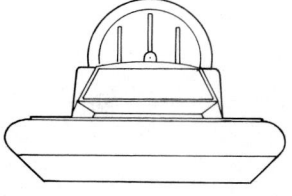
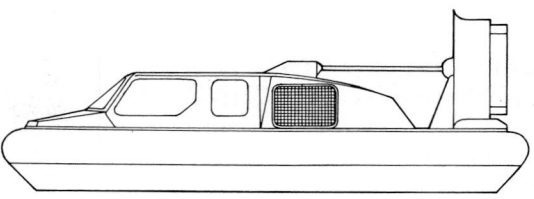
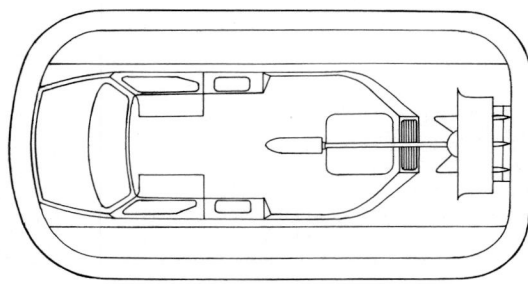

CY-6 Mk III

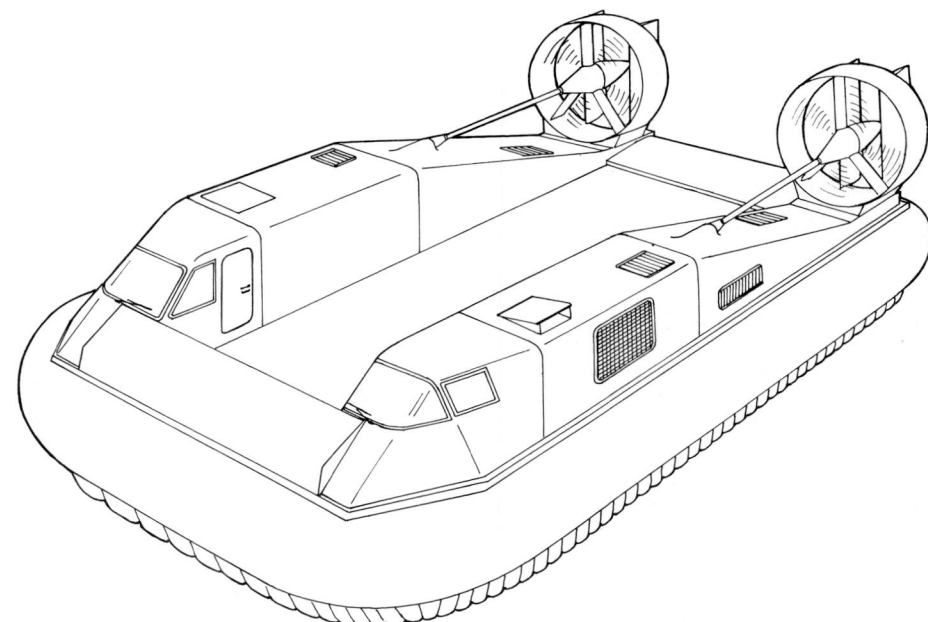

CY-12

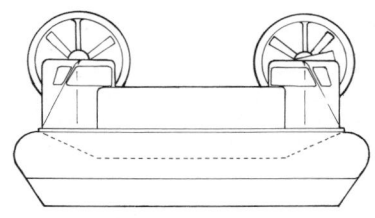
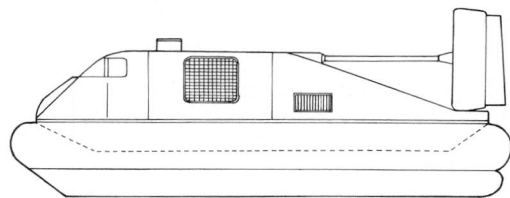
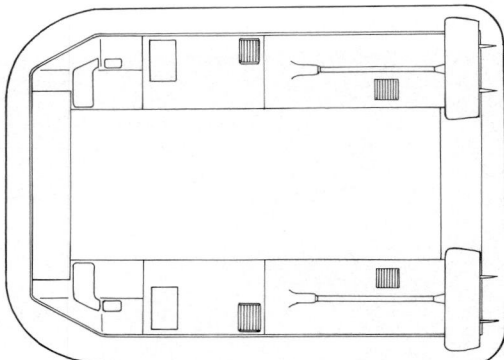

CY-12

UNION OF SOVIET SOCIALIST REPUBLICS

CENTRAL LABORATORY OF LIFESAVING TECHNOLOGY (CLST)

Moscow, USSR
Officials:
Yury Makarov, *Chief Engineer*
A W Gremyatsky, *Project Leader*
Evgeniy P Grunin, *Designer*
N L Ivanov, *Designer*
S Chernyavsky
Y Gorbenko
A Kuzakov, *Consultant*
V Shavrov, *Consultant*
A Baluyev, *Director of Flight Trials*

The Central Laboratory of Lifesaving Technology (CLST), a division of the Rescue Organisation for Inland Waters (OSVOD), has designed a small aerodynamic ram-wing machine, capable of 140km/h (86mph), which will be used to answer distress calls on the Soviet lakes, rivers and canals. The Ekranolyetny Spasatyelny Kater-Amphibya (ESKA), surface-effect amphibious lifeboat is available in several versions. It has been referred to as the Ekranolet and the Nizkolet (skimmer).

Apart from meeting emergency situations on waterways, the craft, which is amphibious, is capable of operating in deserts, tundra, arctic icefields and steppeland. Derivatives are to be employed as support vehicles for geologists, communications engineers and construction groups.

In Soviet publications emphasis has been given to the potential value of such craft in opening up the mineral wealth of Siberia, the Soviet far-east, far-north and other virgin territories.

As with the X-113 Am and other machines of this type, the vehicle operates on the principle that by flying in close proximity to the ground, the so-called image flow reduces induced drag by about 70 per cent. Flight-in-ground-effect inhibits the downwash induced by wing lift, thus suppressing the induced drag. Whereas an average aircraft at normal flight altitude carries about 4kg (9lb) per hp of engine output, the wing-in-ground-effect machine, on its dynamic air cushion carries up to 20kg (44lb), an improvement of more than 400 per cent. Weight efficiency of the craft (ratio of useful load to all-up weight) is 25 to 50 per cent depending on size.

At angles of attack of 2 to 8 degrees near the ground, its lift is 40 to 45 per cent greater than when flying out of ground effect. In addition the supporting surface hinders the vortex flow from the lower wing surface to the upper surface which decreases induced drag.

Control of the ESKA is said to be easy and pilots require no special training. Within ground effect it is no more complicated to control than a car.

The design, which has been strongly influenced by the Lippisch 'aerofoil boat' concept, employs an almost identical short span, low aspect ratio reversed delta wing with anhedral on the leading edge, dihedral tips and wing floats. A description of ESKA-1 follows, together with illustrations of other aerodynamic machines designed at the CLST, including the saucer-shaped E-120 single-seater; the AN-2E, which incorporates the fuselage, engine and cabin of the Antonov

ESKA-1

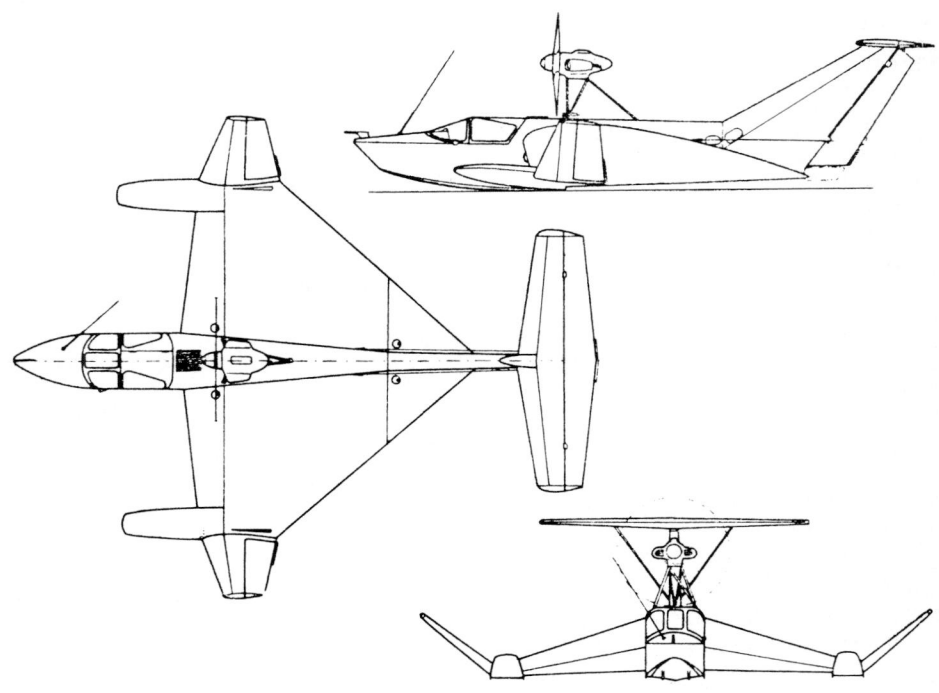

General arrangement of ESKA-1

AN-2W seaplane, and a two-seater powered by a 210hp Walter Minor engine.

One of the Ekranoplan's designers has been quoted as saying: 'Craft of this type are destined to become, in the not-too-distant future, as popular as hydroplanes, hovercraft and helicopters'.

ESKA-1

Research on aerodynamic ram wings began at CLST during 1971. During 1971-72 a series of small scale models were built, followed by the construction of five different full-size craft, including one with a circular planform.

The initial design of the ESKA-1 was prepared by Evgeniy Grunin between September and December 1972. In December 1972 the CLST section specialising in the provision of transport rescue facilities gave the design its full approval and accepted it for construction without additions or alterations.

Several free-flying models of the design were built and tested. In February 1973 A Gremyatsky was nominated leader of the project, and test-flew the first prototype in August of that year. Flight tests were subsequently undertaken by A A Baluyev.

Keynotes of the design were low cost, the use of advanced technology wherever possible and overall reliability in operation. In addition the craft had to be easily broken down for storing and transport by road. Analysis of these and other requirements and conditions led to the decision to build the craft in wood, using 1mm thick aviation ply, plastic foam, glass fibre, glues and varnishes. The resulting machine operated for more than four years in various conditions.

The designers state that although the ESKA-1 is similar aerodynamically to the late Dr Alexander Lippisch's X-112, X-113Am and X-114, the basis of ensuring longitudinal stability and the hydrodynamics at take-off differ. They add, 'In the absence of data on the results of tests for

ESKA-1

those designs, we relied on our own experience and used the results obtained in our own experiments with model ram wings'.

Practical help in the preparation of the initial design was given by A Kuzakov, designer of the MAK-15 glider, and the late V B Shavrov (1899-1976), designer of the Sh-2. Another well-known Soviet aircraft designer, V B Gribovsky acted as a consultant in solving the design problems presented by certain joints and structural members.

The basic aerodynamic design and construction of ESKA-1 has provided sufficient data for it to be recommended as a rescue/patrol and communications craft for certain national assignments. The test results show a case for continuing development work on two or three ESKA-1 prototypes, built with modern materials. It has shown considerable operational potential.

POWER PLANT: Single 32hp M-63 four-stroke two-cycle motorcycle engine drives, via a two-stage reduction gear, a wooden SDW-2 series 1·6m (5ft 3in) diameter constant pitch propeller. Engine is mounted on tubular steel tripod in dorsal position behind the cockpit. ST-4 electric starter mounted on engine block and driving the camshaft via a gear mounted on the extension shaft.

HULL: Built mainly of pinewood frames and longerons, with a box keel in plywood. Structure covered in aviation plywood with exterior clad in glass cloth saturated with ED-6 epoxy resin. Finished with white emulsion and synthetic varnish.

ACCOMMODATION: Cabin contains two aircraft seats in tandem with safety belts and space for parachutes. Rear seat for passenger or observer is placed close to centre of gravity so that no additional trimming is necessary when flying without a passenger.

WINGS: Cantilever shoulder-wing monoplane. Wooden monospar construction with leading edge covered in 1mm ply to form torque box. Dihedral tips each carry a wooden slotted aileron.

TAIL UNIT: Trapezium-shaped, strutted T-tailplane mounted on top of fin by sheet metal fixtures. All-wooden single box spar structure. Fixed-incidence, single full-span elevator. Elevator and tailplane covered with AST-100 glass cloth. Wooden rudder secured to fin at two points.

LANDING GEAR: Wing-tip floats are made in pvc foam and covered with a single layer of ASTT3b/-S1 glass cloth. Each is attached to wing by four steel bolts.

CONTROLS: Single aircraft-type control column, incorporating engine throttle, located in the centre of cockpit ahead of pilot's seat. Conventional foot-operated bar to control rudder.

TESTING AND RECORDING EQUIPMENT: In addition to basic aircraft-type instrumentation, the prototype ESKA-1 carried the following test equipment to record pitch and bank angles of up to 40 degrees: K12-51 oscilloscope; GS-6W equipment to measure pitch and angles of bank; synchronising equipment and an electrical supply pack, comprising an SAM28 27V battery and a PT-0.125-36/100 3F alternator.

RADIO: A modified portable 21 RTN-2-4M transmitter receiver provides a continuous radio link between ESKA-1 and the shore up to a distance of 2·5-3km (1·5-1·75 miles).

DIMENSIONS
Wing span overall: 6·9m (22ft 5·62in)
Length: 7·55m (24ft 7in)
Height: 2·5m (8ft 2·5in)
Wing area: 13·85m² (148·13ft²)
Tail area: 3m² (32·4ft²)
WEIGHTS
All-up weight: 450kg (992lb)
Empty: 230kg (507lb)
Useful load: 220kg (485lb)
Weight efficiency: 48·879%
PERFORMANCE
Speed, displacement condition: 30-40km/h (18-24mph)
   planing on water: 50-60km/h (31-37mph)

ram flight at a height of 0·3-3m (11·75in-9ft 10in): 100-140km/h (62-86mph)
   at altitude, 100-300m: 120-130km/h (74-80mph)
   take-off: 55km/h (34·17mph)
   landing: 50-55km/h (31-34mph)
Take-off run from water: 80-100m (260-300ft)
   from snow: 50-60m (162-195ft)
Landing run on water (without braking parachute): 40m (131ft)
Most effective flying height in surface effect: 0·3-1·5m (1ft-4ft 11in)
Max altitude, with 50% load, for obstacle clearance: up to 50m (164ft)
Range with full fuel supply: 300-350km (186-217 miles)
Wing loading: 32·5kg/m² (6·67lb/ft²)
Power loading: 15kg/hp (33lb/hp)
Limiting weather conditions—can operate in force 5 winds.

CLST ANTONOV An-2E

This adaptation of the An-2 multi-duty 12-seat biplane was built in 1973 to the design of E P Grunin. It incorporates several major components of the Soviet-built floatplane version, the An-2W, including the forward fuselage, cabin and engine—a 1,000hp Shvetsov ASh-621R nine-cylinder radial air-cooled engine, driving a four-bladed variable-pitch metal propeller.

The craft is intended for a range of utility applications in addition to carrying passengers and freight. Like the RFB X-114, which is undergoing trials in the German Federal Republic, the An-2E has a retractable wheeled undercarriage for operation from land as well as rivers, lakes and coastal waters.

DIMENSIONS
Span: 15·75m (51ft 8in)
Length: 18·65m (61ft 2in)

Height: 8·1m (26ft 7in)
Lift area: 94m² (1,011ft²)
WEIGHTS
All-up weight: 7,000kg (15,435lb)

CLST EKRANOLET E-120

No technical details have been released concerning this circular planform WIG single-seater. One of a number of experimental wing-in-ground-effect machines designed by the CLST, it was built in 1971.

PARAWING EKRANOPLANS

The originator of the idea of applying Rogallo-type flexible delta wings to light ekranoplans is Evgeniy Grunin, one of the designers of the ESKA-1. The parawing is well known for its outstanding aerodynamic qualities and stability and is convenient for transport and storage. Grunin, assisted by S Chernyavsky and N Ivanov, fitted a flexible wing to the fuselage of the Czechoslovak Let L-13J Blanik, a powered version of the well known two-seat, all-metal sailplane. Power is supplied by a 42hp Jawa M-150 piston-engine driving a 1·1m (3ft 7·25in) diameter Avia V210 propeller on a tripod mounting aft of the cockpit, an arrangement almost identical to that employed on ESKA-1. The craft was designated the E-0773 Shmiel (Bumblebee). Profiting from the encouraging results of the flight trials, the team has designed a number of small ekranoplan projects incorporating flexible wings, including a modified version of the An-2W, the floatplane version of the Antonov An-2, single-engine general-purpose biplane.

R-1001 MANTA

In 1974 the Central Laboratory of Lifesaving Technology developed a two-seater ekranoplan for light liaison duties with the Soviet fishing fleet.

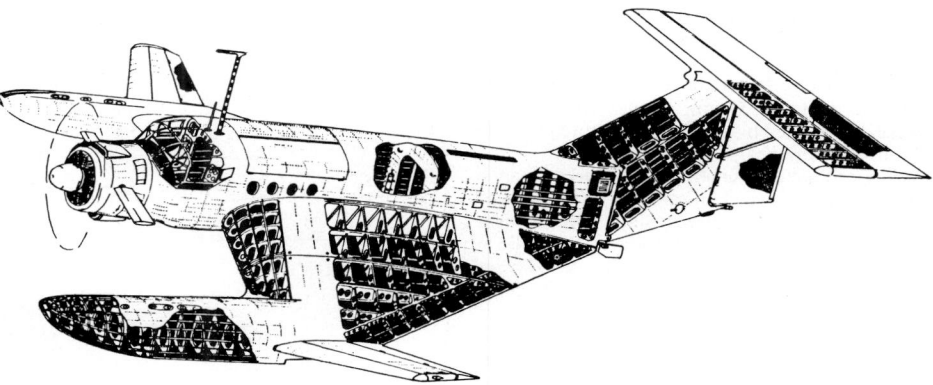

Cutaway of CLST ESKA adaptation of Antonov An-2W

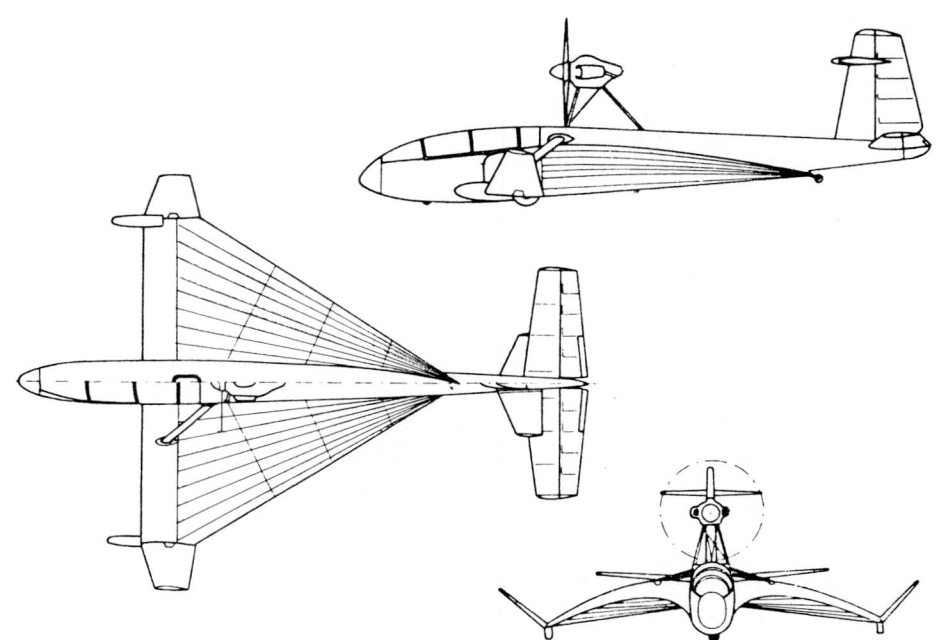

General arrangement of E-0773 Bumblebee 1

Visually the craft shows the influence of the late Dr Alexander Lippisch's design studies for a 300-ton Aerofoil boat, a major departure from the Lippisch concept being the asymmetrically located cabin jutting ahead of the broad aerofoil-shaped hull on the port side. Reports suggest that in building the wings and hull extensive use was made of grp laminate reinforced with carbon fibres.

Power is supplied by a 210hp Walter Minor VI engine of Czechoslovak manufacture, and the craft has an all-up weight of 1,460kg (3,219lb).

Dynamic models were used to gather design data on stability, manoeuvrability and performance.

CLST ESKA EA-06

A developed version of ESKA-1, believed to be a four-seater, began trials in September 1973, one month after ESKA-1 made its first flight. Photographs of a radio-controlled model of the EA-06 indicate that its lines are similar to those of ESKA-1, major differences being a wider cabin with a full-view windscreen and an aft fuselage angled upwards to support the fin and high-mounted tailplane well clear of the water.

The dynamically similar model was built to ¼ scale and had a wing span of 1·75m (5ft 9in). Power was supplied by a two-cylinder motor, developing 1·8hp at 12,500rpm, and driving a 300mm (11·81in) diameter laminated airscrew. Laminated balsawood construction was employed.

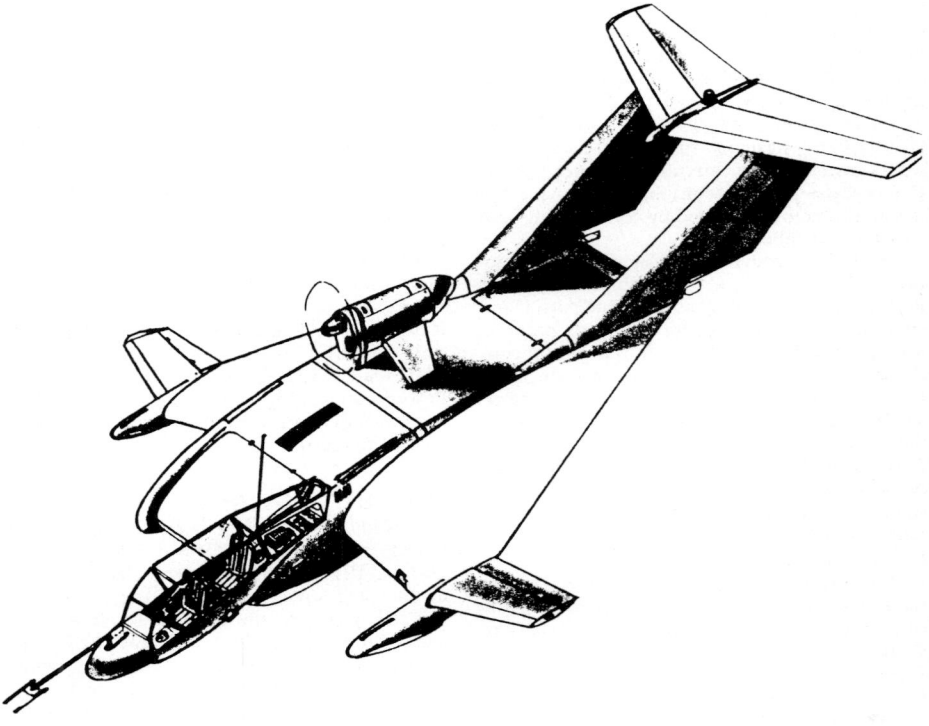

R-1001 Manta

KRASNOYE SORMOVO

Gorki, USSR

This shipyard began work in the ACV field by building a five-passenger air cushion river craft, known as the Raduga, in 1960-61. Since then it has built the Sormovich, a 30-ton peripheral jet ACV for 50 passengers, and the Gorkovchanin, a 48-seat prototype sidewall craft for shallow, winding rivers. It is believed that the Gorkovchanin, Zarnitsa, Orion, Chaika and Rassvet were all designed by the Gorki Institute of Water Transport Engineers.

The production version of the Gorkovchanin, the Zarnitsa, of which more than 100 have been built, is employed on almost all the river navigation lines of the Russian Federative Republic as well as on the rivers of the Ukrainian, Moldavian, Byelorussian and Kazakhstan Soviet Socialist Republics.

The design of an 80-seat rigid sidewall ferry, the Orion, was approved by the Soviet Ministry of Inland Waterways in 1970. Construction of the prototype began in 1972 and trials were successfully undertaken in 1975. The craft is now in series production.

A third sidewall vessel is the Rassvet, designed to carry up to 80 passengers along local sea routes. Like Zarnitsa, the craft is able to run bow-on to flat sloping beaches and does not require piers or specially prepared moorings. The prototype, Chaika-1, is undergoing trials. Work is also in hand aimed at evolving a substantially bigger sidewall ACV ferry which has been given the name, Turist. This craft has a design speed of 36 knots and is intended for shallow waterways unsuitable for hydrofoils. Two variants are projected, a 300-seat passenger ferry and a mixed-traffic model for 15 cars and 100 to 120 passengers.

Work should be completed during the mid-1980s on a variety of sidewall ACV projects including the following:

A 120- to 150-seat river ferry
A passenger ferry for very shallow rivers
A freight vessel for now and major rivers, including rivers with limited navigation seasons
A 120- to 150-seat seagoing craft
A high-speed mixed-traffic ferry for long distance routes

In 1969 prototypes of two fully-skirted hovercraft made their debut: the Briz, a light utility craft and the Skate, a 50-seat passenger ferry

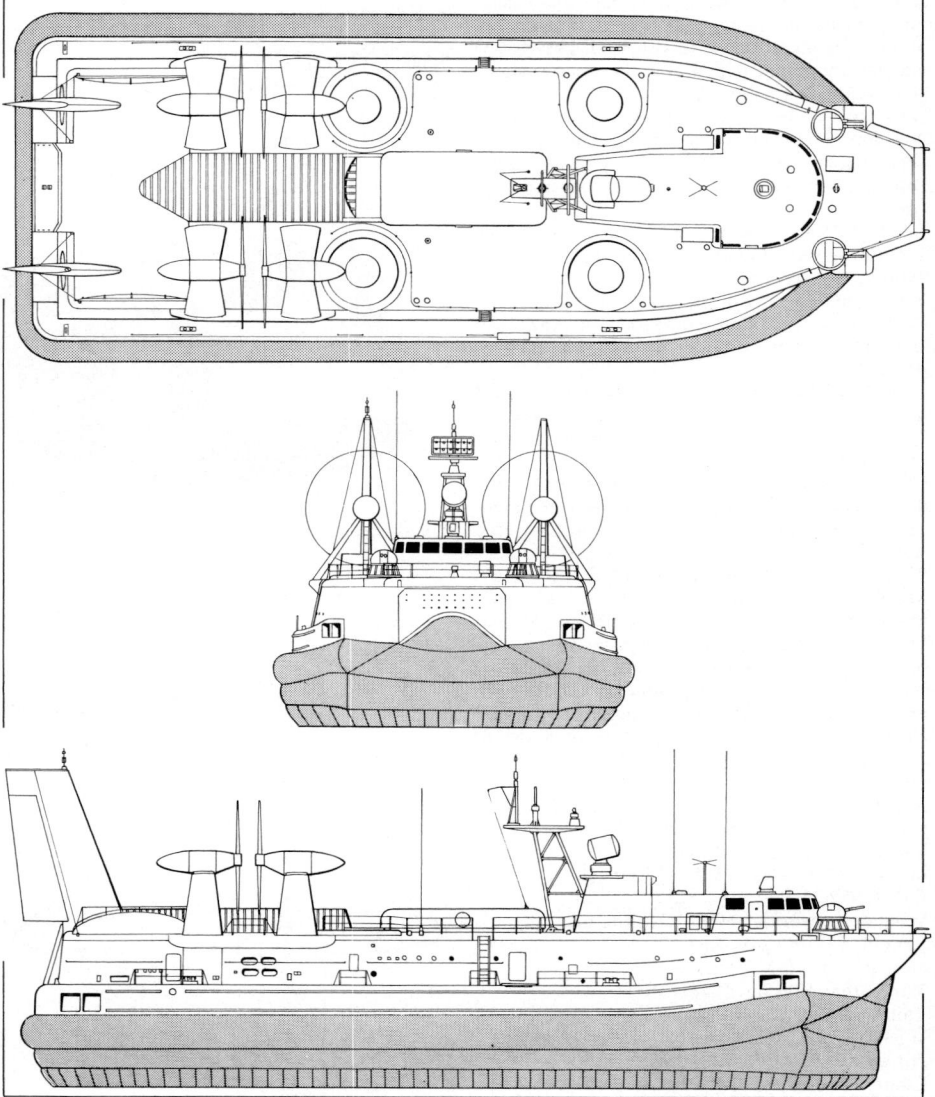

General arrangement of Aist with modified main engine air intakes

with an all-up weight of 27 tonnes and a cruising speed of 57·5 mph. While there is no evidence of the Skate going into production, a military version, known in the West by the NATO code name Gus, is in widespread service with the Soviet marine infantry and army. Gus was designed by a special Soviet Navy High-Speed Ship Design Bureau, in Leningrad, which was also responsible for the design of the Soviet Union's biggest skirted hovercraft, known in the West as Aist. More than 16 are in service with the Soviet Navy as amphibious assault landing craft. Aist can cross water, beaches and marginal terrain to deliver tanks, armoured transporters, equipment and personnel well beyond the shore line. Aist is generally similar in shape, size and performance to the BHC SR.N4 Mk 2.

Among military air cushion vehicles to enter production for the Soviet armed forces are a 90-tonne amphibious assault landing craft, similar in certain respects to the Vosper Thornycroft VT 2 but smaller, and known by the NATO code name Lebed, a craft similar in size and overall appearance to the BH.7 and a successor to Gus with ducted fans. It is likely that the latter will appear in a variety of configurations for military duties including assault craft, reconnaissance and fast attack craft. The Soviet Navy is also examining the potential of surface effect ships and is employing at least one sidewall craft for research and development.

Sormovo is thought to have been responsible for building the world's largest air cushion vehicle, a wing-in-ground-effect machine known by the code name Casp 1 and capable of carrying 800 to 900 troops at speeds up to 300 knots. Plans are in hand to build wing-in-ground-effect machines capable of navigating rivers at a speed of about 250km/h (155mph). A number of these craft are understood to be in experimental service.

Soviet air cushion activity is already massive in

Three-quarter view of Aist

comparison with the efforts of the West. Part of this activity is devoted to meeting Soviet military needs, but in the main it is devoted to the development and construction of amphibious carriers and snowgoing and marshgoing vehicles capable of providing reliable year-round transport in the Soviet north and north-eastern regions where a number of vital development projects are under way including the Siberia-West Europe gas pipeline.

Only a small percentage of the freight required can be delivered to these areas by helicopter. Estimates of the Institute of Integrated Transport Problems, operating under the USSR Gosplan Institute, have indicated that the use of air cushion vehicles, apart from speeding up the construction of important facilities under difficult conditions, will enable haulage costs over difficult routes of the north and north-east to be reduced by one-third. As a result, savings in transport

Aist

expenditure for the work volume forecast for the Eleventh Five-Year Plan will be 1,200 to 1,500 million roubles annually.

The use of amphibious ACVs in agricultural production enables operations including the application of fertilisers, herbicides and weeding to be conducted regardless of weather.

Large-load air-cushion platforms allow the movement of beet, potatoes and other crops from fields regardless of soil conditions. Expenditure for the chemical treatment of fields using self-propelled ACVs is half the cost of employing an AN-2 aircraft for this work and is one-third of the cost of an Mi-2 helicopter.

The Institute of Integrated Transport Problems, in considering under Gosplan the data of 25 Soviet ministries, has ascertained the requirement for transport equipment for developing the north and north-eastern regions of the Soviet Union. It was established that, for the level of haulage forecast for the long term, 6,000 to 6,500 self-propelled and towed amphibious air cushion transport vehicles and about 3,500 fully amphibious ACV ships will be necessary.

From the forecast it is apparent that fully amphibious ACVs will become more common in the Soviet Union than sidewall ACVs which lack all-terrain capability, require waterway depths of at least 1m, and can only be employed seasonally because of winter ice.

Soviet air cushion vehicles will soon be available on the world markets. Oleg Kropotov, Director General of Sudoimport, the organisation responsible for the export sales of Soviet ships and shipping equipment and hydrofoils, has announced that the Soviet Union 'is now prepared to hold negotiations for the sale of licences for the construction of hovercraft'.

270-ton NAVAL ACV
NATO Code Name Aist

The first large amphibious hovercraft to be built in the Soviet Union, Aist is entering service in increasing numbers with the Soviet Navy. Reports suggest that 16 have entered service to date. Built in Leningrad it is similar in appearance to the SR.N4 Mk 2 Mountbatten though giving the impression of being very much heavier than the British craft. It is likely that the bare weight, equipped but with no payload, crew or fuel, is as much as 170 tons. The prototype was launched in 1970 and production began in 1975.

Several variants have been built and differ externally in fin height, overall length, superstructure detail and defensive armament.

An Aist combat mission simulator has been introduced by the Soviet Navy to improve the ability of Aist commanders in operating the craft across sea and beach interfaces and Aist production facilities at Dekabristov, Leningrad, have been doubled. If output is expanded to take full advantage of both old and new production facilities, a new Aist is likely to be launched every 12 weeks.

A modified main engine air intake is being installed on all Soviet Navy Aists which are in service with the Baltic and Black Sea fleets. The intakes are believed to incorporate new filters to

Forward port quarter of Aist showing long bridge superstructure. Emblem in centre indicates amphibious ship, second insignia is combat efficiency award for operational readiness, rating craft an 'outstanding ship of the Soviet Navy'

Aist double bag skirt with finger fringe at base of lower loop

reduce the ingestion of salt water, sand and dust particles into Aist's engines and machinery, limiting the effects of salt corrosion and erosion. Due to high cushion pressure, Aist develops exceptionally heavy cushion spray, especially at low speeds.

Since delivery to the Soviet Navy, craft of this type have been employed largely as an amphibious assault landing and logistic supply craft, delivering naval infantry, its vehicles and weapons, mechanised infantry, self-propelled weapons, and main battle tanks to simulated beach-heads. Alternative military uses for amphibious craft of the Aist type would be mine countermeasures and fast patrol.

LIFT AND PROPULSION: Integrated system with motive power supplied by two NK-12MV marinised gas turbines, each of which is likely to be rated at 24,000shp. Each gas turbine drives

two 3·65m (12ft) diameter variable-pitch axial fans and two identical, pylon-mounted propellers, arranged in a facing pair, with the pusher propeller forward and the puller aft. The propellers, which are of the four-bladed variable- and reversible-pitch type are mounted so closely as to be virtually contraprops. Diameter of each propeller is thought to be about 6m (19ft 8·25in).

Modified engine air intakes are being installed on all Soviet Navy Aists. Several types are being tested. One modification involves the replacement of the original single, curved spine-like trunk above the longitudinal centreline by a mushroom sectioned box forward and a ribbed, shortened arch duct aft. The T-piece running athwartships across the stern superstructure between the twin fins has also been replaced by a ribbed arch duct. Alternative modifications include removing the athwartships T-piece and

Aist in foreground has original main engine intake while second Aist has new split air intake

the shortened arch duct on the centreline leaving the mushroom sectioned box forward. Modified lift fans and new lift fan intakes are also being introduced.

Additional intakes appear to be sited in the sides of the superstructure towards the stern.

An auxiliary gas turbine is at the rear end of the combat information centre (CIC) at the back of the cabin superstructure.

CONTROLS: Deflection of twin aerodynamic rudders aft, differential propeller pitch and fore-and-aft thrust ports provide steering control. Rudders are controlled by a wheel and propeller pitch by levers. All controls are in a raised bridge well forward on the superstructure.

HULL: Built mainly in welded marine corrosion resistant aluminium alloys. Structure appears to follow standard practice for large amphibious ACVs. The main hull is formed by a buoyancy raft based on a grid of longitudinal and transverse frames which form a number of flotation compartments. Two main longitudinal vertically stiffened bulkheads run the length of the craft separating the central load deck from the outer or side-structures, which contain the gas turbines and their associated exhausts, lift fans, transmissions, auxiliary power systems and seating for half a company of troops in cabins in the forward port and starboard quarters.

A full width ramp at the bow and a second at the stern, provide through loading facilities.

Typical vehicle loads include one or two T-62 or T-72 tanks or four PT-76 tanks; mobile radio trucks, armoured troop carriers, supply vehicles and ambulances.

ACCOMMODATION: Crew accommodation includes the control cabin or commander's cabin (Aist is described as being the sole warship type in the Soviet fleet in which the commander himself is responsible for steering), galley, radio room, sleeping and living quarters, engine mechanic's watch room and combat information centre (CIC). Naval infantrymen are seated in cabins on both sides of the central vehicle deck.

SKIRT: 2·5m (8ft 3in) deep double bag type in rubberised fabric with finger fringe beneath. Features include a high bow skirt line to protect the bow loading door against wave impact.

SYSTEMS, WEAPONS: Two twin 30mm fully-automatic dual-purpose mountings, controlled by Drum Tilt radar for close-in AA defence and by optical director and manual control for surface targets, including the suppression of LMG and rifle-fire during beach assaults.

DIMENSIONS (estimated)
Length overall, off cushion: 47·3m
Beam overall, off cushion: 17m
Height, control cabin: 1·98m
Length, control cabin: 10·5m
Width, bow ramp: 4·41m
rear ramp: 4·87m
WEIGHTS (estimated)
Bare weight: 170 tons

Gorkovchanin

Crew, fuel, AFVs or two main battle tanks and ½ company of naval infantry or troops: 90 tons
All-up weight: 260-270 tons
PERFORMANCE (estimated)
Max speed: about 70 knots
Cruising speed: 50 knots
Endurance: about 5 hours
Range, cruising: 350n miles

CHAYKA-1 (GULL-1)

This is the name given to the prototype Rassvet, 80-seat sidewall ACV ferry, designed for service in coastal areas with limited water depth. Details will be found in the entry for the Rassvet.

GORKOVCHANIN

The Gorkovchanin is a waterjet-propelled, 48-seat, rigid sidewall ACV, designed for water-bus services on secondary rivers with a guaranteed depth of 0·5m (1ft 8in). In view of the winding nature of these rivers, the craft operates at the relatively low speed of 30-35km/h (19-22mph). No marked reduction of speed is necessary in water up to 0·5m (1ft 8in) deep.

The craft has been developed from a ten-seat scale model built at the experimental yard of the Institute of Water Transport Engineers at Gorki in 1963, and the pre-production prototype was completed in September 1968. Design was undertaken by a team at the Volgobaltsudoproekt special design office.

Official trials were completed on the Sura river in May and June 1969. During speed tests over a measured mile with a full complement of passengers, 36·6km/h (22·75mph) was attained. The

main engine developed 265hp of which approximately 30hp was used to drive the centrifugal fan.

The craft has covered the journey from Gorki to Moscow (1,016km (622 miles)) and back in 31 and 27 running hours respectively at an average speed of approximately 35km/h (22mph) and has good manoeuvrability when running ahead and astern. In 1970 the Gorkovchanin was succeeded in production by a developed version, the Zarnitsa.

LIFT AND PROPULSION: Integrated system powered by a 3D6H diesel engine rated at 250hp continuous. The engine is mounted aft and drives a 960mm (3ft 1·75in) diameter six-bladed centrifugal fan for lift, and a 410mm (1ft 4·5in) diameter single stage waterjet rotor for propulsion. Fan air is taken directly from the engine compartment. Skirts of rubberised fabric are fitted fore and aft. The bow skirt of production craft is of segmented type. Cushion pressure is 180kg/m².

The waterjet intake duct is 100mm (4in) below the displacement water level to prevent air entry, with a consequent reduction in the navigable draft.

CONTROLS: Vanes in the waterjet stream provide directional control. Thrust reversal is achieved by the use of waterflow deflectors.

HULL: Similar in appearance to that of the Zarya, the hull is in riveted D16 corrosion resistant aluminium alloy. The hull bottom and sides have transverse frames and the sidewalls and superstructure top longitudinal frames. Thickness of plating on sides and bottom is 1·5mm (¹/₁₆in) (2·5mm (³/₃₂in) in the bow section); and on the sidewalls 1mm (³/₆₄in) (up to 5mm (¹³/₆₄in) in the bow section). Deck plates are 1mm (³/₆₄in) thick and the top of the superstructure is in 0·8mm (¹/₃₂in) plating.

Acoustic and thermal insulation includes 100mm (4in) thick foam polystyrene sheeting.

ACCOMMODATION: Seats are provided for a crew of two, who are accommodated in a raised wheelhouse, and 28 passengers. Access to the passenger saloon, which has airliner-type seats, is through a single door at the bow in the centre of the wheelhouse. The craft runs bow-on to flat sloping banks to embark and disembark passengers.

SYSTEMS, ELECTRICAL: One 1·2kW, 24V dc, engine-operated generator and batteries.

COMMUNICATIONS: Car radio in wheelhouse and speakers in passenger saloon.

DIMENSIONS
Length overall: 22·3m (73ft 2in)
Beam overall: 4·05m (13ft 3·5in)
Hull beam: 3·85m (12ft 7·62in)
Height of hull to top of wheelhouse: 3·3m (10ft 9·87in)
Height of sidewalls: 0·45m (1ft 5·75in)
Draught afloat: 0·45m (2ft 1·62in)
cushionborne: 0·65m (1ft 4·87in)

Aist unloading PT-76 tank and armoured troop carrier

Two Lebeds leave floodable well deck of Soviet Navy LPD, *Ivan Rogov*

WEIGHTS
All-up weight with 48 passengers, crew and fuel:
14·3 tons
PERFORMANCE
Normal service speed: 30-35km/h (19-22mph)
Distance and time from full ahead to full astern:
60m (197ft) and 14 seconds

LEBED

Primary roles of this multi-duty hovercraft are as an amphibious initial assault landing craft and high-speed vehicle for LOTS (Logistics-over-the-shore) operations. It provides Soviet naval infantry with a rapid lift capability to move personnel and equipment from the well decks of landing ships across water, beaches and marginal terrain to assembly points well above the shore line.

Smaller than both the US Navy's Jeff (A) and (B) and the Royal Navy's Vosper Thornycroft VT 2, Lebed has an overall length of about 24·4m, a gross weight of 86 tonnes and a maximum speed of 70 knots.

Two Lebeds or three Gus-type craft can be carried in the well deck of the Soviet Navy's LPD, the 13,100-ton *Ivan Rogov*, which also accommodates up to a battalion of naval infantry, 40 tanks and a range of supporting vehicles. Two Lebeds were demonstrated in South Yemen when the vessel called there on the way to the Soviet far east in 1979. The first of the 'Lebed' class was launched in 1973 and the craft entered production in 1976-77. If production rates have been similar to those of Gus (two to four units per year), it is likely that some 18 to 19 units are now operational. For use in the initial assault role, Lebeds would be pre-loaded before the *Ivan Rogov* sailed. Typical vehicle payloads include two PT-76 light amphibious tanks, two BMP-1 armoured personnel carriers, mobile radio trucks or supply vehicles up to a total weight of 35 tonnes. Design of Lebed is thought to have been undertaken by the Soviet Navy's High Speed Ship Design Bureau in Leningrad.
LIFT AND PROPULSION: Integrated system powered by two marinised gas turbines mounted one each side of the cargo deck aft. Engines are two AI-20s, each rated at 4,150 shp continuous. Air for the two main engines appears to be drawn in through two rectangular, filtered intakes then fed aft through a curved spine-like trunk above the longitudinal centreline and terminating between the two fins. The intakes for the axial-flow lift fans are outboard of the two gas-turbine air intakes. Each engine drives via a main gearbox and shaft a variable-pitch axial lift fan in light alloy. The fans deliver air to the cushion via a continuous peripheral loop skirt with segmented fringes. A second shaft from each main gearbox transmits power via bevel gears to a pylon-mounted four-bladed variable-pitch propulsion fan. The two propulsion fans are contained within aerodynamically shaped ducts which are partly submerged in the hull sidestructures. Apart from attenuating noise the ducts protect the fans from accidental damage. Exhaust covers are provided for both gas turbines aft at the rear of the port and starboard sidestructures.

Lebed *(Danish Defence)*

Lebed showing two propulsion fan ducts

Lebed showing details of skirt at bow

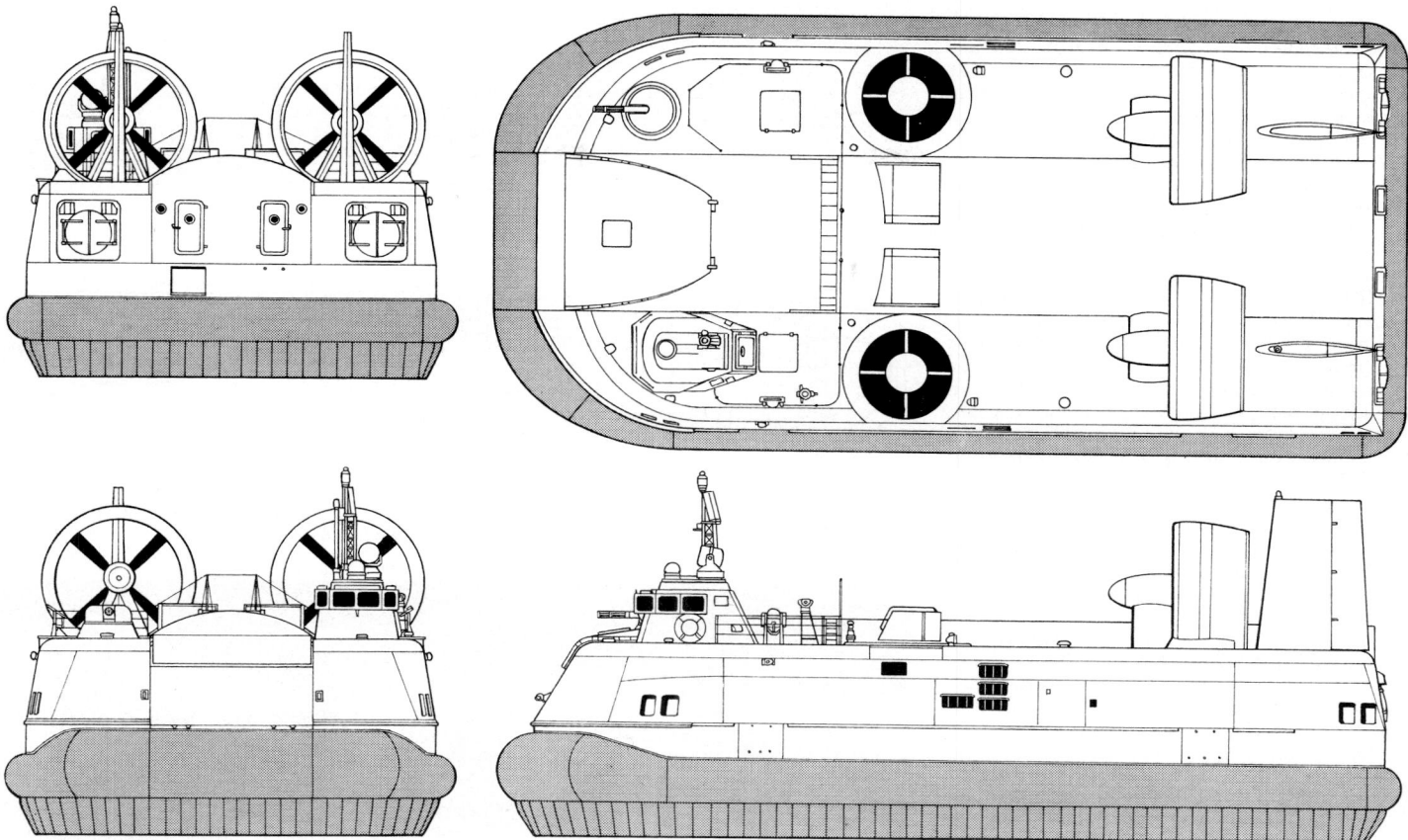

General arrangement of Lebed

CONTROLS: Control cabin is well forward above the port sidestructure and provides a 360-degree view. Directional control at normal operating speeds is by twin aerodynamic rudders aft of the thrust fan ducts and operating in the fan slipstreams. Differential pitch to the propulsion units augments the turning moment provided by rudder operation. Reverse thrust is applied for braking and reversing. Forward and aft thrust ports, port and starboard, aid directional control at low speeds.

HULL: Riveted skin and stringer structure employing alloy sheet. Structure follows standard practice for large and medium size amphibious ACVs. The main hull is formed by a buoyancy raft based on a grid of longitudinal and transverse frames which form a number of flotation compartments. Two main longitudinal vertically stiffened bulkheads run the length of the craft

separating the 4·8m (15ft 9in) central load deck from the outer sidestructures which contain the gas turbines and their associated exhausts, lift fans, transmissions and auxiliary power systems. The freight deck is reinforced for the carriage of tanks, armoured troop carriers, self-propelled guns, rocket launchers and heavy vehicles. Drive-on, drive-off loading facility is provided by a full-width hydraulically-operated bow door/loading ramp. This is hinged from the base and has an overlapping hatch cover. Personnel doors are provided aft. Photographs suggest that six landing pads are built into the craft's undersurface.

SKIRT: Loop and segment type with raised hinge line at bow.

ARMAMENT: One remotely-controlled six-barrel Gatling-action 30mm cannon in barbette on forward quarter of the starboard sidestruc-

ture. Employed in conjunction with fire-control radar for close-in anti-aircraft and anti-missile defence and with optical sighting and manual control for surface targets including suppressing LMG and rifle fire during beach assaults.

It is reported that a new gun is being installed on Soviet 'Lebed' class medium air cushion landing craft. It has a 54cm long tapered barrel, with a 50mm external muzzle diameter and a 100mm diameter base at the gunhouse. As with the previous arrangement, the gun is mounted on a circular barbette on the starboard bow. A periscopic sighting device is fitted for manual operation and the gun can be elevated from about 13 degrees negative to 90 degrees vertical. The gun house is 134cm in diameter and 63cm high.

DIMENSIONS
Length overall: 24·4m (79ft 9·75in)
Beam overall: 10·8m (35ft 5·25in)
WEIGHTS
Max all-up weight: 86 tonnes
Max payload: 35 tonnes
PERFORMANCE
Max speed, calm conditions: 70 knots
Cruising speed, calm conditions: 50 knots

LUCH-1

A new sidewall ACV for river use has been completed at the Astrakhan Shipyard and underwent State trials in September 1983. Designed to replace the eleven-year-old Zarnitsa, the craft, named Luch, will carry two crew and up to 66 passengers, 15 standing. Of all-welded aluminium construction, it has an all-up weight of 20·1 tonnes and a top speed of 44km/h. Its shallow on cushion draught of just over 0·5m allows it to run bow-on to flat sloping river banks to embark and disembark passengers. A ladder is fitted at the bow.

New design features will permit operation on large rivers such as the Don, Kama, Oka and Volga, where high waves are encountered. However, the yard emphasises that it will be used primarily by oil and gas personnel and timber rafters who work on the banks of small rivers.

Among the basic design requirements were: that the Zarnitsa's general characteristics should be preserved; increased reliability; easier maintenance; increased service speed; widened operating potential and improved ride comfort.

Lebed unloading PT-76 tanks

Compared with the Zarnitsa, Luch has a more powerful diesel, the 328kW 3KD12N-520, and uses a lighter form of construction. The overall dimensions of the craft permit rail transport to distant rivers and canals.

During trials before the commissioning of the first of the class it was demonstrated that its operating and technical performance is significantly superior to that of the Zarnitsa. The craft is built to the requirements of the 'R' class of the USSR's River Craft Registry. It is in series production.

LIFT AND PROPULSION: Power provided by single 3KD12N-520 marine diesel with normal service output of 328kW at 1500rpm. The engine is mounted aft and drives, via a transmission shaft, a centrifugal fan for lift and a waterjet rotor for propulsion. The waterjet rotor and its bearing can be replaced while the craft is in displacement condition without having to lift it out of the water.

CONTROLS: Twin rudder vanes in the waterjet stream control craft heading. Thrust reversal achieved by waterflow deflectors.

HULL: The buoyancy structure is built in welded AlMg-61 aluminium alloy. The superstructure is built in D16 alloy. Superstructure and bulkheads are riveted together. Pressed panels are employed throughout the hull to improve the external appearance and reduce the volume of assembly work necessary during construction.

SKIRT: Fingered type at bow, bag-type aft. Bow segments attached to an easily replaceable module.

ACCOMMODATION: Seats are provided for a crew of two, in a raised wheelhouse, and 51 passengers. On route sectors of 1 hour or less, the capacity can be increased to 66 by allowing 15 standing in the passenger cabin. The hull is divided into seven basic sections: a forward platform, the control cabin, service room, vestibule, passenger cabin, auxiliary rooms, engine room and stern platform. The bow platform has a gangway/ladder for embarkation and landing on unequipped stopping points, jetties and for mooring. The location of the control cabin at the bow simplifies handling on narrow waterways. A service room, aft of the control cabin, provides rest accommodation for the relief crew.

The lounge has 51 passenger seats, one seat for a guide and racks for small items of luggage. Large sliding windows ensure good visibility and ventilation. The lounge and crew rooms are air conditioned. The passenger cabin is separated from the engine room by a store room on the port side and a toilet on the starboard side, an arrangement which reduces the noise level. Mooring, refuelling, taking-on oil and water, discharging sewage and oil-contaminated waters to container vessels or shore based containers are all performed from the aft platform. A hatch on the aft platform gives access to the waterjet rotor.

SYSTEMS, ELECTRICAL: One 1·2kW 24V dc engine-operated generator and batteries. During prolonged night stops power can be supplied by a shore based 220V, 50Hz electrical supply.

COMMUNICATIONS: VHF, Kama 'R', marine transceiver. PA and crew command systems.

DIMENSIONS
Length overall: 22·8m
Beam: 3·85m
Height overall: 3·35m
    side: 1·2m
    skegs: 0·45m
Draught, off cushion: 0·63m
    on cushion, bow: 0·1m
    on cushion, stern: 0·5m
WEIGHTS
All up: 20·1 tonnes
Empty: 14·2 tonnes
PERFORMANCE
Speed: 44km/h
Range, with fuel reserves: 300 km

NAVAL RESEARCH HOVERCRAFT

A 15-ton experimental ACV has been employed by the Soviet Navy since 1967 to assess the potential of hovercraft for naval applications and investigate controllability and manoeuvrability. Lift is provided by a single 350hp radial aircraft

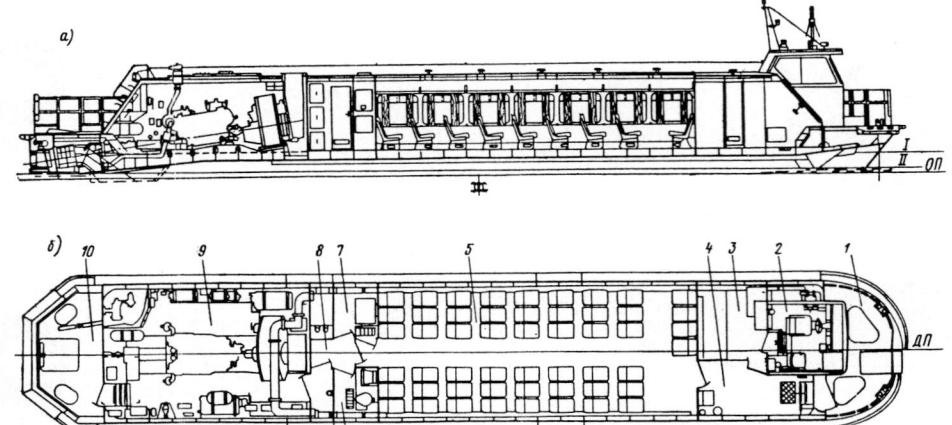

Inboard profile and plan of Luch: **(a)** longitudinal section **(b)** deck plan **(I)** waterline in displacement mode **(II)** waterline when cushionborne **(1)** fore deck **(2)** wheelhouse **(3)** duty compartment **(4)** vestibule **(5)** passenger saloon **(6)** toilet **(7)** storeroom **(8)** vestibule **(9)** engine room **(10)** aft deck

Naval 15-ton research craft

engine driving a centrifugal fan and propulsion by two pylon-mounted radials of the same type driving controllable-pitch airscrews.
DIMENSIONS
Length: 21·33m (70ft)
Beam: 9·14m (30ft)
WEIGHTS
Displacement: 15 tons
PERFORMANCE
Max speed: 50 knots

NAVAL AMPHIBIOUS ASSAULT CRAFT

The latest hovercraft under development for the Soviet Navy is reported to be similar in size, configuration and performance to the BHC BH.7 Mk 4 and incorporates a bow door and central load well. Size constraints would be dictated by the dimensions of the well decks of the *Ivan Rogov* and possible follow-on classes.

Like the BH.7, the craft is fully amphibious and has an all-up weight of 50 to 55 tons.

Gus *(Danish Defence)*

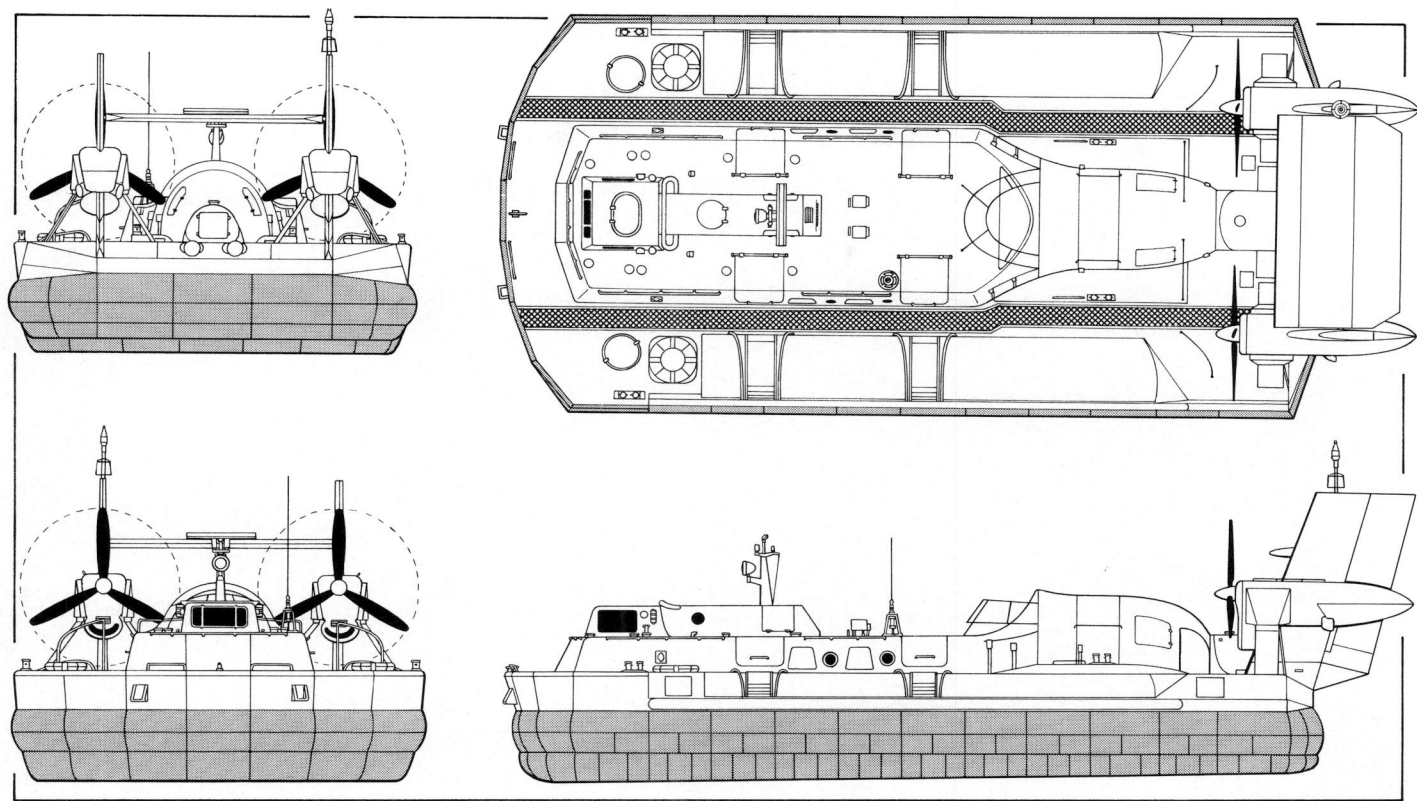

General arrangement of Gus

NAVAL SES TEST CRAFT

The Soviet Navy is testing a small SES with an overall length of about 18·2m (60ft). In general appearance the craft is said to resemble a scaled-down version of the Bell Halter 212A (110 Mk II) Dashboat, with the bridge well forward and a large open deck aft for weapons and other equipment. The craft is thought to be propelled by two marine diesels driving waterscrews. As a result of detailed assessments undertaken in the Soviet Union over a number of years, a range of large sidewall hovercraft is being developed for both military and commercial applications. Designs of 2,000 to 4,000 tonnes are under consideration.

LOGISTIC SUPPORT ACV
NATO Code Name Gus

A variant of the Skate, which was designed as a 50-seat amphibious passenger ferry, but which was not put into production, Gus is now employed extensively by the Soviet Naval Infantry for river patrol, small-unit troop insertion and amphibious assault. The Soviet Navy's amphibious landing ship, the *Ivan Rogov*, can carry three amphibious assault ACVs of the Gus type. Each of these craft can carry a fully-armed platoon onto a landing beach at speeds of up to 60 knots. The prototype was launched in 1969 and it is thought that 31 of these 27-tonne vehicles are in service. Production of this class is thought to have been completed in 1979. A derivative with twin ducted propellers is under development.

LIFT AND PROPULSION: Motive power is provided by three 950hp TVD-10 marine gas turbines mounted aft. Two drive 3m (9ft 10in) diameter three-bladed variable and reversible-pitch propellers for thrust and the third drives an axial lift fan. Cushion air is drawn through a raised intake aft of the cabin superstructure.

CONTROLS: Craft direction is controlled by differential propeller pitch, twin aerodynamic rudders and forward and aft puff ports. Elevator provides pitch trim at cruising speed.

HULL: Hull and superstructure are in conventional corrosion-resistant marine light alloy. Basic structure comprises a central load-carrying platform which incorporates buoyancy tanks and outer sections to support the side ducts and skirt. The cabin, fuel tanks, lift fan bay engines and tail unit are mounted on the platform.

ACCOMMODATION: Air-conditioned cabin for up to 25 troops. Commander and navigator

Gus craft during exercise in eastern Baltic Sea

Training variant of Gus with raised second cabin for instructor

Gus during beach landing exercise

are seated in a raised wheelhouse. Battle crew of six, including two responsible for opening the two entry/exit doors forward and amidship, port and starboard.

DIMENSIONS

EXTERNAL
Length overall, power on: 21·33m (69ft 11·5in)
Beam overall, power on: 7·8m (25ft 7·5in)
Height to top of fin: 6·6m (21ft 8in)
WEIGHTS
Normal operating: 27 tonnes
PERFORMANCE
Max speed: 60 knots
Cruising speed: 43 knots
Range: 200n miles

PLAMYA (FLAME) ACV RIVER FIRETENDER

The Central Design Bureau at Gorki has developed a river-going firetender. The craft is based on the hull of the Orion sidewall-type passenger ferry, but the passenger cabin superstructure has been replaced by an open deck forward to accommodate a tracked or wheeled firefighting vehicle and its crew. Plamya is designed for the fast delivery of an off-the-road firefighting vehicle and its crew to points on lakes, reservoirs and major rivers near forest fires. The craft can be beached bow-on on the river bank and the firefighting vehicle or bulldozer off-loaded across the bow ramp.

Plamya meets the requirements of the Register of Shipping of the USSR and is constructed to class R in the RSFSR Inland Waterways Register. It is in service on the river Kama.

LIFT AND PROPULSION: Integrated system powered by two 520hp 3D12N-520 marine diesels. Each engine drives a Type Ts 39-13 centrifugal fan for lift and, via a cardan shaft, a semi-submerged single-stage waterjet rotor for propulsion.

CONTROLS: Rudders aft of the waterjet inlets and two waterjet deflectors control craft direction.

HULL: All-welded structure in AlMg-61 aluminium-magnesium alloy. Frames, plates, partitions and roof of superstructure in D16 alloy.

SKIRT: Bow, triple-row, fully segmented type; stern, fingered bag type.

ACCOMMODATION: As opposed to the

Gus

Plamya

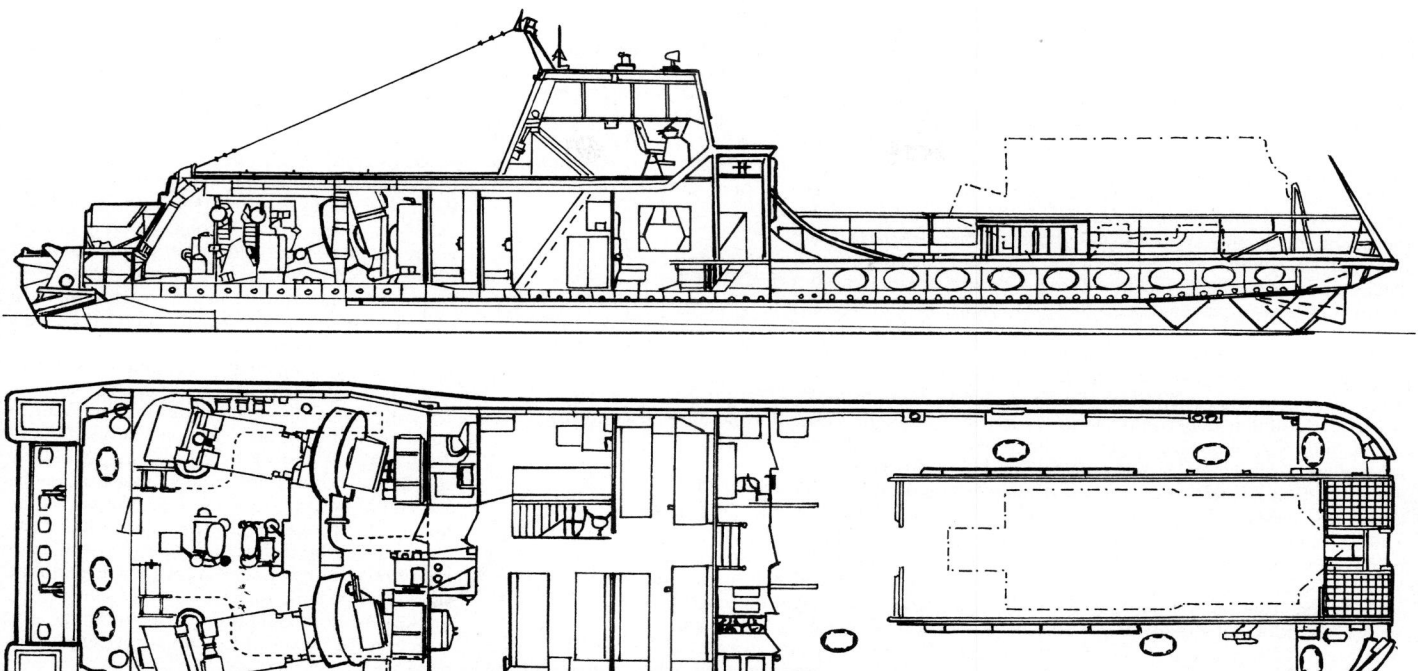

Inboard profile and deck plan of Plamya

'Orion' class the Plamya's pilothouse is amidships, with a large cargo deck forward to facilitate the carriage of a firefighting vehicle or bulldozer and the crew. Alternative loads include an ATsL-3(66)-147 forest firefighting tracked vehicle, a VPL-149 firefighting cross-country vehicle, a truck with portable firefighting equipment and a crew of 18, or a bulldozer with a crew of three. Beneath the pilothouse superstructure are storerooms for portable firefighting equipment, a lounge for the firefighting squad, an off-duty cabin for the crew of three and a toilet. Engine room is aft.

SYSTEMS, ELECTRICAL: 24V dc, supplied by two 1·2kW engine-driven generators linked with two sets of storage batteries.
COMMUNICATIONS: Kama-S UHF radio and PZS-68 passenger announcement system. Granit-M and Groza-2 transceivers for communication with firefighting team.
DIMENSIONS:
Length overall: 26·1m (85ft 8in)
Beam: 6·5m (21ft 4in)
Height overall, amidship: 5·5m (18ft 2in)
Draught displacement condition: 0·88m (2ft 11in)
Draught, on cushion, at stern: 0·7m (2ft 4in)

WEIGHTS:
Fully loaded: 34·5 tonnes
Cargo capacity: 7·3 tonnes
PERFORMANCE:
Max speed: 50km/h (31mph)

ORION-01

Design of the Orion, a rigid sidewall ACV with seats for 80 passengers, was approved in Moscow in autumn 1970. The prototype, built in Leningrad, began trials in October 1973 and arrived at

its port of registry, Kalinin, in late 1974, bearing the serial number 01.

The craft is intended for passenger ferry services along shallow rivers, tributaries and reservoirs and can land and take on passengers bow-on from any flat sloping bank. It is faster than the Zarnitsa and its comfort and performance are less affected by choppy conditions. Cruising speed of the vessel, which is propelled by waterjets, is 53km/h (32·3mph). It belongs to the 'R' class of the Soviet River Register.

Several variants are under consideration,

ORION—Stopping and starting characteristics	Shallow water	Deep water
Distance run by vessel from Full Ahead to Stop		
Metres	136	120
Time in seconds	67	40
Distance run by vessel from Full Ahead to Full Astern		
Metres	84	65
Time in seconds	23	20
Distance necessary for attainment of Full Speed from Stop		
Metres	250	330
Time in seconds	60	80

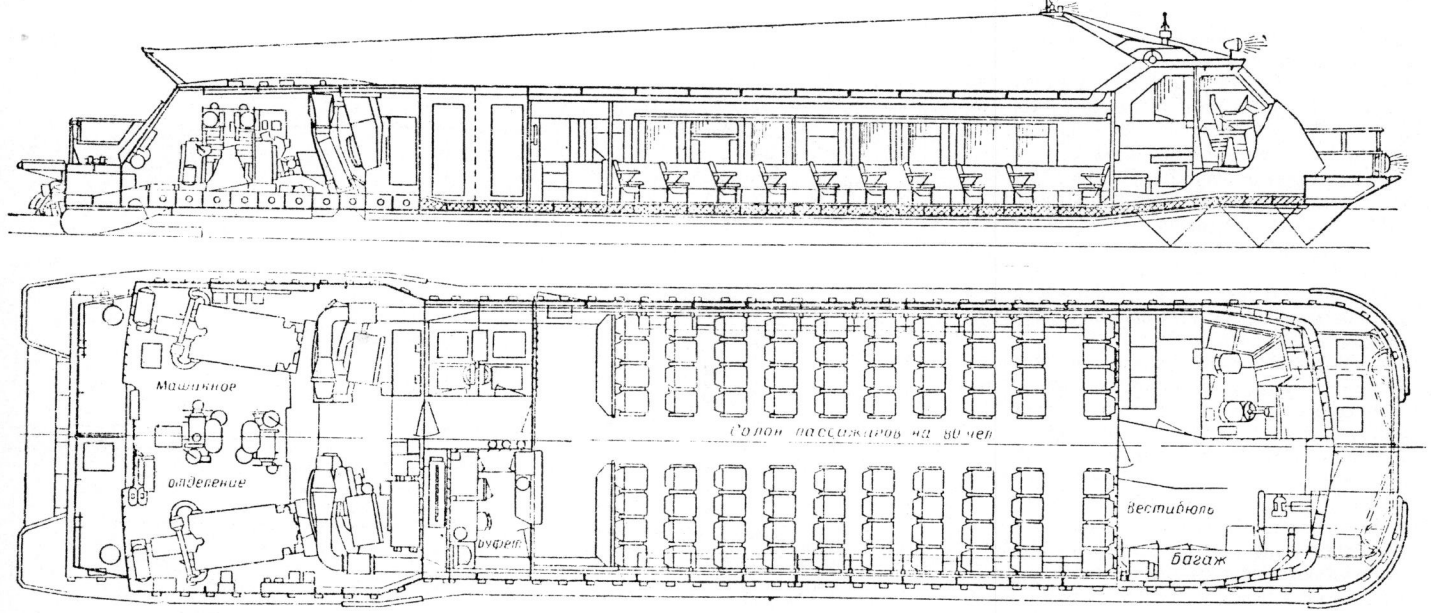

General arrangement of Orion

including a 'stretched' model seating 100 passengers on shorter routes, a mixed passenger/freight model, an all-freight model and an 'executive' version for carrying government officials.

Experimental operation of the Orion-01 was organised by the Port of Kalinin, Moscow River Transport, the initial run being Kalinin—1 May Factory, a distance of 99km (61·5 miles), of which 45km (28 miles) is on the Volga, 42km (26 miles) on the Ivanov reservoir and 12km (7·5 miles) on the shallow waters of the Soz. The first weeks of operation showed that there was an insufficient flow of passengers on this particular route.

The vessel was then employed on public holidays only for carrying holiday makers and day trippers on such runs as Kalinin—Putlivo 31km (19 miles), Kalinin—Kokoshky 19km (12 miles) and Kalinin—Tarbasa 28km (17·3 miles), and subsequently on a regular schedule to Putlivo. Finally, Orion-01 was used on the Kalinin—Kimry run, a distance of 138km (85·7 miles), of which 70km (43·4 miles) passes through the Ivanov reservoir and 68km (42 miles) on the Volga.

Particular attention was paid to skirt reliability. The side sections of the lower part of the bow skirt were badly chafed and split due to contact with the skegs when coming onto the shore. Upper parts of the skirt were not damaged. Problems were also experienced with the aft skirt made from a balloon type fabric. Layers of rubber in the aft part of the segments peeled off; chafing was caused by securing washers and splitting was experienced in the vicinity of the fastenings.

In order to reduce the time spent on repairs, sections of the stern skirt were attached to removable frames. Later a new stern skirt was introduced, based on panels made from a 12mm (0·47in) thick conveyor belt. This enabled the stern draught, on cushion, to be reduced by 10cm (3·87in) and the speed to be increased by 1·5km/h (0·87mph). It also improved the reliability of the craft. During the 200 hours under way from the time the skirt was fitted until the end of the vessel's trials, there was no damage.

It was considered that, in the main, the Orion met the requirements of the Soviet operators for the rapid transport of passengers on 'R' class rivers and reservoirs. The elimination of the defects revealed during the experimental operation will improve the vessel's operational characteristics and increase its reliability.

Series production of this vessel is being undertaken at the Sosnovska Shipbuilding Yard in Kirovskaya Oblast.

LIFT AND PROPULSION: Integrated system powered by two 520hp 3D12N-520 diesels mounted in an engine room aft. Each engine drives a Type Ts 39—13 centrifugal fans for lift, and via a cardan shaft, a semi-submerged single-stage waterjet rotor for propulsion. Fan air is fed via ducts to the bow skirt, a transverse stability slot and to the fingered bag skirt aft. Casing of the waterjet system, which is removable, forms the stern section of the vessel. The waterjets are mounted on shock absorbers to reduce vibration.

HULL: Similar in overall appearance to Zarya and Zarnitsa types. All-welded structure in AlMg-61 aluminium-magnesium alloy. Lateral framing throughout hull with the exception of the bow and stern decks, where longitudinal frames have been fitted. Superstructure and wheelhouse are of welded and riveted duralumin construction on longitudinal framing.

ACCOMMODATION: Seats for operating crew of three, which is accommodated in a raised wheelhouse, a barman, two seamen and 80 passengers. At the aft end of the passenger saloon are two toilet/washbasin units and a bar. An off-duty cabin for the crew. Access to the passenger saloon is via a single door at the bow, in the centre of the wheelhouse. A ram-air intake provides ventilation while the craft is under way. Stale air is drawn out by the lift fans aft.

CONTROLS: Rudders located aft of the waterjet inlets and two waterjet deflectors control craft direction. Rudder and flap movement is by cables.

SYSTEMS, ELECTRICAL: Two G-73Z engine-driven generators, linked with two sets of STK-18M batteries, provide 28V, 1,200W. One battery set is employed for engine starting, the other for supplying current for the ship's systems.

COMMUNICATIONS: Standard equipment comprises an R-809MZ radio-telephone, a Kama-3 UHF radio and an Unja cabin announcement system.

DIMENSIONS
Length overall: 25·8m (84ft 7·75in)
Beam overall: 6·5m (21ft 4in)
Height overall to mast top: 5·27m (17ft 3·5in)
Height to top of wheelhouse: 3·97m (13ft 0·25in)
Draught, displacement condition, fully loaded: 0·84m (2ft 9·12in)
    empty: 0·76m (2ft 5·87in)
Draught, cushionborne, bow: 0·1m (4in)
    stern: 0·5m (1ft 8in)

WEIGHTS
Loaded displacement: 34·7 tonnes
Light displacement: 20·7 tonnes

PERFORMANCE
Max speed: 60km/h (37·25mph)
Cruising speed, full load: 53km/h (33mph)
Max wave height on scheduled runs: 1·2m (4ft)
Range: 400km (249 miles)
Diameter of turn to port: 182m (597ft)
Time to complete turn with rudders at 33 degrees: 187 seconds
Time taken from start of berthing procedure to completion: 1 min approx
Time taken to attain cruising speed from leaving berth: 2 minutes approx

CASP A ('CASPIAN SEA MONSTER')

Trials of Casp A, the 91·4-metre (300-foot) long Soviet experimental wing-in-ground-effect machine, which began on the Caspian Sea in 1965, appear to have stopped and the craft is no longer in use. Tests with Casp B, and a number of proportionally smaller models, are continuing.

A description and artist's impression of Casp A can be found in *Jane's Surface Skimmers 1984* and earlier editions.

CASP B

A new Soviet ekranoplan is reported to be under test. The vehicle is thought to have been developed from the 'Caspian Sea Monster' and could be a pre-production prototype.

Two versions of Casp B are being developed: one for amphibious assault, the other for use as a fast strike craft or sea raider. Reports indicate that the latter variant will carry two or more SS-N-22 long-range, sea-skimming missiles.

Compared with the 'Monster', the new design has been improved aerodynamically and, for greater economy at cruising speed, has a single turboprop at the top of its fin instead of twin gas turbines. Another major difference is the internal mounting of a single or twin gas turbines forward to provide the power augmented ram effect.

During low-speed manoeuvring, take-off and while flying through hump speed, the forward power plant breathes air through flush intakes in the upper nose ahead of the crew cabin and expels its exhaust gases through rotating nozzles at mid-hull height below the crew cabin. At take-off both forward and rear power plants are employed. The exhaust nozzles of the forward unit are rotated downwards to direct their high energy efflux into the plenum formed by the wing undersurface, wing endplates, trailing edge flaps and the water or other supporting surface beneath and within a short distance the craft is lifted bodily out of the water on a cushion of air. After take-off and while accelerating to cruising speed, the nozzles are rotated upwards to the horizontal position to align their efflux with the line of flight. Once cruising speed has been attained and the craft is on course, the wing flaps are retracted, the nozzles are withdrawn into the sides of the hull, the forward gas turbine air intakes are closed and the craft cruises in ground effect on the power of its contra-rotating turbo-prop aft.

The turboprop is almost certainly a Kuznetsov NK-12MV driving two four-blade contra-rotating propellers.

Use of the PAR-WIG technique will enable this type of craft to rise out of the water on an air cushion before take-off and to set down at low speed on an air cushion when landing in rough or calm water. The same capability permits land or shoreline landings.

It is assumed that the new ekranoplan has a shore delivery capability and will be able to operate from suitable beaches, including those with a surf zone. The overall configuration suggests that the nose swings open aft of the crew compartment and forward propulsor bay to allow loading and unloading of cargo. The craft will be beached bow-on and reverse thrust from the tail-mounted contra-rotating turboprop will be employed to withdraw it from the shoreline.

Operating at low altitude at a speed probably approaching 300 knots the craft will give the Soviet Navy the ability to land assault groups on accessible beaches quickly and with maximum surprise.

DIMENSIONS
Length overall, approx: 60·9m (200ft)
Span: 30·4m (100ft)
Aspect ratio: 3·0

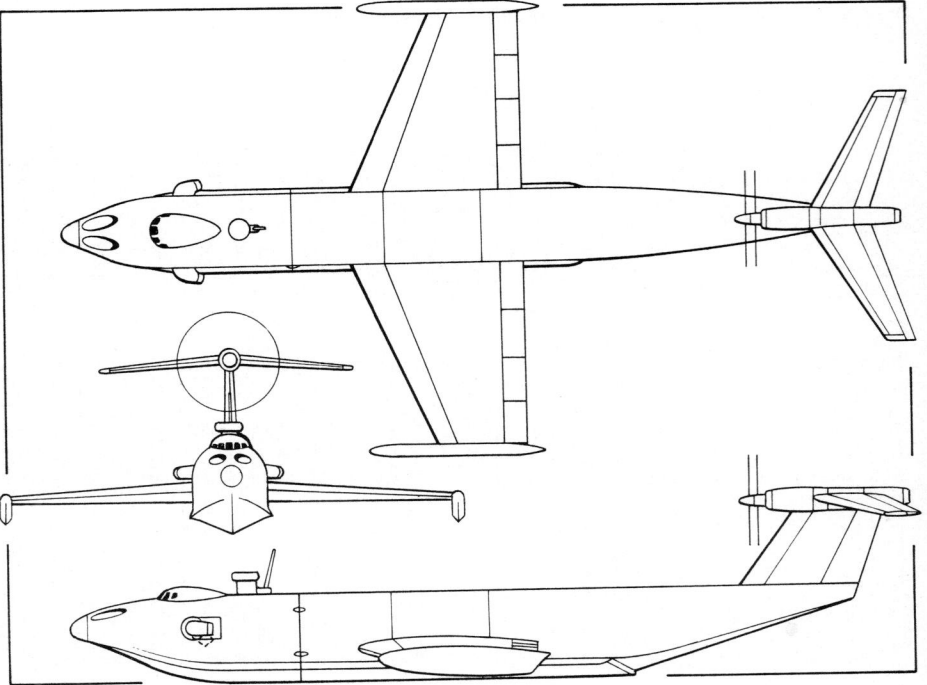

Provisional 3-view drawing of Casp B

PERFORMANCE
Cruising speed: 250-280 knots
Max significant wave height for landing and take-off: (1·2-1·5m) (4-5ft) approx

BARTINI T-WINGS

The Ministry of the River Fleet announced in April 1972 that it planned to build craft of the ekranoplan (WIG) type 'which will travel within several metres of a river surface at speeds of some 250km/h (155mph)'.

It seems probable that in order to avoid navigation problems in busy river port areas these craft will be of smaller overall dimensions than the 40m (131ft 3in) span machine described earlier. Low aspect ratio wings are likely to be employed and it is possible that these early production craft are of 5 to 6 tons displacement. A number of these machines were reported to be in experimental service in 1973.

On Moscow television in July 1973, a programme commemorating Soviet Navy Day traced the progress of high-speed water transport and confirmed that ekranoplans are being developed in the Soviet Union. The craft were described by the commentator as 'ground gliders', capable of operating over land, water, snow and ice. A small machine built in Odessa in the early 1960s was shown to viewers, together with a completely new research craft of much larger size believed to have been designed by the late Robert Oros di Bartini.

The craft, a derivative of an earlier design patented in Bartini's name, is of catamaran configuration and carries up to forty passengers in each of the twin hulls. The crew and operating controls are in a central pod jutting ahead of the wing leading edge.

Thrust is provided by three pairs of pylon-mounted marinised gas turbines, one pair located aft on the vehicle's longitudinal centreline and two mounted forward beneath the leading edge, between the central cabin pod and the inner faces of the two hulls.

The four forward-mounted engines blow air beneath the wing for take-off and landing. By directing the exhaust gases under the wing leading edge, the vehicle is lifted out of the water. The system enables it to take-off and land on both rough and calm water and from dry land.
DIMENSIONS
Length: approx 30·48m (100ft)
WEIGHTS
All-up: 50 tonnes
Payload: 20 tonnes
Empty: 30 tonnes
PERFORMANCE
Max speed: 300-350 knots
Cruising speed: 170-200 knots

RADUGA

This experimental amphibious ACV was completed at the Krasnoye Sormovo shipyard in 1962 and is reported to have attained a speed of 100km/h (62mph). Lengthy trials of the Raduga provided positive results and the data obtained was used as a basis for the design and construction of the 36-tonne Sormovich.

Built originally as a peripheral jet type, it is now being used to develop control techniques, and provide amphibious experience and data on skirt design.
LIFT AND PROPULSION: The craft is powered by two 220hp air-cooled radial engines. One, mounted amidships, drives a 1·8m (5ft 11in) 12-bladed lift fan; the second, mounted on a pylon at the stern, drives a two-bladed propeller for propulsion. The fan delivers air to the cushion via a continuous peripheral skirt, the bow and side sections of which are of the fingered bag type.
CONTROLS: Directional control is provided by an aerodynamic rudder operating on the propeller slipstream.
HULL: Riveted aluminium construction.
ACCOMMODATION: The cabin seats five.
DIMENSIONS
Length: 9·4m (30ft 10in)
Beam: 4·12m (13ft 6in)

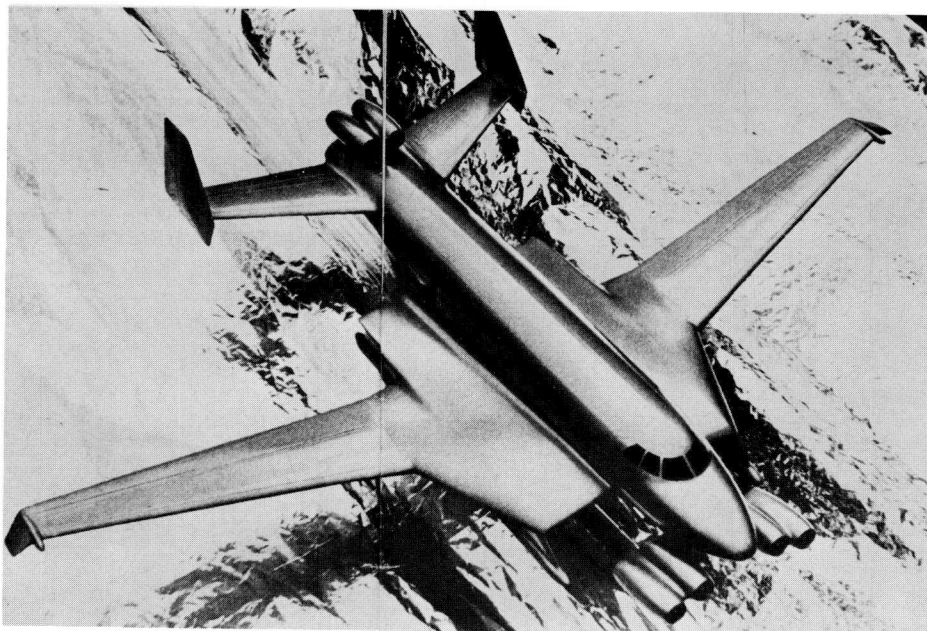
Model of Bartini PAR design

Possible configuration of production version of Bartini concept

WEIGHTS
Operating weight: 3 tons
PERFORMANCE
Max speed: 120km/h (75mph)
Endurance: 3 hours

RADUGA-2

Little is known about this new amphibious ACV, which was first reported in the Soviet press in late spring 1981. Designed at the Krasnoye Sormovo ship and ACV building facility at Gorki, Raduga-2, in common with the Gepard and Klest, is powered by an automotive engine, the Chayka.

RASSVET (DAWN)

A waterjet-propelled sidewall passenger ferry, Rassvet is designed for local sea routes of limited water depth. It is an offshore counterpart to the Orion sidewall ACV. Plans call for the Rassvet to serve resort routes in the Crimea, on the Caspian and Baltic Seas as well as on large lakes and reservoirs. Like the Orion and Zarnitsa, its two predecessors, it can run bow-on to flat, sloping beaches to embark and disembark passengers. Landing on a beach is facilitated by an articulated gangway with a hydraulic drive.

Rassvet's features include shallow draught, good manoeuvrability and relatively simple construction.

Raduga

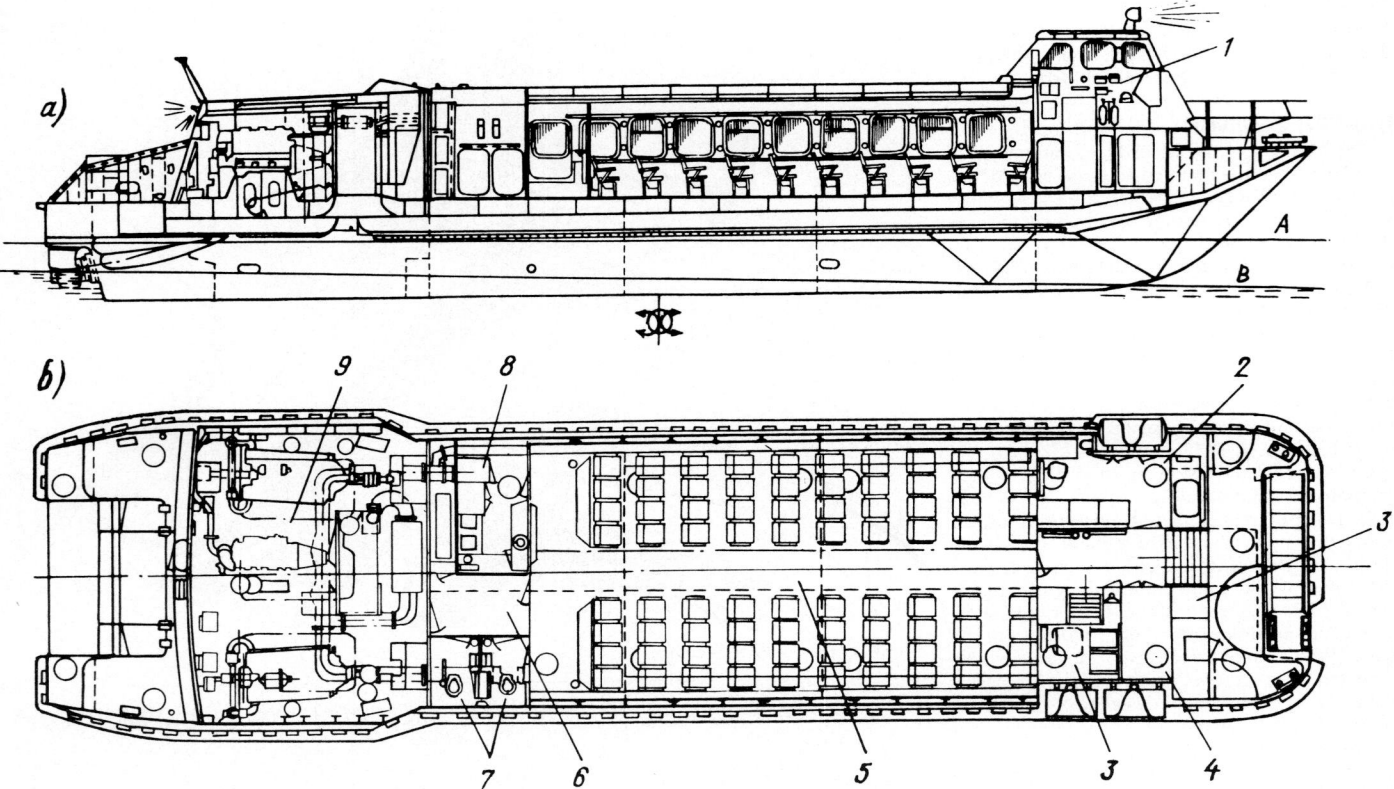

Longitudinal cross section (a) and passenger deck plan (b) of Chayka
(A) waterline in displacement condition; (B) waterline underway on air cushion; (1) pilot house; (2) crew's off-duty cabin; (3) storeroom; (4) baggage compartment; (5) passenger lounge; (6) companionway; (7) toilets; (8) buffet; (9) machinery space

The waterjet reversing/steering system is specially protected to enable the craft to moor alongside existing berths built originally for small conventional displacement ferries.

The Rassvet prototype, named Chayka-1 (Gull-1), is undergoing trials. The Chayka-1 was the first of thirty of its type to be built at the Sosnovska Shipyard in Kirovskaya Oblast for the Black Sea Shipping Line. In January 1976 it was stated that the vessel was the first seagoing passenger ACV to be built in the Soviet Union. The extent of the remote control, automation and monitoring provided for the power plant and systems generally is sufficient to permit the craft to be operated by one person, with intermittent attendance to the machinery space.

Rassvet is designed to carry 80 passengers during daylight hours on coastal routes in conditions up to force 4. It complies with USSR Registration classification KM*II☐ Passenger ACV Class.
LIFT AND PROPULSION: Power for the waterjet system is provided by two 3D12N-520 lightweight (3·54kg/kW) irreversible, high-speed four-cycle V-type marine diesels each with a gas-turbine supercharger and a rated power of

383kW at 1,500rpm. Each powers a two-stage waterjet impeller. Water inlet scoops are arranged in the sidewalls and the pump ports, each of which comprises two rotors and two straightening devices, are installed in the sidewalls behind the transoms. Cushion air is generated by a single 110kW PD6S-150A diesel driving an NTs6 centrifugal fan via a universal joint and a torque-limited coupling.
CONTROLS: Craft direction is controlled by twin balanced rudders operating in the water discharged by each of the two waterjets. Reversal is achieved by applying rotatable deflectors to reverse the waterflow.
SKIRT: Double-row segmented type at bow; two-tier bag type skirt aft. Repair or replacement of sections of the bow skirt can be undertaken with the bow run on to a flat, gently sloping beach. The stern skirt is secured to special hinged sections which permit inspection and maintenance while still afloat.
HULL: Hull and superstructure are built in aluminium magnesium alloy. The hull is of all-welded construction in AlMg-61 and the decks, superstructure, pilot house and partitions are in

AlMg-5 alloy. Hull, superstructure and pilot house have longitudinal frames. Single-piece pressed panels are employed for the lower sections of the sidewalls. Corrugated sheets are used for the hull bottom. Below the passenger deck the hull is sub-divided by transverse bulkheads into seven watertight compartments, access to which is via hatches in the passenger deck. The craft will remain afloat in the event of any one compartment flooding.
ACCOMMODATION: Rassvet seats 80 passengers in a single fully ventilated and heated saloon amidships. Airliner-type seats are provided, beneath each of which a life-jacket is located. Decks in the passenger cabin, pilot house and crew's off-duty cabin are covered with carpet and the floors of the companionways with pvc linoleum. Pavinol aircraft-type leather substitute decorates the deckheads. Large windows give passengers a good view. At the aft end of the cabin are a small buffet and two toilets. At the forward end of the cabin are the wheelhouse, a duty crew restroom and a vestibule. The operating crew of six comprises captain, engineer, motorman, radio operator, seaman and one barman. Passenger embarkation at piers designed for the berthing of small ferries of the local services takes place across the section of open deck forward of the pilot house. Where conventional berthing facilities do not exist the craft runs bow-on to a flat sloping bank where landing facilities are provided by an articulated gangway with a hydraulic drive.

SYSTEMS, ELECTRICAL: Power supply requirements are met by a 28V, KG-2·9kW generator driven by a power take-off shaft from the main engine and three 28V, 1·2kW G-732 charging generators mounted on the main engine. Two banks of storage batteries are installed. One, comprising two Type 6STK-180M storage batteries, supplies dc power when the craft is operating. The second bank, comprising four batteries of the same type, is employed for engine starting and for powering the diesel engine control circuits and emergency alarm systems. An inverter is installed for navigation and other equipment requiring ac supplies. An auxiliary circuit can be connected to shore systems for a 220V single-phase 50Hz ac supply.
SAFETY EQUIPMENT: PSN-10M and PSN-6M inflatable life rafts are installed in containers

Chayka-1

along each side of the craft. The number of rafts is designed to meet the requirements of all passengers and crew. Life raft release is remotely controlled from the landing positions at the bow and stern. Individual lifesaving devices, lifebelts and lifejackets are also provided.
FIREFIGHTING, HYDRAULICS, BILGE, BALLASTING, WATER SUPPLY: Complete systems installed as standard.
COMMUNICATIONS: Lastochka radio telephone transceiver for ship-to-shore and ship-to-ship communications; Kater uhf transceiver and Plot-M portable emergency transceiver. Ryabin passenger announcement and broadcast relay system. Omega radar for navigating along shorelines, in narrow waterways and in poor visibility.
ANCHOR: Single 100kg (220lb) Matrosov anchor operated by a hydraulic winch.
DIMENSIONS
Length overall: 26·7m (87ft 3in)
Beam, max: 7·1m (23ft 3in)
  amidship: 6m (19ft 8in)
Height overall, hull: 2·2m (7ft 3in)
  sidewall only: 1·5m (4ft 11in)
Draught hullborne: 1·27m (4ft 2in)
  cushionborne at bow: 0·1m (4in)
  stern: 0·8m (2ft 7·5in)
WEIGHTS
Loaded displacement: 47·5 tonnes
Passenger capacity: 80 persons
PERFORMANCE
Cruising speed: 23 knots
Max speed: 29 knots
Range: 352km (190n miles)

SIDEWALL PASSENGER FERRIES

Details of two Soviet surface effect ship (SES) passenger ferry projects were published in Leningrad in late 1979, one seating 120 passengers, the other 150. Preliminary specifications of each are given below.

23·5m SES PASSENGER FERRY

LIFT AND PROPULSION: Integrated system, powered by two 1,000hp diesels.
CONTROLS: Craft heading is controlled by water rudders.
HULL: Welded marine aluminium.
ACCOMMODATION: 120 passengers.
DIMENSIONS
Length overall: 23·5m (77ft)
Max beam: 7m (23ft)
Sidewalls, height: 1·5m (4ft 11in)
  breadth: 1m (3ft 3in)
Air cushion, length: 20m (65ft 7in)
  breadth: 5m (16ft 4in)
  area: 100m² (1,076ft²)
WEIGHTS
Empty: 15·3 tonnes
All-up weight: 48·6 tonnes
Displacement tonnes/passenger: 0·406
PERFORMANCE
Max operating speed: 32 knots

25·6m SES PASSENGER FERRY

LIFT AND PROPULSION: Integrated system, probably similar to that employed on Chayka and Turist, powered by two 1,000hp marine diesels.

Chayka-1

CONTROLS: Craft direction is controlled by water rudders.
HULL: Welded marine aluminium.
ACCOMMODATION: Seats are provided for 150 passengers.
DIMENSIONS
Length: 25·6m (84ft)
Max beam: 7m (23ft)
Air cushion, length: 22·5m (73ft 10in)
  breadth: 5m (16ft 5in)
  area: 110m² (1,184ft²)
WEIGHTS
Empty: 18 tonnes
All-up weight: 52·8 tonnes
Displacement tonnes/passenger: 0·354
PERFORMANCE
Max operating speed: 31 knots

TURIST

The Central Scientific Research Institute has completed the design of a new sidewall ACV ferry, the Turist. The vessel, which is based on extensive experience gained from the operation of the Zarnitsa, Orion and Rassvet, is virtually a scaled-up version of the latter. It has a design speed of 36 knots and is intended for use along shallow waterways unsuitable for hydrofoils. Propulsive thrust appears to be supplied by two gas-turbine driven waterjets, one in each

sidewall. Two variants are projected, a 250- to 300-seat passenger ferry and a mixed traffic variant for 10 to 15 cars and 100 to 120 passengers. Turist is due to go into series production at the Nakhodka yard following the completion of shipbuilding facilities there.

Recent reports suggest that, as a result of detailed assessments undertaken in the Soviet Union over a period of years, a range of large sidewall hovercraft is being developed for the conveyance of freight. It appears that designs of 2,000 to 4,000 tons are under consideration.

ZARNITSA

Evolved from Gorkovchanin, the Zarnitsa is a 48- to 50-seat waterjet-propelled rigid sidewall ferry designed to operate on shallow rivers, some less than 0·7m (2ft 3in) deep. Series production is under way, and large numbers have been delivered.

The prototype was put into trial service on the Vyatka river, in the Kirov region, in the summer of 1972, and the first production models began operating on shallow, secondary rivers later in the year. During 1973-74, Zarnitsas entered service on tributaries of the Kama, Lena and Volga. More than 100 are employed on almost all the river navigation lines of the Russian Federative Republic as well as on the rivers of the Ukrainian,

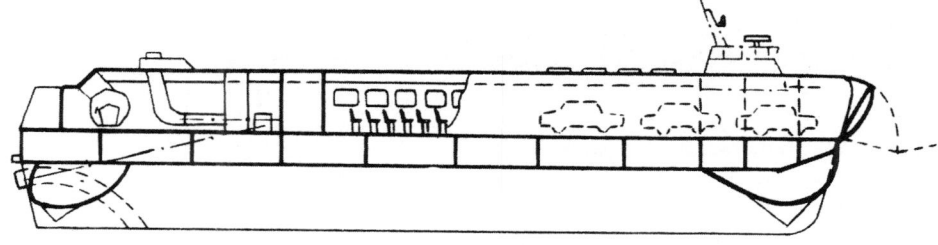

Inboard profile of car-ferry version of Turist showing fingered bag skirts fore and aft

Zarnista

Passenger saloon in Zarnista, looking aft

Zarnista

The object was to develop a vessel for services on shallow waters, with depths of only 0·5m (20in), at speeds of at least 21·5 knots. The prototype Zarya, called the Opytnye-1 (experimental), was put into experimental operation on the river Msta in 1963. During trials the craft attained a speed of 42km/h (26mph) and proved to have a turning radius of 40-70m (44-76 yards). The craft runs bow-on to any flat, sloping bank to embark passengers.

Built with a strong aluminium alloy hull and equipped with a well protected waterjet, the craft is unharmed by floating logs, even when they are encountered at full speed.

Variants include models with a flat load deck in place of the passenger cabin superstructure amidships, and used as light freight vessels. A total of 149 units of the first model of the Zarya were built.

Zarya was designed by a team at the Central Design Office of the Ministry of the River Fleet, Gorki, working in conjunction with the Leningrad Water Transport Institute. Series production is under way at the Moscow Shipbuilding and Ship Repair Yard of the Ministry of the River Fleet.

Given the design prefix P83, Zarya conforms to Class P of the River Register of the USSR.

The latest model is distinguished by its trimaran bow configuration, which gives improved performance in waves and enables the craft to be routed on major waterways. Apart from the large number of Zaryas in service in the USSR, a number have been supplied to Czechoslovakia, Poland and the German Democratic Republic.

Moldavian, Byelorussian and Kazakhstan Soviet Socialist Republics.

LIFT AND PROPULSION, CONTROLS, HULL: Arrangements almost identical to those of the Gorkovchanin.

ACCOMMODATION: Seats are provided for two crew members, who are accommodated in the raised wheelhouse forward, and 48-50 passengers. Access to the passenger saloon is via a single door at the bow in the centre of the wheelhouse. The craft runs bow-on to flat sloping banks to embark and disembark passengers.

DIMENSIONS
Length: 22·3m (72ft 3in)

Beam: 3·85m (12ft 8in)
Skeg depth: 0·45m (1ft 6in)
WEIGHTS
Light displacement: 9 tonnes
All-up weight, with 48 passengers, crew and fuel: 15 tonnes
PERFORMANCE
Service speed: 33-35km/h (20-22mph)

ZARYA (DAWN)

Experiments with high speed 'aéroglisseur' (literally air skimmer) waterbuses, capable of negotiating the many shallow waterways in the Soviet Union, began in 1961.

LIFT AND PROPULSION: Power is provided by a single M401A-1 four-stroke, water-cooled, supercharged, 12-cylinder V-type diesel with a

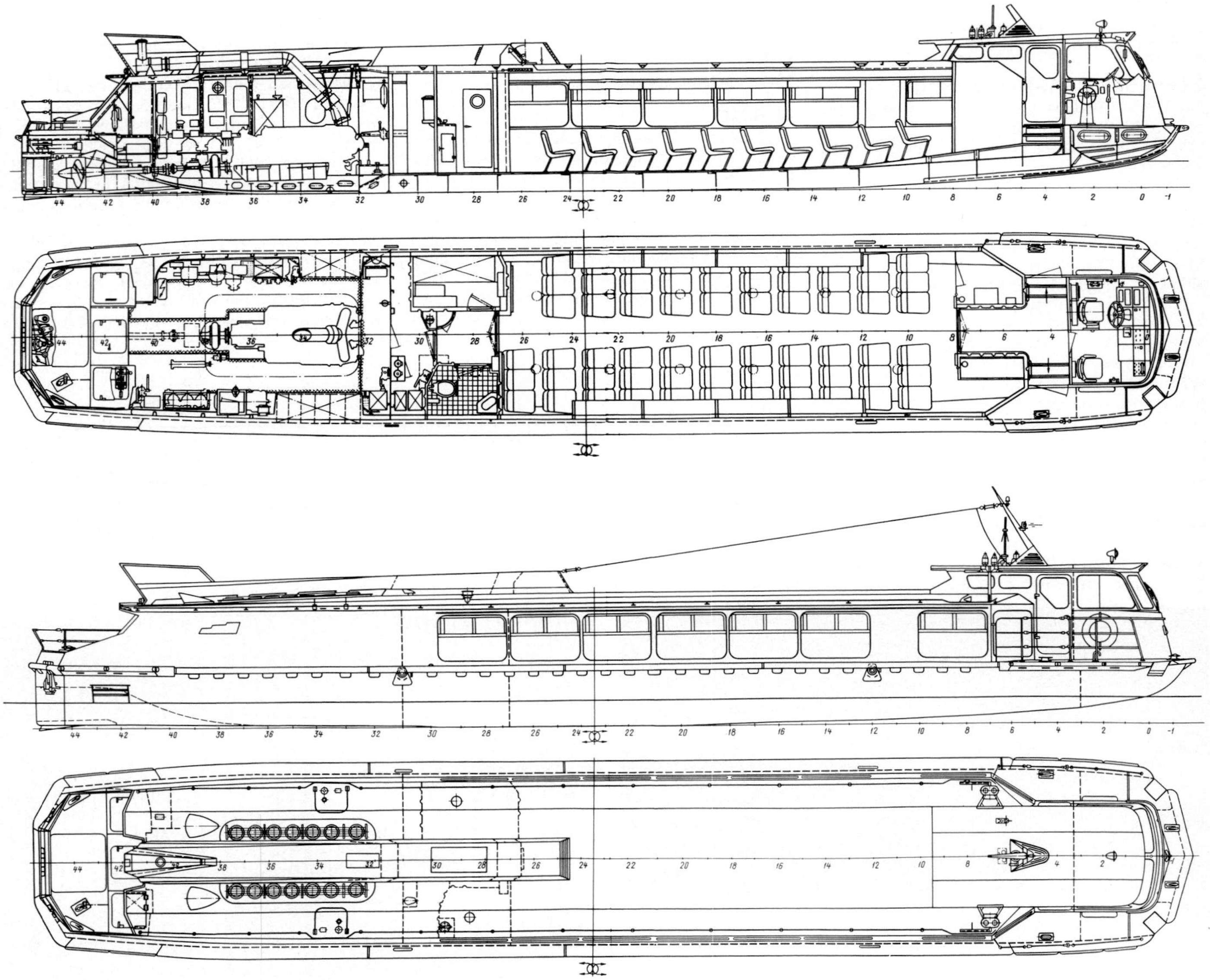

Inboard and outboard profiles and deck views of export model of Zarya

normal service output of 870-900hp at 1,450-1,500rpm and a maximum output of 1,000hp. It has a service life of 3,000 hours before the first overhaul. It has a variable-speed governor and reversing clutch and drives a single 0·7m (2ft 2·5in) diameter variable-pitch, four-bladed waterjet impeller. Fuel consumption is 155kg/h. Lubricating oil consumption at continuous cruising speed is 5kg/h.

The waterjet is of single-stage type with a semi-submerged jet discharge. The brass impeller sucks in water through an intake duct which is covered by a protective grille. The discharged water flows around two balanced rudders which provide directional control. Two reversal shutters, interconnected by a rod and operated by cable shafting, reverse the craft or reduce the waterjet thrust when variations in speed are necessary.

A localised ram-air cushion, introduced by an upswept nose and contained on either side by shallow skegs, lifts the bow clear of the water as the craft picks up speed. The airflow also provides air/foam lubrication for the remainder of the flat-bottomed hull.

CONTROLS: Irrespective of load, the radius of turn is between 30 to 50m (98 to 164ft) with the rudder put hard over at an angle of 30 degrees. This can be decreased by throttling down the engine or closing the valves of the reversing system. At slow speed the craft is capable of pinwheeling. The time required to stop the vessel is 8 to 10 seconds, the coasting distance being between 50 and 60m (164 and 196ft). The craft is able to navigate small winding rivers with waterways of 12 to 15m (39 to 49ft) wide with the radii of windings varying between 40 and 70m (131 and 229ft) without slowing down.

The vessel can easily pull into shore without landing facilities, providing the river bed slope is no steeper than 3 degrees. The time required for pulling in, embarking passengers, then leaving, averages 1½ minutes. Steps for access are at the bow, port and starboard, and lowered by a control in the wheelhouse.

HULL: Hull and superstructure are of all-welded aluminium alloy plate construction, the constituent parts being joined by argon-shielded arc welding. Framing is of mixed type, with transverse framing at the sides and the main longitudinal elements within the hull bottom. The outside shell and bottom plating is 5mm (13/64in) thick, except for the base at the bow where it is 6mm (15/64in) thick. The wheelhouse is in moulded glass-reinforced plastic. The waterjet duct and nozzle are in grade Cr3 steel and are riveted to the hull.

ACCOMMODATION: Three transverse bulkheads and two recesses divide the hull into six compartments. Behind the forepeak and wheelhouse (frames 0-3) is the passenger cabin (frames 3-27) and aft of this is a compartment housing a small bar and toilet (frames 27-30). A soundproof cofferdam (frames 30-31) follows, aft of which is the engine room (frames 31-41) and steering compartment (frames 41 to stern). The raised wheelhouse, located at the bow, gives 360-degree visibility. The latest export model of the Zarya seats 63 in the passenger cabin, plus another four, without luggage, in two recesses. On routes of up to 45 minutes duration an additional 24 standing passengers can be carried. Life jackets for passengers are stowed in lockers in the baggage compartment and under seats at the rear of the cabin.

The crew off-duty room contains a sofa, table, wall-mounted cupboard, folding stool and a mirror. The toilet contains a wash basin, a bowl, mirror and soap tray.

The wheelhouse has rotating seats for the captain and engineer, two sun visors and there are two windscreen wipers.

The passenger cabin and wheelhouse are heated by warm air produced by hot water from the closed circuit main engine cooling system. Warm air is admitted into the passenger cabin and wheelhouse through a perforated chamber at the bulkhead. The engine room is heated by two 1·2kW electric heaters and the crew room by a

Zarya

Zarya

Zarya

0·6kW electric heater. The wheelhouse and its windows are heated by a 330kW electric heater.
SYSTEMS, ELECTRICAL: Main engine driven 3kW, 28V dc generator charges the storage batteries and meets the demands of 24V circuits while the vessel is under way. Four lead-acid batteries supply 24V for monitoring and alarm circuitry and starting the main engine.

Equipment supplied for charging the storage batteries, operating electric heater, engine room and service space heaters from a shore-based 220V source.
FIREFIGHTING: Two tanks containing fire-extinguishing compound and hoses for fighting an outbreak in the engine room. System can be brought into operation either from the engine room or from the wheelhouse. Engine room is also provided with two portable carbon dioxide fire extinguishers. Another of the same type is provided in the wheelhouse and two foam fire extinguishers are standard equipment in the main cabin.
FUEL: Craft is refuelled through a filling hose and a neck on the port side of the superstructure. Fuel is fed to the main engine from a service tank with a capacity of 4·13m³, sufficient to enable a vessel to cruise for 8 hours without refuelling. In addition, there is a 400-litre storage tank which

contains a two-hour reserve to be used in an emergency. The same tank supplies fuel to a water heater.
COMPRESSED AIR: Starting system for main engines comprising three 45-litre air-cylinders, valves (safety, shut-off, pressure reducing and starting) and piping. Pressure 150-75kgf/cm². Two cylinders in operation, one standby.

DIMENSIONS
Length overall: 23·9m (78ft 5in)
Beam overall: 4·13m (13ft 7in)
Freeboard up to undetachable parts at mean draught of 0·44m (1ft 5·5in): 3·2m (10ft 6in)
Mean draught, light: 0·44m (1ft 5·5in)
    loaded: 0·55m (1ft 9·5in)
WEIGHTS
Empty: 16·68 tonnes
Weight with 60 passengers and stores for 8-hour trip: 24·78 tonnes
Max weight of cargo stowed in luggage recesses: 1 tonne
Fuel capacity: 3·8 tonnes
PERFORMANCE
Speed (in channel of 0·8m depth): 45km/h (27·96mph)
Range: suitable for service distances of 150km (93 miles) and above
Endurance at cruising speed: 8 hours

KHARKOV MOTOR TRANSPORT TECHNICAL SCHOOL

AERO-GLIDER

Built by V Kalekin, a teacher at Kharkov Motor Transport Technical School, this five-metre long air-propelled sled has been in use since 1972, during which time it has travelled more than 15,000km, including long stretches of mountain rivers. According to its designers, it has performed particularly well during long-distance journeys over water.

DIMENSIONS
Length overall: 5m (16ft 5in)
Beam: 1·86m (6ft 1in)

WEIGHTS
Payload: 500kg (1,102lb)
Fuel capacity: 260 litres (57 gallons)

Aero-Glider

PERFORMANCE
Range: 1,000km (621 miles)

A M GORKI MEMORIAL MARINE INSTITUTE OF TECHNOLOGY
Mariinsky, Iosha-Ola, USSR
Officials: S F Kirkin *Chief Manager*

The student design group at the Mariinsky Institute of Technology has been involved in ACV development since 1970. It specialises in designing amphibious hovercraft for operation in the less accessible areas of the Soviet Union and has successfully built and tested craft commissioned by the Soviet Union's oil, gas and fisheries authorities. It has also adapted hovercraft for forestry and agricultural roles and for use in establishing communication networks.

Further studies include an investigation into soil damage caused by agricultural machines crossing farmland. The findings are likely to result in the wide scale use of hovercraft for Soviet agriculture. The Institute claims that conventional agricultural machinery is too heavy, and compacts the soil when crossing fields, whether on wheels or tracks. The subsequent disintegration of the soil structure results in a reduction in fertility and a loss of yield. It has been recommended that the size of these vehicles should be greatly reduced and, in some cases, they may be taken out of service.

Extensive use of hovercraft is seen as the answer, since their low pressure on the soil prevents any damage to its structure.

SAV SERIES
SAVR-1M
In 1977 the Institute was awarded a contract by the Soviet Gas Industry for a small snow-mobile/hovercraft to carry a driver and two passengers, plus 500kg of cargo, over snow, ice and water. It also was required to travel over mud to ensure year-round operation on rivers. The first stage of the programme was the design and construction of an experimental model, designated SAVR-1.
LIFT AND PROPULSION: Separate lift and propulsion systems enable the craft to be operated at its maximum clearance height and speed depending on the surface and weather conditions. Two engines are fitted, the propulsion engine, which develops 72kW and the lift engine, developing 3kW. The propulsion engine drives a two-bladed airscrew and the lift engine an axial fan ahead of the cockpit.
WEIGHTS
Total weight: 1·8 tonnes
Load capacity: 0·8 tonnes
PERFORMANCE
Max speed, across snow: 70km/h
    across water: 40km/h

SAVR-1
Built in 1980, this production version of the SAVR-1M is intended for high speed ferrying of personnel and urgent cargoes of up to 1·3 tonnes over roadless areas all year round.
LIFT AND PROPULSION: Cushion air is sup-

SAVR-1

Cutaway of SAVR-2

plied by a 98hp car engine driving two standard centrifugal fans. A clutch between the engine and fans allows the fans to be disconnected during engine startup and idling. Thrust is supplied by a 160hp engine, aft, which drives a 2m diameter propeller.
CONTROLS: Directional control is by two air rudders operating in the slipstream.
HULL: Built in duralumin sheet. Buoyancy chamber of honeycomb construction.

DIMENSIONS
Length: 7·5m
Beam: 3·8m
Height, with propeller vertical: 3·3m
WEIGHTS
All up weight: 2·9 tonnes
Max useful load: 1·3 tonnes
PERFORMANCE
Cruising speed, across snow: 50km/h
    across water: 40km/h

SAVR-2

SAVR-2 made its appearance in 1982. It was designed and built to a specification prepared by the Soviet Ministry of Fisheries for a craft to serve the inaccessible water regions of North and West Siberia.

LIFT AND PROPULSION: Lift is provided by a single petrol engine aft of the crew cabin driving, via a split transverse shaft, two centrifugal fans. Thrust is supplied by a single 224kW (300hp) Ivchenko AI-14ChR air-cooled radial piston engine driving an AV-14 3-blade variable-pitch propeller. Fuel is carried in two 400-litre tanks, one for each engine. Fuel employed is standard automotive petrol. Engine compartment separated from the cabin by thermo-insulating and soundproofing partition.

CONTROLS: Craft heading is controlled by twin vertical aerodynamic rudders aft operating in the propeller slipstream. Reverse propeller pitch is employed for braking and reversing. A horizontal stabiliser is mounted between the twin rudders to adjust pitch trim. By altering its incidence angle the centre of gravity can be moved along the longitudinal axis should an uneven load distribution cause it to move.

HULL: Believed to be a composite light alloy and glass fibre structure. Flotation compartments and basic raft structure filled with plastic foam make hull unsinkable.

ACCOMMODATION: Cabin seats driver with a passenger on each side. Interior lined with layer of polyurethane and PVC for thermal insulation. Passenger module seating 14 to 16 can be fitted on cargo platform aft of lift fan system.

SKIRT: Segmented skirts fore and aft. Bag-type skirts at sides. An experimental model of the SAVR-2 has two flexible side skids replacing the conventional skirt. The skids consist of a number of right-angled plates, hinged together, and fitted with removable stainless steel or polyethylene soles. The plates are fixed to the hull by lever suspension and spring shock absorbers. The area between skid and hull is covered with rubberised fabric. Flexible skids reduce to a minimum the air escaping from the cushion when travelling over rough ground, so reducing the power required from the lift system, as they follow the ground contours more accurately. When the craft is supported by the skids the pressure of the air cushion can be considerably reduced. Flexible skids provide lateral stability when the craft is stationary and when travelling over snow, ice and mud, and surfaces covered in a thin layer of water. The least cushion pressure is required over damp, muddy terrain or land covered with a thin layer of water. To cross open water the pressure must be increased to 1,000 to 1,200Pa (70 to 80 per cent maximum) and over dry soil and ploughland it has to be increased to the maximum, 1,400Pa.

DIMENSIONS
Length: 9·8m
Beam: 4·5m
Height: 3·7m
WEIGHTS
All up: 5,900kg
Payload: 2 tons
PERFORMANCE
Fully laden, maximum speed: 50 km/h

SAVR-3, -5GD, -40

In 1981 the Ministry of Oil and Gas approved a programme for the construction of trackless modes of transport, building machines and pipe-laying equipment for muddy soils. Within this programme, which spans the period 1981-1985, the Institute is constructing three new transport hovercraft with the following load capacities: SAVR-3, 2 tons; SAVR-5GD, 5 tons; SAVR-40, 50 tons.

MP-18

This snowmobile/amphibious hovercraft is designed to carry a 600kg load across snow, water and swamps. Air is fed into the cushion by a forward-mounted engine driving an axial lift fan. Cushion air is contained by a flexible polyethylene skirt forward, by a control flap aft and by rigid skids at the two sides. When partially

SAVR-2

Impression of enlarged derivative of MPI-20

MPI-20

Design project for tractor and hovercraft for carrying oil/gas pipes

cushionborne, craft heading is controlled by movable front skids. Once contact with the supporting surface has ceased, steering is by an air rudder aft of the two-bladed propeller.
WEIGHTS
Payload: 600kg
All-up weight: 1·2 tons
PERFORMANCE
Max speed: 75km/h

MPI-20

This cargo/passenger hovercraft was built in response to specifications prepared by the Ministry for Gas and a Siberian organisation, Sibribprom.

Built in modular form, the craft comprises fore and aft components linked by a coupling unit. It is supplied in two versions with load capacities of three and five tons.

PROJECTS

Current projects at the Institute include the design of new propellers to provide greater thrust and braking power when negotiating steeper inclines, and ride control systems to reduce heave motions when crossing undulating terrain at speed. It is also planned to build a modular hovercraft which can be built up from towed passenger and cargo platforms to suit traffic requirements.

NEPTUN CENTRAL DESIGN BUREAU

Moscow, USSR

Officials:
Igor Alexandrovich Martynov, *Head of Design Bureau*
G Andreyev, *Chief Engineer*
Alexander Sergeyevich Kudryavtsev, *Chief Designer, AKVPR project*
Valeriy V Protsenko, *Designer*
Alexander V Rubinov, *Test Engineer*

The Neptun Central Design Bureau is concerned primarily with the design of small launches, yachts and runabouts for leisure and commercial applications on Soviet inland and coastal waters.

The AKVPR-001 airjet-propelled amphibious ACV, Neptun's first attempt at designing and building a hovercraft, is intended for research only. Several variants are under development including the Barrs-1 which is destined for service in Siberia and other underdeveloped areas of the Soviet Union. A 20-seat derivative has been suggested and the bureau has a four-seater, the Gepard, on the drawing board.

AKVPR-001

NEPTUN AKVPR-001

This multi-purpose amphibious five-seater is being considered for use in geological expeditions, to provide communications in the Soviet far north and Siberia, in river rescue services and for emergency services when ice is forming and breaking up on inland waterways. The nomenclature AKVPR signifies 'Amphibious Air Cushion Craft, Airjet, Rivergoing'. A film of the craft taken during trials in the winter of 1977 and spring of 1978 showed the craft successfully operating across broken ice, negotiating ice hummocks at speed and crossing boggy terrain and marshes.

LIFT AND PROPULSION: Integrated lift/propulsion system, believed to be similar to that of Cushioncraft CC-7. Power is supplied by a single automotive engine, aft of the cabin. Power is transmitted via a gearbox to two transverse shafts at the opposite ends of which are axial fans. Air is fed downwards into the cushion and through circular thrust outlets aft for propulsion.

CONTROLS: Craft heading is controlled by interconnected rudder vanes set in the airjet ducts aft and operated by a wheel. Airflow for braking and reversing is provided by deflecting thrust air upwards and through forward facing roof apertures.

HULL: Built mainly in corrosion resistant light alloy. Basic structure is the main hull which is divided into watertight sub-divisions for safety.

PERFORMANCE: Has achieved 50km/h (31mph) across calm water over a measured mile.

BARRS-1 (SNOW LEOPARD)

The prototype of this enlarged variant of the AKVPR-001 seats a driver and seven passengers. A cargo version carries a load of 650kg (1,433lb).

A feature of the design is the use of a Kamov Ka-26 helicopter piston engine to power the integrated lift/propulsion system. The engine, the M-14V-26, has a rigidly-prescribed operational life and its use in Barrs-1 is the outcome of a search to find a terrestrial application for it once it had reached the end of its airborne career.

Barrs-1 is designed for year-round operation and can be used as a light passenger ferry, light freighter or as a service crews' launch on routes in remote and scarcely-developed regions of western and eastern Siberia, the far north and the far east, which have a thinly developed network for year-round transport of domestic goods.

Trials have shown that Barrs-1 can operate safely in wave heights of up to 0·6m (2ft) and can clear obstacles of up to 0·5m (1ft 8in) in height. It is said to 'ride superbly over sand and snow-covered ice'. During long runs it normally operates with a six-degree bow-up trim. It meets the requirements of Class 'L' in the Inland Waterway Register of the Russian Soviet Federated Socialist Republic (RSFSR).

Barrs-1

LIFT AND PROPULSION: Integrated system powered by a single Vedeneev M-14V-26 air-cooled petrol-driven four-stroke piston engine developing 325hp at 2,800rpm. Power is transmitted via a gearbox to two transverse shafts at the opposite ends of which are axial fans. Air is fed downwards into the cushion and through rectangular thrust outlets aft for propulsion. Cushion pressure, 115kg/m^2.

CONTROLS: Craft heading is controlled by interconnected rudder vanes set in the airjet ducts aft and operated by a wheel. Airflow for braking and reversing is provided by deflecting thrust air upwards and through forward-facing roof apertures.

HULL: Light metal alloy structure. Main hull divided into watertight sub-divisions for safety. Designed for mass production.

DIMENSIONS, EXTERNAL
Length overall: 7·43m (24ft 6in)
Width: 3·95m (13ft)
Height: 2·43m (8ft)
Draught, off cushion: 0·15m (6in)

DIMENSIONS, INTERNAL (CABIN)
Length: 3m (10ft)

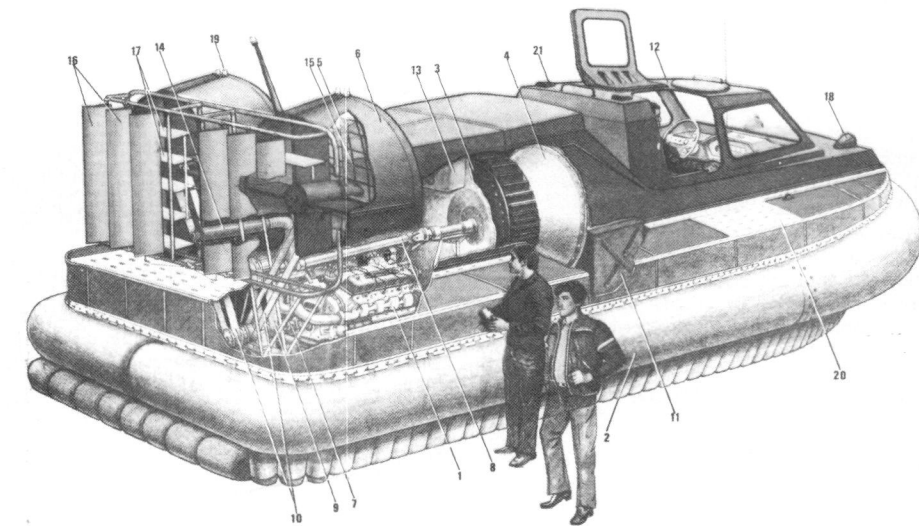

Cutaway of Gepard: (**1**) GAZ-53 power plant (**2**) bag skirt (**3**) fan (**4**) fan air scoop (**5**) thrust fan (**6**) duct (**7**) main (cardan) shaft (**8**) fan drive (cardan) shaft (**9**) fan transmission belts (**10**) airscrew transmission belts (**11**) fuel tank (**12**) deck cabin (**13**) water and oil radiators (**14**) exhaust pipe (manifold) (**15**) fan duct (**16**) vertical rudders (**17**) elevators (**18**) headlights (**19**) navigation and landing lights (**20**) drainage plate (**21**) ventilator heads

Width: 2·6m (8ft 7in)
Height: 1·3m (4ft 4in)
WEIGHTS
Loaded: 2·15 tons
PERFORMANCE
Max speed: 80 km/h (49·6mph)
Cruising speed: 50-60km/h (31-37·2mph)
Endurance: 5 hours

GEPARD (CHEETAH)

A multi-role five-seater introduced in 1981, Gepard has been designed to provide convenient, reliable and inexpensive transport in remoter areas of the Soviet Union. Specialist professions in those areas were questioned about their transport needs before finalising the design. Early in 1983 a Gepard successfully underwent trials at Andreyevskoye Lake, near the centre of the Tyuman Oblast. Gepard is due to go into quantity production.

LIFT AND PROPULSION: Integrated system, powered by a 115hp GAZ 53 lorry engine, aft of the cabin. Output is transmitted to a centrifugal lift fan and two duct-mounted, multi-bladed 0·95m diameter glass-fibre fans for thrust.

CONTROLS: Directional control by inter-

Gepard

connected rudder vanes hinged to the rear of the thrust fan ducts and operated by a wheel.

HULL: Corrosion-resistant light alloy hull. Moulded glass fibre cabin superstructure.

DIMENSIONS
Length, hard structure: 6·25m (20ft 6in)

Width: 2·8m (9ft 3in)
WEIGHTS
Loaded weight: 1·7 tons
PERFORMANCE
Max speed, fully loaded, calm water: 70km/h (43·4mph)

OTTO PETERSON
Riga, USSR

RIGA

This two-seat amphibious runabout is one of a large number of light hovercraft built in the Soviet Union during the past decade.

LIFT AND PROPULSION: Motive power for the propulsion system is provided by a single 12hp Vikhr M air-cooled petrol engine mounted aft. Power is transmitted by two V-belts to a pair of axial fans mounted on a common shaft within a transverse duct aft of the cockpit. Air is drawn in from both sides of the fan housing and expelled aft through a rectangular duct for propulsion. Thrust of 30kg gives a speed of 60km/h (37·2mph) over smooth water. A second engine, at the bow, drives the lift fan. Fuel capacity is 30 litres (6·5 gallons).

CONTROLS: Craft heading is controlled by rudders fitted in the thrust port and actuated by motorcycle-type handlebars.

SKIRT: Bag type, 20cm (7·8in) deep.

DIMENSIONS
Length: 3·7m (12ft 2in)
Beam: 1·8m (5ft 11in)

Freeboard: 0·6m (2ft)
WEIGHTS
Empty weight: 120kg (264·5lb)

PERFORMANCE
Max speed, calm water: 60km/h (37·2mph)
Fuel consumption: 15 litres/h (3·2 gallons/h)

Riga

S ORDZHONIKIDZE AVIATION INSTITUTE
Moscow, USSR

MAI-OS-2

A number of Soviet technical institutions are developing ekranoplans capable of flying-in-ground effect, just above their supporting surfaces. To assist them in their studies, scientists at the S Ordzhonikidze Aviation Institute have designed the MAI-OS-2 ekranoplan scooter.

One of its characteristics is the use of a stern hydrofoil which, in conjunction with hydroskis, raises the stern of the craft during take-off, thus sharply decreasing drag. Maximum speed attained during tests is 180km/h (112mph).

A N TUPOLEV

TUPOLEV A-3 AMPHIBIOUS AEROSLEDGE

The provision of year-round transport in under-developed areas of the Soviet north, far east and Siberia would be impossible without the assistance of special vehicles. To reach communities in some of the more inaccessible regions means traversing deep snow, hummock ice, marshes that never freeze and natural waterways overgrown with reeds.

The diversity of the conditions in which transport has to operate, the demand for increased speed and the ability to cross all types of terrain complicates the development of a suitable vehicle.

In intermediate navigational seasons when the ice is melting and unsafe, during the winter freeze-up when large chunks of ice drift along rivers and when strips of unfrozen water abound in frozen or semi-frozen rivers, there is not, generally speaking, a single means of terrestrial

Tupolev A-3

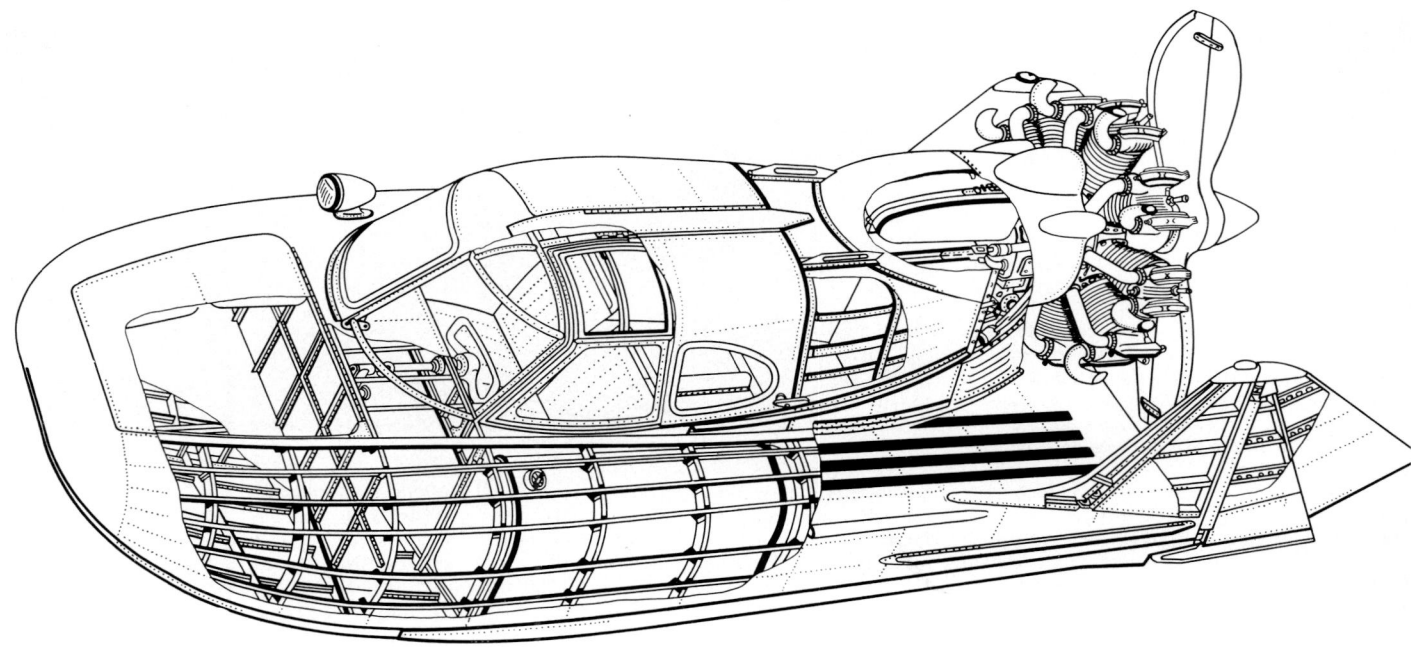

Cutaway showing basic structural components of Tupolev A-3

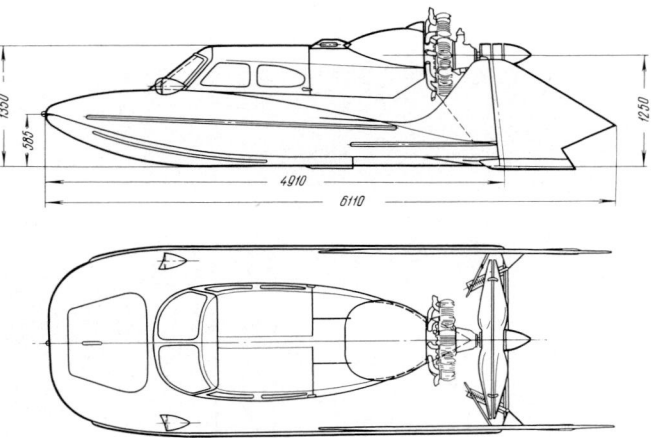

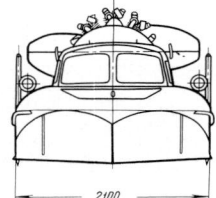

General arrangement of Tupolev A-3

transport which can provide reliable year-round communications.

One answer to the problem is the amphibious aerosledge, designed under the direct control of one of the Soviet Union's best known aircraft designers, A N Tupolev. Employed for the carriage of mail, passengers, light freight, medical supplies and hospital cases, the craft has the appearance of a small speedboat powered by a radial engine driving an airscrew. It can carry a payload of half a ton over a distance of 300 to 500km (186 to 310 miles) at a cruising speed of 50 to 70km/h (31 to 43mph). At speed, when traversing snow, the slightly upturned bow of the hull, together with the difference of pressure between the upper and lower surfaces of the craft, generate an aerodynamic lifting force. At 80km/h (50mph) and above, aerodynamic lift reduces by almost one-third the pressure of the craft on snow. The depth of its furrow becomes negligible and resistance to the motion of the craft decreases accordingly. On water the large area of the hull bottom, with its small keel, makes it a stable, shallow-draught craft.

Additionally, the smooth lines of the hull's underside enable it to cross stretches of water overgrown with water weeds without difficulty and glide across areas of shallow water with a depth no greater than 50mm (2in). More than 200 vehicles of this type are in service with the Soviet Union, and many have been exported to Eastern Europe and elsewhere.

PROPULSION: Early production aerosledges were fitted with a single 100hp, five-cylinder M-11 aircooled radial. This was replaced by the more powerful 260hp AI-14R radial. The engine is mounted aft on a tubular frame with shock-absorbers and drives a two-bladed wooden airscrew. The engine compartment is covered by an easily removable cowling. Above the compartment and beneath the cowling is the oil tank and pipes for the oil system. Fuel is carried in two tanks, concealed one on each side of the cabin. Filler caps are in wells in the decking.

CONTROLS: Craft direction is controlled by twin aerodynamic rudders aft operating in the propeller slipstream. For operation over snow or ice, positive control is obtained by steel runners fitted to the base of the rudders which maintain surface contact. When moving the rudder wheel to make a turn, upper (air) and lower sections of the rudder operate simultaneously. If the wheel is pulled towards the driver the rudders turn outwards to form a brake. If it is turned and drawn towards the driver only one rudder operates—the one on the inside of the turn. This assists turning when the aerosledge is crossing expanses of water overgrown with reeds or weeds.

HULL: Riveted metal alloy construction employing 2mm D-16T plates and profiles. Ribs, stringers and plates are in D-16T duraluminium. A radial chine runs for 66 per cent of the overall length of the craft from the bow. Transverse bulkheads divide the hull into three watertight compartments. The craft will remain afloat in the event of any one compartment flooding. Double plating is employed on the hull bottom to strengthen it for crossing ice, snow mounds and ice hummocks. Low friction 3·5mm polyethylene is stuck to the bottom of the plates which are removable for replacement. Three stainless steel runners are fitted to the hull base, one on the central keel and one on each side. These ensure that the craft is able to hold a given course and prevent it from side-slipping on sheet ice when it is well heeled over.

ACCOMMODATION: In mail-carrying form the Aerosledge carries a driver, postman and mail weighing up to 650kg (1,433lb) in winter and 300kg (661lb) in summer. Driver and passenger sit in swivelling armchairs. As a passenger

Tupolev A-3

vehicle, it carries a driver and up to four passengers. Ahead of the passenger cabin is a hermetically-sealed hatch providing access to a baggage compartment.

DIMENSIONS
Length overall: 6·11m (20ft 1in)
Hull length: 4·01m (13ft 2in)
Beam: 2·14m (7ft)
Cabin height: 1·35m (4ft 5in)
Airscrew diameter: 1·87m (6ft 2in)
WEIGHTS
Empty: 815kg (1,797lb)
Payload: 650kg (1,433lb)
PERFORMANCE
Max speed over snow: 120km/h (74·6mph)
       over water: 65km/h (40·4mph)
Max permitted wave height: 0·6m (2ft)

Tupolev A-3

UFA AVIATION INSTITUTE

Tyumen, USSR

Officials:
F Nuriakhmetov, *Head of Propulsion Systems Group*
I Shalin, *Design Engineer*
S Komarov, *Candidate of Science (Technical)*

Designers at the UFA Aviation Institute have been active in ACV development since the mid-1960s when they exhibited an experimental craft, named Skat, with a circular planform at the USSR National Economy Achievements Exhibition in Moscow.

TAIFUN

The unit's most recent ACV is Taifun, a multi-duty amphibious vehicle designed for all-weather, 24-hour operation. It can carry up to three tonnes of freight or 20 passengers and is extensively used in mineral development projects in the Soviet far north. Due to the Soviet north's changeable weather, aircraft are often grounded for 80 to 100 days a year. Highways and railways to the major mineral deposits have been laid but prospectors and other workers have to travel considerable distances from them in all weathers.

Conventional vehicles can normally be used during winter months only, when frost makes it possible to lay routes along ice-bound rivers and swamps. ACVs, however, can easily cross swamps, rivers and other waterbound or marginal terrain throughout the year and are consequently being used on a much wider scale.

Taifun is claimed to be the only cross-country vehicle capable of negotiating 1-metre (3·2-foot) high obstacles and 35-degree slopes. Designers at the UFA Aviation Institute are designing

Taifun

Dynamic model of ACV to be used as mobile gas-turbine electricity-generating station

another ACV with increased load-carrying capacity.

VOSTOK CENTRAL DESIGN BUREAU

Leningrad, USSR
Officials:
V D Rubtsov, *Chief Designer*
B V Baymistruk
Ye A Meschchanov
S F Gorbachevskiy

KLEST

Development of this small utility hovercraft began at the Vostok Central Design Bureau in 1979. Trials of the prototype, named *Metan 1*, were undertaken in the Gulf of Finland and at Bolshaya Nevka, Leningrad in summer 1981. An integrated lift/propulsion system is employed, powered by a single Volga Automotive Plant (VAZ) automotive engine. Power is transmitted to two ducted propulsion fans and a single lift fan. The fans are scaled-down and modified versions of conventional industrial fans used in Soviet coalmines. Parts for the engine and servicing can be provided by any Zhiguli service station, a network of which now exists in the Soviet Union.

Klest

Series production is proposed. Maximum speed is 80km/h (50 mph).

UNITED KINGDOM

AIR CUSHION EQUIPMENT (1976) LIMITED

15/35 Randolph Street, Shirley, Southampton SO1 3HD, England
Telephone: 0703 776468
Telex: 477537
Cables: Hoverace, Southampton
Officials:
J D Hake, *Chairman (US)*
R C Gilbert
R R Henvest

HOVERSPORT

A new multi-purpose light sports hovercraft, Hoversport combines a top speed of 80km/h over land or water with a simple control system which enables any adult to operate it with complete safety after instruction. It is designed to conform with the requirements of the Hoverclub of Great Britain.

LIFT AND PROPULSION: Integrated system powered by a 500cc Rotax engine. Power is transmitted to a duct-mounted, triple-bladed axial-flow fan, the primary airflow from which is ejected aft through the propulsion slot in the air duct. The secondary airflow, for the cushion, is ducted downwards into the plenum. Fuel capacity is 23 litres. Fuel type recommended is petrol/two stroke oil 50 : 1.

CONTROLS: Triple rudder vanes, hinged to the aft end of the fan duct and operated by handle-bar, provide directional control.

HULL: Large capacity sealed buoyancy tanks are provided to keep the craft afloat, even if waterlogged.

ACCOMMODATION: Open cockpit with upholstered seat for one, or two in tandem.

DIMENSIONS
Length: 3·1m
Beam: 1·93m
Height off cushion: 1·18m
Height on cushion: 1·42m
WEIGHTS
Unladen: 205kg
Max payload: two adults
PERFORMANCE
Cruising speed over land and water: 56km/h
Max speed over land and water: 80km/h
Noise level at cruising power: 82Db at 25m
Fuel consumption, average: 13·4 litres/h

ACE Hoversport showing fan duct and rudder vanes

ACE Hoversport

AIR VEHICLES LIMITED

Head Office and Factory: Unit 4, Three Gates Road, Cowes, Isle of Wight, England
Telephone: (Office) 0983 293194
Telex: 86513 HVWORK G

Officials:
C D J Bland, *Director*
C B Eden, *Director*

Air Vehicles Limited was founded in 1968 and has concentrated on the development of small commercial hovercraft and various systems and special equipment for larger craft.

The company's main product is the Tiger 12-seat hovercraft; customers include the British, French and Canadian Ministries of Defence, the People's Republic of China, the Nigerian Police and the Bahrain Ministry of the Interior. The design is being updated so a diesel engine can be fitted and to improve payload and performance.

Air Vehicles Limited is approved by the Civil Aviation Authority and undertakes modifications to larger craft. These have included flat-deck freight conversions of the SR.N5 and SR.N6, power-assisted rudder packs for both types, and in 1984, the conversion of an SR.N6 Mk 1S for high speed hydrographic surveying.

The company is a leader in the design of low-speed ducted propeller systems and following the success of the propeller duct fitted to an SR.N6, two units have been supplied to the USA for a military hovercraft.

Air Vehicles Limited worked with British Hovercraft Corporation and Hovertravel Limited to produce the new diesel amphibious hovercraft, the AP1-88. Based on an original design undertaken by Air Vehicles Limited in a study for Hovertravel, the company was responsible for the detail design and technical work for this craft. Many of the design features of the AP1-88 are derived from Tiger including ducted propellers, multi rudder controls, aluminium-welded hull and transmission system.

Experience gained with the AP1-88 has contributed to the design of the larger diesel-engined Twin Tiger and Tiger 40.

One of two Tigers operated by British Army

HYDROGRAPHIC SURVEY CRAFT

An SR.N6 Mk 1S has been modified for high speed hydrographic surveying. The cabin is fitted with an air-conditioned computer room, and a control area for the survey crew.

The main external modifications are flat side decks to ease crew movement; two 12·5kVA generators and two hydraulically operated, transducer carrying 'fish' which deploy into the water when taking depth measurements. The craft can operate at 25 knots while measuring depth and records its position by means of a Trisponder system.

A similar conversion has also been provided on a Tiger 12 craft. The cabin is converted to carry the recording instruments and is fully air conditioned. A 2·5kW power supply is provided and the single transducer is mounted on an hydraulically deployed 'fish' at the front of the craft. Positioning is again by Trisponder and surveying is carried out at speeds up to 20 knots.

Operations from the shore in shallower areas are easily undertaken without requiring any prepared docking facilities.

TIGER 12

The standard production craft seats 12 and the non-structural cabin top can be removed for different purposes. Fully amphibious, the craft can operate over a variety of surfaces such as mud, ice, sand and shallow water.

LIFT AND PROPULSION: Motive power for the integrated lift/propulsion system is provided by a single AMC 5,900cc (360in³) petrol engine delivering 180hp at 3,600rpm. Diesel version has a Deutz BF 6L913C delivering 180hp at 2,500rpm. The engine output is transferred to a 12-bladed centrifugal lift fan and a 1·37m (4ft 6in) diameter, four-bladed, ducted propeller through a notched belt system. Normal fuel capacity is 213 litres (47 imperial gallons).

CONTROLS: Multiple rudder vanes hinged at the aft end of the propeller duct provide directional control. Elevators provide trim and, when raised fully, assist braking by reducing thrust by 75 per cent.

HULL: Superstructure and all bulkheads are of marine grade aluminium sheet welded to form a strong rigid box structure. Side members are inflatable, giving additional buoyancy and protection for the craft when mooring. By deflating the side members the vehicle can be trailed behind any large car or small truck. Built-in jacking system provided for loading and maintenance.

ACCOMMODATION: Enclosed cabin for driver and up to 11 passengers. Access via sliding doors, one port, one starboard. Driver's seat forward right; navigator's forward left. Adequate space for radar, radios and navigation equipment ahead of these positions.

SKIRT: Pressurised bag type with separate segments. Inflatable sides and skirt attached to craft with quick-release piano hinges.

SYSTEMS, ELECTRICAL: 12V dc, negative earth, with engine driven 35A alternator and 60Ah battery.

DIMENSIONS
Length: 8m (26ft 2in)
Width, inflated: 3·85m (12ft 6in)
Transport width: 2·44m (8ft)
Height, static: 2·26m (7ft 5in)
Hoverheight: 50-55cm (20-22in)
12-place cabin: 3·9 × 1·8m (12ft 9in × 6ft)
WEIGHTS
Empty: 1,910kg (4,200lb)
Max: 2,865kg (6,300lb)
Disposable load: 955kg (2,100lb)
PERFORMANCE
Max speed: 65km/h (35 knots)
Cruise speed: 46km/h (25 knots)
Max conditions: 46km/h (25 knot) wind, 1m (3ft) sea
Speed in 46km/h (25 knot) wind: 37km/h (20 knots)
Gradient climbing: 1 : 7 (standing start)
Fuel consumption, cruise: 27-45 litres/h (6-10 imperial gallons/h)
Max: 70 litres/h (15·5 imperial gallons/h)

Hydraulically-operated transducer carrier for high-speed hydrographic survey on SR.N6 Mk 1S

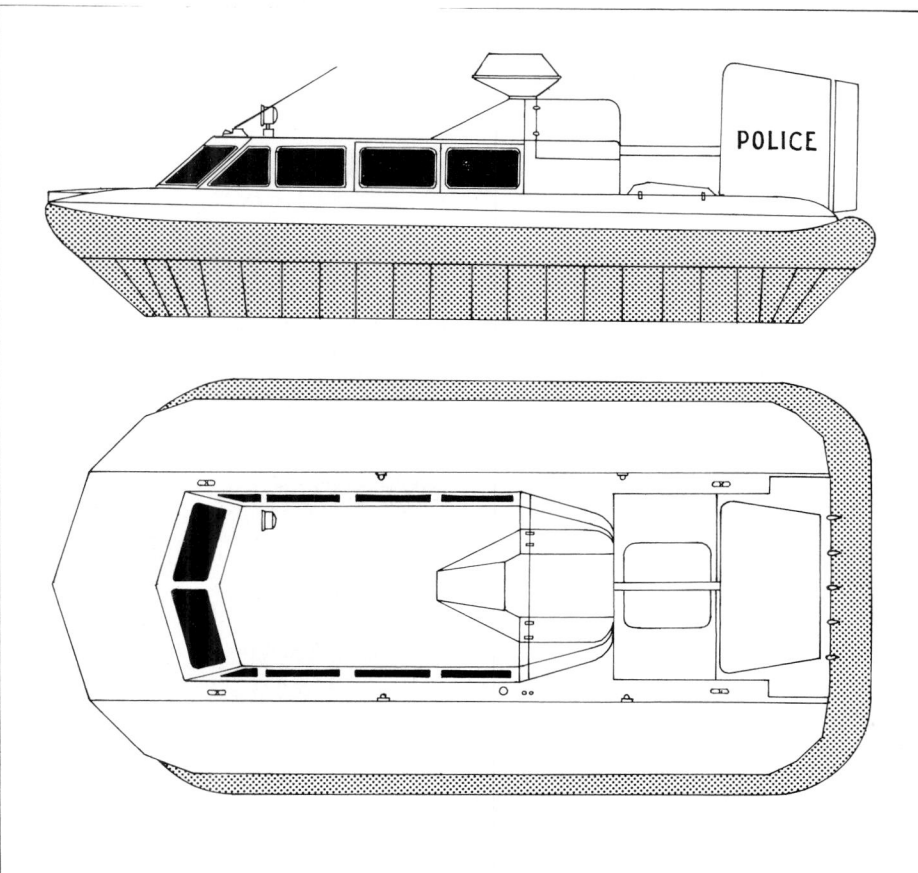

General arrangement of Tiger for Nigerian Police

Tiger rescue version

TIGER 40

The Tiger 40 is a development of the Tiger and Twin Tiger. It uses the same design approach and incorporates many of the features and components of the smaller craft.

The propulsion and lift machinery is in the sidebodies leaving the centre of the craft clear for a variety of accommodation layouts. This arrangement ensures a well balanced craft at any load state, despite its rear engine configuration. Different cabin modules fit the craft for a number of roles, ranging from workboat and patrol craft to cargo carrying and passenger transport.

LIFT AND PROPULSION: Motive power is supplied by four air-cooled Deutz BF 6L913 diesel engines each delivering 180 hp. Two fan units are on each side of the craft. One discharges into the skirt system, the other upwards into the steerable bow thruster unit. A ducted propeller unit is mounted at the rear of each sidebody.

CONTROLS: Multiple rudder vanes hinged at the aft end of the twin propeller ducts provide directional control. Elevators provide rapid pitch trim and the bow thruster units provide reverse thrust, a righting moment when cornering or in a beam wind, and accurate control at slow speed. They also supplement the forward thrust at speed.

HULL: Welded marine grade aluminium alloy in three sections: two sidebodies and a central deck. The two sidebodies form the main longitudinal beams and house the engines, transmission assemblies, lift fans and propulsion units. The central deck assembly comprises floor and buoyancy compartments, with box members at the bow and stern.

DIMENSIONS
Length: 14m (45·93ft)
Width: 6m (19·68ft)
Height on landing pads: 3m (10ft)
Hoverheight: 0·8m (2·75ft)
WEIGHTS
Max all up weight: 11,360kg (25,000lbs)
Payload: 3,180kg (7,000lbs)
PERFORMANCE
Max speed: 38-40 knots
Endurance: 5 hours at cruising speed
Weather: 25 knot wind, 1·5m (5ft) sea

Tiger 40 passenger ferry

Tiger 40 fast patrol craft

Workboat variant, Tiger 40

AVON INDUSTRIAL POLYMERS LIMITED

Flexible Fabrications Division, Bumpers Way, Bristol Road, Chippenham, Wiltshire SN14 6NF, England
Telephone: 0249 656241
Telex: 444557
Officials:
B Stacey, *Managing Director*
D W Wisely, *Director and General Manager, Flexible Fabrications*
A J Bridger, *Commercial Manager, Flexible Fabrications*
Dr S R Harris, *Technical and Manufacturing Manager, Flexible Fabrications*

Avon Industrial Polymers Flexible Fabrications Division, part of Avon Rubber plc, designs and produces a complete range of hovercraft skirt components. Avon has long been established as the major supplier of hovercraft skirt components in the UK. The company has been

Jeff(A) in Alaska

appointed prime supplier of skirt components to the Bell Halter consortium which is developing the range of surface effect ships in the USA. The company also provides skirt components and systems for giant hovercraft barges operating on major construction and civil engineering projects in such different climates as Arabia and the Arctic.

For Bell Halter, Avon has completed many sets of the world's hovercraft skirt components. The Bell Halter 110 demonstration surface effect ship (Model 201A) has a bow seal consisting of 8 fingers, each 7·6 metres wide, 4·5 metres high and weighing 100kg. Its stern seal is 9 metres wide, 3 metres long and weighs 300kg. These craft are in use with the US Coast Guard and Command Marine and on trial with the US Navy.

Avon is also supplying skirt materials and components for the US Navy's landing craft air cushion programme (LCAC). Avon has designed, developed and fabricated the skirt system for Vosper Hovermarine's HM5 series and in the UK the Hoverspeed service employs Avon skirt components for the SR.N4 craft in its original and stretched form. Other products produced by the division include a full range of ISO container flexitanks for the transportation of fluids, dry diving suits for navy and commercial use, inflatable containment booms and jet engine plugs.

The company is approved to the UK Ministry of Defence Defstan 05-21 and approved by the Civil Aviation Authority.

BHC SR.N4 Mk 3 Super 4 with Avon skirt components

BH 110s in service with US Coast Guard

BILL BAKER VEHICLES LIMITED (BBV)

1 Stud Farm Cottages, Adderbury, Banbury, Oxon OX17 3NW, England
Telephone: 0295 810624

Bill Baker Vehicles Limited designs and manufactures multi-purpose hovercraft and also supplies components. The latter include tapered roller-bearing fan hubs, nylon pulleys and other items for racing and two-seat integrated cruising craft. Hirth, Rotax and Rowena motors, Multiwing and Truflo fans are also available.

Since 1979 a range of craft has been developed for manufacture by the company or to be made under licence by suitable UK or foreign manufacturers. This has enabled the company to develop products such as a cab and cab heater for use in sub-zero conditions, tests being undertaken in Finland, Norway and Sweden on various winter surfaces to monitor performance.

The company supports the Hoverclub of Great Britain and international race meetings. Development of racing hovercraft is felt to be important for overall improvement of products from small-engined, integrated pleasure craft to larger four-seater craft.

BBV-1 (THE GNAT)

The smallest craft in the range is a low-price single-seater suitable for a beginner. It has a bag skirt and an 18hp Robin engine. It can also be fitted with the larger 48hp Rotax engine making it highly competitive in European Formula 'S' racing events. (Single engine, any size, single duct of 800mm maximum.) BBV-1 can be carried on a roof rack.
DIMENSIONS
Length: 3m (10ft)
Beam: 1·8m (6ft)
Weight: 20hp motor: 85kg (187lb)
40-50hp motor: 110kg (242·5lb)

BBV-1 Gnat *(Banbury Guardian)*

PRICE: Kit form, approximately £1,000; complete craft, £1,650 (1983)

BBV-1-S

This racing craft, derived from the BBV-1, features a pressure-fed, segmented skirt and a full 800mm duct. Engines of between 20 and 80hp can be installed.
PRICE (dependent on engine type): Kit form, approximately £1,700; complete craft, £2,200 (1983)

BBV-2

Based on the BBV-1, this two-seater has the same simplicity of construction, resulting in an extremely robust, lightweight craft. Features include moulded-in buoyancy foam on the outer edges of the hull as well as the floor. The hull will accept either bag or segmented skirt with minimum modification.

It has pillion- or bench-type seating (folding upholstered seats also available). A removable 22·7-litre (5-gallon) outboard type fuel tank,

BBV-2

spray dodger, engine cover and outer duct skin are standard. Electric start and windscreen are optional.
DIMENSIONS
Length: 3·6m (12ft)
Width: 1·8m (6ft)

BBV CRUISING CRAFT

More efficient hulls and the better matching of fans to installed power has improved the performance of BBV designs over the last few years.

A 2- to 3-seat hull is available which will take a variety of automobile engines with outputs of between 65 to 100hp. This realistically-priced cruising hovercraft can be bought with or without engines, and its features include competent performance, low noise, and low fuel consumption.

BBV-4

This four-seater has a segmented skirt and separate lift and thrust motors enabling it to maintain full hoverheight when stationary or traversing rough surfaces.

A number of thrust options are available. The most efficient is the twin fan unit (similar to that used on the BBV-11 racing craft). A cheaper unit is the single 900mm (35·4in) fan, usually only supplied with the open version of the craft. In its cab form (full or half cab) it can be fitted with various optional items, including electric wipers, plush seats, running lights, cab heater, vented cooling, and full instrumentation.
LIFT AND PROPULSION: Lift is supplied by a single 8hp Rowena Solo two-stroke motor. The thrust motor is a 42hp Hirth driving a single 91·4cm (3ft) diameter Truflo fan or a twin fan system for improved control.
CONTROLS: Tiller-controlled rudders in thrust duct.
HULL: Grp filled with rigid foam buoyancy. The optional cabin, which is removable, is made of coloured grp to match the hull. The front and rear of the cabin are open providing easy access to the lift system at the front, to the thrust motor and for passengers at the rear. Windows are glass or plastic laminated.
SKIRT: Pressure-fed segmented system in neoprene-coated nylon.
DIMENSIONS
Length: 4·82m (15ft 10in)

Beam: 2·13m (7ft)
Hoverheight: 254mm (10in)
WEIGHTS
Unladen: 272kg (600lb)
PERFORMANCE
Max speed with driver and three passengers, depending on conditions: 32-48km/h (20-30mph)

BBV-4 with cab

BBV 1.F1

BBV-1-F1 RACING HOVERCRAFT

Winner of the 1983 Formula One Championship, this craft uses the same hull shape and skirt design as the BBV-1-S, and BBV has also drawn on the experience gained during the development of its earlier Formula One racing craft, the BBV-11. The 9hp Solo lift engine drives a 558mm, 5-blade fan, and the Rotax 48-60hp engine drives two 645mm thrust fans, giving 110 to 140kg of thrust.
CONTROLS: Craft heading is controlled by twin rudders, one hinged to the rear of each thrust duct. Handlebars control rudder movement.
HULL: Two-part grp construction with foam buoyancy and a motorcycle-type seat moulded-in. Hull has full hydrodynamic surfaces and internal-skirt feed ducts.
SKIRT: Pressure-fed segmented system in neoprene-coated nylon.
DIMENSIONS
Length: 3·2m (10ft 6in)
Beam: 1·96m (6ft 6in)
Weight (unladen): 145kg (325lb)

PERFORMANCE
Max speed, calm conditions: 88·51km/h (55mph)
PRICE (approx): £2,550 (1983)

BRITISH HOVERCRAFT CORPORATION (BHC)

East Cowes, Isle of Wight, England
Telephone: 0983 294101
Telex: 86761/2
Officials:
B D Blackwell, MA, BSc(Eng), CEng, FIMechE, FRAeS, FBIM, *Chairman*
A V Reed, BSc(Tech), CEng, FRAeS, AMBIM, *Managing Director*
R L Wheeler, MSc, DIC, CEng, AFRAeS, *Engineering Director*
J McGarity, *Site Director*
P M M Ryan, *Sales Director*
H W Paice, *Secretary*

The British Hovercraft Corporation is the world's largest hovercraft manufacturer. The

capital of the corporation is £5 million, which is wholly owned by Westland PLC.

Formed in 1966, the corporation deals with a wide variety of applications of the air cushion principle, the emphasis being on the development and production of amphibious hovercraft. Other activities include the investigation of industrial applications of the air cushion principle.

BHC established the world's first full-scale hovercraft production line in 1964. BHC produces the 10- to 17-ton 'Winchester' (SR.N6) class craft, the 39-ton AP1-88, the 50-ton 'Wellington' (BH.7) class craft and the 200- to 300-ton 'Mountbatten' (SR.N4) class craft at East Cowes.

Six 'Mountbatten' class craft are in service, as passenger/car ferries on the Dover/Boulogne and

Ramsgate/Calais routes, with Hoverspeed (UK) Limited, the cross-Channel operator, formed as the result of the merger between Hoverlloyd Limited and Seaspeed in October 1981.

Four of the craft have been converted to Mk 2 standard and two have been converted from Mk 1 to Mk 3 (Super 4) standard with a daily capacity of 11,650 passengers and 1,550 cars. By early 1985 the six craft had carried 25 million passengers.

A military variant, the Military 4, can carry a disposable load of up to 165 tons (or 1,000 troops) at a speed of 65 knots and has a maximum endurance of almost 19 hours.

One BH.7 has been in service with the Royal Navy's Naval Hovercraft Trials Unit and six with the Iranian Navy.

Latest variant of the BH.7 is the Mk 20 which

has been 'stretched', re-engined and incorporates the latest skirt technology. Power is supplied by a 4,500 shp Detroit Diesel 570-K marinised gas turbine. Mine countermeasures, fast strike, patrol and logistics variants are available. In September 1983 the UK Ministry of Defence (Procurement Executive) awarded BHC a contract to examine the feasibility of converting the Royal Navy's BH.7 Mk 2 into a Mk 20. It is expected that a contract for conversion will be awarded and that the craft, when completed, will be employed in the development of mine countermeasures and fast exploration techniques.

Military and general duty variants of the 'Warden' and 'Winchester' class hovercraft are now in service with the Egyptian Navy, Iraqi Navy, Iranian Navy, Italian Interservice Hovercraft Unit, and the Canadian and Saudi Arabian Coast Guard.

Winchesters have been employed since 1967 in trials and sales demonstrations in Africa, Canada, Denmark, Finland, India, South America and the Middle and Far East, logging well over 250,000 operating hours.

Commercial general-purpose variants of the Warden and Winchester are in service with the Department of Civil Aviation, New Zealand, Department of Transport, Canada, Hovertravel Limited and Hoverwork Limited. In recent years the Winchester has been used increasingly for general-purpose roles including hydrographic and seismic survey, freighting and search and rescue duties.

Latest addition to the BHC range is the AP1-88 diesel-powered general-purpose hovercraft. Built in welded aluminium alloy employing shipbuilding techniques, it combines a 10- to 12-ton payload with a performance equal to that of the SR.N6. As a fast passenger ferry it will seat up to 101 passengers and in troop-carrying form it will seat up to 60 armed troops.

'MOUNTBATTEN' (SR.N4) CLASS Mk 2

The SR.N4 Mk 2 is a 200-ton passenger/car ferry designed for stage lengths of up to 184km (100n miles) on coastal water routes. It has an average service speed of 40 to 50 knots in waves up to 3·04m (10ft) in height and is able to operate in 3·7m (12ft) seas at a speed of about 20 knots.
LIFT AND PROPULSION: Power is supplied by four 3,400shp Rolls-Royce Marine Proteus free-turbine, turboshaft engines located in pairs at the rear of the craft on either side of the vehicle deck. Each has a maximum rating of 4,250shp, but usually operates at 3,400shp when cruising. Each engine is connected to one of four identical propeller/fan units, two forward and two aft. The propulsion propellers, made by Hawker Siddeley Dynamics, are of the four-bladed, variable and reversible pitch type, 5·79m (19ft) in diameter. The lift fans, made by BHC, are of the 12-bladed centrifugal type, 3·5m (11ft 6in) in diameter.

Since the gear ratios between the engine, fan and propeller are fixed, the power distribution can be altered by varying the propeller pitch and hence changing the speed of the system, which accordingly alters the power absorbed by the fixed pitch fan. The power absorbed by the fan can be varied from almost zero shp (ie boating

SR.N4 Mk 2 *The Prince of Wales*

with minimum power) to 2,100shp, within the propeller and engine speed limitations. A typical division on maximum cruise power would be 2,000shp to the propeller and 1,150shp to the fan; the remaining 250shp can be accounted for by engine power fall-off due to the turbine rpm drop, transmission losses and auxiliary drives.

The drive shafts from the engine consist of flanged light-alloy tubes approximately 2·28m (7ft 6in) long supported by steady bearings and connected by self-aligning couplings. Shafting to the rear propeller/fan units is comparatively short, but to the forward units is approximately 18·27m (60ft).

The main gearbox of each unit comprises a spiral bevel reduction gear, with outputs at the top and bottom of the box to the vertical propeller and fan drive shafts respectively. The design of the vertical shafts and couplings is similar to the main transmission shafts, except that the shafts above the main gearbox are of steel instead of light alloy to transmit the much greater torque loads to the propeller. This gearbox is equipped with a power take-off for an auxiliary gearbox with drives for pressure and scavenge lubricating oil pumps, and also a hydraulic pump for the pylon and fin steering control.

The upper gearbox, mounted on top of the pylon, turns the propeller drive through 90 degrees and has a gear ratio of 1·16:1. This gearbox has its own self-contained lubricating system.

Engines and auxiliaries are readily accessible for maintenance from inside the craft, while engine, propellers, pylons and all gearboxes can be removed for overhaul without disturbing the main structure.

The fan rotates on a pintle which is attached to the main structure. The assembly may be detached and removed inboard onto the car deck without disturbing the major structure.
CONTROLS: The craft control system enables the thrust lines and pitch angles of the propellers to be varied either collectively or differentially.

The fins and rudders move in step with the aft pylons. The pylons, fins and rudders move through ±35 degrees, ±30 degrees and ±40 degrees respectively.

Demand signals for pylon and fin angles are transmitted electrically from the commander's controls. These are compared with the pylon or fin feed-back signals and the differences are then amplified to actuate the hydraulic jacks mounted at the base of the pylon or fin structure. Similar electro-hydraulic signalling and feed-back systems are used to control propeller pitches.

The commander's controls include a rudder bar which steers the craft by pivoting the propeller pylons differentially.

For example, if the right foot is moved forward, the forward pylons move clockwise, viewed from above, and the aft pylons and fins move anticlockwise, thus producing a turning movement to starboard. The foregoing applies with positive thrust on the propellers, but if negative thrust is applied, as in the case of using the propellers for braking, the pylons and fins are automatically turned to opposing angles, thus maintaining the turn. A wheel mounted on a control column enables the commander to move the pylons and fins in unison to produce a drift to port or starboard as required. The control of the distribution of power between each propeller and fan is by propeller pitch lever. The pitch of all four propellers can be adjusted collectively over a limited range by a fore-and-aft movement of the control wheel.
HULL: Construction is primarily of high strength, aluminium-clad, aluminium alloy, suitably protected against the corrosive effects of sea water.

The basic structure is the buoyancy chamber, built around a grid of longitudinal and transversal frames, which form 24 watertight sub-divisions for safety. The design ensures that even a rip from end-to-end would not cause the craft to sink or overturn. The reserve buoyancy is 250%, the total available buoyancy amounting to more than 550 tons.

Top and bottom surfaces of the buoyancy chamber are formed by sandwich construction panels bolted onto the frames, the top surface being the vehicle deck. Panels covering the central 4·9m (16ft) section of the deck are reinforced to carry unladen coaches, or commercial vehicles up to 9 tons gross weight (maximum axle load 5,900kg (13,000lb)), while the remainder are designed solely to carry cars and light vehicles (maximum axle load 2,040kg (4,500lb)). An articulated loading ramp 5·5m (18ft) wide, which can be lowered to ground level, is built into the bows, while doors extending the full width of the centre deck are provided at the aft end.

Similar grid construction is used on the elevated passenger-carrying decks and the roof, where the panels are supported by deep transverse and longitudinal frames. The

SR.N4 Mk 2 *The Prince of Wales*

buoyancy chamber is joined to the roof by longitudinal walls to form a stiff fore-and-aft structure. Lateral bending is taken mainly by the buoyancy tanks. All horizontal surfaces are of pre-fabricated sandwich panels with the exception of the roof, which is of skin and stringer panels.

Double curvature has been avoided other than in the region of the air intakes and bow. Each fan air intake is bifurcated and has an athwartships bulkhead at both front and rear, supporting a beam carrying the transmission main gearbox and the propeller pylon. The all-moving fins and rudders behind the aft pylons pivot on pintles just ahead of the rear bulkhead.

The fans deliver air to the cushion via a peripheral fingered bag skirt.

The material used for both bags and fingers is nylon, coated with neoprene and/or natural rubber, the fingers and cones being made from a heavier weight material than the trunks.

ACCOMMODATION: The basic manning requirement is for a commander, an engineer/radio operator and a radar operator/navigator. A seat is provided for a fourth crew member or a crew member in training. The remainder of the crew, ie those concerned with passenger service or car handling, are accommodated in the main cabins. The arrangement may be modified to suit individual operator's requirements.

The control cabin, which provides nearly 360-degree vision, is entered by either of two ways. The normal method, when the cars are arranged in four lanes, is by a hatch in the cabin floor, reached by a ladder from the car deck. When heavy vehicles are carried on the centre section, or if for some other reason the ladder has to be retracted, a door in the side of the port forward passenger cabin gives access to a ladder leading onto the main cabin roof. From the roof a door gives access into the control cabin.

The craft currently in service carry 282 passengers and 37 cars.

The car deck occupies the large central area of the craft, with large stern doors and a bow ramp providing a drive-on/drive-off facility.

Separate side doors give access to the passenger cabins which flank the car deck. The outer cabins have large windows which extend over the full length of the craft. The control cabin is sited centrally and forward on top of the superstructure to give maximum view.

DIMENSIONS
EXTERNAL
Overall length: 39·68m (130ft 2in)
Overall beam: 23·77m (78ft)
Overall height on landing pads: 11·48m (37ft 8in)
Skirt depth: 2·44m (8ft)

Control cabin of Super 4

INTERNAL
Passenger/vehicle floor area: 539m² (5,800ft²)
Vehicle deck headroom-centre line: 3·43m (11ft 3in)
Bow ramp door aperture size (height × width): 3·51 × 5·48m (11ft 6in × 18ft)
Stern door aperture size (height × width): 3·51 × 9·45m (11ft 6in × 31ft)
WEIGHTS
Normal gross: 200 tons
Fuel capacity: 20,456 litres (4,500 imperial gallons)
PERFORMANCE (at normal gross weight at 15°C)
Max waterspeed over calm water, zero wind (cont power rating): 70 knots
Average service waterspeed: 40-60 knots
Normal stopping distance from 50 knots: 480m (525 yards)
Endurance at max cont power on 2,800 imperial gallons: 2·5 hours
Negotiable gradient from standing start: 1 : 11

SR.N4 Mk 3 SUPER 4

The Super 4 differs from earlier Marks of the SR.N4 primarily in that it is 16·76m (55ft)

longer, increasing the overall length to 56·38m (185ft) with a beam of 28·04m (92ft).

Modification of an SR.N4 Mk 1 to Super 4 standard necessitates adding a new 16·76m (55ft) section amidships, widening the existing superstructure and strengthening the original bow and stern halves to accept the increased stresses resulting from the 40 per cent increase in length. The propeller pylons are raised to allow 6·4m (21ft) diameter propellers to be fitted, the transmission systems are realigned and four uprated 3,800shp Rolls-Royce Marine Proteus gas turbines are installed.

A more efficient low pressure ratio skirt system with larger fingers is fitted, giving a mean air cushion depth of 2·7m (9ft). Passenger cabin trim and seating have been completely revised and sound-proofing increased.

Compared with the SR.N4 Mk 1, the Super 4 has a 70 per cent greater revenue earning capability, but costs only about 15 per cent more to operate. The increased length and advanced skirt system give both a higher performance in adverse weather and greatly improved ride comfort for the passengers.

Craft handling and skirt behaviour have proved completely satisfactory over the entire weight range from 212 to 300 tons in sea conditions up to Force 8 to 9. Measurements taken in the passenger cabins of acceleration forces show a three-fold improvement in ride comfort over the SR.N4 Mk 2. The uprated Rolls-Royce Proteus gas turbines have been trouble-free and the new propellers have substantially reduced external noise when operating into and out of hovercraft terminals.

Super 4 has a payload of 418 passengers and 60 vehicles, a laden weight of 300 tons and a top speed in excess of 65 knots.

LIFT AND PROPULSION: Motive power is supplied by four Rolls-Royce Marine Proteus Type 15M/529 free-turbine turboshaft engines, located in pairs at the rear of the craft on either side of the vehicle deck. Each engine is rated at 3,800shp continuous under ISA conditions and is connected to one of four identical propeller/fan units, two forward and two aft. The propellers, made by Hawker Siddeley Dynamics, are of four-bladed, controllable-pitch type D258/485A/2. The lift fans, made by BHC, are of 12-bladed centrifugal type, 3·5m (11ft 6in) in diameter. Maximum fuel tankage, 28·45 tonnes; normal fuel allowing for ballast transfer, 18·29 tonnes.

AUXILIARY POWER: Two Lucas turboshaft engines driving 55kVA 200V, 400Hz Lucas alternators.

SR.N4 Mk 2 *Sure*

DIMENSIONS
Length overall: 56·38m (185ft)
Beam, hardstructure: 23·16m (76ft)
Height overall, on landing pads: 11·43m (37ft 6in)
Bow ramp door aperture size,
  Height: 3·5m (11ft 6in)
  Width: 5·48m (18ft)
Stern door aperture size,
  Height: 3·51m (11ft 6in)
  Width: 9·45m (31ft)
Car deck area: 631m² (6,790ft²)

WEIGHTS
Max laden: 300 tons
Max disposable load: 112 tons
Typical fuel load: 20 tons
Payload: 54-60 cars, 418 passengers

PERFORMANCE
Typical cruise waterspeeds:
Calm (2ft waves, 5 knots wind): 60-65 knots
Moderate (5ft waves, 20 knots wind): 50-55 knots
Rough (8ft waves, 27 knots wind): 35-45 knots
Endurance per ton of fuel: 0·23 hour

SR.N4 Mk 4
The MCMH version of the SR.N4 is identical in most respects to the Mk 2 commercial craft but has a much larger fuel capacity. A high-speed self-jacking system, which would allow the craft to be raised for skirt inspections and repairs on temporary landing sites, can be installed if required. At its design maximum all-up weight of 220 tonnes it is capable of carrying up to 60 tonnes of role payload in addition to the fuel for a ten-hour mission.

The craft is able to undertake all the mine clearance tasks currently performed by conventional vessels such as a minesweeper with wire or influence sweeps, or a mine hunter using towed sonar and mine disposal equipment. It can therefore operate either independently or as a unit of a mixed-craft MCM force.

The operations room, crew quarters and workshop can be in the twin side cabins or on the central deck area forward of the winch positions. All major installations in the central area can be erected on palletised modules to facilitate changes of MCM equipment and conversion for logistic support duties, enabling individual craft to perform any of the proposed MCM roles at short notice.

As with the standard craft, the SR.N4 MCMH has considerable development potential. Most of

Vehicle deck, Super 4

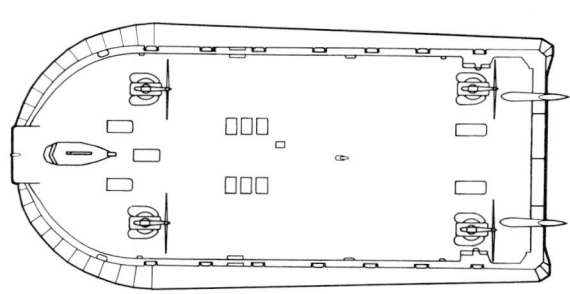

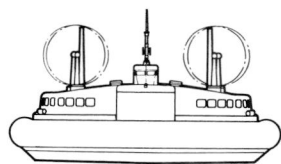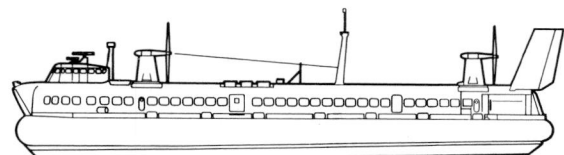
General arrangement of SR.N4 Mk 3 Super 4

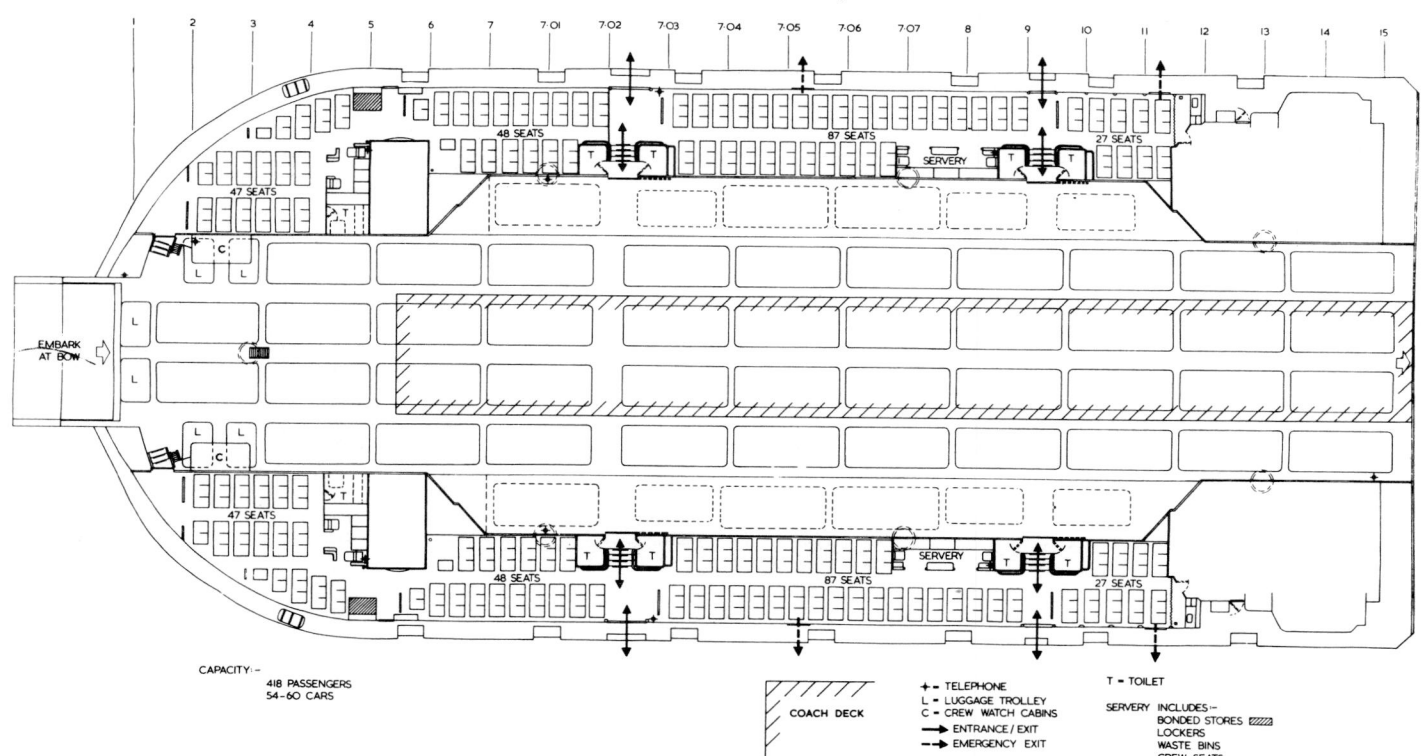
Layout of vehicle deck and passenger cabins on SR.N4 Mk 3 Super 4

the future modifications which may be introduced to improve the efficiency of the civil versions will be applicable to the MCMH, including larger propellers, uprated engines and revised skirts. In particular its payload carrying capability could be increased by lengthening as has been undertaken for the ex-Seaspeed craft.

All types of minesweeping gear used by conventional minesweepers—a wiresweep to cut the moorings of tethered mines or influence sweeps, magnetic and acoustic, to detonate influence mines—can be carried by the SR.N4. Additionally in the minehunting role it can tow sonars to locate mines which cannot normally be swept and carry the equipment to destroy them.

Trials with SR.N4 have shown that it maintains a track in winds of at least 20 knots to within a standard deviation of less than 8 metres. In the minehunting role, position accuracy as well as track keeping accuracy is required, since relocation may be necessary. These requirements can be met by the provision of two navigation modes. In the primary mode, position fixing could be derived from a high accuracy radio navigation aid. Secondary mode sensors could include a navigation radar with auto extraction, possibly by range-range measurement relative to short scope buoys. Decca Navigator could provide a further mode.

It is likely that the SR.N4 MCMH would have an integrated computer-based navigation and action information system. This would have inputs of heading from a gyro compass; velocities from a speed and drift sensor, probably a multi-beam doppler radar; position from Hi-fix 6, Decca Navigator and Inboard navigational radar; target position from a towed sonar.

The SR.N4 MCMH would operate from Forward Support Units (FSU) located in the general area of probable mining targets. One such unit could be the force headquarters, providing training facilities and co-ordinating mine clearance operations including, if necessary, those of conventional craft. In the event of a mining attack it may be desirable to establish an additional MCMH base closer to the area of operations. This could be in the form of a Mobile Advanced Base (MAB) able to support up to three craft for a period of 14 days. It is anticipated that MAB sites would be selected in advance of an attack but not necessarily prepared in any way.

Where the situation did not justify a MAB, fuel, sweep spares and crew could be readily transferred at a Temporary Replenishment Point (TRP) which need be no more than a suitable beach area having vehicular access.

It is envisaged that the MCMH force would be responsible for the establishment of any shore based navigation system such as Hi-fix which might be required for operation in particular areas.

A recent feasibility study for a single role minehunter based on the SR.N4 showed that with some modification and re-engining, all-up weight of 300 tonnes would be possible on the Mk 2 planform.

MULTI-ROLE CRAFT

The SR.N4 MCMH can carry the full range of equipment associated with the mine sweeping, influence sweeping and hunter/disposal roles at the same time. There is adequate deck space for all the items to be stowed—the central through deck area is about 35m long by 10m wide—and the corresponding craft weight of 227·5 tonnes, which includes fuel for 11 hours endurance, is well within operational limits.

In practice the craft is unlikely to be required to carry all the equipment when operating in a specific role. Wire sweeping can be undertaken with the influence sweeping equipment on board since many components are common. The various mine hunting and disposal systems considered are sufficiently portable to be fitted at the Mobile Advanced Base when needed for specific tasks.

The characteristics of the standard SR.N4 are such that the craft can be adapted to other roles and in particular to those of fast attack craft and

Super 4

Super 4, *The Princess Anne*

SR.N4 Mk 3 in fast-attack configuration

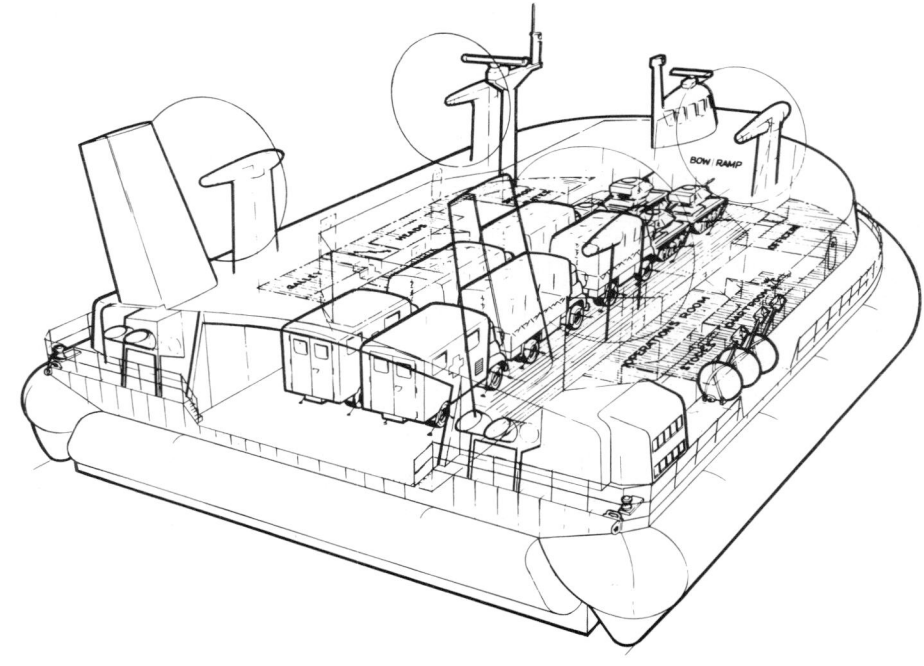
SR.N4 with typical logistic payload

anti-submarine craft. As a fast attack craft a typical weapon fit could include at least four surface-to-surface missiles of Exocet or Harpoon type or similar, a 75mm OTO Melara gun and a twin 30mm gun mount for anti-aircraft defence, together with their associated sensors and control equipment. The anti-submarine version could carry upwards of 60 tonnes of equipment enabling it to operate in the hunter/killer role alone or in conjunction with other craft.

LOGISTIC SUPPORT

Should a situation develop which requires large numbers of troops and their equipment to be transported over water at high speed then the SR.N4 MCMH could, by removal of the bulk of the MCM equipment, be converted for Logistic Support duties.

Typical loadings up to 90 tonnes:

7 GS trucks; 250 troops.

1 battle tank; 2 light tanks; 6 1-tonne Land-Rovers.

4 light tanks; 2 laden trucks; 2 unladen trucks; 2 ambulances.

Operating around the clock over a 30n mile route in moderate conditions, the craft could, over a 24-hour period, transport approximately 1,500 tonnes of military personnel and equipment.

SR.N4 MINELAYER

A high-speed mine laying version of the SR.N4 is now available. This particular variant will carry 110 to 120 ground mines with their trolleys. A feature of the design is a revised stern door arrangement which will permit mine laying to take place at high speed over all depths of water.

'WINCHESTER' (SR.N6) CLASS

Designed primarily as a fast ferry for operation in sheltered waters, the Winchester can accommodate either 38 passengers or 3 tons of freight.

Fully amphibious, it can operate from relatively unsophisticated bases above the high water mark, irrespective of tidal state.

Directional control is achieved by twin rudders and a thrust port system. Two manually actuated elevators provide pitch trim at cruising speed.

Winchesters have been in regular commercial service since 1965. Operators include Hovertravel Limited and Hoverwork Limited. A further Winchester is in service with the Civil Aviation Department, Ministry of Transport, New Zealand, as a crash rescue craft at Auckland International Airport. Both the Winchester and its smaller, 7-ton predecessor, the SR.N5 (see *Jane's Surface Skimmers 1971-72* and earlier editions), are in service with the Canadian Coast Guard.

Military variants are in service with the Egyptian Navy, Iraqi Navy, Iranian Navy, Italian Navy and the Saudi Arabian Frontier Force and Coast Guard.

LIFT AND PROPULSION: Power for the integrated lift/propulsion system is provided by a Rolls-Royce Marine Gnome gas turbine with a maximum continuous rating at 15°C of 900shp. This drives a BHC 12-blade centrifugal 2·13m (7ft) diameter lift fan, and a Dowty Rotol four-blade variable pitch 2·74m (9ft) diameter propeller for propulsion.

DIMENSIONS

EXTERNAL

Overall length: 14·8m (48ft 6in)

Overall beam, skirt inflated: 7·7m (25ft 4in)

Overall height on landing pads: 3·8m (12ft 6in)

Hoverheight: 5m (16ft 6in)

Skirt depth: 1·22m (4ft)

INTERNAL

Cabin size (length × width): 6·62 × 2·34m (21ft 9in × 7ft 8in)

Cabin headroom-centre line: 1·83m (6ft)

Door aperture size (height × width): 1·75 × 0·99m (5ft 9in × 3ft 3in)

WEIGHTS

Normal gross: 10 tons

PERFORMANCE (at normal gross weight at 15°C)

Max water speed over calm water, zero wind, (continuous power rating): 96km/h (52 knots)

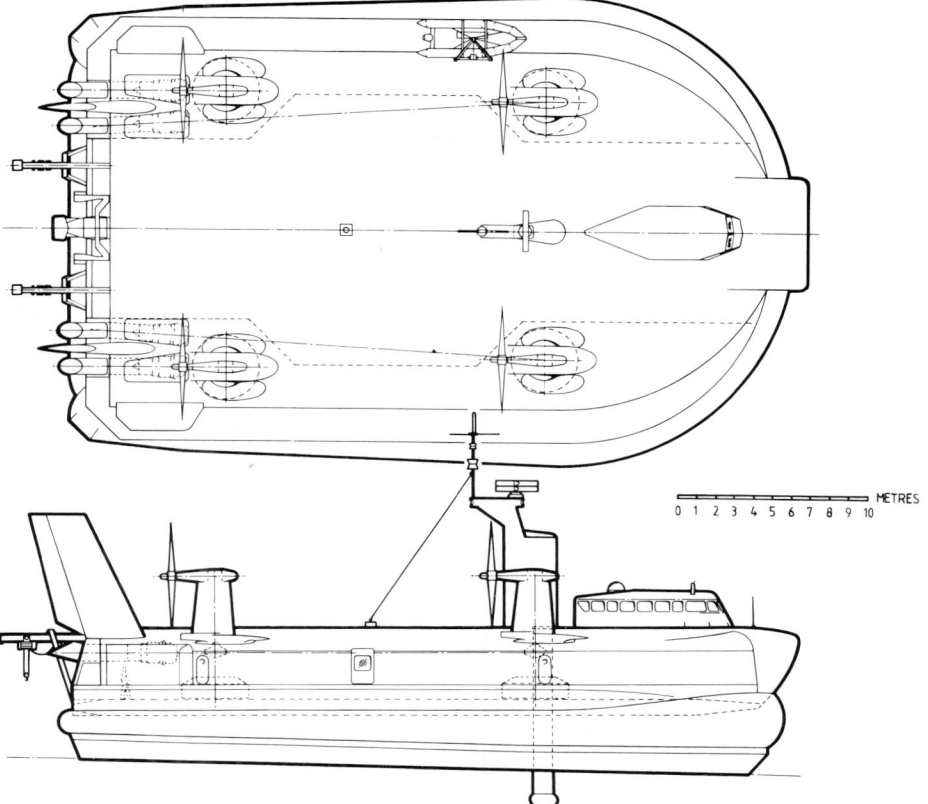

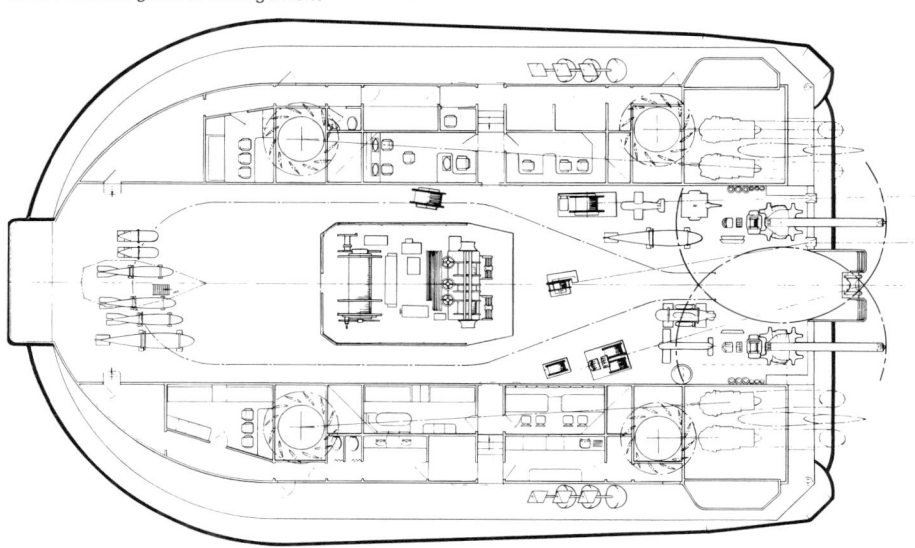

SR.N4 MCMH general arrangement

Deck plan of multi-role version of SR.N4 minesweeper

SR.N6 operated by Canadian Coast Guard Hovercraft units

Average service water speed in sheltered coastal
waters: 55·65km/h (30·35 knots)
Endurance at max continuous power rating on
265 imperial gallons of fuel: 3·6 hours

'WINCHESTER' (SR.N6) CLASS— PASSENGER FERRY/GENERAL PURPOSE

Since the SR.N6 first entered service as a passenger ferry in 1965, it has carried well over three
million fare-paying passengers and is firmly
established in certain areas as an integral part of
surface transport networks.

The popularity of these services led to the
introduction of an SR.N6 with a larger carrying
capacity, designated the SR.N6 Mk 1S. At 17·6m
(58ft), the Mk 1S is 3m (10ft) longer than the
standard craft and can carry up to 58 passengers
as opposed to 35 to 38 in the standard SR.N6.

Other modifications to this craft include additional baggage panniers, emergency exits and
improved cabin ventilation. There is also a significant increase in ride comfort. To ensure that
performance is maintained, the rating of the
Rolls-Royce Marine Gnome gas turbine engine
has been increased by 100 to 1,000shp.

One Mk 1S is in operation on the Ryde/South-
sea route with Hovertravel Limited.

Apart from passenger services, commercial
SR.N6s have also made successful inroads into
other fields of operation in recent years including
freight-carrying, hydrographic/seismographic
survey, offshore support operations, general
communications, crash rescue and firefighting.

To undertake these duties, craft have been
modified either with the fitting of specialised
equipment or by structural alterations such as
flat-decks.

'WINCHESTER' (SR.N6) CLASS— MILITARY

Variants of the SR.N6 are in service with a
number of the world's military and para-military
forces on coastal defence and logistic support
duties.

The SR.N6 Mk 2/3, for logistic support, features a roof loading hatch and strengthened
side-decks for carrying long loads of up to 0·5
ton. Lightweight armour may be fitted to protect
troops being carried in the cabin, the engine, and
other vital systems. Defensive armament is provided by a roof-mounted light machine gun
(7·62mm or 0·5in).

The craft can carry upwards of 20 fully-
equipped troops or supply loads of up to 5 tons. A
small auxiliary generator is installed to provide
power when the main engine is stopped.

The SR.N6 Mk 4 for coastal defence duties
may be fitted with 20mm cannon or short-range
wire-guided surface-to-surface missiles. Communications equipment is concentrated behind
the rear cabin bulkhead.

SR.N6 Mk 6 GENERAL PURPOSE

The SR.N6 Mk 6 is the most recent development in the successful Winchester series and
represents significant steps forward in terms of
increased payload, all-weather performance, and
increased manoeuvrability, especially in high
winds and at low speeds. There is also a significant reduction in the external noise level.

These advances have been achieved by the
introduction of twin propellers for thrust, a more
powerful engine, wider side-decks and a redesigned skirt for better seakeeping capabilities.
The tapered skirt, which is deeper at the bow than
the stern, cushions the effect of operating over
larger waves and surface obstacles and enables
the craft to operate in winds of up to Beaufort
Scale 8 and waves of up to 3·04m (10ft).

The craft, with its large cabin, can carry up to
55 passengers or between 5 and 6 tons of equipment. Options include air-conditioning and VIP
interior trim.

LIFT AND PROPULSION: Motive power is
supplied by a single 1,125hp Rolls-Royce Marine
Gnome GN 1301 gas turbine driving a single
2·13m (7ft) diameter BHC lift fan and two 3·05m
(10ft) diameter Dowty Rotol variable-pitch

SR.N6 Mk 6 general purpose hovercraft showing twin-propeller arrangement and tapered skirt

propellers. Maximum fuel capacity is 4,840 litres
(1,065 imperial gallons).
DIMENSIONS
Length overall: 18·3m (60ft)
Beam overall: 8·5m (28ft)
Height overall, on landing pads: 5·6m (18ft 4in)
   on cushion: 6·7m (22ft)
WEIGHTS
Max operating: 17,010kg (37,500lb)
PERFORMANCE
Max speed over calm water: 60 knots
Fuel consumption: 410 litres/h (90 imperial gal-
lons/h)

SR.N6 Mk 8

Latest military variant of the SR.N6, the Mk 8
has the same overall measurements as the SR.N6
Mk 6 twin-propeller model but has a single propeller only. Another external difference is the provision of two air-conditioning modules on the
cabin roof aft of the driving position.

In the logistic support role the Mk 8 can carry
up to 55 fully-equipped troops or loads of up to 6
tons. Access to the cabin, which measures 9·5 ×
2·3m (31ft 2in × 7ft 7in), is via a bow door. The
floor is fitted with tie-down points for stores and
equipment. Loads up to ½ ton which are too long

SR.N6 Mk 8s

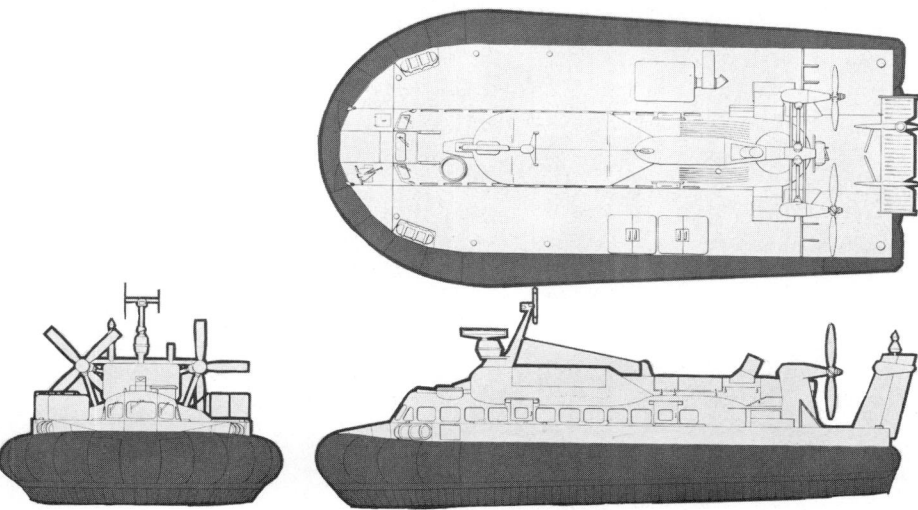

General arrangement of SR.N6 Mk 6

for the cabin may be carried externally on the side-decks.

In the coastal patrol role, the operational flexibility of the SR.N6 is greatly improved by its ability to work from beaches and other unprepared sites and to navigate freely in shallow water. At the same time the craft is sea-worthy and can operate in most weather conditions by day or night.

LIFT AND PROPULSION: Integrated system powered by a single Rolls-Royce GN 1301 marine gas turbine rated at 1,050shp at 15°C. Auxiliary power is supplied by a Lucas SS923 gas turbine driving a three-phase alternator. Main fuel tank capacity is 1,204 litres (265 imperial gallons). Long range tanks can be fitted, giving a capacity of 1,818 litres (400 imperial gallons).

ARMAMENT: Either a ring-mounted machine gun (0·5in or 7·62mm) or short range wire-guided surface-to-surface missiles mounted on the side-decks.

DIMENSIONS
Length overall: 18·3m (60ft)
Beam overall: 8·5m (28ft)
Height overall on cushion: 6·7m (22ft)
PERFORMANCE
Max speed, calm water: 50 knots
Endurance, on main tanks: 2·4 hours
    on long-range tanks: 6 hours
A further 1·8 hours endurance can be obtained by using the fuel carried in the craft's trim system giving a maximum endurance of 7·8 hours

'WELLINGTON' (BH.7) CLASS

BH.7 is a 55-ton hovercraft which was designed specifically for naval and military roles. The prototype, designated BH.7 Mk 2, has been

in service with the Royal Navy since 1970 where it has been evaluated in a number of roles including fishery protection, ASW and MCM work.

The second and third craft, designated Mk 4, and a further four Mk 5As, are in service with the Iranian Navy.

LIFT AND PROPULSION: Power for the integrated lift propulsion system on the Mk 2 and Mk 4 is provided by a Rolls-Royce Marine Proteus 15M541 gas turbine with a maximum rating at 23°C of 4,250shp. On the Mk 5A, a 15M549 is installed with a maximum rating of 4,250shp. In both types the engine drives, via a light alloy driveshaft and bevel drive gearbox, a BHC 12-blade, centrifugal 3·5m (11ft 6in) diameter lift fan and an HSD four-blade, variable-pitch

pylon-mounted propeller. Propeller diameter on the Mk 4 is 5·79m (19ft) and 6·4m (21ft) on the Mk 2 and Mk 5A. Normal fuel capacity is up to 3,000 imperial gallons (13,635 litres).

CONTROLS: Craft direction is controlled by swivelling the propeller pylon angle by a foot-pedal. Thrust ports are fitted at each quarter to assist directional control at low speed, and a hydraulically-operated skirt-shift system helps to bank the craft into turns, thereby reducing drift.

Fuel is transferred between forward and aft tanks via a ring main to adjust fore and aft trim.

HULL: Construction is mainly of corrosion resistant light alloy. Extensive use is made of components which were designed for the N4. The bow structure is a Plasticell base covered with glass fibre.

SKIRT: The fan delivers air to the cushion via a continuous peripheral fingered bag skirt made in neoprene-coated nylon fabric. The skirt provides an air cushion depth of 1·68m (5ft 6in). The cushion is divided into four compartments by a full length longitudinal keel and by two transverse keels located slightly forward of amidships.

ACCOMMODATION: The raised control cabin, located slightly forward of amidships on the hull centre line, accommodates a crew of three, with the driver and navigator/radar operator in front and the third crew member behind. The driver sits on the right, with the throttle and propeller pitch control lever on his right, and the pylon angle pedal and skirt-shift column in front.

The navigator, on the left, has a Decca radar display (Type 914 on the Mk 5) and compass in front and Decometers in an overhead panel.

The large main cabin area permits a variety of operational layouts. In a typical arrangement, the operations room is placed directly beneath the control cabin and contains communication, navigation, search and strike equipment and associated displays.

The craft has an endurance of up to 11 hours under cruise conditions but this can be extended considerably as it can stay 'on watch' without using the main engine.

Provision can be made for the crew to live aboard for several days.

SYSTEMS, ELECTRICAL: Two Rover IS/90 APUs provide, via two 55kVA generators, three-phase 400Hz ac at 200V for ac and dc supplies.

DIMENSIONS
EXTERNAL
Length overall: 23·9m
Beam overall: 13·8m
Overall height on landing pads: 10·36m
Cushion depth: 1·76m
INTERNAL (Main Cabin)
Cabin length: 13·2m
Cabin width: 4·17m
Headroom (on centre line): 2·38m
WEIGHTS
Normal gross: 56 tonnes
Disposable load, inc role equipment: 18·3 tonnes
PERFORMANCE (at max operating weight at 15°C)
Max continuous calm water speed: 58 knots

Wellington BH.7 Mk 5A

WELLINGTON (BH.7) Mk 4 LOGISTIC SUPPORT

ACCOMMODATION: In this role, the main hold floor area of 56m² (600ft²) of the Mk 4 provides an unobstructed space suitable for loading wheeled vehicles, guns and military stores.

Two side cabins, filled with paratroop-type seats, can accommodate up to 60 troops and their equipment.

Access at the bow is through a 'clamshell' door.

Machine guns can be fitted in gun rings on the roof on either side of the cabin and provision can be made for armour plating to protect personnel, the engine and vital electrical components.

TYPICAL MILITARY LOADS: 170 fully equipped troops or three field cars and trailers plus 60 troops or two armoured scout cars or up to 20 NATO pallets.

WELLINGTON (BH.7) Mk 5 COMBAT

Designed for coastal defence operations, the BH.7 Mk 5 carries medium-range surface-to-surface missiles, such as Exocet, on its side-decks. Secondary armament consists of a twin 30mm surface/AA radar controlled mounting situated on the foredeck forward of the main centre cabin.

The main central cabin, employed on the BH.7 Mk 4 for load-carrying, is equipped as an operations and fire-control room. Since it is fully amphibious, the BH.7 Mk 5 can be operated from relatively unprepared bases on beaches and can head directly towards its target on interception missions regardless of the tidal state and marginal terrain. Also, since none of its solid structure is immersed, it is invulnerable to underwater defences such as acoustic, magnetic and pressure mines and to attack by torpedoes.

A full range of electronic navigational aids permits the craft to operate by day or night.

WELLINGTON (BH.7) Mk 5A COMBAT/LOGISTICS

Similar to the Mk 5, with the exception that the bow door is retained, giving the craft a dual fast attack/logistic capability. Secondary armament can consist of two roof-mounted single 20mm guns.

BH.7 Mk 20 MULTI-ROLE AMPHIBIOUS HOVERCRAFT

This new BH.7 variant has been 'stretched', re-engined and incorporates the latest advances in skirt technology. Its chief modifications are as follows.

All-up weight has been increased to 82 tonnes, giving a 75 per cent increase in disposable load.

Cushion length and area have been increased by approximately 25 per cent and the depth by 20 per cent. This brings the length/beam and depth/beam ratios into line with the SR.N6 Mk 8 and the SR.N4 Mk 3, both craft with a good rough water performance and notably more comfortable than earlier unstretched models.

Royal Navy BH.7 Mk 2 equipped for minehunting with Plessey 193M sonar immersed

BH.7 Mk 2 with retracted Plessey 193M sonar tube

The control cabin has been lengthened to provide additional accommodation and to house an overhead-mounted, remotely-operated sight/director. A wider range of missiles can be fitted.

The auxiliary power unit is moved aft to maximise the deck area and accommodate all exhausts aft where their infra-red (IR) signature will be partially masked by spray.

There are two additional structure bays, increasing the hardstructure length by about 4·9m to 28·3m, and the former 3,800hp Rolls-Royce Marine Proteus has been replaced by the more powerful Allison 570-K flat-rated to a continuous output of 4,500shp.

The craft is suitable for the following roles: minehunting/mine disposal, route surveillance, fast exploratory operations, minesweeping, fast attack, logistic support and VIP transport.

The BH.7 Mine Countermeasures Hovercraft is described below.

BH.7 Mk 20 MINE COUNTERMEASURES

Minesweeping is one of the most hazardous of all naval activities. Clearance techniques in the past have been very much on a hit or miss basis with craft operating in pairs, one sweeping and the other hunting and destroying the released mines as they surfaced by rifle and machine-gun fire. Since the precise location of each mine was unknown, it was not unusual for a released mine to surface in the path of or beneath the hull of the hunter craft.

In the USA in recent years, efforts to reduce the tremendous loss in lives and craft led to the introduction of the Edo 105 and 106 foil-equipped catamaran minesweeping systems. These not only speed up the process of mine clearance but, since they are towed by helicopter, considerably reduce the risks to the crews involved.

In the United Kingdom, the Ministry of Defence (Navy) has stated that as hovercraft normally operate clear of the water, they are less

BH.7 Mk 2 during minehunting demonstrations

vulnerable to possible mine explosions than conventional vessels, and with mine countermeasures equipment they have a potential for this type of work.

The British Hovercraft Corporation has announced plans for both sweeper and hunter versions of the BH.7 and the SR.N4. Trials have shown that in comparison with a conventional minesweeper a BH.7 in this role has five times the transit speed, better track-keeping in rough water and, because of its low underwater signatures, magnetic, acoustic and pressure, is unlikely to explode mines.

The BH.7 Mk 20 is a new mine countermeasures system which can carry, deploy and operate all existing and projected mine countermeasures equipment.

LIFT AND PROPULSION: Power for the integrated lift/propulsion system is provided by a single Allison 570-K marinised gas turbine rated at 4,500 shp maximum. Power is transmitted, via a light alloy drive shaft and a bevel drive gearbox, to a BHC 12-bladed 3·5m (11ft 6 in) diameter, centrifugal lift fan and a British Aerospace Dynamics Group 4-bladed, 6·4m (21ft) diameter, controllable-pitch propeller mounted on a swivelling pylon. Air from the lift fan is fed into a low pressure ratio, low-drag, deep-fingered skirt in neoprene rubber-coated fabric with a mean cushion depth of 2 metres. Advances in skirt design have reduced the propulsion and lift power requirements of the BH.7 Mk 20 by almost 50 per cent compared with earlier BH.7 models. Large integral fuel tanks provide a total capacity of 31,800 litres (7,000 imperial gallons).

CONTROLS: Craft direction is controlled by varying the propeller pylon angle by up to ± 35 degrees. Thrust ports in each quarter assist directional control at low speeds and a hydraulically-operated skirt-shift system helps to bank the craft into turns, reducing drift. Fuel is transferred between forward and aft tanks via a ring main to adjust fore and aft trim. Above the main cabin is a large air-conditioned control cabin which provides an all-round view and a comfortable working environment for an operating crew of four and up to three observers. The crew comprises a commander (driver), radar operator (co-driver), radio operator and navigator. Access is normally via a ladder from the main cabin. A door on the port side gives access to the main cabin roof and, via an external ladder, to the main deck.

HULL: The main hull is formed by a buoyancy raft of high strength light alloy, divided into watertight compartments. Above this, and bounded by broad external side-decks, is the main cabin superstructure. The cabin is loaded and unloaded via a bow ramp and door. Handling equipment is provided for loading vehicles and cargo during logistics operations. The craft is designed to carry separate accommodation modules for use as alternative crew quarters, VIP cabin or command information centre (CIC). Crew facilities include a galley, toilets, showers and a mess area. Side-decks are used for search and rescue and similar operations and stowage areas for equipment.

At the forward end, each deck has provision for a stabilised gun mounting. Safety rails can be fitted along the sides and there are mounting points for up to five life rafts in the search and rescue role.

SYSTEMS, MINEHUNTING/MINE DISPOSAL: Key items of equipment required for this mode of operation are as follows:

The Plessey 193M 'search and classify' sonar, the acoustic head of which is mounted on a retractable tube enabling it to be immersed to the correct depth while the craft is cushion-borne.

The PAP 104 remote mine disposal vehicle and its associated magazine module.

A Racal or similar integrated navigation system.

An inflatable dinghy for diving operations.

Command and sleeping modules are fitted within the main cabin. The command module is equipped with navigation, surface and under surface plotting tables, radar and sonar displays, and

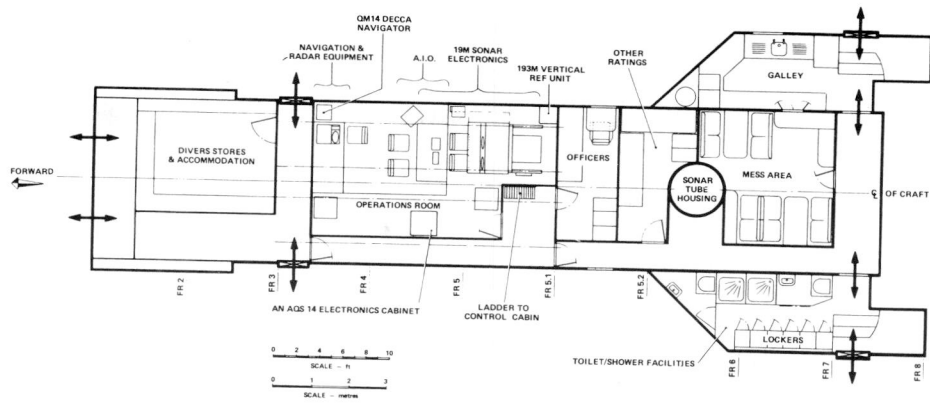

BH.7 Mk 20 minehunter, internal layout

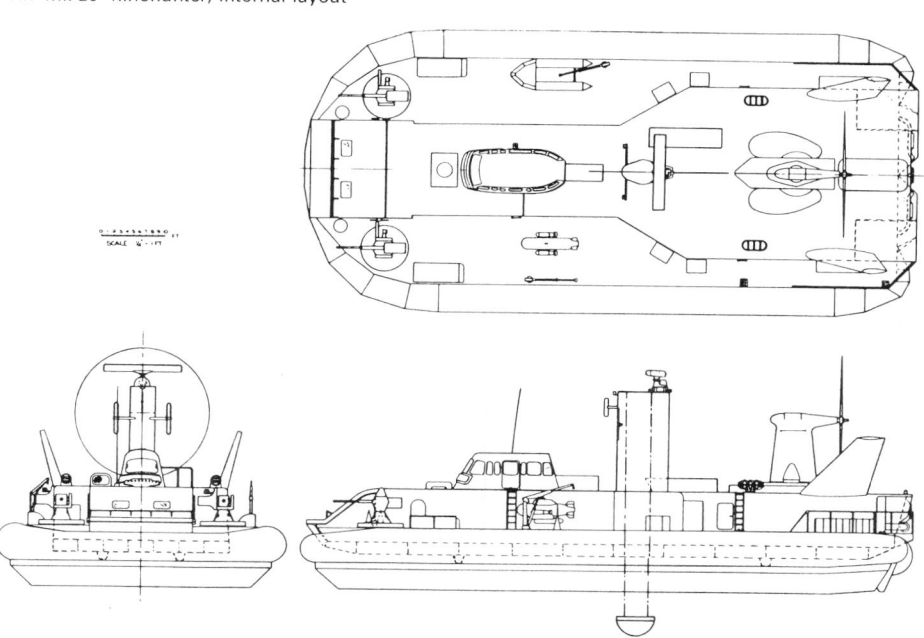

BH.7 Mk 20 equipped for minehunting

BH.7 Mk 20 mine countermeasures hovercraft with PAP 104 remote control mine disposal vehicle and Plessey 193M and 2048 sonars with retractable transducer

data processing equipment. Ahead of the command module is the sleeping accommodation with eight bunks.

In the minehunting/mine disposal mode the craft searches a pre-determined area at 2 to 5 knots. Once a contact has been made, the sonar mode is changed to 'classify' and the object is further investigated. The PAP 104 is armed, deployed and remotely guided to the position of the mine where it drops a charge as close to the mine as possible. After recovery of the PAP, the charge is detonated.

The high transit speed of the BH.7 allows it to refuel, change crews and return to station. Typically, at 100n miles from base the craft would have 16 hours on station. This would enable an area 450m wide and up to 80n miles long to be searched.

MINESWEEPING: The craft is capable of towing the following types of sweepgear developed by the US Navy for use with helicopters: Edo Mk 103 mechanical wire sweep; Edo Mk 104 acoustic sweep (hydrofoil sled); Edo Mk 105 magnetic sweep (hydrofoil sled); Edo Mk 106 combined magnetic and acoustic sweep' (hydrofoil sled).

Equipment for the mechanical and acoustic sweeps is stowed on the side-decks and towed from the stern bridle, the gear being deployed from the aft platforms. The Edo hydrofoil sled can be towed but is too large to be carried aboard.

In addition to the sweepgear, the craft would also be equipped with a command containing navigation equipment and a crew accommodation module.

Deployment and recovery is quick and, except for the magnetic sweep, does not require support from additional craft. Employing the Mk 103 sweepgear, the craft, in a 0·8m maximum wave height sea, would sweep a channel 250m wide by 200m miles long at 100n miles from base. Towing speeds for the various sweeps are: Mk 103, 12 knots; Mk 104, 30 knots; Mk 105/106, 28 knots.

ROUTE SURVEILLANCE: With the addition of Plessey PMS 75 Speedscan, the Plessey 193M 'search and classify' sonar can produce a permanent hard copy map of the sea bed, at speeds up to 12 knots, showing topography and all permanent sonar echo features. Newly laid mines can be detected.

The transducer of the 193M is trained 90 degrees from the head of the craft to port or starboard, and a sonar beam with a constant effective width in the water is produced by electronic processing. Speedscan is portable and interfaces with the 193M operator's console via a cable link.

FAST EXPLORATORY OPERATIONS: Channels, once surveyed and cleared, can be continuously monitored at speeds up to 20 knots using towed sidescan sonars, such as the Westinghouse AN/AQS-14, to make comparative records of the sea bed. Suspect unrecorded contacts can be relocated, classified and, if necessary, destroyed. Accurate track keeping and towed body location is ensured by integrating the sonar with specialised navigation equipment.

The sonar winch and hoist are on the sidedeck. The towing bridle is handled from the aft platform. Typically, the time on station at 100n miles from base would be 17 hours, allowing the survey of a channel 180 metres wide by 280n miles long.

COMMUNICATIONS: Equipment covers the following wavebands: hf 2-30 MHz, vhf, international aero band, 116-151 MHz, vhf marine band, 155-163·6 MHz and vhf, 225-390 MHz.

RADAR: Decca 1290 Clearscan is standard and the system is stabilised in azimuth by a Sperry Gyrosyn compass to provide a clear and stable display unaffected by rapid changes in craft heading. Nine range scales allow operation from 0·25n mile to 48n miles. For fast attack and other roles in which information is required on both air and sea targets, the more powerful Decca 2549 may be fitted at the masthead in place of the Decca 1290. It has two displays, one in the control cabin and a marker display in the command module.

NAVIGATION AIDS: Equipment comprises Loran or similar hyperbolic navigation system, the Sperry Gyrosyn CL2 compass, Smiths E2B standby magnetic compass and a Doppler waterspeed indicator.

DIMENSIONS

EXTERNAL
Length over hard structure: 28·6m (94ft)
Beam over hard structure: 11·2m (36ft 8in)
Beam, skirt inflated: 13·9m (45ft 6in)
Height on landing pads: 10·36m (34ft)
Cushion depth, mean: 2m (6ft 7in)
Cushion area: 255·6m² (2,750ft²)

INTERNAL
Main cabin length: 18·3m (60ft)
   width: 4·2m (13ft 10in)
   height: 2·4m (7ft 10in)

WEIGHTS
Basic equipped weight: 50 tonnes
Disposable load: 32 tonnes

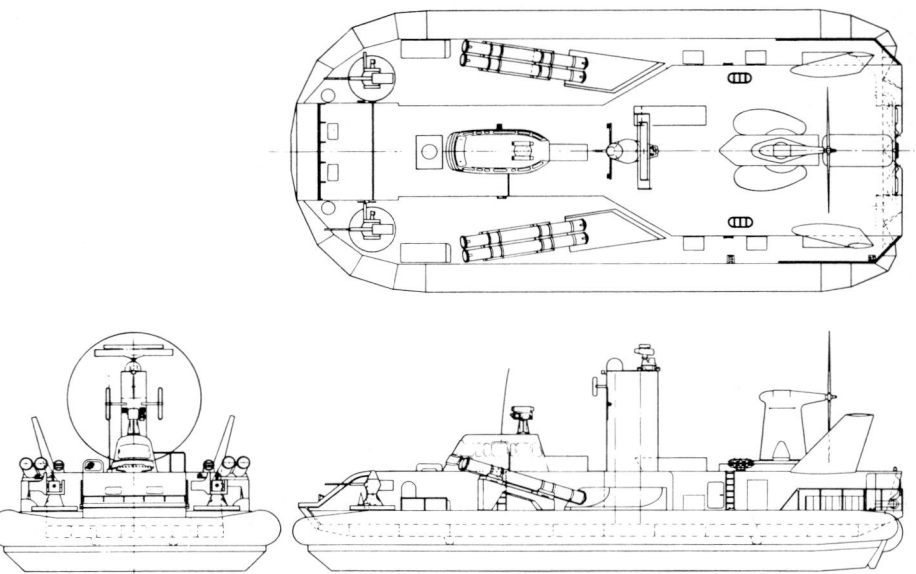

BH.7 Mk 20 equipped for fast attack with twin 30mm Rarden guns and Exocet missiles

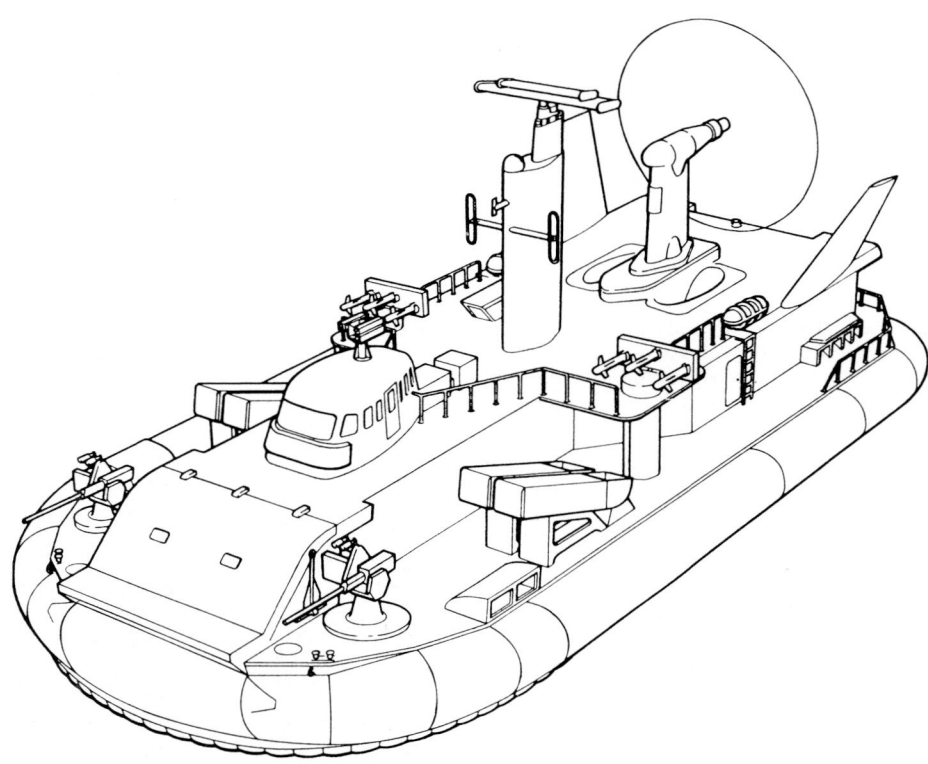

BH.7 Mk 20 fast attack craft with twin Rarden guns, Sea Skua and Sea Cat missiles

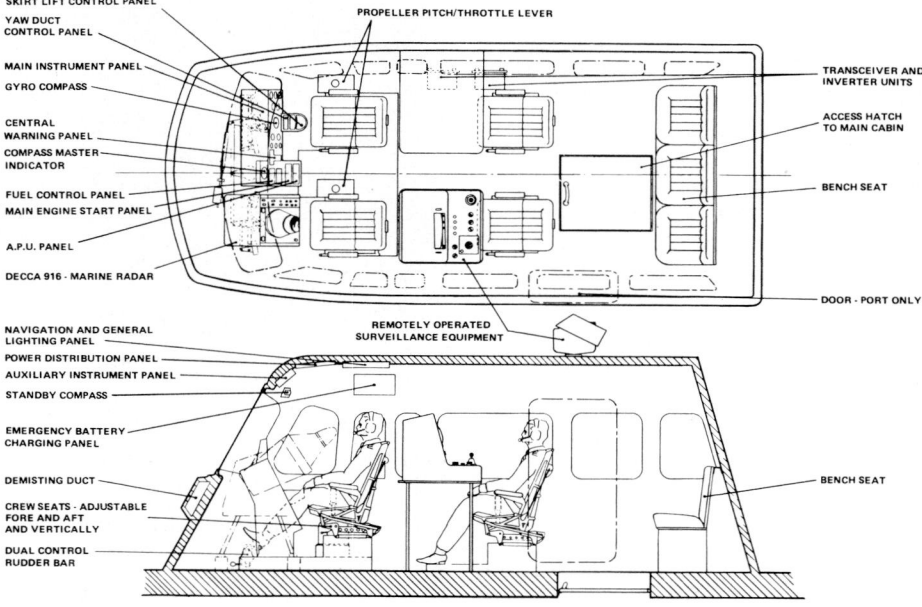

BH.7 Mk 20 control cabin

All-up weight: 82 tonnes
Max fuel (full tanks): 25·4 tonnes
PERFORMANCE
The waterspeed/waveheight and load/range performance of the BH.7 Mk 20 are shown in the accompanying graphs.

BH.7 Mk 20 FAST ATTACK CRAFT

On this craft typical alternative weapon systems are: four Sea Skua surface-to-surface missiles, and six Sea Cat surface-to-air or surface-to-surface missiles, or four Exocet surface-to-surface missiles. With these systems the craft is fitted with a full weapon fire-control system comprising mast-mounted surveillance and electronic warfare antennas, a command information centre and equipment modules, and full navigation and reference systems.

Two 30mm Rarden guns are fitted in the fast attack role, but other guns may be installed to inidividual requirements. The aft MCM platforms can be used as lookout stations to house additional aft firing guns, or ECM, or missile decoy dispensers.

BH.7 Mk 20 LOGISTIC SUPPORT

In this role the craft can carry troops with or without vehicles, or be fitted to transport bulky items of freight. Its load capacity enables it to carry 20 tonnes for 230n miles, or 5 tonnes for 950n miles. Stores can be unloaded directly ashore without transferring them to landing craft, and then manhandling them over the beach.

The large main cabin allows bulky loads to be carried either on 1 metre by 1·2 metre 1-tonne pallets or netted down. Wheeled vehicles with a maximum axle loading of 2,000kg can also be carried.

First 101-seat production AP1-88 showing deeper bow skirt

Four seat rails throughout the length of the cabin floor enable loads to be secured. Joloda roller skates can be used to move freight along the seat rails, the pallets being unloaded from the bow ramp by crane.

BH.7 Mk 20 VIP TRANSPORT

Twenty reclining airline-type seats are provided in a detachable module, the lighting and air conditioning being plugged into the craft system. There are windows along the sides and front, and a public address system is provided.

IMPROVED BH.7 Mk 20

Recent MCM studies have shown a requirement for a craft with higher endurance and towing capabilities than the BH.7 Mk 20. This has led to proposals for an improved version of the Mk 20, lengthened still further and capable of using power ratings of up to 6,000hp (4,480kW) from the DDA 570K marinised gas turbine.
Leading particulars are as follows:
DIMENSIONS
EXTERNAL
Length overall: 30·7m
Beam overall: 15·6m
Height on landing pads: 10·36m
Cushion depth: 2m
INTERNAL
Length, main cabin: 20·34m
Width, main cabin: 4·17m
Height, main cabin: 2·4m
WEIGHTS
Basic equipped weight: 53 tonnes
Disposable load: 33 tonnes
All-up weight: 86 tonnes
PERFORMANCE
Max speed in calm water: 65 knots
Typical speed in 2m sea, beam wind: 35-40 knots
Endurance at continuous power: 15-18 hours

AP1-88 GENERAL-PURPOSE HOVERCRAFT

Major advances in hovercraft technology in recent years have enabled British Hovercraft Corporation to offer an 8- to 9-ton payload craft with a performance equal to that of the well-proven SR.N6. Built in welded aluminium alloy AP1-88 is powered by air-cooled marine diesels. Not only is it substantially cheaper in first and operating costs but it is considerably more robust than many earlier generation craft of this size. Most of its components are commercially available. AP1-88 has low crew and maintenance requirements, footprint pressure and noise levels. It can be employed in a wide variety of commercial, military and para-military roles including passenger ferrying, search and rescue, geographical surveying, anti-smuggling operations, firefighting and logistics.

In its civil passenger form it will seat up to 101 passengers and as a troop carrier, up to 60 armed troops. In the logistics role the AP1-88 will carry two LWB Land-Rovers, a BV202 Snowcat and trailer, or 4,000kg (8,818lb) of stores.

Typical military roles would include amphibious support, logistic support, counter insurgency and police and customs duties. It can also be employed for minelaying and mine countermeasures support. As a fast minelayer it would carry four 1,000kg (2,205lb) mines.

The first two AP1-88s, *Tenacity* and *Resolution*, began operating with Hovertravel between Ryde, Isle of Wight and Southsea, in 1983. These two pre-production prototypes are slightly smaller than the production vehicles, carrying 80 passengers and having 8-cylinder, as opposed to

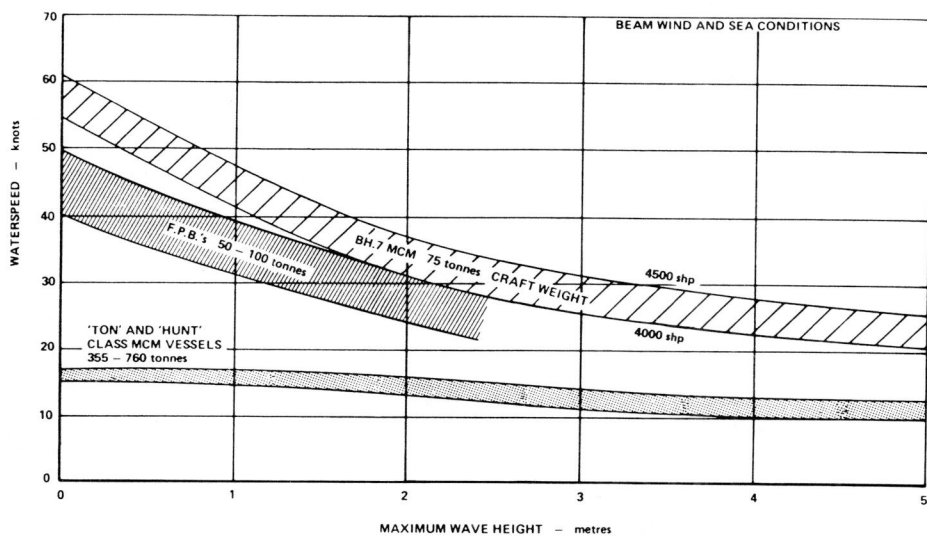
BH.7 Mk 20 waterspeed

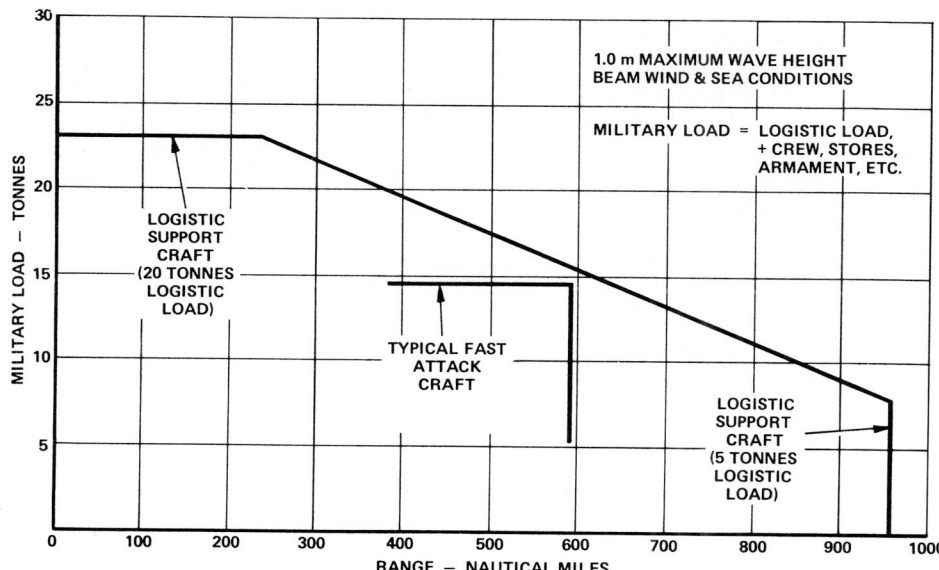
BH.7 Mk 20 load/range performance

12-cylinder, Deutz engines powering the lift system. During 1984 two of the 101-seat production craft entered service with A/C Dampskibsselskabet Oresund (DSO) of Denmark, on a route linking Copenhagen's Kastrup airport and Malmö.

The craft can operate over land or water in winds up to 30 knots, and over rough water with wave heights up to 2·4 metres (1·5 metres significant).

LIFT AND PROPULSION: Lift is provided by two 319kW (428hp) Deutz BF12L413FC air-cooled marine diesels, housed in two box structures flanking the forward end of the cabin superstructure, each driving directly three 0·84m (2ft 9in) diameter double-entry centrifugal fans. Two of the fans discharge into the cushion via the skirt system and the third upwards into the steerable bow thruster. Thrust is supplied by two 319kW (428hp) Deutz BF12L413FC air-cooled marine diesels, each driving a 2·74m (9ft) diameter 4-bladed fixed-pitch Hoffmann ducted propeller via a system of V-belts. The engines are turbo-charged and equipped with a charged air cooler. Alternative types of marine diesel engines can be installed if required, including water-cooled types. The higher engine rating of 367kW (492hp) will increase the speed by about 6 knots. Maximum fuel capacity, including ballast allowance, is 3,600 litres (80 imperial gallons).

CONTROLS: Directional control is provided by two sets of triple aerodynamic rudder vanes mounted on the rear of the propeller ducts, differential propeller thrust and by swivelling bow thrusters. In the straight-aft position, the bow thrusters contribute to forward thrust. Trim is controlled by fuel ballast transfer with additional control available from horizontal surfaces in the propeller ducts.

HULL: Basic hull is formed by a buoyancy tank made almost entirely of very wide aluminium alloy extrusions, one extrusion being used for the I-beams forming the transverse frames and a second for the integrally stiffened planking used for the bottom and deck. The remainder of the rigid structure is built from smaller welded extrusions and plating, with the exception of the roof, made from riveted light gauge corrugated panels and the propulsor ducts which are in moulded grp. Marine alloys are used, including N8 plate and HE30 extrusions. In general, plate thicknesses are 2 or 3mm except for the light gauge roof plating. The structure is welded throughout to eliminate mechanical fastenings which can be sources of corrosion. Detachable panels give easy access for engine and fan removal and facilitate the inspection of ventilation ducting and tail control cable runs. Lifting, for the inspection of the craft underside and skirts, is achieved by three jacks which are fitted and operated from inside the craft. The propeller ducts are in glass reinforced plastic and aluminium alloy. Rudders are mounted on the rear of the ducts.

SKIRT: Low-pressure ratio tapered skirt based on that of the Super 4. Mean cushion depth 1·2m (4ft).

ACCOMMODATION: The superstructure is divided into four main components: a large central accommodation area forward of a propulsion machinery bay and two side bodies containing the lift system machinery. A control cabin is mounted on top of the main cabin. In addition to the full-cabin version, half-cabin and well deck versions are available. The commercial full-cabin version seats 101 passengers and the half-cabin seats 40. The seats are arranged in rows of seven across the cabin. The rows are divided by two gangways 600mm wide which separate the seats into a 2-3-2 configuration. The seats are of the non-reclining aircraft type with Perry foam life jackets beneath the cushion. Two doors, one port and one starboard, are at the aft end of the cabin. Doorways are 1·75 by 0·9 metres. An emergency door 1·06 by 0·9 metres is at the forward end of the passenger cabin. Craft built to standard include a cabin heating and ventilation system adequate for operation in temperate climates. Requirements for more elaborate air-conditioning will result in a reduced disposable

'Tenacity' first prototype AP1-88 in service with Hovertravel

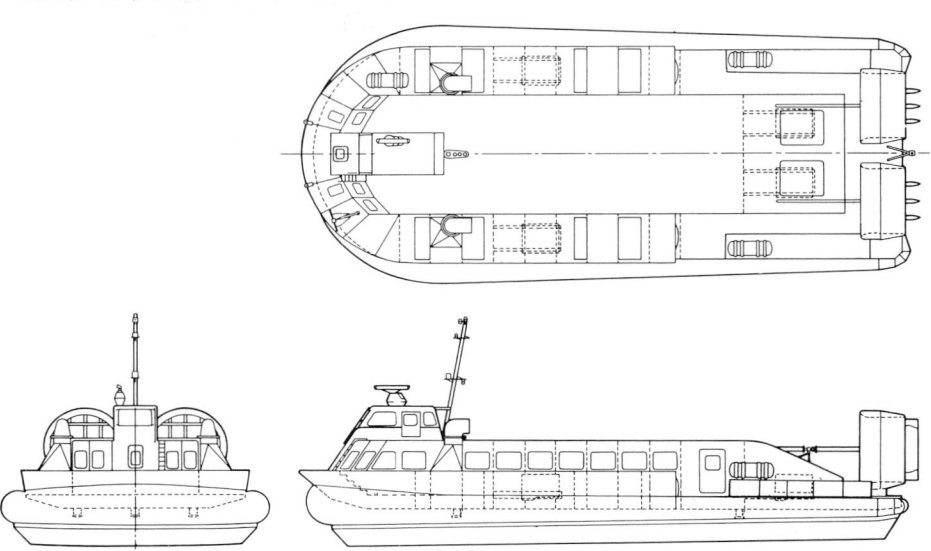

General arrangement of AP1-88 passenger hovercraft

One of production AP1-88s on DSO Malmö-Kastrup route

load. A full air-conditioning system, complete with an APU installation, can be added with a disposable load penalty of approximately 1,000kg.

There are two sets of four luggage panniers, one port and one starboard, on the side-decks aft of the cabin doors. Each set has three doors hinged from the top edge. The doors, which form the outward closing face of the panniers, have a water seal around the periphery and stays to hold them open when loading. Total volume of the eight panniers is approximately 6·6 cubic metres.

COMMUNICATIONS: A Sailor RT 145 vhf international marine band radio or similar equipment.

RADAR: Racal-Decca 914C. Antenna turning

unit and tranceiver on control cabin roof. Display unit mounted in control cabin on port side. Display is north-up stabilised by gyro compass.

NAVIGATION: Remote reading gyro compass; a Lambda T.12 spherical compass. Optional range of automatic and semi-automatic navigational aids.

DIMENSIONS

EXTERNAL

Length overall: 23·55m (77·3ft)
Beam overall: 10·1m (33ft)
Height on landing pads: 7·95m (26ft)
Height on cushion: 8·9m (29ft 2in)
Mean cushion depth: 1·2m (4ft)

INTERNAL

Cabin, length: 14·4m (47·2ft)
Beam: 4·8m (15·7ft)
Headroom: 1·98m (6ft 5in)

WEIGHTS

Basic equipped craft: 28,500kg (62,800lb)
Disposable load (crew, fuel, provisions, fresh water, freight, passengers): 10,000kg (22,000lb)
All-up weight: 38,500kg (85,000lb)

PERFORMANCE

Max calm water speed: 58 knots (114km/h)
Max cruising speed: 50 knots
Total fuel consumption at max power (full throttle): 432 litres/h (95 imperial gallons/h)

AP1-88 TYPE 25 PATROL CRAFT

The Type 25 can work from temporary bases on beaches and river banks. It can operate hull-borne at sea or remain on land, monitoring water traffic with radar or visual aids. Interception is made at speeds up to 50 knots. Boarding vessels is aided by the air-filled peripheral skirt which acts as a fender.

The amphibious capability of the Type 25 enables it to work where the terrain makes defence force operations difficult or impossible. Weapons up to 30 mm, missiles, flare launchers, specialised radar and radio-equipment can be fitted.

AP1-88 Type 25 patrol craft

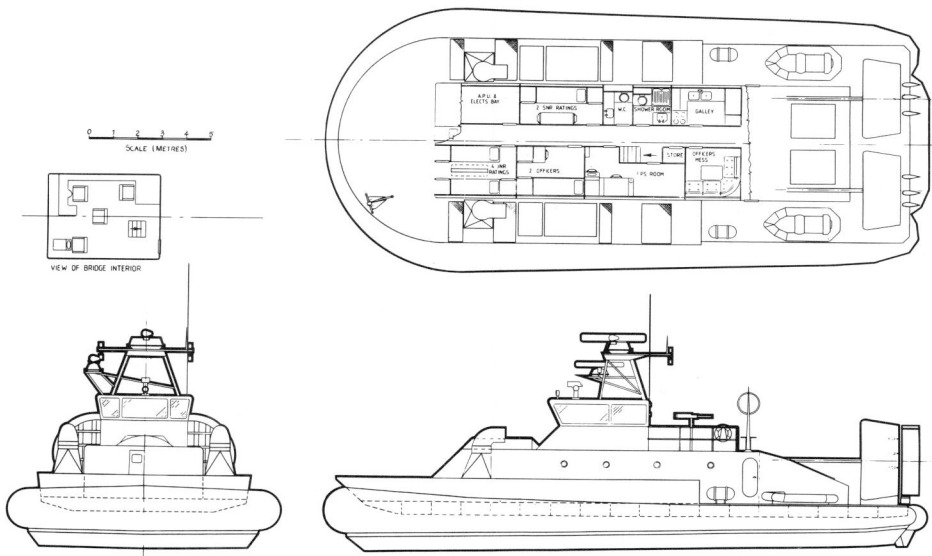

AP1-88 Type 25 patrol craft

AP1-88 Type 25 search and rescue craft

AP1-88 ASSAULT/LOGISTICS

Military logistic versions of the AP1-88 feature a bow ramp for driving vehicles on and off. Troops can also disembark quickly in the landing zone. The logistic support variant has a deck 15 metres long by 4·8 metres wide which can accommodate light vehicles and logistic loads. Equipped to military standards, the full-cabin version seats 70 fully-armed troops. In the half-cabin version there are full mess and accommodation facilities for a crew of ten or, alternatively, 42 troops could be seated.

AP1-88 Type 25 amphibious assault/logistics craft

CHARTMERE SHIPPING COMPANY LIMITED

17 Stratton Street, London W1X 5PD, England
Telephone: 01-493 6803
Telex: 21719

Chartmere has taken over and redesignated the former Tropimere hovercraft range and all craft are now available with diesel engines. The Chartmere 1000 (formerly the K40), previously powered by petrol engines, will now only be available with marine diesels. The Chartmere 340 (formerly the Dash 6) and the Chartmere 170 (formerly Dash 7) will be available with Land-Rover V8 engines or VM diesels.

The craft listed here are either in operation or under construction. The company has received CAA approval to design and build hovercraft up to 35 tonnes avw.

	Chartmere 170	Chartmere 340	Chartmere 1000
NEW DESIGNATION			
OLD DESIGNATION	Dash 7	Dash 6	K40
CONSTRUCTION	Aluminium	Aluminium and grp	Aluminium
LENGTH	8·68m	10·06m	17·35m
BEAM	5·08m	6·1m	9·61m
Height, off cushion	2·1m	3·1m	4·35m
MAX SPEED	30 knots	40 knots	50 knots
PAYLOAD	0·7 tonne	1·5 tonnes	3 tonnes
PASSENGERS	6-10	14	40
ENGINES	1 × Rover V8 or 1 × VM HR692HT/I	2 × Rover V8 2 × VM HR692HT/I	2 × MAN D254MLE
ROAD TRAILER OPTION	YES	YES	NO

Chartmere 170

Chartmere 170

Chartmere 340

Chartmere 1000

CYCLONE HOVERCRAFT

8 Walton Road, Caldecotte, Milton Keynes, Buckinghamshire MK7 8AE, England
Telephone: 0908 64733
Officials:
N R Beale BSc, MSc, *Director*
P J Beale, *Director*

Cyclone Hovercraft has developed a plans, components and design service based on the experience that won the British National Championships for eight consecutive years.

The company is marketing three designs, the Simple Cyclone, the Cyclone Sport and the Cyclone Sprint.

SIMPLE CYCLONE

A single-engined design employing a single ducted fan for its integrated lift and propulsion system. The British hovercraft land-speed record, under 250cc, is held by Simple Cyclone with an average speed of 64km/h (40mph). The craft performs equally well over water.

Simple Cyclone plans give details for constructing three different models, each powered by a single engine of under 250cc: 2·85m (9ft 4in) long mini version for Formula III or junior racing; the standard 3m (9ft 10in) long single-seat trainer or racing craft and a 3·44m (11ft 3in) long cruising or utility model.
LIFT AND PROPULSION: A single Kyoritsu KEC 225cc two-stroke engine, rated at 12·5bhp at 5,550rpm, drives, via a toothed belt, a 600mm (23·62in) diameter Breeza fan. The unit supplies air for both lift and thrust. Any suitable engine of

between 10 and 25bhp may be used. The 4·5-litre (1-gallon) fuel tank gives a cruising endurance of more than one hour. A larger capacity tank may be fitted if desired.
CONTROLS: For the utmost simplicity, only two controls are provided, designed for single-

handed operation. A lever control for the engine throttle is mounted on the control column which operates the twin rudders.
HULL: The hull is constructed from thin exterior-grade plywood with wooden stringers. Polyurethane foam within the hull structure

Simple Cyclone

ensures adequate buoyancy. The fan duct unit is laminated from glass reinforced plastic.

SKIRT: The skirt fitted to the Simple Cyclone is a Cyclone-designed extended segment type employing an individual air feed through the hull to every segment.

DIMENSIONS
Length overall: 3m (9ft 11in)
Width overall: 1·83m (6ft)
Height at rest: 0·9m (2ft 11in)
Hard structure clearance: 180mm (7·09in)
WEIGHTS
Unladen: 80kg (176lb)
Normal payload: 90kg (198lb)
PERFORMANCE
Max speed over land or water: 48·28km/h (30mph)

SIMPLE CYCLONE II

The basic hull of this model is nearly identical to that of the Mk 1, the main differences being a slightly larger fan, a new engine frame and transmission ratio, minor mechanical changes and improved skirt design in the Mk II.

CYCLONE SPORT

A two-seater, Cyclone Sport incorporates many of the features of earlier Cyclone Hovercraft designs. The open cockpit with side-by-side seating can be adapted to carry a stretcher or a bulky payload. A number of engine options are available giving speeds from 40km/h (25mph) with the Kyoritsu KEC 225 to over 64km/h (40mph) with the Robin EC44.

LIFT AND PROPULSION: A single Kyoritsu KEC 225 two-stroke engine, rated at 12·5bph at 5,550rpm, drives, via a tuning belt, a 630mm (2ft 1in) diameter ducted fan. The fan supplies air for both lift and thrust. Any suitable engine between 10 and 46hp may be fitted. Fuel is carried in a single 10-litre (2·2-gallon) tank. Recommended fuel is two-stroke petrol/oil mixture.

SKIRT: Segmented-type with separate air-feed to every segment.

DIMENSIONS
Length overall: 3·63m (11ft 11in)
Beam overall: 1·85m (6ft 1in)
Height overall: 3·46m (11ft 4in)
WEIGHTS
Empty: 120kg (260lb)
Payload: 145kg (320lb)
PERFORMANCE
Speed (KEC 225 engine): 40km/h (25mph)

CYCLONE SPRINT

Cyclone Sprint is a single-seat racing craft designed for Hovercraft Formula III (250cc) and Formula II (500cc) racing. The prototype won the 1980 Formula III UK National Championship. The specification is almost identical to Cyclone Sport's apart from the following:

Simple Cyclone Mk II

Cyclone Sport

DIMENSIONS
Length overall: 3·04m (10ft)
Hull length: 2·88m (9ft 5in)

WEIGHTS
Empty (approx): 100kg (220lb)
Payload (1 adult): 90kg (200lb)

GRIFFON HOVERCRAFT LIMITED

Head Office: Carlton House, Ringwood Road, Woodlands, Southampton SO4 2HT, England
Telephone: (0703) 813461
Telex: 47423 GIFTEK G
Officials:
D R Robertson
E W H Gifford
J H Gifford

Founded in 1976, Griffon Hovercraft has concentrated on the design and development of small commercial vehicles.

Its first design, Griffon, used a four-bladed ducted propeller for propulsion with a centrifugal fan for lift, both driven by a Jaguar engine. This craft was subsequently put into production as the Skima 12, under licence by Pindair Limited. Many of this type of craft have been in service throughout the world in a variety of roles.

The initial choice of a petrol engine was due to its superior power-to-weight ratio, although the advantages of the diesel engine were recognised. The development of the turbo-charged diesel led to the company's decision, early in 1982, that a

Griffon 1000 TDs ready for shipment to China

1000 TD with canvas hood

small commercial diesel-powered hovercraft would be feasible and would carry a realistic payload.

Construction of the Griffon 1000 TD prototype began in June 1982. Performance trials began in May 1983 and exceeded expectations. The prototype is now with the company's US licensees for the 1000 and 1500 models, F W Hake Co Hover Systems Inc of Eddystone, Pennsylvania and is at present being operated by the Maryland Department of Natural Resources Marine Police, for patrol and rescue. Operating hours are in excess of 500. Three craft of this type have been supplied to Geophysical Surveys Inc of Dallas, USA, for use in an oilfield survey on the Yellow River, China. The design has been prepared for production with larger variants, thus providing a range of amphibious hovercraft ranging from one to four tonnes of payload and using the same engine and ducted propeller lift fan units.

The company intends to concentrate on this area to meet the requirement for a low-cost easily maintained craft for use as a workboat in survey, civil engineering and patrol applications and for sheltered water ferries.

1000 TD

The smallest craft in the range, the 1000 TD carries a payload of 1,000kg or 10 passengers.

It has a single diesel engine and is available with a variety of superstructures. Folding sidedecks enable it to be towed on roads and it can be fitted into a 20-foot container, after removal of bow and stern sections.

LIFT AND PROPULSION: Integrated lift/propulsion system powered by a single Deutz BF 6L 913 C air-cooled six-cylinder, in-line, turbo-charged and intercooled diesel rated at 190hp (140kW) at 2,500rpm. This drives from the front of the crankshaft, via an HTD toothed belt, a 760 mm diameter centrifugal lift fan. Power is transmitted from the back of the engine via an automotive clutch to an HTD belt and a 1·36m diameter four-bladed ducted propeller. Enclosed within a pylon, the belt drive is protected from the weather. The engine, transmission, duct and pylon are mounted on a welded alloy subframe attached to the hull via resilient mounts.

Cooling air for the engine passes through a Knitmesh filter to remove spray and is drawn into the front of the engine bay by the engine cooling fan before passing over the cylinders and being drawn out from the rear of the engine bay by the propeller.

CONTROLS: Twin rudders in the grp duct provide directional control. Elevators within the duct provide a degree of fore and aft trim, augmented by a fuel ballast system. The craft is fitted with an HDL-type skirt shift, operated by a small electric winch, that provides responsive control on roll trim, and offsets cross wind effects and banks the craft into turns.

HULL: Main hull and side structures are of bonded marine grade aluminium. Side bodies fold upward for transport and they are locked into running position by five struts on each side.

Removable bow and stern sections reduce the length of the 1000 TD to 5·6m (18ft 6in).

ACCOMMODATION: Seats forward for driver and passenger/navigator. A four-person inward facing bench-type seat on each side. Front two seats and controls are in a grp cabin. Front left-hand seat for driver. Radar can be fitted in front of right-hand seat. Options for remaining accommodation space are: grp cabin; pvc hood over aluminium frame; open area, without cover.

SKIRT: HDL open loop/segment type, with similar segments at bow and sides and cones stern. Segments are attached to loop at outer edge with nylon bolts and to hull at inner end with plastic shackles. Segments can be quickly changed without lifting craft off landing pads.

SYSTEMS: Electrical system is 12V dc standard. Negative earth with 35 amp alternator and 108 amp hour battery.

DIMENSIONS (hard structure)
Length: 8·52m
Width: 3·79m
Height: 2·5m
Hoverheight: 380mm
Cabin,
Length: 3·05m
Width: 1·8m
Height: 1·42m
WEIGHTS
Empty: 2,000kg
Payload: 1,000kg

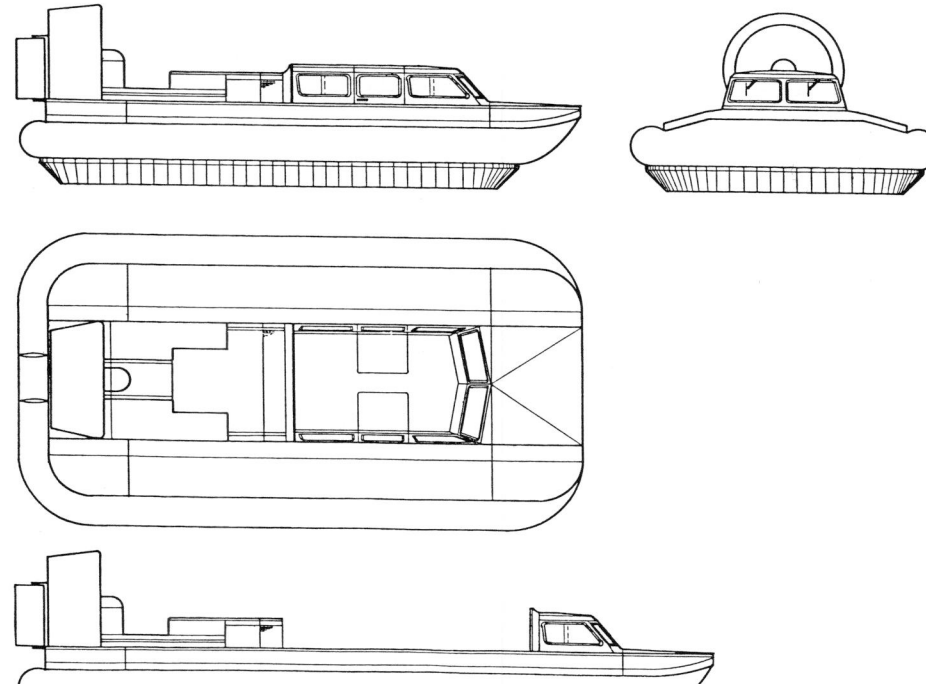

Above: 1000 TD with hard top cabin; below: 1500 TD with open deck

1000 TD showing ducted propeller, engine air intake and lift air intake

PERFORMANCE
Max speed: 35 knots
Cruise speed: 28 knots
Max operating conditions: wind, 25 knots; waves, 1 metre
Fuel consumption, max: 31·8 litres/h
    cruise: 22 litres/h

1500 TD

This variant is 1·8 metres longer than the 1000 TD, but with identical machinery. Capacity is increased to 1·5 tonnes or 16 persons. Bow and stern sections are not removable but folding side-decks allow transportation within a 40ft container.

The first production craft has been completed and is giving demonstrations in the UK for survey, freight and passenger ferry roles.

Details of this craft are as for the 1000 TD with the following exceptions:
DIMENSIONS
Overall length: 10·48m
Cabin length: 5·01m
WEIGHTS
Empty: 2,300kg
Payload: 1,500kg
PERFORMANCE
Max speed: 33 knots
Cruising speed: 27 knots
Fuel consumption, max: 31·8 litres/h
    cruise: 26 litres/h

2500 TD

This twin-engined version of the 1000 TD has a payload of 2·5 tonnes or 32 passengers. Open freight and cabin versions are available. The structure can be divided into sections to fit two 40-foot containers.
LIFT AND PROPULSION: Twin integrated lift/propulsion systems each identical to that of 1000 TD.
CONTROLS: The control surfaces are as for the smaller craft. A fuel ballast system is fitted as well as an HDL skirt shift system.
DIMENSIONS (hard structure)
Length: 12·5m
Width: 5·4m
Height: 2·67m
Cabin,
Length: 6·25m
Width: 3·8m
Height 2·67m
WEIGHTS
Payload 2,500kg
PERFORMANCE
Max speed: 33 knots
Cruise speed: 28 knots
Hoverheight: 0·45m
Fuel consumption, max: 63·6 litres/h
    cruise: 45 litres/h

4000 TD

The largest craft in the range, the 4000 TD carries a payload of 4 tonnes or up to 52 passen-

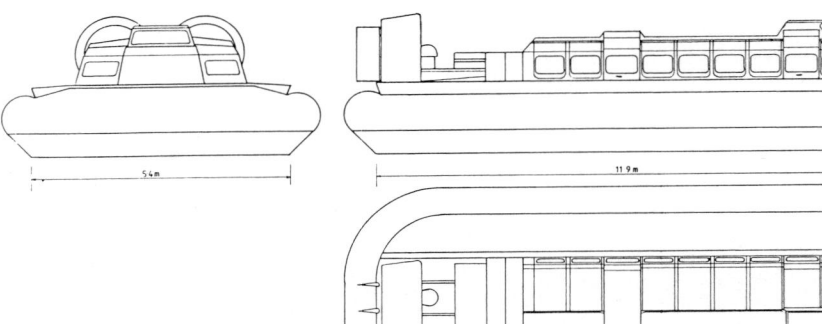

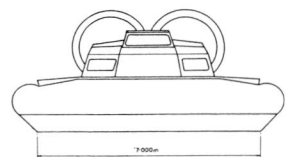

2500 TD

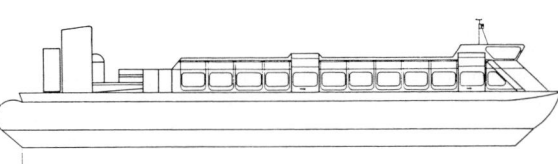

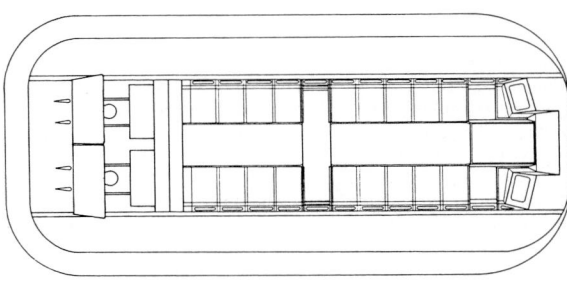

Griffon 4000 TD

gers. Open workboat and passenger cabin versions are available. The structure can be dismantled to fit into three 40-foot containers.
LIFT AND PROPULSION: The same twin-engined concept as the 2500 TD is used but with additional power. Two Deutz BF 8L 573 engines each drive a 1·82m lift fan and a 1·3m ducted propeller. Transmission is the same as for the smaller craft.
CONTROLS: As for the rest of the range.
HULL: Construction techniques identical to smaller craft.
ACCOMMODATION: Small two-person control cabin. Passenger cabin variant seats 52 with forward wheelhouse for two crew. Open version can be supplied with ramp and can carry a Land-Rover and 2-tonne trailer.

SKIRT: HDL open loop-type.
DIMENSIONS
Length: 15·67m
Width: 7m
Height: 3·2m
Cabin,
Length: 9·1m
Width: 3·8m
Height: 1·9m
WEIGHTS
Payload: 4,000kg
PERFORMANCE
Max speed: 33 knots
Cruise speed: 28 knots
Hoverheight: 0·45m
Fuel consumption, max: 100 litres/h
    cruise: 70 litres/h

GP VEHICLES

Worton Hall, Worton Road, Isleworth, Middlesex TW7 6ER, England
Telephone: 01-568 4711/4664
Telex: 477019 GP
Officials:
John Jobber, *Managing Director*
P D Allnutt, *General Manager*

HOVER HAWK

This four-seat utility ACV is intended for survey and patrol duties as well as the leisure industry. Orders have been placed by countries throughout the world including North and South America, Europe, Scandinavia, South Africa, Australia, the Middle and the Far East.
LIFT AND PROPULSION: Integrated system. A single 1,835cc Volkswagen VW4 air-cooled engine drives, via a belt, a ducted fan aft. Propulsion air is expelled rearwards and lift air is ducted into the plenum below. Fuel capacity is 28 litres (6 imperial gallons). Fuel recommended 93 octane.

Hover Hawk

CONTROLS: Single control column operates a single rudder hinged to the rear of the fan duct. Column incorporates a twist-grip throttle for the engine.

HULL: Moulded glass fibre reinforced plastics structure.

SKIRT: Fully-segmented type in neoprene-coated nylon.

ACCOMMODATION: Open cockpit with seating for driver and up to three passengers.

DIMENSIONS
Length overall: 4·12m (13ft 6in)
Width: 2·5m (8ft)
Height: 1·27m (4ft 2in)

WEIGHTS
Empty: 200kg (405lb)
Payload: 249kg (550lb)

PERFORMANCE
Max speed: 64km/h (40mph)
Gradient capability: 1:7 from static hover
Obstacle clearance: 0·3m (12in)
Endurance, max: 3 hours
Fuel consumption, average: 7·79km/litre (22mpg)

PRICE: £6,100 plus VAT. Car trailer for Hover Hawk, £320 plus VAT (1985)

Hover Hawk

HOVERCRAFT DEVELOPMENT LIMITED (HDL)

101 Newington Causeway, London SE1 6BB, England
Telephone: 01-403 6666
Telex: 894397
Officials:
W H Barber, *Chairman*
D J Veasey, *Director*
A M Bone, *Secretary*

Hovercraft Development Limited (HDL) was formed in January 1959 by the National Research Development Corporation (NRDC) which is now part of the British Technology Group. The company uses its portfolio of patents as the basis of licensing agreements with hovercraft manufacturers in the UK and overseas. HDL or its parent, British Technology Group, may, in certain cases, provide financial backing to assist project development.

HDL's principal patents concern craft with segmented skirts. These skirt systems are now used by all major manufacturers of hovercraft. The skirt is a series of pockets arranged around the craft which when inflated seal against each other. The skirt is flexible and conforms to the contours of the surface over which it passes, and has a low drag characteristic both in calm water and waves. Should an individual segment be lost, the performance is not substantially affected.

Licences are available to all companies in the industry.

Skima 12 fitted with HDL skirt shift system

HDL segmented skirt

HOVERCRAFT (INVESTMENT) LIMITED

Felbridge Hotel, East Grinstead, West Sussex
RH19 2BH, England
Telephone: 0342 26992
Telex: 95156
Officials:
R L Fowler, *Managing Director*
P M Browne, *Director*
J S Hart, *Director*

Hovercraft (Investments) Limited specialises in the manufacture of amphibious leisure/utility hovercraft and is now producing two models, Freedom 6 and Freedom 3, as well as continuing marketing of the hoverpallet. These hovercraft descend from a line which began in 1971 with the Cyclone, the first amphibious light hovercraft to be put into production. It was also the first to cross the English Channel and won the British Racing Championship for eight consecutive years.

Freedom 6 and Freedom 3 have been designed as fast open cruising hovercraft or as work craft where conventional transport is unsuitable.

FREEDOM 6

A replacement for Light Hovercraft Company's Phantom, Freedom 6 is a six-seater sports/utility hovercraft. Design features are reliability, ease of maintenance and quiet operation. The craft is easily manhandled onto a trailer for towing. It has also been designed to pull a water skier.

LIFT AND PROPULSION: Integrated system powered by a single 155bhp Rover V8, 3·5-litre SD1 engine. Power is transmitted by toothed belts and shafts to two ducted axial fans, air from which is used for both lift and propulsion. Thrust,

Freedom 3

approximately 180kg (400lb). Fuel capacity, 90 litres (20 gallons).
CONTROLS: Twin aerodynamic rudders hinged at the rear of each thrust duct control heading operated by a steering wheel.
HULL: Glass-fibre reinforced plastic monocoque structure with sealed polyurethane block at base of craft for buoyancy. Storage compartments provided for tools and spares.
SKIRT: Segmented type, in neoprene-coated nylon material.
DIMENSIONS:
Length: 5·5m (18ft)
Beam: 2·75m (9ft)

Freedom 6

WEIGHTS
Payload capacity (approx): 550kg (1,210lb)
PERFORMANCE
Max speed over land and water: 85km/h (45 knots)
Cruising speed: 55km/h (30 knots)
Hard structure clearance: 0·3m (1ft)
Endurance: 4 hours plus

FREEDOM 3

This three-seater is powered by a single 40bhp Reliant engine and is suitable for cruising and sport and leisure activities.
LIFT AND PROPULSION: Integrated system powered by a single fully-enclosed 40bhp 850cc 4-cylinder 4-stroke, driving a ducted 735mm (29in) diameter polypropylene-bladed axial fan, air from which is used for both lift and propulsion. Thrust, 80kg (180lb). Fuel capacity, 46 litres (10 imperial gallons).
CONTROLS: Heading is controlled by twin aerodynamic rudders hinged to rear of thrust duct and operated by steering wheel.
HULL: Glass-fibre reinforced plastic monocoque construction with sealed polyurethane buoyancy block at base. Large storage compartment provided under seat.
SKIRT: Segmented type, 0·396m (1ft 4in) deep, neoprene-coated nylon.
DIMENSIONS
Length: 4·1m (13ft 6in)
Beam: 1·93m (6ft 4in)
WEIGHTS
Payload: 250kg (550lb) plus
PERFORMANCE
Max speed over land and water: 65km/h (35 knots)
Cruising speed: 40km/h (22 knots)
Hard structure clearance: 0·23m (9in)
Endurance: 3 hours plus

HOVERSERVICES SCARAB HOVERCRAFT

24 Hazel Grove, Wallingford, Oxon OX10 0AT, England
Telephone: 0491 37455
Proprietor:
Graham Nutt

Hoverservices was formed in 1972 to market Scarab hovercraft plans and components. The company now offers a range of light hovercraft plans for the single-seat Scarab I and two-seat Scarab II, in addition to plans for other racing craft such as the Snoopy II and Eccles. All of these plans are marketed world-wide.

The company has a wide range of fans, grp ducts, skirt material and other components in stock and provides a complete engineering service.

SCARAB I (Plans)

This is a simple, lightweight craft, ideal for sheltered water operation. It uses low cost

Scarab 8

engines and is a useful craft for beginners. Many craft of this type have been selected for school or group hovercraft building projects. It seats one person.

LIFT AND PROPULSION: A single 3·5bhp Briggs & Stratton engine provides power to an axial lift fan of 482mm (19in) diameter, fitted with Multiwing blades. For thrust the craft employs a JLO 250cc 15bhp engine which drives a 609mm (24in) diameter ducted fan fitted with Multiwing blades.

CONTROLS: There is a single rudder located in the thrust duct and movement of this control is achieved by a joystick in the cockpit. A twist grip gives throttle control for the thrust engine and a simple lever controls the lift engine.

HULL: The hull is constructed using a triangulated plywood box technique on a pine frame and finished with grp tape for extra strength. A full flow skirt of loop design is fitted to the craft.

ACCOMMODATION: Single seat in open cockpit.

DIMENSIONS
Length: 3·05m (10ft)
Width: 1·68m (5ft 6in)
Hoverheight: 228mm (9in)
WEIGHTS
Empty: 72·57kg (160lb)
Normal payload: 90·72kg (200lb)
Normal all-up weight: 163·29kg (360lb)
PERFORMANCE
Over land or water the craft can achieve speeds of 40·2-48·2km/h (25-30mph)

SCARAB II (Plans)

Scarab II is a two-seater light hovercraft designed for cruising in calm coastal or sheltered estuarial waters. With its larger size it will accept a variety of engines for lift and propulsion.

LIFT AND PROPULSION: A typical lift engine for this craft would be a 5bhp Briggs & Stratton, driving a 558mm (22in) diameter axial lift fan fitted with Multiwing blades. For propulsion the craft could use various powerplants up to 42bhp driving either 609mm (24in) or 762mm (30in) diameter ducted Multiwing fans.

CONTROLS: Employs a single rudder positioned in the thrust duct which is activated by a joystick in the open cockpit. A twist grip throttle is used for the thrust engine and a quadrant type lever for lift.

HULL: This is made from triangular plywood boxes upon a framework of pine with grp tape for additional strength for joints etc. A full flow loop skirt is fitted.

ACCOMMODATION: Side-by-side seating for driver and one passenger in open cockpit.

DIMENSIONS
Length: 3·5m (11ft 6in)
Width: 1·83m (6ft)
Hoverheight: 228mm (9in)
WEIGHTS
Empty: 113·4kg (250lb)
Normal payload: 181·44kg (400lb) (two people)
All-up weight: 294·84kg (650lb)

PERFORMANCE
Over land and water Scarab II craft, with propulsion units of 35-42bhp, can achieve speeds of 48·28-56·32km/h (30-35mph)

SCARAB 14 PROTOTYPE

Latest sports hovercraft to comply with British and European Formula III regulations, Scarab 14 can also be used for cruising in sheltered waters. The extremely lightweight hull is made by a new wood/epoxy construction system. The craft is available as a set of plans or as a kit complete with the necessary epoxy materials and tools.

LIFT AND PROPULSION: Power for the integrated lift/propulsion system is provided by a single 18bhp Robin EC24 single cylinder two-stroke, or a Yamaha RD 250LC Twin. A tooth belt reduction drive transmits power to a ducted 609mm (24in) fan that provides both thrust and lift.

HULL: Triangulated box sections formed in epoxy saturated 4mm ply, bonded with epoxy/foam and grp tape.

SKIRT: Segmented pressure-fed system developed for this model.

DIMENSIONS
Length: 3·04m (10ft)
Beam: 1·82m (6ft)
Hoverheight: 228mm (9in)
WEIGHTS
Unladen weight: 68·73kg (150lb)

INGLES HOVERCRAFT ASSOCIATES LIMITED

Ingles Manor, Castle Hill Avenue, Folkestone, Kent CT20 2TN, England
Telephone: 0303 59055
Officials:
S Sendall-King, BSc, CEng, MRAeS, FSLAET, *General Director*
D G Staveley, BSc, *UK Director*
T J R Longley, TEng(CEI), AMRAeS, *Design Consultant*

Ingles Hovercraft Associates Limited administers the design and patent rights relating to the hovercraft developed by the Missionary Aviation Fellowship (MAF).

MAF's first craft was the Missionaire, a general purpose amphibious five-seater. This was succeeded by the six-seat River Rover. Following evaluation trials by the Naval Hovercraft Trials Unit, the River Rover was chosen by the 1978-79 British Joint Services Expedition to Nepal. For a period of four months, two Mk 2 craft were successfully used over a 60 mile stretch of the turbulent Kali Gandaki river in support of a medical aid programme.

One of these craft is now in regular use by a mission in Irian Jaya, Indonesia, on the Baliem river and its tributaries, three are in service on the upper reaches of the Amazon in Peru; one with the Taiwanese Police and one on the tidal flats of South Australia.

RIVER ROVER

Designed as a water-borne counterpart to the Land-Rover utility vehicle, River Rover is a sturdily constructed, six-seat cabin hovercraft which has proved its usefulness and reliability in many parts of the world where navigation by conventional boats is difficult or impossible.

The four main requirements for such a craft are:

Low cost, both of manufacture and of operation;

Positive control characteristics, enabling the craft to follow safely the course of a narrow, winding river with the minimum of sideways skidding;

Simple bolt-together unit construction, facilitating transport and simplifying maintenance and repair;

An efficient and reliable skirt system, combining good wear resistance with ease of repair.

The following information refers to the River Rover Mk 3.

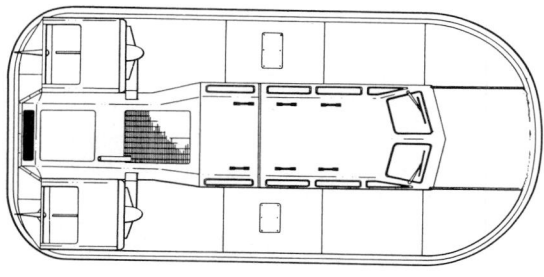
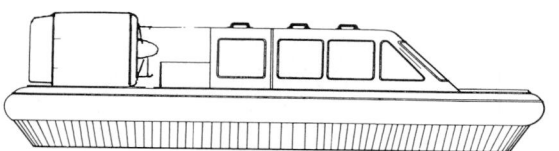
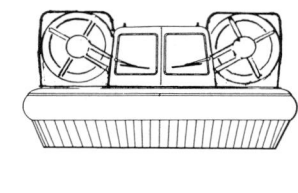

General arrangement of River Rover Mk 3

River Rover Mk 3

LIFT AND PROPULSION: Motive power is provided by a single 100bhp Renault R-20TS automotive engine. This drives a 630mm (25in) diameter lift fan, and two 710mm (28in) thrust fans mounted on either side of the lift fan. Power is transmitted via three Uniroyal HTD toothed belts and pulleys enclosed in streamlined fairings. All three fans are housed in grp ducts. Air from the lift fan is channelled through 90 degrees down beneath the craft via the skirt bag. Fuel consumption at cruising speed is 20·3 litres/h (4·5 gallons/h). Standard capacity 82 litres (18 imperial gallons).

CONTROLS: The primary means of control are two horizontally-pivoted elevons, one in each of the two square-sectioned ducts immediately aft of the thrust fans. Movement of foot pedals rotates the elevons jointly or differentially. Employed together, craft longitudinal trim is adjusted and, when rotated fully, braking is achieved. Used differentially, small deflections of the elevons enable the craft to be banked into a turn, thereby reducing sideways skidding. Greater pedal movement progressively closes the duct on the 'inside' of the turn, the outside duct remaining open. Thus differential thrust is added to the bank initially applied to the craft. Conventional vertically-pivoted aerodynamic rudders, controlled by a steering yoke, are fitted immediately aft of the elevons. These are used during operation in crosswinds, in conjunction with the elevons.
HULL: Aluminium alloy angle frame covered with 6mm (¼in) marine grade plywood panels. Engine bay bulkheads and sides are in aluminium alloy sheet. Structure is bolted together for ease of repair and simplicity of breakdown and re-assembly. The entire hull is surrounded by an

One of three River Rovers employed by 1982 British Joint Services Expedition to Peru

inflatable collar at deck level, providing all-round fendering and additional reserve buoyancy. The sliding cabin canopy is of moulded grp.
ACCOMMODATION: Three bench-type seats. These can be folded flat to provide sleeping accommodation for two persons, or, with cushions removed, for the carriage of freight. Alternatively, a stretcher can be carried aft on the port side of the cabin.
SKIRT: HDL-type loop and segment skirt in neoprene-coated nylon.

DIMENSIONS
Length: 6·19m (20ft 3·75in)
Width: 2·62m (8ft 7·5in)
Height, off cushion: 1·45m (4ft 9·5in)

WEIGHTS
Empty: 780kg (1,716lb)
All-up weight: 1,230kg (2,711lb)

PERFORMANCE
Max speed: 55km/h (34·3mph)
Cruising speed: 40km/h (25mph)

MAXCAT HOVERCRAFT

16 Laurieknowe, Dumfries, Scotland
Telephone; 0387 62452
Officials:
Max Houliston, *Proprietor*

The design specification for the Maxcat Hovercraft called for a cabin accommodating four people, facilities for towing and the use of a single powerplant to power the lift and propulsion systems. Design was undertaken by Paul Davis of Southampton and the construction of the craft was supervised by Ivor Verlander. The prototype is currently operating on the Solway Firth in Scotland.

MAXCAT HOVERCRAFT

Intended primarily for leisure applications, including cruising, the Maxcat Hovercraft is a grp-hulled four-seater powered by a single 150hp aero-engine giving it a maximum speed of 50 knots.
LIFT AND PROPULSION: Power for the integrated lift and propulsion system is provided by a 150hp Lycoming aero-engine mounted behind the cabin. This drives, via a shaft and a 2:1 bevel gear box, a 965mm (38in) HEBA/B AL Alloy centrifugal lift fan and a Hoffman variable-pitch 2m (6ft 7in) diameter pylon-mounted propeller. The propeller is driven from the main shaft by pulleys and toothed belts. A 36-litre (8-gallon) capacity fuel tank is behind the rear starboard seat. A 91/96 octane is used.
CONTROLS: Craft direction is controlled by

Maxcat Hovercraft

twin aerodynamic rudders operating in the airscrew slipstream. Yaw is controlled by thrust ports in the bow of the craft and rudders in the stern.
HULL: Two grp mouldings: lower hull and upper

hull including the cabin. Sections are filled with foam and sealed to provide maximum buoyancy. The pylon and other highly stressed parts are in AL alloy or steel.
SKIRT: HDL closed-loop segment type using black 11551 quality material as produced by the Northern Rubber Company.
ACCOMMODATION: Seats for an operator and three passengers. Two gull-wing doors, one port and one starboard, and the cabin is ventilated. In an emergency the cabin windows can be jettisoned. All the necessary gauges and indicators are provided on the dashboard. Pedals operate the puff ports. A fireproof and sound-proof bulkhead divides the cabin from the engine bay.
SYSTEMS, ELECTRICAL: A 12V system with an engine driven generator supplies power to the engine and lights.
DIMENSIONS
Length: 5·94m (19ft 6in)
Beam: 2·84m (9ft 4in)
WEIGHTS
All-up weight: 1,270kg (2,800lb)
PERFORMANCE
Max speed: 50 knots
Cruising speed: 35 knots
Endurance at cruising speed: 2 hours
Vertical obstacle clearance: 355mm (1ft 2in)

Maxcat Hovercraft

NORTHERN RUBBER COMPANY LIMITED

Victoria Works, Retford, Nottinghamshire
DN22 6HH, England
Telephone: 0777 706731
Telex: 56417 RUBBER G
Officials:
D E P Owen, *Managing Director*
K Richardson, *Works Director*
W J Newbold, *Technical Director*
D Collett, *Chief Textile Technologist*
D S Offord, *General Sales Manager*
K D Bacon, *Commercial and Overseas Sales Manager*

During the past 25 years Northern Rubber Company has been involved with the hovercraft and ACV industry. During this period it has assisted leading manufacturers with solutions to various requirements by extending skirt life, improving craft performance, and producing cost effective skirt fabrics.

As result of development work in conjunction with leading ACV manufacturers, a new range of natural rubber/nylon combinations has been launched to meet the demands of the faster, larger and heavier generation of craft used world wide. These new materials have superior low temperature characteristics, coupled with tough abrasion resistance and excellent adhesion and tear strength properties. These benefits are due to a specially formulated high performance polymer/fabric composite, based on Northern Rubber's manufacturing process.

River Rover fitted with Northern Rubber skirt

In addition to this new range of natural rubbers, Northern Rubber produces successful neoprene/nylon skirt fabrics, well proven in extreme service conditions throughout the world.

Northern Rubber has one of the widest range of skirt materials available for all current air cush-

ion vehicles and heavy lift systems, including military hovercraft, lightweight river craft, hoverbarges and cross channel craft.

The company has SQA approvals including the Ministry of Defence DEF STAN 05/24 plus CAA approval.

OSPREY HOVERCRAFT LIMITED

PO Box 34, Crawley, West Sussex RH10 4TF, England
Telephone: 04446 45791
Officials:
P V McCollum, *Director*
D McCollum, *Director*

This company produces a range of four craft, Kestrel, Kestrel GT, Falcon and Cormorant. These craft recently underwent a modification programme which increased their performance by about 30 per cent. Osprey Hovercraft has also developed the Goshawk, its first model to be specifically designed for Formula I racing.

Osprey Hovercraft has constructed and tested a four- to six-seat sidewall design which will be in single engine integrated form or with twin engines. It is envisaged that the sidewall design could become a leisure product and that it could fulfil specialist roles, including shallow-water surveying.

CORMORANT

This addition to the Osprey range originated as a one-off craft to meet a particular customer requirement. After trials it was decided to include the design in the standard range. The chief difference between the Cormorant and the Falcon is the departure from the integrated lift/propulsion system of the latter by the introduction of a separate lift engine and fan. This arrangement has resulted in a craft with a greater payload capacity and generally increased all-round performance.
LIFT AND PROPULSION: A 10hp one-cylinder two-stroke engine mounted ahead of the cockpit drives a 560mm (22in) diameter polypropylene-bladed axial fan for lift. Thrust is furnished by a 49hp air-cooled twin-cylinder two-stroke driving a ducted 737mm (29in) polypropylene, nine-bladed axial fan via a heavy-duty toothed belt. Fuel capacity is 27 litres (6 imperial gallons). Consumption is 9-16 litres/h (2-3·5 gallons/h).
CONTROLS: Craft heading is controlled by twin aerodynamic rudders hinged to the rear of the thrust duct and operated by a handlebar.
HULL: Monocoque construction in self-coloured glass fibre. Pre-formed sealed polyurethane block at base of craft for buoyancy. Tools and spares compartment provided.
SKIRT: Segmented type in neoprene-coated nylon material.

Cormorant

Falcon

DIMENSIONS
Length: 3·8m (12ft 6in)
Width: 1·83m (6ft)
Height: 1·22m (4ft)
WEIGHTS
Empty: 181·4kg (400lb)
Normal payload: 226·7kg (500lb)

PERFORMANCE
Speed over land and water: 88km/h plus (55mph plus)
Cruising speed: 32-40km/h (20-25mph)
Max continuous gradient, standing start: 1 : 8
Max short gradient, at speed: 1 : 4
Vertical hard obstacle clearance: 200mm (8in)

FALCON

Though intended primarily as a two-seat recreational craft, the Falcon is also suitable for a variety of light commercial and utility roles. Two of the craft are used by the Central Electricity Board on a land-reclamation scheme. A keynote of the design is its simplicity. All maintenance can be undertaken by a competent mechanic or handyman.

Some 50 per cent of Falcons sold are being employed for utility purposes. Several have been purchased as standby emergency craft in tidal areas and one Falcon is employed in Scotland for harvesting 9·65km (6 miles) of salmon nets. This craft is in use twice daily and is often required to operate at night. One Falcon is being evaluated by the West German Army.

A 'stretched' version, with a central driving position forward and a bench seat for two passengers aft, is in the planning stage. This arrangement will increase its ability to carry a larger payload when operating as a utility craft.

LIFT AND PROPULSION: Integrated system powered by a single 49hp air-cooled twin-cylinder two-stroke. This drives, via a heavy-duty toothed belt, a 737mm (29in) diameter polypropylene-bladed ducted fan, air from which is used for both lift and propulsion. Fuel capacity is 27 litres (6 imperial gallons). Fuel recommended is 93 octane, oil mix 25 : 1. Consumption is 11-16 litres/h (2·5-3·5 gallons/h).

HULL: Monocoque construction in self-coloured glass fibre. All components and fasteners are made from marine quality material. Pre-formed sealed polyurethane block at base of craft for buoyancy. Tools and spares compartment provided.

SKIRT: Segmented skirt in neoprene-coated nylon material.

DIMENSIONS
Length: 3·8m (12ft 6in)
Beam: 1·83m (6ft)
Height: 1·22m (4ft)
WEIGHTS
Empty: 172kg (380lb)
Normal payload: 204·1kg (450lb)
Max payload: 294·8kg (650lb)
PERFORMANCE
Cruising speed: 32-40km/h (20-25mph)
Speed over land and water: 72km/h plus (45mph plus)
Max continuous gradient, standing start: 1 : 8
Max short gradient, at speed: 1 : 2 (45 degrees)
Vertical hard obstacle clearance: 200mm (8in)

KESTREL GT

Based on a standard Kestrel hull but fitted with the Falcon's engine and fan system, the Kestrel GT has been designed to meet the need of enthusiasts for a powerful lightweight hovercraft for sport and competitive racing. It is the fastest selling craft in the Osprey range. Due to its high power/weight ratio, it is particularly agile and can

Kestrel

Kestrel GT

negotiate relatively steep slopes with comparative ease.

LIFT AND PROPULSION: Integrated system powered by a single 49hp air-cooled twin-cylinder two-stroke. This drives, via a heavy-duty toothed belt, a 737mm (29in) diameter polypropylene-bladed ducted fan, air from which is used for both lift and propulsion. Also available as a twin-engine model. Fuel capacity is 20·25 litres (4·5 imperial gallons). Fuel recommended is 93 octane, oil mix 25:1.

CONTROLS: Twin aerodynamic rudders, oper-

ated by a handlebar, control craft heading. Engine throttle mounted on handlebar.

HULL: Monocoque construction in self-coloured glass fibre. Pre-formed sealed polyurethane block at base of craft for buoyancy. Tools and spares compartment provided.

SKIRT: Fully-segmented type in neoprene-coated nylon.

ACCOMMODATION: Open cockpit for driver.

DIMENSIONS
Length: 3·2m (10ft 6in)
Width: 1·83m (6ft)
Height: 1·22m (4ft)

WEIGHTS
Empty: 164kg (360lb)
Normal payload: 113kg (250lb)
PERFORMANCE
Speed across land and water: 80km/h plus (50mph plus)
Cruising speed: 32-40km/h (20-25mph)
Max continuous gradient, standing start: 1 : 6
Max short gradient, at speed: 1 : 2 (45 degrees)
Vertical hard obstacle clearance: 200mm (8in)

KESTREL

Designed as a single-seater this fully-amphibious recreational craft has nevertheless operated many times on inland waterways with two aboard in force 5 winds, gusting to force 6. Built on a base of solid foam it will not sink even if badly damaged. Recent modifications to the craft have made it a Formula III competitor.

LIFT AND PROPULSION: Integrated system with a single 22hp air-cooled one cylinder two-stroke driving one 737mm (29in) polypropylene-bladed ducted fan aft. Fuel capacity is 27 litres (6 imperial gallons). Recommended

Goshawk

fuel, 93 octane/oil mix 25 : 1. Consumption, 6·75 to 9 litres/h (1·5-2 gallons/h).
CONTROLS: Twin aerodynamic rudders controlled by handlebars. Engine throttle mounted on handlebars.
HULL: Self-coloured glass fibre structure based on a rigid foam block for strength and buoyancy. Built-in tools and spares compartment.
SKIRT: Segmented system in neoprene-coated nylon.
DIMENSIONS
Length: 3·2m (10ft 6in)
Beam: 1·83m (6ft)
Height: 1m (3ft 3in)

WEIGHTS
Empty: 127kg (280lb)
Normal payload: 113·5kg (250lb)
Max payload: 136kg (300lb)
PERFORMANCE
Cruising speed: 24-40km/h (15-25mph)
Speed across land and water: 56km/h plus (35mph plus)
Max continuous gradient, standing start: 1 : 7
Max short gradient, at speed: 1 : 2 (45 degrees)
Vertical hard obstacle clearance: 200mm (8in)

GOSHAWK
TYPE: Formula I racing craft.
LIFT AND PROPULSION: A 10hp one-cylinder two-stroke engine drives a 560mm (22in) diameter fan for lift. Powered by a 49hp twin-cylinder two-stroke driving two 686mm (27in) diameter polypropylene fans via a flexible coupling driving a toothed belt.

Goshawk showing ducted propulsion fans and skirt detail

CONTROLS: Twin-aerodynamic rudders in each fan duct controlled by handlebars. Engine throttles mounted on handlebars.

HULL: Monocoque construction in self-coloured glass fibre based on a rigid foam block for strength and buoyancy.

SKIRT: Fully-segmented in neoprene-coated nylon.

DIMENSIONS
Length: 3·5m (11ft 6in)
Beam: 1·85m (6ft 2in)
Height: 1·5m (5ft)
WEIGHTS
Empty: 81·4kg (400lb)
PERFORMANCE
Speed across land and water: 96km/h plus (60mph plus)

RTK MARINE LIMITED
Head Office: Lake Road, Hamworthy, Poole, Dorset, England
Telephone: 0202 685581
Telex: 418281 Romarp G
Cables: Rotomar, Poole

Officials:
A Moseley, *Chairman and Managing Director*
D W Smith, *Director*

Formed in March 1966 as Rotork Marine Limited, this company originally developed a simple marine-ply 8-metre planing hull manufactured in grp. The range was extended from 8 to 12 metres in 1973 and the Series 5, with a revised hull configuration, was introduced in 1975. The boats are sold world-wide and are in operation in over 75 countries and in service with 42 nations' defence forces. A key feature of the hull design is the use of air lubrication to reduce hydrodynamic drag. A ram-air cushion, contained by shallow side skegs, raises the bow clear of the water at speed. As the pressurised air flows aft it generates air/foam lubrication for the remainder of the hull, permitting speeds of up to 83·5km/h (52mph) to be achieved. The performance depends on the payload, installed power and sea conditions. A wide choice of power plants is available, and cabin modules can be supplied for passenger and work crew accommodation. Bow loading ramps are fitted for ease of access and operation from beaches.

The company offers a series of fast assault craft and patrol boats, tactical personnel carriers and

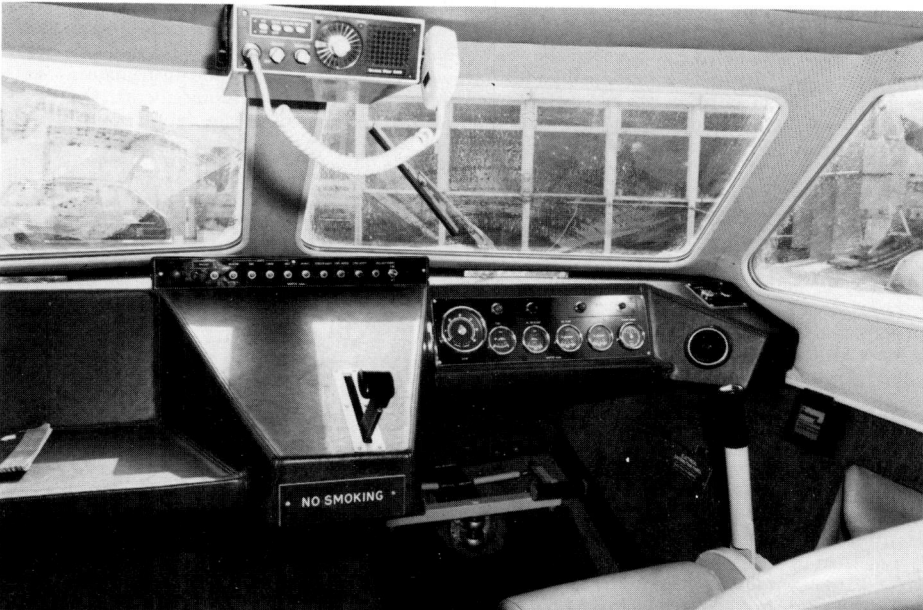
Driving position, Tiger 12

logistic support craft, together with a range of general purpose passenger and vehicle ferries, 7·37m (24ft 2in) to 12·65m (41ft 6in) in length. The four basic craft are the 408, 412, 518 and 512.

In November 1982 RTK Marine Limited undertook the marketing world-wide of the Tiger 12 amphibious hovercraft on behalf of Air Vehicles Limited, Cowes, Isle of Wight. Variants of the Tiger are already in use with many organisations, including the British Ministry of Defence, as firing range safety craft. They are also in service with the Nigerian Police, the Institute of Geological Sciences (UK), the Canadian Armed Forces and the French Ministry of Defence. In addition to marketing the Tiger through its agency network in more than 80 countries, RTK Marine also provides an extensive after sales service. Air Vehicles Limited will continue to design and manufacture its own hovercraft.

RTK TIGER 12
A fully amphibious 12-seater, the RTK Tiger 12 is designed to operate with payloads of up to 1 tonne over mud, sand, swamp, snow, ice and water. Although its speed varies considerably with weather conditions, type of terrain and temperature, it will normally operate on calm

Tiger 12

Performance Guide — UK conditions — RTK Sea Trucks and Multi-Duty Workboats

	Speed Light	50%	Laden	Weight light	Max payload	Draught, laden drive up	drive down
GVF or LSC 512 2 × 143hp diesel/stern drive Volvo Penta AQAD 40/280 (6-cylinder in-line turbocharged)	26 knots	21 knots	17 knots	4,750kg	4,250kg	42cm	89cm
LSC 512 2 × 143hp diesel/waterjet Volvo Penta TAMD 40 (6-cylinder in-line turbocharged)	22 knots	18 knots	15 knots	5,500kg	3,500kg	42cm	42cm
STW 412 2 × 143hp diesel/stern drive Volvo Penta AQAD 40/280 (6-cylinder in-line turbocharged)	28 knots	23 knots	18 knots	4,200kg	3,300kg	28cm	72cm
STW 412 1 × 79hp Deutz air-cooled diesel Schottel rudder	10 knots	9 knots	8·5 knots	4,400kg	3,100kg	28cm	120cm
STW 408 1 × 143hp diesel/stern drive Volvo Penta AQAD 40/280 (6-cylinder in-line turbocharged)	20 knots	16 knots	14 knots	2,500kg	2,000kg	28cm	72cm
FAC 408 2 × 140hp outboard motors OMC (Johnson or Evinrude)	35 knots	30 knots	27 knots	2,300kg	2,200kg	28cm	71cm
FAC 408 2 × 235 hp outboard motors OMC (Johnson or Evinrude)	45 knots	40 knots	36 knots	2,400kg	2,100kg	28cm	71cm
FAC 508 2 × 143hp diesel/waterjet Volvo Penta TAMD 40 (6-cylinder in-line turbocharged)	27 knots	19 knots	10 knots	3,250kg	2,750kg	42cm	42cm

water at 56km/h (35mph) and overland at 32km/h (20mph).

It can be trailed behind a Land-Rover or packed into a container. The designers state that the craft is easy to operate and maintain. A complete novice can be trained to become a competent driver with about 25 hours' tuition. Maintenance is no more complicated than that on a commercial truck. All machinery and spare parts are easy to obtain.

Design variants include load carriers, in which the area aft of the crew can be left completely open for the carriage of bulky items; military and para-military patrol, in which a gun mounting can be provided forward, and survey and civil engineering. On the latter, a variety of racks and carriers can be incorporated on the superstructure for carrying seismographic and general survey equipment, pipework and cables.

LIFT AND PROPULSION: Integrated system powered by a 5·9-litre (360in³) V8 petrol engine developing 200bhp gross at 4,000rpm. Power is transmitted to a 1·37m (4ft 6in) diameter four-bladed, duct-mounted propeller and a 12-bladed centrifugal fan by a toothed belt and shaft mounted in self-aligning bearings bolted to a welded steel frame attached to the main bulkhead. The propeller shaft is in hollow 77mm (3in) stainless steel tube and is mounted in a steel support aft of the propeller. The rear edge of the grp propeller duct has moulded mountings for the rudder and elevator blade shafts. Fuel consumption is approximately 36·3 litres/h (8 gallons/h). Normal fuel capacity, 159 litres (35 imperial gallons, 42 US gallons).

CONTROL: Five rudder blades operated by rudder bar through heavy duty Morse cable provide directional control. Five elevator blades operated by lever with a ratchet system through Morse cable provide trim and when raised fully assist braking by reducing thrust.

HULL: Superstructure and all bulkheads are of marine grade aluminium sheet, welded together to form a rigid box structure.

SKIRT: Inflatable side structures each comprise three separate compartments in hypalon/nylon sheet. Each compartment has an inflation/deflation valve and a pressure relief valve set at 700 grms/cm². Nylon hinges attach the side structure to the hull. The loop skirt, which is also in hypalon/nylon material, is fastened to the side structures by large nylon zips. Skirt segments are in neoprene/nylon.

ACCOMMODATION: Standard model has a

totally enclosed cabin with access through two doors. The driver's seat is forward right, the navigator's forward left. Sufficient space is available ahead of these positions for a radar display unit, radios and navigation instruments. Seats arranged to customer's requirements. A removable soft top is available. A ventilation system is

standard and supplies pressurised air to the cabin or windscreen. A Graviner firefighting system installed in the cabin is capable of being fired into the engine bay. It can also be used as a hand-held cabin fire extinguisher.

LIFTING AND JACKING: Four strongpoints are built into the hull sides, providing eyes for the

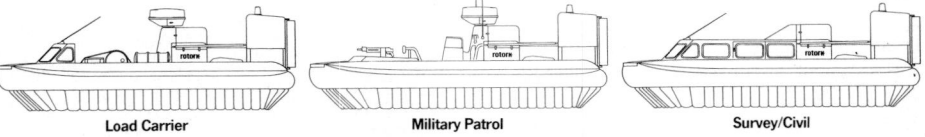

Load Carrier   Military Patrol   Survey/Civil

Tiger 12 variants

Tiger 12s during beaching exercises

lifting harness and four lifting jacks. The jacks allow hull and skirt inspection and loading onto a road trailer (supplied as an optional extra).

ELECTRICAL SYSTEM: 12V dc negative earth with engine driven 35-amp alternator and 60-amp/hour battery. Electrical accessories; collision warning flashing beacon; port and starboard navigation lights; windscreen wipers and washers; instrument illumination; cabin lighting.

DIMENSIONS
Hull:
  Length overall: 7·97m (26ft 2in)
  Beam inflated: 3·81m (12ft 6in)
  Transport width: 2·36m (7ft 9in)
  Height on landing skids: 2·26m (7ft 5in)
Cabin:
  Length: 3·89m (12ft 9in)
  Width: 1·89m (6ft)
WEIGHTS
Empty: 1,727kg (3,800lb)
Disposable load (fuel, passengers and optional items): 900kg (2,000lb)
All-up weight: 2,627kg (5,800lb)

PERFORMANCE
Max speed, calm water, 60°F, ISA conditions: 56km/h (35mph)
Speed over land: 32km/h (20mph)

RTK STW 408 SEA TRUCK WORKBOAT

This is a heavy duty, multi-purpose workboat designed for high performance and low running costs. It can operate safely in only 304mm (1ft) of water and is equipped with a bow ramp to facilitate the loading of passengers, freight or light vehicles from beaches. The maximum payload is 2,500kg, depending on machinery and optional equipment fitted.

POWER PLANT: Dependent upon payload and performance requirements and whether the craft is to be employed for sheltered water or open sea operation. Engines recommended are 85-235hp OMC OBMs fitted in pairs or single 143hp Volvo Penta AQAD 40/280. Supplied as standard with these units are the control console and, depending on the type of power unit, 227-litre (50-gallon) or 455-litre (100-gallon) fuel tanks, together with separate fuel lines.

HULL: Heavy duty glass fibre reinforced plastics. Buoyancy is provided by closed cell polyurethane foam of TD I type. The skegs are in pre-stressed cold drawn galvanised steel tube. The manually operated ramp is in 25·4mm (1in) thick, polyurethane-coated marine ply. It is housed in a galvanised steel frame with galvanised steel capping, and is counter-balanced by a torsion bar.

ACCOMMODATION: As a workboat a grp cabin can be fitted, together with extensions, to

RTK 512 in general purpose launch (GPL) configuration

provide adequate covered crew space and lockers.

SYSTEMS, ELECTRICAL: Heavy duty 12V batteries housed in acid-resistant reinforced plastic battery box mounted at deck level.

FUEL: Fuel is carried in one or more 227·2-litre (50-gallon) tanks positioned to suit customers' layout requirements.

SCUPPERS: Located in the transom. Discharge capacity is 818·27 litres/min (180 gallons/min).

DIMENSIONS
Length, overall: 7·37m (24ft 2in)
  at waterline: 6·09m (20ft)
Beam: 3m (9ft 10in)
Freeboard, unladen, to deck level: 127mm (5in)
  to top of bulwarks: 914mm (36in)
  max load, to deck level: 50·8mm (2in)
  to top of bulwarks: 838mm (33in)
Deck area (with outboard power): 15·81m² (170ft²)
Draught:
unladen, outboard drive up: 203mm (8in)
  outboard drive down: 635mm (25in)
max load, outboard drive up: 280mm (11in)
  outboard drive down: 711mm (28in)
WEIGHTS
Total, light condition, twin OMC OBMs: approx 2,300kg (5,071lb)
  single Volvo Penta AQAD 40 diesel: approx 2,500kg (5,512lb)
Max displacement: 4,500kg (9,922lb)
Payload, dependent on engines and fixed equipment: up to 2,200kg (4,852lb)
PERFORMANCE
  Varies with rig, type of load, installed power and operating conditions.

RTK STW 412 SEA TRUCK

This 12-metre variant of the Sea Truck is available in two versions, the STW workboat and the FAC 412 assault craft. The latter can carry up to 50 men or a Land Rover at speeds up to 25 knots. It can operate in only 304mm (12in) of water and can unload vehicles, personnel and supplies directly on to a beach.

PROPULSION SYSTEMS
  OMC 85-235hp OBMs in pairs
  Single Volvo Penta AQAD 40/280 143hp diesel stern drive unit
  Twin Volvo Penta AQAD 40/280 143hp diesel stern drive units
  Single 79hp Deutz air-cooled diesel with Schottel rudder propeller

HULL: Standard RTK Sea Truck hull in glass fibre reinforced plastics. Reinforcement: E glass chopped strand mat. E glass woven roving. Silane finish. Buoyancy: closed cell polyurethane foam. Deck has a non-slip bonded grit surface applied to a point load integral with the hull structure. Chassis is of star frame type, integral with the hull structure. Fender frames are in hot-dip galvanised welded steel tube 101·6mm (4in) and 127mm (5in) diameter. Rotating fender wheels are fitted as standard at bow and stern. A polyester resin coated and grit bonded 25·4mm (1in) thick marine plywood ramp is fitted at the bow. The ramp is opened and closed manually by galvanised mild steel levers. Fuel tanks are in welded mild steel with zinc spray and polyurethane finish. Tanks have a capacity of 227 litres (50 imperial gallons) and are in pannier form for bulwark mounting. Independent fuel lines are provided.

ACCOMMODATION: A grp covered cabin can be supplied together with an extension of the control position, providing additional crew space and lockers.

DIMENSIONS
Length overall: 11·27m (37ft)
  at waterline: 9·8m (32ft 2in)
Beam: 3m (9ft 10in)
Freeboards, unladen to deck level: 127mm (5in)
  unladen to top of bulwarks: 914·4mm (36in) with max load to deck level: 50·8mm (2in)
  with max load to top of bulwarks: 838mm (33in)
Height, of top rail from deck: 787·2mm (31in)
Deck area, overall: 30·85m² (287ft²)
Draught, unladen, outdrive up: 203mm (8in)
  unladen, outdrive down: 635mm (25in)
  max load, outdrive up: 280mm (11in)
  max load, outdrive down: 723mm (28ft 6in)
WEIGHTS
Total, light condition, twin Volvo Penta AQAD 40/280: approx 4,200kg (9,260lb)
Max displacement: 7,500kg (16,535lb)
Payload, dependent on engines and fixed equipment: up to 4,750kg (10,472lb)

RTK 512 RANGE

Seven principal versions of the 512 (12-metre) craft are in production. The flexibility design concept based on modular layout arrangements

STW 412 Sea Truck workboat

allows variations to meet specific user requirements. The range comprises:
Goods Vehicle Ferry (GVF)
General Purpose Launch (GPL)
Passenger Vehicle Ferry (PVF)
Passenger Ferry (SPV)
Sea Truck Workboat (STW)
Logistic Support Craft (LSC)
Fast Patrol Boat (FPB)

The basic hull is constructed in heavy duty grp to British Admiralty specifications and is foam-filled, resulting in the craft being unsinkable, even when fully laden. Extensive use is made of stainless steel, rubber, nylon and other non-corrodible materials for minimum maintenance.

The PVF 512, which is designed for ferrying vehicles, cargo, livestock and passengers in areas where jetties and other landing facilities are not available, was conceived with international safety requirements in mind, enabling, where applicable, local authorities to issue certificates for the operation of these boats under varying conditions.

HULL: Glass reinforced plastic with non-slip bonded grit surface on deck. Superstructure in integrally coloured grp. Stainless steel rolled section gunwales. Full peripheral fendering at gunwale. Solid rubber strake at waterline. Tubular stainless steel full length skegs, additional beaching skegs at bow. Winch operated reinforced plastic loading ramp with non-slip surface. Scuppers for the removal of deck water located in transom. Fuel is carried in two 200-litre (44-imperial gallon) pannier tanks mounted on internal bulwarks.

ACCOMMODATION: An all-weather grp cabin is provided aft above the gunwale level with a canvas dropscreen giving access to the quarterdeck. Door and steps give access to the welldeck. A seat is provided for the helmsman and a bench seat for two observers. Standard bridge equipment includes navigation lights, searchlight, internal light, klaxon, windscreen wiper, rechargeable fire extinguishers (two) and bilge pump. Personnel accommodation varies according to type. On the SPV 512 it comprises a cabin on deck forward of the bridge, with doors to the bridge and foredecks, a washroom/toilet unit, galley unit with sink, cooker and 90·9-litre (20-gallon) fresh water supply system and ferry seating for 36 passengers.

COMMUNICATIONS: Optional. Fully synthesised, 25W VHF radio transceiver, up to 56 channels. SSB. HF radio telephone.

NAVIGATION: Optional. Illuminated helmsman's compass. Short range radar (Decca 060, range 24n miles).

DIMENSIONS
Length, overall: 12·65m (41ft 6in)
    waterline: 10·75m (35ft 3in)
Beam, overall: 3·2m (10ft 6in)
Overall height, hull: 1·487m (4ft 10in)
    with cabins: 2·501m (8ft 2in)
    with flying bridge: 3·525m (11ft 7in)
Height of gunwale above deck: 1m (3ft 3in)
Deck area: 9 × 2·5m = 22·5m² (29ft 6in × 8ft 3in = 243ft²)
Freeboard with max load to gunwale: 1,052·5mm (41·4in)
Draught, unladen: 268mm (10·5in)
    with max load: 420mm (16·5in)
WEIGHTS
Total, light condition, twin Volvo Penta AQAD 40/280: 4,750kg (10,472lb)
Max allowable displacement: 9,000kg (19,842lb)
Payload, dependent on engines and fixed equipment: up to 5,000kg (11,023lb)

RTK STW 508

Like the RTK 512, the 508 is a second generation craft developed from the successful 412/408 range, but with increased payload and softer ride in rough seas. In common with all RTK craft, the 508 has reserve buoyancy far in excess of the permissible fully laden displacement which makes it unsinkable.

A range of propulsion options are available including outboard motor, diesel waterjet and

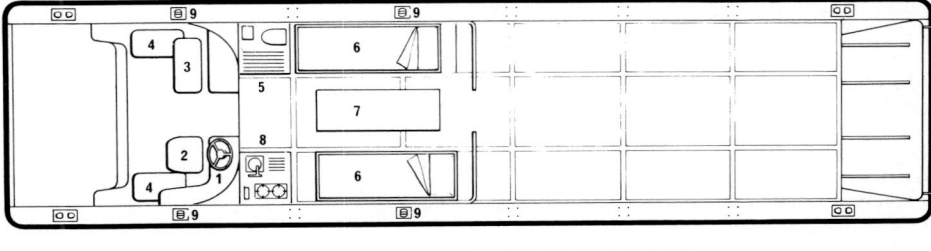

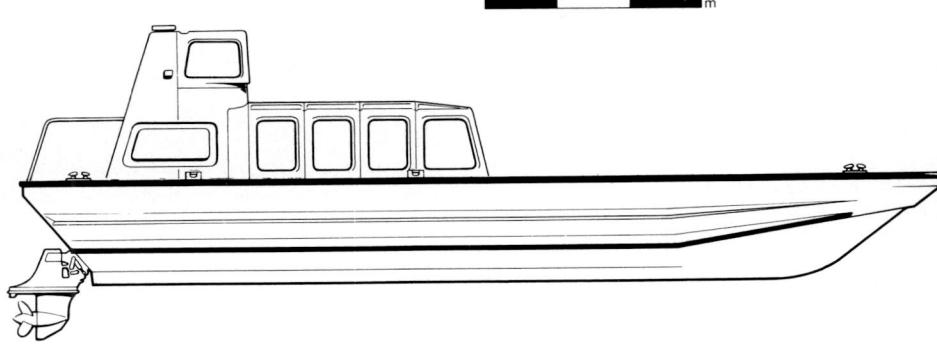

FPB 512 fast patrol boat

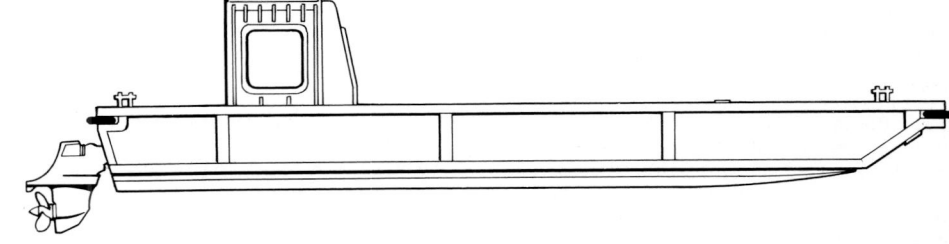

RTK 512, outboard profile and deck plan

diesel sterndrive, enabling it to be used as a versatile utility craft, or in a high speed assault role.
DIMENSIONS
Length, overall: 8·23m
    waterline: 6·5m
Beam, overall: 3·05m
Height, overall hull: 1·24m
Deck area: 15·1m²

Freeboard with max load to gunwale: 800m
Draught max load with waterjets: 420mm
WEIGHTS
Total, light condition, twin Volvo Penta TAMD 40 engines with PP90 waterjets: 3,250kg
Max allowable displacement: 6,000kg
Payload, dependent on engines and fixed equipment: up to 3,500kg

FAC 508 fast assault craft

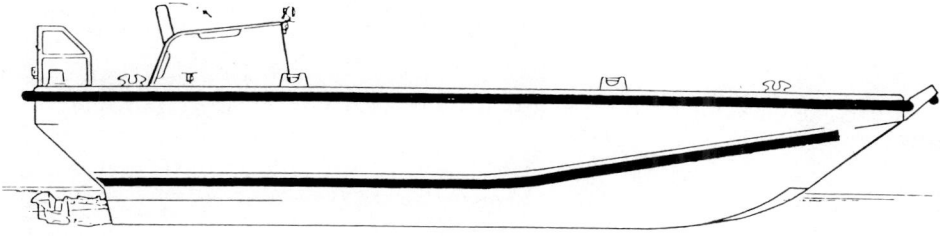

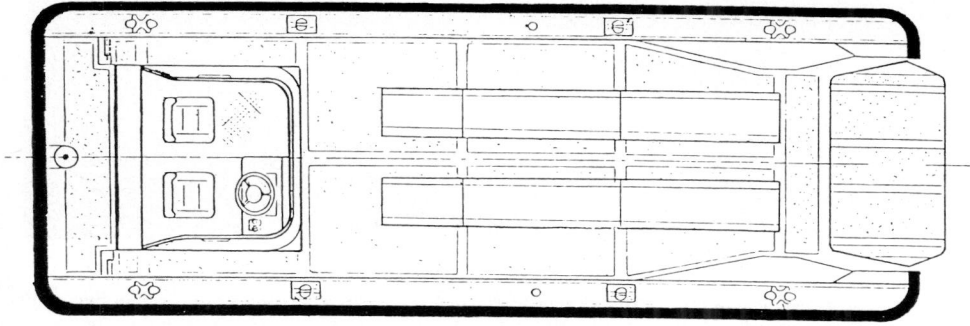

Elevation and deck plan FAC 508 fast assault craft

SKIDADDLE LEISURE PRODUCTS
Division of Fruitree Ltd

Burton-on-the-Wolds, Near Loughborough, Leicestershire, England
Telephone: 0509 880471
Telex: 341023
Officials:
B S Chandler, *Chairman*
B Stairs, FCA, *Director*
R Shaw, *Company Secretary*

Skidaddle Leisure Products has been licensed to build and market throughout the world the Scarab 12, a Bill Baker design which has been renamed Jetstream. It is the intention of the company, with Bill Baker as consultant, to continue the development of the Jetstream and one

or two other craft and eventually mass produce them.

JETSTREAM

This 3·65-metre (12-foot) amphibious two-seater is designed for a range of leisure applications, including fishing, shooting, bathing and touring inland waterways. It can also be employed in under-developed areas for survey work in marginal terrain and as a light transport vehicle to support expeditions.

On the latest model the freeboard has been increased by 153mm (6in), which not only provides a drier craft but, since it required an alteration in hull design, it now has greater structural strength without a large increase in overall weight.

LIFT AND PROPULSION: Integrated system.

A single 40bhp Hirth 276 R.6 2-cylinder air-cooled two-stroke drives via a toothed belt a ducted 71cm (28in) six-bladed Multiwing fan aft. Propulsion air is expelled rearwards and lift air is ducted into the plenum below. An 18·18-litre (4-gallon) capacity fuel tank is built into the seat. Fuel recommended is 25 : 1 petrol oil mix.

CONTROLS: Craft heading is controlled by a single handlebar-operated rudder hinged to the rear of the fan duct. Handlebars incorporate twist grip throttle for the engine. An electric starter is provided as well as a lockable ignition to prevent theft.

HULL: Moulded grp structure with foam buoyancy.

SKIRT: Fully segmented type in neoprene-coated nylon.

ACCOMMODATION: Open cockpit with two

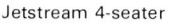

Jetstream 4-seater

Standard Jetstream 4-seater with separate lift and thrust systems

Jetstream 6-seater

Standard Jetstream with large fairing and perspex screen

seats in tandem or with side-by-side seating. In the latter configuration a single central control column is installed enabling the craft to be controlled by either occupant.

DIMENSIONS
Length: 3·68m (12ft)
Beam: 1·98m (6ft 6in)
WEIGHTS
Unladen: 164kg (360lb)
PERFORMANCE
Driver only: 55-65km/h (35-40mph)
Driver and passenger: 40-48km/h (25-30mph)
Max gradient, static conditions: 12·5%
Vertical obstacle clearance: 228mm (9in)

JETSTREAM VARIANTS

A special variant for Scandinavian countries has separate side-by-side seating and increased protection for the face and body through the addition of a higher cockpit moulding and a raised perspex screen. Basic heating is provided by a heat exchanger fitted to the engine exhaust system.

JETSTREAM 4-SEATER

Several custom-built Jetstream 4s have been sold. This particular design is under the direction of Bill Baker, the company's ACV design consultant. A feature of the craft will be separate lift and

Jetstream

thrust motors. Wide interest in this design has already been shown by Scandinavian countries. A small lightweight cabin top can be fitted, together with a heating arrangement similar to that employed on earlier Jetstreams supplied to the Scandinavian market.

SKIMA HOVERCRAFT LIMITED

6 Hamble Close, Warsash, Southampton, Hampshire SO3 6GT, England
Telephone: 04895 3210
Officials:
M A Pinder, *Managing Director*

Pindair Limited's hovercraft are used in 67 countries for a range of applications, although the company ceased trading in September 1983 and Skima Hovercraft Limited has now taken over its designs.

Skima Hovercraft Limited is continuing to develop the Skima range for manufacture by established boatbuilders. Marketing will be undertaken by the builders or by Skima Hovercraft Limited.

All Skima craft incorporate inflatable structures. The advantages of this design feature include low weight, impact resistance, improved obstacle and wave clearance, low cost transport or storage costs and excellent buoyancy and stability. The craft can be easily maintained and spares are readily available. The smaller, portable models are fitted with high performance two-stroke engines, while the larger transportable ones use four-stroke automobile units or diesels.

SKIMA 1 Mk 3

A pleasure craft, Skima 1 Mk 3 was designed with low performance and low cost as the main criteria. It has a circular planform, one-piece grp deck, Torroidal-inflatable and conical skirt. Two- or four-stroke engines can be specified.

SKIMA 2 Mk 3

A low cost two-seat inflatable hovercraft which can be folded and stowed in the luggage compartments of most cars or carried complete on the roof. Skima 2 is intended primarily for the recreation market and will carry two people inshore and inland in moderate weather.

LIFT AND PROPULSION: Integrated system powered by a single-cylinder two-stroke. Engine is fitted with a hand starter and drives a six-bladed plastic fan via a high torque toothed belt. Engine and fan are mounted in a grp duct module. Fuel consumption: 5·9 litres/h (1·3 gallons/h).
CONTROLS: There are only two controls, tiller and throttle, both of which can be operated by either occupant.
HULL: Inflatable structure with three compartments and a raised floor which increases obstacle clearance height. Underside has thick rubber landing pads. Sectional deck locked in place with aluminium extrusions.

Skima 1

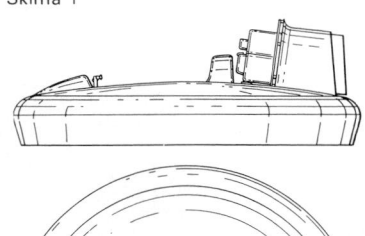
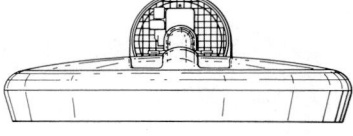

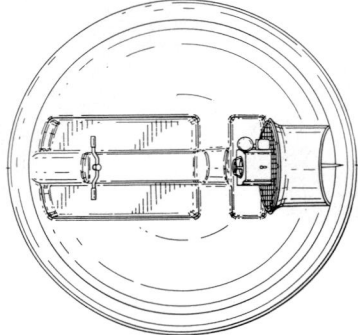

Skima 1

Skima 2

TRANSPORT AND ASSEMBLY: For transport and storage the complete hovercraft can be packed into a box of only 1m³ and can be assembled in less than one hour.

ACCOMMODATION: An adjustable bench seat is supplied and the wrap-around windscreen, low cushion pressure and long bow provide a dry and comfortable ride.

SKIRT: HDL loop and segment type with bolt-on segments.

SKIMA 3 Mk 3

After many successful races in British and European Championships, a Skima 3 took the light hovercraft speed record on Loch Ubnaig in 1976. This latest version incorporates many components used in the Skima 4 Mk 3 and is built to order only.

SKIMA 4 Mk 3

Building on the success of earlier four-seat designs, the Skima 4 Mk 3 incorporates an electric starter and integrated lift and propulsion system for the first time. The design also features markedly-reduced noise levels, more comfortable and spacious passenger accommodation and an improved skirt with bolt-on segments and virtually no bow spray. It can be transported on a light trailer or folded inside a pick-up truck and can be lifted by four people.

It is being evaluated by the Royal Navy, the US Navy and the US Coastguard. Users include the United Nations, UK Overseas Development Administration, Imperial Chemical Industries and a number of water authorities, civil engineers, survey groups and pest control organisations.

LIFT AND PROPULSION: Power is provided by a single Hirth engine, fitted with hand and electric starters and driving a six-bladed plastic fan via a high torque toothed belt. In 1982 a flow straightener was added which greatly improves thrust. Engine and fan are mounted in a grp duct module which also houses the battery. Fuel consumption is approximately 10 litres/h (2·2 gallons/h).

CONTROLS: Craft direction is controlled by a tiller, mounted on the dashboard, which operates four air rudders in the propulsion duct. The engine throttle is mounted on the tiller and a separate lever operates the flow splitter, which varies the proportion of air used for lift and thrust according to conditions.

HULL: The inflatable hull has four compartments and a raised floor, which increases obstacle clearance. The sectional deck is locked in place with aluminium extrusions. The underside is reinforced and fitted with rubber landing skids.

TRANSPORT AND ASSEMBLY: For transport or storage the complete hovercraft can be packed into a space of only 2m³ (70ft³) and can be assembled in about two hours.

ACCOMMODATION: Two adjustable bench seats are supplied. Wrap-around windscreen, low

Skima 3

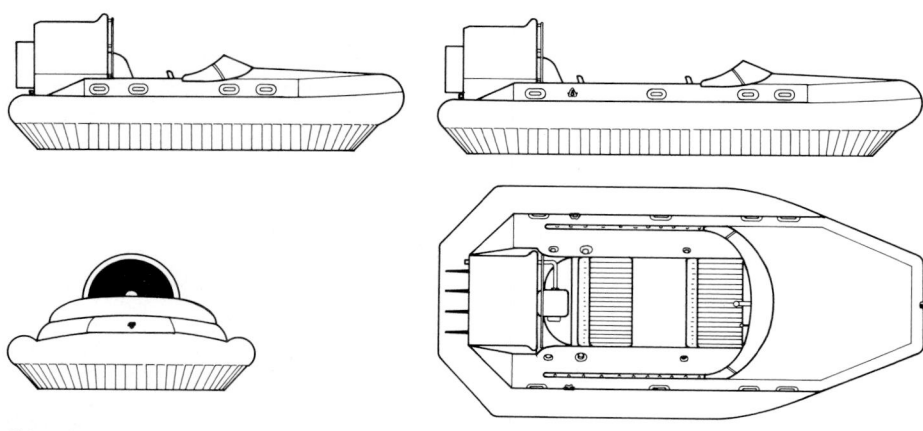

Skima 3   Skima 4

Skima 4s before being shipped to Bangladesh for civil engineering work

cushion pressure and long bow ensure a comfortable and dry ride.

SKIRT: HDL loop and segment type, with bolt-on segments.

SKIMA 5 Mk 2

The first Skima 5 prototype was similar to Skima 4, but it was intended to incorporate a more powerful engine to increase performance and payload. This approach has now changed and Skima 5 fulfils a role midway between Skima 4 and Skima 6, and may replace both craft in the future.

The Skima 5 benefits from recent developments in four-stroke automobile engines and incorporates improvements in the integrated air

PINDAIR SKIMA SPECIFICATIONS AND PERFORMANCE

Craft	Skima 1	Skima 2	Skima 3	Skima 4	Skima 5	Skima 6	Skima 12	Skima 18	Skima 25
Length	3m	3·5m	3·8m	4·8m	5m	6·19m	7·77m	8·88m	9·99m
Width	3m	1·7m	2m	2m	2·25m	2·62m	3·5m	3·5m	5m
Height off cushion	1m	1m	1·2m	1·2m	1·3m	1·45m	2·3m	2·3m	2·3m
Unladen weight	75kg	100kg	200kg	225kg	450kg	670kg	990kg	1,500kg	2,000kg
Hard structure clearance	15cm	25cm	35cm	35cm	35cm	30cm	50cm	50cm	60cm
Shipping dimensions	2·5 × 2·5 × 0·5m	1 × 1 × 0·75m	1·2 × 1·3 × 1·5m	1·2 × 1·3 × 1·5m	2 × 1·3 × 1·5m	6 × 2·3 × 1·3m	6 × 2·5 × 2·5m	7·6 × 2·5 × 2·5m	10 × 3 × 2·5m
Skirt	Cone	HDL	HDL	HDL	HDL	HDL	HDL	HDL	HDL
Engine type	2-stroke	2-stroke	2-stroke	2-stroke	4-stroke	4-stroke	4-stroke	4-stroke	4-stroke
Cooling	Air	Air	Air	Air	Water	Water	Water	Water	Water
Cylinders	1	1	2	2	4	4	V8	V8	2 × V8
Capacity	160cc	250cc	500cc	500cc	1,800cc	2 litres	5·7 litres	5·7 litres	2 × 5·7 litres
Power hp	10	20	45	25	80	100	250	300	500
Max speed km/h	30	50	65	60	60	60	70	70	80
Max wind force, Beaufort	3	4	6	6	6	6	6	6	6
Max range km	50	100	100	100	250	250	250	250	250

system, which was developed for the Skima 4.

The main superstructure is rigid to allow optional weather equipment to be fitted to the cabin. The inflatable side bodies are retained. Cabin and working parts are in similar sized units which can be separated and nested for transport or storage. A standard 20ft shipping container can accommodate four Skima 5s.

Skima 5

SKIMA 6 Mk 3

Conceived as a car-size hovercraft capable of being stored in a domestic garage and towed behind a family car, Skima 6 can carry up to six people at speeds of up to 30 knots over a wide variety of surfaces. Maintenance is simplified by using a Renault R-20TS car engine which has exceptional economy, as well as an excellent power-to-weight ratio. Prototypes (called 'River Rovers') have been tested by the British Joint Services Expedition team on the rapid-strewn Kali Gandaki River in Nepal and several tributaries of the Amazon. They have also been used in Irian Jaya, Indonesia, and by the Royal Navy.

Skima 6 is manufactured on the Isle of Wight by Dodnor Marine Limited.

Recent customers include a police force in the Far East and the Australian Army.

LIFT AND PROPULSION: Motive power is provided by a single 100bhp Renault R-20TS automotive engine, driving a ten-bladed axial lift fan and two five-bladed thrust fans. Power is transmitted via three high torque toothed belts, enclosed in streamlined fairings. All three fans are housed in grp ducts. Air from the lift fan is channelled through 90 degrees down beneath the craft via the skirt loop. Fuel consumption at cruising speed is 20 litres/h (4·3 gallons/h).

CONTROLS: The primary means of control is two horizontally pivoted elevons, one in each of the two square-sectioned ducts immediately aft of the thrust fans. Movement of foot pedals rotates the elevons jointly or differentially. Employed together, craft longitudinal trim is adjusted, and when rotated fully, braking is achieved. Used differentially, small deflections of the elevons enable the craft to be banked into a turn, thereby reducing sideways skidding. Greater pedal movement progressively closes the duct on the 'inside' of the turn, the outside duct remaining open. Thus differential thrust is added to the bank initially applied to the craft. Conventional vertically-pivoted aerodynamic rudders, controlled by a steering yoke, are fitted immediately aft of the elevons. These are used during operation in crosswinds, in conjunction with the elevons.

HULL: Aluminium alloy angle frame covered with 6mm (¼in) marine grade plywood panels. Engine bay deck and sides are in aluminium alloy sheet. Structure is bolted together for ease of repair and simplicity of breakdown and reassembly and is surrounded by an inflatable collar. The sliding cabin canopy is constructed of moulded grp.

ACCOMMODATION: Three bench type seats. These can be folded flat to provide sleeping accommodation for two persons, or with cushions removed, for the carriage of freight. Alternatively, two stretchers can be carried aft of the front seat.

SKIRT: HDL loop-and-segment type in neoprene-coated nylon.

Skima 6 showing elevons

Skima 6 operated by Australian Army

SKIMA 12 Mk 3

A semi-inflatable multi-role hovercraft, Skima 12 is capable of carrying up to 12 people or 1 tonne of freight. It combines features of an off-highway vehicle with those of a high-speed workboat. Skima 12 is easily transported on a trailer with the eight-compartment, inflatable cylindrical tube around the perimeter of the hull furled or detached and can be shipped in a standard 6 × 2·5 × 2·5m (19ft 8in × 8ft × 8ft) container.

It can be built for a variety of applications: police, coastguard, pilot and military uses, pest control, flood relief, air crash rescue and as a passenger ferry or ambulance. It can carry sufficient self-inflatable life rafts for most air crash situations.

A new military variant has controls aft to allow for a variety of weapons to be mounted forward. Recent customers include the Nigerian Police Force, Hovercraft Hire Company, Auckland Airport and ferry operators in the Maldive Islands and South America.

LIFT AND PROPULSION: The engine, tooth-belt transmission and ducted propulsor can be removed quickly for service or repair.

The 5·7-litre GM V8 automobile engine is geared to run at relatively low speed for long life and low noise. The centrifugal aluminium lift fan and ducted four-blade propulsor are also designed to run at low speed to reduce noise and provide more than adequate air flow for good payload and performance.

Open-top version of Skima

Hard top version of Skima 12 Mk 3

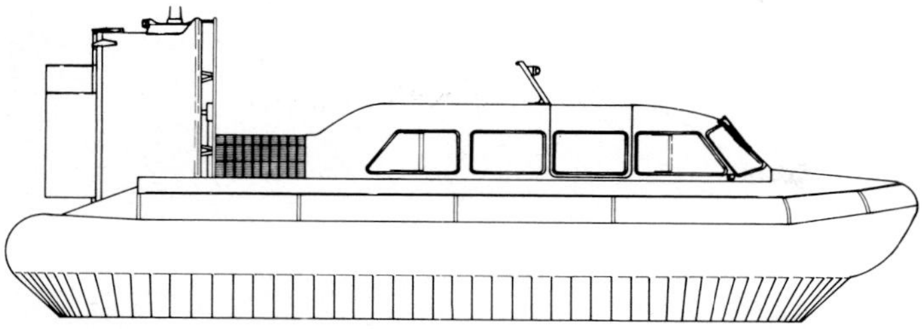

Skima 12 hard top

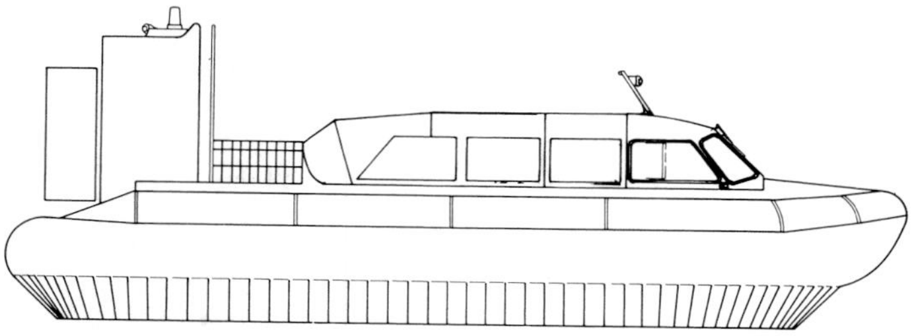

Skima 12 soft top

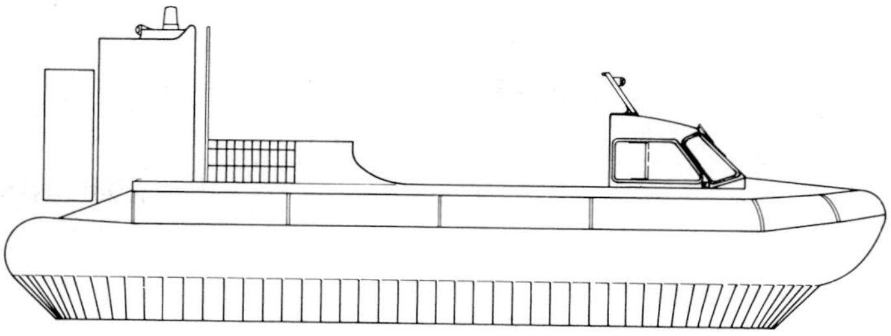

Skima 12 open top

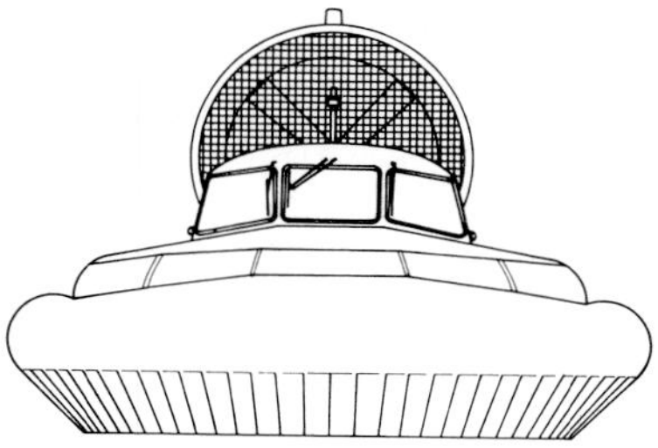

Skima 12 open top

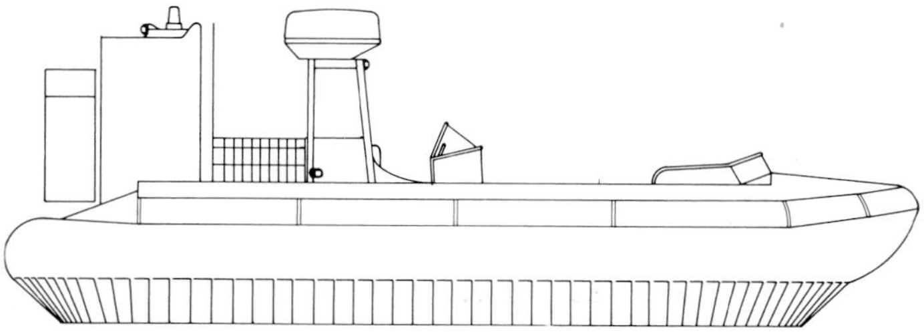

Skima 12 assault

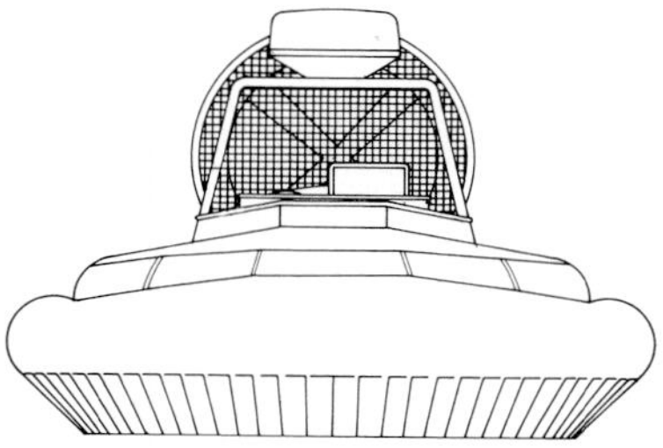

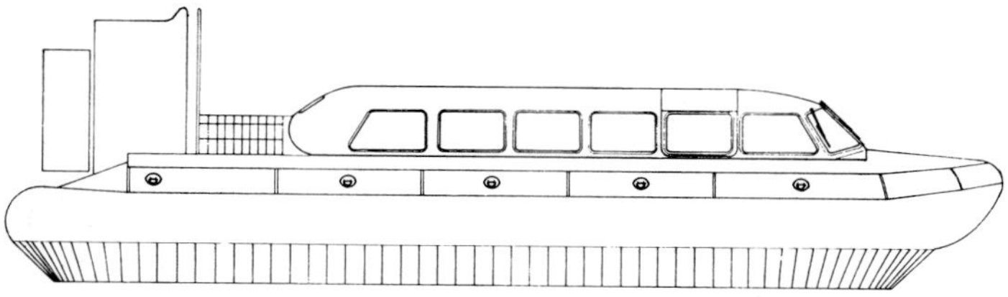

Skima 18 passenger

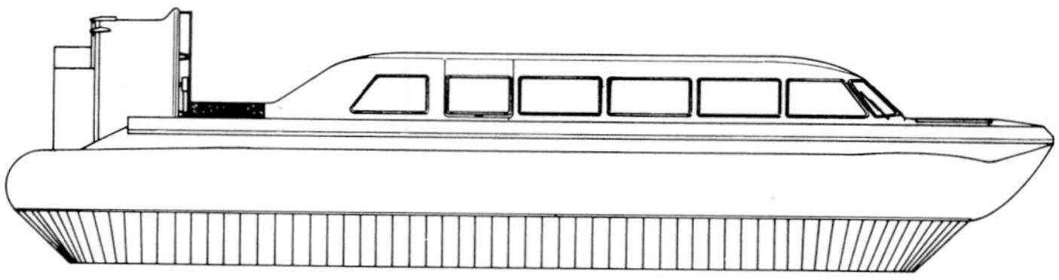

Skima 25 passenger

The low cushion pressure, together with the HDL patented skirt system, generate a low spray pattern, allowing the Skima 12 to be operated with an open cockpit if desired. Individual skirt segments may be quickly replaced when they become worn or damaged without lifting the craft.

HULL: Strong hull built in marine aluminium. It will not corrode or absorb water and if knocked will dent rather than fracture allowing repairs to be made at a convenient time. Separate compartments contain the accommodation, the engine and propulsor, the lift fan, the trim system, batteries, safety equipment and stowage areas.

ACCOMMODATION: The standard craft has accommodation for 11 to 12 passengers and a driver. There are three bucket seats with the driver in the centre at the forward end of the cockpit with a U-shaped bench seat in the cabin. The bench seat is removable to provide a 5m³ load space. Various arrangements can be specified to provide cover for the accommodation. A cruiser-type folding hood with removable sides can be fitted, or a small cockpit cover or an insulated grp hard top with gull-wing doors. Additional equipment such as radio, radar, searchlights, heating and air conditioning can be incorporated. A trailer and lifting gear are available.

SKIMA 18

Skima 18 is a 'stretched' version of the proven Skima 12 capable of carrying 18 people or 1½ tonnes. A workboat model incorporates a six- to eight-seat cabin and an open well-deck with a removable davit for lifting oil drums or similar loads aboard.

Military variant of Skima 12 with control position aft

Skima 12 with hood, operating in Oman

SKIMA 25

This is a projected 25-seat, 2-tonne hovercraft incorporating two proven Skima 12 lift/thrust power units and many other components developed for Skima 12. Alternative layouts are envisaged including versions with a 25-passenger enclosed cabin, an open loadspace with bow ramp for vehicles or freight and various rescue, coastguard patrol, firefighting and military variants.

SKIMA 25 AND 50 DIESEL

As an alternative to the Skima 25 powered by two V8 petrol engines, work has begun on the design of a 25-seater craft with a single diesel power unit and a 50-seater with twin diesels. The latter will have a well deck and bow ramp. Payload will be 4 to 5 tonnes. Various military configurations are envisaged.

Skima 12 operated in New Zealand for air-crash rescue

SLINGSBY AVIATION PLC

Kirkbymoorside, York YO6 6EZ, England
Telephone: 0751 32474
Telex: 57597
Officials:
Air Marshal Sir Peter Wykeham, *Chairman*
J S Tucker, *Managing Director*
S A Cooper
J W Davy
R Dobson
A F White, *General Manager, Hovercraft*

Formed in the 1930s as Slingsby Sailplanes, the company has grown over the years to its present size with around two hundred employees, working on a site with covered factory space of 150,000 square feet.

In the last fifteen years the company has specialised in the fabrication of composite structures and products for both marine and aviation markets. Work has been undertaken for the British Navy, Royal Air Force, Royal Marines, British Army, Airship Industries Ltd, oil companies working in the North Sea and other major companies. In addition a composite aircraft trainer, the Firefly is produced, which is fully certificated by the CAA.

The company has full CAA approval and is also approved under MoD defence standard 05-21. Work is undertaken to meet Lloyds' and other marine regulatory authorities' standards.

Over the last five years the company has identified the hovercraft as a suitable application for its composite engineering skills. An experienced hovercraft design team has been recruited to complement the existing composite design team and the company intends to establish a position in the 10- to 50-passenger seat hovercraft market.

With experience gained on the Firefly trainer the commercial department can arrange lease, charter or outright purchase to meet particular customer requirements. The existing product support department will offer substantial after-sales service for customers world wide.

The first craft in the hovercraft range, the SAH 1500, is under construction.

SAH 1500

This is capable of carrying 17 passengers or 1500kg of disposable load in the logistic support role. The design is such that rapid changes between cargo and passenger versions can be made. Diesel power and a 24-volt electrical supply have been chosen to reduce operating costs and maintenance time to a minimum. The composite structure offers high strength, good fatigue characteristics and low corrosion for long life and low maintenance.

LIFT AND PROPULSION: Integrated system. A single Deutz BF6L913c air-cooled diesel, rated at 190bhp at 2,500rpm, drives a centrifugal lift fan and a ducted propeller. The engine has resilient mounts and all machinery components are easily accessible for maintenance.

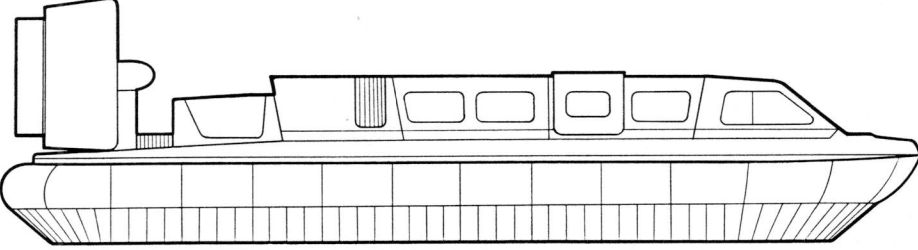

Passenger variant SAH 1500

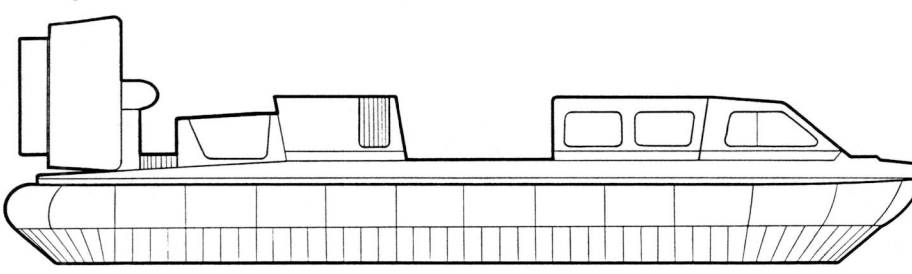

SAH 1500 supply boat

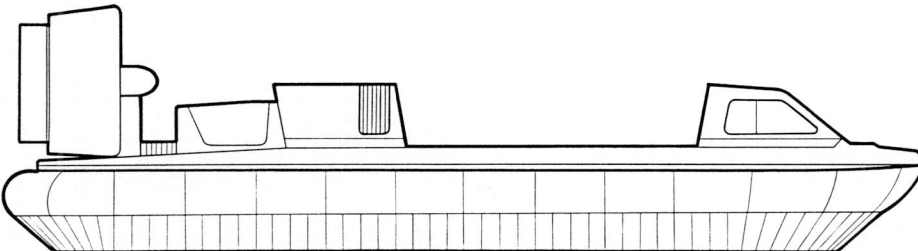

SAH 1500 logistic support craft

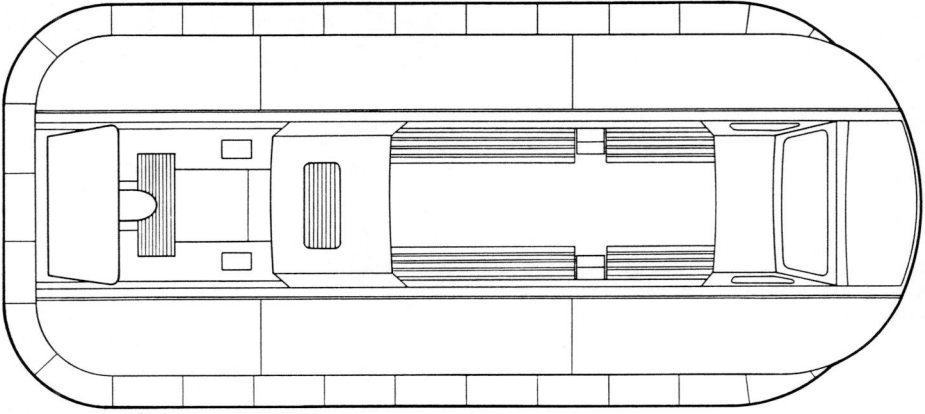

Logistic support variant of SAH 1500 showing removable bench seats

CONTROLS: Aerodynamic rudders mounted in the propeller slipstream provide directional control; similarly mounted elevators provide fore and aft trim. A fuel ballast system is incorporated to counteract adverse loading.

HULL: Heavy duty composite structure strengthened in high load areas. Heavy duty landing skids are provided. Four marine bollards on the deck form lifting rig attachments and guides for the integral jacking system. Sidedecks are rigid and enable large, bulky items to be carried outside the load space. They fold to allow transport of the craft by road vehicles or shipping within a 40-foot container.

SKIRT: Loop and segment type.

SYSTEMS: 24V electrical supply is standard. Provision is made for optional extras such as radar, air conditioning, heating, searchlights and Decca Navigator radar.

ACCOMMODATION: Seats forward for commander and passenger/navigator are in a self-contained wheelhouse. The load space is flexible in layout and two quick release composite canopies allow three options:

PASSENGER VERSION: Bench seating running fore and aft is capable of providing a total of sixteen passenger seats. Access is port and starboard through gullwing doors mounted in the canopies. A further passenger seat is available in the wheelhouse.

SUPPLY BOAT: Covered accommodation for eight passengers with open load space with capacity for up to 700kg of cargo.

LOGISTICS SUPPORT: With canopies and seats removed, integral cargo lashing rails are provided to enable a disposable load of up to 1,500kg to be carried.

In addition to the above, special purpose pods, designed to fit the load space, can carry gear such as survey equipment.

DIMENSIONS (OFF CUSHION)

EXTERNAL
Length overall: 10·6m
Beam: 4·5m
Beam (sidedecks folded): 2·4m

Height overall: 2·7m
Obstacle clearance: 0·5m
CABIN
Length: 5·35m
Beam: 1·8m
Height (inside canopies): 1·45m
WEIGHTS
Disposable load: 1,500kg
PERFORMANCE
Max speed: 36 knots
Cruise speed: 30 knots
Max operating conditions: 1m waves and 25-knot wind
Fuel capacity (max): 360 litres
Fuel consumption (max): 32 litres/h
Fuel consumption (cruise): 18 litres/h
Max endurance (cruise): 20h
Max range (cruise): 600n miles

VOSPER HOVERMARINE LIMITED

Hazel Road, Woolston, Southampton, Hampshire S02 7GB, England

Telephone: 0703 443122

Telex: 47141 VHL G

Officials:
Sir John Rix, *Chairman*
E W Furnell, *Managing Director*
B Smith, *Financial Director*
E G Tattersall, *Technical Director*
P J Hill, *Operations Director*
D P E Shepherd, *Commercial and Sales Director*
K D C Ford, *Director*
R Ducane, *Director*
R L S Blackadder, *Director*
W A Zebedee, *Director*
S J Warren, *Secretary*
N I Gee, *Technical General Manager*

Vosper Hovermarine has sold over 100 surface effect ships (SES) to more than 28 countries and is one of the most experienced designers and builders of these craft. The company is now a wholly-owned subsidiary of Vosper Limited. Vosper Hovermarine has two yards at Woolston, Southampton with an undercover area of more than 13,000m².

Recent designs are the 200 and 500 series craft. The 200 series comprise the HM 216 (16m, 60-seat) and HM 218 (18m, 84- to 103-seat) passenger ferries, 28 of which are in service with the HongKong and Yaumati Ferry Company; the HM 218 multi-role harbour craft, four of which are in service with the Port of Rotterdam Authority; the HM 218 crewboat for the oil industry; the HM 221 (21m) fireboat; the HM 221 (21m) 112- to 135-seat passenger ferry and the HM 221 (21m) crewboat. Other variants of the 200 series craft are offered for hydrographic survey, coastguard and patrol duties. The HM 216 is no longer in production. The HM 500 series comprises the Series 2 (27m, 256-seat) passenger ferry. Other variants (also 27m) are available for the following roles: naval fast strike and patrol craft, crewboat, hydrographic survey and coastguard patrol. All craft are type-approved in the UK by the Civil Aviation Authority and for operating permits issued by the Department of Transport. They have also been certified by Lloyds' Register of Shipping as a Class A1 air cushion vehicle Group 2 LMC and approved by the US Coastguard, the Marine Division of the Japanese Government, the Canadian Coastguard, the Hong Kong Marine Department, the Singapore Marine Department and Norske Veritas.

The prototype of the HM 500 series was launched in January 1982. This is a HM 527 (27m, 200-seat) passenger ferry, capable of speeds above 35 knots. The Series 2 follows the 200-seat design and seats 260. The increased size of the HM 500 series craft improves its seakeeping capability as an offshore crewboat, missile craft, and naval and coastguard patrol boat. The first four HM 527 passenger ferries have been built for Sealink Ferries of Hong Kong and were in service by the end of 1983.

Nine HM 200 series craft operated by HongKong and Yaumati Ferry Company

HM 218 with Seaspeed Transport Canada Ltd

HM 218 operated by Shell Petroleum in Singapore

HM 216 HYDROGRAPHIC SURVEY VESSEL

The HM 216 hydrographic survey vessel features a superstructure and equipment designed specifically for this role. A craft delivered to the Belgian Ministry of Public Works has been used in the River Scheldt estuary since 1972. The HM 216 is no longer in production.

POWERPLANTS

Lift: One 206bhp Cummins V555M marine diesel

Propulsion: Two 445bhp General Motors Detroit Diesel Allison 8V92TI marine diesels

DIMENSIONS

Length overall: 15·24m (50ft)

Beam overall: 5·8m (19ft)

Height overall: 4·1m (13ft 4in)

Draught floating, loaded: 1·49m (4ft 10in)
  on cushion, loaded: 0·87m (2ft 10in)

Bridge/cabin length: 4·3m (14ft)
  beam: 4·3m (14ft)
  height: 2m (6ft 6in)

WEIGHTS

Standard gross: 19,300kg (42,500lb)

Normal disposable payload: 5,600kg (12,300lb)

PERFORMANCE

Cruising speed: 35 knots

Standard range at cruising speed: 250n miles

HM 218 FERRY

The HM 218 ferry represents a 40 per cent improvement in payload over the earlier HM 216 ferry for only a 15 per cent increase in operating costs. It can carry 84 to 103 passengers at cruising speeds of up to 35 knots. An extended bow skirt permits passenger operations in up to 1·5m (5ft) waves. A computerised roll stabilisation system can be fitted to customer order.

The first HM 218 ferry went into service in 1976. A major operator of the type is the Hong-Kong and Yaumati Ferry Company, which has 28 in commuter service within Hong Kong and on an 80n mile international route to Kwang-Chow (Canton) in the People's Republic of China. Other HM 218 ferries operate in Brazil, Canada, the People's Republic of China, Indonesia, Japan, Kuwait, Malaysia, Nigeria, Portugal, Singapore and Venezuela.

LIFT AND PROPULSION: Two General Motors Detroit Diesel Allison 8V92TI V, eight-cylinder marine diesels, each developing 445bhp at 2,300rpm, provide propulsive power. A single Cummins 90-degree V, eight-cylinder V555M marine diesel rated at 206bhp at 2,800rpm drives the 0·6m (24in) diameter centrifugal lift fans.

The lift engine drives two pairs of forward fans through toothed belts and one aft fan through a hydraulic system. Air for the forward fans is drawn through inlets at each forward cabin quarter and in the base of the wheelhouse structure. Air for the aft fan is drawn through an inlet in the rear companionway.

The two propulsion engines each drive a 0·45m (18in) diameter aluminium bronze three-bladed propeller through a reversing gearbox and 1:1 ratio vee box. Fuel is carried in stainless steel tanks, two beneath the aft companionway and one under the main lift fans. Electrical power for instruments, radio, radar, lighting and air conditioning is supplied by ac/dc alternators driven by the lift and propulsion engines.

CONTROLS: Craft direction is by twin balanced stainless steel rudders operated hydraulically by a steering wheel. Additional control is by differential use of the water propellers.

HULL: Built in grp mouldings and various types of sandwich panels. The mouldings consist of the main deck, deck and superstructure centre section, forward intakes and wheelhouse, inner sidelinings, aft companionway and engine bay cowlings. The first three are joined by a system of transverse frames. The floor panels are bonded to the frames and to the longitudinal intercoastal members.

The outer shell of the hull, including the bottom between the sidewalls and under the bow, is moulded in one piece, gunwale to gunwale. The hull moulding incorporates local thickening of the laminate to meet the design load require-

One of 28 HM 218s operated by Hong Kong and Yamauti Ferry Company

ments and to facilitate the incorporation of fittings and apertures. Frames and bulkheads are manufactured from sandwich panels of expanded pvc foam covered with grp. All frames and bulkheads are laminated into the hull.

ACCOMMODATION: The HM 218 ferry can be operated by a crew of two. Controls are in an elevated wheelhouse, with a 360-degree view, at the forward end of the passenger saloon. The saloon can be fitted out with up to 84 aircraft-type seats or 92 to 103 utility seats. These are normally arranged three abreast in banks of three. Toilet and baggage compartments are located aft. Up to six luggage containers, able to hold a total of 1,500kg (3,307lb), may be carried on the saloon roof.

Passenger access to the saloon is via a double width door aft. Crew and emergency access is forward via two hatch doors, one on each side of the wheelhouse. Knock-out emergency windows are fitted in the passenger saloon. Safety equipment includes life rafts, life jackets under the seats, fire detectors and extinguishers.

SKIRTS: The extended bow skirt consists of a single loop extending from the bow chine to a line just below the base of the main hull. 32 segments are attached to the main loop and connected to the underside of the hull by terylene ropes. An inner loop overlaps the fan volute outlet and causes the bow skirt to inflate.

The rear seal consists of a membrane and loop which is suspended front and rear by transverse continuous sheets of material. It is inflated to a

pressure slightly above that of the cushion by the rear fan in the starboard propulsion engine room.

DIMENSIONS

Length overall: 18·29m (60ft)

Beam overall: 6·1m (20ft)

Height overall: 4·88m (16ft)

Draught floating, loaded: 1·72m (5ft 6in)
  on cushion, loaded: 1·07m (3ft 5in)

Saloon length: 9·75m (32ft)
  beam: 4·88m (16ft)
  height: 1·93m (6ft 4in)

WEIGHTS

Standard gross: 27,900kg (61,520lb)

Normal disposable payload: 7,154kg (15,775lb)

Normal fuel capacity: 1,455 litres (320 imperial gallons)

PERFORMANCE

Cruising speed: 34 knots

Acceleration 0-30 knots: 45 seconds

Standard range at cruising speed: 200n miles

Standard endurance at cruising speed: 4 hours

HM 218 CREWBOAT

Since 1979 three HM 218 crewboats have been operating in Venezuela, transporting crew to-and-from oil rigs on Lake Maracaibo. Five more have been delivered to Shell (Eastern) in Singapore. The crewboat is based on the HM 218 passenger ferry but has a substantially reinforced hull to withstand the buffeting which the craft receives alongside offshore installations.

A bow-loading technique has been developed; rollers are fitted to the bow allowing the craft to

HM 218 for Touristic Enterprises Co, Kuwait

HM 218 multi-role harbour craft

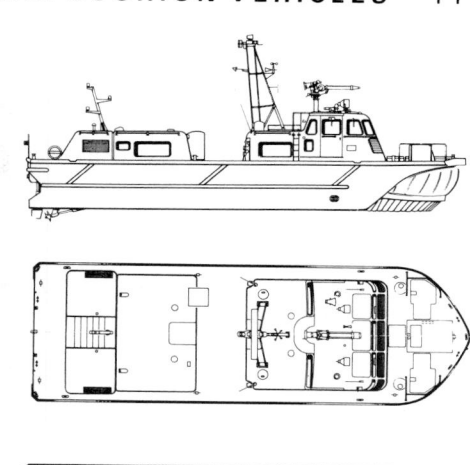

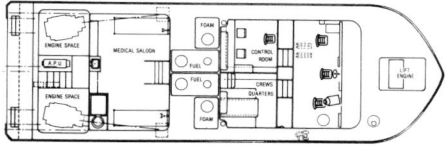

HM 218 multi-role harbour craft

Endurance (max continuous power, half load): 200n miles

HM 218 MULTI-ROLE HARBOUR CRAFT

Four HM 218 multi-role harbour craft were delivered to the Port of Rotterdam Authority in 1979-80. The design retains the standard HM 218 passenger ferry hull fitted with two super-structure modules to house port-monitoring and emergency-service equipment.

LIFT AND PROPULSION: Two General Motors 8V-92TI marine diesels drive fixed pitch propellers through reversing gearboxes and V drive gearboxes. The lift engine, which doubles as a pump engine for firefighting duties, is a Cummins V504M marine diesel. Engine transmission incorporates clutches for on-cushion lift, via four mechanically-driven and one hydraulically-driven centrifugal fans, or fire pump drive. Propulsion, lift and pumping machinery are controlled remotely from the wheelhouse. Engines are electrically started.

ACCOMMODATION: Utility standard accommodation for crew of commander, navigator, fire-control officer, medical attendant and one seaman. Crew's mess cabin with bunk and galley area is forward and medical room and toilet are aft. There are fan-assisted heaters.

EQUIPMENT: Firefighting equipment capable of delivering seawater, aspirated protein foam, high-pressure fog and dry powder. A remote control monitor with foam and seawater nozzles has a range of 46m (151ft) and flow rate of 2,270 litres/minute (500 gallons/minute) for water or water/foam mix. The two deck hydrants can be supplied with water or water/foam mix. Each has four low-pressure outlets and one high-pressure outlet for fog generation.

HM 218 multi-role harbour craft

approach installations and transfer crew over the bow. This is safer than the conventional stern transfer system as the captain can view the whole operation.

Grp luggage containers may be fitted above the superstructure for extra baggage. An alternative version of the HM 218 crewboat accommodates 25 passengers, with a well deck for three tonnes of cargo.

LIFT AND PROPULSION: Two General Motors 8V-92TI marine diesels driving fixed pitch propellers through Capitol reversing gear-boxes and BPM V-drive gearboxes. Lift is by one Cummins V555M marine diesel driving two pairs of forward fans through toothed belts and one aft fan through a hydraulic system.

HULL: Shell mouldings, sub-mouldings, frames, bulkheads and major attachments in grp, using polyester resins and pvc foam. Construction is to Lloyds' survey requirements.

ACCOMMODATION: Air-conditioned accommodation for up to 99 passengers in airline-type seats. Toilet compartment in stern.

DIMENSIONS
Length overall: 18·29m (60ft)
Beam overall: 6·1m (20ft)
Height (underside of propeller to top of mast light): 7·4m (24ft 4in)

Draught off cushion: 1·72m (5ft 8in)
  on cushion: 1·07m (3ft 6in)
PERFORMANCE
Max speed (fully loaded, calm water): 34 knots

HM 221 firefighting craft

Hull and superstructure are protected by a waterskirt drenching system. Other ancillary equipment includes wind speed and direction meters, explosive gas detection apparatus, water temperature monitoring and compressed air breathing equipment. For emergencies requiring medical aid, they are equipped with racks for four stretchers, oxygen respiratory equipment and a resuscitation unit.

The HM 218 port patrol boat can be operated on patrol by the commander and a navigating officer. For full duties, there are manning positions for a fire officer, traffic control officer and a working crew of four. Dimensions and powerplants are similar to the HM 218 ferry.

FENDERING: Fitted at the gunwale with three diagonals from gunwale level to below the waterline around both sidewalls and transom.

DIMENSIONS
Length overall: 18·29m (60ft)
Beam overall: 6·1m (20ft)
Height (including radar, mast, above water, off cushion): 6·5m (21ft 4in)
Draught off cushion: 1·52m (5ft)
  on cushion: 0·91m (3ft)
LOGISTICS
Fresh water storage: 91 litres (20 gallons)
Fuel storage: 2,500 litres (550 gallons)
Firefighting protein foam storage: 2,545 litres (559·9 gallons)
PERFORMANCE
FULLY LOADED, CALM WATER
Max speed: 30 knots
Endurance (max speed): 280n miles

HM 218 MEDICRAFT

A variant based on the HM 218 hull, the HM 218 medicraft is available as a rapid-intervention vessel able to provide emergency medical facilities in areas where local conditions necessitate approach by water. The standard design offers an examination/treatment clinic for medical or dental work, fitted out with an operating table and a comprehensive range of equipment.

HM 221 FIREFIGHTING CRAFT

Two HM 221 firefighting craft were ordered by the city of Tacoma, Washington, USA in 1978. The first of these was delivered in May 1982 and the second late in 1982. They are fitted with a comprehensive range of firefighting, rescue, navigation and communications equipment.

LIFT AND PROPULSION: Two General Motors 8V-92TI marine diesels drive fixed pitch propellers via direct-drive reversing gearboxes and V-drive gearboxes. Lift power is from one General Motors 6V 92TI marine diesel which is also used as a pump engine. A second pump engine is provided by a General Motors 6V-92TI marine diesel. Propulsion, lift and pumping machinery is controlled from the wheelhouse. All engines electrically started.

ACCOMMODATION: Utility-standard crew accommodation comprises six-berth cabin with cooker, sink and toilet compartment.

EQUIPMENT: Two remotely-controlled

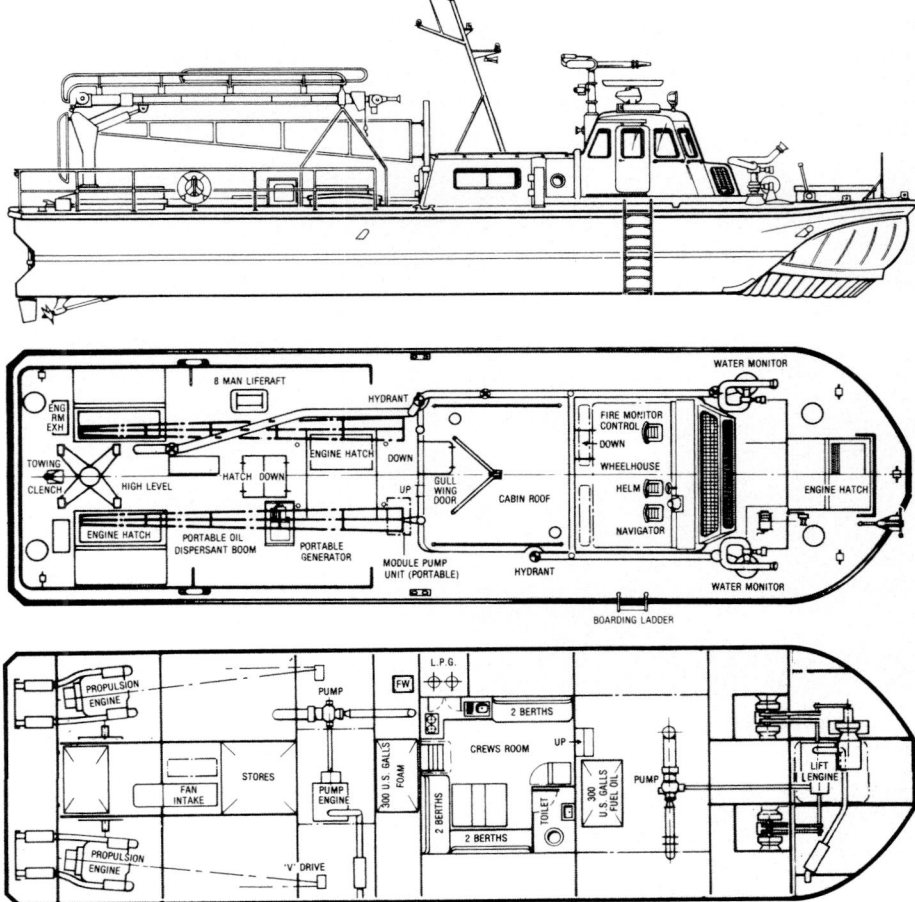

HM 221 firefighting craft

bow-mounted monitors each of 9,400 litres/minute water flow rate; one wheelhouse-mounted monitor of 20,800 litres/minute water flow rate; two under-wharf monitors of 9,400 litres/minute water flow rate and one remotely-controlled 5,600 litres/minute foam/water monitor fitted to the telescopic end of a high-level (10·5m) ladder which doubles as a crane. The monitors are remotely controlled for rotation and elevation from a console in the wheelhouse. The ladder is controlled from its base. All fire monitors, except the wheelhouse monitor, can be controlled from a straight stream to 90-degree fog.

FENDERING: Hardwood fendering fitted to the gunwale.

DIMENSIONS
Length overall: 20·9m (68ft 7in)
Beam overall: 6·1m (20ft)
Height above water, off cushion: 6·3m (20ft 9in)
Draught off cushion: 1·55m (5ft 1in)
  on cushion: 1·1m (3ft 8in)

LOGISTICS
Fresh water storage: 90 litres (19·7 gallons)
Fuel storage: 2,950 litres (649 gallons)
Allowance for miscellaneous firefighting equipment: 500kg
Firefighting AFFF foam: 1,136 litres (249·9 gallons)
PERFORMANCE
FULLY LOADED, CALM SEA
Max speed: 30 knots
Endurance, max speed: 120n miles, including 5½ hours continuous pumping at rated capacity, plus a fuel allowance of 426 litres for station-keeping

HM 221 CREWBOAT

The HM 221 crewboat is based on the 21-metre HM 221 fireboat hull. Designed for offshore oil industry, it has a flat cargo-deck area aft. Rollers are fitted to the bow for passenger transfer.

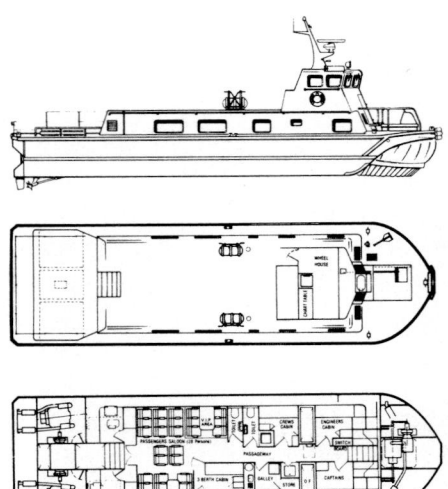

HM 221 crewboat for 28 passengers

HM 221 crewboat operated by Gray MacKenzie in Arabian Gulf

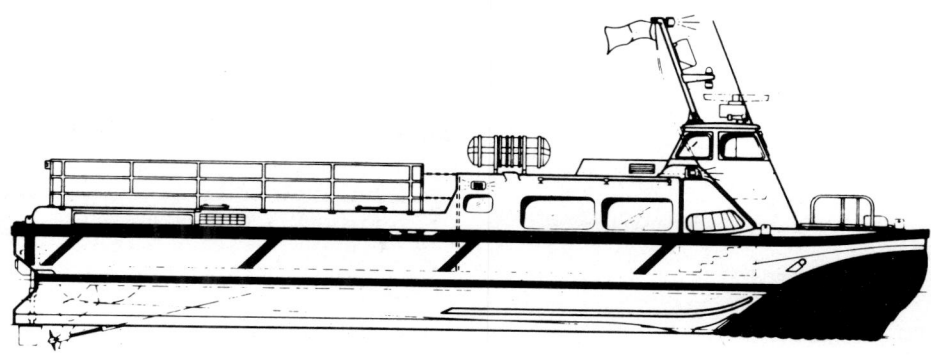

LIFT AND PROPULSION: Two 510bhp General Motors 8V-92 MTI marine diesels, driving fixed pitch propellers through reversing gearboxes and V-drive gearboxes, provide the main propulsion. Lift power is provided by one 356bhp General Motors 6V 92 MTI marine diesel. The lift and propulsion engines are controlled from the wheelhouse. The engines are electrically started. Fuel capacity is 3·4 tonnes (900 imperial gallons).

ACCOMMODATION: Air-conditioned accommodation for 28 passengers and crew. Crew accommodation comprises cabins for captain, engineer and crew, galley and two toilets.

DIMENSIONS
Length overall: 21·4m (70ft 3in)
Beam overall: 6·1m (20ft 1in)
Height (wheelhouse top): 5·35m (17ft 7in)
Draught off cushion: 1·75m (5ft 9in)
on cushion: 1·06m (3ft 6in)

LOGISTICS
Fresh water storage: 1·35 tonnes
Fuel storage: 3·4 tonnes (900 imperial gallons)

PERFORMANCE
FULLY LOADED, CALM CONDITIONS
Max speed: 30 knots
Endurance: 400n miles

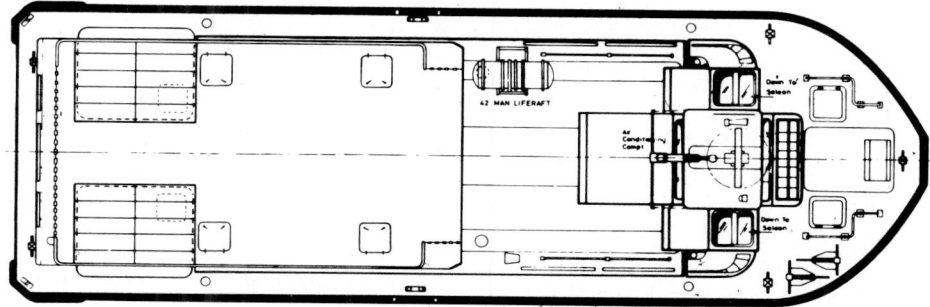

HM 221 PASSENGER FERRY

Based on the HM 221 (21-metre) hull, this new variant will seat 112 to 135 passengers depending on route requirements. It has a continuous speed in excess of 31 knots in calm conditions and an endurance of 140n miles. The structure is designed to Lloyds' Register Classification A1, Air Cushion Vehicle, Group 2 LMC.

Firefighting and crewboats based on this hull are already in service and a medical treatment variant is available.

LIFT AND PROPULSION: Power for the lift system is provided by a single Cummins VT-555BC marine diesel with a continuous rating of 270bhp at 2,800rpm. Propulsive power is supplied by two General Motors 8V 92 T1 marine diesels, each rated at 490bhp at 2,300rpm continuous. Lift and propulsion systems are controlled from the wheelhouse. Fuel capacity is 1,450 litres when 95 per cent full.

HULL: Single shell grp mouldings, with sub-mouldings, frames, bulkheads and other attachments bonded together.

ACCOMMODATION: Within the saloon of the 112-seat variant there are two toilet compartments, each with a WC and washbasin. Seats have a depth of 419mm, breadth of 430mm and a seat pitch of 457mm. Aisle width is a minimum of 457mm. Saloon and wheelhouse are air-conditioned. The air-conditioning plant is belt driven off the lift engine.

CONTROLS: Power assisted manual hydraulic system operating twin rudders with a hard over angle of 30°-0-30° when set with a zero rudder divergence. Power assisted hydraulic pump mechanically operated from the lift engines.

SYSTEMS ELECTRICAL
SYSTEM VOLTAGE: 24V dc nominal negative earth.

GENERATION/CHARGING EQUIPMENT: Two propulsion engine driven ac/dc alternators rated at 27·5V, 100A. One lift engine driven ac/dc alternator rated at 27·5V, 100A.

BATTERIES: Two 24V lead acid batteries, each with sufficient capacity to provide six starts for each engine.

LIGHTING
Normal: 18watt fluorescent tubes supplied from 24-volt dc system via invertors.
Emergency: 24-volt incandescent fittings sited throughout craft.

COMMUNICATIONS: PA system between wheelhouse and passenger saloon.
External: one VHF(FM) Sailor RT146/C401 radio telephone, frequency range 155·4 to 162·6mHz. Output 25/1 watt.

NAVIGATION: One Marinex Meteor transmitting magnetic compass. One emergency magnetic compass, Smith's type E2B. One Firebell Blipper radar reflector on mast.

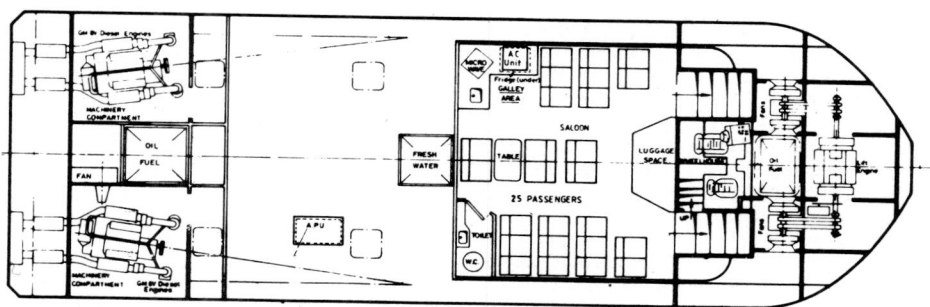

HM 218 crewboat for 25 passengers

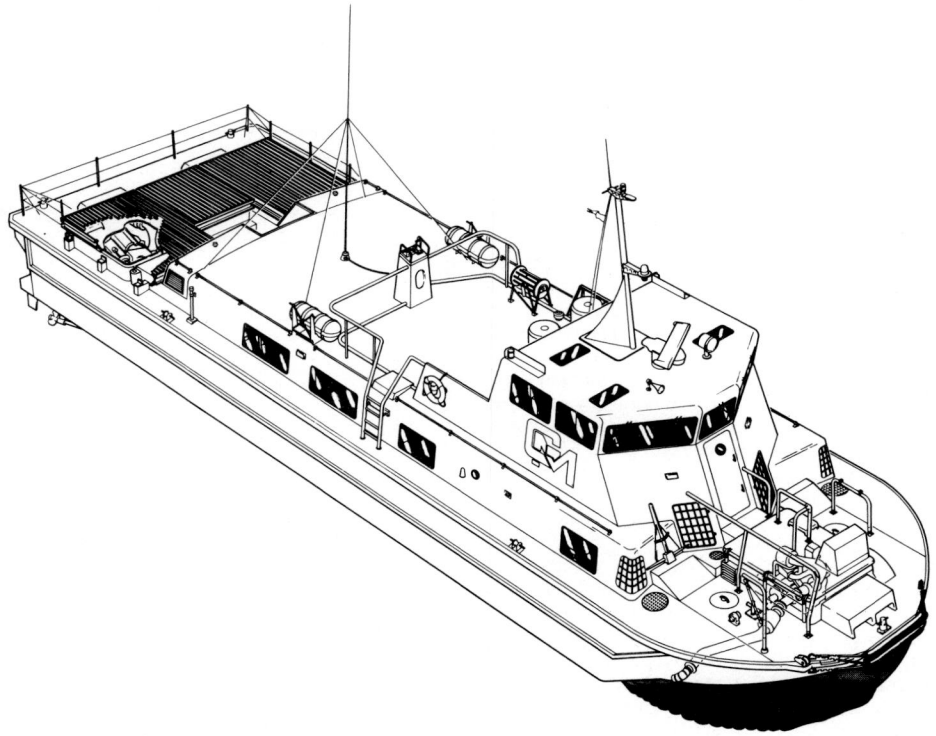

HM 221 crewboat

RADAR: One Furono relative motion radar.
NIGHT VISION: Vistar 301, comprising camera, main control and slave display.
CONTAINERS: Four grp luggage containers.
HEATING: Recirculating warm air heating system employing propulsion engine hot coolant.
BOW LOADING: Flush foredeck, guardrails

and bow fenders arranged for bow loading of passengers.
DIMENSIONS
Length overall: 21·4m
Beam overall: 6·1m
Height (underside of propeller to top of mast anchor light): 7·4m

Draught off cushion: 1·75m
  on cushion, aft, loaded: 1·07m
WEIGHTS
Passengers, 112 × 67kg: 7,504kg
Baggage, 112 × 2kg: 224kg
Crew, 3 × 67kg: 201kg
Oil fuel: 1,100kg
Payload: 9,029kg
PERFORMANCE
Cruising speed, calm conditions: in excess of 31 knots
Endurance: 140n miles

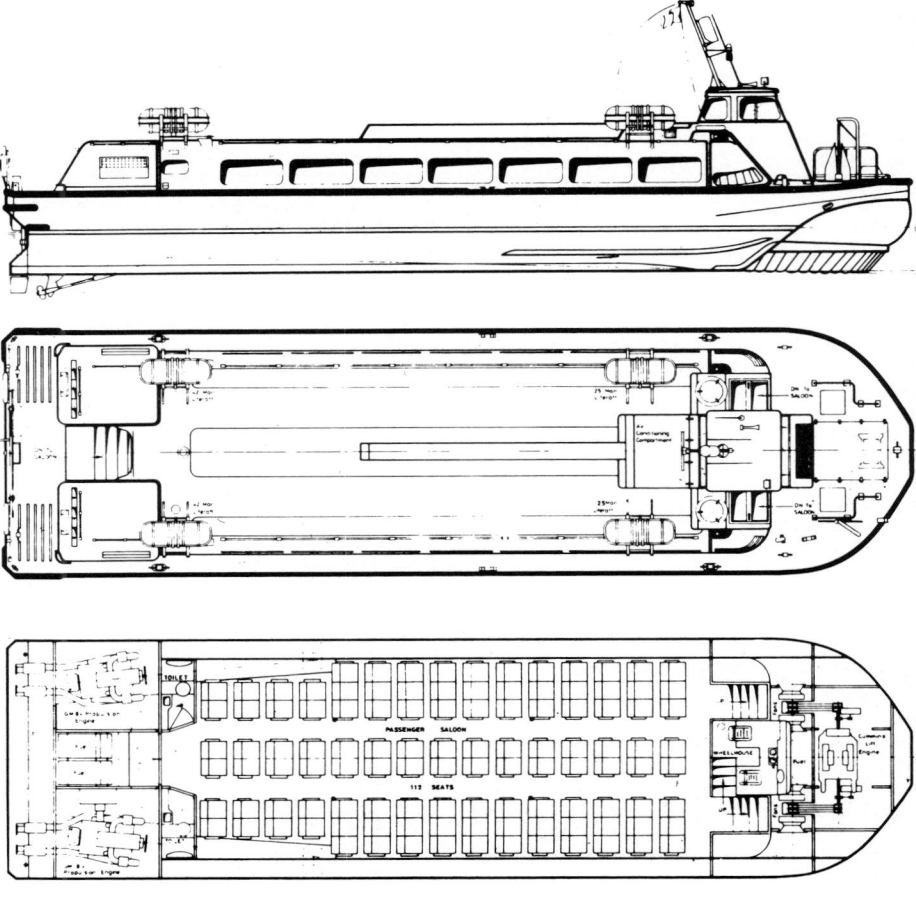

HM 527 FERRY

The prototype HM 527 was launched in January 1982. It carries 200 passengers at a cruising speed of 36 knots and has been designed to operate on coastal and inland waters in wave heights of up to 3m (9ft 10in) with a payload of 21,000kg (20·7 tons). Normal range is 200n miles. A computerised roll stabilisation system is fitted as standard. The first four craft, ordered by Sealink Ferries Limited, were delivered before the end of 1983. Other designs based on the HM 527 hull include a hydrographic survey vessel and all-passenger crewboats and mixed payload supply boats for the offshore oil industry.

LIFT AND PROPULSION: The marine diesels are in two amidships engine rooms. Both accommodate one lift engine, one propulsion engine and one auxiliary power unit. The lift engines are General Motors Detroit Diesel Allison 8V92TIs rated at 332kW at 2,300rpm. Each drives a lift fan, via a gearbox, to provide plenum air and, via a hydraulic pump and hydraulic motors, two secondary fans for skirt inflation. The propulsion engines are MTU 12V 396 TB83 diesels rated at 1,050kW at 1,800rpm. Each incorporates a ZF BW 455 reverse-reduction gearbox and drives a single three-bladed propeller via transmission shafting inclined at 13 degrees. The outward rotating propellers operate at up to 900rpm. Two Perkins 4·236M marine diesels rated at 27·2kW, 50Hz, 220V drive the ac alternators and compressors for the air-conditioning system.

Fuel is carried in two tanks in the transom bay, in-line athwartships. Fuel capacity is 4·2 tonnes. Separate salt-water ballast tanks are provided with a capacity of 5 tonnes.

CONTROLS: Vessel heading is controlled by power-operated twin water rudders. Additional control is provided by differential use of the propellers. An automatic roll-stabilisation system operates through inclined independent rudders.

HULL: Single shell grp moulding with sub-moulding, frames, bulkheads and cabin sole panels bonded together. Materials used include expanded pvc foam, glass fibre, polyester resins, wood and aluminium alloy.

ACCOMMODATION: The bridge normally accommodates the commander, navigator and engineer. Passenger access is via doors port and starboard in the forward saloon and rearward double door for aft saloon. Emergency exits are located in both saloons. Four toilet/washbasin units are provided plus luggage space. Eight luggage containers can be mounted on the roof of the craft. Safety equipment includes life rafts, inflatable life jackets, lifebuoys and line-throwing apparatus.

SKIRTS: Main plenum chamber receives air from two lift fans via ducts located amidships port and starboard. Bow and stern skirts receive air from port and starboard fans, driven hydraulically by lift engine gearbox pumps, via ducts forming part of the superstructure.

Bow skirt is made up of two tailored neoprene/nylon loops suspended in 180-degree arcs sidewall to sidewall and joined at their lower edges to form an irregularly shaped inflatable compartment. When inflated, the loops support 20 single fabric segments, attached at the loop joint line, and absorb wave impact shock to a degree. Four additional corner segments are attached on each side by ropes and shackles.

Three similar tailored loops are suspended under the stern. These are joined to form a single inflatable compartment.

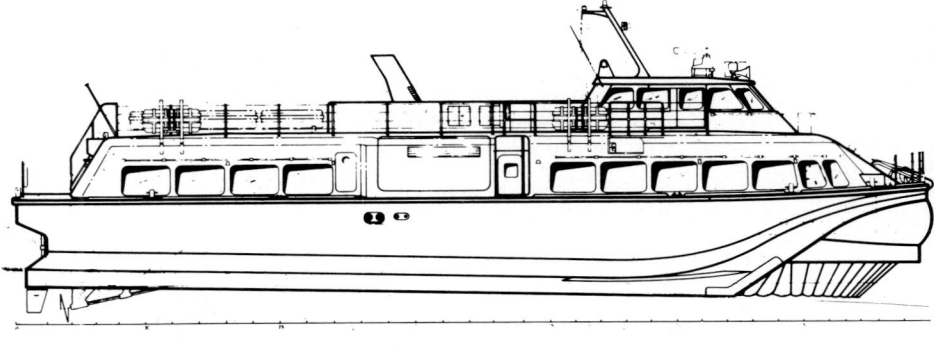

HM 221 fast ferry

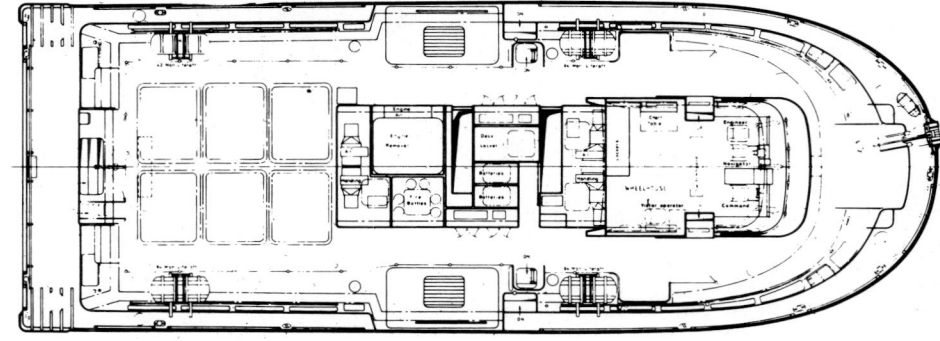

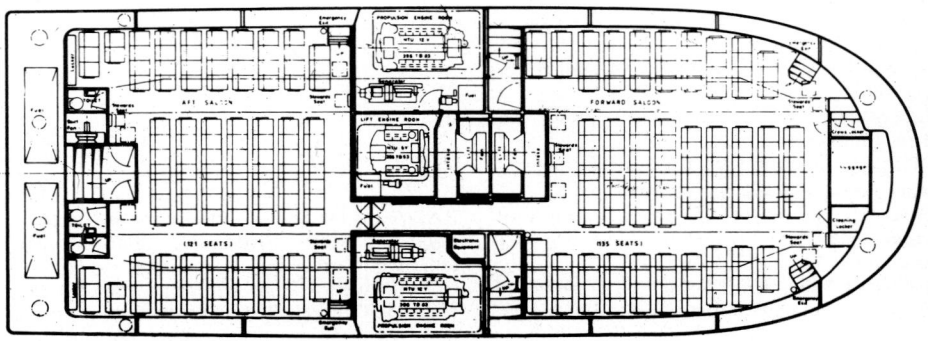

HM 527 Series 2 passenger ferry

DIMENSIONS
Length overall: 27·2m (89ft 3in)
Beam overall: 10·2m (33ft 5in)
Height overall: 4·9m (16ft)
Draught floating, loaded: 2·55m (8ft 4in)
on cushion, loaded: 1·7m (5ft 6in)
Standard passenger capacity, forward saloon: 84
aft saloon: 116
WEIGHTS
Max gross: 87,000kg

HM 527 SERIES 2 PASSENGER FERRY

The refinements incorporated into this new production variant of the HM 527 result from experience gained with the Series 1 craft. The Series 2 design maintains the same performance levels, with increased seating capacity. It can carry up to 260 passengers with hand baggage. A single 332kW (445bhp) diesel lift engine is fitted.
LIFT AND PROPULSION: Power is supplied by three marine diesels amidship in separate engine rooms in-line athwartships. The two outer engine rooms each accommodate one propulsion engine and one auxiliary power unit, the central engine room housing the lift engine. Lift is provided by a 550kW MTU 6V 396TB53 driving, via a flexible coupling and Cardan shaft, two 1·22m (48in) diameter HEBA B centrifugal fans and, via a hydrostatic system, a secondary fan for aft skirt inflation. The propulsion engines are MTU 12V 396TB83 diesels rated at 1,150kW at 1,800rpm continuous. Each incorporates a ZF BW 455 reverse-reduction gearbox and drives a single three-bladed propeller via transmission shafting inclined at 13 degrees. The outward rotating propellers operate at up to 900rpm. Fuel is carried in two tanks in the transom bay and fuel capacity is 4·2 tonnes. Machinery is monitored by a programmable controller and visual display.
CONTROLS: Lift and propulsion machinery controls in the wheelhouse meet Lloyds' requirements for unmanned machinery spaces. All diesel engines are electrically started. A plug-in portable unit provides bridge wing control of the propulsion gearbox clutches. Craft heading is by power-operated twin water rudders with a hard-over angle of 26°-0-26° when set with a zero rudder divergence. Additional control is by differential use of the propellers. Provision is made for emergency control from the aft deck. A Marconi Avionics automatic roll-stabilisation system operates through inclined independent rudders.
HULL: Grp structure comprising shell mouldings, sub-mouldings, frames, bulkheads and major attachments built from glass fibre weaves and mats using polyester resin matrix. Frame and bulkhead cores are end grain balsa or polyvinyl chloride foam.
ACCOMMODATION: Seats for 260 passen-

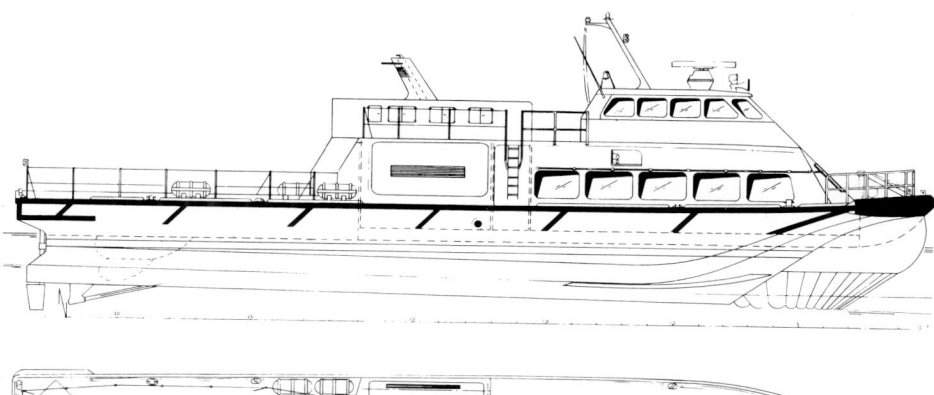

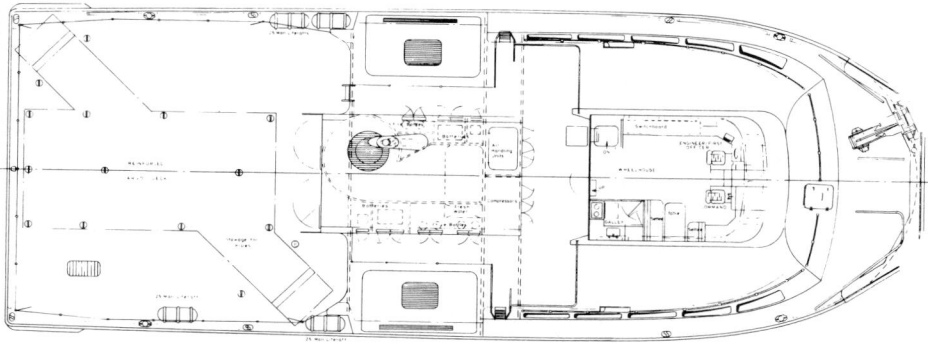

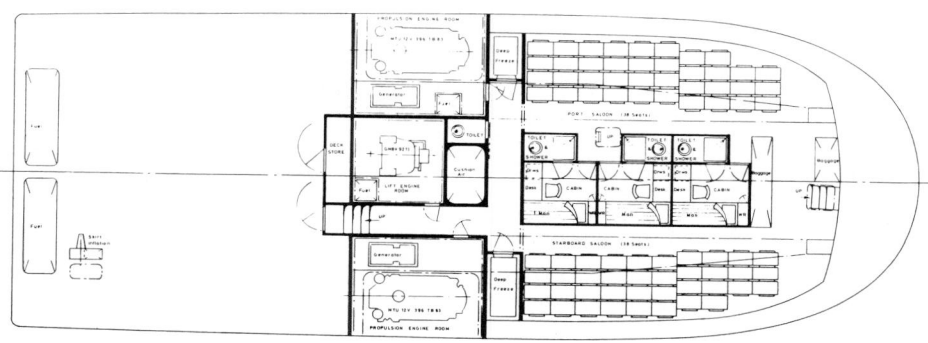

HM 527 Series 2 crewboat/offshore supply vessel

gers in two saloons, forward and aft. Passenger access via doors, port and starboard, aft of forward saloon and double door at rear of aft saloon. Two emergency exits in both saloons. Bridge normally accommodates commander and navigator/engineer. Each passenger saloon has three hinging seats with safety belts for stewards/stewardesses. Safety equipment includes life rafts, inflatable life jackets, lifebuoys and line-throwing apparatus.

VENTILATION: Fresh air ventilation for passenger saloons, wheelhouse and toilet.
HEATING: Warm air heating.
FIRE SAFETY: Engine rooms: fire detection and extinguishing systems. Wheelhouse: two CO_2 portable fire extinguishers. Passenger areas: four AFFF portable fire extinguishers.
SYSTEMS, ELECTRICAL: Ship's service electrical plant comprises two diesel-driven, brushless, air-cooled ac generators rated at 45kVA, 36kW at 0·8 power factor lagging. Each machine can supply the normal running load. Medium voltage supply is 220 volts, 3-phase, 50Hz, 3 wire. Supply for engine starting, essential services and exit point illumination is provided by 24-volt batteries.

COMMUNICATIONS
INTERNAL: Two-way amplified speech between wheelhouse, navigation positions, machinery compartments and steward's positions. Public address system.
EXTERNAL: One vhf (fm) radio telephone Type 145. Frequency range 155 to 163·2 MHz. Power output 25/1 watt. One Marconi Marine Survivor 3 emergency portable radio.
NAVIGATION
RADAR: Racal Decca RM 1216 relative motion radar with combined antenna/transceiver unit and one 12-inch master and one 9-inch slave displays.
COMPASS: Marinex transmitting magnetic compass with tape repeater and input to navigation radar displays. Smiths Type E2B emergency compass.
LOG: Chernikeeff Aquacatch EM Log with transducer and master unit.
DIMENSIONS
Length overall: 27·2m (89ft 3in)
Beam overall: 10·2m (33ft 5in)

First of four HM 527s delivered to Sealink Ferries Limited, Hong Kong

Height (wheelhouse top): 4·9m (16ft)
Draught off cushion: 2·7m (8ft 10in)
  on cushion: 1·7m (5ft 7in)
WEIGHTS
Oil fuel: 3,500kg (7,718lb)
Passengers and baggage, 256 × 75kg (165lb):
  19,200kg (42,240lb)
Crew, 7 × 75kg: 525kg (1,158lb)
Fresh water: 180kg (396lb)
Total payload: 23,405kg (51,512lb)
PERFORMANCE
Max speed (fully loaded, zero wave height, zero
  wind speed): 36 knots
Speed, 85% continuous power: 28·5 knots
Endurance (at 85% continuous power and one
  generator running at 70% rated load): 300n
  miles

HM 527 SERIES 2 CREWBOAT

Success with the HM 218 crewboats in Venezuela has led to the HM 527 crewboat. Its larger
size will improve its seakeeping capabilities,
extend the operational capability of SES crewboats and provide greater capacity and endurance. Fully loaded, the craft can carry 76 passengers, 3 crew members, up to 7 tonnes of cargo
(including 40ft long pipes) and fuel for a range of
250 nautical miles at 34 knots.
LIFT AND PROPULSION: Two MTU 12V 396
TB83 marine diesels, each rated at 1,050kW at
1,800rpm continuous, drive fixed-pitch propellers through ZF BW 455 reverse reduction gearboxes. Lift power is provided by one MTU 6V
396TB53 diesel rated at 525 kW at 1,800rpm.
Lift and propulsion machinery are controlled
from the wheelhouse. All diesel engines are electrically started.
HULL: Structure of shell mouldings, sub-
mouldings, frames, bulkheads and major attachments in grp, using a polyester resins and pvc
matrix. Frame and bulkhead cores in end grain
balsa or polyvinyl chloride (pvc) foam.
Wheelhouse in marine-aluminium alloy.
ACCOMMODATION: Port and starboard
saloons on main deck beneath wheelhouse each
seat 38 passengers. Craft is designed for bow
loading and access is via a forward door. Baggage
stowage at forward end of saloon. Single toilet
equipped with wc and washbasin. Three crew
cabins beneath wheelhouse, each with bunk,
wardrobe, desk and chair, shower, toilet and folding washbasin. Wheelhouse contains galley with
cooker, basin and refrigerator, and mess area
with table and bench seats. Air-conditioned passenger saloons, wheelhouse and crew accommodation.
AFT DECK: Clear deck space aft, 9m wide × 8m
long (29ft 6in × 26ft 3in), for cargo. Centre
section, 4m wide × 8m long (13ft 1in × 26ft 3in),
reinforced for loads up to 1 tonne/m² and up to 7
tonnes total cargo load. Diagonal area, 1·6m
wide × 21·1m long (5ft 3in × 69ft 2in), for pipes.
Deck protected against chafe and provided with
cargo docking points.
CONTROLS: Electro-hydraulic proportional
power steering operating twin rudders with a
hard-over angle of 26°-0-26° when set with zero
rudder divergence. Control from steering position in wheelhouse and emergency control sta-
tion on aft deck.
FENDERING: Around gunwale. Fendering
around bow reinforced to permit bow docking.
DIMENSIONS
Length overall: 27·2m (89ft 3in)
Beam overall: 10·2m (33ft 5in)
Height (wheelhouse): 4·9 m (6ft)
Draught off cushion: 2·7 m (8ft 10in)
  on cushion: 1·7 m (5ft 7in)
WEIGHTS
Oil fuel required for endurance: 3,700kg
  (8,157lb)
Passengers and baggage, 76 × 75kg: 5,700kg
  (12,566lb)
Crew, 3 × 75kg: 225kg (496lb)
Fresh water: 280kg (617lb)
Cargo: 7,000kg (15,432lb)
Refrigerated cargo: 900kg (1,984lb)
Crew provisions: 150kg (330lb)
Total payload: 17,955kg (39,583lb)

HM 527 fast patrol craft

PERFORMANCE
Max speed (fully loaded, zero wave height, zero
  wind speed, specified propulsion engine ratings): 36 knots
Endurance: (at max continuous speed, one
  generator running at 70% rated load): 200n
  miles

HM 500 SERIES FAST PATROL AND FAST ATTACK CRAFT

Military variants of the HM 527 are now available in patrol and attack configurations for
coastal patrol duties.
The HM 527 fast patrol boat mounts a twin
30mm cannon forward and is intended for EEZ
duties. The fast strike craft for coastal defence
carries four British Aerospace Dynamics Sea
Skua anti-ship missiles.
In-service trials with the passenger version
confirmed the craft's suitability for military operations. Design changes in the military version
include hull strengthening to accept the weapons
fit and uprated lift and propulsion engines to
accommodate the increased weight and improve
performance.
Features of these craft include fuel economy,
an improved ride and a high standard of accommodation. The craft are propelled by military-
rated MTU diesels driving variable-pitch propellers, giving a half-load cruising speed in excess of
35 knots and a top speed of over 40 knots.
LIFT AND PROPULSION: The fast patrol boat
and the fast strike craft have identical machinery
arrangements with four diesels in two amidship
engine rooms above the sidewalls. Both accommodate one lift engine, one propulsion engine
and one auxiliary power unit. The lift engines are
two General Motors Detroit Diesel Allison 8V
92 TI marine diesels rated at 346kW (465bhp) at
2,300rpm. Each drives a lift fan via a gearbox to
provide plenum air, plus two separate fans for
skirt inflation via a hydraulic pump and hydraulic
motors. The two lift engines can drive a supplementary propulsion system when the craft
operates in displacement condition and the main
engines are not in use. The propulsion engines
are two MTU 12V 396 TB93 diesels rated at
1,310kW at 2,100 rpm maximum and 1,090kW
at 1,975rpm continuous. Each incorporates a ZF
BU 455 reverse-reduction gearbox and drives a
single three-blade controllable-pitch propeller.
All engines are electrically operated and controlled from the wheelhouse. The two fuel tanks are
in the transom bay, in-line athwartships. Fuel
capacity in the fast patrol variant is 14·25 tonnes
and for the fast strike craft, 3·4 tonnes.
CONTROLS: Craft direction is by power-
operated twin water rudders. Additional control
is provided by differential use of the twin propellers and variation of the propeller pitch. An
automatic roll stabilisation system operates two
inclined independent rudders.

HULL AND SKIRT: As for HM 527 Series II
passenger ferry.
ACCOMMODATION: Designed for a complement of 15 for six days. Working areas
comprise combined wheelhouse, radio and operations room (the FSC variant has separate operations room) and open conning position. Single
berth cabin for commanding officer, two-berth
cabin, toilet, shower, and wardroom for officers.
Six-berth cabins for NCOs and seamen with
separate toilet and shower. Galley, for officers
and ratings, equipped with electric cooker,
domestic refrigerator/freezer and double sink.
AIR CONDITIONING: Air conditioned living,
working, messing and berthing areas. Machinery
rooms and galley ventilated by forced exhaust,
natural air supply. Toilets ventilated by forced
exhaust, conditioned air supply. Stores have
natural ventilation.
LIFESAVING: One 20-man marine life raft
with survival pack. Four lifebuoys with lines,
lights and smoke markers. Twenty marine lifejackets.
BOATS: One Avon W400 inflatable rubber raft
with 30hp outboard motor, launched by
manually-operated crane.
COMMUNICATIONS
INTERNAL
Intercommunication system for machinery
control, weapons and navigation. Main broadcast
net for relaying orders and alarms. Crew enter-
tainment net in all accommodation areas. Speakers carry orders and alarm broadcasts.
Loudhailer controlled via the main broadcast net.
Telephone emergency system for communication
on a single channel basis for damage control.
EXTERNAL
Operators console contains: two hf transmitter
receivers, frequency range 1·5 to 30MHz. Modes
of operation: AM, CW, SSB (USB or LSB),
AME. Output 100 watts. Vlf/lf/mf/hf receiver,
frequency range 15KHz to 30MHz. Modes of
operation: AM, CW, LSB or USB. Vhf (fm)
transceiver, frequency range 156·025 to
163·1MHz. Mode of operation: F3. Power output 25 watts or 1 watt. Control from wheelhouse
and communications office. Two uhf (AM) transceivers, frequency range 225 to 399·975MHz.
Mode of operation: A3. Power output 20 watts.
Two remote voice control positions hf/uhf. Survival craft radio (SOLAS), Frequency range:
transmit, 500KHz, 2,182KHz, 8,364KHz;
receive, 500KHz, 2,182KHz. Mode of operation: MCW, DSB. Power output 2 watts nominal.
Two hand-held vhf (fm) transceivers, 2 crystal
controlled channels. Mode of operation: fm.
Power output 1 watt (adjustable). Automatic mf
direction finding receiver, frequency range
70KHz to 3·99MHz. CRT display.
DIMENSIONS
Length overall: 27m
Beam overall: 10·2m

Under side of prop to top of mast: 11·3m
Draught, off cushion: 2·7m
  on cushion: 1·7m
PERFORMANCE
Speed: At a mean load condition with ambient conditions not exceeding 45°C air, 32°C sea water temperatures.
Max speed, intermittent (2 hours in 12 hours), zero sea state, zero wind speed: 40 knots
Max speed, continuous, zero sea state, zero wind speed: 35 knots
ENDURANCE: Range at a mean load condition in zero sea state and zero wind speed with one generator running at 80% capacity.
FAST PATROL CRAFT, at 13 knots: 840n miles
  at 24 knots: 790n miles
FAST STRIKE CRAFT, at 13 knots: 660n miles
  at 24 knots: 590n miles
Using overload tank capacity of the vessel in the above conditions, the range can be extended to:
FAST PATROL CRAFT, at 13 knots: 1,500n miles
  at 24 knots: 1,300n miles
FAST STRIKE CRAFT, at 13 knots: 1,400n miles
  at 24 knots: 1,200n miles

HM 527 FAST PATROL CRAFT

SYSTEMS, ELECTRICAL: Medium voltage: ac 380-volt 3-phase/220V single phase, 60Hz, 4-wire. Low voltage: ac 115-volt single phase, 400Hz, 2-wire. Low voltage: dc 24-volt two wire insulated.
GENERATION AND CONVERSION: Two diesel-driven, brushless, ac generators, each rated at 50kVA, 40kW at 0·8 power factor lagging. Solid state inverter, 115-volt single phase 400Hz for general weapons and computer systems with capacity of 1kW. Two air cooled transformer rectifier units providing float/boost charging facilities. Output 24 volts dc with capacity of

HM 527 fast strike craft

1kW. Two 24-volt nickel cadmium batteries, one in each machinery compartment with capacity to supply essential services for 30 minutes. Two main engine driven ac/dc alternators. Output 24 volts, capacity 80 amps.

NAVIGATION
Racal Decca Cane 100 computer-assisted navigation system with automatic plotting table. Anschutz standard 6 gyro compass with associated repeaters. Chernikeef electromagnetic log with fixed probe and master display unit, plus bridge repeater. Krupp Atlas DESO 20 echo sounder. Two Plath Jupiter magnetic compasses.
WEAPONS
Gun mountings: 30mm Oerlikon twin mounting type GCM-A02. Two spigots for 7·62mm GPMG.
Radar: Racal Decca F/I band surveillance/navigation radar.
Display: Racal Decca 12-inch main navigation display.
Optronic director: PEAB 9LV 100.
WEIGHTS
Ammunition: 776kg
Provisions and stores for 6 days: 160kg
Fresh water: 750kg
Naval stores & spares: 500kg
Standard oil fuel storage capacity (inclusive of service tanks): 11,230kg
Lubricating oil storage capacity: 300kg
Total payload: 13,716kg
Less half fuel and fresh water: 5,990kg
Payload for mean load condition: 7,726kg
Additional overload fuel capacity: 7,750kg

HM 527 FAST STRIKE CRAFT

SYSTEMS, ELECTRICAL: Medium voltage: ac 440-volt, 3-phase, 60Hz, 3-wire.
Low voltage: ac 115-volt, 3-phase, 60Hz, 3-wire.
Low voltage: dc 24-volt, two-wire, insulated.
GENERATION AND CONVERSION: Two diesel-driven, brushless, ac generators, each rated at 75kVA, 60kW at 0·8 power factor lagging. 10kVA air cooled transformer, output 118 volts, 3-phase, 60Hz for general lighting and small power consumers. Two air cooled transformer rectifier units providing float/boost charging facilities. Output 24 volts dc with capacity of 1kW. Two 24-volt nickel cadmium batteries, one sited in each machinery compartment with capacity to supply essential services for 30 minutes.
NAVIGATION
Anschutz standard 6 gyro compass with associated repeaters. Chernikeef electromagnetic log with fixed probe and master display unit, plus repeater. Krupp Atlas DESO 20 echo sounder. Two Plath Jupiter magnetic compasses. Wind speed and direction system.
WEAPONS
Missile launchers: Two twin box Sea Skua anti-ship missile launchers.

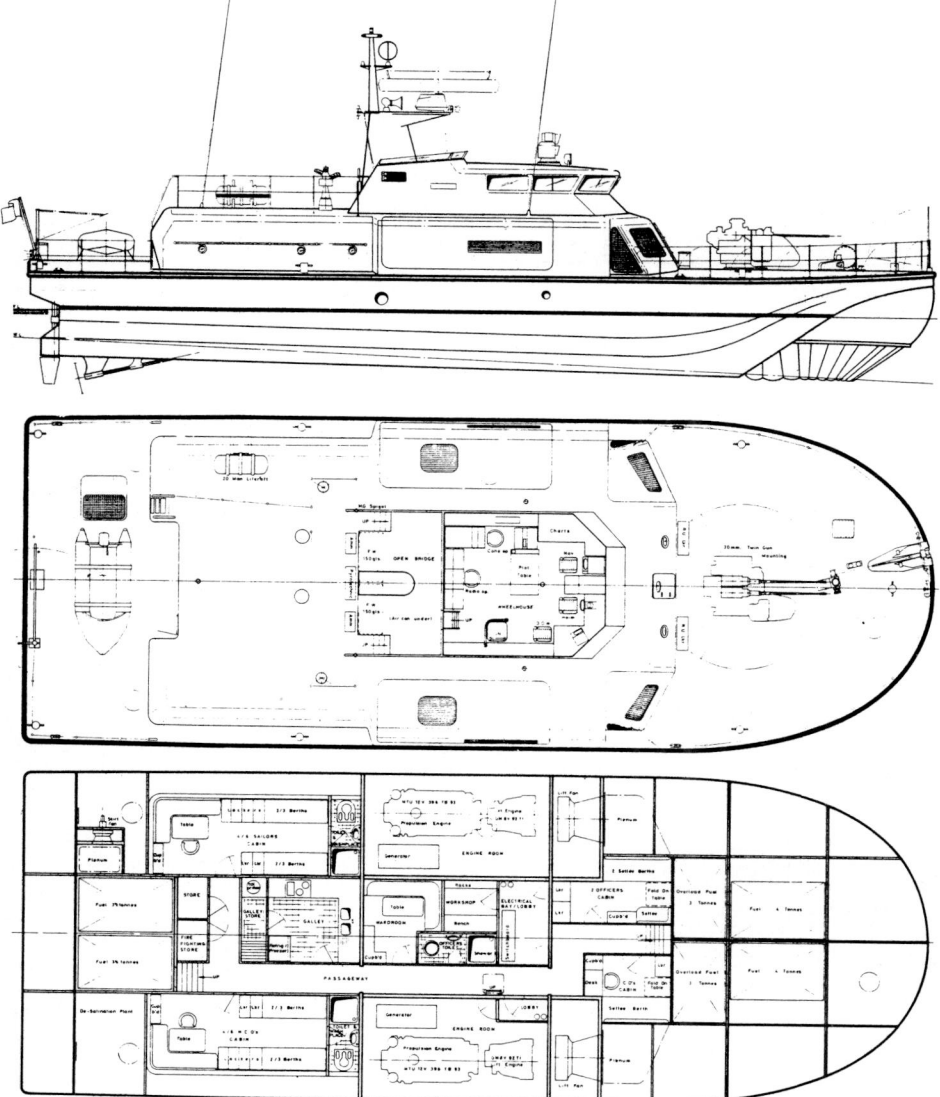

HM 527 fast patrol craft

Gun mountings: 30mm remotely operated Oerlikon twin gun mounting Type GCM-AO3. Two
spigots for 7·62mm GPMG.
Stowages: For 640 rounds of 30mm ammunition
and small arms ammunition. Pyrotechnic and
demolition stores in pyrotechnics locker.
Director: PEAB 9LV 100.
Radar: Racal-Decca F/I band surveil-
lance/navigation radar. Ferranti Seaspray surveil-
lance/tracking.
Display: Decca main navigation display in
wheelhouse. Seaspray control console in opera-
tions room.
Tactical display: Cane 100 AIO system with
plotting table in operations room.
WEIGHTS
Ammunition: 3,550kg
Provisions and stores for 6 days: 160kg
Fresh water: 750kg
Naval stores and spares: 500kg
Standard oil fuel storage capacity (inclusive of
    service tanks): 8,427kg
Lubricating oil storage capacity: 300kg
Total payload: 13,687kg
Less half fuel, fresh water and gun ammunition:
    5,589kg
Payload for mean load condition: 8,098kg
Additional overload fuel capacity: 7,750kg
ADDITIONAL OPTIONS, HM 527 FAST PATROL AND
FAST STRIKE VARIANTS
Navigation: Magnavox MX 1105 combined satel-
    lite/Omega navigator. Decca Navigator and/or
    Loran C receiver.
Esm: Esm sensor and control system.
Chaff: Two Wallop Stockade launchers.
Heating: In ambient temperatures below 20°C,
    accommodation and wheelhouse spaces
    heated to 20°C by conditioned air.

HM 700

Vosper Hovermarine is developing an open-
water craft with an all-up weight of approximately 700 tonnes. The vessel, the HM 700, will
have a cushion depth in excess of 6m (20ft) and
will be fully stabilised to cope with sea conditions
up to that severity. It is envisaged that as a quick
response emergency vessel it would be powered
with high speed diesel engines to provide on-
cushion speeds in excess of 50 knots and enable it
to maintain 40 knots in conditions of up to 4m
(13ft) seas. A slower patrol speed in displacement mode would be provided for speeds of 17 to
20 knots. This craft would be capable of patrolling for long periods at sea and would have a
range capability in the patrol mode in excess of
5,000 miles (about 2,000 miles on cushion at
speeds in excess of 40 knots). With this capability

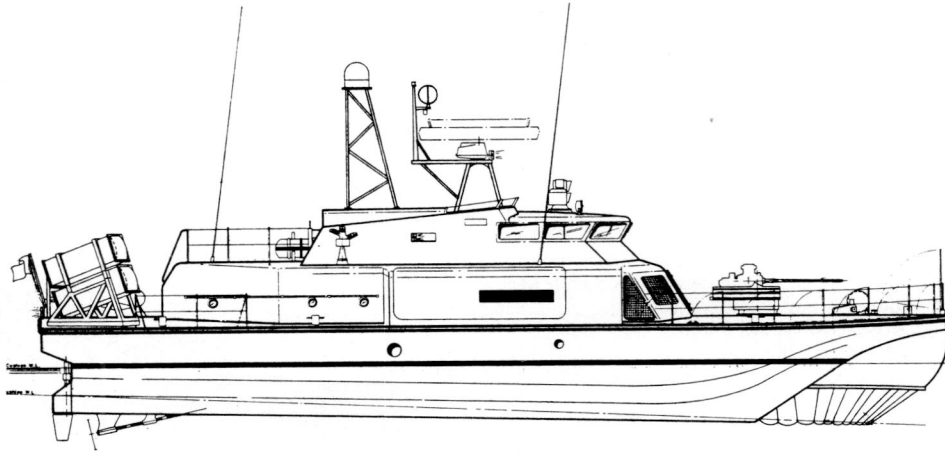

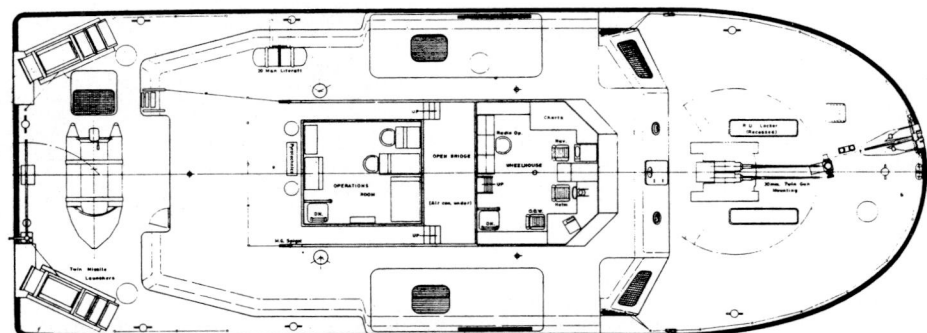

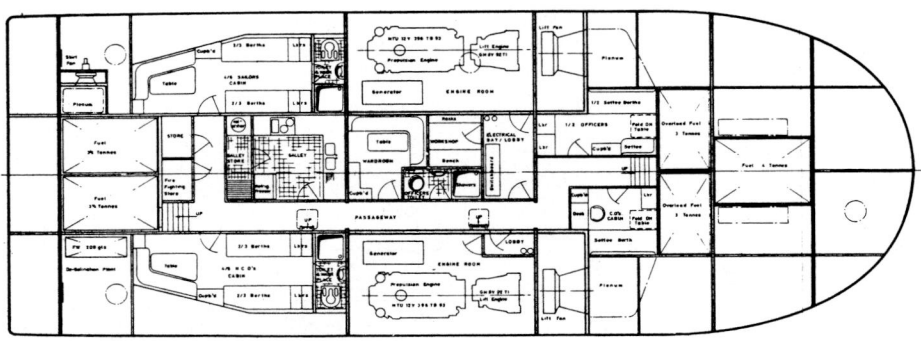

HM 527 fast strike craft

it should be possible to locate vessels quickly in a
large area of operation. The passenger variant is
designed to carry 500 passengers and up to 76
cars at over 50 knots.

VOSPER THORNYCROFT (UK) LIMITED

Head Office: Fareham House, East Street,
Fareham, Hants PO16 0BW, England
Telephone: 0329 283411
Telex: 86669 VT FARE G
Cables: Repsov, Portsmouth
Officials:
J E Steele, *Chairman*

P J Usher, *Managing Director*
G W Cameron, *Products and Support Projects
    Director*
B Chapman, *Production Director*
A L Dorey, *Technical Director*
J B Gray, *Finance Director*
E J Grisley, *Commercial Director*
P D G Hares, *Non-Executive Director*
A O Lambie, *Non-Executive Director*
M A Phelps, *Non-Executive Director*
B Stobart Hook, *Sales Director*

Vosper Thornycroft (UK) Limited, a subsidiary of British Shipbuilders, continues the
shipbuilding business established over a century
ago by two separate companies, Vosper Limited
and John I Thornycroft & Co Ltd. These companies merged in 1966 and the organisation has
continued the design and construction of warships from fast patrol boats to large frigates. The
company was nationalised in July 1977 and is
now part of British Shipbuilders.

The company's main activities embrace the
design and construction of warships and hovercraft intended primarily for military purposes.
However, two 62-metre, 28-knot fast passenger
ferries are under construction. Diversified
engineering work is also undertaken including
the design and manufacture of ship stabilisers and
specialised electrical and electronic control
equipment for marine and industrial use.

VT 2

VT 2 has an overall length of 30·1m (99ft) and
an all-up weight of 100 to 110 tonnes, according
to role.

A number of variants are available. In addition
to a strike version, there is a logistic version for
carrying troops, vehicles and guns; a multi-
purpose configuration combining both weapons
and a logistic capability and a mine countermeasures variant.

VT 2 hovercraft (P234)

VT 2 (P234) during underwater shock trials

VT 2-001 (P234)

A VT 2 craft in a logistic support configuration has seen service with the Royal Navy.

To extend the VT 2's overall capabilities before participating in exercises in 1978, VT 2-001 was modified under Ministry of Defence contract to permit palleted cargo to be handled for transport from ship-to-shore. Modifications included the fitting of a loading hatch in the superstructure roof and laying roller tracking on the deck below.

In the spring of 1977 the VT 2 took part in trials and exercises with the West German and Danish navies. The VT 2 (P234) underwent a series of trials to examine the effect of underwater shock. This was the first such trial of a hovercraft while carrying a full crew.

Following an extensive refit, VT 2-001 (P234) returned to Royal Naval service for further evaluation in the mine countermeasures support role. Modifications and additions include: Avon Sea Rider 5·4m runabout; Atlas 5002 hydraulic crane; a large roof hatch; improved internal payload-handling system incorporating roller tracks; radio equipment and antennas compatible with that of the 'Hunt' class MCV. Following the closure of the Naval Hovercraft Trials Unit, VT 2 was sold to Hoverspeed (UK) Ltd.

LIFT AND PROPULSION: Motive power for the integrated lift/propulsion system is supplied by two Rolls-Royce Proteus marine gas turbines, each rated at 4,250shp maximum. The two gas turbines are installed in port and starboard engine rooms amidships and each powers two drive shafts via a David Brown gearbox. One shaft transmits power to a bank of four centrifugal lift fans, which absorbs about one third of the output, the other drives a ducted propulsion fan via an inclined shaft.

The two variable-pitch fans, each 4·1m (13ft 6in) in diameter, have seven blades and each rotates in a duct of streamline section. Manufactured by Dowty Rotol Limited, the blades are of foam-filled glass-reinforced plastics. In comparison with air propellers, ducted fans offer increased efficiency and substantial reductions in noise levels. The noise reduction results from the low fan tip speed of 150m/s (500ft/s). Other advantages offered are reduced diameter for a

given thrust and power, and less danger to crew working in their vicinity. The variation in pitch provides differential thrust for manoeuvring. Downstream of the fan blades are stator blades, sixteen in each duct, ensuring uniformity of thrust and of the directional control provided by rudders mounted at the aft ends of the ducts.

The ducted fans are mounted with their shaft axes at an angle to the horizontal of about 13·5 degrees, avoiding the need for right-angle gearbox drives. This entails some slight loss in efficiency, but this is offset by savings in the losses in the right-angle boxes themselves and in the additional power for air cooling which would be needed for their lubricating oil.

Gas turbines, main gearboxes and lift fans are housed in machinery spaces on either side of the craft outboard of the main longitudinal webs. The engines are mounted with their shaft axes parallel to those of the propulsion fans, so that normal gearing can be used for the 75 per cent or so of the engine output which is transmitted to the propulsion fans. This arrangement also directs the turbine exhausts upwards, thereby simplifying the ductwork.

The remaining 25 per cent of engine power is applied to the lift fans which are accommodated in separate compartments of the machinery spaces, two each side, with their axes horizontal. A V-drive gear system effects the change in shaft axis at the output from the main gearbox to the lift fans. The fans draw air through grilled areas in the upper outboard part of the craft's superstructure amidships and discharge down to the cushion loop. A quantity of cushion air is diverted via a filtration system to remove salt and sand contamination to the Proteus gas turbine intakes, and a further quantity is ducted to bow thrusters for manoeuvring at low speeds.

CONTROLS: The pilot and engineer are accommodated atop the superstructure in a control cabin which has an all-round view. Rudder pedals provide steering via the control surfaces in the fan slipstream. Twin levers between pilot and engineer control fan pitch, and hence speed, and can be moved differentially to provide additional turning moments. To give close lateral control at low speeds side thrusters are fitted which utilise pressurised cushion air to provide side thrust. Hydraulically-actuated doors direct air from the ducts to port or starboard as required, in response to movement of a combined selector control at the pilot's position. Rapid trim adjustment is provided by elevators in the fan slipstream. A ballast control provides slow trim adjustment by pumping reserve fuel, totalling 3 tonnes, from one compartment to another. This is done electrically by means of a switch. Engine throttle levers are available to both pilot and engineer. Communications are normally operated by the pilot. Full navigational and machinery instrumentation is provided.

HULL: Marine aluminium alloys with bolted or riveted joints. The main structural elements are the buoyancy raft, of egg-box form, providing 26 watertight compartments and a buoyancy reserve of more than 100%, and two deep vertical webs, forming fore-and-aft bulkheads enclosing the central bay of the craft. On the underside of the buoyancy raft are three pads on which the craft is supported when at rest on dry land. A lighter shell structure attached to the periphery of the raft and the main longitudinal webs encloses accommodation and machinery spaces and the central bay. In logistic support configuration a door with loading ramp is provided at the bow, extending across the full width of the central bay. A door can be incorporated aft if through loading is required. The design allows substantial flexibility in the choice of superstructure arrangement.

SKIRT: Peripheral skirt contains a 1·58m (5ft 6in) deep air cushion at a pressure of about 31mb (65lb/ft²). Cushion is in the form of a single undivided cell. It provides a comfortable ride in rough seas, and enables the craft to clear obstacles overland up to 1·1m (3ft 7in) high.

The skirt is of nylon-reinforced neoprene and consists of two main parts, loop and segments. The loop forms a continuous duct around the periphery of the craft, contained between inner and outer bands of skirt material attached to the

VT 2-001 showing Sea Rider installation, hydraulic crane and communications antennas

VT 2 preparing to tow minesweeping gear. Note protection to personnel by fan ducts and ample deck space aft

Impression of mine countermeasures craft based on VT 2

raft structure. The lift fans deliver air to the loop through apertures in the raft plating. The segments are attached to the lower edges of the loop, and consist of 157 sets of inner and outer scoop-shaped pieces. The inner segments direct air flow outwards and downwards into the outer segments, and have holes which allow a controlled proportion of the air flow to pass directly into the main cushion under the craft. The outer segments turn the airflow from the inner segments downwards and inwards.

The flexible skirt assembly is stabilised by cables connecting every junction between adjacent pairs of segments and the inner loop to the raft structure. The outer segments are the only ones subject to wear and are attached with special fasteners so that they can be changed in a few minutes with hand tools, without having to lift the craft. Quite severe damage to the skirt, the loss of 30 per cent of segments or 15 per cent of the loop for example, can be accepted without seriously affecting the manoeuvrability of the craft.

SYSTEMS, ELECTRICAL AND HYD-RAULIC: Auxiliary machinery includes diesel or gas turbine alternator sets for electrical supplies, a hydraulic system for fan pitch control, loading ramp and door actuation, and side thruster doors.

DIMENSIONS (Typical)
Length overall: 30·17m (99ft)
Width overall: 13·3m (43ft 6in)
Cushion height: 1·58m (5ft 6in)
Cushion pressure: 31mb (65lb/ft²)

WEIGHTS
All-up weight: 100-110 tonnes, according to role

PERFORMANCE
The basic VT 2 vehicle can carry a load of up to 32 tonnes for 550km (300n miles) at speeds of more than 60 knots (111km/h, 69mph) over sea, river shallows, shoals, mudflats, ice and snow. It can also travel over dry land reasonably free from obstructions. It can operate in rough seas and accept a substantial amount of damage.

MINE COUNTERMEASURES

Extended trials were undertaken by the Naval Hovercraft Trials Unit (now disbanded), which was primarily concerned with the development of hovercraft for mine countermeasures duties. Interest in amphibious hovercraft for this application stems from its relative invulnerability to underwater explosions compared with displacement vessels, and its low magnetic and underwater noise signatures. The accompanying artist's impression shows one possible arrangement of a VT 2 for this particular role. The VT 2 is of suitable size for this work and the picture shows the sweepdeck space with sweepgear stowed. The gear illustrated is either in current use or readily available commercially.

The craft has an extended rear deck equipped with davits and MCM gear. The bow ramp is retained and this, together with the use of containerised MCM equipment modules, allows some multi-role characteristics to be retained.

UNITED STATES OF AMERICA

AIR CUSHION SYSTEMS

25975 SW 182nd Avenue, Homestead, Florida 33030, USA
Telephone: (305) 248 4795
Officials:
John Van Veldhuizen

Air Cushion Systems has been building air cushion vehicles since 1960. The craft employ an air bearing system invented by John Van Veldhuizen. The object of the system is to provide improved stability and control and also to reduce cushion pressure. Beneath the hardstructure are up to five longitudinal trunks which divide the air cushion into four separate chambers. Air is fed into each chamber via multiple feeding holes running the length of each chamber. Flexible seals are fitted at the bow and stern. Features of the designs can be seen in the accompanying photographs.

Five longitudinal trunks divide air cushion into four separate chambers

18ft 6in (5·64m) air-bearing ACV

AIR CUSHION SYSTEMS X16

The company's latest design is a six-seat glass fibre leisure craft. Four longitudinal trunks will be beneath the hardstructure. Power for the integrated lift/propulsion system will be provided by a 180hp Lycoming piston engine driving a Kevlar 7-bladed axial fan. Twin rudders will provide directional control.

DIMENSIONS
Length overall: 4·8m (16ft)
Beam overall: 2·28m (7ft 6in)

5·64m (18ft 6in) air-bearing ACV powered by 500in³ Cadillac engine

AIR CUSHION TECHNOLOGIES INTERNATIONAL INC

1601E 84th Court, No 105, Anchorage, Alaska 99501, USA
Telephone: (907) 344 0733/349 1814
Officials:
Henry G Saylor Jr, *President*
Mike January, *Vice President*
Mina K Saylor, *Secretary/Treasurer*

Air Cushion Technologies International was founded in 1981 by Henry G Saylor Jr, who had previously started Alaska Hovercraft Inc. The company is concentrating on the development of the 9-metre Corsair and 6·4-metre Falcon III amphibious multi-duty hovercraft. Eight Corsairs and 18 Falcons have been built and further craft are on order. Future plans include the design and construction of larger hovercraft of up to 24·38m (80ft). The company has also developed a single-seat recreational machine, the Sand Piper, which is sold in kit form, and is designing a four-seater runabout.

CORSAIR MARK 1

Corsair is a fully-amphibious eight-seater designed specifically for operations in arctic terrain. It can carry a payload of up to 1,133kg (2,500lb) and has a maximum speed of 48 knots.
LIFT AND PROPULSION: Lift is provided by a single Ford Marine LSG 42·3L industrial engine driving, via a cog belt, two 0·76m (2ft 6in) diameter centrifugal fans generating a flow of 67,000cfm. Thrust is supplied by a GMC 454 marine engine driving, via a cog belt, a 1·87m (6ft 2in) diameter two-bladed propeller. Total fuel capacity is 189·26 litres (50 US gallons). Long-range tanks can be provided with a capacity for a further 189·26 litres (50 US gallons). Both engines run on standard petrol or 80·87 aviation fuel. Fuel consumption is 12·8 US gallons/h.
HULL: Marine-grade aluminium.
CONTROLS: Heading is controlled by triple vertical rudders operated by a steering wheel. An elevator, mounted between two fixed vertical stabilisers, provides longitudinal trim.
SKIRT: Loop and segment type by Air Cushion Equipment Limited.
DIMENSIONS
Length overall: 8·99m (29ft 6in)
Length hull: 7·62m (25ft)
Hull width: 3·5m (11ft 6in)
Hull width, prepared for transport: 2·84m (9ft 4in)
Height, on cushion: 3·07m (10ft 1in)
    off cushion: 2·66m (8ft 9in)
WEIGHTS
All-up weight: 3,696·77kg (8,150lb)
Payload: 1,133·98kg (2,500lb)
PERFORMANCE (zero wind, standard craft)
Max speed over land: 45 knots
    over water: 45 knots
Cruising speed over land: 35 knots
    over water: 30 knots
Vertical obstacle clearance: 406mm (1ft 4in)
Standard fuel consumption, zero wind: 12·8 US gallons/h
Max range, standard tanks, no reserve: 225km (140 miles)
Max range, long-range tanks, no reserve: 450km (280 miles)

FALCON III

This addition to the Air Cushion Technologies

Corsair Mk 1

Corsair Mk 1

Falcon III

International range is designed to compete in size, payload and price with 20ft waterjet-powered speedboats. Falcon III seats five and has a top speed in calm water of 45mph. An automatic cushion relief system developed by the company is said to give a smooth ride, even in rough water.

LIFT AND PROPULSION: Integrated system powered by a single GMC 305 V8 marine petrol engine. Lift and thrust power are controlled independently by an automotive clutch which engages the thrust propeller and drives a 30-inch diameter centrifugal lift fan from the front of the engine crankshaft. Lift power is developed via a vernier control that adjusts the foot throttle to raise craft to full hoverheight with the propeller disengaged. Total fuel capacity is 40 US gallons. Long range tanks give an extra capacity of 24 US gallons. The engine runs on standard petrol or 80·87 aviation fuel. Standard fuel consumption, in zero wind conditions, is 6·8 US gallons/h.

CONTROLS: Craft heading is by twin vertical rudders operated by a steering wheel. An elevator mounted between the two fixed vertical stabilisers provides longitudinal trim.

HULL: Marine-grade aluminium hull with glassfibre canopy.

SKIRT: Loop and segment type.

ACCOMMODATION: Enclosed cabin seats driver and four passengers.

DIMENSIONS
Length overall: 6·4m (21ft)
  hull: 5·7m (19ft)
Hull width, prepared for transport: 2·4m (8ft)
Height, on cushion: 2·4m (8ft)
  off cushion: 2·1m (7ft)

WEIGHTS
All-up, standard craft: 1,564kg (3,450lb)
Payload: 544kg (1,200lb)

PERFORMANCE
Max speed, zero wind, over water: 72·4km/h (45mph)

Falcon III

Cruising speed, zero wind, over water: 62·7km/h (39mph)
Max range, standard tank, no reserve: 200 miles

Max range, long range tanks, no reserve: 320 miles
Obstacle clearance: 0·3m (1ft)

AIR RIDE MARINE INC

15840 SW 84th Avenue, Miami, Florida 33157, USA
Telephone: (305) 233 4306
Officials:
Donald E Burg, *President*
James G Seat, *Vice President*

The Air Ride concept combines the appearance and simplicity of construction of conventional hulls with the low hydrodynamic drag of surface effect ships, but without heavily stressed structures or flexible skirts. Inventor of the Air Ride concept is Donald E Burg, whose experience in high speed marine craft includes work on the applications of Pratt & Whitney gas turbine-powered waterjets for US Navy hydrofoils and surface effect ships.

The hulls of the Air Ride vessels incorporate a long, shallow plenum chamber for pressurised air in the underside. Air is fed into the chamber by a fan and is retained by two shallow sidewalls and transverse frames fore and aft. Efficiency is claimed to be comparable to an SES or sidewall hovercraft. The ride is better than that of conventional boats at speed as there is less wetted hull impact area. In the same way as the bow of a conventional vessel, the structural bow of the Air Ride vehicle shapes the waves, permitting the use of a shallow air cushion. As Air Ride vehicles do

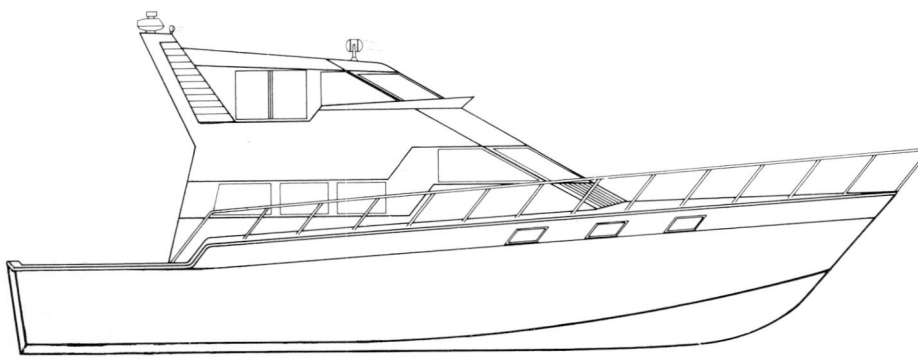

56ft Sports Fisherman

not have a high centre of gravity, they do not need wide sidehull spacing for stability.

The company claims there is virtually no size restriction on craft employing the concept. Preliminary studies show that craft with lengths of 150 to 300ft, and larger, are as effective in speed and economy as smaller craft.

Air Ride Marine was incorporated in 1979 as a technical services company to develop and market the design, and it intends to make its invention available to users or qualified builders.

In October 1984 the company revealed that it

is working in conjunction with Swiftships Inc, Morgan City, Louisiana, USA, on both commercial and military aluminium-hulled Air Ride designs of up to 200ft, and also Lantana Boatyard, Lantana, Florida, USA, on similar craft of up to 150ft and with speeds of up to 50 knots. In Hong Kong the company is with Cheoy Lee Shipyards Ltd to develop fibreglass-hulled craft, initially in the 75ft class. Considerable interest is being shown in the Pacific and other areas in passenger ferry variants.

The following designs can use other engines, and can achieve speeds in excess of 40 knots with increased power. Waterjets or semi-submerged propellers will reduce draught requirements.

AIR RIDE EXPRESS

This 65ft crew/supply boat has been developed from a 42ft aluminium-hulled prototype first tested in October 1980. Satisfactory test results led to the design of a 65ft hull for the offshore industry. Air Ride Express is under long-term lease to Getty Oil Company, Mobile, Alabama, and operates in the Gulf of Mexico. Further 65ft crew/supply boats will be in operation by 1985. Other Air Ride craft likely to begin operation in

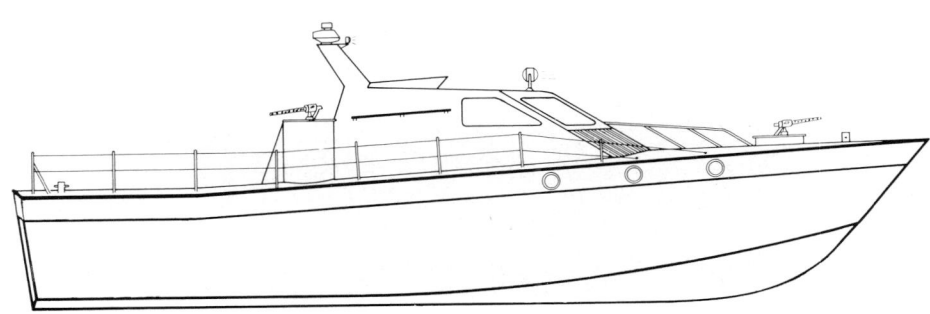

56ft fibreglass coastal patrol boat

1985 include a 110ft crew/supply boat, and a 35-knot, 65ft, 140-passenger ferry. Interest is also being shown in a 53-metre fast attack craft.
LIFT AND PROPULSION: Power for the mixed-flow lift fan is supplied by a General Motors Detroit Diesel GM 6V53T, capable of 265hp but only required to operate at 125hp constant. Power is transmitted directly to the fan through a simple flexible coupling. To ensure maximum operational life the fan is designed for 5g shock loadings although loadings in operation should not exceed 0·5g. The fan air inlet is an angled grille next to the stairway aft of the crew cabin. The main engines are two 590hp 12V71TI General Motor Detroit Diesels each driving a single three-bladed Columbian Bronze Company bronze 36/44 crewboat propeller via a Twin Disc 514C 2·5:1 gearbox. The main shafts are 3-inch diameter ARMCO Aquamet 17s. Standard fuel capacity is 4,542 litres (1,200 gallons).
CONTROLS: Hydraulically operated steering units at helm and stern. Morse single lever controls engine and each engine has a Murphy low water monitor alarm that sounds in the pilothouse. A water ballast system trims uneven loads fore or aft, port or starboard. Ballast tanks, controlled from the pilothouse, have a total capacity of 9,463 litres (2,500 gallons).
HULL: All-welded aluminium structure by Atlantic and Gulf Boat Building, Florida.
ACCOMMODATION: Passenger cabin seats 32. Pilothouse equipped with heavy duty offshore captain's and mate's chairs. Carrier Traniscold air conditioning and heating. 3-ton marine commercial unit supplied by Thermo Air Inc, Miami. Full below deck living quarters for crew of 2 to 4, with 290ft² floor space and 6ft 8in headroom. Accommodation includes three bunks, stove, refrigerator, freezer, shower, colour television and storage for two weeks' provisions. Below deck area can be converted to seat 30 additional passengers. Portable water capacity, 1,250 litres (275 gallons). Cargo deck area in excess of 450ft² (17ft 6in × 26ft). Design is certified by US Coast Guard for operations 100 miles offshore.
SYSTEMS, ELECTRONICS/NAVIGATION: Furuno FR 360 radar. Si-Tex/Koden 767 Loran C, Motorola Triton 55/75vhf. Raytheon SSB. Datamarine DL 2480 depthsounder.
DIMENSIONS
Length: 19·8m (65ft)
Beam, max: 6·4m (21ft)
Draught, hull only, lift fan on: 0·38m (1ft 3in)
    lift fan off: 0·69m (2ft 3in)
Draught, including appendages, lift fan on: 1·37m (4ft 6in)
    lift fan off: 1·67m (5ft 6in)
WEIGHTS
Displacement, light: 27,216kg (60,000lb)
Displacement, max: 43,092kg (95,000lb)
Payload and fuel: 15,876kg (35,000lb)
Fuel capacity: 4,542kg (1,200 gallons)
Portable water capacity: 1,040 litres (275 gallons)
Ballast water capacity: 9,463 litres (2,500 gallons)
PERFORMANCE
Fast cruising: 25-32 knots (46-59km/h)
Fuel consumption at 26 knots, moderate load: 235 litres/h (62 gallons/h)
Range: 500n miles (927km)
PRICE: Approximately US$700,000, fob (1983).

AIR RIDE 65ft VARIANTS

Variants of the Air Ride Express include a motor yacht, a sports fishing vessel, a fireboat, a 120- to 150-seat passenger ferry and a fast patrol boat. Overall dimensions of each design are the same as the Air Ride Express and the standard models employ the same lift and propulsion systems. Differences in superstructure detail are seen in the accompanying outboard profiles of several of these variants.

AIR RIDE 53m FAST ATTACK CRAFT

The stability of the Air Ride hull allows it to be used as a weapons platform. Increased performance of the missile-firing version described

HULL TYPES

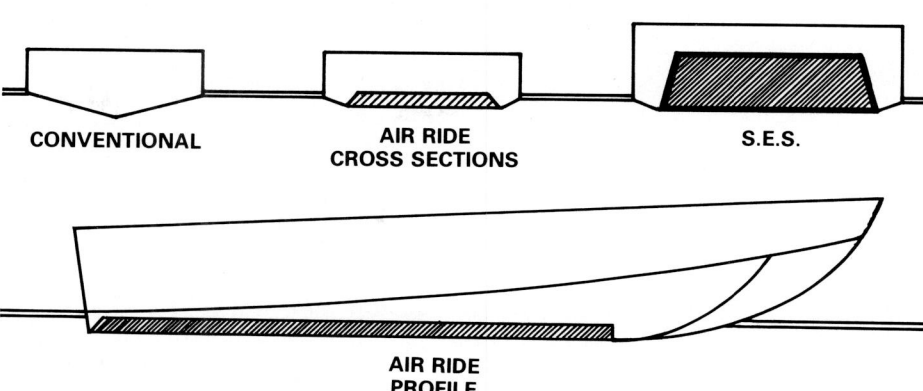

CONVENTIONAL   AIR RIDE CROSS SECTIONS   S.E.S.

AIR RIDE PROFILE

Air Ride hull profile

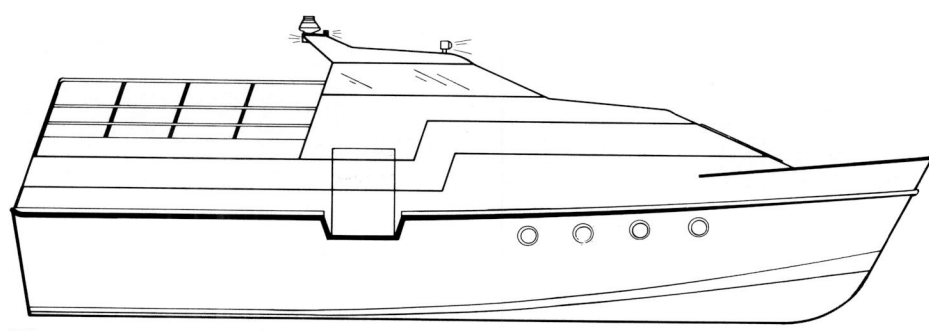

65ft passenger ferry

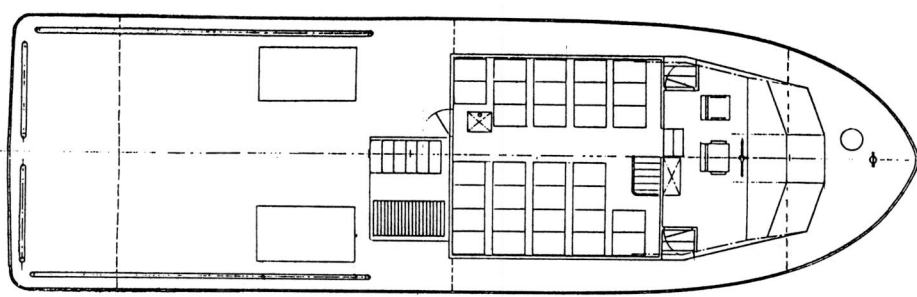

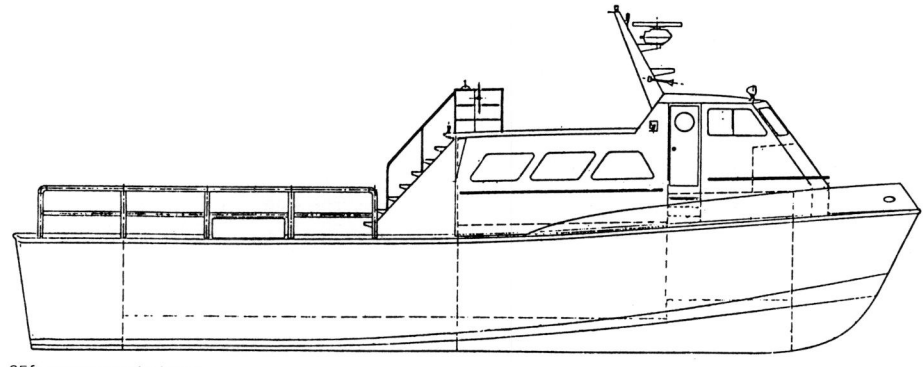

65ft crew/supply boat

65ft crew/supply boat

65ft crew/supply boat

below can be achieved by installing more powerful engines or employing four 1,600shp GM 12V92TI diesels instead of the two engines specified below.

LIFT AND PROPULSION: Cushion air is generated by a mixed-flow fan powered by a single 800shp General Motors 12V92TI diesel. Fan and engine are aft of the pilothouse superstructure. Fan air is inhaled through an angled grille at the rear of the deckhouse. Main engines are two 1,600shp GM 16VI49TI diesels, each driving a 40/52in three-blade bronze Columbian crewboat propeller. Power from each engine is transferred via a Reintjes WAV 800 gearbox and an Aquamet 17, 4in diameter shaft. Fuel capacity is 45,420 litres (12,000 gallons).

CONTROLS: Hydraulic steering with units at helm and stern. Morse MD 24 single lever engine controls. Water ballast trim system. Ballast water capacity, 37,850 litres (10,000 gallons).

HULL: All-welded structure in Type 5086 aluminium.

ACCOMMODATION: Air conditioned pilothouse and crew quarters.

SYSTEMS, ELECTRICAL: Radar, Decca 914. Loran C, Si-Tex Koden. Depth sounder, Datamarine DL 2480. Vhf, Decca STR 25. SSB, Drake TRM.

DIMENSIONS
Length: 53m (175ft)
Beam: 9m (30ft)
Draught, hull only, fan on: 1·5m
    fan off: 2·5m
    to base of standard propeller, fan on: 1·68m
    fan off: 1·99m
WEIGHTS
Displacement, light: 94 long tons (210,000lb)
Gross operating displacement: 229 long tons (514,000lb)
Payload and fuel: 135 long tons (304,000lb)
Fuel capacity: 45,420 litres (12,000 gallons)
PERFORMANCE
Speed, 229 tons: 30 knots
    120 tons: 34 knots
Fuel consumption at 26 knots and 200 long tons: 643 litres/h (170 gallons/h)

AIR RIDE 110

Primary uses for Air Ride 110 are crew/supply vessel, fast patrol craft, motor yacht and 250- to 300-seat passenger ferry.

LIFT AND PROPULSION: Power for the lift fan is provided by a 590hp Detroit Diesel 12V1TI. Main engines are four 590hp Detroit Diesel 12V71T1s, each driving a conventional subcavitating bronze propeller via a reverse-reduction gearbox. Fuel capacity, 22,710 litres (6,000 gallons).

CONTROLS: As for Air Ride 53m and 65ft craft.

HULL: All-welded structure in Type 5086 aluminium.

DIMENSIONS
Length overall: 33·5m (110ft)
Beam, max: 8·5m (28ft)
Draught, including appendages, fan on: 1·52m (5ft)
    fan off: 1·83m (6ft)
WEIGHTS
Displacement, light: 68,040kg (150,000lb)
Displacement, max: 108,864kg (240,000lb)
Payload and fuel: 40,284kg (90,000lb)
Potable water capacity: 3,785 litres (1,000 gallons)
Ballast water capacity: 18,925 litres (5,000 gallons)

PERFORMANCE
Speed range, fast cruise: 26-33 knots
Fuel consumption, at 26 knots, moderate load: 435 litres/h (115 gallons/h)
Range: 2,500km (1,350n miles)

AIR RIDE 175

As with the Air Ride 110, this 53·3m (175ft) variant is suitable for a range of military and commercial roles, including naval patrol craft and fast passenger ferry.

LIFT AND PROPULSION: Lift system comprises two Detroit Diesel 8V92T1 marine diesels each driving a mixed-flow fan via a gearbox and flexible coupling. Main engines are two 1,600hp Detroit Diesel 16V149T1s, each driving a conventional subcavitating bronze propeller via a reverse-reduction gearbox. Fuel capacity is 45,420 litres (12,000 gallons).

CONTROLS: As for Air Ride 53m and 65ft craft.

HULL: All-welded structure in Type 5086 aluminium.

DIMENSIONS
Length overall: 53·3m (175ft)
Beam, max: 9·8m (32ft)
Draught, hull only, fan on: 0·46m (1ft 6in)
    fan off: 0·76m (2ft 6in)
Draught, including appendages, fan on: 1·68m (5ft 6in)
    fan off: 1·98m (6ft 6in)
WEIGHTS
Displacement, light: 95,256kg (210,000lb)
Displacement, max: 233,150kg (514,000lb)
Payload and fuel: 137,894kg (304,000lb)
Fuel capacity: 45,420 litres (12,000 gallons)
Potable water capacity: 3,785 litres (1,000 gallons)
Ballast water capacity: 30,280 litres (8,000 gallons)
PERFORMANCE
Speed range, fast cruising: 26-33 knots (48-61km/h)
Fuel consumption at 26 knots, moderate load: 681 litres/h (180 gallons/h)
Range: 3,150km (1,700n miles)

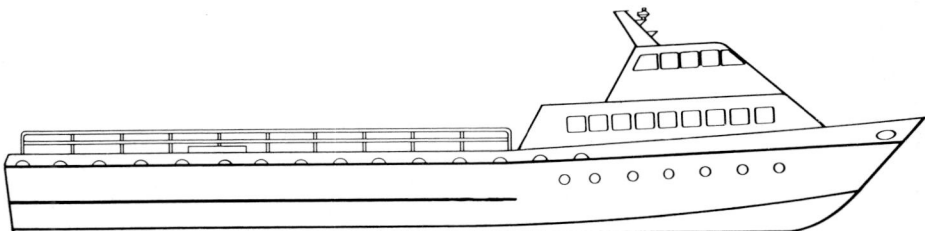

110ft crew/supply boat

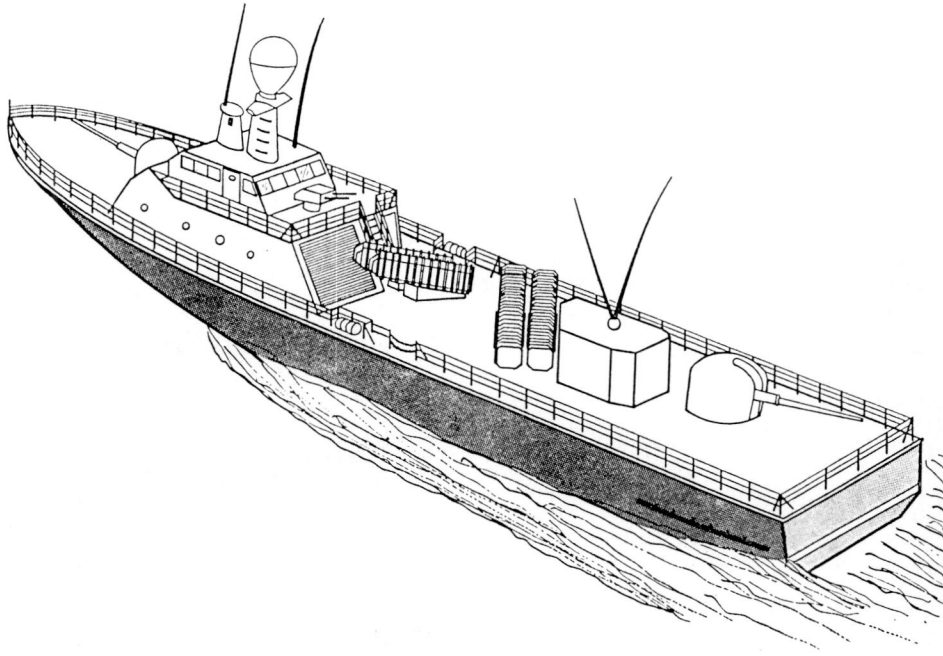

53m fast attack craft

BELL AEROSPACE TEXTRON
Division of Textron Inc

New Orleans Operations: 6800 Plaza Drive, New Orleans, Louisiana 70127-2596, USA
Telephone: (504) 245 6600
TWX: (810) 951 5028
Cables: BELLHAL NLN

Officials:
John J Kelly, *Senior Vice President and General Manager*
John B Chaplin, *Vice President, Engineering*
Roland Decrevel, *Vice President, LCAC Project*
Clarence L Forrest, *Vice President, Test and Training Directorate*
Donald E Kenney, *Controller*

Jeff(B)

Bell Aerospace began its air cushion vehicle development programme in 1958. Craft built by the company range in size from the 18ft XHS3 to the LCAC (Landing Craft, Air Cushion), currently in production for the US Navy.

The first LCAC was shipped to Panama City, Florida, in May 1984 for checking out and builders' trials. Acceptance trials and delivery took place in late 1984.

The company has rights to manufacture and sell in the USA machines employing the hovercraft principle through a licensing arrangement with the British Hovercraft Corporation and Hovercraft Development Ltd.

In addition to importing seven BHC SR.N5s, three of which were employed by the US Navy and later by the US Coast Guard for use and evaluation, Bell built three SK-5 Model 7255s—the company's first production ACVs—to a US Army specification. The craft were airlifted to Viet-Nam, where they performed a variety of missions, including high-speed troop/cargo transport and patrol.

In January 1969 the US Surface Effect Ships Project Office awarded Bell a contract for the detailed design of a 100-ton surface effect ship test craft. Construction began in September 1969 and a test and evaluation programme began in February 1972.

In January 1974 the company announced the successful completion of tests by the SES-100B, which confirmed the suitability of the design technology required for a 2,000-ton ocean-going surface ship.

In March 1971 the company was awarded a Phase II contract by the US Navy to start work on a programme covering the detail design, construction and test of an experimental 160-ton AALC (amphibious assault landing craft), designated Jeff(B).

Built at the NASA Michoud Assembly Facility, New Orleans, the craft was later transferred to the Naval Coastal Systems Center, Panama City, Florida. After preliminary testing the craft was delivered to the US Navy's Experimental Trials Unit at Panama City for crew training and operational trials.

In July 1974 the Naval Material Command awarded Bell a US $36 million 18-month contract to conduct an advanced development programme for a 2,000-ton, high-speed, ocean-going operational warship—the 2KSES. The company continues to support surface effect ship development through studies in advanced systems in lift and propulsion.

In October 1977 Bell linked with Halter Marine Inc, the New Orleans-based shipbuilders in a joint venture to develop and build a range of commercial surface effect ships.

In autumn 1979 Bell signed a US $21 million contract with the US Army Mobility Equipment R & D Command (MERADCOM) for the first four of twelve LACV-30s (lighter, air cushion vehicles — 30 short ton payload) with the first deliveries made in 1981. In January 1981 an additional four craft were ordered and in autumn 1982 a further 12. Production is at Bell's Niagara Frontier Operations, Wheatfield, New York.

Bell Aerospace Canada (see Canadian section) has built several prototypes of the Bell Model 7380 Voyageur heavy haul ACV, the second of which is in use by the Canadian Coast Guard. Production of additional Voyageurs is in hand.

Jeff(B) unloading 60-ton main battle tank

Two Voyageurs, 001 and 003, began operation in a US Army personnel training programme at the ACV/SES Test and Training Centre in 1975. Voyageur 004 was transferred to Panama City, Florida, in late 1980 for use in an ACV training programme for US Navy personnel.

The company initiated a programme for the US Air Force that covers the design, development, installation and test of an air cushion landing system aboard a de Havilland XC-8A Buffalo transport aircraft. The first ACLS landing of the XC-8A took place at Wright-Patterson Air Force Base, Dayton, Ohio, on 11 April 1975.

On 5 June 1981 Bell signed a US $40 million contract with the US Navy for the detail design and long-lead materials for an amphibious assault landing craft designated by the Navy as the LCAC (Landing Craft, Air Cushion). The LCAC is the production version of the Jeff craft. The contract contained two options for the later construction of six craft. One option was for US $81 million and the other for US $51 million, a total contract value of US $172 million. In February 1982 the US Navy exercised the first option for the production of three lead craft and in October 1982 it ordered a further three craft.

In March 1984 Bell was awarded a $102 million contract to build six more LCACs with a $197 million option to construct an additional 12 craft. Bell now holds contracts to produce a total of 24 LCACs. The first production craft was rolled out on 2 May 1984.

The LCAC contract is being undertaken by Bell's New Orleans operations.

The corporation's current ACV and SES activities are divided among its plants and associate companies as follows:

Bell Aerospace Textron
Niagara Frontier Operations
Buffalo, New York: LACV-30

Bell Aerospace Canada Textron
Grand Bend, Ontario, Canada: Voyageur and AL-30

Bell Aerospace Textron
New Orleans Operations
New Orleans, Louisiana: Jeff(B), LCAC, Voyageur 004, SES-100B and MSH

Bell Halter Inc
New Orleans, Louisiana: Bell Halter SES and LCAC

SK-5 MODEL 7255

Details of the SK-5 Model 7255 and its predecessor, the Model 7232, will be found in *Jane's Surface Skimmers 1972-73* and earlier editions.

AALC JEFF(B)

In March 1971 US Naval Ship Systems Command awarded Bell's New Orleans Operations a contract for the detail design, construction and testing of an experimental 160-ton, 50-knot air cushion amphibious assault landing craft.

Bell and Aerojet-General developed ACV test craft to the 68,038kg (150,000lb) payload, 50-knot specification. Both craft operate from the well-decks of landing ships and alongside cargo ships.

The Bell project, designated Jeff(B), involved mathematical and scale model investigations, interface and support system design, sub-system and component testing and design and systems analysis.

The 160-ton Amphibious Assault Landing Craft Jeff(B) was completed in March 1977. Full-scale testing began with static hovering trials in October 1977. First overwater operation was in December 1977. Completion of contractor trials and handing over of the craft to the Navy was in July 1978. Naval evaluation of the Jeff(B) began with a series of system trials. Mating trials have been completed with the Landing Ship Dock USS *Spiegel Grove* (LSD-32) and the Amphibious Transport Dock USS *Austin* (LPD-4). By June 1984, the Jeff(B) had undertaken 300 missions and had accumulated approximately 953 hours of underway testing, a large part at full payload gross weight. Operational demonstrations played a key role in the US Navy's acquisition plan for the Landing Craft, Air Cushion (LCAC), the operational version of the Jeff craft. Between 1978 and 1982 Jeff(B):

   operated consistently at full gross weight;
   demonstrated operations at maximum overload weight;
   operated at full weight with two of its six engines shut down;
   exceeded 75 knots;
   operated in the Gulf of Mexico in sea state 3; repeatedly transitioned from water to land over beaches in the area and operated over sand dunes.

During November and December 1983, the Jeff(B) underwent cold weather/arctic tests in the climatic chamber at Eglin Air Force Base, Fort Walton Beach, Florida. The craft was subjected to blowing snow, freezing rain and icing at 10°F (−12·2°C), and blowing snow at −30°F (−34·4°C). All major equipment and systems operated satisfactorily throughout the tests.

Jeff(B) is designed to operate at a nominal speed of 50 knots in sea state 2 and accommodate 60 to 75 tons in palletised supplies and/or equipment. In simulated beach attacks Jeff(B) has car-

Jeff(B) being moved into well-deck of Landing Ship Dock USS *Spiegel Grove* (LSD-32) using ship's amphibious in-haul device (AID)

ried ashore to a drop point a 60-ton main battle tank, a jeep and a detachment of US Marines. To ensure adequate world-wide operational capability, the specification calls for operation in temperatures from 0 to 100°F and requires that the performance criteria can be met with a 25 knots headwind on a 100°F day.

LIFT AND PROPULSION: Motive power is supplied by six 2,800hp Avco Lycoming gas turbines, driving four 1·52m (5ft) diameter double-entry centrifugal impellers for lift, and two four-bladed 3·58m (11ft 9in) diameter, Hamilton-Standard variable pitch, ducted propellers, for thrust. Fuel capacity is 29,094 litres (6,400 gallons).

CONTROLS: Deflection of two aerodynamic rudders hinged at the rear of the propeller duct exits, differential propeller pitch, and the deflection of bow thrusters atop the side structures provide steering control. All controls are in a raised bridge well forward on the starboard superstructure. The helmsman's raised platform provides 360-degree vision for the two helmsmen, who have within easy reach all the necessary controls, navigation equipment and instruments. Two more seats are provided at this level for additional crew members. On a lower level in the bridge is an engineer's station with monitoring instrumentation and a radar operator/navigator station. The crew will normally comprise four operating personnel and two deck supervisors.

HULL: Overall structural dimensions of the craft, 24·38 × 13·1 × 5·79m (80 × 43 × 19ft), have been dictated by the well deck dimensions of the US Navy's LSDs (Landing Ship Dock) and LPDs (Amphibious Transport Dock).

The main hull is a 1·37m (4ft 6in) deep buoyancy raft with port and starboard side structures. The main deck between the side structures forms the cargo deck, which is 20·11m long by 8·02m wide (66ft by 26ft 4in), and provides an unobstructed cargo area of 161·46m² (1,738ft²). A full width ramp is provided at the bow and a narrower ramp, capable of taking the main battle tank, at the stern.

The bottom and deck structures of the hull are separated by longitudinal and transverse bulkheads to form a buoyancy raft with a number of watertight flotation compartments. Fuel tanks and the bilge system are contained within these compartments.

Plating at the bottom and side of the hull is stiffened by aluminium extrusions, and the main cargo deck is in mechanically fastened hollow truss-type core extrusions. The transverse bulkheads are sheet webs of aluminium alloy integrally-stiffened extrusions, with upper and lower bulkhead caps, also of aluminium extrusions.

The basic framing of the sidestructures is aluminium back-to-back channels, which coincide with the transverse bulkheads and are spaced apart to straddle the hull bulkheads.

Each sidestructure contains three Avco Lycoming gas turbines, and their associated air intakes, exhausts, lift fans, transmissions and auxiliary power system.

SKIRT: Peripheral bag and finger type, with a 1·52m (5ft) high cushion compartmented by longitudinal and transverse keels. The upper seal bag attachment hinge line is raised high over the bow ramp area and the vertical diaphragm contains non-return valves similar to those fitted to the SR.N4.

DIMENSIONS
Length overall: 26·43m (86ft 9in)
   stowed: 24·38m (80ft)

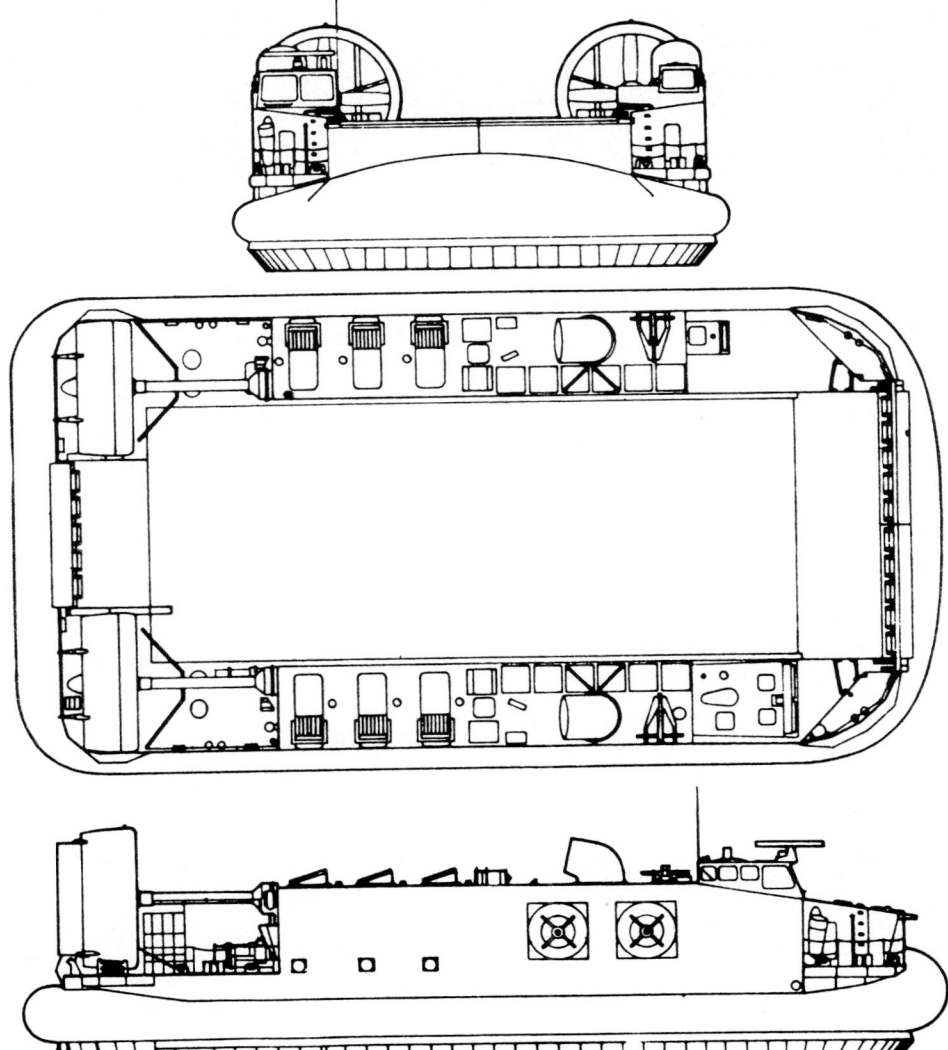

Amphibious Assault Landing Craft (AALC) Jeff(B)

Beam overall: 14·32m (47ft)
  stowed: 13·1m (43ft)
Height: 7·16m (23ft 6in)
Cargo area: 160·71m² (1,738ft²)
Bow ramp width: 8·53m (28ft)
Stern ramp width: 4·41m (14ft 6in)
WEIGHTS
Normal gross: 149,688kg (330,000lb)
Normal payload: 54,431kg (120,000lb)
Overload payload: 68,038kg (150,000lb)
PERFORMANCE
Design operational speed: 50 knots in sea state 2
Range: 200n miles
Max gradient continuous: 13%

LCAC

On 5 June 1981 the US Navy announced a programme to modernise its amphibious forces. Bell Aerospace Textron was awarded a US $40 million contract for the detail design and long-lead material procurement for a new type of amphibious landing craft.

The craft, designated LCAC (Landing Craft, Air Cushion) is the operational version of the Jeff (B) amphibious assault landing craft. The contract contained two options for the later construction of six craft. In February 1982 the US Navy exercised the first option for the production of the three lead craft and in October 1982 it ordered a second batch of three craft.

In March 1984 Bell was awarded a $102 million contract to build six more LCACs, with a $197 million option to construct an additional 12 craft. Bell currently holds contracts to produce a total of 24 LCACs. The first production craft was rolled out on 2 May 1984. A second LCAC is due for completion in late 1984, three are to be delivered in 1985, and seven are scheduled for completion in 1986. The LCACs are being produced at the Bell Halter shipyard in eastern New Orleans, Louisiana.

SES-100B TEST CRAFT

A description of the SES-100B 100-ton sidehull SES test craft can be found in *Jane's Surface Skimmers 1984* and earlier editions.

MINESWEEPER HUNTER (MSH)

In November 1983 it was announced that the US Navy had awarded a $1,000,000 contract to Bell Aerospace for the final phase of the design of a 450-ton minesweeper hunter (MSH) that will ride on an air cushion.

Bell Aerospace was one of four companies to receive an initial design contract for the minesweeper in April 1983 and, following Navy evaluation of submitted designs, was one of two companies contracted to work on the second phase of the programme.

The MSH, which is based on the hull of the Bell Halter SES-200, will be a new class of minesweeper designed to maintain access to US ports and coastal waterways in the event of a mine threat. It will be more resistant to underwater shock from mine explosions than conventional minesweepers as the use of air cushion technology will allow most of the hull to be lifted clear of the water surface. The air cushion also reduces the underwater acoustic and pressure signatures, thereby reducing the risk of triggering mines before they can be detected by the systems aboard the minesweeper.

Machinery arrangements are understood to be similar to those of the SES-200 with diesel engines powering the lift and propulsion systems.

To test the shock resistance of the SES hullform, Bell Aerospace and Bell Halter subjected the BH 110 Mk II SES *Swift Command* to a series of underwater explosions. The tests were conducted about 19 miles southwest of Panama City, Florida, during February and March 1984. Explosive charges were detonated at various stand off distances relative to the SES. All systems operated satisfactorily, even after the most severe shock test on cushion.

A $27·3 million contract for the detail design and construction of the MSH lead ship was awarded by the US Navy at the end of 1984. The contract also gives the US Navy two additional options to acquire eight more MSHs for $126·6 million. These would be awarded in groups of four in 1985 and 1986. The final design of the MSH will be undertaken at Bell's New Orleans Operations and the lead vessel will be built at the Bell Halter Shipyard in New Orleans.

Jeff(B) inside *Spiegel Grove's* well deck

First production Landing Craft, Air Cushion (LCAC-1)

Artist's impression of projected minesweeper hunter (MSH)

BELL AEROSPACE TEXTRON
Division of Textron Inc

Head Office and Works: PO Box 1, Buffalo,
New York 14240, USA
Telephone: (716) 297 1000
TWX: (710) 524 1663
Telex: 91-302
Officials:
Norton C Willcox, *President*
Robert A Norling, *Senior Vice President and
General Manager (Niagara Frontier Opera-
tions)*
Dr Clifford F Berninger, *Vice President (Opera-
tions)*
John R Clark Jr, *Vice President (Eastern Region)*
John J Kelly, *Senior Vice President and General
Manager (New Orleans Operations)*
Joseph R Piselli, *Vice President (Vehicle Prog-
rams)*
Donald F Bonhardt, *Vice President (Product
Assurance)*
John W McKinney, *Vice President (Finance)*
Robert L Cockrell, *Vice President (Business
Development)*

LACV-30

MODEL 7467 LACV-30

This stretched version of the Voyageur has
been designed to meet the US Army's requirements for a high-speed amphibious vehicle for
LOTS (lighter-over-the-shore) operations.

In 1975 Bell built two prototypes as a joint
development between the company's Niagara
Frontier Operations near Niagara Falls, New
York and Bell Aerospace Canada Textron at
Grand Bend, Ontario. The prototypes, owned by
the US Army, are being refurbished by Bell.
Delivery of the first 12 production craft, forming
the US Army 331st Transportation Company at
Fort Story, Virginia, was completed in 1983.
Twelve additional LACV-30s are now in joint
production at the two plants with completion
scheduled for mid-1986.

The chief modifications are a 3·35m (11ft)
lengthening of the deck ahead of the raised control cabin to facilitate the carriage of additional
Milvan containers; the siting of a swing crane at
the bow, which gives the craft a self-discharge
capability in areas where materials handling
equipment is not available; also the provision of a
surf fence and a bow loading ramp.

The LACV-30 (lighter, air cushion vehicle –
30 short tons (60,000lb) payload) is employed
primarily by the US Army as an amphibious

LACV-30

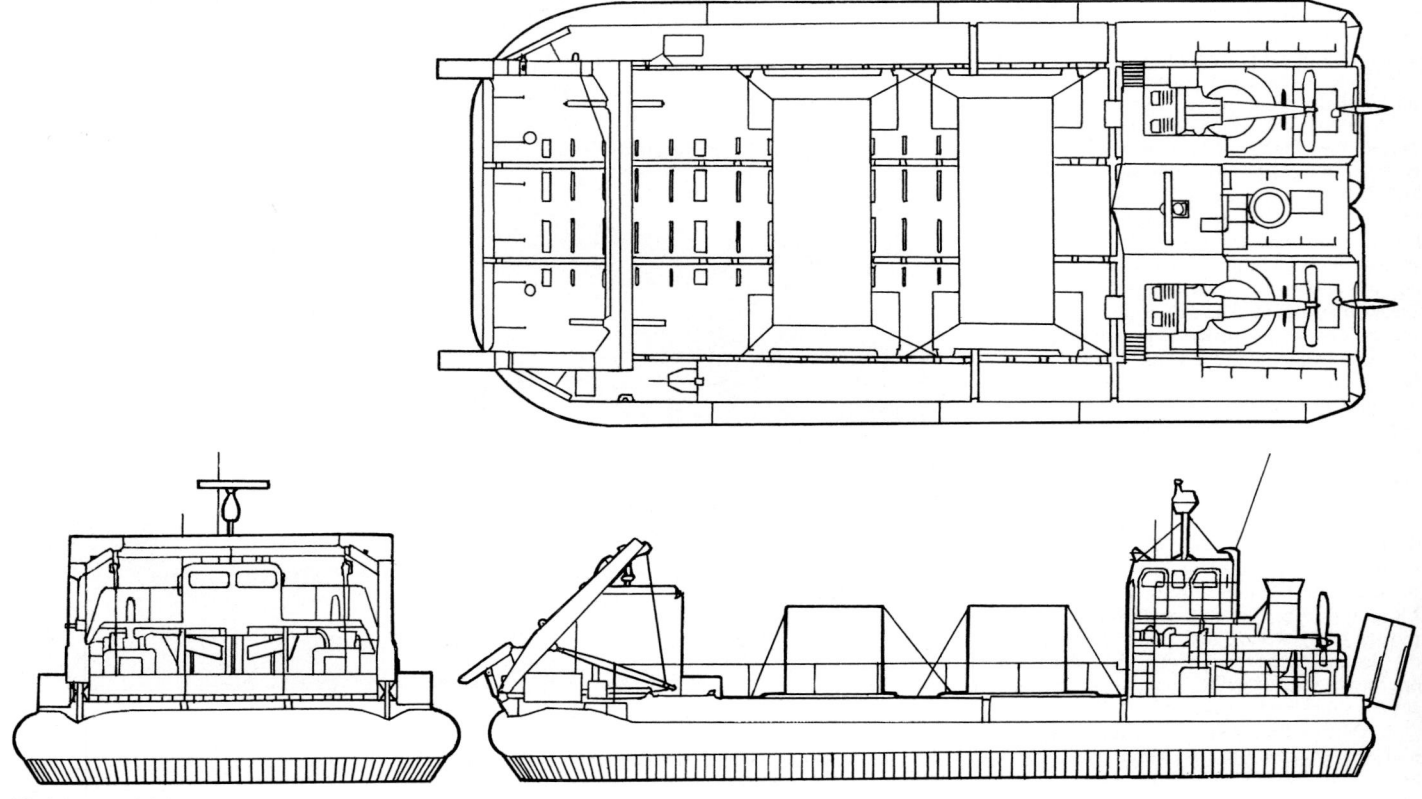

Model 7467 LACV-30

lighter for efficient cargo removal from ship to shore and inland when no port facilities exist. It can travel at 62 miles per hour (99km/h), and operates over water, land, snow, ice, marshes, swamps and low brush, through 8ft surf and over 4ft obstacles. It hauls a variety of containerised cargo, wheeled and tracked vehicles, engineer equipment, pallets and barrels.

The craft can be used on 70 per cent of beaches compared to the 17 per cent accessible to conventional lighterage craft. It permits dry landings for many payloads. Its air cushion makes it an effective icebreaker. It operates in harsh environments, from arctic to tropical conditions, including sand beaches and salt water. It has achieved the best productivity per craft of all the US Army lighterage systems.

The LACV-30 can be carried, fully assembled, on containerships and break-bulk cargo ships,

launched by the ships' crews and readied for service in a few hours. It disassembles into 15 sections, including structural and power modules, side decks, landing pads, flexible skirts and cabin, for transport by truck, rail or aircraft. It does not require dock or berthing facilities.

The LACV-30 will replace the amphibious LARC-5 and LARC-15.

Endurance at cruising speed depends on the configuration/role in which the craft is used. For the drive-on cargo and Milvan cargo roles the craft can carry payloads of 30 short tons with an endurance of two hours. In the self-unload Milvan cargo role the payload is reduced to 26·5 short tons for the same endurance. Other configurations give endurance figures of between 5 hours and 9 hours 6 minutes with varying payloads.

The craft is also suitable for a number of sec-

ondary roles such as coastal, harbour and inland waterway patrol, search and rescue, medical evacuation, water and fuel supply, vehicle, personnel and troop transport, augmentation of fixed ports, pollution and fire control.

LIFT AND PROPULSION: Integrated system, powered by two Pratt and Whitney ST6T Twin-Pac gas turbines mounted aft, one at each side of the raised control cabin. Each engine is rated at 1,800shp maximum and 1,400shp at normal output. The output of each is absorbed by a three-bladed Hamilton Standard 43D50-367 reversible-pitch propeller and a 2·13m (7ft) diameter, twelve-bladed, fixed-pitch light aluminium alloy, centrifugal lift fan.

FUEL: Recommended fuel is standard aviation kerosene-Jet A-1, JP4, JP5, JP8 or light diesel fuel oil. Main usable fuel capacity is 9,419 litres (2,272 gallons). Fuel ballast/emergency fuel capacity 6,960 litres (1,531 gallons).

SYSTEMS, ELECTRICAL: Starter generators: four gearbox-driven, brushless, 28V dc, 200A each. Batteries: two nickel cadmium, 28V dc, 40Ah each.

DIMENSIONS

Length overall, on cushion: 23·3m (76ft 6in)
Beam overall, on cushion: 11·2m (36ft 8in)
Height overall, on cushion: 7·52m (24ft 8in)
  off cushion: 6·56m (21ft 6in)
Skirt height, nominal: 1·21m (4ft)
Height, cargo deck, off cushion: 1·16m (3ft 10in)
Cargo deck: 15·69 × 9·9m (51ft 6in × 32ft 6in)

WEIGHTS

Design gross: 52,163kg (115,000lb)

PERFORMANCE (estimated)

Standard day, zero wind, calm water, at gross weight of 52,163kg (115,000lb):
  Normal rating: 74km/h (46mph)
  Max rating: 99km/h (62mph)
Estimated fuel consumption during lighterage missions: 1,159 litres/h (260 gallons/h)

LACV-30

BELL HALTER INC

6800 Plaza Drive, New Orleans, Louisiana 70127-2596, USA
Telephone: (504) 245 6699
TWX: (810) 951 5028
Cables: BELLHAL NLN
Officials:
John J Kelly, *President*
John B Chaplin, *Vice President, Engineering*
James W Steadman, *Vice President, Operations*
John W Hedges, *Secretary*
Donald E Kenney, *Treasurer*
John W McKinney, *Vice President*
John K Lyons, *Assistant Treasurer*
Charles R Le Blanc, *Controller*

Bell Halter Inc is jointly owned by Bell Aerospace Textron, Division of Textron Inc, and by Halter Marine Inc. The corporation was founded in 1979, replacing a joint venture established in 1977 to produce a 110ft SES demonstration vessel. It combines Bell's technical background in air cushion craft with Halter's 20 years' experience as boat builders. Bell Aerospace Textron has been in the forefront of air cushion vehicle and surface effect ship development since 1958. Halter Marine is one of the world's largest builders of

offshore supply vessels, over 1,000 of which have been delivered to United States and overseas operators, and has extensive experience in steel, aluminium and fibreglass construction. Halter has also built a large number of fast patrol boats for navies in the Middle East, South America and the Far East.

Bell Halter has the largest team of engineers experienced in the design of air cushion craft in the USA which is aided by an extensive data base from model and full-scale trials. State-of-the art CAD/CAM (computer-aided design and computer-aided manufacturing) systems are in use for the production of high quality drawings and high accuracy cutting and welding of aluminium plate.

Bell Halter's ACV/SES manufacturing facility, completed in 1982, is a 15-acre site alongside an existing Halter Marine shipyard in eastern New Orleans, Louisiana and has direct access to the Intercoastal Waterway, the Mississippi River and the Gulf of Mexico. The building covers 168,000ft², and it is planned that an additional 110,000ft² will be added as the production of SESs and US Navy LCACs (Landing Craft, Air Cushion) increases.

Bell Halter offers a range of surface effect ships

for commercial and military applications. Each of several basic hulls can be fitted with production marine diesel engines to offer speeds in the 30- to 50-knot range, with exceptional efficiency and fuel economy. Higher power diesels or gas turbines in combination diesel or gas turbine (CODOG) or combination diesel and gas turbine (CODAG) arrangements can be fitted to some models, producing speeds in the 50- to 70-knot range. Vessels are in service with the US Army Corps of Engineers, the US Navy, the US Coast Guard and a commercial crewboat operator, and have accumulated many thousands of hours of service.

BELL HALTER MODEL 720A HYDROGRAPHIC SURVEY BOAT (RODOLF)

Rodolf was built in 1979 and delivered to the US Army Corps of Engineers (Portland District) in early 1980.

The vessel operates as a displacement catamaran at low speeds and as an air-cushion-assisted planing catamaran at high speeds. With the lift system shut down, speeds in excess of 24km/h (15mph) are possible, with the sidehulls supporting 100 per cent of the weight through a combination of buoyancy and planing forces. The lift system can be employed at any speed to support part of the weight of the boat. At high speeds, up to 85 per cent of the weight can be supported by the air cushion, with a resulting increase of lift-to-drag ratio from 5 to approximately 11. The maximum speed is thereby increased to 56·32km/h (35mph). Over the complete speed range, from 24 to 56km/h (15 to 35mph) approximately, total power requirements, and hence fuel consumption, can be reduced by selecting the appropriate lift fan rpm settings.

LIFT AND PROPULSION: The lift system is powered by a single Detroit Diesel 4-53N rated at 105shp at 2,600rpm. Propulsive thrust is supplied by twin Detroit Diesel Allison 8V92N marine diesels rated at 360hp at 2,100rpm, each driving a propeller via a standard Allison M reduction gear with a ratio of 1·52:1. Fuel is

Bell Halter hydrographic survey boat, *Rodolf*

carried in four tanks, each with a capacity of 1,325 litres (350 US gallons).

CONTROLS: Directional control is provided by twin water rudders aft, one on each sidehull, in addition to the differential use of propeller thrust for slow speed manoeuvring.

HULL: Primary structure is built of welded marine aluminium alloy 5086. The structure is of catamaran configuration and consists of two sidehulls, separated by decks and the cabin structure. The sidehull shell plating varies between ⅛ and ¼ in thick, depending on local pressures, and is stiffened by T-section longitudinals. Sidehull shape is maintained by frames and bulkheads, spaced generally at 0·91 to 1·52m (3 to 5ft), that support the hull longitudinals.

Three watertight bulkheads are used in each sidehull and across the centre section between the hulls. Two are at the forward and aft ends of the cabin and one is forward of the helmsman's platform. The latter also forms a collision bulkhead. The bulkheads provide transverse bending and torsional continuity to the hull structure. There are also longitudinal watertight bulkheads running the full length of the craft aft of the collision bulkhead.

SKIRT: Flexible skirts at bow and stern. The bow seal consists of six fingers, each approximately 3·96m (13ft) long, 0·6m (2ft) wide and 1·95m (6ft 6in) high. All fingers are identical.

The stern seal has a constant cross-section and consists of two inflated lobes of coated-fabric material, with a horizontal diaphragm to sustain pressure loads. End caps, which bear partly on the sidehulls, contain the air at the ends of the seal. Principal dimensions of the stern seal are length 2·13m (7ft) and height 1·21m (4ft). Each lobe has a radius of approximately 304mm (1ft).

ACCOMMODATION: Deckhouse structure contains pilothouse, cabin and lift system housing. Pilothouse is in forward portion with pilothouse deck slightly higher than weather deck elevation. Main cabin deck is recessed below weather deck between sidehulls. Main cabin profile is lower than pilothouse to allow visibility directly aft through rear-facing pilothouse windows. Two interior stairways lead from main cabin deck level; one to pilothouse level and one to the aft section of weather deck. Provision is made for complement of seven crew and/or observers.

DIMENSIONS

EXTERNAL
Length overall: 14·63m (48ft)
Beam overall: 7·31m (24ft)
Height overall: 4·72m (15ft 6in)
Draught, max static: 1·6m (5ft 3in)
Skirt depth, bow: 1·82m (6ft)
    stern: 1·21m (4ft)
Cushion area: 62·92m² (677ft²)

INTERNAL
Length: 7·01m (23ft)
Max width: 3·65m (12ft)
Max height: 2·13m (7ft)
Floor area: 25·64m² (276ft²)

WEIGHTS
Normal empty: 18·6 long tons
Survey equipment: 1·2 long tons
Fuel capacity: 4·4 long tons
Normal gross: 24·2 long tons

PERFORMANCE
Max speed over calm water, max continuous power: 33 knots (29°C (85°F))
Cruising speed, calm water: 23 knots
Water speed in 1·22m (4ft) waves and 15 knot headwind: 24 knots
Still air range and endurance at cruising speed: 1,090n miles and 50 hours
Max speed, over calm water, hullborne at 18·7 long tons displacement: 17 knots

BELL HALTER MODEL 410A HARBOUR UTILITY BOAT OR FIREBOAT

The Bell Halter Model 410A is a derivative of *Rodolf* and designed for use as a harbour patrol vessel or, when suitably equipped, as a small fireboat. The overall dimensions are the same as those of *Rodolf*, but the hull lines have been revised to increase cushion area and reduce

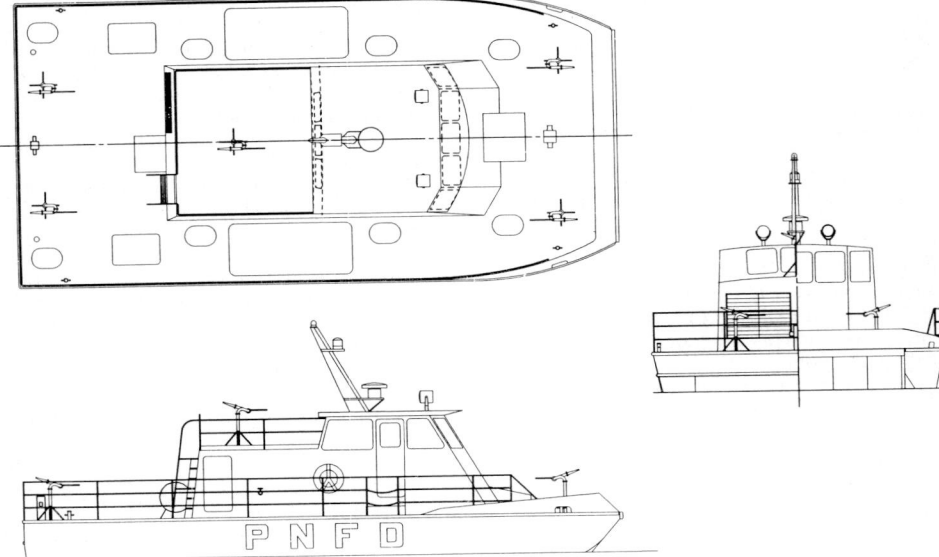

BH Model 410A harbour utility boat or fireboat

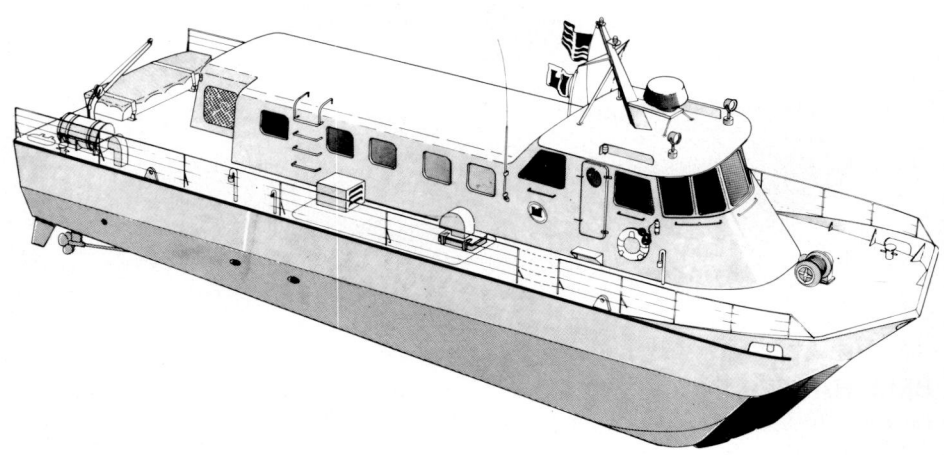

BH Model 415A utility boat or fishing vessel

sidehull drag. Propulsion engines of between 250 and 400hp can be installed giving cruising speeds between 25 and 40 knots. High speed, fuel efficiency, and low wave making characteristics make it ideal for harbour security where a long waterfront has to be protected with limited resources.

BELL HALTER MODEL 415A UTILITY OR FISHING VESSEL

The Bell Halter Model 415A is a derivative of the BH 410A, with overall length increased to 19·8m (65ft) for added payload capacity. The vessel has a wide range of applications, including harbour security and hydrographic survey, when more equipment and/or personnel are required. A version can be offered as a charter fishing vessel and, in comparison with conventional boats, improvements include reduced travel time to fishing grounds, improved ride, larger deck area and greater stability on site.

PROPULSION: Two 8V92TI Detroit Diesel marine engines, rated at 430hp, each driving two 635mm (25in) diameter, four-bladed, stainless steel propellers.

LIFT: One 4-53T Detroit Diesel marine engine, rated at 155hp, driving one Bell Aerospace Textron 838mm (33in) diameter centrifugal fan.

SYSTEMS, ELECTRICAL: Generators: Two Onan, 15kW

DIMENSIONS
Length overall: 19·8m (65ft)
Beam overall: 7·92m (26ft)
Depth moulded: 2·92m (9ft 7in)
Draught, off cushion: 1·82m (6ft)
    on cushion: 1·21m (4ft)

WEIGHTS
Displacement, light ship: 28,086kg (62,000lb)
Payload: 3,171kg (7,000lb)
Fuel capacity: 1,950 US gallons
Displacement, full load: 37,146kg (82,000lb)

PERFORMANCE
Speed: 32 knots
Range: 1,000n miles

BELL HALTER MODEL 210A (110 Mk I) DEMONSTRATION SES

Launched in late 1978, the BH 110 demonstration boat has undergone extensive successful testing by both commercial operators and the US Coast Guard. The basic hull and machinery layout permits modification of the deckhouse and arrangement of the deck space for a number of alternative applications, from crew boat and 275-seat passenger ferry to fast patrol boat.

In September 1980 the US Navy purchased the Bell Halter Demonstration SES (110 Mk I) to be used in a joint US Navy/US Coast Guard programme. The US Coast Guard, designating the boat the USCG *Dorado* (WSES-1), conducted an operational evaluation of the craft for the first six months of the programme. Bell Halter modified the craft to conform to US Coast Guard requirements for an operational evaluation vessel. The US Coast Guard has completed its evaluation and Bell Halter has added a 15·24m (50ft) hull extension to the boat for the US Navy to assess the performance of a higher length-to-beam vessel. The craft has been designated the SES-200 by the US Navy (see later entry).

LIFT AND PROPULSION: Cushion lift is provided by two 445hp Detroit Diesel Allison 8V92TI diesels each driving identical Bell-designed fans constructed in aluminium. Fan air inlets are in a housing aft of the deckhouse. Cushion air is discharged into two longitudinal ducts between the second and wet decks. Some is released into the cushion for pressurisation, the remainder is programmed between the bow and stern seals.

Motive power for the propulsion system is supplied by two Detroit Diesel Allison 16V149TI diesels, each rated at 1,600hp at 1,900rpm. Each engine drives a 1·07m (42in) diameter Gawn-Burrill propeller via a Reintjes marine reduction gearbox. One right- and one left-hand rotating propellers are used. Seven fuel tanks, with two integral tanks within the sidehulls, provide a total capacity of 26,224 litres (6,928 US gallons). Refuelling is through fillers on the main deck, port and starboard sides. Oil is integral with the engines and gearboxes.

CONTROLS: Craft direction is controlled by twin rudders, one aft on each sidehull. Differential propeller thrust is employed for slow-speed manoeuvring. The steering system is electro-hydraulic and can be operated from any of the control stations in the pilothouse and the wing bridges.

HULL: Primary structure is built in welded marine aluminium alloy 5086. The structure is of catamaran configuration and consists of two sidehulls separated by decks and transverse bulkheads. The sidehull shell plating varies between ¼ and ½in depending on local pressures, and is stiffened by T-section longitudinals. The spacing of the longitudinals is 457mm (1ft 6in) on the bottom plating and 381mm (1ft 3in) on the side plating. Sidehull shape is maintained by bulkheads spaced generally at 2·44m (8ft) which support the hull longitudinals. Bulkheads have ⅛in webs with T-section and flat bar stiffening and flat bar caps sized appropriately for each bulkhead.

Four of the bulkheads in each sidehull and also across the centre section between the hulls are watertight. Two are in the accommodation area, and one is forward of the deckhouse. The latter also forms a collision bulkhead. The bulkheads provide the transverse bending and torsional continuity to the hull structure.

The cabin superstructure consists of T-section frames fabricated from flat bars and spaced as the frames on the hull. T-stiffened plate is welded to the framing.

SKIRT: The bow seal consists of eight equally spaced fingers, each of which is attached to the underside of the centre hull. The stern seal, which has a constant cross section, consists of inflated horizontal lobes of coated-fabric material.

ACCOMMODATION: Deckhouse structure comprises pilothouse on 01 level and crew quarters for seven on main deck. Pilothouse contains controls, navigation and communications systems. Second deck has additional crew quarters for seven, galley, messroom and lounge.

ARMAMENT: Two 50 calibre machine guns mounted on bridge deck, one port, one starboard.

SYSTEMS, ELECTRICAL: Ac and dc electrical systems provide electrical power. The prime system is a Detroit Diesel Allison diesel/generator set. The prime mover is rated at 86hp at 1,800rpm. Electrical output is 60Hz at 1,800rpm. Voltage is 208/240 three-phase with a 55kW rating. A back-up 40kW generator can be driven off the port lift engine.

DIMENSIONS

EXTERNAL
Length overall: 33·52m (110ft)
Beam overall: 11·88m (39ft)
Height, on cushion: 12m (39ft 5in)
off cushion: 10·26m (33ft 8in)
Draught, on cushion: 1·67m (5ft 6in)
off cushion: 2·51m (8ft 3in)
Skirt depth, bow: 2·28m (7ft 6in)
stern: 1·52m (5ft)

INTERNAL
Control cabin
Length: 4·57m (15ft)
Max width: 3·35m (11ft)
Max height: 2·13m (7ft)
Main cabin
Length: 8·53m (28ft)
Max width: 9·14m (30ft)
Max height: 2·13m (7ft)
Floor area: 78·04m² (840ft²)

WEIGHTS
Light ship displacement: 105 long tons
Max displacement: 150 long tons
Max payload: 20 long tons

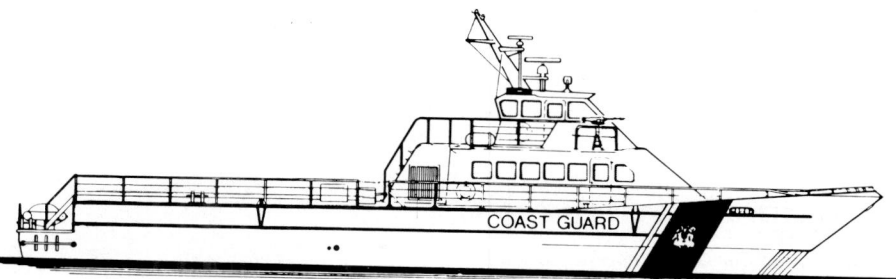

Outboard profile of USCG *Dorado* (WSES-1)

USCG *Dorado* (WSES-1), formerly BH 110 demonstrator SES

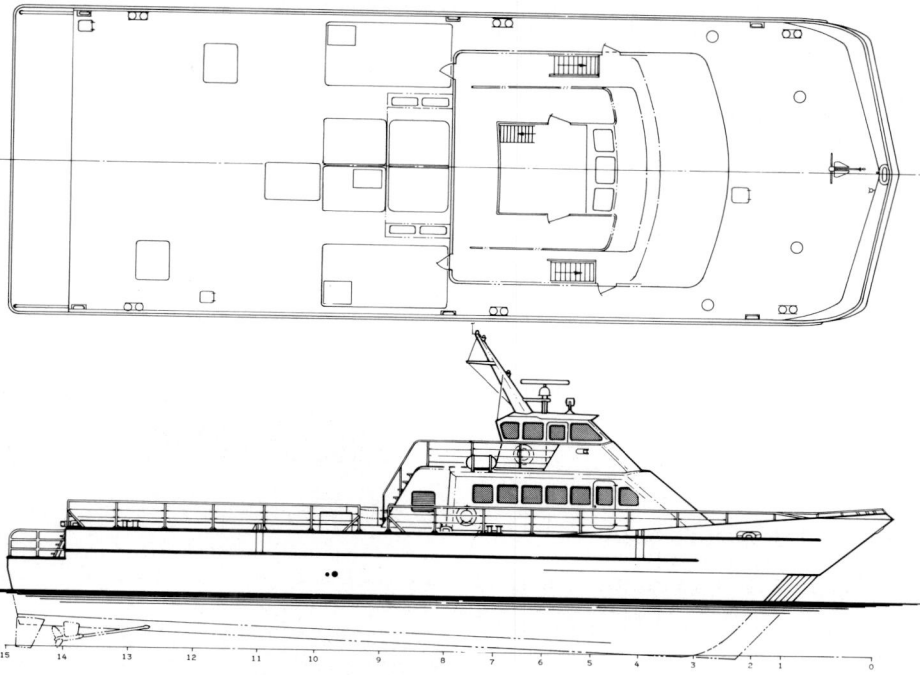

Original outboard profile and plans of BH 110 demonstration SES

BH 110 demonstration SES

PERFORMANCE (16V149TI engines)

	sea state 0	sea state 3
Cruising speed,		
on cushion:	35 knots	30 knots
off cushion:	19 knots	15 knots

Range: 1,000n miles in sea state 3

BELL HALTER MODEL 212A (110 Mk II) DASHBOATS

Command Marine Inc, Lafayette, Louisiana, has taken delivery of two Bell Halter Model 212A Dashboats (crewboats) for transporting personnel and priority cargo between operating bases and oil drilling sites in the Gulf of Mexico.

In overall design the Dashboat is very similar to the Bell Halter 110 prototype. The vessel is able to carry up to 127 passengers or 30 tons of cargo at 32 knots in calm seas and 28 knots in sea and weather conditions in which conventional marine transport cannot operate.

The first Dashboat, *Speed Command*, completed trials in January 1981 and was delivered in February 1981. The second vessel, *Swift Command*, completed trials and was delivered in July 1981.

LIFT AND PROPULSION: Cushion lift is provided by two Detroit Diesel Allison 8V92N marine diesels, each driving a double-inlet centrifugal lift fan. Motive power for the propulsion system is furnished by two SACM 175V12 RVR marine diesels each rated at 1,330hp at 1,500rpm. Each drives a fixed-pitch propeller. Maximum fuel load is 7,500 gallons.

CONTROLS, HULL AND SKIRT: As for Bell Halter 110 demonstration SES.

ACCOMMODATION: Deckhouse superstructure contains pilothouse, with passenger cabin below on main deck. Additional passenger seating on second deck. Command Marine vessels seat 127 passengers, with alternative arrangements for specific customer requirements. Second deck has living accommodation for 10 crew.

DIMENSIONS: As for BH 110 prototype.

WEIGHTS

Max displacement: 150 long tons
Normal displacement: 126 long tons
Light ship displacement: 98 long tons
Max deck load: 40 long tons

RANGE

Sea state 0: 1,650n miles
Sea state 3: 1,450n miles

PERFORMANCE

Sea state	0 (calm)	3 (wave height to 4·6ft)
Speed,		
on cushion:	32 knots	28 knots
off cushion:	19 knots	15 knots

BELL HALTER MODEL 522A US COAST GUARD SES

In June 1981 the US Coast Guard awarded Bell Halter a contract for the purchase of three Bell Halter Model 522A (110 Mk II) high-speed cutters, the first two of which were delivered in October 1982.

The craft, known as the 'Seabird' class, are designated *Sea Hawk* (WSES-2), *Shearwater* (WSES-3) and *Petrel* (WSES-4). *Petrel* was delivered in June 1983. These vessels are based at Key West, Florida, at a new Coast Guard facility, and are being used to intercept illegal drug runners operating in the Gulf of Mexico and in the Caribbean Sea.

LIFT AND PROPULSION: Cushion lift is provided by two Detroit Diesel Allison 8V92N marine diesels each driving a double-inlet centrifugal fan. Motive power for the propulsion system is furnished by two GM 16V149TI marine diesels each rated at 1,600 hp at 1,900 rpm. Each drives a 1·06m (42in) diameter three-bladed, fixed-pitch propeller. Maximum fuel load is 34,050 litres (7,500 gallons).

CONTROLS, HULL and SKIRT: As for Bell Halter Model 212A Dashboats.

ACCOMMODATION: Deckhouse superstructure contains pilothouse at 01 level with com-

BH 110 Mk II *Swift Command* during underwater explosion test

munications and navigation equipment. Auxiliary aft-facing control station is provided plus additional controls on each wing bridge. Main deckhouse contains ship's office, armory, captain's stateroom, quarters for three officers and three men. Second deck accommodation includes galley and additional quarters for 12 crew.

ARMAMENT: Two 50-calibre machine guns on the foredeck.

DIMENSIONS: As for Bell Halter Model 212A Dashboats.

WEIGHTS

Max displacement: 150 long tons
Normal displacement: 134 long tons
Light ship displacement: 105 long tons

PERFORMANCE

Speed,	sea state 0	sea state 3
on cushion:	30 knots	28 knots
hullborne:	19 knots	16 knots

RANGE

Sea state 0: 1,550n miles
Sea state 3: 1,250n miles

US Coast Guard cutter *Petrel*

Sea Hawk and *Shearwater*, the first two Model 522A cutters to be delivered to US Coast Guard

BELL HALTER MODEL 340 PASSENGER FERRY

The Bell Halter Model 340 is a derivative of the Bell Halter Model 210 crewboat, with an extended superstructure and seating for 276 passengers on the main deck. Second deck spaces can be used as passenger lounges, snack bars, or game rooms, according to customer requirements.

The overall dimensions are the same as those of the Model 210, and the same machinery could be used providing speed performance in the 30- to 32-knot range. Higher power diesels and variable-pitch propellers can be installed to provide cruising speeds between 40 and 50 knots.

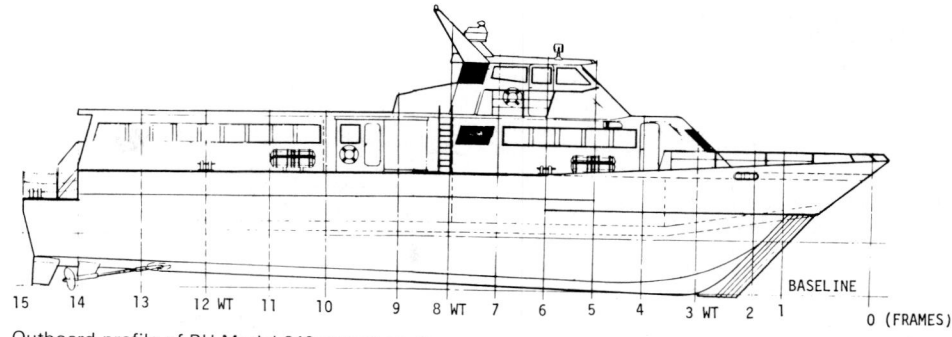

Outboard profile of BH Model 340 passenger ferry

SES-2000 BELL HALTER MODEL 730A HIGH LENGTH-TO-BEAM (L/B) TEST CRAFT

The original 110ft SES demonstration boat is now owned by the US Navy. Bell Halter modified the boat by adding a 50ft (15·24m) hull extension. The hull was cut amidships; the lift fans and engines remaining in the bow and the main engines remaining in the stern. Bow and stern sections were then moved apart and a 50ft (15·24m) plug section inserted between them. All major systems remained the same as they were in the original vessel, including the GM 16V149TI engines.

In this configuration, the vessel has a 60 per cent greater disposable load than the demonstration boat, while its maximum speed is only reduced by 3 to 4 knots. At intermediate speeds, the power requirements are lower than for the shorter vessel, despite the greater displacement.

The engine rooms of the SES-200 can accommodate larger diesels, or CODOG/CODAG arrangements of diesels and gas turbines, to extend the speed capability up to the 50-knot range. Simple modifications have been made to reinforce the aft deck for helicopter operations. In this configuration, the beam of the vessel and the forward location of the superstructure results in a flight deck as large as those normally found on multi-thousand-ton naval combatants.

DIMENSIONS
Length overall: 48·7m (160ft)
Beam overall: 11·88m (39ft)
Height, on cushion: 12m (39ft 5in)
WEIGHTS
Displacement, light ship: 125 long tons
Fuel capacity: 80,128 litres (17,630 US gallons)
Displacement, full load: 200 long tons
PERFORMANCE (typical operating displacement)

Speed,	sea state 0	sea state 3
on cushion:	32 knots	27 knots
off cushion:	16 knots	14 knots

RANGE
Sea state 0: 2,950n miles at 30 knots
3,850n miles at 20 knots
Sea state 3: 2,400n miles at 25 knots
2,900n miles at 20 knots

BELL HALTER MODEL 350 PASSENGER FERRY

The all-welded-aluminium construction of Bell Halter SESs permits the tailoring of hull length to match specific payload capacity and performance requirements. The Model 350 is a high capacity passenger ferry based on the proven 110ft series of SESs, with a hull length of 48·7m (160ft). Seating for 450 passengers can be provided on the main deck, with spacious lounge areas, casino, or passenger service facilities on the second deck. A smaller first-class cabin can be provided on the 01 level behind the pilothouse giving greater comfort and outside visibility to passengers.

As with all Bell Halter designs, the make and type of power plants can be selected to comply with operator preference. The standard vessel is powered by SACM 195V16RVR main engines driving fixed-pitch propellers, providing cruising speeds of up to 40 knots.

DIMENSIONS
Length overall: 48·7m (160ft)

BH Model 350 passenger ferry

Model 730A (SES-200) operated by US Navy

Beam overall: 11·88m (39ft)
Height overall: 12·03m (39ft 6in)
WEIGHTS
Light ship: 152 long tons
Payload: 42 long tons
Normal fuel: 10 long tons

Gross weight: 204 long tons
PERFORMANCE
Speed,
   sea state 0: 40 knots
   sea state 3: 36 knots
Range: 340n miles

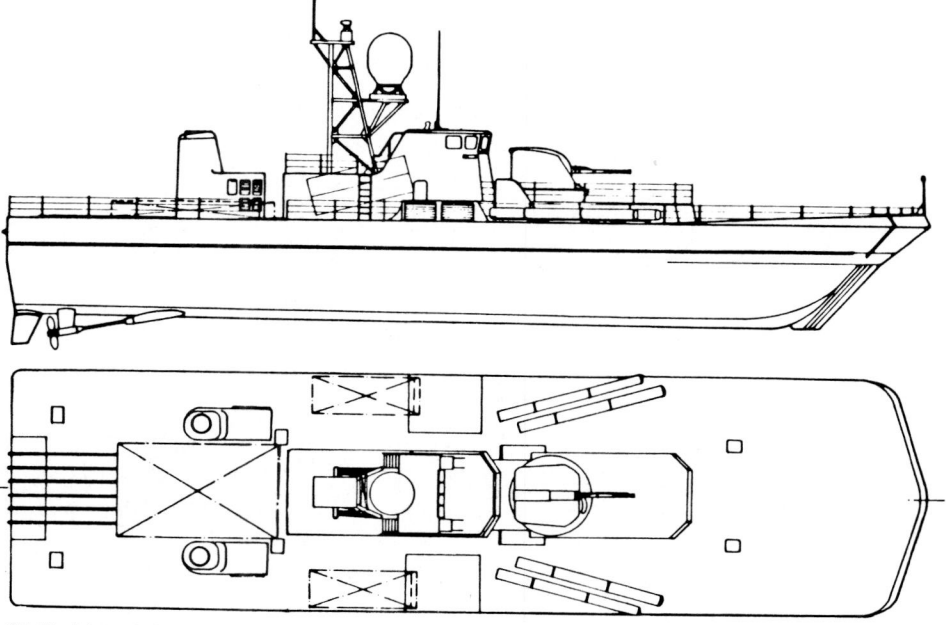

BH Model 511A fast patrol craft

BELL HALTER MODEL 511A
FAST PATROL CRAFT

The Bell Halter Model 511A fast patrol craft uses the basic hull form of the 110ft SES and the overall length is increased to 45·72m (150ft). Construction is of welded 5086 marine aluminium, with T-stiffened plating for the exterior shell and bulkheads. The hull is divided into seven watertight compartments for safety in the event of hull damage. The second deck provides accommodation for a ship's complement of 28 officers and crew, together with wardroom, galley and mess facilities. A wide range of weapons systems, electronic warfare and countermeasures can be accommodated on the main deck. A high degree of computerised control and integration of the weapons systems with the ship systems can be provided.

DIMENSIONS
Length overall: 45·72m (150ft)
Beam overall: 11·88m (39ft)
Draught, on cushion: 1·82m (6ft)
    off cushion: 2·74m (9ft)

MEDIUM DISPLACEMENT
COMBATANT

Bell Halter is continuing its research to extend the design technology of its existing range of surface effect ships to the 1,000- to 1,500-ton class ocean going naval combatant. The vessel would be of high length-to-beam configuration and would use high displacement sidehulls for efficient operation in the hullborne mode. The propulsion system would use partially submerged supercavitating propellers driven by CODOG machinery for high efficiency at all speeds. The vessel is fully air capable, with flight deck and hangar accommodation for two LAMPS helicopters.

ARCTIC SUPPLY ACV

The Arctic Supply ACV has been designed for operation in the coastal and offshore regions of the Beaufort Sea, off the northern shores of Alaska and Canada. It employs marine diesel engines for propulsion and lift and can carry payloads of up to 100 tons across 2·28 to 2·43m high ice ridges while cruising at speeds of up to 20 knots. The craft can also operate over water, snow, marsh, and tundra.

LIFT AND PROPULSION: Two Caterpillar 3512 diesel engines provide motive power for the lift system. Each is rated at 1,200hp continuous and drives a 1·4m diameter Bell-designed centrifugal fan. Thrust is supplied by four Caterpillar 3516 diesel engines each driving a 5·02m controllable pitch air propeller. The propulsion engines are rated at 1,900hp maximum and 1,600hp continuous. Power is transmitted to the propellers through right-angle speed-reducing gearboxes. The lift and propulsion engines have

PERFORMANCE		
	3,200 hp diesels	CODOG (GE LM500 or Allison 570-KF)
Speed,		
calm:	39 knots	54 knots
sea state 3:	32 knots	45 knots
sea state 5:	27 knots	38 knots
RANGE		
High speed:	1,140n miles	860n miles
Low speed:	1,420n miles	1,500n miles

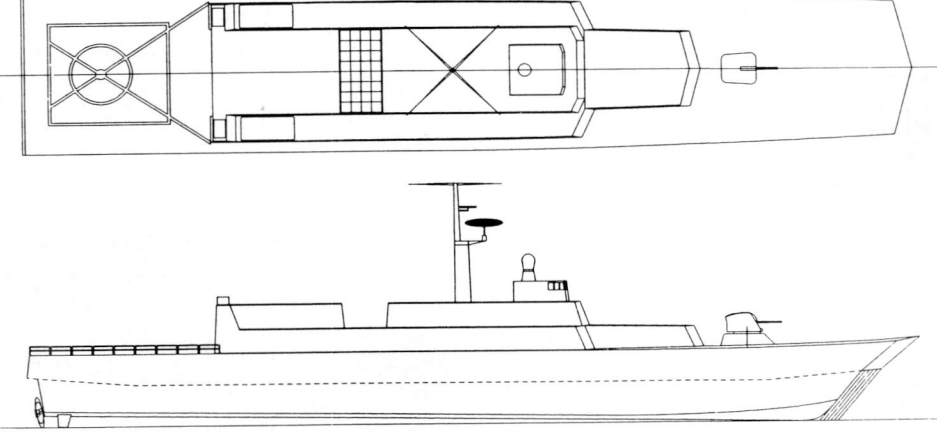

SES-1500 medium displacement combatant

closed-loop liquid coolant systems with standard heat exchangers.

Two 2·43m diameter retractable wheels, each driven by a 150hp hydraulic motor, are installed near the midship position to improve low-speed control in winds, as well as to improve grade-climbing ability.

CONTROLS: Primary control is provided by the four air propellers each of which is fully controllable from maximum positive to maximum negative pitch. Collective variation of pitch and/or rpm applies forward or reverse thrust, while differential variation, port and starboard, applies yawing moments. Secondary control for low speed operation is supplied by hydraulically powered low pressure wheels, which also can be controlled collectively for thrust or braking, or differentially for yaw control.

HULL: All welded 5456 marine aluminium with a double-bottom construction for protection against ice-ridge impacts. The buoyancy box consists of the bottom plating (wet deck) and the cargo deck separated by 19 full-width transverse bulkheads, two full-length longitudinal bulkheads, and the outer edges of the vessel. The cargo deck, 8·53m wide, extends the full length of the craft. A hydraulically operated ramp at the stern permits roll-on and roll-off loading and

unloading of cargo with fork lift trucks and transport of wheeled vehicles. The craft can also be loaded over the bow from fixed ground-based loading ramps, and over the side by overhead cranes.

ACCOMMODATION: The control station, aft of the amidship position, extends 6·09m above the cargo deck. This provides the operating crew of three with unlimited visibility in all directions from an eye-level height of 11·27m when operating cushionborne.

Main hull provides living accommodation for six crew and comprises four staterooms and galley, mess, and lounge.

SKIRT: A full peripheral skirt, comprising 1·21m wide by 3·04m high open fingers around bow and sides and closed fingers at the stern, provides 3·04m hull clearance for operation over 2·28 to 2·43m ice ridges at cruising speed.

DIMENSIONS
Length overall (including ramp): 52·12m
Beam overall: 20·42m
Height overall, on cushion: 11·88m
    off cushion: 8·6m
Cargo deck: 45·41m × 8·53m
WEIGHTS
Light ship displacement: 258 long tons
Design load: 352 long tons
Max load: 372 long tons
PERFORMANCE
Max speed, over rough ice: Greater than 20 knots
    Sea State 2: 11·5 knots
Range over rough ice: 300n miles

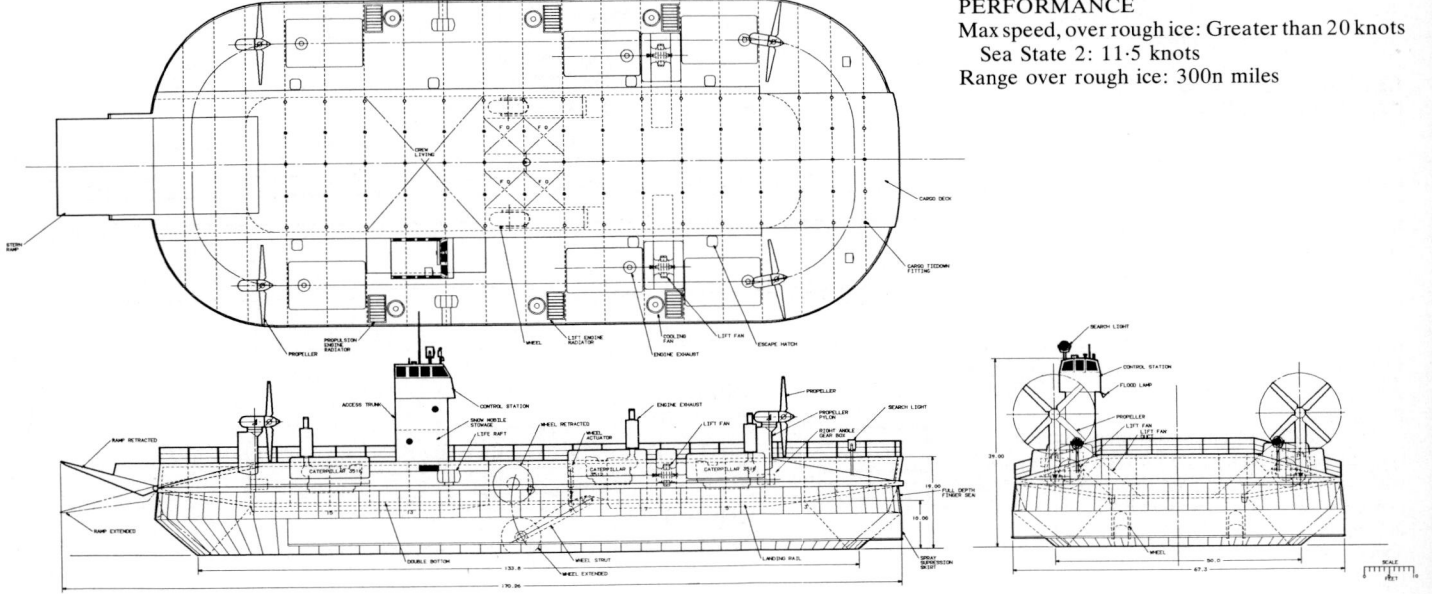

372-ton Arctic Supply ACV

BELL AVON INC

Picayune, Mississippi, USA

Officials:
David Miller, *General Manager*

This new company is a joint venture between Avon Industrial Polymers, part of the Avon Rubber Group and Bell Aerospace Textron. Initially the company will manufacture and maintain hovercraft skirt components for existing US Navy and commercial craft, using the technology and materials developed and manufactured at Avon's Chippenham plant in the UK.

The ground breaking ceremony for the new plant took place in October 1984. The first phase is the construction of an air-conditioned 20,000sq ft building on a six-acre site. During the next four years it is anticipated that the workforce will grow to 80.

Avon has been supplying materials and components for the first twelve LCACs, currently under construction at Bell Halter's New Orleans Shipyard for the US Navy. It also fabricates skirts for Bell Halter's Model 522A (110 Mk II) 'Seabird' class high speed SES cutters, now in service with the US Coast Guard at Key West, Florida.

BERTELSEN INC

Head Office: 210 W 22nd Street, Oak Brook, Illinois 60521, USA
Telephone: (312) 920 9748
Works: 113 Commercial Street, Neponset, Illinois 61345, USA
Officials:
William R Bertelsen, *Chairman of the Board, Vice President and Director of Research*
William C Stein, *President and Treasurer*
Charles A Brady, *Secretary*

Dr William R Bertelsen, a general practitioner and talented engineer, was one of the first to build and drive an air cushion vehicle.

Dr Bertelsen designed his first Aeromobile air cushion vehicle in 1950, and has since built and tested 16 full-scale vehicles, ranging from simple plenum craft to ram-wings. The 5·4m (18ft) long Aeromobile 200-2 was a star exhibit at the US Government's Trade Fairs in Tokyo, Turin, Zagreb and New Delhi in 1961. Descriptions of the Aeromobile 14 and 15 can be found in *Jane's Surface Skimmers 1980* and earlier editions. An Aeromobile system of rapid transit, based on the Aeromobile 13, is described in the section devoted to Tracked Skimmers in this edition.

Dr Bertelsen's two earliest vehicles, the Aeromobile 35 and the Aeromobile 72, were acquired by the Smithsonian Institution's National Air and Space Museum in January 1981.

During 1984 the company concentrated on improving the operating efficiency of the Mercury V6 150hp outboard engines in a 40in diameter duct driving a new computer-designed 12-blade axial lift/propulsion fan. The lift fan has been designed by the Turbo Machinery Engineering Faculty at the University of Illinois to produce 581lb thrust at 2,900rpm or at a 2 : 1 reduction from engine rpm of 5,800 at 150hp.

The company is developing an ACV crawler tractor which overcomes the problems of hill climbing, steering and obstacle clearance. It is designed to carry substantial loads at very low ground pressures.

AEROMOBILE 16

Interest in this 7·82m (25ft 8in) long utility vehicle, the largest to be constructed by Bertelsen, is being shown by potential customers throughout the USA and Canada. It employs a lift, propulsion and control system similar to that of the earlier Aeromobile 15. The craft is being retrofitted with 1·01m (40in) diameter spun aluminium ducted fans powered by two 150hp Mercury outboard engines for increased thrust and efficiency. The icebreaking capabilities of the A-16 were demonstrated during the winter of 1978-79. The craft can operate on cushion with one engine only, the other being employed for full propulsion and steering. It is one of the few air cushion vehicles capable of sidehill operation.

LIFT AND PROPULSION: Power is supplied by two duct-mounted, 150hp, 122in³ displacement Mercury V-6 outboard engines, each driving a 1·01m (40in) diameter axial fan fabricated in spun aluminium. Each duct is spherical and gimbal-mounted at its centre so that it can be tilted and rotated in any direction. When the fan shaft is vertical the total airflow is discharged into the cushion. By tilting the gimbal the operator allows air from the fan to escape across the stern to provide propulsive thrust.

The thrust force is instantly available throughout 360 degrees and, metered finely by degree of tilt, provides propulsion, braking or yaw torque.

Aeromobile 16

Aeromobile 16

Aeromobile 16 lift/propulsion unit under test

The maximum available force is equal to 100 per cent of the propulsion force.

Under test is a variant with new HTD belt drive. Fan tip speed will be only 121·9m/second (400ft/second). Thrust is expected to be 1,162lb per unit, nearly double that of the earlier system. About 30 per cent of this is employed for lift at 90 degrees tilt.

Fuel is carried in two 90-litre (24-US gallon) tanks, one behind the forward engine and one forward of the aft engine. Type of fuel recommended is regular automobile petrol. Fuelling points are on deck above tanks.
HULL: Basic structure built in mild steel tubing. Designed to carry 907kg (2,000lb) payload. Total buoyancy 6,803kg (15,000lb).
ACCOMMODATION: Enclosed cabin with driver's seat forward and midship and rear bench seats behind, each seating three to four passengers. Access is via two doors, one each side. Seats

are removable should the craft be required to undertake light utility roles. Cabin may be heated or air conditioned.

SYSTEMS, ELECTRICAL: Two 12V alternators and two 12V storage batteries.

DIMENSIONS

EXTERNAL

Length overall, power off: 7·44m (24ft 5in)
    skirt inflated: 7·82m (24ft 8in)
Beam overall, power off: 4·31m (14ft 2in)
    skirt inflated: 5·48m (18ft)
Structure width, power off, folded: 2·28m (7ft 6in)

Height overall, on landing pads: 1·82m (6ft)
    skirt inflated: 2·23m (7ft 4in)
Cushion area: 24·15m² (260ft²)
Cushion height (hardstructure clearance): 406mm (1ft 4in)

INTERNAL

Cargo bay
Length: 3·35m (11ft)
Max width: 1·82m (6ft)
Max depth: 0·68m (2ft 3in)
Deck area total: 27·78m² (299ft²)

WEIGHTS

Normal empty: 1,587kg (3,500lb)

Normal all-up weight: 2,267·96kg (5,000lb)
Normal payload: 680kg (1,500lb)

PERFORMANCE

Max speed, calm water, max power: 96·56km/h (60mph)
Cruising speed, calm water: 80·46km/h (50mph)
Turning circle diameter at 30 knots: 152·4m (500ft) estimated
Max wave capability: 1·21m (4ft)
Max survival sea state: 1·82m (6ft) waves
Still air endurance at cruising speed: 8 hours
Max gradient, static conditions: 10 degrees
Vertical obstacle clearance: 406mm (1ft 4in)

DOBSON PRODUCTS CO

2241 South Ritchey, Santa Ana, California 92705, USA
Telephone: (714) 557 2987
Officials:
Franklin A Dobson, *Director*

Dobson Products Co was formed by Franklin A Dobson in 1963 to develop and market small ACVs either in complete, factory built form, or as kits for private use. His first model, the Dobson Air Dart, won the first ACV race in Canberra in 1964. The company's Model F two-seater was described and illustrated in *Jane's Surface Skimmers 1973-74* and earlier editions.

The first Dobson craft designed for quantity production is the Model H, the test development of which is described here. Since good results have been obtained with the Dobson six-bladed variable-pitch propeller and more positive control is desirable at low and negative speeds, Model K has been developed using two side-by-side thrust units. This gives powerful yaw control at all speeds in addition to a very considerable increase in positive as well as negative thrust.

DOBSON AIR CAR, MODEL H

This is a simplified and slightly larger machine than the original Model H. It is being used to test a number of ideas which are to be incorporated in a new model. The accompanying photograph shows the Model H with a fixed-pitch ducted fan with a thrust reverser instead of the original variable-pitch fan. It also has a simplified skirt, with air introduced at both the bow (by a gear-driven fan) and aft, by bleed from the thrust fan.

LIFT AND PROPULSION: Integrated system powered by a single JLO engine rated at 18hp at 5,500rpm. The lift fan is a Multiwing 24-9-32, driven by a long shaft and a Dobson right-angle gearbox with a 2:1 reduction. The thrust unit is a Dobson six-bladed variable-pitch propeller driven at about 2,000rpm via a single V-belt. The propeller is mounted in a specially-designed abbreviated duct and produces more than 40·8kg (90lb) static thrust or 13·6kg (30lb) reverse thrust from 13hp, since 5hp is used by the fan. As the fan is driven separately only 13hp is carried by the V-belt. A centrifugal clutch is used on the engine.

CONTROLS: Lateral motion of a control stick operates twin rudders, while fore-and-aft motion controls the propeller pitch, forward for thrust, aft for braking. The control stick also incorporates a motorcycle type twist-grip throttle.

HULL AND SKIRT: Hinged floats are used for buoyancy and these also support a flexible skirt which gives about a 203mm (8in) obstacle clearance. With the floats hinged upwards or removed, the overall width is less than 1·21m (4ft).

DIMENSIONS

Length: 3·35m (11ft)
Width: 2·28m (7ft 6in)
Height: 1·29m (4ft 3in)
Folded width: 1·14m (3ft 8in)
Obstacle clearance: 203mm (8in)
Cushion area: 5·11m² (55ft²)

WEIGHTS

Empty: 104·32kg (230lb)
Tools and miscellaneous: 4·52kg (10lb)
Fuel (6·75 US gallons): 18·14kg (40lb)
Pilot: 72·57kg (160lb)
Passenger: 72·57kg (160lb)
Max gross: 272·12kg (600lb)

Air Car Model H

Model K on first trial run

Air Car Model K

AIR CAR MODEL K

Franklin Dobson's Model K Air Car design is among the first light hovercraft to employ variable-pitch ducted fans for thrust, braking and control. Plans are being made for limited production.

Modifications, as a result of development testing, included the substitution of specially-designed blades in the variable-pitch thrust units. This has provided a substantial increase in reverse thrust as well as some increase in forward thrust. Control and braking have been improved. Another change has been the installation of a variable-pitch lift fan. This allows the division of power between lift and thrust to be varied, according to prevailing conditions.

Planned changes, including the use of two variable-pitch lift fans and a new skirt and lift system to reduce momentum drag, are incorporated in the Model K (modified) described below.

LIFT AND PROPULSION: Integrated system powered by a single Briggs and Stratton four-stroke opposed twin, of 688cm³ (42in³) displacement, rated at 18hp at 3,600rpm. This particular engine is much quieter than the two-stroke engines formerly used, in addition to which it incorporates a governor, an important safety feature. Power is transmitted to two 0·63m (25in) diameter thrust fans by V-belts. The 0·56m (22in) diameter lift fan, mounted in a recessed duct ahead of the open cockpit, is driven via a shaft and right-angle gearbox. Thrust is about 36·3kg (80lb), with a noise level below 80dB.

CONTROLS: Because the engine is governed at a constant speed only a single control is required. Forward-and-aft movement of the control stick gives thrust or braking from the two variable-pitch thrust fans, while lateral movement produces differential thrust for steering.

SKIRT: Segmented type.

ACCOMMODATION: Open cockpit seating two side-by-side.

DIMENSIONS

Length overall: 3·68m (12ft 1in)

Beam overall: 2·28m (7ft 6in)

WEIGHTS

Gross: 272kg (600lb)

Empty: 118kg (260lb)

PERFORMANCE: Details not received

AIR CAR MODEL K (MODIFIED)

During 1984, Air Car Model K was redesigned and a prototype of the modified craft was constructed. Features of this craft are shown in the accompanying photographs.

The new craft has the same overall dimensions as the original Model K, but has a larger passenger compartment and is more streamlined.

LIFT AND PROPULSION: Integrated system powered by an 18hp two- or four-stroke engine. Power is transmitted to two variable-pitch fans for propulsion and direction control as on the Model K, but the lift system has been developed

Air Car Model K (modified)

Air Car Model K (modified)

from that used on the Model H. Instead of the segmented skirt used formerly, the new model has one with conical segments, based on the original Dobson patents. Pressurised air for the cushion is generated by a variable-pitch fan forward and a fixed-pitch fan at the rear. Employed in conjunction with other design features, this gives pitch stability without surface contact, in addition to trim control. The forward fan is also a very powerful control to prevent plough-in or pitch-up. Air for the rear fan is drawn through a slot aft of the passenger compartment. Removal of the boundary-layer air has a beneficial effect on drag, while drawing air past the engine improves the cooling sufficiently to permit the engine to be totally enclosed. Gross weight is 600lb. Positive thrust over 100lb. Negative thrust about 60lb.

HAKE HOVERING SYSTEMS
Member of the Hake Group
PO Box 531, Media, Pennsylvania 19063, USA
Telephone: (215) 876 8241
TWX: 510 669 3625
Officials:
J D Hake, *President*
J Zador, *Vice President*
R G Longaker, *Vice President & General Manager*

Frank W Hake Inc is the parent company of Hover Systems Inc and Air Cushion Equipment (1976) Ltd of Southampton, UK. Until 1984, the major activity of these companies was the relocation of oil storage tanks and similar structures by air cushion handling techniques.

Hover Systems has a manufacturing facility at Media, Pennsylvania, for large flexible structures based on the techniques developed by Air Cushion Equipment.

Since 1984 the company has begun the design, assembly and marketing of self-propelled hover-

Hake Husky MK-O during trials on Delaware river

craft, including the 42ft long, diesel-powered Husky MK-O and the two-seat Hoversport leisure craft. It has also concluded an agreement with Griffon Hovercraft of Southampton, UK, as the exclusive US licensee for the construction and marketing of the Griffon TD-1000 and TD-1500, renamed Husky MK-1 and Husky MK-2 respectively. The first of these craft was delivered to the state of Maryland Natural Resource Police in May 1984. Further orders are pending from several other states, municipalities and associated organisations.

HUSKY MK-O

This utility hovercraft can be quickly converted from an enclosed 20-seat passenger ferry to an open well deck freighter. Powered by three Ford V-8 marine diesels it has a calm water speed of 56·32km/h (35mph).

LIFT AND PROPULSION: Lift is supplied by a single 302 CID Ford V8 marine engine, rated at 200hp continuous, driving a 1·52m (5ft) diameter horizontally-mounted fan. Thrust is provided by two 302 CID Ford V8 marine engines, also rated at 200hp continuous, each driving a 1·52m (5ft) diameter, four-bladed, wooden, fixed-pitch, ducted fan via a toothed belt drive. Maximum fuel capacity is 229 US gallons and fuel consumption, at continuous power, is 29 US gallons per hour.

CONTROLS: Craft heading is controlled by duct-mounted rudders, differential propeller thrust and bow thrust ports. Trim attitude is controlled by liquid ballast tanks at the extremities of each sidebody, pump controls in the control cabin and two duct-mounted elevators.

HULL: The main hull and sidebodies are built in heavy gauge marine-grade aluminium. Transverse frames, formers and bulkheads are combined with longitudinal channels and vertical side frames welded together and also to the double bottom and single side plates. Reserve buoyancy,

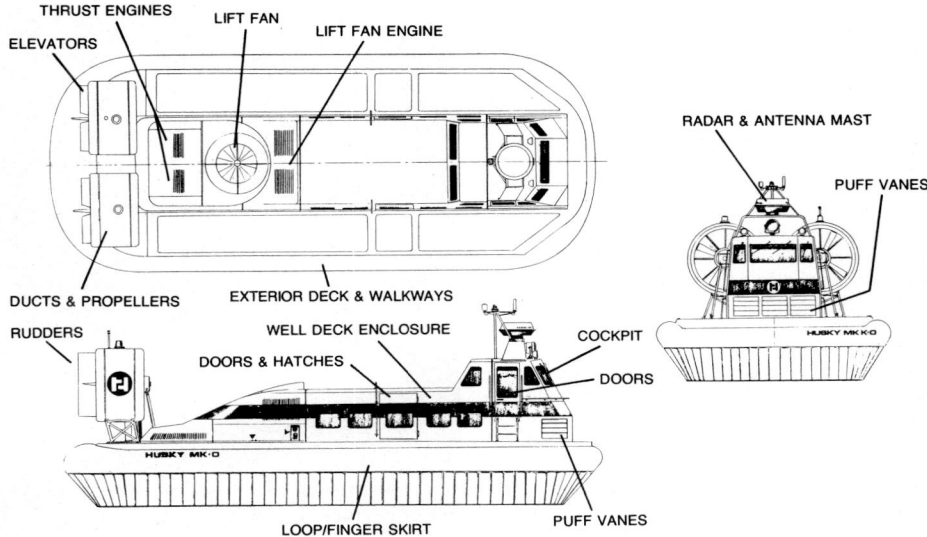

Hake Husky MK-O

in excess of 150%, is supplied by five watertight compartments in each sidebody, plus three compartments in the main hull.

SYSTEMS
ELECTRICAL: 12V dc. Two 120 amp systems with emergency crossover. 100V ac shore power jack with on-board 100ac to dc transformer and 12V dc to 110ac convertor.

FIREFIGHTING: Automatic fusing-engine shutdown; automatic halon extinguishers. Electrical with manual overrides and test facilities. Five manual extinguishers.

DIMENSIONS
Length, hardstructure: 11·73m
  on cushion: 12·75m
Beam, hardstructure: 4·57m
  on cushion: 6·45m

Height, on landing pads: 4·21m
  on cushion: 4·95m
Well deck, length: 4·47m
  beam: 2·13m
  headroom (enclosure on): 1·93m
  depth from exterior deck: 0·81m
Control cabin, length: 2·13m
  width: 2·28m
Dual level control cabin headroom, seated: 0·96m
  standing: 1·9m
WEIGHTS
Max operating weight: 9,072kg
Max disposable load: 2,812kg
PERFORMANCE
Speed, calm water: 56·32km/h (35mph)
Obstacle clearance: 0·55m (1ft 10in) approx
Max operating condition: Force 5

LANDING CRAFT, AIR CUSHION (LCAC) ACQUISITION PROGRAMME

US Naval Sea Systems Command, Washington DC 20362, USA
Telephone: (202) 692 8511

Officials:
Capt Charles H Piersall Jr, *Project Manager*
Frank P Quarto, *Deputy Project Manager*
Col Carl R Ariola, *USMC, Marine Corps Advisor*
Richark W Kenefick, *Program Manager*
Cdr Andrew C Arje, *Fleet Introduction Manager*
Capt Jon F Fantin, *Production, Test and ILS Manager*

The results of US Navy trials with prototype Jeff craft in an assault role have provided the technology base for the Landing Craft, Air Cushion (LCAC) programme. LCAC is similar to Jeff(B) and incorporates many of its features. Bell Aerospace Textron is now building the first LCAC under contract to the US Navy. The AALC programme continues to support the LCAC production programme through product improvements and through LCAC design and hardware validation/verification testing. Jeff craft have also demonstrated alternative amphibious assault mission capabilities, most notably as a coastal zone mine-sweeping platform.

The US Navy initiated the Amphibious Assault Landing Craft (AALC) programme in 1969. The aim was to create the technology to prove the effectiveness of hovercraft in the amphibious assault role. Aerojet-General and Bell Aerospace were selected to manufacture Jeff(A) and Jeff(B) respectively. These 50-knot, 60-ton payload craft were delivered to the US Navy Experimental Trials Unit at Panama City, Florida for development testing in 1976.

Single point management for the AALC research and development programme and the

Jeff(B) entering well deck of LSD-32

LCAC production programme is the responsibility of PMS377, the US Navy Amphibious Ship Acquisition Project office. PMS377 is also responsible for the design acquisition and integration of the Landing Ship Dock ('LSD-41' class), the new Amphibious Assault, General Purpose ('LHD-1' class) as well as the US Navy's Fast Logistics Ship, Maritime Prepositioning Ship and Merchant Ship Augmentation programmes.

LCAC production was officially launched by the US Navy with the release of RFPs for System Design Specifications in February 1980. Bell Aerospace Textron and Rohr Marine Inc were awarded contracts in June 1980. Proposals for

the LCAC Sub-system Design and Lead Production were submitted by both companies in early 1981.

After an extensive US Navy/Marine Corps evaluation of these production proposals, an award was made to Bell Aerospace Textron on 5 June 1981. This award of US $40 million was for the detail design and long-lead material procurement of six LCAC craft. The contract contained two options for the initial craft construction. The first option for three craft was exercised in February 1982 costing US $80·9 million.

The production craft is most accurately described as a production version of the prototype Jeff(B). Actual production of the first craft began in August 1982 at Bell Aerospace Textron's building plant in New Orleans. The facility was specifically designed and equipped to produce LCACs on an assembly line basis.

The first production LCAC craft came off the assembly line on 2 May 1984. The first six craft, when delivered to the fleet, will provide the initial operating capability.

LCAC-02 was due to be completed in late 1984, three are due to be delivered in 1985, and seven are scheduled for completion in 1986. Contracts have been awarded to Bell so far to produce a total of 24 LCACs.

Current planning for follow-on production is in excess of 100 craft. As craft are delivered, assault craft units will be activated at sites on the East and West Coasts of the USA. With the arrival of this craft in numbers, the Amphibious Forces of the Navy and Marine Corps will achieve the first fundamental change to amphibious capabilities since the Second World War. While the helicopter brought important changes to amphibious practices, there continued a lingering dependence on slow conventional displacement landing craft to conduct the heavy lift surface portion of the assault from ships a few hundred yards offshore. Historically, beaches were likely to be heavily defended as an enemy was aware that conventional landing craft can only assault a small percentage of the world's shorelines because of beach gradients and other considerations. This permitted an enemy to concentrate its forces on the few assaultable beaches. The assault itself was frequently delayed by the slow movement of men and material ashore between the surfline and the high water mark.

The percentage of shorelines accessible to LCACs is approximately four times those assaultable by conventional displacement craft, more nearly complementing the capabilities of the helicopter. The craft will be launched at distances well over the horizon and will deliver its payload at points inland of the high water mark.

The initial squadron will be available in the mid-1980s and will be assigned to the Pacific Fleet. A support facility will be constructed at Camp Pendleton, a Marine Corps base near San Diego, California, to support this and subsequent squadrons. A similar facility will be constructed on the East Coast of the USA. Squadrons will be deployed in both existing and new construction amphibious shipping. Each squadron will have its own maintenance section. The 'LSD-41' class of

Jeff(B) carrying US Marine Corps M-60 tank onto beach

Artist's impression of LCAC

amphibious ships, currently under construction at Lockheed Shipbuilding and Construction Company in Seattle, Washington, has been specifically designed to lift and support LCACs.

LANTANA BOATYARD
Lantana, Florida, USA

Lantana Boatyard is working in conjunction with Air Ride Marine Inc, of Miami, Florida, to develop commercial and military craft based on Air Ride Marine designs. Initially the craft will be up to 150 feet in length. An entry for Air Ride Marine Inc will be found on page 122 in this edition.

LOCKHEED-GEORGIA COMPANY
(Division of Lockheed Aircraft Corporation)

86 South Cobb Drive, Marietta, Georgia 30063, USA
Telephone: (404) 424 9411

PAR/WIG PROJECT

Lockheed's PAR/WIG (power-augmented ram-wing/wing-in-ground-effect) is a design study for a logistics vehicle for the US Navy with a cruising speed of Mach 0·40 and a range of 4,000n miles. It would cruise at an average height of 1·16m (3ft 9in) in sea state 3, increasing to 1·62m (5ft 4in) in sea state 4.

Characteristics of the craft include PAR lift augmentation for take-off and landing and all payload contained in the wing, thus obviating the need for a hull. Maximum payload capability of the craft would be 200,038kg (441,000lb), based on carrying four M60A3 main battle tanks with the necessary shoring and restraint hardware.

A design constraint imposed on the study was a span limitation of 32·91m (108ft) to allow the use of facilities designed for the majority of contemporary naval vessels.
LIFT AND PROPULSION: Power is supplied by four turbofan engines, each delivering 95,600lb st maximum at sea level. The engines would be similar to the STF477 turbofan designed by Pratt & Whitney Aircraft as a low energy consumption turbofan for the 1990s. The selected engine thermodynamic cycle is assumed to be similar to a low rotor modification of the STF477. The high-pressure compressor, the combustor and the high-pressure turbine characteristics of the basic STF477 core would be retained while the low-pressure spool is modified to meet the selected bypass and fan pressure ratios. The resulting engine configuration is assumed scaleable to the design point maximum thrust level of 95,600lb.

A dual rotor configuration is assumed with a variable-pitch, single-stage 1·15 pressure ratio fan and booster compressor stages gear-coupled to a low-pressure turbine and a high-pressure compressor driven by an air-cooled turbine. Performance and geometry characteristics of the variable-pitch fan would be similar to those available from an advanced Hamilton Standard 'Q-Fan'. A low emission two-stage vortex-burning and mixing combustor will provide 1,430°C (2,600°F) maximum average combustor exit temperature. The engines are mounted on the forward fuselage. A continuous torque box spans the fuselage width and supports all four engines. Engine rotation is accomplished by actuating the torque box which rotates all engines as a single unit.

The PAR/WIG thrust vector permits the entire engine/nacelle/pylon system to rotate to provide the powered ram for take-off and landing and the thrust vectoring for low-speed craft pitch control.
CONTROLS: PAR lift augmentation is employed during take-off and landing. The engines are rotated so that the primary propulsion efflux is directed towards the cavity beneath the wing formed by the wing undersurface, endplates, trailing edge flaps and the water surface. Use of this technique provides lift of up to six times the installed thrust, while still recovering 70% of the thrust for acceleration. Twin vertical fins, the wing flaps, ailerons and a variable-incidence tailplane provide aerodynamic control. A hydrofoil provides hydrodynamic lift and drag during landing. Flying in ground effect close to the water surface prevents the aircraft from banking into a turn, obstacle avoidance therefore has to be undertaken by sideslipping.
WING AND FUSELAGE: Because PAR lift would be employed during take-off and landing the contact speed between the water and the primary structure is reduced to about 60%. Consequently there is no need for a conventional hulled undersurface and the structural weight of the aircraft can be reduced. The basic structural

components are the very low aspect ratio wing fuselage protruding ahead of the wing, twin boom and twin fins and single high-set tailplane aft of the wing, four rotatable pylon-mounted engines forward on the fuselage and the hydrofoil. The basic wing includes wing endplates and flaps and the static flotation structure.

In order to meet the requirements for an efficient low subsonic cruising speed, a spacious cargo compartment for spanwise loading and a flat undersurface for PAR lift augmentation, a modified Clark Y aerofoil design is employed. Wing flaps are of hinged split-surface type and are employed as both control surfaces and as hydrodynamic drag surfaces when landing. A load relief system is incorporated into the flap system to prevent excessive loads should the maximum allowable water contact speed be exceeded during landing. The outer panels also act as ailerons.

The hydrodynamic and structural configuration of the wing endplate is integral to the feasibility of the craft since it is the only structure required to impact the water at cruising speed. It is 27·73m (91ft) long, 2·77m (9ft 1in) high and has a beam width of 0·76m (2ft). The leading edge, which is wedge-shaped, has a sweepback angle of 30 degrees. The endplate design was determined from the results of analysis of endplate loads due to drag and side forces at a speed of M = 0·4, using towing tank data.

Static buoyancy is provided by the displacement volume located beneath the wing cargo compartment floor and the forward fuselage crew compartment floor. Both buoyancy compartments are divided into watertight subdivisions to ensure that the craft remains afloat should the wing or fuselage lower surface suffer impact damage from floating debris.

PAR/WIG design model

A hydrofoil located beneath the centre of the fuselage provides both lift and drag during landing. Lift and drag co-efficients are 0·3 and 0·1 respectively. When landing, the engine vector angle is rotated to 30 degrees, flaps are set at 40 degrees and the power setting is reduced to 70%. This provides sufficient lift from the PAR system. However, the horizontal thrust available is more than sufficient to maintain a speed of 89 knots and it becomes necessary to increase drag by use of the hydrofoil. At speeds of less than 37 knots, the wing endplates and flaps are allowed to touch the water and provide additional drag. Not until the speed has been reduced to 16 knots is the primary structure, wing or fuselage lower surface allowed to impact the water. The hydrofoil is constructed in titanium plate supported by heavy reinforcement structure.

A major proportion of the PAR/WIG structure will be in graphite epoxy composites in primary structural components. The remainder of the craft is in aluminium and steel alloys with the exception of those which have to be in contact with the water, such as the endplates and hydrofoil, which are constructed entirely in titanium for strength and corrosion resistance.

CARGO COMPARTMENT: The dimensions of the cargo compartment are designed to accommodate either of two alternative payloads. The first is to transport standard commercial sea/land containers 2·44m (8ft) wide, 2·9m (9ft 6in) high and 6·1 or 12·2m (20 or 40ft) in length at a gross payload density goal of 160kg/m³ (101lb/ft³). The second payload requirement includes the transport of standard vehicles for the US Army or US Marine Corps. A compartment height of 4·11m (13ft 6in) is required to accommodate a launcher with bridge, the maximum height of the tallest vehicle to be carried. The maximum payload capability of 200,038kg (441,000lb) is based on the requirement to transport four main battle tanks.

The span of 32·91m (108ft) is of sufficient length (spanwise) to accept five 6·1m (20ft) containers and the width of the aerofoil is sufficient to accommodate six rows, thus providing the volume necessary for 30 6·1m (20ft) containers.

PAR/WIG spanloader concept

DIMENSIONS
Span: 32·91m (108ft)
Length: 72·6m (238ft 6in)
Height, wing undersurface to
  tip of tail: 10·36m (34ft)
Wing area: 913·05m² (9,828ft²)
Endplate, length: 27·73m (91ft)
  width: 0·61m (2ft)
  height: 2·74m (9ft)
Geometric aspect ratio: 1·19
Effective aspect ratio: 5·70

WEIGHTS
Operating: 162,340kg (357,900lb)
Fuel: 255,420kg (563,100lb)
Payload: 200,038kg (441,000lb)
Gross: 617,850kg (1,362,000lb)
Wing loading: 678kg/m² (139lb/ft²)
Thrust/weight: 0·2808

PERFORMANCE
Cruising speed: Mach 0·4
Cruising height: sea level
Note: Cruising height is based on clearing the one-tenth highest wave crest and impacting the one-thousandth wave crest to a depth of 206mm (0·63ft) and 459mm (1·4ft) for sea states 3 and 4 respectively. A minimum clearance of 0·91m (3ft) is maintained between the one-thousandth wave crest and the wing lower surface primary structure during cruise operations in either sea state.

MARITIME DYNAMICS INC
4515N Lexington, Tacoma, Washington 98407, USA
Telephone: (206) 759 1709

Officials:
William C House, President
MariDyne has developed a prototype SES/ACV Ride Control System (RCS) and has

pioneered the use of optimal control for developing SES ride control algorithms. This work has been funded by the US Navy SES Office and all testing has taken place at the US Navy Surface

Effect Ship Test Facility, Patuxent River, Maryland.

The system reduces craft heave motions caused by waves pumping the cushion volume. This is accomplished by using an electronic control unit in conjunction with cushion vent valves or variable-flow fans to regulate the mass of air in the cushion.

The control unit employs a 16-bit microprocessor and will accept one to four pressure or accelerometer signals for control law feedback. It performs a sampled data control algorithm with these signals and transmits control signals to each vent valve or variable-flow fan selected for active control. Fault monitoring of the system's electronic, hydraulic and mechanical components is performed between each control algorithm computation.

The control unit can be used on any SES/ACV craft equipped with either vent valves or variable-flow fans by programming it with control algorithms. MariDyne has developed a systematic technique based on optimal control theory, plus experimental testing for deriving these control algorithms.

Design work continues on ACVs for arctic applications.

ART-1

The ART-1 arctic roller transport has been designed for use as a school bus and also for carrying mail and freight in south-western Alaska. It is an air-cushion supported truck employing low pressure tyres or rollers for propulsion. When traversing solid surfaces, including ice, it is supported and propelled solely by its rollers. But when the bearing strength of the surface is insufficient to support the footprint pressure of the rollers, or for operation over water, the skirts are dropped and air cushion assistance is provided. Propulsion is still provided by the rollers and, if required, additional thrust can be provided by selective venting of the cushion air.

Advantages claimed for the roller transport concept over air-propelled vehicles are a reduction in noise and improved propulsive efficiency. When the lift system is not required fuel consumption is greatly reduced. Since the rollers are in constant contact with the surface, directional control of the craft is good, including in strong crosswinds and when negotiating side gradients.

The design incorporates many developed components and can carry a useful load of one tonne. Modular construction enables the vehicle to be dismantled into easily handled units for transporting by air in the C-130 Hercules.

A number of studies of the arctic roller transporter air cushion vehicle have been undertaken in sizes ranging from 1 to 100 tons payload. Initially, studies were concentrated on 10- to 40-ton payload vehicles in the belief that they were the more practical sizes for freight operations and would be more cost-effective when the anticipated freight market opened up.

More recently the company has considered the need for a school bus-type air cushion vehicle in Alaska which also could be employed to transport mail or freight.

A study was conducted based on a small army vehicle which could easily be converted to a 17-student bus configuration. By removing the seats, the vehicle could be used in off-duty hours as a truck.

The basic vehicle can tow a second 25-passenger ART-1 trailer across reasonably level ground. The trailer would have a lift engine and fans for air cushion support but would not have a propulsion engine.

LIFT AND PROPULSION: Lift is supplied by a single 65hp Volkswagen air-cooled automotive engine, driving, via a right-angle bevel gearbox, two centrifugal fans. Fan air is ducted fore and aft into a loop and pericell skirt system similar to that designed for Jeff(A). The entire lift system is located aft in order to simplify centre of gravity movement for widely varying loads. The propulsion system comprises a second Volkswagen engine of the same type and output driving four Rolligon-type low-pressure tyres mounted on

standard Volkswagen differentials with shortened axles. This size of vehicle can be fitted with 1·21m (4ft) diameter rollers and could therefore be capable of clearing 609mm (2ft) obstacles.
CONTROLS: Craft direction is controlled by the differential application of brakes and power to the four wheels. The cushion pressure can be reduced to allow a proportion of the weight to be

borne by the rollers. The percentage borne by the rollers will depend on the strength of the supporting surface and the amount of traction needed. In this way, the operator can vary the craft operating mode to suit the nature of the terrain.
HULL: All-welded marine aluminium structure.
SKIRT: Pericell type, comprising a loop (the upper semi-circular duct) and peripheral cells.

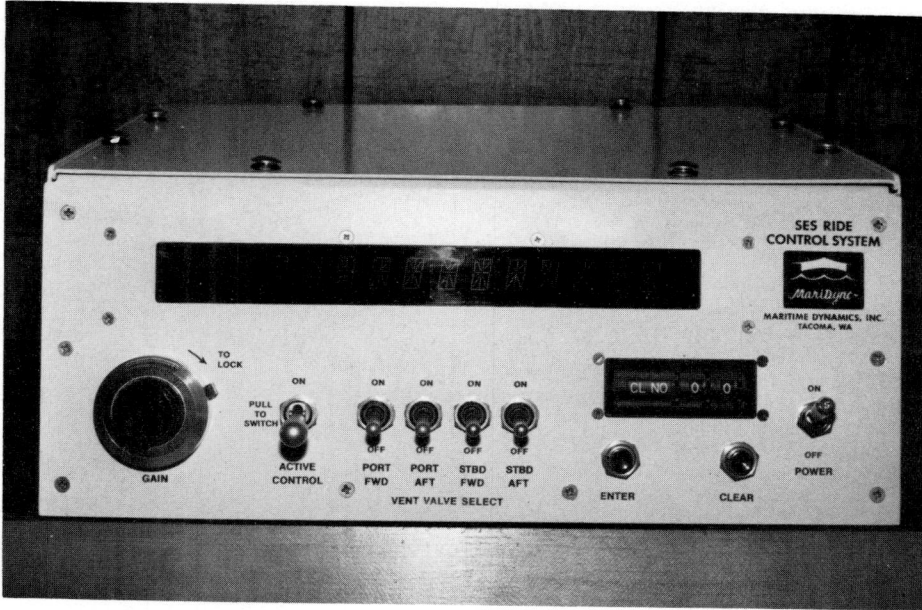

SES ride control system

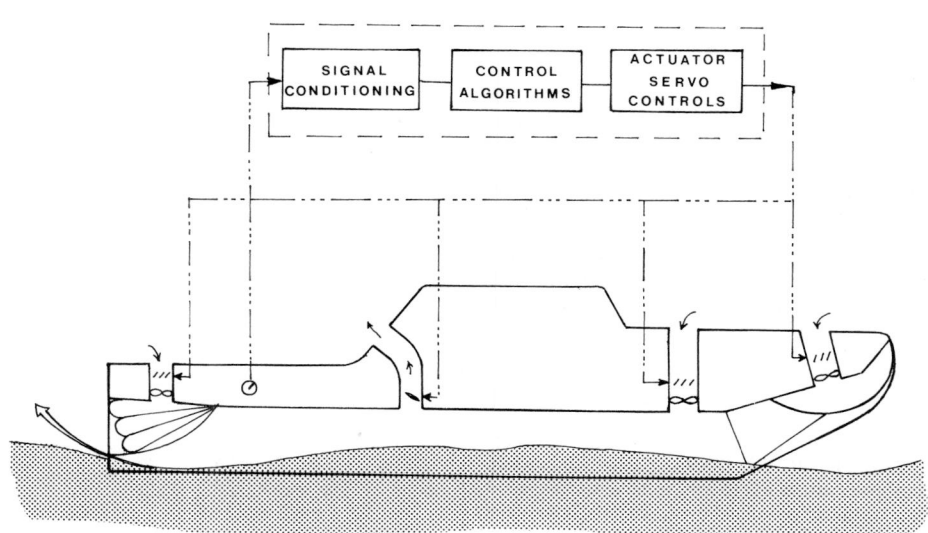

Ride control system to reduce SES/ACV heave motions

ART-1 arctic roller transport

Loop and cells are in rubber-coated fabric. Fingered bag skirt can be employed as an alternative. Transverse and longitudinal dividers are not required.

DIMENSIONS
EXTERNAL
Length, power off: 6·09m (20ft)
   skirt inflated: 7·92m (26ft)
Beam, power off: 3·04m (10ft)
   skirt inflated: 4·87m (16ft)
Height, power off: 1·93m (6ft 4in)
   skirt inflated: 2·89m (9ft 6in)
Hard structure draught in water: 228mm (9in)
INTERNAL
Load space: 3·04 × 2·74m (10 × 9ft)
WEIGHT (Tractor)
Gross: 3,822kg (8,425lb)
Payload: 907·18kg (2,000lb)
Fuel: 409 litres (90 gallons)
Empty: 2,268kg (5,000lb)
PERFORMANCE
Max speed across firm terrain: 40 knots
   with trailer: 25 knots
Max water speed, on cushion: 35 knots
   with trailer: 20 knots
Max range, hard ground or ice, off cushion:
   800km (500 miles)
   with trailer: 482km (300 miles)
Water, on cushion: 362km (225 miles)
   with trailer: 161km (100 miles)
Obstacle clearance: 609mm (2ft)

ART-10

This is an enlarged version of the ART-1. At the behest of the Alaska State Board of Education, it was considered for possible use as a school bus as well as a freighter. Since school bus operation alone would not offset the amortisation costs, it was decided to design a removable school bus module to fit the truck bed space of the vehicle. The module measures 6·09 × 6·09m (20 × 20ft) and provides seating for 90 to 100 students. Assuming that the freight portion of the ART-10's application would contribute, together with the school bus role, an annual utilisation of 3,600 hours per year, then the cost per seat mile as a school bus would be about 8 cents for a 100 per cent load factor. An operation depending on only a 50 per cent load factor would double the cost.
LIFT AND PROPULSION: The lift system comprises a single ST6 gas-turbine engine driving, via a right-angle bevel gearbox, two centrifugal fans. Fan air is ducted fore and aft into a loop and pericell skirt system similar to that designed for the Jeff(A) AALC (amphibious assault landing craft). The propulsion system comprises a second ST6 gas turbine driving, via a reduction gearbox, four Rolligon-type low pressure tyres mounted on standard truck tandem differentials with shortened axles. This size of craft could accommodate 1·82m (6ft) diameter rollers and thus would be capable of clearing 0·91m (3ft) obstacles.
CONTROLS, HULL, SKIRT: As for ART-1.
ACCOMMODATION: The ART-10 will carry a crew of two, an operator and an observer, who will alternate their duties. The crew cab will be a modified transport truck cab with basic bunking, toilet and messing facilities.
DIMENSIONS
Hard structure,
   length: 12·19m (40ft)
   beam: 6·09m (20ft)
   height, including gearbox: 2·59m (8ft 6in)
Air cushion duct and skirt,
   length: 14·02m (46ft)
   beam: 7·92m (26ft)

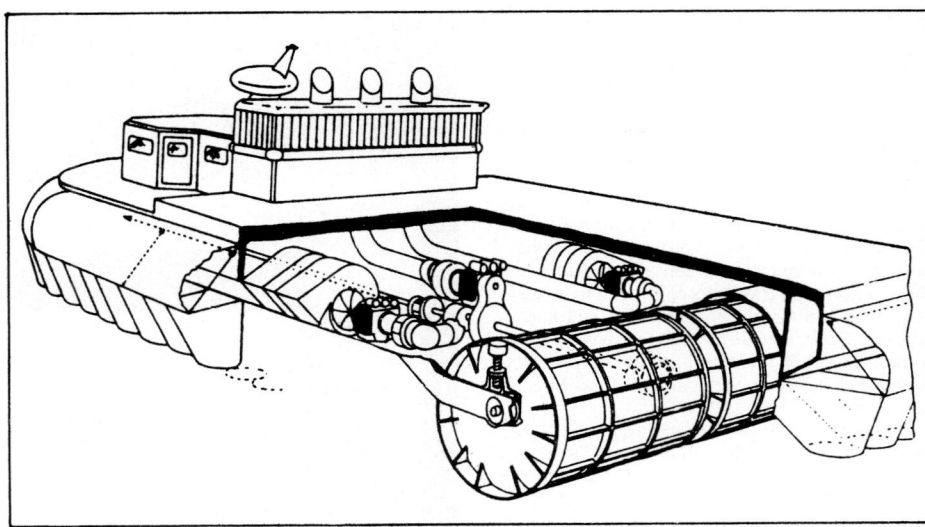
ART-1 lift and propulsion arrangements

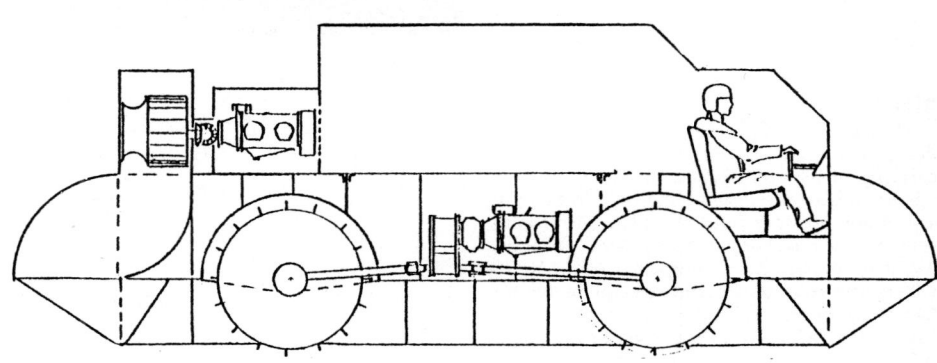
Inboard profile of arctic roller transporter

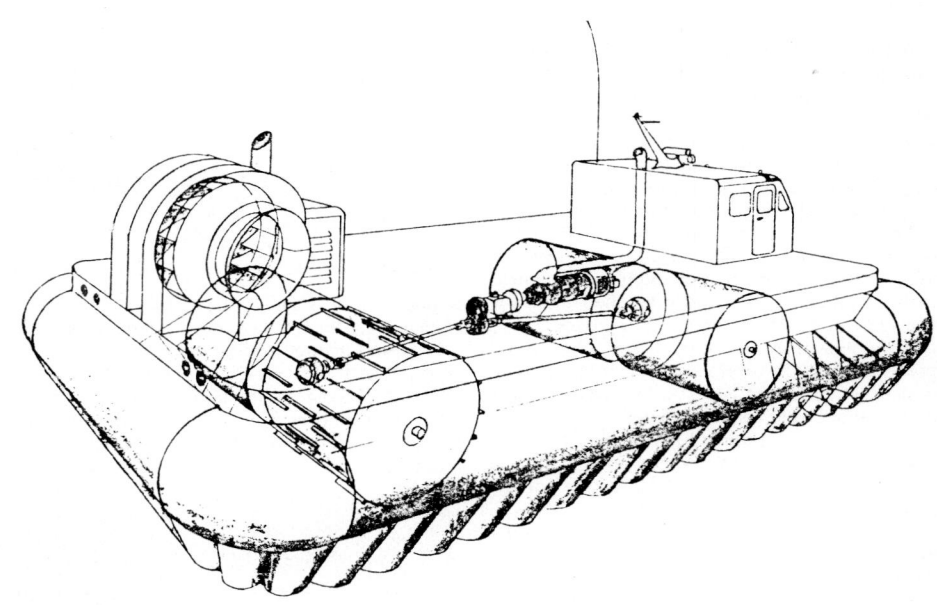
ART-10 machinery arrangement

   height, on rollers or skirt: 3·65m (12ft)
Load area: 6·09 × 6·09m (20 × 20ft)
WEIGHTS
Gross: 20,411kg (45,000lb)
Payload: 9,071kg (20,000lb)
Fuel (300 US gallons): 907·18kg (2,000lb)

Empty: 10,432kg (23,000lb)
PERFORMANCE
Range, overland, at 40 knots
   into a 20-knot wind: 290n miles
   overwater (calm) at 37 knots: 120n miles
   overwater (rough) at 32 knots: 90n miles

NEOTERIC—USA— INCORPORATED

Fort Harrison Industrial Park, Terre Haute, Indiana 47804, USA

Telephone: (812) 466 2303

Officials:
Chris Fitzgerald, *President*
Donald Brown, *Secretary*

Neoteric—USA—Incorporated was formed in 1975 by three of the founders of Neoteric Engineering Affiliates Pty Ltd, Melbourne, Australia (see separate entry). The Neova range of two-seat ACVs, which is now being manufactured and marketed by Neoteric USA, was first introduced by the Australian associate. The fully amphibious Neova is available in kit or ready-built form. Other businesses may manufacture the Neova range under licence.

NEOVA II

A highly-manoeuvrable light ACV, the Neova is an amphibious two-seater intended primarily for recreational use. Neova II is supplied in kit form in two versions, Standard and Super. The Standard model comprises four basic modules: the fibreglass base, machinery, ducts and controls and skirt system. The Super model includes two additional modules: fibreglass-moulded upper hull and hatch and a trailer. Individual components are also supplied, enabling the homebuilder to assemble any part of the complete vehicle.

The overall dimensions of the machine—2·13 × 4·27m (7 × 14ft)—allow it to be transported by road on a flat trailer.

LIFT AND PROPULSION: Integrated system powered by a 1,600cc, 124A or 126A Volkswagen engine. The company has developed a new timing belt drive transmission. The new drive features a centrifugal clutch and an all-aluminium pod structure. Maintenance is reduced substantially and the life of the drive is increased. In addition assembly time is further reduced. Assembly time of the complete kit is now 350 hours as opposed to 700 hours for the original design with a wooden structure. Airflow is ducted into the plenum for lift and two outlets aft for thrust. The power module, comprising engine, transmission and axial-flow fans, is mounted on a rubber-seated frame, secured to the main hull by three bolts. It is totally enclosed and when operating is impossible to touch. A large hatch provides ready access to the engine and all components. Fuel consumption, full throttle is 13·6 litres/h (3·6 US gallons/h).

CONTROLS: Back and forward movement of a dual stick control column operates two thrust buckets which vary the power and the direction of the thrust. The column is pulled back for reverse thrust and moved ahead for forward thrust. Differential use of the two columns, with one stick forward and the other back, is used for changing craft direction. The aerodynamic rudders at the rear of the propulsion ducts are normally used only for small corrections in heading at cruising speeds.

HULL: Fibreglass structure with solid foam buoyancy. Safety skids beneath. An integral siphon system prevents the collection of excessive water within the hull. Buoyancy is 150%. The skirt module is removable as two single units.

ACCOMMODATION: Side-by-side seating for two.

DIMENSIONS
Length overall: 4·27m (14ft)
Beam overall: 2·13m (7ft)
Height overall, skirt inflated: 1·4m (4ft 7in)
WEIGHTS
Normal all-up weight: 454kg (1,000lb)
Payload, maximum: 196kg (430lb)
PERFORMANCE
Speeds: 48-96km/h (30-60mph)
Hard, beach: 56km/h (35mph)
Water: 51km/h (32mph)
Land: 48km/h (30mph)
Ice: 72km/h (45mph)
Firm, snow: 65km/h (41mph)
Max gradient from standing start: 1 : 10
Vertical obstacle clearance: 203mm (8in)
Endurance on full power: 3 hours with 34-litre tank
Range with 34-litre (9-gallon) tank: 128km (80 miles)

LÉMERE

This new addition to the Neoteric range is an all-terrain, two-seater built in glassfibre and pvc foam. It is not yet available in kit form. Maximum speed is about 64km/h (40mph). The craft can be towed behind a standard car on a single axle.

LIFT AND PROPULSION: Lift is provided by a single 8hp Briggs & Stratton four-cycle petrol engine driving an axial flow fan. Thrust is supplied by a single 55hp liquid-cooled two-cycle engine driving a ducted fan.

HULL: Composite structure in glass fibre and pvc foam.

SKIRT: Bag type in neoprene/nylon material.

ACCOMMODATION: Side-by-side seating for two.

DIMENSIONS
Length, hardstructure: 3·5m (11ft 6in)
Width, hardstructure: 2·03m (6ft 8in)
Height, on landing pads: 0·91m (3ft)
WEIGHTS
Empty, with 26 litres (7 gallons) fuel in tank: 194kg (428lb)
Payload: 227kg (500lb)
Range: 64km (40 miles)
Clearance height: 152mm (6in)

Neova II two-seater

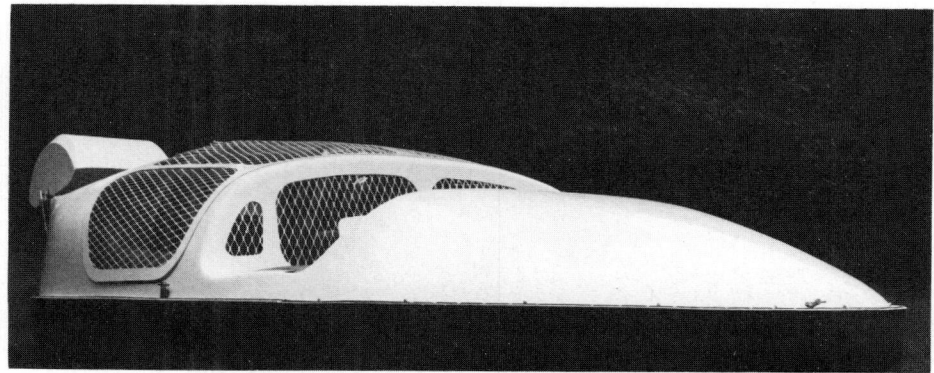

Neova II

Neova II's engine

NEORACER

Introduced in late 1984 for hoverclub racing and cruising events, the Neoracer is a glass fibre hulled two-seater powered by a 50hp Fuji engine and capable of 80km/h. It is available in kit or ready-built form.

LIFT AND PROPULSION: Integrated system powered by 37kW (50hp) Fuji 44pm air-cooled, two-cycle engine. Alternative engines of similar output are acceptable on craft built from kits.

Fuel capacity is 82 litres. Recommended fuel is two-cycle mix.

CONTROLS: Handlebar operates rudders at rear of propulsion duct. Throttle on handlebar.

HULL: Composite structure in glass fibre and pvc foam.

SKIRT: Bag type in neoprene nylon material.

ACCOMMODATION: Seating for two in tandem.

DIMENSIONS
Length: 3,505mm
Width: 2,032mm
Height: 940mm
WEIGHTS
Empty: 123kg
Payload: 227kg
PERFORMANCE
Speed: 80km/h
Hover height: 152mm
PRICE, on November 1st, 1984, US $3,499

Lémere two-seater

Lémere two-seater

Neoracer

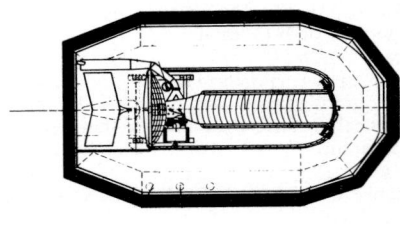

NORTH AMERICAN HOVER-CRAFT CORPORATION

One World Trade Center, New York, NY 10048, USA
Telephone: (212) 775 1415
Officials:
George Dagher, *President*

North American Hovercraft Corporation has built seven AV Tigers in the USA under licence. Negotiations between the company and Air Vehicles Ltd of Cowes, Isle of Wight, were completed early in 1978. Air Vehicles Ltd supplies a number of components for the craft.

In April 1982 the company filed an application for a waiver on the Jones Act to import AP1-88s. At the time of going to press the company was intending to import six AP1-88s to operate commuter ferry services in the New York, New Jersey and Connecticut areas.

PANTHER AIR BOAT CORPORATION

300 Wilson Avenue, Cocoa, Florida 32922, USA
Telephone: (305) 632 1722
Officials:
L A Bell, *President*
Allen H Gaffney, *Vice President and General Manager*
D C Dempsey, *International Sales Manager*

Panther Air Boat Corporation has developed a range of airboats capable of traversing snow, ice, rivers and swamps at speeds up to 88·5km/h (55mph). Thrust is provided by a large two-blade airscrew above the transom.

The company is concentrating on the construction of craft of 3·6 to 6m (12 to 20ft) long and 2·1 to 2·4m (7 to 8ft) wide, built in heavy duty 4·76mm (³/₁₆in) thick all-welded marine grade

aluminium alloy. Craft of different dimensions and built in glass fibre can be made to order.
POWER PLANT: Modified and remanufactured General Motors automotive engines of 220hp (350in³) or 300hp (450in³) are normally fitted except on the 3·6m (12ft) models. Four- or six-cylinder Lycoming air-cooled aircraft engines are an optional alternative. Fuel consumption, depending on payload and horsepower, varies

from 18·1 to 36·3 litres (4 to 8 gallons) per hour at cruising speed. Fuel capacity of the standard 35 US gallon alumimium tank provides an endurance of between 4½ and 9 hours and an operating range of 289·6 to 547·1km (180 to 340 miles).

CONTROLS: Heading controlled by single or twin rudders in the propeller slipstream. Standard instrument panel includes a tachometer, hour meter, ammeter, oil pressure and either water or oil temperature gauges. An electric starter, alternator, fuel pump, in-line fuel filter and a heavy duty 70-amp/hour battery are as standard.

WEIGHTS

Payload (according to model): 680·3-1,474·1kg (1,500-3,250lb)

PERFORMANCE (according to model)

Max speed, normal load: 48·2-88·5km/h (30-55mph)

Cruising speed (according to model): 56·3-64·3km/h (35-40mph)

Panther airboat in recreational configuration

Panther in use as light patrol craft

Automobile-style configuration

POWER BREEZE

8139 Matilija, Panorama City, California 91402, USA

Telephone: (213) 785 0197

Officials:

Dan W Henderson Jr, *President/Designer*

Power Breeze Air Cushion Vehicle Systems

was founded to increase public interest in ACVs, and is currently selling plans to home builders for a small, easily assembled amphibious single-seater.

A set of plans costs US $5 and a ready made skirt costs US $35.

Weight of the craft is 113kg (250lb) and the maximum speed is approximately 40·23km/h (25mph). The latest model of this circular platform single-seater folds to a width of 1·21m (4ft) to simplify storage and to permit it to be carried by a light truck or pick-up van.

A number of craft have been built to this design in the United States and Australia.

In addition to selling plans, the company is engaged in the sales of second-hand ACVs, and specialises in finding craft to meet the individual needs of its clients.

RMI, INC

Head Office: 225 West 30th Street, National City, California 92050, USA

Telephone: (619) 235 7005

Telex: 695212 (RMIMARINE NTCY)

Officials:

Wilfred J Eggington, *Chairman and Chief Executive Officer*

F Patrick Burke, *Executive Vice President*

Darrell L Reed, *Executive Vice President*

Robert Derusha, *Vice President, Shipyard Operations*

John H Barker, *Director of Engineering*

Robert S Cramb, *Director of Business Development*

Jack J Edwards, *Director of ACV Programs*

Charles M Lee, *Director of SES Programs*

George Luedeke, Jr, *Director of SWATH Programs*

Richard Thomas, *Director of Repair Programmes*

Directors:

Wilfred J Eggington, *Chairman*

Francis P Burke, *Secretary*

Darrell L Reed, *Treasurer*

Stephen R Haessler

Hon Edward Hidalgo

Hon Barry J Shillito

Hon Robert C Wilson

Adm Elmo E Zumwalt, Jr, USN (Ret)

Washington Representative: W C Beckwith Associates, 205 Pennsylvania Avenue SE, Washington DC 20003, USA

Telephone: (202) 671 4528

RMI, Inc designs, builds, and operates surface effect ships, air cushion vehicles and other advanced marine vehicles including small waterplane area twin hulled (SWATH) boats. The company has successfully developed a number of advanced marine subsystems, such as seals, skirts, waterjet inlets, low drag hull forms, lift fans, ride control systems and lightweight hull structures.

The RMI team was formed between 1970-1972 to participate in the United States Navy's Surface Effect Ship Program. In December 1976, after competition with three large, high technology companies, the company was awarded a contract to design and build the US Navy's projected 3,000-ton surface effect ship, the 3KSES. The 3KSES had an overall length of 81·07m (266ft) and a maximum beam of 32·3m (106ft). A top speed in excess of 80 knots and a range in excess of 3,000n miles were specified in Sea State 3. Research, development, design, and manufacturing demonstrations costing more than US$170 million were completed by RMI on the SES programme before its termination for budgetary reasons in January 1980.

Throughout 1970 to 1981, the company was under US Navy contract to provide design, construction, test and analysis services in support of the XR-1, SES-100A, and the SES-100B test and demonstration programmes. These craft were in almost continuous use as testbeds for SES development. Critical subsystem improvements were evaluated, including planing seals, waterjet propulsion, and ride control.

RMI, Inc, formerly Rohr Marine, Inc, a subsidiary of Rohr Industries, Inc, became an independently owned company in January 1981. In 1982 RMI was one of two companies contracted to prepare a system design and specification for the US Navy's Landing Craft, Air Cushion (LCAC) programme. RMI has also broadened its business base while continuing as a US Government prime contractor for advanced marine products.

In 1983 RMI leased the Jeff(A), a 160-long ton amphibious assault landing craft prototype from the US Navy and subsequently time-chartered it to Sohio Alaska Petroleum Company to support Sohio's arctic petroleum operations. The craft successfully completed a three-phase test programme and carried nearly two million pounds of cargo over both solid and rotten ice, operating at temperatures as low as 50 degrees below zero with an operational availability of over 90 per cent. In addition, RMI is providing programme management, engineering, and construction supervision for the development of Sohio's ACV 300 for use in the Arctic.

RMI is participating in the US Navy's SES programme as prime contract for the Patrol Boat Multi-Mission (PBM). Instructions to proceed with the construction of the first craft of this class, which has been redesignated Special Warfare Craft, Medium (SWCM), was given in November, 1984. The company also is supporting several US Navy Concept Formulation (CONFORM) studies, evaluating future SES applications and is the programme integration manager for the upgrading of lift systems on the US Navy's SES 200 craft.

In 1983 RMI completed the design and tow tank testing of a 60-foot small waterplane area twin hull (SWATH) boat for demonstration as a patrol boat, work boat, fishing boat, or yacht. Designated the SD-60, the craft was launched by RMI in San Diego in December 1984.

RMI is continuing to develop and market its family of Light Multi-purpose Surface Effect Ships (LMSES) in the displacement range of 70 to 500 long tons as ferries, patrol boats, and military transports.

In 1983, to provide its customers with a complete engineering, manufacturing, and operations capability, RMI acquired the Lockheed Ocean System Tow Basin and the Atkinson Marine Shipyard, both in San Diego. Now designated the RMI Hydrodynamic Laboratory and Tow Basin, the laboratory includes a sophisticated 320ft × 15ft × 6ft tow channel. The RMI Shipyard, formerly the Atkinson Marine Shipyard, a 15-acre site on San Diego Bay, was built in 1977 for construction of advanced marine vessels up to 500 long tons displacement. In May

XR-1, seen in D configuration

Impression of 3KSES

SES-100A before and after modification

100 Series

1984, RMI was awarded a Master Ship Repair Agreement by the US Navy. The RMI Shipyard is now performing MSR contract work to supplement ongoing advanced marine construction programmes.

SPECIAL WARFARE CRAFT, MEDIUM (SWCM)

During 1983, the US Navy conducted competitive design studies between four companies to define the SWCM. Two planing hull design teams and two SES design companies were selected for this competition. Vehicle design was constrained by the requirement that the craft should fit the well deck of an amphibious transport ship and that it should be able to achieve high speed in waves.

In April 1984, a contract was awarded to RMI as the prime contractor for the detailed design of the SWCM. This was followed by instructions to build the first of class in November 1984. Technical and operational evaluation of the first craft will take place early in 1986. Follow-on construction of 18 craft is anticipated.

The SWCM is designed for high-speed operation in rough water with excellent ride quality. Compared to other hull types, it requires less total installed power and so offers economy in terms of acquisition and in-service costs. The relatively short length and large width of the SES platform has helped to provide an efficient topside and internal space arrangement. The SES hull also provides excellent stability characteristics to enable the craft to survive accidental or battle-inflicted damage.

The performance, seaworthiness, and stability predictions were validated by extensive model tests at both the RMI Towing Basin and the David Taylor Naval Ship Research and Development Center (DTNSRDC).

The state-of-the-art sub-systems and components have demonstrated reliable service in marine or closely analogous industrial applications. The systems are designed for simplicity and to provide a high measure of modularity and standardisation. As far as possible performance critical systems incorporate a measure of redundancy to increase reliability.

HULL: The hull structure is built in welded marine grade aluminium alloy (5456). The hull construction technique is compatible with factory as well as shipyard production.

POWER PLANT: The main engines are two Detroit Diesel Allison 16V-149 TIB diesels rated at 1,800bhp at 1,900rpm. Power is transmitted to two fixed-pitch propellers for propulsion and six fans, which supply air to the air cushion and bow and stern seals.

ACCOMMODATION: A modular CIC/radio room and pilot house installation is outfitted before incorporation in the craft assembly. The major electronic systems will be installed and fully tested in a controlled environment without being disrupted by, or disrupting, other craft assembly operations.

DIMENSIONS

Length overall: 23·93m

Max beam: 10·67m

Height, baseline to top of mast: 9·14m
  mast folded, fire control antenna retracted:
  5·72m

Cushion length: 21·34m

Cushion beam: 7·01m

Draft at FLD, off-cushion: 1·52m
  on-cushion, midships: 0·61m

WEIGHTS

Max full load displacement with margins: 112·4 tonnes

Light ship displacement with margins: 84·4 tonnes

PERFORMANCE

Speed: In excess of 35 knots

SERIES 80 SES

The RMI Series 80 surface effect ship has diesel engines and a modular design approach which can be adapted to various customer requirements. Typical variants include commuter craft, patrol, and crew boats, all using the same machinery and structural arrangements.

70-knot fast strike craft

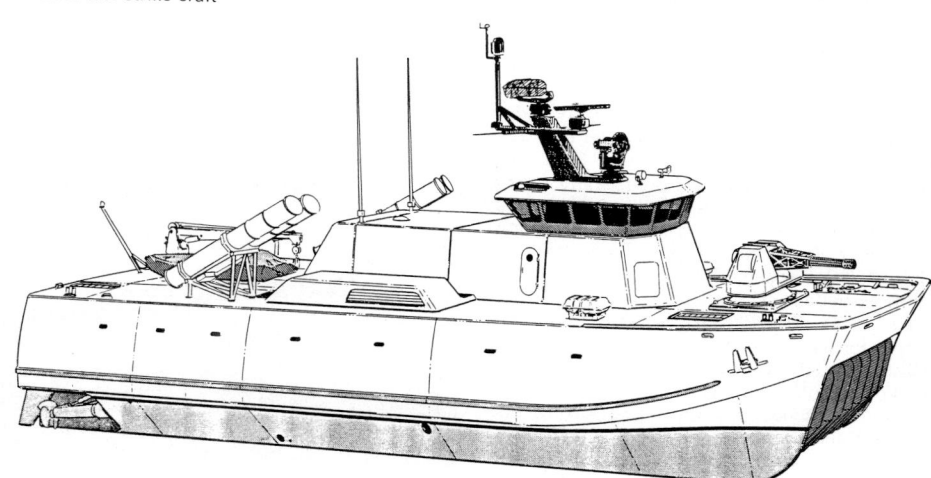

Series 80 patrol boat

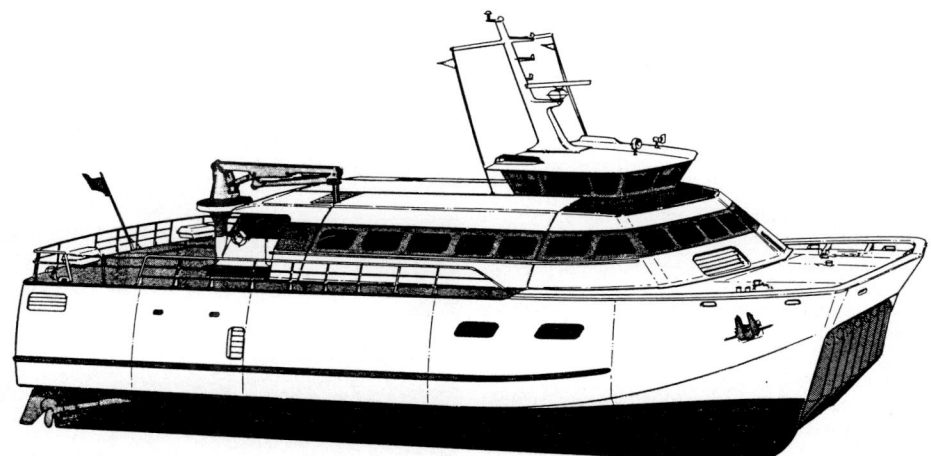

Series 80 crewboat

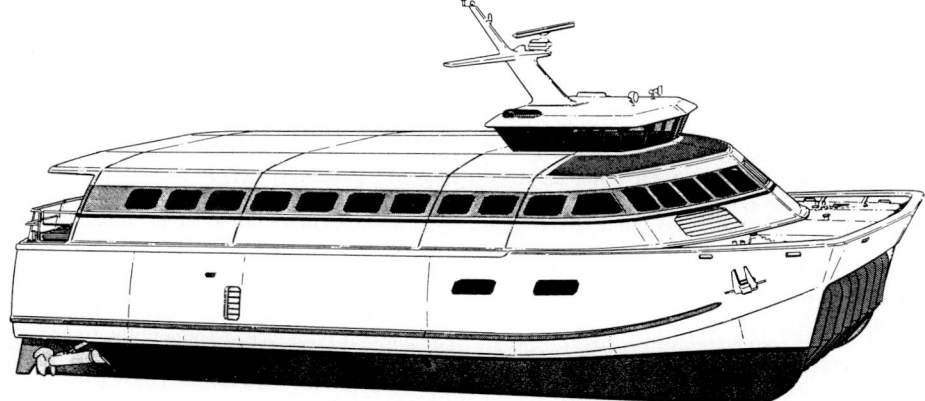

Series 80 commuter

Principal characteristics are:
Length overall: 25·6m
Max beam: 10·67m
Height, baseline to top of mast: 11·58m
Cushion length: 21·03m
Cushion beam: 7·01m
Draft at FLD, off-cushion: 1·68m
  on-cushion, midships: 0·61m
Light ship displacement: 72 tonnes
Wet deck height above baseline: 1·83m
Crew: 3-4 operating personnel
Passengers: 300 minimum
Main engines: Two Detroit Diesel Allison 16V-149 TIB diesels rated at 1,800bhp at 1,900rpm
Propellers: Two controllable pitch propellers
Auxiliary engines: Two Detroit Diesel Allison 8V-92TA diesels rated at 330bhp at 1,900rpm

SES-100A DERIVATIVE

A very high speed surface effect patrol boat design was based directly on the successful US Navy SES-100A, one of two 100-ton testcraft developed by the US Navy between 1969 and 1981 to expand SES technology. Dockside testing of the SES-100A began in August 1971, deep water trials in May 1972. Official Navy Test and Evaluation Trials begun in September 1972 were completed in July 1974. Subsequently the RMI team, under contract to the Navy, incorporated a number of major modifications and sub-system improvements (seals, hulls, lift system), including the fabrication and installation of an entirely new bow section from midships forward. RMI continued the development test programme during 1981, operating both the SES-100A and its sister ship, the SES-100B. The craft established new speed records for naval surface vehicles. The SES-100A exceeded 75 knots, while the SES-100B exceeded 90 knots.

LIFT AND PROPULSION: Power for the propulsion system is provided by two 6,000shp Allison 570 KF gas turbines. Propulsors are two Rocketdyne PJ-24 waterjet pumps in the port and starboard sidehulls. Lift is provided by one Pratt & Whitney ST6T-76 gas turbine (1,400shp) and one Pratt & Whitney ST6T-76 gas turbine (550shp), driving three 1·04m diameter centrifugal fans.

DIMENSIONS
Length overall: 25·45m
Maximum beam: 13·41m
Height (baseline to top of mast): 12·95m
Cushion length: 18·75m
Cushion beam: 9·14m
Draught at FLD, off-cushion: 1·52m
  on-cushion: 0·3m
WEIGHTS
Design displacement: 110 tonnes
Light ship displacement: 85 tonnes
Long range displacement: 126 tonnes
PERFORMANCE
Speed, design displacement with 15·24 tonnes fuel
  Sea State 2: 76 knots
  Sea State 3: 72 knots
Long range displacement with 30·48 tonnes fuel
  Sea State 2: 71 knots
  Sea State 3: 68 knots
Range, design displacement with 15·24 tonnes fuel
  Sea State 2: 350n miles
  Sea State 3: 650n miles
Long range displacement with 30·48 tonnes fuel
  Sea State 2: 660n miles
  Sea State 3: 650n miles

2K/3KSES DERIVATIVES

During the 1970s, RMI, as the prime contractor for the US Navy's 2000/3000-ton surface effect ship (2K/3KSES) programme, developed an extensive and unique data base for an ocean-going combatant SES. Over $100 million was expended on development tests, design drawings, and production planning.

Prior to the completion of the 3KSES programme, RMI uses its own funds to develop ferry and patrol boat SES designs in the 300- to 500-ton range, using the 3KSES data. Tow tank and development model tests were rescaled to the

LMSES-148

LMSES 180 long-range passenger/car ferry

LMSES-180 commuter

LMSES 300- to 500-ton range. These designs represent 'scaled-down' geosymmetric 3KSES designs, and are called Light Multipurpose Surface Effect Ships (LMSES). They have welded aluminum hull structures and propulsion machinery options, and can be adapted for commercial and military uses.

The 148 Series are gas turbine powered, waterjet-propelled craft of approximately 300 tons displacement. They have a speed of 60 knots and a range of approximately 800n miles with average payload weights of 25 tons. Craft in this series are suitable for high-volume passenger-commuter service, ocean-going utility transport, and military coastal patrol roles.

The 180 Series has a full load displacement of approximately 500 tons and is propelled by gas turbine-powered waterjets. The military version

can transport 250 troops and 522·2m² of vehicles, equipment, and supplies. This payload can be discharged to portside facilities or unprepared beach areas. Light weapon systems, limited armour protection, and helicopter landing facilities are also provided.

Alternative 180 Series commercial ferries have been developed for potential customers on the Atlantic coast of the USA, Nigeria, Saudi Arabia, and other countries. One high-speed, all-passenger commuter version can carry 1,000 passengers at a speed of 70 knots over a 100 to 150n mile route. A second long-range, all-passenger ferry can carry 1,000 passengers at a speed of 50 knots over a 1,000n mile route. Another long-range, passenger and vehicle ferry can carry 350 passengers and 34 cars at a speed of 48 knots over approximately 1,000 miles.

INTRA-THEATER LOGISTICS TRANS-PORT

The Intra-Theater Logistics Transport (ITLT) is a roll-on/roll-off SES transport for military equipment and supplies, including tanks, trucks, artillery, munitions and fuel. It has high displacement sidehulls to provide a long-distance hullborne cruising range and can unload equipment directly on an unimproved beach via a bow ramp. It can carry a US infantry battalion and oversized or non-air transportable cargo.

DIMENSIONS
Length overall: 111·25m
Max beam: 22·25m
Deck area: 3,041·83m²
WEIGHTS
Full load displacement: 1,830 tonnes
Cargo/payload: 453,592kg
PERFORMANCE
Speed: 45 knots
Range with 10% fuel reserve and cargo rated: 1,100n miles

Intra-Theater Logistics Transport

JEFF(A) ARCTIC PROGRAMME

Jeff(A), an experimental 160-ton amphibious assault landing craft, is one of two prototypes developed by the US Navy in preparation for the Landing Craft, Air Cushion (LCAC) production programme. The Jeff(A) operates at 50 knots in Sea State 2 and can carry up to 75 tons of palletised supplies and equipment.

Originally designed and built by the Aerojet General Corporation, it was delivered to the US Navy test facility in Panama City, Florida, in September 1977. US Navy trials and evaluations were completed in 1982.

In June 1983, RMI, Inc leased the Jeff(A) from the US Navy and entered into a time charter with Sohio Alaska Petroleum Company (SAPC), to operate, maintain, and repair the Jeff(A) for SAPC on the North Slope of Alaska.

Data collected relative to the operation of the Jeff(A) in an arctic environment includes:

The effects of an extreme, low-temperature environment on ACV systems and materials
Operational guidelines for ACV employment in low visibility and arctic weather conditions
Maintenance procedures and schedules for maximum ACV availability in extremely low temperatures
Cargo loading and unloading procedures in arctic conditions
Modifications and the selection of fuel, grease, oil and hydraulic fluid
Warming-up procedures for craft systems in use daily in moderate (−26°C to −40°C) and extremely low temperatures (−40°C to −54°C)
The effectiveness of base camp maintenance support facilities, including hangar, shops, and parts storage
Training of ACV operators
The effectiveness of personnel in ACV maintenance and repair, outside and within protective shelters
Emergency procedures, should difficulties occur with an ACV.

With one drilling season complete, the Jeff(A) has an operational record which includes over 300 hours of over-ice and ice/water operating time, over 1·8 million pounds of cargo hauled, and an operational availability of over 90 per cent.

Operational and design data and criteria for larger or follow-on arctic ACVS:
LIFT AND PROPULSION: Cushion lift is provided by two 3,750hp Avco Lycoming TF40 gas turbines, one in each of the two sidestructures, driving two sets of four, 1·21m diameter fans through lightweight transmission and shafting connections.

Thrust is supplied by four 3,750hp Avco Lycoming TF40 gas turbines, each driving a 2·26m diameter, pylon-mounted, shrouded propeller, mounted above the sidestructure and outside the cargo deck area to provide access and uninterrupted air flow. Each propeller pylon rotates to provide propulsion and directional control.

Jeff(A) during Arctic operations

HULL: Marine aluminium with corrugated structures to minimise total craft weight. The main hull is formed by a buoyancy raft with port and starboard sidestructures. Each sidestructure contains three Avco Lycoming gas turbines with associated air intakes, exhaust, shrouded propellers, lift fans, transmissions, and auxiliary power systems. The bottom and deck structures of the hull are joined by longitudinal and transverse bulkheads to form watertight flotation compartments. Cargo deck area is 211·82m². Bow ramp opening width is 6·55m. Aft ramp width is 8·33m.
SKIRT: 1·52m deep Pericell loop and cell type.
ACCOMMODATION: Two air-conditioned, sound-insulated compartments, each seating three crew or observers. Access is via cargo deck.

Jeff(A) modifications required to improve arctic operations include:
Natural rubber skirts and spray aprons
Insulation of control and navigation cabins and installation of heated window
Reconstruction of the stern ramp to enable

cargo trailers to be driven onto the cargo deck
Change in gas turbine and gearbox lubrication oil used
Insulation and heating of hydraulic and fuel systems
Incorporation of features to meet US Coast Guard safety and certification requirements
Additional high intensity lighting
Fire retardant, closed cell urethane foam and plywood sheathing on the cargo deck and external areas of the machinery enclosure.

ACV-90

The ACV-90 is a diesel-powered, welded aluminium, self-propelled air cushion vehicle designed to carry 50 passengers and up to 40 tons of cargo. Bow and stern ramps facilitate ro-ro cargo operations. Six feet of on-cushion ground clearance together with a lower temperature design limit of −40°C make the craft ideal for operation in the Arctic.

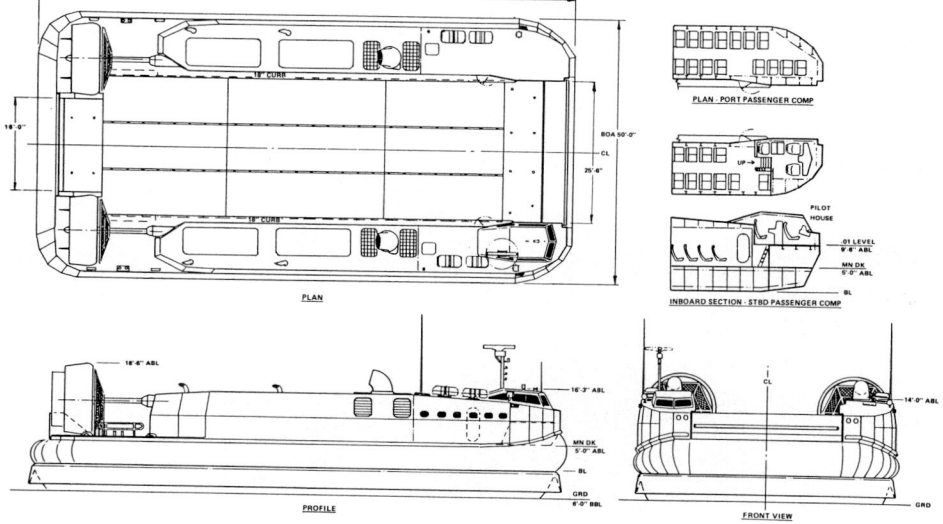

ACV-90

DIMENSIONS
Length overall: 24·99m
Breadth overall: 14·63m
Height on landing pads: 6·1m
Cushion height: 1·83m
Propulsion engines: 2 at 1,250hp
Propulsors: 0·61-2·74m diameter shrouded pro-
pellers, 2 bow thrusters
Lift engines: 2 at 1,250hp
Max operating weight: 113 tonnes
Cargo: 34 tonnes
Max calm water speed: 35 knots

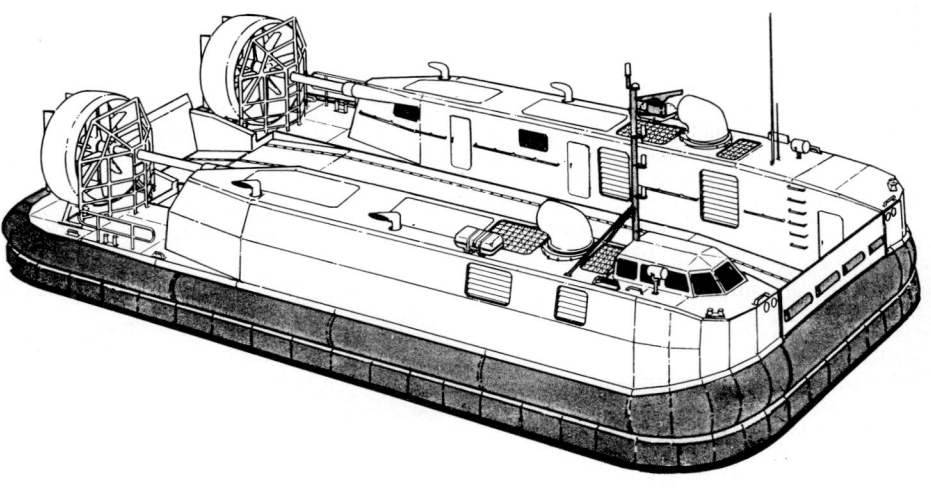

ACV-90

SWIFTSHIPS INC
Morgan City, Louisiana, USA

Swiftships Inc is working in conjunction with Air Ride Marine Inc, of Miami, Florida, to develop commercial and military craft based on Air Ride designs. The craft will exceed 200ft in length and in several cases will operate at speeds up to 50 knots. An entry for Air Ride Marine Inc will be found on page 122 in this edition.

UNITED STATES HOVERCRAFT MANUFACTURING CO INC

Box 1191, Lynwood, Washington 98036, USA
Telephone: (206) 481 8468
Cables: Hoverco, Box 1191, USA 98036
Officials:
Gerald W Crisman, *President*
E Wood Peabody Jr, *Vice President*
Sharron E Crisman, *Secretary*
Henry A Roche, *Financial Adviser*

Formed in 1961 as Gemco Incorporated, United States Hovercraft Manufacturing Co has built a number of light and ultra-light craft, including the first hovercraft to cross the Mississippi. The company is concentrating on the production of a two-seater, the 6300 Hoverbird, a six-seater, the Model 5501 Eagle, and a light utility variant, the Model 5502 Crane. In the planning stage are two larger vehicles, the Alaskan, an amphibious utility craft with a payload capacity of 10-12 tons and the Pioneer, a 30-seat passenger ferry. In 1979 the company was appointed as a representative for Space Hovercraft Ltd of Ottawa, Canada. It is also marketing and selling the Odyssey 700 four-seater, designed by Space Hovercraft, in the Seattle area.

MODEL 5501 EAGLE

The prototype of this glass fibre-hulled six-seater completed its trials in 1974. Hulls for both the Eagle and a light utility version, the Model 5502 Crane, are being built by Mirical Marine in Taiwan.
LIFT AND PROPULSION: Integrated system employing a single Ford 429 automobile engine which drives a stainless multibladed fan for lift and a Hartzell variable and reversible-pitch

Model 5502 Crane

propeller for propulsion. Total fuel capacity is 151·5 litres (40 US gallons).
CONTROLS: Deflection of triple rudder vanes mounted at the aft end of the propeller duct, together with thrust ports, forward and aft, provide heading control. Reverse propeller pitch for braking.
HULL: Moulded fibreglass with honeycomb aluminium reinforcement at stress points. Buoyancy boxes filled with expanded polyurethane.
SKIRT: Simple bag type in Hypalon material.
ACCOMMODATION: Fully enclosed cabin for driver and five passengers. Access via two central gull-wing doors, one port, one starboard. Air-conditioning optional.
SYSTEMS, ELECTRICAL: 12V for starting and services.

DIMENSIONS
Length overall: 6·4m (21ft)
Beam overall: 3·35m (11ft)
Height overall, on cushion: 2·74m (9ft)
    off cushion: 2·13m (7ft)
Cabin: 2·13 × 1·83m (7 × 6ft)
WEIGHTS
Empty: 635kg (1,400lb)
All-up weight: 1,125kg (2,700lb)
Disposable load: 499kg (1,100lb)
PERFORMANCE
Max speed: in excess of 60 knots
Endurance: 4 hours
Normal range: 386km (240 miles)
Stopping distance: 106·68m (350ft)
Obstacle clearance: 609mm (2ft)
Max wave capability: 0·914-1·2m (3-4ft)

MODEL 5502 CRANE

This multi-duty version is almost identical to the Model 5501 Eagle apart from a well deck immediately aft of its cabin. The Crane's cabin measures 1·2 × 1·83m (4 × 6ft) and seats three, with the driver in the central position. Access to the cabin is via a gull-wing door at the rear, leading from the well deck.
Machinery arrangement, dimensions, weight and performance are similar to those of the Eagle.

MODEL 6300 HOVERBIRD

The Hoverbird is a fibreglass-hulled utility two-seater with twin ducted thrust fans. The company reports that orders have been placed for more than 200 machines.
LIFT AND PROPULSION: Cushion air is supplied by a 28hp Kohler engine mounted ahead of the cockpit and driving a multibladed fan. Thrust

Model 5501 Eagle

is by a single 46hp Fiat automotive engine driving via a belt transmission two ducted fans aft.

HULL: Moulded fibreglass structure.

SKIRT: A simple bag skirt is standard. A segmented skirt can be supplied if required.

ACCOMMODATION: Open cockpit with tandem seating for driver and one passenger. Fold-down seat backs provided for comfort and safety.

DIMENSIONS

Length overall: 3·65m (12ft)

Width: 2·13m (7ft)

Height, on cushion: 1·49m (4ft 11in)
   on landing pads: 1·21m (4ft)

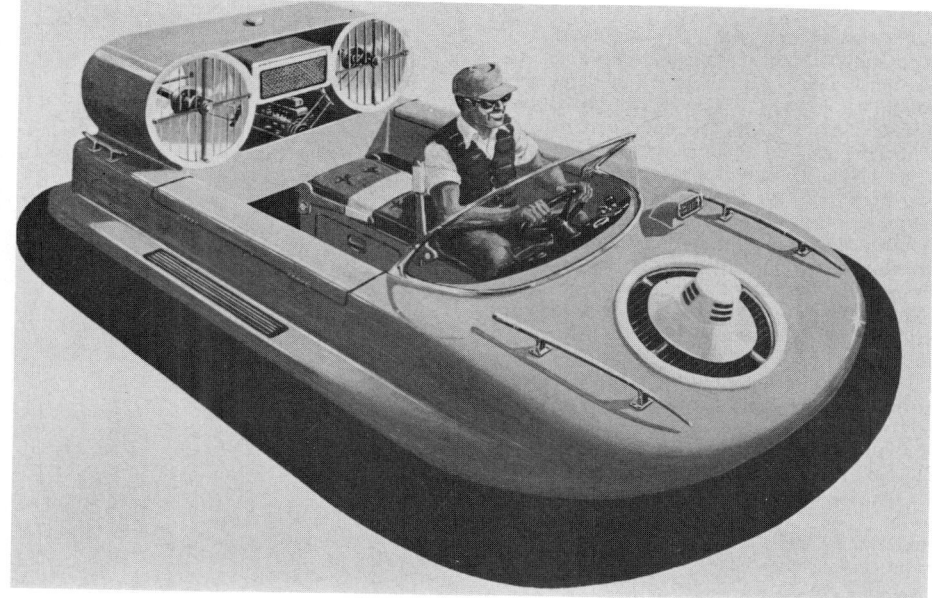

Hoverbird

UNIVERSAL HOVERCRAFT

1204 3rd Street, Box 281, Cordova, Illinois 61242, USA

Telephone: (309) 654 2588

Officials:

R J Windt, *Director*

Formed in 1969, this company has designed and built over 80 different sports and utility ACV prototypes, ranging from an ultra-light single-seater to the 12-seat UH-26 powered by a 225hp automotive engine. Plans for some of these designs are available to homebuilders. It has recently developed three new single-engined amphibious craft: a 3·65m (12ft) two-seater, a 3·96m (13ft) four-seater and a 5·48m (18ft) six-seater.

Work has also been undertaken on air cushion vehicles propelled by waterjets, outboard motors and sails.

Descriptions of the UH-10C, UH-11S and UH-11T will be found in *Jane's Surface Skimmers 1980* and earlier editions.

UH-10T

Designed specifically for amateur hovercraft builders, UH-10T can be built in between 90 and 180 hours at a cost of approximately US $150 (1984).

LIFT AND PROPULSION: A single 2·5 to 5hp vertical-shaft lawnmower engine, mounted ahead of the open cockpit, drives the lift fan. Thrust is supplied by a 5 to 8hp horizontal-shaft lawnmower engine driving a two-bladed propeller direct.

CONTROLS: A single rudder hinged to the rear of the propeller guard provides directional control.

HULL: Frame built from fir ribs and stringers and covered in 3·1mm (⅛in) plywood.

ACCOMMODATION: Open cockpit with seat for driver.

DIMENSIONS

Length: 3·32m (10ft 11in)

Beam: 1·93m (6ft 4in)

WEIGHTS

Empty: 102-131·53kg (225-290lb)

Payload, max: 124·73kg (275lb)

PERFORMANCE

Max speed over water: 32-48km/h (20-30mph)

Max speed over snow and ice: 40-56km/h (25-35mph)

Max gradient: 8-16%

PRICE: Complete set of plans for homebuilding, US $10. Full-size rib outlines US $4 (1984)

UH-12S

This lightweight two-seater is capable of carrying two adults and their camping or fishing equipment at 56·32km/h (35mph) over water.

LIFT AND PROPULSION: A single JLO 340

UH-10T

or 440 engine drives the lift fan and the thrust propeller via a V-belt system. The 0·61m (2ft) diameter fan turns at a maximum of 3,500rpm, while the 1·21m (4ft) diameter thrust propeller turns at 2,200rpm at full throttle.

CONTROLS: Three aerodynamic rudders behind the propeller provide directional control.

HULL: Construction is of fir ribs and stringers and 3·1mm (⅛in) plywood covering. Fibreglass applied to all joints and edges.

ACCOMMODATION: Tandem arrangement with passenger seated behind driver on a sliding seat.

DIMENSIONS

Length: 3·91m (12ft 10in)

Width: 1·82m (6ft)

Height: 1·52m (5ft)

WEIGHTS

Empty: 147kg (325lb)

Normal payload: 158·75kg (350lb)

Max payload: 204·1kg (450lb)

PERFORMANCE

Max speed, over land: 72·42km/h (45mph)
   over water: 56·32km/h (35mph)

Gradient at 450lb gross weight: 23%

PRICE: Plans US$15 (1984)

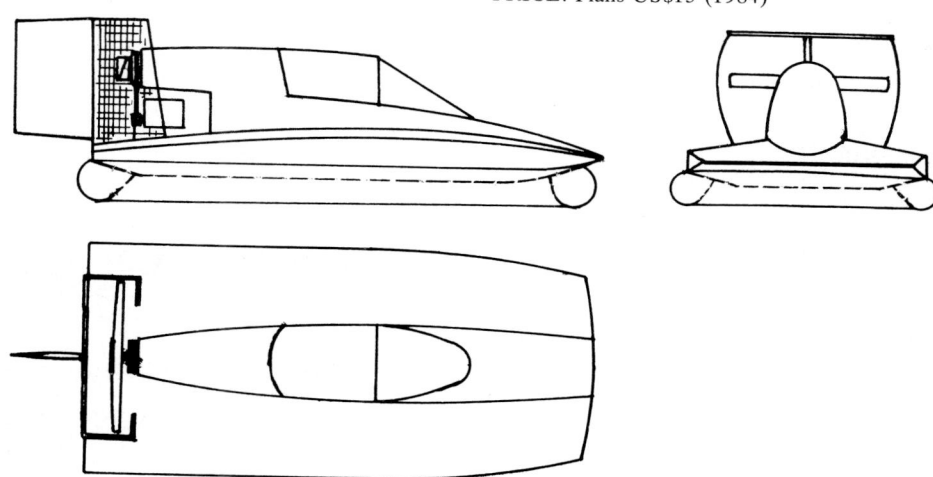

UH-12S

UH-12T2

This two- to three-seat, easily constructed craft is powered by standard lawnmower engines. The low rpm of these engines ensures quiet operation and a long engine life. Construction costs range from US $200 to $500, depending on the quality of the engines and the materials used.

LIFT AND PROPULSION: Lift is supplied by a 5hp Briggs and Stratton engine driving a 0·6m (24in) diameter, 0·3m (14in) pitch four-bladed wooden fan at 3,000rpm. Maximum cushion pressure is 11lb/ft². Thrust is provided by a 10hp Briggs and Stratton engine driving a 1·06m (42in) diameter, 40cm (16in) pitch two-bladed propeller aft. Total fuel capacity is 6·15 litres (1·5 US gallons).

CONTROLS: Triple rudders hinged to the rear of the propeller guard control craft handling.

HULL: Wooden structure built from pine ribs and struts and covered with 3·1mm (⅛in) plywood skin. The structure is designed to survive a 64km/h (40mph) plough-in in choppy water.

SKIRT: 177mm (7in) deep, 304mm (12in) diameter bag skirt, in 16oz/yd² neoprene-coated nylon.

ACCOMMODATION: Enclosed cabin seating driver and two passengers on a movable tandem seat.

DIMENSIONS
EXTERNAL
Length overall, power off: 3·93m (12ft 11in)
Beam overall, power off: 1·82m (6ft)
  skirt inflated: 2·03m (6ft 8in)
Cushion area: 6·03m² (65ft²)
Skirt depth: 177mm (7in)
INTERNAL
Cabin length: 1·21m (4ft)
Max width: 0·6m (2ft)
WEIGHTS
Normal empty: 136·07kg (300lb)
Normal gross: 272·14kg (600lb)
Normal payload: 136·07kg (300lb)
Max payload: 181·44kg (400lb)
PERFORMANCE
Max speed, calm water: 56·32km/h (35mph)
Max wave capacity: 304mm (12in) chop
Max gradient, static conditions: 12 degrees at 600lb
Vertical obstacle clearance: 152mm (6in)
PRICE: Plans US $15 (1984)

UH-12T3

The UH-12T3, twin-engine light ACV is intended primarily for the first-time builder. It has side-by-side seating with room for storage or a seat for a child. Payload is 136-226kg (300-500lb), depending on power installed.

LIFT AND PROPULSION: Lift is supplied by a 5hp four-cycle lawnmower engine driving a four-bladed wooden fan. Thrust is provided by any suitable four-cycle horizontal-shaft lawnmower engine in the 8 to 16hp range or a two-cycle engine of up to 440cc with a maximum weight of 34kg (75lb).

CONTROLS: Twin-rudders hinged to the rear of the propeller guard control craft direction.

HULL: Wooden structure built from pine ribs and struts and covered with 3·1mm (⅛in) plywood skin.

ACCOMMODATION: Open cockpit with side-by-side seating for two in front with room for child's seat behind.

DIMENSIONS
Length: 3·93m (12ft 11in)
Beam: 1·98m (6ft 6in)
WEIGHTS
Empty: 136-181kg (300-400lb)
Payload: 181-226kg (300-500lb)
PERFORMANCE
Max speed over water: 40-72km/h (25-45mph)
Max speed over land, snow and ice: 48-80km/h (30-50mph)
PRICE: Complete plans, US $12·75. Full-size rib outline, US $5·75 (1984)

UH-13SA

The prototype of this craft was built in 1974 from 25mm (1in) thick urethane foam fibreglass

UH-12S amphibious two-seater

UH-12T2

UH-12T3

UH-13SA

laminate. This type of construction proved too difficult for the homebuilder and so the craft was redesigned for wooden construction. The structure is built in fir or pine ribs and stringers, covered with 3·1mm (⅛in) plywood. An integrated lift/propulsion system is employed. Once engine speed is above idling the correct amount of lift is automatically maintained throughout the entire engine speed range by a patented system.

LIFT AND PROPULSION: Motive power is provided by a single JLO 440 driving a 0·63m (2ft 1in) diameter four-bladed lift fan and a 1·21m (4ft) diameter propeller via a V-belt reduction drive.

CONTROLS: Craft heading is controlled by twin rudders behind the propeller.

HULL: Construction is similar to that of UH-12T.

ACCOMMODATION: Two bench-type seats for two adults and two children.

DIMENSIONS
Length: 4·21m (13ft 10in)
Width: 1·98m (6ft 6in)
WEIGHTS
Empty: 181·42kg (400lb)
Normal payload: 181·42kg (400lb)
Max payload: 272·14kg (600lb)
PERFORMANCE
Max speed, over land, snow, ice: 96·56km/h (60mph)
  over water: 80·46km/h (50mph)
Max gradient: 26%
PRICE: Complete plans, US $9. Full-scale outline US $3 extra (1984)

UH-13T

UH-13T

This derivative of the UH-13 employs the same basic hull as the UH-13S, but exchanges its automatic lift system for a separate lift engine.

The 13T can carry 136-181kg (300-400lb) even when powered by 10 to 16hp four-cycle lawnmower engines.

LIFT AND PROPULSION: Recommended engines: lift, 8hp four-cycle vertical shaft mower engine or equivalent; thrust, two-cycle 20-55hp (295-760cc) or 10-16hp four-cycle engine weighing under 45kg (100lb).

DIMENSIONS
Length: 4·21m (13ft 10in)
Beam: 1·98m (6ft 6in)
WEIGHTS
Payload: 317kg (700lb)
Empty: 192-215kg (425-475lb)
PERFORMANCE
Max speed over water: 64-96km/h (40-60mph)
  land, ice and snow: 72-112km/h (45-70mph)
Hoverheight: 203mm (8in)
Max gradient: 15-33%

UH-14B

UH-14B

An amphibious four-seater, the UH-14B has a maximum payload capacity of over 362·85kg (800lb). Employment of a large slow-turning propeller for thrust permits high-speed cruising while generating very little noise.

LIFT AND PROPULSION: A JLO 230 two-cycle engine turns a four-bladed fan for lift. Alternatively, an 8hp vertical shaft lawnmower engine may be used for lift. Thrust is supplied by a JLO 440 two-cycle engine driving a 1·21m (4ft) diameter propeller through a V-belt speed reduction system.

CONTROLS: Heading is controlled by multiple aerodynamic rudders aft of the propeller.

HULL: Construction is of fir or pine ribs and stringers, which are covered with 3·1mm (⅛in) plywood.

UH-14T

DIMENSIONS
Length: 4·52m (14ft 10in)
Width: 2·13m (7ft)
Height off cushion: 1·52m (5ft)
WEIGHTS
Empty: 204kg (450lb)
Normal payload: 226·78kg (500lb)
Max payload: 362·85kg (800lb)
PERFORMANCE
Max speed, over land, snow, ice: 96·56km/h (60 mph)
  over water: 88·51km/h (55mph)
Max gradient at 650lb gross weight: 28%

UH-15P

PRICE: Complete plans US $14. Full-scale outline US $5 (1984)

UH-15P

A high-speed derivative of the UH-13, the UH-15P has an arrow-head planform which reduces air drag. It is one of the fastest craft in the Universal Hovercraft range and has attained 83mph during test runs. Roll and pitch stability are about the same as on the UH-13T. Some experimental work is being undertaken with ducted propellers employing the UH-15P as a test vehicle. The craft won the Canadian National Championships Rally in 1983 and 1984.

LIFT AND PROPULSION: Recommended engines: lift, 8 to 10hp four-cycle vertical shaft mower engine weighing 18·1 to 22·6kg (40 to 50lb) or equivalent; thrust, 10 to 20hp four-cycle mower engine for direct drive, or 20 to 60hp two-cycle for belt drive, high-performance application.

CONTROLS: Heading is controlled by triple aerodynamic rudders aft of the propeller.

ACCOMMODATION: Open cockpit for driver and up to two passengers.

HULL: Structure is of fir or pine ribs and stringers, covered with 3·1mm (⅛in) ply. Drainage system incorporated.

DIMENSIONS
Length: 4·82m (15ft 10in)
Width: 1·98m (6ft 6in)
WEIGHTS
Empty: 158·7-204·1kg (350-450lb)
Payload: Up to 362·8kg (up to 800lb)
PERFORMANCE
Across water: 64·3-112·6km/h (40 to 70mph)
  ice, snow and land: 72·4-133·5km/h (45 to 83mph)
Max gradient: 15-40%
Hoverheight: 203·2mm (8in)
PRICE: Complete plans, US $15. Full-size rib outline, US $6 (1984)

UH-16S

First introduced in 1980, the UH-16S seats five to six and has a maximum speed over land, snow and ice of 104km/h (65mph).

LIFT AND PROPULSION: Integrated system, employing the same type of automatic lift control as fitted to the 13S, 18S and 26S. Motive power is by a 1,500cc or larger Volkswagen, Corvair or any other four-cylinder water-cooled automotive engine weighing less than 150kg (350lb). Thrust, 68 to 158kg (150 to 350lb).

CONTROLS: Heading is controlled by triple-aerodynamic rudders aft of the propeller.

ACCOMMODATION: Enclosed cabin seating five to six.

DIMENSIONS
Length: 5·15m (16ft 11in)
Width: 2·28m (7ft 6in)
WEIGHTS
Empty: 340-453kg (750-1,000lb)
Payload: 340kg (750lb) with 1,500cc VW engine and over 454kg (1,000lb) with 2,300cc four-cylinder Ford engine
PERFORMANCE
Speed over water: 88·51km/h (55mph)
  land, snow and ice: 104km/h (65mph)
Clearance height: 177-304mm (7-12in)
Gradient: 15-25%

UH-17S

Construction of the prototype UH-17S, which has an integrated lift/propulsion system powered by either a Volkswagen or Corvair engine of 50-140hp, was completed in May 1970. The craft, which seats a driver and three passengers, is said to be extremely quiet and control is precise. It is capable of towing water or snow skier, sleds or ski boards.

LIFT AND PROPULSION: A single 75hp Corvair automobile engine drives a 1·06m (3ft 6in) diameter centrifugal fan mounted vertically on a shaft inside a transverse duct. Air is drawn by the fan from each end of the duct. Propulsion air is expelled through outlets at the stern and lift air is ducted into a plenum below. The fan feeds air

UH-15P which won Canadian National Championship Rally in 1983 and 1984

UH-15Ps fitted with ducted propellers

UH-15P

into the cushion at 6·79m³/s (240ft³/s) and provides 68kg (150lb) thrust.

ACCOMMODATION: Enclosed cabin seating driver and three passengers on two bench-type seats.

DIMENSIONS
Length: 5·43m (17ft 10in)
Beam: 2·41m (7ft 11in)

WEIGHTS
Empty: 430·89kg (950lb)
Normal loaded: 725·71kg (1,600lb)
Max loaded: 861·78kg (1,900lb)

PERFORMANCE
Max speed, over land: 67·59km/h (42mph)
over water: 56-64km/h (35-40mph)
Continuous gradient at 1,200lb: 12%

UH-18S

This was the first hovercraft to complete the journey from Los Angeles to San Diego, a distance of 169·98km (105 miles) across open seas. It accommodates up to seven people on three bench-type seats. Normal payload is 544·28kg (1,200lb). An automatic lift system similar to that

used on the UH-13S simplifies driving, improves reliability and decreases maintenance costs.

LIFT AND PROPULSION: Motive power is supplied by a single Corvair automotive engine, rated at 90hp at 3,600rpm, driving a 0·914m (3ft) diameter four-bladed fan for lift via the automatic lift system, and a 1·87m (6ft 2in) diameter two-bladed propeller through a V-belt speed reduction system. The lift fan turns at a constant 2,400rpm while the propeller turns 1,700rpm at full throttle.

Range of engines which can be used on this craft includes any air-cooled engine from 60-150hp and any four- to six-cylinder water-cooled unit weighing under 181·42kg (400lb).

CONTROLS: Heading is controlled by triple aerodynamic rudders behind the propeller.

HULL: Construction is similar to that of the UH-18T.

DIMENSIONS
Length: 5·63m (18ft 6in)
Width: 2·43m (8ft)
Height: 1·82m (6ft)

WEIGHTS
Empty: 498·92kg (1,100lb)
Normal payload: 544·28kg (1,200lb)
Max payload: 635kg (1,400lb)

PERFORMANCE
Max speed, over land, snow, ice: 104·6km/h (65mph)
over water: 88·51km/h (55mph)
Max gradient: 30%
PRICE: Complete plans, US $21. Full-scale outline US $5 (1984)

UH-18T

The prototype of this amphibious six-seater was built in 1971 and has accumulated over 400 operating hours, mainly on open seas.

It was the first hovercraft to visit Catalina Island, 41·84km (26 miles) off the coast of California. It has also been employed extensively for water and snow skiing.

The aerofoil-shaped hull is similar to that of the UH-12T and UH-14T.

In 1983 the design was revised to incorporate the latest hull design and drainage systems.

LIFT AND PROPULSION: Lift is provided by a 25hp JLO 395 two-cycle engine driving a 762mm (2ft 6in) diameter four-bladed fan at 3,200rpm. Alternatively, an 18hp Briggs & Stratton mower engine is recommended. About 5% of the air is employed to inflate the bag skirt. Propulsive thrust is supplied by an 85hp Corvair automobile engine driving a 1·52m (5ft) diameter two-bladed propeller at up to 2,800rpm. Recommended alternatives are 1,200 to 2,400cc 4-cylinder water- or air-cooled engines of less than 300lb.

UH-16S light amphibious hovercraft

UH-17S

UH-18S operating in surf zone

UH-18S

UH-18S

UH-18T light utility ACV

CONTROLS: Craft heading is controlled by a single rudder operating in the propeller slipstream and two auxiliary rudders hinged to the rear of twin fins, one each side of the propeller guard. All three rudders are operated by a steering wheel. Separate throttles provided for lift and thrust engines.

HULL: Mixed wood and grp construction. Hull frame is built from fir ribs and stringers and covered with 6·3mm (¼in) plywood. Highly stressed areas covered with glass fibre.

SKIRT: 0·46m (1ft 6in) diameter bag type, providing 0·304m (1ft) vertical clearance.

ACCOMMODATION: Driver and five passengers seated on two three-place bench seats. Cabin enclosed by canopy in cold weather.

DIMENSIONS
Length: 5·63m (18·5ft)
Beam: 2·43m (8ft)
Height, off cushion: 1·82m (6ft)
  on cushion: 2·13m (7ft)

WEIGHTS
Empty: 476·27kg (1,050lb)
Payload: 498·95kg (1,100lb)
Max loaded: 1,088kg (2,400lb)

PERFORMANCE
Max speed, over land: 104·6km/h (65mph)
  over water: 88·5km/h (55mph)
Max gradient: 20-35%

PRICE: Complete set of plans for homebuilding, US $25, including full-scale outline (1984)

UH-19P

UH-19P

This new design is similar to the UH-15P but is larger. It has slightly less stability in roll than a craft with a rectangular hull, but has greater pitch stability and lower drag, giving it higher speeds. Seating is three in the front and two in the aft of the open cockpit. With an enclosed cabin the craft can attain 90mph across ice and snow. Construction time is approximately 200 to 350 hours. Cost is between US$1,000 to $2,000 (1984).

The craft is being employed in attempts to establish a new water craft speed record between New Orleans and St Louis, a distance of 1,027 miles along the Mississippi.

Two attempts had been made up to November 1984 on the present record of 23 hours 9 minutes. One was foiled by a storm which damaged the craft, the second was completed in 25 hours. Difficulties encountered on the journey are rough water created by up to 150 barges encountered, each creating several miles of rough water; bad weather and the avoidance of obstacles at night. Further attempts are to be made during the summer of 1985.

LIFT AND PROPULSION: Motive power for the lift system is provided by an 18hp Briggs & Stratton vertical shaft mower engine driving an axial fan. Thrust is supplied by almost any automobile engine of up to 1600cc, weighing less than 300lb. The craft would still be very fast with the smaller 1100cc Datsun and Toyota engines.

DIMENSIONS
Length: 5·91m (19ft 5in)
Width: 2·28m (7ft 6in)

WEIGHTS
Empty: 935lb (424kg)
Payload: 1,000lb (453·5kg)

PERFORMANCE
Max speed, ice and snow, with closed cabin: 90mph
Max speed, calm water: 80mph
Max gradient capability: 30°-45°
Clearance height: 8in

UH-26S

This 12- to 16-seat ACV is the largest homebuilt craft available. Ribs and stringers are in fir and pine and covered with a 6·3mm (¼in) plywood skin. The driver's seat is placed high and forward for good visibility. The passenger compartment can seat 16 or eight plus 544kg (1,200lb) of cargo. The craft may also be equipped for touring with sleeping space for four to seven persons. In the hands of its designer, Bob Windt, the UH-26S completed a 4,409km (2,740 mile) trip from Cordova, Illinois to New Orleans, Louisiana and back in three weeks.

UH-19P

LIFT AND PROPULSION: Integrated system. Power supplied by a standard V-8 283-400in³ automobile engine driving a 1·06m (3ft 6in) diameter, four-bladed fan for lift and a 2·43m (8ft) diameter two-bladed propeller for thrust. Maximum recommended installed power is 225hp.

The lift fan is driven off the pulley end of the engine, employing a double Auto-lift system, drive shaft and right-angle drive gearbox. The two-bladed propeller is belt-driven from the flywheel end of the engine.

DIMENSIONS

Length: 7·92m (26ft)

Width: 3·65m (12ft)

WEIGHTS

Empty: 1,133·92kg (2,500lb)

Payload: 1,133·92kg (2,500lb)

Max weight capacity: 1,359kg (3,000lb)

PERFORMANCE

Max speed, over land: 104·6km/h (65mph)
over water: 88·5km/h (55mph)

Hoverheight: 355mm (14in)

Max gradient: 25%

PRICE: Complete set of plans available US $45.
Full size rib outline $10 (1984)

UH-26S

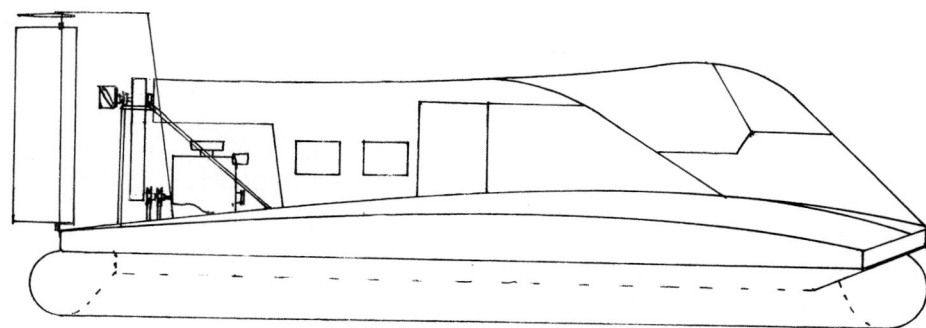

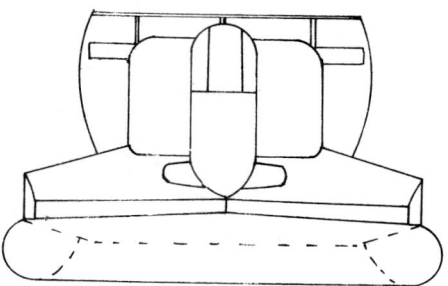

Outboard profile and head-on view of UH-26S

UH-26S, 12-16 seater

VENTURE AERO-MARINE

871 Moe Drive, Unit A-2, Akron, Ohio 44310, USA

Telephone: (216) 836 8794

Officials:
Paul W Esterle, *Proprietor*

Venture Aero-Marine is a major supplier of kits for homebuilt hovercraft in the United States. It will also supply partially or fully assembled hovercraft, custom built to order, and offers a wide range of components from engine mountings and fan ducts to skirts and steering systems.

In 1981 the company began marketing its own hovercraft designs, the first two of which are the Hoverbike and the Spectre III.

In response to a demand from young enthusiasts who cannot afford full-scale craft, the company offers a line of five radio-controlled and free flight model hovercraft kits.

In addition the company publishes *The Hoverlog*, a comprehensive annual catalogue of sports hovercraft and accessories.

HOVERBIKE

The Hoverbike has been designed for the first-time amateur hovercraft builder. The thrust unit may be removed, allowing the hull to be carried on top of a car.

LIFT AND PROPULSION: Lift is provided by a 5-8hp, four-cycle, vertical-shaft lawnmower engine driving a 0·6m (2ft) diameter five-bladed fan. Propulsive thrust is supplied by an 8-11hp, four-cycle lawnmower engine driving, via a belt, a 1·21m (4ft) diameter two-bladed propeller.

CONTROLS: Heading is controlled by twin-aerodynamic rudders hinged to the rear of the propeller guard.

HULL: Lightweight plywood structure assembled from flat sheets by a sewing process using light wire or fishing line. Buoyancy, 408kg (900lb).

ACCOMMODATION: Snowmobile-type seat for one in open cockpit.

DIMENSIONS
Length: 3·35m (11ft)
Beam: 2·05m (6ft 9in)
Height: 1·98m (6ft)
WEIGHTS
Empty: 88·44kg (195lb)
Payload: 124·73kg (275lb)
PERFORMANCE
Hoverheight: 177mm (7in)

SPECTRE III

Spectre III has been designed to meet the demand for a two-seater with sufficient fuel and storage space to undertake weekend cruises on sheltered waterways. It can be fitted with an open-top sports windshield or a lightweight closed 'bubble' canopy is available.

LIFT AND PROPULSION: Motive power is supplied by a single 1,200 or 1,300cc Volkswagen automotive engine driving via belt transmissions a 0·96m (3ft 2in) diameter five-bladed fan for lift and a 1·82m (6ft) diameter two-bladed propeller. Standard Volkswagen and Dune Buggy components are used and the engine requires no special machining. The engine, lift fan and propeller are incorporated in a compact machinery module to facilitate servicing and transport.

CONTROLS: Heading is controlled by triple-aerodynamic rudders hinged to the rear of the propeller guard. Electrically-operated elevator aft provides pitch trim.

HULL: Wooden structure covered in marine-grade plywood. Buoyancy, 907kg (2,000lb).

ACCOMMODATION: Side-by-side seating for two. Can be equipped with canopy.

DIMENSIONS
Length: 4·19m (13ft 9in)
Beam: 2·38m (7ft 10in)
Height: 2·13m (7ft)
WEIGHTS
Empty: 265·33kg (585lb)
Payload: 226·78kg (500lb)
PERFORMANCE
Hoverheight: 203mm (8in)
Max gradient: 15-25%

Hoverbike

1·06m (3ft 6in) Cyclone

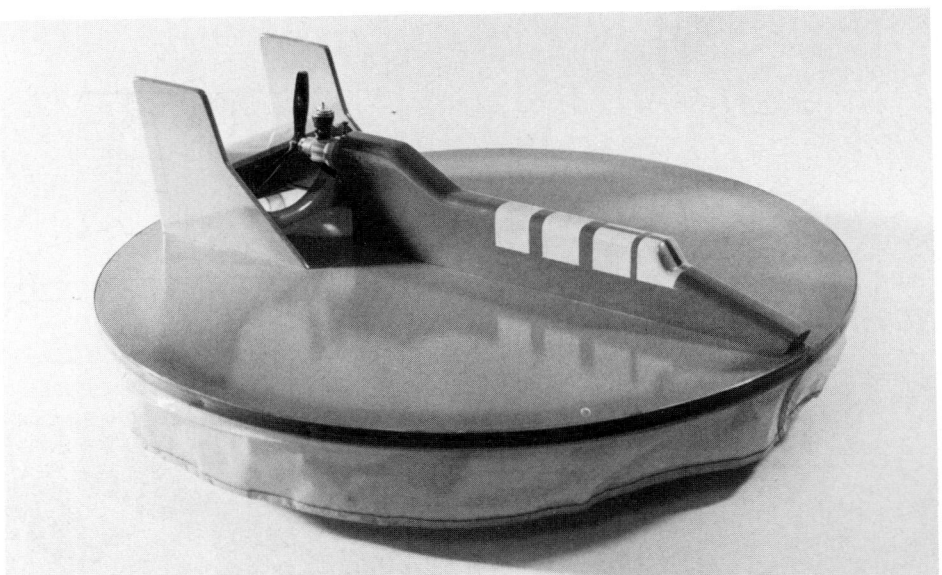

Hoverbird model hovercraft sold in kit form

Spectre III fitted with winter cockpit canopy

Spectre III

WATER RESEARCH COMPANY

3003 North Central Avenue, Suite 600, Phoenix, Arizona 85012, USA

Telephone: (602) 265 7722

Officials:
Richard R Greer, *President*

The Water Research Company was formed in 1972 to consolidate activities surrounding the patents held or applied for by Richard R Greer relating to various aspects of water-borne vehicles. The company has subsequently prepared conceptual studies on a class of winged surface effect vessels (WSEV) intended to fill a variety of US Navy and commercial freight applications.

The conclusions of this study were published in *Naval Engineer's Journal*, April 1974, and further comprehensive conclusions also setting forth energy savings and use of alternate fuels were published in *Jane's Surface Skimmers 1975-76*. Present efforts are directed towards providing assistance in related research activities and further research studies.

ACV OPERATORS

AUSTRALIA
AUSTRALIAN ARMY

A Skima 6 is in operation on tidal flats in Southern Australia with the Australian Army.

BAHRAIN
GRAY MACKENZIE MARINE SERVICES

A Vosper Hovermarine HM 221 was delivered to Gray Mackenzie Marine Services in September 1982. The craft, which has living quarters for seven, can carry 28 passengers and up to five tonnes of cargo on an aft deck. It is currently being operated on oil industry support duties throughout the Arabian Gulf.

MINISTRY OF THE INTERIOR

An AV Tiger is employed in Bahrain as a quick response rescue hovercraft for the Bahrain Coast Guard.

BELGIUM
MINISTRY OF WORKS
Antwerp, Belgium

An HM 216 *Kallo* is employed as a River Scheldt survey craft.

EUROSENSE

An SR.N61S previously operated across the Solent by Hovertravel has been sold to Eurosense, a company specialising in hydrographic survey and remote sensing work. Previously named *Freedom*, the craft is now named *Beasac*, an acronym for Belfotop-Eurosense Acoustic Sounding Air Cushion platform. It was delivered in April 1984 and is being operated out of Zeebrugge on behalf of the Belgian Ministry of Works.

BRAZIL
AEROBARCOS DO BRASIL, Transtur

Transportes Máritimos e Turismo SA, Transtur, Avenida Amaral Peixoto 71-11th floor, Niteroi-R-J, Brazil
Telephone: 719-7070
CRAFT OPERATED
Three Hovermarine 216s.

CANADA
CANADIAN ARMED FORCES

One AV Tiger is based at Cold Lake, Alberta for overland evaluation.

CANADIAN COAST GUARD HOVER-CRAFT UNITS

Headquarters: Transport Canada, Canadian Coast Guard, Fleet Systems Branch, Tower A, Place de Ville, Ottawa, Ontario K1A 0N5, Canada
Unit Addresses: Canadian Coast Guard Hovercraft Unit, PO Box 23068, AMF Int'l Airport, Vancouver, British Columbia V7N 1T9, Canada
Telephone: (604) 273 2556
Canadian Coast Guard ACV Laurentian Region, ACV Unit, 850 Nuns Island Boulevard, Nuns Island, Montreal, Quebec H3E 1H2, Canada
Telephone: (514) 283 7882
Administration: Vancouver Unit: Regional Director, Canadian Coast Guard, PO Box 10060, Pacific Centre, 700 West Georgia Street, Vancouver, British Columbia V7Y 1E1, Canada
Montreal Unit: Director, Canadian Coast Guard, 2 Place Quebec, Room 212, Quebec G1R 2O5, Canada

The Canadian Coast Guard Hovercraft Unit in Vancouver was formed in 1968 for hovercraft evaluation in search and rescue and other coast guard duties.

Delivery of SR.N6 039 in 1977 increased the search and rescue capabilities. A second SR.N6, 031 joined the Vancouver fleet in 1981.

SR.N61S *Beasac* operated out of Zeebrugge by Eurosense

OPERATIONS: Patrol area is the Straits of Georgia and Gulf Islands (500 square miles), although search and rescue duties are undertaken outside this area. The average patrol distance is 80 miles.

Since April 1969, the unit has carried out over 10,000 missions including marine, aircraft distress and mercy missions. The unit is now operational 24 hours a day.

In early in 1982 a second base was opened at Parksville, Vancouver Island.

Other operations include: checking, servicing and repairing marine navigational aids within the patrol area; transporting men and materials for aids construction; laying underground cables in marshy terrain; aircraft accident inspection; water pollution investigation; safety checks of tugs. Exercises with police departments and the Canadian Armed Forces vessels; training of government personnel; experimental work with government agencies.

EQUIPMENT: One SR.N5 serial No 021 and two SR.N6s, Nos 031 and 039, modified to CCG requirements.

Equipment includes navigation and communications equipment, such as radar, HF and VHF direction finder, HF/MF, VHF/FM and VHF/AM radio-telephone, two Nightsun 65 million candle power searchlights, two six-person inflatable life rafts, two 100-gallon (454·5-litre) auxiliary fuel tanks (extending endurance to nine hours at maximum power), stretchers, first-aid kit, firefighting equipment, towing gear and other search and rescue equipment.

The delivery of a refurbished Voyageur in 1974 formed the equipment of the CCG's Development and Evaluation Unit, whose task was to evaluate the vehicle in various CCG roles. In 1980 the unit was reformed as the Laurentian Region ACV Unit, thus becoming an integral part of the CCG's operational fleet. The ACV has proved to be suitable for operations requiring high response speed, operations across water/land interface, and in shoal conditions. Roles include: navigation aids servicing, supply of light stations, construction support, pollution control, inshore icebreaking, search and rescue and regulation enforcement.

The unit has one Bell Aerospace Voyageur (Serial No 002, registration CH-CGA), fitted with navigation and communications equipment. It can carry a portable crew module to enable the crew to stay aboard for extended periods.

CANADIAN HOVERWAYS

CRAFT OPERATED
North American Tiger based at Moosonee, Ontario for charter.

CHURCHILL WILDERNESS ENCOUNTER
PO Box 9, Churchill, Manitoba R0B 0F0, Canada

CRAFT OPERATED
One North American Hovercraft Tiger for charter.

DEPARTMENT OF ENVIRONMENT AND NATIONAL RESEARCH COUNCIL

CRAFT OPERATED
Towed trailers and air cushion assist transporters undergoing evaluation in logging and heavy transport.

RIVTOW, VANCOUVER, BRITISH COLUMBIA

CRAFT OPERATED
PSL 003 Angevinière, three-seat utility craft.

CHINA, PEOPLE'S REPUBLIC

ACVs are used for a variety of military and civil applications, including the operation of fast passenger ferry services over river networks with route distances of up to 240 to 320km (150 to 200 miles). One of a number of test craft is operating from Chungking on a passenger ferry service. Largest hovercraft to be built in China is a 65-ton multi-duty design for use as an amphibious assault craft or high-speed passenger/vehicle ferry. The craft, which was launched at Tianjin in August 1979, resembles a scaled-down BHC SR.N4. The prototype is undergoing evaluation.

CHANGJIANG SHIPPING ADMINIST-RATION BUREAU

The bureau, which is based in Shanghai, purchased two Hovermarine 218s from the Hongkong and Yaumati Ferry Company in 1983. They are being operated on ferry services along the Yangtse River.

DENMARK
A/S DAMPSKIBSSELSKABET ØRESUND

Havnegade 49, DK-1058, Copenhaghen, Denmark
Telephone: 01 14 77 70, 01 12 80 88
Telex: 45-27502 Sundet DK

DSO introduced a new route in June 1984 employing two BHC AP.1-88s to link Copenhagen Airport and Malmö. The two hovercraft, which are leased to the Scandinavian Airlines System, are named *Liv Viking* and *Freja Viking*.

EGYPT
EGYPTIAN NAVY

Alexandria, Egypt

Three SR.N6s, one Mk 1 and two Mk 2s have been operated on coastal defence patrols since 1976.

OFFSHORE GAC SERVICES

A Bell Halter 110, *Margaret Jill*, has been chartered from the manufacturers by GAC Services for oil industry support duties in the Gulf of Suez. It was due to begin operations in late 1984.

FINLAND
BOARD OF ROADS AND WATERWAYS

A 25-tonne payload capacity passenger/vehicle ferry, the PUC 22-2500SP, was delivered to the Finnish Board of Roads and Waterways by the Wärtsilä Helsinki Shipyard in December 1982. The vehicle, which can carry 16 cars or two buses and 50 passengers, is operated in the Finnish archipelago, particularly in winter conditions.

FRANCE
FRENCH NAVY

Toulon, France

The French Defence Ministry has undertaken studies of fully amphibious and sidewall hovercraft including projects with SEDAM and DCN. It is not clear whether there will be any requirement announced by the French Government in the near future, but there are signs that the French Navy is interested in the anti-submarine warfare and mine countermeasure potential of SES and ACV craft. A 5-tonne SES test craft, Molenes, was completed by DCN in 1981 and is undergoing trials. The craft is a dynamic model of a projected 4,000-tonne escort vessel.

LANGUEDOC-ROUSSILLON REGIONAL DEVELOPMENT BOARD

Montpellier and Perpignan, France
CRAFT OPERATED
2 × N 102

MINISTRY OF DEFENCE

An AV Tiger entered service in one of France's overseas territories during 1982.

HONG KONG
HONGKONG AND YAUMATI FERRY COMPANY LIMITED

This company, which is the world's biggest operator of passenger-ferry hovercraft, has a fleet of four Hovermarine 216s and 24 Hovermarine 218s. They are operated on cross-harbour services, longer commuter routes and an international service between Hong Kong and Canton in the People's Republic of China.

SEALINK FERRIES LIMITED

This company was formed in 1981 to operate on the Kowloon-Macao route with the Hongkong and Yaumati Ferry Company as majority shareholder and Far East Hydrofoil Company as a minority shareholder. Services began in September 1983 with four Vosper Hovermarine HM 527s.

AP.1-88 operated by DSO between Copenhagen Airport and Malmö

IRAN
IRANIAN NAVY

Hovercraft base: Khosrowabad, Iran

Eight SR.N6s, two Mk 3s and six Mk 4s, were delivered to the Iranian Navy in 1968-69. Two BH.7 Mk 4s were introduced in 1971 and four BH.7 Mk 5s in 1975-76. Some of the craft are believed to be still operational and two of the Mk 5s are being refitted.

IRAQ
IRAQI NAVY

Six SR.N6 Mk 6Cs were delivered to the Iraqi Navy during 1983. It is understood that they are operational on internal policing patrols out of Basra.

ISRAEL
ISRAELI NAVY

The Israeli Navy has two SH.2 Mk 5 nine-seater hovercraft for use as support craft.

JAPAN
FUKE KAIUN CO LTD

3-3-25 Honmachi, Sumoto, Hyogo, Japan
Telephone: 07992 4 1144

Officials
M Oda, *President*

The company purchased a 65-seat HM 216, *Hovstar* from Hovermarine Pacific Company Limited in July 1981. It operates an all-year-round passenger ferry service from Sumoto to Fuke, near Osaka.

JAPANESE NATIONAL RAILWAYS

Kokutetsu Building, 6-5 Marunouchi 1-chome, Chiyoda-ku, Tokyo 100, Japan

A service between Uno in Okayama Prefecture and Takamatsu in Kagawa Prefecture began in 1972, using MV-PP5, *Kamome (Sea Gull)*. In 1980 it was succeeded by *Tobiuo (Flying Fish)*, a 66-seat version of the MV-PP5 Mk II. Route distance is 21km; journey time 23 minutes. *Tobiuo* has an annual utilisation of 2,400 hours.

MEITETSU KAIJO KANKOSEN CO

18-1 Sanbonmatsu-cho, Atsuta-ku, Nagoya, Japan

Regular services began across the Mikawa and Ise Bays between Gamagori and Toba in 1969, with an intermediate stop at Nishiura and Irako. Routes: Gamagoori to Nishiura, 11·5km (15 minutes), Nishiura to Irako, 33·6km (30 minutes), Irako to Toba, 23·2km (20 minutes). These routes are not serviced at present.

MV-PP5 Mk II *Tobiuo (Flying Fish)*, operated by Japanese National Railways

NIPPON KAI KANKO FERRY CO LTD

This company began operating two PP15s, PP15-01 *Cygnus* and PP15-02 *Cygnus No 1*, in April 1978.
Route(s): Manao-Ogi, 150km (2 hours 15 minutes); Ogi Suzu, 105km (1 hour 25 minutes); Suzu-Manao, 60km (50 minutes). These routes are not serviced at present.

OITA HOVERFERRY CO LTD

1-14-1 Nishi-shinchi, Oita, Japan

Oita operates four MV-PP5s converted to Mk 2 standard: 03, 04, 06 and 15, named *Hakucho 3, Hobby 1, Hobby 3* and *Angel 5,* and one MV-PP5, 10, *Angel 2.*
Route(s): Oita Airport to Oita City, 29km (24 minutes), Oita Airport to Beppu City, 31km (26 minutes), Oita City to Beppu City, 12km (10 minutes). Annual utilisation, about 1,500 hours per craft.

JORDAN
JORDAN VALLEY AUTHORITY

Amman, Jordan

The Jordan Valley Authority has two Hovermarine 218s based on the Dead Sea.

KUWAIT

Two 82-seat Hovermarine 218s were delivered to Touristic Enterprises Company KSC during 1983 and were joined by a third craft of the same type at the end of 1984. They operate on a 10 n mile route linking Kuwait City and the island of Failaka.

NETHERLANDS
ROTTERDAM PORT AUTHORITY

The Rotterdam Port Authority operates four HM 218 multi-role harbour craft in the Europort area. The craft are based on the standard HM 218 hull, with provision for port monitoring and emergency services in two separate superstructure modules.

NEW ZEALAND
DEPARTMENT OF CIVIL AVIATION

The New Zealand Department of Civil Aviation has one SR.N6 Winchester for crash rescue services at Mangere Airport, Auckland. A Pindair Skima 12 was introduced as reserve craft in 1982.

ROTORUA AERO CLUB INC

PO Box 118, Rotorua, New Zealand

One Riverland Surveyor 8 Mk 2 is operated on Lake Rotorua.

AIR BORNE HOVERCRAFT SERVICES

PO Box 11034, Dunedin, New Zealand

One Riverland Surveyor 8 is operated on Lake Wakatijou and also on the Kawarau and Shotover rivers.

NIGERIA
FEDERAL MINISTRY OF TRANSPORT (IND)

19th Floor, Western House, Broad Street, Lagos, Nigeria

Two Hovermarine 218s owned by the Federal Ministry of Transport are based in Lagos harbour.

NIGERIAN POLICE

Five AV Tigers were delivered to the Nigerian Police in 1983. The craft are to be used on patrol duties in Lagos harbour.

PORTUGAL
SOCIEDADE TURISTICA PONTA DO ADOXE SARL

Apartado 114, Setubal, Portugal

This company has one Hovermarine 216 for ferry services linking Setubal, Troia and Sesimbra.

SAUDI ARABIA
SAUDI ARABIAN COASTAL AND FRONTIER GUARD

Ministry of the Interior, Airport Road, Riyadh, Saudi Arabia

The Saudi Arabian Coastal and Frontier Guard operates 16 SR.N6s on patrol, contraband control, search and rescue and liaison duties. The craft are based at Jeddah and Aziziyah on the east and west coasts.
The original fleet of eight SR.N6 Mark Is was increased by the delivery of six SR.N6 Mark 8s in 1981 and a further two in 1982.

SINGAPORE
SHELL EASTERN PETROLEUM (PTE) LIMITED

Head Office: Shell Tower, Singapore
Five HM 218s were introduced during 1983. They are operated on support operations between Singapore and the Shell refinery on Pulau Bukom.

UNION OF SOVIET SOCIALIST REPUBLICS
MINISTRY OF THE RIVER FLEET

The most widely used commercial ACV at present is the 48- to 50-seat Zarnitsa sidewall craft, well over 100 of which have entered service since 1970. This is being followed into production by the enlarged, 80-seat Orion, the Rassvet, 30 of which are being built for the Black Sea Shipping Line, and Luch.
Over 100 Zarya air-lubricated hull craft have been completed and many are in service on shallow rivers in the eastern areas of the Soviet Union.

SOVIET ARMY

Gus, a military version of the Skate 50-seat fast ferry, is in service with the Soviet Army.

SOVIET NAVY

Several experimental ACVs are being evaluated by the Soviet Navy and a 27-tonne amphibious assault landing craft, which bears the NATO code name Gus, is in service with the Soviet naval infantry. It has been joined in service by the 90-tonne Lebed initial amphibious assault landing craft which operates from the well docks of LSDs and carries up to two PT-76 amphibious tanks. Largest air cushion vehicle in service is the 270-ton Aist, similar in many respects to the SR.N4 Mountbatten and employed to carry tanks and mechanised infantry. About 35 Gus-type craft, 18 Lebeds and 16 Aists are in service in the eastern Baltic, Black Sea and Soviet far east.

UNITED ARAB EMIRATES
MARINE TRANSPORT SERVICES CO

This organisation operates a Tropimere SH2-4 which was delivered in September 1977.

UNITED KINGDOM
HOVERCRAFT HIRE

Officials:
Anthony H E France, *Managing Director*

Hovercraft Hire owns a Pindair Skima 12 which is available for charter in the United Kingdom and overseas.

HOVERSPEED (UK) LIMITED

Head Office and Reservations: The International Hoverport, Ramsgate, Kent CT12 5HS, England
Telephone: 0843 55555
Operations Base: The International Hoverport, Dover, Kent CT17 9TG, England
Telephone: 034 20813
01 499 9481
Telex: 96323
Officials:
J P Cumberland, *Managing Director*
K Hilditch, *Personnel Manager*
T Redburn, *Finance Director*
R Wilkins, *Sales and Marketing Director*
P Yerbury, *Technical Director*
D Meredith, *Operations Manager*
D Wise, *Projects Manager*

Hoverspeed was formed as a result of a merger between the two cross-Channel operators, British Rail Hovercraft Limited (Seaspeed) and Hoverlloyd. Operations began in October 1981.
British Rail, former owner of Seaspeed, and the Broström Group, former owner of Hoverlloyd, each have a 50 per cent shareholding in the company.
A year-round service is operated between Dover and Boulogne/Calais. The city-link coach and rail services between London and major European cities are retained.
Both former companies made significant contributions to the successful operation and technical development of the SR.N4 hovercraft and the merger is a natural progression to consolidate and improve the market position of hovercraft over the short Channel routes.
British Rail Hovercraft Limited was formed in March 1966 and launched its first commercial

Hoverspeed terminal at Western Docks, Dover

service in July 1966, between Southampton and Cowes. The cross-Channel service for passengers and cars between hovercraft terminals at Dover and Boulogne began in August 1968 using an SR.N4 *The Princess Margaret*. A year later the service was augmented by the introduction of a sister craft, *The Princess Anne* and in October 1970 a service began between Dover and Calais.

During 1978 the first of the two stretched SR.N4 Mk III craft came into operation. *The Princess Anne*, formerly a Mk 1 craft, had a 16·7m (55ft) midships section inserted at the British Hovercraft Corporation's factory at Cowes, Isle of Wight. The largest hovercraft in the world, it is driven by four uprated Marine Proteus gas turbine engines of 3,800shp, each driving a fan unit and a 6·4m (21ft) propeller. Craft motion is considerably less than that experienced on the standard N4 and operating limitations have been extended to cope with waves of up to 3·5m. The car deck cabins have been incorporated into large, outward facing passenger decks. These widened compartments have been improved with the introduction of new overhead ventilation, underseat heating, improved hand luggage storage and lighting. An improved skirt design with lower pressure ratio, deeper fingers and increased air cushion depth at the bow, has improved passenger comfort and reduced crossing times in adverse weather. Seaspeed's second N4, *The Princess Margaret*, rejoined the Seaspeed fleet in May 1979, after being stretched.

In July 1978, Seaspeed took delivery of the French-built SEDAM N.500-02. The craft was operated by SNCF (French Railways). Extensive modifications to improve seakeeping and manoeuvrability of the N.500 were completed in late 1982.

The craft returned to commercial service with Hoverspeed in March 1983 but was withdrawn in July 1983 as a result of technical unreliability. Hoverspeed's commercial operation is now entirely serviced by British-built SR.N4 hovercraft. A new purpose-built terminal complex was opened at Dover in 1978, on 15 acres of reclaimed land between the Prince of Wales Pier and the North Pier in Western Docks. Independent of the conventional ferry operations it contains its own passport control and immigration services. Passengers arrive via a landscaped terminal approach and enter a spacious arrival concourse. Facilities include duty and tax free shops, licensed bars, a cafeteria, snack bar, bureau de change and a nursing mothers room. Motorists check into a multi-lane arrival area with space for 178 cars.

In 1977 the Boulogne Chamber of Commerce and Industry, which controls the port installations for ships and hovercraft in the area, decided to go ahead on the first phase of work for the reception of the N.500. The ramp was widened and the hoverpad extended to take three hovercraft. The car parking area was enlarged and a visitors' car park was provided. A maintenance block and repair area were built for servicing the N.500 craft, which is based at Boulogne.

In 1978, work started on the second phase, the building of a new passenger terminal complex. It has two distinct buildings; an hexagonal tower which houses the administrative offices and the control tower and a single storey building for passenger traffic. A footbridge connects the two buildings.

The reception lounge has a ticket counter, ticket office, bureau de change, cafeteria for 150 people, newsagent's shop, car hire desks and other passenger amenities including public telephones and toilets. Beyond the customs, immigration and ticket control points, passengers enter a large departure lounge which has a licensed bar and a duty-free shop.

Autorail trains leave from the railway platform at Boulogne Hoverport for Paris all-year-round. The hoverport complex at Boulogne was opened to the public in May 1979.

Hoverlloyd was formed by two shipping companies, Swedish Lloyd and Swedish American Line (now both members of the Broström group), to operate a cross-Channel car and

HM 216 operated by NMI Limited

passenger-ferry service between Ramsgate and Calais. The company operated four BHC SR.N4 Mk II widened Mountbattens.

In May 1969 the company opened coach-hovercraft-coach services between London and Paris. In April 1974 Hoverlloyd opened coach-hovercraft-coach services between London/Kortrijk and Brussels. Another coach-hovercraft-coach service, linking London with Amsterdam, began in April 1979.

Covering an area of 9 hectares at the northern end of Pegwell Bay, the International Hoverport at Ramsgate is on a site raised 2·4m (8ft) above the beach, so that operations are unaffected by tides. The hoverport houses customs and immigration, administrative departments and a large engineering section, as well as a wide range of modern passenger facilities, including a visitors' observation platform. There is a large car-parking area alongside the main building. In front of the hoverport, facing the sea, is a large concrete apron on which the hovercraft land and load/unload. Large ramps give access to the apron from the beach. Between the buildings and the cliffs nearby are the car park and car reception area which are joined to the main road which connects with the Thanet Way and the M2 motorway to London.

Hoverspeed did not operate from Ramsgate in 1983, and is operating only from Dover to Calais and Boulogne. Reservations, accounts department and technical workshops are still based at Ramsgate.

HOVERTRAVEL LIMITED

Head Office: 12 Lind Street, Ryde, Isle of Wight, England
Telephone: 0983 65181
Telex: 86513-Hoverwork
Terminal Offices: Quay Road, Ryde, Isle of Wight (Tel: 0983 65241); Clarence Pier, Southsea (Tel: 29988)
Officials

C D J Bland, *Chairman and Managing Director*
E W H Gifford, *Director*
D R Robertson, *Director*
J Gaggero, *Director*
A C Smith, *Director*
R G Clarke, *Director and General Manager*
G W Black, *Director*
J E H Davies, *Director*
G M Palin, *Company Secretary*

Hovertravel Limited was formed in 1965 to operate two SR.N6 Winchester hovercraft across

AP.1-88 *Resolution* operated by Hovertravel

the Solent between Ryde, Isle of Wight and Southsea and Gosport. The Gosport route was discontinued some years ago.

Journey time is about 7 minutes on the Ryde to Southsea route. Approximately 450,000 passengers are carried each year on the route together with many tons of mail and freight parcel packages. By September 1984 the total number of passengers carried exceeded 9·5 million.

Two AP.1-88 80-seat hovercraft were introduced into service by Hovertravel in 1983.

The combined fleet operated by Hovertravel and Hoverwork includes: Two AP.1-88s, *Tenacity* and *Resolution*; and SR.N6 Mk 1s.

The company also builds AP.1-88s by agreement with BHC.

HOVERWORK LIMITED

(Wholly-owned subsidiary of Hovertravel Limited)

12 Lind Street, Ryde, Isle of Wight, England
Telephone: 0983 65181
Telex: 86513
Officials:
C D J Bland, *Managing Director*
E W H Gifford, *Director*
A C Smith, *Director*
R G Clarke, *Director*
G M Palin, *Secretary*

Hoverwork Limited was formed in 1966. The company provides crew training and charter facilities for all available types of ACVs, thus bridging the gap between the operators and manufacturers.

The company has trained over 50 hovercraft captains and has received some 40 charter contracts, including film sequences and the operation of the SR.N6 craft for mineral surveys throughout the world. The company operated the hovercraft passenger service during Expo' 67 at Montreal and a service at the 1970 and 1976 Algiers Expositions.

Hoverwork is the largest international operator of hovercraft, having access to Hovertravel's 56- and 38-seater SR.N6s, and the newly acquired AP.1-88 80-seat passenger craft. It has undertaken operations in areas from the Arctic to the equator, including logistics exercises in the northern part of Svalbard and in equatorial parts of South America. To date Hoverwork has operated in the following areas: Canada, South America, Mexico, Brunei, Netherlands, Bahrain, Kuwait, the United Arab Emirates, Saudi Arabia, Algeria, Tunisia, English North Sea, Spitzbergen, Australia, Iraq and Egypt.

MINISTRY OF DEFENCE

Two AV Tigers were delivered to the Ministry of Defence during summer 1982. They are operated on patrol and support duties at the Proof and Experimental Establishment in Essex.

NMI LIMITED

St Johns Street, Hythe, Hampshire SO4 6YS, England

An HM.216, based at Hythe, is operated by NMI Limited as a support craft for marine trials.

UNITED STATES OF AMERICA

CITY OF TACOMA

Two HM 221 firefighting craft were delivered to the city of Tacoma, Washington State, in 1982. Based on a HM 200 series hull, they are equipped with a wide range of firefighting, rescue, navigational and communications equipment designed to cope with ship and harbour installation fires in Tacoma harbour.

COMMAND MARINE INC

Lafayette, Louisiana, USA

Command Marine operates two Bell Halter BH 110 Mk II Dashboats to service offshore rigs and platforms in the Bay of Campeche, Mexico.

SR.N6 modified by Hoverwork for seismic survey in Iraq and Egypt

Jeff(A) during offshore oil industry support operations in Beaufort Sea

SOME TYPICAL HOVERWORK OPERATIONS

Year	Location	Type of Operation	Type of Terrain
1972	Tunisia— Sfax	Seismic survey	Very shallow water and shoreline land work
	North West Territories, Canada	Seismic survey	Shallow water, ice
	UK—The Wash	Logistics	Mud, shallow water
1973	UK— Maplin Sands	Geological survey for London's third airport	Tidal sands, shallow water
1974-1976	Saudi Arabia	Seismic survey	Shallow water, reefs, uncharted areas
1975	Australia— Thursday Island	Casualty evacuation and general transport	Shallow water and reefs. No conventional docking facilities
	UK—The Wash	Transportation of men and materials	Tidal areas, half mud, half water
1976	UK	Seismic survey	Tidal area of Liverpool Bay and Blackpool
	Algiers	Passengers	Transport from Algiers Port to Fair Site including half a mile down a specially prepared road
1977-80	United Arab Emirates	Seismic survey	Very shallow water combined with coral reefs and sand bars
1981-82	Iraq	Seismic survey	Inland lakes; in part mud banks and reeds
1983-84	Egypt	Seismic survey	Very shallow water, coral reefs and sand bars

HARBOR BAY ISLE ASSOCIATES

Alameda, California, USA

A Vosper Hovermarine 218 SES has been chartered by Harbor Bay Isle Associates to operate demonstration services between various points in San Francisco Bay, including central San Francisco, and an estate development at Bay Farm Island in Alameda, near Oakland Airport.

The demonstration services are intended to operate for six months. If the programme proves successful several more HM 218s will be ordered and a permanent service will be established.

HOVERCRAFT TRANSPORT SERVICES INC

PO Box 10-1023, Anchorage, Alaska 99511, USA
Telephone: (907) 272 2954
Officials:
Skip Freeman, *President*

This company specialises in the operation of hovercraft in Alaska. It provides Alaska Hovercraft Contenders on a leased basis, complete with drivers. Operations are being conducted in the Prudhoe Bay oilfield on a joint venture basis with Veco Inc, an oilfield support company.

RMI INC

National City, San Diego, California 92050, USA

RMI successfully completed Arctic operations with the Jeff(A), a US Navy ACV, leased by RMI, Inc, and chartered to Sohio Alaska Petroleum Company. The operation was to provide ACV design engineering data and logistics support for offshore drilling operations in the Beaufort Sea. The craft was winterised by RMI at Prudhoe Bay, Alaska, by 36 engineering changes, primarily to incorporate heating or insulation on critical craft systems. The operating phase began November 1, 1983, and continued until July 1984. Three engineering test series directed at gathering craft performance data (manoeuvering, ridge crossing ability, drag and thrust; ice-breaking and towing capability; and above-and-below-ice acoustic information) were undertaken.

SEAFLITE

Pier 8, 155 Ala Moana Blvd, Honolulu, Hawaii 96813, USA
Telephone: (808) 536 0861
Officials
Lee Martin, *President*
Jan Baccigaluppi, *General Manager*

Seaflite plans to acquire a new 400-passenger surface effect ship to recommence inter-island routes in Hawaii. The route network will subsequently be expanded to include the islands of Kauai and Hawaii.

US ARMY CORPS OF ENGINEERS

The first of the Bell Halter 48 hydrographic survey boats was delivered to the US Army Corps of Engineers in 1980. Named *Rodolf*, it is operated out of Portland, Oregon.

US ARMY MOBILITY EQUIPMENT R & D COMMAND (MERADCOM)

In September 1979 a US $40 million contract was placed with Bell Aerospace Textron by MERADCOM for the first eight of twelve LACV-30s (lighter, air cushion vehicle–30 short ton payload). In January 1981 the contract was amended to include an additional four craft, which together with contract modifications increased the contract value to US $61 million. All 12 were delivered by the end of 1983. A second batch of 12 LACV-30s will enter service during 1984-86.

US NAVY LCAC ACQUISITION PROGRAMME

Competitive contracts for the LCAC system design were awarded in June 1980 to Bell Aerospace Textron and Rohr Marine Inc.

AP.1-88-002 *Resolution*, employed in Florida to train US Navy personnel to operate hovercraft

One of twelve LACV-30s ordered by US Army

First LCAC to be delivered to US Navy

In June 1981 a contract was awarded to Bell Aerospace Textron by the US Navy for the detailed design and long lead material purchase for its Landing Craft, Air Cushion (LCAC) programme. Bell Aerospace has six LCACs under construction. In addition to the rollout of the first LCAC in May 1984, a second craft was due to be completed before the end of the year. Three more LCACs will be completed in 1985 and a sixth craft is scheduled to be rolled out in 1986. As well as the craft under production, Bell Aerospace was awarded a $100 million contract in 1984 to build six additional LCACs, with a $194 million option for 12 more craft. This increases the number of LCACs to be built by Bell to 24. Under the new contract the second six LCACs are scheduled for delivery in 1986.

In November 1984, the BHC/Hovertravel AP.1-88-002 *Resolution*, formerly operated by Hovertravel, was delivered to the US Navy base at Panama City, Florida, where it is operated by Bell Aerospace as an *ab initio* trainer for LCAC commanders.

US NAVY

Bell Halter's 33·52m (110ft) SES demonstrator has been purchased by the US Navy. The craft was employed initially by the US Coast Guard, designated *USCG Dorado* (WSES-1). Following this evaluation at the end of 1981, the SES was returned to Bell Halter to add a 15·24m (50ft) hull extension. This enabled the US Navy to assess the performance of a higher length-to-beam SES.

US NAVY, SPECIAL FORCES

In December 1984 a keel-laying ceremony was held at the RMI Shipyard, National City, San Diego, for the first 110-ton Special Warfare Craft, Medium (SWCM), a diesel-powered SES designed to operate from the well decks of the US Navy's LSDs and LPDs. The craft will be employed in multi-mission roles, including missile strike, patrol, transport and search and rescue. Technical and operational evaluation of the first craft will be undertaken early in 1986. Follow-on orders for up to 18 craft are expected.

US COAST GUARD

The US Coast Guard introduced two Bell Halter 110s, *Sea Hawk* and *Shearwater*, at the end of 1982 and a third, *Petrel*, in mid-1983. These craft are fitted out for patrol work in the Gulf of Mexico.

VENEZUELA
MARAVEN SA

Apartado 175, Lagunillas, Estado Zulia, Venezuela

Maraven SA operates three Hovermarine 218 crewboats on support duties for offshore oil platforms on Lake Maracaibo.

ZAIRE
SOCIETE MINIERE DE BAKWANGA

Mbujimayi, R C Lulubourg 10,424, Zaire
CRAFT OPERATED
CC.7 002

ACV TRAILERS AND HEAVY LIFT SYSTEMS

CHINA, PEOPLE'S REPUBLIC

HEILONGJIANG MARINE TRANSPORT RESEARCH INSTITUTE

Two hoverbarges, built by the above institute, have been supplied to the Ministry of Communications. Between May 1981 and June 1982, they carried 6,000 tonnes of cargo, travelled 24,000km and during trials recorded fuel savings, compared with conventional barges, of 20 to 30 per cent.

FINLAND

OY WÄRTSILÄ AB

Wärtsilä Helsinki Shipyard, PO Box 132, SF-00151 Helsinki 15, Finland

Towed amphibious barges and self-propelled amphibious lighters have been under development at Wärtsilä's Helsinki Shipyard since 1976. The vessels are designed to help transfer heavy cargoes from ship-to-shore in areas such as the Soviet arctic regions where problems are created by the lack of harbour facilities, difficult ice conditions and shallow coastal waters.

The company's first self-propelled amphibious lighter, Vector 4, was introduced in 1983. Two larger derivatives, the Vector 75 and the Vector 200, with payloads of 75 tonnes and 200 tonnes respectively, were announced in 1984.

TAV 40

A contract for nine TAV (Towable Air-Cushion Vehicle) 40s was signed in Moscow early in 1981 and was followed by an order for a further five. The craft will operate in conjunction with 14 20,000-tonne, icebreaking, multi-purpose cargo ships designed by Wärtsilä. They were delivered during 1982 and 1983.

The overall dimensions of the TAV 40 and its self-propelled variants allow them to be carried in holds or on decks of SA-15-type icebreaking cargo ships.

The craft are based on a Soviet licence and are on long-term product development at Wärtsilä. Experience gained by Wärtsilä during the construction and testing of the TAV 40 will be shared with the Soviet organisation, Licensiutorg.

The Soviet counterpart to the TAV 40 is the MPVP-40, a vehicle of similar overall design, construction, power and dimensions, described later in this section. The main difference between the two vehicles, both of which are intended for operation in arctic conditions, is that the Soviet craft is designed for bow loading while the Finnish vehicle is designed for side loading.

TAV 40s can be equipped with a range of propulsion systems for operation in differing terrain and climatic conditions. Systems tested and available to order include air and water screws, wheels, crawler track units, paddle wheels and screw rotors.

LIFT: One 590kW (790shp) marinised diesel mounted in an engine room at the bow drives two centrifugal fans in two volutes, one each side of the elevated bridge aft.
HULL: Buoyancy raft-type structure in all-welded steel with light alloy superstructure.
SKIRT: Loop and segment type.
CONTROLS: All controls are in an elevated bridge on the centreline aft.

TAV 40

TAV 40

DIMENSIONS
Length overall: 20·7m (68ft)
Beam, max: 9·9m (32ft 6in)
Height, hull sides: 1m (3ft 3in)
WEIGHTS
Useful load: 40 tons
PERFORMANCE
Speed (dependent on tow vehicle): self-propelled variant achieves 5 knots in open waters and 15km/h (9-10mph) over land
Vertical obstacle clearance: 0·6m (2ft)

VECTOR 4

Derived from the TAV 40, Vector 4 is self-propelled and fitted with steerable outrigged crawler tractor units forward and aft. It is designed for carrying heavy cargoes on firm ground, swamps, across water, snow or ice. Accommodation is for a driver and an assistant. As with the TAV 40, larger versions are under development to carry loads of up to 100 tonnes.
DIMENSIONS
Length, overall: 27m
Length, waterline: 18m
Beam: 8·5m
PERFORMANCE
Speed across even ground: 20km/h
  across calm water: 4 knots
Gradient capability: 6 degrees

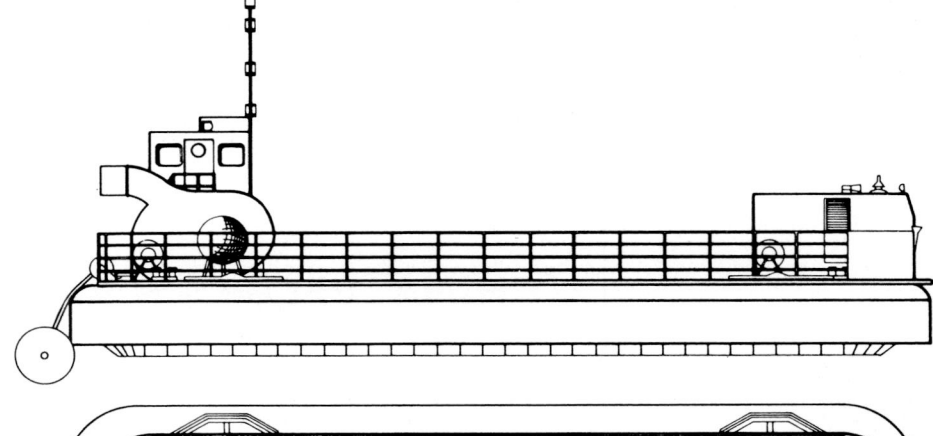

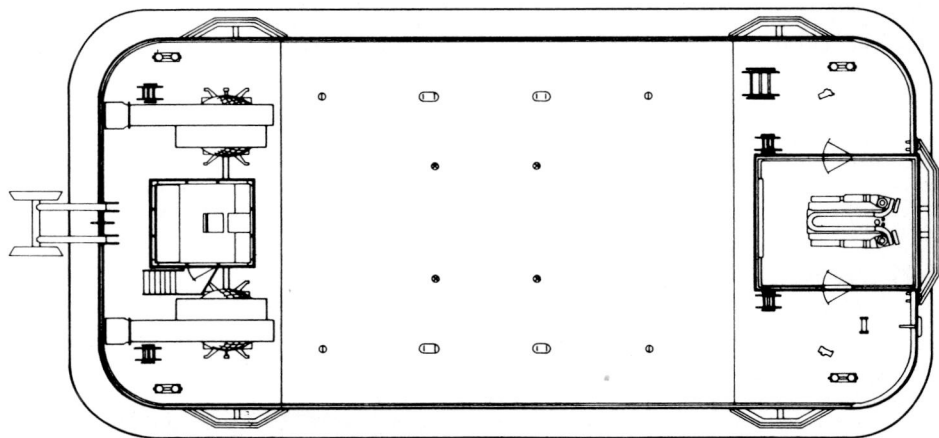

Profile and deck plan, TAV 40

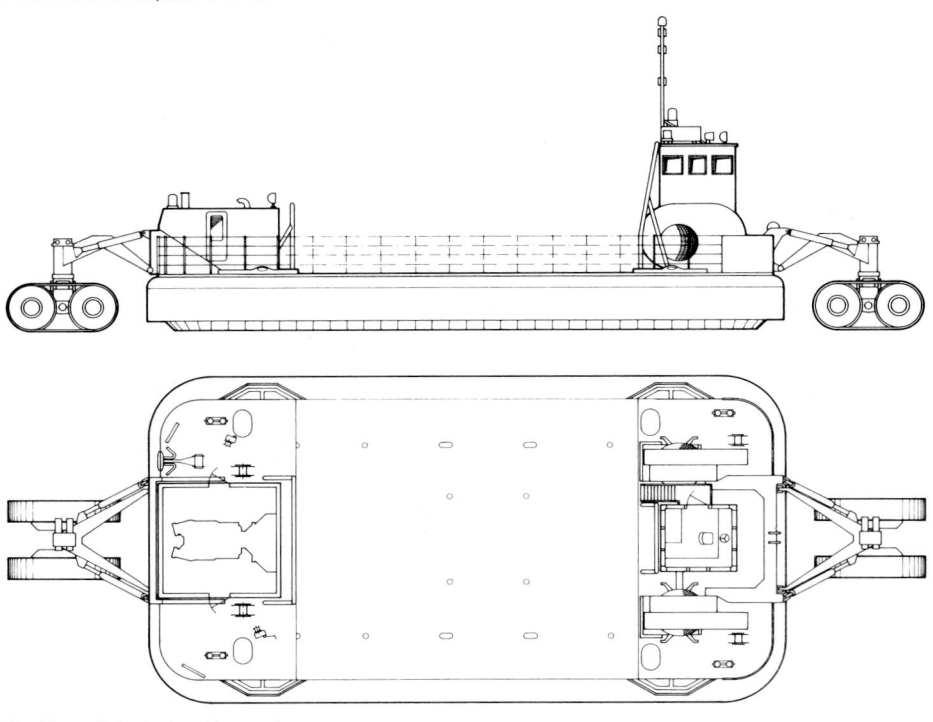

Profile and deck plan, Vector 4

Vector 4 showing forward tracked propulsion unit

VECTOR 75

A derivative of the Vector 4, Vector 75 is a self-propelled, year-round, heavy cargo transporter. It can be built in all-welded steel or aluminium and has a payload of 75 tonnes. The brief specification at the end of this entry applies to the steel version.

LIFT AND PROPULSION: Motive power is supplied by two 625kW marinised diesels mounted transversely, one forward, one aft. Each drives two centrifugal fans mounted vertically on a common shaft and housed in two separate volutes. Power from the diesels is also transmitted to hydraulic pumps which drive outrigged crawler track-drive units forward and aft. Rubber wheels drive the crawler tracks. The pressure of the tracks on the supporting surface beneath is adjustable.

CONTROLS: Craft heading is controlled by the forward track drive which is steerable.

DIMENSIONS
Length, on cushion: 37·5m
  hull: 28m
Beam, hull: 12m
WEIGHTS
Payload: 75 tonnes
PERFORMANCE
Speed, even ground: 16·09km/h (10mph)
  open water: 3 knots
  astern: 3·21km/h (2mph)
Slope capacity, track drive: 8°
  towing winch: 15°

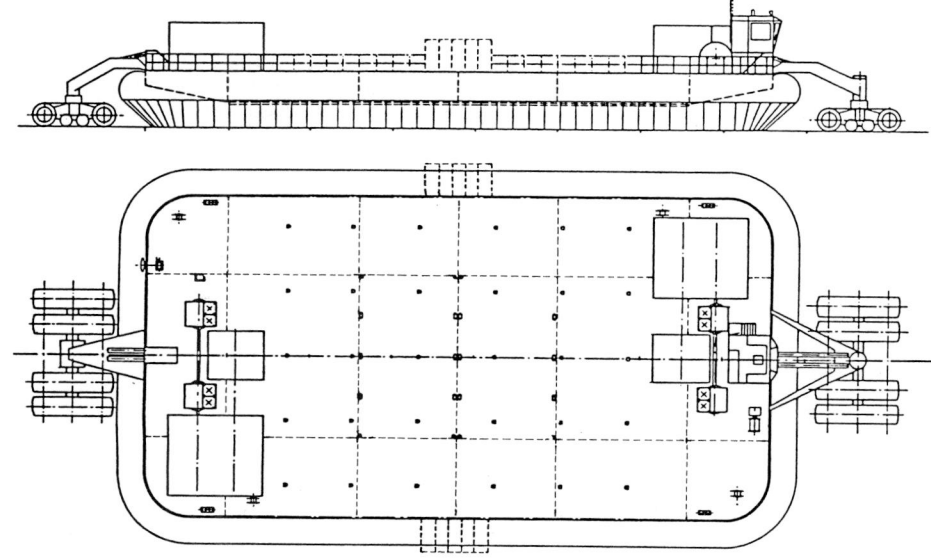

Vector 75

VECTOR 200

The layout of the Vector 200 is similar to that of the Vector 75, but the hardstructure is 10 metres longer and 8 metres have been added to the beam, giving overall hull dimensions of 38 × 20 metres. The vehicle is fitted with four 625kW diesels to cope with the additional structural weight and payload.

The brief specification at the end of this entry applies to the welded steel version.

LIFT AND PROPULSION, CONTROLS: Motive power is supplied by four 625kW diesels driving eight centrifugal lift fans and, via hydraulic pumps, outrigged crawler tracks as on the Vector 75.

HULL: Built in all-welded steel or aluminium.
DIMENSIONS
Length, on cushion: 48m
  hull: 38m
Beam, hull: 20m
WEIGHTS
Payload: 200 tonnes
PERFORMANCE
Speed, even ground: 9·65km/h (6mph)
  open water: 2·5 knots
  astern: 3·21km/h (2mph)
Slope capacity, track-drive: 3°
  towing winch: 5°

Vector 200

Vector 200

JAPAN

MITSUI ENGINEERING & SHIPBUILDING CO LTD

6-4, Tsukiji 5-chome, Chuo-ku, Tokyo 104, Japan
Officials:
See ACV section

SEP-1

Mitsui has designed a 310-ton hoverbarge for use in deep or shallow waters. A feature of the craft, designated SEP-1, is the provision of jackup legs similar to those employed on some offshore oil rigs. These enable the craft to be positioned above test or survey sites in shallow waters or in areas of marsh or tundra.

SEP-1 hoverbarge

UNION OF SOVIET SOCIALIST REPUBLICS

ALL-UNION OIL MACHINERY RESEARCH INSTITUTE, WEST SIBERIA (VNII neftmash)

Tyumen, USSR

Officials:
A V Vladimirskii, *Director*
V A Shibanov, *Head of Air Cushion Vehicle Department*

Air cushion platforms with load capacities of up to 400 tonnes have been under development in the West Siberian lowlands since 1965. 80 per cent of the gas and petroleum sites in this area are amid almost impassable swamps, salt marshes, taiga and stretches of water.

In the Tyumensk area, where deep wells are being drilled, more than 200 tons (448,000lb) of support equipment are required at each site in addition to between 130 and 180 tons of drilling gear. In 1965 a group of ACV engineers and designers, headed by V A Shibanov, left the Urals for Tyumen to design a hover platform capable of carrying a complete oil rig across tundra and taiga, and also to design and construct an all-terrain vehicle for towing the drilling rig, on hover, to the drilling sites.

Small-scale models were used during the development stages, and several attempts were made before a completely satisfactory design was conceived.

The most successful arrangement, the BU-75-VP, is illustrated. It comprises a rectangular, all-metal buoyancy raft (the load carrying member), with side structures to carry a bag-type skirt. A derrick, derived from a standard BU-75 drilling rig, was mounted on the central raft, and the drilling pump, usually delivered to sites separately, was also installed on board. Apart from specialist items of oil drilling gear, the platform is equipped with lift fans and drilling engines which serve a dual purpose by driving the lift fans when the platform is changing location.

Two tractors are normally required to tow the platform in a fully loaded condition.

Transport and routeing problems are now greatly simplified as the need to detour virtually

Towed PVP-60 cushion platform employed in Urengou area

impassable lakes, marshes, and snow or water-filled ravines no longer arises. The rig has been employed in oilfields at Shaimskoye, Urai and Samotlor.

Two more multi-ton cargo-carrying ACV platforms have been completed at the Tyumen Ship Repair yard. One platform, which began service in 1974, has a load capacity of 203·2 tonnes.

A more recent design has been undergoing tests at the Strezhevoye workings at the Alexandrov field in the Tomsk region. Large ACV rigs with a capacity of several thousand tons are under development to aid the exploitation of oil and gas in Siberia and the Soviet far north.

The latest ACV product of the research institute is a 400-tonne oil pumping station ordered by the Sibkomplektmontazh Association for the Lyantorskoye oilfield, 200km north of Surgut, western Siberia. Cushion lift was supplied by two fans powered by two 800hp diesels. The skirt was made from 1,500m² of rubberised fabric supplied by the Lisichansk Industrial Fabrics Plant, working in conjunction with the Rezinotekhnika Association which specialises in industrial rubber products and waterproofing fabrics. The skirt was

attached directly to the body of the pumping unit, obviating the need for a platform.

The pumping station reached the Lyantorskoye field via two rivers, the Ob' and the shallower Pim. Throughout the journey it was towed by either a shallow draught tugboat or swamp tractor.

Builders, timber workers, geologists and other specialist workers in western Siberia are advocating the use of large air cushion platforms in the area as they would enable many rivers to be used in those areas which are too shallow for use by conventional displacement vessels.

BU-75-VP

DIMENSIONS
Length: 30m (98ft 5in)
Width: 20m (65ft 7in)
WEIGHT
All-up: 170 tonnes
PERFORMANCE
Speed (depending on towing vehicle): about 9·65km/h (6mph)

ACV TRAILERS

Three ACV trailers have been developed by the organisation: a 6-ton platform; the PVP-40 with a cargo capacity of 40 tonnes; and the PVP-60 with a capacity of 60 tonnes.

The PVP-40 is powered by a single diesel engine driving two centrifugal fans. Its 60-tonne counterpart is powered by a single gas turbine driving twin axial-flow fans. Discs or wheels fitted to swinging arms at the rear provide directional control when reversing. 'Trains' of ACV trailers can carry heavy loads and a further development is an articulated trailer, several times the length of platforms like the PVP-40, with one tractor forward and another at the rear.

A total of 550 PVP-40 and PVP-60 hover platforms had been put into service in Siberia, the Soviet far east and far north by the end of 1980. Another 560 were completed by the end of 1981. All-up weight of the PVP-40 is 58 tonnes and the PVP-60, 84 tonnes. Total installed power for the PVP-40 is 305kW and the PVP-60, 390kW. Position of the lift fan/engine modules can be altered to suit load requirements.

UVP 400-TONNE CAPACITY, TRANSPORTABLE HOVER PLATFORM

An all-purpose, towed air cushion platform for carrying extra-heavy loads has been built at Tyumen for the Sibkomplektmontazh Association. It differs from conventional air cushion platforms in that it is attached to the object to be carried.

During tests, which took place on the shore of the Ob' river, near Surgut, West Siberia, the 32-tonne vehicle was mounted on a 400-tonne high-pressure pumping station for pumping oil from a well into a pipeline. Its two diesel engines, each developing 800hp, and four fans lifted the station, and the whole structure, described as being as high as a three-storey building, was

BU-75-VP oil rig mounted on air cushion platform

hauled by two tractors. Following trials, the equipment carried the pumping station from Surgut to the Lentorskoye oilfield, 220km to the north of Surgut. The platform and its tractors negotiated forests, marshes and rivers during the five-day operation.

To simplify transport, the platform breaks down into about six basic components, none of which weighs more than 6 tonnes. These can be carried to a site by truck, tractor, boat or helicopter.

It is claimed that the platform can be applied to even heavier loads, and it is proving successful in moving large fully-assembled units, particularly power station equipment, into areas without roads or technical facilities.

DIMENSIONS
Length: 36·21m
Width: 25·8m
Track width: 50m
WEIGHTS
Structure only: 32 tonnes
Load carrying capacity: 400 tonnes plus
PERFORMANCE
Towing speed: 10km/h
Clearance height: 200mm

PVP-40 under tow across Siberian swamp

ACV TRACTORS

Towing requirements for the rigs and ACV trailers built in Tyumen were initially met by conventional GTT amphibious crawler tractors. Since these were unable to cope with very soft terrain, development of a true multi-terrain tractor was undertaken, and this led to the construction of the Tyumen I. This was the first of a completely new ACV type with combined crawler propulsion and air cushion lift. The first model, now in the Tyumen's ACV museum, carried a 2-tonne load at speeds up to 40km/h (25mph) in off-road conditions. It is described as a broad, squat vehicle on long narrow caterpillar tracks, with a flexible skirt between its crawlers. The second was the MVP-2 which was upgraded soon afterwards to the MVP-3 5-tonne capacity model. The MVP-3 uses extremely narrow crawler tracks for propulsion, steering and support on hard surfaces. As with the Bertin Terraplane series of wheel-assisted ACVs, the weight transfer to the crawler track is variable according to the nature of the terrain being crossed and the gradient. It is said to be capable of 80·46km/h (50mph) over swamps with 1·01m (40in) high hummocks, and cruises at 48·28km/h (30mph). At the time of its first demonstration to the Soviet press in July 1974, it had completed 96·56km/h (60 miles) over Siberian swamps.

Operation of the vehicle appears to be relatively simple. Main controls are an accelerator for the single engine, which has an automatic clutch, and two standard tracked vehicle steering levers which skid-steer through the differential use of the tracks.

PVP-60 under tow

6-ton capacity ACV trailer towed by 5-tonne capacity MVP-3 combined ACV/crawler tractor

The policy at Tyumen is to standardise on composite crawler ACV systems rather than air propeller or endless-screw type propulsion.

MINISTRY OF THE MERCHANT MARINE, LENINGRAD CENTRAL DESIGN BUREAU
Leningrad, USSR
Official:
V Vladimirtsev, *Project Chief Designer*

MPVP-40

During 1977-1980, the Leningrad Central Design Bureau, in conjunction with the Northern Shipping Line, undertook a research and development programme for the construction of a 40-tonne capacity seagoing hoverbarge to be employed as a lighter at landing points along the Northern Sea Route between Murmansk and Uelen.

Designated MPVP-40, the craft is intended to operate in conditions up to sea state 4. Under normal conditions the craft is towed by tugs over water and by tractors over land. Provision has been made, however, for the craft to be propelled independently by air expelled through thrust nozzles which can be fitted aft of the fan casings. These provide a speed of 2·5 knots over calm

MPVP-40

water and ice and permit the craft to operate over shallow stretches of water.

The craft are in production at several Soviet shipyards and are intended primarily for operation from SA-15 type 20,000dwt, arctic multipurpose icebreaking cargo vessels, 28 of which are under construction for Soviet shipping operators at yards in Finland and the Soviet Union. Each will carry two MPVP-40s or its Finnish-built counterpart, the TAV 40.

LIFT: Cushion air is supplied by a single 600hp (441·3kW) V2-800TK-S3 marine diesel driving via a reduction gear two VTsD-II fans, each of 1,800m³/minute capacity. The engine compartment contains the essential accessories and pumps as well as a dc generator. Also included in the power pack are a PZhD-600 preheater and VTI-4 air filters. Engine cooling is of closed type, with radiator. Rotor of the VTsD-II fan, which is 1·1m in diameter and develops 5kPa static pressure, is built in welded stainless steel. Blades are in hollow stainless steel filled with foam plastic.

Fan transmission comprises a flexible coupling,

friction clutch, reduction gear, neck bush and three jointed shafts.

CONTROLS: Rotating thrust ports control craft direction when operating independently of tugs and tractors. Twin metal wheels keep the platform on course during towing at sea or over ground.

HULL: Ribbed, carbon steel structure. Cargo deck and side plates, 4mm thick; deck and bottom, 3mm thick. Hull divided into three watertight compartments. The craft will remain afloat in the event of any one compartment flooding.

The engineer's cabin is on the port side in line with the engine. On the starboard side are the battery box and a heater used to preheat the lubricant and the liquid coolant during cold weather. A demountable signal mast is installed above the engineer's cabin. A deflection system protects the fan housing against spray. Both sides of the platform are enclosed by rope railings. At the bow are anchor and ramp equipment, bollards, cable chocks, and mallets and pulleys for moving the load on the deck. The platform is

equipped with a 50kg Matrosov anchor, two hand windlasses for weighing the anchor, lifting and lowering the ramps, and for mooring. Four separate ramps are fitted for cargo transhipment as well as the loading and offloading of wheeled and tracked vehicles.

SKIRT: Fingered bag type with transverse stability trunk and longitudinal stability keel in rear section. Cushion area, 14m².

DIMENSIONS
Length: 20·2m
Deck width: 8·5m
Structure height: 1m
Designed draught: 0·64m

WEIGHTS
Empty: 29 tonnes
Loaded: 69 tonnes

PERFORMANCE
Cruising endurance: 24 hours
Max permissible sea state: 4
Max speed, independent air-jet propulsion: 2·5 knots

UNITED KINGDOM

AERO-DOCKS LIMITED

Brooklands, Landford, Nr Salisbury, Wiltshire SP5 2AA, England
Telephone: 0794 390213
Telex: 47106 AERODS G
Official:
A Haikney, *Chairman*

Aero-Docks Limited and Hover Systems are members of the Brookland Management Holdings Group of Companies. Aero-Docks specialises in the development, construction and marketing of industrial and agricultural hover platforms, aircraft recovery systems and other related aircraft maintenance and access products.

HOVER PLATFORMS

Industrial hover platforms built by this company are designed to operate across undeveloped terrain, particularly marshes, bogs, mudflats and pipeline construction wayleaves. They may be used for a variety of applications including civil engineering, pipe- and cable-laying, forestry work, geological and mineral surveying, and agricultural, conservation or drainage schemes.

The basic structure is a rigid-steel platform with a strong welded sub-frame to which a flexible skirt is added. Lift is from a centrifugal fan driven by either a petrol or diesel engine mounted on the platform. The engines are standard units used in a wide range of construction and commercial vehicles. The centrifugal fans are in everyday use and require little maintenance. Engine and fan units are matched to give the optimum speed and power required for the supply of air to the cushion system.

The drive from the engine to fan is direct, via a clutch and flexible coupling. This arrangement dispenses with complicated gearing systems and reduces maintenance. Engine/fan units are usually mounted together with all ancillary equipment on a separate frame which is attached to the hover platform by four bolts. The complete unit may, in the event of a breakdown, be removed for repair and replaced immediately by a spare unit.

Special wheels are fitted to swinging arms at the rear of the platform to give directional control on side slopes and when reversing. Hover height of the platforms varies according to design and size. Load capacities of the general-purpose hover platforms range from 10 to 100 tonnes.

The standard 12m pipe carrier is designed to carry pipes of up to 1·25m diameter. It can be operated on any normal pipeline route. Overall length of the vehicle is over 18m and, to enable it to operate on wayleaves of the normal width, it is equipped with directional-control wheels at both ends so that it may be towed in either direction. After the platform has been loaded with pipes, it is towed with the engine/fan unit at the front and the front wheels locked clear of the ground. When unloaded, the towing vehicle is unhitched

Hover trailer pipe carrier

and moved to the other end. The position of the directional-control wheels is then reversed and the vehicle is towed back to the pipe dump with the engine/fan unit at the back.

This unit has enabled pipeline contractors in Europe to increase the rate of pipe stringing in areas where it is difficult or even impossible to

operate conventional pipe-stringing vehicles.

AIRCRAFT RECOVERY SYSTEMS

The Mk III Aircraft Recovery System is the result of extensive research into low-cost methods of recovering disabled aircraft and it meets the requirements formulated in consultation with airlines, air forces and airport

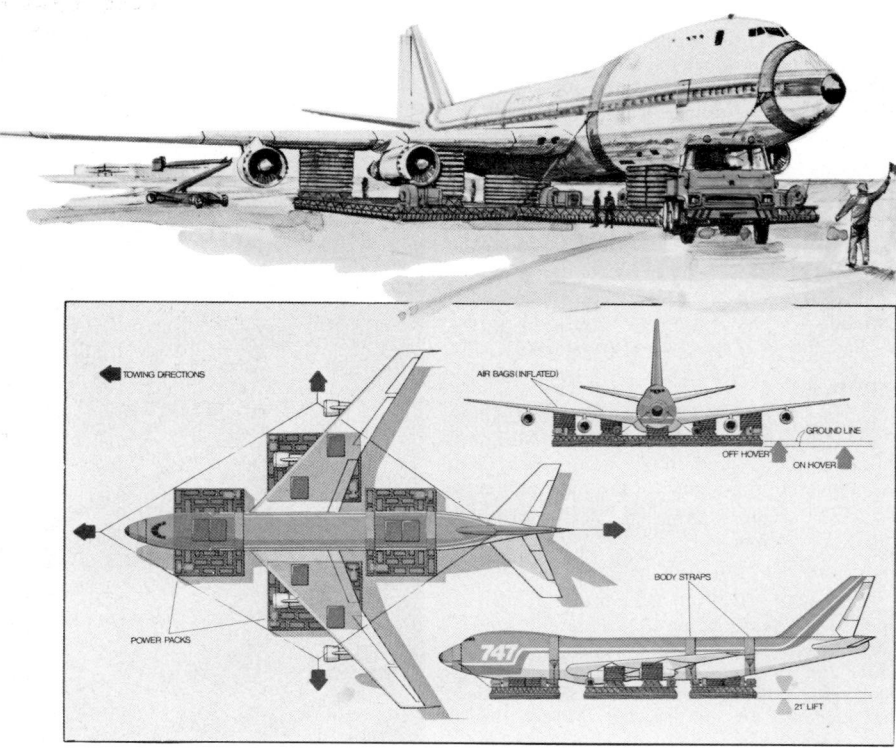

Aircraft Recovery System

authorities. The system helps overcome the considerable difficulties involved in recovering wide-bodied aircraft, eliminates much unnecessary handling and, with a normal air-cushion pressure of less than 1psi, it can hover across all types of terrain, leaving the ground surface undisturbed regardless of the load being carried.

Built on a modular system, the Mk III Aircraft Recovery System is completely air-transportable, making it suitable for most airfields. Each standard aircraft recovery module weighs 190kg (86lb), can be handled by four men and nest-packed for air transport. Linked together these modules form the main structure of the platforms, 15 modules being needed to move 15,000kg (33,000lb), four sets of 40 modules to move a Boeing 747 and a maximum system capacity of 227,000kg (500,000lb).

Modular skirt frames are attached to the periphery of the assembled hover platform and lifting power is provided by a power/fan unit mounted on a mild-steel frame which weighs 3,175kg (7,000lb) (including an air compressor and 181·8-litre (40-gallon) fuel tank).

Once the modular units are assembled under the aircraft, they are linked by tow wires with adjustable stays in between each platform. A conventional winch or tractor is then used for

Rice Harvester

pulling the platforms while on hover. There are two power/fan engines per 40-module platform, one set up to maximum rpm to provide lift, the other engine running more slowly to provide control. Specially-designed body straps locate the aircraft fuselage and prevent the superstructure from being damaged as often occurs when hawsers are used. The body straps help maintain aircraft stability during movement and prevent oscillation.

Following the recovery in 1977 at Kano, Nigeria of a Fokker F28 using a Mk II Aircraft Recovery System, the Nigerian Civil Aviation Authority has purchased two of the more versatile Mk III systems.

RICE HARVESTER

The Rice Harvester is another example of a hover platform designed to meet a specific need. The Harvester is a unit mounted on a self-propelled tracked hover platform, with a normal air-cushion pressure of less than 1psi, enabling it to move freely across the soft surfaces of paddy fields.

The unit can harvest rice and rice-straw swiftly and, when used in conjunction with small hover platforms as collection vehicles, can substantially reduce the harvest time. It is claimed that the use of this vehicle will make second and third harvests possible.

Aircraft Recovery System

AIR CUSHION EQUIPMENT (1976) LIMITED

15-35 Randolph Street, Shirley, Southampton, Hampshire SO1 3HD, England

Telephone: 0703 776468
Telex: 477537

Officials:
J D Hake, *Chairman*
R C Gilbert, *General Manager*
R R Henvest, *Works Manager*

Air Cushion Equipment (1976) Limited is involved in the design, development and manufacture of air and water cushion systems. Main products are skirt systems for hovercraft and industrial applications, special skirt systems for use with water as a cushion fluid, the 'Water Skate' heavy load carrying module system, low pressure air pallets, lifting bags and flexible drinking water containers.

A service offered world-wide is the movement of heavy loads using either air or water cushions. The best known of the services offered by this company is the design and production of equipment used for moving oil storage tanks.

The technology and skirt types developed by the company are based on the original work carried out by Hovercraft Development Ltd and developed to suit the special requirement and specification of the client.

16 Water Skate pallets moving 1,200-tonne oil rig jacket

Much research and development has been undertaken into the behaviour of skirt systems under widely varying operating conditions and the company has skirt systems for use in tropical and Arctic conditions.

Cushion pressure investigations range from the low pressure amphibious hovercraft requirement through to 225psi achieved during the development of the 'Water Skate' system.

The company accepts contracts for all aspects of air cushion engineering and manufacturing.

LOW PRESSURE AIR SYSTEMS

Design services are offered in the application of the hover principle utilising low-pressure air (2psi and below) for the movement of heavy and awkward loads over unprepared ground. This includes air cushion systems engineering and the design and manufacture of skirts.

'WATER SKATE' LOAD-CARRYING PALLET AND HIGH PRESSURE WATER SYSTEMS

The 'Water Skate' load-carrying pallet uses water as the cushion fluid and has been tested up to 225psi. Modular in application the total system can be used in multiples of the required number of three sizes of pallet of 5, 35 and 100 tonnes capacity. The equipment uses normal contractors' pumps to give water at the required pressure and flow. One pump can feed several modules via a control manifold and console. The manifold can vary the pressures to each module thus eliminating the need to present equipment symmetrically about the centre of gravity. The pressure gauges can be calibrated in weight enabling the operator to weigh a bulky structure and to identify the centre of gravity to verify practical readings against calculation.

The areas of use for this product are diverse but include the movement of oil rig jacket structures and deck modules, concrete caissons, transformers, ship sections and hulls, plant and machinery, bridge sections and the launching of structures, ships and boats.

The high pressure water cushion system is offered to those companies which require a low cost system of dense and large load movement. The principle is similar to that of the modular skirt system and tank moving system but uses a water feed system similar to that used for the 'Water.Skate' modules.

TANK MOVING

Tank moving, using an air cushion for support, has now become a well established procedure. The method offers many advantages over the older conventional forms of movement such as water flotation, mechanical skidding, cranes or bogies. Route preparation is kept to a minimum and it is seldom necessary to reinforce the tank. A tank move can usually be completed in about seven to ten days, depending on the size of the tank and the distance to be moved. Once the skirt has been assembled on the tank and the tank has been lifted from its foundation, the distance that it can be moved is infinite and only requires the provision of an appropriate means of propulsion and a clearway of adequate width. With all other methods movement is normally limited to comparatively short distances, or the time for the move becomes very extended.

As air is ducted from the fan to the cushion area it percolates through the tank foundation until sufficient pressure is built up to lift the tank. No jacking is required. Once on cushion the tank can be towed or winched to its new location. The air cushion system allows omni-directional mobility, hence to change direction or rotate the tank about its vertical axis requires only the application of towing forces in the appropriate direction. Location to dimensional tolerances of ± 2in can easily be obtained. The towing force required is usually in the order of 1% of the weight of the tank.

Tanks of all types can be moved on air including those with floating, fixed and column supported roofs and welded or riveted construction. A 700-tonne floating roof tank moved in Pauillac

16 Water Skate pallets moving 700-tonne container crane

With mobile blower unit suspended from tank inflating skirt, Hover Systems Inc moved this storage tank to prepared site

for Shell France was the largest tank moved on air to date and on this occasion an added innovation was used, floating the roof on a second cushion of air during the move. This not only reduces the possibility of damage to the roof but also reduces the pressure differential developed across the bottom of the tank.

Tank moving on air cushion is undertaken by licensed contractors as follows:

UK, Western Europe—Mears Construction Ltd
Canada and USA—Hover Systems Inc
Japan—Nippon Kensan Co

Water Skate pallets moving crane in France

BRITISH HOVERCRAFT CORPORATION

Osborne, East Cowes, Isle of Wight, England
Officials:
See ACV section

HOVERBARGES

In recent years BHC has made several heavy lift design studies including two for the US Army. The earliest of these studies considered a range of hoverbarges of the logistics-over-the-shore-operation (LOTS) type. More recently BHC has studied the use of SR.N4 and BH.7 components as craft to meet the LAMP(H) requirement. This has a civil counterpart in the recent sale of SR.N4 pylons to Sohio for a self-propelled air cushion barge project.

BHC has a contract to design a towed air cushion barge, to be based on an existing dumb barge, for the CEGB. For more general use it has designed a series of standard modules which can, in various combinations, be used to construct modular hoverbarges catering for a wide range of payloads.

AIR CUSHION HEAVY LOAD TRANSPORTER (AIR CUSHION EQUIPMENT SERIES I AND II)

Transformer units now in service weigh between 155 and 250 tons, and 400-ton units are in prospect. On occasion the Central Electricity Generating Board (CEGB) has been involved in the heavy expense of strengthening and even rebuilding bridges to accept these loads when no alternative route has been available.

The use of air cushion equipment, however, provides a practical and economic alternative. By providing an air cushion under the centre section of an existing transporter it is possible to support a high proportion of its gross weight. Distributing the gross load over the whole length of the transporter reduces the bending moments and sheer force imposed on bridges so that these heavy transformers can be transported without risk over existing bridges.

The transporter illustrated has a length of 27·4m (90ft) and a maximum width of 5·13m (16ft 10in). The payload is normally supported between two bogies each of which may have up to 48 wheels.

The skirt containing the air cushion is an easily handled unit which is fitted under the load and side beams of the trailer. Any spaces between the load and trailer frame are 'timbered-in' to take the upward thrust.

This type of skirt system can be built to suit any size of transporter and the one illustrated measures 9·57 × 4·26m (32 × 14ft). It is constructed largely of nylon/neoprene sheet extending across the underside of the load platform and formed into a bellows around its periphery. To the bottom of the bellows is attached a series of plates, each about 0·3m (1ft) long, which make contact

135-short ton payload non-self-propelled hoverbarge designed for US Army MERADCOM

Proposed LAMP(H) craft

Hoverbarge based on existing dumb barge (CEGB)

with the road surface. Thus the only escape route for air from the cushion is through the small gap formed between the plates and the ground by the roughness of the surface.

Any general unevenness of the surface, such as the camber of a road or the hump of a bridge, causes the bellows of the 'skirt' to flex so that the plates can remain in contact with the road.

The cushion was designed for a 155-ton lift, when the cushion pressure reaches 5·4psi. At this pressure, when moving over the roughest road surfaces, the volume of air escaping from underneath the shoes is approximately 373·5m³/min (13,200ft³/min) (free air volume flow).

In the Series I equipment, the power to maintain the air cushion is provided by four Rolls-Royce B81SV petrol engines delivering 235hp (gross) at 4,000rpm. Each engine drives, through a gearbox, its own centrifugal compressor, with engine, gearbox and compressor mounted together on a steel underbed as a complete working unit. The four units supplying the power are built onto a road vehicle chassis. This vehicle, which also contains stowage space for the folded cushion container, is attached to the rear of the transporter train whenever it is required for a bridge crossing. It is connected to the air cushion through four 1ft diameter air ducts, each con-

nected to a power unit. The ducts are connected by sections of flexible hose to allow for relative movement between the vehicles.

The first commercial load carried by the transporter was a 155-ton transformer for delivery to the Central Electricity Generating Board's sub-station at Legacy, near Wrexham, from the AEI Transformer Division Works at Wythenshawe, Manchester. The route involved crossing the Felin Puleston Bridge which, under normal circumstances, was incapable of withstanding the combined weight of the transporter and the transformer. By using the air cushion to relieve the load on the transporter's wheels the stress on the bridge was reduced by about 70 tons.

Had a conventional transporter been used the bridge would have had to be strengthened at a cost equal to about half the cost of developing and equipping the transporter.

Optimum relief is obtained by taking up about one-third of the gross load in the skirt and transferring this proportion from the bogies to a position under the piece being carried. Current requirements are for redistribution of between 85 and 125 tons of the gross load in this manner and to date over 870 bridges have been crossed using the air cushion with savings in bridge strengthening costs estimated to be well in excess of £4 million.

Future movements of larger plants are likely to call for relief up to 200 tons. Recognising this potential requirement, and also the fact that the existing equipment has already had a considerable part of its operating life, the Board decided in 1973 to order a second set of equipment, designated Series II, which would cover all present and anticipated requirements whilst allowing the Series I equipment to be held for back up and stand by duties. The latter has become particularly important in view of the substantial increase in air cushion assisted movements recently.

Series II equipment incorporates new features and design improvements made in the light of operating experience with the original system; the main differences being centred around the air supply units.

Air is supplied by four 200hp gas turbines running on diesel fuel and each directly coupled to an axial compressor to give an output potential up to 7·3psi with a 20% increase in air capability. The gas turbines, supplied by Noel Penny Turbines Ltd, are mounted together on a module on the swan necks of the heavy load trailer. The swan necks also carry the control cabin, fuel tanks, batteries, and battery charger so that no separate air supply vehicle is required. The trailer can now operate as a single unit when the air cushion is in situ. The need for flexible air duct sections is avoided, also the loss of time in connecting or disconnecting flexible sections and replacing the rear tractor by the blower vehicle as is required for Series I equipment.

Since becoming operational the transporter has assisted in the movement of more than 40 pieces of heavy electrical plant to the CEGB's power stations and transmission sub-stations and with the movement of plant destined for export. During these movements the equipment has been used to give loading relief at 1,000 bridges that would otherwise have needed to be strengthened or rebuilt at an estimated cost of more than £3 million.

The Series II equipment is in full commercial service. Similar equipment is available on a world-wide hire basis to other users.

Four 200hp gas turbines mounted as module on swan necks of heavy load trailer

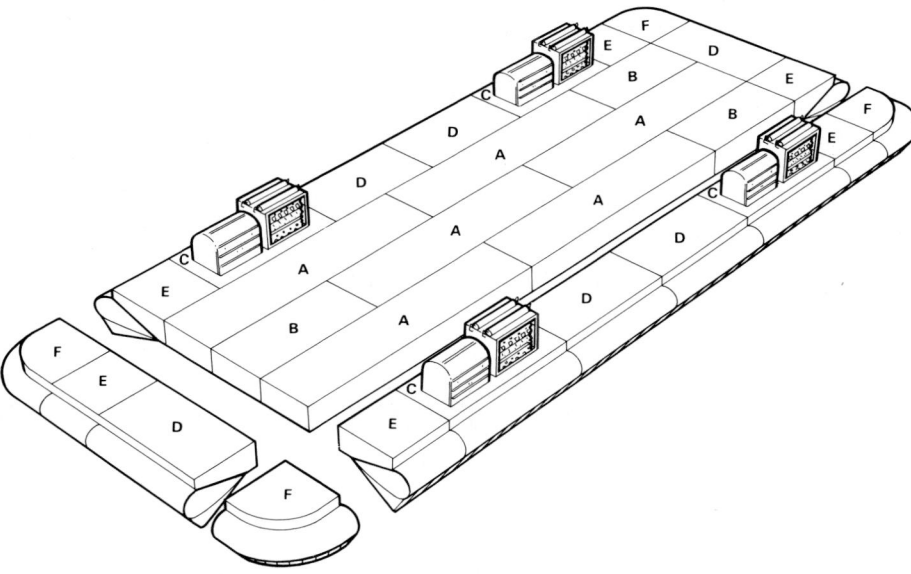

Components of typical modular hoverbarge: (A) 12 × 3 × 1·5m flat deck pontoon (B) 6 × 3 × 1·5m flat deck pontoon (C) 6 × 3 × 1·5m peripheral lift fan unit (D) 6 × 3 × 1·5m peripheral flat deck unit (E) 3 × 3 × 1·5m peripheral flat deck unit (F) 3 × 3 × 1·5m peripheral corner unit

---

MEARS CONTRACTORS LIMITED

Dorcan House, Dorcan Way, Swindon, Wiltshire SN3 3TS, England
Telephone: 0793 40111
Telex: 449824 (G)

Air Cushion Division:
Marsham House, 12-14 Albion Place, Maidstone, Kent ME14 5DZ, England
Telephone: Maidstone (0622) 679661
Telex: 966318

Officials:
R W Bale, *Managing Director*
D G Kinner, *Manager, Air Cushion Systems*

Mears Contractors Limited holds the franchise for Air Cushion Equipment (1976) Limited's system of tank moving throughout the United Kingdom and western Europe.

Tanks moved by the company range in size between 48m (157ft 4in) diameter, 700 tonnes weight; 68m (223ft) diameter, 530 tonnes weight and 6m (19ft 6in) diameter, 7 tonnes weight.

The equipment consists of a segmented skirt system, diesel-driven air supply fans and interconnecting ducting, all of which can be readily shipped to any location in the above areas.

Site surveys are undertaken by a Mears engineer in conjunction with an appointed associate company, in countries outside the United Kingdom, which provide non-specialist plant and equipment for the move. Mears provides the lift equipment and specialist supervision.

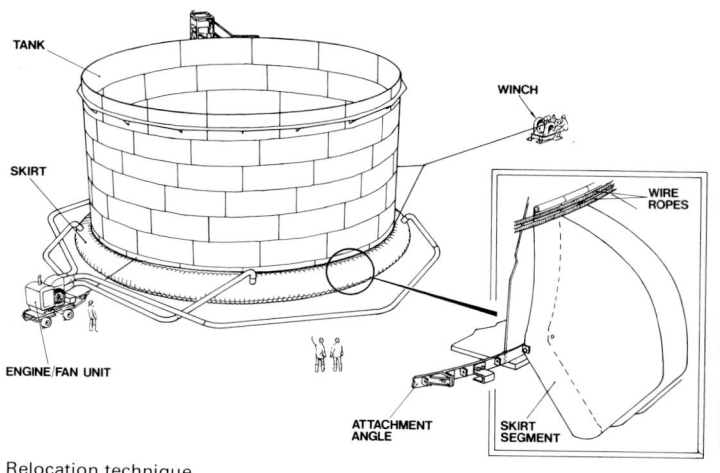

TANK
WINCH
SKIRT
WIRE ROPES
ENGINE/FAN UNIT
ATTACHMENT ANGLE
SKIRT SEGMENT

Relocation technique

Relocating 68m diameter tank

SKIMA HOVERCRAFT LIMITED

6 Hamble Close, Warsash, Hampshire SO3 6GT, England
Telephone: 04895 3210
Officials:
M A Pinder *Managing Director*

Mike Pinder conceived and patented a process for moving oil tanks on air cushions while working in the oil industry in 1966 and has retained a keen interest in low speed applications of the air cushion principle. Although mainly involved in the design, manufacture and marketing of small hovercraft, Skima Hovercraft Limited is interested in designing small platforms, trailers, lighters and agricultural equipment embodying air cushions and various methods of propulsion.

Particular concepts under study are as follows:

Agricultural air cushion platforms: Simple bolt-together air cushion platforms using lightweight diesel engines and centrifugal fans in sizes up to 10 tonnes payload, enabling equipment and crops to be transported over soft or wet ground. These platforms are conceived as having optional bolt-on propulsion and guidance systems to suit the particular application.

Rigid amphibious air cushion platforms: Similar to the above, but incorporating buoyancy and suitably marinised. Particularly suitable for ship-to-shore lightering work where harbours are not available.

Inflatable amphibious air cushion platforms: Similar to the above, but designed to be quickly packed into a smaller size for transport or storage. It is envisaged that a vehicle such as a

Skima Barrow 250

Land-Rover could be made fully amphibious by adding this equipment, giving it greater versatility in military and exploratory applications.

SKIMA BARROW 250

This platform is designed to carry quarter tonne loads with minimum effort over soft or rough ground and without damaging crops. It can be used in the construction and maintainance of power and telephone lines over open country and has many agricultural applications including handling straw bales, spraying equipment and

land drainage. It can be carried on a pick-up or trailer.
DIMENSIONS
Length: 3·04m (10ft)
Width: 1·82m (6ft)
Height off cushion: 0·6m (2ft)
WEIGHT
Unladen: 181kg (400lbs)
SKIRT: Extended segment type
Hard structure clearance: 0·25m (10in)
SYSTEMS: Air-cooled. One cylinder. Power: 11bhp

UNITED STATES OF AMERICA

GLOBAL MARINE DEVELOPMENT INC (GMDI)

777 W Eldridge, Houston, Texas 77210, USA
Telephone: (713) 596 5100
Telex: 76 5558
Officials:
R C Crooke, *President*
R B Thornburg, *Vice President*
S B Wetmore, *Vice President, Advanced Development*

Associated Company:
Arctic Systems Ltd, Calgary, Alberta, Canada
Officials:
R A Bennett, *Vice President, Commercial Products*
S Dietrich, *Vice President, Administration and Control*

Global Marine Development Inc (GMDI), a wholly owned subsidiary of Global Marine Inc of Houston, Texas, is primarily concerned with the development of marine related systems for oil and gas extraction, generally those having a significant element of advanced or new technology. One of these systems involves the use of air cushion vehicles in conjunction with oil and gas

ACT-100

exploration and production programmes in Arctic regions.

ACT-100

Construction of the prototype ACT-100 was completed in April 1971. The craft is essentially an ACV barge designed to transport 100-ton payloads throughout the year across Arctic tundra and marsh without unduly disturbing the soil

and vegetation. It will also traverse offshore ice and open water.

Five months of testing under arctic winter conditions on the Great Slave Lake at Yellowknife during 1971-72 demonstrated that the craft is able to operate in temperatures of −45·6°C (−50°F) without difficulty. It proved extremely stable and manoeuvrable when travelling over level terrain, slopes, water, and over varying thicknesses of ice. It also showed unusual ice-breaking ability in thicknesses up to 660mm (26in) and had no difficulty in traversing broken ice.

The Canadian Ministry of Transport employed the ACT-100 under contract to investigate the feasibility of operating air cushion ferries in the Mackenzie River highway system. Initial trials were conducted at Tuktoyaktuk, NWT, in November 1972. The craft was towed 322km (200 miles) up the Mackenzie for final ferry trials at Arctic Red River in June 1973.

In December 1973 the ACT-100 was employed by Imperial Oil Ltd to transport drill rig supplies and equipment from Langley Island to Adgo Island. Adgo is an expendable artificial island constructed by Imperial in the Beaufort Sea to support an exploratory drilling operation. The ACT-100 carried loads of up to 99·8 tons over ice, broken ice, and water.

LIFT: Cushion air is supplied by two 640hp Caterpillar D-348 diesel engines driving two 1·37m (4ft 6·25in) diameter Joy 5425 NOL steel centrifugal fans. Air is fed directly into the cushion without ducting. Cushion pressure is 144lb/ft². Diesel is contained in a single 500 US gallon integral tank in the main hull amidships.

CONTROLS: Towing cables to pull vehicle and wheels beneath centre of hull. A liquid ballast is provided for trim.

HULL: Box-type hull in A537 low temperature alloy steel, designed to support a 100-ton payload.

SKIRT: 1·52m (5ft) deep fully segmented skirt in rubber-coated nylon.

CREW: Control cabin for one operator and assistant. A third member of the operating crew is the towing vehicle operator.

ACCOMMODATION: A 'habitat' unit, with complete camp facilities for 35-40 men and storage facilities, can be mounted on the hull.

SYSTEMS: 110/220V, 60Hz 30kW generator for lighting, control and pumping.

COMMUNICATIONS: None permanently installed.

DIMENSIONS
Length, power off: 23·71m (75ft 3·37in)
  skirt inflated: 24·15m (79ft 3in)
Beam overall, power off: 17·38m (57ft 0·37in)
  skirt inflated: 18·59m (61ft)
Height overall, power off: 1·98m (6ft 6in)
  skirt inflated: 3·2m (10ft 6in)

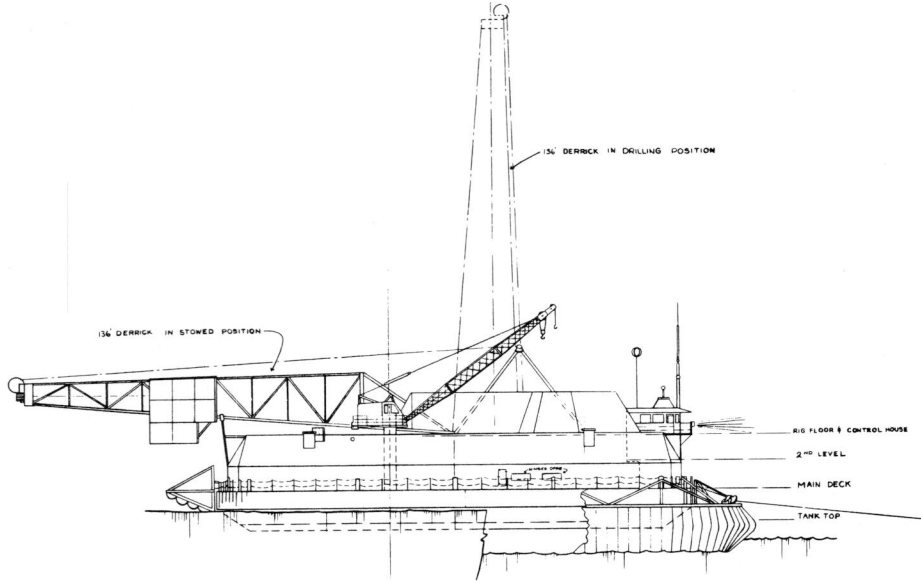

Smaller version of ACDS

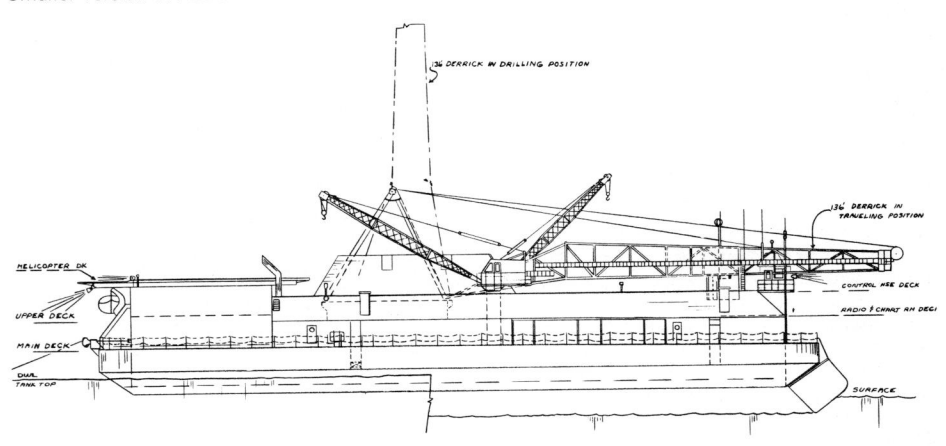

Profile of ACDS showing derrick in travelling and drilling position, control house and helipad

Draught afloat: 1·04m (3ft 5in)
Cushion area: 308·068m² (3,316ft²)
Skirt depth: 1·52m (5ft)

CONTROL CABIN
Length: 2·43m (8ft)
Max width: 2·74m (9ft)
Max height: 2·43m (8ft)
Floor area: 6·89m² (72ft²)
FREIGHT HOLDS: Open deck, with tankage available beneath
WEIGHTS
Normal empty: 150 US tons
Normal all-up: 250 US tons
Normal payload: 100 US tons
Max payload: 130 US tons
PERFORMANCE (at normal operating weight)
Speed (dependent on tow vehicle): 9·65km/h (6mph) plus
Still air range and endurance at cruising speed:
  12h at average speed of 9·65km/h (6mph) = 115·87km (72miles)
Vertical obstacle clearance: 1·21m (4ft)

ACDS

The latest design of an ACV drilling rig is the air cushion drilling system (ACDS) which was initially designed for use in offshore arctic regions but also has been considered for drilling in marshlands and swamp areas where its amphibious ability is equally useful.

The system offers two important advantages in its arctic configuration: the complete drilling system can be moved between locations at any time during the summer or winter, and the unit can remain over the wellhead even with moderate ice movement.

The ACDS is a two unit system consisting of an air cushion drill platform (ACDP) and an air cushion support platform (ACSP). Both units consist of identical hulls, 64 × 52·7 × 3m (210 × 173 × 10ft) overall, one of which contains the complete drilling equipment package and the other (ACSP) contains the accommodation,

ACT-100

ACT-100

additional pipeline equipment and consumables. The latter unit also serves as a back-up drill rig as the accommodations are portable, modular units which can be removed and a standard land rig installed on the main deck to allow a relief well to be drilled if required.

LIFT: A 3,500kW common-bus ac power generating system, with silicon-controlled rectifiers, supplies power to the drilling equipment and three of the four lift fan drive motors on the ACDP. The fourth lift fan is powered by 1,275hp direct drive diesel engine. All lift fans on ACSP are similarly powered by diesel engines.

The fans deliver a maximum pressure of 1·5psi or an all-up weight of 3,100 tons. For normal rig moves the cushion pressure is 1·1 psi providing a total lift of 2,300 short tons.

SKIRTS: 2·4m (8ft) hover height is provided by retractable, fully segmented HDL-type skirts of rubber-coated nylon fabric (99oz/yd²).

PROPULSION: Moving the ACDS will be accomplished by use of two onboard traction winches and logistic support vehicles which will both handle the 31·8mm (1·25in) wire line and also act as dead men. Alternatively, the winch line can be secured to ice anchors providing a maximum tractive effort of 72,700kg (160,000lb). The ACDS will have a minimum velocity of 6·4-8km/h (4-5mph).

LOGISTIC SUPPORT: Candidate vehicles include icebreaking workboats; self-propelled, 50-ton hovercraft; conventional barges frozen-in near the drilling locations; fixed-wing aircraft; tracked vehicles and large rubber-tyred vehicles. The selection will be determined by specific conditions, economics, availability and other operator requirements.

ACCOMMODATION: A totally enclosed and heated working environment for maximum crew efficiency during the coldest arctic weather. Modern crew quarters for 70 are included.

A preliminary specification for the 3,100-ton ACDS is given below.

DIMENSIONS
Length. 64m (210ft)
Beam: 52·7m (173ft)
Depth of hull: 3m (10ft)
WEIGHTS AND CAPACITIES
Gross weight: 3,100 short tons
Casing: 210 short tons
5in drill pipe: 15,000ft
Liquid mud: 1,425bbl
Fuel oil: 1,700bbl
Max variable load, ACDP: 1,325 short tons
  ACSP: 1,675 short tons

ICEATER-I

The icebreaking characteristics of the ACT-100 led to the development of a new vehicle designed specifically to aid a conventional ship through ice-bound waters.

The craft, known as the VIBAC (Vehicle, Icebreaking, Air Cushion) system, is attached to the bow of the ship as soon as it enters an ice-field. Close visual observation and films have revealed what happens when the air cushion platform approaches an ice sheet, and how the air cushion icebreaking phenomenon takes place.

On making contact with the ice sheet the skirt rises up over the ice while continuing to maintain its air seal. The ice sheet then penetrates the zone

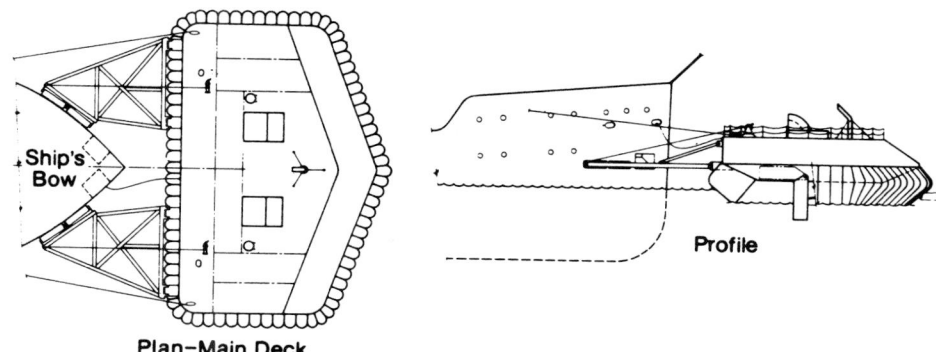

Plan–Main Deck
Early VIBAC air-cushion icebreaker concept

Profile

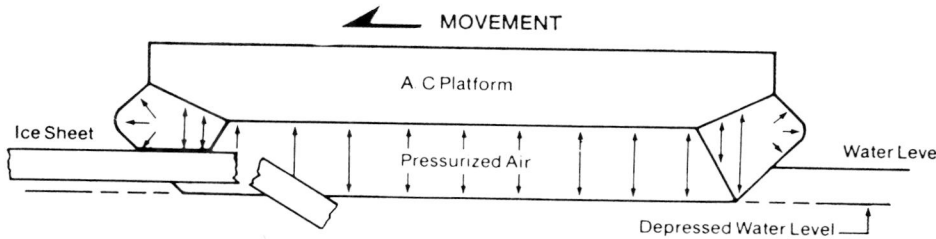

Action of air cushion platform when ice sheet is encountered

of pressurised air beneath the craft, where the water level within the skirt area is depressed to a lower level than the bottom of the ice layer. The ice has now become a cantilevered ledge without water support beneath. When the cantilevered section reaches its critical length, failure occurs and the overhanging section breaks off and falls into the depressed water below.

Under the sponsorship of Transport Canada, the ACT-100 was modified into an icebreaking system and named Iceater-I. It was first demonstrated during the 1975-76 winter season at Thunder Bay, Ontario. Scoring an impressive first in the history of icebreaking and transiting, it maintained continuous headway through ice up to 0·812m (32in) thick at speeds up to 9 knots.

A 4·2m (14ft) deep 'V' notch was cut into the stern of the ACT-100 to accommodate the bow of the *CCGS Alexander Henry*. The Thunder Bay tests began on 15 January 1976 in temperatures of –30°C. They continued for three and a half months, with the *Alexander Henry* and Iceater-I coupled together as a single unit.

A notch plug was built in the winter of 1977-78 to fit the 4·2m (42ft) deep 'V' cutout in Iceater-I. The purpose of the plug is threefold: to permit the Iceater to be pushed by a flat-bow tug; to further break up ice cusps in the after end of the plenum and to divert broken ice outboard as far and as quickly as possible.

Maximum speed of the icebreaking operations undertaken so far has been 9 knots in 431mm (17in) thick ice and the maximum thickness of ice broken continuously has been 0·812m (32in). Channel clearing has been significantly simplified and speeded-up by the system and it has been found that because of the method employed and its configuration, Iceater can work alongside locks, piers, docks and other vessels without fear of damage.

LIFT: Air pressure is generated by two Caterpillar D-348 diesels, each directly coupled to a 1·37m (4ft 6in) Joy A-1670 Airfoil centrifugal fan. Each engine develops 440hp at 1,850rpm. The fans develop 170,000ft³/min air flow within the plenum at a nominal pressure of about one

	Length	Beam	Displacement	Horsepower
ASL Iceater-1 has now operated with four different vessels:				
Thunder Cape, harbour tug	32m (105ft)	8·11m (26ft 7in)	600 tons	1,440shp
CCGS Alexander Henry	57·91m (190ft)	13·2m (43ft 6in)	2,240 tons	3,550shp
CCGS Griffon	65·22m (214ft)	14·93m (49ft)	2,793 tons	4,250shp
MV Imperial St Clair	122·49m (415ft)	22·55m (74ft)	16,450 tons	6,500shp

Iceater-I coupled with *MV Imperial St Clair*

psi, or 0·73m (29in) water pressure gauge. Consequently, water below the ice sheet is depressed by an equal amount, 0·73m (29in).

HULL: Box type structure in ASTM A537 low temperature alloy steel.

SKIRT: 1·52m (5ft) deep fully segmented skirt in natural rubber coated nylon fabric, 99oz/yd².

GENERATOR: Single Perkins/Bemac II, 30kW

BALLAST PUMP: 10hp Viking, 200 gallons/min

DIMENSIONS

Length: 23·77m (78ft)

Beam: 17·37m (57ft)

Height (on landing pads)
   to main deck: 1·21m (4ft)

WEIGHTS

Light: 190 tons

Gross: 270 tons

PACT-50

Following the successful operation of the ACT-100 under a wide variety of environmental conditions, a second generation air cushion transporter was designed with a ground drive and water propulsion system. The self-propelled air cushion transporter (PACT) was initially conceived to work in conjunction with the ACDS, though it can function equally effectively as an independent cargo/personnel carrier or as a lighter in remote areas.

The payload of the PACT is a direct function of its logistic support requirements, and for ACDS operations under study, a 50-ton payload was optimum. However, should the need arise the payload can be increased by a factor of two to four without difficulty.

Power is provided by two Detroit 16V-149Tl diesel engines, each driving one lift fan (87,000ft³/min at approximately 1psi) and two hydraulic pumps (350hp each) which drive two hub-mounted hydraulic motors on each drive wheel.

A preliminary specification for the PACT-50 is given below.

DIMENSIONS

Length: 29·56m (97ft)

Beam: 21·34m (70ft)

Depth of hull: 1·83m (6ft)

Hoverheight: 1·83m (6ft)

WEIGHTS

Payload: 50 tons

Light weight: 165 tons

Gross weight (dry): 215 tons

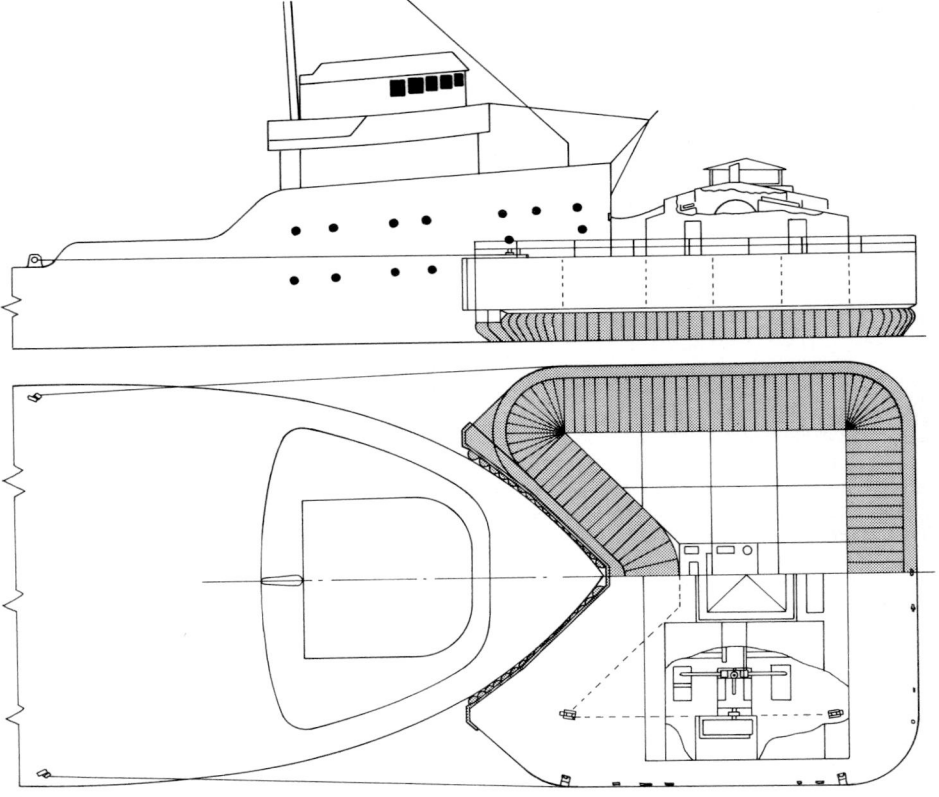

Iceater-I

4·2m (14ft) deep 'V' notch being raised from lowered to stowed position

HOVER SYSTEMS INC

PO Box 531, Media, Pennsylvania 19063, USA
Telephone: (215) 876 8241
TWX: 510-669-3265
Officials:
J D Hake, *President*
J Zador, *Vice President*
R G Longaker, *Vice President*

This organisation is the parent company of Air Cushion Equipment (1976) Ltd of Southampton, UK, and its major activity is the relocation of oil storage tanks and similar structures by the air-cushion method in the USA, Canada and South America.

Hover Systems Inc has a manufacturing facility at Media for large flexible structures based on techniques developed by Air Cushion Equipment Ltd.

A 50·8-tonne capacity amphibious ACV transporter was designed and constructed in Pennsylvania in early 1980 and put into service by HSI at Bethel, Alaska, towards the end of that year. It delivered oil and essential provisions to outlying villages along the Kuskokwin River.

During summer 1984, HSI's ACV transporter, D-PAAC (Demonstration Program, Alaskan Air Cushion), operated as successfully over open water as it had during winter conditions. The craft continued to deliver fuel oil to Eskimo villages (12,000 gallons from internal tanks, pumped and metered to village storage tanks), together with lumber and construction material loaded on to the deck.

The average distance of a summer (or winter) voyage was over 200 miles, servicing four villages on three separate routes every three weeks. The average continuous hover time each trip was 28 hours, with no shutdowns or overnight stops.

The paddle wheels, seen in the accompanying photographs, provided a speed equivalent to that of shallow draught Alaskan river tug-barges. Two grounded barges and one tug were pulled to safety during the annual low river water period in August.

D-PAAC underway on paddle wheels on Kokosquinn river, Alaska

D-PAAC during winter operations on frozen river near Bethel, Alaska. One of Hover Systems' Air Vehicles Tigers is in foreground

---

MARIDYNE

1169 East Ash Avenue, Fullerton, California 92631, USA
Telephone: (714) 992 1620

MARIDYNE ACV-4000 BACKHOE

The Backhoe is an air cushion platform equipped with a hydraulically-operated backhoe. The prototype has been designed and built for the mechanised harvesting of oyster beds in the trial areas within Puget Sound, requiring raking, light digging and lifting, but it can also be employed for trenching, dredging or light excavating on mudflats, marshes or shoreline areas which cannot be reached by conventional machines because the footing is too soft. On level surfaces the craft, which is 5·5m (18ft) long and weighs 1,814kg (4,000lb), can be moved without difficulty by two men.

LIFT: Cushion air is supplied by a single Wisconsin petrol engine, developing 37hp at 2,400rpm, driving a 60·96cm (24in) diameter Rotafoil centrifugal fan. Cushion pressure is 17lb/ft² and the airflow is 12,000ft³/min. Fuel is carried in a single 72·7-litre (16-gallon) tank.
PROPULSION: Tests have shown that the backhoe itself can be employed for locomotion. Alternative methods of propulsion include one or two persons pushing; the use of a winch or hydraulically-driven capstan with a 913kg (2,000lb) maximum line pull for steep slopes; hydraulically-driven rear-mounted wheels fitted with soft tyres and, for overwater use, a 50hp

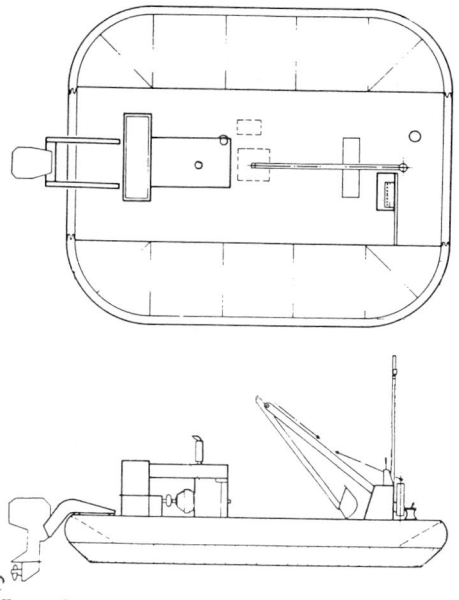
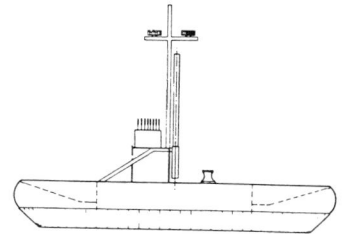

General arrangement ACV-4000 Backhoe

outboard motor fitted on a retractable mounting bracket.
CONTROLS: All air cushion, propulsion and backhoe controls at operation console.
HULL: Raft type structure in aluminium with foam for additional buoyancy. The side sections are of fibreglass construction and are removable to reduce the overall width for transport by road.
SKIRT: Loop and segment type in neoprene on nylon fabric. Hull clearance 305mm (12in). Total of 120 peripheral fingers, all independently replaceable.

DIMENSIONS
Length: 5·5m (18ft)
Width: 4·57m (15ft)
Height: 2·44m (8ft)
Reach from swing mast: 4·27m (14ft)
Digging depth (max): 2·13m (7ft)
Swing arc: 270°
Transport width, side sections removed: 2·39m
  (7ft 10in)

ACV-4000 Backhoe

RMI, INC

Head Office: 225 West 30th Street, National
City, California 92050, USA
Telephone: (619) 235 7005
Telex: 695212 RMIMARINE NTCY
Telefax: (619) 474 1046
Officials:
Wilfred J Eggington, *Chairman and Chief Executive Officer*
F Patrick Burke, *Executive Vice President*
Darrell L Reed, *Executive Vice President*
John H Barker, *Director of Engineering*
Robert S Cramb, *Director of Business Development*
Jack J Edwards, *Director of ACV Programmes*
Charles M Lee, *Director of SES Programmes*
George Luedeke, Jr, *Director of SWATH Programmes*
Washington Representative: W C Beckwith
Associates, 205 Pennsylvania Avenue, SE
Washington DC 20003, USA
Telephone: (202) 671 4528

ACV 300

Sohio Alaska Petroleum Company is developing a self-propelled 1,000-ton hover platform to lift 300-350 tons of cargo and equipment during oil well drilling operations in northern Alaska. RMI is under contract as design manager for the project. British Hovercraft is providing the propulsor pylons and British Aerospace Corporation is supplying the air propellers. The skirt system is being manufactured by Avon Industrial Polymers from a design by HCL. The vehicle has four propulsion units for operation at a minimum speed of 3 to 5 knots even when breaking 24 inches of ice in shallow water, carrying a 300-ton load and operating against a 23-knot headwind. In more typical conditions of solid ice with scattered ridges and a 12-knot wind, the vehicle will be able to maintain an average speed in excess of 15 knots. Minimum obstacle clearance will be 6ft 6in to the base of the HDL loop and segment-type skirt. A separate spray skirt will be fitted.

DIMENSIONS
Length overall: 56·69m (186ft)

Beam overall: 33·52m (110ft)
Deck height: 5·48m (18ft)
  floating (32in draught): 2·21m (7ft 3·5in)
  landing pads on solid surface: 3·5m (11ft 6in)
Clear unobstructed deck: 929m² (10,000ft²)
  17·98 × 54·86m (59 × 180ft)

WEIGHT
Empty: 564 short tons
Fuel for 20 hours plus ballast: 92 short tons
Payload (no deck dunnage): 355 short tons
Internal cargo fuel: 100 short tons
Design auw: 1,011 short tons

PERFORMANCE
Minimum operating temperature: −45°C
  (−42·8°F)
Max propulsion thrust (−10°C),
  static, calm air: 24,829kg (54,740lbs)
  30 knot relative headwind:
  21,772kg (48,000lbs)
Max allowable operating speed,
  open water: 5-10 knots
  breaking ice up to 2ft 6in: 3-7 knots
  rough ice, ridging to 6ft: 10 knots
  smooth ice, 3ft thick: 20 knots

ACV 300

AIR CUSHION LANDING SYSTEMS

CANADA

BELL AEROSPACE CANADA TEXTRON (BACT)
Grand Bend, Ontario, Canada
in conjunction with:

AEROSPACE INDUSTRIES DIRECTORATE, INDUSTRY, TRADE AND COMMERCE
235 Queen Street, Ottawa, Ontario K1A 0H5, Canada
Telephone: (613) 995 3201

Bell Aerospace Canada Textron (BACT) is developing, with Canadian Government assistance, a new air cushion landing system for light aircraft which will allow operations from land, snow, water and swampland. It will also enable pilots to land in cross-wind conditions that would defeat a conventional aircraft.

The practicality of the air cushion landing gear was first demonstrated in 1967 with a Lake LA-4 light amphibious aircraft fitted with an inflatable, doughnut-shaped trunk. A fan, powered by a separate engine, forces air into the trunk. The air

escapes through hundreds of small holes on the underside, providing a cushion of air to support the weight of the craft. In addition to pressurising the air cushion cavity, the escaping air also provides air bearing lubrication between the trunk and its supporting surface. The trunk is fabricated from multiple layers of stretch nylon cloth for strength, layered with natural rubber for elasticity and coated for environmental stability. When deflated during flight its elasticity ensures that it retracts tightly against the underside of the hull.

The converted LA-4 performed its first take-off and landing in August 1967. In subsequent tests it performed well on ice, snow, grass and water, in addition to conventional runways. It also completed taxi tests over mud and ploughed fields.

In November 1970, Bell was awarded a US Air Force contract to install similar equipment on a de Havilland CC-115 Buffalo transport aircraft. The aircraft, redesignated XC-8A, was delivered to the US Air Force in November 1973. XC-8A was conceived as a tactical transport which could fly into front-line airfields. In 1971 interest

moved onto high-performance aircraft and an ACLG was fitted, under US Air Force sponsorship, to an Australian Jindivik drone. Modification was undertaken at the Wright Patterson Air Force Base in the USA and test flights were undertaken in Australia, proving the feasibility of high-speed flight and landing.

LIGHT AIR CUSHION TRIPHIBIOUS CRAFT (LACTA)
LACTA, a completely new vehicle, optimises the advantages of the air cushion landing gear (ACLG).

It is a wide body design and will be equipped with a large area, wide-track, ovoid-shaped air cushion trunk. It will have a low-wing layout and high mounted engine with rudder in the airscrew slipstream for cushionborne control. A 400hp engine, mounted above the fuselage on a pylon, drives a 208·2cm diameter three-bladed Hartzell propeller. A dihedral of 10 degrees on the inner section of the wings provides stability when operating hullborne or floating on water. The ACLG, which is fabricated in elastic and conforms with the fuselage profile in flight, is inflated by a fan driven by the main engine through a hydraulic transmission.

The first phase in this programme was a feasibility study of the LACTA air cushion landing gear which demonstrated that operating costs would be no more than for a conventional wheeled undercarriage. During this limited ACLG, proof-of-concept stage, a converted LA-4 was used as a test bed for the LACTA landing gear. A plywood and fibreglass LACTA shell, representing the LACTA central fuselage section into which the LA-4 was fitted, was built by J & J Nash Company, Strathroy, Ontario. The shell incorporates the LACTA landing system which was tested by taxiing the combination over a variety of surfaces.

The ACLG doughnut is perforated with more than 2,000 holes. Air escapes through many of these to create the air cushion supporting the aircraft. The remaining holes on the underside of the trunk are fitted with small, chlorobutyl rubber pads which are brought into contact with the surface after landing or during taxiing, and act as braking skids.

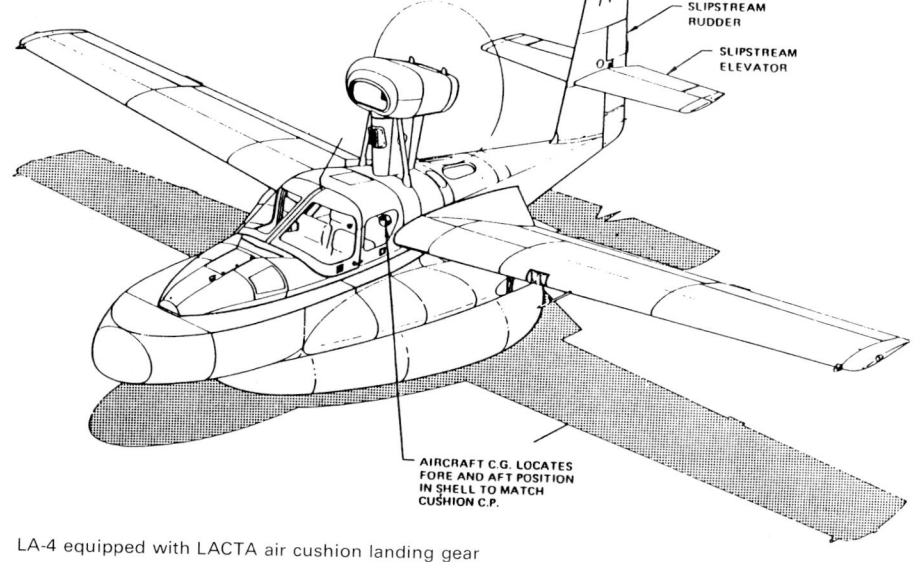

LA-4 equipped with LACTA air cushion landing gear

UNION OF SOVIET SOCIALIST REPUBLICS

BARTINI

The late Robert Oros di Bartini indicated that air cushion landing systems were under development in the Soviet Union and would possibly replace conventional wheeled undercarriages on a number of aircraft type machines by the end of the century.

Bartini's Stal-6, of 1933, was the first in the Soviet Union to be equipped with a completely retractable undercarriage.

Bartini was head of the group of designers at the Scientific Research Institute of the Civil Air Fleet. His Stal-7 was shown at the Fifteenth Paris Aviation Salon and achieved a world speed record in 1939. He worked with Lavochkin and Myasishchev on fighter development and his later designs included the ER-2 long-range night bomber. He also participated in the development of VTOL aircraft.

During the Sixteenth Soviet Antarctic Expedition in summer 1970-71, an initial test programme employing a towed ACLS test rig was undertaken at Molodezhnaya Station, Antarctica. The air cushion test rig, which was towed

SEN UT-2 conversion with air cushion landing gear

behind a GAZ-47 oversnow truck, took the form of a small air cushion trailer.

Tests included runs over a series of courses, including slopes and surfaces with natural

irregularities. Performance over a variety of surfaces was studied, including powdered snow, ice and compacted ice.

It was later stated that the rig was operated

successfully over terrain from which ski-equipped aircraft could neither take-off nor land. Another advantage was that the skirt did not freeze to the surface, a not infrequent problem with conventional ski-equipped aircraft.

Stage two of the tests involved mounting sensors employed on the ACLS rig on one of the expedition's IL-14s equipped with skis.

Take-offs, landings and taxiing were performed, mainly under extreme conditions of wind, temperature and surface states, and the recorded data was compared with the rig results.

Instrumentation was provided on the test rig to record vertical and angular accelerations plus pressures in the air-cushion plenum.

One of the first photographs to show a Soviet air cushion landing system attached to an aircraft was published in 1982. The accompanying text stated: 'It is also worth remembering the SEN experimental aircraft of 1939-41, with an early ACV undercarriage. This was a UT-2 trainer in which the air cushion was generated by an 18kW (25hp) motorcycle engine. After successful trials the air cushion undercarriage was adapted, in 1941, for the Pe-2 twin-engine bomber; the modified aircraft were used for reconnaissance. The construction of a prototype of a new twin-engined bomber with an air-cushion undercarriage was interrupted by the outbreak of war with Germany in 1941.'

AIR CUSHION APPLICATORS, CONVEYORS AND PALLETS

AUSTRALIA

FLOMAT (AUST) PTY LIMITED
18 Rowe Street, Eastwood 2122, New South Wales, Australia

Flomat (Aust) Pty is a licensee of Jetstream Systems Company of Hayward, California. Details of the conveyor system built by the company can be found under the entry for Jetstream Systems Company, USA.

CANADA

SAILRAIL
(Division of E B Eddy Forest Products Limited)
60 Rayette Road, Concord, Toronto, Ontario L4K 1B1, Canada
Telephone: (416) 665 2974
PO Box 3521 Station C, Ottawa, Canada
Telephone: (819) 595 6194

The Sailrail storage system uses a thin layer of compressed air to reduce sliding friction so that pallets on a level plane can be easily pushed, or move unassisted, down a slope of as little as 1·75 degrees.

Each pallet is supported on two compliant tubular cushion shoes in high-impact plastic tracks. The tracks can be built into trailer floors, warehouse racking, loading docks and other material flow systems. Small jets in each track supply compressed air which elevates the shoes sufficiently to permit the load to glide under control easily and safely. When the compressed air is not released, the load stops.

Features include a trailer level override control with air-bag springing to maintain pressure dock level alignment for load transfer operations. The slight tilt of a trailer can move loads mounted on Sailrail by gravity to the front or rear when the compressed air is being supplied.

Sailrail trailer tracks are approximately 1·5 tons lighter than an equivalent conventional rollerbed system. The reduction in weight means a greater payload can be carried and fuel saved. One-piece Sailrails can be installed flush with trailer floors. If required, manual and forklift operations can be undertaken over the rails.

The cushion shoes under each pallet absorb road vibrations, protecting fragile loads through their dampening action.

Low-profile tracks fit into floors or rack

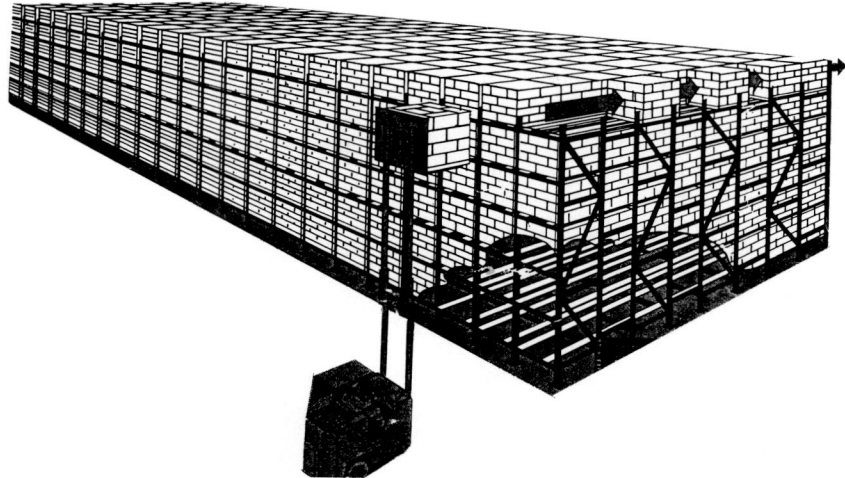

Sailrail storage system

troughs. Rack components are standard and adaptable. When required they can be easily extended using spacers and slotted-end cross beams.

When in use, a 200ft (60·9m) length of trailer requires only 30 to 50cfm at a pressure of only 15 to 20 psi. One tonne of material can be floated on ⅛hp. Sloped tracks optimise the use of gravity thrust and minimum air flow requirements. Sectionalisation of track control permits the use of tractor air.

Sailrail offers a rack system which can double the storage capacity of a warehouse by reducing the number of aisles normally required for forklift movement. Tracks are easily installed and

compressed air is released through non-closable jets in the tracks when needed. The pallets are elevated and guided and move by gravity. They have virtually no moving parts, resulting in less maintenance, noise and damage. Pallets are loaded at one end of the storage rack system and are automatically indexed at the other end, thus ensuring normal stock rotation. A simple automatic control allows one or, at the most, two people to operate an entire warehouse racking flow.

The system adds a new dimension to material handling offering high-density storage to companies previously unable to justify buying a traditional mechanical system.

FRANCE

SOCIÉTÉ BERTIN & CIE
Head Office and Works: BP 3, 78370 Plaisir, France
Telephone: (3) 056 25 00
Telex: 696231 F
Officials:
Eric Barsalou, *President Director General*
Michel Perineau, *Director General*
Georges Mordchelles-Regnier, *Director General*
M Croix-Marie, *Head of Air Cushion Department*

Research into ground effect and air cushion principle applications has been undertaken by Bertin & Cie since 1956. The company developed the original technique of separately fed plenum chambers surrounded by flexible skirts (see entry for Dubigeon-Normandie Shipyards/SEDAM (ACVs)). The same technology is applied extensively to industrial materials handling.

Past developments in this field have mainly covered special applications, but standard

equipment can now be made available for a large number of handling applications.

Bertin supplies standard components and, according to the type of problem to be solved, offers clients 'do-it-yourself-kits', plus advice, technological assistance or full design services.

Standard kits
These 'do-it-yourself' kits are available in the following configurations:

Circular Cushions
These form the basis of the handling platforms.

Standard Bertin circular cushion

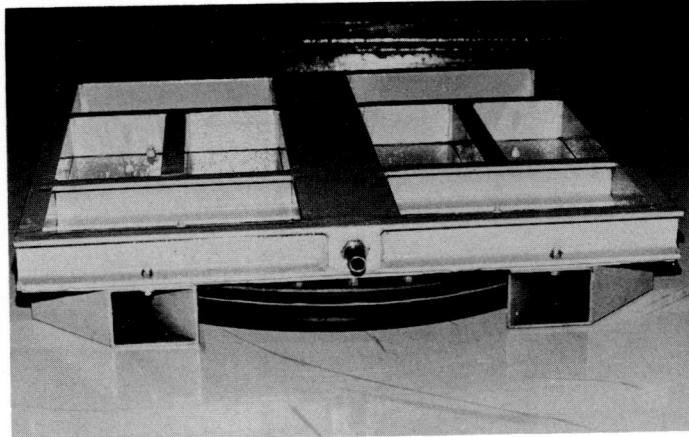

Lift pad

Soft air pad

Their positioning and number is determined by function, and the weight and nature of the loads (height, position of centre of gravity etc).

Three cushions at least must be employed to ensure stability.

The cushions can be fitted on to a chassis with spring fastenings.

The flexible lips will not suffer wear under normal conditions but are interchangeable in cases of accidental damage.

Circular cushions are produced as standard units in three sizes: Ø 300, Ø 450, Ø 600.

General characteristics are given in the accompanying table.

Lift Pads

Lift pads, complete with chassis and based on the standard circular cushions, are available in a variety of sizes and lifting capacities. Lifting capacity of these pads is comparable to that of the corresponding circular cushion.

Rigid Air Cushions

These metal air cushion skids can be used across even surfaces and operate without surface contact on an air film a few hundredths of a millimetre deep. Applications include a 3,000kg payload platform for feeding a press mounted on seven 200mm diameter skids. This unit can withstand a pressure of 26,000kg when at rest beneath the press.

Water Cushions

Circular water cushions are available for very heavy loads. Power required for lift with water cushions is 20 to 30 times less than with standard air cushions.

Soft Air Pads

Small square air pads (100 × 100 × 25mm) with a 100kg load capacity. These pads are designed especially for moving tools on press tables.

Fluid Skis

Bertin fluid skis are designed to pass over slits or grooves where normal air cushions will deflate. The main applications of these units include moving and positioning tools on grooved press tables, positioning parts to be machine tooled over working tables, and moving loads from a lift table to a working table.

SPECIFICATIONS
Dimensions: 160 × 44mm
Weight: 350 grams
Thickness, unloaded, unfed: about 28mm
    loaded, unfed: about 23mm
    loaded, air fed: about 30mm
Max payload per unit: 100kg
Air requirements: Pressure 6 bars max
    Flowrate 4N litres/s loaded at 100kg
Performance: 10mm wide groove is cleared with motion effort increased by about 3kg

Machinery handling in factories

Major applications of Bertin air cushions to solve machinery and material handling problems

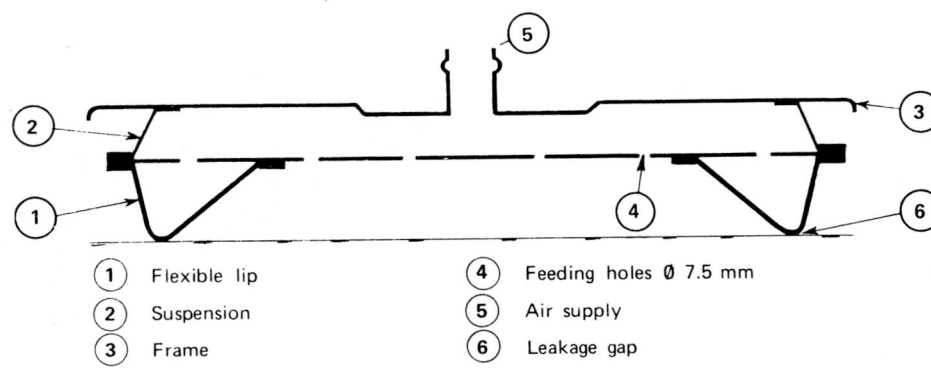

1	Flexible lip	4	Feeding holes Ø 7.5 mm
2	Suspension	5	Air supply
3	Frame	6	Leakage gap

Basic configuration and components of circular cushion

Tripods fitted with air cushion lift pads positioning Airbus

Air cushion pads moving jet engine along assembly line

within factories, listed in past issues of *Jane's Surface Skimmers*, include:

air film cushion sheer tables (1966);
air cushion platforms to install 40,000lb machinery units within factory buildings (1966);
air cushion chassis for moving machinery (1968);
air cushion conveyors adapted to specific loads (1969);
air film conveyors for the transfer of soft or tacky sheet material (1970);
loading platform for lorries (1970);
cast mould press feeding platform on air cushions (1971);
transfer of 12-ton spinning mills on air cushions (1972);
permanent air cushion platforms for the transfer of 5-ton diesel engine cooling units from the assembly line to the dispatching area (1972);
air cushion platforms for precise positioning of metal blanks under a magnetic unstacking unit (1973);
permanent air cushion platforms fitted under 30-ton profiling machines facilitating the use of alternative machines along a production line (1973);
50-ton capacity platform to introduce loads within an X-ray control room through staggered protection walls (1974);
air cushion turntable for 50-ton loads of glass-ware (1974);
space-saving air cushion system to rotate railway trucks along assembly line (1975);
shipyard air cushion platforms to facilitate positioning of large hull sections (1976);

metal sheet handling platforms and two-tier mobile lifting table for transfers in stores (1976); positioning heavy parts for assembly in the car industry (1977);
moving ceiling structures on building sites (1979).

The most recent applications are mainly in the field of assembly lines. Bertin air cushions are

extensively used to move machinery and assembled units.

Since the first air cushion system was supplied in 1975 to rotate railway trucks, several similar systems have been manufactured. In 1978 a full size swivel bridge traversing table on air cushions with a load capacity of 150 tons was designed and supplied.

Fluid ski

Type		Capacity (tonnes)	Lift Pad Characteristics								Lift (mm)
			Air Flowrate (l/s)			Dimensions (mm)					
			Metal sheets	Epoxy	Smooth cement	A	B	C	D	E	
Series 300	300-1	0·3	2·5	4	6	78	350	350	250	330	15±5
	300-2	0·5	3	5	8	78	350	350	250	330	15±5
	300-R	1·25	5	7	12	78	350	350	250	330	15±5
Series 450	450-1	0·75	5	8	12	93	520	520	420	500	20±5
	450-2	1·25	5	8	12	93	520	520	420	500	20±5
	450-R	2·5	7	9	17	93	520	520	420	500	20±5
Series 600	600	2·5	4	7	8	93	660	660	560	640	25±5
	600-R	4	6	10	12	93	660	660	560	640	25±5
	600-RS 6	6	9	15	18	93	660	660	560	640	25±5
	600-RS 10	10	15	25	30	93	660	660	560	640	25±5
	600-RS 20	20	30	50	60	93	660	1,340	465	1,110	25±5
	600-RS 30	30	45	75	90	93	660	2,000	—	—	25±5
	600-RS 40	40	60	100	120	93	1,340	1,340	—	—	25±5

ETABLISSEMENTS NEU

Division B, Sac Postal 2028, 59013 Lille Cedex, France

Etablissements NEU is a licensee of Jetstream Systems Co of Hayward, California, USA. Details of the conveyor system built by the company can be found under the entry for Jetstream Systems Company, USA.

UNION OF SOVIET SOCIALIST REPUBLICS

LENINGRAD INSTITUTE OF ENGINEERING AND CONSTRUCTION

Leningrad, USSR

An air cushion vibrating platform designed to improve the rate of setting and uniformity of concrete has been designed and built by the Leningrad Institute of Engineering and Construction. It oscillates vertically, horizontally and diagonally.

The idea of employing an air cushion in constructing vibrating platforms for the production of prefabricated reinforced concrete was proposed and introduced by technologists in the Byelorussian Ministry of Construction.

Conventional vibrating platforms require considerable quantities of metal in their construction and costly foundations, the weight of which can be 18 to 20 times the load capacity of the platform. The concentrated dynamic loads fre-

quently lead to the breakdown of the platform's framework, and during operation the vibration and noise can cause severe discomfort to plant personnel.

The operating principle of vibrating platforms using air cushions is as follows.

Beneath the vibrating platform, which is a framework with a metal bottom, air is fed by a fan to form an air cushion between the foundation and the bottom of the vibrating platform. As a result, the vibrating platform (along with a form filled with mixed concrete) is lifted into the air. The vibrating system is then switched on and the mixture is allowed to set under the influence of vertical oscillations with an amplitude of 0·3 to 1mm. To limit power expenditure, the cushion forms a closed system with an elastic apron. The pressure in the air cushion is 600 to 800kg/m² with a lift of 6 to 10 tons.

These platforms have a load capacity of 2 to 3 tons. They do not require special concrete foundations and are mounted on a sandy base 100 to

150mm thick. The power consumption of existing mass-produced platforms with load capacities of 4, 6 and 8 tons are 14, 20 and 40 kW, respectively, in contrast to 10, 14 and 28 kW for air cushion vibrating platforms. Use is made of the ability of an air cushion to distribute pressure evenly over the entire reaction surface, and of its outstanding shock absorbing qualities.

NOVOCHERKASSK POLYTECHNIC

The Novocherkassk Polytechnic has developed a series of air pads and platforms capable of supporting loads of up to 12·5 tonnes. The air supply is from a compressor or the factory air supply.

A platform with a load capacity of 40–80 tonnes is in the design stage and a feature is an automatic load relief should the air supply be cut off. A diagram showing the system can be found in *Jane's Surface Skimmers 1981* and earlier editions.

UNITED KINGDOM

AIRMATIC ENGINEERING (UK) LIMITED

King Street, Sileby, Loughborough, Leicestershire LE12 7LJ, England
Telephone: 050 981 2816
Officials:
R D Owen, *Managing Director*
P Lucas, *Commercial Manager*

This company manufactures and markets the Pneu-Move air bearing systems for manual movement of loads of up to approximately 10 tonnes.

TURNTABLES AND WORK TRANSFER SYSTEMS

Both turntables and linear systems can be stopped and effectively locked in any position by turning off the compressed air supply. At this point the metal bearing pads settle onto their tracks, resulting in a firm, robust working surface, sturdy enough for high precision work, such as in the optics industry.

Another advantage of Pneu-Move systems is that they are self-cleaning, exhaust air being constantly expelled onto the bearing track. They are also extremely adaptable; the control valves may be automatic, remote, foot or hand operated, to meet individual requirements.

Pneu-Move turntables consist of a base plate with fixed air-flotation bearing pads (usually three) on which rests the rotating table top. The latter has a protective skirt. Each pad is connected to a common air-line supply through an operating valve.

Turntables are available in a range of sizes, either free-standing or flush floor fitted, with a machined surface, checker plate, 'T' slots or other arrangements by request. Linear systems are normally designed to suit the particular applications.

INSPECTION ROTARY AIR TABLE

An addition to the Pneu-Move air bearing range is the inspection rotary air table. Four sizes of inspection table are available and these are supplied in two grades of accuracy, according to application. Optional features for the table top include 'T' slots, drilled and tapped holes, and jig-bored location holes. The basic table may be supplied with indexing by shot-pin location and also a lock and fine angular adjustment as well as a digital readout system.

The table can be used while supported on an inspection surface plate or granite table top and a linear translation facility of the air flotation type for these surfaces.

The table consists of a base casting onto which are fixed air bearing pads. The rotating top is supported on these pads, each of which is connected to the common air supply through the control console. When no air is supplied to the lift bearings the table top sits firmly on the base casting which has been machined to fine limits, thus the base acts as a reference spacer between the top and the surface it stands on.

TRI-GLIDE

Tri-Glide is a three-pad air bearing system for moving loads over any precision surface, for example a surface plate or a machine tool table. Where these surfaces have holes, or T-slots, Tri-Glide will pass over them, but with a slightly reduced load capacity. Tri-Glide is virtually frictionless, floating heavy work-pieces or measuring equipment over expensive precision surfaces without damage or wear.

Where accurate work is to be performed, eg marking out or measuring, Tri-Glide can be supplied optionally with the top surface of the three pads precision ground to equal height within ±0·005mm (±0·0002in).

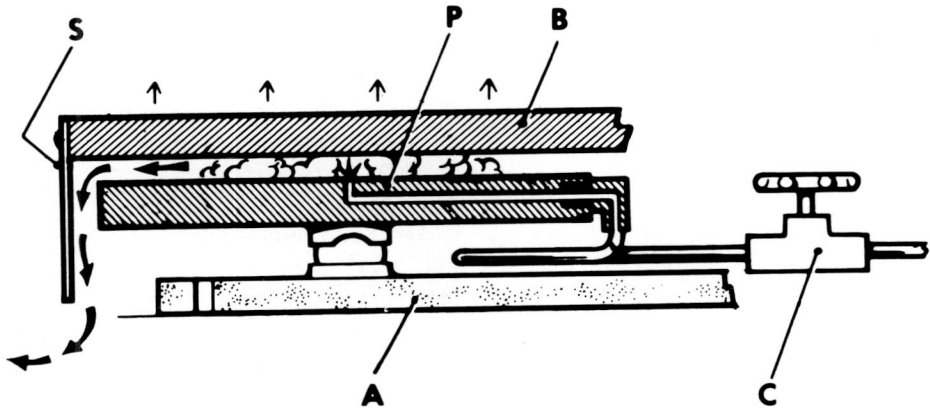

Pneu-Move turntable. Air supply valve C is opened to allow compressed air to pass through flotation pads P. Pressure lifts turntable top B on cushion of compressed air to permit rotation. Exhaust air is expelled sideways. When new position is reached, air supply is closed, allowing table top to settle onto bearing pads P

Inspection rotary air table

Tri-Glide

AIR CUSHION EQUIPMENT (1976) LIMITED (ACE)

15-35 Randolph Street, Shirley, Southampton, Hampshire S01 3HD, England
Telephone: 0703 776468
Telex: 477537
Officials:
J D Hake, *Chairman*
R C Gilbert, *General Manager*
R R Henvest, *Works Manager*

ACE WATER SKATE LOAD-CARRYING PALLET

Two sizes of pallet are available: Module A, with 35-tonne maximum capacity at 6 bar, and Module AA, with 100-tonne maximum capacity at 6 bar. Both have a rise height of 75mm and use water as the cushion fluid.

Due to the modular concept of the system, loads of many thousands of tonnes can be moved. A simple flexible skirt system retains water under pressure while allowing sufficient water to escape to lubricate the surface between the skirt and the ground. For movement of heavy loads on sloping surfaces a restraining line is recommended.

The type of flexible seal used in the pallet facilitates the lifting and movement of a load without the use of complex hydraulic jacking systems or heavy cranes. The equipment will operate over any surface from rough concrete to compacted soil with the minimum of ground preparation and the use of supplementary sheeting.

Water is usually provided via water pumps and distributed through normal flexible hoses. Each pallet is controlled by a standard gate valve. When the valve is opened water is supplied to the pallet and the lift of 75mm is achieved.

The load is normally moved by towing, winching or a combination of both. The drag coefficient, which is very low especially when using a running sheet, is generally between 2 and 3 per cent of the total weight.

The heaviest load movement to date using the AA modules was a 10,000-tonne capacity barge destined for operation in the North Sea, weighing 1,800 tonnes. Twenty-one AA modules were arranged in five lines and operated along five temporary tracks over a beach to the low water line. Water was supplied in two stages via two delivery pumps feeding a four pump system giving the required operating pressure of 6 bar.

One of the most difficult moves attempted was the loading of a railway locomotive onto a roll-on, roll-off cargo vessel. The lack of head room in the ship and the requirement for a single load moving system to move the locomotive from the rail track into the ship, then from the ship to the new location and rail track, presented problems with equipment specification. The Water Skate

Four Water Skates moving 160-tonne reinforced concrete pumping chamber

Six A pallets moving ship sections weighing 65 to 110 tonnes

Close-up of Water Skate pallet in position below ship section

Sixteen AA pallets moving 240-tonne grain barge

system, however, enabled the locomotive to be jacked from and onto the trackway while maintaining a low profile for entry between decks.

Another unusual marine loading took place when a 320-tonne Link Span Bridge, destined for a cross-Channel ferry service, was loaded onto a sea-going barge which carried it to Boulogne. Other marine associated work included the slipway launching of a 240-tonne grain barge and a 180-tonne trawler.

On land, Water Skate operations have ranged from moving six oil production modules of 400 tonnes average weight destined for the North Sea, to the transfer of a dockside crane from one rail track to another.

The Water Skate is operated under licence from Air Cushion Equipment Limited by Lifting Services International, a division of Taylor Woodrow Construction Limited, except in North America, where Hover Systems Inc, of Media, Philadelphia, is the agent.

The equipment is normally hired by the client, who is also given technical assistance, although contract movements are also undertaken. Companies also have the option of purchasing Water Skate equipment for operation by their own personnel.

Eight A Water Skates launching 180-tonne trawler

Module size

'A'

'AA'

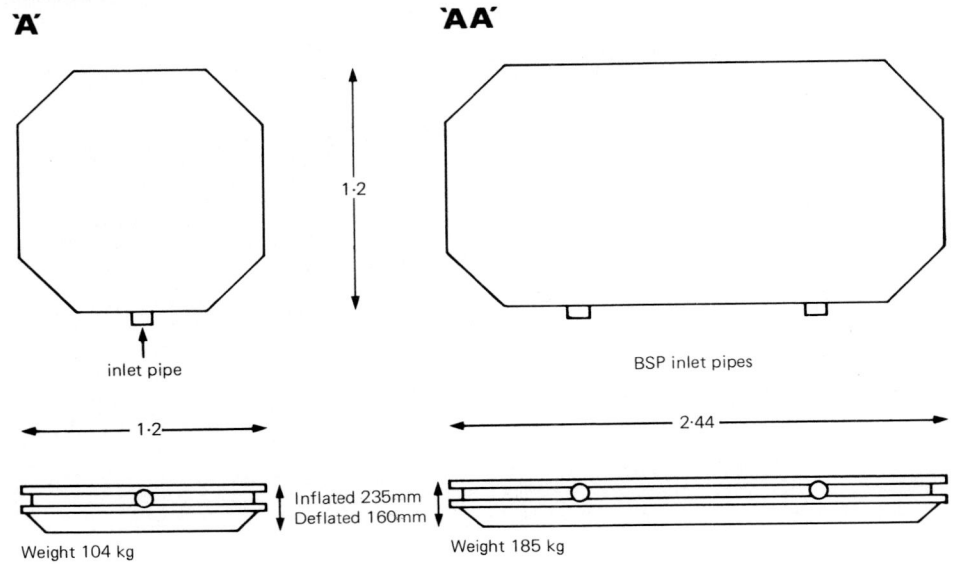

1·2

inlet pipe

BSP inlet pipes

1·2

2·44

Inflated 235mm
Deflated 160mm

Weight 104 kg

Weight 185 kg

MINI WATER SKATE

To meet a growing demand from industrial users with heavy or dense 'problem' loads, Lifting Services International has introduced a Mini Water Skate load-bearing module. Working at a water pressure of 6 bar each module will lift 10 tonnes and on smooth concrete will use 100 litres of water per minute.

The skates can be used in multiples of three or more to form a load movement system to suit individual applications and, because they are omni-directional, heavy loads can be manoeuvred in confined spaces. The force needed to move a load is approximately 2 to 5 per cent of the deadweight.

Lift pressure ratio

Maximum working pressure 6 Bar (87 psi)

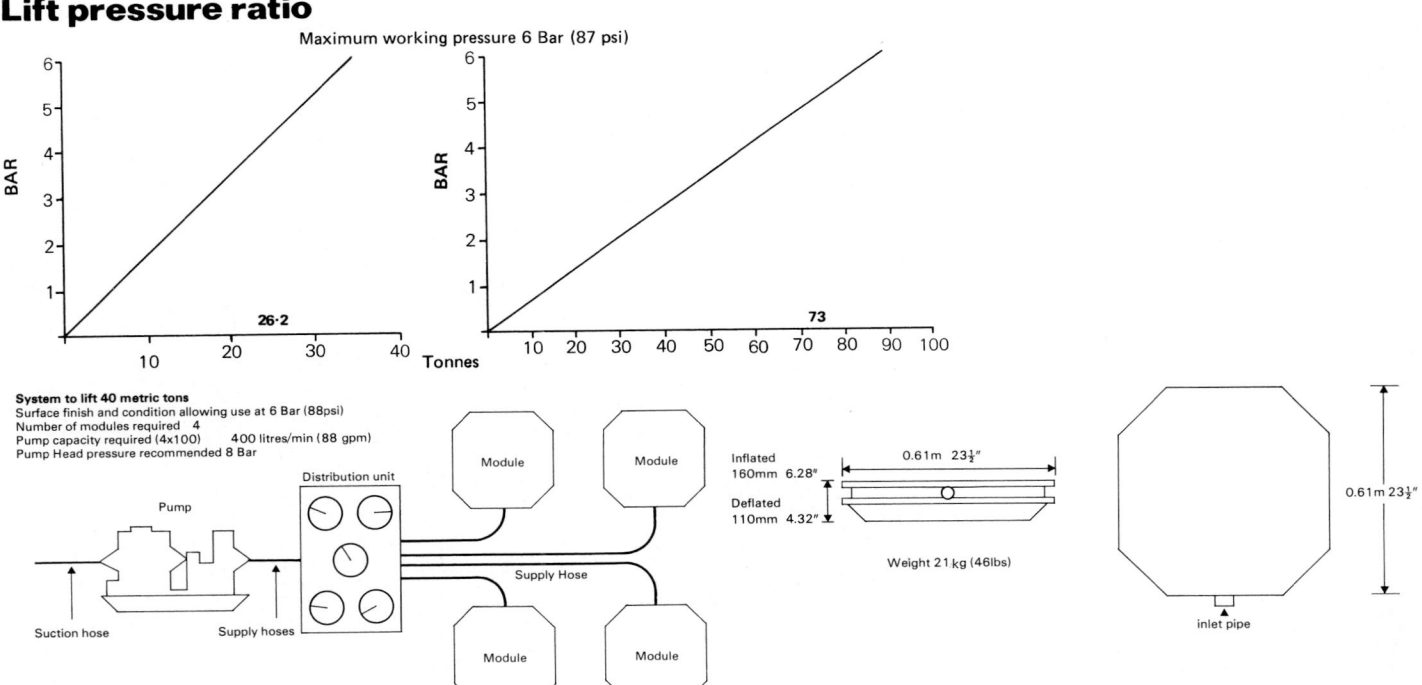

BAR

6
5
4
3
2
1

26·2

10   20   30   40   **Tonnes**

BAR

6
5
4
3
2
1

73

10 20 30 40 50 60 70 80 90 100

System to lift 40 metric tons
Surface finish and condition allowing use at 6 Bar (88psi)
Number of modules required   4
Pump capacity required (4x100)   400 litres/min (88 gpm)
Pump Head pressure recommended 8 Bar

Distribution unit

Module   Module

Pump

Supply Hose

Module   Module

Suction hose   Supply hoses

Inflated
160mm 6.28"

Deflated
110mm 4.32"

0.61m 23½"

Weight 21 kg (46lbs)

0.61m 23½"

inlet pipe

Diagram of Water Skate system

BRITISH HOVERCRAFT CORPORATION (BHC)

East Cowes, Isle of Wight, England
Officials:
See ACV section

HOVERPADS

BHC Hoverpads are fitted beneath a load carrying platform and connected by air-line via a control valve to the factory mains. Two sizes of hoverpad are currently available, 38 and 66cm diameter (15 and 26in). These can be used in multiples to move loads in the range of 0·5 to 5 tons per pad. Air consumption is dependent on the load and the smoothness of the floor surface. Typically, a 1,000kg (1 ton) load can be floated with 1m³/min (40ft³/min) air supply from a 6 bar (80psi) compressed air line.

Manoeuvring 2½-ton diesel engine using BHC hocrpads in conjunction with scissor lift table

Helicopter being moved across flight shed with BHC hoverpads

HOVAIR SYSTEMS LIMITED

Ampere Road, London Road Industrial Estate, Newbury, Berkshire RG13 2AE, England
Telephone: 0635 49525
Telex: 847015 HOVAIR G
Officials:

B H Wright, RD, BSc, BCom, CEng, MIEE,r hairman and Managi director
D L Campbell, MC, *Director*
R H Lacey, CEng, MIMechE, *Director*
J F Cownley, TEng (CEI), MITE, *Director*
J C Cutler, CEng, MIMechE, MRAeS, *Sales Manager*
M A Pinder, BSc, CEng, MIMechE, *Technical Sales Manager*

The compliant air bearings manufactured by Hovair Systems Ltd are made of abrasion resistant elastomeric urethane, and are incorporated into a wide range of industrial equipment.

Hovair transporters are produced in a standard range with payload capacities ranging from 1 to 240 tonnes. They can be fitted with pneumatic drives, lifters, remote or onboard pilot-operated controls and a wide range of additional equipment. The transporters can be built with tandem operation, and multiple and directional drives according to specific requirements. The largest system built to date is a multiple-drive twin-transporter with a combined capacity of 600 tonnes.

12-tonne capacity transporter for movement of nuclear equipment

Air Skates, with individual capacities from 1 to 60 tonnes, are normally used in sets of four or six as rigging tools or for fitting permanently to customers' equipment.

The company also manufactures turntables ranging from 1 tonne, 1 metre diameter, to 250 tonnes, 13·5 metres diameter. The turntables, while usually for continuous rotation, can be supplied with automatic controls for accurate indexing. The controls can be manual or automatic, and are housed within a console next to the turntable. Vehicle turntables have been supplied to supermarkets, city centres and workshops, and Hovair also produces Cranes-on-Air, with capacities ranging from 1 to 25 tonnes.

Recent applications of Hovair equipment in the United Kingdom include: nuclear flask and shielding block movements; generator and transformer movements; ship-section transporters; omni-mobile cranes; standard transporters for interbay movements; steel-ladle transfer cars; turntables for steel-ladle movements; rotating furnaces; paint booths; fettling shops and vehicle turntables; oil-rig maintenance equipment; printing machinery; stage and television seating and scenery movements; production lines for diesel engines; machine tools and other industrial applications.

Two 90-tonne capacity transporters moving 180-tonne rotor

220-tonne capacity carousel carrying five gas-fired furnaces

HOVERCRAFT (INVESTMENT) LIMITED

Felbridge Hotel, East Grinstead, West Sussex RH19 2BH, England
Telephone: 0342 26992
Officials:
R L Fowler, *Managing Director*
P M Browne, *Director*
J S Hart, *Director*

This company markets a pedestrian-controlled hoverpallet which has a payload capacity of 152kg (336lb).

Lift power is provided by an 8hp Briggs and Stratton petrol engine which drives a plastic/alloy axial fan mounted beneath a close mesh safety guard. Since the power unit is of the lawn mower type, the general noise level is low.

The pallet, which is built in glass fibre, can be used over a wide range of unprepared surfaces including snow, ice, mud, water, grass, swamp and sand. Ploughed fields with ridges of up to 152mm (6in) can be traversed with a reduced payload. The over-water and swamp applications are restricted by the degree to which the operator is prepared to become immersed, or to what

extent control of the vehicle is impaired. Machines can be winched across areas of deep water. Working under these conditions, however, applications such as wildfowling, reed collection,

slurry control and insect spraying in swamp areas are possible.

Two directional wheels are fitted and these can be adjusted or removed according to the degree

Assembled hoverpallets ready for despatch

of directional control or ground contact pressure required.

A clip-on spraying unit, manufactured by E Allman & Co Ltd, Birdham Road, Chichester, Sussex, has been developed for use in conjunction with the pallet.

Skirt is of HDL segmented type in nylon-coated polyurethane.

SPECIFICATIONS
Length (with handle): 2·89m (9ft 6in)
Width: 1·21m (4ft)
Height (with handle): 0·91m (3ft)
Weight (approx): 72·57kg (160lb)
Skirt depth: 127mm (5in)
Fuel capacity: 3·4 litres (6 pints)
Engine: 4-cycle (319cc)
Endurance (approx): 2 h/gallon
Payload: 152kg (336lb)
Payload area: 2·6m² (28ft²)

Hoverpallets fitted with clip-on spraying unit

LIFTING SERVICES INTERNATIONAL
Division of Taylor Woodrow Construction Limited

345 Ruislip Road, Southall, Middlesex UB1 2QX, England
Cables: Taywood Southall
Telex: 24428
Telephone: 01 578 2366 (Switchboard)

Lifting Services International sells, hires and operates Water Skate load carrying pallets for the movement of heavy loads. Water Skate systems have been used to move ships, dockside cranes, steel and concrete structures and other loads weighing between 20 to 20,000 tonnes.

Four typical operations include:

Movement of 1,200-tonne oil rig jacket

A tubular steel jacket 105m long, weighing 1,200 tonnes and with a 30m² base, was moved from the construction area to load-out position.

The movement, in three separate directions, was by the use of 16 AA Water Skates operating on temporary tarmac and steel plate tracks. A crawler crane provided the motive power of 36 tonnes and a second crane steered the jacket along the track. During construction, Water Skates were also used for the movement and alignment of the jacket side frame.

Oil rig jacket being moved on Water Skates

Ship movement and launching

An oil rig supply vessel, 52 metres long by 11 metres and with a launch weight of 600 tonnes, was moved from the construction area to the float-off position at the bottom of an inclined slipway. Eight AA Water Skates, with a total 800-tonne carrying capacity, were used in pairs under pivoting steel structures beneath the ship. The Water Skates were inflated by pump to lift the vessel clear of its build supports. A winch then towed the ship onto the slipway where a second winch, acting as a brake, lowered it to its float-off position. A guide beam, secured to the centre of the slipway, provided position alignment of the Water Skates on the narrow concrete trackways.

Relocation of container crane

16 AA Water Skates positioned beneath temporary steelwork supports attached to the crane's pivoting bogies moved a container crane weighing 700 tonnes from one quayside to another. A mobile crane provided the pulling force of 21 tonnes. Pumps, mounted on a pontoon floating in the harbour, supplied water to the skates. The crane was moved 100 metres back from the quayside, rotated through 90 degrees, and then moved another 100 metres to its new position on the adjacent quayside.

Movement of 500-tonne tug

Movement of oil platform modules

Eight AA Water Skates moved 350-tonne deck section modules from the construction area to the quayside load-out area.

The four-legged, 10-metre high sections were towed 200 metres by a mobile crane. The Water Skates enabled two of the deck sections to be

Movement of 350-tonne oil platform module

rotated through 180 degrees to the loadout position and allowed directional changes to be made so as to avoid obstacles.

A high pressure pump, drawing water from the River Seine, operated the Skates.

Relocation of container crane

LING SYSTEMS LIMITED

Little End Road, Eaton Socon, St Neots, Huntingdon, Cambridgeshire PE19 3JH, England

Ling Systems Limited is the exclusive licensee in the United Kingdom, Ireland and the Netherlands for the Jetstream air cushion conveyor system. Equipment is in use to handle a wide range of scrap materials (metal, paper, board and plastic); many types of unit loads including boxes, both full and empty; plastic bottles; cap closures; can ends and pressed and moulded parts.

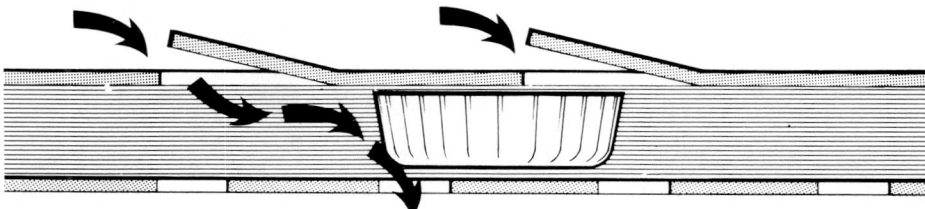

High-speed conveying system for caps and lids

CAP, LID AND CLOSURE CONVEYOR

A high-speed conveying system for caps, lids and other types of closure is available from Ling Systems Limited. Based on the JetStream air-cushion conveying principle, it is designed for high-volume conveying in food processing, bottling or finishing plants. It can achieve throughputs of 2,000 units a minute, transferring closures safely and without surface damage or abrasion of enamelled or printed finishes.

The system can be configured to use redundant areas along walls or in roofs, thus saving floor space and providing live storage away from production areas.

The system transports closures of any material on a bed of high-speed air in single file and in any required number of lanes. It can operate vertically and horizontally and can fit in with existing process plant, without production disruption or any structural alterations.

Maintenance requirements are low as the only moving parts are the centrifugal fans, the number of which depends on the extent of the system which can operate over extremely long distances. Automatic transfer devices, or diverters, can be linked up with other production machinery.

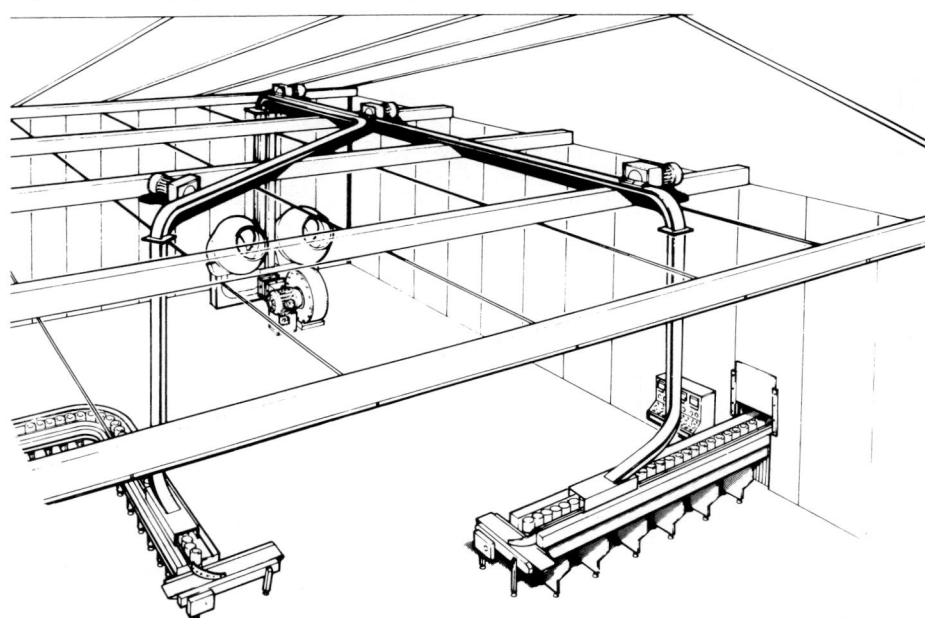

Cap, lid and closure conveyor

SCRAP HANDLING CONVEYOR

JetStream air-cushion scrap handling conveyors provide a safe, efficient, and cost-effective method of scrap removal from production areas, particularly paper, cardboard and press scrap.

The JetStream conveying principle uses very low pressure air, directed through a series of specially-designed louvres in a steel surface plate, to provide lift and high-speed propulsion. Air pressure is generated by centifugal fans and is carried to the louvred conveying surface by a plenum duct. The resulting laminar layer of high-velocity air keeps the conveyed material close to the surface plate. Shape, size, distribution and direction of the louvres control the motion and speed of the scrap.

JetStream installations are made to suit individual needs. Systems can fit in with existing production layouts with minimum disruption and can incorporate bends, junctions, diversions and inclines. High-level or under-floor layouts can also be constructed. Systems can be easily

Scrap handling conveyor

extended to accommodate increased production requirements. Maintenance is minimal as the fans are the only moving parts, and their number depends on the extent of the installation.

ROTARY BUFFERING/SORTATION TABLE

This air-cushion rotary buffering/sortation table is for small circular items such as jar lids and round packs.

Called Rotastream, the unit accepts items en masse in multiple conveyor lanes from production machines, and diverts them automatically into a single lane for high-speed feeding to filling/cap-closing equipment; 1,200 caps per minute is a typical feeding rate.

The diameter of a Rotastream air table can be made to suit the size of circular product to be handled. An air-cushion is created by directing low-pressure air through a pattern of holes on the specially-domed table surface, and the products then float from the input to the output conveyors, while being automatically put into single file, with little possibility of damage.

Rotary buffering/sortation table

UNITED STATES OF AMERICA

AERO-GO INC

1170 Andover Park West, Seattle, Washington 98188, USA
Telephone: (206) 575 3344
Cable: Aerogoseattle
Telex: 152596
Officials:
Kurt Kosty, *President*
William A Shannon, *Vice President*
Gerald A Vice, *Sales Manager*
Cheryl Gagne, *Sales Co-ordinator*

Overseas
Aero-Go Europe
Tullastrasse 19, 6900 Heidelberg-Rohrbach, Federal Republic of Germany
Jayant Khirwadkar, *Field Manager*

Associated companies:
Moving AB
Box 18, S-265 01 Astorp, Sweden
Bjorn Ohlsson, *Product Manager*

Aero-Go (UK) Ltd
Chiddingstone Causeway, Tonbridge, Kent TN11 8JU, England
M Fitzcharles, *Managing Director*

Avio-Diepen BV
Vliegeld Ypenburg, 2280 HZ Rijswijk ZH, Netherlands
R de Rooij, *Director*

M Claessens
Kloosterstraat 107, B-2070 Ekeren, Belgium
R Metzelaar, *Sales Manager*

Dr Hans Kraus Ges mbH & Co KG
9210 Portschach, Austria
Dr Brigette Enzenhofert, *Manager*

International Marketing Services
22 rue de Vintimille, 75009 Paris, France
J H Maillon, *Manager*

Pfingstweid AG
Box 773, Pfingstweidstrasse 31A, 8037 Zurich, Switzerland
B Maechler, *Director*

Aero-Go Italia, SRL
Via Statuto 18, 20100 Milan, Italy
Leonardo Desenzani, *Manager*

Erice
Organizacion Technica Nacional
Apartado 437, Alda Recalde 35-6, Bilbao, Spain
Jaime Erice, *Manager*

Transgrua
Representacoes E Aluguer De Gruas LDA
Av Ressano Garcia 39 7, 1000 Lisbon, Portugal
Fernando Antunes, *Sales Manager*

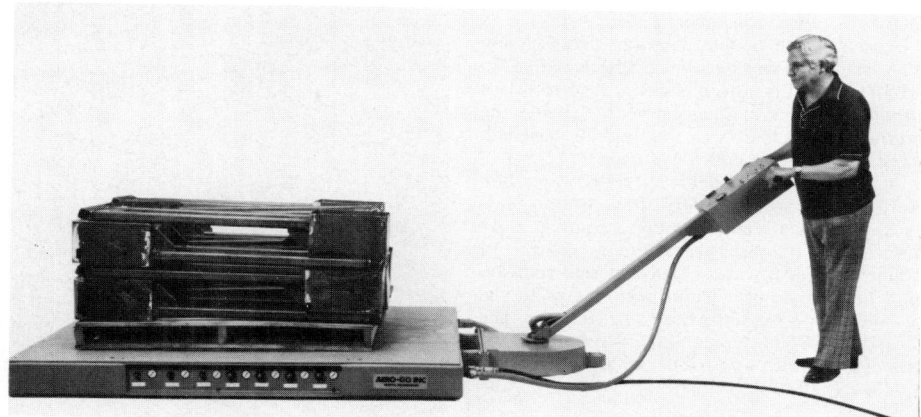
Steerable Aero-Pallet

Aero-Go Inc manufactures fluid film load movement equipment and systems for general industrial applications. It provides a broad range of standard equipment complemented by complete complex materials handling systems based on fluid film technology. Founded in 1967 to market new developments in dual chamber air film bearings pioneered by the Boeing Company, Aero-Go holds exclusive rights to extensive developments in the industry.

Aero-Go fluid film systems support heavy loads and simultaneously provide nearly zero friction and omni-directional movement. This results in low initial and operating costs as the source of compressed air is normally the existing factory air system.

AERO-CASTER LOAD MODULES

The air film Aero-Caster is manufactured in seven sizes ranging from 20·3cm (8in) diameter, with a 227kg (500lb) lift capacity, to 121·9cm (48in) diameter with a 36,300kg (80,000lb) capacity. Individual load modules are used in sets of three or more of one size, and are normally slipped beneath a load in a triangular or square pattern with the centre of gravity of the load placed over the pattern's geometric centre.

Within the rated limit of each caster's lift capacity, a load is lifted in direct proportion to the air pressure applied. A 53·3cm (21in) unit with a face area of 1,808cm² (280in²) will lift 3,182kg (7,000lb) maximum at 1·76kg/cm² (25psi). Four model K21Ns will therefore float loads up to 12,700kg (28,000lb) maximum at an air pressure of 1·76kg/cm² (25psi).

Load module systems are available complete with interconnecting hoses, air-regulation control console and fittings as required by a customer, such as a popular rigging tool for the movement of loads between crane bays, into tight storage areas, or installing new machinery into a plant.

The heaviest load was moved on air film in September 1977 at Beynes, near Paris, France. A new 2,000-tonne concrete boxbridge was moved 34 metres (112 feet) into a precise location under an overhead railway line in half an hour. Two truck winches pulled the load floating on 54 units of the 121·9cm (48in) load module size. The National French Railways (SNCF) has been using them to install bridges throughout France since March 1976.

AERO-PALLETS

Load moving platforms can be supplied with built-in Aero-Casters. Lightweight aluminium extrusion is used for distributed loads up to 18,500kg (40,000lb). Structural steel construction is employed for higher weights and concentrated loading.

Options include drive and guide wheels to facilitate large load movement and to provide positive directional control.

Detachable or permanently mounted drive systems can be internal or external to the pallet, and the controls can be integrated in the drive or remotely located. Travel speed is controllable from 0 to 12 metres (0 to 39 feet) per minute in forward or reverse directions.

The systems have low-lift height, large support

surfaces and self-regulating valves to adapt to changing load weights and shifting centres of gravity. Aero-Pallets will not damage floors and can be used safely in factories using volatile gases or liquids.

AERO-GO TURNTABLES

Standard Aero-Go turntables rotate through 360 degrees. One pound (0·5kg) of thrust rotates 1,000lb (453·6kg). Optional-drive motors are available to assist turning heavy loads.

Aero-Caster flotation elements beneath the ribbed-steel turntable have no moving parts. A pressure regulator, gauge and adjustable flow-control valves are standard. Decks can be fitted with conveyor rolls, rails or other devices specified by the customer to handle various load shapes and sizes. It can be installed on the floor or in a pit.

Standard turntable sizes range from 2 to 12ft (60·96 to 365·76cm) diameter and rotate loads from 500 to 160,000lb (226·8 to 72,576kg) depending on model capacity.

'WATER FILM' AERO-CASTERS

In 1971 Aero-Go introduced 'Water Film' casters which convey high-tonnage loads on water film. A number are in use at several major shipyards and offshore oil-drilling platform docks. To date, the largest ship constructed with the use of Aero-Caster load modules is a 3,400-ton ferry, built by Vancouver Shipyards Co, Canada.

The largest and heaviest single load yet moved on a water film system is a 4,500-ton grandstand section added to the outdoor sports stadium in Denver, Colorado in spring 1977.

Seating 23,000 people, the three-tiered section is 163m (535ft) long by 60m (200ft) deep by 42m (135ft) high. It is moved backwards or forwards 44m (145ft) several times per year to change the central playing field area for football, baseball, soccer and other outdoor events.

A total of 163 Model 48NHDW water film Aero-Casters are in clusters of two to four units each, under the section's support framing at 47 different lift points. The casters move over 14 2-metre (6-foot) wide sealed-concrete runways with built-in drains. Water recirculates to the system from a 60,000-gallon storage tank. The thrust of hydraulic rams employed to push the grandstand into position is approximately 3,628kg (8,000lb).

MOBILE MACHINE TOOL BEDPLATES

Aero-Go introduced the mobile machining bedplate concept in 1974. This air film product line greatly increases efficiency when using large machine tools. The mobility of an air film pallet is mated with the accuracy and precise positioning required for locating parts in front of large machine tools. Two of these special pallets, working in sequence, enable the time consuming 'set-up' of parts to be done whilst machining is under way. Typical efficiency improvements of 30 per cent or more in machine time use have been achieved. Aero-Go is now supplying complete systems including the accurate positioning components for a variety of customers.

ENGINE INSTALLATION

Jet engines can be quickly and safely installed or changed using the Aero-Go engine installation fixture. Almost all underwing aircraft/engine combinations are covered by one unit, which lifts the jet engines while still cradled in their shipping dollies. Lift, roll and pitch functions allow full control of engine attitude. The superstructure of the fixture floats on Aero-Go air bearings to provide yaw control and eliminate side forces on the engine mounts. A time saving of 10 to 1, compared with conventional systems, is possible.

COIL TRANSPORTERS

In-plant transport of steel coils weighing up to 35 tonnes is facilitated by Aero-Go's automated coil transporter. The transporter incorporates a lift table enabling the loading and unloading of coils at transfer points. A guided-wire steering system is employed. Two steerable drive units are computer controlled, as are other functions. Control signals are transmitted by radio using full

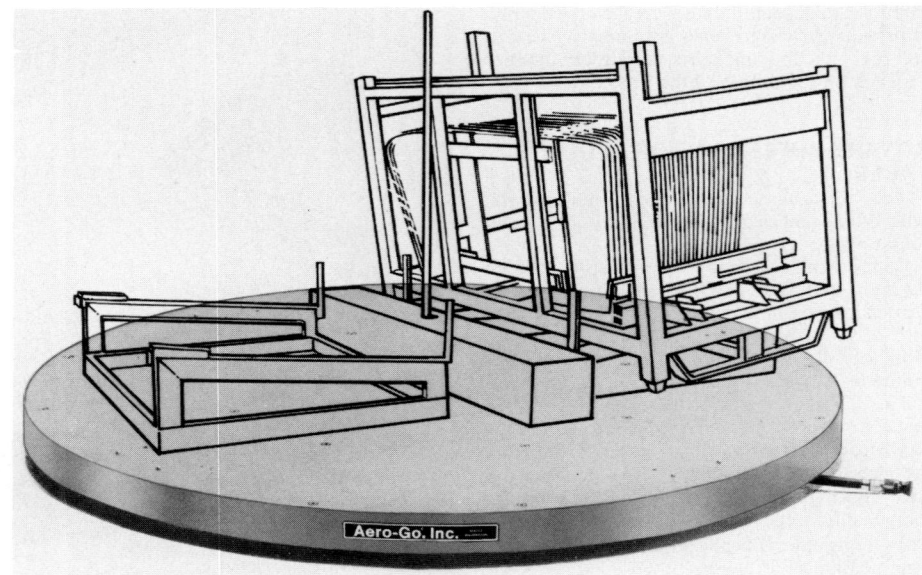

Aero-Go turntable

Brown and Root transport system lifts and floats 2,000-ton drill platforms. Water elevators distribute loads between platform legs during transfer from land to barges. 16 water film transporters incorporate 32 heavy-duty water Aero-Casters

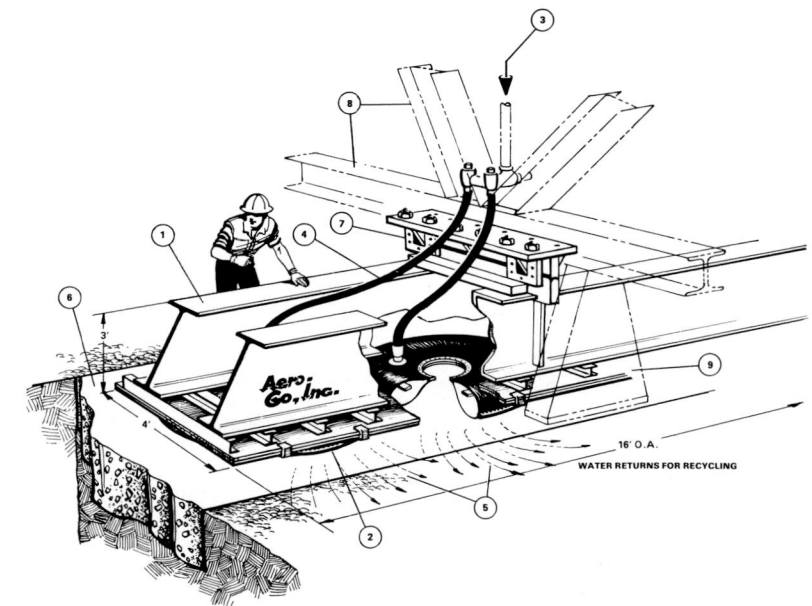

Typical lifting point beneath grandstand at Denver: (1) 160-ton capacity transporter (2) Aero-Caster tray mounted—40-ton capacity each (3) water supply service—80 gpm total (4) water hose to Aero-Caster (5) water film (6) coated concrete runway (7) hinged stadium attachment (8) stadium structure (9) static support

'hand shaking' protocols. Alternative communications methods can be used if required.

Layout of the travel path and the number of stations is unrestricted. Linear distance is unlimited as the transporter carries its own power source, such as a diesel engine. Multiple vehicle operation is accomplished through the use of a 'block' system.

The hard-to-handle coils are carried by the transporter which floats on Aero-Go air bearings.

ROLLMOVER

Large rolls of paper can be easily moved with Aero-Go Rollmovers. The 'C'-shaped units are inserted under each end of the roll, and the two pieces are then linked with a length of self-coiling hose. Advantages of this system include improved directional control, ease of movement and the elimination of damage.

Another important factor is the alignment capability when loading a press, re-wind stand or other device. Since the roll is free floating, it will self-align when contacted by shaftless chucks, thereby eliminating side forces on the chucks and arms of the machine.

Roll movers are available in sizes to handle 61cm to 183cm diameter rolls, weighing up to 3,632kg and 3·7m in length.

AERO-GO DIE TRANSFER PALLET

The Aero-Go Die Transfer Pallet has facili-tated the insertion and removal of large die sets. This mechanised system is designed to manipulate dies weighing up to 45,400kg (100,000lb).

A lower base unit incorporates a horizontally-mounted powered screw jack on each side. These drive a draw-bar forward and backward. A drive motor, Aero-Casters and a positioning/anchoring system lock the transfer pallet in place when moving a load. The height of the base unit matches the lower platen of a press and also the level of a storage rack.

A separate Aero-Caster system operates on top of this lower unit, and floats the die into and out of both the press and the storage area. Large dies can be changed quickly and safely with minimum labour.

AIRBARGE COMPANY

Head Office: 26807 Spring Creek Road, Palos Verdes Peninsula, California 90274, USA
Telephone: (213) 378 2928

AirBarge Company supplies load-bearing platforms and containers that float on air cushions. These units provide virtually frictionless movement in any direction and can lift loads of almost any size when powered by a standard shop air supply. Standard AirBarge casters can be installed on a variety of structural components including air pads, air cells, air tables, air pallets and air vans. The range includes pneumatic lifting units called Air Jacks which allow precise vertical positioning and angular tilt of a load even while being moved.

AirBarge seals have a flexible wear foot mounted on the underside of a completely-protected inflatable hanger. Since this inflated seal hanger cannot come in contact with the surface over which the seal is operated, all wear is taken by the wear foot which can be replaced when necessary without replacing the remainder of the seal assembly. A number of alternate-wear foot materials are available to match different operating surfaces. AirBarges have been produced to operate over surfaces ranging from smooth vinyl tiles to weathered asphalt.

AIRBARGE MODULAR SYSTEM

The AirBarge modular system is based on a family of standard air casters. Six sizes of air casters span the total load range. They can be directly attached to a variety of loads either singly or in multiples. Air caster equipped pallets can also be floated under a skid-mounted load at reduced height and then lift the load off its skids by increasing air flow into the air casters.

Single air casters are attached to round structural plates to form air pads. These air pads are stressed to support concentrated loads at their centres such as the support legs of machine tools, tooling fixtures and maintenance scaffolds.

The family of standard air cells consists of single-caster units stressed for distributed loads. These air cells have flat-top surfaces to facilitate their positioning under any flat-bottomed structural load.

Air pallets are produced by installing standard air casters in multiples under compatible load-bearing structural pallets. Four, six and eight caster air pallets are available.

Air vans are standard-size cargo containers with built-in AirBarge air casters.

MOVING JET AIRLINER COMPONENTS

The Lockheed L-1011 Tri-Star wide-bodied jet employs the largest bonded skin structures to be used in an aircraft. These skin sections are stored in holding fixtures in a clean room, picked up by overhead crane and transported in a mobile carrier to an autoclave for curing of the adhesive. For the most efficient use of the autoclave up to four skin assemblies should be cured simultaneously. For this purpose Lockheed built several transporters, each capable of carrying four skin-bonding fixtures weighing up to 25,000 pounds.

The transporters roll into the autoclave on six steel wheels which ride on flush steel rails built

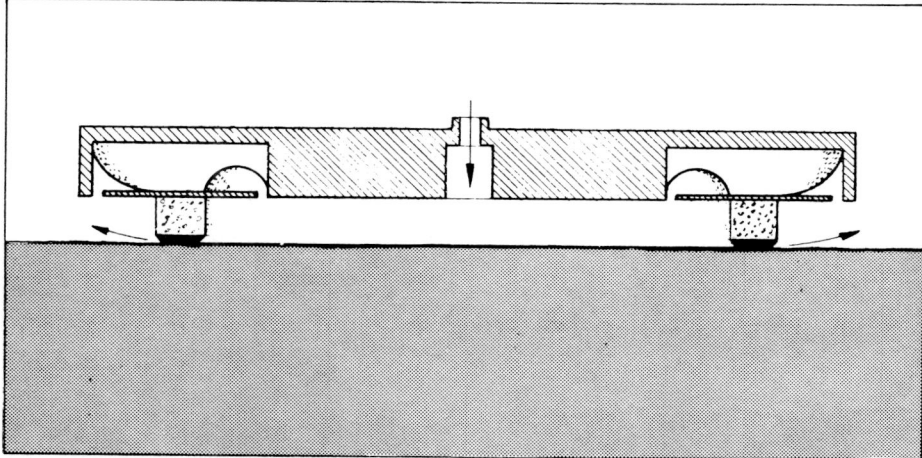

Cross-section of standard AirBarge caster. When flotation air flow is shut off, non-inflatable, flexible wear ring presses against supporting surface acting as brake shoe to halt moving load

AirBarge lifting casters

AirBarge pallet has air casters with non-inflated wear feet

into the floor. While one transporter is inside the autoclave, several others are being loaded or unloaded and it is necessary to be able to manoeuvre the transporters freely around the work area. Initially, the non-castering steel wheels of the transporters could not be moved sideways, and the rolling loads imposed by the wheels exceeded the floor's bearing strength. The installation of a large overhead crane was envisaged in order to move the transporters. However, this costly alternative was avoided by the use of four small air cushion pallets to float the transporter across the floor in any direction.

The AirBarge pallets are pushed under the load at reduced height; when air flow is increased, they raise the transporter's wheels and it can then be moved freely in any direction, the air cushions distributing the weight to avoid overloading the floor. The air pallets are equipped with a patented air caster which employs a non-inflated wear foot as its air seal. The seals cannot be damaged by any loose shop debris on the floor. The units, with their original seals, have been in continuous service at Lockheed for over five years. Purchase of this equipment obviated the need for an investment in cranes and installation estimated in excess of US$250,000.

JETSTREAM SYSTEMS COMPANY

3486 Investment Boulevard, PO Box 4177, Hayward, California 94540, USA
Telephone: (415) 785 9360
Officials:
Stanley Lenox, *President*
Peter F Loveland, *Vice President, Marketing*
Eugene S Batter, *Vice President, Operations*

Jetstream Systems Company holds the world-wide rights for Jetstream air film conveyors and processing equipment.

Jetstream uses low-pressure air delivered to a plenum by a fan or fans and introduced to the conveyor surface through various types of orifices along the full length of the conveyor to maintain a film of air flowing close to the conveyor surface. This air film both lifts and moves the objects being conveyed. It conveys packages of various types; small items which must be kept properly oriented; scrap metal; plastic; paper; and granular materials.

The air can be heated or cooled to condition the product while it is being conveyed. A rectangular fluid bed using the air film principle is available where longer retention times are required.

The system provides constant controlled power around curves and up inclines including vertical faces. Entry points and spurs, inputs and outputs, can be added easily anywhere along the conveyor. Maintenance and wear are greatly reduced because no moving parts are in contact with the product. Objects can be accumulated on the conveyor with very low back-pressure since they are riding on an air film and no belts or chains are dragged across the bottom.

POWER SUPPLY: Pressure of air necessary: 2·54mm (0·2in) water gauge to ½psi. Air ducting and centrifugal fans are generally fitted as an integral part of the conveyor.

CONVEYOR SYSTEM: Units are designed to suit product. The length can run to 304·8m (1,000ft) or more, and the width from 2·54cm to 3m (1in to 10ft) or more as necessary.

ROLAIR SYSTEMS INC

PO Box 30363, Santa Barbara, California 93105, USA
Telephone: (805) 968 1536
Telex: 658433
Officials:
L P Cabot, *Chairman*
T M Baker, *President*
S F Ecker, *Secretary/Treasurer*
Licensee:
Marubeni Corporation, Japan

Rolair Systems Inc manufactures a range of equipment making use of compliant air bearings for moving heavy or large loads. Key personnel with the company were engaged in the same field with General Motors between 1962 and 1968. The company was incorporated in 1968 as Transocean Air Systems Corporation. In 1971 its name was changed to Rolair Systems Inc.

The company's products include standard catalogue items and unlimited custom-engineered systems. Government, military and industrial use of Rolair air film systems is world-wide. Systems now operating range in weight handling capacities up to 14 million pounds.

The basic compliant air bearing device comprises a membrane holding compressed air which conforms to the floor. Controlled escape of this air in a thin layer between membrane and floor forms a frictionless air film which 'floats' the load, enabling it to be moved in any horizontal direction by a force only one-thousandth of the weight of the load. Air pressure is self-regulating according to the bearing size and its load. Typically a 0·6m (2ft) diameter bearing will lift 1,814kg (4,000lb); four 0·6m (2ft) bearings will carry a truck.

A number of the company's air bearing products and typical applications are described as follows:

AIR BEARINGS AID SHIP STORAGE

A programme for reverse ship storage and upkeep for the US Navy has resulted in over $1 million savings in both money and man hours.

The US Navy's ship repairing facility on Guam operates a reserve craft branch, responsible for the security, maintenance and upkeep of out-of-service-in-reserve Navy vessels. The problem was to store effectively and protect ten 300-ton YFUs, a landing-craft type vessel, against Guam's hostile tropical environment including typhoons.

In this first application of its kind the problem was solved by using four Rolair air film transporters. The 120-ton capacity transporters, each equipped with four air bearings, enabled the craft to be floated on dry land to a 'high and dry' area, safe from the problems inherent in water storage.

Air film transporters with keel or bilge blocks being floated beneath crane-supported YFU

Boat transfer system

Previous experiments had used heavy equipment and grease on steel plate, but it took four days and 714 man hours to store one YFU. With air film transporters, two a day can be positioned, each requiring 76 man hours, using very little in the way of equipment.

Manoeuvrability was another problem solved with air film transporters as they allowed the manoeuvring of the craft in any direction with little difficulty.

The air film transporters, topped with interfacing keel or bilge blocks, are positioned under the YFU after the craft is lifted onto the dock from the water by two floating cranes. A 30·4 × 121·9m (100 × 400ft) steel-trowelled concrete slab is provided at the dockside for storage. Two lift trucks are used to tow and manoeuvre the craft to their storage position.

After trying both compressed air and water as the fluid for the air bearings, water was determined to be the best fluid for this particular operation. Rolair supplied transporters with both air and water inlets so either could be used.

To remove the air film transporters, a second set of keel or bilge blocks, 1·97m (6·5ft) high was built-up between the concrete slab and the hull.

Using wedges, the hull was raised a few inches so that the transporters could be simply moved. The 1·97m (6·5ft) block height was chosen to permit personnel and vehicle access under the hulls for periodic hull inspection.

Securely-anchored, protected bay storage is the normal storage procedure practised by the Navy for other than small boats. It was recognised that there are a number of economic disadvantages with this method. For example, there is the need for cathodic hull protection; periodic dry-docking for barnacle removal; expensive electronic flooding alarm surveillance as well as regular visual waterline checks by each watch. In addition expensive anchors are lost from time to time during the typhoon season.

It is estimated that the ten YFUs stored at SRF Guam by the 'high and dry' method have saved the US Navy over $100,000 per craft, an amount continually increasing due to the reduced inspection necessary.

BOAT TRANSFER SYSTEM

The 150-ton boat transfer system provides an economical and efficient method of moving large boats into drydock or repair stations. The air cushion transfer system is equipped with X-Y axis pneumatic drive units for precisely-controlled omni-directional movement. This allows accurate positioning of the vessels in the limited areas of the service bays. The transfer system is designed to handle boats of any length or size. The boats are lifted from the water on checks via an elevator.

The transfer system, which is equipped with pneumatic lifters, is floated under the boat and checks. The lifters are actuated, freeing the load for movement to the service area. Once in position, the lifters are lowered and the transfer system removed making the system available to lift another vessel.

All lifting, floating and drive functions are controlled by a single remote-control pendent.

MINE-HUNTER ASSEMBLY LINE

Aluminium air cushions are being used to convey grp-hulled mine hunters through an assembly line. The shipyard concerned, Van der Giessen-der-Noord-Alblasserdam, Netherlands, is building between 50 and 60 mine hunters in a tripartite arrangement between the navies of the Netherlands, Belgium and France.

To solve the problem of handling and moving the hulls, each of which weighs about 750,000kg, a controlled assembly line has been introduced employing air film technology. This is flexible and relatively inexpensive. The components for one ship are: fourteen 122 × 183cm air cushions which elevate the load through the use of elliptical, compliant urethane diaphragms; a steel structure called a keel block, supplied by the customer, into which the cushions slide; and an umbilically-operated, remote-control unit which allows precise control of the ship's movement.

Once a ship reaches the end of the assembly line, the cushions can be removed from beneath the keel blocks and reused. Since not more than four ships are processed at any one time, 60 ships can be handled with four sets of cushions and remote-control units.

ASSEMBLY LINE FOR CRAWLER TRACTORS

One of the most advanced air film systems in operation is at the Caterpillar Tractor plant at Gosselies, Belgium, where an automatic assembly line has been installed by Rolair for Model 225 Excavators.

The first line for these vehicles was installed at the company's plant at Aurora, Illinois, USA. Experience with the Aurora plant led to certain improvements on the Gosselies plant. For example, air tools are used throughout the line, allowing the air-powered transporters to serve as the air supply for the tools. This enables assemblers to connect their tools at the start of the assembly and leave them connected throughout the line.

The assembly operation begins on a 175ft (53·3m) long section of track immediately preceding the air pallet area. There, drive assemblies are built on manually-propelled transfer carts.

First, the tractor's two planetary gears are aligned on a stationary fixture. A housing is then lifted into position by an overhead crane. After the housing has been connected to the axles, the unit is lifted onto a transfer cart. Small components are then added to the housing as the cart is moved to the end of the track. The sub-assembly and cart now weighs about 18,000lb (8,154kg) and requires two men to push it. At this point the sub-assembly is lifted by the overhead crane and positioned on one of the air pallets. Now one man can easily move the 9-ton load.

Components are brought to the air pallet line on flat-bed trucks and lifted by crane onto the pallets. Workers climb portable step ladders to perform the necessary welding and bolting operations. The same air source that supplies the pallets is used to power air-articulated assembly tools.

Each transporter has a 45ft (13·7m) hose mounted on a retractable reel. Air hose connectors are installed below the surface every 25ft (7·6m) along the assembly line. This allows the

Section of mine-hunter hull on assembly line

Caterpillar Tractor plant at Gosselies

transporter 90ft (27·4m) of travel before changing air connectors.

When air is fed into the system, each bearing diaphragm inflates, traps a shallow bubble of air and lifts the load slightly off the floor. Controlled leakage around the edge of the bearings creates a lubricating layer of air between the transporter and floor. Friction is practically eliminated and the transporter can be moved with a minimum of force.

A master clock controls the complete assembly line. Magnetic sensors are on the bottom of the transporters and, using a series of electromagnets embedded every 10ft (3m) along the assembly line floor, the transporter can be directed to move from station to station. The electromagnets are normally energised. When the control clock de-energises a specific electromagnet, the sensor on the transporter opens, providing an air supply to the air bearing, causing the transporter to advance toward the next energised electromagnet. Since each electromagnet is individually controlled, the air transporter can be moved any distance along the line.

At the same time as the air system is activated, two guide wheels automatically lock onto a V-type floor rail and guide the transporter down the assembly line. As a safety factor a 25-second delay is provided between air activation and initial machine movement, allowing ample time for assemblers to move from the path of the transporter.

Although the major portion of the line is automatic, some manual movement remains. At the end of the line, where the assembly floor is wide enough for two machines on transporters to operate side-by-side, excavators undergo flushing and computer testing of the hydraulic system. Advancing from the assembly line, the transporter's guide wheels are retracted and two men simply 'float' the 20-ton load into the test area.

With the air film transporter system the assembly line can be easily altered. It can be lengthened over a weekend simply by laying more concrete. A turn can be added the same way, and if the line has to be shortened, the section no longer required is simply abandoned. Relocation can be effected by simply picking up the whole system and setting it down on a new strip of concrete.

MOBILE CRANE

Rolair cranes offer the added dimension of omni-directional mobility. The 15-ton mobile crane can be moved fully loaded in any direction for precise positioning of the weight. It is driven by an optional steerable drive unit capable of moving the loaded crane at speeds of up to 30fpm and which will stop the moving crane in less than 2·5ft (0·76m).

AIRCRAFT GROUND TESTING INSTALLATION

An air flotation system has been installed by Vought to allow quicker positioning of each plane for testing operational equipment. The system uses an air film and replaces hand-operated tripod-type jacks. It has provided not only a saving in time, but a safer environment for testing. Twelve Corsair II light attack aircraft can be closely positioned within a single hangar.

Three air bearings, connected directly to a T-shaped dolly, make up the casters for each of six 'sets' of bearings in use in the hangar. Their design is such that they easily handle the 19,000lb (8,607kg) aircraft. On-off air valves for the bearings are operated quickly by a single employee. The bearings have their own stabilising chamber, eliminating any throttling of incoming air. Inlet air pressure is supplied at 75psi from standard 1in plant lines.

MOVING STEEL PRESSURE VESSELS

Pressure vessels for refineries, nuclear generators and the chemical industry represent one of the most difficult types of material handling problems for their manufacturers. The vessels are massive, bulky and hard to handle.

At Kobe Steel's plant in Takasago, Japan, the problem of transporting 1,000-ton pressure vessels from the assembly floor to the X-ray facility for weld examination was solved by the use of four 250-ton capacity air transporters. The transporters, based on designs by Rolair Systems, are manufactured by its Japanese licensee, Marubeni Corporation.

In the Kobe Steel plant, overhead cranes are used for loading and unloading the 1,000ft (304·8m) long pressure vessel fabrication line. The task of transporting the vessels between the fabrication line and the weld X-ray building, some hundreds of feet away for safety reasons, had been assigned to multi-axle, heavy-duty flatbed trucks at a round-trip cost of approximately $10,000 and a frequency of as much as twice a day. The new system, while representing a six-figure investment, provided Kobe Steel with an economical solution that was expected to pay for itself within the first year with ease.

The Rolair transporters are completely air-operated, using existing shop air supplies. Underneath each 10in (254mm) high structural steel transporter are eight disc-like air bearings which are specially compounded elastomeric compliant diaphragms.

When air is applied to the system through flexible hoses connected to the shop air supply, the bearings inflate. Controlled leakage creates a lubricating layer of air between the bearings and the floor. Friction is completely eliminated and the transporter can easily be moved in any horizontal direction by means of a built-in air motor drive system.

Each 250-ton capacity transporter contains four air motor drives mounted in tandem on opposite axes. By selective activation of the drives, the load can be moved as the operator wishes, including a full 360-degree turn around the load's vertical axis.

Wall-mounted retractable hoses permit easy movement between the fabrication line and the X-ray building at slow walking speeds. The system is designed for one-man operation for loads up to 500 tons. Two operators, one for each pair of transporters, are required for heavier loads, with maximum system capacity at 1,000 tons.

Once in position, the load is lowered gently to the floor by simply shutting off the air supply. With this ability of frictionless movement, a 1 : 1,000 force : load ratio results which means simple lightweight air motors can move the unwieldy pressure vessels very easily and with precise positioning.

SPACE SHUTTLE SOLID ROCKET BOOSTERS

The use of air film movement systems in the production and operation of the solid rocket boosters (SRB) for the US Space Shuttle Programme represents an unmatched in-depth integration of air film into production. Air film equipment is used from the first phase of production to recovery and remanufacture.

Primary solid rocket booster elements are the

Mobile crane

Omni-Mobile crane of travelling-bridge type

Centre deck of tractor-trailer transporter moving on 12 air bearings

motor, which includes the case, propellant, igniter and nozzle; forward and aft structures; and separation, recovery, electrical and thrust vector control sub-systems. Each booster is 45·41m (149ft) long and 3·65m (12ft) in diameter, weighs approximately 1,293,000lb and produces 2,900,000lb static thrust.

The solid rocket motor, the primary component of the booster, contains 1,100,000lb of solid propellant. The motor is built in four casting segments: a forward segment, two centre segments, and the aft segment. To these segments the nozzle assembly is added. Each of the casting segments is manufactured independently and transported, together with the nozzle exit cone assembly, to the launch site, where they are assembled.

For the first time rocket motors will be routinely recovered and re-used. When the spent boosters are separated from the shuttle vehicle external tank they will descend to the ocean by parachutes. Towed back to the Kennedy Space Center (or later to Vandenberg Air Force Base), the boosters are disassembled and the motors returned to the manufacturer, Thiokol Corporation. Residue is washed from the case segments, which are then refurbished, reinsulated and again loaded with propellant. Each case segment is designed to be used 20 times over. Some parts of the nozzle, igniter hardware and the safe and arming devices will also be refurbished and re-used.

Rolair Systems Inc designed and built the air film equipment for Thiokol Corporation.

Production cycle: Use of air film begins at sub-contractor level and spans the production process from Thiokol's Utah-based Wasatch Division to NASA's operations at Marshal Space Flight Center and Kennedy Space Center.

For example, Standard Tool and Die Company uses Rolair bearings to position 22-ton mandrels during machining operations. The mandrels are used in casting the solid rocket fuel into the proper shape within the casting segment. What is unique about Standard Tool and Die's application of air film is that the air bearings remain with air-on for over 24 hours continuously to provide friction-free precision alignment during machining.

Utility handling equipment: Air film utility handling equipment is used throughout Thiokol. Examples include a standard air film transporter for handling such parts as nozzle flexible bearings to specially designed dollies to handle case segments weighing up to 4,988kg (11,000lb) throughout the plant with ease.

Shot blast turntable: New segments are grit-blasted at one of Thiokol's sub-contractors, Rohr. As a part of the refurbishment after recovery, expended case segments are processed through grit blasting before painting and reprocessing. Rolair provided an air film turntable for this operation. The turntable rotates on inverted air bearings and has a low height and very few moving parts for high reliability. The turntable drive system is synchronised with the automatic grit-blasting equipment to avoid damage to the case segments.

Painting turntable: 9·75m (32ft) long casting segments are lowered into a pit by crane onto an air film turntable for automatic painting inside and out. Since the painting equipment moves only up and down, the rotational drive system of the Rolair turntable is designed for highly accurate and repeatable control to ensure uniform application of paint. The hydraulic drives have a digital readout to indicate speed accurately.

Empty case handling and rotation: When the case segments are joined into casting segments the innovation of the air film system becomes pronounced. At this stage 3·65m (12ft) diameter cylinders, 9·75m (32ft) long and weighing up to approximately 25 tons, must be manoeuvred throughout the plant. But, more important, they must be rotated around the horizontal axis of the cylinder as insulation and other components are added to the evolution of the solid rocket booster.

For movement over the floor in confined quarters Rolair designed a drive system with umbilical

Turntable in use for grit-blasting and painting booster skirt of NASA space shuttle

Air film system dolly showing one casting segment in background

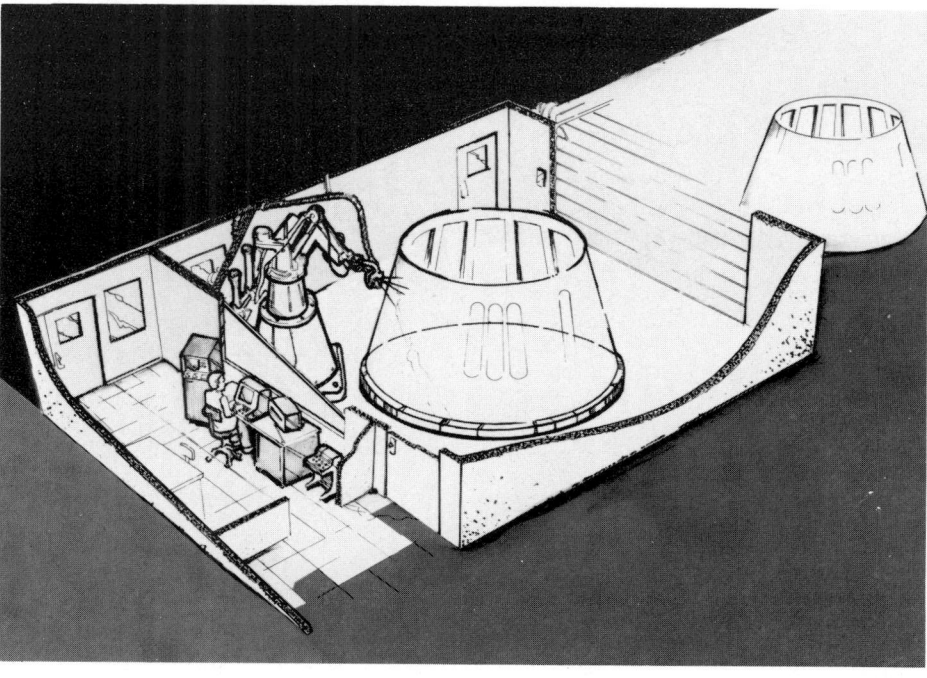

System for applying and removing space shuttle's protective coating

operator control. The operator first selects the mode of movement by a dial selector on the control. Then the left thumb depresses a dead-man protected button to actuate the air bearings, and the right thumb causes the drive mode selected to be activated. The release of either thumb causes movement to cease automatically.

As insulation and other components are added to the casting segments horizontal rotation is necessary. To accomplish this curved air bearings were perfected which conform to the perimeter of the 3·65m (12ft) diameter casting segments.

For rotation the same umbilical control selector switch is positioned to either clockwise, counter-clockwise, or free float. The same thumb-operated actuators implement the desired motion.

Air-bearing usage in the case processing areas has provided very efficient use of the existing floor space and enables these large space shuttle segments to be moved between work stations with minimum effort. The ability to rotate these large hardware items during various process operations without additional tooling established a very streamlined process.

180-ton loaded case handling and rotation: Before incorporation of the solid-rocket fuel itself the empty casting segment weighs about 31,751kg (70,000lb). It is then moved horizontally to the casting pits on a specially-designed trailer, installed vertically into the casting pits and cast with approximately 131,370kg (290,000lb) of solid fuel.

A tractor-trailer transporter 42·3m (139ft) long, 4·2m (14ft) wide and with a capacity of 200 tons arrives at the casting pit. On arrival the centre deck of the trailer is lowered to the ground by built-in jacks and the 58-wheeled front and rear wheeled jeep dollies are unhitched from the centre deck and moved away. The centre deck weighs 24,915kg (55,000lb) and moves over the ground on 12 air bearings. In addition, 30 curved air bearings are shaped to support the solid rocket motor segments when loaded with propellant.

Using a similar but higher capacity drive and control system than the unloaded case dollies, the centre deck and empty casting segment are floated across a temporarily covered crane rail and into a 200-ton capacity breakover fixture. The breakdown raises the empty centre deck in preparation to receive a loaded socket motor segment.

A vertical loaded segment lifting beam attached to a 200-ton capacity gantry crane removes the loaded segment from the casting pit and places it onto the breakover fixture. The breakover process is reversed, the air bearings float the total system, weighing approximately

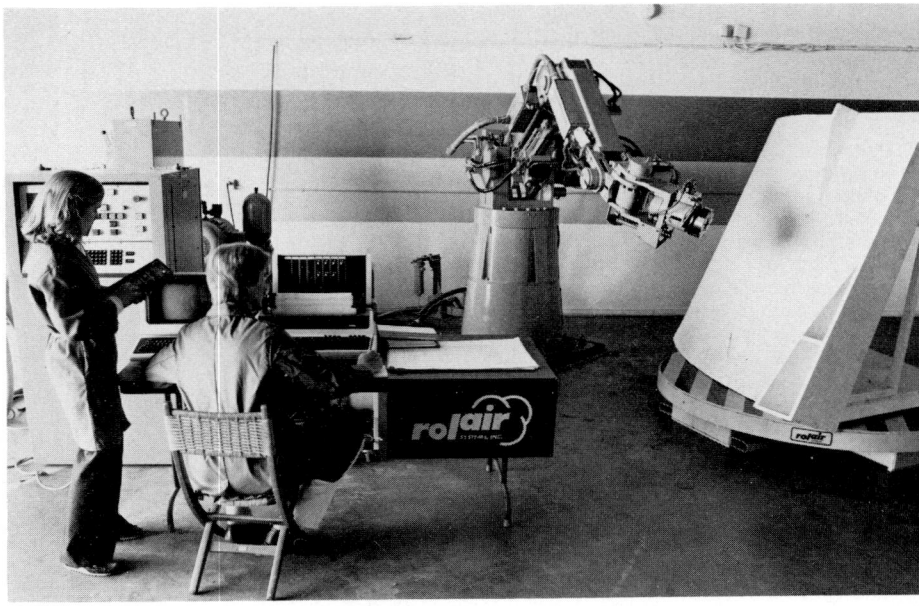
Applying thermal protective coating to space shuttle

200 tons, back across the temporary crane rail covers and into position to hook to the tractor-trailer transporter.

When the loaded case segment and centre deck are re-united with the 58-wheeled trailer they are moved by road to the next manufacturing operation. At each location, the centre deck is again lowered and over-the-ground and rotation motion is accomplished using air film.

Air bearings have simplified the entire handling of loaded segments. The tractor-trailer transporter length prohibited it from being positioned between the casting pits, where the segment could be handled with the 200-ton gantry crane. Other methods considered for moving the segment to the crane, such as a rail system, exceeded the allotted budget for facility modification and re-arrangement. Air bearings require only a level concrete pad thick enough to withstand the total load and bridges for crossing over the gantry rails.

At other assembly buildings where crane capacity is limited to that required for tooling there was no other way to handle the segments short of expensive building modifications to provide drive through capabilities. Now, it is simply a matter of driving straight to the front of the building, lowering and disconnecting the air bearing dolly from the transporter, and floating it into the building.

SPACE SHUTTLE'S THERMAL PROTECTIVE SHIELD

One of Rolair's projects is a totally-integrated system using air cushion products and highly-sophisticated robot and support components. The purpose is to apply an epoxy-base glue and a layer of cork-like material to the space shuttle aft-skirt before launching and then to remove the burnt material and reapply it before relaunch.

Precision indexing turntables are being built which accurately interface with robot and hydrolaser units for both the removal and application of the space shuttle's thermal protective shield. One task the system performs is to support and accurately position a water spray with a force of 1,100 atmospheres. It also programmes the interface between the robot and the 3·6m diameter turntable on which the shuttle rests. Accuracy is essential to the successful functioning of the system.

ALUMINIUM AIR CUSHIONS

Rolair aluminium air cushions are available in 12, 24, 36 and 48in² (0·77, 1·54, 2·32 and 3·09cm²) configurations and with capacities ranging from 1,000 to 36,000lb (454 to 16,329kg). Their lightweight construction and low profile are suitable for situations which require the frequent movement of heavy and unwieldy loads.

In common with many of the other air film applicators in the Rolair range, the aluminium air cushions have diaphragms which slide out for replacement.

CURVED AIR BEAMS

A system has been evolved for moving a fragile 12·75-ton (13,000kg) load inside a pipe measuring 8ft 2in (2·5m) in diameter. The curved beam is a welded steel structure shaped like a sector of a circle with a diameter of approximately 7ft 10in (2·4m). Attached to the bottom of the curved plates are three air cushions, each with a 2ft 3in (70cm) diameter. When inflated, these cushions form a radius of 3ft 11in (120cm), which float inside the pipe and move the load horizontally along its length. Hoses supply air to each of the three cushions through needle valves which adjust the flow in each. The cushions have separate internal chambers which dampen out pressure-induced oscillations.

This use of air film technology has solved a number of potential problems for heavy but fragile loads needing careful transporting. The curved road way posed a problem for the pipe-to-support interface. It was solved by the use of compliant urethane diaphragms which form the underside of the cushions. The inaccessibilty of the pipe necessitated a handling system requiring low maintenance; with few moving parts, the curved beams are virtually maintenance free.

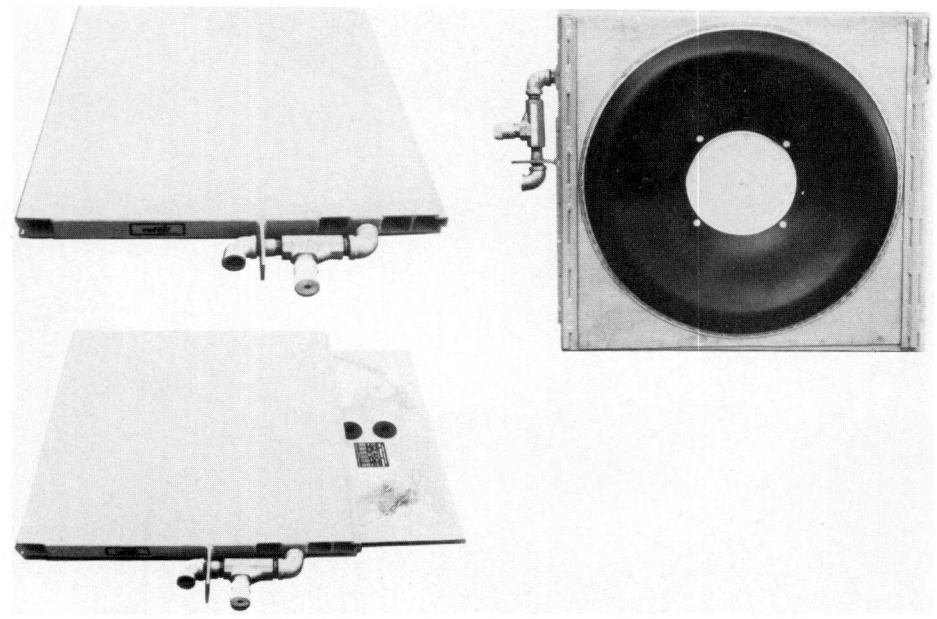
Aluminium air cushion. Top left: upper surface of applicator showing adjustable orifice valve. Bottom left: slide-in diaphragm which can be exchanged without removing load. Top right: base of applicator showing urethane diaphragm

Their use has proved to be a major advantage over conventional material-handling systems.

ALUMINIUM AIR BEAMS

Using standard shop air, aluminium air beams are equipped with standard Rolair air cushions and have capacities up to 72,000lb (32,659kg) per pair; with a coefficient of friction of 0·001 (1lb of force to move 1,000lbs). They are available in widths from 13 to 48in (330mm to 1·21m) and lengths as required. Built to the same standards as the structural steel air beams which have been a standard product of Rolair Systems for several years, the beams are available in an extruded aluminium shape or an aluminium tube construction. Their low profile facilitates positioning under a load and because they operate on a thin film of air with no moving parts, maintenance is virtually eliminated. Compressed air inflates the air cushions on the beam's underside. Communication holes in the cushions allow a release of the pressurised air on which the beams and their load float.

ROLAIR TURNTABLE

A mobile turntable has been added to the company's range of air bearings. It rotates on a frictionless film of air and there is no need to remove its payload if an alternative position is required on the factory production line or floor. Capacities and sizes are identical to those of the standard low-profile air film turntables manufactured by Rolair Systems. The smallest is a 36in (914mm) diameter model with a 5,000lb (2,268kg) capacity. Larger sizes range up to a 12ft (3·65m) diameter, 70,000lb (31,752kg) payload. Custom-designed sizes, capacities and configurations are available. All mobile turntables can be floated from one place to another while fully loaded. Compressed air inflates the air cushions, raising the load. Small holes in the cushions allow a release of pressurised air to create a thin layer of lubrication on which the turntables and their load float. The turntables can be moved or rotated with 1lb of force per 1,000lb load.

ROTARY TABLE FOR PLATE GLASS HANDLING

The Rolair rotary table provides a computer-operated cutting table with a fast and steady supply of plate glass. The unstacking machine loaded with heavy, fragile glass comprises a square table rotating on a thin cushion of air.

Each side of the table supports a vertical stack of plate glass so that sheets can be unloaded by the machine on one side while the other sides are being restocked. The table has a maximum capacity of 45,455kg (100,000lb), can support any configuration from 0 to 11,364kg per side and is capable of handling two sizes of glass: 3·3 × 4·3m and 3·3 × 5·2m. The table is operated by a remote-control station.

Curved air beam for conveying loads within pipe

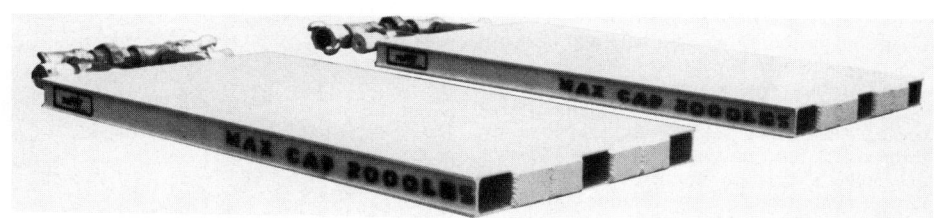

Aluminium air beams

Mobile turntable

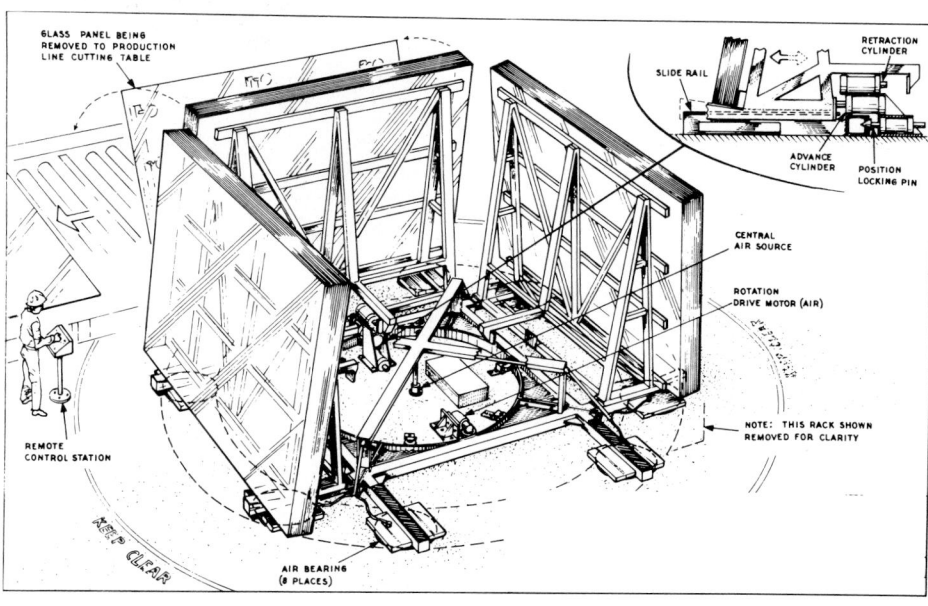

Rotary table for plate glass handling

TRACKED SKIMMERS

FRANCE

SOCIÉTÉ BERTIN & CIE

Département Aérotrain, BP 3, F 78370 Plaisir,
France
Telephone: (3) 056 25 00
Telex: 696231
Officials:
Eric Barsalou, *President Director General*
Michel Perineau, *Director General*
Georges Mordchelles-Regnier, *Director General*
Jean Cayla, *Head of Aérotrain Department*

This department was created in December
1980 when Société de l'Aérotrain was absorbed
by Bertin & Cie so the Aérotrain concept could
benefit from the support of a larger organisation
with a long experience of Aérotrain technology
and an extensive development task force. Société
de l'Aérotrain was founded in April 1965 to
develop a high-speed transport system based on
air cushion support and guidance principles conceived by Bertin & Cie.

Jean Bertin, chairman of the company from
1971 until he died in December 1975, is known
as the father of the Aérotrain. His name will
remain attached to a number of outstanding
inventions in the air cushion field and in many
others, including aeronautics.

The Aérotrain has completed its experimental
phase as far as the air cushion technique is concerned. The 01 half-scale prototype, after nearly
three years of test runs at speeds up to 346km/h
(215mph), successfully attained its phased design
requirements, namely the verification of dynamic
behaviour, the development of integrated suspension systems, and the accumulation of data
for the design and costing of full-scale operational vehicles.

The 02 half-scale prototype has undergone
similar tests in order to produce data for vehicles
operating at speeds above 322km/h (200mph). A
speed of 423·26km/h (263mph) was attained by
the vehicle in January 1969.

There are three families of Aérotrain systems:
Interurban, with speeds of 280 to 400km/h (175
to 250mph); Suburban, with speeds of 160 to
200km/h (100 to 125mph) and the Tridim
system, designed for speeds of up to 80km/h
(50mph), as the distance between suburban stations generally ranges between several hundred
yards and one or two miles.

The speeds selected will be based on economic
considerations. Suburban systems will cover a
variety of routes from city centres to airports and
city centres to satellite towns and suburban areas.
The size, speed and control system of each vehicle will be decided according to the route.

Current studies are aimed primarily at
developing associated techniques including
propulsion modes for the various speeds and
environments, controls, signals and stations.

A mathematical model has been developed in
order to computerise the various parameters for
both families of applications. This enables
operating costs to be obtained, in an optimised
form, for given traffic requirements.

Two full-scale vehicles, the 80-seat Orleans
inter-city Aérotrain and the 40- to 44-seat suburban Aérotrain, have undergone extensive trials. Between 1969 and 1971, the 80-seat I-80
Orleans Aérotrain completed more than 700
hours of operation on its 18km (11·2 mile) track
north of Orleans, carrying more than 10,000
people at a speed of 260km/h (160mph). In
January 1973, the vehicle was taken to the UTA
maintenance facility at Le Bourget airport where
it was equipped with a 15,000lb st JT8D-11 turbofan, permitting its speed to be studied in the
360 to 400km/h (220 to 250mph) range.

In November 1973, a speed of 400km/h
(250mph) was attained and by May 1974, 150
hours of operation had been logged in this
configuration, during which 2,000 professionally
interested passengers had been carried.

Rohr-built Aérotrain

28·6m (94ft) long Rohr Aérotrain

Turntable at end of Aérotrain test track

Impression of Aérotrain variant designed for Europole project

All these programmes, completed or under
way, represent a financial development effort of
roughly US $22 million. The French Govern-
ment extended its support at every stage by
means of various loans, subsidies and orders.

In November 1969, the company formed a US
subsidiary, Aérotrain Systems Inc, to build and
market Aérotrains in the USA and Mexico. Initially, this company was jointly held by Rohr
Industries Inc, Bertin & Cie and Société de
l'Aérotrain. Since 1976, it has been held by the
two latter companies. A 60-seat, 140mph, LIM-
propelled prototype was completed in December

1972 and was successfully tested in 1975-76 on
an experimental line built at the US Department
of Transport centre at Pueblo, California. In May
1976 the 28·6-metre (94-foot) long Aérotrain
attained a speed of 230km/h (144mph), a world
record for LIM-propelled, all-electric TACV.

In 1971 another subsidiary was formed,
Aérotrain Scandinavia AB, in which the Salén
Group has a 50 per cent interest. A third com-
pany, formed in Brazil with the support of four
French banks, is Aérotrain Systemas de Trans-
porte.

In December 1973 an agreement was signed

Prefabricated concrete beams of Orleans track *(P M Lambermont)*

between Bertin & Cie, Aérotrain, Spie-Batignolles, Jeumont-Schneider, SGTE MTE and Francorail-MTE to co-operate with the promotion and operation of Aérotrain systems and various aspects of production of French projects.

Since 1974, feasibility studies have been under way for the Marseilles metropolitan area including connections between the airport and Aix-en-Provence, for the Europole project linking Brussels to Geneva (via Luxembourg, Metz, Nancy, Strasbourg, Basle, Berne and Lausanne) and for several projects in Argentina. A 360km/h (223mph) Aérotrain variant, fan-jet propelled with seating for 144, has been designed for this project.

EXPERIMENTAL AÉROTRAIN 01

An experimental, half-scale prototype, this vehicle was operated along a test track 6·7km (4·2 miles) long. The track has an inverted T cross section, the vertical portion being 55cm (1ft 10in) high and the horizontal base 1·8m (5ft 11in) wide. Turntables, which would not normally be used on operational lines, are fitted at each end. In service Aérotrains will be able to manoeuvre independently on the flat-floor surface of stations.

The vehicle is of light alloy construction. The slender body has seats at the front for six people, and an engine compartment at the rear. Lift and guidance are provided by two centrifugal fans, driven by two 50hp Renault Gordini motor car engines, linked by a shaft. The fans supply air to the guidance and lift cushions at a pressure of about 25g/cm² (0·35lb/in²), the maximum airflow being 10m³/s (350ft³/s). Propulsion is provided by a 260hp Continental aero-engine, mounted at the top of a 1·2m (3ft 11in) tail pylon and driving a reversible-pitch propeller, which is also used for normal braking. There are brake pads at the rear of the vehicle which grip the vertical track section like a disc brake.

The first test run on the track was made on 29 December 1965. The prototype was intended to evaluate and demonstrate the Aérotrain principle on a small scale, and was developed with the active support of the French Government and French Railways.

Although the vehicle was designed for a maximum speed of 200km/h (125mph) tests have been undertaken at higher speeds with the help of booster rockets to supplement the propulsive airscrew. In December 1967, the vehicle reached the top speed of 345km/h (215mph) several times with a jet engine assisted by two booster rockets.

DIMENSIONS
Length overall: 10m (32ft 10in)
Width overall: 2m (6ft 7in)
Height overall: 3·7m (12ft 2in)
Height to top of body: 1·6m (5ft 3in)
WEIGHTS
Basic: 2,500kg (5,500lb)
PERFORMANCE
Cruising speed: 200km/h (125mph)
Top speed: 303km/h (188mph)

EXPERIMENTAL AÉROTRAIN 02

Aérotrain 02 is an experimental half-scale prototype designed for high speed tests on the track at Gometz used by the first prototype.

Due to the track's relatively short length, a more powerful thrust engine, a Pratt & Whitney JT 12, is installed in order to maintain high speeds over a distance of 2km (1·3 miles) for performance measurements.

Aérotrain 01

Aérotrain 02

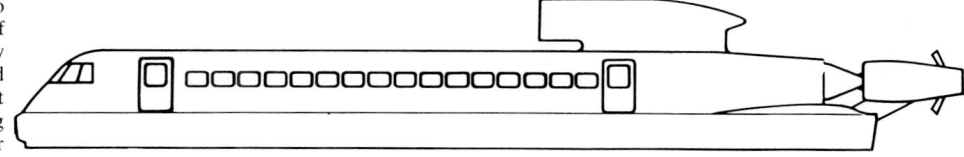

Side view showing revised configuration of I-80V Aérotrain with turbofan thrust unit

I-80HV Aérotrain with turbofan thrust unit

During its first series of test runs, the Aérotrain 02 attained 378km/h (235mph). A booster rocket was then added, and a series of tests followed, culminating in a record speed of 422km/h (263mph). The average speed recorded over the 2 to 3 mile track was 411km/h (255mph).

The air cushions for lift and guidance are provided by fans driven by a Turboméca Palouste gas turbine. At high speed, the dynamic pressure is sufficient to feed the air cushions.

The internal space has been devoted in the main to test instrumentation. Seats are provided only for the pilot and a test engineer.

Aérotrains 01 and 02 were both equipped with propulsion engines which were readily available from the aviation market and capable of giving high speed on a short test track. Operational vehicles use quieter power arrangements.

FULL-SCALE AÉROTRAIN I-80 ORLEANS INTERCITY PROJECT

This medium-range inter-city vehicle (the Orleans-Paris line will be 113km (70 miles) long) was designed originally with airscrew propulsion for speeds up to 300km/h (186·41mph), but has now been equipped with a silenced turbofan engine which has increased its speed to 400km/h (250mph). The vehicle carries 80 passengers, in airline comfort, in an air-conditioned and sound-proofed cabin.

The lift and guidance air cushions are fed by two axial fans driven by a 400hp Turboméca Astazou gas turbine. At high speeds, they will be fed by dynamic intake pressure.

On the original model thrust was supplied by a shrouded propeller, driven independently by two 1,300hp Turmo III gas turbines.

SIDE VIEW

PLAN VIEW

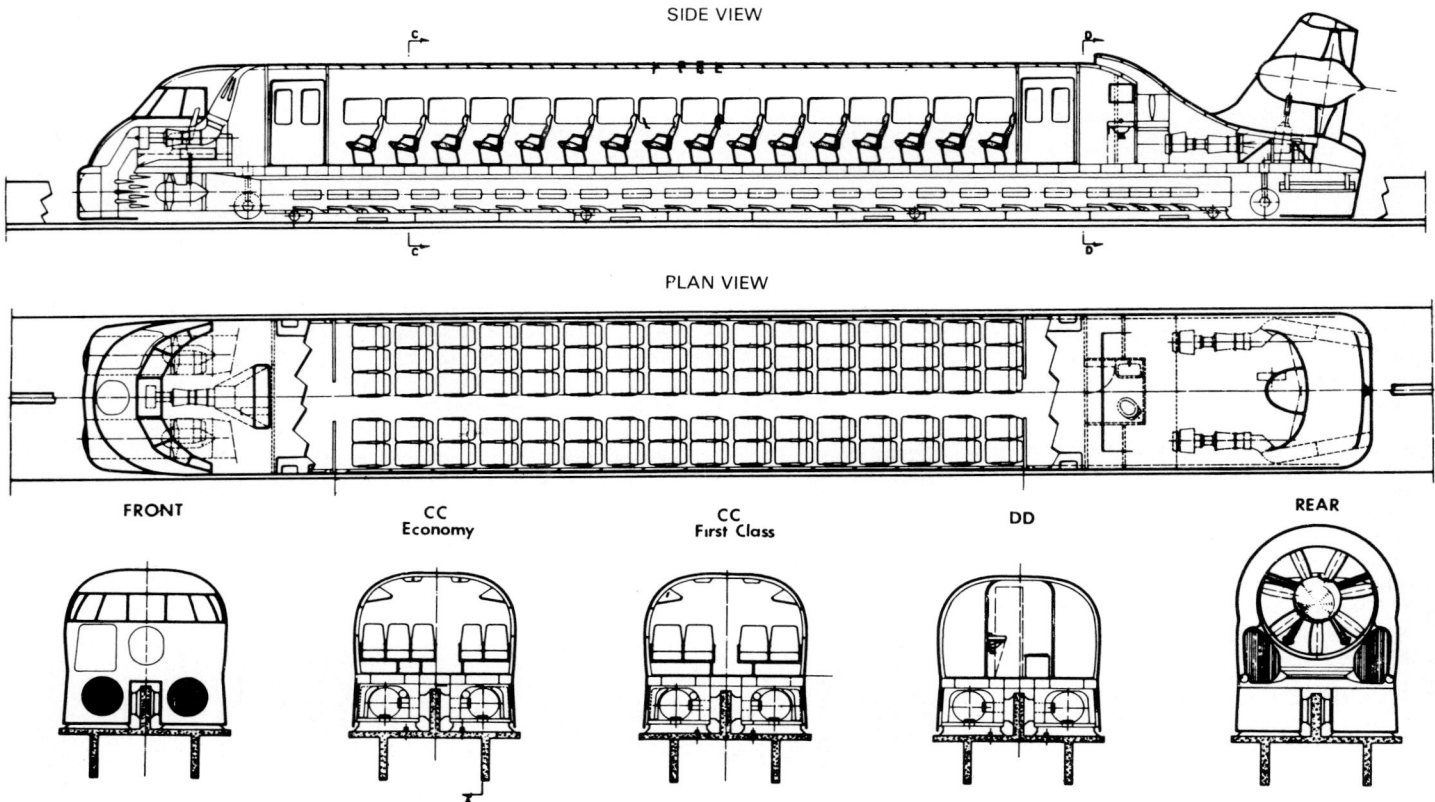

FRONT   CC Economy   CC First Class   DD   REAR

Aérotrain I-80 configuration for medium-range inter-city traffic

In January 1973, the vehicle was taken to the UTA maintenance facility at Le Bourget, where it was fitted with a 15,000lb thrust Pratt & Whitney JT8D-11 turbofan, which permitted the systematic study of the I-80 and its components at speeds in the 354 to 426km/h (220 to 250mph) range.

The air intake has been designed for maximum effectiveness and a special high-dilution ejection system suppresses the noise of the exhaust gases.

Hydraulically retractable tyred wheels are incorporated to help to achieve silent operation near and in stations, and also to assist in manoeuvring and switching the vehicle on station floors. The vertical rail of the inverted T track is unnecessary at low speeds.

A very low empty-weight-to-payload ratio has been possible because of the lack of concentrated loads inherent in the vehicle. This permits the use of lightweight supporting structures—tracks and stations.

Vehicles will not be coupled, so that very high frequency services can be maintained throughout the day. With headways as low as one minute, simple or articulated vehicles offer a range of capacities which largely cope with the peaks of traffic expected in known inter-city lines.

Two articulated cars with seats for up to 160 passengers and luxury models with a wider aisle and reduced seating capacity are being considered in feasibility studies being undertaken for several projected routes.

DIMENSIONS
Length overall: 30·5m (101ft 8in)
Length at track level: 27·75m (92ft 6in)
Width: 3·2m (10ft 8in)
Height at fan jet air intake: 5·1m (17ft)
WEIGHTS
Gross: 24 tonnes
PERFORMANCE
Test speed range: 354-426km/h (220-250mph)

GUIDEWAY

The first leg of the Orleans to Paris line (a track 18·5km (11·5 miles) long) was completed in July 1969. It included turntables at both ends and a central platform for manoeuvring and switching.

In mid-1973 the French Government confirmed that the line is to be completed in due course, but did not announce details.

The track has been designed for a service speed of 402km/h (250mph). It is mounted on pylons along the entire route. The prefabricated concrete beams, of 20m (67ft) span, have a minimum ground clearance of 4·81m (16ft). This allows the track to be constructed across roads and cultivated land.

Due to the low stresses produced by the Aérotrain vehicles it has been possible to design a lightweight elevated track structure, which is less expensive than an equivalent ground track. Local ground subsidence, which may occur during the first years after erection, will be countered by adjusting the pylon heads. This will be limited to a simple jacking operation using built-in devices in the pylon structure.

The radii of curves and gradient angles will depend upon the accelerations admissible without causing discomfort to passengers. Banking can be provided, and banking of seven per cent is incorporated in three curves in the Orleans track. The radius requirements are therefore the same as for other guided systems of transport for similar speeds. The advantage of the Aérotrain track is that there are no gradient limitations and it can therefore be constructed with a much smaller number of curves.

TESTS

Speed, acceleration and braking characteristics have confirmed expectations, and the riding comfort has proved to be highly satisfactory. Under all operating conditions, including propeller reverse braking, negotiating curves and in cross winds of 50km/h (31mph), the average accelerations were less than 0·6m/s² at all times, with values of 0·3 to 0·5m/s² during normal cruising conditions.

Since the interior noise level in the passenger compartment is between 75 and 78 dBA, it is possible to converse in normal tones. A level of 70 to 72 dBA will be reached on series production vehicles. External noise, 90 to 95 dBA at 60m (65yds), compares favourably to that of a modern electric train, with a much shorter duration.

During the 850 hours of operation there was no breakdown which caused the vehicle to stop on the guideway, with the exception of a single incident involving hydraulic circuits to the propeller, which were repaired in less than an hour. Only three items have necessitated a major repair since the vehicle was put on the guideway, and the air cushions have been completely trouble-free.

The third phase of the test programme consisted of an endurance, or accelerated service test involving 200 hours of running time. 36 operating days with a daily average of 6 hours continuous operation were completed. The cruising speed established was 250km/h (154·33mph). Since this involved acceleration and deceleration between 0 and 250km/h (154·33mph) every six minutes, a commercial operation of 1,000 to 2,000 hours or 200,000 to 400,000km in terms of wear on the vehicle was simulated. The rate of air cushion lip wear experienced indicates a useful lip life of 40,000 to 50,000km and a practically negligible cost factor of 0·001 to 0·002 francs per passenger/kilometre.

It is to be noted that cultivation has been resumed around and underneath the guideway which, in sharp contrast with the high permanent way maintenance costs experienced by the railways, has required no maintenance whatsoever since it was built.

HIGH-SPEED I-80 HV 'ORLEANS' AÉROTRAIN

In November 1973, the I-80 'Orleans' Aérotrain began a series of tests with a new propulsion system. The two Turmo III gas turbines, which powered a shrouded propeller, were replaced by a 15,000lb thrust Pratt & Whitney JT8D-11 turbofan, fitted with a sound suppressor system designed by Bertin & Cie. The ride characteristics remained outstanding at speeds up to 416km/h (260mph) in spite of the size of the new propulsion unit which resulted in the vehicle being 4 tons over weight.

The compressors and air feeders remained unchanged.

On 5 March 1974, the vehicle attained 430km/h (270mph), with an average speed (in each direction) of 418km/h (263mph) over a distance of 1·86 miles. The sound insulation has been extremely effective resulting in a noise level 2dBA lower than the original propulsion system.

In 1976, the Orleans vehicle was still in use for demonstrations. By May 1976, it had completed 925 hours of operation including 212 hours with its JT8D-11 turbofan. During this time it has carried 13,500 passengers, 3,280 of whom have been carried at speeds in excess of 400km/h (250mph).

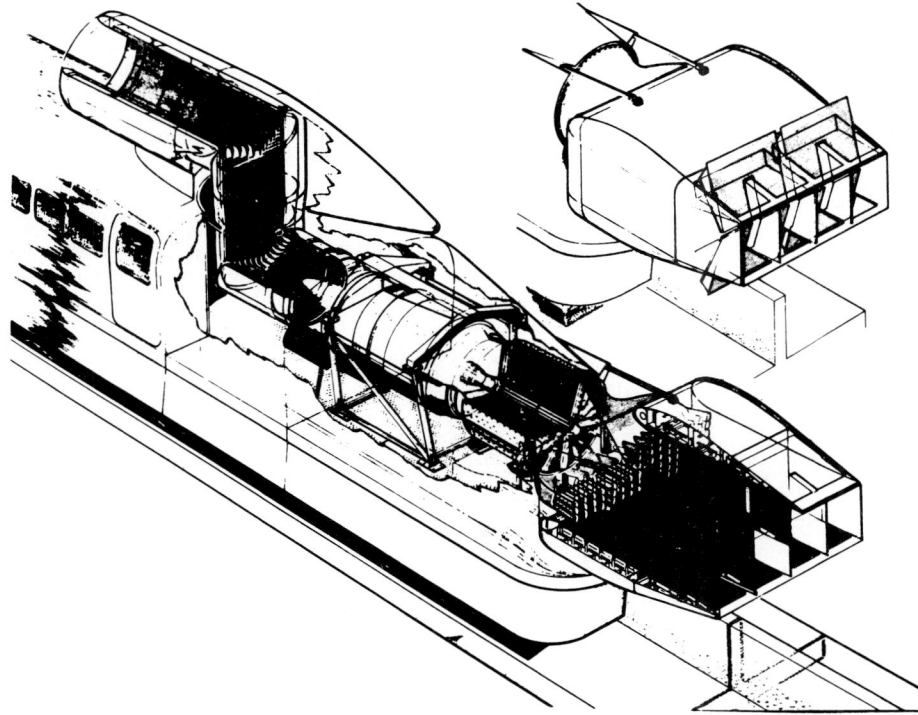

I-80HV Orleans Aérotrain showing air intake and high-dilution ejection system

SUBURBAN AÉROTRAIN
AÉROTRAIN S-44

The prototype 40- to 44-passenger suburban vehicle is equipped with a linear induction motor. The vehicle underwent trials at Gometz between 1969 and 1972, where its 3km (1·9 mile) test track ran parallel to that used by the Aérotrain 01 and 02 experimental vehicles. During its test programme the vehicle was operated at speeds up to 170km/h (105mph).

The power for the two axial lift fans is provided by a 525hp GM Chevrolet V8 car engine. Virtually silent operation is achieved since there is no noise of rolling wheels. No vibration is communicated to the track structure which can therefore be erected in urban areas without fear of any noise disturbing local communities, even if steel is used for the longer spans of the guideway.

This vehicle is equipped with an electrical linear motor developed by the Société Le Moteur Linéaire (Merlin & Gerin Group). It provides a thrust of 18,000N at 137km/h (85mph) and has been currently operated at speeds above 160km/h (100mph). Electric current is collected from the three-phase 1,000V powerline set alongside the track.

Braking performance is particularly efficient. During normal operation, braking is obtained either by dephasing the linear motor supply (or in the case of failure of this supply by feeding it with dc current from the battery), or by a hydraulic braking system equipped with friction pads which grip the vertical portion of the track.

The passenger cabin is divided into four 10-seat compartments, each provided with two doors. An additional half-compartment forward can accommodate four passengers seated on folding seats.

Automatic doors on both sides of each passenger compartment reduce stopping time. The coupling of several of these vehicles will be possible, but this should be necessary only at peak hours for heavy commuter traffic.

The seating arrangement is optional; each of the various layouts is optimised to provide the maximum possible space for passengers.

DIMENSIONS
Length: 14·4m (47ft)
Beam: 2·75m (9ft 4in)
Height: 3·1m (10ft 2in)
WEIGHTS
Loaded, linear motor: 11,500kg (25,000lb)
automotive version: 10,000kg (22,000lb)
PERFORMANCE
Cruising speed: 180km/h (113mph)

A lower speed system is being designed for urban lines with stations only ½ mile apart.

GUIDEWAY

In this programme the track is at ground level. The horizontal support is an asphalt carpet and the upright is an aluminium beam which is used for both guiding the vehicle and as an induction rail for the linear motor. A 3km (1·9 mile) long track has been constructed at the company's base at Gometz.

Operational suburban lines will generally be supported on pylons in order to leave the ground free. The use of an elevated track will reduce the construction time and avoid costly tunnelling on many sections of urban/suburban projects.

PROJECT STUDIES

Société de l'Aérotrain conducted detailed

Artist's impression of suburban Aérotrain

Prototype of 40- to 44-seat S-44

studies of a dozen projects. The technical and operational characteristics of the vehicles may substantially differ from those of the two prototypes, particularly as regards capacity and cruising speed.

The mathematical model, which has enabled the company to examine technico-economical optimisation procedures, an approach to operations, station design, and baggage handling, has produced data based on a number of projected situations. The two major fields which are being investigated are inter-city services and suburban links, mainly between city centres and airports.

Suburban links require, in some cases, a higher capacity than the one provided by the Gometz-type vehicle. Capacity can be increased by widening the vehicles, or coupling them, to provide an hourly capacity of around 10,000 passengers each way.

TRIDIM URBAN TRANSPORT SYSTEM

The Tridim system has been designed to solve the transportation problem in urban areas or suburbs where the distance between stations ranges from a few kilometres down to several hundred metres.

It is believed that the solution to this problem lies in an overhead transport system adapted to passenger flows ranging from a few thousand to 10-15,000 per hour and offering appreciable comfort, speed and frequency. To transport 6,000 passengers per hour, trains of three vehicles of 50 seats each every 90 seconds will be sufficient. If a larger module is adopted, 20,000 passengers can be carried hourly.

The Tridim system is designed to meet these requirements through the use of an air cushion for suspension and a flexible rack-and-pinion system, rubber-tyred traction-wheels, or linear induction motor for propulsion.

It consists of small-size, self-powered air cushion vehicles moving on a lightweight overhead track.

The capacity of each vehicle can be between four and 100 seats according to customer requirements. The required capacity can be obtained by varying the width and the length of the vehicles or grouping any number of vehicles to form a train. Since June 1973, a four to six seat prototype vehicle has been under test at a research centre of the French National Electricity Company (EDF) at Les Renardières, near Fontainebleau, on a 305m (1,000ft) track which includes a straight section, grades, curves and points.

Characteristics of this vehicle are as follows:
Loaded weight: 1·2 tons
Nominal propulsion power: 15kW
Lifting power: 4kW
Max speed: 50km/h (31mph)
Max slope: 20%
Power supply: 160V dc
Number of air cushions: 8
Air pressure: 900kg/m² (184·33lb/ft²)

The Tridim vehicle is built on a modular basis, with additional modules being added as required to provide the desired capacity.

In the case of the type VM 1 (designed for a specific client), the passengers are transported in modules measuring approximately 3 × 1·8m (10 × 6ft) and equipped with nine seats placed along the longitudinal walls. There is also room for a maximum of four standing passengers, which brings the rush-hour capacity to 13 passengers for each module, ie 52 per vehicle, 36 of whom are seated (the vehicle consists of four modules).

Propulsion and lift are obtained from electric

Three-phase powerline alongside track at ground level

energy collected from a 'third' rail (direct-current power supply).

The vehicle is guided by a low metal rail fixed on the track in line with the vehicle axis. This is the inverted-T track fundamental to the Aérotrain technique. Besides its guidance function, this rail carries the propulsion rack and keeps the vehicle retained on the track, which makes overturning impossible in the event of incident or abnormal operating conditions.

LIFT: The basic advantages of employing the air-cushion principle are: suspension of concentrated loads and shocks, hence possibility of a lightweight vehicle structure on the one hand,

and of the overhead track on the other; the absence of rolling noise and vibration; vehicle maintenance drastically reduced, and virtually non-existent for the track; and, finally, low total cost of the transport system due to the simplicity and the low weight of the track.

The air cushion system requires a power supply of only 4 to 5hp per supported metric ton. This is expected to be reduced to the order of 2hp per metric ton. The air cushion supply is operated by sound-insulated electric fans.

PROPULSION: In the case of the VM 1 the vehicle is propelled by a patented rack-and-pinion system. But alternative methods include

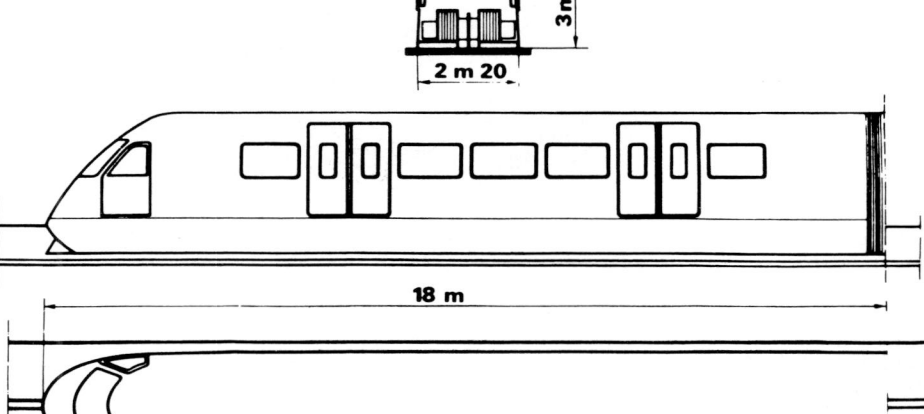

Unit of suburban Aérotrain

Tridim urban transport vehicle

Four- to six-seat Tridim

rubber-tyred traction wheels acting on the centre guidance rail or linear induction motor, according to requirements. The former consists of a dual rack fixed on the guiding rail and two pinions carried by the vehicles and driven by electric propulsion motors. It allows operation on tracks with steep slopes and maintains acceleration and braking performance in any weather including conditions of snow and ice.

The ability to climb steep slopes enables the stations to be built at street level or at the level of another transportation system for ease of transfer.

OVERHEAD TRACK: The system is intended primarily for an overhead track but it can also be used at ground level or as an underground system. In the case of an overhead track, the viaduct can be made of metal or reinforced concrete, depending on the line layout.

The line consists of pylons supporting beams of 20 to 30m (66 to 100ft) span carrying the guide-

way which has a width of about 2·23m (7ft 4in) for single track or 4·72m (15ft 6in) for dual track in the case of the VM 1 system. The track itself consists mainly of the guiding rail with its rack.

The absence of concentrated loads, either static or dynamic, allows the use of a light viaduct, which leads to lower costs.

As an example, with metal construction, a dual track viaduct weighs approximately 590kg/m (1,300lb/m) (VM 1).

VM 1 SPECIFICATION

The system can be adapted to client specification.

Capacity of the VM 1 is 52 passengers, 36 of whom are seated.

DIMENSIONS
Length: 16·26m (53ft 4in)
Width: 1·93m (6ft 4in)
Height: 2·59m (8ft 6in)

WEIGHTS
Empty: 5,900kg (13,000lb)

Loaded: 9,900kg (21,800lb)

PERFORMANCE
Nominal speed: 64-80km/h (40-50mph)
Max speed: 80-104km/h (50-65mph)
Average acceleration between 0 and 40mph: 0·12g
Emergency deceleration: 0·2g
Allowable slope at 40mph: 3%
Max allowable slope at reduced speed: 15% to 25%
Minimum turning radius: 24·4m (80ft) approx

MOTOR POWER
For propulsion: 150kW approx
For cushion: 35kW

OVERHEAD TRACK
Span: 20-30m (66-100ft) for normal span
Height above ground: 4·88m (16ft) on average
Width of track, single track: 2·23m (7ft 4in) dual track: 4·72m (15ft 4in)
Electrical power supply by conductor rail

GERMANY, FEDERAL REPUBLIC

TRANSRAPID INTERNATIONAL (TRI)

Steinsdorfstr 13, D-8000 Munich 22, Federal Republic of Germany
Telephone: (089) 23729 117
Telex: 529463 mbbes

In April 1974, it was announced that Krauss-Maffei (KM) and Messerschmitt-Bölkow-Blohm (MBB) were to develop jointly a high-speed transport system.

In June 1982, the joint venture group, known as the Arge Transrapid EMS, was expanded to include Thyssen Henschel Company, and renamed Transrapid International (TRI).

TRI's main objective is to advance development of the maglev train technology and to prepare and implement its introduction, particularly in other countries, through a variety of application studies.

The companies included in TRI have all been active in the area of rail vehicles, such as locomotives and passenger cars for both short- and long-distance traffic, and have contributed significantly to its development. All are pioneers of maglev train technology. Between 1971 and 1979 they individually and jointly constructed and tested successfully several systems with a total of six vehicles.

As members of the 'Konsortium Magnetbahn Transrapid', Krauss-Maffei, MBB and Thyssen Henschel, together with AEG-Telefunken, Brown, Boveri and Cie, Dyckerhoff & Widmann and Siemens, are engaged in building the Transrapid Test Facility in the Emsland region. This project is supported by the German Federal Ministry for Research and Technology. The trial runs of the Transrapid 06 began at the Emsland test facility in mid-1983, with speeds reaching 400km/h.

A feasibility study is also being undertaken for the application of a maglev system between Las Vegas and Los Angeles.

TRACK

The track for a rapid transit system based on the principle of magnetic suspension and guidance would consist of the supporting concrete pylons and beams, or steel girders, the ferromagnetic support and guidance rails, the secondary part of the linear motor and the power rails.

In order to ensure the safe operation of a rapid transit system, and yet not to endanger the environment by its operation, the track will be supported on pylons spaced approximately 24m (78ft) apart with the elevation (clearance) of the track being at least 4·5m (14ft 9in). This eliminates to a large extent the need for special structures at intersections with roads, rail tracks, etc.

A fast and reliable switching system for traffic diverging from and merging with the main line is

necessary for smooth and safe operation of a rapid transit system.

Experiments with an electromagnetic switch with no moving parts revealed that special devices were needed on board which added weight and increased aerodynamic drag, therefore a mechanical switch has been developed.

Rotary test track to study operational behaviour of synchronous linear machines (SLIM)

MBB's basic experimental craft

PRINCIPLE OF MAGNETIC LEVITATION

In the selected principle of magnetic attraction, the vehicles are supported and guided by controlled electromagnets along armature rails fastened to the guideway. Sensors continuously measure the air gap between the vehicle magnets and the armature rails (10 to 20mm). The data measured is transmitted to control units which control the attractive forces of the magnets and thus keep the vehicle hovering.

In addition to the development of the magnetic levitation and guidance system, vehicle development also includes other components, such as linear motor propulsion energy transfer, vehicle frame, braking, emergency gliding and safety systems. The design of cost-saving, elevated guideways and planning of the necessary stationary facilities, such as stations, power supply, etc are of equal significance for the overall system.

Knowledge and experience gained and substantiated through extensive testing on various test stands formed the basis for the construction of experimental vehicles and test tracks in Ottobrunn, München-Allach and Manching.

TEST STANDS

Static, dynamic and rotating magnet test stands were built for the purpose of defining and optimising magnets for the levitation and guidance system and various control techniques. Support force losses and braking forces on magnets as a result of eddy current effects at high speeds can be measured and power transmission methods tested on rotation test stands. Switching tests with magnetically levitated vehicles are performed on switch test stands. Linear motor test stands are used to determine thrust and lateral forces on single- and double-sided linear motors and to measure temperature, current and voltage.

BASIC VEHICLE

MBB began work on the vehicle and the test track in July 1970. In February 1971, the first suspension tests of the experimental vehicle took place in the test laboratory. In April 1971, the first test runs were made on MBB's special test track.

In May 1971, the experimental vehicle was presented to the public for the first time in the presence of the Federal Minister for Educational Science and the Federal Minister for Transportation.

It demonstrated the feasibility of magnetic suspension and guidance with linear motor propulsion, and provided information on those parameters not covered during simulation of the system, and development of the components.

Weighing 5·6 tonnes and with a length of 7m (23ft), it has an asynchronous linear motor with 200kW nominal power which is capable of accelerating the vehicle on the 700m (766yd) test track to a speed of 100km/h (62mph).

Four controlled suspension magnets and two guidance magnets on each side of the vehicle lift and guide it during operation with a nominal air gap of 14mm (0·5in) between the magnets and the rails.

TRANSRAPID 02 RESEARCH VEHICLE

In October 1971 Krauss-Maffei started operating an experimental 12m (39ft 4in) long vehicle on a 930m (1,017yd) test track. It reached a maximum speed of 164km/h (101·9mph). A novel power pick-up system ensures troublefree transmission of electric energy at high speeds. A secondary suspension system with pneumatic shock absorbers and vibration dampers constitutes the link between the vehicle superstructure and the hovering chassis.

Guideway and vehicle concepts provide realistic test data. The test results obtained so far have revealed that the system requirements can be fulfilled without difficulty.

TRACK
Length: 930m (1,017yds)
Radius of curvature: 800m (875yds)
EXPERIMENTAL VEHICLE
Length: 11·7m (38ft 4·5in)
Width: 2·9m (9ft 6in)
Height above track surface: 2·05m (6ft 8·75in)
Number of seats: 10
Weight: approx 11,000kg (24,250lb)
Payload: 2,000kg (4,409lb)
Design speed of vehicle: approx 350km/h (220mph)

Transrapid research vehicle in 02 configuration

PROPULSION BY LINEAR INDUCTION MOTOR
Thrust (transient): approx 32kN
Present vehicle speed (due to short track length): approx 160km/h (100mph)
Synchronous speed LIM at 50Hz: approx 180km/h (112mph)
SERVICE BRAKES
Brake retardation by LIM: approx 2·5m/s²
  by jaw brake: approx 8·5m/s²
  by friction brake: approx 8m/s²
ELECTROMAGNETIC SUPPORT AND GUIDANCE SYSTEM
Air gap: 10-25mm (0·5-1in)
POWER SUPPLY
Support and guidance system: Voltage 380V three-phase current, 50Hz
Power: 32kW

TRANSRAPID 03 RESEARCH VEHICLE

In October 1971, Krauss-Maffei started operating a dual-purpose test facility which allowed a comprehensive system comparison between magnetic cushion and air cushion techniques using the same vehicle specifications and the same track with identical operating conditions. Vehicles and track have been designed for a maximum speed of approximately 140km/h (87mph). The track length is 930m (1,017yds) allowing the attainment of a speed of about 160km/h (100mph), which has already been reached with the magnetic cushion vehicle. This

experimental system provided realistic information since it subjected the support, guidance and propulsion system to extreme loads during straight runs and cornering.

Transrapid 03 is the basic Transrapid 8-ton research vehicle adapted for tests as a tracked air cushion vehicle. The payload of two tons and overall dimensions are identical to those of the vehicle in its earlier configuration. The programme, which is supported by the Federal Ministry of Research and Technology, enables the TACV and maglev concepts to be compared under identical conditions for the first time.

Tests with air cushion support began at the end of 1972 and finished in 1973.

As a TACV, the vehicle is supported and guided by a total of 14 air cushion pads. Six, each with a cushion area of 3m² (32·29ft²), support the vehicle on its elevated concrete guideway, and eight, mounted in pairs, each of about 1m² (10·76ft²) cushion area, provide lateral guidance along the LIM reaction rail. The air cushion lift system is of plenum type and each pad has a rubber skirt. Cushion air is supplied by a two-stage compressor.

The vehicle is propelled by a French-made LIM system, which accelerates the vehicle to 145km/h (90mph) on its 930m (1,017yd) guideway.

Comparisons covered the following areas: vehicle dynamics; weight; load tolerances; vertical air gap tolerances; specific power requirements

Transrapid 03 research craft

for support and guidance; effects on the environment (noise level); reliability; life; reaction to weather influences; maximum speed; aerodynamic drag; investment, operating and maintenance costs.

Results of the comparison showed that magnetic levitation technology is superior.

TRACK
Length: 930m (1,017yds)
Radius of curvature: 800m (875yds)
EXPERIMENTAL VEHICLE
Length: 11·7m (38ft 4·5in)
Width: 2·9m (9ft 6in)
Height above track surface: 2·05m (6ft 8·5in)
Number of seats: 10
Weight: 9,600kg (21,200lb)
Design speed of vehicle: approx 140km/h (87mph)
PROPULSION BY LINEAR INDUCTION MOTOR
Thrust (transient): approx 2·9 Mp
Vehicle speed (due to short track length): approx 160km/h (100mph)
Synchronous speed LIM at 50Hz: approx 180km/h (112mph)
SERVICE BRAKES
Brake retardation by LIM: approx 2·3m/s²
    by jaw brake: approx 8·5m/s²
    by friction brake: approx 8m/s²
POWER SUPPLY
Support and guidance system: 380V three-phase current, 50Hz
Power: 235kW
LIM: voltage 1·7 kV three-phase current, 50 Hz
Output: 3MVA

MAGNET TEST VEHICLE

Operation of the magnet test vehicle started on the Ottobrunn test track in 1972. The vehicle consists of a platform supported and guided by wheels and accelerated by a hot water rocket.

It was used to test magnets and acceleration sensors at different speed levels up to 225km/h (140mph). The components were tested in conjunction with an instrumented test rail mounted in the guideway.
TECHNICAL DATA
Vehicle length: 3·6m (11ft 9·75in)

KOMET COMPONENT TEST VEHICLE

Komet was an unmanned, magnetically levitated and guided vehicle with a mounting rack for testing components at speeds up to 400 km/h. This mounting rack allowed the installation of magnets, linear motors and power pick-ups of various designs, which could be tested in combination with instrumented rails, which could also be easily replaced. The test data was transmitted to a fixed receiving station via a telemetry system. The Komet was accelerated by a thrust sled with up to six hot water rockets to achieve the desired high speeds on only 1,300m (4,265ft) length of test track. Komet achieved a world speed record for maglev vehicles of 401·3km/h (249·1mph) on its guideway in February 1976.

Technical data can be found in *Jane's Surface Skimmers 1983* and earlier editions.

TRANSRAPID 04

The Transrapid 04 was one of the largest passenger-carrying magnetically levitated and LIM-propelled experimental vehicles.

The elevated guideway, with curves of different radii, represented a further development on the way to future applications. Different design principles and materials, such as concrete and steel, were used to test various alternatives. For the first time, a LIM reaction rail was mounted horizontally on the guideway beam.

The 2,400m (1·5mile) test track allowed the testing of different system components under realistic conditions and at higher speeds. The results of the test programme are being employed as the basis for the definition of future test vehicles and large-scale test facilities.
TECHNICAL DATA
Vehicle
    length: 15m (49ft 2·5in)
    width: 3·4m (11ft 2in)
    height: 2·8m (9ft 2in)

Magnet test vehicle

Komet

Transrapid 04

weight: 16,500kg (36,376lb)
max speed: 250km/h (155mph)
propulsion: asynchronous linear motor
max thrust: 50,000N
Guideway
    track gauge: 3·2m (10ft 6in)
    length: 2,400m (1·5 miles)
    radii of curvature: 800-3,100m (875-3,390yds)
    span: 17-20m (55ft 8in-65ft 7in)
    max guideway inclination: ±11 degrees

TRANSRAPID 05

Transrapid-EMS (Krauss-Maffei and Messerschmitt-Bölkow-Blohm) and Thyssen

Henschel Company were awarded a contract from the German Federal Ministry of Research and Technology to build a demonstration facility for a magnetically-levitated transport system for the International Transport Fair, IVA 79, in Hamburg. During the Fair the vehicle carried more than 40,000 visitors. This was the first limited-scale public demonstration of a magnetically-levitated vehicle.

Transrapid-EMS had the responsibility for building the 26-metre (85·3-foot) long, two-section vehicle which seats 68 passengers. This was the fifth maglev vehicle to be constructed by the Krauss-Maffei, MBB, and Transrapid-EMS consortium. The levitation and guidance system

Transrapid 05

has four bogies with individually spring-suspended electromagnets using a decentral, hierarchical control system.

A synchronous, iron-backed linear long stator motor serves as propulsion unit. With this version of a linear motor the primary coils are mounted in the track while the levitation magnets serve as its secondary.

Within the joint programme, Thyssen Henschel and the Braunschweig Technical University are responsible for the guideway (length approximately 1,000m), the track-mounted primary of the motor and other stationary installations. Sponsored and financed by the Federal Ministry of Research and Technology, the chief aim of the project is to demonstrate to a broad public the advanced state of development of the high-speed maglev system in West Germany.

TECHNICAL DATA
Train: 2 sections
Length: 26m (85ft 3in)
Width: 3·1m (10ft 2in)
Height: 2·7m (8ft 10in)
Capacity: 68 passengers
Total weight: 36 tonnes
Max speed: 80km/h (50mph)
Propulsion: synchronous linear long stator motor

TRANSRAPID 06

The Federal Ministry of Research and Technology is constructing a 31km (19·25mile) test track in the Emsland district in northern Germany; 20·5km have so far been completed. The facility is being constructed in several stages and tests with the Transrapid 06 began in summer 1983.

Transrapid 06 is equipped with an electromagnetic levitation and guide system, the levitation system being a part of the synchronous long-stator propulsion. In size, configuration, interior arrangements and performance the vehicle approximates the actual requirements of an inter-city high-speed system.

The vehicle comprises two mechanically and electrically coupled units and is designed aerodynamically for a maximum speed of about 400km/h (250mph).

Built in sandwiched structure, the body is supported by secondary springs over four maglev bogies, which in turn embody 32 levitation magnets and 28 guide magnets. Suspension and supply systems, mechanical brakes and sliding skis are also incorporated.

Highly reliable levitation is ensured by the mechanical attachment of the magnet feed with two self-sufficient battery and distributing systems.

On-board energy requirements of about 400kW are transmitted without contact with the vehicle via linear generators, temporary storage being supplied by two batteries.

Propulsive thrust and braking are supplied by a synchronous linear motor, the moving magnetic feed being generated in the levitating rails of the guideway. The magnetic field of the levitating magnets also serves as the excitation field employing the long stator principle.

In this type of propulsion the inverters required for the voltage and frequency control are housed in stationary sub-stations, obviating the need for them to be carried aboard the vehicle.
CONTROLS: System controls and monitors the main components, depending on the selected mode of operation: automatic, semi-automatic or manual. It also maintains communication with the driving position, ensuring that the vehicle does not exceed its design performance and contributes to the data acquisition system.
TECHNICAL DATA
Length: 54m (176ft 5in)
Width: 3·7m (12ft)
Height, outer/inner: 3·8/2·2m (12ft 6in/7ft 3in)
Number of sections: 2
Seats: 192
Operating weight: 122 tonnes
Max thrust: 86kN
Max acceleration: 0·8m/s^2
Nominal speed: 300km/h (186mph)

Section of Emsland concrete guideway

Transrapid 06 levitation bogie undergoing payload tests

Transrapid 06 unit with levitation bogie at Emsland test facility

Transrapid 06 cabin interior

Max speed: 400km/h (250mph)
Levitation system: controlled electromagnets
Guiding system: controlled electromagnets
Propulsion: electric long-stator linear motor with
levitating magnets as exciting part
Braking: electrically with linear motor/mechanical emergency brake
Energy transfer: electric linear generator with
windings in the levitation magnet

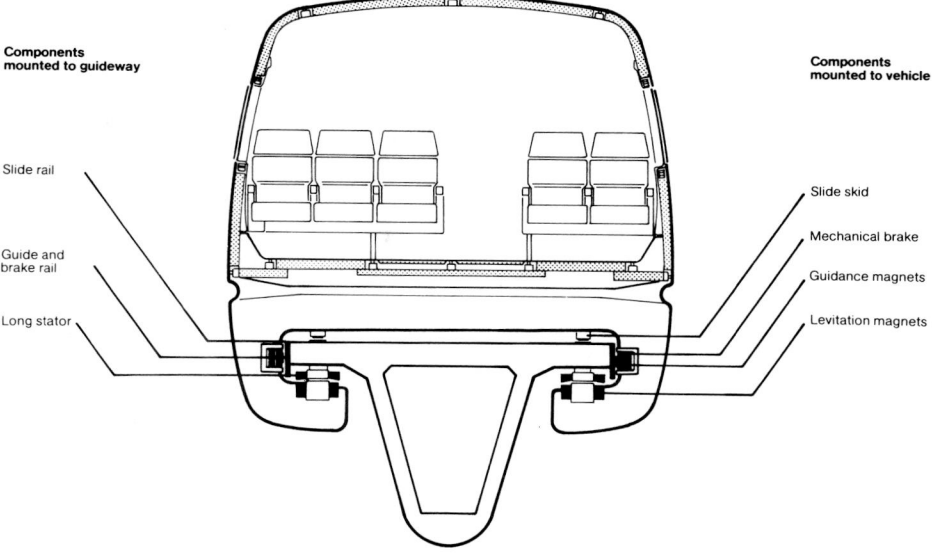

Transrapid 06 cross section

JAPAN

JAPAN AIR LINES (JAL)

HSST Development Department, Engineering and Maintenance, Japan Air Lines Maintenance Center Building, 9-1 Haneda Kuko 1 Chome, Ohta-ku, Tokyo 144, Japan
Telephone: Tokyo (03) 747-2295
Officials:
Mitsuo Kitamoto, *General Manager, HSST Development Department, Engineering and Maintenance*

Japan Air Lines has completed a number of successful test runs with manned and unmanned test vehicles which are levitated by electromagnetic force and powered by linear induction motors. The vehicle, known as the High Speed Surface Transport (HSST), is being developed to provide air travellers with rapid ground transport between cities and airports. Japan's first commercially-operated HSST could carry 400 passengers, plus their luggage, the 60km (40 miles) between Tokyo and Tokyo International Airport at Narita in 14 minutes.

HSST DEVELOPMENT
Stage 1 (1973-75): Basic studies and bench tests of components for HSST-01 test vehicle.
Stage 2 (1976): Low-speed tests initiated on 189m track to obtain information on linear induction motors and electromagnets.
Stage 3 (1977-79): Testing of electromagnets and linear induction motors at higher speeds on 1,300m track.
Stage 4 (1977-79): Completion of HSST-02 and start of tests with this vehicle.
The test track was then extended to 1,600m (5,249ft) and two curved tracks were added (radii 280m (918ft) and 2,000m (6,560ft)). High-speed runs were repeated up and down the track without any problems.
Stage 5 (1982-): Design and manufacture of the HSST-03, which was due to be demonstrated at the Expo '85 world science exhibition at Tsukuba, Ibaragi prefecture, Japan in 1985.

HSST LEVITATION AND PROPULSION
The HSST uses the principle of electromagnetic levitation with onboard magnets which are prevented from coming into contact with the track by an electronic sensing device that maintains the gap between the magnet and the rail at 10mm (0·39in).
Loss of wayside power is overcome by the use of onboard batteries which in an emergency would provide levitation for several minutes while the vehicle gradually touched down on the rails on its emergency sliding shoes.
Propulsion is by a linear induction motor that produces a propelling force without any form of

link between the rails and the vehicle. This can produce speeds of up to 300km/h (186mph). No totally new technology is required in the development of the HSST since all the components in the system have been proved in principle. The track is designed to avoid the deep shadow normally associated with the areas below conventional roads or railways.

HSST-01
The HSST-01 test vehicle is the first test vehicle of its kind to be designed and built by JAL

engineers. Built at the company's engineering centre at Haneda airport, Tokyo, it has been tested at a special site at Higashi-Ogishima, Kawasaki. Modifications during its development included fitting wings to increase its aerodynamic stability at high speeds.
Although operating on a relatively short track only 1·3km (now extended to 1·6km) in length, the vehicle has achieved a speed of 307·8km/h (191·25mph) with the assistance of booster rockets. Highest speed attained without rocket assistance is 220·6km/h (137mph). On tracks long

HSST track

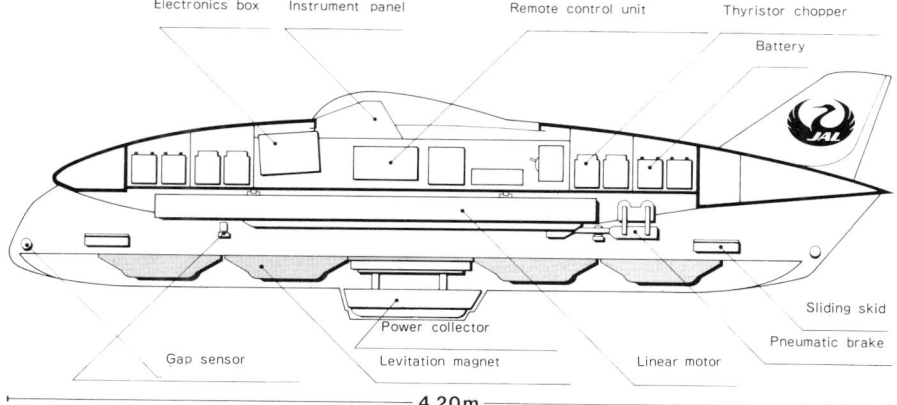

General arrangement of HSST-01 test vehicle

enough for the vehicle to be braked safely, speeds of around 300km/h (186mph) should be attainable without booster rockets. Total distance recorded on test runs amounted to 1,519km (944 miles) (HSST-01) and 3,802km (2,363 miles) (HSST-02) by the end of March 1981.

LEVITATION SYSTEM: Eight electromagnets, four on each side, attached to the 'wrap around' sections of the bodywork. Onboard batteries supply 150V dc for levitation.

PROPULSION SYSTEM: Asynchronous single-sided, short stator linear induction motor onboard and a horizontal aluminium reaction plate in the middle of the track. Power from the motor is picked up from each of three power rails (which run alongside the track) by carbon shoes on the vehicle's power collector.

Max thrust: 340kg (750lb)
Power source: three-phase variable voltage and variable frequency
Max power: 200kVA
Voltage: 0-600V
Frequency: 0-350Hz
DIMENSIONS
Length overall: 4·2m (13ft 9in)
Width: 2·6m (8ft 6in)
Height: 1·1m (3ft 7in)
WEIGHTS
Empty: 1,000kg (2,204lb)
PERFORMANCE
300km/h (186mph) on a 1·3km (1,421 yards) track

HSST-02

JAL's second test vehicle was designed to operate at speeds up to 100km/h (62mph) on a 1·6km (1,750yd) track. Its primary uses are to gather design data and assess the ride quality of vehicles of this type. Seats are provided for up to eight passengers. The body is of semi-monocoque light alloy construction. Secondary suspension is provided between the body shell and the electromagnets of the levitation system. HSST-02 has been operating since May 1978.

LEVITATION SYSTEM: Basically the same as that for the HSST-01. Ac electric power supply for the linear induction motor is rectified to 120V dc for levitation by inboard rectifier. The power rails and power collectors are basically the same as those for HSST-01.

PROPULSION SYSTEM: A single-sided short stator linear induction motor is installed.

Max thrust: 300kg (661lb)
Power source: three-phase variable voltage and variable frequency

HSST-01

HSST-02

HSST-03

Max power: 200kVA
Voltage: 0-600V
Frequency: 0-120Hz

HSST-03

JAL's HSST-03 is designed to operate at about 30km/h on a 400m track in the grounds of the Tsukuba Expo '85 world science exhibition. The maximum speed has been limited by the short track length. The primary purpose of the HSST-03 is to demonstrate the excellent ride quality of this system of transport.

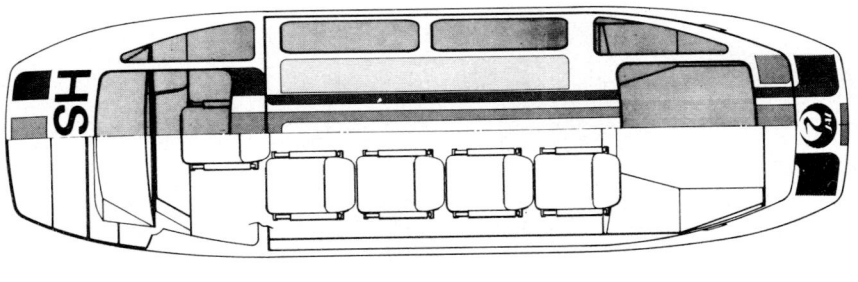

|← 6.84m →|

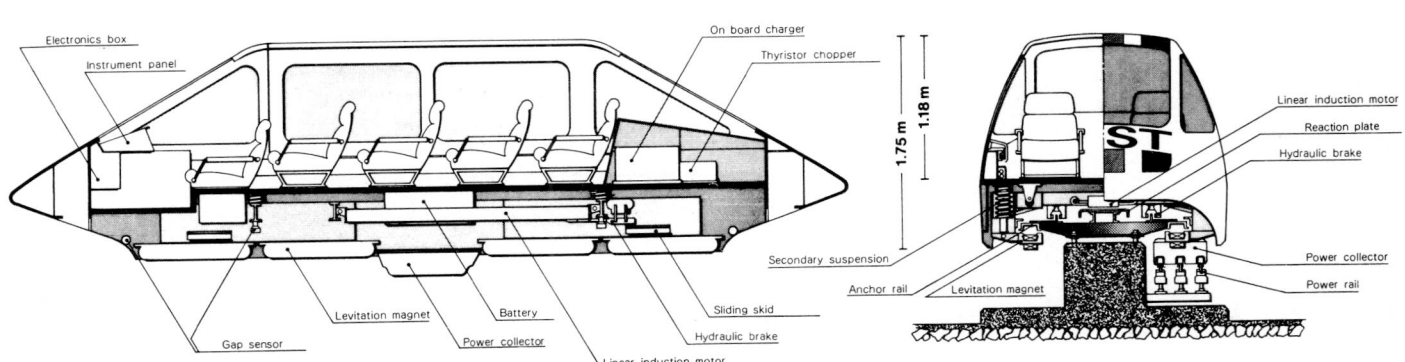

Electronics box
Instrument panel
On board charger
Thyristor chopper
1·75 m
1·18 m
Linear induction motor
Reaction plate
Hydraulic brake
ST
Secondary suspension
Anchor rail
Levitation magnet
Power collector
Power rail
Gap sensor
Levitation magnet
Battery
Power collector
Linear induction motor
Sliding skid
Hydraulic brake

External view and seating arrangements of HSST-02

An important feature of this vehicle is its modular maglev arrangement. Six modules are attached to the underside symmetrically in two rows, as seen in the accompanying three-view drawing. Each module incorporates four electromagnets for levitation and guidance, one linear induction motor for propulsion, a mechanical brake system and a suspension structure.

The suspension structure connects the body shell with the levitation modules. It dampens the motions of each module relative to the vehicle body, but permits a limited degree of freedom for vertical, lateral, pitching and yawing motion.

LEVITATION AND GUIDANCE: Similar to HSST-02.
Power source: 210V dc

PROPULSION: Similar to HSST-02
Max thrust: 1,020kg
Power source: Three-phase variable voltage and variable frequency
Max power: 400kVA
Voltage: 0-550V
Frequency: 0-70Hz
VEHICLE
Construction: Semi-monocoque aluminium structure
Suspension: Air system
Length: 13·8m
Width: 2·95m
Height: 3m
Accommodation: 44 passenger and two crew seats
WEIGHT
(without passengers): 12 tonnes
(with passengers): 15 tonnes
PERFORMANCE
Operating speed: about 30km/h
Max speed: 60km/h

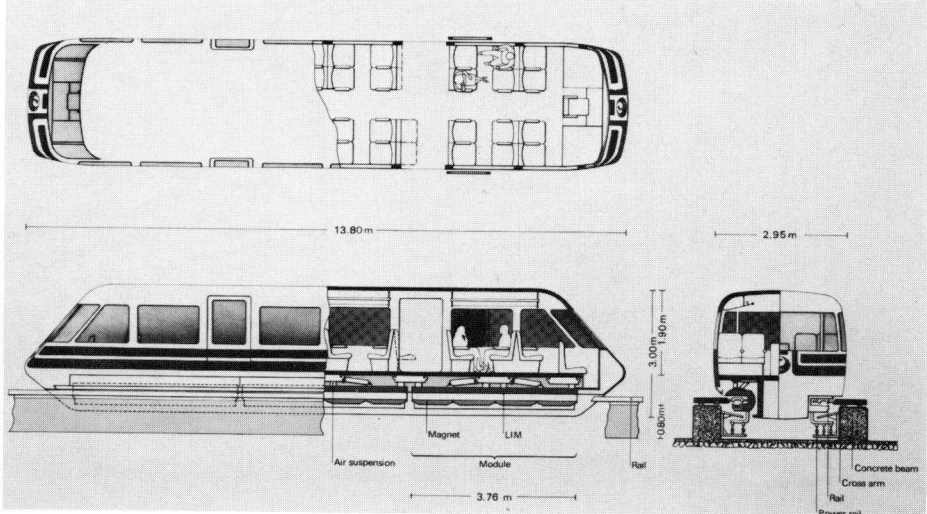

General arrangement of HSST-03

Likely appearance of HSST in commercial operation

COMMERCIAL HSST

JAL's proposed commercial HSST, designed to provide air travellers with fast ground transport between cities and outlying airports, will have a body shape resembling the fuselage of the Douglas DC-8 jet airliner with similar interior styling. The minimum size train would comprise two streamlined end vehicles, each seating 112 passengers. Standard 'mid-train' or middle vehicles, each seating 120 passengers, would be added according to passenger load demand.

Cruising speed would be about 300km/h (186mph) and the standard acceleration 0·1g, approximately the same as a standard electric train. Power used at cruising speed would be in the region of 5kW per passenger. Levitation and propulsion arrangements would be the same as those for the HSST-01.

DIMENSIONS
Length, streamlined end vehicle: 21·8m (71ft 6in)
    standard middle vehicle: 18·2m (59ft 9in)
Width: 3·8m (12ft 6in)
Height: 3·2m (10ft 6in)
Seats, streamlined end vehicle: 112
    standard middle vehicle: 120

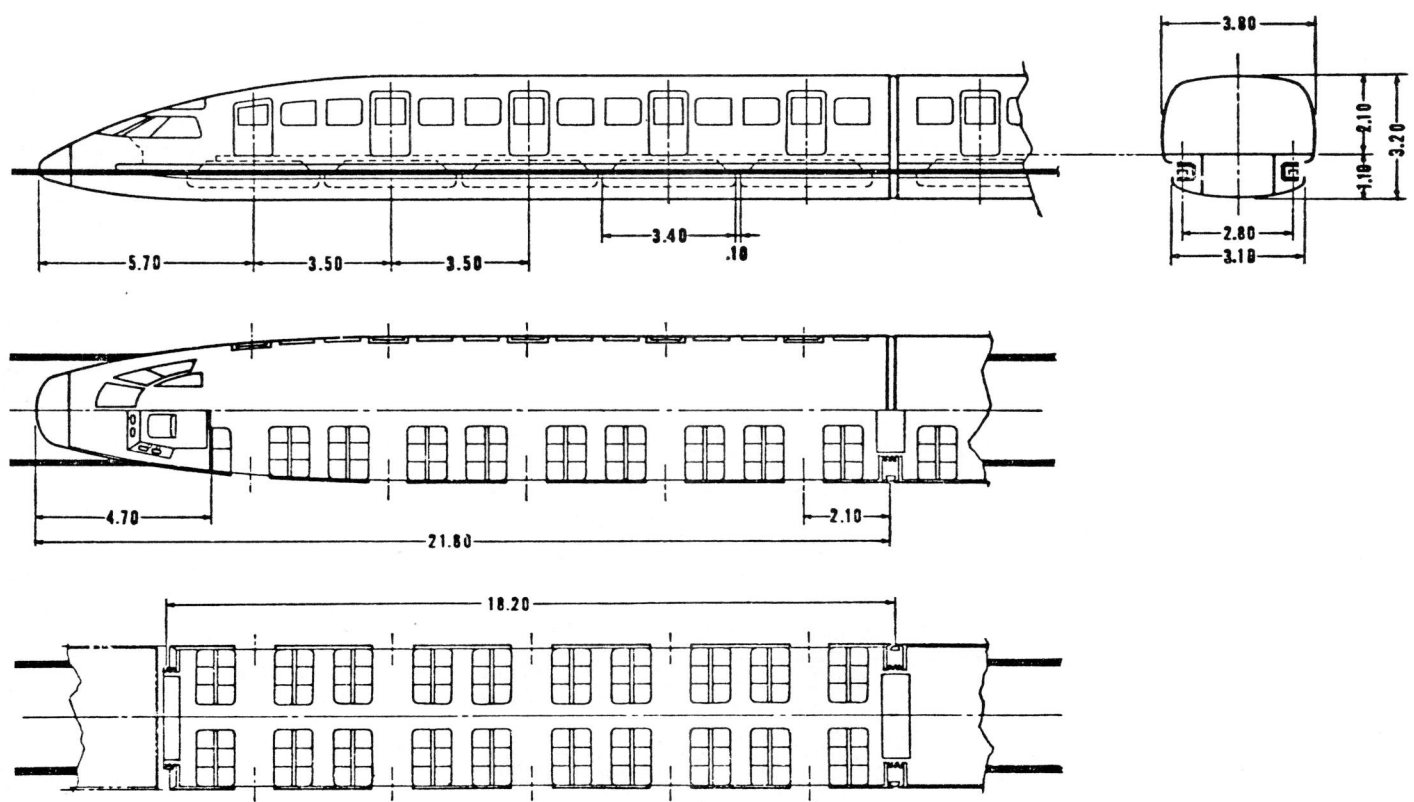

Commercial HSST concept

UNION OF SOVIET·SOCIALIST REPUBLICS

INSTITUTE OF DIESEL LOCOMOTIVE ENGINEERING, MOSCOW

The design of tracked skimmers started in Moscow during the five-year plan period 1971-75. Professor Alexander Zolotarsky announced in May 1972 that the technical and economic assessment of TACV systems was being undertaken at the Institute of Diesel Locomotive Engineering at its research establishment near Moscow.

It appeared from his statement that the first vehicles were to be powered by gas turbines and would operate on concrete tracks. Construction of prototype vehicles capable of speeds in excess of 300km/h (186mph) was due to start 'in the nearest future'. Professor Zolotarsky foresaw the use of TACVs to link densely populated industrial centres and resort areas where conventional railways are usually overloaded. They could also be operated successfully in the marshy areas of Siberia and in the North, as well as in permafrost areas.

Research undertaken jointly by the VNII Wagonbuilders, the Design Bureau for Aviation Research of AS Yakovlev and the Kalinin Wagon Factory led to the construction of a high-speed, jet-propelled research locomotive, the VNIIVOS-KOROST.

Thrust for the vehicle, which was designed to travel on wheels on a conventional track at speeds up to 250km/h (155mph), was provided by two Ivchenko AI-25 turbofans of the type employed on the Yak-40 airliner and normally rated at 1,500kg (3,300lb st). These are sited above the cabin of the locomotive.

Data gathered from the Korost was employed in the design of primary and secondary suspensions systems, magnetic rail disc and air brakes and other features.

Full-scale facilities for research into trains powered by linear induction motors have also been provided at a new transport research centre, a few miles from Kiev, capital of the Ukraine. It is intended to make a thorough investigation of the possibilities opened up by modern technology, including propulsion systems and original methods of suspension including air and magnetic cushions.

In 1982, it was announced that work was nearing completion on the first section of a proving ground for linear electric motors. It includes a stretch of experimental track 2km (1·25 miles) long.

One of the aims of the Soviet railway authority is to provide maglev trains capable of speeds of 300 to 500km/h (186 to 310mph) suitable for the rapid transport of long-distance, commuter and airport services.

Impression of Soviet maglev vehicle

In 'Young Technician', March 1979, reference was made to the Soviet maglev system as follows:

The magnetic suspension arrangement is relatively simple. The track is laid with magnetic slats. Permanent magnets of the same polarity are also fixed to the base of the carriage. The repellent faces of the line magnets keep the carriage in suspension, creating a gap between it and the slats of about 1 to 1·5cm. The motor in this transport system is also unusual.

A traditional electric alternating motor has a stator—a steel ring with windings. In this maglev system it is effectively cut in half and unwound, with the stator conductors laid out on the bottom of the carriage. The rotor is an aluminium slat placed along the axis of the track. The name 'rotor' is in this instance a matter of convention; it does not move, and is generally called the 'reactive rail'. The working principle of a linear electric motor is essentially the same as in a traditional one: an electric current taken up by a special 'shoe' with three contact conductor wires parallel to the track supplies energy to the stator. A magnetic wave begins to run along the conductors, bringing vertical currents to the reactive rail. The complementary action of the rotor and stator induce magnetic forces which impel the carriage along the track. Electrical energy is directly converted into translational movement. The magnetic suspension and linear motor system is simple, reliable and silent in operation because there are no moving parts. Nevertheless, wheels are fitted to the prototype.

This is because the permanent magnetic suspension system does not have a lateral carriage stabilisation system. At bends in the track or in high cross-winds the coach lacks directional control. For this reason the first experimental model has rollers which transfer lateral forces into channels in the track. The rollers only fulfil an auxiliary function and do not limit the speed (up to 100km/h). The permanent magnets with which the complete track must be "paved" are suitable for laboratory conditions. In the case of the experimental track the suspension principle is a little different, being electromagnetic.

An operational passenger-carrying track will be mounted on pylons, which will allow the track to be constructed across roads without impeding road traffic. On both sides of the supports will be skegs which will run along the complete length of the track. Two strips of steel will be attached to the skegs. The carriage itself will carry a powerful electro-magnetic suspension system. The desired air gap and carriage stabilisation both in the vertical and horizontal planes will be provided by automatic current regulators supplying the electromagnets.

The attraction forces to the steel strips will be generated in the same manner. Movement along the track will be effected by a linear electric motor.

The first section of the Soviet maglev railway will come into operation during the current five year plan.

Soviet maglev prototype

NOVOCHERKASSK LOCOMOTIVE TECHNICAL INSTITUTE

The Novocherkassk Locomotive Technical Institute is one of the main centres for the design of high-speed ground transport systems in the USSR.

A model of a maglev system has been constructed in a large hangar with a 30m (99ft) track. A 40kW motor propels a magnetically-levitated and propelled model train at speeds in excess of 48·3km/h (30mph). The model is automatically held at a constant gap of 15mm (0·59in) above the track. In August 1983 it was reported that the Novocherkassk Electric Locomotive Works had designed a 3-tonne maglev vehicle, known as the 'magneto plane'.

On the basis of the tests now being made, it is hoped to provide data for the design of a 40-tonne train, carrying 100 passengers at 500km/h.

UNITED STATES OF AMERICA

BERTELSEN INC

Head Office: 9999 Roosevelt Road, Westchester, Illinois 60153, USA
Telephone: (312) 681 5606
Works: 113 Commercial Street, Neponset, Illinois 61345, USA

Dr William R Bertelsen, Director of Research, Bertelsen Inc, has proposed the use of a vehicle based on the twin-gimbal Aeromobile 13 for a tracked skimmer system. It is described in US Patent No 3,845,716 issued in November 1974.

Dr Bertelsen suggested that the system, based on the use of ACVs in simple, graded earth grooves, would be ideal for mass transport in developing countries where no large investments have been made in roads, railways or airlines. The fuel can be petroleum in oil-rich areas or hydrogen in depleted or polluted areas. Whereas in densely populated countries new rights of way will inevitably be elevated or underground, there should be little difficulty in obtaining rights for the guideways in developing countries. In large countries with relatively empty interiors, the low-cost surface groove will be ideal.

Current or abandoned railway rights-of-way can be used for the Bertelsen Aeromobile-Aeroduct system, since rail gradients are acceptable to the Aeromobile. Hills can be climbed by the use of steps on which the vehicle is on the level or slightly inclined uphill most of the time. It climbs simply by lifting its mass in ground effect up each step, each of which would be slightly lower than its skirt height. Relatively low propulsive power is required to climb a hill in this manner and no increase in lift power is necessary.

The Aeromobile vehicles employed for the system would be fully automated. Journey data would be fed into an onboard mini-computer and the vehicles would follow the route through signals emitted at junction points. A tape could guide the car across the country with a sleeping or reading driver. Dr Bertelsen states that the car would move from low- to high-speed lanes automatically and remain in high-speed lanes until the signals at junctions told it to move down into a slower lane before turning off. This process would be repeated automatically until the car left the automatic guideway system.

AERODUCT SYSTEM

The air cushion vehicle, so unquestionably superior for off-road and amphibious transport of heavy loads, can also carry loads, as do trucks and trains, on rights-of-way. However, the right-of-way for the ACV will be different. It should be wider due to modern loads and because the length and width of the base of the vehicle determines the lift area and the total ACV hauling capacity. The ACV right-of-way should be semi-circular in cross section or a cylindrical tube to provide guidance and yaw stabilisation of the frictionless craft. There should be steps up and down grades to facilitate grade climbing and descent by frictionless but massive craft.

The system has the attributes of being frictionless; it has a high speed; provides a very soft, shockless, self-damped ride; offers a heavy load carrying capacity; and a low ground pressure which renders it amphibious.

Because the ACV is frictionless, a cylindrical groove provides perfect guidance for high speed translation longitudinally down the track. It also allows the craft to centrifugate up the wall on a curve, which obviates side forces on passengers or loads.

The low ground pressure makes the right-of-way very inexpensive to build and maintain. Whether of sodded or lightly paved earth, ploughed, ice-coated snow or in the form of a sheet metal tube or groove, all are far less expensive than the high pressure of conventional roads or railways (30 to 100psi in tyres, up to 10,000psi on rails).

The groove (or tube) can be located on, along, next to, above, or below existing roads or rails, requiring no further acquisition, and will not interfere with existing road drainage. The new ACV modality can be compatible with all existing surface transport. It will cost far less per mile to build and maintain than its conventional counterpart.

ACVs and Aeroducts can be adapted to massive loads of 44·7 tonnes (100,000lb) or more per vehicle, and adaptation of the vehicle beds to flat surface for loading, unloading, storing, staging,

servicing, etc, is also possible. The loaded 'trailers' may be moved singly or in trains down the hollow path at high speed. Tractors or pushers for these loads would have similar adaptability to flat or semi-cylindrical surfaces. The tractors would probably be powered by turbine-driven gimbal fans, capable of full manoeuvrability with 100 per cent of propulsive force available for forward thrust, braking, lateral force, or for steering torque. Only a gimbal type of handling vehicle or 'tug' could manage the 44·7-tonne (100,000lb) ACVs on 'flat' surfaces and against winds and gusts. Crawlers or tyre wheel tractors could attempt the flat surface handling of the massive carriers, but experience shows that paving becomes necessary for repeated traverse of ground by any land vehicle. However, grass is often adequate for ACVs. The air cushion 'tug' will be irreplaceable in the sodded or otherwise lightly prepared mileages of grooves between important shipping centres, with, for example, grain elevators, mines, stockyards, factories, cities, forests, oil and gas fields.

The system is designed to be all-inclusive, providing every type of transport need, from personal transit, 'mass' transit, taxis, police, fire and emergency service, mail, freight, parcel, grocery and milk delivery to refuse collection.

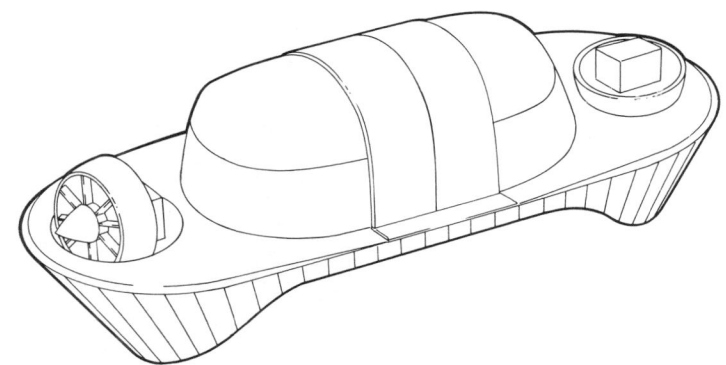

Tracked ACV based on Aeromobile 13

Impression of tracked ACV based on Aeromobile 13

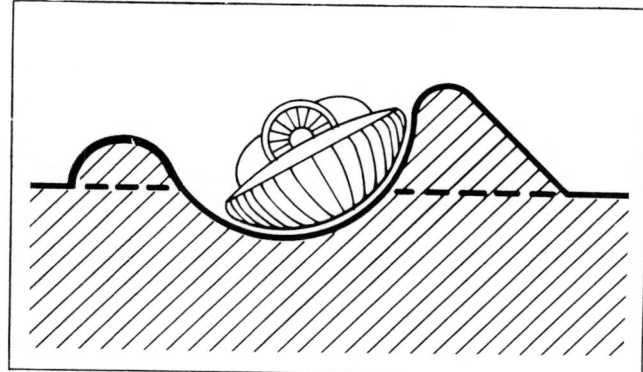

Aeromobile shown in graded groove at speed in left curve

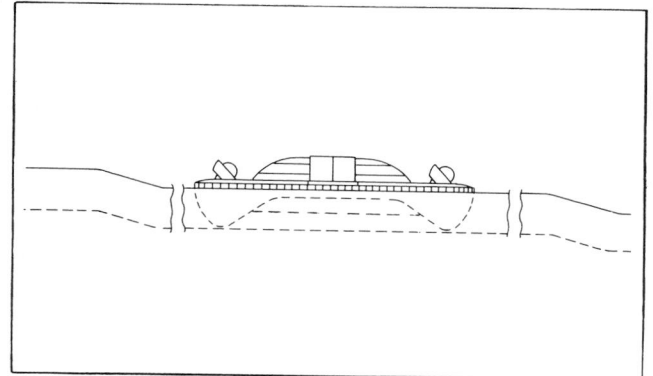

Side view, stepped aeroduct for grade climb and descent

BOLIVIA

HELMUT KOCK

4125 West Point Loma Blvd, Apartment 209,
San Diego, California 92110, USA
Telephone: (619) 224 6657

Helmut Kock, designer of the Honald Albatross hydrofoil, which operated New York's first
commercial hydrofoil service, and former chief
engineer of International Hydrolines Inc, has
designed and built a 15·27m (50ft) hydrofoil
ferry for Crillon Tours of La Paz, Bolivia. The
craft, the *Bolivia Arrow*, was built during 1976 at
Huatajata, on the shore of Lake Titicaca
(3,700m; 12,000ft) and entered service in February 1977.

All materials, equipment, engines, tools and
machinery were imported from the USA. The
entire craft is of welded aluminium and was built
by Helmut Kock with the aid of a few Bolivian
Indians who, in order to undertake the work,
were taught how to use modern hand and electric
tools and automatic welding techniques.

He has been responsible for modifying the
three Sea World hydrofoils to improve their load
capacity and performance.

BOLIVIA ARROW

Crillon Tours Ltd, La Paz, Bolivia, has operated four of Helmut Kock's 20-seat Albatross
craft on tourist routes across Lake Titicaca since
the late 1960s. The need to cope with increasing
tourist traffic and to provide a craft capable of
crossing the full length of the lake led to a decision by Darius Morgan, Crillon's chief executive,
to build a craft tailored to the company's
requirements on the shore of the lake. Construction of the *Bolivia Arrow* began in December
1975 and it was launched in September 1976.
The craft entered service in February 1977. It is
designed for medium range fast ferry services on
rivers, bays, lakes and sounds.
FOILS: Surface-piercing trapeze foil system with
'W' configuration pitch stability subfoil. Welded
aluminium construction designed by Helmut
Kock, US patent no 3, 651, 775.
POWER PLANT: Twin Cummins VT8-370
diesels, each developing 350shp at sea level and
oversize to compensate for loss of power due to
altitude. Each engine drives its own propeller via
an inclined shaft. Engine room is amidships, after
the third row of seats.
ACCOMMODATION: Crew comprises a cap-
tain, deckhand and a tourist guide. The captain is
accommodated forward in a raised wheelhouse.
His seat is on the hull centreline with the wheel,
engine controls and main instrumentation in
front. Passengers are accommodated in a single
saloon with seats for 40. Seats are arranged in ten
rows of two abreast, separated by a central aisle.
A washbasin/WC unit is provided and also a lug-
gage compartment. All void spaces are filled with
polyurethane foam.
DIMENSIONS
Length overall: 15·24m (50ft)
Hull beam: 3·55m (11ft 8in)
Width across foils: 5·79m (19ft)
Draft, hullborne: 2·28m (7ft 6in)
WEIGHTS
Displacement fully loaded: 14 tons
PERFORMANCE
Cruising speed: 32 knots

Bolivia Arrow

Bolivia Arrow showing foil system

Sea World II

CANADA

WATER SPYDER MARINE LIMITED

157 Richard Clark Drive, Downsview, Ontario
M3M 1V6, Canada
Telephone: (416) 244 5404
Officials:
J F Lstiburek, *President*
A Lstiburek, *Vice President*
J F Lstiburek, *Designer*

Water Spyder Marine Limited is a wholly-owned Canadian company operating under charter issued by the Government of the Province of Ontario. It produces two fibreglass-hulled sports hydrofoils which are available ready-built or in kit form.

WATER SPYDER 2-B

The Water Spyder 2-B is a two-seat sports hydrofoil powered by a long-shaft outboard of 20 to 35hp.
FOILS: The foil system comprises a split W-type surface-piercing main foil supporting 98 per cent of the load and an adjustable outrigged trim tab which supports the remaining 2 per cent.
HULL: This is a two-piece (deck and hull) moulded fibreglass structure and incorporates buoyancy chambers. Standard fittings include a

curved Perspex windshield and regulation running lights, fore and aft.
ACCOMMODATION: The craft seats two. The trim tab assembly is adjustable from inside the cockpit.
POWER PLANT: Any suitable outboard engine of 20 to 35hp (Mercury 200L or 350L Chrysler Evinrude) with long-shaft extension.
CONTROLS: Controls include steering wheel with adjustable friction damper and trim tab control.
DIMENSIONS
Length overall, hull: 3·6m (12ft)
Beam overall, foils retracted: 1·6m (5ft 4in)
 foils extended: 2·2m (7ft 4in)
WEIGHTS
Empty: 99·7kg (220lb)
PERFORMANCE
Max speed: up to 64km/h (40mph)
Max permissible wave height in foilborne mode: 457·2mm (1ft 6in)
Turning radius at cruising speed: 3m (10ft) approximately
PRICE: Standard craft and terms of payment, US $4,500 (1983); terms, cash. Delivery, three weeks from date of order, fob Toronto.

WATER SPYDER 6-A

An enlarged version of the Water Spyder 2,

Model 6-A is a six-seat family pleasure hydrofoil boat, with a two-piece moulded fibreglass hull. The main foil, trim-tab support and engine fold upward so the craft can be floated on-and-off a trailer.

The seats, which are immediately over the main foil, are arranged in two rows of three abreast, one row facing forward, the other aft.

Power is supplied by a long-shaft outboard motor of 60 to 115hp.
DIMENSIONS
Length overall, hull: 5·79m (19ft)
Beam overall, foils retracted: 2·5m (8ft 3in)
 foils extended: 3·96m (13ft)
Height overall, foils retracted: 1·37m (4ft 6in)
Floor area: 2·78m² (30ft²)
WEIGHTS
Gross tonnage: 1 ton approx
Empty: 444kg (980lb)
PERFORMANCE
Max speed: 56-64km/h (35-40mph)
Cruising speed: 51km/h (32mph)
Max permissible wave height in foilborne mode: 0·76m (2ft 6in)
Turning radius at cruising speed: 6·09m (20ft)
PRICE: Standard craft and terms of payment, US $8,500 (1983); terms, cash. Delivery, three weeks from date of order, fob Toronto.

Water Spyder 6-A

CHINA, PEOPLE'S REPUBLIC

HUTANG SHIPYARD
Shanghai, People's Republic of China

Hydrofoil torpedo boats of the 'Hu Chwan' (White Swan) class have been under construction at the Hutang Shipyard since about 1966. Some 130 to 150 are in service with the Chinese Navy and another 32 have been lent or leased to the Albanian Navy, four to Pakistan, four to Tanzania and three to Romania.

20 others, of a slightly modified design, have been built in Romania since 1973.

HU CHWAN (WHITE SWAN)
FOILS: The foil system comprises a bow subfoil to facilitate take-off and a main foil of trapeze or shallow V configuration set back approximately one-third of the hull length from the bow. At high speed in relatively calm conditions the greater part of the hull is raised clear of the water. The main foil and struts retract upwards when the craft is required to cruise in displacement condition.

HULL: High speed V-bottom hull in seawater resistant light alloy.

POWER PLANT: Three 1,100hp M-50 type, water-cooled, supercharged 12-cylinder V-type diesels, each driving its own inclined propeller shaft.

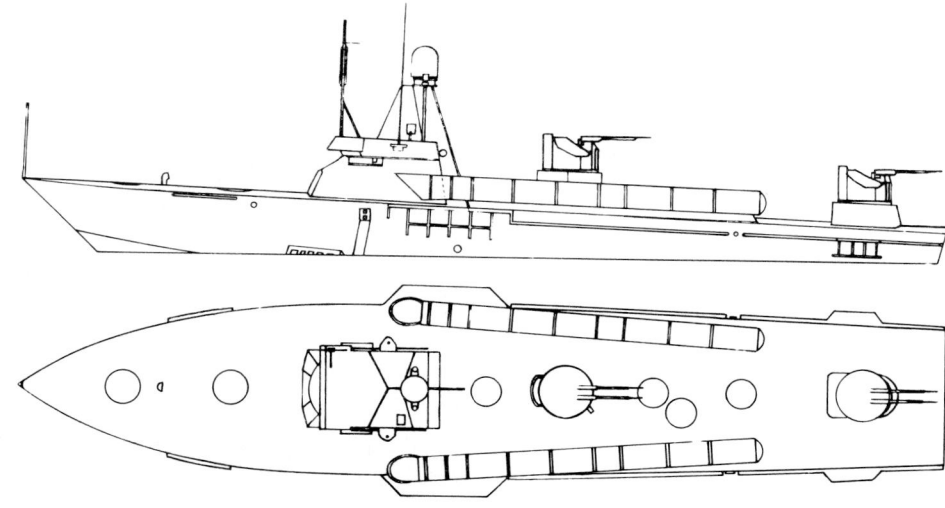
One of four 'Hu Chwan' class torpedo/fast attack craft supplied to Pakistan Navy

ARMAMENT: Two 53cm (21in) torpedo tubes, plus four 15mm machine guns in two twin mountings.
DIMENSIONS (approx)
Length overall: 22m (72ft 2in)
Width across foils: 5·1m (16ft 9in)
Hull beam: 3·96m (13ft)

Draught hullborne: 1m (3ft 3in)
WEIGHTS
Displacement full load: 40 tonnes
PERFORMANCE
Max speed foilborne calm conditions: 50-55 knots
Range: 100-150n miles

HEMA

Hema, the latest hydrofoil to enter service with the Chinese Navy, is a derivative of the 'Hegu' class FAC (missile) which is based on the Soviet Komar but has a steel hull. Hema differs from Hegu in that it is fitted with bow foils in a similar way to the Hu Chwan, Matka and Turya, it has a slightly longer hull and a second twin 25mm AA mount aft. The prototype was launched in 1970.

FOILS: Single main foil of surface-piercing con-figuration set back approximately one third of the hull length from the bow.

HULL: High-speed, V-bottom hull. Steel construction.

POWER PLANT: Four 1,100hp M-50 type, water-cooled, supercharged 12-cylinder V-type lightweight marine diesels each driving an inclined propeller shaft.

ARMAMENT: Two SS-N-2A Styx missile launchers, one each side of the aft superstructure. Two twin 25mm AA mounts, one forward, one aft. Radar: Square Tie, IFF, High Pole A.

DIMENSIONS
Length overall: 29m (95ft 2in)
Beam, hull: 6·5m (21ft 4in)
WEIGHTS
Displacement, full load: 95 tonnes
PERFORMANCE
Max speed, foilborne, calm conditions: 40-45 knots
Cruising speed, hullborne: 25 knots

Hu Chwan torpedo/fast attack hydrofoil of Chinese Navy

FRANCE

DCN
(Direction des Constructions Navales)
Officials:

R V Balquet, *Head of Special Naval Division*

DCN has been undertaking a hydrofoil research and development programme since the mid-1960s. In 1970 an order was placed for an experimental 4·5-tonne hydrofoil, the H890, built by the helicopter division of the Société Nationale Industrielle Aérospatiale. It was launched in 1972 and by 1974 had solved a variety of problems relating to autopilot systems and flight safety.

DCN began to develop a high-performance propulsion system for a projected 170-tonne hydrofoil missile-armed patrol vessel, the H74. In 1975 DCN, with Aérospatiale's assistance, undertook the modification of the H890 experimental hydrofoil to convert it to a test-bed for the new propulsion system which incorporates a base-ventilated propeller. Trials of the modified craft, designated H891, were completed in 1979, the performance of the propeller (at fixed pitch) having proved satisfactory under all sea conditions enabling the craft to achieve a maximum speed of 54 knots.

DCN is developing the Saphyr programme, a 185-tonne hydrofoil patrol vessel derived from the H74, and is preparing preliminary designs for higher-tonnage hydrofoils, including one of 2,000 tonnes.

SAPHYR

Saphyr, a fast patrol hydrofoil, is designed for a wide range of duties in coastal waters, inland seas and archipelagoes. A variety of weapon systems can be installed and the operational range modified to suit the application. Research has been mainly concentrated on patrol and coast-guard models, but a passenger-ferry variant is projected.

FOILS: Fully-submerged subcavitating canard system, with 80 per cent of the weight supported by the aft foils and 20 per cent by the bow foil. All three foils retract for hullborne operation. Lift control is achieved by varying the incidence angles of all three foils. Camber of the aft foils is varied by the use of flaps, giving greater lift at take-off and in low-speed flight to increase the range of foilborne speeds and improving take-off performance in heavy seas. Heading hold and turn are achieved by rotation of the bow foil.

AUTOMATIC PILOT: Foils and struts are constructed in 17·4PH high-strength stainless steel. When foilborne, the hydrofoil is controlled by an autopilot system which converts the flight mode smoothly from platforming to contouring when in deteriorating sea conditions. The autopilot comprises three completely segregated systems of which two provide redundancy and the third a simplified emergency system. All sensors, computers and interfaces of each system are dupli-cated. The controls are electro-hydraulic servo-actuators

PROPULSION: Foilborne propulsion is by two identical but independent systems working in parallel. Each system comprises a 4,750kW Allison 570 KA gas turbine driving a four-bladed base-ventilated propeller through a mechanical Z-drive transmission. The propellers, designed for high-thrust performance by Bassin d'Essais des Carenes, are in titanium alloy. Air ventilation is delivered to the base of the propeller hub. For hullborne operation Saphyr has an independent auxiliary propulsion system comprising two Schottel-type Z-drive propeller units, which can be rotated for manoeuvring and are retractable to avoid stress on take-off and landing. Each propeller is driven by a 200kW diesel engine.

HULL: Constructed in light welded alloy 5083 and 6082. Characteristics include a deep V-bow designed to minimise structural load due to wave impact and a flat W-section aft for improved directional control when hullborne.

ACCOMMODATION: Air-conditioned accommodation for a complement of 14 can be altered to suit operational requirements.

SYSTEMS, ELECTRICAL: Two generators, a 110kW diesel alternator set and a 60kW gas-turbine alternator set, produce an alternating current of 440V, 60Hz. Battery chargers, producing 28V dc, are also installed.

HYDRAULICS: Independent system. Reliability and safety are guaranteed by redundancy of distribution systems, pumps and actuators. Hydraulic fluid used is PHS-standard AIR 3420 A, pressure regulated at 207 bars.

WEAPONS: Dependent on operational role. Weapons on the patrol model would normally comprise: two twin MM40 missile mounts; a single automatic 76mm OTO Melara gun with optical and radar fire control; Triton MTI and Decca 1226 radars and electronic warfare equipment.

DIMENSIONS
Length overall, waterline: 32·7m (104ft 9in)

Impression of Saphyr hydrofoil missile craft

Length overall,
  foils extended: 35·8m (115ft)
  foils retracted: 39·7m
Hull beam: 8·5m (28ft 11in)
Beam overall: 14·81m (48ft 7in)
Draught hullborne, foils retracted: 1·95m (6ft
  5in)
  foilborne: 2·3m (7ft 7in)
WEIGHTS
Displacement, fully loaded: 185 tonnes
PERFORMANCE
Max speed, fully loaded, calm sea: 54 knots
  sea state 5-6: 52 knots
Cruising speed: 40 knots
Range at 40 knots: 1,000n miles
Hullborne speed: 10·5 knots
Range at 10·5 knots: 3,600n miles

2,000-TONNE HYDROFOIL PROJECT

In 1979 DCN studied a proposal for a high-tonnage hydrofoil which would meet requirements outlined by the Chiefs of Staff of the French Navy for a vessel to be used in the 1990s.

The proposal was for an anti-submarine vessel with a displacement of 2,000 tonnes, a foilborne speed in calm seas in excess of 50 knots and the ability to operate in sea state 6. The foilborne range was 2,000n miles.

Various hull and foil designs were examined, initially in conjunction with Aérospatiale. These studies led to the selection of a vessel with the following characteristics:
FOILS: Fully-submerged canard configuration with approximately one-third of the dynamic lift provided by the bow foil and two-thirds by the aft foil.

A sonic autopilot system controls the incidence angles of both the bow and rear foils. Each aft strut has an auxiliary foil surface, installed above the main foil and operated differentially to provide roll control. The main aft foil is fitted with slotted flaps. For hullborne operation the bow foil retracts forward and the aft foils rearwards. Foils and struts are in high-strength 17·4PH stainless steel.
HULL: Catamaran-type structure, comprising two welded light alloy lateral keels linked by a buoyancy tank.
POWER PLANT: Foilborne propulsion is supplied by two FT9 gas turbines, each rated at 30,000kW maximum continuous. Each drives a fixed-pitch base-ventilated propeller through a mechanical Z-drive transmission. The hullborne propulsion system comprises two 1,600kW diesels each driving a fixed-pitch propeller. Foilborne and hullborne power plants are installed in the lateral keels.
ACCOMMODATION: Working and living quarters for a complement of 92 officers and ratings.
SYSTEMS, ELECTRICAL: Two generator sets each comprising two diesel alternators, one of 480kW and the other of 320kW, produce 440-60Hz three-phase alternating current. An emergency turbo-alternator is in the superstructure.
ARMAMENT: Basic armament would comprise two ASW helicopters, six MM40 sea-to-sea missiles and a 100mm cannon.
DIMENSIONS
Length overall,
  foils retracted: 102·1m (334ft 9in)
  foils extended: 92·8m (304ft 4in)
Hull beam: 22·8m (74ft 8in)
Beam overall: 23·9m (78ft 4in)
Draught hullborne, foils retracted: 4·8m (15ft
7in)
  hullborne, foils extended: 16·3m (53ft 4in)
  foilborne: 4·8m (15ft 7in)
WEIGHTS
Displacement fully loaded: 1,940 tonnes
PERFORMANCE
Max speed foilborne,
  calm conditions: 53 knots
  sea state 6: 50 knots
Max speed hullborne,
  calm sea: 16·5 knots
  sea state 6: 14 knots

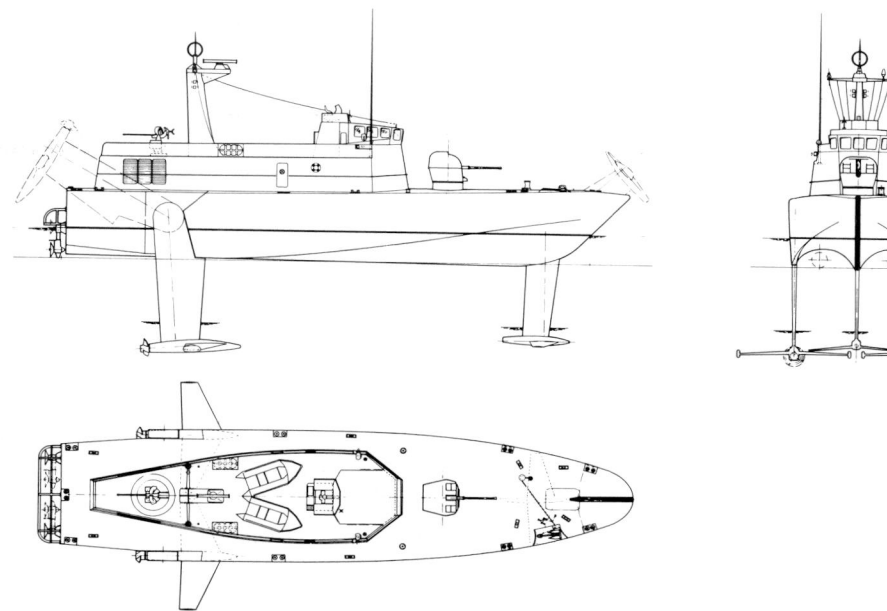
General arrangement of Saphyr fast patrol craft

General arrangement of Saphyr 11b coastguard patrol craft

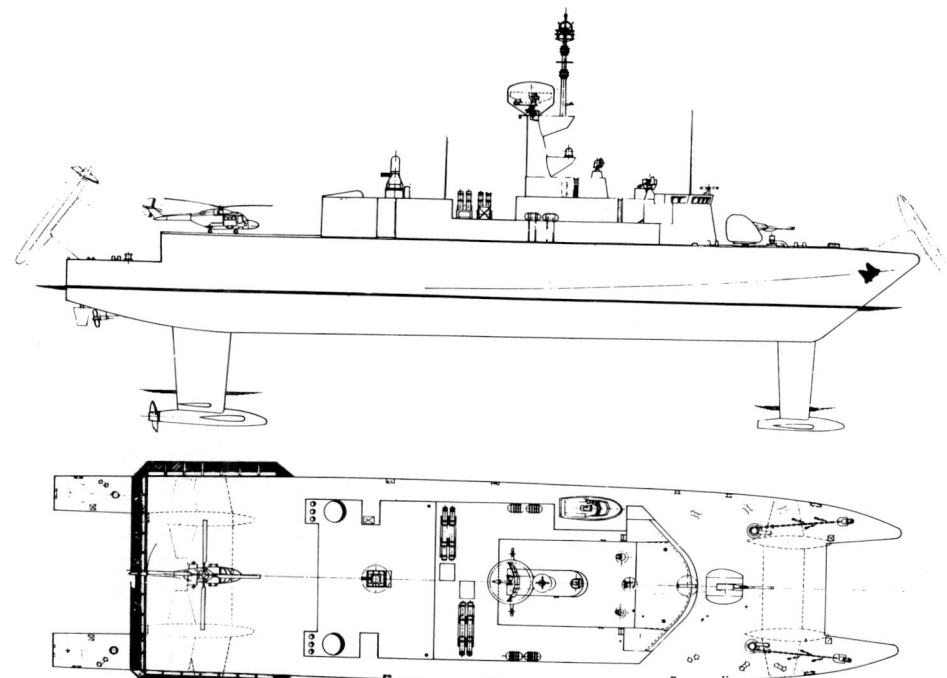
Outboard profile and weather deck plan of 2,000-tonne hydrofoil escort vessel

RANGE
Foilborne, calm conditions: 2,200n miles
Hullborne, at 14 knots: 7,700n miles

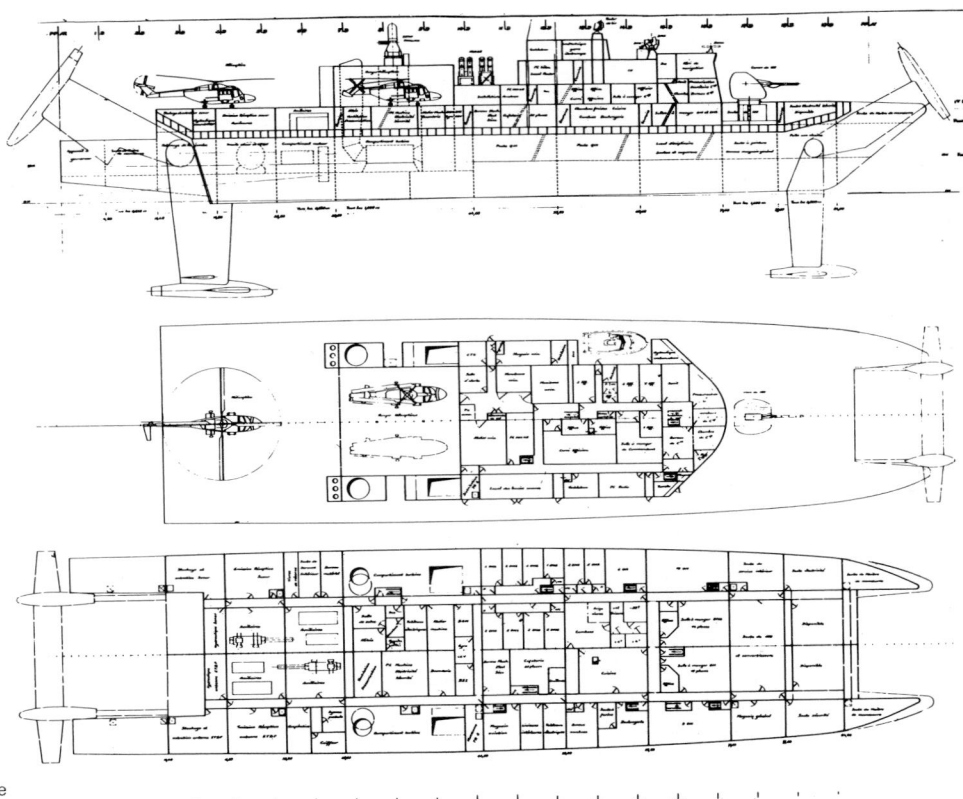

Inboard profile and deck plans of 2,000-tonne
hydrofoil escort vessel

GEORGES HENNEBUTTE
**Société d'Exploitation et de Développe-
ment des Brevets Georges Hennebutte**
Head Office: 43 avenue Foch, 64200 Biarritz,
France
Works: 23 impasse Labordotte, 64200 Biarritz,
France
Telephone: 23 03 70
Telex: 22128
Officials:
G Hennebutte, *Managing Director*

Etablissements Georges Hennebutte was
founded in 1955 to design and build inflatable
dinghies. Its Espadon series of sports craft is employed by lifeguard patrols in France and elsewhere in the world and also by the French Navy.

Development of the Espadon to meet a range
of special requirements led to the construction of
a number of experimental craft, including one
with an inflatable parasol delta wing and another
with a Lippisch-type wing for aerodynamic lift
while operating in ground effect. Preliminary
descriptions of these craft appeared in *Jane's Surface Skimmers 1977-78* and earlier editions.

In another approach, hydroskis have been
fitted to the Etel 422 Swordfish, a winged version
of which is under construction.

Etel 422 Swordfish

ETEL 422 SWORDFISH
This variant of the Etel 422 employs the same
basic inflatable hull but is equipped with hydroskis, wings and a ducted fan. The Etel 422 is the
only inflatable craft to have crossed the Etel barrier, a feat accomplished during a severe storm in
1967. The accompanying photograph shows an
earlier experimental version of the Etel 422
equipped with hydroskis and a marine outboard
engine driving a water propeller. A speed of
112km/h (70mph) was achieved during trials.
LIFT AND PROPULSION: Aerodynamic lift at

cruising speed and above is provided by a wing.
Thrust is supplied by an RFB SG85 fan-thrust
pod, combining a 50hp Wankel air-cooled rotary
engine with a three-bladed, ducted propeller.
HULL: Catamaran type hull with rigid central
frame and inflatable, nylon-coated neoprene
outer sections.
ACCOMMODATION: Open cockpit for driver.
DIMENSIONS
Length overall: 4·22m (13ft 10in)
Beam overall: 2·5m (8ft 2in)

SOCIÉTÉ NATIONALE INDUSTRIELLE AÉROSPATIALE

Head Office: 36 boulevard de Montmorency,
75781 Paris (2) Cedex 16, France
Telephone: 524 43 21
Telex: AISPA 620 059F
Works: BP13, 13722 Marignane, France
Telephone: (91) 89 90 22

In 1966 the Direction des Recherches et
Moyens d'Essais (Directorate of Research and
Test Facilities) initiated a basic hydrofoil design
and research programme with the object of building a prototype hydrofoil ferry with a displacement of 55 tons and a speed of 50 knots.

The companies and organisations co-operating
in this programme are: Aérospatiale, project
leader; STCAN, the hull test centre; several
French government laboratories of DCN;
Alsthom—Techniques des Fluides—and Constructions Mécaniques de Normandie.

H.890

The main headings of the programme are: hydrodynamics (foils, struts and hull); foil hydroelas-
ticity data and flutter phenomenon; automatic

pilot; material technology relative to foils, struts
and hull.

The design and research programme is nearly

complete and the results will be processed and refined using a 4·5-tonne submerged foil test craft, the H.890, designed by Aérospatiale. The comprehensive test programme is under the control of Aérospatiale and DCN, a French government agency.

In addition to the SA 800 55-ton hydrofoil ferry, preliminary designs have been completed for a missile-carrying 118-ton hydrofoil combat vessel, the H.851, and a commercial variant, intended for mixed-traffic ferry services. The latest project is a 174-tonne missilecraft with a speed of 54 knots and capable of operating in Force 5 weather at 50 knots. Armament would comprise four Exocet missiles and one rapid-fire automatic cannon.

H.890

This 4·5-tonne seagoing test vehicle is being employed to gather data for foil systems and accelerate the development of autopilot systems for large hydrofoils.

The combination of catamaran hull and pure jet propulsion allows the foils to be arranged in conventional configuration—two foils forward and one aft—or canard configuration, with one foil forward and two aft.

The vessel was developed and built under contract to the French government agency DCN by Aérospatiale's Helicopter Division in conjunction with Constructions Mécaniques de Normandie and Alsthom—Techniques des Fluides—of Grenoble. It has been undergoing tests on the Etang de Berre since it was launched in June 1972. A speed of 52 knots has been reached during trials.

FOILS: Fully submerged system with facilities for changing from conventional (aeroplane) to canard configuration as required. In aeroplane configuration about 70 per cent of the weight is supported by the twin bow foils, which are attached to the port and starboard pontoons, and 30 per cent by the single tail foil, mounted on the central hull section aft.

The stern foil rotates for steering and all three struts are fixed (non-retractable). Lift variation of the three foils is achieved by an autopilot system, developed by Aérospatiale and SFENA, which varies the incidence angles of all three foils. During the first series of tests the foils were tested in conventional configuration. During the second series the canard configuration was adopted.

HULL: Catamaran type in corrosion-resistant light alloys. Central hull incorporates control cabin, engine bay and test instrumentation and is flanked by two stepped pontoons.

ACCOMMODATION: Seating for pilot and test observer.

POWER PLANT: Twin 480 daN Turboméca Marboré VIc gas turbines, mounted in the central hull structure aft of the cabin, power the craft when foilborne. Hullborne propulsion is supplied by a 20hp Sachs 370 engine driving, via a hydraulic transmission, a folding-blade Maucour waterscrew located at the top of the aft foil strut. The waterscrew rotates through ±90 degrees for steering.

DIMENSIONS

Length, overall: 10·66m (34ft 11·5in)
waterline: 9·3m (30ft 6in)
Beam, overall: 3·9m (12ft 9·5in)
Draught, afloat: 1·72m (5ft 8in)
foilborne: 0·37m (1ft 3in)

WEIGHTS

Normal take-off: 4·5 tonnes

PERFORMANCE

Cruising speed, foilborne, calm conditions: 50 knots
hullborne, calm conditions: 6 knots
Craft is designed to cross waves up to 0·8m (2ft 8in) high without contouring.

H.891

This modified version of the H.890 underwent its first trials programme in 1976. The hull is the same as that employed for the H.890 but the foils are arranged in canard configuration instead of the earlier conventional or 'aeroplane' configuration.

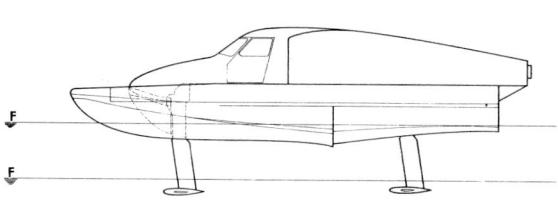
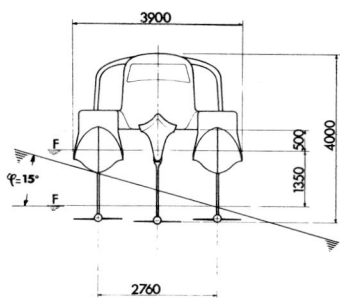
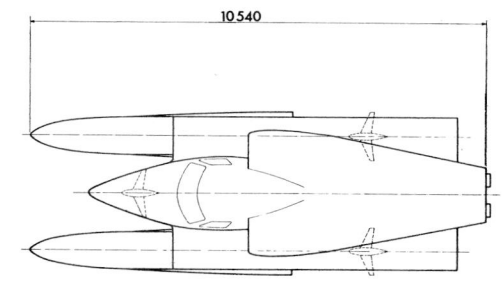

H.891

H.891

Artist's impression of SA 800

Accommodation is provided for a pilot and two test engineers.

It is powered by a single Turboméca Turmo IIIC₃ marinised gas turbine delivering 1,100kW. The power available is nearly five times that required by the H.890 to attain 50 knots. One of the primary reasons for providing the craft with an excess of power is to enable it to be employed as a test-bed for new types of propulsion, including Z-drives.

Modifications to the craft were undertaken by Aérospatiale under the direction of STCAN (Service Technique des Constructions et Armes Navales) which designed the experimental propulsion system.

WEIGHTS

Weight operational, with 2½ hours fuel: 4·7 tonnes approx

PERFORMANCE

Cruising speed foilborne, calm conditions: 54 knots
Speed over waves of up to 0·8m (2ft 8in) without contouring: 50 knots
Cruising speed, hullborne: 6 knots

SA 800

The SA 800 is a design study for a mixed-traffic hydrofoil powered by two Turmo IIIC turbines driving a waterjet propulsion unit. Conventional marine light alloy construction is employed and the craft will have incidence-controlled, fully-submerged foils operated by a sonic/electronic sensing system.

Variants of the basic design are being studied for alternative applications, including prospecting, marine research, coastal surveillance and naval patrol. Trials with dynamic models have been successful and are continuing. Preliminary design studies are now complete.

FOILS: The foil system is fully submerged and of 'aeroplane' configuration. All three foil struts retract hydraulically completely clear of the water. An SNIAS sonic autopilot system controls the incidence angle of the two bow foils and adjustable control flaps on the rear foils.

HULL: The hull is of conventional marine corrosion-resistant aluminium alloys. Features include a deep V bow, designed to minimise structural loading due to wave impact, and a flat W section aft for good directional control when hullborne.

POWER PLANT: Foilborne propulsion is supplied by two 1,300shp Turboméca Turmo IIIC gas turbines driving a SOGREAH waterjet propulsion unit mounted at the base of the aft foil strut.

Output from the transmission shafts of the two turbines, which are mounted end-to-end, intakes outwards, athwart the stern, passes first to a main bevel drive gearbox, then to a drive shaft which extends downwards through the aft foil strut to a waterjet pump gearbox located in a nacelle beneath the aft foil. Air for the turbines is introduced through intakes at the top of the cabin aft. Filters are fitted to the intakes to prevent the ingestion of water or salt spray into the gas turbine. There is a separate hullborne propulsion system, with a 400hp diesel driving twin water propellers beneath the transom.

ACCOMMODATION: The elevated wheelhouse forward of the passenger compartment seats the captain and engineer. All instrumentation is located here for easy monitoring. Navigation and collision avoidance radar is fitted. Accommodation is on two decks, each arranged with three seats abreast on either side of a central aisle. As a passenger ferry the craft will seat 200; 116 on the upper deck and 84 on the lower; and in mixed traffic configuration it will carry 8 to 10 cars on the upper deck with the lower deck seating capacity remaining at 84. Cars are loaded via rear door/ramps. Baggage holds are provided forward of both upper and lower saloons.

DIMENSIONS
Length overall: 26·88m (88ft)
Max beam, deck: 5·4m (18ft)

WEIGHTS
Displacement, fully loaded: 56 tonnes (55 tons)
Payload (200 passengers with luggage or 84 passengers with luggage and 8-10 cars): 18,300kg (40,300lb)

PERFORMANCE
Max speed, calm conditions: 55 knots
Cruising speed: 50 knots·
Cruising speed, sea state 5: 48 knots
Range, at 50 knots, calm sea: 250n miles
   at 48 knots, sea state 5: 200n miles
   Craft is designed to platform over 3m (10ft) high waves, crest to trough, and contour 4m (13ft) high waves.

ISRAEL

ISRAEL SHIPYARDS LIMITED

POB 1282, Haifa 31000, Israel
Telephone: 749111
Telex: 45132 YARD IL
Cables: Israyard
Officials:
D Yallon, *Company Secretary*

Israel has negotiated with the US Government for the purchase of two Flagstaff multi-duty naval hydrofoils from Grumman Aerospace Corporation, together with the acquisition of a licence for the series production of these craft in Israel. The contract signed between Israel and Grumman permitted the construction of at least ten craft for the Israeli Navy without licence fees. Israeli-built craft would also be made available for export. Israel Shipyards Limited has non-exclusive export rights to all countries except the USA and one Asian nation, but the US State Department has veto rights on all prospective Israeli export sales.

M161 SHIMRIT (GUARDIAN)

In 1977 the US Government announced that agreement had been reached on the joint development of hydrofoils by two countries and Grumman Aerospace Corporation stated it had 'received its first order for the Flagstaff from an overseas client'. Later, the Corporation confirmed that the country concerned was Israel. In May 1979 it was reported that two 105-tonne derivatives of the Flagstaff II, known by their

M161

Grumman design number M161, were under construction, one at Lantana, Florida, the other in Israel. The first craft to be completed, *Shimrit* (Guardian), was launched in May 1981, followed by equipment tests and sea trials in the Atlantic.

The Israeli-built vessel, *Livnik* (Heron), followed six months behind the lead vessel. It is identical to the US-built craft and will have identical performance tests. It was launched during the latter half of 1982 and began sea trials in July 1983.

It is understood that up to 14 M161s may be built under licence.

The M161 has been designed for a wide range of naval and military roles and can be fitted with a variety of weapons. Variants are available with differing payloads and endurances for applications including gunboat, troop transport, surveillance craft, missile boat, inshore ASW patrol, EEZ patrol and search and rescue.

It was agreed originally that all struts and foils, transmission, the main propeller unit and the foil automatic control system would be supplied by Grumman for all Israeli-built craft. However, at the time of going to press Grumman has closed its Advanced Marine Systems Division in the USA, but is to continue supervision of the construction of this design in Israel. It will be built for the Israeli Navy with possible exports to clients of Israel Shipyards Limited in South Africa and South America.

FOIL SYSTEM: Fully-submerged system of conventional configuration, comprising twin inverted T-foils forward and single inverted T-foil aft. Approximately 70 per cent of the load is supported by two forward foils and 30 per cent by the aft foil. All three foils are subcavitating. They have an identical span of 5·23m, area of 4·97m² and aspect ratio of 5:5, and are machined from forged aluminium 6061-T652. All three foils are incidence-controlled and operated by Hamilton Standard automatic control system (ACS) employing electro-hydraulic actuators. Inputs are height, supplied by twin TRT radio altimeters in the bow, vertical acceleration, pitch and pitch rate, roll and roll rate and yaw rate. Pitch and roll attitudes are controlled by a vertical gyro. The system has an autopilot facility for heading hold. The stern foil power strut, together with the propeller, rotates ±5 degrees for steering and all three foil/strut units retract completely clear of the water for hullborne manoeuvring. Break joints are incorporated on the two forward struts so that if either of them hit floating debris each would break clean at the point of its connection to its yoke. A shear bolt releases the aft strut permitting it to rotate rearwards and upwards aft of the transom.

HULL: Fabricated in 5086 and 5456 aluminium alloys. Frames and bulkheads are welded assemblies. Bottom, side and deck plating consists of large panels of wide-ribbed extrusions welded to the frames and bulkheads.

ACCOMMODATION: Size of the crew varies with the mission and weapons fitted. Minimum operating crew normally comprises three to four: helmsman, engineer, deck officer/navigator and, if necessary, a lookout. Stations and messing facilities for a crew of 15 on the Israeli craft. The

Grumman M161 *Shimrit* built for Israeli Navy

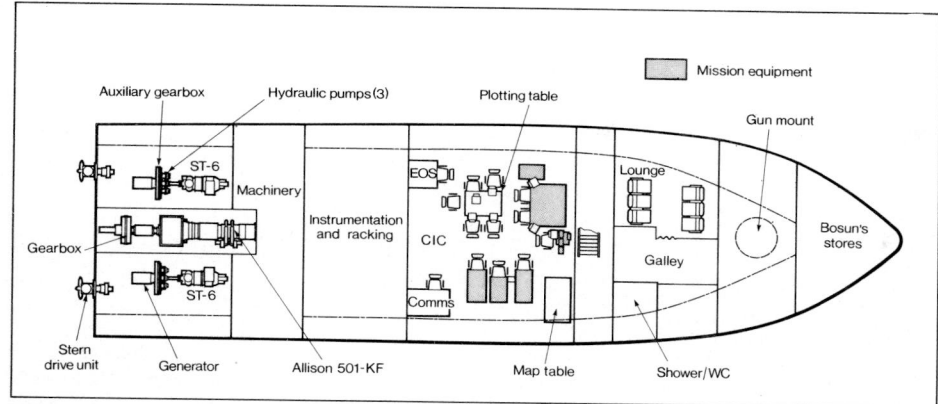

M161 deck plan *(Defence Attaché)*

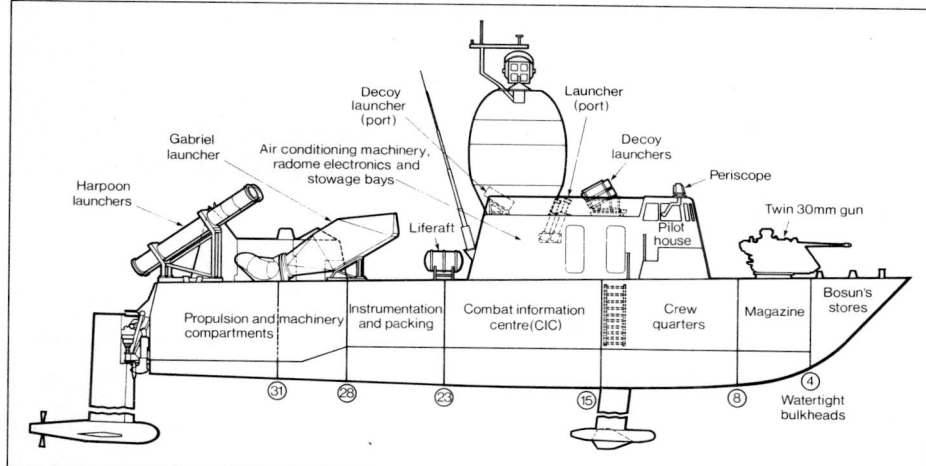

Inboard profile of M161 *(Defence Attaché)*

pilothouse has three seats, the port position is occupied by the helmsman, the centre by the gunner operating the twin 30mm Emerlec cannon and the starboard by the commander, who sits in front of a radarscope. The CIC occupies the full width of the craft between hull frames 15 and 23. Stations are provided within the CIC for 13 of the 15 crew, all being involved in the operation of the weapon systems apart from the engineering officer who sits in front of an engineering operating station (EOS) which incorporates a one-person centralised and computerised engineering monitoring and control system (EMCS). All manned spaces are heated and air-conditioned by an Airscrew Howden system which comprises two Freon modules, each of 15-ton capacity. The forward superstructure accommodates the bridge, which contains steering and engine control consoles and is elevated to give a 360-degree view. Entry to the deckhouse is via two 660mm × 1·52m (2ft 2in × 5ft) watertight doors, one port, one starboard. There is an emergency exit aft, behind the pilothouse on the weatherdeck. Escape hatches are provided in the living spaces.
POWER PLANT, FOILBORNE: A 5,400hp Allison 501-KF marine gas turbine is installed. Power is transmitted to a 1·32m supercavitating four-bladed controllable-pitch propeller via a Western Gear transmission with a reduction ratio of 14:1 and a Grumman Z-drive transmission.
HULLBORNE: Twin 130hp Maritime Industries retractable and steerable outdrives. Three-bladed stainless steel 660mm (26in) fixed-pitch propellers driven through geared transmission by integrally-mounted Rexroth hydraulic motors.
FUEL: All installed prime movers operate on VP-5 or diesel No 2 or equivalent fuel. Maximum

fuel tankage is 21 tonnes. Under way refuelling facilities can be provided.
SYSTEMS, ELECTRICAL: Two 200kW, 120/208V, 400Hz three-phase generators driven by two 660shp Pratt and Whitney ST-6 gas turbine APUs. Each generator is capable of supplying normal ship electrical load and can be operated in parallel during battle conditions.
HYDRAULICS: 3,000 psi system driven by four pumps on both the hullborne and foilborne prime movers provides control power for hullborne and foilborne operation and turbine starting.

CONTROLS: An automatic control system stabilises the craft in foilborne operations. This comprises dual radar height sensors, an inertial sensor, a digital processor, displays and controls. Both flat or co-ordinated turns and platforming or contouring modes can be selected by the helmsman.
FIRE EXTINGUISHING: A Spectronix fire detection and suppression system is installed.
ARMAMENT: Typical armament kit comprises four McDonnell Douglas Harpoon ship-to-ship missiles in two pairs of launchers aft, and two IAI Gabriel Mk III ship-to-ship missiles immediately ahead of them. Anti-ship missile and aircraft defence is provided by a twin 30mm Emerlec remote-controlled cannon on the foredeck. Chaff launchers are mounted on the deckhouse roof.
ELECTRONICS: Large radome on deckhouse, built by Brunswick Corporation, houses the antenna of an Elta search radar. This is reported to employ horizontally polarised X-band for surface search and vertically-polarised S-band for air alert with selectable fast and slow rates of antenna rotation. Fire control radar: ECCM/ESM.

DIMENSIONS
Length, overall (hull moulded): 25·62m (84ft)
  between perpendiculars: 23·4m (76ft 9in)
  overall (foils retracted): 31·79m (104ft 4in)
  overall (foilborne): 29·81m (97ft 10in)
Beam, hull moulded: 7·32m (24ft)
  foils retracted (extreme): 12·95m (42ft 6in)
  foilborne (extreme): 12·45m (40ft 10in)
Draught (full load)
  foil system retracted: 1·45m (4ft 9in)
  foil system, extended: 4·83m (15ft 10in)
  foilborne (nominal) 1·7m (5ft 7in)
Surface search radar height, hullborne: 9·99m (32ft 10in)
  foilborne: 12·13m (39ft 10in)

WEIGHTS
Light displacement: 71 tonnes
Full load displacement: 105 tonnes
Normal fuel load: 16 tonnes
Max fuel load: 21 tonnes

PERFORMANCE
Max intermittent speed: 52 knots
Most economical speed: 42 knots
Foilborne operating envelope (normal): 35-48 knots
Max hullborne speed: 9·5 knots
Range at 42 knots: 750-1,150n miles
Specific range at 42 knots: 47-55n miles/tonne

M161 *Shimrit (Defence Attaché)*

ITALY

CANTIERI NAVALI RIUNITI SpA (CNR)
(Fincantieri Group)
Via Cipro 11, 16129 Genoa, Italy
Telephone: 0039 10 59951
Telex: 270168 CANTGE 1

Officials:
Enrico Bocchini, *Chairman and Managing Director*
Antonio Fiori, *Deputy Chairman*
Pietro Orlando, *General Manager (Naval Vessels and Mechanical)*

Sergio Castagnoli, *Deputy General Manager (Commercial)*
P Giorgio Teodorani, *Deputy General Manager (Technical, Naval Vessels)*
Michele Diaz Satta, *Director, Marketing & Sales, (Naval Vessels)*

Cantieri Navali Riuniti SpA has taken over the interests of Alinavi which was formed in 1964 to develop, manufacture and market advanced military marine systems.

Under the terms of a licensing agreement, CNR has access to Boeing technology in the field of military fully-submerged foil hydrofoil craft.

In October 1970, the company was awarded a contract by the Italian Navy for the design and construction of the P 420 Sparviero hydrofoil missilecraft. This is an improved version of the Boeing PGH-2 Tucumcari. The vessel, given the design name Sparviero, was delivered to the Italian Navy in July 1974. An order for a further six of this type was placed by the Italian Navy in February 1976.

The first of the series production craft, P 421 *Nibbio*, was commissioned in 1981. *Falcone* (P422), *Astore* (P423) and *Grifone* (P424) were commissioned in 1982, and *Gheppio* (P425) and *Condor* (P426) were commissioned in 1983.

SPARVIERO

The Sparviero missile-launching hydrofoil gunboat displaces 60·5 tonnes and is designed for both offensive and defensive missions. Its combination of speed, firepower, and all-weather capability is unique in a ship of this class.

The vessel has fully-submerged foils arranged in canard configuration and an automatic control system. A gas-turbine powered waterjet system provides foilborne propulsion and a diesel-driven propeller outdrive provides hullborne propulsion. A typical crew comprises two officers and eight enlisted men.

Sparviero's advanced automatic control system considerably reduces the vertical and transverse acceleration normally experienced in rough seas. In sea state 4 the maximum vertical acceleration likely to be found is in the order of 0·25g (rms), while the maximum roll angle is not likely to be greater than ±2 degrees.

In the lower sea states 'Sparviero' class hydrofoils have a maximum continuous speed of 44 knots, decreasing to 40 knots in sea state 4.

FOILS: Fully-submerged canard arrangement, with approximately one-third of the dynamic lift provided by the bow foil and two-thirds by the two aft foils. The aft foils retract sideways and the bow foil retracts forwards into a recess in the bow. Bow doors preserve the hull lines when the forward hydrofoil is either fully extended or

Turning radius of Sparviero hydrofoils at 40 knots is under 125m (137yds)

Three Sparviero hydrofoil missilecraft at Cantiere Navale Riuniti yard at Muggiano

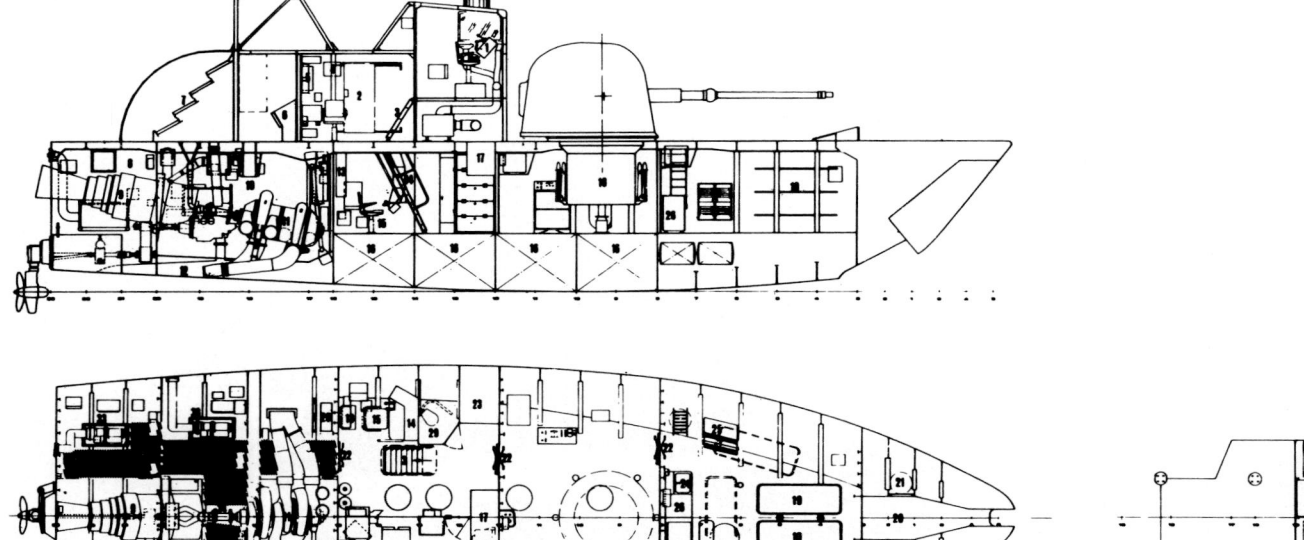

Inboard profile and deck plan of Sparviero: **(1)** helm/main control console **(2)** combat operations centre (COC) door **(3)** companionway ladders **(4)** COC electric power distribution panel **(5)** COC **(6)** air intake forward machinery room **(7)** filtering panels for combustion air **(8)** aft machinery room **(9)** gas turbine engine: foilborne propulsion **(10)** forward machinery room **(11)** waterjet pump **(12)** waterjet nozzle (P/S) **(13)** main electrical power distribution panel **(14)** engineer's console **(15)** engineer's station **(16)** fuel oil tanks **(17)** automatic control system **(18)** cannon revolving feeding machine **(19)** crew berths **(20)** forward hydrofoil retraction well **(21)** rope locker (P/S) **(22)** watertight doors **(23)** galley stores locker **(24)** lavatory **(25)** crew lockers **(26)** refrigerator **(27)** folding mess table with benches **(28)** main electrical switchboard **(29)** water closet **(30)** electronic equipment bay **(31)** gyrocompass **(32)** diesel engine: hullborne (unmanned) propulsion **(33)** turbine generator set **(34)** pump drive coupling **(35)** conning station **(36)** helm station

retracted. Foils and struts are built in high resistance stainless steel.

Anhedral is incorporated in the aft foils to enhance the directional stability of the craft at shallow foil depths. In addition, the anhedral assures positive roll control by eliminating tip broaching during rough water manoeuvres.

CONTROLS: Automatic system incorporating two aircraft-type gyros, one to sense pitch and roll and the other to sense yaw, plus three accelerometers to sense vertical movements (heave) of the craft. Ultrasonic height sensors detect and maintain flying height above the water surface. Information from the sensors is sent to a hermetically-sealed solid-state computer, which calculates movement of the control surfaces necessary to maintain boat stability and/or pre-selected flying height, and sends appropriate commands to the servo-mechanisms that control trailing edge flaps on bow and stern foils.

Foilborne steering: Helm-commanded automatic control system controls hydraulic servo-actuated hydrofoil flaps and steerable forward hydrofoil strut to produce co-ordinated (banked) turns in design sea conditions. Forward foil strut is steerable through 10 degrees, port and starboard.

Hullborne steering: Helm-commanded steerable retractable outdrive unit driven by 160hp Isotta Fraschini diesel via toothed belt transmission. Outdrive unit can be steered through 360 degrees for maximum manoeuvrability when hullborne. Manual emergency hullborne steering is provided on the aft deck.

HULL: Hull and superstructure are built in corrosion-resistant aluminium, the hull being welded and the superstructure riveted and welded.

ACCOMMODATION: Ten berths are provided in the forward crew space. One toilet and one sink. A folding table with benches in the forward crew space.

POWERPLANT, FOILBORNE: Power for the waterjet is supplied by one 4,500shp Rolls-Royce Proteus 15M/553 gas turbine.

Engine output is transferred to a single double-volute, double-suction, two impeller centrifugal pump. Water is taken in through inlets on the nose of each aft foil at the foil/strut intersection and passes up through the hollow interiors of the struts to the hull, where it is ducted to the pump. From the pump, the water is discharged through twin, fixed-area nozzles located beneath the hull under the pump.

POWERPLANT, HULLBORNE: An Isotta Fraschini ID 38N6V marine diesel, rated at 2,600rpm, drives via a toothed belt a steerable propeller outdrive unit, which is mounted on the centreline of the transom. The unit is retractable and rotates through 360 degrees. Propeller is fixed-pitch. Continuous speed, hullborne, is 8 knots.

P421 *Nibbio*

P422 *Falcone*

APUs: Two, each comprising a 150hp Solar T-62-T-32 gas turbine driving one 208V 400Hz three-phase 75kVA alternator, one 30V dc 200 amp starter generator and one hydraulic pump for ships services.

Craft may be refuelled through main deck connection at dock or at sea. The fuel tanks are equipped with fuel level indicators and vents.

ARMAMENT: A typical military payload consists of:

one dual purpose 76mm/62 calibre automatic OTO Melara gun and 110 rounds of ammunition

two fixed missile launchers and two ship-to-ship missiles, eg Sea Killers, Otomat or Exocet

one Elsag NA 10 mod, 3 fire-control system

one Orion 10X tracking radar

one SMA MM SPQ 701 search and navigation radar

A variety of other payloads may be carried according to customer needs.

FIRE CONTROL SYSTEM: SPG 73 tracking radar, SXG 75 low light level tv and 2AC50C console. Console includes tv monitor and 12in PPI screen for search radar video presentation.

DIMENSIONS

Length overall: 22·95m (75ft 4in)
 foils retracted: 24·6m (80ft 7in)
Width across foils: 10·8m (35ft 4in)
Deck beam, max: 7m (23ft)

WEIGHTS

Max displacement: 60·5 tonnes

PERFORMANCE

Exact craft performance characteristics depend on the customer's choice of foilborne gas turbine and operating conditions which can affect the quantity of fuel carried. Performance figures shown below, therefore, are representative.

Foilborne intermittent speed in calm water: 50 knots
 continuous speed in calm water: 44 knots
 continuous speed in sea state 4: 38–40 knots
Hullborne continuous speed, foils down: 8 knots
Foilborne range at max continuous speed: up to 400n miles
Hullborne range: up to 1,000n miles
Turning radius at 45 knots: less than 150m
Rate of turn at max continuous speed, foilborne: 10 degrees/s

P420 *Sparviero*

RODRIQUEZ CANTIERE NAVALE SpA

Via S Raineri 22, 98100 Messina, Italy
Telephone: (090) 7765
Telex: 980030 RODRIK I
Officials:
Cav Del Lavoro Carlo Rodriquez, *President*
Dott Leopoldo Rodriquez, *Vice President*
Dott Riccardo Rodriquez, *Managing Director*
Dott Gaetano Mobilia, *Managing Director*
Dott Ing Giovanni Falzea, *Technical Manager*

Rodriquez Cantiere Navale SpA, formerly known as Cantiere Navaltecnica SpA and as Leopoldo Rodriquez Shipyard, was the first company to produce hydrofoils in series, and is now the biggest hydrofoil builder outside the Soviet Union. On the initiative of the company's president, Carlo Rodriquez, the Aliscafi Shipping Company was established in Sicily to operate the world's first scheduled seagoing hydrofoil service in August 1956 between Sicily and the Italian mainland.

The service was operated by the first Rodriquez-built Supramar PT 20, *Freccia del Sole*. Cutting down the port-to-port time from Messina to Reggio di Calabria to one-quarter of that of conventional ferry boats, and completing 22 daily crossings, the craft soon proved its commercial viability. With a seating capacity of 75 passengers the PT 20 has carried between 800 and 900 passengers a day and has conveyed a record number of some 31,000 in a single month.

The prototype PT 20, a 27-ton craft for 75 passengers, was built by Rodriquez in 1955 and the first PT 50, a 63-ton craft for 140 passengers, was completed in 1958.

The company has built and delivered more than 140 hydrofoils. The RHS models, the only craft now built by the company, are fitted on request with a Hamilton Standard electronic stability augmentation system.

In the autumn of 1984 the company had three RHS 160s under construction.

Apart from these standard designs, the company offers a number of variants, including the M 100, M 150 and M 200 fast patrol craft, the M 300 and 600 fast strike craft and the RHS Hydroil series of mixed passenger/freight hydrofoils, based on the RHS 70, 140 and 160, but adapted for servicing offshore drilling platforms.

RHS 70

This is a 32-ton coastal passenger ferry with seats for 71 passengers. Power is supplied by a single 1,430hp MTU diesel and the cruising speed is 32.4 knots.
FOILS: Surface-piercing type in partly hollow welded steel. During operation the angle of the bow foil can be adjusted within narrow limits from the steering position by means of a hydraulic ram operating on a foil support across the hull.
HULL: V-bottom hull of riveted light metal alloy construction. Watertight compartments are below the passenger decks and in other parts of the hull.
POWER PLANT: A single MTU 12V331 TC 82 diesel, developing 1,430hp at 2,340rpm, drives a three-bladed bronze aluminium propeller through a Zahnradfabrik W 800 H 20 gearbox.
ACCOMMODATION: 44 passengers are accommodated in the forward cabin, 19 in the rear compartment and 8 aft of the pilot's position, above the engine room, in the elevated wheelhouse. A wc/washbasin unit is provided in the aft passenger compartments. Emergency exits are provided in each passenger compartment.
SYSTEMS, ELECTRICAL: 24V generator driven by the main engine; batteries with a capacity of 350Ah.
HYDRAULICS: 120kg/cm³ pressure hydraulic system for rudder and bow foil incidence control.
DIMENSIONS
Length overall: 22m (72ft 2in)
Width across foils: 7.4m (24ft 3in)
Draught hullborne: 2.7m (8ft 10in)
   foilborne: 1.15m (3ft 9in)

RHS 70 *Freccia delle Magnolie,* operated by Ministero di Transporti

WEIGHTS
Displacement fully loaded: 31.5 tons
Useful load: 6 tons
PERFORMANCE
Cruising speed, half loaded: 32.4 knots
Max speed, half loaded: 36.5 knots

RHS 110

A 54-ton hydrofoil ferry, the RHS 110 is designed to carry a maximum of 110 passengers over routes of up to 485.7km (300 miles) at a cruising speed of 37 knots.
FOILS: Surface-piercing type, in partly hollow welded steel. Hydraulically operated flaps, attached to the trailing edges of the bow and rear foils, are adjusted automatically by a Hamilton Standard stability augmentation system for the damping of heave, pitch and roll motions. The rear foil is rigidly attached to the transom, its incidence angle being determined during tests.
HULL: V-bottom of high-tensile riveted light metal alloy construction, using Peraluman plates and Anticorrodal profiles. The upper deck plates are in 3.5mm (0.137in) thick Peraluman. Removable deck sections permit the lifting out and replacement of the main engines. The superstructure, which has a removable roof, is in 2mm (0.078in) thick Peraluman plates, with L and C profile sections. Watertight compartments are below the passenger decks and other parts of the hull.
POWER PLANT: Power is supplied by two 12-cylinder supercharged MTU MB 12V 493 Ty 71 diesels, each with a maximum output of 1,350hp at 1,500rpm. Engine output is transferred to two three-bladed bronze-aluminium propellers through Zahnradfabrik W 800 H20 gearboxes. Each propeller shaft is 90mm (3.5in) in diameter and supported at three points by seawater lubricated rubber bearings. Steel fuel tanks with a total capacity of 3,600 litres (792 gallons) are aft of the engine room.
ACCOMMODATION: The wheelhouse/observation deck saloon seats 58 and the lower aft saloon seats 39. Additional passengers are

accommodated in the lower forward saloon, which contains a bar.

In the wheelhouse, the pilot's position is on the port side, together with the radar screen. A second seat is provided for the chief engineer. Passenger seats are of lightweight aircraft type, floors are covered with woollen carpets and the walls and ceilings are clad in vinyl. Two toilets are provided, one in each of the lower saloons.
SYSTEMS, ELECTRICAL: Engine driven generators supply 220V, 50Hz, three-phase ac. Two groups of batteries for 24V dc circuit.
HYDRAULICS: Steering, variation of the foil flaps and the anchor windlass operation are all accomplished hydraulically from the wheelhouse. Plant comprises two Bosch pumps installed on the main engines which convey oil from a 60-litre (13-gallon) tank under pressure to the control cylinders of the rudder, foil flaps and anchor windlass.
FIREFIGHTING: Fixed CO_2 plant for the main engine room, portable CO_2 and foam fire extinguishers of 3kg (7lb) and 10-litre (2-gallon) capacity in the saloons, and one water firefighting plant.
DIMENSIONS
EXTERNAL
Length overall: 25.6m (84ft)
Width across foils: 9.2m (30ft 2.25in)
Deck beam, max: 5.95m (19ft 2in)
Draught hullborne: 3.3m (10ft 9.87in)
   foilborne: 1.25m (4ft 1in)
WEIGHTS
Displacement, fully loaded: 54 tons
PERFORMANCE
Max speed: 40 knots
Cruising speed: 37 knots
Range: 485.7km (300 miles)

RHS 140

This 65-ton hydrofoil passenger ferry seats 125 to 140 passengers and has a cruising speed of 32.5 knots.
FOILS: Surface-piercing V foils of hollow welded steel construction. Lift of the bow foil can

RHS 110

be modified by hydraulically-operated trailing-edge flaps.

HULL: Riveted light metal alloy design framed on longitudinal and transverse formers.

ACCOMMODATION: 125 to 140 passengers seated in three saloons. The belvedere saloon, on the main deck above the engine room, can be equipped with a bar. Wc washbasin units can be installed in the forward and aft saloons.

POWER PLANT: Power is provided by two MTU 12V 493 Ty 71 12-cylinder supercharged engines, each developing 1,350hp at 1,500 rpm. Engine output is transmitted to two, three-bladed 700mm diameter bronze propellers through Zahnradfabrik gearboxes.

SYSTEMS, ELECTRICAL: Two engine-driven generators supply 24V dc. Two battery sets each with 350Ah capacity.

HYDRAULICS: Steering and variation of foil flap incidence is accomplished hydraulically from the wheelhouse. Plant comprises two Bosch pumps installed on the main engines and conveying oil from a 70-litre (15·4-gallon) tank under pressure to the control cylinders of the rudder and foil flaps.

FIREFIGHTING: Fixed CO_2 plant for the engine room; portable CO_2 and foam fire extinguishers in the saloons. Water intake connected to bilge pump for fire hose connection in emergency.

DIMENSIONS
Length overall: 28·7m (94ft 1·5in)
Width across foils: 10·72m (35ft 2·25in)

RHS 140 operated by Condor Ltd between Guernsey, Sark, Jersey, St Malo and Alderney

Draught hullborne: 3·5m (11ft 5·75in)
  foilborne: 1·5m (4ft 11in)
WEIGHTS
Displacement, fully loaded: 65 tons
Carrying capacity, including 3 tons bunker, and 5 tons fresh water, lubricating oil and hydraulic system oil: 12·5 tons
PERFORMANCE
Max speed, half load: 36 knots
Cruising speed: 32·5 knots
Range at cruising speed: 550km (340 miles)

RHS 150

Combining features of both the RHS 140 and the RHS 160, the RHS 150 hydrofoil passenger ferry is available in two versions: a seagoing model with seats for 150 and a variant developed for services across the Italian lakes, seating 180. Power is supplied by two 1,430hp MTU supercharged 4-stroke diesels which give the craft a cruising speed of 32·5 knots and a cruising range of 130n miles.

FOILS: Surface-piercing W foils of hollow

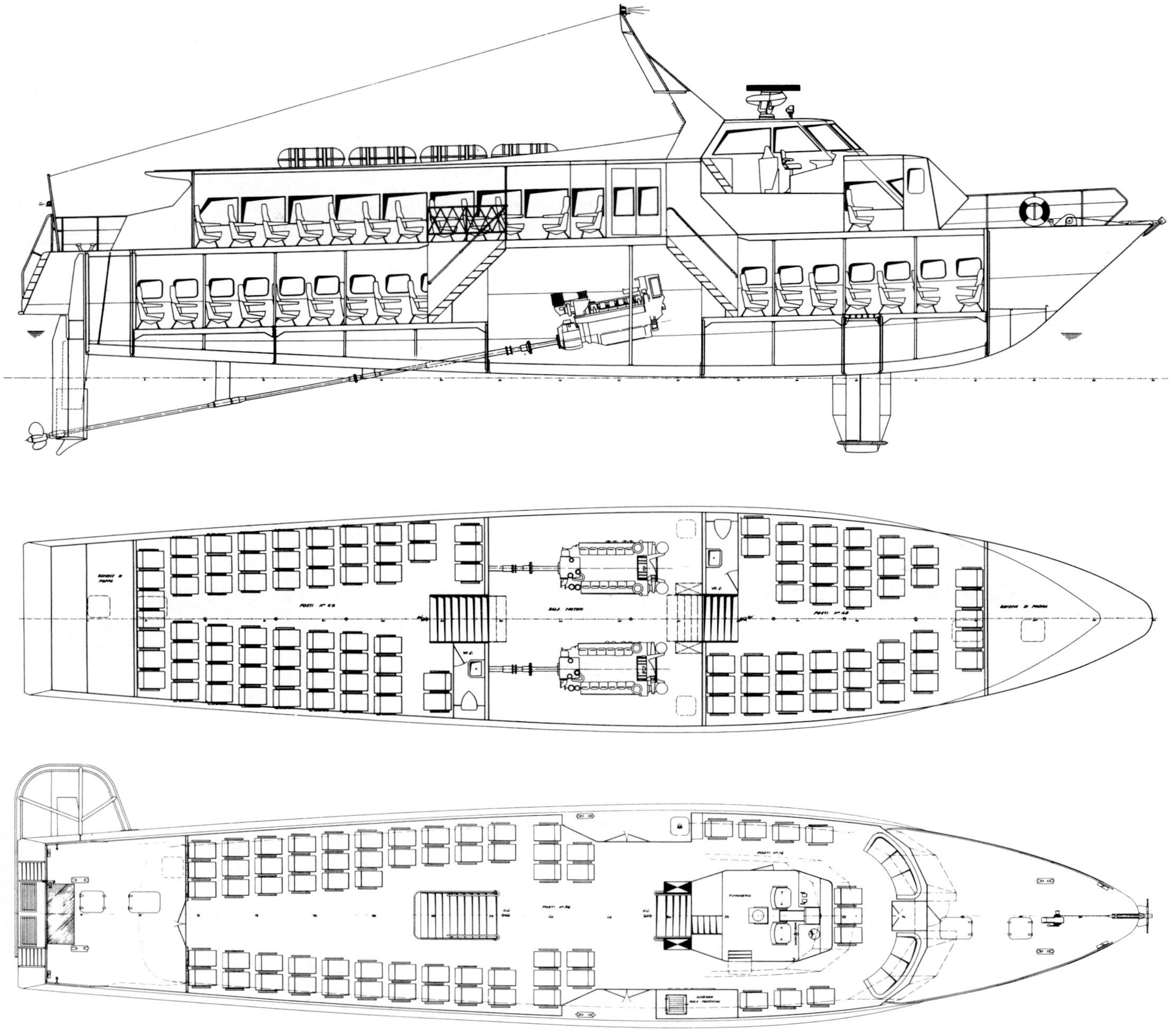

RHS 150

welded steel construction. Lift of the bow foil can be modified by hydraulically-operated trailing edge flaps.

HULL: Riveted light metal alloy design framed on longitudinal and transverse formers.

ACCOMMODATION: The standard model seats 150 in three saloons. High density model design originally for services on the Italian lakes seats 180: 63 in the aft saloon, 45 in the forward saloon and 72 in the belvedere. The forward and stern saloons each have a toilet/wc unit.

POWER PLANT: Motive power is furnished by two supercharged MTU MB 12V 331 TC 82 four-stroke diesels each developing 1,430hp at 2,140rpm continuous. Engine output is transmitted to two bronze propellers via two Zahnradfabrik BW 255L gearboxes.

SYSTEMS, ELECTRICAL: Two 1,300W engine-driven generators supply 24V dc.

DIMENSIONS
Length overall: 28·7m (94ft 1·5in)
Width across foils: 11m (36ft 1·87in)
Draught hullborne: 3·1m (10ft 2in)
      foilborne: 1·4m (4ft 7·87in)
WEIGHTS
Displacement, fully loaded: 65·5 tons
PERFORMANCE
Cruising speed, fully loaded: 32·5 knots
Cruising range: 240km (130n miles)

RHS 160F

One recent addition to the Rodriquez range is the RHS 160F, a 90-ton passenger ferry with seats for 210 passengers and a cruising speed of 36 knots.

FOILS: Surface-piercing W foils of hollow welded steel construction. Craft in this series feature a bow rudder for improved manoeuvrability in congested waters. The bow rudder works simultaneously with the aft rudders. Hydraulically-operated flaps, attached to the trailing edges of the bow and rear foils, are adjusted automatically by a Hamilton Standard electronic stability augmentation system, for the damping of heave, pitch and roll motions in heavy seas.

HULL: Riveted light metal alloy longitudinal structure, welded in parts using inert gas. The hull shape of the RHS 160F is similar to the RHS 140

Seagoing version of RHS 150F

RHS 150 *Freccia del Giardini,* operated by Navigazione Lago Maggiore GG

Outboard profile and upper deck plan of RHS 160

series. In the manufacture of the hull, plates of aluminium and magnesium alloy of 4·4 per cent are used while angle bars are of a high-resistant aluminium, magnesium and silicon alloy.

ACCOMMODATION: 210 passengers seated in three saloons. 58 passengers are accommodated in the forward cabin, 63 in the rear compartment and 89 in the belvedere. Forward and aft saloons and belvedere each have a toilet with wc washbasin units and toilet accessories.

POWER PLANT: Power is provided by two supercharged MTU 16V 396 TB 83 four-stroke diesel engines each with a maximum output of 1,530kW at 2,000rpm under normal operating conditions. Engine starting is accomplished by compressed air starters. Engine output is transmitted to two, three-bladed bronze propellers through two Zahnradfabrik BW 7505 gearboxes, or, alternatively, through two Reintjes WV5 1032V gearboxes.

SYSTEMS, ELECTRICAL: Two 35kVA generating sets, 220V, 60Hz, three-phase. Three insulated cables for ventilation, air-conditioning and power. Two insulated cables for lighting, sockets and other appliances, 24V dc for emergency lighting, auxiliary engine starting and servocontrol. A battery for radio telephone supply is installed on the upper deck. Provision for battery recharge from ac line is foreseen.

HYDRAULICS: Hydraulic steering from the wheelhouse. Plant comprises a Bosch pump installed on the main engines and conveying oil from a 45-litre (10-gallon) tank under pressure to the control cylinders of the rudder and anchor windlass, whilst a second hydraulic pump, which is also installed on the main engines, conveys oil under pressure to the flap control cylinders.

FIREFIGHTING: Fixed CO_2 plant of four CO_2 bottles of about 20kg each for the engine room and fuel tank space; portable extinguishers in various parts of the craft. Water intake connected to fire pump for connection in emergency.

DIMENSIONS
Length overall: 31·2m
Width across foils: 12·6m
Draught hullborne: 3·76m
    foilborne: 1·7m
WEIGHTS
Displacement, fully loaded: 91·5 tons
Payload, passengers and luggage: 17·8 tons

RHS 160F undergoing sea trials

Interior of RHS 160 belvedere cabin

PERFORMANCE
Max speed: 37 knots

Cruising speed: 34 knots
Cruising range: 100n miles

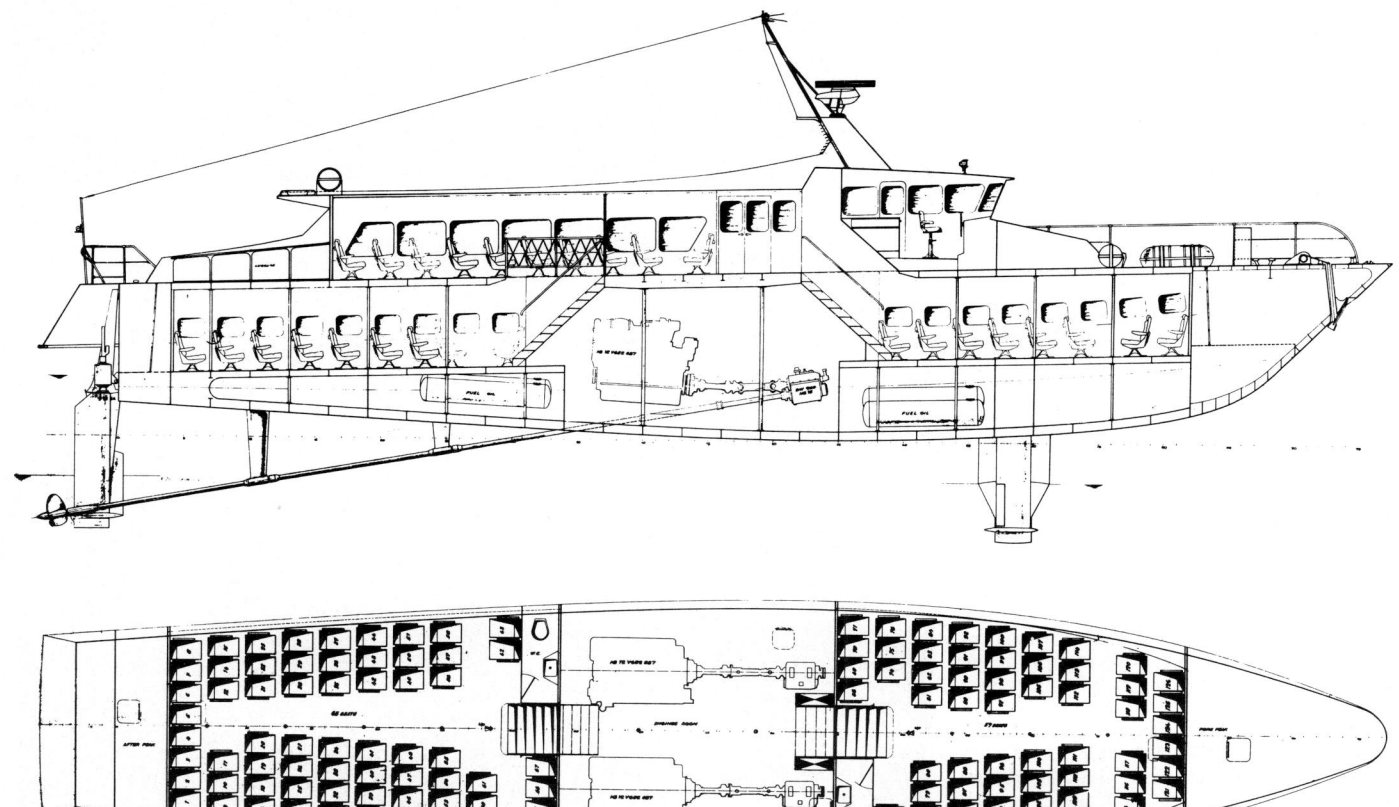
Inboard profile and lower deck plan of RHS 160F

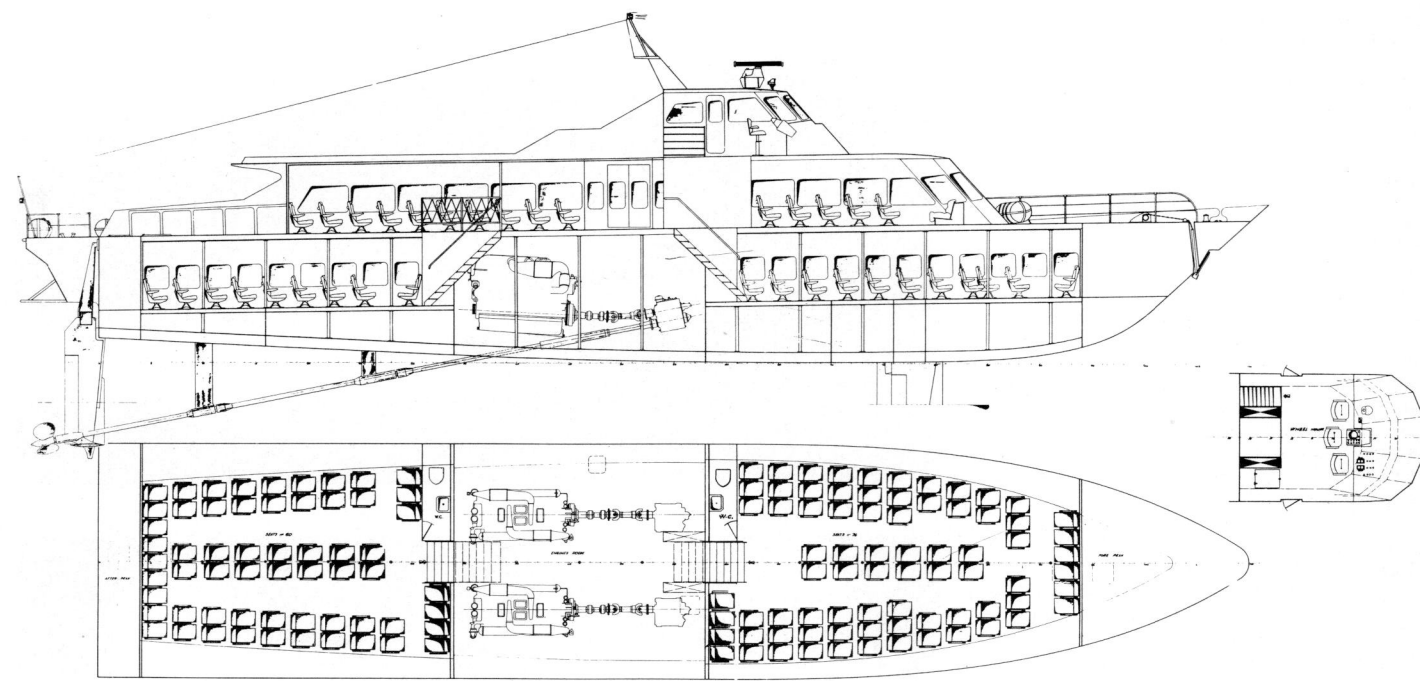

Inboard profile and lower deck arrangement of RHS 200

RHS 200

Construction of this 125-ton, 254- to 400-seat fast ferry began in 1978. Powered by two super-charged MTU MB 16V 652 TB 71 four-stroke diesel engines, the cruising speed is 36 knots.

FOILS: Surface-piercing W foils of hollow welded steel construction. Craft in this series feature a bow rudder for improved manoeuvrability in congested waters. The bow rudder operates simultaneously with the aft rudders. An advantage of the W configuration bow foil is its relatively shallow draught requirement in relation to the vessel's overall size. Hydraulically-operated flaps are fitted to the trailing edge of the bow foil to balance out longitudinal load shifting, assist take-off and adjust the flying height. The craft can also be equipped with the Hamilton Standard electronic stability augmentation system, which employs sensors and servomechanisms to position flaps automatically on the bow and stern foils for the damping of heave, pitch and roll motions in heavy seas.

HULL: V-bottom hull of high tensile riveted light metal alloy construction, employing Peraluman plates and Anticorrodal frames. The rake of the stem is in galvanised steel.

ACCOMMODATION: Seats for up to 400 passengers, according to the route served. In typical configuration there are three main passenger saloons and a bar. The standard seating arrangement allows for 127 in the main deck saloon, 55 in the aft lower saloon and 72 in the bow passenger saloon. Seating is normally four abreast in two lines with a central aisle. The bar, at the forward end of the wheelhouse belvedere superstructure, has either an eight-seat sofa or 19 seats.

The wheelhouse, which is raised to provide a 360-degree view, is reached from the main deck belvedere saloon by a short companionway. Controls and instrumentation are attached to a panel on the forward bulkhead which extends the width of the wheelhouse. In the centre is the steering control and gyro-compass, on the starboard side are controls for the two engines, gearboxes and controllable-pitch propellers, and on the port side is the radar. Seats are provided for the captain, chief engineer and first mate. In the wheelhouse are a radio-telephone and a chart table.

POWER PLANT: Motive power is supplied by two supercharged MTU MB 16V 652 TB 71 4-stroke diesel engines, each with a maximum output of 2,530hp at 1,460rpm under normal operating conditions. Engine output is transferred to two supercavitating, controllable-pitch propellers.

SYSTEMS, ELECTRICAL: Two generating

Forward cabin of RHS 200

Belvedere cabin of RHS 200

sets: one 220V, three-phase ac, for all consumer services, the second for charging 24V battery sets and operating firefighting and hydraulic pumps. Power distribution panel in wheelhouse for navigation light circuits, cabin lighting, radar, RDF, gyro compass and emergency circuits.

FIREFIGHTING: Fixed CO_2 self-contained automatic systems for power plant and fuel tank spaces, plus portable extinguishers for cabins and holds.

DIMENSIONS
Length overall: 35·8m (117ft 5in)
Width across foils: 14·5m (47ft 7in)
Draught hullborne: 4·55m (15ft 1·75in)
    foilborne: 2·05m (6ft 8·33in)

WEIGHTS
Displacement fully loaded: 125 tons

PERFORMANCE
Cruising speed: 36 knots
Max speed: 41 knots
Cruising range: 200n miles

RHS ALIYACHT

A luxury hydrofoil yacht of light alloy construction, the RHS Aliyacht is derived from the

RHS 200 *Superjumbo*

RHS 110 passenger ferry. It is powered by two 1,350hp MTU MB 12V 493 Ty 71 diesel engines and has a cruising speed of 38 knots.

The craft is equipped with the Hamilton Standard electronic stability augmentation system, which is designed to provide a smoother ride in

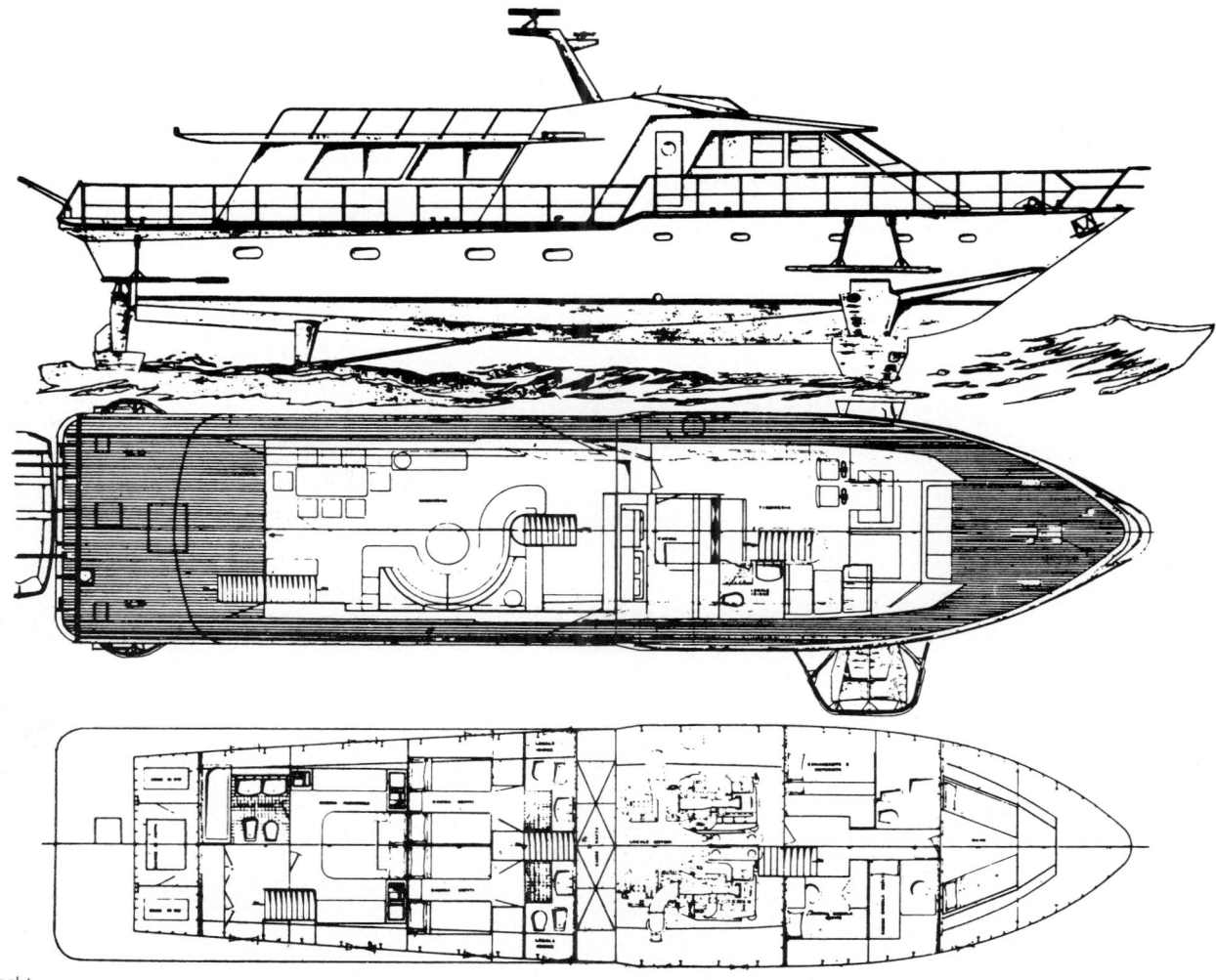

RHS Aliyacht

RHS Aliyacht

heavy seas. The system uses sensors and servo-mechanisms to position foil flaps automatically for the maximum damping of heave, pitch and roll motions.

FOILS: Bow and rear foils are of surface-piercing type and constructed in partly hollow welded steel. Two hydraulically-operated flaps, attached to the trailing edges of the bow foil, are adjusted automatically by the stabilisation system for the damping of heave, pitch and roll motions. The rear foil is rigidly attached to the transom, its incidence angle being determined during tests.

HULL: The V-bottom hull is of high-tensile riveted light metal alloy construction, using Peraluman (aluminium and magnesium alloy) plates and Anticorrodal (aluminium, magnesium and silicon alloy) profiles. The rake of the stem is in 3·5mm (0·137in) thick galvanised steel. The superstructure is constructed in 2mm (0·078in) Peraluman plate, and the roof is detachable to facilitate the removal and replacement of the main engines.

ACCOMMODATION: Main deck accommodation comprises the wheelhouse and radio cabin, a saloon and a galley. The saloon can be fitted with two four-seat sofas, armchairs, tea-table, a metal table with four chairs, and a bar. Below deck, from aft peak forward, is a large cabin for the owner, with its own bathroom and small private drawing room; two double cabins for guests with adjacent wc/washbasin/shower units and, beyond the engines, a cabin for the captain and engineer, and two single cabins for guests.

The wheelhouse is reached via a companion-way from the saloon and is connected by a door with the upper deck. The pilot's position, controls and instruments are on the port side, together with the radar screen.

POWER PLANT: Power is supplied by two supercharged 12-cylinder MTU MB 12V 439 Ty 71 diesels, each rated at 1,350hp at 1,500rpm. Engine output is transferred to two three-bladed bronze-aluminium propellers through Zahnrad-fabrik BW 800 H20 gearboxes.

SYSTEMS, ELECTRICAL: Two 10kW, 220V, three-phase Onan generating sets, coupled to batteries, provide 24V dc for engine starting, instruments, lighting, radio, etc.

DIMENSIONS
EXTERNAL
Length overall: 24·5m (78ft 9in)
Beam overall: 6·1m (20ft)
Hull beam: 5·85m (19ft 2·25in)
Draught hullborne: 2·95m (9ft 8·125in)
    foilborne: 1·25m (4ft 1·25in)
WEIGHTS
Displacement, loaded: 52 tons
PERFORMANCE
Max speed: 41 knots
Cruising speed: 38 knots
Range: 644km (400 miles)

RHS HYDROILS

These are derivatives of RHS passenger-carrying hydrofoils, and are designed to ferry personnel, materials and equipment between offshore oil rigs and shore bases. Vessels in the series feature an open cargo deck aft of the bridge superstructure instead of an aft passenger saloon. The three main types are the RHS 70, the RHS 140, and the RHS 160 Hydroil.

RHS 70 HYDROIL

The first of the series of RHS 70 Hydroil offshore drilling platform supply vessels was built for ENI Oil Corporation, which employs the craft, called *Porto Corsini*, in the Adriatic. A mixed passenger/cargo version of the RHS 70 passenger ferry, this variant has an open cargo deck aft of the bridge superstructure. Dimensions of the cargo deck are: length 7·5m (24ft 7in); width 3·5m (11ft 6in) and height 1·05m (3ft 5in).

FOILS: Bow and rear foils are of surface-piercing V configuration, with about 66% of the weight supported by the bow foil and 34% by the rear foil. Each foil, together with its struts and horizontal supporting tube, forms a rigid framework which facilitates the exchange of the foil structure. The foils are of hollow-ribbed construction and fabricated from medium Asera steel. The forward foil can be tilted within narrow limits by means of a hydraulic ram acting on the foil strut supporting tube. The angle of attack can therefore be adjusted during operation to assist take-off and counteract the effect of large variations in loading.

HULL: The hull is of riveted light metal alloy (Peraluman) and framed on a combination of longitudinal and transverse formers. Watertight compartments are provided in the bow and stern, and a double-bottom runs from immediately aft of the engine room, beneath the full length of the cargo deck, to the after peak. Contained within the double-bottom are six cylindrical aluminium fuel tanks with a total capacity of 2,250 litres (495 gallons). Access to the fore and aft compartments is via removable deck hatches. The deck is of 5mm (0·196in) Peraluman, reinforced to withstand heavily concentrated loads. Two 125mm (4·9in) diameter scuppers are provided aft for rapid drainage. Heavy rubber fenders are provided at the bow and stern.

ACCOMMODATION: The craft has a crew of two, and seats up to 12 passengers in a saloon, immediately aft of the wheelhouse. Passengers have a choice of six armchairs and two, three-place settees, one of which converts into a bed for transporting sick or injured personnel. All seats are equipped with safety belts. Aft of the saloon is

RHS 70 Hydroil *Porto Corsini*

a fully equipped galley with refrigerator, a gas cooker with two gas rings, cupboards, plate rack and sink unit. Two folding wooden tables permit up to eight passengers to take meals at one sitting. A toilet/washbasin unit is provided opposite the galley on the port side. The engine room, wheelhouse and passenger saloon are fully heated and ventilated. A full range of safety equipment is carried including inflatable rafts and lifebelts for each passenger and crew member.

POWER PLANT: Power is supplied by a 12-cylinder supercharged MTU 12V 331 TC 82 with a maximum output of 1,430hp at 2,340rpm. Engine output is transferred to a three-bladed 700mm (27·5in) bronze-aluminium propeller through a Zahnradfabrik BW 800 H20 gearbox. The propeller shaft is 90mm (3·5in) in diameter, and supported at three points by seawater lubricated rubber bearings. In an emergency, hullborne propulsion is provided by a 105hp Mercedes OM 352 diesel with a Mercruiser Z-drive. The engine is installed in the aft peak and propels the craft at about 5 knots.

SYSTEMS, ELECTRICAL: 220V 50Hz three-phase ac, 24V dc; provision for 220V 50Hz three-phase shore supply. The dc supply is from a 24V generator driven by the main engine and

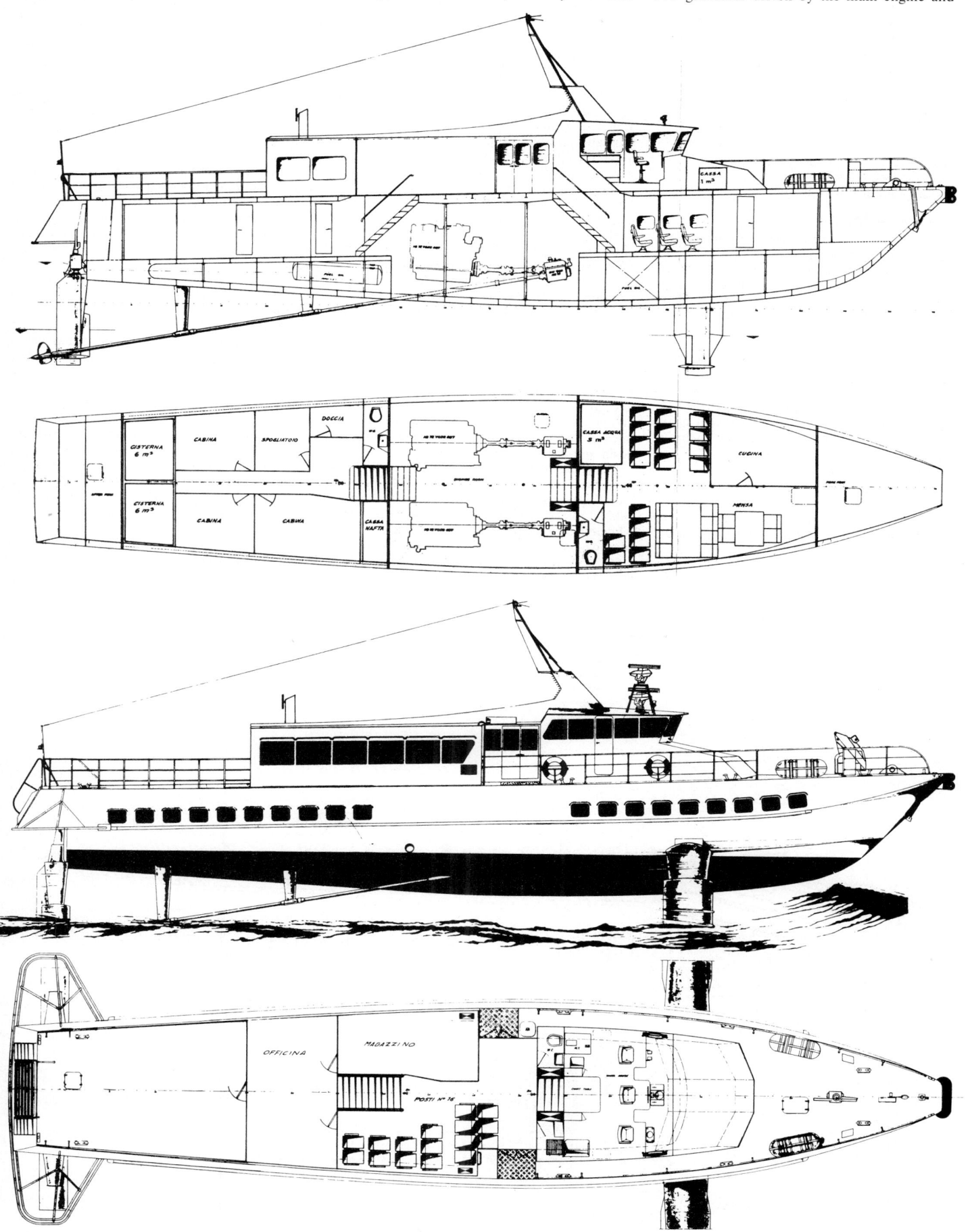

RHS 160 Hydroil

feeding a 235Ah battery. Ac supply is derived from a four-stroke Onan diesel generator set, located in the engine room.

HYDRAULICS: One Bosch Hy/ZFR 1/16 AR 101 for steering and bow foil incidence control.

COMMUNICATIONS AND NAVIGATION

Radio: VHF radio-telephone to customers' requirements.

Radar: Decca, Raytheon etc, to customers' requirements.

DIMENSIONS

Length overall, hull: 20·95m (68ft 9in)
Hull beam: 5·06m (16ft 7in)
Width over foils: 7·4m (24ft 3in)
Draught hullborne: 2·7m (8ft 10in)
  foilborne: 1·14m (3ft 9in)

WEIGHTS

Max take-off displacement: 33·12 tons
Max load on open cargo deck: 3 tons

PERFORMANCE (with normal payload)

Cruising speed: 32 knots
Range: 480km (300 miles)

RHS 140 HYDROIL

The second in the Rodriquez Hydroil range is a mixed passenger/cargo version of the 65-ton RHS 140. As with the smaller RHS 70 Hydroil, the main passenger saloon is replaced by a large open cargo deck for loads up to 6 tons. The deck is 9·5m (31ft 2in) long, 4·8m (15ft 9in) wide and 1·19m (3ft 11in) high.

The craft will carry a crew of two and up to 14 passengers. Two variants are available, one equipped with seats for 23 passengers and with a cargo capacity of 5 tons and the other with seats for 60 passengers and a cargo capacity of 3 tons. Power will be supplied by two 12-cylinder super-charged MTU 12V 493 Ty 71 engines, each with a maximum output of 1,350hp.

DIMENSIONS

Length overall, hull: 28·5m (93ft 6in)
Hull beam: 6·1m (20ft)
Width over foils: 10·72m (35ft 2in)
Draught hullborne: 3·5m (11ft 6in)
  foilborne: 1·5m (4ft 11in)

WEIGHTS

Normal take-off displacement: 64 tons

PERFORMANCE

Cruising speed: 32-34 knots
Range at cruising speed: 480km (300 miles)

RHS 160 HYDROIL

Largest member of the Rodriquez range of offshore oil rig support vessels, the RHS 160 features an open cargo deck aft of the bridge superstructure and additional fuel and water tanks in the place of the lower aft passenger saloons. The vessel carries a crew of 5 and 42 passengers, plus 10 tons of cargo, at a cruising speed of 35 knots.

FOILS: Surface-piercing W foils of hollow welded steel construction. Craft in this series feature bow and aft rudders, both of which operate simultaneously. Hydraulically-operated flaps attached to the trailing edges of the bow and rear foils are adjusted automatically by a Hamilton Standard electronic stability augmentation system for the damping of heave, pitch and roll motions in heavy seas.

HULL: V-bottom hull of high tensile riveted light metal alloy construction. In the manufacture of the hull, plates of aluminium and magnesium alloy of 4·4% are used, whilst angle bars are of a high resistant aluminium, magnesium and silicon alloy. Inert gas welding (Argon) is used for strengthening beams, web frames, keelsons and stringers. Steel and rubber fenders are fitted aft and in the sides of the main deck to protect the foils when docking.

ACCOMMODATION: Forward saloon seats 37 passengers, and the upper belvedere saloon seats 5. The seats, designed for maximum comfort, have arms and each is provided with an ash tray and magazine holder. The toilet, finished in Formica or similar laminate, is provided with a wc basin and normal accessories.

Crew members are accommodated in two cabins forward, that on the starboard being provided with two berths and a locker, while the port cabin has three berths and lockers. The wheelhouse is located well forward and has seats for the master in the centre, chief engineer on the starboard side and radar operator on the port side. All steering and other controls are located in the wheelhouse, including a circuit control panel for the navigation lights, craft lighting, radar, gyro-compass and other electrical consumer and emergency circuits.

POWER PLANT: Power is provided by two supercharged MTU MB 12V 652 TB 71 4-stroke diesel engines, each with a maximum output of 1,950hp at 1,460rpm. Engine starting is accomplished by compressed air starters. Output is transmitted to two three-bladed bronze propellers through two Zahnradfabrik 900 HS 15 gearboxes.

SYSTEMS, ELECTRICAL: Two 35kVA generating sets, 220V, 50Hz, three-phase for ventilation and air-conditioning; 220V, 50Hz single-phase, for lighting and other appliances; 24V dc for auxiliary lighting, engine starting and servocontrol.

HYDRAULICS: Hydraulic steering from the wheelhouse. Plant comprises a Bosch pump installed on one of the main engines and conveying oil under pressure from a 45-litre (10-gallon) tank to the control cylinders of the rudder and anchor windlass, whilst a second hydraulic pump, which is installed on the other main engine, conveys oil under pressure to the flap control cylinders.

The two systems are interchangeable and equipped with safety valves, manometers and micronic filters.

FIREFIGHTING: Fixed CO_2 plant for engine room and fuel tank space; portable appliances include two 6kg powder extinguishers and one 5kg CO_2 extinguisher in the engine room; two 10-litre water extinguishers in the passenger saloons and one 6kg powder extinguisher in the wheelhouse.

Two water extinguishing systems are provided, one driven by the main engine and the other by a motor driven pump. The system can supply a monitor on the upper deck at the bow and two fire hose water outlets located amidships on the upper deck. A dual-purpose water/foam nozzle can be supplied on request.

DIMENSIONS

Length overall: 31·3m (103ft)
Moulded beam: 6·2m (20ft 4·125in)

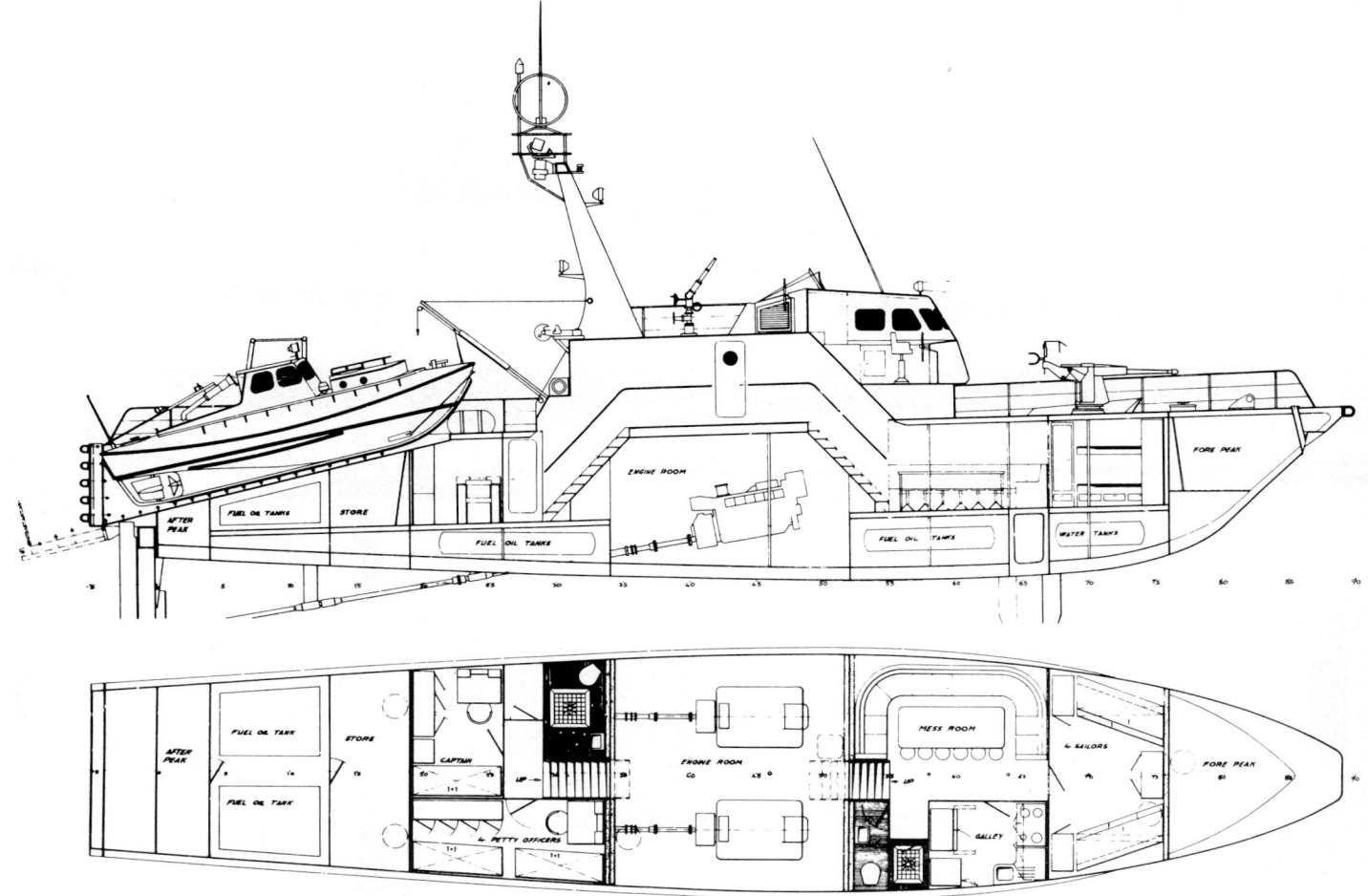

Inboard profile and deck plan of M-RHS 150

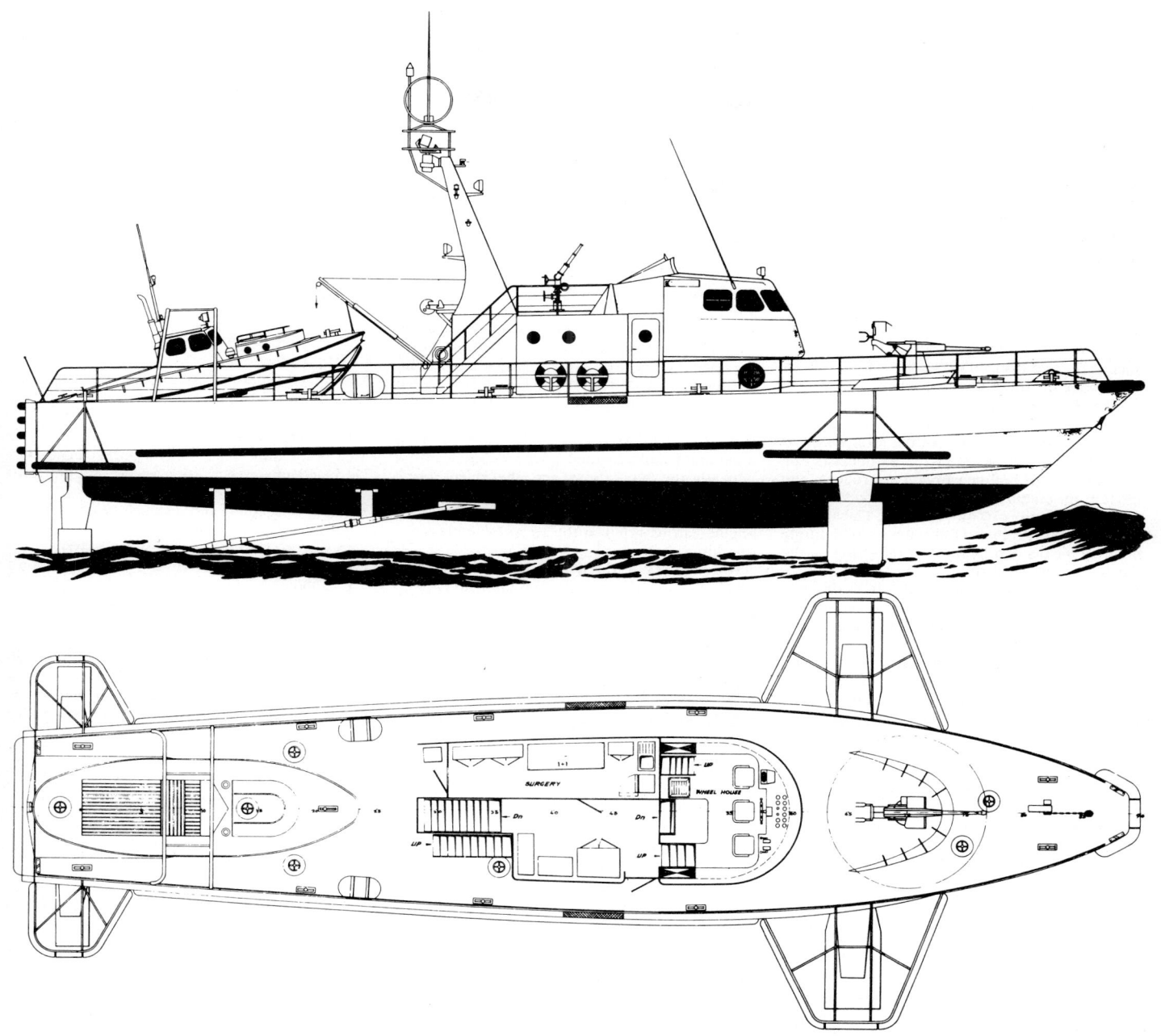

M-RHS 150 search and rescue craft

Width across foils: 12·6m (41ft 4in)
Draught, hullborne: 3·7m (12ft 6in)
  foilborne: 1·35m (4ft 6in)
WEIGHTS
Displacement, fully loaded: 85 tons
PERFORMANCE
Cruising speed: 35 knots
Cruising range: 322km (200 miles)

M-RHS 150 SEARCH AND RESCUE CRAFT

This variant of the well-known RHS 140 is a multi-purpose rescue craft equipped for a full range of search and rescue duties, including firefighting and wreck marking. It has a top speed of 36 knots and can operate in heavy seas at a considerable distance from its shore base. A Merryweather dual-purpose water/foam monitor is located on the foredeck and an 8·5m launch is carried on the upper deck aft.

A sick bay is provided and can be fitted out to accommodate 30 to 40 survivors.

A feature of the design is the filling of the double bottom with expanded polystyrene to provide sufficient buoyancy to make it unsinkable, even with the watertight compartments flooded.

FOILS: Surface-piercing W foils of hollow welded steel construction. Foil lift is varied by flaps operated by an electronic/hydraulic system developed by Rodriquez in conjunction with

Hamilton Standard. Under calm sea conditions, the flaps can be operated manually.
HULL: Riveted light metal alloy design framed on longitudinal and transverse formers. Areas of the attachment points of the bow and rear foils are reinforced with steel. Steel is also used for the rake of the stem, the stern tube for the propeller shaft and the propeller shaft attachment.
ACCOMMODATION: Berths, lockers and living accommodation for a crew of eleven, comprising the captain, two officers, two petty officers and six seamen. Seats are provided in the wheelhouse for an operating crew of three. A 'flying bridge' with a duplicated set of instruments and controls provides improved visibility during search operations. A ten-berth sick bay, with a small office for the doctor, is provided aft. A large roof hatch is provided in the sick bay through which stretcher casualties can be lowered. The sick bay can be fitted out to accommodate 30 to 40 survivors.
POWER PLANT: Power is provided by two MTU 12V 331 TC 82 12-cylinder supercharged diesel engines, each developing 1,430hp at 2,340rpm. Engine output is transmitted to two three-bladed, 700mm diameter bronze propellers through Zahnradfabrik gearboxes.
SYSTEMS, ELECTRICAL: Two engine-driven generators of 24V dc supply essential services and emergency lights. An ac system, powered by a generator set, supplies lighting and all other on

board consumers. Two battery sets are provided for starting the main engines and generators.
HYDRAULICS: Hydraulic steering and variation of foil flap incidence from the wheelhouse. Plant comprises two Bosch pumps installed on the main engines and conveying oil from a tank under pressure to the control cylinders of the rudder and foil flaps.
AIR CONDITIONING: Provided on request.
FIREFIGHTING: Fixed CO_2 plant for the engine room and fuel oil bays; portable CO_2 and foam fire extinguishers at various parts of the craft. One Merryweather dual purpose foam/water monitor.
DIMENSIONS
Length overall: 28·7m (94ft 1·5in)
Width across foils: 10·9m (35ft 9in)
Draught hullborne: 3·15m (10ft 4in)
  foilborne: 1·2m (3ft 11in)
WEIGHTS
Displacement, fully loaded: 65 tonnes (64 tons)
PERFORMANCE
Max speed: 36 knots
Cruising speed: 32·5 knots
Endurance at cruising speed: 18 hours, 600 miles
  at low speed: 50 hours, 600 miles
Cruising range: 1,110km (600n miles)

M-RHS 150 PATROL CRAFT

The patrol variant of the M-RHS 150 is designed for fisheries law enforcement, patrolling and customs operations against ships offshore. It has a similar specification to the Search and Rescue variant but a fully loaded displacement of only 64 tonnes. Accommodation is provided for a crew of twelve, comprising the captain, three officers, four petty officers and four seamen.

M PATROL CRAFT

Derived from RHS passenger vessels, the M series craft are designed for coast guard and anti-contraband patrol. Suitably armed, they can undertake various naval duties, ranging from patrol to minelaying. The armament shown in the accompanying drawings can be augmented or substituted by surface-to-air and surface-to-surface missiles according to requirements.

M 100

The M 100 is similar in design and performance to the two PAT 20 patrol hydrofoils built by Rodriquez for the Philippine Navy.

FOILS: Bow and rear foils are surface-piercing V configuration and identical to those of the standard RHS 70. About 59% of the total weight is borne by the bow foil and 41% by the rear foil. The foils are of hollow ribbed construction and made from medium Asera steel.

Total foil area is 10·4m² (112ft²). The angle of incidence of the forward foil can be varied during flight by means of a hydraulic ram acting on the foil strut supporting tube.

HULL: The hull is of riveted light alloy construction with Peraluman (aluminium and magnesium alloy) plates and Anticorrodal (aluminium, magnesium and silicon alloy) profiles.

ACCOMMODATION: The crew comprises a captain, two officers and eight NCOs and ratings. The pilot's position is on the left of the wheelhouse, with the principal instrumentation;

the radar operator sits on the right with the auxiliary instrumentation. The pilot is provided with an intercom system connecting him with the officers' cabin, engine room and crew cabin. The internal space has been divided as follows:

the forward or bow room, subdivided into two cabins, one for the captain, the other for two officers, and including a wc with washstand and a storeroom with a refrigerator;

the stern room, with eight berths for the NCOs and ratings, a wc with washstand and a galley equipped with a gas stove and an electric refrigerator;

the deck room, aft of the wheelhouse, with tilting sofa and table for R/T equipment.

Air conditioning is installed in the captain's and officers' quarters.

POWER PLANT: Power is supplied by a supercharged 12-cylinder MTU 12V 331 TC 82 with a max continuous output of 1,430hp at 2,340rpm. Engine output is transferred to a three-bladed bronze aluminium propeller through a Zahnradfabrik BW 800/S reversible gear. Fuel (total capacity 2,800kg) is carried in ten cylindrical aluminium tanks located in the double bottom beneath the bow room and the stern room. Dynamic and reserve oil tanks in the engine room give a total oil capacity of 120kg. An auxiliary engine can be fitted in the stern for emergency operation.

ARMAMENT AND SEARCH EQUIPMENT: Single 12·7mm machine gun mounted above well position in bow, and two searchlights or one 8cm Oerlikon 3Z8DLa rocket launcher.

SYSTEMS, ELECTRICAL: 220V, 10kW, diesel generator with batteries supplies instruments, radio and radar and external and internal lights, navigation lights and searchlights.

HYDRAULICS: 120kg/cm² pressure hydraulic

system for steering and varying forward foil incidence angle.

APU: Onan engine for air conditioning when requested.

DIMENSIONS
Length overall, hull: 20·89m (68ft 6in)
Hull beam: 4·79m (15ft 8·75in)
Beam overall: 7·4m (24ft 4in)
Draught hullborne: 2·76m (9ft 1in)
  foilborne: 1·2m (4ft)
Height overall,
  hullborne: 6·44m (21ft)
  foilborne: 8m (26ft 3in)
WEIGHTS
Net tonnage: 28 tons
Light displacement: 26 tons
Max take-off displacement: 32·5 tons
Useful load: 7·6 tons
Max useful load: 8·1 tons
PERFORMANCE
Max speed foilborne: 38 knots
  hullborne: 13 knots
Cruising speed foilborne: 34 knots
  hullborne: 12 knots
Max permissible sea state, foilborne: Force 4
Designed range at cruising speed: 869km (540 miles)
Number of seconds and distance to take-off: 20 seconds, 100m (328ft)
  to stop craft: 12 seconds, 50m (164ft)
Fuel consumption at cruising speed: 145kg/h (320lb/h)
  at max speed: 180kg/h (397lb/h)

M 150

This is the fast patrol boat version of the RHS 110 passenger ferry. Modifications include a revised cabin superstructure with an upper bridge; the installation of eight Sistel Sea Killer

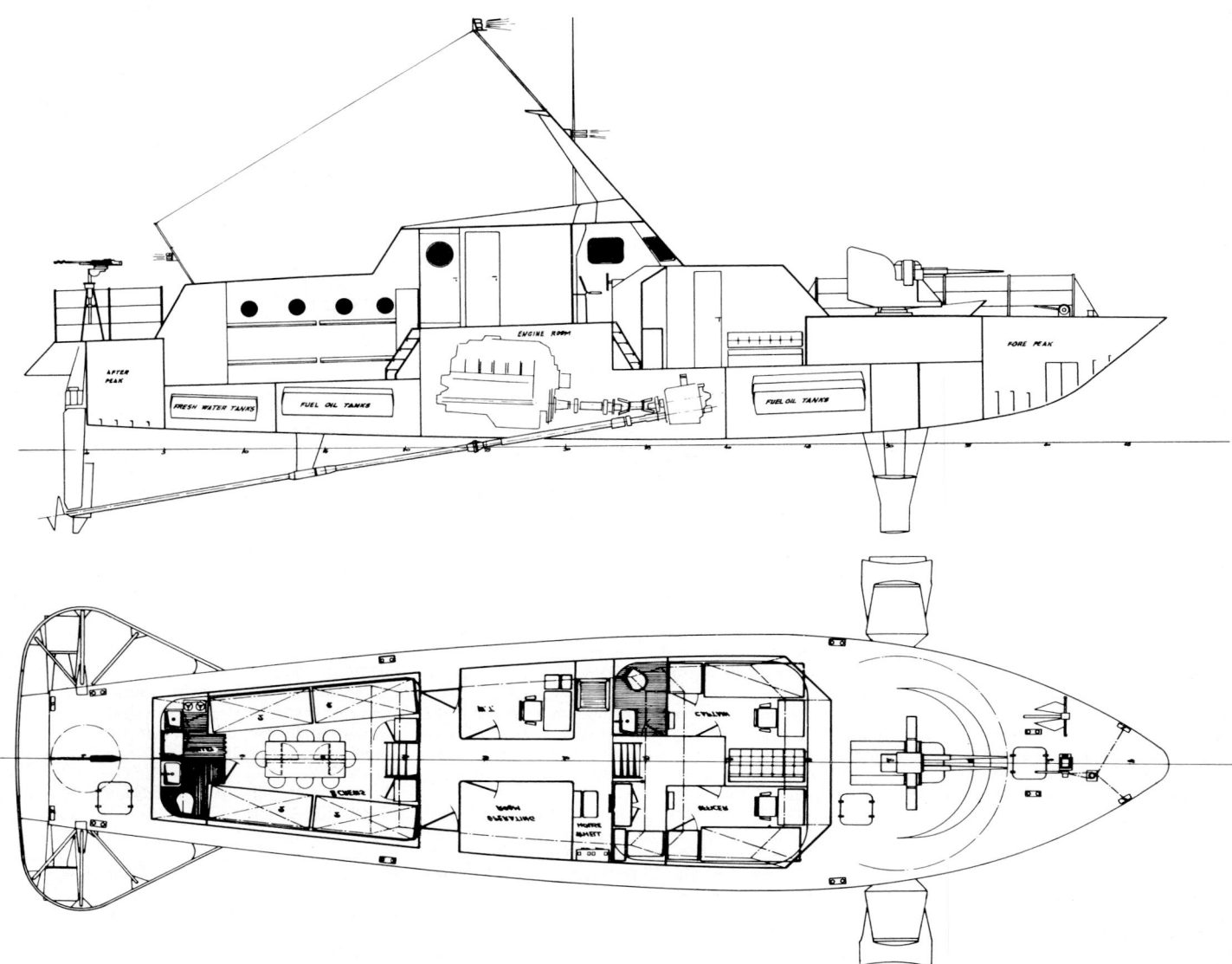

Inboard profile and deck plan of M 100

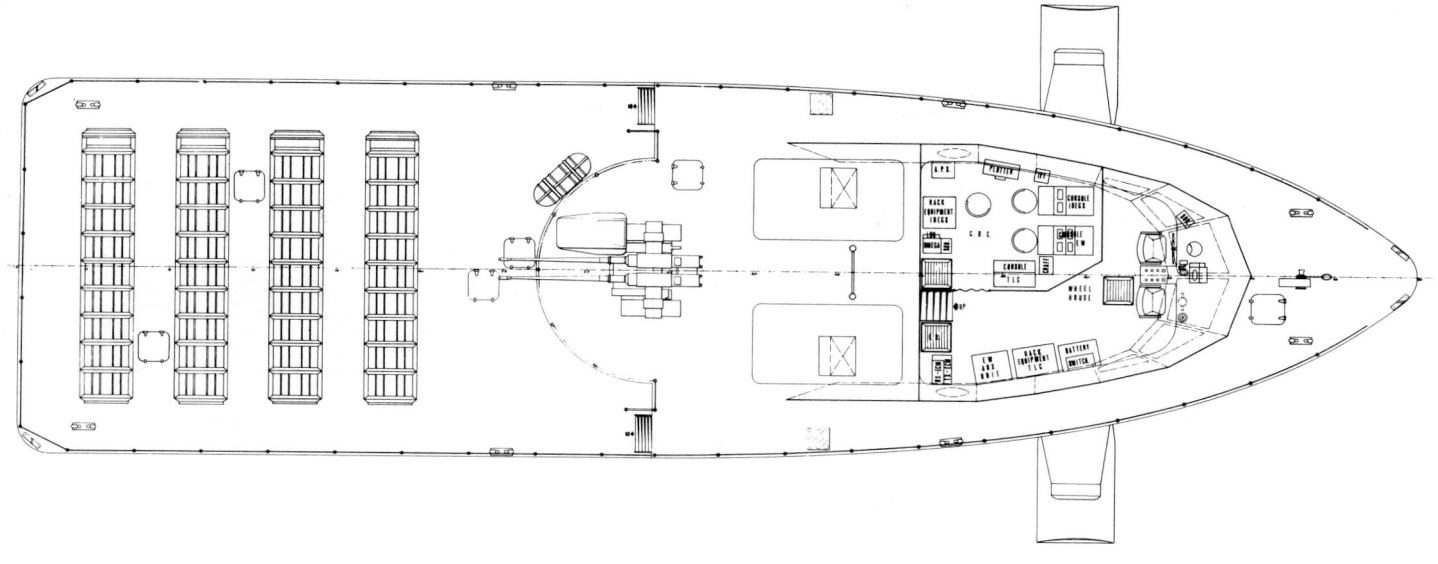

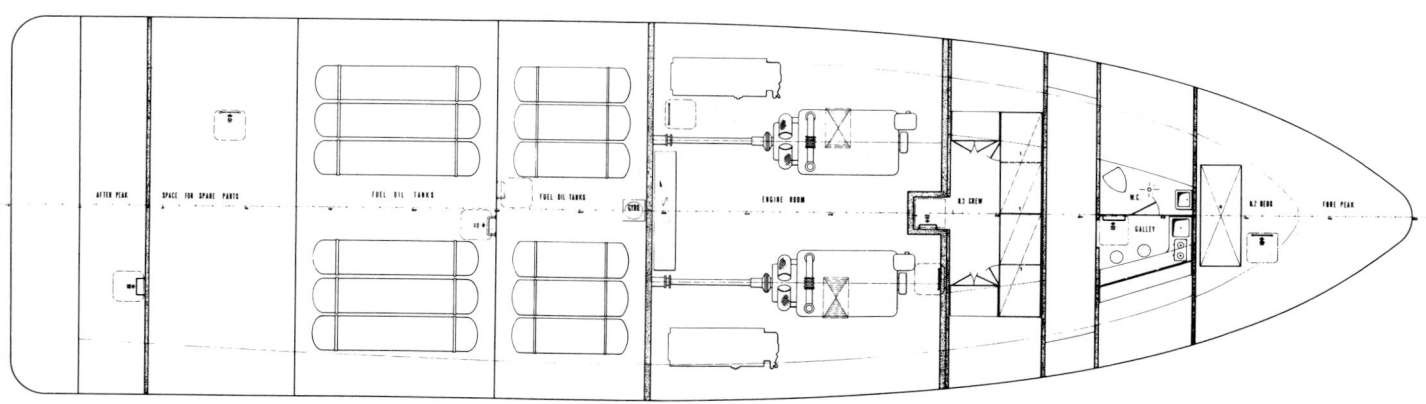

Deck views of M 150

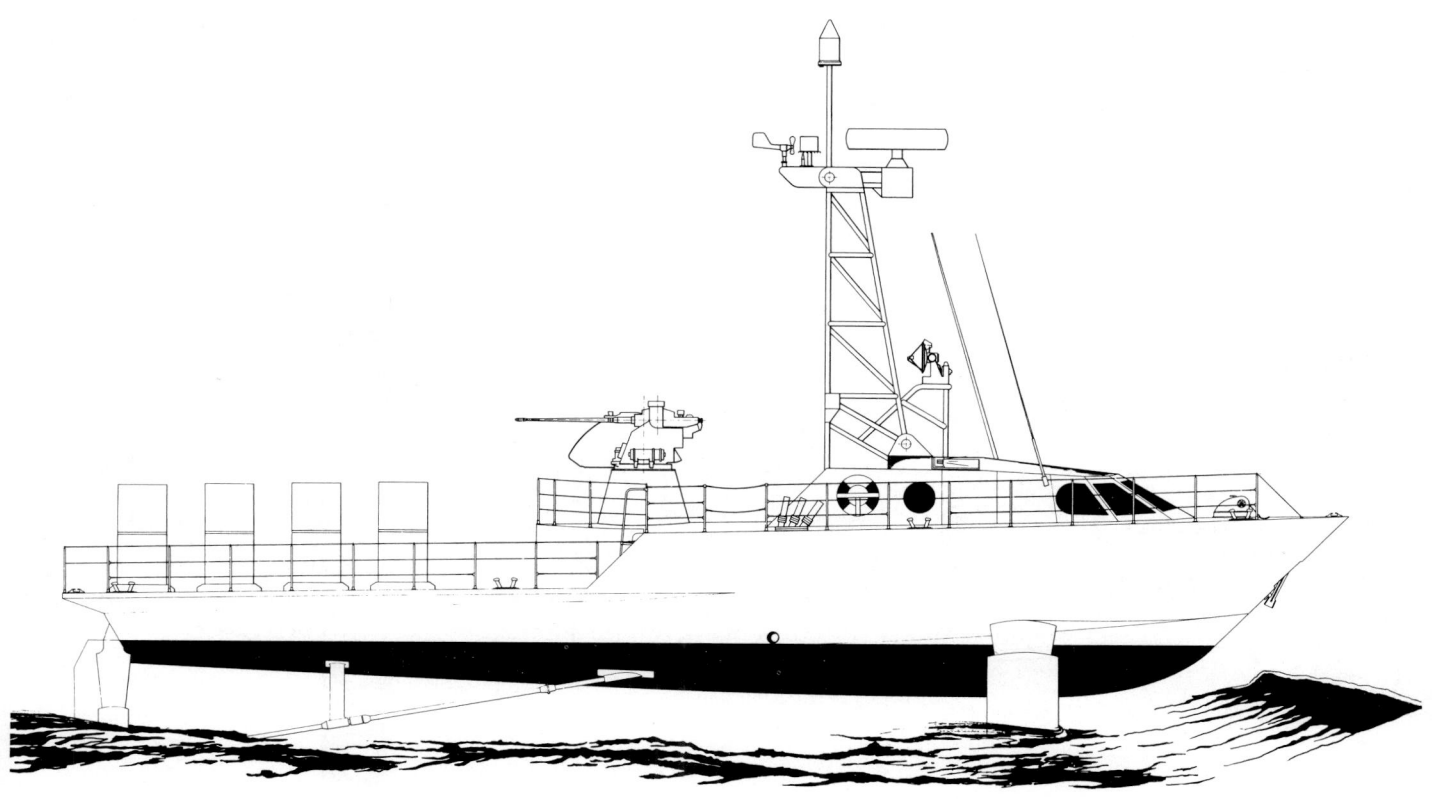

Outboard profile of M 150

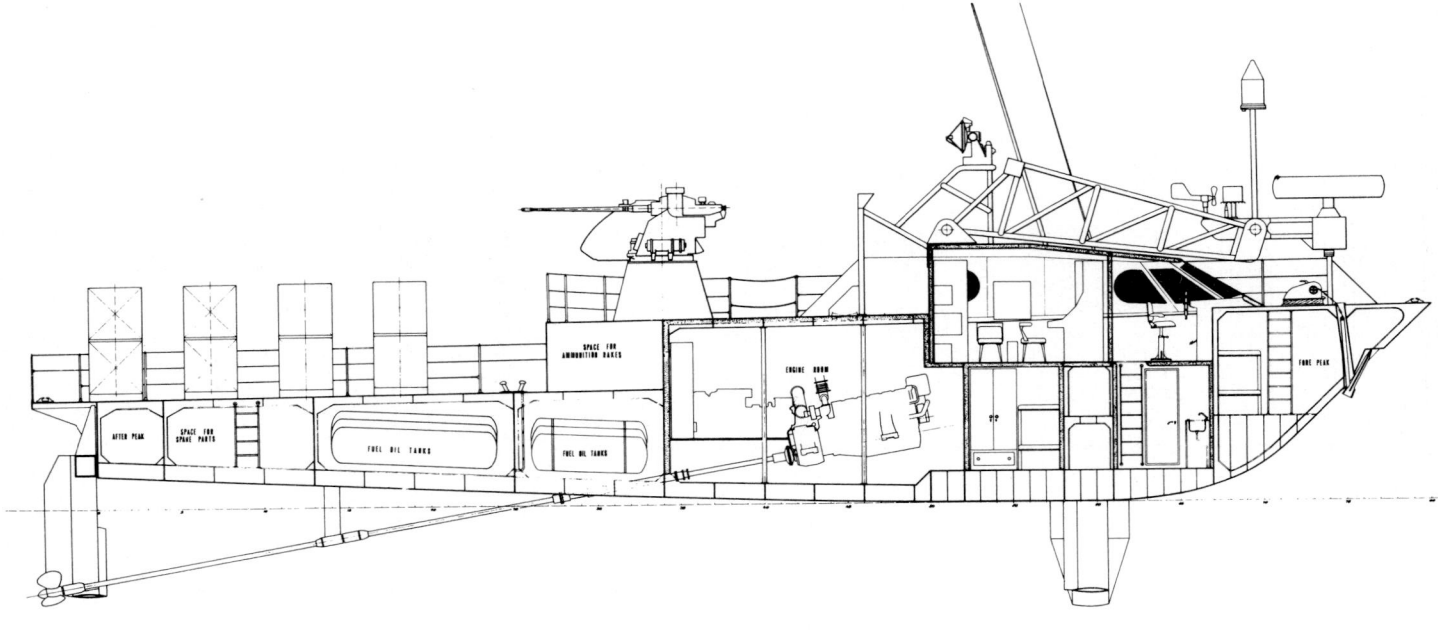

M 150 inboard profile

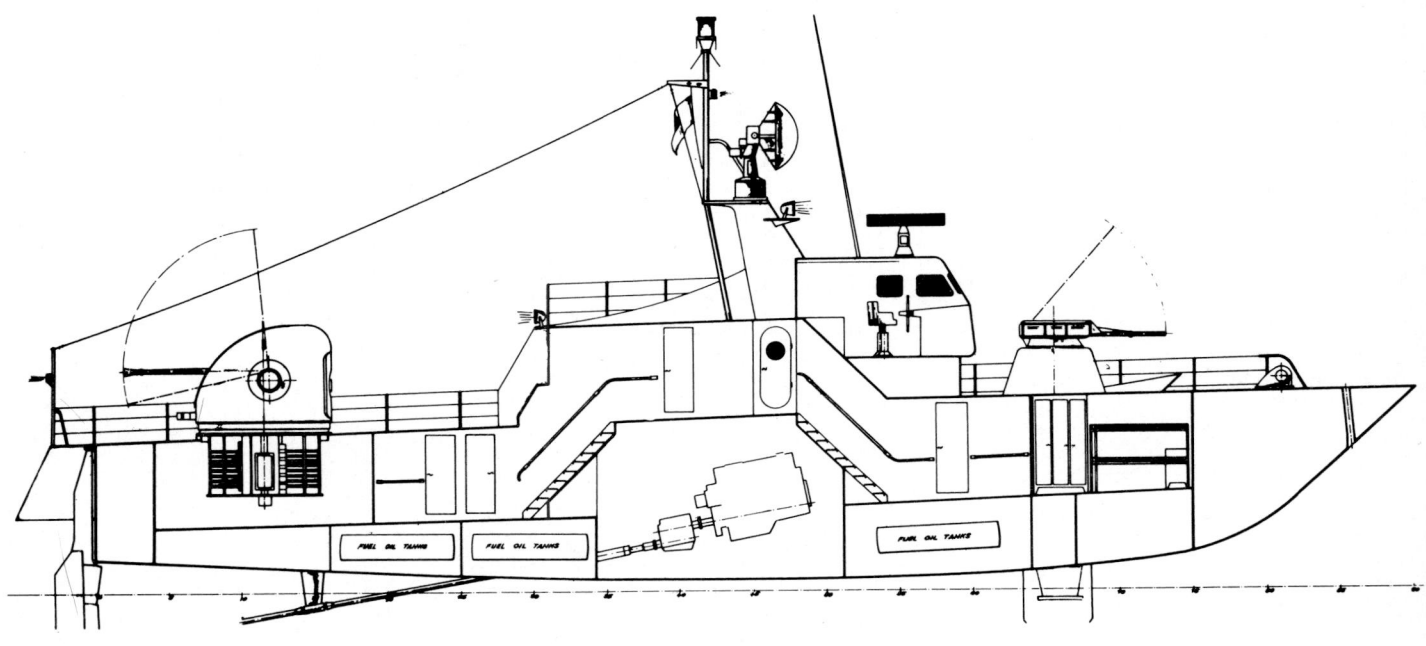

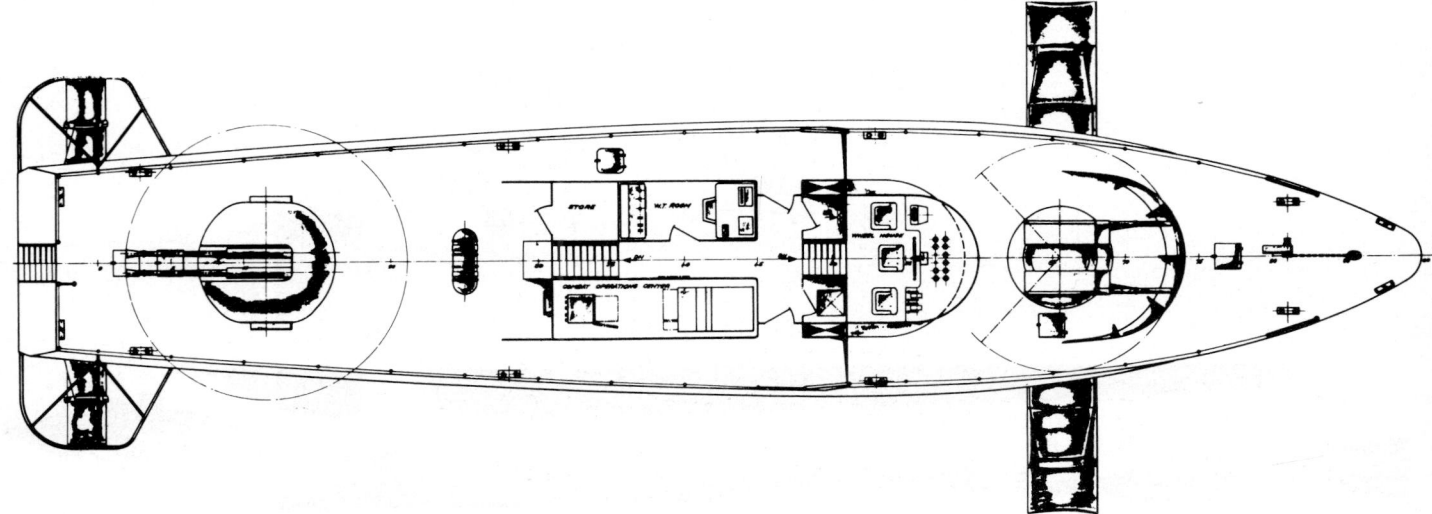

General arrangement of M 200

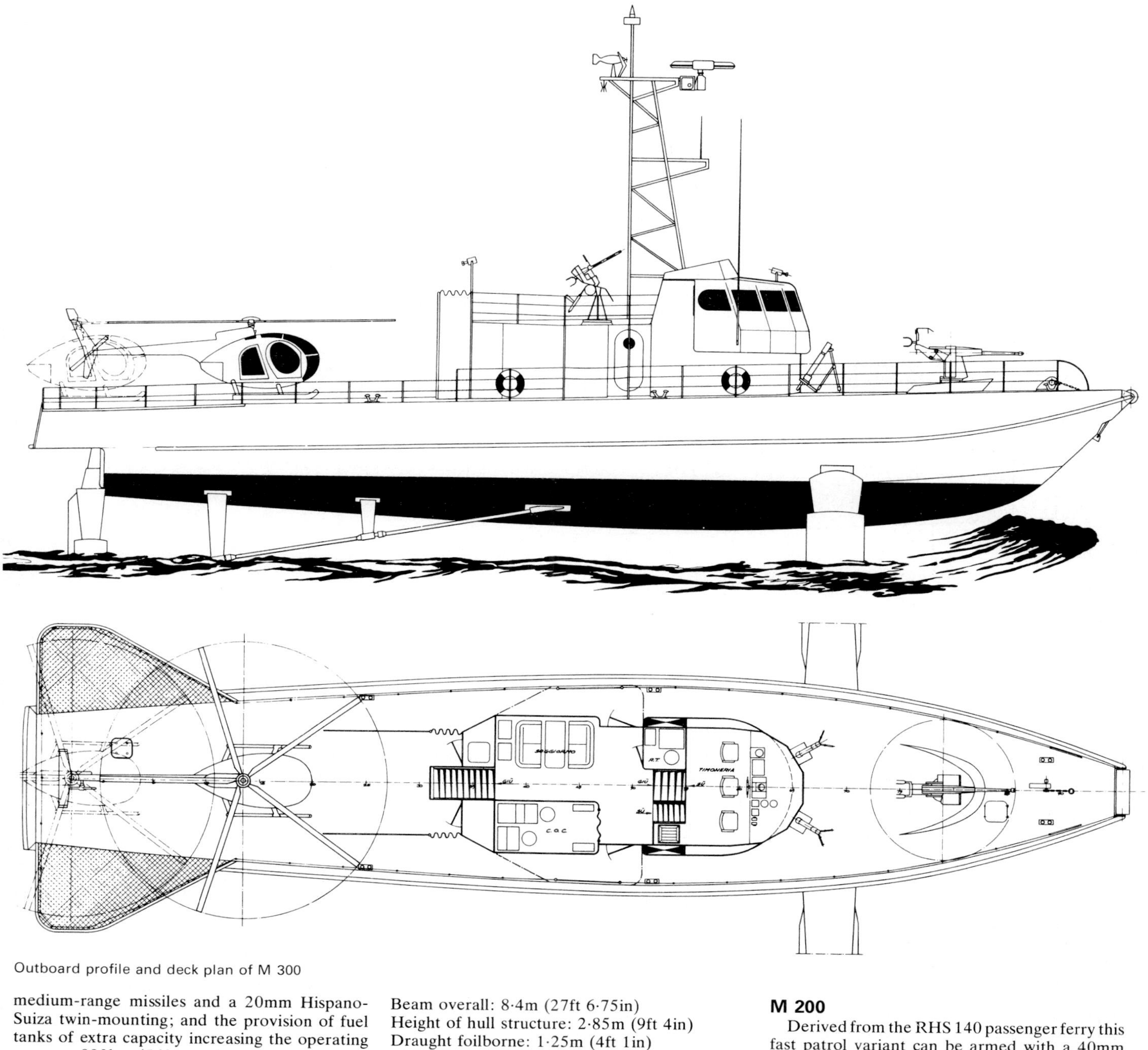

Outboard profile and deck plan of M 300

medium-range missiles and a 20mm Hispano-Suiza twin-mounting; and the provision of fuel tanks of extra capacity increasing the operating range to 900km (560 miles).
FOILS, HULL, POWER PLANT: Arrangements similar to those of the RHS 110.
ACCOMMODATION: Berths provided for eight officers and non-commissioned officers and eight ratings.
DIMENSIONS
Length overall: 25·4m (83ft 2in)

Beam overall: 8·4m (27ft 6·75in)
Height of hull structure: 2·85m (9ft 4in)
Draught foilborne: 1·25m (4ft 1in)
 hullborne, fully loaded: 3m (9ft 10in)
WEIGHTS
Displacement, empty: 36 tons
 loaded: 50 tons
PERFORMANCE
Max speed: 41 knots
Cruising speed: 38 knots
Cruising range: 900km (560 miles)

M 200

Derived from the RHS 140 passenger ferry this fast patrol variant can be armed with a 40mm Breda-Bofors twin naval mounting and one 8cm Oerlikon 2Z8DLa rocket launcher, and has a maximum speed of 37 knots. Above the wheelhouse is an open bridge with duplicate steering, engine controls and instrumentation.
WEIGHTS
Displacement loaded: 64 tons
 empty: 50 tons
PERFORMANCE
Max speed foilborne: 37 knots
Cruising speed: 34 knots
Minimum foilborne speed: 23·3 knots
Range: 1,127km (736 miles)

M 300 AND 600 FAST STRIKE CRAFT

The 90-ton M 300 and 125-ton M 600 are two hydrofoil missilecraft designed to augment the existing range of Rodriquez fast patrol boats.

Though differing in size, the two craft are almost identical in terms of overall design, construction and internal arrangements. Both are equipped with the SAS stability augmentation system, which stabilises the vessels in bad weather, and the Breda-Bofors twin 40mm/L 70 or similar rapid-fire cannon. In addition the M 300 will carry two Otomat or similar missile launchers and the M 600 will carry four.

Power for the M 300 is provided by two 1,950hp MTU 12V 652 TB 71 diesels, while the M 600 has two MTU 16V 652 TB 71 diesels each rated at 2,600hp. Maximum speed of both craft is in excess of 38 knots.

M 150

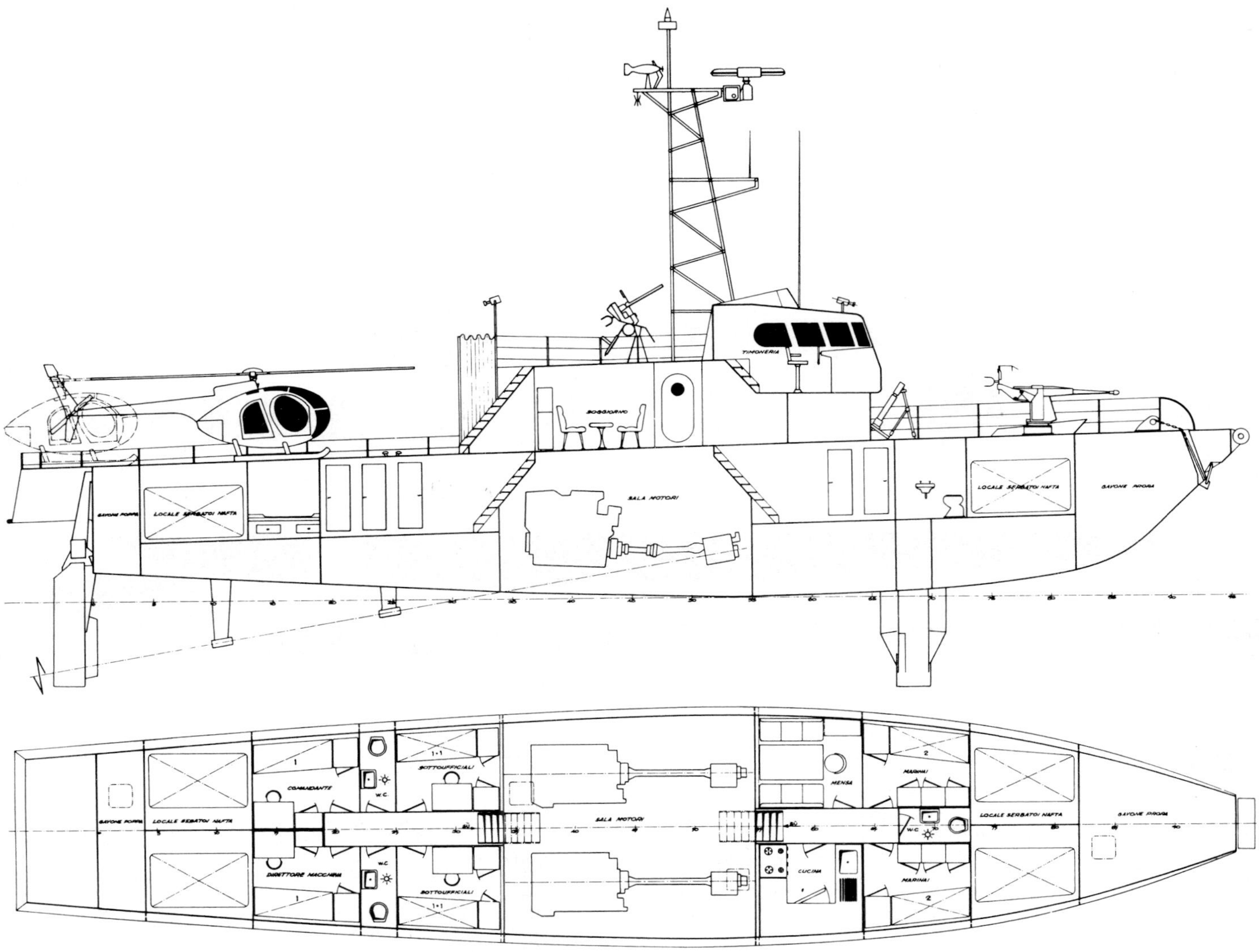

Inboard profile and deck plan of M 300

Dimensions, weights and performance figures are given at the end of the summary. The following characteristics apply to both designs.

FOILS: Surface-piercing W foils of hollow welded steel. Craft in this series have a bow rudder for improved manoeuvrability which works simultaneously with the aft rudders to provide fully co-ordinated turns. Hydraulically-operated flaps, attached to the trailing edges of the bow and rear foils, are adjusted automatically by an SAS electronic stability augmentation system for

the damping of heave, pitch and roll motions in heavy seas.

HULL AND SUPERSTRUCTURE: V-bottom hull of high tensile riveted light metal alloy construction. Argon gas welding employed on strengthened beams, web frames, keelsons and stringers. Basic hull structure is longitudinal; forepeak and after peak are transverse type structures. Steel is employed for the stern, fore and aft foil attachment points, propeller struts and foils. Cadmium plated rivets are used for joining steel

and light alloy components. Side plating ranges in thickness from 3·5 to 5mm; the upper deck varies from 3 to 4mm and plating on the stem and stern platforms is 2mm thick.

The superstructure is built on transverse frames with stanchions and beams every 300mm.

ACCOMMODATION: Berths, living and working accommodation and full wc washroom facilities for complement of 12, including commissioned and non-commissioned officers and ratings. The wheelhouse, all living spaces and fire control room are air-conditioned. Ventilation system provided for the engine room.

PROPULSION

M 300

Two MTU 12V 652 TB 71 four-stroke diesels, each delivering 1,950hp at 1,460rpm.

M 600

Two MTU 16V 652 TB 71 four-stroke diesels, each delivering 2,600hp at 1,460rpm.

On both designs engine output is transferred via a short intermediate shaft, universal joint and Zahnradfabrik 900 HS 15 gearboxes to two hollow, stainless steel propeller shafts operating two, three-bladed bronze-aluminium propellers. The drive shafts are supported by brackets and on the aft foils by rubber bearings lubricated by the water coolant system.

Stainless steel controllable-pitch propellers are available as an alternative to the fixed-pitch bronze-aluminium type.

FUEL OIL: Diesel fuel oil is carried in fibreglass-reinforced, welded aluminium tanks in the double bottom. All tanks are connected to a service tank from which oil is delivered to the injection pumps. Each engine has two suction and two engine pumps. Before reaching the injection pumps, fuel is fed through two filters in parallel, with replaceable filter elements, and water drain cocks. Injection excess fuel is piped back to the service tank.

Dynamic model of M 300

Inboard profile of M 600

Tanks are refuelled through necks on the main deck, each equipped with air vents and fuel level calibrated in kilograms and gallons.

SYSTEMS: Two systems are employed, each pressurised by a gear pump installed on one of the main engines. The first is used for the steering system and anchor winch, the second supplies the cylinder operating the lift control flaps and the bow rudder. The two systems are interchangeable and equipped with safety valves, manometers and micronic filters. Hydraulic pressure is also used for operating the weapons systems.

DRAINAGE AND FIRE CONTROL: Bilge pumps, operated by the main engines, can empty water from any compartment. Drain valves can be operated from the engine room or the deck. One pump can also supply water for fire hoses located on the amidship and aft sections of the vessels, port and starboard.

CO_2 system installed for fuel bays and engine room. Portable dry chemical and foam extinguishers also fitted.

ELECTRICAL: Two systems, dc and ac. 24V dc system operates navigation lights, radio and starts auxiliary engines. Ac system, for all the other requirements, comprises two diesel generating sets delivering 70kVA, 220V, three-phase 50Hz. Meters for monitoring voltage, amperage, frequency and power of ac systems are on main switchboard in engine room, from which isolated or parallel operation of the two alternators is controlled. Also on board are circuit breaker and switches for the transformer when the craft is connected to shore power, and distributing panels for the power and lighting system.

SAFETY: Smoke, fire and high temperatures in various parts of the craft, as well as the malfunctioning of machinery, auxiliary systems and hydraulics automatically sets off an electric alarm.

NAVIGATION AND COMMUNICATIONS: The craft are equipped with all navigation lights as well as an electrically operated horn and signal lights. Communications and navigation systems (radio, Decca Navigator and Flight Log etc) are available options.

M 300

DIMENSIONS
Length, overall: 30·95m (101ft 6in)
    waterline: 26·25m (86ft 1in)
Beam, moulded: 6·2m (20ft 4in)
    across foils: 12·5m (41ft 4in)
Draught, hullborne: 3·7m (12ft 1in)
    foilborne: 1·4m (4ft 7in)

WEIGHTS
Displacement: 92 tonnes (90 tons)
Military payload: 15 tonnes (14·76 tons)
Liquids, fuel oil and water: 11·7 tonnes (11·52 tons)

PERFORMANCE
Max speed: in excess of 68·5km/h (37 knots)
Cruising speed: 66·5km/h (36 knots)
Cruising range: 925km (500n miles)

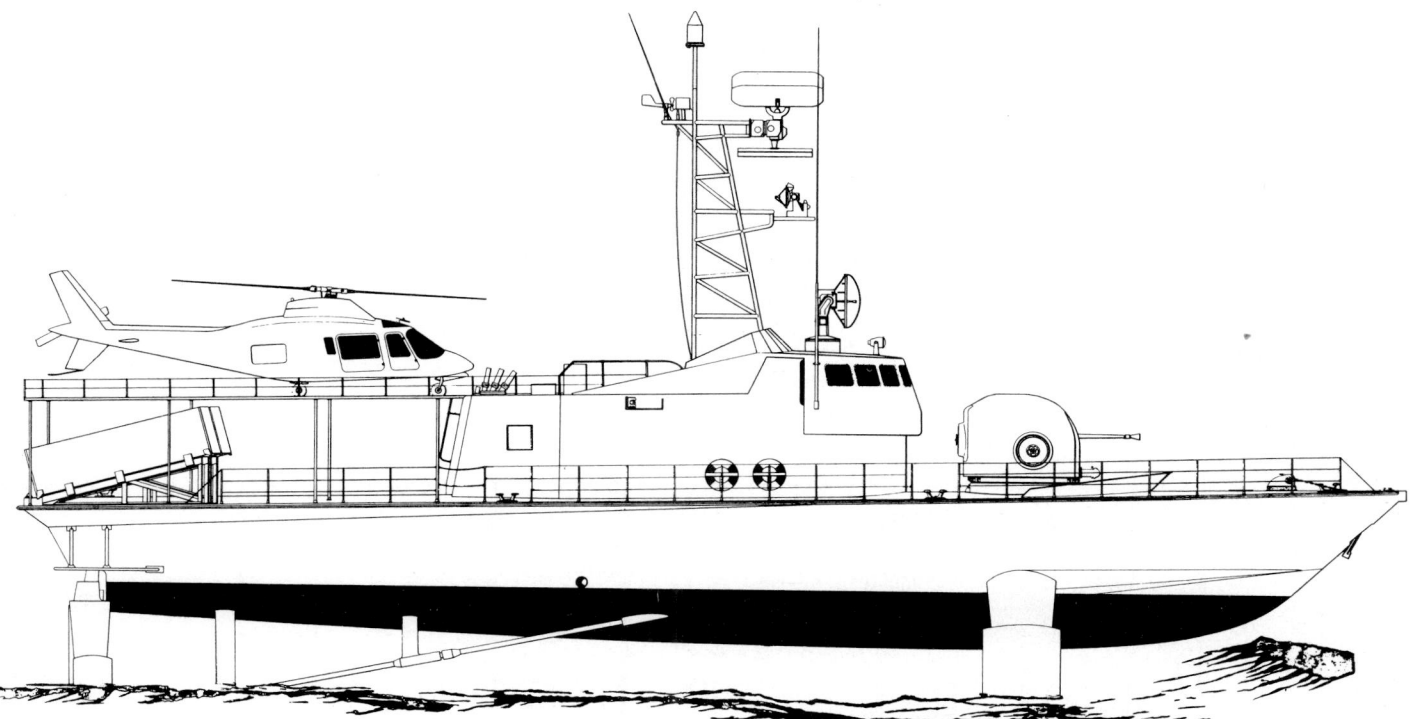

Outboard profile of M 600

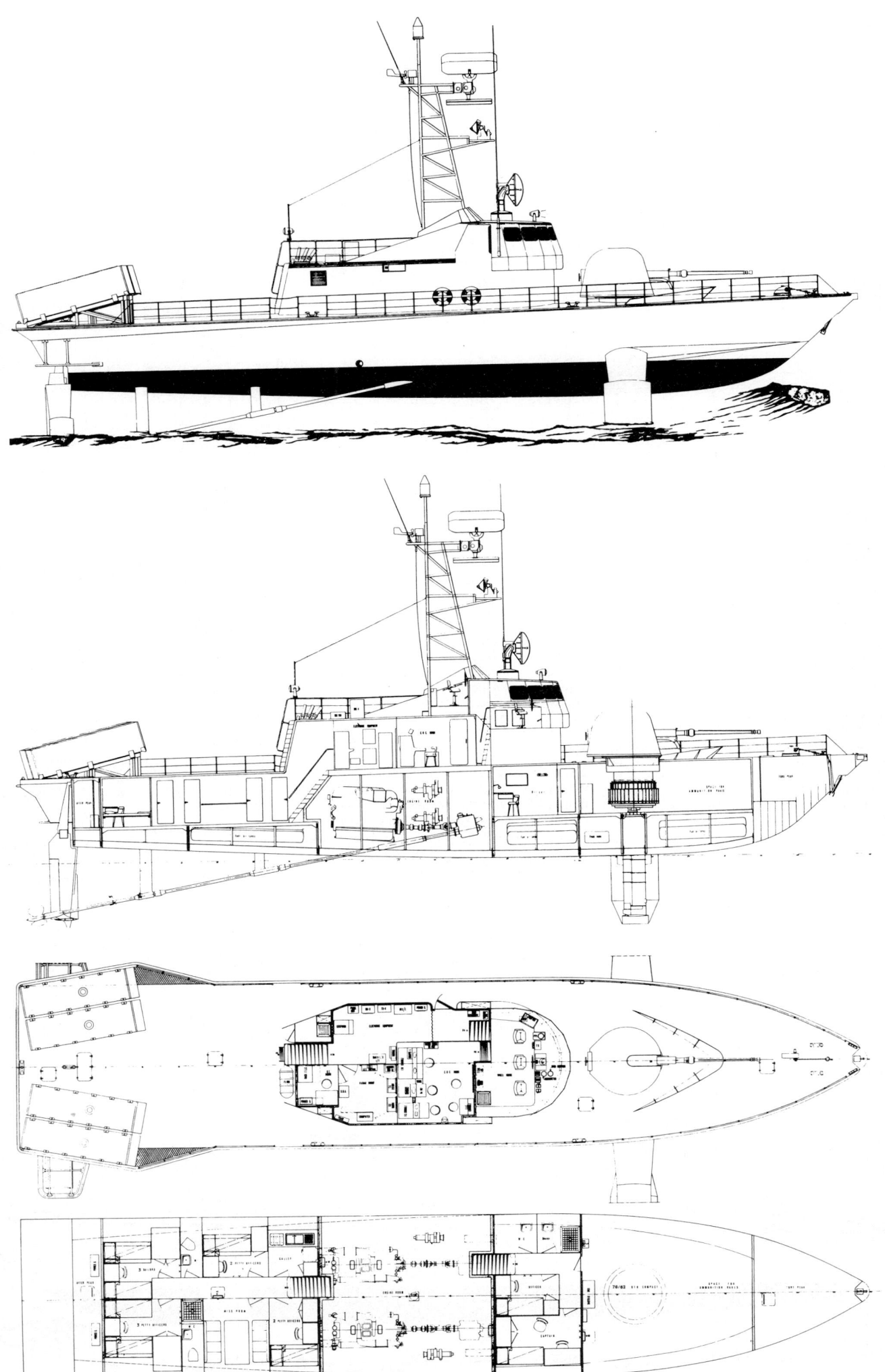

M 600 variant with four missiles and single dual-purpose naval gun mount forward

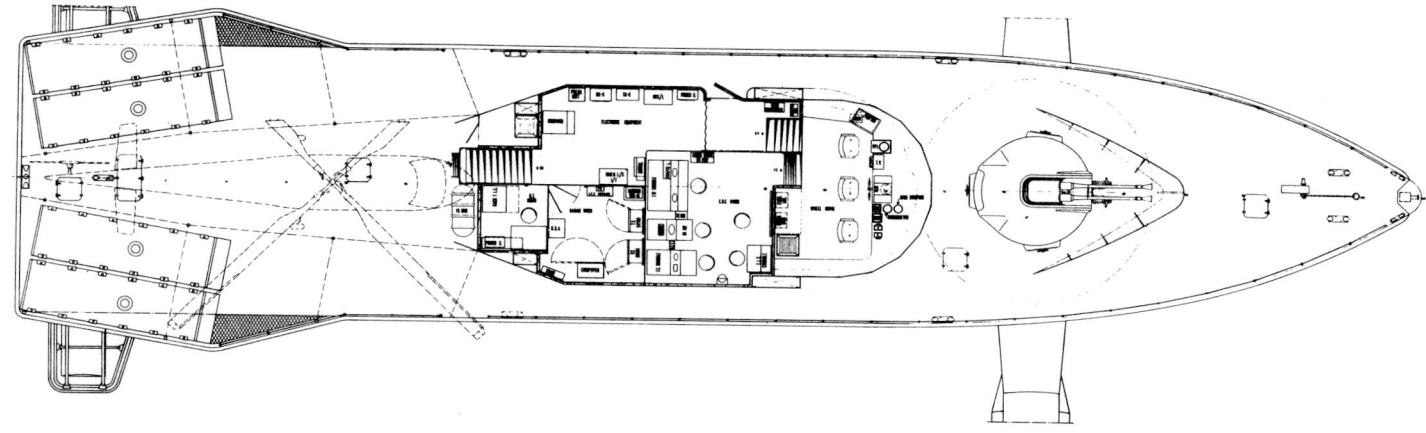

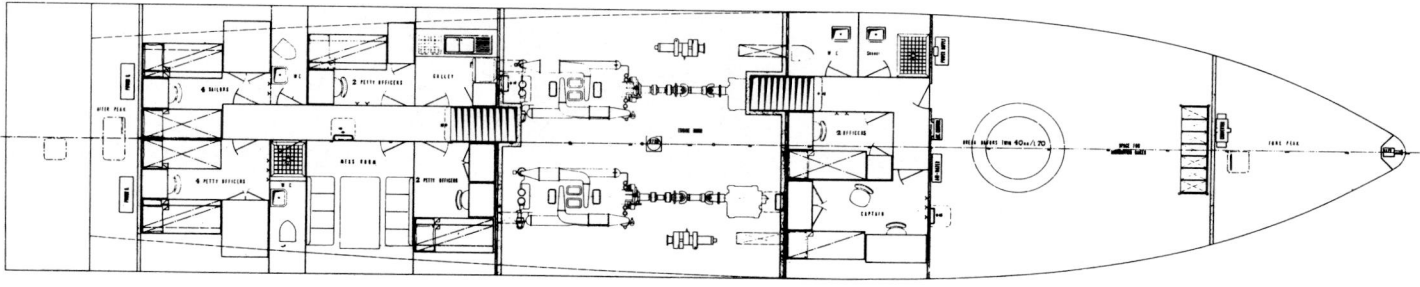

M 600 variant with helicopter landing pad above missile launchers aft. Breda Bofors twin 40mm/L70 or similar dual-purpose rapid-fire cannon mounted forward

M 600

DIMENSIONS
Length, overall: 35m (114ft 9in)
 waterline: 30·1m (98ft 9in)
Beam, moulded: 7m (23ft)
 across foils: 14·4m (47ft 3in)

Draught, hullborne: 4·55m (14ft 11in)
 foilborne: 2·15m (7ft)
WEIGHTS
Displacement: 125 tonnes
Military payload: 21·45 tonnes

Liquids, fuel, oil and water: 16·3 tonnes
PERFORMANCE
Max speed: 70·5km/h (38 knots)
Cruising speed: 68·5km/h (37 knots)
Cruising range: 925km (500n miles)

Impression of M 600

JAPAN

HITACHI ZOSEN

Head Office: 6-14 Edobori 1-chome, Nishi-ku, Osaka, Japan
Telephone: Osaka 443 8051
Telex: J 63376
Works: 4-1 Mizue-cho, Kawasaki-ku, Kawasaki, Kanagawa Pref, Japan
Telephone: Kawasaki 288 1111
Officials:
Takao Nagata, *Senior Representative Director*
Masaru Hattori, *Chairman of the Board of Directors*
Toshio Murayama, *President*
Shojiro Okada, *Executive Vice President*
Azuma Hasegawa, *General Manager, Kanagawa Works*

Hitachi Zosen, the Supramar licensee in Japan, has been building PT 20, PT 32 and PT 50 hydrofoils since 1961. The majority of these have been built for fast passenger-ferry services across the Japanese Inland Sea, cutting across deep bays which road vehicles might take two to three hours to drive round, and out to offshore islands. Other PT 20s and 50s have been exported to Hong Kong, Australia and South Korea for ferry services.

Specifications of the PT 32 (*Jane's Surface Skimmers 1967-68*), PT 20 and PT 50 will be found under Supramar (Switzerland). The Hitachi Zosen craft are identical apart from minor items.

In 1974 the company completed the first PT 50 Mk II to be built at its Kawasaki yard. The vessel, *Hikari 2*, is powered by two licence-built MTU MB 820Db diesels, carries 123 passengers plus a crew of seven and cruises at 33 knots. It was delivered to Setonaikai Kisen Co Ltd of Hiroshima in March 1975. Hitachi Zosen has constructed 25 PT 50s and 17 PT 20s.

In conjunction with Supramar, Hitachi Zosen is developing a new roll stabilisation system for the PT 50. The first PT 50 to be equipped with this new system was completed in January 1983 and is now in service. A schematic drawing showing the operation of the system is included in this entry.

ROLL-STABILISED PTS 50 Mk II

Housho, the first PTS 50 Mk II to be equipped with this new system, was delivered to Hankyu Kisen Co Ltd on 19 January 1983 and is operating on the Kobe-Naruto route. The system, which

PT 20 *Ryusei*

PTS 50 Mk II *Housho*

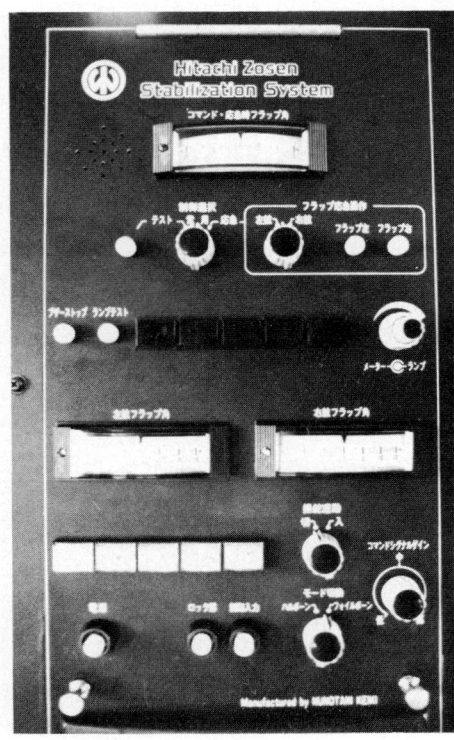
Roll-stabilisation control panel

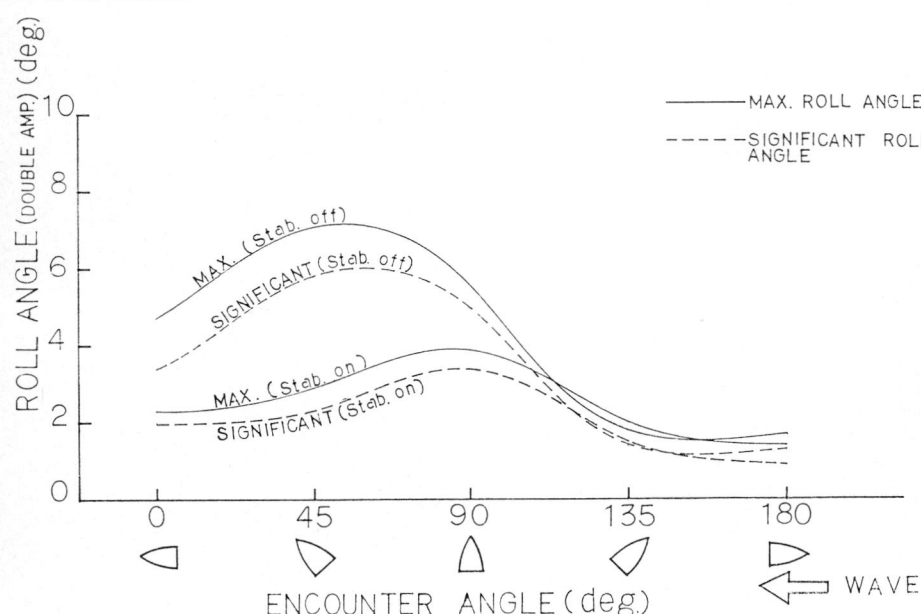
Stabiliser test results

was developed by Hitachi Zosen in conjunction with Supramar, reduces the PTS 50's rolling motion by between one-half and one-third.

The underside of the bow foil is fitted with two flapped fins to improve riding comfort. Operated by automatic sensors, the fins augment stability and provide side forces to dampen rolling and transverse motions.

Housho is powered by two MTU 12V 331 TB82 marine diesels, each rated at 1,380Ps at 2,150rpm. It seats 123 passengers and has a maximum speed of about 38 knots.

DIMENSIONS
Length overall: 27·55m
Beam, hull: 5·84m
Width across foils: 10·8m
Draught hullborne: 3·5m
  foilborne: 1·4m
WEIGHTS
Displacement, loaded: 62 tonnes
Gross tonnage: 128 tonnes
PERFORMANCE
Maximum speed: about 38 knots

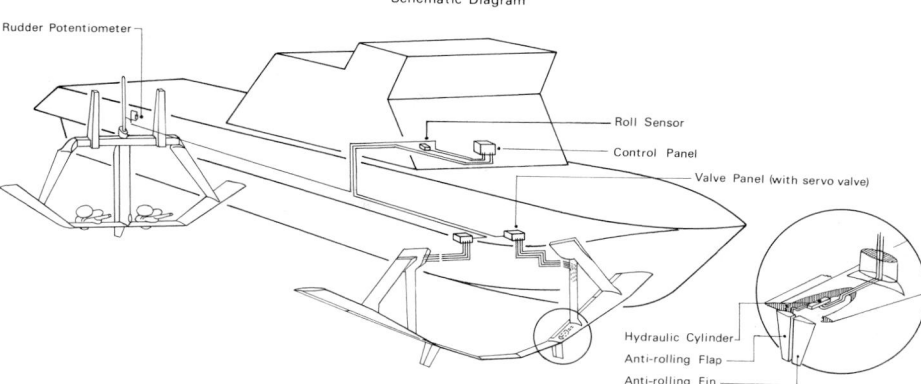

PT 50 Roll-Stabilizing System
Schematic Diagram

PTS 50 Mk II roll-stabilising system

Flapped roll-stabilisation fin on *Housho*

POLAND

GDANSK SHIP RESEARCH INSTITUTE

Technical University, Gdansk, Poland
Telephone: 414712

Research on problems connected with hydrofoil design and construction has been conducted by the Department of Theoretical Naval Architecture at Gdansk Technical University since 1956.

Experience with various dynamic test models led to the construction of the K-3 four-seat runabout which, powered by an FSC Lublin con-

verted auto-engine, has a top speed of 50km/h (27 knots).

In 1961 the Department was invited by the Central Board of Inland Navigation and United Inland Shipping and River Shipyards Gdansk to design a hydrofoil passenger ferry for service in the Firth of Szczecin. Designated ZRYW-1 the craft seats 76 passengers and cruises at 35 knots. It was completed in 1965.

During 1966 the Ship Research Institute designed two hydrofoil sports craft, the WS-4 Amor and the WS-6 Eros. The prototypes were completed in 1967 and were put into series pro-

duction during 1972.

In 1971 a catamaran-hulled research hydrofoil, the Badacz II, was built for the Ship Hydrodynamics Division of the Institute. The vessel is employed to tow models of ACVs and hydrofoils in coastal waters and provide data and performance measurements. It is also being employed to test new propulsion systems.

The largest hydrofoil craft to be designed by the Institute is a 300-ton passenger/car ferry.

Details of the ZRYW-1, Amor, Eros and Badacz II can be found in *Jane's Surface Skimmers 1974-75* and earlier editions.

ROMANIA

The Romanian Navy operates about 20 Chinese-designed 'Hu Chwan' (White Swan) class hydrofoil torpedo boats. The first three were shipped from the Hutang Shipyard, Shanghai, complete, while the remaining craft were constructed locally under a building programme started in 1973.

Although the Romanian craft are identical outwardly in most respects to the imported models, there are minor differences in defensive armament and superstructure design.
FOILS: System comprises a bow subfoil to stabilise pitch and facilitate take-off and a main foil of trapeze or shallow V configuration set back approximately one-third of the hull length from the bow. At high speed in relatively calm conditions the greater part of the forward hull is raised clear of the water. The mainfoil and struts retract upwards when the craft cruises in displacement conditions.

Romanian-built, Chinese-designed Hu Chwan hydrofoil torpedo boat

HULL: High speed V-bottom hull in seawater resistant light alloy.
POWER PLANT: Three 1,100hp M50 or M401 watercooled, supercharged 12-cylinder, V-type diesels, each driving its own inclined propeller shaft.
ARMAMENT: Two 534mm (21in) torpedo tubes, plus four 14·5mm cannon in two twin mounts.
DIMENSIONS (approx)
Length overall: 21·8m (71ft 6·5in)
Beam overall: 5·02m (16ft 6in)
Hull beam: 3·96m (13ft)
Draught, hullborne: 1m (3ft 3in)
WEIGHTS
Displacement full load: 40 tons
PERFORMANCE
Max speed foilborne, calm conditions: 50-55 knots
Cruising speed: 30-35 knots
Range: 926km (500n miles) approx

SWITZERLAND

SUPRAMAR HYDROFOILS AG

Ausserfeld 5, CH-6362 Stansstad, Switzerland
Telephone: (041) 61 31 94
Telex: 78228 Supra CH

Officials:
Baron Hanns von Schertel, *President*
Dipl Ing Harry Trevisani, *General Manager*
Dipl Ing Eugen Schatté, *Research and Development*
Jürg Bally, *Board Member*
Ernst Schneider, *Board Member*

Supramar was founded in Switzerland in 1952 to develop on a commercial basis the hydrofoil system introduced by the Schertel-Sachsenberg Hydrofoil Syndicate and its licensee, the Gebruder Sachsenberg Shipyard. Supramar AG was reorganised in April 1980 under the name of Supramar Hydrofoils AG.

The co-operation between the companies started in 1937 and led to the development of the VS6, a 17-ton hydrofoil, which in 1941 attained 47·5 knots, and the VS8, an 80-ton supply hydrofoil completed in 1943, which attained 41 knots. The inherently stable, rigid V-foil system used on these and subsequent Supramar vessels, stems from experimental work undertaken by Baron Hanns von Schertel between 1927 and 1937.

In May 1953 a Supramar PT 10, 32-passenger hydrofoil began the world's first regular passenger hydrofoil service on Lake Maggiore, between Switzerland and Italy. In August 1956 the first Rodriquez-built Supramar PT 20 opened a service across the Straits of Messina and became the first hydrofoil to be licensed by a marine classification authority for carrying passengers at sea.

Supramar employs a staff of highly qualified scientists and engineers specialising in hydrodynamics, marine engineering, foil design, propulsion and shipyard production. In addition to building its own hydrofoils it licenses other shipyards to produce its hydrofoil designs.

Supramar hydrofoils being built by these companies are referred to elsewhere in this section under the respective company headings.

A recent Supramar design is the PTS 75 Mk III, a development of the PT 50 with increased engine power and full air stabilisation. The prototype was constructed by Vosper Thornycroft at the company's Portchester yard and delivered to Hong Kong in 1974. The second vessel of this type was completed in 1976 by Supramar's licensee in Hong Kong. The company has also completed designs for a modernised PT 50 which is available as the PT 50 Mk II. A new version of the PTS 150 Mk II has been operating between Toronto and Youngstown, New York, near Niagara Falls. This is the PTS 150 Mk III, a second generation craft with improved performance and greater passenger comfort.

The company is also developing a fully submerged foil system with air stabilisation. First craft to use this system is the Supramar ST 3A, a 4·9-ton experimental boat built under a US Navy contract. During tests in the Mediterranean it demonstrated promising stability and seakeeping qualities and reached a speed of 54·5 knots. Military and para-military versions of all Supramar commercial hydrofoils are now available. In addition Supramar has completed the design of a patrol boat hydrofoil which meets the tactical requirements of the NATO navies. The vessel, the MT 250G, has an operational displacement of 250 tons and a maximum intermittent speed of 60 knots.

Supramar's latest hydrofoil concept is the CT 70, a hydrofoil catamaran designed for use in shallow waters where draught limitations preclude the use of conventional hydrofoil craft.

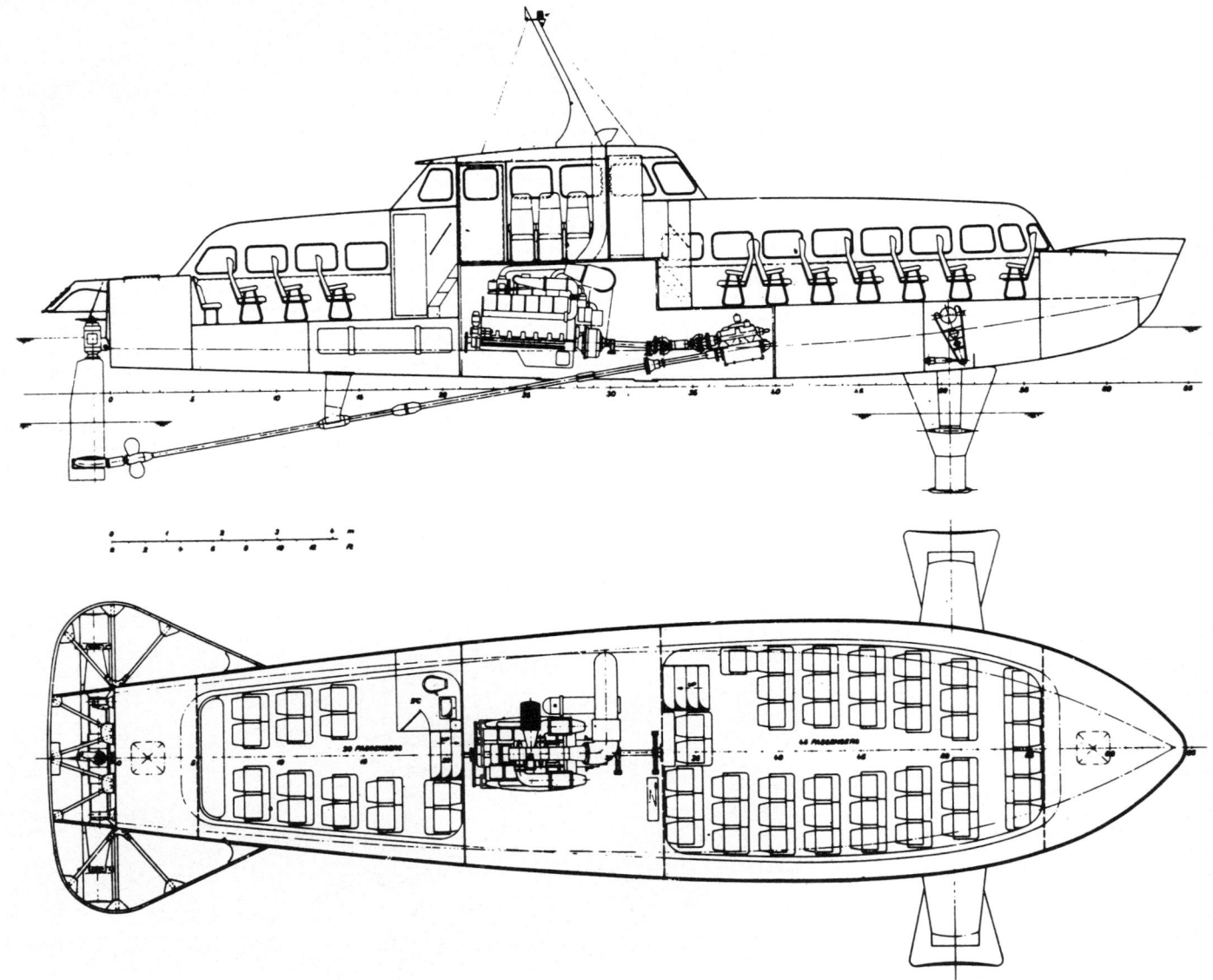

Inboard profile and main deck plan of PT 20

INHERENTLY STABLE FOIL SYSTEM

Supramar is planning to introduce a new foil system which will combine the comfort of the fully-submerged system with the features of stability, simplicity, reliability and low construction and maintenance costs inherent in the surface-piercing system.

The new system is said to have a wider range of flying modes than fully-submerged systems and can operate in higher wave conditions. Trials have been undertaken on test craft and in a towing tank. The system can contour or platform waves as required and compensates for orbital motions.

PT 20 Mk II

The PT 20 Mk II, a 27-ton boat for 72 passengers, is considered by Supramar to be the smallest size hydrofoil suitable for passenger-carrying coastal services. The first of this very successful series was built by the Rodriquez shipyard at Messina in 1955 and since then nearly 70 PT 20s of various types have been built in Japan, Netherlands, Norway and Sicily. The design has been approved by almost every classification society. Fast patrol boat variants are also available.

FOILS: Foils are of standard Schertel-Sachsenberg, surface-piercing type, with 58 per cent of the load supported by the bow foil and the remaining 42 per cent by the rear foil. Submerged foil area in foilborne condition is 5·5m². Together with the struts and a horizontal guide, each foil forms a uniform framework which facilitates the exchange of the foil elements. The medium steel foils are of partly hollow, welded construction. The angle of incidence of the bow foil can be adjusted within narrow limits from the steering stand by means of a hydraulic ram operating on a foil support across the hull. To counteract the effects of large variations in passenger load and to ensure optimum behaviour in sea waves the angle of attack can be adjusted during operation.

HULL: The hull has a V-bottom with an externally added step riveted into place. Frames, bulkheads, foundations, superstructure and all internal construction is in corrosion-proof light alloy. Platings are of AlMg 5 and the frames, bars and other members are made in AlMgSi. Watertight compartments are provided below the passenger decks and in other parts of the hull.

POWER PLANT: Power is supplied by an MTU 12V 396 TB 83 diesel with an exhaust turbocompressor. Maximum continuous output is 1,050kW at 1,800rpm. A BW 800/HS 20 reversible gear, developed by Zahnradfabrik Friedrichshafen AG, is placed between the engine and the drive shaft.

ACCOMMODATION: The boat is controlled from the bridge which is above the engine room. 46 passengers are accommodated in the forward cabin, 20 in the rear compartment and six aft of the pilot's stand in the elevated wheelhouse. There is an emergency exit in each passenger compartment and the craft is equipped with an inflatable life raft and life belts for each person. A crew of four is carried.

SYSTEMS, ELECTRICAL: 24V generator driven by the main engine; batteries with a capacity of approximately 250Ah.

HYDRAULICS: 120kg/cm² pressure hydraulic system for rudder and bow foil incidence control.

COMMUNICATIONS AND NAVIGATION: VHF ship-shore radio is standard equipment. Radar is optional.

DIMENSIONS

EXTERNAL

Length overall, hull: 20·75m (68ft 1in)
  over deck: 19·95m (65ft 6in)
Hull beam, max: 4·99m (16ft 4in)
Width across foils: 8·07m (26ft 5in)
Draught hullborne: 3·08m (10ft 1in)
  foilborne: 1·4m (4ft 7in)

INTERNAL

Aft cabin (including wc): 13·5m² (145ft²)
Volume: 27m³ (954ft³)
Forward cabin: 26m² (280ft²)
Volume: 50m³ (1,766ft³)
Main deck level (including wheelhouse): 12m² (129ft²)
Volume: 24m³ (847ft³)

Supramar PT 20 built by Hitachi Zosen

WEIGHTS

Gross tonnage: approx 56 tons
Max take-off displacement: 32 tons
Light displacement: 25 tons
Deadweight (including fuel, oil, water, passengers, baggage and crew): 7 tons
Payload: 5·4 tons

PERFORMANCE (with normal payload)

Cruising speed, foilborne: 63km/h (34 knots)
Max permissible wave height in foilborne mode: 1·29m (4ft 3in)
Designed range at cruising speed: 400km (216 miles)
Turning radius: 130m approx (427ft)
Take-off distance: 150m approx (493ft)
Take-off time: 25 seconds
Stopping distance: 70m (230ft)
Fuel consumption at cruising speed: 150kg/h (330lb/h)

SEA TESTS: Prototype tests were undertaken in the Mediterranean in every kind of sea condition, and further tests have taken place off Japan. Acceleration measurements have shown maximum values below 0·5g when accelerometer had been fitted above the bow foil. Maximum lateral acceleration was 0·32g. Measurements were made in wave heights of approximately 1·2–1·5m. These are the maximum measurements obtained and subsequent tests have seldom equalled these figures.

PT 20B Mk II

In this model of the PT 20, the engine room and bridge are arranged in the foreship. This improves the pilot's vision in waters likely to have an influx of driftwood and provides a large main passenger cabin with seats for 55 and an upper deck cabin with seating for 16 passengers.

PT 20B

The layout of this craft has been based on experience gained with the Supramar PT 27 which was designed for servicing the offshore drilling platforms on Lake Maracaibo. This design has been slightly modified to meet the requirements of passenger services.

FOILS: The foil design is similar to that of the PT 20 Mk II. About 66% of the total weight is borne by the bow foil and 34% by the rear foil. Submerged foil area in foilborne condition is 6·2m². The forward foil can be tilted within narrow limits by means of a hydraulic ram acting on the foil strut supporting tube. The angle of attack can therefore be adjusted during operation to assist take-off and to counteract the effect of large variations in passenger loads.

HULL: This is of riveted light metal alloy design and framed on a combination of longitudinal and transverse formers. Watertight compartments are provided below the passenger decks and in other parts of the hull, and some are filled with foam-type plastic.

POWER PLANT: Power is supplied by a supercharged 12-cylinder MTU 12V 396 TB 83 diesel with a maximum continuous output of 1,050kW at 1,800rpm. Average time between major overhauls is approximately 10,000 hours. Engine output is transferred to a three-bladed 700mm diameter bronze subcavitating propeller through a BW 800/H 20 reversible gear made by Zahnradfabrik. The propeller shaft is supported at three points by seawater lubricated rubber bearings.

ACCOMMODATION: The PT 20B Mk II has a crew of four and seats 71 passengers. The main passenger compartment seats 55, and the small cabin behind the pilot's stand seats a further 16. Access to the main compartment is through two doors, located port and starboard, to the rear of the wheelhouse. An emergency exit is provided at the rear of the main passenger compartment.

The PT 20B Mk II can also be delivered with fully integrated air-conditioning equipment. The total passenger capacity will then be reduced to 69.

A full range of safety equipment is carried, including inflatable rafts and lifebelts for each passenger and crew member.

SYSTEMS, ELECTRICAL: 24V generator driven by the main engine, batteries with a capacity of approximately 250Ah.

HYDRAULICS: 120kg/cm² pressure hydraulic system for operating rudder and bow foil angle of incidence control.

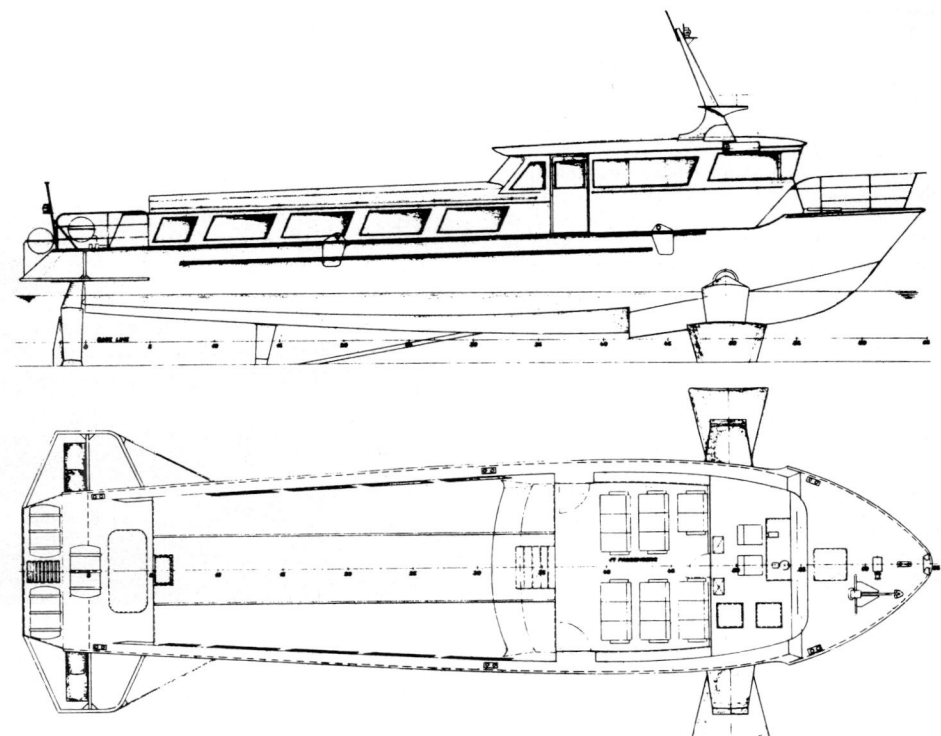

Outboard profile and plan of PT 20B Mk II

COMMUNICATIONS AND NAVIGATION: A VHF ship-shore radio is supplied as standard equipment. Radar is an optional extra.

DIMENSIONS
EXTERNAL
Length overall, hull: 20·85m (68ft 5in)
  over deck: 19·5m (64ft)
Hull beam, max: 5·16m (16ft 11in)
Width over foils: 8·6m (28ft 3in)
Draught hullborne: 3m (9ft 10in)
  foilborne: 1·3m (4ft 3in)
INTERNAL
Main passenger compartment (including w/c):
  Length: 9·3m (30ft 7in)
  Width: 3·8m (12ft 6in)
  Height: 2m (6ft 7in)
  Floor area: 22·1m² (237ft²)
  Volume: 44m³ (1,553ft³)

WEIGHTS
Gross tonnage: 50 tons approx
Max take-off displacement: 32·5 tons
Light displacement: 25·4 tons
Deadweight (including fuel, oil, water, passengers, luggage, crew): 7·5 tons
Payload: 5·8 tons
PERFORMANCE (with normal payload)
Cruising speed: 63km/h (34 knots)
Max permissible wave height in foilborne mode: 1·29m (4ft 3in)
Turning radius: approx 130m (426ft)
Take-off distance: approx 150m (492ft)
Take-off time: approx 30 seconds
Stopping distance: approx 70m (231ft)
Stopping time: approx 10 seconds
Fuel consumption at cruising speed: 150kg/h (330lb/h)

PT 20 Mk IIs and PT 20B Mk IIs

These are high-speed versions of the PT 20 Mk II and PT 20B Mk II. Each is powered by a single supercharged MTU 12V 396 TB 83 diesel with a continuous output of 1,050kW at 1,845 rpm.
PERFORMANCE
Cruising speed: 72km/h (39 knots)

PTL 28

The PTL 28 is derived from the PT 27 utility and oil rig supply vessel, three of which have been in service for 20 years with the Shell Oil Company on Lake Maracaibo, Venezuela.

Features of the craft include facilities for loading across the bow as well as the stern, twin rudders for improved manoeuvrability, and a variety of structural and mechanical modifications to simplify and reduce maintenance. The Schottel drive now has only two bevel gears, the hull is of welded construction, and the foil and propeller mounting arrangements have been redesigned to facilitate servicing. All non-essential components have been omitted.

Normally seats are provided for 54, but the number of passengers can be increased if the range is reduced. The weather deck above the engine room is available for cargo; heavy loads are compensated for by a reduction in passenger capacity. A cargo compartment can be made available at the rear of the passenger cabin (up to frame 17), a typical load being 1,825kg (4,023lb) of cargo combined with 33 passengers.

FOILS: Schertel-Sachsenberg surface-piercing

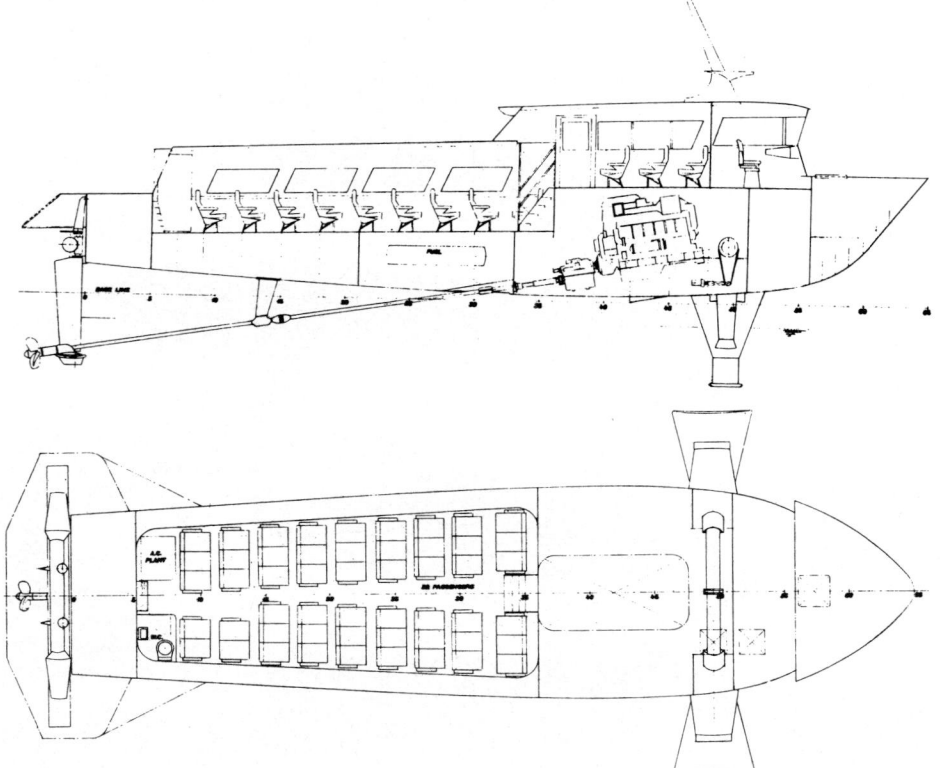

Inboard profile and passenger deck of PT 20B Mk II

PTL 28 servicing offshore oil platforms on Lake Maracaibo

system similar to that of the PT 20 Mk II. Bow foil of hollow welded stainless steel. Foil, vertical struts, inclined fins and horizontal supporting tube form a framed structure which can easily be detached when necessary. The complete assembly divides into two to facilitate transport. Once the angle of incidence is adjusted no further alteration is necessary.

The rear foil is similar to the bow foil in type and construction. The complete system is mounted on its bearings at the transom by four bolts.

HULL: Constructed in seawater-resistant light metal alloy, the V-bottomed hull is of hard chine type and framed longitudinally. All joints are welded. Hoist fittings facilitate maintenance.

POWER PLANT: Power is supplied by a 12-cylinder MTU 12V396 TB 83 diesel, rated at 1,050kW at 1,800rpm continuous.

Engine output is transferred to a three-bladed bronze propeller through a Zahnradfabrik BW 800 H20 reverse gearbox. Hullborne propulsion is provided by a 150hp diesel engine directly coupled to a Schottel Z-drive unit which can be

Guia, Hitachi-built PT 50, operated by Far East Hydrofoil Co Ltd on Hong Kong-Macao route

rotated through 360 degrees. During take-off and when foilborne, the lower bevel gear and hullborne propeller are retracted hydraulically into a recess in the hull bottom.

ACCOMMODATION: The PTL 28 has a crew of three and seats 54 passengers in a single saloon aft of the engine room. The bridge is forward and provides a 360-degree view. The captain's seat,

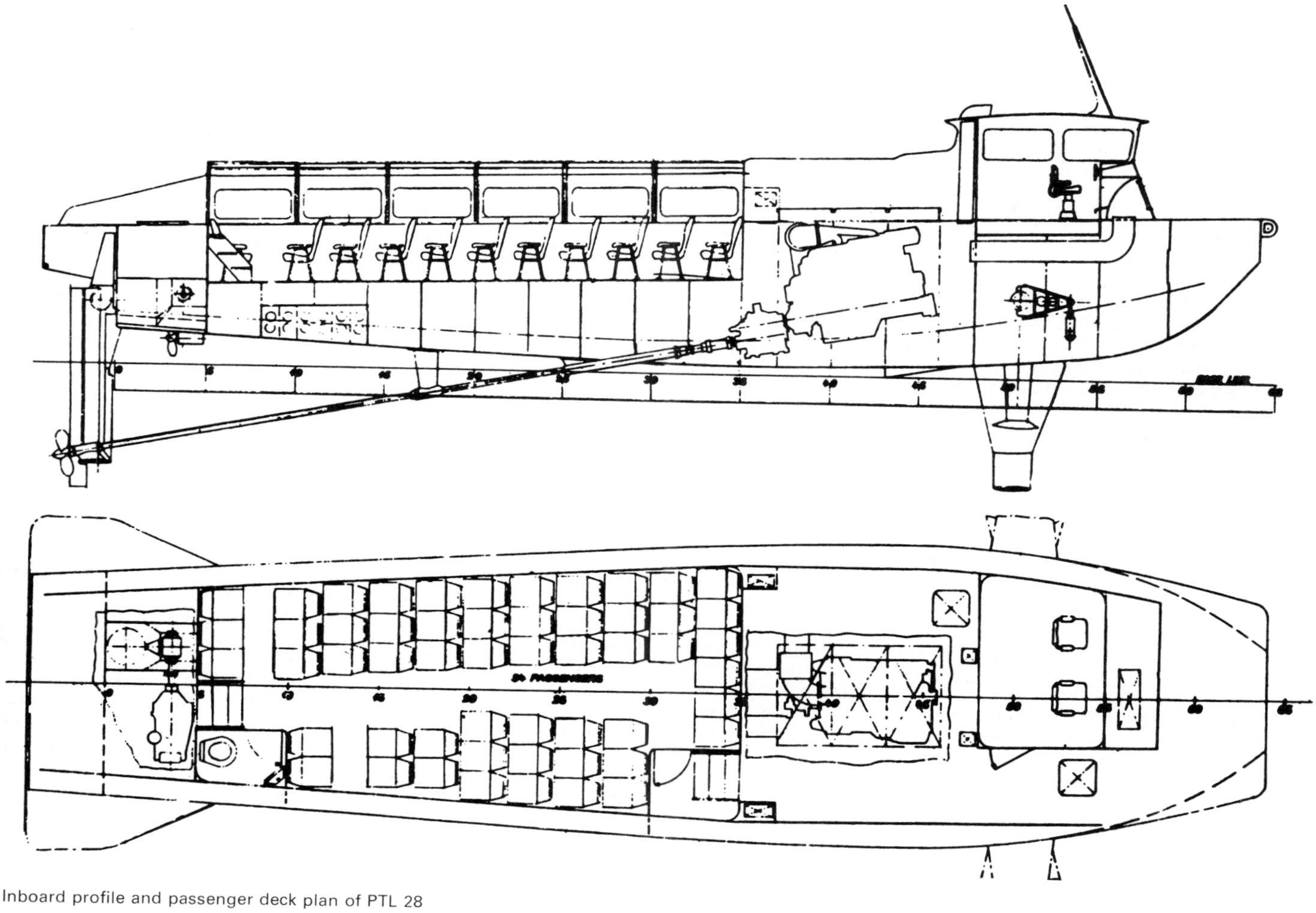

Inboard profile and passenger deck plan of PTL 28

together with the operating controls and instrumentation, is on the hull centreline.

DIMENSIONS

EXTERNAL

Length overall, hull: 20·75m (68ft 1in)
  over deck: 19·95m (67ft 6in)
Hull beam, max: 4·99m (16ft 4in)
Width over foils: 8m (26ft 3in)
Draught hullborne: 2·95m (9ft 8in)
  foilborne: 1·5m (4ft 11in)

WEIGHTS

Displacement fully loaded: 28 tonnes (27·56 tons)
Disposable load: 5·6 tonnes (5·51 tons)
Light displacement: 22·4 tonnes (22·05 tons)

PERFORMANCE

Max speed: 72km/h (39 knots)
Cruising speed: 65km/h (35 knots)
Range: 260km (140n miles) approx

PT 50 Mk II

The successful and profitable operation of the PT 20 led to the development of the PT 50, a 63-ton hydrofoil passenger ferry designed for offshore and inter-island services. The prototype was completed in 1958 and more than 30 are operating regular passenger services in areas ranging from the Baltic and Mediterranean Seas to the Japanese Inland Sea.

The craft has been approved by almost every classification society including Registro Italiano Navale, Germanischer Lloyd, Det Norske Veritas, American Bureau of Shipping and the Japanese Ministry of Transport. The requirements of the SOLAS 1960 convention for international traffic can be met by the type if required.

FOILS: Rear and forward foils are rigidly attached to the hull but the lift of the forward foil can be modified by hydraulically operated flaps, which are fitted to assist take-off and turning and for making slight course corrections and adjustment of the flying height. The foils are of hollow construction using fine grain and MSt 52-3 steel throughout. Foils in stainless steel construction are optional.

The bow foil comprises the following elements:
two fins, forming connecting links between the foil and the supporting structure which is riveted to the hull;
the hydrofoil, which (according to its foil section characteristics) generates the lift and, with the stern foil, provides transverse stability in foilborne conditions;
two struts, which transmit the main lift loads to the supporting structure.

The rear foil system comprises the following elements:
the hydrofoil, which generates the lift;
two side struts;
a single rudder which transmits the lift to the supporting structure.

For improved passenger comfort the PT 50 Mk II can be provided with a roll stabiliser on the bow foil. The system, including the motion sensing device, has been developed by Supramar.

HULL: Of hard chine construction, the hull is of partly riveted, partly welded light metal alloy design and framed on longitudinal and transverse formers. Steel is used only for highly stressed parts such as the foil fittings, and the shaft brackets and exits.

ACCOMMODATION: The PT 50 Mk II is available in three interior configurations:
For 111 passengers, including bar and catering facilities.
Standard version, with seats for 122 passengers.
Commuter version, seating 136 passengers.
The crew varies from 6 to 8 members, depending mainly on local regulations.
Passenger seats are a lightweight aircraft type and the centre aisle between the seat rows has a clear width of 76cm (30in). Ceilings are covered with lightweight plastic material and the walls, including web frames, are clad in luxury plywood or artificial wood. Toilets are provided in the rear and forward passenger spaces. Floors in the passenger compartments have thick carpets. Each passenger compartment has an emergency exit. Inflatable life rafts and lifebelts are provided for

Inboard and outboard profiles and deck plans of PT 50 Mk II

110 per cent of the passenger and crew capacity.

POWER PLANT: The craft is powered by two MTU 12V 396 TB 83 turbocharged diesels, each developing 1,050kW at 1,800rpm continuous. Engine output is transmitted to two three-bladed 700mm diameter bronze propellers through two inclined stainless steel propeller shafts, each supported at four points by seawater-lubricated runner bearings. Reverse and reduction gear with built-in thrust is manufactured by Zahnradfabrik Friedrichshafen AG, West Germany. The reverse clutches are solenoid-operated from the bridge.

Eight cylindrical fuel tanks with a total capacity of 3,650 litres are in the aft peak and below the tank deck. Oil capacity is 320 litres.

SYSTEMS, ELECTRICAL: Engine driven generator; 24V battery set.

HYDRAULICS: 120kg/cm² pressure hydraulic system for operating twin rudders and front foil flaps.

AIR CONDITIONING: Optional.

COMMUNICATIONS AND NAVIGATION: Standard equipment includes UHF and VHF radio-telephone. Radar and Decca Navigator are optional.

DIMENSIONS

EXTERNAL

Length overall: 27·75m (91ft)
  over deck: 26·4m (86ft 7in)
Hull beam max: 5·84m (19ft 2in)
Beam over deck: 5·46m (17ft 11in)

Width over foils: 10·8m (35ft 5in)
Draught hullborne: 3·55m (11ft 8in)
  foilborne: 1·55m (5ft 1in)
INTERNAL
Aft passenger compartment (including wc):
  Length: 9m (29ft 7in)
  Width: 4·9m (16ft)
  Height: 2m (6ft 7in)
  Floor area: 44·1m² (474ft²)
  Volume: 88m³ (3,108ft³)
Forward passenger compartment (including wc):
  Length: 7·1m (23ft 3·5in)
  Width: 5·4m (17ft 9in)
  Height: 2m (6ft 7in)
  Floor area: 37·3m² (412ft²)
  Volume: 67·6m³ (2,703ft³)
Main deck foyer:
  Length: 3·9m (12ft 9·5in)
  Width: 4m (13ft 1·5in)
  Height: 2m (6ft 7in)
  Floor area: 15m² (161ft²)
  Volume: 57·6m³ (2,030ft³)
WEIGHTS
Max take-off displacement: 63·3 tons
Light displacement: 49·3 tons
Deadweight (including fuel, oil, water, passengers, baggage and crew): 14 tons
Payload: 9·5 tons
PERFORMANCE (with normal payload)
Max speed foilborne: 67·5km/h (36·5 knots)
Cruising speed foilborne: 63km/h (34 knots)
Range: 600km (325n miles)
Turning radius: 470m (1,542ft)
Take-off distance: 250m (819ft)
Take-off time: 35 seconds
Stopping distance: 80m (264ft)
Time to stop craft: 10 seconds
Fuel consumption at cruising speed: 300kg/h
  (710lb/h)

ROLL-STABILISED PTS 50 Mk II

The first of this new variant of the PTS 50 Mk II, built by Hitachi Zosen, entered service in January 1983.

In order to improve seaworthiness and riding comfort, the underside of the bow foil is fitted with two flapped fins. Controlled by automatic sensors, these augment stability and provide side forces to dampen rolling and transverse motions.

PTS 75 Mk III

The Supramar PTS 75 Mk III is an advanced derivative of the PT 50. It seats 160 passengers and is designed for higher speed, improved seaworthiness and greater riding comfort. By increasing the specific PT 50 engine power of 43hp/ton to 50hp/ton a top speed of about 38 knots is obtained with the vessel fully loaded, and sufficient power is provided for operation in tropical waters.

An improved Schertel-Supramar air stabilisation system is fitted and this, combined with a new W-foil configuration, considerably reduces rolling, pitching and vertical accelerations. The vessel can operate foilborne in 1·82m (6ft) high waves with full power.

The prototype was completed at the Vosper Thornycroft, Paulsgrove, Portsmouth yard in May 1974. The second craft of this type was completed in early 1976 by Supramar's licensee in Hong Kong, Supramar Pacific Shipbuilding Co Ltd. It was ordered by Far East Hydrofoil Co for the Hong Kong-Macao service.
FOILS: The foil configuration is surface-piercing and incorporates the Schertel-Supramar air stabilisation system. The bow foil assembly forms a rigid framework which facilitates the exchange of the foil structure. The foil is of hollow steel construction. It has three supporting struts, one on the centre line and one on either side. These are bolted to welded steel suspension points on the keel and chine respectively. Hydraulically operated flaps are fitted to the trailing edges to assist take-off, facilitate course corrections and provide automatic stabilisation when low frequency disturbances are encountered.

The rear foil is of surface-piercing Schertel-Supramar type and attached to the transom.

PTS 75 Mk III operating on Hong Kong-Macao service

Method of construction is the same as that employed for the bow foil. The complete assembly—foil, rudder sternpost, rudder, and two inclined struts—forms a rigid frame unit which is attached or detached as necessary. The aftermost propeller bearings are attached to the foil, the propellers being sited aft of the foil.
HULL: Hard chine type, constructed in partly riveted, partly welded corrosion resistant light metal alloy. A longitudinal frame system is employed, with transverse frames 900mm apart. Steel is used only for highly stressed parts such as the foil fittings and shaft exits. A new hull construction method is being employed for this design. The hull is built in the inverted position and turned upright after the plating is completed.
ACCOMMODATION: Depending on operating requirements, between 130 and 160 passengers can be accommodated in three saloons. In the standard version airliner-type seats are provided for 135 passengers, 19 in the upper aft saloon, 61 in the lower aft saloon and 55 in the lower forward saloon.

Ceilings are covered with lightweight plastic material, walls, including web frames, are clad in luxury ply or artificial wood and the floors have thick carpets.

Three toilets are installed on the upper deck, within easy reach of all three saloons.

Passengers board the craft through wide side doors on the upper deck opening to a central foyer from which companionways lead to the lower passenger saloons. A promenade deck is available aft of the upper saloon and can be reached by passengers from the lower saloons via the foyer. Sufficient space for luggage is provided in the foyer. The upper aft saloon can be modified into a small dining room, if required, reducing the passenger capacity by 19.

All passenger saloons have emergency exits. A lifebelt is stowed beneath each seat and most of the inflatable life rafts are stowed aft and on the forward main deck.
POWER PLANT: Power is supplied by two 12-cylinder, MTU MB12V 652 SB70 supercharged diesels, each with a normal continuous output of 1,650hp at 1,380rpm, and 1,950hp at 1,460rpm maximum. Under tropical conditions normal continuous rating is 1,590hp at 1,380rpm and 1,810hp at 1,460rpm maximum. Engine output is transferred to two 950mm (3ft 1·37in) diameter three-bladed bronze propellers through a Zahnradfabrik BW 900 HS 15 reversible gearbox, which is hydraulically operated and remotely controlled from the wheelhouse. The propeller shafts are in stainless steel and supported at four points by seawater lubricated rubber bearings. Fuel is carried in integral tanks beneath the lower deck in the bottom compartments.
SYSTEMS, ELECTRICAL: Two 37kVA water-cooled 60Hz diesel-driven 380V generators installed in the engine room. An emergency generator of similar capacity is provided at main deck level.
HYDRAULICS: 120kg/cm² pressure hydraulic system for operating all hydraulic driven consumers.
AIR CONDITIONING: An air conditioning system is provided. Capacity is sufficient for adequate temperature and humidity conditions in all passenger saloons and on the bridge when operating in tropical conditions.
COMMUNICATIONS AND NAVIGATION: UHF radio, VHF radio-telephone and magnetic compass are standard. Radar, Decca Navigator and gyro compass to customer's requirements.
DIMENSIONS
EXTERNAL
Length overall, hull: 30m (98ft 6in)
  deck: 29·2m (96ft)
Hull beam max: 5·8m (19ft 1in)
Width across foils: 11·6m (38ft 1in)
Draught hullborne: 4m (13ft 1in)
  foilborne: 1·96m (6ft)
INTERNAL (standard version)
Aft lower saloon
  Length: 9m (29ft 6in)
  Width: 4·6m (15ft 1in)
  Height: 2·15m (7ft 1in)
  Floor area: 42m² (452ft²)
  Volume: 92m³ (3,249ft³)
Forward lower saloon
  Length: 8·1m (26ft 7in)
  Width: 4·7m (15ft 5in)
  Height: 2·15m (7ft 1in)
  Floor area: 37m² (398ft²)
  Volume: 82m³ (2,896ft³)
Upper aft saloon
  Length: 4·5m (14ft 9in)
  Width: 4·2m (13ft 9in)
  Height: 2·1m (6ft 11in)
  Floor area: 18m² (193ft²)
  Volume: 38m³ (1,342ft³)
Foyer
  Length: 5·1m (16ft 9in)
  Width: 4·2m (13ft 9in)
  Height: 2·1m (6ft 11in)
  Floor area: 20m² (215ft²)
  Volume: 42m³ (1,483ft³)
WEIGHTS
Max take-off displacement: 85 tons
Light displacement: 68·5 tons
Disposable load (including fuel, oil, water, passengers, luggage and crew): 16·5 tons
PERFORMANCE (with normal payload)
Cruising speed: 66·5km/h (36 knots)
Max speed: 72·5km/h (39 knots)
Range: 333km (180n miles)
Turning radius: approx 700m (2,350ft)
Take-off distance: approx 500m (1,600ft)
Take-off time: approx 50 seconds
Stopping distance: approx 100m (330ft)
Time to stop craft: approx 20 seconds
Fuel consumption at cruising speed: approx
  600kg/h (1,323lb/h)

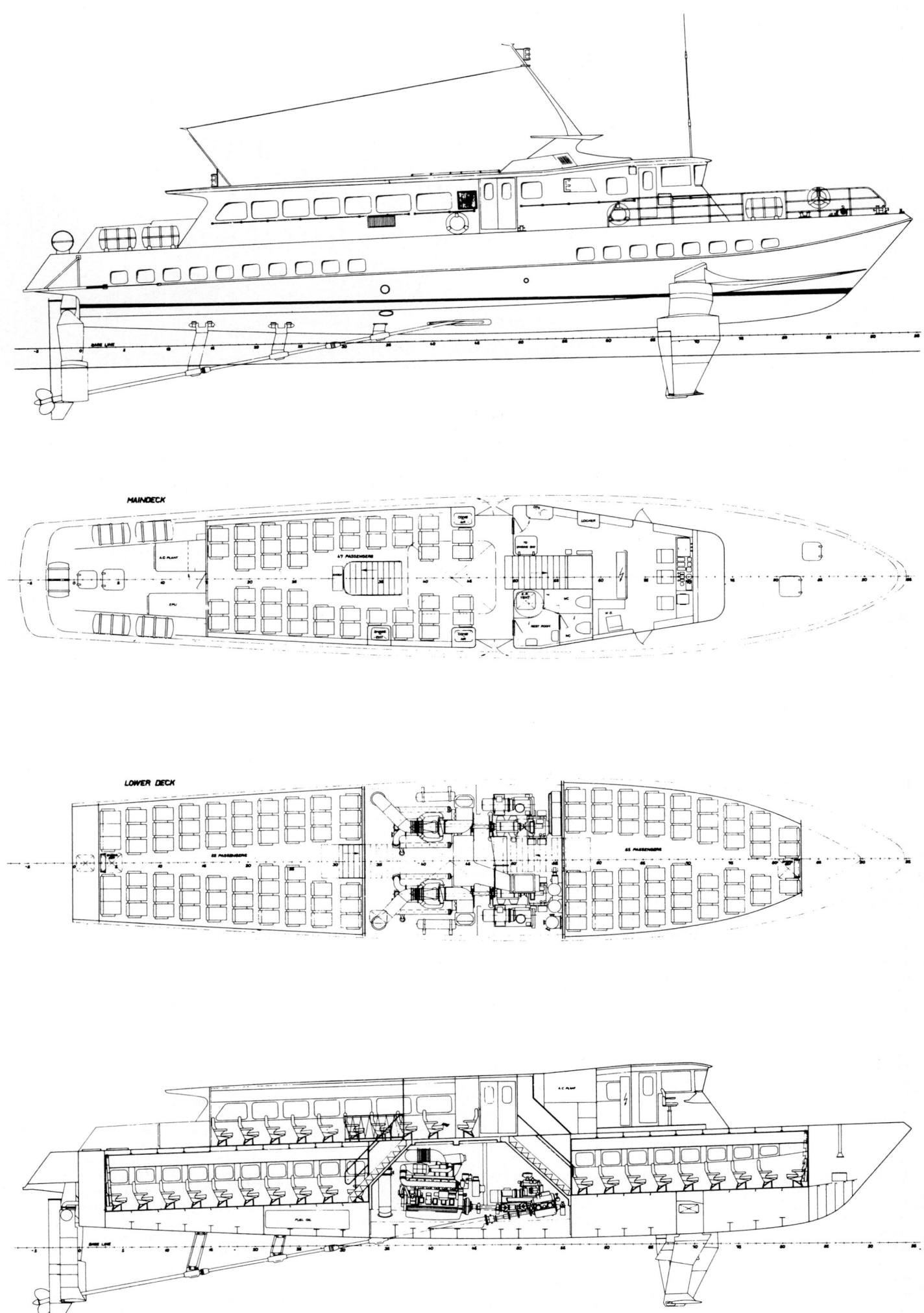

Inboard and outboard profiles and deck views of PTS 75 Mk III

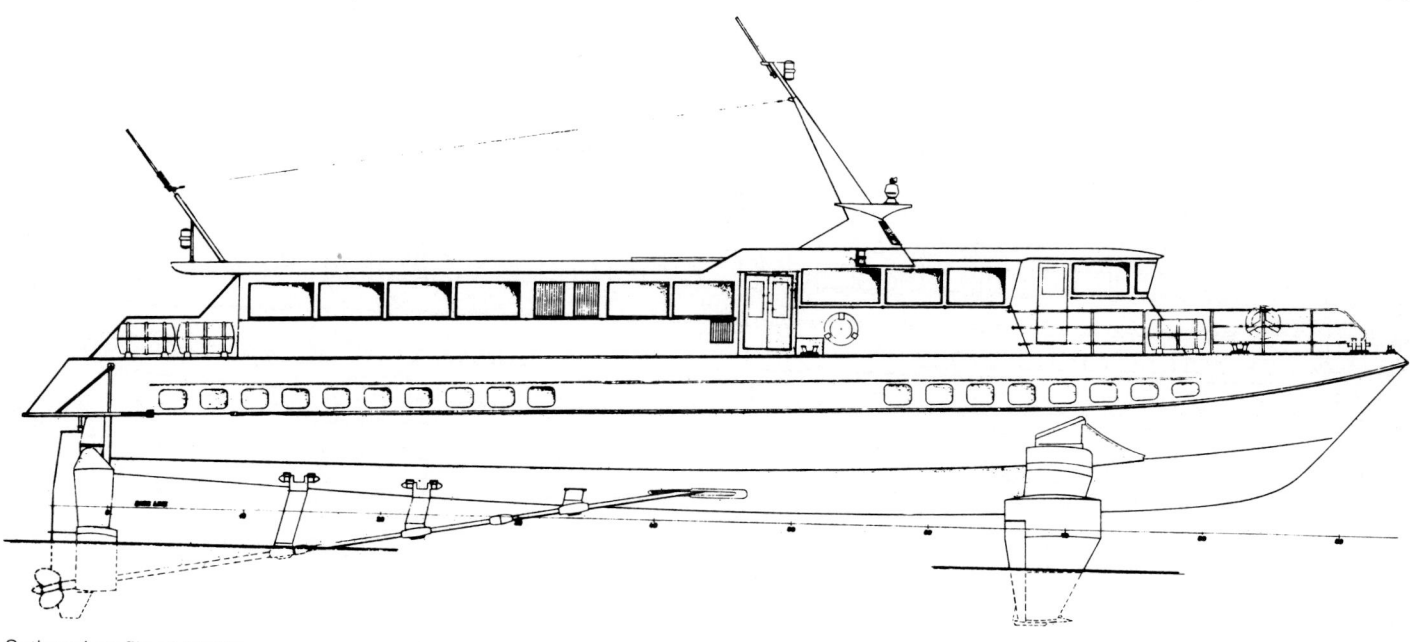

Outboard profile of PT 100

SUPRAMAR PTS 100

A variant of the PTS 75 Mk III, the PTS 100 seats 200 passengers and is designed for short-haul commuter routes.

FOILS: New Supramar system combining features of surface-piercing and fully-submerged systems.

POWER PLANT: Two 16-cylinder MTU 16V 396 TB83 high-speed marine diesels, each rated at 1,400kW at 1,800rpm normal continuous output.

DIMENSIONS

Main dimensions and characteristics are identical to those of the PTS 75 Mk III, seen in the accompanying general arrangement drawing.

WEIGHTS

Fully loaded: 90 tons

PERFORMANCE

Cruising speed: 37 knots

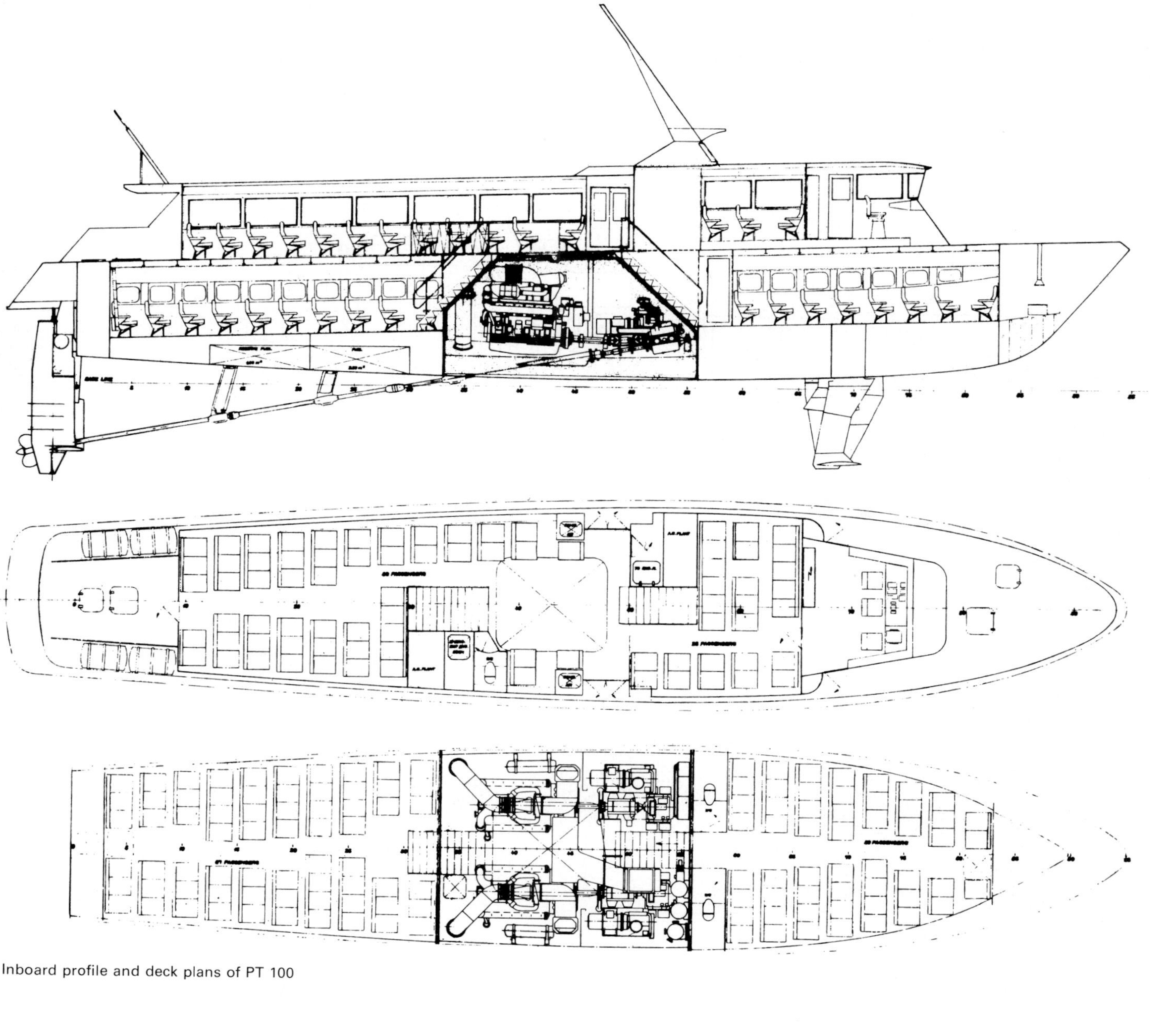

Inboard profile and deck plans of PT 100

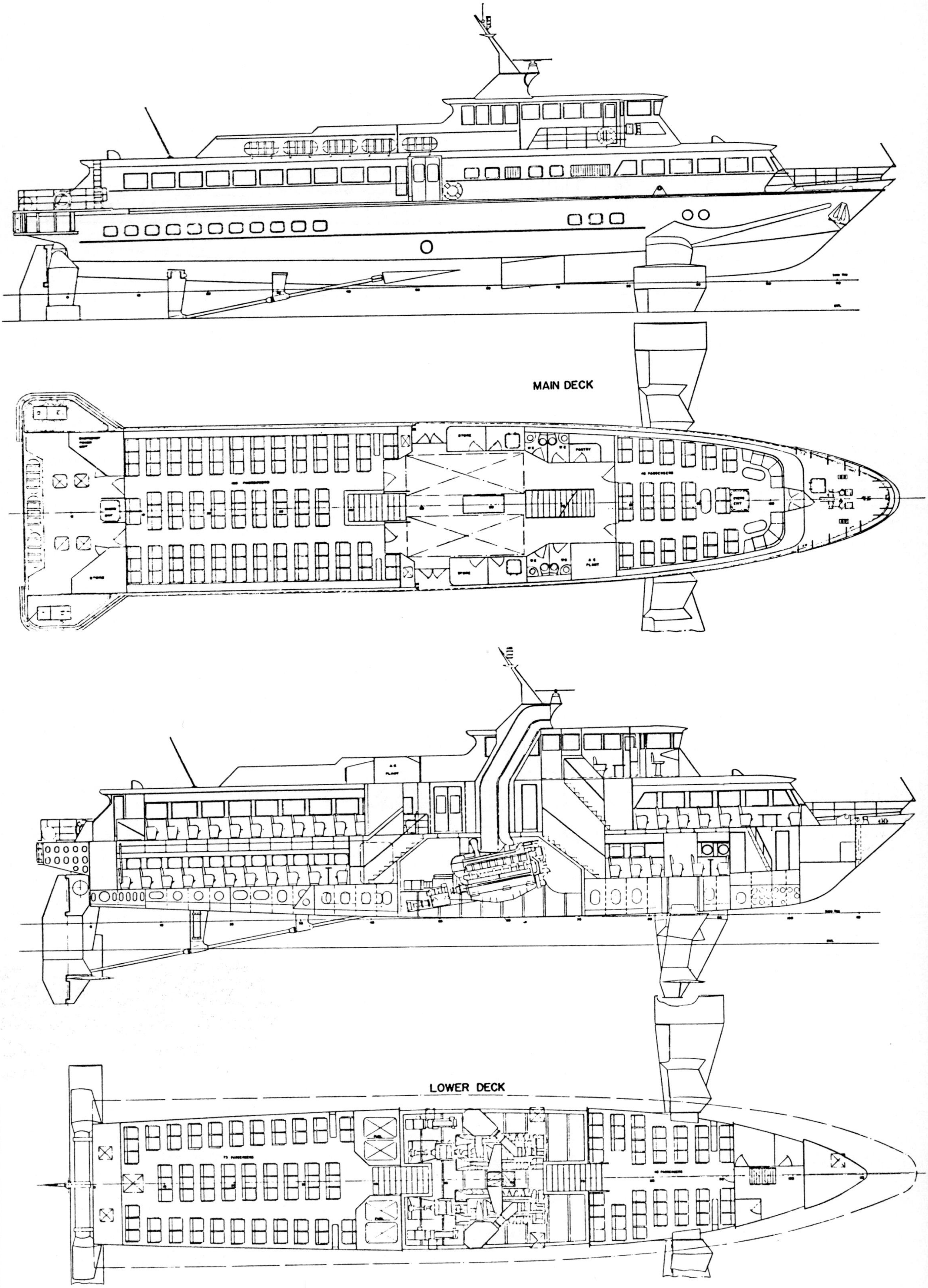

MAIN DECK

LOWER DECK

Inboard and outboard profiles, main deck and lower deck arrangements of PTS 180 Mk III

PTS 180 Mk III

The Supramar PTS 180 Mk III is an improved version of the PTS 150 Mk II.

FOILS: New Supramar inherently stable design combining the advantages of the fully-submerged system with the simplicity and reliability of the surface-piercing type.

The new Supramar stabilisation system improves the seakeeping qualities and enables the boat to cope foilborne with waves up to 3m (10ft) high at full power and up to 3·6m (12ft) at reduced speed.

Apart from the augmentation of effectiveness of the stabilisation resulting from speed increase, the new system generates higher motion reducing moments than obtained by the existing PTS 150s.

HULL AND SUPERSTRUCTURE: Partly riveted and partly welded construction employing a system of longitudinal and transverse frames. It has high deadrise and hard chine sections for performance as a planing hull and for structural impacts in a seaway while foilborne. A step is provided to facilitate take-off. While the main or structure deck is continuous from bow to stern, the lower deck is interrupted by the engine room, sited amidships. The superstructure, which is also longitudinally and transversally framed, is not included in the load bearing structure, several expansion joints have therefore been provided.

The subdivision of the hull can be seen on the general arrangement drawing. The hull is subdivided by four watertight bulkheads (continuous from bottom to main deck) into five watertight main compartments. The double bottom frame 8 to frame 44 and from frame 71 to frame 102 is further subdivided separately by four watertight floor frames into six double bottom cells. The superstructure extends from frames 8 to 102 and is subdivided by transverse walls at frames 45 to 78 into three main compartments. The aft main deck forms a partly roofed open air deck.

ACCOMMODATION: The PTS 180 Mk III carries 270 passengers in four saloons, two on the main deck and two on the lower deck. The forward compartment main deck seats 46, and the aft compartment 105. On the lower deck the forward compartment seats 46 and the aft compartment 73.

Passengers board the craft through double doors to the single centralised foyer, from which doors and companion ladders lead to the respective passenger saloons on the upper and lower decks.

Provision is made for all passengers to be served in their seats with cold meals and drinks.

Passenger seats are of lightweight aircraft type. Floors and ceilings are covered with lightweight plastic materials and the walls are clad in luxury plywood. Each passenger saloon has fitted carpets. Each room has an independent ventilation unit. Four toilets are provided.

The bridge, which is on a separate level above the main deck, slightly forward of midships, is reached by a companion ladder at the aft of the forward passenger compartment. All passenger saloons have emergency exits.

The craft carries 13 inflatable RFD life rafts (for 110 per cent of the classified number of passengers and crew) which are stowed along both sides of the superstructure deck, and on the aft maindeck. Lifejackets are arranged beneath the seats.

POWER PLANT: Power is supplied by two 16-cylinder MTU 16V 1163 TB 83 diesels with a maximum output of 4,335kW at 1,210rpm and a continuous output of 3,300kW.

Lightweight Zahnradfabrik BW 1500 HS 22 hydraulically-operated reverse and reduction gears incorporate the propeller thrust bearings. The gears are pneumatically remote controlled from the wheelhouse. The propeller shafts are made of a heat-treated stainless steel and each is supported by five seawater lubricated rubber bearings. Two three-bladed propellers of approximately 1·3m are placed behind the rear foil.

SYSTEMS, ELECTRICAL: The following main systems are used:

For power, permanently installed heating and cooking apparatus: 380V rotary current, 50Hz three-wires, insulated from the ship's structure.

PT 180

For light sockets and instrumentation: 220V ac, 50Hz two-wires, insulated from the ship's structure.

For remote control and monitoring: 24V dc, two-wires, insulated from the ship's structure.

Two shore connections are provided, both on the superstructure deck. The main shore connection is for the supply of the bus bar of the main switchboard. The second shore connection is exclusively for the heating of the boat and preheating of the main engine.

HYDRAULICS: Steering, variation of the front foil flap angle and the angle of the rear foil flap are all operated hydraulically. Each system has its own circuit which is monitored by a pressure-controlled pilot lamp.

CONTROLS: Starting, manoeuvring and operation of the craft is controlled from the bridge, but in cases of emergency the main engines may be controlled from the engine room.

The two main engines are each controlled by an operating lever designed for singlehanded control. Propeller reversal is also by means of these levers, the reverse gear being actuated by pneumatic remote control between bridge and main engines.

To start the boat both operating levers must be put in the 'full ahead' position simultaneously. Foilborne speed can be regulated by fine adjusting of the operating levers. No other control devices are necessary for the main engines.

Levers for variation of the front foil flap angle and the angle of the rear foil flap are actuated only before and after starting. During foilborne operation these can be used for trim compensation. All instrumentation and monitoring equipment is installed on the bridge.

AIR CONDITIONING: The vessel is equipped with an air conditioning and heating plant which guarantees a room temperature of between 20 and 25°C, dependent on the relative humidity. Air rate is 25m³/h/person.

COMMUNICATION AND NAVIGATION: Standard navigation equipment includes a gyro master compass with transformers, rectifiers and one multiple steering repeater positioned ahead of the helmsman, Loran or Decca Navigator and radar.

Communications equipment includes radio telephone equipment for normal and emergency use.

DIMENSIONS

EXTERNAL

Length overall, hull: 37·9m (124ft 3in)
  deck: 37·1m (121ft 10in)
Hull beam, max: 7·5m (24ft 7in)
Deck beam, max: 7·4m (24ft 3in)
Width across foils: 16m (52ft 5in)
Draught hullborne: 5·6m (18ft 4in)
  foilborne: 2·4m (7ft 9in)

WEIGHTS

Displacement, fully loaded: 180 tons
Disposable load (payload plus consumable stores): 35 tons
Passenger capacity: 270

PERFORMANCE

Cruising speed at 6,600kW: 42 knots
Range: 460km (250n miles)
Max permissible wave height in foilborne mode at full power (head seas) for passenger acceptability: 3m (10ft)

ST 3A FULLY SUBMERGED FOIL RESEARCH CRAFT

In 1965 the US Navy awarded Supramar a contract for the construction and testing of a 5-ton research craft with fully submerged air stabilised foils. The objectives of the tests were the investigation of the effectiveness and reliability of the Schertel-Supramar air stabilisation system under a variety of wave conditions.

FOIL SYSTEM: The craft was fitted with two fully-submerged bow foils and one fully-submerged rear foil. The load distribution was 62% on the bow foils and 38% on rear foil. A rudder flap was attached to the end of the rear foil strut.

AIR FEED SYSTEM: Lift variation was achieved without movable foil parts. Each foil has two air ducts with outlets on the suction side. Air was drawn through these apertures from the free atmosphere via the foil suspension tube and the hollow struts. Air valves, controlled by sensors, governed the quantity of air admitted to the respective ducts.

ST 3A

CONTROLS: The signals of a depth sensor, a rate gyro and damped pendulum were added and amplified. The pneumatic follow-up amplifier drew its propulsion power from the subpressure which was produced at a suction opening at the strut near the foil. The amplifier output was connected with the air valve. The depth sensor probed the submergence depth digitally by means of suction orifices at the front struts. No motor-driven power source was required for the control system which, as well as the air feed system for lift variation of the foils, was designed for simplicity and reliability.

HULL: The hull, of hard chine construction, was basically that of a standard Supramar ST 3, modified to accommodate the new foil system, gas turbine and test equipment. To facilitate take-off, a step was provided and a ram wedge was fastened to the stern bottom. The hull clearance (tip of step to water surface) of only 36cm (1ft 2·5in) was due to the requirement that an existing ST 3 hull, with an inclined propeller shaft, was to be used for the tests.

POWER PLANT: The craft was powered by a single 1,000hp GE 7 LM100 PG 102 gas turbine. Engine output was transferred to a 0·38m (1ft 3in) diameter S-C bronze propeller through a reduction gear, a V-drive and an inclined stainless steel shaft. A 35hp Mercury outboard was installed on the port side of the transom to provide auxiliary propulsion. To feed the stabilisation gyros a 6hp petrol engine was installed in the forepeak and coupled to a three-phase ac generator.

DIMENSIONS
Length overall, hull: 10·32m (33ft 10in)
Width over foils: 3·6m (11ft 10in)
    over hull: 2·7m (8ft 10in)
Draught hullborne: 1·55m (5ft 1in)
    foilborne (front foil): 0·5m (1ft 7·5in)
Hull clearance: 0·36m (1ft 2·5in)
WEIGHTS
Displacement: 4·9 tons
PERFORMANCE
Max measured test speed: 101km/h (54·5 knots)
Max speed (design): 104km/h (56 knots)
Take-off time: 14·5 seconds
Stopping distance: 50-5 knots: 120m (390ft)
Turning radius at 40 knots: 230m (750ft)
SEA TEST: Sea trials along the Mediterranean coast revealed that the craft, despite a small hull clearance, was capable of taking waves 0·9 to 1·2m (3 to 4ft) high, and with a minimum length of about 30·4 to 36·4m (100 to 120ft), at 45 knots in all courses from head to beam seas, partially contouring. In waves over 1·2m (4ft) the hull periodically touched wave crests, which was accompanied by a marked speed reduction (very high Froude number) during water contacting. In a following sea, and in all courses up to about 60 degrees to a following sea, foilborne operation was limited to 0·76m (2ft 6in) waves due to the control system, which at that time had no heave sensor. At a wave height of 0·91m (3ft) (a tenth of boat length), vertical accelerations of only 0·08g had been measured, which compares very favourably with the sea test results of other craft with fully submerged foils.

NAVAL HYDROFOILS

Derived from Supramar's range of commercial vessels, this range of military hydrofoils is designed for naval defence duties, coast guard and anti-contraband patrol.

SUPRAMAR PAT 20

This military version of the Supramar PT 20B Mk II is in service with several navies for patrolling coastal and sheltered waters. It has good seakeeping capabilities for a craft of this size.
FOILS: Schertel-Sachsenberg surface-piercing type in structural steel.
POWER PLANT: The main propulsion engine is an MTU Type 331 12-cylinder, four-stroke diesel, developing 1,430hp maximum intermittent and 1,300hp continuous. Engine output is transferred to a three-bladed propeller via an inclined shaft.
HULL: Riveted seawater-resistant light metal alloy structure.

ARMAMENT: Two 40mm Bofors L/70 automatic guns, one forward, one aft. Ammunition stored in compartments beneath.
DIMENSIONS
Length overall: 21·75m (71ft 4in)
Width over foils: 8·6m (28ft 2in)
Draught hullborne: 3·1m (10ft 2in)
    foilborne: 1·4m (4ft 7in)
WEIGHTS
Displacement loaded: 31 tons
Disposable load (fuel, consumable stores, crew, provisions, armament and ammunition): 6·3 tons
PERFORMANCE
Cruising speed: 35 knots
Range: 536km (300n miles)

PAT 70

The PAT 70 is similar in design and construction to the PT 50 Mk II.
FOILS: Bow and rear foils are of surface-piercing V configuration and fabricated in structural steel.
HULL: Riveted light alloy construction.
POWER PLANT: Power is provided by two MTU MB 12V 652 12-cylinder four-stroke diesels, each rated at 1,725hp continuous and 1,950hp maximum intermittent. Engine output is transferred to two three-bladed propellers via twin inclined propeller shafts.
ARMAMENT: A typical weapon fit would comprise two 40mm Bofors L/70 automatic mounts, one forward, one aft.
DIMENSIONS
Length overall: 29·5m (96ft 9in)
Width over foils: 10·7m (35ft 1in)
Draught hullborne: 3·8m (12ft 6in)
    foilborne: 1·7m (5ft 7in)
WEIGHTS
Displacement loaded: 69 tons
Disposable load (fuel, consumable stores, crew, provisions, armament and ammunition): 14 tons
PERFORMANCE
Cruising speed: 39 knots

Range: 536km (300n miles)
Max permissible wave height foilborne: 1·8m (6ft)

NAT 85

Derived from the PTS 75 Mk III passenger ferry, this fast patrol boat variant is armed with a 40mm Breda Bofors twin naval mounting and Otomat guided missiles.
FOILS: Surface-piercing configuration, incorporating the Schertel-Supramar air stabilisation system.
HULL: Hard chine type, constructed in partly riveted, partly welded corrosion resistant light alloy.
POWER PLANT: Power is supplied by two MTU MB 16V 652 16-cylinder four-stroke diesels, each rated at 2,300hp continuous and 2,610hp maximum. Engine output is transferred to two three-bladed propellers through a Zahnradfabrik reversible gearbox.
ARMAMENT: Anti-ship missiles: Two Otomat Mk I missile launchers aft. Guns: 40mm Breda Bofors L/70 twin naval mounting on the foredeck, ahead of the superstructure.
ELECTRONICS: Thomson-CSF Canopus C fire control system.
DIMENSIONS
Length overall: 30·4m (99ft 9in)
Width over foils: 12m (39ft 4in)
Draught hullborne: 4·3m (14ft 1in)
    foilborne: 2·3m (7ft 6in)
WEIGHTS
Displacement loaded: 85 tons
Disposable load (fuel, consumable stores, crew, provisions, armament and ammunition): 16 tons
PERFORMANCE
Cruising speed: 42 knots
Range: 741km (400n miles)
Max permissible wave height: 2·3m (7ft 6in)

NAT 90

Based on the PTS 75 Mk III, this alternative fast strike missile craft variant has waterjet propulsion and fully retracting foils. It is intended for

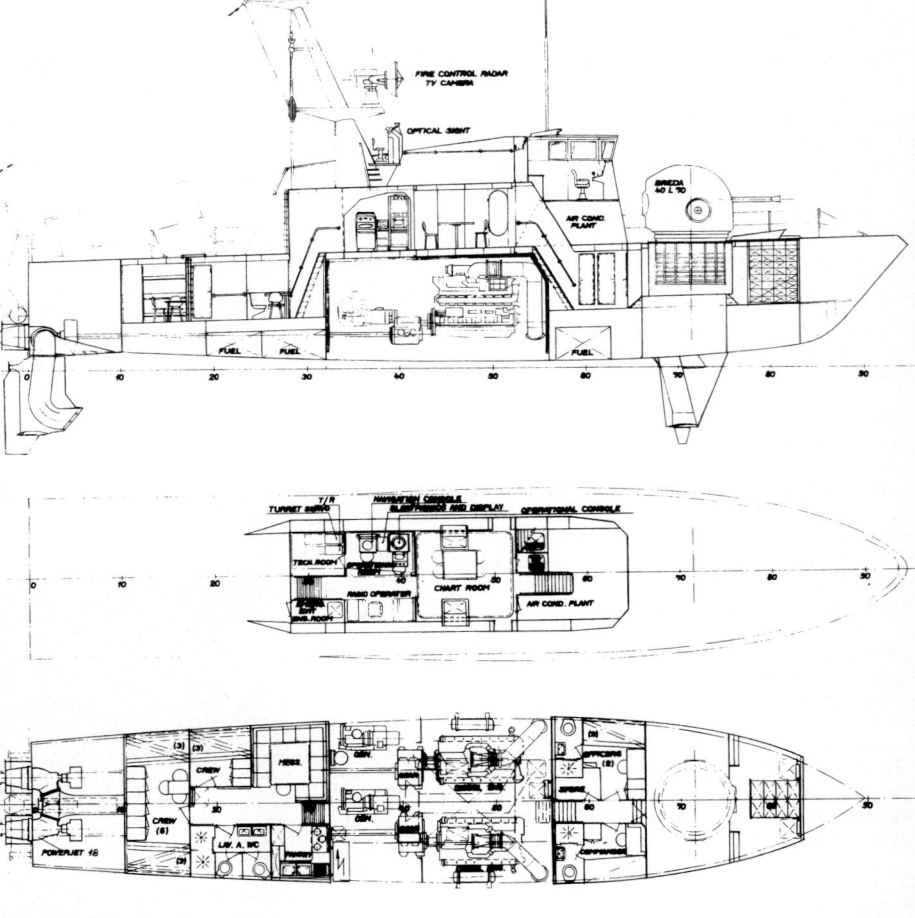

Inboard profile and deck plans of NAT 90

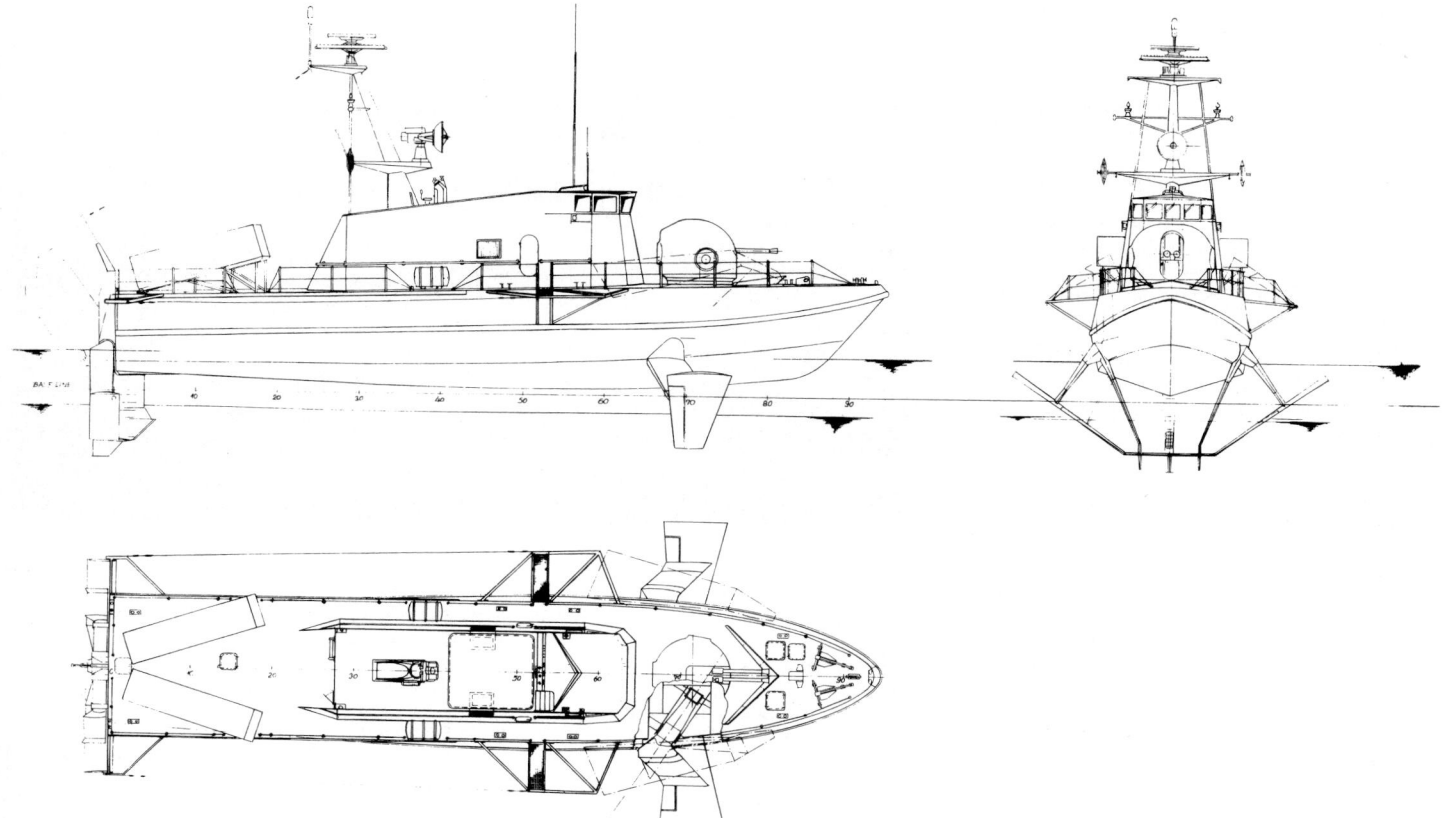

Outboard elevations and weatherdeck plan of Supramar NAT 90 fast strike missile craft

operations in areas where the hullborne draught would be too deep for satisfactory navigation, particularly in sheltered waters. The foils are retracted hydraulically above the waterline.

FOILS: Surface-piercing V configuration. Bow foil is 'split' to permit the two halves to swivel upwards hydraulically. The aft foil assembly is built as a single unit and comprises the foils, a central rudder/water strut, to which the rudder flap is attached, and two side struts.

HULL: Hull and superstructure in combined riveted and welded seawater resistant light metal. All compartments are air-conditioned, including the bridge.

POWER PLANT: Power for the waterjet propulsion system is supplied by two MTU MB 16V 652 16-cylinder, four-stroke diesels, each rated at 2,300hp continuous and 2,610hp maximum intermittent. Each is connected to a Rocketdyne Powerjet 18 single-stage, axial-flow waterjet. During foilborne operation water enters through an inlet at the forward lower end of the aft centre foil strut. When the craft is operating in hullborne mode, with foils retracted, water enters the propulsion system through an inlet in the bottom of the hull. Hullborne speed (foils retracted), with a single Powerjet 18 in use, is 15 knots, with both Powerjets in use, 25 knots.

ARMAMENT: A typical weapons fit would be one Breda Bofors L/70 twin 40mm mounting forward of the superstructure and two Exocet missile launchers aft.

DIMENSIONS
Length overall: 29·9m (98ft 1in)
Width across foils: 11·8m (38ft 8in)
Draught hullborne: 4·1m (13ft 5in)
    foils retracted: 1·3m (4ft 3in)
    foilborne: 1·9m (6ft 3in)
WEIGHTS
Displacement loaded: 85 tons
Disposable load (fuel, consumable stores, crew, provisions, armament and ammunition): 15 tons
PERFORMANCE
Max cruising speed: 39 knots
Range: 741km (400n miles)
Max permissible wave height: 2·3m (7ft 6in)

NAT 190
NAT 190 is the designation given to the military version of the Supramar PTS 180. As a fast

strike craft its main armament would comprise two 40mm Bofors L/70 automatic twin mounts and three Exocet MM 38 missile launchers.

FOILS: Fixed surface-piercing foils of Schertel-Supramar air stabilised type. In the event of the air stabilisation system failing, the craft is able to continue operating in foilborne mode although foil submergence would be increased moderately.

POWER PLANT: Foilborne propulsion is supplied by two MTU 16V 956 TB 82 16-cylinder diesels each driving a three-bladed propeller via an inclined shaft. Each engine is rated at 3,800hp continuous at 27°C.

ARMAMENT: Typical weapons fit would comprise two 40mm Bofors L/70 automatic dual purpose guns, one forward and one aft, and three Exocet MM 38 anti-ship missile launchers.

ELECTRONICS: Thomson-CSF Vega-Pollux tactical information unit and fire control system.

DIMENSIONS
Length overall: 37·9m (124ft 4in)
Width over foils: 16·6m (54ft 6in)
Draught hullborne: 5m (16ft 5in)
    foilborne: 2·1m (6ft 11in)
WEIGHTS
Displacement loaded: 180 tons
Disposable load (fuel, consumable stores, crew, provisions, armament and ammunition): 40 tons
PERFORMANCE
Cruising speed: 39 knots
Foilborne range: 1,072km (600n miles) at 36 knots

Hullborne range: 1,850km (1,000n miles) at 10 knots
Endurance at sea: 3-5 days
Max permissible wave height: 2·8m (9ft)
    at reduced speed: 3·5m (11ft 6in)

SUPRAMAR MT 250
This is a design concept for a 250-tonne patrol boat hydrofoil which meets the tactical requirements established by the West German and other NATO navies. It conforms to the fast patrol boat standards of the West German Navy and has a maximum intermittent speed of 60 knots.

Main dimensions of the vessel are similar to those of the Swedish 'Spica' class, Vosper 'Tenacity', Israeli 'Sa'ar' class and the West German Type 148. It is designed for all-weather operation in the western Baltic, the Skagerrak and other areas with similar operational conditions.

Foilborne propulsion is supplied by gas-turbine powered waterjets. The foil system is of fully-submerged type employing the Schertel-Supramar air stabilisation system.

As a significant part of the total operating time will be in the hullborne mode, a separate hullborne propulsion plant is provided which guarantees adequate speed in the two hullborne modes: foils retracted and foils extended.

FOILS: Canard system with a single fully-submerged bow foil and two fully-submerged rear foils. The foils are of welded hollow shell construction in stainless steel. All three are hydraulically retracted clear of the waterline. The

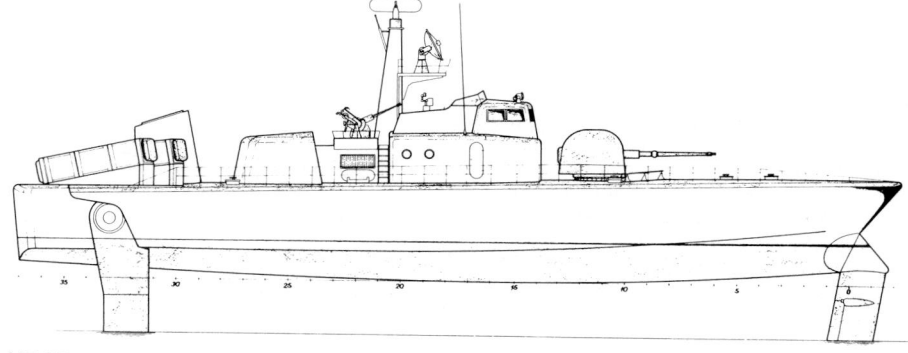

MT 250

design avoids the use of hinged doors or panels to raise the bow foil.

CONTROLS: The stabilisation system is a combined automatic control process employing flaps for damping low frequency motions and air-control for high frequency motions. Roll stabilisation is effected by air control of the outer rear foil and the rear foil struts, also by the operation of flaps on the outer rear foil.

Pitch and heave are controlled by flaps on the bow foil and flaps in the centre section of the aft foil.

The stabilisation system consists of four units: the sensors, a computer (for automatic flight control), a command unit and the transactuators.

HULL: Hull and superstructure is of partly riveted, partly welded seawater-resistant light metal alloy. There are seven watertight transverse bulkheads.

INTERNAL LAYOUT/ACCOMMODATION: Accommodation and operations rooms are almost entirely below deck leaving a relatively large free deck area. Crew would normally comprise 21, officers and ratings. Operating and control rooms are all fully air-conditioned. Minelaying equipment, conforming to NATO standards, can be installed as an alternative to missile launchers. Stand-by space is available for a substantial number of Mk 55 mines. There are three officers' cabins and two crew rooms, two toilets with wash basins, one pantry, store rooms, operating and control rooms for ship and machinery. The control and operations rooms have direct access to the bridge and the radio room. All facilities are provided for an intended sea endurance of three to five days.

POWER PLANT, FOILBORNE: The main propulsion plant consists of a slightly modified version of the Rolls-Royce Marine Olympus TM 3, with the following ratings:

   performance: 25,350ps
   power turbine speed: 5,450rpm
   spec fuel consumption: 0·219kg/PSh
   ambient air temperature: 15°C

This comprises an Olympus gas-generator and a single-stage long-life power unit mounted on a common base. The forward end of the gas-generator mates with the air-intake plenum chamber, which has a cascaded bend to give an undisturbed airflow to the engine intake. Flexible joints are applied to the faces of the air-intake and exhaust system to allow relative movement between the module and the ship's uptakes and downtakes. At the engine ratings given, estimated time between overhaul for the gas-generator is 2,000 hours.

A Metastream M 4000 elastic coupling of approximately 1,500mm length connects the power turbine output shaft with an Allen epicycle gear box. The latter is flanged directly to a Rocketdyne Powerjet 46 pump. The Allen gear box has a reduction ratio of approx 1:5·5.

The Rocketdyne Powerjet 46 pump has twin side water intakes and is rigidly mounted to the ship's structure. It transmits thrust via three points.

AUXILIARY PROPULSION PLANT: The auxiliary propulsion plant comprises two 8-cylinder MTU 8V 331 TC 71 diesel engines driving via REINTJES WAV 500 A reverse and reduction gears and inclined propeller shafts two variable-pitch KAMEWA propellers. The propellers are arranged in a duct at the transom.

The MTU 8V 331 TC 71 diesel has the following ratings and characteristics:

   output continuous: 750 PS at 2,055rpm
   output intermittent: 815 PS at 2,120rpm
   number of cylinders: 8 in V form

ARMAMENT: Optional, but can comprise surface-to-surface missiles of Exocet, Otomat or similar types or OTO Compact gun mount and additional 20mm anti-aircraft guns. Provision has been made for various types of combat systems including Vega II-53 or Mini-Combat-System WM 28.

DIMENSIONS
Length overall, foils extended: 43·7m (143ft 4in)
Beam max over deck: 9·4m (30ft 9in)
Max width over foils: 15·8m (51ft 11in)

MT 250

Draught foilborne: 3·35m (11ft)
Draught hullborne,
   foils extended: 6·95m (22ft 9in)
   foils retracted: 2·2m (7ft 2in)
WEIGHTS
Operational displacement: 250 tonnes
PERFORMANCE
Speed max continuous,
   foilborne: 55 knots
   hullborne, foils retracted: 13 knots
   hullborne, foils extended: 9·5 knots
Range,
at max continuous speed foilborne: 741km (400n miles)
at max continuous speed hullborne, foils extended: 3,340km (1,800n miles)
at max continuous speed hullborne, foils down: 2,400km (1,300n miles)
Max permissible sea state, foilborne: 3·6m (12ft) waves

SUPRAMAR MT 80

The MT 80 is designed for operation in coastal waters. A fully submerged retractable foil system enables it to operate under adverse weather conditions. It can be equipped with a variety of weapons and control systems.

The hull and superstructure are of combined riveted and welded light metal alloy construction. The foils are of high tensile structural steel. The main propulsion system consists of one Rolls-Royce Proteus gas turbine driving either a water-jet pump, or a propeller via a double bevel gear arrangement. The armament and weapon control system is optional.

DIMENSIONS
Length overall: 29m (95ft 2in)
Beam max: 5·8m (19ft)
Width over foils: 8·9m (29ft 2in)
Draught hullborne, foils extended: 4·4m (15ft 5in)
   foils retracted: 1·5m (4ft 11in)
   foilborne: 2·1m (6ft 10in)

WEIGHTS
Displacement: 85 tons
PERFORMANCE
Speed: 53 knots
Range: 741km (400n miles)
Crew: 8–12
Sea endurance: 3 days
Max permissible sea state, foilborne: 2·7m (9ft) waves

SUPRAMAR 500-SEAT PASSENGER FERRY

In August 1972 Supramar revealed that it was undertaking studies for the design of a 500-seat passenger ferry.

SUPRAMAR CT 70 CATAMARAN HYDROFOIL

The Supramar hydrofoil catamaran has been designed for operation in shallow and sheltered waters, where draught limitations preclude the use of conventional hydrofoil craft. Berthing is possible at any existing pontoon or quay facility without adaption, as the foils are well within the hull beam and thereby fully protected against damage while drawing alongside.

One of the major applications foreseen for this new class of hydrofoil is that of fast water bus on urban passenger services. Other likely roles include those of oil-rig support vessel, leisure craft and water sports, especially fishing.

About 80 to 90 per cent of the lift is produced by the foils, and the remainder by the partly immersed hull planing surfaces forward, which also provides stability. The arrangement permits the placing of the foils below the water surface at a depth generally free of floating debris.

In the case of partial foil ventilation, the planing surfaces prevent high angles of list and also impede deep immersion in the waves of a following sea. In cases where retractable foils are required a simple method of retraction can be incorporated.

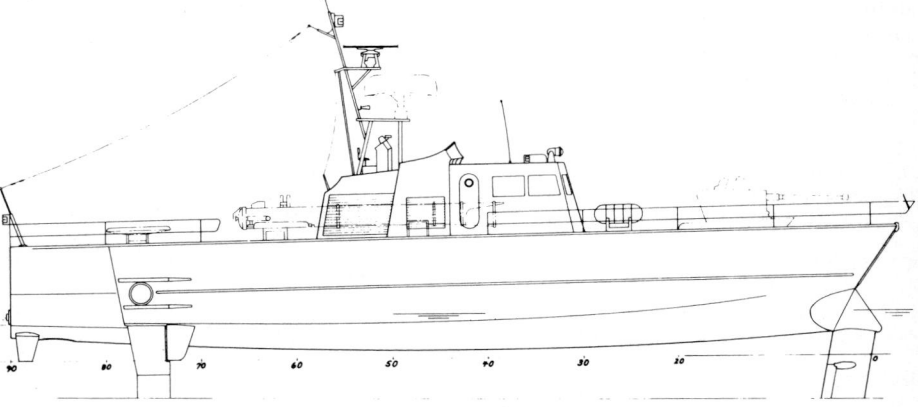

Outboard profile of MT 80

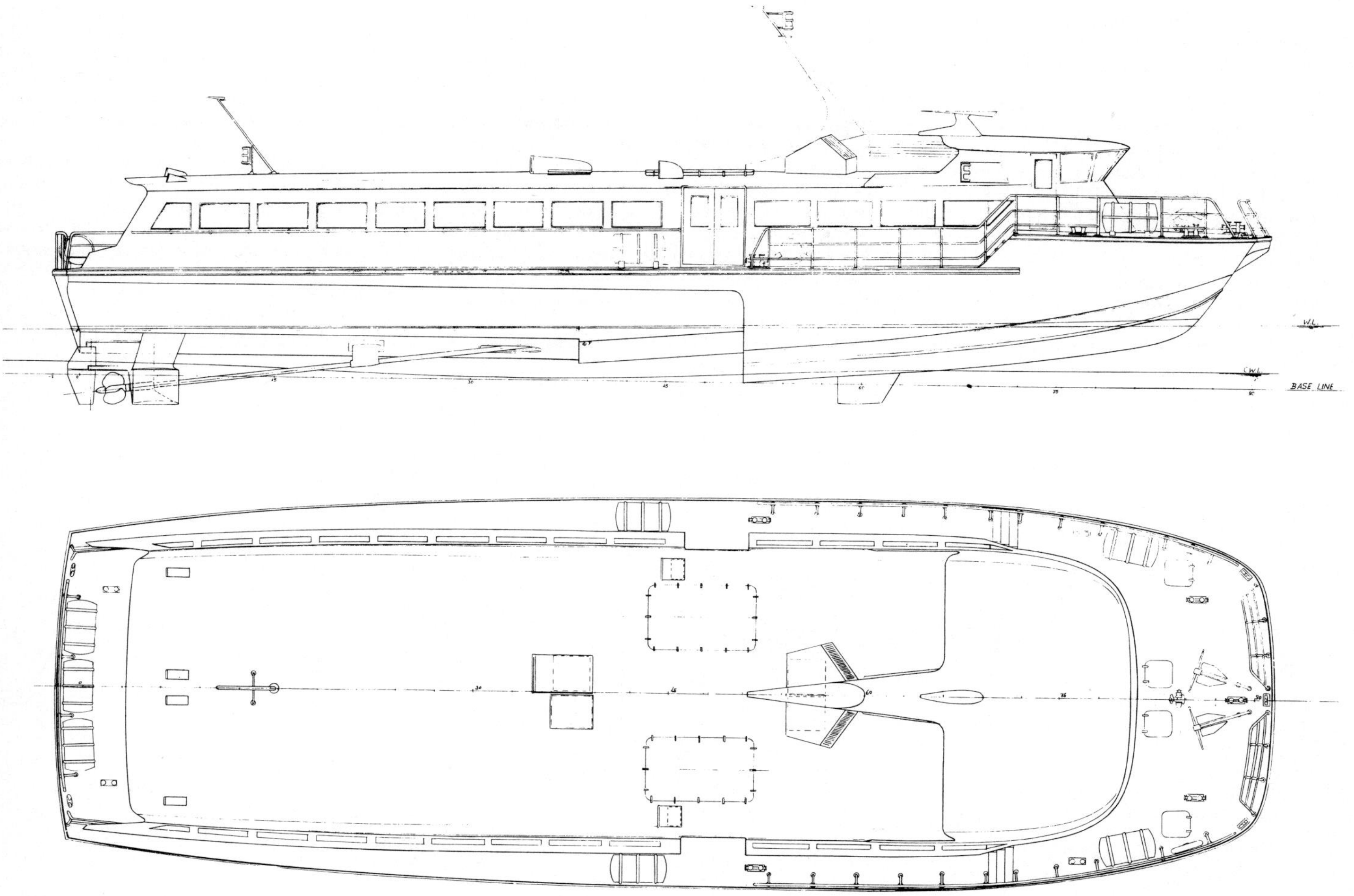

Supramar CT 70 catamaran hydrofoil

General arrangement of CT 70

Because of the uncomplicated nature of the concept and the ease of foil retraction, it is felt that it could be successfully applied to outboard craft.

FOILS: System comprises two Supramar type foils arranged in tandem. The bow foil is located at frame 60 and the rear foil at frame 6.

When foilborne 65% of the weight is supported by the bow foil and the side keels while the remaining 35% is supported by the rear foil. Flying height is adjusted by hydraulically-operated flaps on the bow foil. Foils are in St 52-3 high tensile structural steel.

HULL: The hull, which is of hard chine construction, comprises two side hulls and one central hull. Its design is based on experience gained from the construction of a wide variety of hydrofoil craft.

All members included in the longitudinal strength of the vessel, such as longitudinals, shell and deck plating, are of riveted construction. Transverse members, including web frames and bulkheads, are welded but the connections with main deck, side and bottom shell, are riveted.

POWER PLANT: Motive power is provided by two MTU 331-type 12-cylinder four-stroke diesel engines, each rated at 1,100ps continuous and 1,300ps maximum intermittent. Each drives a propeller via an inclined shaft. The engines are rated for 45°C air intake temperature and 32°C seawater temperature.

ACCOMMODATION: Total seating capacity is for 159 to 166 passengers in one large saloon. Major obstructions, like staircases, have been avoided. Windows are in safety glass and tinted anti-sun grey. On the standard version passenger seats are each fitted with arm rests, an ashtray and a number plate. Four toilets are in the aft of the saloon.

On the short-haul model the passenger seats are more simple and two toilets are provided. There are three luggage compartments, one adjacent to the embarkation doors leading to the passenger saloon, and two at the aft of the saloon.

DIMENSIONS
Length overall: 28m (91ft 10in)
Beam, max moulded: 9·3m (30ft 6in)

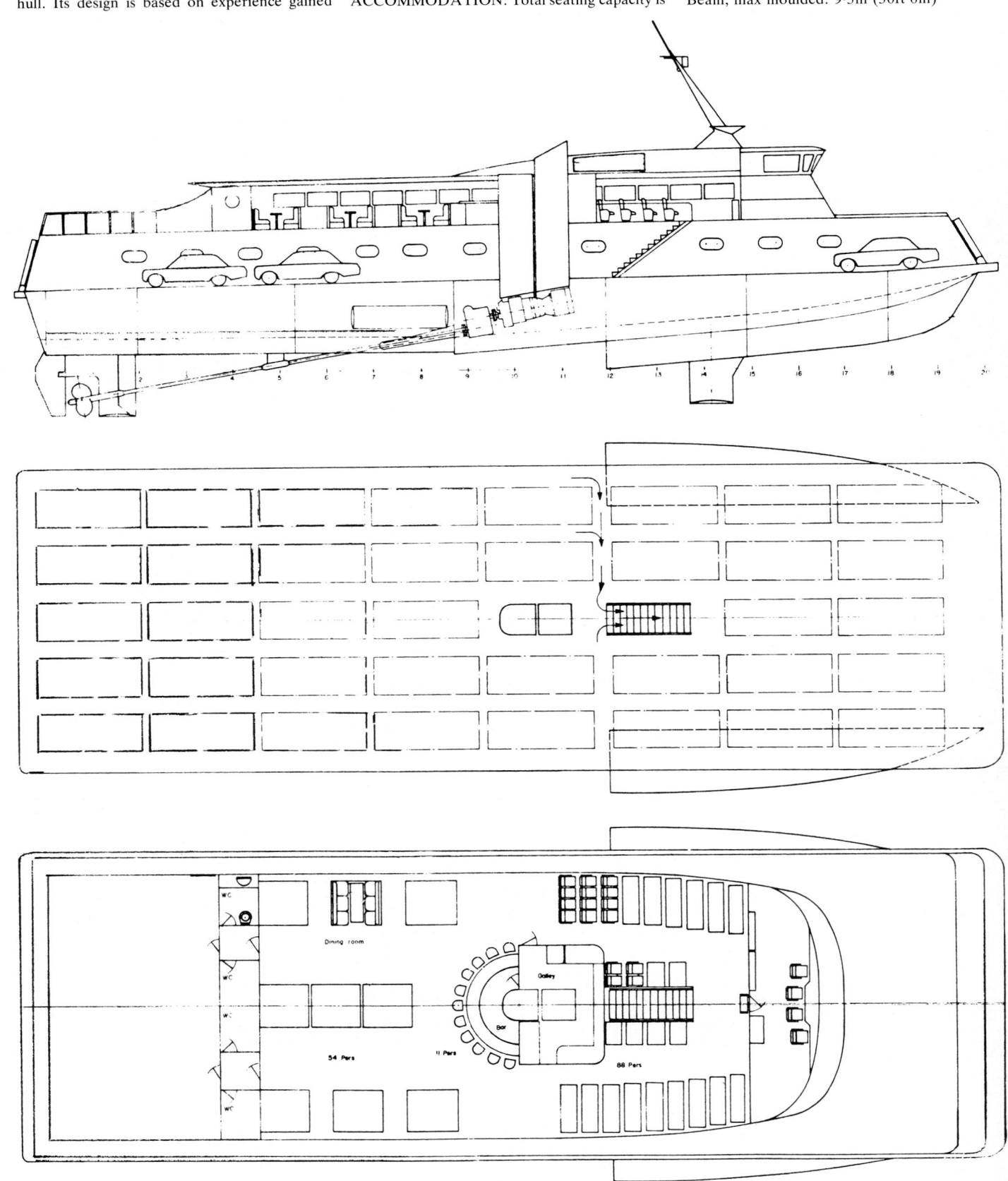

200T hydrofoil catamaran car ferry

Draught hullborne: 1·8m (5ft 11in)
  foilborne: 1m (3ft 3in)

WEIGHTS
Displacement, fully loaded: 68·5 tonnes (67·45 tons)
  unloaded: 51·7 tonnes (50·9 tons)
Disposable load: 16·8 tonnes (16·56 tons)
Payload: 13·6 tonnes (13·4 tons)
Driving fuel and crew: 3·2 tonnes (3·15 tons)

PERFORMANCE
Max speed, foilborne: about 61·5km/h (33 knots)
Cruising speed, foilborne: about 57·5km/h (31 knots)
Number of seated passengers: 159-166

SUPRAMAR 200T HYDROFOIL CATAMARAN CAR FERRY

This projected mixed-traffic ferry is intended mainly for commuter services on lakes. It has twice the speed of conventional displacement ferries and economical performance.

HULL: Lightweight design using partly riveted and partly welded seawater-resistant aluminium alloys. Highly stressed parts such as fittings for the foils, shaft, struts etc are in steel.
FOILS: Tandem arrangement. The fully-submerged front foil is well protected by the partly immersed planing surfaces, from floating debris. Electro-hydraulically actuated flaps are fitted for adjusting the flying height. Rear foil is fully submerged.
POWER PLANT: Propulsive power is provided by two marinised gas turbines each rated at 3,700kW (5,000hp) continuous at 27°C air intake temperature. The propellers are placed behind the rear foil and are driven via reverse and reduction gears and two inclined shafts.
ACCOMMODATION: The lower deck carries 38 cars. Large stern and bow doors provide roll-on/roll-off facilities.

Passengers are accommodated on the upper deck which has adequate space to seat 260. A companion stair connects the passenger compartment directly with the car deck. Four toilets and/or luggage rooms are located in the aft part. The accompanying plan shows a configuration for long distance services with a passenger compartment for 88, a bar for 11 and a cafeteria for 54 persons. Total seating is for 153 persons. Food is prepared in a centrally located galley.
DIMENSIONS
Length overall: 42m (137ft 10in)
Width over hull: 15·6m (51ft 2·62in)
Draught hullborne: 3·6m (11ft 9·75in)
  foilborne: 2·5m (8ft 2in)
WEIGHTS
Displacement loaded: 200 tons
Disposable load: 83 tons
PERFORMANCE
Cruising speed: 40 knots
Range: 425km (264 miles)
Passenger capacity: 153-260
Car capacity: 38

UNION OF SOVIET SOCIALIST REPUBLICS

KRASNOYE SORMOVO SHIPYARD

Head Office and Works: Gorki, USSR
Officials:
M Yuriev, *Shipyard Director*
Ivan Yerlykin, *Chief Hydrofoil Designer*
Export Enquiries: Sudotransport (V/O Sudoimport), 5 Kaliayevskaya str, Moscow 103006, USSR
Telephone: 251 05 05, 299 52 14
Telex: 411272 SUDO SU, 411387 SUDO SU

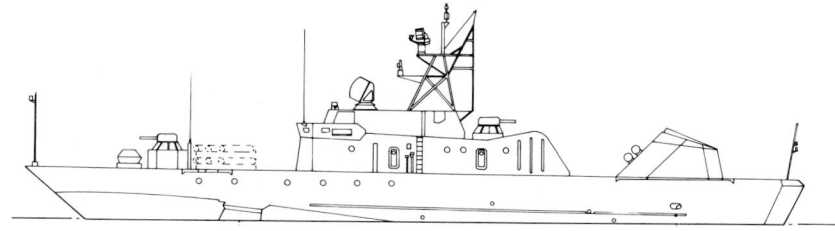

Outboard profile of Babochka

Krasnoye Sormovo is one of the oldest established shipyards in the Soviet Union. In addition to building displacement craft of many kinds for the Soviet River Fleet, the yard constructs the world's widest range of passenger hydrofoils, many of which are equipped with the Alexeyev shallow draught submerged foil system. The late Dr Alexeyev started work at the end of 1945 on the design of his foil system which had to be suitable for operation on smooth, but open and shallow rivers and canals. He succeeded in making use of the immersion depth effect, or surface effect, for stabilising the foil immersion in calm waters by the use of small lift coefficients.

The system comprises two main horizontal lifting surfaces, one forward and one aft, with little or no dihedral, each carrying approximately half the weight of the vessel. A submerged foil loses lift gradually as it approaches the surface from a submergence of about one chord. This effect prevents the submerged foils from rising completely to the surface. Means therefore had to be provided to assist take-off and prevent the vessel from sinking back to the displacement condition. The answer lay in the provision of planing sub-

foils of small aspect ratio in the vicinity of the forward struts arranged so that when they are touching the water surface the main foils are submerged approximately to a depth of one chord.

The approach embodies characteristics of the Grunberg principle of inherent angle of attack variation, comprising a 'wing' and a stabiliser system. When the Alexeyev foils drop below the shallow draught zone, the craft converts momentarily to the Grunberg mode of operation, duplicating its configuration. The otherwise inactive sub-foils, coming into contact with the water surface, become the Grunberg stabilisers and cause the foils to climb up into the shallow draught zone where they resume normal operation in the Alexeyev mode.

The foils have good riding characteristics on inland waters and in sheltered waters.

The system was first tested on a small launch powered by a 77bhp converted car engine. Three more small craft were built to prove the idea, then work began on the yard's first multi-seat passenger craft, the Raketa, the first of which was

launched in June 1957 and has completed more than 25 years of service.

The yard also co-operates with the Leningrad Water Transport Institute in the development of seagoing craft with fully submerged V-type and trapeze-type surface-piercing foils, similar in configuration to those of the Schertel-Sachsenberg system. Craft employing V or trapeze foils are generally described as being of the Strela-type, Strela being the first operational Soviet design to use trapeze foils. Seating 82 to 94 passengers, the vessel is powered by two M-50 diesels and in appearance is a cross between the PT 20 and the PT 50, though smaller than the latter. A military derivative, the Pchela (Bee), is employed by the Soviet frontier police for coastal patrol in the Baltic and Black Seas.

The first hydrofoil vessels to enter service with the Soviet Navy were the 75-ton 'P 8' class, wooden-hulled torpedo boats which were equipped with bow foils and gas-turbine boost. These have now been retired.

Included in this entry are illustrations of the latest Soviet military hydrofoil to enter production, the 260-tonne Matka, which has been designed to replace the 25-year-old Osa missile-craft. Like the Turya fast-attack torpedo craft, also based on an Osa hull, Matka has a bow foil only. Powered by three 5,000hp radial-type diesels it has a top speed of 40 to 45 knots under calm conditions. Military hydrofoil designs under development are a 330-tonne fast strike craft, known to NATO by the code name Sarancha, and a 400-tonne fast patrol boat known as Babochka. The Sarancha, armed with four SS-N-9 missiles and capable of speeds in excess of 50 knots, is currently undergoing trials.

With an overall length of 50m (164ft) and an all-up weight of 400 tonnes, Babochka is the biggest military hydrofoil in operational service in the world.

Among new Soviet passenger hydrofoils in production or being prepared for series production at yards on the Baltic and Black Seas are: the Zenit, designed to replace Meteor; and the Albatros and Kolkhida, Kometa derivatives with seats for 120, stability augmentation and speeds of 36 knots; and the waterjet-propelled, 250-seat, 45- to 50-knot Cyclone. Smaller hydrofoils

Stern view of Babochka

Babochka (Butterfly)

are also under development including the 50-seat Polesye at the river-craft shipyard at Gomel and Lastochka, which has been designed to supercede Voskhod.

Substantial numbers of Soviet hydrofoils are being exported, especially Kometas, Meteors, Raketas, Voskhods and Volgas. Countries in which they are being operated include Austria, Bulgaria, Czechoslovakia, Finland, Yugoslavia, Italy, Iran, France, Cyprus, Greece, East Germany, Morocco, Spain, West Germany, the Philippines, Poland, Romania and the United Kingdom.

Plans are being prepared to build a new generation of hydrofoil passenger ferries with a loaded displacement of 500 to 600 tons. Mixed passenger/cargo hydrofoils of up to 1,000 tons are also envisaged. These will be operated on routes of up to 1,250 miles and would successfully compete with conventional ships.

Soviet commentators state that although today's hydrofoils attain top speeds of 40 to 45 knots, this figure will rise to 65 to 75 knots in the near future. Although this will call for considerably more powerful engines, experimental vessels which can attain these speeds are said to exist already.

BABOCHKA

The world's largest and most powerful operational hydrofoil warship, this unexpected addition to Soviet sea power is designed for anti-submarine warfare. Motive power for its foilborne propulsion system appears to comprise three NK-12MV marinised aircraft gas turbines, each delivering between 12,000 to 15,000shp.

Combustion air for the three gas turbines is fed through a large inlet occupying the aft end of the deckhouse. Exhaust discharge to atmosphere is via three angled funnels on the aft deck. Judging from its size, the craft is almost certainly intended for operation on the open seas. If propeller driven, either V- or Z-drives are likely to have been employed so as to provide as great a clearance height as possible.
FOILS: Conventional configuration, with a surface-piercing bow foil and fully-submerged rear foil, and an automatic sonic/electronic control system operating trailing edge flaps on each foil.
ARMAMENT: Two six-barrelled 30mm Gatling-action guns for AA defence, activated by a Bass Tilt fire control radar or a remote optical director and eight 40cm AS torpedoes in two quadruple mounts immediately ahead of the superstructure between the deckhouse and the forward 30mm mount. Dipping sonar is also installed. Electronic equipment includes High Pole B IFF, Square Head and Peel Cone radar.
DIMENSIONS
Length overall: 50m (164ft)
WEIGHTS
Normal take-off displacement: about 400 tonnes
PERFORMANCE
Max speed foilborne: 50 knots plus

SARANCHA

The forerunner of a new class of formidable fast strike missile craft, the 330-tonne Sarancha is one of the world's biggest naval hydrofoils. Designed and built at Petrovsky, Leningrad, the craft is armed with four SS-N-9 anti-ship missiles, an SA-N-4 ship-to-air missile system and a 30mm Gatling-type rapid-fire cannon. The foil system is fully retractable to simplify slipping and docking. Autostabilisation equipment is fitted as well as an autopilot and the latest navigation, target detection and fire control systems.

Operational evaluation trials with the Soviet Navy began in the eastern Baltic in mid-1977. Sarancha is the NATO code name for the vessel.
FOILS: Combined surface-piercing and submerged system. The bow foil, which provides the necessary transverse stability, is of split-V surface-piercing type and carries about 60% of the load and the single fully submerged rear foil supports the remaining 40%. The rear foil is supported by two vertical struts, each of which carries a twin propeller pod assembly at its base. The struts also carry the vertical shafts and second bevel gears of the Z-drive systems which transmit power from the gas turbines in the hull to the propellers. A sonic/electronic autopilot system controls lift by operating trailing edge flaps on the aft foil. Single rudders, which act individually for port or starboard turns, are fitted to the trailing edges of the aft foil struts. All three foil/strut units retract completely clear of the water, the two elements of the 'split V' bow foil sideways and the aft foil rearwards and upwards.
POWER PLANT: Foilborne power is believed to be provided by two NK-12MV marinised gas turbines, each delivering 12 to 15,000hp. Power is transmitted to the two propellers at the base of each strut through two sets of bevel gears and two vertical shafts to the nacelle. The central compartment of this contains the lower reduction gear which transmits power from the vertical shafts to the propeller shafts. The power trans-

mission system is thought to have been derived from that employed on the Typhoon commercial hydrofoil, also built in Leningrad.
ARMAMENT: Four SS-N-9 Siren anti-ship missiles on four lightweight launchers amidship, one twin SA-N-4 surface-to-air missile launcher with 15 to 20 missiles on forward deck and one 30mm Gatling-type rapid fire AA cannon aft. The SS-N-9s are activated by a Band Stand radar, the SA-N-4 launcher is controlled by a Pop Group radar and the 30mm cannon has a Bass Tilt fire control. The SA-N-4 may have limited surface-to-surface capability. The craft also carries Fish Bowl fire-control radar, a Band Stand radar for air search, one High Pole transponder and one Square Head interrogator for ECM/ESM. A new type of navigation and surface radar is carried.
DIMENSIONS
Length overall: 45m (147ft 8in)
Length, foils extended: 51m (167ft 4in)
Width, foils extended: 23m (75ft 6in)
Hull beam: 10m (32ft 9·5in)
Width across foils: 24m (78ft 9in)
Draught hullborne, foils retracted: 2·5m (8ft 3in)
 foilborne: 3·5m (11ft 6in)
WEIGHTS
Estimated normal take-off displacement: 330 tonnes
PERFORMANCE
Max speed foilborne: 50 knots plus

VOSKHOD-2

Designers of the Voskhod, which has been gradually replacing craft of the Raketa series, drew on engineering experience gained with the Raketa and also the more sophisticated Meteor and Kometa. Voskhod, in turn, is due to be succeeded by the new 50-seat Lastochka.

Among the basic requirements were that the Raketa's general characteristics should be preserved; foilborne operation should be possible in 1m (3ft 3in) high waves, with a 3 per cent safety factor; accommodation should be acceptable

Sarancha, 330-tonne missile armed fast attack craft *(DpA)*

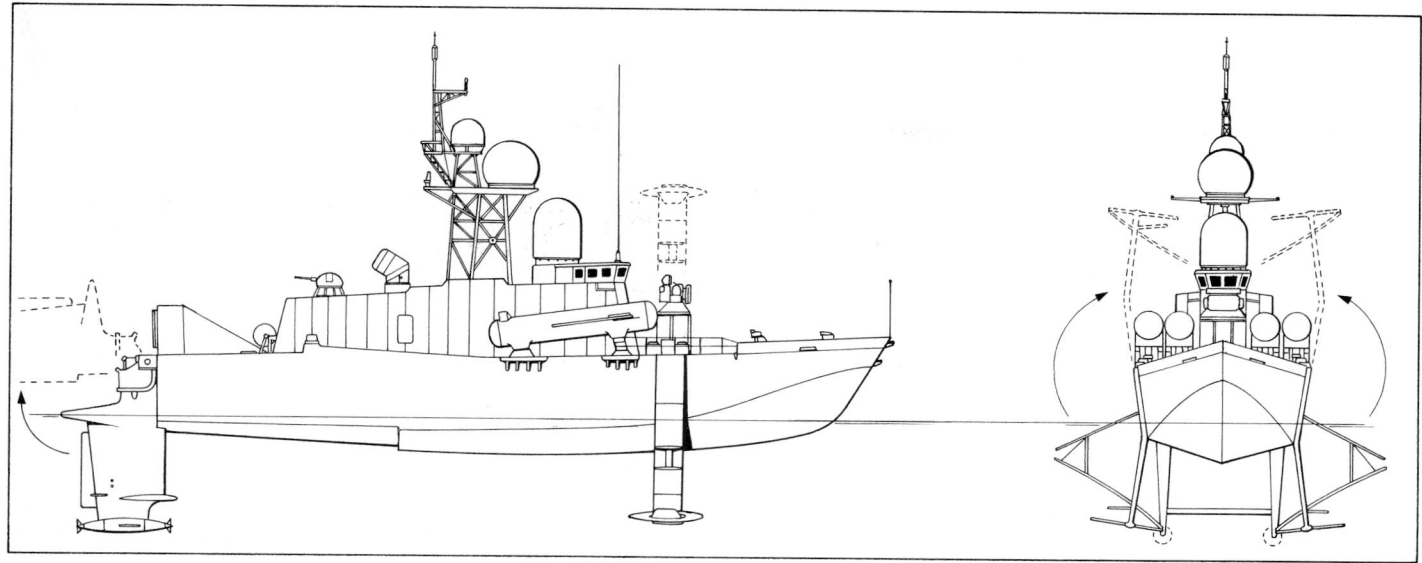

Provisional elevation and bow-on view of Sarancha

from health and safety viewpoints; noise levels should be significantly reduced, and the maximum use should be made of standard mechanical, electrical and other components and fittings proven on the Raketa.

In fact, the end product bears little resemblance to its predecessor. Visually the Voskhod is more akin to a scaled-down Kometa with its engine room aft, replacing the rear passenger saloon.

In June 1974 Voskhod 2-01 began service on the Gorki-Kineshma route, across the vast Gorki reservoir which cannot be navigated by the Raketa because of its limited seaworthiness. It continued in service until the end of the 1974 navigation season. During this time it was demonstrated that its operating and technical performance was significantly superior to that of the Raketa.

Experience accumulated during this experimental service indicated the need for minor modifications which have been incorporated in the first series of production craft.

Voskhod 14 was launched in June 1980 and delivered to the Amur Line for summer services along the Amur river.

At the time of its inception, it was announced that the Voskhod would be available in a number of versions to suit local navigation and traffic requirements. Voskhod 3 will be powered by a gas turbine.

The vessel is designed for high-speed passenger ferry services during daylight hours on rivers, reservoirs, lakes and sheltered waters. It meets the requirements of Soviet River Register Class 'O' with the following wave restrictions (3% safety margin): foilborne, 1·3m (4ft 3in); hullborne, 2m (6ft 7in).

The passenger saloons are heated and provided with natural and induced ventilation. Full air-conditioning can be installed in craft required for service in tropical conditions. The crew comprises a captain, engineer, motorman and barman.

FOILS: Fixed foil system, comprising one bow foil with a pitch stability sub-foil immediately

behind, one aft foil, plus an amidship foil to facilitate take-off. Bow and amidship foils appear to be of shallow V configuration and each has four vertical struts. The fully submerged stern foil has two side struts and is supported in the centre by the end bracket of the propeller shaft. The surface and lower parts of the foil struts and stabiliser are in Cr18Ni9Ti stainless steel, while the upper parts of the struts and stabiliser and also the amidship foil are in AlMg-61 plate alloy.

HULL: Similar in shape to the Kometa and earlier models of the Sormovo hydrofoil series, with a wedge-shaped bow, raked stem and spoon-shaped stern. A single step is provided to facilitate take-off. In fabricating the basic structure, which is largely in AlMg-61 aluminium magnesium alloy, extensive use has been made of arc and spot welding. The hull is framed on longitudinal and transverse formers. Below the deck it is divided into eight watertight compartments by transverse bulkheads. It will remain afloat with any one compartment or the machinery space flooded. Access to the forepeak, which houses the anchor capstan, is via the forward passenger saloon and then through a rectangular hatch on the forecastle. Aft of the main passenger saloon is an area split into three compartments by two longitudinal bulkheads. The lower central space contains the reduction gear and V-drive,

the starboard compartment contains the sanitary tank and the port compartment forms part of the double-bottom. Entrance to the engine compartment is via a door on the port side of the main deck. An emergency exit is provided starboard aft.

POWER PLANT: Power is supplied by a single M-401A four-stroke water-cooled, super-charged 12-cylinder V-type diesel, delivering 809·6kW (1,100hp) at 1,600rpm maximum and 736kW (1,000hp) at 1,550rpm cruising. The engine, which has a variable-speed governor and a reversing clutch, is sited aft with its shaft inclined at 9 degrees. Output is transferred via a flexible coupling to a single six-bladed variable-pitch propeller via an R-21 vee-drive gearbox. Guaranteed service life of the engine before the first overhaul is 3,000 hours. Specific fuel consumption, including attached units, is not more than 6gr/ehp/h. Specific oil consumption is not more than 6gr/ehp/h. The engine room is insulated with fire-retardant, heat and sound-insulating materials. Perforated aluminium alloy sheet is laid over the insulating materials.

CONTROLS: Single semi-balanced rudder in AlMg plate provides directional control. Operation of the engine, rudder, reverse gear and fuel supply is effected hydraulically from the wheelhouse.

Voskhod-2 operated on Danube by Mahart Magyar Hajozasi

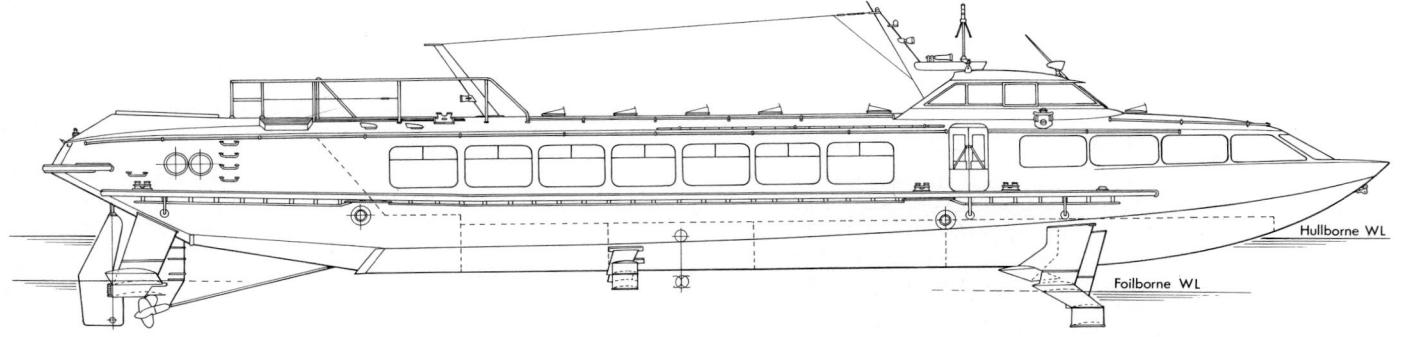

Voskhod-2, outboard profile

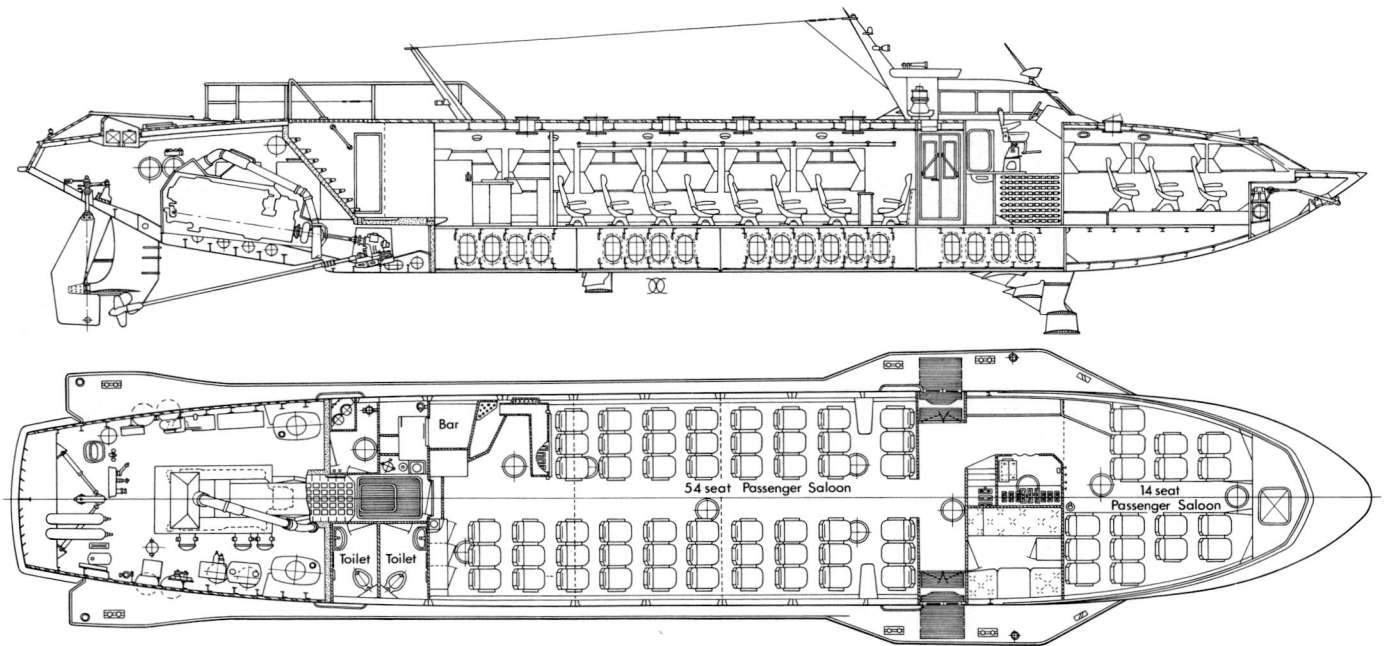

Voskhod-2, inboard profile and deck plan

ACCOMMODATION: Voskhod-2 carries an operating crew of three, comprising captain, engineer and motorman, plus a barman. Embarkation platforms immediately below the wheelhouse provide passenger and crew access. Passengers can embark from both sides and from the stern.

The captain and engineer are accommodated in a raised wheelhouse located between the forward and main saloon. Main engine controls are in both the wheelhouse and the engine room.

Passengers are accommodated in two saloons, a forward compartment seating 17 and a main saloon seating 54. The main saloon has three exits, two forward, leading to the embarkation platforms, and one aft, leading to the stern embarkation area. Between the two saloons, on the starboard side, is a crew rest cabin. The saloons are fitted with upholstered seats, racks for small hand-luggage and coat pegs. Spacing between seats is 900mm and the central aisle is 800mm wide.

At the rear of the main saloon is a small buffet and bar and aft of the main saloon, at the foot of the rear embarkation steps, are two wc/wash-basin units.

SYSTEMS, ELECTRICAL: Power supply is 24-27V dc. A 3kW generator is attached to the engine and supplies 27·5V while the craft is operating. Four 12V storage batteries, each of 180Ah capacity and connected in series-parallel to form a single bank, supply power during short stops. An auxiliary circuit can be connected to shore systems for 220V, single-phase, 50Hz ac supply.

FIREFIGHTING: Four carbon dioxide and four foam fire extinguishers for the passenger saloons and wheelhouse. Remote-controlled system employing '3·5' compound in the engine room.

HEATING AND VENTILATION: Heating in the saloons is provided by pipes circulating water from the internal cooling circuit of the engine. Ventilation is natural, using the dynamic pressure of the approaching air flow, and induced, by means of electric fans.

During the spring and autumn, the temperature of the ventilating air can be heated to 21°C.

DRINKING WATER: Hot and cold water supplies. An electric boiler supplies hot water for washbasins and the small kitchen behind the snackbar. Drinking water tank has a capacity of 138 litres.

BILGE WATER: System designed for bilge water removal by shore-based facilities or service vessels.

ANCHOR: Matrosov system, weighing 35kg (77lb), attached to an anchor cable 8·4mm (0·33in) in diameter and 80m (262ft) long, and operated by hand winch in the forepeak.

DIMENSIONS
EXTERNAL
Length overall: 27·6m (90ft 7in)
Hull length: 26·3m (86ft 3·5in)
Beam overall: 6·2m (20ft 4in)
Height above mean water level, foilborne, including mast: 5·7m (18ft 8in)
Draught hullborne: 2m (6ft 6·75in)
  foilborne: 1·1m (3ft 7·25in)

INTERNAL
Deck area: 105m² (1,130ft²)
  per passenger: 1·48m² (15·35ft²)
WEIGHTS
Displacement, fully loaded: 28 tonnes
Light displacement: 20 tonnes
Passengers per displacement tonne: 2·55
Payload, passengers and buffet/bar equipment: 5·9 tonnes
Payload/displacement ratio: 21·2%
PERFORMANCE
Max speed, calm water, wind not in excess of force 3,
  at 1,550rpm (1,000hp): 70km/h (43·49mph)
  at 1,450rpm: 60km/h (37·28mph)
Turning circle diameter
  hullborne: 106m (348ft)
  foilborne: 380m (1,246ft)
Range, based on normal fuel supply of 1,400kg: 500km (310·68 miles)
Max wave height, with 3% safety margin
  hullborne: 2m (6ft 7in)
  foilborne: 1·3m (4ft 3in)

TURYA

Based on the well-proven Osa missile-firing FPB hull, Turya is equipped with a fixed, surface-piercing V or trapeze foil set back approximately one-third of the hull length from the bow. At 25 knots, in relatively calm conditions, the foil system generates sufficient lift to raise the forward hull clear of the water, providing a 'sprint' speed of 40 to 45 knots.

In addition to improving the maximum speed, the foils reduce the vessel's wave impact response, thus enhancing its performance as a weapon platform.

The installation of a dipping sonar on the transom suggests that the primary duty of Turya is anti-submarine patrol. The main armament appears to comprise four 53cm ASW or anti-ship torpedoes in single fixed tubes, a forward 25mm twin mount and a twin 57mm AA mount aft.

The first of this class was launched in 1972 and a series production programme is under way, involving more than one yard in western Russia and one in the Soviet far east. Output is estimated at between four and five units per year and about 30 are in service. Eight have been supplied to the Cuban Navy.

Latest version of Turya is equipped with semi-retractable foils permitting the overall width to be reduced, thus enabling craft to be taken alongside conventional berthing facilities.

FOILS: Single main foil of trapeze configuration set back one-third of hull length from bow. Raises greater part of hull bottom clear of the water in calm conditions at speed of about 25 knots depending on sea conditions and loading.

Voskhod

Turya

Similar system employed earlier on Soviet 'P 8' class, now retired, and on the highly successful Chinese 'Hu Chwan' class.

HULL: Standard Osa hull, welded steel construction.

POWER PLANT: Three M-504 high performance radial-type diesels, each developing 5,000hp and driving variable-pitch propellers through inclined shafts.

ARMAMENT: One twin 57mm dual-purpose gun with Muff Cob radar control and one remote optical director and one twin 25mm AA mount with local control. Mounts for SA-7 Grail light AA missile launcher and four 53cm ASW or anti-ship torpedoes. Latest variants fitted with twin 30mm fully-automatic dual purpose mount forward.

Navigation radar: Pot Drum
Fire-control radar: Muff Cob
Sonar: One dipping-type
ECM/ESM: One High Pole transponder and one Square Head interrogator

DIMENSIONS
Length: 39·3m (128ft 11in)
Beam: 7·7m (25ft 1in)
Width across foils: 12·3m (40ft 5in)
Draught, hull: 3m (9ft 11in)
 foils: 3·8m (12ft 6in)
WEIGHTS
Max loaded displacement: 250 tonnes
Standard: 200 tonnes
PERFORMANCE
Max speed foilborne: 40-45 knots

TYPHOON

The Typhoon, a gas-turbine powered fast ferry for 98 to 105 passengers, was launched in Leningrad in December 1969. During trials it completed the journey from Leningrad to Tallinn, the Estonian capital, in 4½ hours.

It is understood that the craft is no longer in service and has not entered production.

A full description can be found in *Jane's Surface Skimmers 1984* and earlier editions.

BUREVESTNIK

First Soviet gas turbine hydrofoil to be designed for series production, the Burevestnik

Two of latest Turya variants en-route to Cuba where eight are in service

has two 2,700hp marinised aircraft gas turbines driving two two-stage waterjets. The prototype was launched in April 1964 and it was intended to build two models: one for medium-range, non-stop inter-city services, seating 130 passengers, the other, for suburban services, seating 150.

After extensive trials and modifications, the prototype Burevestnik began operating on the Gorki-Kuibyshev route, about 700km (435 miles), on 26 April 1968. It is understood that the vessel is no longer in service and has not entered production.

A full description of the Burevestnik can be found in *Jane's Surface Skimmers 1983* and earlier editions.

BYELORUS

This craft was developed from the Raketa, via the Chaika, for fast passenger services on shallow winding rivers less than 1m (3ft) deep and too shallow for conventional vessels.

It was put into series production at the river shipyard at Gomel, Byelorussia in 1965. Byelorus is expected to be succeeded in service by the new 50-seat Polsye, now in the final design stage.

FOILS: The shallow draught submerged foil system consists of one bow foil and one rear foil.

HULL: Hull and superstructure are built in aluminium magnesium alloy. The hull is of all-welded construction and the superstructure is riveted and welded.

ACCOMMODATION: Aircraft type seats for 40 passengers. The prototype seated only 30.

POWER PLANT: Power is supplied by an M-50 F-3 or M-400 diesel rated at 950hp maximum and with a normal service output of 600hp. The wheelhouse is fitted with an electro-hydraulic remote control system for the engine and fuel supply.

DIMENSIONS
Length overall: 18·55m (60ft 6in)

Hull beam: 4·64m (15ft 2in)
Height overall: 4·23m (13ft 11in)
Draught foilborne: 0·3m (1ft)
  hullborne: 0·9m (2ft 11in)
WEIGHTS
Light displacement: 9·6 tons
Take-off displacement: 14·5 tons
PERFORMANCE
Cruising speed: 60km/h (34 knots)

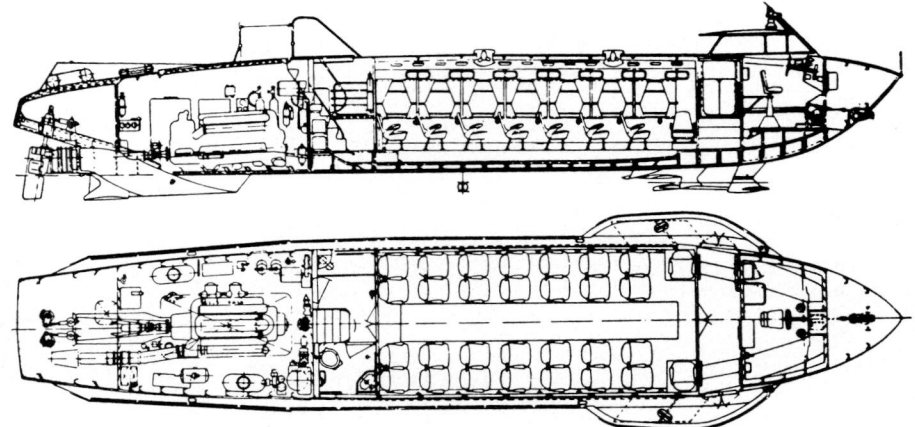

KOMETA

Derived from the earlier Meteor, the Kometa was the first seagoing hydrofoil to be built in the Soviet Union. The prototype, seating 100 passengers, made its maiden voyage on the Black Sea in 1961, after which it was employed on various passenger routes on an experimental basis. Operating experience accumulated on these services led to the introduction of various modifications before the craft was put into series production.

Kometas are built mainly at Gorki and Poti, one of the Black Sea yards.

Kometa operators outside the Soviet Union include Inex-Nautical Touring, Split, Yugoslavia; Empresa Nacional de Cabotage, Cuba; Achille Onorato, Naples, Italy; and Transportes Touristiques Intercontinentaux, Morocco. Other vessels of this type have been supplied to Bulgaria, German Democratic Republic, Greece, Iran, Poland, Romania and Turkey. More than 50 have been exported.

Export orders have mainly been for the Kometa-ME, designed for service in countries with a moderate climate, which was introduced in 1968. Two distinguishing features of this model are the employment of new diesel engines, with increased operating hours between overhauls, and a completely revised surface-piercing foil system, with a trapeze bow foil instead of the former Alexeyev shallow draught submerged type.

A fully tropicalised and air-conditioned version is now in production and this is designated Kometa-MT.

The present standard production Kometa-ME seats 116 to 120. Because of the additional weight of the Kometa-MT's air-conditioning system and other refinements, the seating capacity is reduced in the interest of passenger comfort to 102.

Profile and deck plan of Byelorus

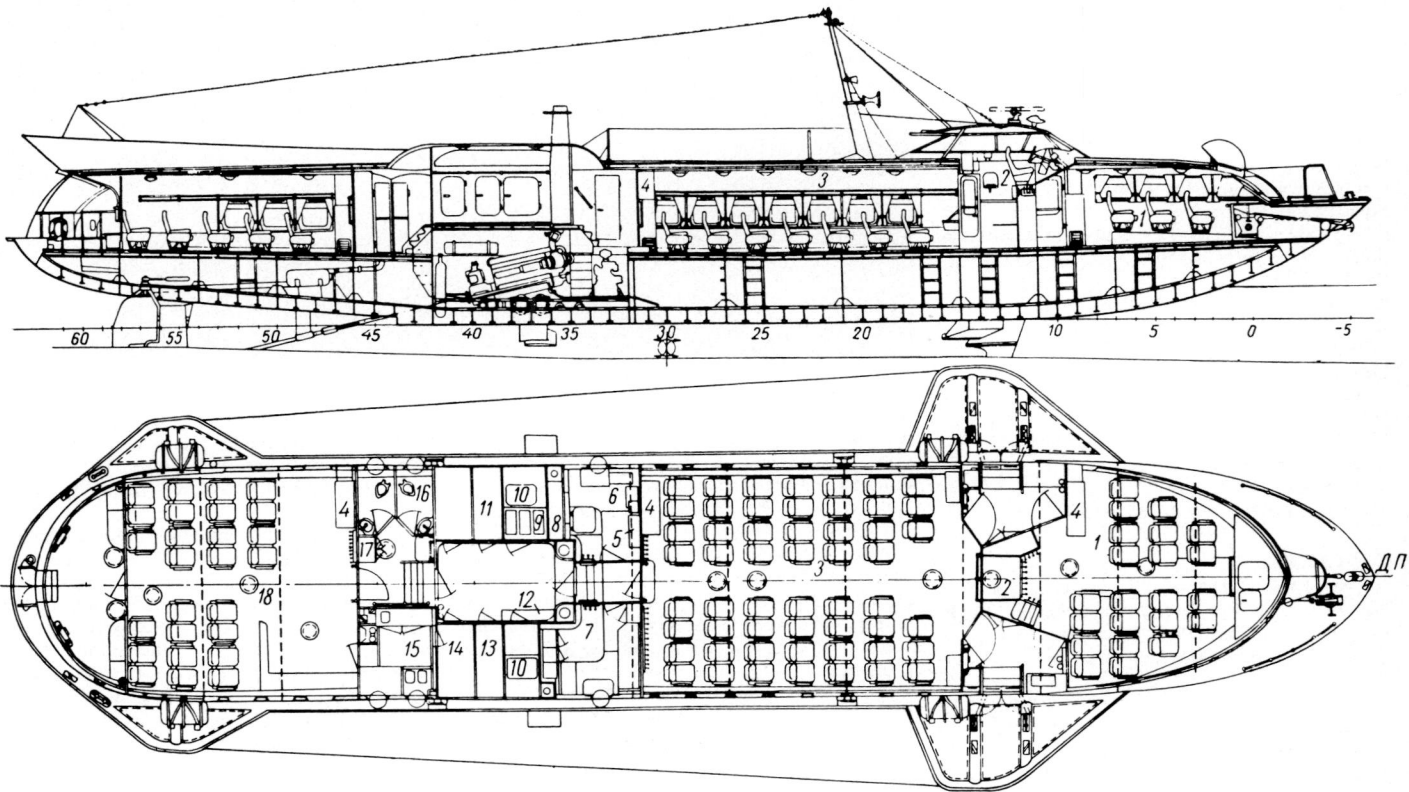

Byelorus on Karakum Canal, Turkmenia

Official designation of the Kometa in the USSR is Hydrofoil Type 342. The craft meets the requirements of the Rules of the Register of Shipping of the USSR and is constructed to Hydrofoil Class KM ★ 2 11 Passenger Class under the Register's technical supervision. IMCO recommendations on fire safety are now being taken into account and non-flammable basalt fibres are being employed for sound and heat insulation and the engine room is clad with titanium plating. The craft is designed to operate during daylight hours on coastal routes up to 81km (50 miles) from ports of refuge under moderate climatic conditions.

The standard craft has proved to be exceptionally robust and has a good, all-round performance. On one charter, a Kometa-ME covered 5,310km (3,300 miles) by sea and river in 127 hours. It can operate foilborne in waves up to 1·7m (5ft 7in) and travel hullborne in waves up to 3·6m (11ft 10in).

One of the features of the latest models is the relocation of the engine room aft to reduce the noise in the passenger saloons and the employment of a vee-drive instead of the existing inclined shaft. The arrangement is expected to be similar to that on the Voskhod-2. The revised deck configuration allows more seats to be fitted.

Internal arrangement of Kometa-MT, designed for tropical operation: **(1)** 22-seat forward passenger saloon **(2)** wheelhouse **(3)** 54-seat main passenger saloon **(4)** luggage rack **(5)** engine room door **(6)** control position **(7)** duty cabin **(8)** liquid fire extinguisher bay **(9)** battery room **(10)** engine room **(11)** boiler room **(12)** installation point for portable radio **(13)** store **(14)** provision store **(15)** bar **(16)** wc washbasin units **(17)** boatswain's store **(18)** 26-seat aft passenger saloon

These modifications are also incorporated in the recently announced Kometa derivative, the Kolkhida, which will be fitted with two 1,500hp engines. In future, development of the Kometa and Kolkhida is likely to continue in parallel.

FOILS: Employment of a surface-piercing trapeze-type bow foil provides the Kometa-ME with improved seakeeping capability in waves. The foil system comprises a bow foil, aft foil, and two auxiliaries, one (termed 'stabiliser') located above the bow foil for pitch stability, the other sited amidship near the longitudinal centre of gravity to assist take-off. The foils are connected to the hull by struts and brackets. Middle and side struts of the bow foil are of the split type. The lower and upper components of each strut are connected by flanges and bolts. The upper sections are connected to the hull by the same means.

The bow and stern foils are of hollow welded stainless steel construction. The midship and pitch stability foils and the upper components of the foil struts are in aluminium-magnesium alloy.

HULL: Similar in shape to that of the earlier Meteor, the hull has a wedge-shaped bow, raked stem and a spoon-shaped stern. Hull and superstructure are built in AlMg-61 and AlM-6g alloys. Hull and superstructure are of all-welded construction using contact and argon arc welding. The hull is framed on longitudinal and transverse formers, the spacing throughout the length of the hull is 500mm and in the superstructure 1,000mm.

Below the freeboard deck, the hull is divided by watertight bulkheads into thirteen compartments, which include the engine room, fuel compartments, and those containing the firefighting system, tiller gear and fuel transfer pump.

ACCOMMODATION: The Kometa-MT seats 102 passengers. It carries an operating crew of six, comprising captain, engineer, motorman, radio-operator, seaman, and one barman. Embarkation platforms immediately below the wheelhouse provide passenger and crew access.

The captain and engineer are accommodated in a raised wheelhouse located between the forward and main saloons, and equipped with two seats, a folding stool, chart table, sun shield and a locker for signal flags. The wheelhouse also contains a radar display and radio communications equipment.

Main engine controls are installed in both the wheelhouse and engine room.

Passengers are accommodated in three compartments, a forward saloon seating 22, and central and aft saloons seating 54 and 26 respectively. The central saloon has three exits, two for-

Kometa ME

ward, leading to the embarkation platforms, and one aft, leading to the promenade deck. This is located in the space above the engine room and is partially covered with a removable metallic awning.

In the current production model of the Kometa-ME, the forward saloon seats 24, the central saloon 56 and the aft saloon 36.

To the starboard side is a crew's off-duty cabin, hydraulic system pump room, bar store and bar, and to the port are two toilets, boiler room, battery room and fire extinguishing equipment.

The aft saloon has two exits, one forward leading to the promenade deck, the other aft, leading to the weather deck, which is used for embarking and disembarking when the vessel is moored by the stern.

Floors of the passenger saloons, crew's cabins, bar and wheelhouse are covered in linoleum and the deckhead in the passenger saloons, as well as bulkheads and the sides above the lower edge of the windows, are finished in light coloured Pavinol. Panels of the saloons beneath the windows are covered with plastic.

Passenger saloons are fitted with upholstered chairs, racks for small hand luggage and pegs for clothing. The middle and aft saloons have niches for hand luggage and the former is fitted with cradles for babies. The bar is fully equipped with glass washers, an ice safe, an automatic Freon compressor, electric stove, etc.

SAFETY EQUIPMENT: A full range of lifesaving equipment is carried including five inflatable life rafts, each for 25 persons, 135 life jackets, and four circular life belts with life lines and self-igniting buoyant lights. There are two life rafts on the forward sponsons and two on the aft sponsons . When thrown into the water the life

rafts inflate automatically. Life jackets are stowed under the seats in all saloons, and the circular life belts are stowed on the embarkation and promenade platforms. Kometas for export are provided with life jackets on the basis of 25 persons per raft.

FIRE FIGHTING EQUIPMENT: An independent fluid fire fighting system is provided for the engine room and fuel bay. An automatic light and sound system signals a fire outbreak. The fire fighting system is put into operation manually from the control deck above the engine room door. Boat spaces are equipped with hand-operated foam and CO_2 fire extinguishers, felt cloths and fire axes.

POWER PLANT: Power is supplied by two M-401A water-cooled, supercharged 12-cylinder V-type diesels, each with a normal service output of 1,000hp at 1,550rpm and a maximum output of 1,100hp at 1,600rpm. Guaranteed service life of each engine before first overhaul is 2,500 hours. Each engine drives via a reverse gear its own inclined shaft and the twin propellers are contra-rotating. The shafts are of steel and are parallel to the craft. Guaranteed service life of the M-401A before each overhaul is 2,500 hours.

The propellers are of three-bladed design and made of brass.

Main engine controls and gauges are installed in both the wheelhouse and the engine room. A diesel-generator compressor-pump unit is provided for charging starter air bottles; supplying electric power when at rest; warming the main engines in cold weather and pumping warm air beneath the deck to dry the bilges.

Diesel oil tanks with a total capacity of 3,000kg (6,612lb) for the main engines and the auxiliary unit are located in the afterpeak. Two lubricating oil service tanks and one storage tank located at the fore bulkhead of the engine room have a total capacity of 250kg (551lb). Diesel and lubricating oil capacity ensures a range of 370km (230 miles).

CONTROLS: The wheelhouse is equipped with an electro-hydraulic remote control system for the engine reverse gear and fuel supply, fuel monitoring equipment, including electric speed counters, pressure gauges, lubricating and fuel oil gauges. The boat has a single, solid aluminium magnesium alloy balanced rudder, which is controlled through a hydraulic steering system or a hand-operated hydraulic drive. In an emergency, the rudder may be operated by a hand tiller. Maximum rudder angle is 35 degrees in hullborne conditions and 5·6 degrees foilborne. In the event of the steering gear failing the craft can be manoeuvred by differential use of the main engines, the rudder being locked on the centre line. The vessel can be pinwheeled in hullborne condition by setting one engine slow ahead, the other slow astern and turning the rudder hard over.

SYSTEMS, ELECTRICAL: Power supply is 24V dc. A 1kW dc generator is attached to each of the two engines and these supply power during operation. A 5·6kW generator is included in the auxiliary unit and supplies power when the craft is at rest. It can also be used when under way for supplying the heating plant or when the 1kW

Kometa under construction at Ordzhonikidze shipyard, Poti, in 1980

generators are inoperative. Four 12V acid storage batteries, each of 180Ah capacity and connected in series to provide 24V, supply power during short stops.

HYDRAULICS: The hydraulic system for controlling the main engines and reverse gear consists of control cylinders located in the wheelhouse, power cylinders located on the engines, a filler tank, pipe lines and fittings.

ANCHORS: The craft is equipped with two Matrosov anchors: a main anchor weighing 75kg (165lb) and a spare anchor weighing 50kg (110lb). The main anchor is raised by an electric winch located in the forepeak. The cable of the spare anchor can be heaved in manually and is wound over a drum fitted with a hand brake.

COMMUNICATIONS: A radio transmitter/receiver with r/t and w/t facilities is installed in the wheelhouse for ship-to-shore and inter-ship communications on SW and MW bands. A portable emergency radio and automatic distress signal transmitter are also installed in the wheelhouse. A broadcast system is fitted in the passenger saloons and a two-way crew communications system is installed in the wheelhouse, engine room, anchor gear compartment and mooring stations.

NAVIGATION: The following navigation aids are standard: a gyro compass, magnetic compass (reserve) and log.

DESIGN 342
KOMETA-ME
DIMENSIONS
Length overall: 35·1m (115ft 2in)
Beam overall: 11m (36ft 1in)
Height, foilborne from waterline to tip of mast: 9·2m
Draught, hullborne: 3·6m (11ft 9·75in)
  foilborne: 1·7m (5ft 6·87in)
WEIGHTS
Light displacement: 44·5 tonnes
Fully loaded displacement: 60 tonnes
Gross register tonnage: 142·1 gross tonnes
PERFORMANCE
Max speed, intermittent: 66·8km/h (36 knots)
Cruising speed: 58km/h (32 knots)
Fuel consumption: 172g/hp/h
Oil consumption: 4·5g/hp/hr
Max sea state: Speed of the Kometa-M at full load displacement in sea states 0-2 and wind conditions up to force 3 is 32 knots. Under the worst permissible conditions under which the craft is able to navigate (sea state 5, wind force 6) it will operate hullborne at 10 to 12 knots. Sea states up to 4 and wind conditions up to force 5 are considered normal for Kometa operation.

DESIGN 342
KOMETA-MT
DIMENSIONS
Length overall: 35·1m (115ft 2in)
Beam: 11m (36ft 1in)
Height, foilborne, waterline to tip of mast: 9·2m (30ft 2·25in)
Draught, hullborne: 3·6m (11ft 9·75in)
  foilborne: 1·7m (5ft 6·87in)
WEIGHTS
Light displacement: 45 tonnes
Fully loaded displacement: 58·9 tonnes
PERFORMANCE
Max speed: 61km/h (34 knots)
Service speed: 58km/h (32 knots)
Fuel consumption: 180g/hp/h
Oil consumption: 5g/hp/h
Range: 240km

Development of the Kometa is continuing. Current research is aimed at the introduction of a stability augmentation system employing either control flaps on the bow foil or air stabilisation on the stern foil and struts; the reduction of labour involved in construction; the introduction of design improvements through the use of grp and sandwich construction; noise reduction in the saloons and the extension of the cruising range.

LASTOCHKA
In May 1981 it was announced that this new craft is being built to succeed the 71-seat Vos-

khod. Design speed is given as 90km/h (50 knots).

MATKA
Latest of the Soviet Navy's hydrofoils to go into production is the Matka, a missile-equipped fast strike craft built at the Izhora Yard, Leningrad. Matka is designed to replace the 20-year-old Osa fast patrol boat and is based on the standard 39·3m Osa steel hull. A fixed surface-piercing trapeze foil is fitted at the bow to increase its speed in the lower sea states and reduce its wave impact response thereby improving its performance as a weapon platform. At a speed of between 24 to 28 knots, depending on sea conditions and loading, the bow foil generates sufficient lift to raise a substantial part of the forward hull clear of the water thus reducing hydrodynamic drag and providing a 'sprint' speed of 40 to 45 knots.

The Matka prototype was launched in 1977 and series production began in the spring of 1978. At least eight are in service.

FOILS: Single main foil of trapeze configuration, set back one-quarter of hull length from bow, raises much of the hull clear of the water in relatively calm conditions at speeds of 24 to 28 knots depending on sea conditions and loading. Similar to system proven on Chinese 'Hu Chwan' class and Soviet Turya. Latest version of Turya is equipped with semi-retractable foils, thereby reducing the overall width and enabling craft to be taken alongside conventional jetties, piers and other vessels without damaging the foil tips. Matka is likely to employ similar foil arrangement.

HULL: Standard Osa hull, welded steel construction.

POWER PLANT: Three 3,700kW (5,000hp) M-504 radial-type high-performance diesels,

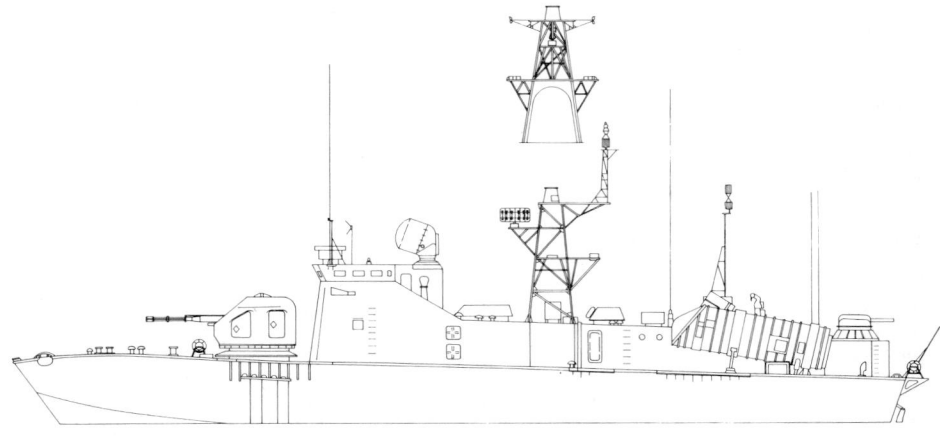
Outboard profile of Matka

Matka in Baltic Sea

Matka foilborne *(Danish Defence)*

each driving a variable-pitch propeller through an inclined shaft.
ACCOMMODATION: Living, messing and berthing spaces for crew of 33.
ARMAMENT: Two SS-N-2C surface-to-surface missiles; one 76mm dual-purpose cannon; one six-barrelled ADMG-630 Gatling-type 30mm cannon for close-in AA defence and one mount for SA-7 Grail light AA missile launcher to counter attacks by low-flying subsonic aircraft.
CHAFF: Two 16-tube chaff launchers.
NAVIGATION RADAR: Cheese Cake.
SURFACE SEARCH: Plank Shave.
FIRE CONTROL: Bass Tilt.
ECM/ESM: One High Pole transponder and one Square Head interrogator.
COMMUNICATIONS: Cage Bear.
DIMENSIONS
Length: 39·3m (128ft 11in)
Hull beam: 7·7m (25ft 3in)
Width across foils: 12·3m (40ft 5in)
Draught, hull: 3m (9ft 10in)
    foils: 3·8m (12ft 6in)
WEIGHTS
Displacement, full load: 260 tonnes
    standard: 225 tonnes
PERFORMANCE
Max speed foilborne: 40-45 knots
Range: 750n miles at 24 knots

METEOR

Dr Alexeyev's Meteor made its maiden voyage from Gorki to Moscow in 1960, bringing high performance and unprecedented comfort to river boat fleets, and setting the pattern for a family of later designs.

The craft is intended for use in daylight hours on local and medium-range routes of up to 600km (373 miles) in length. It meets the requirements of Class O, experimental type, on the Register of River Shipping in the USSR.

Accommodation is provided for a crew of five and 116 passengers. Cruising speed at the full load displacement of 54·3 tonnes across calm water and in winds of up to Beaufort force 3 is about 65km/h (35 knots).

Outside the Soviet Union Meteors are operated in Bulgaria, Hungary, Poland and Yugoslavia.

FOILS: The foil arrangement comprises a bow foil and a stern foil, with the struts of the bow system carrying two additional planing subfoils. The foils are attached to the struts, which are of split type, by flanges and bolts. The foils are in stainless steel, and the subfoils in aluminium magnesium alloy. The foil incidence can be adjusted when necessary by the insertion of wedges between the flanges and the foils when the vessel is in dock.

HULL: With the exception of the small exposed areas fore and aft, the Meteor's hull and superstructure are built as an integral unit. The hull is framed on longitudinal and transverse formers and both hull and superstructure are of riveted duralumin construction with welded steel members. Below the main deck the hull is sub-divided longitudinally into eight compartments by seven bulkheads. Access to the compartments is via hatches in the main deck. The craft will remain afloat in the event of any two adjacent compartments forward of amidship flooding or any one compartment aft of midship. Frame spacing in the hull is about 500mm while that in the superstructure is 1,000mm.

POWER PLANT: Power is supplied by two M-50 12-cylinder, four-stroke, supercharged, water-cooled diesels with reversing clutches. Each engine has a normal service output of 1,000hp at 1,700rpm and a maximum output of 1,100hp at 1,800rpm. Specific consumption at rated output g/bhp/h is not more than 193, and oil, not more than 6. Guaranteed overhaul life is 1,000 hours. Each engine drives its own inclined propeller shaft through a reverse clutch. Propeller shafts are in steel and the propellers, which are five-bladed, are in brass. The drives are contra-rotating.

Refuelling is via filler necks on each side of the hull. Fuel is carried in six tanks located in the

Matka on patrol in Baltic Sea *(Royal Swedish Air Force)*

engine room. Total fuel capacity is 3,200kg. Lubricating oil, total capacity 370 litres, is carried in two service tanks and a storage tank located on the forward bulkhead in the engine room. Fuel and lubricating oil are sufficient for a cruising range, foilborne, of not less than 600km (373 miles).
AUXILIARY UNIT: 12hp diesel for generating electrical power when the craft is at its moorings, warming the main engines in cold weather and operating drainage pump.
CONTROLS: Control of the engines, reverse gear and fuel supply is effected remotely from the wheelhouse with the aid of a hydraulic system comprising transmitter cylinders in the wheelhouse, and actuators on the engine. The

engines can also be controlled from the engine room.

Craft heading is controlled by two balanced rudders, the blades of which are in solid aluminium magnesium alloy. The rudders are operated hydraulically from the wheelhouse, the rudder angle being checked by an electric indicator in the wheelhouse. In an emergency, with the craft in hullborne conditions, the rudder is put over with the aid of a detachable hand tiller fitted to the rudder stock.

At low speed the craft can turn in its own length by pinwheeling—employing both engines with equal power in opposite directions—one ahead, the other astern.

Minimum diameter of the turning circle is

Meteor operating in Leningrad

Meteor operated on Danube by Mahart Magyar Hajozasi

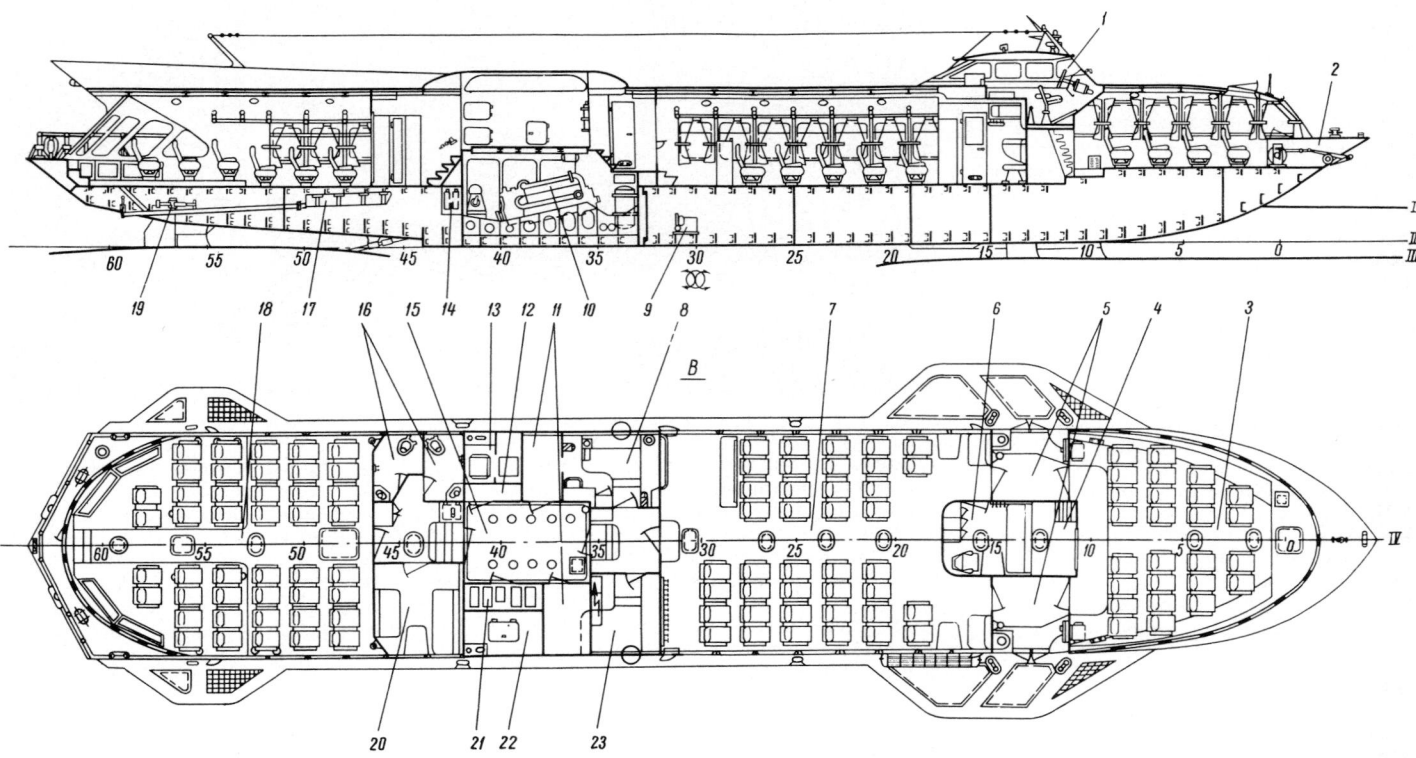

Meteor:
(A) inboard profile **(B)** main deck plan **(I)** waterline hullborne **(II)** hull base line **(III)** waterline foilborne **(IV)** longitudinal centreline **(1)** wheelhouse **(2)** anchor compartment **(3)** forward passenger saloon, 26 seats **(4)** luggage rack **(5)** embarkation companionway **(6)** crew duty room **(7)** midship passenger saloon, 42 seats **(8)** bar **(9)** refrigeration unit **(10)** engine room **(11)** pantry **(12)** boatswain's store **(13)** calorifier **(14)** fire fighting equipment **(15)** promenade deck **(16)** wcs **(17)** tank **(18)** aft passenger saloon, 44 seats **(19)** tiller gear **(20)** four-seat passenger cabin **(21)** storage batteries **(22)** hydraulic units **(23)** main switchboard

approximately 250m (819ft) with the engines running at low speed (700-750rpm) and with the rudder put through an angle of 35 degrees. Turning circle diameter when operating foilborne with the rudder at an angle of 10 degrees is approximately 750m (2,460ft).

The vessel takes off for foilborne flight in 120 to 140 seconds, ie within a distance of 25 to 28 lengths of its hull.

Landing run, with engines reversed, ranges from 1·5 to 2 hull lengths, while the braking distance without reversing the engines is within 3 to 4 lengths of the hull.

ACCOMMODATION: Passengers are accommodated in three compartments, a forward saloon seating 26, and central and aft saloons seating 46 and 44 passengers respectively. The central saloon has three exits, two forward leading to the embarkation platforms and one aft leading to the promenade deck above the engine room. On the port side of the central saloon, aft, is a small buffet/bar. Beneath the wheelhouse is a duty crew room and a luggage compartment which opens into the forward saloon.

The aft saloon has two exits, one leading to the promenade deck above the engine room and one to the weather deck aft. Forward and aft on both sides of the craft are sponsons to protect the foil systems during mooring. The forward pair are used as embarkation and disembarkation platforms.

SYSTEMS, ELECTRICAL: 24 to 28·5V dc from the vessel's power supply or 220V ac, 50Hz, from shore-to-ship supply sources.

RADIO: Ship-to-shore radio telephone operating on any of ten pre-selected fixed frequencies. Also passenger announcement system and crew intercom.

NAVIGATION: Magnetic compass.

COMPRESSED AIR: System comprises two 40-litre air storage bottles for starting the main engines, operating emergency stop mechanism, closing feed cocks of the fuel tanks, recharging the hydraulic system accumulator and the ship's siren.

FIRE FIGHTING: Remote system for fighting outbreak in engine room, with automatic light and sound indicator operating in wheelhouse. Hand-operated foam and CO_2 extinguishers provided in passenger saloons and wheelhouse.

DIMENSIONS
Length overall: 34·5m (112ft 2·25in)
Beam overall: 9·5m (31ft 2in)
Height foilborne above water surface: 6·8m (22ft 3·75in)
Draught hullborne: 2·4m (7ft 10·5in)
   foilborne: 1·2m (3ft 11·25in)
WEIGHTS
Light displacement: 37·2 tonnes
Fully loaded: 54·3 tonnes
PERFORMANCE
Cruising speed, calm water: 65km/h (35 knots)
Limiting sea states,
   foilborne: Beaufort Force 3
   hullborne: Beaufort Force 4

MOLNIA

This popular six-seat hydrofoil sports runabout was derived from Alexeyev's original test craft. Many hundreds are available for hire on Soviet lakes and rivers. In slightly modified form, and renamed Volga, the type is being exported to 44 countries. The craft is navigable in protected off-shore water up to 2 miles from the land and has particular appeal for water-taxi and joy-ride operators.

Molnia is no longer in production, having been replaced by the Volga. Details of the Molnia can be found in *Jane's Surface Skimmers 1976-77* and earlier editions.

NEVKA

This light passenger ferry and sightseeing craft is in series production at a Leningrad shipyard and the first units have been supplied to Yalta for coastal services on the Black Sea. A multi-purpose runabout, it is intended to cope with a variety of duties including scheduled passenger services, sightseeing, VIP transport and crew-boat. The standard version seats a driver and 14 passengers.

The craft, which is designed to operate in waves up to 1m (3ft) high, is the first small hydrofoil in the Soviet Union to employ surface-piercing V foils, and also the first to employ a diesel engine in conjunction with a Z-drive.

In December 1971 a waterjet-propelled variant made its first cruise along the Crimean coast. The 16-mile trip from Yalta to Alushta was made in half an hour.

FOILS: Bow and stern foils are of fixed V surface-piercing configuration and made of solid aluminium magnesium alloy.

HULL: Glass fibre reinforced plastic structure

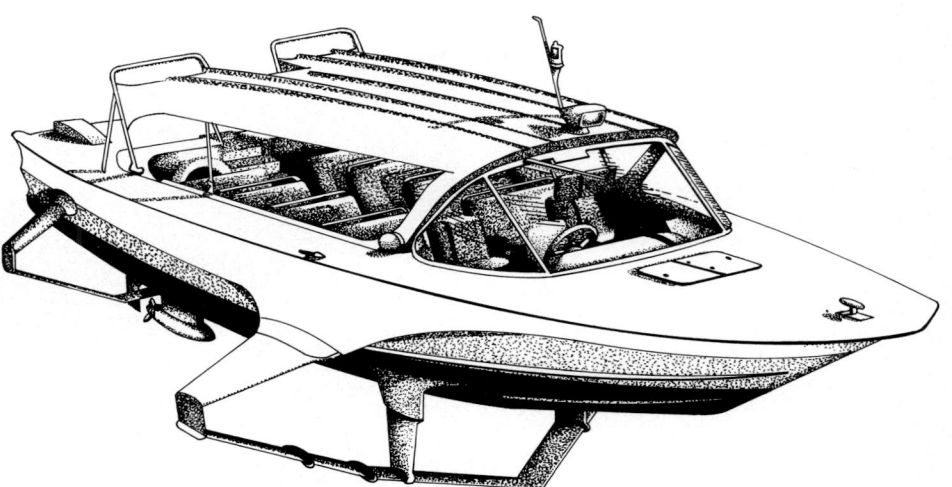

Perspective drawing of export model of Nevka showing foil details

assembled in four basic sections. The outer hull is assembled with the transom, the deck with the rib of the windscreen, the cabin/cockpit with the engine air intakes and afterpeak, and the inner hull with the companionway at the aft of the cabin.

The lower hull is subdivided by watertight bulkheads into four compartments.

The hull contours are designed to facilitate easy transition from hull to foilborne mode and minimise structural loadings due to wave impact. Two transverse steps are incorporated.

ACCOMMODATION: The craft can be supplied with an open cockpit and folding canopy, as a cabin cruiser with a solid top or as a sightseeing craft with a transparent cabin roof. As a cabin cruiser, the craft is equipped with bunks, a galley and toilet. The driver's stand can be located either at the forward end of the cabin or in a raised position amidships.

POWER PLANT: Power is supplied by a single 3D20 four-cycle, six-cylinder diesel, developing 235hp at 2,200rpm. The engine, located aft, drives a three-bladed propeller via a DK-300 Z-drive.

CONTROLS: Craft heading is controlled by a single balanced rudder in solid aluminium alloy mounted aft of the rear foil main strut and operated by a steering wheel via a mechanical linkage. Other controls include a footpedal to control engine speed, and a reverse lever.

SYSTEMS, ELECTRICAL: Power is 24V dc. A 1kW engine-mounted generator supplies power while the craft is operating. Two 12V acid storage batteries, each of 180Ah capacity and connected in series to give 24V, supply power during stops.

FIRE FIGHTING: An independent fluid fire fighting system of aircraft type is installed in the engine bay and is operated remotely from the driving seat.

DIMENSIONS
Length overall: 10·9m (35ft 11in)
Hull beam: 2·7m (8ft 11in)
Beam overall: 4m (13ft 2in)
Draught, hullborne: 1·7m (5ft 3in)
    foilborne: 0·9m (2ft 9in)
WEIGHTS
Max take-off displacement: 5·9 tons
Displacement unloaded: 4·1 tons

Model of Nevka fitted with trapeze foils instead of V-foils which appear to be standard on export models

Payload: 1·05 tons
PERFORMANCE
Cruising speed: 30 knots
Normal cruising range: 160 miles
Diameter of turn at max speed: 109m (357ft)
Take-off time: approx 30 seconds
Max permissible wave height in foilborne mode:
    1m (3ft 3in)

Fuel and lube oil endurance: 6 hours
Fuel consumption per hp at cruising rating: 178g/h

PCHELA (BEE)

This military derivative of the Strela is in service with the KGB for frontier patrol duties in the Baltic and Black Seas. 25 were built between

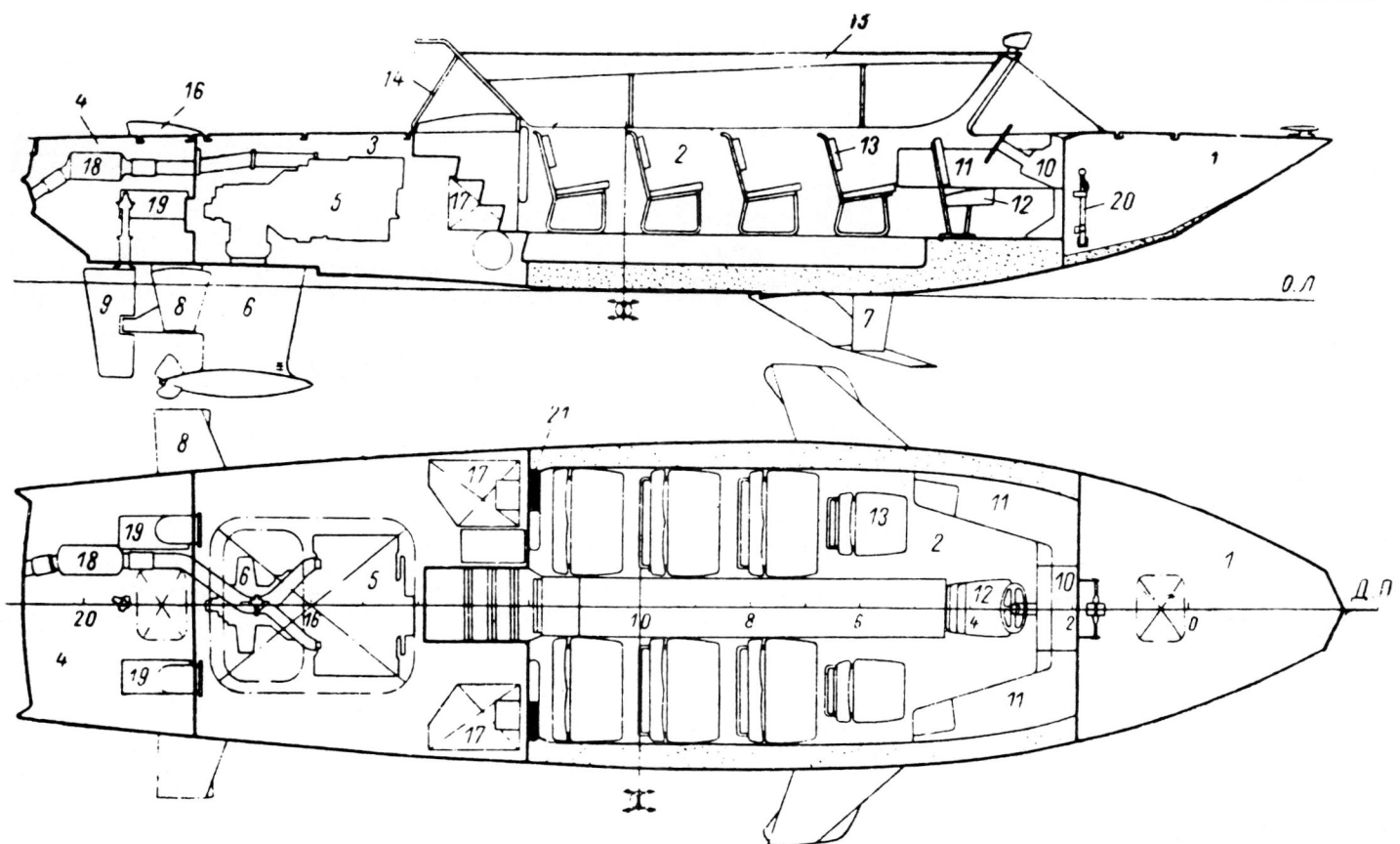

Inboard profile and deck plan of standard Nevka:
(1) forepeak **(2)** passenger cabin **(3)** engine bay **(4)** afterpeak **(5)** 235hp 3D20 four-cycle six-cylinder diesel **(6)** DK-300 Z-drive **(7)** bow foil **(8)** rear foil **(9)** rudder **(10)** control panel **(11)** lockers **(12)** driver's seat **(13)** passenger seat **(14)** guard rail **(15)** detachable awning **(16)** engine air intakes **(17)** fuel tank **(18)** silencer **(19)** storage batteries **(20)** anchor **(21)** lifebelt

1968 and 1972, but it is believed that only about eight remain in service.
POWER PLANT: One 4,000bhp M-503 diesel.
ARMAMENT: Two twin 23mm AA mounts with remote optical director and two to four depth charges.
RADAR: Surface search and navigation, Pot Drum. IFF, High Pole B.
SONAR: dipping type
DIMENSIONS
Length overall: 27m (88ft 7in)
Hull beam: 6m (19ft 8in)
Width across foils: 8m (26ft 3in)
Draught, hull: 1m (3ft 4in)
   foils: 2·6m (8ft 7in)
WEIGHTS
Fully loaded: 75 tonnes
Standard: 60 tonnes
PERFORMANCE
Max speed: 42 knots

POLESYE

Designed to replace the Byelorus shallow-draught fast ferry, Polesye will have the same cruising speed of 34 knots but will accommodate 50 passengers, ten more than its predecessor. Like Byelorus, it will be operated on winding rivers less than 1m deep which are too shallow for standard-type vessels.

Building has begun at the '50 Letiya USSR' Shipbuilding and Repair Yard, Gomel. The hulls will be welded rather than riveted. Chief designer is P Khanayev.

RAKETA

The prototype Raketa was launched in 1957 and was the first multi-seat passenger hydrofoil to employ the Alexeyev shallow draught submerged foil system. Several hundred are now in service on all the major rivers of the Soviet Union.

In August 1982 it was announced that the prototype is still in service and has carried more than two million passengers. The distance travelled by the craft during the period was stated to be equal to '52 voyages around the equator'.

More than 300 Raketas are being operated on rivers and lakes in the Soviet Union, including 66 in service with the Volga United River Shipping Agency.

Variants include the standard non-tropicalised Raketa M, seating 64 passengers; the 58-seat Raketa T, which is both tropicalised and air-conditioned, and finally the Raketa TA, modified in London by Airavia Ltd and licensed by the UK Department of Trade to carry up to 100 passengers (58 seated) on high-density commuter and tourist routes on sheltered waters such as Westminster-Greenwich. On short-range commuter services additional passengers are seated around the promenade deck aft and others can stand.

A substantial number of Raketas have been exported. Examples are in service in Austria, Bulgaria, Czechoslovakia, Finland, the Federal Republic of Germany, Hungary, Poland, Romania and Yugoslavia.

Production of the Raketa has now stopped and yards previously involved in their construction are building Voskhod and other designs.

The description that follows applies to the Raketa T, the standard export variant, powered by an M-401A diesel and with a cruising speed of about 58km/h (32 knots).

The vessel is designed for high-speed passenger ferry services during daylight hours on rivers, reservoirs and sheltered waters in tropical climates. It meets the requirements of the Soviet River Register Class 'O' with operation restricted to 0·8m (2ft 7in) waves when foilborne and up to 1·5m (4ft 11in) when hullborne.

The passenger saloon is provided with natural and induced ventilation and seats 58. The crew comprises a captain, engineer, deckhand and barman.
FOILS: The foil system comprises one bow foil, one aft foil and two dart-like planing sub-foils, the tips of which are attached to the trailing edges of the outer bow foil struts. Foils, sub-foils and struts are in welded stainless steel. The bow foil,

Nevka

Pchela

Pchela fast patrol boat. Note surface-piercing trapeze foils

which incorporates sweepback, and the straight aft foil, are both supported by three vertical struts.

The base of the centre strut aft provides the end bearing for the propeller which is beneath the foil.
HULL: The hull is framed on longitudinal and transverse formers and all the main elements—plating, deck, partitions, bulkheads, platforms and wheelhouse—are in riveted duralumin. The stem is fabricated in interwelded steel strips. Below the freeboard deck the hull is divided into six watertight compartments employing web framing.
ACCOMMODATION: The passenger saloon seats 58 in aircraft-type, adjustable seats. At the aft end of the saloon is a bar. The saloon has one exit on each side leading to the promenade deck

and one forward, leading to the forecastle. Aft of the saloon is the engine room, promenade deck with additional seats, two toilets, a storeroom and a companionway leading up to the wheelhouse.

The craft carries a full range of life-saving and fire fighting equipment. There are 62 life jackets stowed in the passenger saloon and four for the crew in the wheelhouse and under the embarkation companionway. Two lifebelts are provided on the embarkation platform and two on the promenade deck. Fire fighting equipment includes four foam and four CO_2 fire extinguishers, two fire axes, two fire buckets and two felt cloths.
POWER PLANT: Power is supplied by a single M-401A water-cooled, supercharged 12-cylinder V-type diesel, with a normal service output of 900hp. The engine drives, via a reverse

gear and inclined stainless steel propeller shaft, a three-bladed cast bronze propeller. The fuel system comprises two fuel tanks with a total capacity of 1,400kg, a fuel priming unit, and a hand fuel booster pump. A compressed air system, comprising a propeller shaft-driven air compressor and two 40-litre compressed air bottles, is provided for main engine starting, emergency stopping, operating the foghorn and scavenging the water intake.

The diesel generator unit comprises a Perkins P3.152 diesel engine employed in conjunction with a Stamford C20 alternator.

CONTROLS: The wheelhouse is equipped with a hydraulic remote control system for the engine, reverse gear and fuel supply. The balanced rudder, made in aluminium-magnesium alloy, is controlled hydraulically by turning the wheel. A hand tiller is employed in an emergency. Employment of gas exhaust as a side-thruster to assist mooring is permitted at 850rpm.

SYSTEMS, ELECTRICAL: A 3kW generator, rated at 27·5V and coupled to the main engine, is the main source of power while the vessel is under way. A 50Hz, 230V, 1,500rpm three-phase alternator supplies ac power. Four 12V acid storage batteries, each with a 132Ah capacity and connected in series to give 24V, supply power during short stops.

HYDRAULICS: The hydraulic system for controlling the main engine, reverse gear and fuel supply, consists of control levers located in the wheelhouse and on the main engine, power cylinders located on the engine, a filler tank, pipelines and fittings.

HEATING AND VENTILATION: Passenger saloon and wheelhouse are provided with natural ventilation, using ram inflow when the boat is in motion. Norris Warming air-conditioning is fitted for use in hot weather. One conditioner is installed in the wheelhouse and eight are installed in the passenger saloon and bar. The cooled air is distributed throughout the saloon by electric fans installed on the ceiling. One is provided in the wheelhouse. A radio-telephone with a range of about 30km (19 miles) is installed for ship-to-shore and ship-to-ship communication. The vessel also has a public address system and intercom speakers linking the engine room, wheelhouse and forecastle.

DIMENSIONS
Length overall: 26·96m (88ft 5in)
Beam amidships: 5m (16ft 5in)
Freeboard: 0·8m (2ft 7·5in)
Height overall (excluding mast): 4·46m (14ft 8in)
Draught, hullborne: 1·8m (5ft 11in)
    foilborne: 1·1m (3ft 7·25in)
WEIGHTS
Displacement, fully loaded: 27·09 tonnes
    light: 20·31 tonnes
PERFORMANCE
Service speed: about 58km/h (32 knots)
Max wave height, foilborne: 0·8m (2ft 8in)
    hullborne: 1·5m (4ft 11in)
Turning diameter, hullborne: 3-4 boat lengths
    foilborne: 15-16 boat lengths

SPUTNIK

The 100-ton Sputnik was the first of the Soviet Union's large hydrofoils. On its maiden voyage in November 1961, the prototype carried 300 passengers between Gorki and Moscow in 14 hours. Although a heavy autumn storm was encountered en route the craft was able to continue under way at a cruising speed of 40 knots through several large reservoirs with waves running as high as 8ft.

Full details of the craft can be found in *Jane's Surface Skimmers 1984* and earlier editions.

STRELA

Developed from the Mir and intended for services across the Black Sea, the prototype Strela (Arrow) completed its acceptance trials towards the end of 1961. The craft, which was designed and built in Leningrad, was first put into regular passenger service between Odessa and Batumi, and later between Yalta and Sevastopol. More

Bow foil and planing stabiliser foils of Raketa

Raketa operating as fire tender in Leningrad

Raketa M

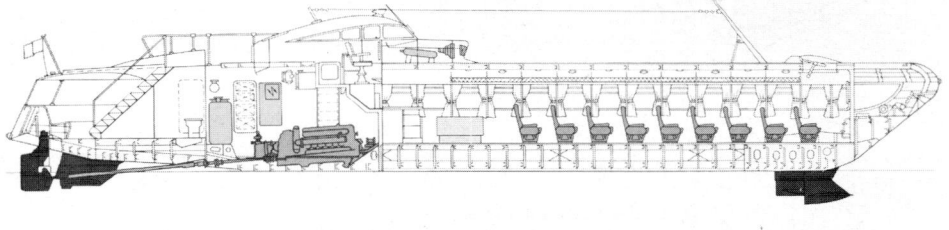

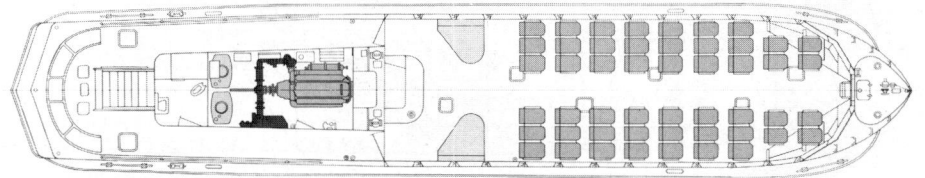

Inboard profile and plan view of standard 50-seat Raketa

recently a Strela has been operating a service between Leningrad and Tallinn. It covers the distance in 4 hours, 90 minutes faster than the express train service connecting the two ports. Only two craft of this type have been built.

Two 970hp 12-cylinder V-type M-50 F3 diesels driving twin screws give the Strela a cruising speed of 75km/h (40 knots). The craft has trapeze type surface-piercing bow foils with a horizontal centre section between the main struts, and can operate in sea state 4.

It carries 82 to 94 passengers in airliner-type seats.

DIMENSIONS
Length overall: 29·3m (96ft 1in)
Beam overall: 8·3m (26ft 4in)
Draught, hullborne: 2·25m (7ft 7in)
    foilborne: 1·2m (3ft 11in)
WEIGHTS
Displacement, fully loaded: 46 tons
PERFORMANCE
Cruising speed: 40 knots
Sea state capability: 1·22m (4ft) waves
Range of operation: 740km (460 miles)
Time to reach service speed from stop: 130 seconds
Distance from full speed to stop: 234m (768ft)
Full speed ahead, to full speed astern: 117m (383ft)

VIKHR (WHIRLWIND)

Seagoing version of the 100-ton Sputnik, Vikhr employs the same hull and is one of the most powerful passenger hydrofoils operating today. Described as a 'Coastal liner', it is designed to operate during hours of daylight on inshore services on the Black Sea up to 50km (31 miles) from the coast. The craft was launched in 1962. It is understood that it is no longer in service. Full details can be found in *Jane's Surface Skimmers 1984* and earlier editions.

VOLGA 70

First export version of the Molnia sports hydrofoil, the Volga 70 incorporates various design

Prototype Strela during trials off Yalta coast

refinements including a completely redesigned bow foil.

Powered by a 90hp Volvo Penta diesel engine it was introduced at the end of 1972. The cruising speed is 4 km/h slower than that of the earlier model, but engine maintenance is easier and the acquisition of spares is simplified in many parts of the world. This model has been purchased by companies and individuals in the USA, West Germany, Sweden, Netherlands and Singapore.

A new export model of the Volga is due to be introduced. It will succeed both the Volga 70 and the Volga-275 described in *Jane's Surface Skimmers 1978*.

FOILS: The foil system consists of a bow foil with stabilising sub-foil and a rear foil assembly. The foils are of stainless steel.

HULL: Built in sheet and extruded light alloy, the hull is divided into three compartments by metal bulkheads. The forepeak is used for stores, the midship compartment is the open cockpit and the aft compartment houses the engine and gearbox.

ACCOMMODATION: Seats are provided for six: a driver and five passengers. The controls, instruments, magnetic compass and radio receiver are grouped on a panel ahead of the

driver's seat. A full range of safety equipment is provided, including six life jackets, life line, fire extinguisher and distress flares. A folding awning can be supplied.

POWER PLANT: Power is supplied by a single Volvo Penta AQD 32A/270TD diesel with a steerable outboard drive delivering 106hp at 4,000rpm. Fuel capacity is 120 litres (26·4 gallons), sufficient for a range of 150 miles.

SYSTEMS, ELECTRICAL: 12V dc. Starting, instrument and navigation lights and siren, are provided by an engine-mounted generator and an acid storage battery.

DIMENSIONS
Length overall: 8·55m (28ft 1in)
Beam: 2·1m (6ft 10·62in)
Height above water when foilborne: 0·98m (3ft 2·62in)
Draught hullborne: 0·92m (3ft)
    foilborne: 0·52m (1ft 8·5in)
WEIGHTS
Loaded displacement: 1,930kg (4,255lb)
Light displacement: 1,350kg (2,977lb)
PERFORMANCE
Max speed: 30 knots
Cruising speed: 28 knots
Range: 241km (150 miles)

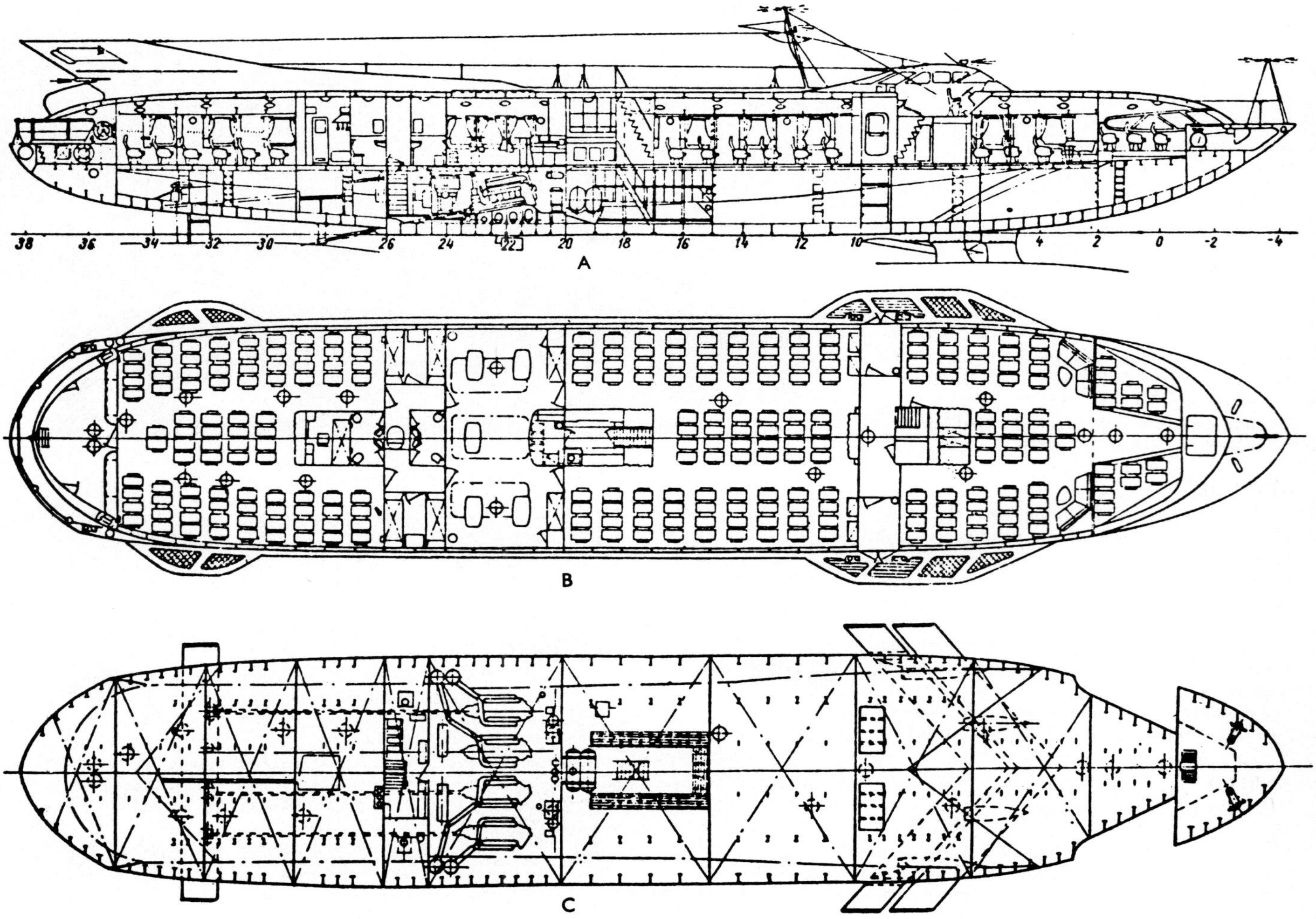

Internal arrangement of Vikhr. (**A**) profile (**B**) main deck (**C**) holds

ZENIT

Described as 'a second-generation fast passenger ferry', Zenit is being developed to replace Meteor. Design speed of the new craft is 90km/h (50 knots) compared with the 65km/h (35 knots) cruising speed of Meteor.

Volga. Production is officially stated to have run into 'several thousand'

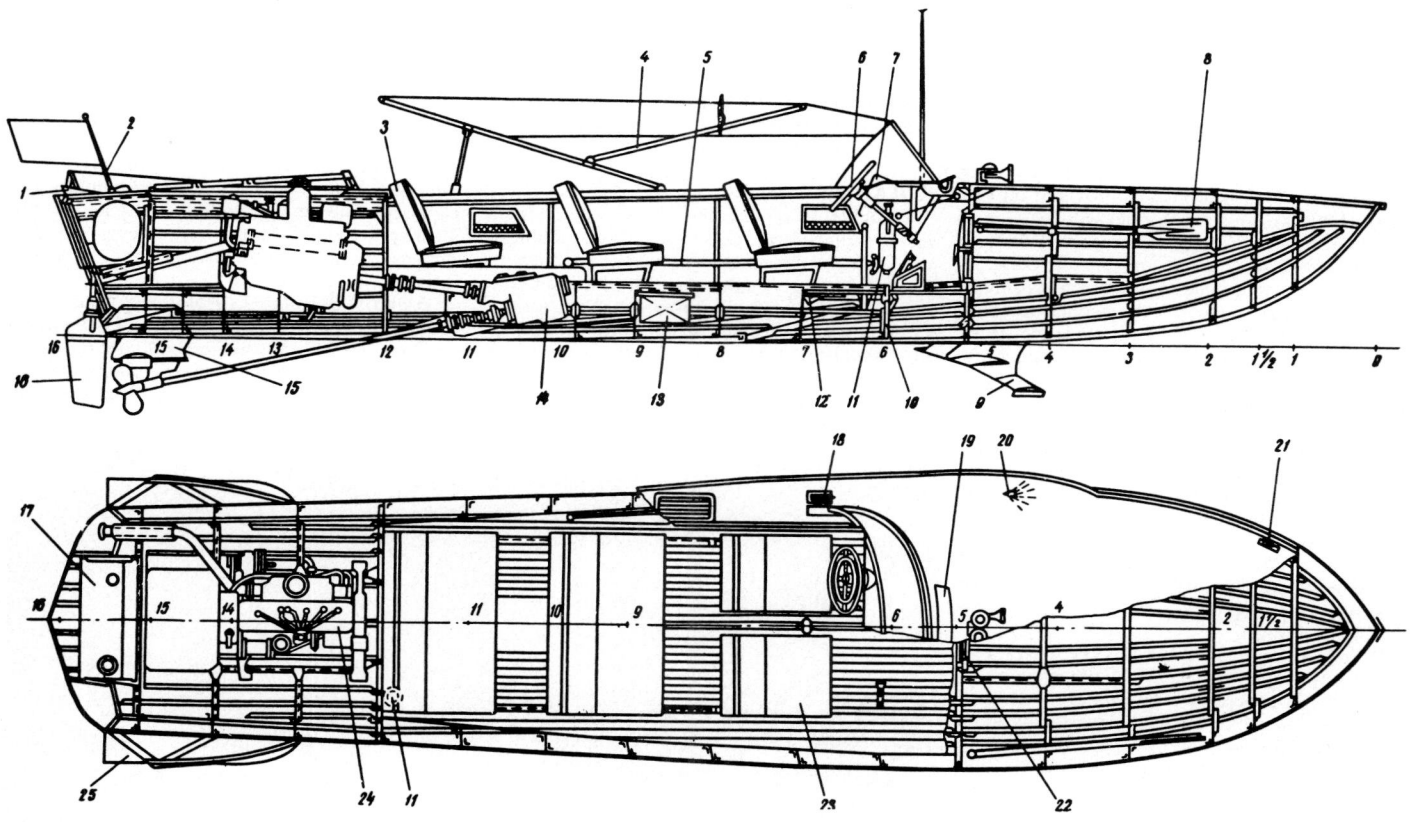

Inboard profile and plan of Volga 70:
(1) stern light **(2)** flag pole **(3)** bench seat **(4)** awning **(5)** dog hook **(6)** steering column **(7)** instrument panel **(8)** oar **(9)** bow foil assembly **(10)** anchor line **(11)** fire extinguisher OY-2 **(12)** anchor **(13)** storage battery **(14)** reduction and reverse gear **(15)** rear foil assembly **(16)** steering and rudder gear **(17)** fuel tank **(18)** cleat **(19)** air intake **(20)** side running light **(21)** fairlead **(22)** cover of first bulkhead hatch **(23)** seat **(24)** M652-Y six-cylinder automotive engine **(25)** foilguard

Ś ORDZHONIKIDZE SHIPBUILD-ING AND REPAIR YARD

Head Office and Yard: Poti, Georgia, USSR
Officials:
Z N Archaidze, *Yard Director*
I Ye Malechanov, *Chief Designer*
Yu Golubkin, *Deputy Chief Designer*
B Pavlyuk, *Chief Engineer*
G A Terentyeb, *Manager, Sea Trials*

CYCLONE

An enlarged, double-deck derivative of the Kometa, the Cyclone seats 250 passengers and is propelled by waterjets driven by two 5,000hp gas turbines, making it the most powerful Soviet commercial hydrofoil to date. Maximum speed is 45 to 50 knots and the cruising speed is 42 knots.

On completion of trials, the vessel will be put into series production at the S Ordzhonikidze Shipbuilding and Repair Yard at Poti. Export models are planned and it is probable that these will be fitted with imported gas turbines and waterjet systems. In May 1982 it was announced that completion of the Cyclone prototype was expected in 1985.

The craft complies with the requirements of Class KM 2MA2 of the USSR Passenger Register. It also meets all the conditions of the Stability Specifications, USSR Shipping Register. It is designed to operate foilborne in waves up to 3m (9ft 10in) regardless of wave direction, and can operate hullborne in conditions up to sea state 5. Foilborne range, fully-loaded, is 300n miles.

FOILS: Surface-piercing system of conventional configuration comprising two main foils, one at the bow and one at the stern; an amidship foil to assist take-off, a pitch stability sub-foil immediately aft of the bow foil, and the associated struts by which the foils are attached to the hull. A sonic/electronic autopilot system controls lift by operating trailing edge flaps on the central section of the bow foil and at both ends of the stern foil. Flap angles are variable in flight and provide a variation in the lift generated by the bow foil of ±35% and ±85% by the stern foil. The foil flaps are adjusted automatically to dampen heave, pitch, roll and yaw motions in heavy seas. A rudder is fitted to the central bow foil strut for improved manoeuvrability in congested waters. Main and stability foils are of welded construction. Bow and stern foil surfaces, flap tie-rods, the lower ends of the bow and stern foil struts, and the central bow foil strut are built in steel alloy. The amidship foil and struts, pitch stability foil and the upper sections of the bow and stern foil struts are in aluminium-magnesium alloy.

HULL: Twin-deck structure. All-welded construction, similar to that employed on Kometa series. Extensive use is made of pressed panels and rolled aluminium-magnesium alloy strip. Hull is framed on longitudinal and transverse formers. Below the main deck the hull is subdivided by 11 watertight bulkheads into 12 compartments. The craft will remain afloat with any two adjacent compartments flooded up to a total length of 9m—or 21 per cent of the craft's overall length. To retard corrosion below the waterline, magnesium protectors are provided.

POWER PLANT: Power for the waterjet propulsion system is supplied by two marinised gas turbines, each rated at 5,000hp maximum and 4,500hp continuous. Each unit has a gas-discharge device and the reduction gear rate of rotation at the power take-off shaft is 950rpm. The shafts of both gas turbines are each connected via flange couplings to the reduction gear of an axial-flow waterjet pump, each of the two pumps receiving water from a common intake. Fuel consumption per horsepower at continuous

Outboard profile of Cyclone

rating is 225g/h. Oil consumption of each gas turbine is 1·5kg/h and that of the reduction gear is 0·5kg/h. The service life of each gas turbine is 10,000 hours before the first overhaul.

ACCOMMODATION: Standard model is designed to carry a crew of 6 and 250 seated passengers. Three saloons are provided on the main deck: a 46-seat bow saloon, a 66-seat amidships saloon and a 74-seat aft saloon. A further 64 are seated in a saloon on the top deck. A separate cabin is provided for the crew. Facilities include a luggage locker, a three-sided refreshment bar, a smaller bar and a promenade deck. Passenger saloons are fully air-conditioned and equipped with airliner-type seats arranged three abreast (32) and two abreast (77). Extensive use is made of heat, sound and vibration absorbing and insulation materials. Decks and serving spaces are overlaid with deep pile carpets. Captain and navigator are accommodated in a raised wheelhouse providing a 360-degree view. A remote control console in the wheelhouse is equipped with the necessary controls and instrumentation for the main and auxiliary engines, the autopilot system, manual steering and fire-fighting.

SYSTEMS, ELECTRICAL: APU drives two 14kW turbogenerators for 28·5V dc service and a 75kW diesel-generator set supplies alternating current at 230V and 50Hz. Two-wire, group-bus type distribution system.

HYDRAULICS: Three separate systems, the first for control of reversing gear, rudder and anchor winch; the second for control of the main engines and water jet nozzles and the third for flap control.

COMMUNICATIONS: R/T simplex/duplex single-band transceiver operating on 18 preselected frequencies in the 1·6 to 8·8 mHz band and transmitting distress signals on 2,182 kHz and 3,023·5 kHz; VHF R/T transceiver operating on seven channels in the 156·3-156·8 mHz band; portable lifeboat type radio, and a PA system.

NAVIGATION: Navigational radar, course indicating system with a steering repeater which automatically provides the course to be steered and transmits data to the repeater, magnetic compass, a log and an automatic steering and stabilisation system.

SAFETY EQUIPMENT: Ten 26-seat inflatable life rafts with provision for the automatic release of five (one side) at a time.

DIMENSIONS
Length overall: 49·9m (163ft 9in)
Width across foils: 13·2m (43ft 6in)
Hull beam: 8m (26ft 3in)
Height above water,
    foilborne (with folded mast): 9m (29ft 7in)
    hullborne: 6·4m (21ft)
Draught foilborne: 1·9m (6ft 3in)
    hullborne: 4·5m (14ft 9in)
WEIGHTS
Loaded displacement: 140 tonnes
Light displacement: 96·4 tonnes
Deadweight: 43·6 tonnes
PERFORMANCE
Max speed, foilborne: 45-50 knots
Cruising speed, foilborne: 42 knots

Endurance: 8 hours
Max wave height,
    foilborne: 3m (9ft 10in)
    hullborne: sea state 5
Range: 300n miles

KOLKHIDA

Designed to replace the 20-year-old Kometa fast passenger ferry, Kolkhida will be available in two versions: the Albatros, which will operate on domestic services within the Soviet Union, and the Kolkhida, intended for export. Keel for the prototype was laid at a ceremony attended by the First Secretary of the Central Committee of the Georgian Communist party in May 1980. The occasion also marked the entry of the craft into series production.

Kolkhida is faster than Kometa, seats more passengers, uses less fuel and can operate foilborne in higher sea states. Among the various design innovations are a new foil system with automatic lift control, the use of new materials in the hull structure and a more rational cabin layout, permitting a substantial increase in seating capacity. The engine room is aft, as on the Voskhod, to reduce the noise level. Overall dimensions are almost identical to those of Kometa-M.

Trials of the Kolkhida prototype took place in the Baltic between March and June 1981. Series production is under way and will continue until 1985. The craft meets the requirements of the Register of Shipping of the USSR and is constructed to Hydrofoil Class KM★ 2 A1A

Kolkhida, main cabin

Kolkhida

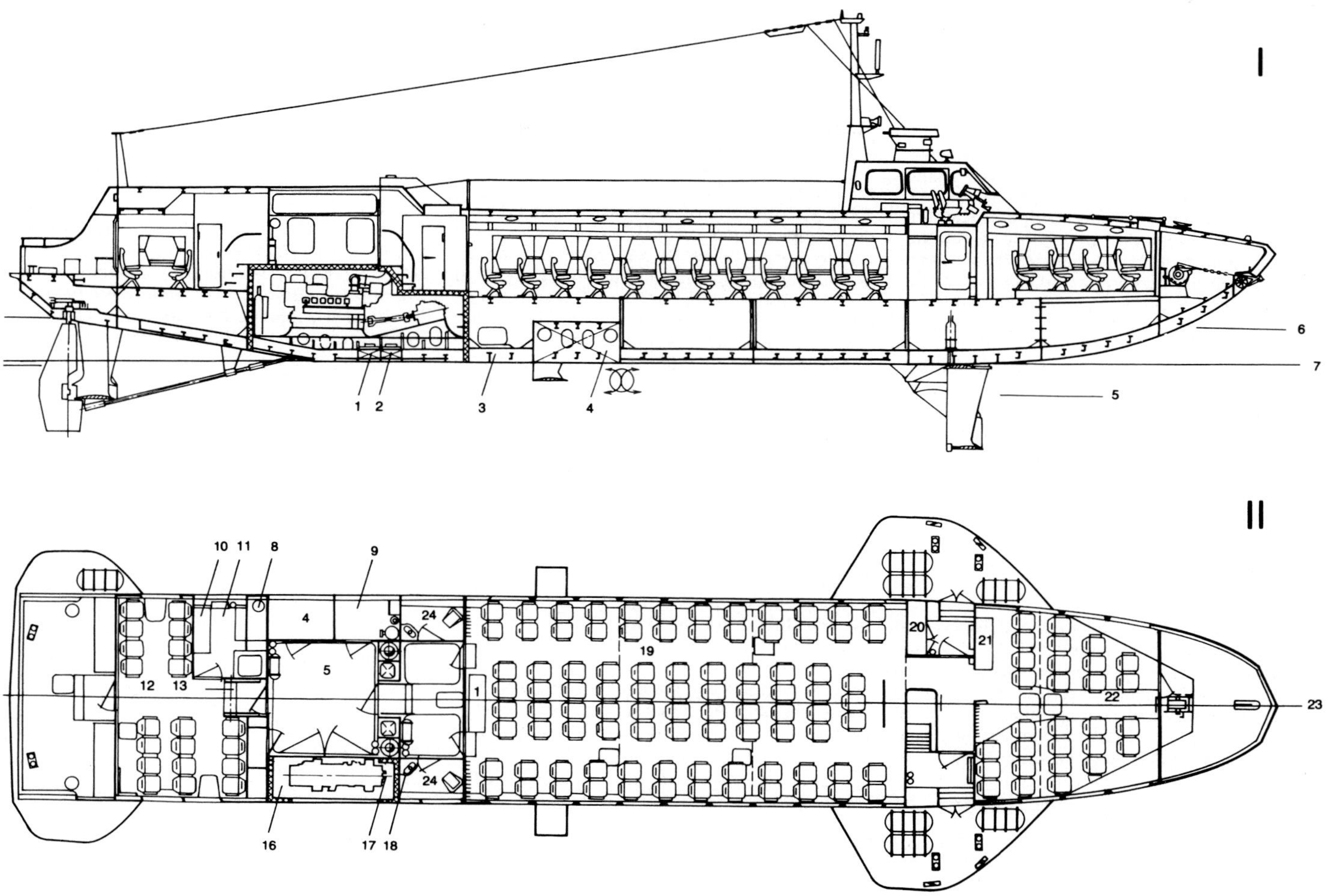

I

II

Kolkhida
Longitudinal section: (1) waste oil collection tank (2) oil-containing water tank (3) sewage water tank (4) fuel tank (5) waterline when foilborne (6) waterline when hullborne (7) base line
Main deck plan: (8) hydraulic station (9) fuel and oil filling, waste water scavenging, fire-fighting station (10) conditioner (11) control post (12) 20-seat passenger saloon (13) VP (14) luggage room (15) promenade platform (16) auxiliary unit room (17) gas exhaust trunk (18) air intake trunk (19) 91-seat passenger saloon (20) Aggregate room (21) conditioner (22) 29-seat passenger saloon (23) central line (24) toilet

Passenger Class under the Register's technical supervision. It complies fully with IMCO's Code of Safety for Dynamically Supported Craft.

It is designed to operate under tropical and moderate climates up to 50 miles from a port of refuge in open seas and up to 100 miles from a port of refuge in inland seas and large lakes, with a permissible distance between two ports of refuge of not more than 200 miles.

Foilborne, the craft can operate in waves up to 2m and winds up to force 5; hullborne it can operate in waves up to 3m and winds up to force 6.

FOILS: The foil system, which is similar to that of Kometa, comprises a trapeze-type bow foil, an aft and an amidship foil, close to the longitudinal centre of gravity to assist take-off. The foils are connected to the hull by struts and brackets. A sonic/electronic autopilot controls lift by operating trailing edge flaps on the centre section of the bow foil and on the inner sections of the aft foil. The foil flaps are adjusted hydraulically to dampen heave, pitch, roll and yaw motions in heavy seas and provide co-ordinated turns. Bow and stern foil surfaces and the lower ends of the bow and stern foil struts are in steel alloy. The amidship foil, struts, upper sections of the bow and stern foil struts are in aluminium-magnesium alloy. A cast, balanced rudder in 40mm thick aluminium-magnesium alloy is fitted. Total blade area is 2·75m². Rudder movement is controlled hydraulically by any one of three systems: push-button, manual or via the autopilot.

HULL: Double-chine, V-bottom type, with raked stern and streamlined superstructure. Hull and superstructure are built in aluminium-magnesium alloys. Framing is based on T and T-angle webframes. Frame spacing is 600mm. Longitudinal framing of the sides, decks and hull bottom is based on stiffening ribs, keelson, stringers and deck girders. Below the main deck the hull is subdivided by watertight bulkheads into

Kolkhida showing surface-piercing bow and stern foils

Kolkhida

nine compartments. The craft will remain afloat with any two adjacent compartments flooded.

POWER PLANT: Power is supplied by two MTU 12V 396 TS 82 water-cooled, supercharged 12-cylinder V-type four-stroke marine diesels, each with a normal service output of 960kW (1,300hp) and 1,050kW (1,430hp) maximum. Guaranteed service life of each engine before first major overhaul is 9,000 hours; maximum service life is 12 years. Output is transferred to twin 740mm diameter contra-rotating fixed-pitch propellers through reversible gearboxes which are remotely controlled from the wheelhouse. The propeller shafts are inclined at 14 degrees and supported by rubber and metal bearings.

ACCOMMODATION: Standard passenger-ferry version is designed to carry an operating crew of six and 120 passengers. A tourist sightseeing version seats 140. Crew comprises a captain/engineer, two motormen, one seaman, one seaman/radio operator and a barman. On the tourist version, no barman is carried. Embarkation platforms immediately below the wheelhouse provide access for passengers and crew. Captain and engineer are accommodated in a raised wheelhouse between the forward and main saloon.

The wheelhouse contains a radar display and radio-communications equipment. Main engine controls are installed in both the wheelhouse and engine room. Passengers are accommodated in three air-conditioned compartments, a forward saloon seating 29, a middle saloon seating 91 and an aft saloon with 20 seats. Facilities include two promenade decks, one immediately aft of the main saloon above the engine room, the other on the weather deck at the stern, toilets and a buffet/bar. Passenger saloons are equipped with airliner-type, reclining-back seats arranged four, three or two abreast. Extensive use is made of heat, sound and vibration absorbing and insulating materials. Decks in saloons and serving places are carpeted.

APU: Combined unit comprises a four-cylinder diesel engine rated at 33kW, a six-cylinder freon compressor, a 4·5kW 27·5 dc generator, a self-priming pump and a starting air compressor. Unit supplies electric power to shipboard consumers, operates air-conditioning system and replenishes starting bottles with compressed air.

SYSTEMS, ELECTRICAL: Engine-driven generators supply power while the craft is operating. The 4·5kW generator included in the auxiliary unit supplies power when the craft is at rest. Acid storage batteries connected in series supply power during short stops.

ANCHOR: Single Matrosov 75kg main anchor and LGY 20 M1 hydraulic windlass. Also appropriate mooring, towing and anchoring equipment.

COMMUNICATIONS: Radio transmitter/receiver with r/t and w/t facilities is installed in the wheelhouse for the ship-to-shore and inter-ship communications on SW and MW bands. Unified communications and relay equipment provides simplex command communication between wheelhouse, engine room, stern, control post, forward embarkation platforms and anchor winch compartment as well as relaying broadcasts and information announcements to the passenger saloons.

NAVIGATION: Gyro compass, magnetic compass and log are standard.

AIR-CONDITIONING: Anton Kaiser-type module, comprising 33kW four-cylinder diesel, six-cylinder Freon compressor, 4·5kW dc generator, self-priming circulating pump and starting compressor, all mounted on a single frame.

HYDRAULICS: System for operating rudder, foil flaps and windlass.

SAFETY EQUIPMENT: Six 25-seat inflatable life rafts in addition to life jackets, life belts, life lines and self-igniting buoyant lights. Chemical- and foam-type fire-extinguishing system installed throughout vessel.

DIMENSIONS
Length overall: 34·5m (113ft 3in)
Beam overall: 10·3m (33ft 10in)
  hull: 5·8m (19ft)
Height overall from water level, hullborne: 8·9m (29ft 3in)
  foilborne: 10·8m (35ft 10in)
Draught, hullborne: 3·5m (11ft 6in)
  foilborne: 1·9m (6ft 3in)
WEIGHTS
Light displacement: 52·3 tonnes
Fully-loaded displacement: 68 tonnes
Gross register tonnage: 143 tonnes
PERFORMANCE
Cruising speed, fully loaded: 35 knots
Take-off time: 20-40 seconds
Hullborne speed: 12 knots
Range: 120n miles

UNITED STATES OF AMERICA

BOEING MARINE SYSTEMS
A Division of the Boeing Company
Head Office: PO Box 3707, Seattle, Washington 98124, USA
Telephone: (206) 237 0220
Officials:
Robert E Bateman, *Vice President and General Manager, Boeing Marine Systems*

Boeing Marine Systems, a separate operating division of the Boeing company, was formed in 1958 to conduct research, development, design, manufacture and the testing of high performance marine vehicles systems. Boeing's entry into the hydrofoil field was announced in June 1960, when the company was awarded a US $2 million contract for the construction of the US Navy's 120-ton PCH-1 High Point, a canard design which was the outcome of experiments with a similar arrangement in the US Navy test craft, Sea Legs.

Boeing has also built a jet-driven hydroplane, the HTS, for testing foil models at full-scale velocity; the Fresh-1, a manned craft for testing superventilating or supercavitating foils at speeds between 60 and 100 knots, and a waterjet test vehicle, Little Squirt. Descriptions of Fresh-1 and Little Squirt appear in *Jane's Surface Skimmers 1970-71* and earlier editions. The company also completed a highly successful waterjet-propelled gunboat, the PGH-2 Tucumcari, for the US Navy's Ship Systems Command. Its operational trials included several months of combat evaluation in Viet-Nam as part of the US Navy's coastal surveillance force. Data provided by the vessel assisted the design and development of the NATO/PHM, which is a 'scaled-up' Tucumcari, and the Jetfoil commercial hydrofoil.

High Point was modified by Boeing during 1972 to incorporate a new automatic control system, modified struts and foils, a new diesel for hullborne propulsion and a steerable forward strut for improved manoeuvrability. The craft was returned to the US Navy as Mod-1 configuration. In its revised form it is employed as a testbed for hydrofoil weapons compatibility.

In April 1975, the PCH was operated by the US Coast Guard for one month as part of a continuing research and development programme to

PHM-1 *Pegasus* hullborne, with foils extended

evaluate high-speed water craft for the US Coast Guard. Operating in Puget Sound and around San Francisco, the craft was employed on fisheries patrol, marine environmental protection and search and rescue missions.

In 1979 the PCH-1 was selected as the research and development vehicle for demonstrating the feasibility of the US Navy's Extended Performance Hydrofoil (EPH) project.

In January 1973 the keel was laid for the first 110-ton 250-seat Model 929-100 Jetfoil passenger ferry. The hull was assembled in a former 727 assembly building at Renton, Washington, and the first craft was launched in March 1974 on Lake Washington, which is adjacent to the plant. Ten Jetfoils of this type are in commercial service. Jetfoil 0011, which was launched in June 1978, is the first Jetfoil of improved design. This version, known as the Model 929-115, has improved performance, payload and reliability. 17 of the craft are in service, with additional Model 929-115s scheduled to begin services in 1983.

An order for the first fast patrol craft version of the Jetfoil was placed by the Royal Navy in 1978. This was a modified commercial Jetfoil, named HMS *Speedy,* and built on the commercial Jetfoil production line. Two Allison 501-K20A gas turbines are installed in this variant for foilborne operation and two Allison 8V92T1 diesels for hullborne operation, giving added time on-station and increased endurance. HMS *Speedy* was commissioned by the Royal Navy in June 1980 but was subsequently decommissioned in April 1982 due to defence cuts.

The company is examining the possibility of exporting civil and military versions of the Jetfoil on a modular basis, with the customer purchasing a basic hull, which would contain all the essential systems, and installing his own superstructure.

In April 1973 US Naval Ship Systems Command awarded the company a US $42,602,384 contract for the design and development of the 235-tonne NATO/PHM missile-equipped patrol boat, under the terms of which Boeing was to build the lead craft for the US Navy for evaluation.

The PHM was the first US Navy craft to be

designed on the basis of a co-operative technical interchange between the USA and its allies within NATO.

The first PHM, *Pegasus,* was launched in November 1974. Delivery to the US Navy took place in late 1976 and the craft completed its acceptance trials at Seattle in early June 1977.

In August 1977 it was announced by the US Defense Secretary that the US Navy would receive five more PHMs, the last of which was delivered in September 1982. The five production craft are assigned to a PHM squadron operating out of Key West, Florida.

Interested observers in the PHM programme include the navies of Canada, Australia, Denmark, the Netherlands, France, Greece, Turkey and the United Kingdom.

Design studies are now being completed for bigger and faster hydrofoils including the 1,300 to 1,500-ton Destroyer Escort Hydrofoil (DEH), a vessel capable of open ocean missions and of crossing the Atlantic without refuelling.

PCH-1 HIGH POINT

The PCH-1 High Point was accepted by the US Navy in August 1963 and used to evaluate the performance of an inshore hydrofoil ASW system. During April 1975 it was employed by the US Coast Guard in Puget Sound and off San Francisco. A full description of the craft can be found in *Jane's Surface Skimmers 1984* and earlier editions.

PCH-1 HIGH POINT EPH FEASIBILITY DEMONSTRATOR

The EPH (extended performance hydrofoil) combines buoyant lift, in the form of a long, slender and submerged body, with the dynamic lift generated by a fully-submerged foil system.

Initial investigation has shown that a suitably-designed buoyancy/fuel tank below the foils would provide about 50 per cent of the total foilborne lift and extend the craft's range beyond that of any comparable hydrofoil. This is achieved without a substantial reduction in foilborne speed. The range improvement, which increases with ship size, is from an increased fuel/weight fraction and higher weight-to-drag ratios, especially at lower foilborne speeds. The lower end of the foilborne speed range can be extended to 20 to 25 knots while maximum speeds of above 40 knots are still attainable.

Development of the EPH is being undertaken at the David W Taylor Naval Ship Research and Development Center. PCH-1 High Point was selected in 1979 as the research and development vehicle for feasibility demonstration of the

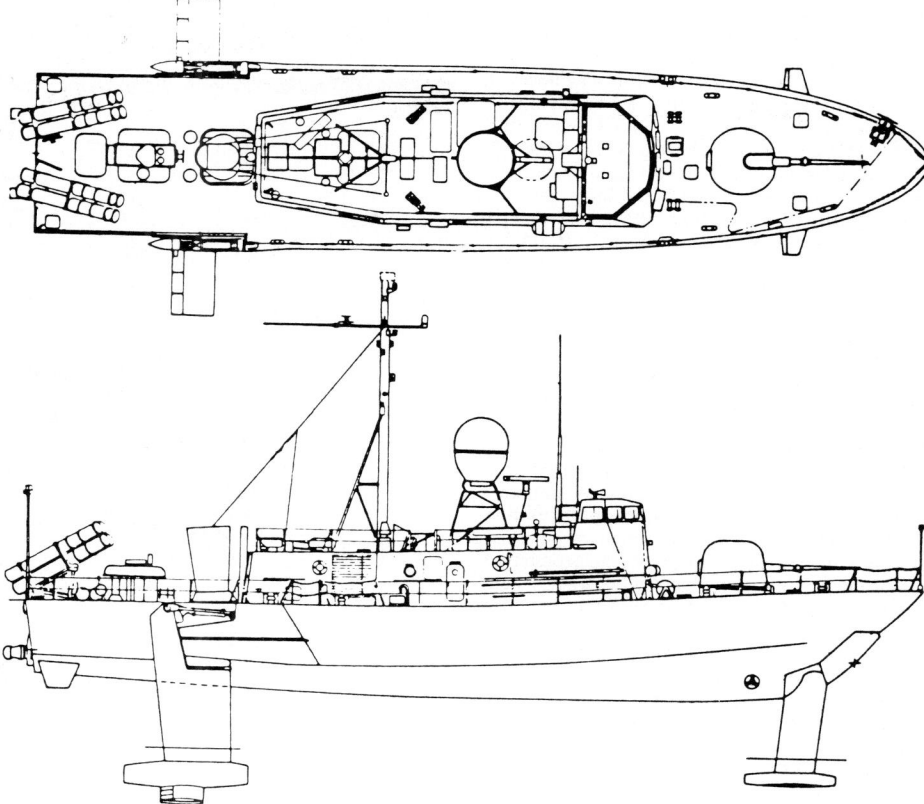

Outboard profile and deck plan of PHM-3

Extended Performance Hydrofoil (EPH) concept under the US Navy's exploratory development programmes. On completion of the detail design of major components for the craft, construction of the buoyancy/fuel tank and modification of the PCH-1 hull will begin at Puget Sound Naval Shipyard.

Objectives of the trials are: to demonstrate the feasibility of operating the EPH in hullborne and foilborne modes in waves up to mid-sea state 5, maximum foilborne speed is expected to be about 40 knots in calm water; verify technical analyses and model experiments; acquire data on EPH tank loads as well as the usual parameters measured during PCH-1 trials for a data base to design and operate projected larger EPH ships.

Studies recently focused on a multi-mission EPH combatant projected for 1990 to 1995. Due to its high speed, long endurance and combat

payload an EPH, with a dynamic lift system of approximately 1,350 tons, is considered to have potential as an escort for high-speed and high-value convoys and naval forces. Despite its small size the EPH equipped with advanced ASW and AAW systems could perform a number of escort missions at higher speeds than modern frigates.

With the addition of a 66-ton buoyancy/fuel tank to the craft, the draughts and displacement for the PCH-1 EPH demonstrator are:
Draught: foils extended: 6·81m
Displacement, light: 132 tons
full load: 200 tons

PGH-2 TUCUMCARI

A 58-ton waterjet-propelled hydrofoil gunboat, the PGH-2 was ordered from Boeing by the US Navy's Ship Systems Command in 1966, under a US $4 million, fixed price PGH (Patrol Gunboat Hydrofoil) programme. The craft was delivered to the US Navy in March 1968.

The craft operated with the US Navy Pacific Fleet Amphibious Command, San Diego, and the Atlantic Amphibious Forces, Norfolk, Virginia. Its operational trials included several months of combat evaluation in Viet-Nam as part of the US Navy's 24-hour coastal surveillance force in Operation Market Time.

In 1971 the craft was deployed to Europe for operation with the US Sixth Fleet in the Mediterranean following a series of demonstrations for officials of NATO navies.

In November 1972 Tucumcari ran aground in the Caribbean, 7 miles east of Puerto Rico, while conducting night-time operations with amphibious forces. No crewmen were killed or seriously injured. Due to damage sustained while removing the craft from the coral reef, the craft was struck from the list of active US Navy vessels and sent to the US Naval Research and Development Center where it has been employed for structural evaluation and fire containment tests. A full technical description of the vessel appeared in *Jane's Surface Skimmers 1974-75* and earlier editions.

BOEING NATO/PHM

The NATO Hydrofoil Fast Patrol Ship Guided Missile (NATO/PHM) originated in mid-1969 when C-in-C South presented to NATO a requirement for a large number of fast patrol

PCH-1 High Point EPH feasibility demonstrator

boats to combat the threat posed by missile-armed fast patrol boats in the Mediterranean.

The concept of a common fast patrol boat was studied, and in September 1970 it was decided that the submerged foil craft of 140 tons proposed by the US Navy was the vessel most suited to NATO mission requirements. In October 1971 the USA indicated that it would proceed at its own expense with the design of the vessel and share the results of the studies with those nations wishing to purchase PHMs. It also offered to conduct all aspects of design and development, contracting and management in co-operation with governments entering into project membership. Costs would be reimbursed only by those nations engaged in the project.

Letters of intent, acknowledging design and cost scheduled obligations, were provided by Italy and West Germany in April and May 1972, respectively. Sudden and extreme changes in the US Government's attitude regarding PHM production in recent years had a markedly negative effect on the continued programme participation by West Germany. Tentative moves were made by Congress to delete four of the five production craft from the programme early in 1976. When, in February 1977, the new Secretary of Defense announced to the West German Government that the USA was terminating the PHM programme, the West German Navy decided it had no option but to terminate participatory effort in production design, called back its project office personnel and embarked on the ordering of conventional fast patrol craft. By the time Congress had completed its 1977 action refusing to rescind prior year appropriated PHM funding, the situation was irreversible and West Germany was no longer an active partner.

Statements made in mid-1978 suggest, however, that the US Departments of Defense and State are currently seeking to promote renewed participation in the PHM Programme by the USA's NATO allies. Although only three governments decided to participate actively in the initial stages, future project membership is not restricted. Interested observers include Canada, Denmark, the Netherlands, France and the United Kingdom. Greece and Turkey have also considered participation. Japan is also expressing interest in purchasing or building PHMs.

In November 1971 the US Navy awarded Boeing a US $5·6 million contract for the preliminary design of a 230-ton craft and the purchase of mechanical and electronic components for at least two of the vessels. 17 months later, Boeing was awarded a US $42,607,384 contract for the design and development of the PHM for NATO navies. Under the terms of the contract the first craft, the *Pegasus,* was built for the US Navy.

Pegasus was launched in November 1974 and made its first foilborne flight in February 1975. It achieved its classified designed speed, completed the Navy-conducted phase of testing its weapons and then began operational evaluation in the San Diego area in autumn 1975.

It completed its acceptance trials during the

PHM-3 USS *Taurus*

Port quarter view of PHM-2 USS *Hercules*

first week of June 1977 and was commissioned into service in July 1977, becoming the first hydrofoil officially designated a United States Ship (USS *Pegasus*). Rear Admiral John Bulkeley, USN, President, Naval Board of Inspection and Survey, recorded that it had demonstrated 'superb reliability throughout her trial with no major or significant breakdowns or failures'.

The first squadron of PHMs consists of the USS *Pegasus* and its five sister ships, *Taurus, Aquila, Aries, Gemini* and *Hercules,* plus the PHM Mobile Logistic Support Group (MLSG) and the Squadron Commander's staff. An interim MLSG was established to support *Pegasus* and comprised one officer and 28 enlisted personnel operating from six standard 40ft (12·1m) containers and three roadable trailers fitted to provide shop, office and training space and stowage for spares and food stores. During the second phase of the squadron build-up a converted 1178 Class LST, to be known as a Hydrofoil Support Ship (AGHS), was to be made available. This would have provided all the facilities available from the van complex plus the basic fuel and other services now provided from ashore.

However, the AGHS has been deleted from the US Navy budget and a mobile complex comprising 2·4 × 2·4 × 6m (72·8 × 8 × 20ft) ISO standard vans has been procured and installed at Key West. The vans are equipped to provide maintenance, workshops, equipment stores, training classrooms and on-shore messing facilities.

Four of the production craft are armed with a 75mm OTO Melara dual-purpose rapid fire cannon and eight Harpoon anti-ship missiles in two four-tube lightweight canister launchers. Armament for the fifth craft will be installed after delivery. Construction of PHM-2 *Hercules* began in May 1974 but was stopped in 1975. This was the last to be delivered in September 1982. PHM-3 was delivered in October 1981, followed

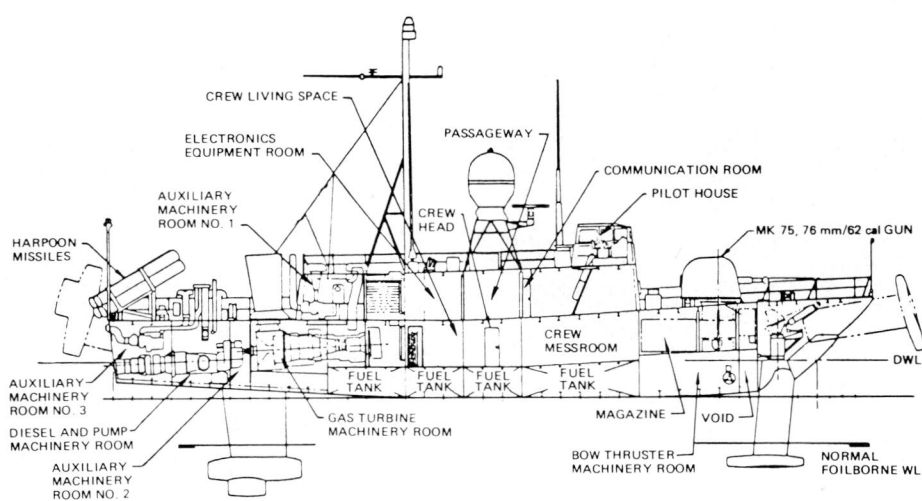

Inboard profile of PHM-3

by PHM-4 in January 1982, PHM-5 in May 1982 and PHM-6 in July 1982. All five craft were built by Boeing Marine Systems at its hydrofoil assembly plant at Renton, Washington, adjacent to Lake Washington. USS *Pegasus* was operationally assigned to the Atlantic Fleet at Key West, Florida in July 1980.

The PHM has sufficient design flexibility to allow for individual variations by any country. These variations will be primarily in the weapons systems installed, and the participating nations, current and future, can acquire the standard PHM carrying whatever combat equipment is determined necessary to meet national requirements.

PHM's potential in terms of strategic mobility was demonstrated between 30 September and 1 October 1975, when *Pegasus* completed the 1,225 nautical miles from Seattle to San Diego in the record-breaking time of less than 34 hours, which included a refuelling stop at Eureka, California.

With the aid of midway refuelling the craft is capable of crossing oceans with fast carrier task groups, convoys of merchant ships and amphibious assault groups. With three under way refuellings, it can cross the Atlantic from Massachusetts to the United Kingdom at an average speed of 30 knots in 4·2 days, or it could cross from Norfolk, Virginia to Cadiz in 4·6 days with four under way refuellings.

PHM is designed to be self-supporting at sea for a period of five days. For extended periods, or during intensive operations, it is refuelled under way with either JP-5 or Naval Distillate (DFM) by oilers, major combatants and carriers.

It can be easily adapted for such roles as anti-submarine warfare, fisheries law enforcement and the protection of offshore resources.

The standard PHM is approximately 40·5m (132ft 10in) long, has a beam of 8·6m (28ft 2in) and a full load displacement of about 241 tonnes (238 tons). Foilborne range is in excess of 500n miles at speeds in excess of 40 knots in 2·4 to 3·6m (8 to 12ft) seas. The hull form and size, the major structural bulkheads and decks, foils and struts, waterjets, pumps, controls and main propulsion machinery are identical. The auxiliary equipment and arrangements, deckhouse and crew accommodation are also of standard design, but variations in the latter are possible to suit the manning requirements of individual countries.

PHM-3 USS *Taurus*

FOILS: Fully-submerged canard arrangement with approximately 31·8 per cent of the dynamic lift provided by the bow foil and 68·2 per cent by the aft foil. The aft foil retracts rearwards and the bow foil retracts forward into a recess in the bow. Bow doors preserve the hull lines when the forward foil is either fully extended or retracted. The foils and struts are in 17-4 PH martensitic, precipitation hardening stainless steel. Both forward and aft foils are welded assemblies consisting of spars, ribs, and skin. Flaps are fitted to the trailing edges to provide control and lift augmentation at take-off and during flight. The bow foil system incorporates a strut that rotates to provide directional control and reliable turning rates in heavy seas.

The shallow M or inverted double pi configuration of the aft foil is designed for improved hydroelastic and turning characteristics. The primary strut structure consists of spars, ribs and skin welded into watertight assemblies. The struts are designed as beam columns, and rigidly attached to the foil support structure at the hull.

The struts are attached to the hull with pivot pins that allow the foils to rotate clear of the water. Hydraulic actuators are used for retraction and extension, mechanical stops and position locks being employed to secure the foils in either position.

CONTROLS, FOILBORNE: The helm, throttle and an automatic control system (ACS) provide continuous dynamic control during take-off, foilborne operation and landing. Once take-off is complete, the ACS requires no attention by the crew. It controls the craft by sensing craft attitude, motion rates and acceleration, then comparing them electronically with desired values. Any deviations are processed by analogue control computer which generates electrical commands causing hydraulic actuators to reposition the control surfaces, thus minimising detected errors. The foilborne control surfaces are trailing edge flaps on each of the foils, plus the rotating bow foil strut which acts as the foilborne rudder.

Manual controls and displays for both hullborne and foilborne conditions are concentrated at the helm station and include the wheel, a foil-depth selector, a foil-depth indicator, a ship-heading indicator and a heading holding switch.

CONTROLS, HULLBORNE: Steering control in the hullborne mode is provided by steerable nozzles which rotate electro-hydraulically in response to the wheel. An automatic heading control, similar to that employed for foilborne operation, is incorporated, together with the necessary heading reference provided by the gyrocompass.

POWER PLANT, FOILBORNE: The foilborne propulsion system comprises a single 17,000shp, coaxial two-stage, two-speed waterjet, driven through two sets of reduction gears by a single General Electric LM 2500 marine gas turbine, developed from the GE TF39, which powers the US Air Force's C-5 transport and the DC-10 Trijet.

PHM-1 uses only 16,200hp from the engine while production craft use 17,000hp. Full use of the 30,000hp potential is possible in the future, although the gearbox will have to be redesigned to absorb this power.

Both the foilborne and hullborne propulsion systems were designed by Aerojet Liquid Rocket Company, Sacramento, California, under a Boeing contract.

The single foilborne propulsion pump is capable of handling 90,000 gallons/minute and the two hullborne pumps will each operate at approximately 30,000 gallons/minute.

Engine installation and removal for overhaul is accomplished through hatches in the main deck between the deckhouse and exhaust outlet.

Normal fuel is diesel oil MIL-F-16884 (NATO F-76) or JP-5 MIL-J-5624 (NATO F-44).

POWER PLANT, HULLBORNE: Twin Aerojet waterjet pumps powered by two 800hp Mercedes-Benz 8V331TC80 diesels propel the vessel when hullborne. Each waterjet propulsor has nozzle steering and reversing buckets. The hullborne system provides long-range cruising and slow speed manoeuvring, while the gas turbine is available when required for high-speed foilborne operation.

HULL: Hull and deckhouses are all-welded structures in AL 5456 alloy.

Wheelhouse of PHM-3 *Taurus*

ACCOMMODATION: Crew will average 21 officers and men, but will vary according to the armament carried up to a total of 24. Accommodation on the US Navy version is provided for five officers—the commanding officer has a separate cabin—four chief petty officers and 15 enlisted men. The superstructure accommodates the bridge, which contains steering and engine control consoles and is elevated to provide a 360-degree view. A short ladder from the bridge leads down to the command and surveillance deckhouse that accommodates the fire-control, radar, communications and navigation equipment. The size of the deckhouse provides flexibility in accommodating various national equipment requirements. The space aft of the superstructure and forward of the foilborne engine exhaust is used to erect rigging for replenishment and refuelling.

Below the main deck, about one third of the PHM's length is devoted to crew accommodation, the forward third is occupied by the primary gun, automatic loader mechanism, ammunition storage and forward foil, and the after third is occupied by the unmanned machinery spaces.

All manned spaces are equipped with a recirculating air conditioning system to give a maximum air temperature of 27°C at 55 per cent relative humidity in summer, and a minimum inside temperature of 18°C in winter. The officers' staterooms, crew quarters and lounge/messing area are fully air-conditioned, the temperature being controlled by individual thermostats in the spaces concerned.

SYSTEMS, ELECTRICAL: Ship's service electric plant comprises two AiResearch Ship Service Power Units (SSPUs), with ME831-800 gas turbines as prime movers driving 250kVA, 400Hz, 450V generators. Each SSPU also drives an attached centrifugal compressor for starting the LM2500 engine and two hydraulic pumps for the ship's hydraulic system. One is capable of handling the entire electrical load, the second is provided as a standby. Through the use of static power conversion equipment, limited three-phase, 60Hz ac power and 28V dc is available for equipment requirements. In port, the craft can utilise shore power or use its own auxiliary power unit for this purpose, as well as battery charging and emergency use of navigation and radio equipment.

HYDRAULICS: 3,000psi to actuate the hullborne and foilborne controls, foil retraction and hullborne engine starting. Dual hydraulic supply is provided to each service with sub-system isolation fore and aft in the event of major damage.

FIRE EXTINGUISHING: Dry chemical equipment throughout craft, and a fixed total flooding-type Freon 1301 system.

WEAPONS/FIRE CONTROL: Either WM-28 radar and weapons control system or US model, the Mk 92 (Mod 1). Both systems embody a combined fire control and search antenna system, mounted on a single stabilised platform and enclosed in a fibreglass radome. The Italian Argo system can also be installed.

TARGETING/MISSILE WARNING: Automatic classification ESM (electronic warfare support measures) set is installed for missile warning and over-the-horizon targeting of enemy surface units.

GUNS: Standard primary gun is the OTO Melara 76mm gun, which is unmanned and automatically controlled by the fire control system. The craft can also be delivered with secondary guns. If specified two Mk 20 Rh 202 20mm AA cannon can be provided, one each, port and starboard, adjacent to the fire control antenna structure.

MISSILES: The prototype carries eight Harpoon missiles in two four-tube lightweight canister launchers, but Exocet, Otomat, Tero or any smaller missile system can be installed. Space is provided aft to accommodate the four launchers, port and starboard, in parallel pairs. The launchers are deck-fixed in elevation and azimuth.

Armament of the standard US Navy version will be eight McDonnell Douglas RGM-84A Harpoon anti-ship missiles in lightweight container launchers; one Mk 75 76mm/62cal OTO Melara gun with 400 76mm rounds, and two Mk

US Navy's six PHMs during operational exercise off Key West, Florida

135, Mod 0, 4·4in launchers, together with 24 Mk 171 chaff cartridges, small arms, ammunition and pyrotechnics.

COMMAND, CONTROL AND COMMUNICATIONS: True motion navigation radar; OMEGA navigation equipment; gyro compass; dead reckoning tracer; Tactical and Navigation Collision Avoidance System (TANCAV); speed log; depth sounder/recorder; AN/SPA-25B repeater consoles (2); integrated intercom/announcing/exterior communications system; HF, UHF and VHF communications (teletype and voice) IFF system, ESM system.

The basic PHM design allows for a growth of approximately 5 tons in full load displacement to enhance mission capability. Areas under consideration include sonar, torpedoes, improved surface-to-surface missiles and low-light-level TV, all of which appear to be feasible without having an adverse effect on its current capabilities.

The following details apply to the model under construction for the US Navy.

DIMENSIONS
Length overall,
  foils extended: 40·5m (132ft 10in)
  foils retracted: 44·3m (145ft 4in)
Beam max, deck: 8·6m (28ft 2in)
Max width across foils: 14·5m (47ft 6in)
Draught,
  hullborne, foils retracted: 1·9m (6ft 3in)
  hullborne, foils extended: 7·1m (23ft 2in)
  foilborne, normal: 2·5m (8ft 2in)

WEIGHTS
Displacement, full load including margins: 241 tonnes

PERFORMANCE
Max speed foilborne: in excess of 50 knots
Cruising speed,
  foilborne, sea state 0–5: in excess of 40 knots
  hullborne: 11 knots

Sea state: can negotiate 10ft seas at speeds in excess of 40 knots

Range, foilborne: in excess of 600n miles
hullborne: in excess of 1,800n miles

BOEING JETFOIL 929-100

This is a 110-ton waterjet-propelled commercial hydrofoil for services in relatively rough waters. It employs a fully-submerged, automatically-controlled canard foil arrangement and is powered by two 3,710hp Allison 501-K20A gas turbines. Normal foilborne cruising speed is 42 knots.

Typical interior arrangements include a commuter configuration with up to 350 seats and a tourist layout for 190 to 250 plus baggage.

The company is also evaluating various utility models with open load decks suitable for search and rescue duties, offshore oil-rig support and firefighting. Two utility derivatives for offshore rig crew and priority/emergency cargo support are showing great potential. They are 50 and 100 seat crew/supply boat versions with considerable cargo capacity for supporting rigs within 50 to 250n miles from shore.

Commercial Jetfoils in service include 12 with Far East Hydrofoil Co Ltd, Hong Kong; two with Sado Kisen Kaisha, Japan; two with Trasmediterranea SA in the Canary Islands and two with RMT, the Belgian state-owned ferry company between Dover, England and Ostend, Belgium.

The Indonesian Government has purchased a Jetfoil for the Agency for the Study and Application of Technology in roles including customs' duties, offshore oil operations, ocean resource control and commercial passenger transport. Boeing is working with a Norwegian company on the development of an offshore Jetfoil and a relative motion transfer system for transferring crews between oil rigs and the Jetfoil in rough water.

Additionally, HMS *Speedy*, an Ocean Patrol Hydrofoil (OPH) derivative of the Jetfoil has been operated by the Royal Navy in a protection role in the North Sea. HMS *Speedy* was launched in July 1979, and, on completion of outfitting by Vosper Thornycroft (UK) Ltd, was commissioned by the Royal Navy in June 1980. Due to budgetary reasons, HMS *Speedy* was decommissioned by the Royal Navy in April 1982.

By 30 June 1984 Jetfoils had logged 1,150 million passenger miles during 205,000 under way hours with a dispatch reliability of 99 per cent.

Keel-laying of the first Jetfoil took place at the company's Renton, Washington, plant in January 1973 and the craft was launched in March 1974. After testing on Puget Sound and in the Pacific, the craft was delivered to Pacific Sea Transportation Ltd for inter-island services in Hawaii. High speed foilborne tests began in Puget Sound in mid-July and it was reported that the vessel attained a speed of 48 knots during its runs.

During a rigorous testing programme to prove the boat's design and construction, Jetfoil One operated for 470 hours, including 237 hours foilborne. The latter phase of testing was conducted in the rough waters of the straits of Juan de Fuca and the Pacific Ocean, where it encountered wave swells as high as 9·1m (30ft), winds gusting up to 60 knots and wave chop averaging 1·8m (6ft) high.

The first operational Jetfoil service was successfully initiated in April 1975 by Far East Hydrofoil Co Ltd, of Hong Kong, with Jetfoil 002, *Madeira*. Before this, the Jetfoil received its ABS classification, was certificated by the Hong Kong Marine Department and passed US Coast Guard certification trials, although a US Coast Guard certificate was not completed as the craft would not be operating in US waters.

The first US service began in Hawaii in June 1975 with the first of three Jetfoils, 003 *Kamehameha*, starting inter-island runs. By the end of the summer all five Jetfoils were in service. The tenth Jetfoil was launched in May 1977. An active world-wide marketing programme is under way to sell these high-speed craft, which are priced at US $12·5 million (1983).

Jetfoil 0011, launched in June 1978, is the first

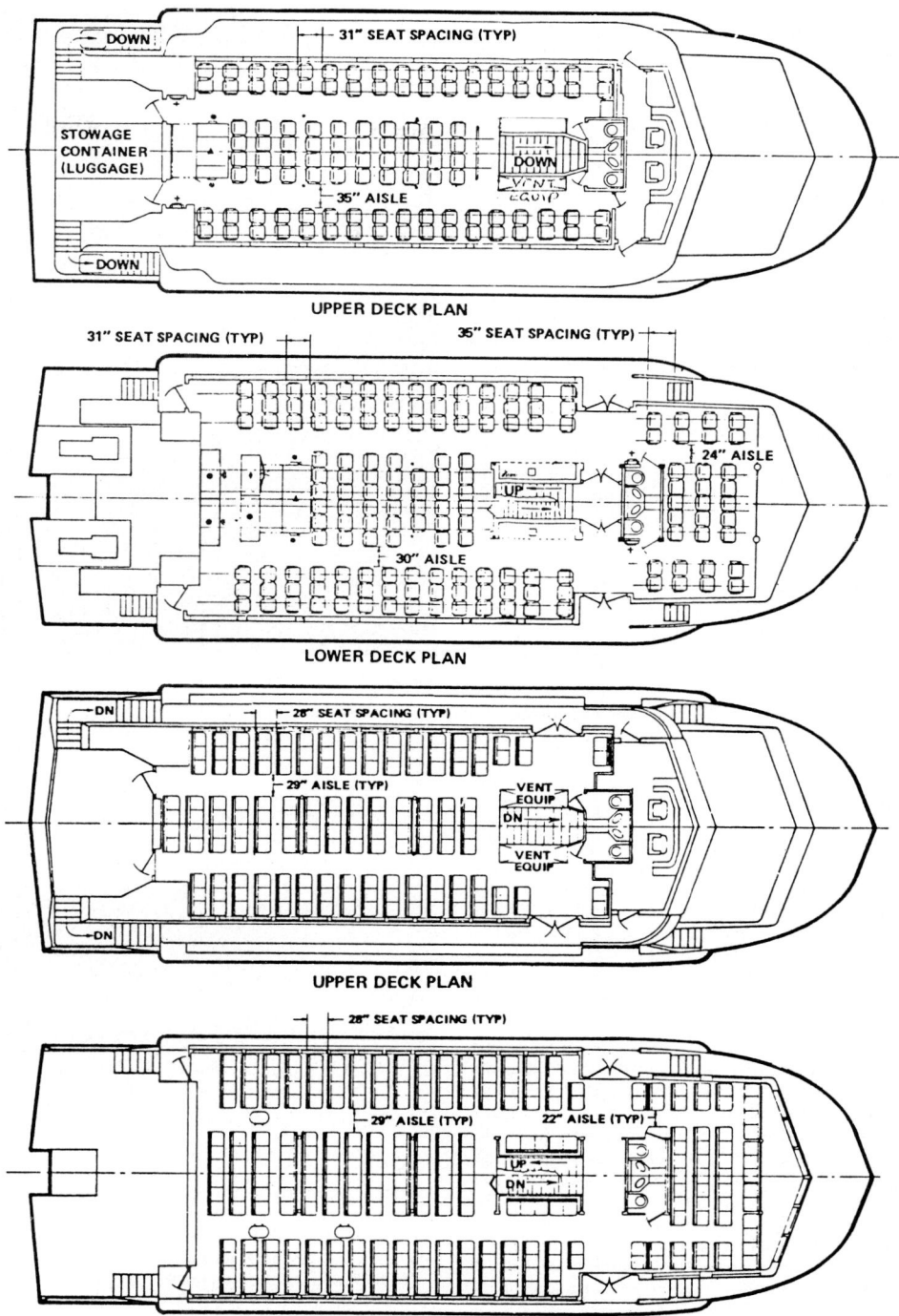

Jetfoil 929-100 interior arrangements

Jetfoil of improved design. Many of the modifications incorporated in this version, the Model 929-115, are based on operating experience and increase the Jetfoil's performance, payload and reliability.

FOILS: Fully-submerged canard arrangement with a single inverted T strut/foil forward and a three-strut, full-span foil aft. The forward foil assembly is rotated hydraulically through 7 degrees in either direction for steering. All foils have trailing-edge flaps for controlling pitch, roll and yaw and for take-off and landing. Hydraulically-driven foil flap actuators control the variation in flap positions through linkages between actuators and flap hinge points. Foils and struts retract hydraulically above the waterline, the bow foil forward, and the rear foil aft. All structural components of the foil/strut system are in 15·5PH corrosion resistant all-welded steel construction.

CONTROLS: The craft is controlled by a three-axis automatic system while it is foilborne and during take-off and landing. The system senses the motion and position of the craft by gyros, accelerometers and height sensors, signals from which are combined in the control computer with

manual commands from the helm. The resulting computer outputs provide control-surface deflections through electro-hydraulic servo actuators. Lift control is by full-span trailing edge flaps on each foil. Forward and aft flaps operate differentially to provide pitch variation and height control. Aft flaps operate differentially to provide roll control for changes of direction.

The vessel banks inwardly into all turns to ensure maximum passenger comfort. The ACS introduces the correct amount of bank and steering to co-ordinate the turn in full. Turn rates of up to six degrees per second are attained within one second of providing a heading change command at the helm.

Three basic controls are required for foilborne operation: the throttle is employed to set the speed, the height command lever to set the required foil depth, and the helm to set the required heading. If a constant course is required, a 'heading hold' circuit accomplishes this automatically.

For take-off, the foil depth is set, the two throttles advanced, and the hull clears the water in about 60 seconds. Acceleration continues until the craft automatically stabilises at the command

UPPER DECK PLAN

LOWER DECK PLAN

UPPER DECK PLAN

LOWER DECK PLAN

depth and the speed dictated by the throttle setting. The throttle setting is reduced for landing, the craft settling as the speed drops. The speed normally diminishes from 45 knots (cruising speed) to 15 knots in about 30 seconds. In emergencies more rapid landings can be made by the use of the height command lever to provide hull contact within two seconds.

HULL: Hull and deckhouse in marine aluminium. Aircraft assembly techniques are used, including high-speed mechanised welding processes.

POWER PLANT: Power for the waterjet propulsion system is supplied by two Allison 501-K20A free-power gas turbines, each rated at 3,300shp at 27°C (80°F) at sea level. Each is connected to a Rocketdyne Powerjet 20 axial-flow pump through a gearbox drive train. The two turbine/pump systems are located in their own bays, port and starboard, separated by the slot in the hull into which the central water strut retracts for hullborne operation. The system propels the craft in both foilborne and hullborne modes. When foilborne, water enters through the inlet at the forward lower end of the aft centre foil strut. At the top of the duct, the water is split into two paths and enters into each of the two axial flow pumps. It is then discharged at high pressure through nozzles in the hull bottom.

The water path is the same during hullborne operations with the foils extended. When the foils are retracted, the water enters through a flush inlet located in the keel. Reversing and steering for hullborne operation only are accomplished by reverse-flow buckets located immediately aft of the water exit nozzles. A bow thruster is provided for positive steering control at low forward speeds.

A 15,140-litre (4,000-gallon) integral fuel tank supplies the propulsion turbine and diesel engines. Recommended fuel is Diesel No 2. The tank is fitted with a 5cm (2in) diameter fill pipe and fittings compatible with dockside refuelling equipment. Coalescent-type water separating fuel filters and remote-controlled motor-operated fuel shut-off valves provide fire protection.

ACCOMMODATION: Air-conditioned passenger accommodation on two decks connected by a wide, enclosed stairway. Seats are track-mounted to facilitate spacing changes, removal or replacement. The cabins have 914mm (3ft) wide aisles and 2·06m (6ft 9in) headroom. In the commuter configuration 1·58m³ (56ft³) per passenger is provided and 1·87m³ (66ft³) in the tourist configuration. Floors are carpeted and 61cm (2ft) seats are provided. Lighting is indirect and adjustable from the wheelhouse. Interior noise is near conversation level (below 68 dB SIL) and there is a public announcement system. Each deck level has two wc/washbasin units. There are drinking water dispensers on each passenger deck.

Quality of the ride in the craft is comparable with that of a Boeing 727 airliner. The vertical acceleration at the centre of gravity is very low and depends on sea state. For example, at 2 metres significant wave height the vertical acceleration is only 0·05g RMS. Lateral acceleration is substantially less than vertical. Angles of pitch and roll are less than 1 degree RMS. A structural fuse is provided which limits deceleration to less than 0·4 g longitudinally and 0·8 g vertically. In the event of the craft striking a major item of floating debris at full speed, the structural fuse, when actuated, allows the foil and strut to rotate backwards, protecting the system from sustaining significant damage.

Crew comprises a captain and first officer plus cabin attendants.

SYSTEMS, ELECTRICAL: 60Hz, 440V ac electrical system, supplied by two diesel-driven generators each rated at 62·5kVA. Either is capable of supplying all vital electrical power. 90kVA capacity shore connection facilities provided, and equipment can accept 50Hz power. Transformer rectifier units for battery charging provide 28V dc from the ac system.

HYDRAULICS: 210·9kg/cm² (3,000psi) system

Jetfoil 929-115 *Bima Samudera*

Jetfoil 929-115 operated by RMT (Sealink)

to actuate control surfaces. Each pump is connected to a separate system to provide split system redundancy in the event of a turbine, pump, distribution system or actuator malfunctioning.

EMERGENCY: Craft meets all applicable safety regulations of the US Coast Guard and SOLAS. Hull provides two-compartment subdivision and a high degree of stability. Life rafts and life jackets are provided.

NAVIGATION: Equipment includes radar. A low-light-level television system covering potential collision zone is available as an optional extra.

DIMENSIONS
Length overall, foils extended: 27·4m (90ft)
   foils retracted: 30·1m (99ft)
Beam overall, max: 9·5m (31ft)
Draught hullborne,
   foils retracted: 1·5m (4ft 10in)
   foils extended: 5m (16ft 4in)
WEIGHTS
Displacement: 110 tons
PERFORMANCE
Max speed: 50 knots
Normal service speed: 42 knots
Turning radius at 45 knots: less than 304·8m
   (1,000ft)
Normal endurance at cruising speed: 4 hours
Max endurance: 8 hours
Max wave height foilborne: 3·65m (12ft)

BOEING 929-115

The last of the Jetfoil 929-100 series was the 0010 *Flying Princess II*. The first of the improved 929-115 series, Jetfoil 0011 *Mikado*, was launched at Renton, Washington in June 1978, and is now operated by Sado Kisen in the Sea of Japan.

A number of detail changes have been made in order to comply with the international naval craft code, but most have been made as a result of operating experience with the earlier model. The improved model Jetfoil has an increased payload, greater reliability and is easier to maintain. Some of the modifications are listed below.

FOILS: External stiffeners on the foil struts have been eliminated and the bow foil has been changed from constant section to tapered planform for improved performance. Stress levels have been reduced for extended life.

CONTROLS: Heading hold (autopilot) installed as basic equipment. Automatic control system 'Autotrim' is improved to reduce steady state pitch and depth errors to negligible values. This reduces or eliminates the need for foil angle of incidence adjustments. A higher thrust bow-thruster is fitted and the navigation radar is now installed on a pedestal between the captain and first officer so that it can be swivelled for viewing from either position.

HULL: The bow structure design has been simplified to provide equivalent strength with increased payload and bulkhead 2 has been revised for decreased stress levels. Based on a seven-minute evacuation time in case of fire the following fire protection provisions have been made:

Fibreglass is used for thermal insulation where required throughout the passenger accommodation areas.

Aluminium ceiling panels, window reveals and air conditioner sleeves are employed throughout, together with aluminium doors and frames.

One-half inch thick Marinite is employed in machinery spaces, with US Coast Guard-type felt added wherever required for insulation to comply with 30-minute fire test.

Carpet, seat fabrics and lining materials meet low flame spread, toxicity and smoke requirements of US Coast Guard and Department of Trade, United Kingdom.

POWER PLANT: The propulsion system has been uprated to operate at 2,200 maximum intermittent pump rpm with an increase of 3 tons in maximum gross weight.

ACCOMMODATION: Seats of revised design are fitted; environmental control unit has been located forward to increase payload and aid servicing, stairway to upper deck has a round handrail for better grip.

SYSTEMS, ELECTRICAL: Dc system is now in the wheelhouse to comply with new dynamically-supported craft rules. Ac panels relocated to be closer to equipment served to reduce wire runs. Redundant power sources are provided from either diesel generator for services to 24V dc emergency loads and loads essential for foilborne operation. Emergency 24V dc lights have been added in lavatories and aft machinery areas. Daylight signalling lamps with self-contained batteries are provided.

HYDRAULICS: System is consolidated with one manifold and reduced piping.

AIR CONDITIONING: Machinery moved forward to space above the main stairway and forward machinery space to improve operation and servicing.

DIESEL FUEL SYSTEM: Separate fuel systems supply the propulsion engines and diesel generators. This allows alternate fuels to be used in the turbines and greatly simplifies the plumbing system.

SEAWATER SYSTEM: Cooling water for the propulsion system has been separated from the remainder of the system. This simplifies the system and improves its reliability.

MISCELLANEOUS: Originally the hull corrosion prevention system was based on the isolation of dissimilar metals and ship-to-shore grounding. The new approach uses dockside impressed current, resistance-controlled shorting of struts and foils to the hull, additional pod anodes and elec-

trical isolation. Other changes include a changeover to titanium seawater piping, a change in seawater pump materials and protective painting added to the hydraulic system.

DIMENSIONS
Length overall, foils extended: 27·4m (90ft)
Beam, max: 9·5m (31ft)
Draught,
  foils extended: 5·2m (17ft)
  foils retracted: 1·7m (5ft 6in)
Height (without retractable mast),
  hullborne, above mean waterline: 12·8m (42ft)
  foilborne, at 2·4m (8ft) foil depth: 15·5m (51ft)

WEIGHTS
Fully loaded displacement: 115 long tons
PERFORMANCE
Design cruising speed: 43 knots (80km/h; 50mph)

BOEING MODEL 929-120

Indonesia has reached agreement with Boeing Marine Systems for the purchase of four Boeing Jetfoil hydrofoils and has taken an option on six additional Jetfoils.

The initial contract, valued at approximately US$150 million, is for the purchase of four Jetfoils for coastal patrol. Boeing will assist P T Pabrik Kapal (P T Pal), the Indonesian

Impression of Boeing Jetfoil 929-120 hydrofoil fast patrol boat for Indonesian Navy

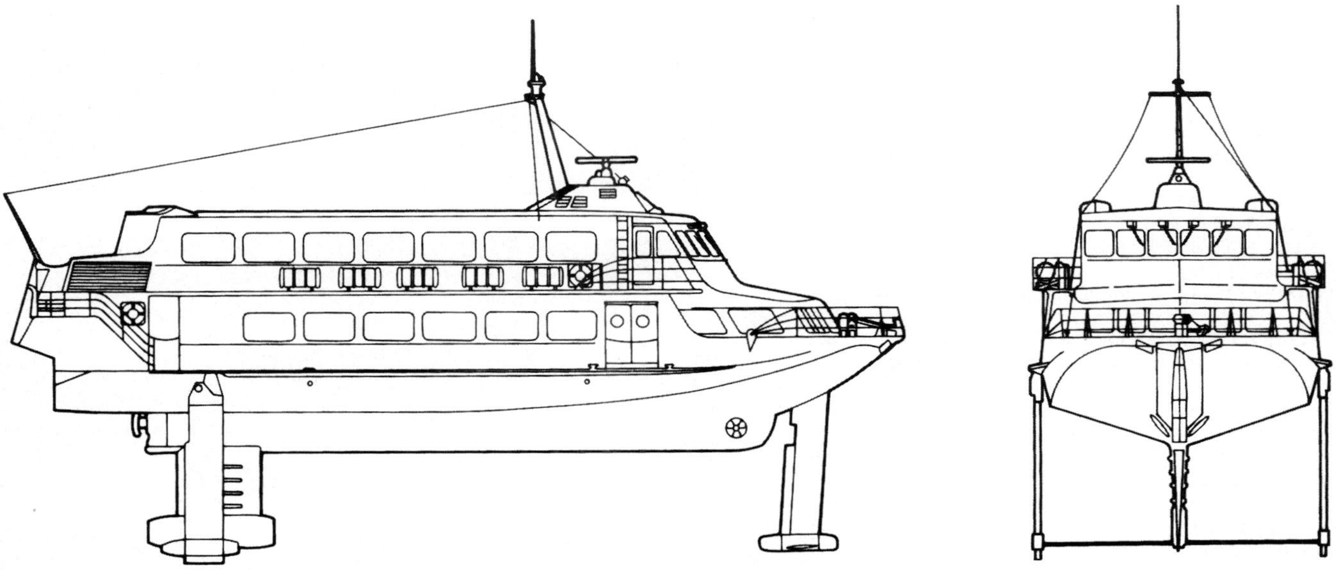

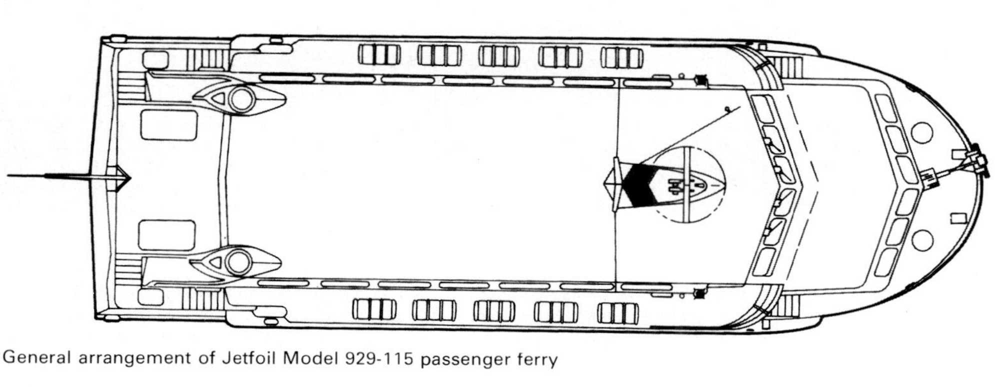

General arrangement of Jetfoil Model 929-115 passenger ferry

national shipbuilding facility, in developing its capability for high technology hydrofoil manufacture. During these preparations Boeing will manufacture and supply to Indonesia components for the struts, foils and the automatic control system.

The rate of programme expansion will depend on Indonesia's economic growth, which is moderate at present due to reduced world oil prices. If Indonesia takes up the option on a further six Jetfoils, the contract value to Boeing would total US$330 million.

The first two Jetfoils, Model 929-119s, were to be delivered in 1984 for use as personnel transport, followed by one Model 929-120 fast patrol boat in 1985 and one in 1986. These will be structurally complete and P T Pal will fit them out.

A Boeing Jetfoil, *Bima Sumudera 1,* was purchased by Indonesia in 1981 and used to evaluate hydrofoil potential for coastal patrol and commercial applications. During evaluation the Jetfoil established several records, including a continuous foilborne operation of 11 hours, 8 minutes.

The Indonesian trials covered nearly 10,000 nautical miles during 245 hours underway and proved the Jetfoil's stability and reliability. As a result, the Indonesian Navy has identified a long-term requirement for up to 47 Jetfoils. Commercial passenger-carrying Jetfoils would be in addition to that order.

Boeing Marine Systems anticipates there will be an increase in the number employed on the programme from the current 420 to a peak of 650 in 1985. An additional 20 Boeing employees will be required to give on-site support in Indonesia.

JETFOIL 929-320

The first Jetfoil 929-320 was delivered to the Royal Navy in June 1980 for use in offshore protection in the North Sea. Named HMS *Speedy,* the craft was a modified Model 929-115 commercial Jetfoil and was built on the commercial Jetfoil production line. Due to defence cuts, the craft was decommissioned by the Royal Navy in April 1982. This concept has now evolved into a new model, 929-320, incorporating the well-tested commercial Jetfoil systems into a basic military platform. Power for foilborne operation is provided by two Allison 501-K20A gas turbines and two Allison 8V92T1 diesels are installed for hullborne operation, giving increased on-station time and endurance.

Externally the Model 929-320 resembles the projected Boeing Offshore Jetfoil, with the top passenger deck removed to provide an open deck measuring 4·87 × 7·31m (16 × 24ft) which accommodates two semi-inflatable dinghies on davits. Light weapons will be carried. Displacement is 117 tons.
DIMENSIONS: As for Jetfoil Model 929-115.

BOEING 929-202 OFFSHORE JETFOIL

The offshore crew model of the Jetfoil is based on the Boeing 929-115 but incorporates a number of modifications, some of which are described below.
DECKHOUSE: The aft section of the upper deckhouse has been removed to provide a working deck for a personnel transfer system and light priority cargo.
FUEL: Tanks of increased capacity for longer routes.
AUXILIARY CONTROL STATION: A stern-directed hullborne auxiliary control station has been added to help position the vessel and control the personnel transfer system.
BOW THRUSTER CONTROL: An integrated hullborne joystick control co-ordinates the operation of a new bow thruster and an improved main thrusting control. Main thruster steering and reversing deflectors can be splayed in a similar way to split rudder control and provide lateral thrusting.
COMMUNICATIONS: Navigation and communications equipment for offshore service, including dual radar, Decca positioner, radio direction finder, dual VHF radios and MF radio-telephone.

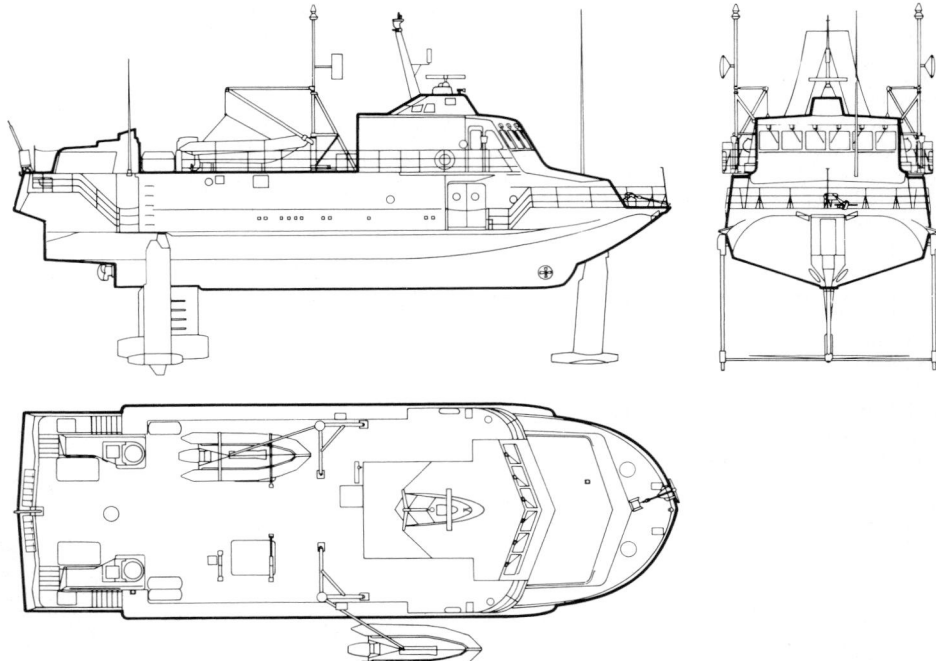

General arrangement of Jetfoil Model 929-320

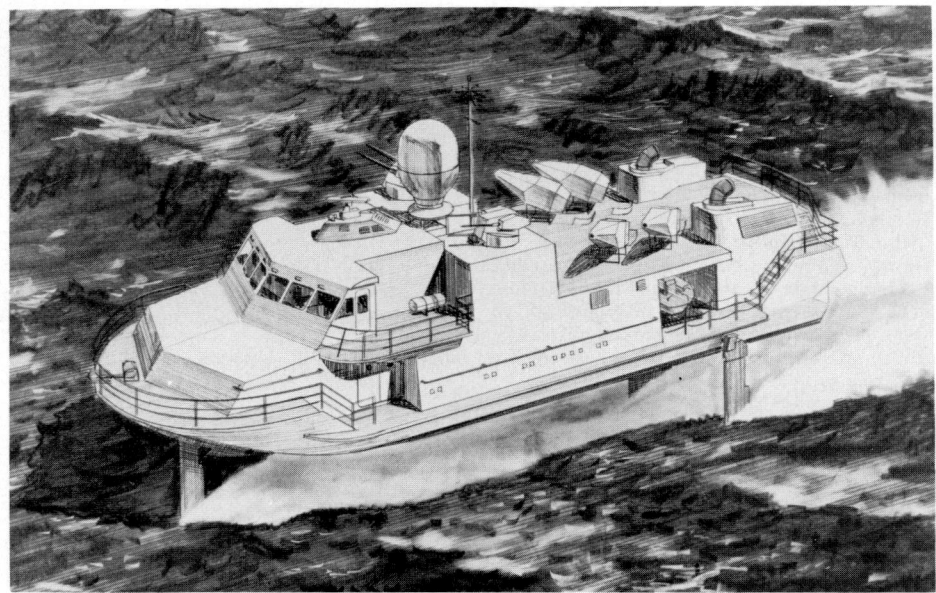

Boeing 929-320 in anti-ship/coastal patrol configuration

Boeing 929-320 Jetfoil in hydrofoil gunboat configuration

ROLL ATTENTUATION: A paravane roll attentuation system reduces hullborne roll motions by about 30 per cent during transfer operations.

ACCOMMODATION: In typical configuration the main deck seats 159 in reclining aircraft-type seats. Two washrooms forward and galley units aft. The internal stairway forward leads to the upper cabin and the upper deck, from where passengers are transferred. The upper cabin contains deluxe seating for eight on the port side, aft of the primary control station. Passenger capacity is 167, the crew requirement is six, comprising two operators, two deckhands and two cabin attendants.

TRANSFER SYSTEM: This comprises a cab or gondola for the batch transfer of passengers, which the crew controls by adjusting the tension forces applied to the connecting cables. With the gondola above the maximum heave elevation of the Jetfoil, the rig-platform crane operator takes over, hoisting and slewing the gondola onto the platform deck. During descent the rig-platform crane operator lowers the gondola to approximately 6m (20ft) above the Jetfoil's mid-heave elevation and holds. The Jetfoil operator pulls the gondola down onto the deck at controlled speed. The gondola matches the deck-heave motion as it approaches the landing cushion. There is provision for communication and emergency release from inside the gondola between the Jetfoil and the rig crane.

DIMENSIONS
Hull length: 27·2m (89ft)
Hull width: 9·2m (30ft)
Hullborne draught,
    foils extended: 5·2m (17ft)
    foils retracted: 1·8m (5ft 11in)
Hullborne height,
    mast up: 12·8m (42ft)
    mast retracted: 8·2m (27ft)
Passenger accommodation: 4·9 × 7·3m (16 × 24ft)

WEIGHTS
Max foilborne displacement: 117,000kg (115 tons)
Useful load: 40,950kg (40 tons)
Fuel capacity,
    volume: 30·3m³ (8,000 gallons)
    weight: 25,450kg (25 long tons)

PERFORMANCE
Speed,
    foilborne: 43 knots
    hullborne: 10 to 15 knots
Range, calm water 30% reserve: 475n miles

MILITARY JETFOIL

New configurations evolving from the construction of HMS *Speedy* include the following variants:

TROOP TRANSPORT

In this configuration the Jetfoil can fly 250 troops and their equipment 300n miles in seven hours. Since it draws only 1·8m in the hullborne mode with foils retracted, it can use most docking facilities.

CARGO CARRIER

Up to 35 tons of high-priority cargo can be flown up to 600n miles without refuelling. With seats and carpeting removed the lower deck provides 230m³ of storage space. Access is through forward and aft doors on both sides of the superstructure. The forward doors are 2m high by 1·5m wide and the aft doors 2m high by 1m wide. A special door 2m high by 3·5m wide is optional. In addition to lower deck cargo, up to 96 troops can be seated on the upper deck.

MEDICAL EVACUATION

Up to 213 litter cases with their attendants can be evacuated at a time. Special facilities are provided for the treatment of emergency cases while under way. Conversion from the standard Jetfoil configuration can be accomplished in 4 hours. Seats are removed and replaced with litter stanchions from a medical evacuation kit which can be stowed aboard for emergency use.

FISHERIES AND OFFSHORE RESOURCES PROTECTION

This version, which can be sea- or shore-based, can be equipped for search and rescue duties, law and treaty enforcement, anti-smuggling patrol and similar missions.

Boeing 929-202 Offshore Jetfoil showing rig crew transfer system

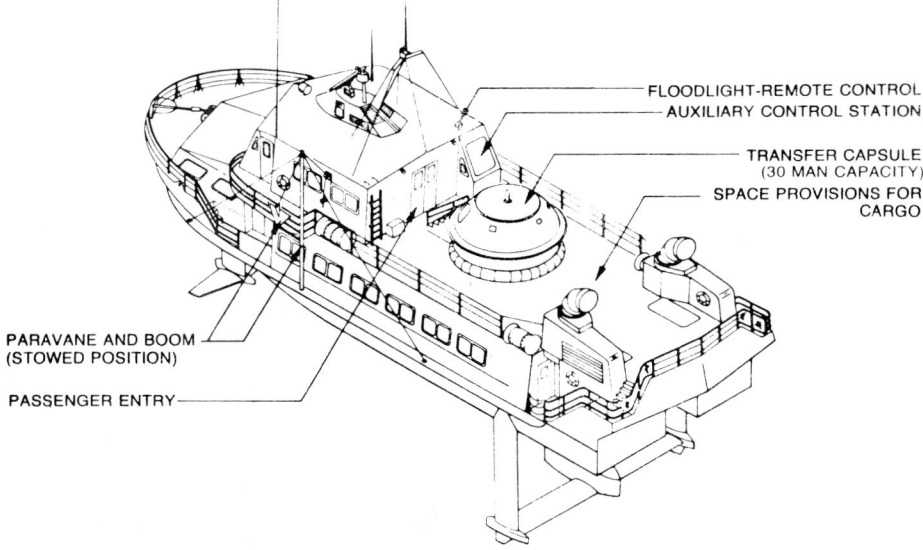

FLOODLIGHT-REMOTE CONTROL
AUXILIARY CONTROL STATION
TRANSFER CAPSULE (30 MAN CAPACITY)
SPACE PROVISIONS FOR CARGO
PARAVANE AND BOOM (STOWED POSITION)
PASSENGER ENTRY

Boeing 929-202 Offshore Jetfoil

COUNTER INSURGENCY VEHICLE

Two fully equipped 12-man patrols, complete with inflatable dinghies, can be carried by this variant. Its defensive armament, mounted above bridge level for maximum field of fire, comprises a twin 30mm rapid-fire cannon.

ANTI-SHIP/COASTAL PATROL CRAFT

Intended as a fast, economical weapons platform, this version is armed with six anti-ship missiles on two triple-tube lightweight launchers plus a single OTO Melara 76mm rapid fire cannon for air defence, together with launchers for rapid blooming off-board chaff (RBOC). The combat system level of automation, similar to that of the PHM, allows one man, unassisted, to engage simultaneously air and surface targets with guns and missiles respectively. A crew of 12 would be carried.

MODULAR JETFOIL

Boeing is considering the export of Jetfoils on a modular basis. One approach would be to supply commercial and military operators with the basic Jetfoil hull, complete with foils, powerplant and control system and the operator would install his own superstructure.

This would give them access to craft embodying the latest developments in hydrofoil technology and permit them to add superstructure tailored to their own particular needs. Variants would range from passenger ferries and utility craft for offshore marine operations, to coast-guard patrol vessels and missile gunboats.

The modular concept is expected to appeal in particular to lesser developed countries, since by completing the craft locally, a useful saving in hard currency could be realised. A substantial amount of the superstructure could be riveted together by fairly low-skilled labour.

Maintenance requirements are expected to be reasonably low. The Allison 501-K20A gas turbines have a life of 18,000 hours. The Boeing Automatic Control System, one of the most complex components of the design, is modularly built and maintained on an 'on condition basis' by removing and replacing circuit cards.

Allison is willing to negotiate contract rates for servicing the gas turbines at a fixed-rate per operating hour.

Boeing states that modifications could be made to the design to allow the installation of alternative engines, such as the Rolls Royce Tyne or Proteus, should countries like the United Kingdom prefer them.

Weapons suitable for the military models include the OTO Melara 76mm rapid fire cannon and the Emerson 30mm cannon, the Argo control system and the Otomat, Exocet, Penguin and Gabriel anti-ship missiles.

Another Boeing concept is the regional final assembly centre, a number of which would be established around the world to supply customers with complete vessels made up from imported hulls and superstructures. This arrangement would also meet the growing demand in lesser developed areas for greater participation in industrial programmes.

The centres, which would not be owned or operated by Boeing, would simply be involved with their importation, assembly and marketing. Likely areas for the establishment of these centres include the Caribbean, Greece, Iran, Japan, Taiwan, Indonesia and Scandinavia.

Boeing 929-202 Offshore Jetfoil

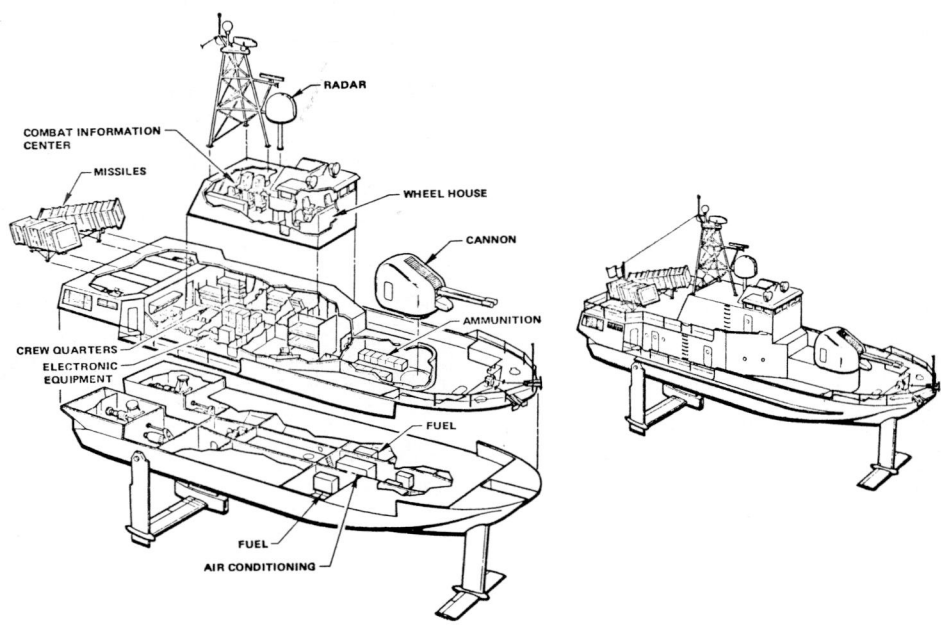

Projected 117-ton fast patrol boat modular version of Jetfoil

CALKINS

15819 SE 50th Street, Bellevue, Washington 98006, USA

Official:

D E Calkins, *DEng, PE, Proprietor*

D E Calkins, research associate professor at the University of Washington, has developed a hybrid hydrofoil catamaran concept which combines a planing catamaran hull with two constant chord foils mounted in tandem fore and aft of the longitudinal centre of gravity. The objective has been to develop a fast craft with a sea state performance midway between that of a surface-piercing and a fully-submerged hydrofoil. Smooth and rough water tests of the concept, known as HYCAT for HYdrofoil CATamaran, have been conducted in the towing tank at the Institute of Technological Research of the University of São Paulo, Brazil. A 1/22·5 scale free-running dynamic model is under construction. Powered by twin 0·2hp electric motors and radio-controlled, it will be used to assess the free-running manoeuvring characteristics of the craft in its current configuration.

HYCAT

The design objectives during the development of this concept were to produce a simple, low-cost advanced marine vehicle for the mass transport market. It has been based on existing technology developed by the US Navy and its contractors. FOILS: Tandem configuration with two constant chord foils mounted fore and aft of the longitudinal centre of gravity. Although flat foils are used in the initial design, dihedral can be incorporated in the outer panels for improved roll stability and

HYCAT showing fixed-pitch propellers

rough water handling. Additionally, streamlined fuel pods can be fitted in the sidehull keels for increased range. The structural weight of the pods plus the fuel weight would be slightly less than the pod buoyancy. As the size of the craft increases, outer hydrofoil panels can be added to optimise the foil loading. Dynamic lift is by the hydrofoils and the spray strips, while the immersed portion of the sidehulls provides buoyancy to support the craft's weight. Stability in heave, pitch and roll is given by the lift from sidehull buoyancy and the displacement dependent lift developed by the foils and spray strips. Dynamic stability is thereby achieved passively, without an automatic control system. Incidence angle of the forward foil can be controlled hydraulically to assist take-off and trim.

POWER PLANT: Powered by two General

Motors 16V149 T1 Detroit Diesels, each rated at 1,600shp maximum and 1,335shp continuous. Output is transferred to a standard fixed-pitch sub-cavitating propeller, the shafts of which are housed in the sidehulls to avoid appendage drag.

ACCOMMODATION: The prototype will seat 302 passengers assuming a seat pitch of 839mm (33in).

DIMENSIONS
Length overall: 24·6m (80ft 9in)
Beam, max: 9·1m (30ft)
Draught hullborne: 2·3 m (7ft 7in)
  foilborne: 1·7m (5ft 7in)
Height above mean waterline,
  hullborne: 7·6m (25ft)
  foilborne: 8·8m (29ft)
WEIGHTS
Displacement: 99·5 tons
Light ship: 65·3 tons
Useful load: 34·2 tons
PERFORMANCE
Max speed: 38·1 knots
Cruising speed, calm water: 32·5 knots
Range at cruising speed: 700n miles
Fuel (normal): 12,726 litres (2,800 gallons)
Fuel consumption at cruising speed: 636·4 litres/h (140 gallons/h)

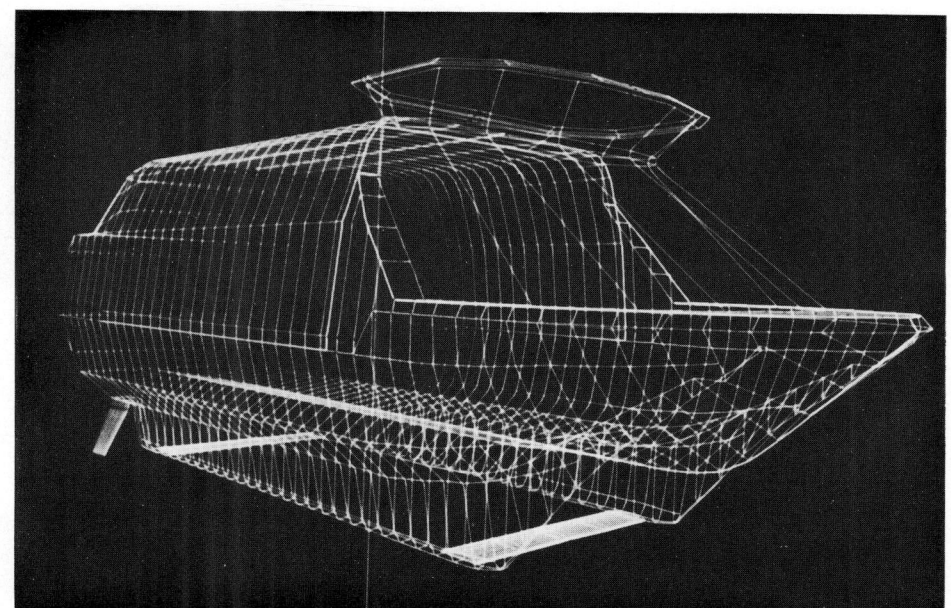

Wire-frame computer graphics image of HYCAT

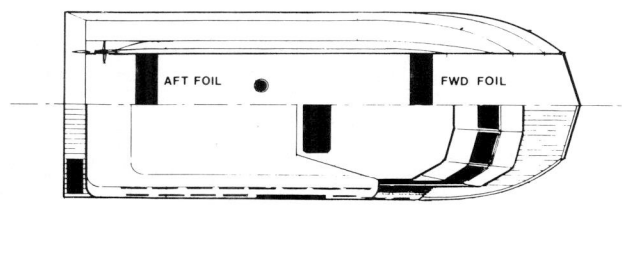

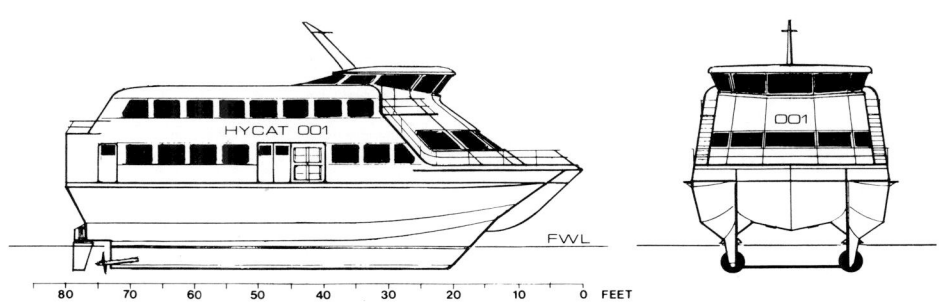

HYCAT 100-ton prototype

HYCAT showing constant chord bow foil

DAK HYDROFOILS

526 Third Avenue, San Francisco, California
94118, USA
Telephone: (415) 752 8748
Official:
David A Keiper, *Proprietor and Chief Designer*

Dak Hydrofoils is currently designing and
developing simple low-cost hydrofoil conversion
kits for outboard powerboats. These are based on
those available from the company for existing
racing catamarans.

The arrangement employs identical lateral
foils, positioned in a similar location, plus a
fully-submerged stern foil. Lighter craft will have
a simple foil beneath the outboard engine.
Heavier craft, of up to 680·38kg (1,500lb) loaded
weight, have a retractable 152mm (6in) chord
foil supported by twin struts.

12ft dinghy equipped with DAK hydrofoils and powered by 9·5hp engine

The propeller is lowered by a combination of
engine shaft extension or extensions, and/or lowering the engine by means of parallel bars.

DYNAFOIL INC

881 West 16th Street, Newport Beach, California
92663, USA
Telephone: (714) 645 3201
Officials:
David J Cline, *Chairman*
James M Dale, *Secretary/Treasurer*
Paul D Griem, *Executive Vice President*

Dynafoil, Inc was formed in December 1971 to
develop the Dynafoil sport craft. The development of this vehicle began in late 1970 with the
construction of IRMA 1, the foil configuration of
which has been the foundation for all subsequent
work. Patents for the foil configuration have been
applied for in all the main consumer countries,
and have been granted in the USA.

DYNAFOIL MARK I

This fibreglass-hulled sports hydrofoil is a
marine counterpart to the motorcycle and snow-
mobile. The bow foil is mounted at the base of a
handlebar-equipped steering head and the handling characteristics are similar to those of a
motorcycle. Production began in June 1975.
FOILS: Canard configuration with a fully submerged main foil located aft and bearing 60 per
cent of the load and small incidence-controlled
twin-delta foil forward. The angle of incidence is
controlled mechanically by a curved planing control foil to achieve a constant flying height. The
control foil and the bow foils rotate on pitch axes
located forward of their centre of hydrodynamic
lift. In normal flight the trailing edge of the control foil skims the water surface, while the twin
delta bow and foil maintains its designed angle of
incidence. If the bow rises too high above the
mean water line, the control foil pitches upwards,
allowing the foils to operate in a neutral position,
in which it generates little or no lift. Conversely,
downward pitch at the bow decreases the angle of
attack of the control foil which, through a linkage
system, causes the bow foils to increase its incidence angle, thus restoring normal flight. The aft
foil has anhedral to prevent tip breeching and
ventilation and is set above the propeller. The
foils are in cast 356-T6 aluminium while the
struts are of fibreglass. Both foils retract fully, the
bow foil rotating upwards and rearwards, the aft
foil rearwards and upwards against the transom.
CONTROLS: Steering is accomplished by turning the front foil strut. All turns enter a fully
co-ordinated bank.
HULL: Two-stage deep V hull comprises two
fibreglass mouldings bonded together at the belt-
line. After bonding, all voids not employed for
functional components are filled with 2lb density
polyurethane foam providing 600lb of buoyancy.
ACCOMMODATION: Open cockpit with a
motorcycle pillion-style seat for two.
POWER PLANT: The Mark I is available with a
choice of two engines—either a 340cc, 26hp, or a
high performance 440cc, 36hp, two-cylinder,
two-stroke Xenoah engine. Power is delivered to
the outdrive through a 90-degree gearbox
mounted inboard. The overall gear ratio is
1·75:1. Final drive is through a bevel gear at the
base of the rear strut. The propeller, made by

Dynafoil Mk I

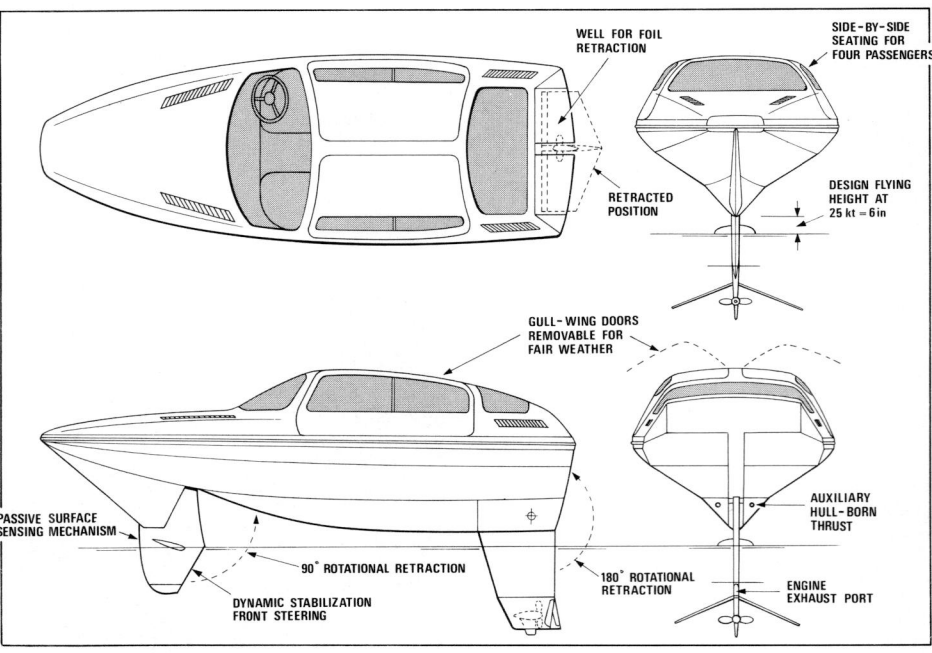

Dynafoil Mk II

Michigan Wheel, is of three-bladed subcavitating
design in cast aluminium. A single 18·92-litre
(5-US gallon) fuel tank is located amidships, with
a refuelling neck on the outside hull at the bow.
DIMENSIONS
Length overall, hull: 2·13m (7ft)
  foils retracted: 2·43m (8ft)
  foils extended: 2·13m (7ft)
Beam overall,
  foils retracted: 1·06m (3ft 6in)
  foils extended: 1·06m (3ft 6in)
Draught hullborne,
  foils retracted: 304mm (1ft)
  foils extended: 914mm (3ft)
Draught foilborne: 457mm (1ft 6in)
Freeboard: 355mm (1ft 2in)
Height overall: 1·06m (3ft 6in)
  hullborne: 609mm (2ft)
WEIGHTS
Light displacement: 158·75kg (350lb)
Normal take-off displacement: 272·14kg (550lb)
Max take-off displacement: 362·85kg (800lb)

PERFORMANCE
Max speed, foilborne: 64·36km/h (40mph)
  hullborne: 8·04km/h (5mph)
Cruising speed,
  foilborne: 48·28km/h (30mph)
  hullborne: 8·04km/h (5mph)
Designed endurance and range at cruising speed, approx: 104·6km (65 miles)
Turning radius at cruising speed: 4·57m (15ft)
Fuel consumption at max speed: 9–22·7 litres/hour (2–5 gallons/hour)

SEA TEST: Craft has been tested in 0·9 to 1·2m (3 to 4ft) chop and 2·4 to 3m (8 to 10ft) swells.

PRICE: $1,995, plus options (1983).

MILITARY DYNAFOIL

Tentative interest has been shown in a military version of the Dynafoil Mk II. Feasibility studies are being undertaken by the company but no construction timetable has yet been established. A four-seater, it would employ the same basic foil configuration as Dynafoil Mk I. Power would be supplied by a 700hp turbocharged V-8 automotive engine. Hydraulic foil retraction is envisaged.

DIMENSIONS
Length overall: 7·62m (25ft)
WEIGHTS
Max take-off displacement: 2,722kg (6,000lb)
Light displacement: 1,814kg (4,000lb)

PERFORMANCE
Cruising speed: 96km/h (60mph)

MARK III

As an intermediate step towards construction of the larger Mark II, the company is operating a 12ft (3·65m) development prototype using a hydrofoil configuration identical to the Mark I. Known as Mark III, this vehicle is undergoing evaluation trials to ascertain performance characteristics before construction of the Mark II. It has already achieved its design goal of foilborne operation at 453·57kg (1,000lb) gross vehicle weight, and has reached a speed of 35mph when powered by a 45hp engine.

EDO CORPORATION, GOVERNMENT PRODUCTS DIVISION

13-10 111th Street, College Point, New York 11356, USA
Officials:
L M Swanson, *Director, Air MCM Applications*

Edo Corporation has developed a foil-equipped catamaran MCM system which speeds the process of magnetic mine clearance and reduces the hazards of mine sweeping operations. The system, the Edo Mark 105, is designed to be towed by the US Navy's RH-53D Sea Stallion and other heavy-lift helicopters of similar size and performance. The first unit formed to operate Mk 105 Airborne Minesweeping Gear was the HM-12 helicopter mine countermeasures squadron, which operated off North Viet-Nam to clear mines from the entrance to the port of Haiphong and undertook the aerial sweeping of the Suez Canal during the spring of 1974. The operation, code named Nimbus Star, was said to have been a complete success.

It has been stated that a mine can be detonated almost immediately beneath the Mk 105 without the craft sustaining major structural damage.

If required, the equipment can be towed behind a BHC BH.7 Mk 20 Minehunter/Disposal hovercraft or other suitable amphibious ACV. Tests with this arrangement have been undertaken in the United Kingdom and USA.

It is reported that ten RH-53D Sea Stallions, together with towed sweeping equipment, have been supplied to the Naval Air Transport Battalion, Iran.

Advantages claimed for the system include: lower acquisition and maintenance costs; fewer operating personnel; low equipment vulnerability and bigger areas cleared within a given time.

Normally the helicopter/seasled combination is conveyed to the affected area aboard an amphibious assault craft. The helicopter lifts-off with the sled at the end of a line, lowers it into the water, extends its foils, and sets off to sweep the minefield.

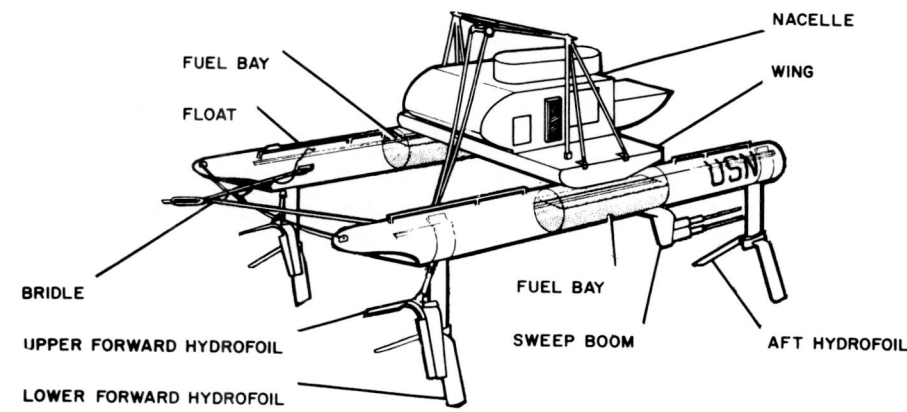

Surface-piercing tandem foil system of Edo Mk 105 and high-riding pitch-control subfoils

The towline, which is 137·16m (450ft) long, also serves as an electric cable for carrying control signals to the sled, and as a fuel transfer line in the case of extended operations.

A portable winch in the helicopter handles the craft, the sweep cables and the towing cable during launching and retrieval. The system can be operated from ships or shore bases equipped with crane facilities and small boats for handling the sweep cables which stream out behind the seasled.

In 1978 it was announced that Edo engineers are working on a system called the Lightweight Magnetic Sweep (LMS). Development is being undertaken for US Naval Air Systems Command. The Edo LMS is designed to improve the US Navy's airborne minesweeping capabilities now provided by the Edo Mk 105. It is said to offer a substantial advance in performance compared with previous systems.

Mk 105 AIRBORNE MINESWEEPING GEAR

The Mk 105 is a helicopter-towed, magnetic minesweeping system mounted on a 8·38m (27ft

6in) long catamaran seasled. Foils are fitted for high speed operation and provide improved seakeeping performance. Aboard the craft a turbogenerator provides energy for the magnetic sweep cables and powers a hydraulic pump for foil retraction.

FOILS: Surface-piercing tandem configuration with two inverted V foils forward and two aft, balancing the loading between them. High-riding pitch control subfoils of similar configuration are located ahead of the two bow foils. Bow and stern foils are rotated for retraction and extension by a self-contained hydraulic system.

HULL: Catamaran hull comprising two tubular pontoons of light metal alloy construction, connected by an aerofoil section platform on which is mounted a gas-turbine powered electric generator set and the retrieval rig structure to which handling lines are attached. The two ends of the towing bridle are attached to the inward faces of the twin pontoon hulls forward of the platform. Wheels are attached to the underside of the pontoons to facilitate deck handling. Fuel for the turbogenerator set is carried in two centrally located tanks, one in each pontoon.

Edo Mk 105

Edo Mk 105

Edo Mk 105 towed by RH-53D Sea Stallion

TOWING AND OPERATION: The 137·16m (450ft) long towing cable terminates in an electrical connector and fuel fitting. As well as providing the towing links between the platform and the helicopter, all electrical commands and supplementary fuel pass through the cable. The cable consists of an electrical core containing 19 individual conductors around which is a double layer of steel wire. Surrounding this is a hose and fuel flows through the annular space between the inner diameter of the hose and the steel wire reinforcement.

The 8·3m (27ft 6in) long sled is generally carried aboard an Amphibious Assault Ship (LPH) or Amphibious Transport Dock (LPD), which also act as a mobile base for the helicopters. The helicopter lifts the sled off the deck then lowers it into the water for completion of the sweepgear streaming operation.

The tow cable is then picked up and the sled is towed, foilborne, into the sweep area. Once in the area, the sled can be towed at lower speeds, hullborne, to simulate a displacement vessel and its magnetic (or in the case of the Mk 106, combined magnetic and acoustic) signature.

SYSTEMS: A gas-turbine generator set, mounted within a nacelle on the platform provides energy for the generation of the magnetic field. The complete power pack comprises a gas-turbine driven ac generator, a rectifier, a controller containing the waterborne electronics and batteries to power the electronics system.

MAGNETIC SWEEP CABLE: This is attached to the after end of the sweep boom located on the underside of the port pontoon. It comprises an upper electrode attached to the end of a trailing cable and a lower electrode fitted to the boom fin. The potential between the electrodes, employing the water as a conductor, produces a magnetic field which simulates that of a ship.

CONTROL PROGRAMMER: Located in the helicopter this is the only manned station employed in the system. It contains the airborne electronics and all the necessary controls and instrumentation.

The console contains the fuel transfer control panel, turbine indicators, hydrofoil and sweep boom actuators and the generator controls and indicators.

From the console the operator can start and stop the turbine, raise and lower the foils and control the magnetic influences generated through the conductor cables trailed behind the sled.

DIMENSIONS
Length overall: 8·38m (27ft 6in)
Beam,
   catamaran structure only: 3·53m (11ft 7in)
   across foils: 6·4m (21ft)
Height, foils extended,
   to top of retrieval rig: 5·26m (17ft 3in)
   to top of nacelle: 4·11m (13ft 6in)
   foils retracted, to base of wheels: 3·5m (11ft 6in)
WEIGHTS
Empty: 2,504kg (5,522lb)
Gross: 2,917kg (6,432lb)
PERFORMANCE
Towing speeds and sea state capability: not available

Mk 106

An earlier airborne minesweeping system was the Mk 104, which can also be carried, towed and recovered by helicopters. This is used to detonate acoustic mines. It comprises a venturi tube and a water-activated turbine which rotates a disc to reproduce a ship's acoustic signature. The latest model in the series combines the duties of the Mk 104 and 105 to provide both acoustic and magnetic influences and is known as the Mk 106.

GRUMMAN AEROSPACE CORPORATION

Bethpage, New York 11714, USA
Telephone: (516) 575 9691, Management and technical staff

Grumman has closed down its Advanced Marine Systems Division in order to concentrate its resources on aviation projects. However, a team of hydrofoil specialists from the division will continue to work in Israel under a technology exchange contract enabling Israel Shipyards, Haifa, to build 10 to 14 Grumman M161 Flagstaff II missile craft for the Israeli Navy and other clients.

The first Israeli-built M161, *Livnit* (Heron), began sea trials in July 1983. It is identical to the first of this class, which was built in the United States, and is undergoing identical performance tests. It is understood that no firm decision has been taken as to the number of M161s to be constructed and that the final figure is dependent on economic and political considerations.

Details of the M161 will be found on page 224. Descriptions of other Grumman hydrofoil designs will be found in *Jane's Surface Skimmers 1983* and earlier editions.

SAILING HYDROFOILS
JAPAN

KANAZAWA INSTITUTE OF TECHNOLOGY

Department of Mechanical Engineering, 7-1 Ogigaoka Nonoichimachi, Ishikawa 921, Japan
Telephone: 0762 48 1100
Official:
Yutaka Masuyama, *Researcher*

The Hydrodynamic Department of Mechanical Engineering, Kanazawa Institute of Technology, has been studying sailing hydrofoil craft since 1975. Three experimental craft have been built. Ichigo-Tei was completed in 1975 and tested in 1976. Employing data obtained from this craft, Hi-Trot II was built and tested in 1977 and Hi-Trot III was tested in 1979.

ICHIGO-TEI

This is a basic test rig to investigate the manoeuvrability, stability and balance of sails and foil systems. The Ichigo-Tei has a specially-designed catamaran hull, to which two surface-piercing bow foils and one stern foil are attached.
FOILS: The bow foils are of three-rung ladder configuration with removable outer rungs. The stern foil is of trapeze configuration with the rudder mounted immediately aft. Foil loading during a normal take-off is bow foils 60 per cent and stern foil 40 per cent. The foils, struts and rudder are in glass fibre and polyester resin. Foil section throughout is Göttinger 797, with 170mm (6·7in) chord.
HULL: Marine plywood sheathed with glass fibre and polyester resin.
SAIL: Sloop rig with a 10·2m² (110ft²) mainsail borrowed from the Hobie-cat 14, and a jib sail of 3·7m² (40ft²) borrowed from the Snipe.
DIMENSIONS
Length overall: 4·46m (14ft 8in)
    waterline: 4·2m (13ft 9in)
Hull beam: 2·2m (7ft 3in)
Width overall across foils: 4·3m (14ft 1in)
Draft afloat (fixed foils): 0·96m (3ft 2in)
    foilborne: 0·5-0·4m (1ft 8in-1ft 4in)
WEIGHTS
Empty: 140kg (309lb)
PERFORMANCE
Take-off speed: 6 knots with 11-knot wind
Max speed foilborne: 9 knots with 14-knot wind

HI-TROT II

Employing data gathered during the test programme conducted with Ichigo-Tei, the Kanazawa Institute of Technology design team built the Hi-Trot II. The hull is longer than that of the earlier craft, but the chief difference, apart from the adoption of a simpler foil system, is the use of a rotating sail rig.
FOILS: The split bow foil is of surface-piercing V-type, with cantilevered extensions, set at 40 degrees dihedral, at the apex. The bow foil section is ogival, with 250mm (9·8in) chord and a 12 per cent thickness-to-chord ratio. The aft foil is of inverted T type and the complete foil and strut assembly rotates for use as a rudder. About 80 per cent of the load is carried by the bow foils and the remaining 20 per cent by the stern foil. Foils, struts and rudder are in glass fibre, carbon fibre and epoxy resin.
HULL: Plywood structure sheathed with glass fibre and epoxy resin.
SAIL: Comprises three sail panels, each 4·2m², mounted in parallel. An air rudder automatically adjusts the attack angle of the sails to the wind. Each panel has a wing section and, though the section is symmetrical, it can form a camber on either side by bending at 40 per cent chord length. The leading edge of each wing is covered with thin aluminium sheet while the trailing edges are covered with terylene cloth. Wing frames are of plywood and polystyrene foam sandwich and provide the necessary buoyancy to prevent the craft from capsizing should it turn on its side. The surface of each wing is spray painted with polyurethane paint.

Ichigo-Tei

Hi-Trot II foilborne showing air rudder attached to central sail panel

Hi-Trot III during trials

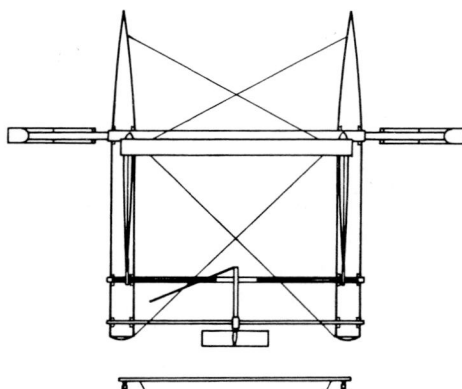

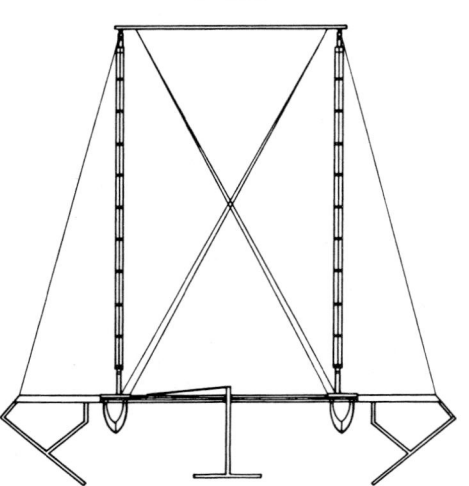

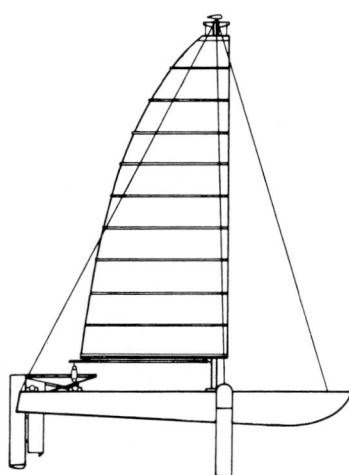

General arrangement of Hi-Trot III

DIMENSIONS
Length overall: 5·1m (16ft 9in)
 waterline: 4·95m (16ft 3in)
Hull beam: 2·68m (8ft 10in)
Beam, overall (fixed foils): 5·45m (17ft 11in)
Draught afloat (fixed foils): 1·1m (3ft 7in)
 foilborne: 0·55-0·4m (1ft 10in-1ft 4in)
WEIGHTS
Empty: 250kg (551lb)
PERFORMANCE
Take-off speed: 7 knots with 15-knot wind
Max speed foilborne: 11 knots with 17-knot wind
SEA TEST: The craft has been tested in 10-20
knot winds. Due to mechanical problems, tests could not be undertaken in wind speeds exceeding 20 knots. Improvements are being made to remedy this.

HI-TROT III

During 1978 the Kanazawa Institute of Technology design team constructed and tested a third craft, Hi-Trot III. The major difference between it and Hi-Trot II is the use of two parallel soft wing sails.
FOILS: The split bow foil is of surface-piercing Y-type, and the aft foil is of inverted T type as on the Hi-Trot II. Up to 90 per cent of the load is carried by the bow foils, and the remaining 10 per cent by the stern foil. Foils are of GFRP sandwich construction with polyurethane foam core and reinforced by carbon fibre.
HULL: Plywood structure sheathed with glass fibre and epoxy resin.
SAIL: Two parallel soft wing sails developed for Hi-Trot III, each 8m². Total sail area, 16m².
DIMENSIONS
Length overall: 5·08m (16ft 8in)
 waterline: 4·95m (16ft 3in)
Hull beam: 0·3m (1ft)
Beam overall, foils retracted: 3·74m (12ft 3in)
 foils extended: 6·84m (22ft 5in)
Draught afloat, foils retracted: 0·2m (8in)
 foils extended: 1m (3ft 3in)
Draught foilborne: 0·4m (1ft 4in)
WEIGHTS
Empty: 255kg (562lb)
PERFORMANCE: Hi-Trot III takes-off at 8 knots in a 15-knot wind and accelerates to 15 knots rapidly. The maximum speed attained during trials was 21 knots in an 18-knot wind (1·2 times wind speed).

UNION OF SOVIET SOCIALIST REPUBLICS

LENINGRAD SHIP DESIGN CENTRE
Leningrad, USSR

Experiments are being made in Leningrad with rigid wing-type sails with slotted flaps. Preliminary analysis indicates that the Kometa passenger hydrofoil, converted into a sailing trimaran, could well prove a passenger ship of the future. The sail system would not merely be an auxiliary source of propulsion, but would constitute the main source.

The system would comprise two vertically-inclined sail wings with a total area of 1,100 square metres. Estimated speed, with favourable winds, would be up to 32 knots. The craft would also be equipped with turbojet engines for generating the necessary thrust for take-off and foilborne operation. Length of the craft would be 39·5m, beam 50m and displacement 58 tonnes. Seats would be provided for 90 passengers.

Impression of Kometa sailing trimaran conversion

UNITED KINGDOM

BEN WYNNE

Glyn Artro Farm, Llanbedr (Mer), Gwynedd LL45 2LY, Wales

MAYFLY

In 1972 the Royal Yachting Association inaugurated the Sailing Speed Record competition and since then has held this event annually in Portland Harbour, England. One of the successful craft to emerge from these trials has been the one-person hydrofoil catamaran, *Mayfly*. It was originally designed and built by Philip Hansford to compete in the 'A' class sail area category (up to 13·94m²) and was sailed in early competitions by James Grogono, who pioneered hydrofoil sailing in the UK with his converted 'Tornado' class catamaran, *Icarus*, in 1969. *Mayfly* was acquired by Wynne for the 1976 event during which it raised the record for the class to 21·1 knots. It was taken to workshops at the University of Newcastle-upon-Tyne where, with the help of Dr V Hill, new bow foils were designed and built for the 1977 competition. In April 1982 *Mayfly* was purchased by the Science Museum, Kensington, London, for permanent exhibition in the Water Transport Gallery. Variants of the *Mayfly* design continue to compete in high-speed sailing events under the name *Seafly*.

FOILS: Aeroplane configuration with surface-piercing bow foils and a single fully-submerged inverted-T rudder foil strut assembly aft. All foils are made of aluminium and retract. The cantilever member of the bow foils has a design lift coefficient of 0·4 and was machined from solid by numerical control to a low drag aerofoil section. The turned down tips reduce leeway at high speeds. The inverted-T rudder/foil assembly is of hollow construction fabricated from aluminium plates rolled to form a symmetrical bi-ogival section 10 to 12 per cent thick. All foils are fitted with full chord anti-ventilation fences.

HULLS: Purpose-built with low freeboard to reduce weight and windage and lightly constructed from 3mm plywood forming a round bilge hull, with joints held by fibreglass tape. The hulls are joined by a forward and an aft tubular aluminium cross beam. A specially tailored sail cloth 'trampoline' is stretched between the beams and hulls to give an aerofoil section bridge deck. The bow foils are mounted directly onto the forward crossbeam and may be retracted or lowered in one minute. They are rotated forwards and upwards for hullborne sailing, and set down in deep water with wire and bottle screw to fix the angle of incidence. The rear foil is mounted centrally on a third cross beam and swings forwards and upwards to retract. Sitting out 'wings' are fitted to enable the helmsman to move his weight further to windward, thus permitting a sail sideforce of up to 85 per cent of the all-up weight including crew.

RIG: A single soft sail with an area of 13·2m² (142ft²). It is fully battened and is set on an over rotating wingmast.

DIMENSIONS
Length overall: 4·8m (15ft 9in)
Beam overall: 5·1m (16ft 8·75in)
Draught hullborne: 1m (3ft 3in)
    foilborne: 0·6m (1ft 11in)
Mast height: 7m (22ft 11in)
WEIGHTS
All-up (less crew): 118kg (260lb)
PERFORMANCE: *Mayfly* requires a 12- to 14-knot breeze to fly. Once foilborne in marginal conditions, it has little difficulty in staying up and is highly manoeuvrable. At speed it takes on an aeroplane-like sensitivity to control movements and the only sounds are a whine from the rig and the hiss of water rushing past the foils. In flat water, foiling to windward is possible on courses to within approximately 60 degrees of the true wind. However, the maximum speed is reached on a course about 120 degrees to the true wind when, under favourable conditions with smooth water and a medium breeze, it can reach twice the windspeed.

Mayfly

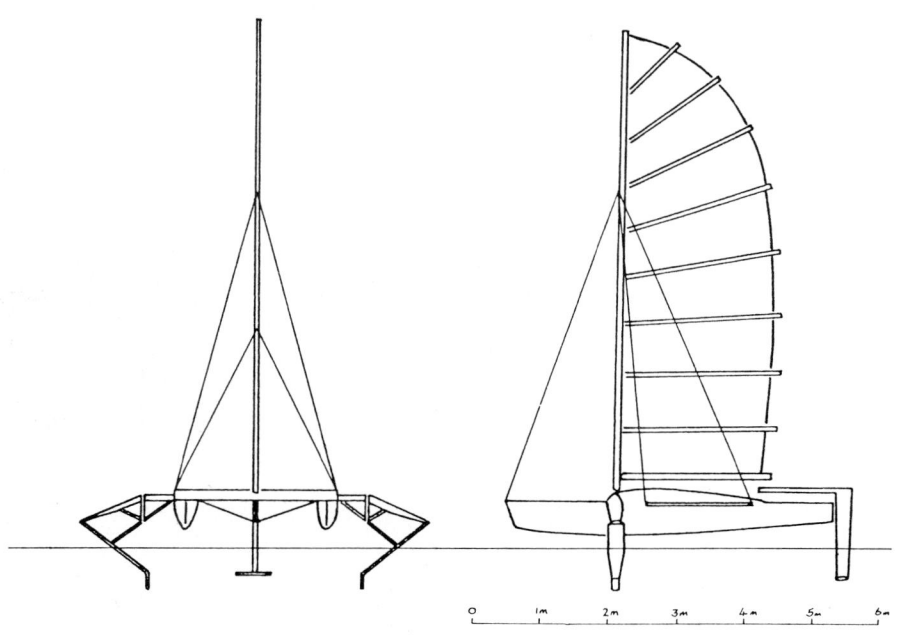

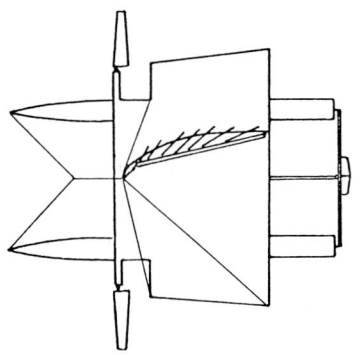

Mayfly, catamaran sailing hydrofoil

Mayfly has held the 'A' class World Speed Record since its inception and established the record of 23 knots in 1977.

UNITED STATES OF AMERICA

DAK HYDROFOILS

526 Third Avenue, San Francisco, California
94118, USA
Telephone: (415) 752 8748
Official:
David A Keiper, *Proprietor and Chief Designer*

Design of the 32ft Williwaw, the world's first
seagoing sailing hydrofoil, began in 1963. Construction of the craft, which is based on a specially
designed trimaran hull, began in May 1966 and
tests started in November 1967.

After nearly three years of trials along the
California coast, Williwaw, manned by David
Keiper and one other crew member, successfully
completed a 16-day passage between Sausalito,
California and Kahului Harbour, Maui, Hawaii,
in September 1970—the first ocean crossing by
the hydrofoil sailboat.

Heavy seas and strong winds were encountered
on the first two days of the voyage, during which
the craft made 200 miles per day. At times the
craft attained 25 knots, but light winds in mid-
ocean prevented the craft from making the
passage in record time.

The craft entered chartered sailing yacht service in March 1971, operating from Hanalei,
Hawaii and, before returning to Sausalito,
California, completed about 2,000 miles of
inter-island sailing around Hawaii, mainly in
open sea conditions.

Williwaw was entered in the Pacific Multihull
Association speed trials held in Los Angeles
Harbour in May 1975. Average speed was
determined over a 229m (250yd) course, planned so that the true wind was approximately 10 to
20 degrees aft of the beam. On one run, with a
reasonably steady wind of 17 knots, Williwaw
averaged 17·5 knots over the course. On another
run, with a stronger wind of 24 knots, under gusty
and turbulent conditions with 1·5ft (0·45m) very
short wave chop, Williwaw averaged 18·5 knots.

The foils stabilised the craft perfectly. The bow
kept up high in all runs, while various racing
catamarans of 4·2 to 11·5m (14 to 38ft) experienced serious problems with bow burying.

Various modifications to the craft were undertaken during 1974-75, followed by a second
series of sea trials in the summer of 1975, in the
South Pacific.

Williwaw sailed to Hawaii again in June 1975.
Wind was generally light until deep within the
tradewind region. In heavy tradewind squalls
with the boat running down steep 4·5m (15ft)
seas, the foils stabilised perfectly and the bow was
never submerged.

On a run from Hanalei, Hawaii to Whangaroa,
New Zealand, made between November and
December 1975, with stopovers in Samoa and
Tonga, moderate trade winds were experienced
during the first 2,000 miles of the voyage and
generally light winds during the last 2,000 miles.
During the first 12 days of the voyage, the foils
were left set continuously. Over one ten-day
period, the craft completed 1,650 miles, including a doldrums crossing. Self-steering was used
for most of the way, with the helm tied. Only the
working sail area of 35·3m² (380ft²) was used.

The return trip from New Zealand to Hawaii
was made via Rarotonga and Penrhyn in the
Cook Islands. When the craft left New Zealand, a
disturbed south west air stream was generating
35-knot squalls, day and night. Seas were very
irregular and the boat would occasionally slam
into walls of water at speeds in excess of 20 knots.
About 500 miles from the New Zealand coast
one freak wave encountered was 10·6 to 12m (35
to 40ft) high, and had a slope greater than 45
degrees. The trough was flat-bottomed, with no
rounding between the slope and the trough.
Descending the slope, the bow was well above the
surface. After impact there was no tendency for
the stern to lift. The bow remained under for
about two seconds before it emerged and the boat
started moving again. Waves such as this have
been known to pitchpole yachts, monohull and

multihull, but the hydrofoil trimaran showed no
such tendency.

Williwaw operated sailing excursions from
Hanalei, Hawaii, during the summers of 1971,
1975 and 1976. By the end of August 1976, it had
completed 19,000 miles of sailing.

In 1984, David Keiper began the design of a
40ft racing catamaran. His most recent craft is a
14ft hydrofoil trimaran, the Stormy Petrel, which
can be carried on the roof of a small car.

WILLIWAW

Williwaw has a specially designed trimaran hull
attached to which are four foils: a deep V-foil at
the bow, a ladder foil at the stern, and one laterally outboard of each of the port and starboard
pontoons. The stern foil pivots and serves as a
rudder when hullborne.

The craft accommodates two to three passengers, together with cruising supplies.

It can remain fully foilborne for unlimited distances in moderate seas as long as there is adequate wind power.

Modifications made to the craft during 1974-
75 included the addition of streamlined fairings
at the four main intersections of the lifting surfaces and struts on the bow foil, the installation of
a retractable leeboard for improved windward

performance in light airs, and the facing of various aluminium foil fittings with stainless steel to
prevent wear and tear around the shear/fastening
bolts.
FOILS: The bow foil, of surface-piercing V-
configuration, is mounted between the pontoon
bows and that of the main hull. Foils, supporting
struts and sub-foil elements, are of welded
aluminium with a protective vinyl coating. Foil
section is NACA 16-510 with 152·4mm (6in)
chord throughout the system. The foils have
fairly high aspect ratio. Foil loading during a
normal take-off is: bow foil 40 per cent, stern foil
20 per cent and leeward lateral foil 40 per cent,
depending on sail heeling forces. Dihedral of the
bow foil is 30 to 50 degrees.

The lateral foils, which are not as deep as the
bow and stern foils, are of four-rung ladder type,
and have 35 degrees dihedral. The stern foil is of
three-rung ladder configuration with zero
dihedral at rest, but craft heel gives it 10 to 15
degrees dihedral. Under most conditions the
rungs are fully submerged. The entire stern foil
pivots for steering action. Shear bolts protect bow
and stern foils from damage if debris is struck.

Foil retraction arrangements are as follows:
After the removal of shear bolts the bow foil
swings forward and upwards through 90 degrees;

Williwaw in Auckland harbour, with foils retracted

Williwaw sailing in San Francisco Bay

the lateral foils swing outwards and over, and are laid flat on the deck through a second pivot axis, and the stern foil swings aft and over through 180 degrees. Retraction of the bow and lateral foils is achieved through the use of a simple block and tackle.

CONTROL: A tiller-operated, combined stern foil and rudder controls direction in foilborne mode; paired struts, also tiller operated, provide rudder control when hullborne.

HULL: Lightweight, but robust trimaran hull with small wing deck to avoid aerodynamic lift. Marine ply structure sheathed with glass fibre. Built-in attachment points for foils. Mast supported by main frame.

ACCOMMODATION: The craft is designed for two to three people, with cruising supplies, but has flown with nine aboard. The deep cockpit accommodates the helmsman and one crew member. The cockpit, which provides adequate shelter from the strong winds developed by high-speed sailing, forms the entrance to main and stern cabins. The main cabin seats four comfortably. There are two berths in the main cabin and one in the stern cabin. The main cabin also includes a galley, shelving and a marine head. There is generous stowage space in the pontoon hulls.

SAIL AND POWERPLANT: Sail power on prototype, but a small outboard auxiliary engine can be fitted if required. Total sail area is 35·3m² (380ft²).

SYSTEMS, ELECTRONICS: Radio direction finder normally carried.

DIMENSIONS

EXTERNAL

Length overall, hull: 9·54m (31ft 4in)
   waterline, hull: 8·53m (28ft)
   overall, foils retracted: 10·05m (33ft)
   overall, foils extended: 9·75m (32ft)
Hull beam:
   main hull at water line: 0·91m (3ft)
   hull overall, foils retracted: 4·97m (16ft 4in)
Beam, overall, foils extended: 7·62m (25ft)
Draught afloat, foils retracted: 0·4m (1ft 4in)
   foils extended: 1·21m (4ft)
Draught foilborne: 0·45-0·76m (1ft 6in-2ft 6in)
Freeboard: 0·61m (2ft)
Pontoon deck: 0·47-0·76m (1ft 6in-2ft 6in)
Main hull deck: 0·76-1·06m (2ft 6in-3ft 6in)
Height overall to masthead: 11·88m (39ft)

INTERNAL

Cabin (wheelhouse, galley, toilet included):
   length: 8·53m (28ft)
   max width: 4·87m (16ft)
   max height: 1·62m (5ft 4in)
   volume: 13·78m³ (480ft³)

WEIGHTS

Light displacement: 997·88kg (2,200lb)
Normal take-off displacement: 1,360kg (3,000lb)
Max take-off displacement: 1,632kg (3,600lb)
Normal payload: 362·8kg (800lb)
Max payload: 635kg (1,400lb)

PERFORMANCE (in steady wind and calm water, with normal payload)

Take-off speed: normally 12 knots. Craft is able to take-off with a 12-knot beam wind and accelerate to 18-20 knots
Max speed foilborne: 30 knots
Cruising speed foilborne: 12-25 knots
Max permissible sea state and wave height in foilborne mode: sea state almost unlimited at 12-knot average speed with wind aft of beam. Foils well behaved in all conditions met so far. Sails reefed down in heavy conditions to maintain comfort and ease of handling. Craft shows no tendency to pound.
Turning radius at cruising speed: 45·72m (150ft)
Number of seconds and distance to take-off: 5 seconds in strong wind, two boat lengths
Number of seconds to stop craft: 8 seconds, turning dead into wind
   Speed is significantly more than wind speed in conditions of steady wind and calm water. The craft can match wind speed in moderate seas, but not in heavy seas. In heavy seas, broad reaching or beam, it has averaged 15 knots for hours at a time, winds gusting to Force 5 and 6. Speeds may climb to 30 knots or drop to 5 knots, depending

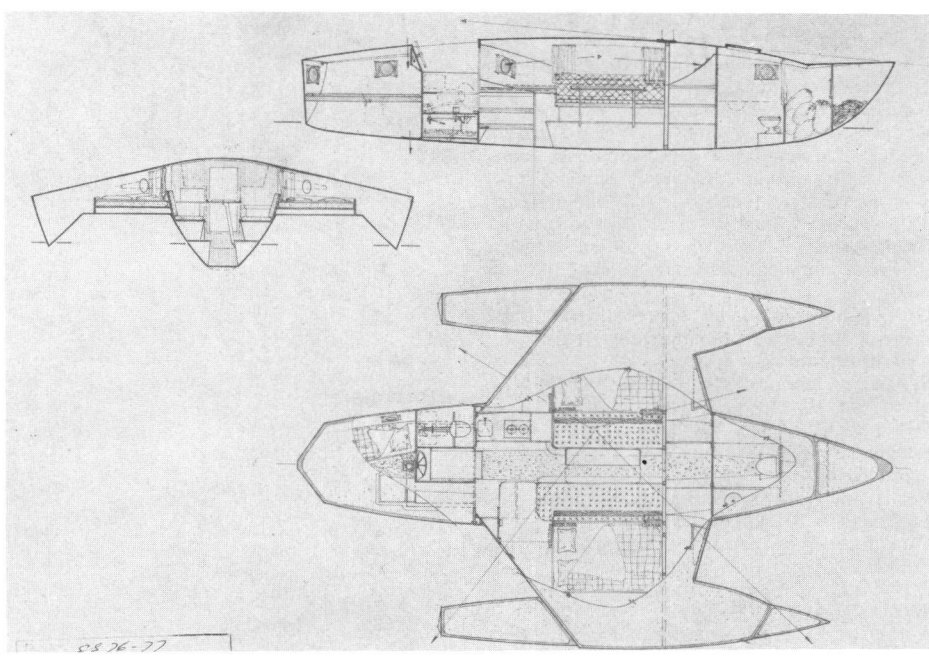

Inboard profile and deck plan of Pacific Express 35

upon local wind and waves. Acceleration and decelerations are gradual and not objectionable. The ride is far smoother than that of displacement multihulls.

PACIFIC EXPRESS 35

Successor to Williwaw, the Pacific Express is a second generation hydrofoil cruising trimaran. It is designed to be sailed solo when necessary, and avoids many of the problems inherent in conventional trimarans: pounding, broaching, tunnel interference, quick motion, pitchpoling, poor control and poor self-steering in heavy seas.

The craft is wider than its predecessor, has fully buoyant float hulls, is equipped with a more efficient hydrofoil system and has a slightly greater load-carrying capacity.

It is designed to operate in a variety of conditions, from heavy storm seas to light airs. In heavy seas, with foils set, it is exceptionally stable and capable of high speeds.

The length, 10·66m (35ft), is the shortest in which it is possible to have full standing headroom as well as a flush deck. Through its proportionately wider hulls, it should be able to exceed true wind speed more substantially than Williwaw and be able to fly fully foilborne at about 50 degrees from the true wind. The boat should be

Stormy Petrel achieving 25 knots during 30-knot wind gust. Most of spray is emanating from leeward lateral foil which is carrying about 90 per cent of weight

able to beat to windward with complete comfort for the crew.

In light airs and calms, with foils retracted, the craft makes the most of the available wind.

FOILS: Configuration similar to that of Williwaw. Foils have a 152mm (6in) chord and are fabricated in heavily anodised aluminium extrusions. Bolts, washers, etc, are in stainless steel. Bow and lateral foils are fixed while sailing. Tiller-operated combined stern foil and rudder controls craft direction when foilborne. All four foils retract manually after the removal of sheer bolts.

HULL: Main hull bottom and topside, triple diagonal wood strips, remainder in plywood. All wood saturated with epoxy.

SAIL: Sail area as a cutter, 60·3m² (650ft²). Sloop working sail area, 45m² (485ft²).

DIMENSIONS
Length, overall: 10·66m (35ft)
  waterline, static: 9·65m (31ft 8in)
Beam, foils retracted: 6·7m (22ft)
Mast height: 12·19m (40ft)
Draught, foils retracted: 0·45m (1ft 6in)
  (static) foils extended: 1·52m (5ft)
Outboard projection of lateral foils: 1·21m (4ft)
WEIGHTS
Normal loaded displacement: 1,814kg (4,000lb)
PERFORMANCE
Top speed, strong wind, flat water: 45 knots
Normal foilborne speed range: 13-30 knots
Speed to become fully foilborne: 13 knots
Speed to become half foilborne: 9 knots
Wind required to become fully foilborne, in flat water: 11-12 knots
  in average seas: 12-15 knots
Average hull clearance at high speed: 0·6m (2ft)
Max sea state for foilborne operation: unlimited
In heavy seas, sails are reefed to obtain a good balance between speed, comfort and safety.

STORMY PETREL

A 14-foot hydrofoil catamaran, Stormy Petrel is capable of 40 knots in ideal conditions and can be easily handled by a single occupant. It can be carried on the roof of a small car and erected and launched from a beach. The foils are retracted for sailing in light winds, in very shallow water, for beaching and for paddling against adverse tides in a calm.

When the wind is up, it can fly on its foils carrying one heavy occupant or two of medium weight. The helmsman sits on the aft deck and the second crew member, if carried, sits in a semi-protected cockpit.

The prototype was build in mid-1982 and tested during the 1982 and 1983 sailing season in all weathers. During sharp 30-knot wind gusts it accelerated to 25 knots. It has attained 30 knots in foggy 20-knot wind puffs and long sea swells in the Golden Gate region.

During tests, take-off has taken place on a close reach with the boat accelerating increasingly as it was turned away from the wind. Its top speed was reached with the true wind on the quarter with the sails close-hauled and the boat tight against the apparent wind. In choppy waters the speed is reduced but the ride is smooth.

FOILS: The lateral foils have a two-inch chord and a 13-inch span, with six rungs on each ladder. Dihedral angles are 30 and 45 degrees. Clark Y section lifters are used and NACA 16012 section struts. The aluminium extrusions, joined with tapped screws and epoxy, are the same as used previously in DAK hydrofoil conversion kits.

Stormy Petrel with foils retracted, enabling craft to sail off beach. Note how lateral foils alternate with 30 and 45 degrees of dihedral to strengthen foil units

ASSEMBLY: Four wingnuts clamp the crossarm unit to the main hull. Foil retraction is by rotating the crossarm through 180 degrees. For carrying on a car roof, the crossarm is laid parallel to the main hull.

MATERIALS: Plywood-epoxy hulls. Aluminium crossarm, mast, lateral foils and fittings.

SAIL AREA: 9·29m², including rotating mast area.

DIMENSIONS
Length, main hull deck: 4·27m
Beam overall: 4·27m
Float hulls, length: 1·52m
Max cross sectional area: 0·093m²
Draught, main hull: 20·32cm

rudder, with foils retracted: 25·4cm
foils: 60·96cm on both lateral foils and stern rudder foil
WEIGHTS
Rigged: 81·65kg
Main hull only: 31·75kg
Crossarm unit, including floats and lateral foils: 31·75kg
PERFORMANCE
Take-off speed and wind requirement: 10 knots in flat water or long swells. Increased by short wave chop, when main hull cannot completely clear tops of waves, although boat may still travel at high speed
Top speed: 40 knots in ideal conditions (limited by onset of cavitation)

DONALD NIGG

7924 Fontana, Prairie Village, Kansas 66208, USA
Telephone: (913) 642 2002

Development of the Flying Fish began in 1963 at Lake Quivira, an inland lake in Kansas. Donald Nigg believed that if the pitchpole moment and vertical stability problems could be solved, the front-steering three-point suspension system, typical of the modern ice-yacht, offered several advantages. Previous craft had often used

three-point suspension, but all appear to have used rear steering. To develop this new approach Exocoetus, an experimental platform, was built. It was evolved through three distinct versions during 1964-67 and established the basic feasibility.

Interest in the experiments resulted in numerous requests for plans, but although the craft was ideal as a development platform, it was not a suitable design for home construction. In response to these requests the Flying Fish was

developed.

To minimise costs, the craft is designed to carry a sail area of 9·2 to 13·9m² (100 to 150ft²). It was anticipated that most of those interested in building a sailing hydrofoil would be small boat sailors, owning a boat carrying a mainsail of this size. The design thus allows the builder to share the sail and rigging with an existing dinghy.

A true development class of sailing hydrofoil has been slow to emerge, but the Flying Fish may mark the beginning of such a class.

Sets of plans for the Flying Fish have been supplied to potential builders throughout the world.

FLYING FISH

Built mainly in wood and with an overall length of 5·02m (16ft 6in), the Flying Fish has a maximum foilborne speed of more than 30 knots.

The estimated cost of constructing a craft of this type, excluding sail and rigging (the 11·61m² (125ft²) mainsail and rigging from a Y-Flyer were used for the prototype illustrated), is US $350 (1983).

FOILS: Surface piercing and non-retractable configuration with 16 per cent of the weight supported by the V bow foil and the remaining 84 per cent by the outrigged main foils. The latter are also of the V type, with cantilevered extensions at the apex. Total foil area is 1·42m² (15·3ft²) and the foil loading is 300lb/ft² max at 30 knots. The front foil and its supporting strut are built in aluminium and oak, and the main foil is in oak only.

STEERING: A basic feature of the design is the use of front rather than rear steering. Directional control is provided by the movement of the hinged bow foil.

HULL: All-wooden structure in fir plywood, ¼in thick and sealed. Torque load is carried by the skin, and bending loads are carried by the skin and the internal beam structure.

The crossbeam provides stability when in dock and in a displacement condition at low speeds. At 2-3 knots the horizontal safety foils at the top of the V of the rear foils provide interim foil stabilisation up to the take-off speed of 5 knots and prevent dragging an end of the crossbeam in the water. At foilborne speeds the safety foils preclude the possibility of an end of the crossbeam being driven into the water by sudden heeling.

RIG: A cat rig of 9·2 to 13·9m² (100 to 150ft²) area is recommended.

DIMENSIONS

Length overall, hull (plus boom overhand at rear, dependent on sail plan): 5·02m (16ft 6in)
    waterline, hull: 4·87m (16ft)
Beam: 6·09m (20ft)
Draught afloat (fixed foils): 1·06m (3ft 6in)
    foilborne: 304-762mm (12-30in) over operating speed range
Height, approx: 7·3m (24ft)

PERFORMANCE

Max speed foilborne: over 30 knots
    design cruise range: optimised for 20-30 knots
Max speed hullborne: 5 knots
Minimum wind for take-off: 10 knots
Number of seconds and distance to take-off (theoretically approx): 3s with 15·2m (50ft) run in favourable wind
Number of seconds and distance to stop craft (theoretically approx): can land from 20 knots in 45·6m (150ft) in about 6 seconds
SEA TEST: The craft has been tested in 10-25 knot winds, on sheltered inland lakes and on ocean bays, with a maximum chop of about 45·72cm (18in). Speeds up to approximately 30 knots have been attained.

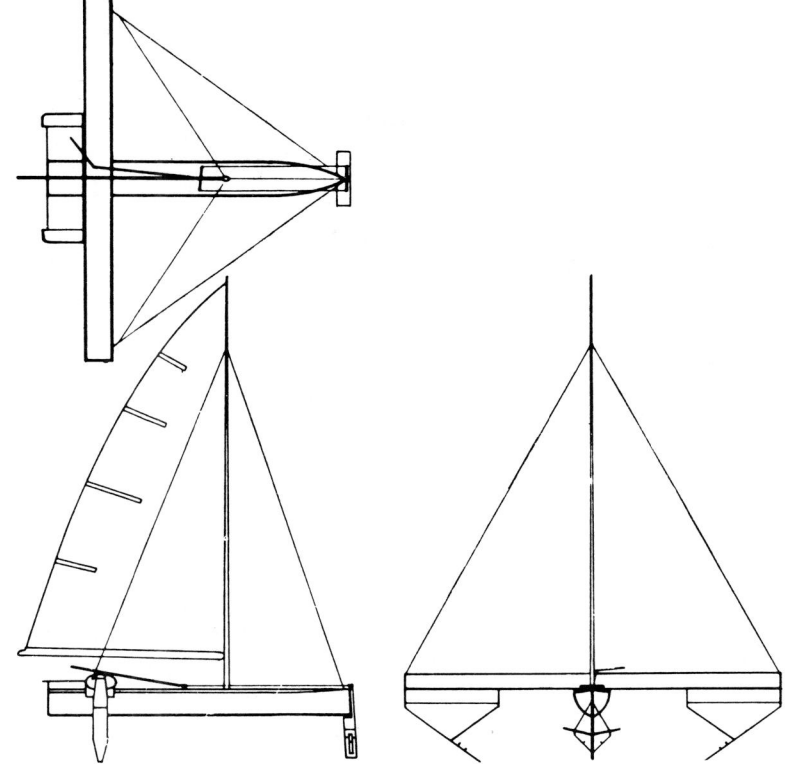

Flying Fish

Flying Fish exceeding 20 knots on close reach in light wind

HYDROFOIL OPERATORS

ALBANIA
ALBANIAN NAVY

Type(s): 'Hu Chwan' (White Swan) class, 32 (Shanghai)
Operational areas: Coastal waters

ARGENTINA
ALIMAR SanciyF

Avda Córdoba 1801 (Esq Callao), Código Postal 1120, Buenos Aires, Argentina
Telephone: 42-4498/3924
Telex: 121510 Almar
Cables: Alimar
Type(s): PT 50, 3 (Rodriquez)
Route(s): Buenos Aires-Colonia (1 hour); Buenos Aires-Montevideo (3 hours)

AUSTRALIA
THE URBAN TRANSIT AUTHORITY OF NEW SOUTH WALES

Head Office: Ferry Division, No 2 Jetty, Circular Quay, Sydney, New South Wales 2000, Australia
Telephone: 27 9251
Telex: NSWTC AA25702
Terminal Offices: No 2 Jetty, Circular Quay
Telephone: 27 9251
Manly Wharf, Manly
Telephone: 977 3028
Officials:
T F Gibson, *General Manager*
W Heading, *Superintendent Engineer*

OPERATIONS: Sydney to Manly, 7 miles, every 20 minutes between 7am and 7pm
1·93 million passengers carried during year.
CRAFT OPERATED
PT 50 (Rodriquez) *Fairlight*, 140 passengers, built 1966
PT 50 (Rodriquez) *Long Reef*, ex *Freccia di Mergellina*, 140 passengers, built 1968
PT 50 (Rodriquez) *Palm Beach*, ex *Patane*, 140 passengers, built 1969
PT 50 (Rodriquez) *Dee Why*, 140 passengers, built 1970
RHS 140 (Navaltecnica) *Curl Curl*, 140 passengers, built 1972

AUSTRIA
SCHIFFSWERFT KORNEUBURG

Korneuburg, Austria
Type(s): Raketa, 1 (Sormovo)
Route(s): Danube

BELGIUM
REGIE TRANSPORTES MARITIME (RTM)

Type(s): Jetfoil 929-115, 2
Route(s): Ostend-Dover
This state operator of Belgian ferry routes operates two Boeing Jetfoil 929-115s, *Princesse Clementine* and *Princesse Stephanie*, between Ostend (Belgium) and Dover. The route length is about 64 nautical miles and takes about 1 hour 40 minutes. RTM already operates several car ferries on this route and the adjacent Folkestone/Ostend route.

BOLIVIA
CRILLON TOURS SA

PO Box 4785, Av Camacho 1223, La Paz, Bolivia
Telephone: 350363, 374566/67
Telex: BV 2557
Cables: Critur
Officials:
Darius Morgan, *General Manager*
Helmut Kock, *Hydrofoil Designer and Consultant*
Type(s): Albatross (Honold) 4, modified by Helmut Kock; Bolivia Arrow (Kock-Crillon Tours) 1; Seaflight H-57, 1
Route(s): Lake Titicaca

BRAZIL
AEROBARCOS DO BRASIL, TRANSPORTES MARITIMOS E TURISMO SA—TRANSTUR

Avenida Amaral Peixoto, 71—11o andar, Niterói-RJ, Brazil
Telephone: 719-7070
Type(s): PT 20, 8 (Rodriquez); RHS 110, 1 (Navaltecnica)

BULGARIA
NAVIGATION MARITIME BULGARE

128 D Blagoev Blvd, Varna, Bulgaria
Type(s): Kometa, 11; Raketa, 1; Meteor, 4 (Sormovo)
Route(s): Bourgas-Nesetow-Varna; Danube, between Rousse and Silistra

CHINA, PEOPLE'S REPUBLIC
NAVY OF THE CHINESE PEOPLE'S REPUBLIC

Type(s): 'Hu Chwan' class, 130 to 150 (Shanghai)
Operational areas: Coastal waters
Type(s): Hema, 1 (Shanghai)
Operational areas: Coastal waters

CUBA
CUBAN NAVY

Type(s): 'Turya' class fast-attack craft, 9 (Soviet Admiralty Shipyards).
Operational areas: Coastal waters

MAR-PORT

Calle 21 y O, Vedado, Havana, Cuba
Type(s): Kometa M, 5 (Sormovo)
Route(s): Batabanó-Nueva Gerona

CYPRUS
NATIONAL SHIPPING

Type(s): Kometa, 1 (Sormovo)
Route(s): Larnaca - Limassol - Beirut - Tripoli - Latakia

DENMARK
A/S DAMPSKIBSSELSKABET ØRESUND

Havnegade 49, DK-1058 Copenhagen, Denmark
Telephone: 01 14 77 70, 01 12 80 88
Telex: 45-27502 Sundet DK
Type(s): PT 50, 3 (Rodriquez); Westamaran W95, 3 (Westermarin)
Route(s): Copenhagen-Malmö, Sweden

EGYPT
THE GENERAL NILE COMPANY FOR RIVER TRANSPORT

39 Kasr El-Nil Street, Cairo, Egypt
Telephone: 54517/18
Cables: Naknahri Cairo
Type(s): PT 20, 3 (Rodriquez)
Route(s): Abu Simbel-Asswan

FINLAND
PÄIJÄANTEE KANT

Type(s): Raketa, 1 (Sormovo)
Route(s): Lahti-Jyvaskyla, across Lake Paijane

FRANCE
VEDETTES ARMORICAINES

Ier Eperon, 56 rue d'Aiguillon, Brest Cedex, France
Type(s): Kometa, 1 (Sormovo)

GERMANY, FEDERAL REPUBLIC
WATER POLICE

Type(s): PT 4, 3 (West German shipyard)
Route(s): Patrol service on the Rhine

KÖLN DÜSSELDORFER SHIPPING CO (KD German Rhine Line)

Frankenwerft 15, D-5000 Cologne 1, Federal Republic of Germany
Telephone: 0221 20880
Telex: 08882 723
Type(s): Raketa, 1 *Rhine Arrow* (Sormovo)
Route(s): Cologne, Koblenz and Mainz

PT 20 operated by Aerobarcos do Brasil

Raketa, *Rheinpfiel,* operated by Köln-Düsseldorfer German Rhine Line

GREECE
CERES HELLENIC SHIPPING ENTERPRISES LTD

Akti Miaouli 69, Piraeus, Greece
Companies: Ceres Flying Hydroways Ltd, Ceres Hydrofoils Limited and Ceres Express Ltd.
Type(s): Kometa-M, 15 (Sormovo)
Route(s): Piraeus to islands in the Saronic group

SOLAM HELLAS

Piraeus, Greece
Type(s): Kometas (Sormovo)
Route(s): Piraeus to Hydra, Spetiai, Syros, Paros, Antiparos, Amagos, Asypalea, Nissyros, Symi and Rhodes.

HONG KONG
HONGKONG MACAO HYDROFOIL COMPANY LIMITED

New World Tower, 33rd Floor, 16-18 Queen's Road Central, Hong Kong
Telephone: 5 218302
Telex: 74493 HMHCO HK
Type(s): PT 50, 3 (Rodriquez); RHS 140, 5 (Navaltecnica)

FAR EAST HYDROFOIL CO LTD

36th Floor, Connaught Centre, Connaught Road, Hong Kong
Telephone: H-243176
Telex: 74200 SEDAM HX
Officials:
Stanley Ho, *Managing Director*
K B Allport, *Group Manager*
D Hill, *Technical Manager*
H Chan, *Fleet Operations Manager*
Type(s): PT 50, 4, *Guia, Penha, Taipa, Balsa* (Hitachi Zosen)
PTS 75 Mk III, 2, *Rosa* (Vosper Thornycroft) *Patane* (Supramar Pacific Shipbuilding Co Ltd). Laid up
Jetfoils, 12, *Madeira, Santa Maria, Flores, Corvo, Pico, Sân Jorge, Acores, Urzela, Ponta Delgada, Terceira, Horta, Funchal* (Boeing)
Route(s): Hong Kong-Macao, distance 36n miles by the Southern Route. Services half-hourly sunrise to sunset, ie 23,000 trips per annum. Twelve Jetfoil services are operated each way between sunset and 2 am. Total number of passengers carried per year exceeds 5 million. Since the Jetfoil was introduced into service in April 1975, the craft have carried (up to 31 May 1984) 22,169,110 passengers.

HUNGARY
MAHART MAGYAR HAJÓZÁSI RT

Apáczai Csere János utca 11, H-1052 Budapest V, Hungary
Type(s): Raketa; Meteor, 1; Voskhod (Sormovo)
Route(s): Budapest-Vienna, Dunaújváros-Budapest, Budapest-Esztergom

INDONESIA
MINISTRY OF RESEARCH AND TECHNOLOGY, AGENCY FOR THE DEVELOPMENT AND APPLICATION OF TECHNOLOGY

A Jetfoil 929-115, *Bina Samudera I*, was delivered to this ministry in March 1982 to evaluate the possible use of the craft in civil and military roles.

INDONESIAN NAVY

Indonesia has ordered four Boeing Jetfoils for delivery in 1984-86 and has taken options on a

further six craft. They are likely to be operated on offshore patrol and logistics support duties.

SUNDAHARYA CORP, JAKARTA

Type(s): PT 20 (Rodriquez)
Route(s): Indonesian coast

IRAN
MINISTRY OF DEFENCE

Type(s): Kometa, 2 (Sormovo)
Operating area: Persian Gulf

ISRAEL
ISRAELI NAVY

Type(s): M161 Flagstaff II, 2 (1 Grumman, 1 Israel Shipyards)
Duties: Coastal patrol, convoy escort
A licence for the series production of these craft in Israel has been acquired. Once Israel's own needs have been met, Israeli-built craft will be made available for export.

ITALY
ITALIAN NAVY

Type(s): 'Sparviero' class, 7 (Alinavi)
Operational areas: Coastal patrol

ALISCAFI SNAV, SpA

Via S Raineri 22, 98100 Messina, Italy
Type(s): PT 20, 10; PT 50, 10; RHS 160, 1; RHS 200, 1 (Rodriquez)
Route(s):
Anzio-Ponza-Ischia
Brancaleone-Naxos
Cefalu-Eolian Islands
Eolian Islands-Milazzo

Terceira, Jetfoil Model 929-115, operated by Far East Hydrofoil Co

Meteor operated by Mahart Magyar Hajózási RT

Maratea-Eolian Islands
Messina-Stromboli (Eolian Islands)
Messina-Vulcano (Eolian Islands)
Naples-Capri-Ischia-Sorrento
Naples-Eolian Islands
Naples-Ustica-Palermo
Vibo Marina-Eolian Islands

SAS, TRAPANI

Via Evrialo 9, 91100 Trapani, Italy
Type(s): PT 50, 1; PT 20, 3 (Rodriquez)
Route(s): Trapani-Egadi Islands

ADRIATICA DI NAVIGAZIONE SpA

Zattere 1411, 30123 Venice, Italy
Telephone: 704322
Telex: 410045 Adrnav
Type(s): PT 50, 1 (Rodriquez); RHS 160, 1 (Navaltecnica)
Route(s): Termoli-Isole Tremiti; Ortona-Vasto-Isole Tremiti; Peschici-Isole Tremiti; Rodi Garganico-Isole Tremiti

ALILAURO ALISCAFI DEL TIRRENO SpA

Via Caracciolo 13, 80122 Napoli, Italy
Type(s): Kometa, 5 (Sormovo); PT 50 (Rodriquez)
Route(s): Naples-Ischia; Naples-Forio; Naples-C/Volturuo; Naples-Sorrento; Sorrento-Capri; Sorrento-C/Mare S; Capri-Ischia; Capri-Positano-Amalfi; Maiori-Salerno

MINISTRY OF TRANSPORT, MILAN

Via L Ariosto 21, 20145 Milan, Italy
Type(s): PT 20, 2 (Rodriquez); RHS 70, 10 (Navaltecnica); RHS 150, 3 (Navaltecnica)
Route(s): Lake Garda, Lake Como, Lake Maggiore

NAVIGAZIONE LAGO MAGGIORE—GG

Viale F Baracca 1, 28041 Arona, Italy
Type(s): PT 20, 2 (Rodriquez); RHS 70, 2 (Navaltecnica); RHS 150, 1 (Rodriquez)
Route(s): Lake Maggiore

RHS 140 *Fabrica* operated by Toremar

COMPAGNIA DI NAVIGAZIONE

Piazza Volta 44, 22100 Como, Italy
Type(s): PT 20, 2 (Rodriquez); RHS 70, 2 (Navaltecnica); RHS 150 SL, 1 (Navaltecnica)
Route(s): Lake Como

G & R SALVATORI, NAPLES

Type(s): PT 50, 2 (Westermoen)
Route(s): Naples-Capri

CAREMAR
COMPAGNIA REGIONALE MARITIMA SpA

Molo Beverello 2, Naples, Italy
Type(s): RHS 140, 1; RHS 160, 2 (Navaltecnica)

SIREMAR
SICILIA REGIONALE MARITIMA SpA

Via Crispi 120, Palermo, Sicily
Telephone: 240801/211916
Telex: 91135 Siremar
Type(s): RHS 160, 2 (Navaltecnica)
Route(s): Palermo-Ustica

TOREMAR
TOSCANA REGIONALE MARITIMA SpA

Scali del Corso 5, Livorno, Italy
Type(s): RHS 140, 1 (Navaltecnica)

AGIP SpA

S Donato Milanese, Milan, Italy
Telephone: 53531
Telex: 31246 ENI
Type(s): PT 20, 1; PT 50, 1 (Rodriquez)

JAPAN
BOYO KISEN CO LTD

134-6, Yanai, Yanai-shi, Yamaguchi, Japan
Type(s): PT 50, 1 (Hitachi); PT 20, 1 *Shibuki No 2* (Hitachi)
Route(s): Yanai-Matsuyama

ISIZAKI KISEN CO LTD

Fukae, Ohaki-cho, Saeki-gun, Hiroshima-ken, Japan
Type(s): PT 50, 1 *Kosei* (Hitachi)
Route(s): Hiroshima-Kure-Matsuyama
Type(s): PT 50, 1 (Hitachi)
Route(s): Hiroshima-Kure-Matsuyama
Type(s): PT 20, 1 *Kinsei* (Hitachi)
Route(s): Onomichi-Matsuyama
Type(s): PT 20, 1 *Tsobasamaru* (Hitachi)
Route(s): Hiroshima-Kure-Matsuyama
An additional PT 50 was delivered to the company during 1977.

MAYEKAWA TRADING CO LTD

3-22-1 Aobadai, Meguru-ku, Tokyo, Japan
Type(s): Kometa, 1 (Sormovo)

MEITETSU KAIJO KANKOSEN CO

99-1, Shinmiyasaka-cho, Atsuta-ku, Nagoya, Japan
Type(s): PT 50, 2 *Osyo* and *Kaio* (Hitachi)
Route(s): Gamagori-Nishiura-Irako-Toba, and Nagoya-Shinogima-Irako-Toba (summer)
Type(s): PT 20, 1 *Hayabusamaru* (Hitachi)
Route(s): Gamagori-Nishiura-Irako-Toba and Kowa-Himagajima-Shinojima (summer)

NICHIMEN CO LTD
(KINKOWAN FERRY CO LTD)

Type(s): PT 50, 1 *Otori No 3* (Hitachi)
Route(s): Kajiki-Kagoshima-Ibusuki

RHS 160, *Diomedea*, operated by Adriatica di Navigazione

RHS 150 *Freccia del Giardini* operated on Lake Maggiore by Navigazione Lago Maggiore-GG

NISSHO-IWAI CO LTD
(HANKYU LINES CO LTD)
Type(s): PT 50, 2 *Zuiho* and *Houo* (Hitachi)
Route(s): Koke-Tokushima

HANKYU LINES CO LTD
Type(s): PT 20, 2 *Amatsu* and *Kasugano* (Hitachi)
Route(s): Kobe-Naruto

HITACHI ZOSEN
Type(s): PT 20, 1; ST 3, 1 (Rodriquez)
Route(s): Japanese coast

SADO KISEN KAISHA
353, Oazaminato, Ryotsu-shi, Niigata, Japan
Type(s): Jetfoil 929-100, 1, *Okesa*; Jetfoil 929-115, 1, *Mikado* (Boeing)
Route(s): Niigata, Honshu Island and Ryotsu, Sado Island, Sea of Japan
Route distance: 63km (34n miles)

SETONAIKAI KISEN CO LTD
Ujinakaigan 1-12-23, Minami-ku, Hiroshima, Japan
Telephone: 082 255 3344
Telex: 653 625
Type(s): PT 50, 3, *Condoru, Condoru 2, Condoru 3* (Hitachi)
Route(s): Hiroshima-Kure-Matsuyama
Type(s): PT 50, 2, *Ohtori, Hikari 2* (Hitachi)
Route(s): Hiroshima-Kure-Imabari
Type(s): PT 50, 2, *Ohtori 2, Ohtori 3* (Hitachi)
Route(s): Onomichi-Setoda-Omishima-Imabari
Type(s): PT 50, 1, *Ohtori 5* (Hitachi)
Route(s): Miyajima-Hiroshima-Omishima-Setoda

KOREA, REPUBLIC
HAN RYEO DEVELOPMENT CO LTD
25-5 1-Ka, Chungmu-Ro, Chung-ku, Seoul, Republic of Korea
Telephone: 28-7145/28-8889
Telex: HANRYEO K24856
Type(s): PT 20, 1 *Angel* (Rodriquez); PT 20, 1 (Hitachi); RHS 110, 1 (Rodriquez)
Route(s): Busan-Yeosu

MEXICO
SECRETARIA DE TURISMO
Av Pdte Masarik 172, Mexico, 5 DF
Telex: 1777566 SETUME
Type(s): RHS 150, 1 (Rodriquez)
Route(s): Cancun-Cozumel

PT 50, *Teisten,* operated by Hardanger Sunnhordalanske Dampskibsselskab

MOROCCO
CIE MARITIME D'HYDROFOILS 'TRANSTOUR'
4 rue Jabha Al Ouatania (ex rue Rembrandt), Tangier, Morocco
Telephone: 340-04; 340-05
Telex: 336-08
Type(s): Kometa, 3 (Sormovo)
Route(s): Tangier-Algeciras, Tangier-Gibraltar, Tangier-Tarifa

NEW ZEALAND
HYDROFOIL CRUISES LTD
PO Box 58, Queenstown, New Zealand
Type(s): PT 4, *Meteor III* (Supramar)
Route(s): Lake Wakatipu, South Island

NORWAY
BRAATHENS SAFE
Oslo, Norway

Braathens SAFE has options on two Boeing Jetfoils for offshore oil rig support in the North Sea. A joint Braathens-Boeing study will determine the best configuration of the Jetfoil Model 929-115 for safe and comfortable crew transportation to the oil platforms. The Jetfoils will also be employed in the transfer of high priority cargo to the rigs. They will operate in conjunction with a new system of transferring crews to and from oil rigs developed by Kongsberg Engineering A/S of Norway.

DE BLA OMNIBUSSER A/S
Type(s): PT 20, 2 (Westermoen)
Route(s): Oslofjord

HARDANGER SUNNHORDALANDSKE DAMPSKIBSSELSKAB
Box 2005, N-5011, Nordnes, Bergen, Norway
Telephone: 315070
Telex: 42607 HSD N
Type(s): PT 50, 1 (Rodriquez)
Route(s): Bergen-Sunnhordland-Haugesund

PAKISTAN
PAKISTAN NAVY
Type(s): 'Hu Chwan' class, 6 (Shanghai)
Duties: Coastal patrol and strike missions

PHILIPPINES
TOURIST HOTEL AND TRAVEL CORPORATION
Type(s): PT 20, 2 (Rodriquez)
Route(s): Manila-Corregidor

PHILIPPINE NAVY
Headquarters, Roxas Boulevard, Manila, Philippines
Type(s): PT 20, 2 (Rodriquez); PT 32, 2 *Bontoc, Baler* (Hitachi)
Operational areas: Coastal patrol

POLAND
ZEGLUGA GDANSKA
This company operates a fleet of Kometa hydrofoils in north-east Poland.
Type(s): Kometa, 6 (Sormovo)
Route(s): Gdynia-Hel-Wladyslawowo; Gdynia-Jastarnia; Gdynia-Sopot; Sopot-Hel; Gdansk-Hel

ZEGLUGA SZCZECINSKA
Type(s): Kometa, 7 (Sormovo); Meteor, 4 (Sormovo)
Route(s): Szczecin-Swinoujscie

ROMANIA
ROMANIAN NAVY
Type(s): 'Hu Chwan' class, 19
Operational areas: Coastal waters

PT 50 *Ohtori 5* operated by Setonaikai Kisen Co Ltd

SPAIN
TRANSMED
COMPANIA TRASMEDITERRANEA SA

Plaza de Manuel Gomez Moreno s/n, Edificio
Bronce, Madrid 20, Spain
Type(s): Jetfoil 929-115, 2, *Princesa Guayarmi-
na, Princesa Guacimara* (Boeing)
Route(s): Las Palmas-Santa Cruz

TANZANIA
TANZANIA NAVY

Dar es Salaam, Tanzania
Type(s): 'Hu Chwan' class, 4 (Shanghai)
Duties: Coastal patrol

TURKEY
SEJIR DENIZYOLLARI LTD

34-A Canbulat, Sokak, Girne, Mersin 10, Tur-
key
Type(s): PT 20, 1; PT 50, 1 (Rodriquez)
Route(s): Turkey-Cyprus

MED SHIPPING

Type(s): Kometa-M, 2 (Sormovo)
Route(s): Turkey-Cyprus

UNION OF SOVIET SOCIALIST REPUBLICS
MINISTRY OF THE RIVER FLEET

The Soviet Ministry of the River Fleet operates
hydrofoil passenger ferries on almost all the
major rivers, lakes, canals and reservoirs from
central Russia to Siberia and the Soviet far east.

In 1958, when hydrofoils were first introduced
to the rivers of the Soviet Union, they carried
10,000 passengers. By 1968 the number of passengers carried had grown to 3 million. During
the 1969-70 navigation season there were 80
hydrofoil services on the Volga alone, operated
by vessels of the Raketa, Meteor, Sputnik and
Burevestnik series. There are now more than 150
hydrofoil passenger services in the Soviet Union.
During the 1981 navigation season Soviet commercial hydrofoils carried in excess of 100 million
passengers.

In addition to craft on inland waterways
employing the Alexeyev shallow draught submerged foil system, Strela-type craft, with
surface-piercing foils, operate in the Gulf of Finland and, supported by Kometas and Vikhrs,
provide year-round services between ports on the
Black Sea.

In July 1981 further second generation hydrofoils were stated to be under development.

New hydrofoil passenger-ferry designs either
in or about to be put into production include the
Cyclone, a seagoing, waterjet-propelled ferry
with seats for 250 and capable of 40 knots and the
Voskhod (Sunrise), a Raketa replacement. The
Voskhod provides greater comfort and improved
facilities for passengers and crew. As with the
Raketa, a family of variants will be available to
suit operating and traffic conditions.

The new Kolkhida has the same overall dimensions as the Kometa, which it will replace, but its
engines are mounted aft, its foils are controlled
by an ACS and the standard version seats 120
passengers.

Smaller hydrofoils which have entered production include the 50-seat Polesye and the Lastochka 50-knot passenger ferry.

The Raketa has given excellent service and has
low operating costs. The cost of carrying passengers is stated to be lower than that of either
displacement-type passenger ferries or
automobiles. Similar low-cost operation is
demonstrated by the 260-passenger Sputnik on
the Moscow-Astrakhan route. It has been found
that the cost of operating a Sputnik on this service
is only 8 per cent of that of the latest
displacement-type passenger ferry of the United
Volga Steamship Line. Time saving is one of the
most important considerations. In many cases,
hydrofoils take passengers to their destinations
faster than trains. For example, a Raketa service
covers the 800km (516 miles) from Gorki to

Kazan in 12 hours, while trains take 20 hours for
the same journey. The price of the ticket is the
same, however, by hydrofoil or rail.

The Meteor service from Moscow to Sormovo
takes 13 hours 40 minutes to cover 900km (559
miles). A conventional passenger ship requires
about three days to cover this distance.

In 1976 sea trials confirmed that the Kometa
can operate successfully in Arctic waters. Tests
conducted off the Kola Peninsula and Kam-
chatka, in the Soviet far east, demonstrated that
the craft can navigate through areas of broken ice
without sustaining damage.

A number of Soviet commercial hydrofoils are
equipped for night operations.

In 1977 it was announced that the number of
hydrofoils operating on Soviet waterways
exceeded 3,000. Nearly two-thirds of these are
likely to be Molnia, Volga and Nevka hydrofoils
which are used throughout the Soviet Union as
water taxis.

SOVIET FRONTIER POLICE

Some eight Pchela patrol hydrofoils, derived
from the Strela passenger ferry, are in service
with the KGB Frontier Police in the Baltic, Caspian and the Black Sea areas.

SOVIET NAVY

First hydrofoil warship to enter service with the
Soviet Navy was the wooden-hulled 'P 8' class
torpedo boat, which was equipped with bow foils
and a gas-turbine booster engine. These have
now been retired. In the spring of 1973, the first
sightings were made of a larger craft, a 230-ton
fast patrol boat given the NATO code name

Turya. This vessel, which is equipped for ASW
work, is based on the hull of the Osa missile craft.
The design employs a fixed surface-piercing bow
foil only. Powered by three 5,000hp diesels it has
a top speed of about 45 knots under calm conditions. Production is in hand at three Soviet naval
shipyards.

Latest hydrofoils to be built for the Soviet
Navy are the Sarancha, a 330-tonne missile-
armed fast strike craft, the Babochka, a 400-
tonne fast patrol boat equipped for anti-
submarine warfare, the 220-ton Matka, a
replacement for the Osa II displacement missile
craft, and a 220-tonne craft with a similar foil
configuration to that of Babochka and probably
designed as a replacement for the Pchela.

UNITED KINGDOM
CONDOR LTD

4 North Quay, St Peter Port, Guernsey
Telephone: 0481 24604
Telex: 4191275 (a/b DILIG G)
Type(s): RHS 140, 1, *Condor 4* (Navaltecnica);
RHS 160, 1, *Condor 5* (Navaltecnica)
Route(s): Guernsey-Sark-Jersey-St Malo-
Alderney

RED FUNNEL FERRIES

12 Bugle Street, Southampton, Hampshire SO9
4LJ, England
Telephone: 0703 333042
Telex: 47388 Chamcom G (Attn Red Funnel)
Type(s): RHS 70, 4, *Shearwater 3, 4, 5,* and *6*
(Rodriquez)
Route(s): Southampton-West Cowes
Journey time: 20 minutes in each direction

Boeing Jetfoil 929-115, *Princesa Guayarmina,* operated by Compania Trasmediterranea

RHS 140 *Condor 4* operated by Condor Ltd

UNITED STATES OF AMERICA
DEPARTMENT OF THE NAVY, NAVAL SEA SYSTEMS COMMAND (NAVSEA)

The Boeing/NATO PHM, Patrol Hydrofoil, Guided Missile, is a NATO project sponsored by the US Navy. It is being developed by NAVSEA PMS 303.

The first craft, the PHM-1 *Pegasus*, was accepted by the US Navy's Board of Inspection and Survey in June 1977 and is now serving with the Atlantic Fleet. A further five PHMs were delivered to the US Navy during 1981-82. All six vessels are fully operational and based in Key West, Florida.

SEA WORLD

1720 South Shores Road, Mission Bay, San Diego, California 92109, USA
Telephone: (714) 222 6363

This company operates three 28-seat hydrofoils, *Sea World II, III* and *IV* (Sprague Engineering Co) on 7-minute sightseeing tours around Mission Bay. The craft were the first built on the West Coast to be licensed by the US Coast Guard for commercial use.

In 1981 the craft were modified by Helmut Kock to increase their load capacity and improve their performance.

US NAVAL SHIP RESEARCH AND DEVELOPMENT CENTER

Type(s): High Point, PCH-1; Plainview AGEH-1 (de-activated June 1978)
Purpose: US Navy hydrofoil development programme

URUGUAY
BELT SA

Head Office: Rincon 467, 4th B Montevideo, Uruguay
Types: RHS 140, 2 (Navaltecnica)
Routes: Colonia-Buenos Aires

YUGOSLAVIA
SPLIT AIRPORT/INTEREXPORT

Split, Yugoslavia
Type(s): Kometa, 11 (Sormovo)
Route(s): Adriatic coastal services; tourist and passenger ferry services between Italy and Yugoslavia

CENTROTOURIST

Beograd, Yugoslavia
Type(s): Raketa, 2 (Sormovo)
Route(s): Adriatic coastal services

RUDNAP

Beograd, Yugoslavia
Type(s): Meteor, 4 (Sormovo)
Route(s): Adriatic coastal services

ZAIRE
NAVAL FORCE

Bases: Matadi and Lake Tanganyika
Type(s): 'Hu Chwan' class, 3 (Shanghai)

PHM-1 *Pegasus* test firing Harpoon anti-ship missile

FAST CATAMARANS

AUSTRALIA

INTERNATIONAL CATAMARANS

1 Secheron Road, Battery Point, Tasmania 7000, Australia
Telephone: (002) 34 8021/34 3296
4 Help Street, Chatswood, New South Wales 2067, Australia
Telephone: (02) 411 1725
Telex: AA 72710 INCAT

Formed in 1978, International Catamarans has designed 18-metre, 20-metre, 22-metre and 29-metre vessels. Catamarans are built at the company's yard in Hobart and under licence in Hong Kong, New Zealand, Singapore and elsewhere in Australia.

Fitting out and diesel engines vary according to customers' specifications. The 20-metre, 21-metre and 22-metre designs each carry over 200 passengers. A 29-metre ferry and three 29-metre supply boats have also been built. At the end of 1983, almost 20 catamarans had been delivered.

20-METRE CATAMARAN

Length overall: 20·5m
Beam overall: 8·2m
Draught: 1·5m
Engines: 2 × 550hp
Max speed: 28 knots
Cruising speed: 24 knots

22-METRE CATAMARAN

Length overall: 23m
Beam overall: 8·7m
Draught: 1·7m
Engines: 2 × 800hp
Max speed: 29 knots
Cruising speed: 25 knots

Mingzhu Hu, one of four International Catamarans 21m craft operated by People's Republic of China

Quicksilver, an International Catamarans 20m craft

FINLAND

VALMETIN LAIVATEOLLISUUS

A new series of catamaran fast ferries, the MXA range, is to be built in Finland by Valmetin Laivateollisuus. The craft are being marketed by the MXA Consulting organisation. They will be built in welded aluminium, are being offered with diesel or gas turbine powerplants and propeller or waterjet propulsion.

The basic MXA 3000 is powered by two MTU 1,310kW diesels and will carry 150 to 250 passengers at 28 to 30 knots. Overall length of the craft will be 29·7 metres, beam 9·2 metres and maximum draught 1·9 metres.

Included in the series is the MXA 3300, an offshore variant with an overall length of 32·7 metres, a beam of 9·4 metres and draught of 1·2 to 2·2 metres. It will carry up to 112 passengers and 20 tonnes of cargo.

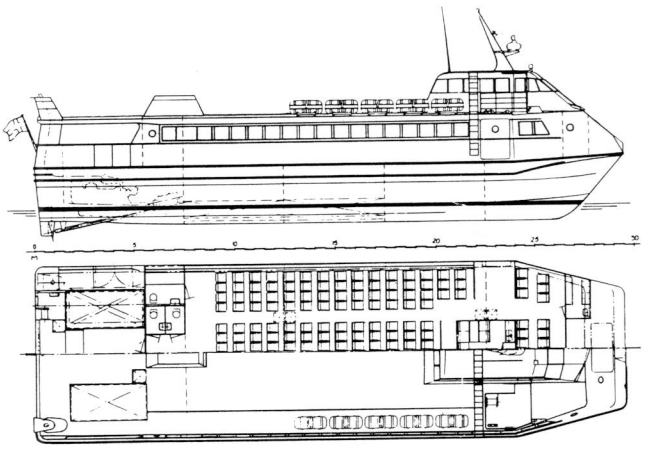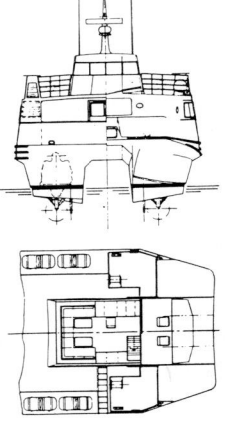

MXA 3000 catamaran fast ferry

JAPAN

MITSUI ENGINEERING & SHIPBUILDING CO LTD

6-4, Tsukiji 5-chome, Chuo-ku, Tokyo 104, Japan

Telephone: (03) 544 3451/3910
Telex: J22821/J22924

Officials:
See ACV section

Under a licensing agreement concluded in 1973 with Westamarine A/S, Mandal, Norway, Mitsui built three Super Westamaran CP20s. The craft, which carries up to 182 passengers, has a cruising speed of about 25 knots and is comparable to the Norwegian-built Westamaran 86. It can operate in waves 1·2 to 1·5 metres high.

In 1978 Mitsui, employing its own design team, developed the Supermaran CP20HF, seating 192 passengers and with a cruising speed of about 30 knots. This craft has been redesigned for better seaworthiness. It can operate in a maximum wave height of 2·5 metres when comfortable service can be provided with no loss of speed. Two had been delivered by the end of 1983.

The first Supermaran CP30 has been recently delivered to the Nankai Ferry Company Limited in Japan. It carries 280 passengers at a cruising speed of 28 knots. Not only has this craft been improved for operational economy, with increased passenger capacity and comparatively less power, but also in seaworthiness. Maximum operable wave height is three metres and comfortable service is assured at a wave height of 2·5 metres or less with no loss of speed.

Dimensions	Super Westamaran CP20	Supermaran CP20HF	Supermaran CP30
Length overall	26·46m	32·8m	40·9m
Breadth	8·8m	9·2m	10·8m
Draught	1·18m	1·2m	1·3m
Gross tonnage, approx	192 tons	275 tons	283 tons
Passengers	182	195	280
Crew	5	5	4
Main engine	MTU 12V331TC82	Fuji Pielstic	Fuji Pielstic
	2 sets	12PA4V185-VG 2 sets	12PA4V185-VG 2 sets
MCO	1,240ps × 2,270rpm	2,540ps × 1,475rpm	2,540ps × 1,475rpm
CSO	1,125ps × 2,200rpm	2,280ps × 1,425rpm	2,280ps × 1,425rpm
Max speed	28·5 knots	30·7 knots	approx 29 knots
Service speed, approx	25 knots	30 knots	28 knots
Cruising range, approx	9 hours	9 hours	10 hours

Mitsui Catamaran CP30

NORWAY

FJELLSTRAND AS

N-5632 Omastrand, Norway
Telephone: 4755 61 100
Telex: 42 148

Fjellstrand AS built its first catamaran, Alumaran 165, in 1976. It has since built three further craft of this type, as well as ten 31·5-metre vessels from a design introduced in 1981. Both craft are for use as passenger ferries and mixed traffic/supply boats. Superstructure, diesel engine and performance options are available according to customers' requirements.

31·5-METRE CATAMARAN

There are several versions of the 31·5-metre catamaran, ranging from a 292-seat passenger ferry to a supply boat which can carry 96 men and,

Helgeland, Fjellstrand 31·5m catamaran

on an aft deck, 15 tonnes of cargo. Depending on the type of engines used, speeds of up to 32 knots can be attained.

HULL: Welded aluminium, with pointed V-frames at bow to reduce slamming and pitching stresses in rough seas. Hulls are divided into watertight compartments by transverse webs and longitudinal stiffeners. Main and superstructure decks are continuous and have transverse webs and longitudinal stiffeners. Tunnel height between the hulls at the bow is raised to increase buoyancy and to prevent waves from reaching the top of the tunnel.

31·5-METRE FERRY M/V LYGRO

Length overall: 31·5m
Max beam: 9·4m
Draught: 2·05m
Approx tonnage: 314 tonnes
Fuel capacity: 9,000 litres
Average fuel consumption: 480 litres/h
Engines: 2 × MTU 16V 396 TB63s delivering 1,650rpm
Max speed: 30 knots
Cruising speed: 26 knots
Cruising range: 560n miles

31·5-METRE OFFSHORE SUPPLY BOAT M/V NORSUL CATAMARAN

Length overall: 31·5m
Max beam: 9·4m
Draught: 1·85m
Approx tonnage: 190 tonnes
Fuel capacity: 9,800 litres
Average fuel consumption: 480 litres/h
Engines: 2 × MTU 12V 396 TB63s delivering 1,330hp at 1,650rpm
Max speed: 30 knots
Cruising speed: 26 knots
Cruising range: 510n miles

31·5-METRE OFFSHORE CATAMARAN M/V ANAHITRA

Length overall: 31·5m
Max beam: 9·4m
Draught: 2·3m
Approx tonnage: 270 tonnes
Fuel capacity: 14,000 litres
Engines: 2 × 5 ACM 195 V12 RVR delivering 2,000hp at 1,400rpm
Max speed: 31 knots
Cruising speed: 28 knots
Cruising range: 525n miles

Norsul Catamaran, Fjellstrand 31·5m offshore catamaran

M/V Lygro

Anahitra, Fjellstrand 31·5m offshore catamaran

WESTAMARIN A/S

PO Box 143, 4501 Mandal, Norway
Telephone: 042-62 222
Telex: 16514

Westamarin A/S was established in 1960, under the name of Westermoen Hydrofoil, to produce, develop and market high-speed surface vessels for commercial and military uses. In 1970 the company introduced the Westamaran, an asymmetric catamaran based on a semi-planing hull of welded marine aluminium. Three versions, the Westamaran 86, 95 and 100, have been built. Larger models for passenger and offshore support duties are projected.

WESTAMARAN 86

24 Westamaran 86s have been built. Most are in service in Scandinavia, fitted out for 140 to 167 passengers. Three of the vessels operating in

Stern view of W86 *Highland Seabird*

Norway are equipped to carry 94 to 100 passengers and up to 6 tonnes of freight. The main powerplants are two MTU 1,100hp diesels.
DIMENSIONS
Length: 26·7m (89ft)
Beam: 9m (29ft)
Draught: 1·2m (4ft)
WEIGHTS
Gross tonnage: 200 tons
Net tonnage: 135 tons
PERFORMANCE
Max speed: 28 knots
Range: 235n miles

WESTAMARAN 95

A longer version of the Westamaran 86, the Westamaran 95 can carry up to 218 passengers. Two SACM 1,800hp diesels give the 29·1m (95ft 6in) vessel a maximum speed of 32 knots. 15 Westamaran 95s have been delivered to operators in Norway, Denmark, Italy, Spain and Yugoslavia. A 30m (98ft 6in) Westamaran 95 has also been developed. Powered by two Avco Lycoming 3,350hp gas turbines driving waterjet units, it can carry 205 passengers at speeds up to 40 knots.

Westamaran W95 *Alisur Amarillo*

WESTAMARAN 100T

The largest Westamaran vessel so far built, the Westamaran 100T can seat up to 260 passengers. Two Avco Lycoming TF40 gas turbines, each producing 4,000hp, driving Rocketdyne PJ24 waterjet units give the vessel a maximum speed of 38 knots. Three are in service in Norway and a diesel-powered version is also available.

POLAND

A Polish-built fast catamaran ferry has entered service in the Soviet Union, operating between the main towns along the Black Sea coast of the Caucasus. The craft, named *Iveruja*, seats four hundred passengers and is the first of a series of five.

SWEDEN

MARINTEKNIK INTERNATIONAL LIMITED

33/F New World Tower, 16-18 Queen's Road, C Hong Kong
Telephone: 5-218302
Telex: 74493 HMHCO HX
Marinteknik Verkstads AB
PO Box 7, S-740 71 Oregrund, Sweden
Telephone: (0) 173 30460
Telex: 76182 MARTAB S

Marinteknik Shipbuilders (S) Pte Ltd
Lot A, 6961 Pioneer Sector 1, Jurong, Singapore 2262
Telephone: 8614178/9; 8611706/7
Telex: RS 38890 BAY

Established in 1968, the companies in the Marinteknik Group specialise in the design and construction of high-speed catamarans. A range of diesel-powered, waterjet-propelled vessels is produced to suit particular customer requirements. Craft with speeds up to 40 knots are offered, seating from 200 to 500 passengers or in passenger plus cargo carrying layouts.

Craft are constructed in specially designed, corrosion-resistant aluminium alloy extrusion, giving great strength and overcoming problems caused by flexing and stressing of the hulls.

JETCAT JC-F1

The Jetcat JC-F1 is mainly constructed in specially-designed corrosion-resistant aluminium alloy extrusions welded together to form the hull plating, bulkheads and frames.
PROPULSION: Two MTU 12V 396 TB 83 1,542bhp diesels drive KaMeWa S-62 waterjets with steering nozzles able to deflect the waterjet stream ±30 degrees. All propulsion machinery is housed within the hulls, assisting in the provision of a low centre of gravity.
HULL: The very narrow hulls are symmetrical and interchangeable, being mounted to the underside of the bridging structure by anti-vibration mountings. Both hulls are divided into the required number of watertight compartments as stipulated by the classification and regulatory authorities.
ACCOMMODATION: Seating for normal ferry operations is provided for 197 passengers.

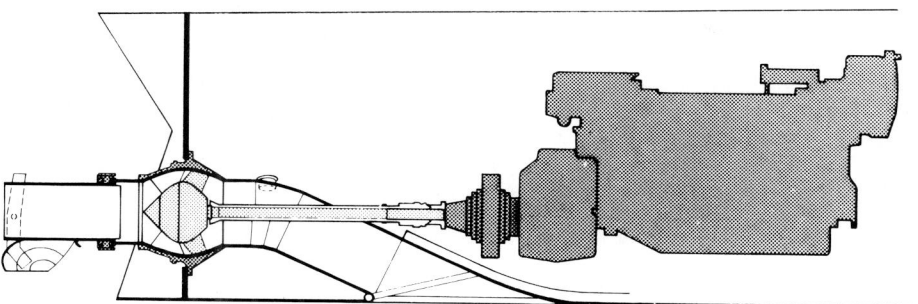

Propulsion arrangement on Jetcat JC-F1

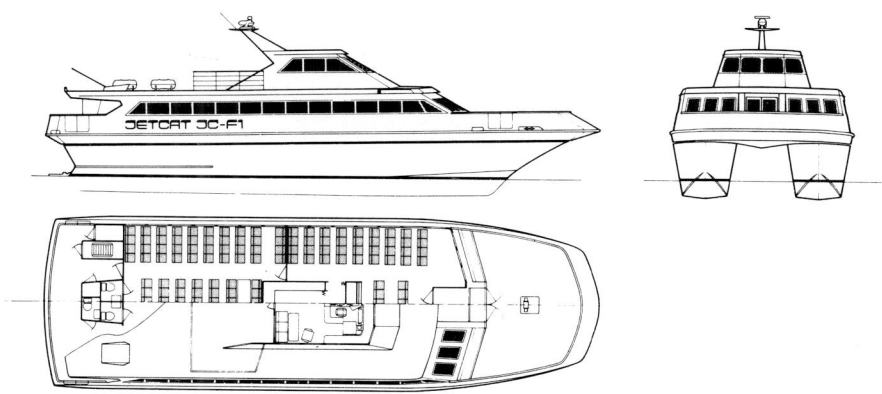

General arrangement of standard Jetcat JC-F1

Jetcat JC-F1 001

DIMENSIONS
Length: 29·8m (97ft 9in)
Beam: 9·4m (30ft 10in)
Height: 7m (23ft)
Draught: 1·2m (3ft 11in)
WEIGHTS
Displacement: 84 tonnes
Nominal max payload: 16·75 tonnes
Fuel, max capacity: 6·02 tonnes
PERFORMANCE
Cruising speed: 30 knots
Range with max payload: 355n miles

MARINJET PV 2400 PASSENGER FERRY

The PV 2400 is a semi-planing catamaran, designed as a 252-seat, high-speed ferry for use in coastal and sheltered waters. It is also available in a double-deck configuration seating up to 368 passengers.

The two hulls, passenger deck and control bridge superstructure are manufactured as one coherent unit. The hulls are symmetrical and narrow, with a sharp stem and transom. The complete craft is made from salt water resistant aluminium alloy extrusions and plates, welded together.

Power is provided by two MTU 12V 396 TB 83 diesels producing 1,180kW at 1,940rpm. These drive two electro-hydraulically controlled KaMeWa 60/S62/6 mixed flow waterjets. Steering is by deflecting the waterjet nozzles, reversing by introducing guide vane buckets into the jetstreams, thereby reversing the direction of thrust.

DIMENSIONS
Length, overall: 33m
Beam, overall: 9·4m
Draught, loaded: 1·2m
WEIGHTS
Disposable load: 24 tonnes
Operating weight: 98 tonnes
PERFORMANCE
Max speed: 35 knots
Cruising speed: 32 knots
Fuel capacity: 7,000 litres
Fuel consumption, cruising: 567 litres/h
Range: 700km

MARINJET PV 3100 PASSENGER FERRY

This is available as either a single- or double-deck ferry. Overall dimensions are identical to

Jetcat JC-F1 001

Apollo Jet, one of four PC 3000s operating in Hong Kong

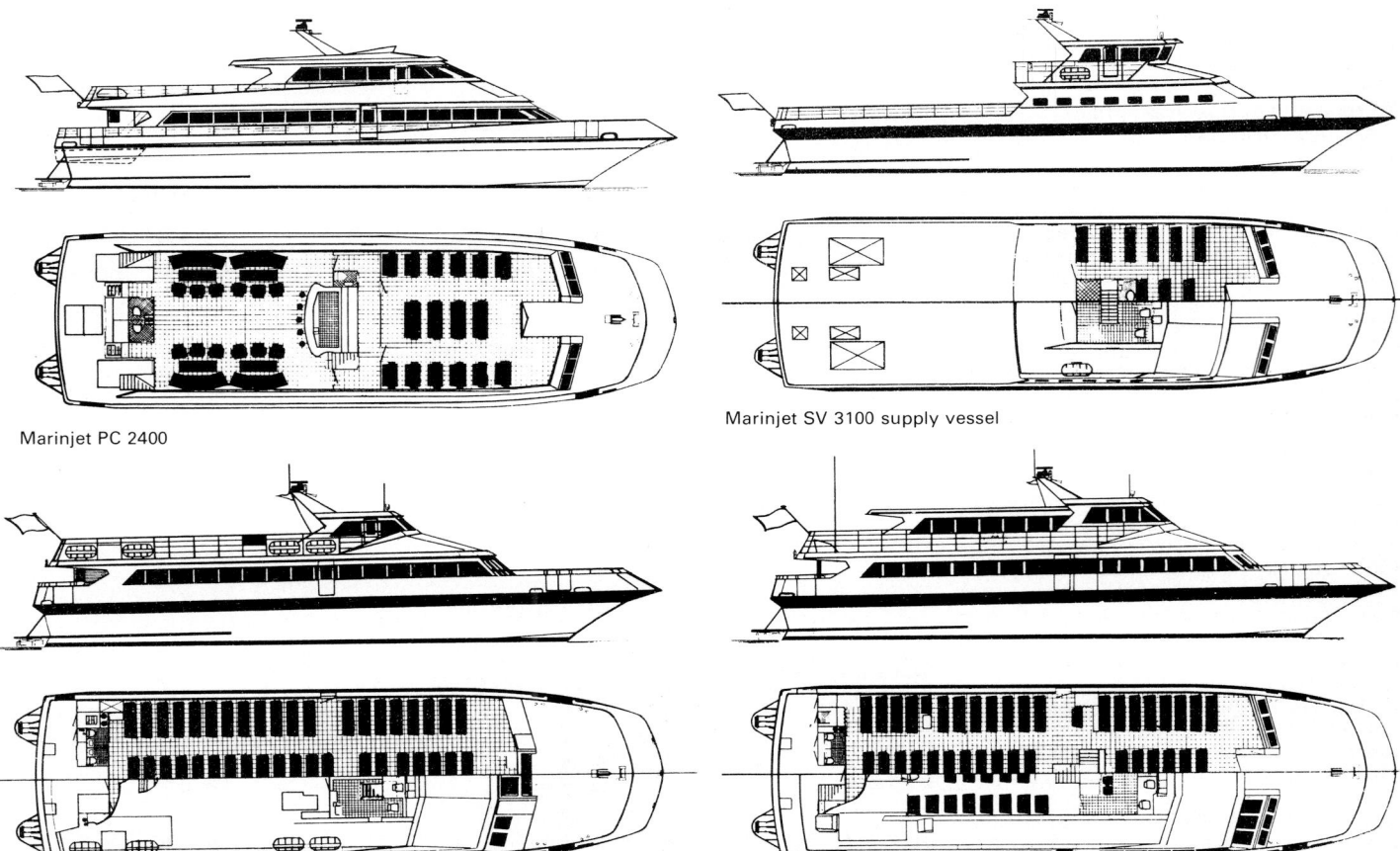

Marinjet PC 2400

Marinjet SV 3100 supply vessel

Marinjet PV 2400

Marinjet PV 3100 passenger vessel in double deck configuration

those of the PV 2400. The two MTU 16 V 396 TB 83 diesels produce 1,540kW at 1,940rpm and drive two electro-hydraulically controlled KaMeWa 63/S62/6 mixed flow waterjets. The higher rated engines and waterjets give improved performance, otherwise all details are as for the PV 2400.

PERFORMANCE
Max speed: 40 knots
Cruising speed: 37 knots
Range: 700km

MARINJET SV 3100 CREW BOAT

This is a high performance crew boat, able to carry up to 30-tonne payloads at speeds of up to 40 knots. It is a low-resistance, semi-planing catamaran with very shallow draught and high stability features.

Power is provided by two MTU 16 V 396 TB 83 diesels, producing 1,180kW at 1,940rpm. These drive two electro-hydraulically controlled KaMeWa 63/S62/6 mixed flow waterjets.

Marinjet PV 2400

DIMENSIONS
Length, overall: 34m
Beam, overall: 9·4m
Draught, loaded: 1·2m

PERFORMANCE
Max speed: 40 knots
Cruising speed: 37 knots
Range: 700km

USSR

A prototype catamaran river cruiser has been completed at a Soviet shipyard in Odessa. The craft is reported to have accommodation for 300 passengers, refreshment facilities and a swimming pool. Series production is planned.

UNITED KINGDOM

VOSPER THORNYCROFT (UK) LIMITED

Head Office: Fareham House, East Street, Fareham, Hampshire PO16 0BW, England
Telephone: 0329 283411
Telex: 86669 VT FARE G
Cables: Repsov, Portsmouth
Officials: See main entry in ACV section

44-METRE CATAMARAN PATROL CRAFT

The first catamaran warship designed by a major UK shipbuilder, Vosper Thornycroft's new 44-metre craft is suitable for EEZ surveillance, offshore patrol and fast attack roles. For normal patrol duty, it is equipped with a single 30 mm cannon, machine-gun and a Lynx helicopter.

The aluminium hull is based on that of a projected ferry and commercial variants will be available.

Advantages of the catamaran configuration over conventional monohull warships of similar length include a much larger payload area on the main deck as a result of the rectangular planform; greatly improved lateral stability, and better manoeuvrability due to the wide separation of the twin propellers.

The twin hulls will not be of conventional planing type, but they will begin to plane at high speed. Static draught of the 44-metre vessels will be less than two metres.

Two versions of the 44-metre naval catamaran are envisaged: an EEZ craft with helicopter and an endurance of about 7 days, and an ASuW missile craft with a slightly wider beam.
POWER PLANT: Two Paxman 16RP200 or similar diesels, each developing 1,500shp.
HULL: Marine-grade aluminium alloy.
ACCOMMODATION: Air-conditioned working and off-duty accommodation for crew of 23.
DIMENSIONS
Length overall: 43·7m
Length waterline: 40m
Beam overall: 12·7m
PERFORMANCE
Depending on power plant and equipment,
Top speed, craft illustrated: about 30 knots

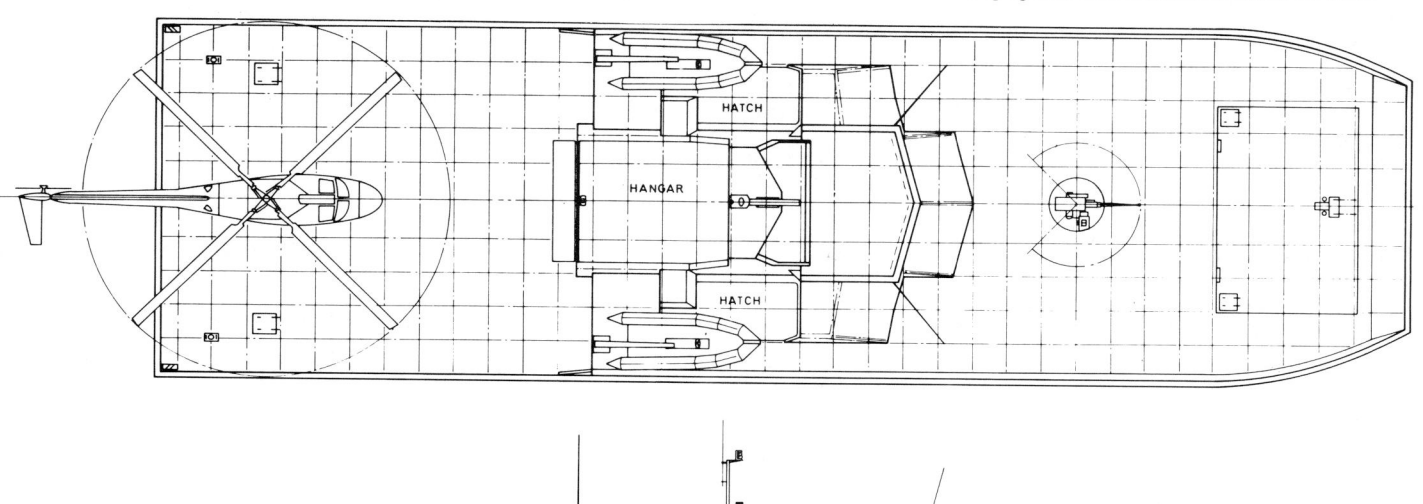

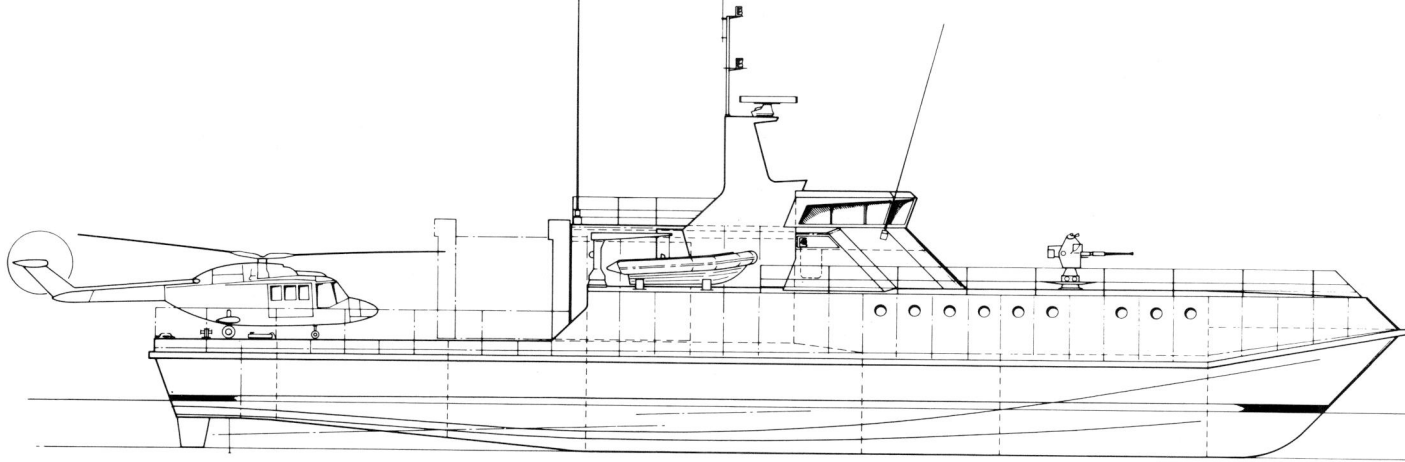

General arrangement of Vosper Thornycroft (UK) 44m fast catamaran patrol craft

CATAMARAN OPERATORS

Australia
Operator: Outer Barrier Reef Cruises
Route(s): Port Douglas-St Crispins Reef
Vessels: *Quicksilver* (International Catamarans 20m)

Operator: Telford South Middle Islands Ltd
Route(s): Whitsunday Islands, North Queensland
Vessels: *Telford Reef* (International Catamarans 22m)

Operator: McLeans Roylen Cruises Pty Ltd
Route(s): Mackay-Brampton Island, North Queensland
Vessels: *Spirit of Roylen* (International Catamarans 29m)

Brazil
Operator: Norsul Offshore
Base: Macal
Vessels: *Norsul Catamaran* (FAY 31·5m)

Cameroon
Operator: SURF
Base: Douala
Vessels: *Anahitra* (FAY 31·5m)

China, People's Republic
Operator: People's Republic of China
Route(s): Jiang Men-Hong Kong
Vessels: *Mingzhu Hu* (International Catamarans 21m)
Yinzhou Hu (International Catamarans 21m)
Liuhua HJ (International Catamarans 21m)

Denmark
Operator: A/S D/S Øresund
Route: Copenhagen-Malmø
Vessels: *Tumleren* (W95)
Tunen (W95)
Tranen (W95)

France
Operator: Service Maritime
Route: Carteret-Jersey
Vessels: *Pegasus* (W86)

Operator: Vedettes Vertes Granvillaises
Route: Granville-Jersey
Vessels: *Belle de Dinard* (W86)

Hong Kong
Operator: Hongkong Macao Hydrofoil Company
Route(s): Hong Kong-Macao
Hong Kong-Khukai
Vessels: *Apollo Jet* (Jetcat)
Hercules Jet (Jetcat)
Janus Jet (Jetcat)
Triton Jet (Jetcat)

Italy
Operator: Libra Navigazione Lauro di Agostino Lauro SA
Route(s): Naples-Ischia-Capri
Vessels: *Amarischia* (W95)
Celestina (W95)

Japan
Operator: Dong-hae Kosokchun Co
Route(s): Imwon-Chodong
Vessels: *Dong-hae Kosok I* (CP 20)

Operator: Nankai Ferry Co
Route(s): Wakaayama-Komatsujima
Vessels: *Marine Hawk* (CP 30)

Operator: Setonaikai Kisen Co
Route(s): Mihara-Imabari
Vessels: *Marine Star* (CP 20)

Operator: Showa Kaiun Co
Route(s): Mihara-Imabari
Vessels: *Blue Hawk* (CP 20)

Operator: Tokushima Kosokusen Co
Route(s): Osaku-Tokushima
Vessels: *Sunshine* (CP 20HF)
Blue Sky (CP 20HF)

Korea (Republic)
Operator: Dong-hae Kosokchun Co
Route(s): Imwon-Chodong
Vessels: *Dong-hae Kosok I* (CP 20)

Netherlands
Operator: BV Terschellinger Stoomboot Mij
Route(s): Terschellinger-Harlingen
Vessels: *Koegelwieck* (W86)

Norway
Operator: Bergen Nohordland Rutelag
Base: Bergen
Vessels: *Lygra* (FAY 31·5m)

Operator: A/S Haanes Rederi
Base: Kristiansand
Vessels: *Gimle Belle* (W100T)
Gimle Bird (W100T)
Gimle Bay (W100T)

Operator: A/S Haugesund D/S
Route(s): Haugesund-Bergen
Haugesund-Stavanger
Vessels: *Haugesund* (W86)*
Storesund (W86)
*Passenger/cargo version

Operator: Helgeland Trafikkselskap
Base: Traen Fjord
Vessels: *Traena* (Alumaran 165)
Helgeland (FAY 31·5m)

Operator: A/S Troms Fylkes D/S
Base: Tromso
Vessels: *Fjorddronningen* (W86)
Fjordkongen (W86)
Fjordprinsessen (W86)
Tromsprinsen (W95)

Operator: Det Stavangerske D/S
Route(s): Stavanger-Sauda
Stavanger-Sanneid
Vessels: *Fjorddrott* (W86)
Mayflower (W86)
Sauda (W86)
Fjordbris (W86)

Operator: DSD/Hardanger Sunnhordalandske D/S (Flaggruten)
Route(s): Stavanger-Bergen
Vessels: *Draupner* (W86)
Sleipner (W95)
Vingtor (W95)

Operator: Finnmark Fylkesrederi & Ruteselskap
Route(s): Hammerfest-Loppa
Hammerfest-Masøy
Vessels: *Brynilen* (W86)*
Hornøy (W86)
*Passenger/cargo version

Operator: Fosen Trafikklag A/S
Route(s): Trondheim-Sula
Vessels: *Hertugbussen* (W86)
Kongsbussen (W86)
Olavsbussen (W86)

Operator: Fylkesbaatane i Sogne og Fjordane
Route(s): Bergen-Årdalstangen
Bergen-Nordfjordeid
Vessels: *Fjordglytt* (W86)
Fjordtroll (W86)

Operator: Hardanger Sunnhordalandske D/S
Route(s): Bergen-Tittelsnes
Bergen-Ølen
Vessels: *Sunnhordaland* (W95)
Tedno (W86)

Operator: Oygarden & Sotra Rutelag
Route(s): Rognøysund-Bergen
Vessels: *Øygar* (W86)*
*Passenger/cargo version

Operator: Saltens D/S
Route(s): Bodø-Skutvik
Vessels: *Steigtind* (W86)

Spain
Operator: Alisur SA
Base: Fuerteventura
Vessels: *Alisur Azur* (W95T)
Alisur Amarillo (W95)

United Kingdom
Operator: Western Ferries (Argyll)
Base: Glasgow
Vessels: *Highland Seabird* (W86)

Yugoslavia
Operator: Union Dalmacijou Ooura Flota
Base: Split
Vessels: *Mediteran* (W96)
Marina (W84)

SEMI-SUBMERGED CATAMARANS

FINLAND

OY WÄRTSILÄ AB

Wärtsilä Helsinki Shipyard, PO Box 132, SF-00150, Helsinki 15, Finland

Wärtsilä is designing a large ocean-going semi-submerged catamaran for cruises in the Carribean Sea. The vessel will be capable of 16 knots and will be equipped with a large lift, about 500 square metres in area, which will permit the launching of sightseeing craft from the above-water platform when required. Each sightseeing craft will carry up to 150 passengers and all three craft can be raised or lowered simultaneously. The vessel will also carry a range of water sports equipment for use when at anchor or from a mooring.

Power will be supplied by four Wärtsilä Pielstic 8PCZL diesels, each developing 4,222hp. The engines will be mounted in pairs, one pair in each sub-sea hull. Each pair will drive two low revolution variable-pitch propellers through reduction gearboxes.

As a cruise liner, the configuration offers a number of advantages: excellent seagoing qualities, low noise and vibration and a wide range of possibilities for the layout of the below-deck spaces.

DIMENSIONS
Length: 165m
Beam: 62m
Height (to boat deck): 34m
Draught: 11m
PERFORMANCE
Speed: 16 knots

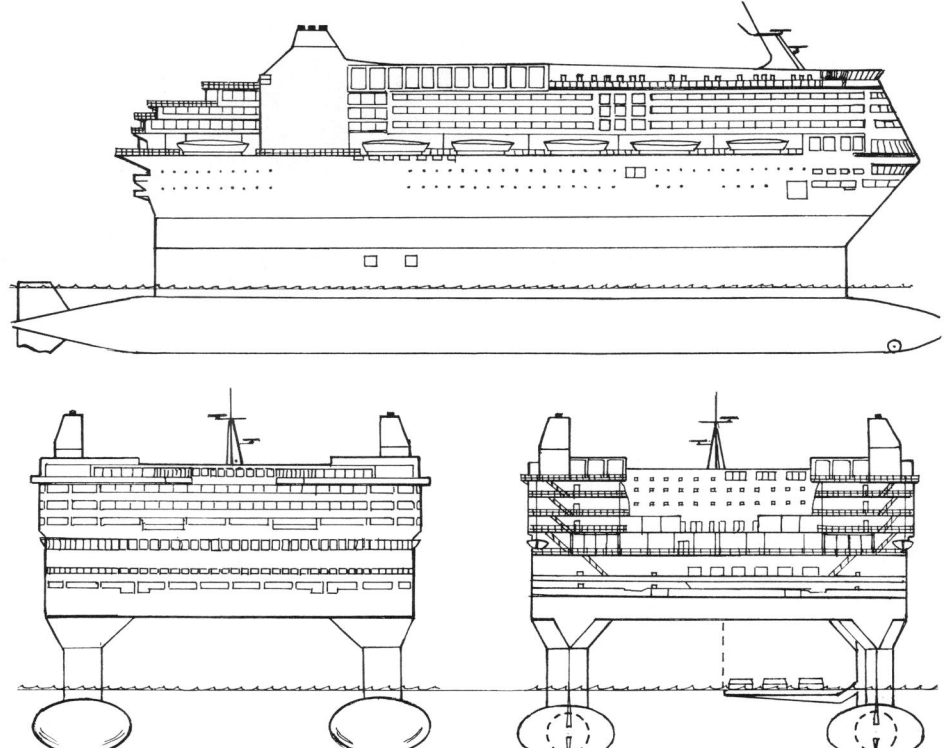

Wärtsilä's projected semi-submerged catamaran cruise liner

JAPAN

MITSUI ENGINEERING & SHIPBUILDING CO LTD

6-4, Tsukiji 5-chome, Chuo-ku, Tokyo 104, Japan
Telephone: (03) 544-3451/3910
Telex: J22821/J22924

Mitsui began its high-speed semi-submerged catamaran development programme (SSC) in 1970. Since 1976, the programme has been operated in conjunction with the Japanese Marine Machinery Development Association (JAMDA). In 1977, following extensive research and model tests, Mitsui built the experimental 18·37-tonne Marine Ace in order to obtain practical experience with this hull form. In 1979 the first SSC high-speed passenger vessel was launched under the provisional name Mesa 80. After extensive trials it was completed in 1981 and renamed Seagull. It has since been operated by Tokai Kisen Co Ltd on a passenger ferry service between Tokyo and Oshima and Niijima on Izu island during the summer and Atami and Oshima during the off-seasons. It was only the second such vessel to be built, the first being the US Navy's SSP Kaimalino range support vessel, designed to operate in the rough seas off the Hawaiian islands.

The company has also developed and built a SSC hydrographic survey vessel, Kotozaki, for the Fourth District Port Construction Bureau of the Japanese Ministry of Transport. The vessel was completed in 1981.

Semi-submerged catamarans can be built to suit a wide variety of applications from passenger ferries to offshore rig-support vessels.

MARINE ACE

Mitsui's first experimental SSC, Marine Ace, is built in marine-grade aluminium alloy and can operate in sea states 2 to 3. Its automatically-controlled fin stabilisers reduce ship motion in waves.
PROPULSION: Motive power for Marine Ace is supplied by two sets of V-type four-cycle petrol engines, each developing 200bhp at 3,700rpm. Each drives, via a vertical intermediate transmission shaft and bevel gear, a three-bladed fixed-pitch propeller; one at the end of each of the two torpedo-like hulls.
tank capacity:
ballast: 11·01m³ (2,420 gallons)
Fuel oil: 1·45m³ (320 gallons).

18·37-tonne Marine Ace

AUTOMATIC MOTION CONTROL SYS-
TEM: Four sets of fin stabilisers, driven by hydraulic servo motors, reduce ship motion in heavy
seas.

DIMENSIONS
Length overall: 12·35m (40ft 6in)
  registered: 11·95m (39ft 2in)
Beam max: 6·5m (21ft 4in)
  at load line: 5·8m (19ft)
Designed full load draught: 1·55m (5ft 1in)
WEIGHTS
Full load displacement: 18·37 tonnes
  (*about 22 tonnes)
Gross tonnage: 29·91 tonnes
  (*31·56 tonnes)
PERFORMANCE
Speed, max cruising revolutions, full load
  draught: about 18 knots
(*about 14 knots)
*after modification in 1978

Seagull

SEAGULL

Developed jointly by Mitsui Engineering &
Shipbuilding Co Ltd and the Japanese Marine
Machinery Development Association (JAM-
DA), the 27-knot Seagull is the world's first
commercial semi-submerged catamaran. Despite
its small size, the overall length is just under 36m
(118ft), the vessel provides a stable ride in seas
with 3·5m (11ft 6in) waves.

During the first ten-month long commercial
run in a service between Atami and Oshima,
Seagull established an operating record of 97 per
cent. The incidence of seasick passengers was
very low, 0·5 per cent or less, proving the exceptional riding comfort.
PROPULSION: Main engines are two Fuji-
SEMT marine diesels, each developing 4,050hp
at 1,475rpm. Each drives, via a vertical transmis-
sion shaft and bevel gear, a three-blade fixed-
pitch propeller. Two 206·25kVA generators
provide electrical power.
HULL: Built in marine grade aluminium alloy.
ACCOMMODATION: Crew of eight. Pas-
senger seats provided for 402.
AUTOMATIC MOTION CONTROL SYS-
TEM: Four sets of fin stabilisers driven by hyd-
raulic servo motors reduce ship motion in heavy
seas.
DIMENSIONS
Length overall: 35·9m (117ft 9in)
Beam: 17·1m (56ft 1in)
Depth: 5·84m (19ft 2in)
Designed draught: 3·15m (10ft 4in)
WEIGHTS
Gross tonnage: 672·08 tonnes approx
PERFORMANCE
Max speed: about 27 knots

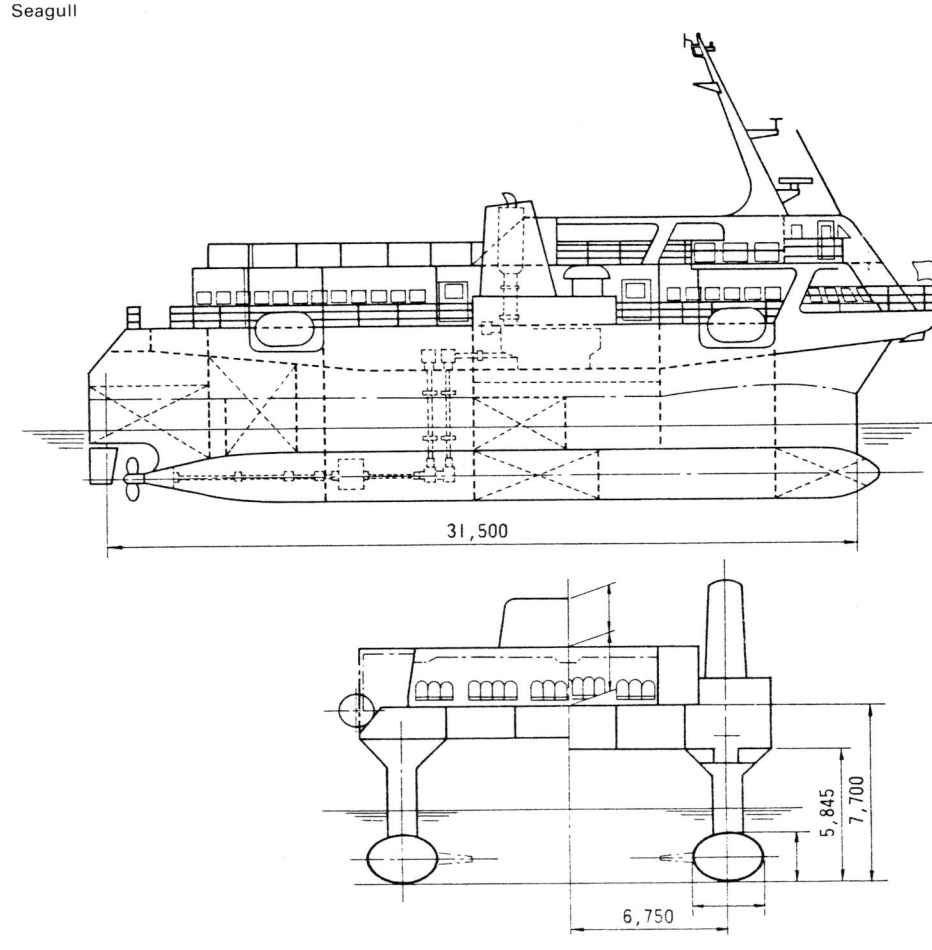
General arrangement of Seagull

KOTOZAKI

The world's first hydrographic survey vessel of
the SSC type, Kotozaki is operated by the Fourth
District Port Construction Bureau of the
Japanese Ministry of Transport.

Kotozaki provides a stable platform from
which data can be gathered and its rectangular
decks allow ample space for hydrographic
equipment, laboratory facilities, working and
living accommodation.
PROPULSION: Main engines are two Fuji-
SEMT marine diesels, each developing 1,900ps
at 1,475rpm. Each drives, via a vertical transmis-
sion shaft and bevel gear, a controllable pitch
propeller.
HULL: Hybrid structure built in steel and
marine-grade aluminium alloy.
ACCOMMODATION: Complement of 20.
MOTION CONTROL SYSTEM: Controllable
pitch propellers and manually-operated fin
stabilisers.
DIMENSIONS
Length overall: 27m (88ft 6in)
Beam: 12·5m (41ft)
Depth: 4·6m (15ft 1in)
Designed draught: 3·2m (10ft 5in)
WEIGHTS
Gross tonnage: 253·67 tonnes
PERFORMANCE
Max speed: about 20·5 knots

Kotozaki

2,800-TON SSC

Mitsui is constructing a 2,800-ton, experimental semi-submerged catamaran for the Japanese Marine Science and Technology Centre. The vessel is due to be completed in May 1985 and is intended as a divers' support craft and also as an offshore testing base for various types of observation and surveying equipment.

It will be equipped with a submersible decompression chamber, a deck decompression chamber for 300m and 500m diving, a precision position finding system and a dynamic positioning system.

2,800-ton SSC

UNION OF SOVIET SOCIALIST REPUBLICS

SEMI-SUBMERGED CATAMARAN PROJECTS

As indicated by the accompanying illustration, Soviet government ship-design bureaus are examining the potential of the semi-submerged catamaran. A number of designs and models have been prepared and tank tests undertaken.

Among the advantages foreseen by Soviet shipbuilders are the deeply-submerged hulls which will reduce wave resistance, require less motive power and lower fuel consumption. The rectangular planform of the above water hull will permit a more straightforward approach to siting the cabins, car decks and recreational areas.

The sub-sea hulls would accommodate cars or containers loaded via lifts. In the forward upper sections of the sub-sea hulls, small viewing lounges would be provided to enable passengers to see the underwater world.

Soviet SSC passenger/car-ferry design

UNITED STATES OF AMERICA

RMI, INC

Head Office: 225 West 30th Street, National City, California 92050, USA

Telephone: (619) 474 8885

Telex: 695212 RMIMARINE NTCY

Officials:
Wilfred J Eggington, *Chairman and Chief Executive Officer*
F Patrick Burke, *Executive Vice President*
Darrell L Reed, *Executive Vice President*
Robert Derusha, *Vice President, Shipyard Operations*
John H Barker, *Director of Engineering*
Robert S Cramb, *Director of Business Development*
George Luedeke, Jr, *Director of SWATH Programmes*
Jack J Edwards, *Director of ACV Programmes*
Charles M Lee, *Director of SES Programmes*
Richard Thomas, *Director of Repair Programmes*
Washington Representative:
W C Beckwith Associates, 205 Pennsylvania Avenue, SE Washington DC 20003, USA
Telephone: (202) 671 4528

SWATH yacht cruiser concept

SD 60 HALYCON

RMI has designed and built a 60ft Small Waterplane Area Twin Hull (SWATH) boat, designated SD 60. The boat was launched for trials in December 1984, and is undergoing builders trials and demonstrations.

The SD60 SWATH offers advantages over conventional craft in transporting passengers and cargo. For example, pitch and roll motions will be significantly less than those of comparable small monohulls over the full range of anticipated sea conditions, and this will give an improved ride. Its increased speed performance in heavy seas will enable it to maintain headway at design speed through and beyond Sea State 4; an important advantage in commercial service operations. The wide separation between its water propellers will allow precise manoeuvring within ports, channels and rivers, and positioning alongside ships or offshore oil platforms.

The deckhouse has a galley, head and berthing accommodation for the crew and space for 20 passengers. The passenger space can be converted to living quarters for 9 additional crew members. The pilot house can accommodate a full range of commercial communications and marine navigation systems. Microprocessor ship control systems and vessel management systems are fitted, as well as fire fighting, diving support and hydrographic survey equipment. Oceangoing ships or Lighter-Aboard-Ship (LASH) barges will be able to carry the boat on deck.

Propulsion power is by twin Caterpillar 3408 DITA marine diesels each driving, via a reduction gear and Eaton V-belt drive, a 45in diameter VPO FR-H Hundested variable-pitch propeller. The electric plant features twin Model 4.236M (25kW) Perkins marine diesel electric generator sets. The design meets USCG safety requirements and certification as a commercial passenger boat under 100 gross tons in displacement.

DIMENSIONS
Length overall: 18·28m (60ft)
Max beam: 9·14m (30ft)
Navigational draught: 2·13m (7ft)
Available cargo deck area: 54·71m² (589ft²)
WEIGHTS
Cargo payload: 5·25 long tons
Passengers and crew: 1·95 long tons
Full load displacement: 62 long tons
Light ship displacement: 44 long tons
PERFORMANCE
Max speed: 21 knots
Cruising: 18 knots
Cruising range (no fuel reserve and payload): 600n miles

SWATH PATROL BOAT

DIMENSIONS
Length: 75ft
Max beam: 30ft
Navigational draught: 7ft
Helicopter platform: 729ft²
Available cargo deck area: 700ft²
WEIGHTS
Full load displacement (inc fuel and helicopter): 18·6 long tons
Light ship displacement: 58·9 long tons
PERFORMANCE
Max speed: over 18 knots
Cruising: 16 knots
Cruising range (with 10% fuel reserve): 1,400n miles

SD-60 SWATH hull nearing completion

SD 60 SWATH under construction

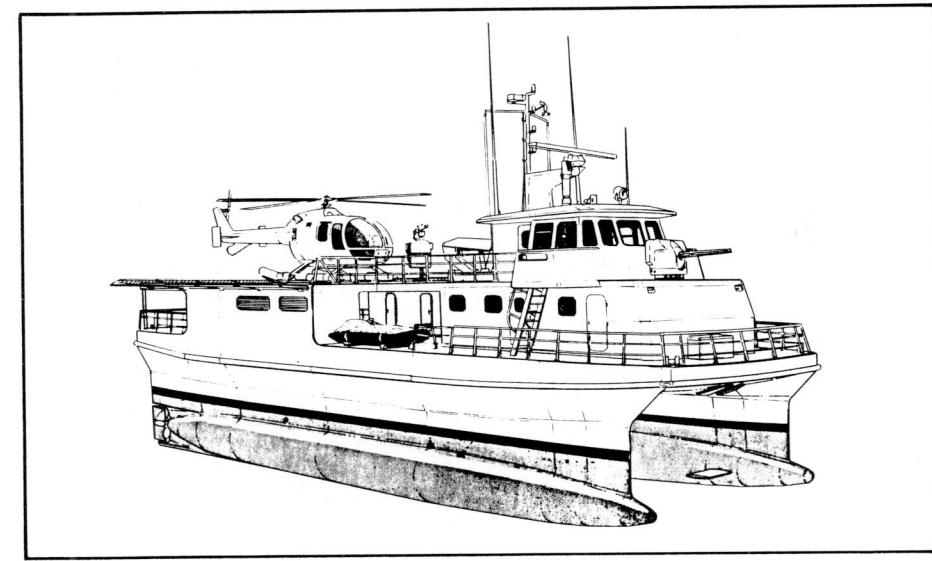

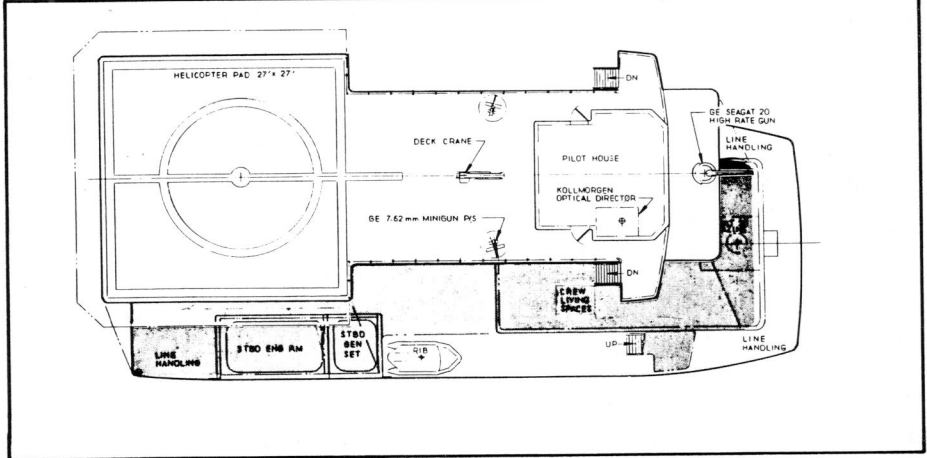

SWATH patrol boat

SWATH EXCURSION BOAT
DIMENSIONS
Length: 60ft
Max beam: 30ft
Navigational draught: 7ft
WEIGHTS
Full load displacement: 57 long tons
Light ship displacement: 51·2 long tons
PERFORMANCE
Max speed: over 20 knots
Cruising: 12 knots
Cruising range (with 10% fuel reserve): 165n
  miles

SD 60 SWATH demonstrator

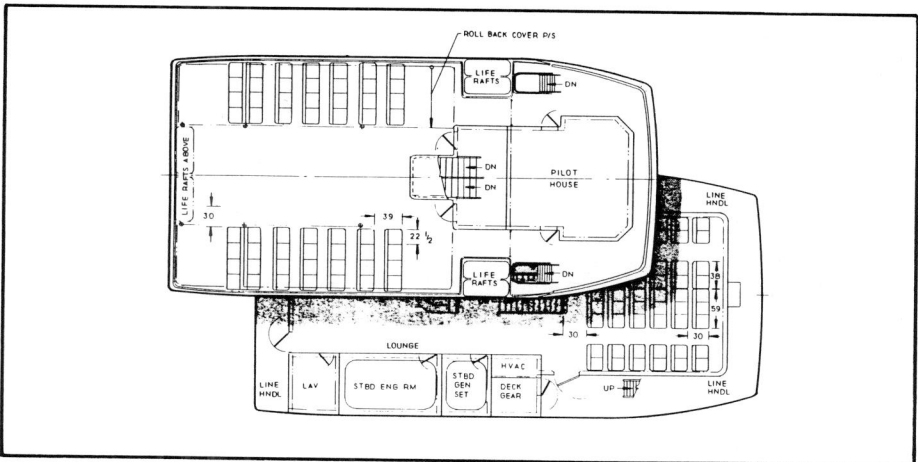

SWATH excursion boat

SEMI-SUBMERGED SHIP CORPORATION (SSSCO)
417 Loma Larga Drive, Solana Beach, California
92075, USA
Telephone: (619) 481 6417
Telex: 695077
Officials:
Dr Thomas G Lang, *President*

SSSCO was founded by Dr Thomas G Lang,
the inventor of the semi-submerged ship (S³).
Basically, the S³ consists of two parallel torpedo-
like hulls attached to which are two or more
streamlined struts which pierce the water surface
and support an above-water platform. Stabilising
fins are attached near the after end of each hull
and a pair of smaller fins are located near their
forward ends.

Semi-submerged ship technology has been
proved over the past five years by the 190-ton
SSP *Kaimalino*, a US Navy developed range-
support vessel which has been operating in the
rough seas off the Hawaiian islands since 1975.
Following private development, Dr Lang introduced the concept into the US Navy in 1968 and
holds several basic patents in the field. He led the
Navy's first research work, and initiated and
developed the hydrodynamic design for the
stable semi-submerged platform (SSP), the
world's first high-performance, open-ocean,
semi-submerged ship.

The US Navy's present SWATH (Small
Waterplane Area Twin Hull) ship programme is
based on the S³ concept. The performance features that distinguish S³s from conventional vessels are greatly reduced motions with sustained

speed even in heavy seas, lower hydrodynamic drag and reduced power requirements at moderate to high speeds, and far superior course-keeping characteristics at all sea headings. S³s have excellent manoeuvrability at speed, when operating in confined harbours and when station-keeping.

The control surfaces of the S³ designs enable them to ride smoothly through the water. Controllable bow and stern fins can be operated collectively or differentially. Used together, the four fins control heave, pitch and roll. Twin rudders provide directional control at high speed. Twin screws and thrusters provide differential thrust at low speed, to help in delicate, close-in manoeuvres. The screws may have variable and reversible-pitch blades.

Typical vessel designs include: crew change vessels, ferries, intervention vessels, multifunction support vessels and diving support vessels, etc, from 100 to 10,000 tons and more. SSSCO has an exclusive agreement with British Shipbuilders covering the development of the S³ in European and Mediterranean areas.

SSP KAIMALINO

SSP *Kaimalino*, a US Navy range-support vessel has operated from near calm conditions to beyond sea state 6 at speeds of up to 25 knots. Its motion is small relative to a conventional monohull either when at rest or under way. The SSP has made smooth transits in 4·57m (15ft) swells without any impacts; however, in short, steep 3·66m (12ft) waves, occasional bow impacts have occurred. No structural damage has occurred, even during storm conditions when 7·62 to 9·14m (25 to 30ft) high waves were encountered.

DIMENSIONS
Length: 27m (88ft)
Beam (at mid section): 14m (46ft)
Height: 9·7m (32ft)
WEIGHTS
Displacement: 217 tons
Max payload (including fuel): 50 tons
PERFORMANCE
Max speed: 25 knots
Range at max speed and payload: 400n miles

CREW CHANGE VESSEL (CCV)

One of the recent projects proposed by Semi-Submerged Ship Corporation is a 1,900-ton displacement vessel designed to service offshore oil and gas deposits. A smooth ride is anticipated in 6·7m (22ft) waves at 35 knots in the North Sea. Its high-speed capability would also help the vessel to participate in the emergency evacuation of personnel. Additionally, vessels of this type have characteristics which make them ideal for transferring passengers when station-keeping with offshore installations.

PROPULSION: Propulsive power would be furnished by two 27,000hp marinised gas turbines, probably installed in the lower hulls. This location would be favourable, not only from the point of view of weight distribution, but also because it would reduce noise and vibration levels for the passengers. For servicing and replacement the powerplants would be removed from the lower hulls via the air intake ducting in the aft struts. Each gas turbine would drive a controllable and reversible-pitch propeller (CRP). Not only would these eliminate the need for reversing clutches and clutch brakes, but they would make a substantial reduction in the stopping time and greatly enhance manoeuvrability and docking capabilities. Maximum engine efficiency could be maintained for varying sea states, wind and load conditions by adjusting the propellers for optimum pitch. It also permits the operation of only one engine in an emergency and for slow speed operation.

AUTOMATIC MOTION CONTROL SYSTEM: If waves are restricted to the strut region the resulting changes in buoyancy due to their passing is small. Automatically controlled bow fins or canards and stabilising fins at the stern are operated collectively or differentially to dampen heave, pitch and roll. Since there will always be some speed and heading in which resonance will

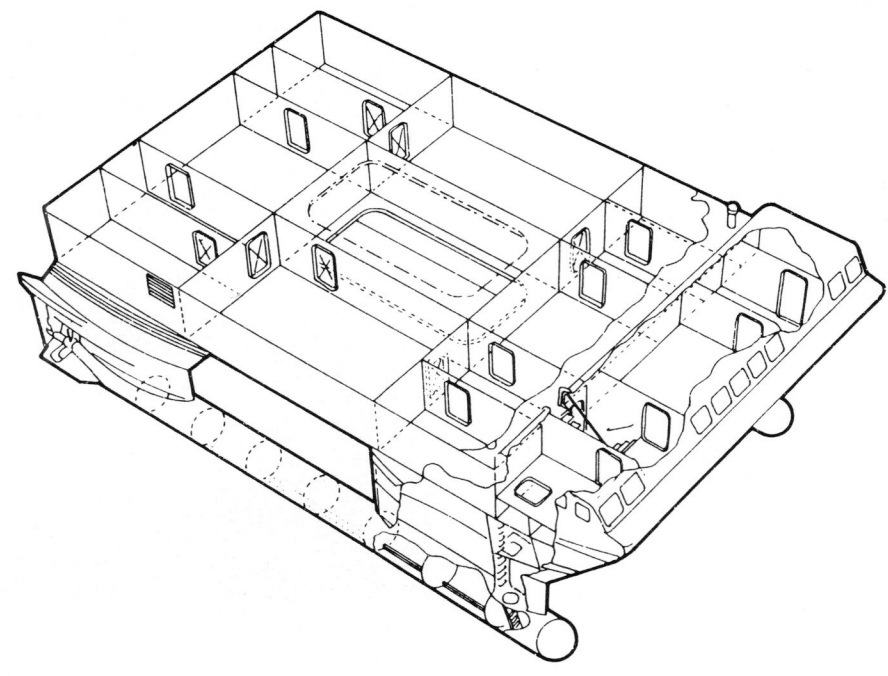

Cutaway showing basic hull configuration of SSP *Kaimalino*

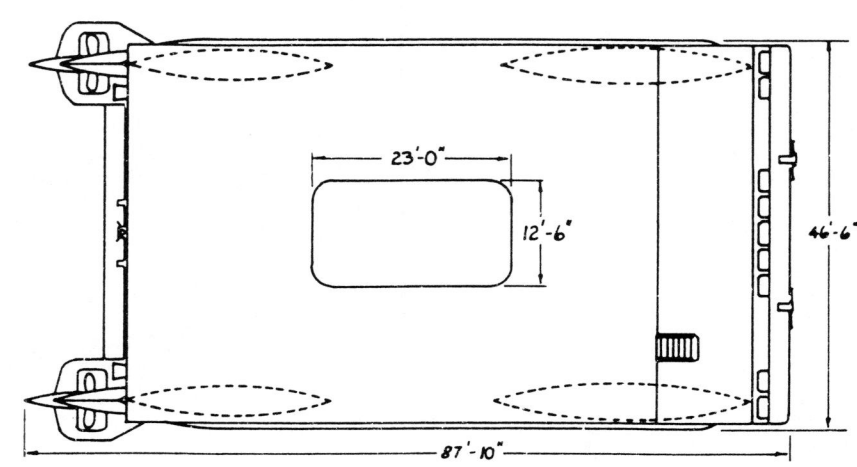

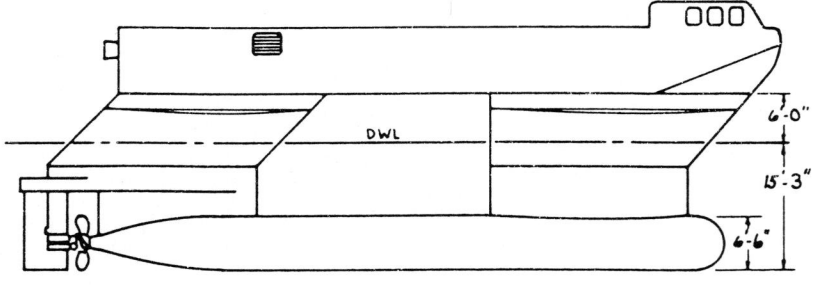

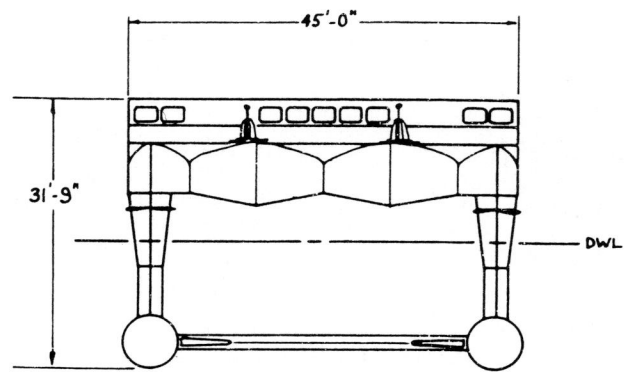

General arrangement of SSP *Kaimalino*

occur in each of the heave, pitch and roll motions, an automatic motion control system has been developed to minimise resonance problems in comparison to those encountered by monohulls and other types of semi-submerged ships which lack fins. Signals are supplied to a central computer unit by a gyrostabilised inertial reference platform, static pressure taps on the lower hull and manual inputs from the helmsman control unit. The helmsman control unit allows the captain to select the desired heading, to trim the vessel in pitch and roll and to engage or disengage the AMCS at will. Manual override is available at any time. The automatic control system is effective at speeds as low as 8 knots.

Canards and fins are attached between the lower hulls and extend inboard. This avoids the need for their retraction while drawing alongside berths and other vessels and while manoeuvring in harbour.

HULL: The hull cross-structure, bow and bottom sides are designed to accept and minimise the force of impacts. It is possible to flood or loose either or both sub-sea hulls without experiencing anything worse than becoming an unpowered barge which will float quite adequately.

ACCOMMODATION: Arrangements to suit the requirements of the operator and the particular service for which the vessel is intended. In typical configuration, accommodation would be provided for a total complement of 25 in single berth cabins. Single class saloons would be provided for up to 400 passengers. Since the vessel is designed to operate on short haul routes, no sleeping accommodation is provided. Features will include a 49-seat cinema and a large refreshment lounge.

The vessel will be able to accommodate a Sikorsky S-61N helicopter which can be used to transfer passengers to and from offshore structures or for the transport of injured personnel. It is claimed that it is an ideal emergency vessel and can respond to disasters in severe weather conditions and at a speed which no other vessel in the North Sea can duplicate.

DIMENSIONS
Length: 74·5m (245ft)
Beam: 27·1m (89ft)
Height: 15·2m (50ft)
Draught: 6·7m (22ft)
WEIGHTS
Displacement: 1,900 tons
PERFORMANCE
Cruising speed: 35 knots
Max speed: 38 knots
Range: 500-1,000n miles
Endurance: 7 days

HIGH-SPEED FERRY CONCEPT

An S³ ferry would provide a smooth, level ride through sea state 5 and into sea state 6 for up to 600 passengers and 130 vehicles. In rough water operations, passengers would experience far less rolling and pitching motions than at present. There should be little, if any, incidence of seasickness. The S³ ferry design is highly manoeuvrable and is easy to dock.
DIMENSIONS
Length: 103m (340ft)
Beam: 39·5m (130ft)
Height: 25·8m (88ft)
WEIGHTS
Displacement: 3,200 tons
PERFORMANCE
Cruising speed: 25 knots

RAPID INTERVENTION VESSEL (RIV)

Because of its high speed, an S³ RIV would be able to reach potential disaster areas extremely quickly. During a full scale emergency, due to the vessel's excellent seakeeping qualities, seriously injured personnel could be air lifted to shore hospitals even under severe weather conditions. The S³ RIV would be fitted with fire monitors to meet international safety requirements.
DIMENSIONS
Length: 74·5m (245ft)
Beam: 27·1m (89ft)
Height: 15·2m (50ft)

SSP *Kaimalino*

Impression of 1,900-ton crew change vessel

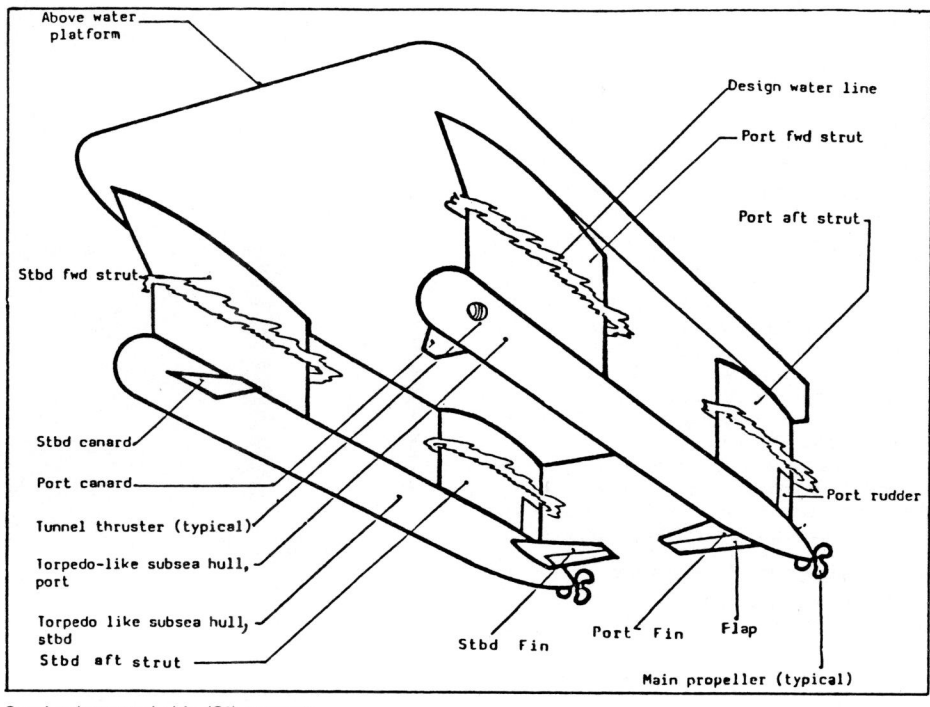

Semi-submerged ship (S³) concept

WEIGHTS
Displacement: 2,100 tons
PERFORMANCE
Cruising speed: 16 knots
Max speed: 25 knots

S³ MULTIFUNCTION SUPPLY AND SUPPORT VESSEL (MSSV)

The S³ MSSV is designed to operate as a supply vessel servicing the offshore complexes in the North Sea during the winter season. Able to operate in 10·6 to 12·2m (35 to 40ft) seas, it could deliver vital supplies when no other type of supply vessel (except possibly conventional slow semi-submersibles) could operate. Available deck area would be 2,500m² (26,900ft²). A central well would be provided to handle equipment such as look-out/observation submersibles, transfer modules and underwater remote control vessels (RCVs) during the summer season.
DIMENSIONS
Length: 93·3m (307ft)
Beam: 40·1m (132ft)
Draught: 10·6m (35ft)

WEIGHTS
Displacement: 6,000 tons
PERFORMANCE
Cruising speed: 16 knots

DIVING SUPPORT VESSEL DESIGN

The diving system of the S³ DSV may have a depth capability of up to 500m (1,650ft) for up to eight divers. A hyperbaric rescue lifeboat is provided on deck. Diving bell handling is through a diving moonpool in the front starboard strut. A central well can support observation/look-out submersibles, RCVs, ADS etc. A fully redundant DP system is provided.
DIMENSIONS
Length: 74·5m (145ft)
Beam: 27·1m (89ft)
Draught: 6·7m (22ft)
WEIGHTS
Displacement: 2,000 tons
PERFORMANCE
Cruising speed: 16 knots
Endurance: 2 weeks

POWER PLANTS AND PROPULSION SYSTEMS

CANADA

PRATT & WHITNEY CANADA

PO Box 10, Longueuil, Quebec J4K 4X9, Canada
Telephone: (514) 677 9411
Officials:

E L Smith, *Chairman and Chief Executive Officer*
L D Caplan, *President and Chief Operations Officer*
R F Steers, *Vice President, Finance*
R H McLachlan, *Vice President, Aircraft Power-plant Marketing*
G P Ouimet, *Vice President, Operations*
J P Beauregard, *Vice President, Materials and Procurement*
C J Pascoe, *Vice President, Counsel*
R C Abraham, *Vice President, Production*
J B Haworth, *Vice President, Industrial and Marine Division*
R J Losch, *Vice President, Product Support*
C B Wrong, *Vice President, Engineering*
B F Duffy, *Vice President, Personnel*
R M Sachs, *Director of Marketing, Industrial and Marine Division*
P Henry, *Vice President, Communications*

In addition to its wide range of small aircraft turbines (for example the PT6A turboprop, PT6B, PT6T and T400 turboshafts, and JT15D turbofan), Pratt & Whitney Canada also manufactures a marine derivative of the PT6, the ST6 series of turboshafts. These engines are rated at 550shp and upwards and are installed in a number of ACV and hydrofoil vessels. The US test craft surface effect ship SES-100B is equipped with three ST6J-70s to power its eight lift fans, and two ST-60 series engines power the Canadian research hydrofoil Proteus. Two ST6T-75 Twin-Pac turbines power the Bell Aerospace Canada Voyageur hovercraft and a single ST6T-75 provides power in that company's Viking craft. A series of larger Voyageurs for the US Army, designated LACV-30, is powered by ST6T-76 engines.

Including aero-engine installations, over 22,000 of this series of gas turbines have been delivered. Between them they have accumulated running experience in excess of 61 million hours.

ST6 MARINE GAS TURBINE

ST6 marine gas turbines are designed and manufactured by Pratt & Whitney Canada.

Details of the engine specifications are given below:

TYPE: A simple cycle free turbine engine with a single spool gas generator and a multi-stage compressor driven by a single-stage turbine. Burner section has an annular combustion chamber with downstream injection. The single- or two-stage (L series) free turbine is connected to the output shaft via a reduction gearbox.

The ST6T-75 and ST6T-76 Twin-Pac are dual engines with the two engines mounted side-by-side and coupled to a twinning reduction gear.

AIR INTAKE: Annular air intake at rear of engine with intake screen.

COMPRESSOR: Three axial-flow stages, plus single centrifugal stage. Single-sided centrifugal compressor with 26 vanes, made from titanium forging. Axial rotor of disc-drum type with titanium stator and rotor blades. Stator vanes are brazed to casing. The rotor blades are dove tailed

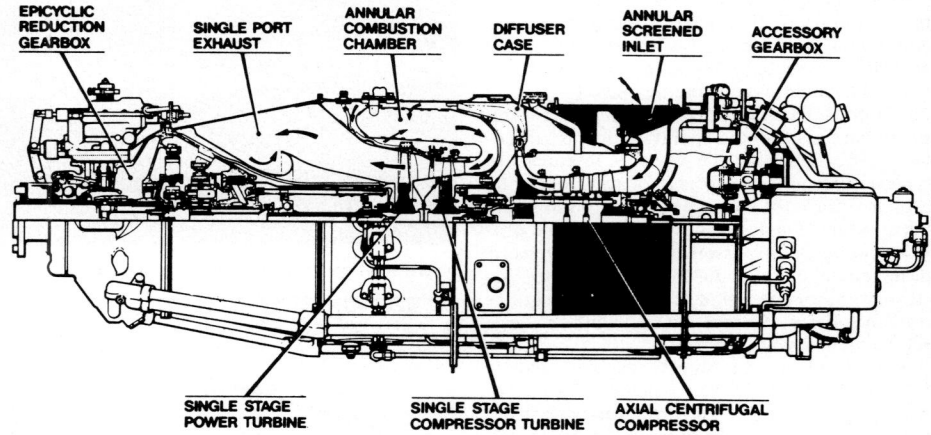

ST6 gas flow

ST6 gas turbine

ST6 ENGINE DATA SUMMARY
Sea Level Standard Pressure at 15°C (59°F) Inlet Temperature

IMPERIAL MEASURE

Model	Maximum		Intermediate		Normal		Output	Length	Width	Height	Weight
	shp	sfc*	shp	sfc*	shp	sfc*	rpm (max)	(in)	(in)	(in)	(lb)
ST6L-77	811	0·59			654	0·62	33,000	52·2	19	19	306
ST6J-77	750	0·61	650	0·63	550	0·66	2,200	62	19	19	379
ST6K-77	690	0·62	620	0·64	550	0·66	6,230	60	19	19	350
ST6L-80	1,065	0·58	955	0·6	840	0·62	30,000	59·4	19	19	360
ST6T-76	1,850	0·615	1,645	0·63	1,440	0·65	6,600	66·4	44·4	31·6	730

METRIC MEASURE

Model	Maximum		Intermediate		Normal		Output	Length	Width	Height	Weight
	kW	sfc*	kW	sfc*	kW	sfc*	rpm (max)	(mm)	(mm)	(mm)	(kg)
ST6L-77	605	0·358			488	0·377	33,000	1,326	483	483	139
ST6J-77	560	0·371	485	0·384	410	0·401	2,200	1,575	483	483	172
ST6K-77	515	0·377	463	0·389	410	0·401	6,230	1,524	483	483	159
ST6L-80	794	0·353	712	0·365	627	0·377	30,000	1,509	483	483	164
ST6T-76	1,380	0·374	1,227	0·381	1,074	0·395	6,600	1,687	1,128	803	332

*sfc = lb/hp/h (imperial)
    = kg/kWh (metric)

to discs. Discs through-bolted with centrifugal compressor to shaft. One-piece stainless steel casing and radial diffuser.

COMBUSTION CHAMBER: Annular reverse-flow type of stainless steel construction, with 14 Simplex burners. Two spark plug igniters.

ST6J-77 seen from above

GAS GENERATOR TURBINE: Single-stage axial. Rotor blades of sulphidation-resistant material mounted by fir tree roots. Cooled vanes in some models.

POWER TURBINE: Single- or dual-stage axial. Rotor blades mounted by fir tree roots.

BEARINGS: Gas generator and power turbine each supported by one ball bearing and one roller bearing.

SHAFT DRIVE: Single- or two-stage planetary reduction gear or direct drive, depending on engine model. Torque measuring system incorporated with reduction gearing.

FUEL GRADE: Diesel Nos 1 and 2 and Navy diesel or aviation turbine fuel.

JET PIPE: Single port exhaust discharging vertically upwards or at 30, 60 or 90 degrees port or starboard of vertical. Models available with twin ports discharging horizontally.

ACCESSORY DRIVES: Mounting pads on accessory case including for starter or starter-generator and tacho-generator. Also tacho-generator drive on power section.

LUBRICATION SYSTEM: One pressure and three scavenge gear type pumps driven by gas generator rotor. Integral oil tank.

OIL SPECIFICATIONS: Type 2 synthetic lube oil PWA-521 MIL-L-23699.

FRANCE

CLUB FRANÇAIS DES AÉROGLISSEURS

41 and 43 rue Aristide Briand, 45130 Meung sur Loire, France

Club Français des Aéroglisseurs markets special propulsion units for high performance lightweight air cushion vehicles. The units, given the name Diagloo, comprise adapted 600 and 1200cc Citroen air-cooled, automotive engines, driving a 1·4m (4ft 7·12in) diameter, two-bladed Merville propeller via a reduction and reverse gearbox. Engine outputs are 32·5bhp (33cv) and 56cv at 5,750rpm.

The 33cv units weigh 100kg (220lb) and the 56cv unit 160kg (352 lb). Each is supplied complete with an aerodynamically profiled hood. Series production has begun.

Diagloo propulsion unit

SOCIÉTÉ TURBOMÉCA

Head office and works: Bordes 64320 Bizanos (Pyrénées Atlantiques), France
Paris office: 1 rue Beaujon, 75008 Paris, France
Telephone: 32 84 37
Telex: 560928

Officials:
J R Szydlowski, *President and Director General*
G Pertica, *Vice President*
M Tavernier, *General Director*
R Deblache, *Technical Director*
P Vauterin, *Deputy Commercial Director*

The Société Turboméca was formed in 1938 by Messieurs Szydlowski and Planiol to develop blowers, compressors and turbines for aeronautical use.

In 1947 the company began development of gas turbines of low power for driving aircraft auxiliaries and for aircraft propulsion.

Many of Turboméca's production series aircraft turbines have been adapted to industrial and marine duties including installation in various French air cushion vehicles. General descriptions follow of the main Turboméca turbine engines in production or under development. Reference is also made to air cushion vehicle and hydrofoil installations.

TURBOMÉCA ARTOUSTE

The Artouste is a single-shaft turboshaft engine which has been manufactured in quantity in two versions, the 400shp Artouste IIC and the 563shp Artouste IIIB. The 590shp Artouste IIID has also been developed. A total of 2,474 Artouste engines had been built by October 1982. The Artouste II had a single-stage centrifugal compressor, annular reverse-flow combustor and two-stage axial turbine. In the second generation Artouste III, in which the pressure ratio is increased from 3·88 : 1 to 5·2 : 1, a single-axial stage compressor has been added ahead of the centrifugal impeller. The turbine also has an additional stage.

A single Artouste drives the two propulsion airscrews on the Naviplane BC 8.

The following description refers to the Artouste IIIB.

TYPE: Single-shaft axial-plus-centrifugal turboshaft.

COMPRESSOR: Single-stage axial plus single-stage centrifugal compressor. Two diffusers, one radial and the other axial, aft of compressor. Pressure ratio at 33,500rpm at S/L 5·2 : 1. Air mass flow 4·3kg/s (9·5lb/s) at 33,500rpm at S/L.

COMBUSTION CHAMBER: Annular type, with rotary atomiser fuel injection. Torch igniters.

TURBINE: Three-stage axial type. Blades integral with discs. Row of nozzle guide vanes before each stage.

JET PIPE: Fixed type.

STARTING: Automatic with 4,000W starter-generator. Two Turboméca igniter plugs.

DIMENSIONS
Length: 1,815mm (71·46in)
Width: 520mm (20·47in)
Height: 627mm (24·68in)

WEIGHT: Dry equipped: 182kg (401lb)

PERFORMANCE RATING: 563shp at 33,500rpm

FUEL CONSUMPTION at T-O and max continuous rating: 322g (0·71lb) ehp/h

TURBOMÉCA TURMO

The Turmo is a free-turbine engine available in turboshaft and turboprop versions spanning the 1,200 to 2,000shp power bracket. First generation Turmo IIIC and E series have a single-stage axial plus single-stage centrifugal compressor, annular reverse-flow combustor, two-stage axial compressor-turbine, and mechanically-separate single- or two-stage power turbine. Second-generation Turmo XII engines have an additional axial compressor stage and other refinements.

Main versions of the Turmo in production or under development include:

Turmo IIIC₇. Derived from the Turmo IIIB, this model (with two-stage power turbine) has a 1,610shp at maximum contingency rating and powers early Sud-Aviation SA 321 Super-Frelon three-engined military helicopters. Two will power the projected Aérospatiale 46-ton patrol boat hydrofoil under development for the French Navy.

The Turmo IIIF also powers the Turbotrains of SNCF.

Turmo IVC. Based on the Turmo IIIC, this is a special version with a single-stage power turbine and powers the Sud-Aviation SA 330 Puma twin-engined military helicopter. The engine has a maximum contingency rating of 1,558shp.

Turmo IIIC₇. This model (which reverts to the standard two-stage power turbine) is in the same series as the Turmo IIIC and E and has a maximum emergency rating of 1,610shp. It is installed in Sud Aviation SA 321 F and J Super-Frelon civil three-engined helicopters.

Turmo IIIC₂. Embodies new materials for the gas generator turbine, and offers an emergency rating of 1,610shp.

Turmo IIIE₃. Two, each rated at 1,282shp, power the Société Bertin and Cie Orléans 250-80 tracked air cushion vehicle. Both engines drive a ducted seven-bladed 2·3m (7ft 7in) diameter Ratier-Figeac FH-201 hydraulically operated reversible-pitch propeller for propulsion. The Turmo IIIE is rated at 1,580shp.

Two Turmo IIIC series engines, with a combined installed power of 2,564shp, are to power the projected Aérospatiale SA 800 second-generation hydrofoil.

TURMO IIIC₇

TYPE: Free-turbine axial-plus-centrifugal turboshaft.
AIR MASS FLOW: 6·2kg (13·7lb)/s
DIMENSIONS
Length: 1,976mm (77·8in)
Width: 693mm (27·3in)
Height: 717mm (28·2in)
WEIGHT
Dry with standard equipment: 325kg (715lb)
PERFORMANCE RATINGS
T-O: 1,550shp
Max continuous: 1,292shp
FUEL CONSUMPTION
At T-O rating: 273g (0·6lb)/shp/h
At max continuous rating: 291g (0·64lb)/shp/h

TURBOMÉCA MARBORÉ

The Marboré single-shaft turbojet has been built in greater numbers than any other Turboméca engine. By 31 December 1982 a total of 4,353 Marboré IIs of 400kg (880lb) had been delivered by Turboméca and a further 12,000 by its US licensees, Continental Aviation and Teledyne CAE. By 31 December 1982 1,301 Marboré VI turbojects of 480kg (1,058lb) had been built. Production by Turboméca is now complete. In both these versions of the Marboré the engine comprises a single stage centrifugal compressor annular reverse-flow combustor and single-stage axial turbine.

Two Marborés power the H.890 hydrofoil test platform currently under development by Aérospatiale for the French Ministry of National Defence.

A Marboré II powers the lift system of the SEDAM Naviplane BC 8 marine ACV. The exhaust gases are ducted along channels designed to entrain additional air to augment the efflux.

MARBORE VI

DIMENSIONS
Length, with exhaust cone but without tailpipe: 1,416mm (55·74in)
Width: 593mm (23·35in)
Height: 631mm (24·82in)
WEIGHT Dry equipped: 140kg (309lb)
PERFORMANCE RATINGS
T-O: 480kg (1,058lb) st at 21,500rpm
Cruising: 420kg (925lb) st at 20,500rpm
SPECIFIC FUEL CONSUMPTION
At T-O rating: 1·09
At cruising rating: 1·07

Turmo IIIC

Turmo IIIC₄ turboshaft

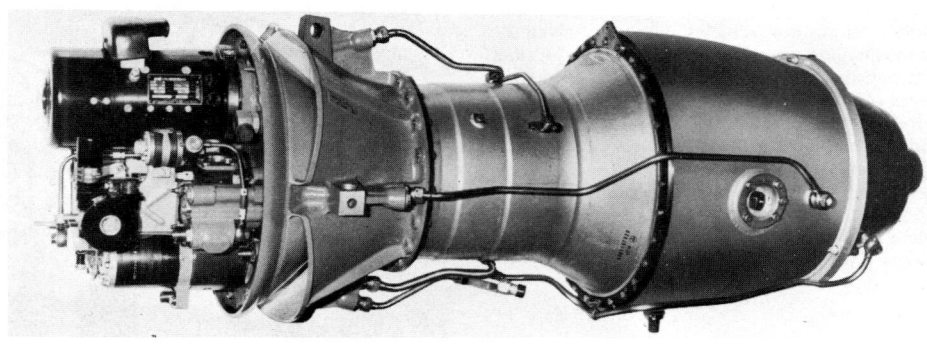
Arbizon IIIB expendable turbojet

TURBOMÉCA ARBIZON

Announced in 1970, the Arbizon is a simple single-shaft turbojet, known originally as the TR281 and derived from the Turmo IIIC₃ turboshaft. It is intended for the propulsion of missiles and RPVs and has single-stage axial and centrifugal compressors and a single-stage turbine.

The original version was the Arbizon IIIB built for Otomat cruise missiles. Four-lobed bell-mouth inlet ducts surround front face carrying electric starter and other accessories. Mass flow 6kg (13·2lb)/s; pressure ratio 5·5. A total of 472 had been built by 31 December 1982.

The following data refers to the Arbizon IIIB.
DIMENSIONS
Diameter of combustion chamber: 405mm (15·95in)
Length overall, with accessories: 1,361mm (53·58in)
WEIGHT, dry: 115kg (253lb)
PERFORMANCE RATINGS
T-O: 3·73kN (727lb st) at 33,000 rpm
Max continuous: 3·24kN (727lb st) at 32,000 rpm
SPECIFIC FUEL CONSUMPTION
Max continuous rating: 31·44mg/Ns (1·11lb/h/lb st)

TURBOMÉCA ASTAZOU

The Astazou is another of the later generation Turboméca engines, incorporating the experience gained with earlier series and making use of new design techniques. It has an extremely small gas-producer section and has been developed as a turboshaft and as a turboprop driving a variable-pitch propeller.

The compressor consists of one or two axial stages followed by a centrifugal stage, with an annular combustion chamber and three-stage turbine. Accessories are mounted on the rear of the main intake casing. Pressure ratio is 6:1 and air mass flow 2·5kg/s (5·5lb/s) for the two-stage compressor engines, and 8 : 1 and 3·4kg/s (7·4lb/s) for the three-stage compressor engines respectively. In the turboshaft version, the rpm of the output shaft is 5,922.

The following are the main Astazou variants:

Astazou IIA. A 390kW (523shp) turboshaft (two-stage compressor) version powering the Aérospatiale SA 318C Alouette II Astazou helicopter. A 450 shp Astazou provides power for the integrated lift and propulsion system of the SEDAM Naviplane N 102 marine ACV. The engine drives a 1·7m (5ft 7in) diameter axial lift fan and two three-bladed variable-pitch propellers for propulsion.

Astazou IIIN. Rated at 592hp, this is the definitive version (two-stage compressor).

Astazou IV. New version designed for industrial duty and in particular to form, in association with a Jeumont-Schneider ac generator, a 300kW generating set. It is installed in the RTG turbotrains made in France, USA, Iran and Egypt. It is also being tested by the French Navy. By end of 1981 166 had been produced.

Astazou XIV (alias AZ14). Current major production turboshaft version (with three-stage compressor) rated at 852shp. The engine is the standard power plant for the Naviplane N 102.

The B version is installed in the Alouette III helicopter and the H version in the SA 342 Gazelle helicopter.

Astazou XVI (alias AZ16). First Turboméca production engine to embody the company's new air-cooled turbine. Rated at 913shp for Jetstream aircraft and the FMA IA 58 Pucará counter-insurgency aircraft of the Argentine Air Force.

ASTAZOU IIIN
DIMENSIONS
Length: 1,433mm (56·3in)
Basic diameter: 460mm (18·1in)
WEIGHT Dry equipped engine: 147·5kg (325lb)
PERFORMANCE RATINGS
T-O: 592shp at 43,500rpm
Max continuous: 523shp at 43,500rpm
FUEL CONSUMPTION
At T-O rating: 284g (0·627lb)/shp/h
At max continuous rating: 292g (0·644 lb)/shp/h

TURBOMÉCA TM 333
This turboshaft engine rated at an initial 625kW at take-off is under development to power twin engined 4-ton class helicopters and particularly the up-rated versions of the Dauphin family. It is a new technology engine which achieves the compromise of mechanical simplicity and high performance. This is obtained through the introduction of new components which have been subjected to in-depth research and the use of the most recent results of technological and metallurgical research at Turboméca.

The engine programme was launched in July 1979. Gas generation testing began in August 1981. The first complete TM 333 ran in September 1981. Flight development began in April 1982 on a Dauphin SA 365C.
TYPE: Free turbine turboshaft.
AIR INTAKE: Annular and fed by a scroll.
COMPRESSOR: One pre-rotation grid; 2 axial stages; 1 evolutive centrifugal compressor.
COMBUSTION CHAMBER: Annular with inverted flow.
GAS GENERATOR TURBINE: Single stage with attached blades.
POWER TAKE-OFF: At the front with reduction gear giving drive at 6,000 rpm.
FUEL SYSTEM: Full authority digital electronic system acts as metering valve.
ACCESSORIES: Filled on gearbox mainly; fuel pumps; starter; oil pumps.

Turmo XII

Turmastazou XIV

PERFORMANCE RATINGS
Max contingency: 680kW
Max take-off: 625kW
Max continuous power: 560kW

SPECIFIC FUEL CONSUMPTION
Max contingency: 318g/kW/h
Max take-off: 322g/kW/h
Max continuous power: 330g/kW/h

GERMANY, FEDERAL REPUBLIC

KLOCKNER-HUMBOLDT-DEUTZ AG (DEUTZ)

D-5000 Cologne 80, Deutz-Mülheimer Str 111, PO Box No 80 05 09, Cologne, Federal Republic of Germany

Deutz air-cooled diesel engines of the 413 series have been in large-scale production for many years. The 413F series is the latest variant and the higher cylinder outputs attained in this uprated model mean that a wider power range is now available.

Engines of the B/FL 413F series are used in a wide range of applications in industry, agriculture, road transport and shipping.

Consisting of 5- and 6-cylinder in-line and 6-, 8-, 10- and 12-cylinder V engines, the B/FL 413FR/F/FC series covers a comprehensive output range from 64kW (87hp) to 386kW (525hp). Turbocharged versions of the 6-cylinder in-line and 8-, 10-, 12-cylinder V models are available. The turbocharged and after-cooled 12-cylinder automotive version delivers a maximum output of 386kW (525hp).

Four Deutz BF12L413FC air-cooled marine diesels are installed in the BHC AP.1-88 general purpose hovercraft, two for lift and two for propulsion. Similar Deutz diesels have been specified for two other hovercraft under development in the United Kingdom, the Griffon 100TD and the Tropimere TAC 1000.

BF12L413FC

DEUTZ B/F 6/8/10/12L413F/FC V ENGINES
TYPE: Air-cooled four-stroke diesel with direct fuel injection (alternatively, two-stage combus-

tion), naturally aspirated or (as BFL 413F) supercharged by two turbochargers; BF12L413FC with air-charge cooling system.
CYLINDERS: Individually removable cylinders

made in grey cast iron and arranged at V-angle of 90 degrees. Cylinder heads in light alloy, each with one inlet and one exhaust valve, overhead type. The valves are controlled via tappets and pushrods by a camshaft running in three-metal bearings in the upper part of crankcase. Camshaft is crankshaft-driven via helical spur gears arranged at the flywheel end of the engine. Crankcase is grey cast-iron. The main journals are supported after each throw in three-metal bearings, one of each is designed as a locating bearing.

PISTONS: Each is equipped with two compres-

sion rings and one oil control ring and are splash-oil cooled. Turbocharged engines and engines with two-stage combustion have pistons with additional cooling galleries.

COOLING SYSTEM: Mechanically-driven axial type cooling air blower with optional load-dependent hydraulic control.

LUBRICATION: Force feed type by gear type pump. Oil is cleaned by full-flow paper filters. If the blower is hydraulically controlled, a centrifugal filter is installed in the hub as secondary-flow filter.

BF12L413FC

Number of cylinders: 12
Bore/Stroke: 125/130mm
Capacity: 19·144 litres
Compression ratio: 16·5 : 1
Rotational speed: 2,500rpm
Mean piston speed: 10·83m/s
Specific fuel consumption (automotive rating and max torque): 210g/kWh (154g/hph)
Shipping volume: 3·16m³
DIMENSIONS
Length: 1,582mm (62·25in)
Height: 1,243mm (48·94in)
Width: 1,196mm (47·06in)

MTU
Motoren-und Turbinen-Union Friedrichshafen GmbH

Olgastrasse 75, Postfach 2040, 7990 Friedrichshafen 1, Federal Republic of Germany
Telephone: (07541) 291
Telex: 734280-0 mtd
Officials:
Dr Oec pupl Ernst Zimmermann, *President*
Dr Ing Hans Dinger, *Executive Vice President*
Dr Ing Peter Beer, *Director*
Hubert Dunkler, *Director*
Dr Ing Wolfgang Hansen, *Director*
Gunther Welsch, *Director*

The MTU group of companies, formed in 1969 by MAN AG and Daimler-Benz AG, consists of MTU München and MTU Friedrichshafen.

MTU Friedrichshafen comprises the two plants of the former Maybach Mercedes-Benz Motorenbau GmbH at Friedrichshafen and is owned by MTU München. MTU München in turn is owned equally by MAN and Daimler-Benz.

The areas of responsibility of the two MTU companies are as follows:
MTU München:
Development, production and support of lightweight, advanced-technology gas turbines mainly for aircraft applications.
MTU Friedrichshafen:
Development, production and application of high-performance diesel engines.

MTU Friedrichshafen is the development and production centre for high-performance diesel engines of Maybach, MAN and Mercedes-Benz origin and embodies the experience of these companies in diesel engine technology. In addition to diesel engines, MTU Friedrichshafen is responsible for sales and application of industrial and marine gas turbines.

For applications in hydrofoils and hovercraft, MTU offers the following engines:
331 engine family
396 engine family
652 engine family
538 engine family
The table provides some details of the various engines with regard to speed, output and weight. The listed outputs are guideline figures only and depend on the application (military or commercial), its operating profile etc, and will therefore be specified for each case individually.

The stated outputs are based on following ambient conditions:
Air intake temperature 27°C
Seawater temperature 27°C
(up to 32°C seawater temperature for 331 type engines)
Barometric pressure: 1,000mb
In addition, MTU projects and delivers complete propulsion systems, including gear shafts and propellers, as well as combined power plants such as CODOG and CODAG systems.

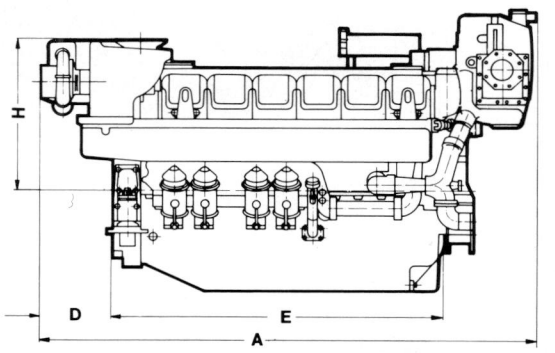
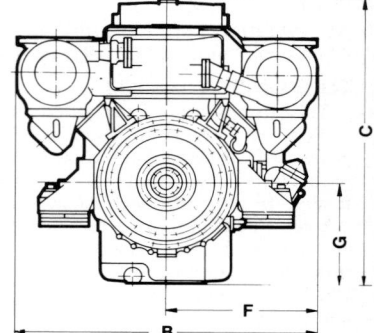

Outline Dimensions (mm)

Engine type	A	B	C	D	E	F	G
6V 331 TC 82	1,620	1,400	1,280	260	1,025	710	475
8V 331 TC 82	1,850	1,400	1,280	260	1,250	720	475
12V 331 TC 82	2,450	1,450	1,440	320	1,710	720	535
6V 396 TB 83	1,720	1,460	1,420	375	1,025	735	475
8V 396 TB 83	1,950	1,440	1,420	375	1,250	720	475
12V 396 TB 83	2,550	1,510	1,510	435	1,710	760	535
16V 396 TB 83	3,200	1,580	1,700	435	2,165	760	590

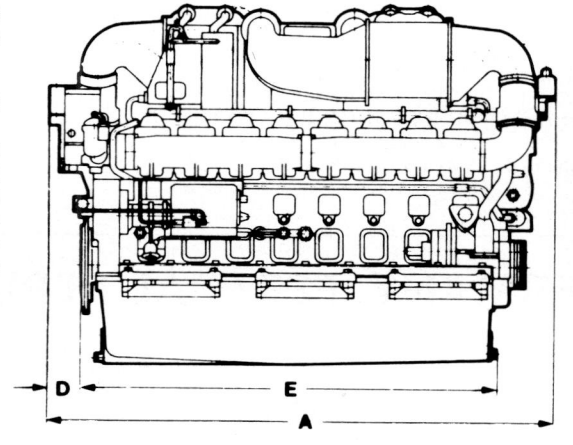
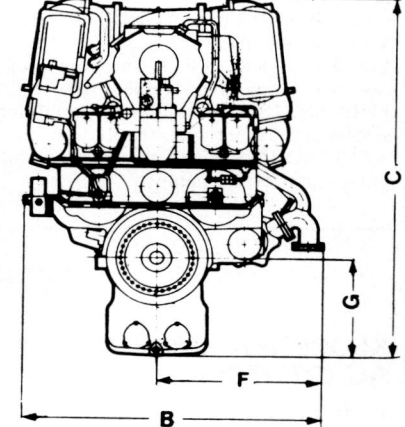

Outline Dimensions (mm)

Engine type	A	B	C	D	E	F	G
16V 652 TB 81	3,122	1,707	2,256	275	2,498	807	625

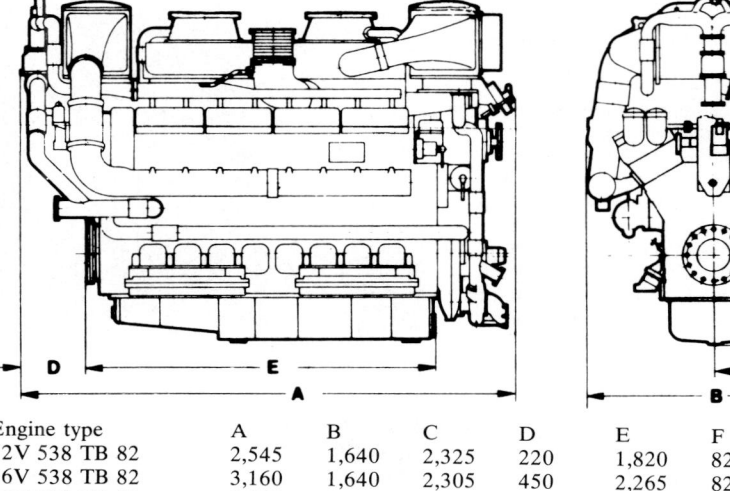
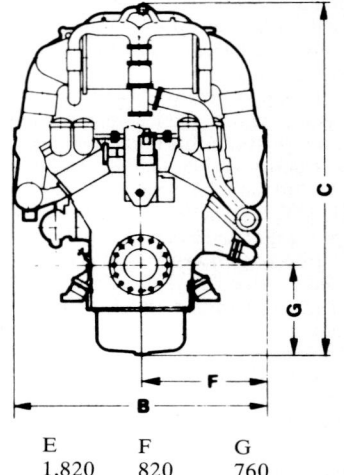

Engine type	A	B	C	D	E	F	G
12V 538 TB 82	2,545	1,640	2,325	220	1,820	820	760
16V 538 TB 82	3,160	1,640	2,305	450	2,265	820	595
20V 538 TB 82	3,800	1,640	2,320	400	3,230	820	665

MTU diesel engines for hydrofoil and hovercraft propulsion

Engine type	Speed rpm	Overload Power (available for limited time during take-off)		Engine weight (dry) (basic engine)	
		kW	hp (metric)	kg	lb
6 V 331 TC 82	2,250	525	715	1,850	4,080
8 V 331 TC 82	2,250	700	950	2,310	5,100
12 V 331 TC 82	2,250	1,050	1,430	3,210	7,080
6 V 396 TB 83	2,000	630	855	2,060	4,540
8 V 396 TB 83	2,000	840	1,140	2,570	5,670
12 V 396 TB 83	2,000	1,260	1,710	3,570	7,870
16 V 396 TB 83	2,000	1,680	2,285	4,800	10,580
16 V 652 TB 81	1,460	1,920	2,610	6,520*	14,380*
12 V 538 TB 82	1,760	1,780	2,420	5,230	11,530
16 V 538 TB 82	1,760	2,380	3,240	6,700	14,770
20 V 538 TB 82	1,760	2,980	4,050	9,000	19,840

*Weight of engine with light alloy housing

RHEIN-FLUGZEUGBAU GmbH (RFB)

Postfach 408, D-4050 Mönchengladbach 1, Federal Republic of Germany
Telephone: (02161) 66 20 31
Telex: 08 525 06
Officials:
Dipl Volksw W Kutscher, *Commercial Director*
Dipl Ing A Schneider, *Technical Director*

RFB has developed a fan thrust pod module (SG 85) for wing-in-ground-effect machines, gliders, air cushion vehicles and air-propelled boats.

By combining rotary engines of the Wankel type with a ducted fan, the company has produced an extremely compact power unit which can be mounted on either a fuselage or a wing in much the same way as gas-turbine pods. The air cooling system permits prolonged ground running when necessary with full throttle.

The system has been fitted to the L13 Blanik glider and also to boats.

SG 85

Length: 1,200mm (3ft 11·5in)
Width max: 750mm (2ft 5·5in)
Height, including 200mm connection: 1,000mm (3ft 3·37in)
Inside shroud diameter: 650mm (2ft 1·37in)
Weight: 58kg (127·8lb)
Power: 50hp
Static thrust at 5,400rpm (with muffler installed): 90kg (198·4lb)
Noise level with full throttle at 304·8m (1,000ft) altitude: 54 dB (A)
Rotor: 3-blades-rotor in fibre-reinforced plastic with erosive protection.
Shroud: plastic.
Engine cowling: glass fibre reinforced plastic.
Engine: Rotary engine KM 914/2V-85 ('Wankel' system; two coupled engines 25hp each) with electric starter 12V, generator, exhaust-gas system and complete assembly sets ready for installation.
Connection: Metal-construction as pylon having a connection-part.
Fuel: mixture 1:30
Fuel consumption:
   full throttle 5,500rpm: 15 litres/h (3·3 gallons/h)
   cruising speed 5,000rpm: 11·5 litres/h (2·5 gallons/h)

SG 85 mounted on Espadon Canot 422 inflatable dinghy, built by Etablissements Georges Hennebutte

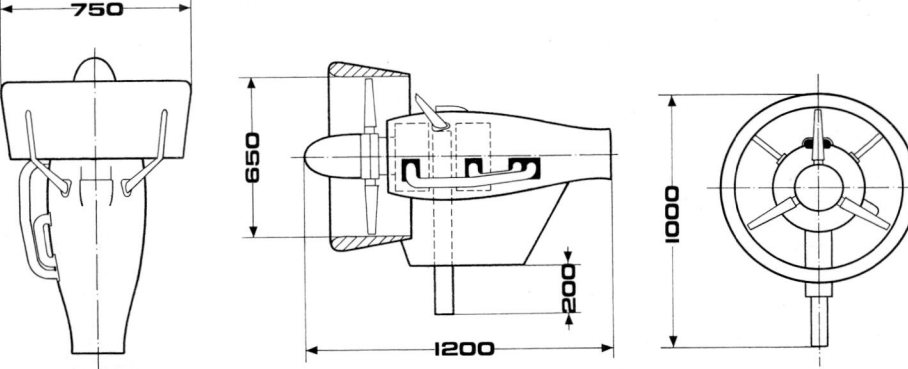

SG 85, incorporating Wankel rotary engine, dimensions given in mm

SG 85

VOLKSWAGEN
VAG (UNITED KINGDOM)
LIMITED

Yeomans Drive, Blakelands, Milton Keynes,
Buckinghamshire MK14 5AN, England
Telephone: 0908 679121
Telex: 825318
Cables: VOLKSAUDI MILTON KEYNES

TYPE 122

The air-cooled petrol engines powering over
20 million Volkswagen cars and vehicles are also
produced as industrial power units in which role
they have been proved reliable and economical in
millions of running hours. There are three versions available, the Type 122 developed from the
1,192cc Volkswagen car engine; the 1,584cc
Type 126A developed from the 1,500cc van
engine; and the 1,795cc Type 127 developed
from the 1,700cc car engine.
TYPE: Air-cooled four-cylinder, horizontally-
opposed four-stroke petrol engine available with
or without governor.
CYLINDERS: Four separate cylinders of special
grey cast iron, with integral cooling fins. Cast
aluminium heads, one for each two cylinders,
with shrunk-in sintered steel valve seats and
bronze valve guides. Bore 77mm (3·032in).
Stroke 64mm (2·52in). Cubic capacity 1,192cc
(72·74 in³). Compression ratio 7·3 : 1.
CRANKCASE: Two-part magnesium pressure
casting with enclosed oil sump and flange for
mounting the engine on machine or pedestal.
CRANKSHAFT: Forged, with hardened journals, mounted in three aluminium bearings and
one three-layer, steel-backed bearing (No 2).
CONNECTING RODS: Forged steel, I-section
shank. Three-layer, steel-backed, lead-bronze
big-end bearing shells with white metal running
surfaces.
PISTONS: Aluminium with steel inserts, two
compression rings and one scraper ring.
CAMSHAFT: Grey cast iron, with three steel-
backed, shell-type bearings in crankcase, driven
by helical gears.
VALVES: One inlet and one exhaust valve per
cylinder. Exhaust valves have special armoured
seating surfaces. 'Rotocap' valve rotating devices
can be fitted on request.
COOLING: Radial fan, driven by belt from
crankshaft. Protective grille on fan intake.
LUBRICATION: Forced feed gear-type pump.
Full flow, flat tube oil cooler in fan airstream. Oil
capacity 2·5 litres (4·4 pints).
CARBURETTOR: Downdraft Solex 26 VFIS
on engine with governor. Downdraft Solex 28
PCI with accelerator pump, on engine without
governor. Both have choke for cold starting.
IGNITION: Magneto, fully waterproofed and
suppressed.
PLUGS: Bosch W145 T1.
FUEL: RON 87.
STARTING: Hand cranking lever or electric
starter.
GOVERNOR: Centrifugal type, operating on
carburettor throttle, driven by toothed belt.
EXHAUST SYSTEM: Cylindrical muffler
located transversely at bottom of engine, with
exhaust pipes from cylinders and damper pipe
with short tail pipe.
MOUNTING: Four bolts in the crankcase flange.
COUPLING: Engine is connected to driven shaft
by a clutch or flexible fixed-coupling.
PEDESTALS AND TRANSMISSIONS: Suit-
able flange pedestals, with or without couplings
or clutches, can be supplied as well as gearboxes
with direct drives or drives of various ratios for
clockwise or anti-clockwise rotation.
DIMENSIONS
Length: 740·5mm (29·2in)
Width: 748mm (29·4in)
Height: 665·5mm (26·2in)
WEIGHT Dry with standard equipment: approx
93·5kg (205lb)
PERFORMANCE RATINGS: Continuous rat-
ing: 34bhp DIN at 3,600 output rpm
FUEL CONSUMPTION
At 20bhp at 2,000 output rpm: 242g
(0·534lb)/bhp/h

At 30bhp at 3,600 output rpm: 268g
(0·59lb)/bhp/h
OIL CONSUMPTION: Approx 20 to 35cc/h at
3,000 output rpm

TYPE 126A

TYPE: Air-cooled four-cylinder, horizontally-
opposed four-stroke petrol engine available with
or without governor. Construction similar to
Type 122 with following exceptions:
CYLINDERS: Bore 85·5mm (3·54in). Stroke
69mm (2·72in). Cubic capacity 1,584cc
(96·5in³). Compression ratio 7·7 : 1.
CARBURETTOR: Downdraft Solex 26 or 28
VFIS on engine with governor. Downdraft Solex
32 PCI on engine without governor.
DIMENSIONS
Length: 723mm (28·5in)
Width: 760mm (29·9in)
Height: 675·5mm (26·5in)
WEIGHT Dry with standard equipment: approx
100kg (220lb)
PERFORMANCE RATINGS: Continuous rat-
ing: 46bhp DIN at 3,600 output rpm
FUEL: 90 octane minimum
FUEL CONSUMPTION
At 28bhp at 2,000 output rpm: 225g
(0·496lb)/bhp/h
At 44bhp at 3,600 output rpm: 255g
(0·562lb)/bhp/h
OIL CONSUMPTION: Approx 25 to 40 cc/h at
3,000 output rpm

TYPE 127

TYPE: Air-cooled, four-cylinder, horizontally-
opposed four-stroke petrol engine of low profile
design.
CYLINDERS: Bore 93mm (3·74in). Stroke
66mm (2·165in). Cubic capacity 1,795cc
(109·53in³). Compression ratio 7·3 : 1.
CRANKCASE: Aluminium, pressure die cast.
COOLING: Radial fan on crankshaft.
CARBURETTOR: Downdraft Solex 32 PCI or
two Downdraft Solex 34PDSIT.
IGNITION: 12V battery.
DIMENSIONS
Length: 829mm (32·64in)
Width: 960mm (37·8in)
Height, without air cleaner: 556mm (21·89in)
WEIGHT Dry with standard equipment: 124kg
(273lb)
PERFORMANCE RATINGS
Max continuous ratings at 4,000rpm:
   single carburettor: 62bhp DIN
   twin carburettor: 68bhp DIN

FUEL: 90 octane minimum
FUEL CONSUMPTION
At 3,000 output rpm: 230g (0·506lb)/bhp/h
At 4,000 output rpm: 255g (0·561lb)/bhp/h

1,600cc WATER-COOLED DIESEL

TYPE: Four-cylinder, diesel in-line engine with
overhead camshaft (OHC). The swirl chamber
ensures optimal combustion. Valves operated
directly by camshaft via bucket tappets. Distributor injection pump and camshaft driven via a
toothed belt. Numerous versions are available for
a wide range of operating and installation conditions.
CYLINDERS: Bore: 76·5mm (3in). Stroke:
86·4mm (3·4in). Capacity: 1,588cc. Compression ratio: 23:1.
COOLING: Pumped liquid cooling (sealed pressurised system). Cooling liquid: water/anti-
freeze.
LUBRICATION: Forced-feed lubrication with
gear pump. Main-flow oil filter.
OIL CAPACITY: When changing filter 3·5
litres, otherwise 3·0 l.
FUEL GRADE: Diesel fuel according to DIN
51601.
INJECTION PUMP: BOSCH distributor injection pump with revolution-speed limiter and
electric cut-out device, or, at extra charge, with
variable speed governor.
ELECTRIC SYSTEM: Twelve-volt system with
alternator 45A and starter 1·5kW (2 HP).
WEIGHT, dry: 129kg (284·3lb)
INCLINATION: 20 degrees to the right when
facing the flywheel.

Power Output (DIN 70020)

Speed rpm	DIN kW	DIN HP	Max torque
2,000	20	27	
2,500	25	34	95 Nm
3,000	30	41	(9·5 mkp)
3,600	35	48	at
4,000	37	50	1,700 rpm

2,400cc WATER-COOLED DIESEL

TYPE: Six-cylinder, diesel, in-line engine with
overhead camshaft (OHC). The swirl chamber
ensures optimal combustion. Valves operated
directly by the camshaft via bucket tappets. Distributor injection pump and camshaft driven via a
toothed belt. Many variants are available for a
wide range of operating and installation conditions.

Type 127 industrial engine

CYLINDERS: Bore: 76·5mm (3in). Stroke: 86·4mm (3·4in). Capacity: 2,383cc. Compression ratio: 23:1.
COOLING: Pumped liquid cooling (sealed pressurised system). Cooling liquid: water/antifreeze.
LUBRICATION SYSTEM: Forced-feed lubrication with rotor-type pump. Main-flow oil filter.
OIL CAPACITY: When changing filter 6·5 litres, otherwise 6·01.

FUEL GRADE: Diesel fuel according to DIN 51601.
INJECTION PUMP: BOSCH distributor injection pump with variable speed governor and electric cut-out device.
ELECTRIC SYSTEM: Twelve-volt system with alternator 45A and starter 2kW (2·7HP).
WEIGHT, dry: 191kg (421lb)
INCLINATION: 5 degrees 30 minutes to the right when facing the flywheel.

Power Output (DIN 70020)

Speed rpm	DIN kW	HP	Max torque
2,000	29	39	
2,500	37	50	144 Nm
3,000	44	60	(14·4mkg)
3,600	52	71	at
4,000	54	73	2,500rpm

ITALY

CRM FABBRICA MOTORI MARINI

Via Manzoni 12, 20121 Milan, Italy
Telephone: 708 326/327
Telex: 334382 CREMME
Cables: Cremme
Officials:
G Mariani, *Director*
Ing B Piccoletti, *Director*
Ing S Rastelli, *Director*
Ing G Venturini, *Director*

CRM has specialised in building lightweight diesel engines for more than 30 years. The company's engines are used in large numbers of motor torpedo boats, coastal patrol craft and privately-owned motor yachts. The engines have also been installed in hydrofoils.

During the 1960s the company undertook the development and manufacture of a family of 12- to 18-cylinder diesel engines of lightweight high-speed design, providing a power coverage of 600 to 1,335kW.

These comprise the 12-cylinder 12 D/S2 and 12 D/SS and the 18-cylinder 18 D/S-2, 18 D/SS and BR-1/2000. All are turbocharged with different supercharging ratios. The 12 cylinders are arranged in two banks of six and the 18 cylinders are set out in an unusual 'W' arrangement of three banks of six.

All engines are available in non-magnetic versions, the perturbation field is reduced to insignificant amounts when compensated with the antidipole method.

CRM 18-CYLINDER

First in CRM's series of low weight, high-speed diesel engines, the CRM 18-cylinder is arranged in a 'W' form. Maximum power is 993kW at 2,075rpm for the 18 D/S-2; 1,213kW at 2,075rpm for the 18 D/SS and 1,335kW at 2,075rpm for the BR-1/2000. The following description relates to all three engines.
TYPE: Eighteen-cylinder in-line W type, four-stroke, water-cooled, turbocharged with different supercharging ratios: 1·85 (18 D/S-2); 2·4 (18 D/SS) and 2·6 (BR-1/2000).
CYLINDERS: Bore 150mm (5·91in). Stroke 180mm (7·09in). Swept volume 3·18 litres (194·166in³) per cylinder. Total swept volume 57·3 litres (3,495in³). Compression ratio 14 : 1. Separate pressed-steel cylinder frame side members are surrounded by gas-welded sheet metal water cooling jacket treated and pressure-coated internally to prevent corrosion. Cylinders are closed at top by a steel plate integral with side wall to complete combustion chamber. Lower half of cylinder is ringed by a drilled flange for bolting to crankcase. Cylinder top also houses a spherical-shaped pre-combustion chamber as well as inlet and exhaust valve seats. Pre-combustion chamber is in high-strength, heat and corrosion resistant steel. A single cast light alloy head, carrying valve guides, pre-combustion chambers and camshaft bearings bridges each bank of cylinders. Head is attached to cylinder bank by multiple studs.
PISTONS: Light alloy forgings with four rings, top ring being chrome-plated and bottom ring acting as oil scraper. Piston crowns shaped to withstand high temperatures especially in vicinity of pre-combustion chamber outlet ports.

CRM 18 D/SS marine diesel

	18 D/S-2	18 D/SS	BR-1/2000
DIMENSIONS			
Length:	2,305mm (90·74in)	2,305mm (90·74in)	2,305mm (90·74in)
Width:	1,352mm (53·22in)	1,400mm (55·11in)	1,400mm (55·11in)
Height:	1,303mm (51·29in)	1,303mm (51·29in)	1,303mm (51·29in)
Reverse gear:	621mm (24·44in)	621mm (24·44in)	621mm (24·44in)
WEIGHTS			
Engine dry:	1,735kg (3,845lb)	1,760kg (3,880lb)	1,760kg (3,880lb)
Reverse gear:	340kg (750·5lb)	340kg (750·5lb)	340kg (750·5lb)
Reduction gear:	150 ÷ 300kg	150 ÷ 300kg	150 ÷ 300kg
RATINGS			
Max power:	993kW (1,350hp) at 2,075rpm	1,213kW (1,650hp) at 2,075rpm	1,335kW (1,815hp) at 2,075rpm
Continuous rating:	919kW (1,250hp) at 2,020rpm	1,103 (1,500hp) at 2,020rpm	1,213 (1,500hp) at 2,020rpm
Specific Fuel Consumption	0·238 ± 5% kg/kW/h (0·175kg/hp/h)	0·224 ± 5% kg/kW/h (0·165kg/hp/h)	0·23 ± 5% kg/kW/h (0·169kg/hp/h)
Specific Oil Consumption	0·004 ± 5% kg/kW/h	0·004 ± 5% kg/kW/h	0·004 ± 5% kg/kW/h

CONNECTING RODS: Comprise main and secondary articulated rods, all rods being completely machined I-section steel forgings. Big-end of each main rod is bolted to ribbed cap by six studs. Big-end bearings are white metal lined steel shells. Each secondary rod anchored at its lower end to a pivot pin inserted in two lugs protruding from big-end of main connecting rod. Both ends of all secondary rods and small ends of main rods have bronze bushes.
CRANKSHAFTS: One-piece hollow shaft in nitrided alloy steel, with six throws equi-spaced at 120 degrees. Seven main bearings with white metal lined steel shells. 12 balancing counterweights.
CRANKCASE: Cast light alloy crankcase bolted to bed plate by studs and tie bolts. Multiple integral reinforced ribs provide robust structure. Both sides of each casting braced by seven cross ribs incorporating crankshaft bearing supports. Protruding sides of crankcase ribbed throughout length.
VALVE GEAR: Hollow sodium-cooled valves of each bank of cylinders actuated by twin cam-

shafts and six cams on each shaft. Two inlet and two outlet valves per cylinder and one rocker for each pair of valves. End of stem and facing of exhaust valves fitted with Stellite inserts. Valve cooling water forced through passage formed by specially-shaped plate welded to top of cylinder.
FUEL INJECTION: Pumps fitted with variable speed control and pilot injection nozzle.
PRESSURE CHARGER: Two turbochargers Holset type on 18 D/S-2, and Brown-Boveri on the 18 D/SS and BR-1/2000.
ACCESSORIES: Standard accessories include oil and fresh water heat exchangers; fresh water tank; oil and fresh water thermostats; oil filters, fresh water, salt water and fuel hand pumps; fresh water and oil temperature gauges; engine, reverse gear and reduction gear oil gauges; pre-lubrication, electric pump and engine rpm counter. Optional accessories include engine oil and water pre-heater, and warning and pressure switches.
COOLING SYSTEM: Fresh water.
FUEL: Fuel oil having specific gravity of 0·83 to 0·84.

LUBRICATION SYSTEM: Pressure type with gear pump.
OIL: Mineral oil to SAE 40 HD, MIL-L-2104C.
OIL COOLING: By salt water circulating through heat exchanger.
STARTING: 24-volt 15hp electric motor and 85A, 24-volt alternator for battery charge, or compressed air.
MOUNTING: At any transverse or longitudinal angle tilt to 20 degrees.
REVERSE GEAR: Bevel crown gear wheels with hydraulically-controlled hand brake.
REDUCTION GEAR: Optional fitting with spur gears giving reduction ratios of 0·561 : 1, 0·730 : 1 and 0·846 : 1. Overdrive ratio 1·18 : 1.
PROPELLER THRUST BEARING: Incorporated in reduction gear. Axial thrust from KN 29·5 to KN 39·5 (3,000 to 4,000kgf).

CRM 12-CYLINDER

Second in the CRM series of low weight diesels, the CRM 12-cylinder is a unit with two blocks of six cylinders set at 60 degrees to form a V assembly. The bore and stroke are the same as in the CRM 18 series and many of the components are interchangeable including the crankshaft, bedplate, cylinders and pistons. The crankcase and connecting rod-assemblies are necessarily of modified design; the secondary rod is anchored at its lower end to a pivot pin inserted on two lugs protruding from the big-end of the main connecting rod. The fuel injection pump is modified to single block housing all 12 pumping elements located between the cylinder banks.

TYPE: Twelve-cylinder V type, four-stroke, water-cooled, turbo-supercharged with medium supercharging ratio (1·8 for 12 D/S-2) and light supercharging ratio (2·85 for 12 D/SS).
PRESSURE CHARGER
Two Holset type on 12 D/S-2 and Brown Boveri type on 12 D/SS.

	12 D/S-2	12 D/SS
DIMENSIONS		
Length:	1,909mm (75·15in)	2,147mm (84·52in)
Width:	1,210mm (47·63in)	1,210mm (47·63in)
Height:	1,204mm (47·4in)	1,310mm (51·57in)
Reverse gear:	621mm (24·44in)	621mm (25·44in)
WEIGHTS, dry		
Engine:	1,310kg (2,891lb)	1,560kg (3,443lb)
Reverse gear:	340kg (750lb)	340kg (750lb)
Reduction gear:	150 ÷ 300kg (331 ÷ 662lb)	150 ÷ 300kg (331 ÷ 662lb)
PERFORMANCE RATINGS		
Max power:	687kW (900hp) at 2,035rpm	1,010kW (1,374hp) at 2,075rpm
Continuous rating:	625kW (850hp) at 2,000rpm	918kW (1,248hp) at 2,020rpm
FUEL CONSUMPTION:	0·245kg/kW/h ± 5% (0·18kg/hp/h)	0·238kg/kW/h ± 5% (0·175kg/hp/h)
OIL CONSUMPTION:	0·004kg/kW/h	0·004kg/kW/h

FIAT AVIAZIONE SpA

Marine & Industrial Products Department, Via Nizza 312, Turin, Italy
Telephone: 63311
Telex: 221320 FIATAV

The LM500 gas turbine is a compact high performance marine and industrial power unit in the 3,000 to 6,000 shaft horsepower class. General Electric's Marine and Industrial Engine Division and Fiat Aviazione SpA, in a co-operative undertaking, initiated the design programme in July 1978. In January 1980 the first engine began full load testing and the LM500 is now in production.

The LM500 is a simple-cycle, two-shaft gas turbine engine with a free power turbine. It incorporates a variable stator compressor, with excellent stall margin capability, driven by an air-cooled, two-stage turbine. It is derived from the TF34 high bypass turbofan aircraft engine which was designed for marine operation in the US Navy's S-3A aircraft and later incorporated in the US Air Force's A-10 aircraft, with the same materials and marine corrosion protection as employed in the very successful LM2500 marine gas turbine. The LM500 incorporates the latest in proven design technology and corrosion-resistant materials to provide a mature design with maximum reliability, component life and time between inspections and overhaul. The LM500 demonstrates higher efficiency than currently available gas turbines in its class and is suited for marine applications requiring low weight and fuel economy.

General Electric Company and Fiat Aviazione SpA have designed the LM500 gas turbine to produce power for marine applications requiring significant fuel economy, compactness, light weight, minimum maintenance, high tolerance to fouling/deposits, and reliable operation. Such applications include military land craft, hydrofoils, air cushion vehicles, fast patrol boats, cruise power propulsion and on-board electric power generators.

LM500

The LM500 is a simple-cycle, two-shaft gas turbine engine. The single shaft gas generator consists of a 14-stage high pressure compressor with variable inlet guide vanes and variable stator vanes in the first five stages, an annular machined ring combustor with 18 externally mounted fuel injectors and an air-cooled, two-stage HP gas generator turbine. The free power turbine has four stages and the output shaft connecting flange is at the air inlet end of the engine.
AIR INTAKE: The LM500 offers, as optional equipment, an air inlet collector to guide the inlet air from the customer's intake ducting into the engine. The inlet duct is made from aluminium and provides the structural connection for the forward engine mounts or for the reduction gearbox containing the forward mounts.

An off-engine inlet screen is also offered to prevent objects from entering the compressor.
COMPRESSOR: The compressor is identical to the TF34 and consists of the front frame, accessory drive assembly, compressor rotor and case/vane assembly. The front frame is an uncomplicated four strut aluminium casting and is designed to provide the compressor inlet flowpath, the forward structural support for the engine, support the forward bearings and seals for the gas generator and power turbine rotors, and support the accessory gearbox.

COMBUSTOR: The LM500 combustor is of the TF34 flight engine design. It is an annular through-flow combustor using a machined ring liner construction for long life. Metered fuel is distributed and introduced through 18 central, individually replaceable injectors.
HIGH PRESSURE TURBINE: The LM500 high pressure turbine is a two-stage, fully air-cooled design, identical to the TF34 turbine except for minor changes to improve performance and meet the requirements for marine and industrial applications.
POWER TURBINE: The LM500 power turbine is a four-stage, uncooled, high performance

LM500

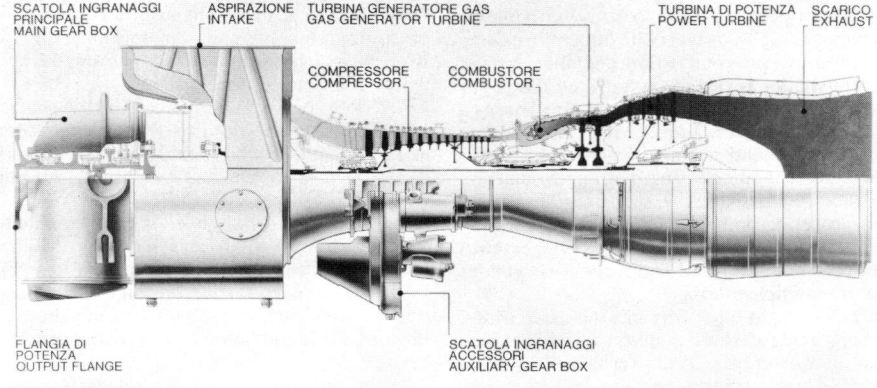

Cutaway of LM500

design incorporating aerodynamic and mechanical features and materials identical to the TF34 low pressure turbine. The power turbine rotor structural components are made of inconel 718 material. The four turbine discs carry tip shrouded turbine blades that are attached to the discs with single tang dovetails. The blades are made of René 77 material with the first stage Codep coated. The durability of René 77 alleviates the need for coatings on the other stages. At operating gas temperatures 111°C (200°F) less than the TF34, the LM500 blades have virtually infinite stress rupture life. The structural integrity of the power turbine rotor has been demonstrated to a speed of 9,030rpm, 29 per cent over the normal rated speed of the LM500 engine.

LUBRICATION: The LM500 lubricating oil system provides the following functions: lubricates and cools the gas turbine main bearings;

supplies hydraulic fluid for the variable geometry actuation system and fuel metering valve actuator.

The main engine bearings are lubricated from an accessory gearbox-driven lube pump. The scavenge circuit is based on a dry sump system and each bearing sump is scavenged by a separate pump or pump elements driven off the accessory gearbox. All scavenge oil is filtered (coarse screens) prior to entry into the pump elements.

FUEL: The LM500 is designed to operate with marine diesel, diesel, and JP fuels. The fuel system consists of on- and off-engine components. Filtered fuel is supplied by the customer to the fuel pump, which is mounted on the accessory gearbox, where the fuel pressure is increased by a centrifugal boost element and then ported externally to an on-engine last chance fuel filter. From the filter the fuel is routed to an off-engine fuel regulating assembly (FRA) which meters the

engine fuel flow according to signals received from the off-engine main electronic control assembly (MECA). Also included in the FRA are two fuel shut-off valves mounted in series for redundancy which are used to shut off the fuel to the engine during normal shutdowns and automatic shutdowns. Fuel is then routed to the on-engine fuel distributor which divides the fuel through separate hose assemblies to 18 fuel injectors.

SPECIFICATION
BASIC ENGINE:
Length overall: 2,184mm (86in)
Width: 864mm (34in)
Weight: 580kg (1,276lb)
WITH OPTIONAL INLET AND AXIAL EXHAUST DUCT, STARTER KIT AND OUTPUT GEARBOX:
Length overall: 3,307mm (130·2in)
Width: 1,179mm (46·4in)
Weight: 1,031kg (2,269lb)

UNION OF SOVIET SOCIALIST REPUBLICS

A IVCHENKO (AI)

This design team, which was headed by the late A Ivchenko, is based in a factory at Zaporojie in the Ukraine, where all prototypes and pre-production engines bearing the 'AI' prefix are developed and built. Chief designer is Lotarev and chief engineer, Tichienko. The production director is M Omeltchenko.

First engine with which Ivchenko was associated officially was the 55hp AI-4G piston-engine used in the Kamov Ka-10 ultra-light helicopter. He later progressed via the widely used AI-14 and AI-26 piston-engines, to become one of the Soviet Union's leading designers of gas-turbine engines.

Two AI-20s in de-rated, marinised form and driving two three-stage waterjets power the Burevestnik, the first Soviet gas-turbine hydrofoil to go into series production, and a single AI-24 drives the integrated lift/propulsion system of the Sormovich 50-passenger ACV. Two AI-20s, each rated at about 3,600shp continuous, are also thought to power the Lebed amphibious assault landing craft.

IVCHENKO
AI-20

The Ivchenko design bureau is responsible for the AI-20 turboprop engine which powers the Antonov An-10, An-12 and Ilyushin Il-18 airliners and the Beriev M-12 Tchaika amphibian.

Six production series of this engine had been built by the spring of 1966. The first four series, of which manufacture started in 1957, were variants of the basic AI-20 version. They were followed by two major production versions, as follows:

AI-20K. Rated at 3,945ehp. Used in Il-18V, An-10A and An-12.

AI-20M. Uprated version with T-O rating of 4,190ehp (4,250 ch e). Used in Il-18D/E, An-10A and An-12.

Conversion of the turboprop as a marine power unit for hydrofoil waterjet propulsion (as on the Burevestnik) involved a number of changes to the engine. In particular it was necessary to hold engine rpm at a constant level during conditions of varying load from the waterjet pump. It was also necessary to be able to vary the thrust from the waterjet unit from zero to forward or rearwards thrust to facilitate engine starting and vessel manoeuvring.

Constant speed under variable load was achieved by replacing the engine's normal high pressure fuel pump with a special fuel regulator pump. The waterjet pump was modified to have a variable exit area and was fitted with an air valve enabling a variable amount of air to be passed into the intake just ahead of the pump rotor. With less air passing through the waterjet, unit load on the engine increased, and vice versa if the air flow was increased by opening the air valve.

The fuel regulator pump was designed to maintain engine rpm constant and to regulate output while the AI-20 was driving the waterjet unit. Steady running conditions were shown to be satisfactorily maintained by the engine under all operating conditions—and rpm and turbine temperature were held within the limits laid down for the aircraft turboprop version: engine rpm did not fluctuate outside ±2·5% of its set speed when loading or unloading the waterjet unit.

During development of the marinised AI-20, the normal aircraft propeller and speed governor were removed and the turboprop was bench tested over the full range of its operating conditions. This demonstrated stable engine performance throughout, from slow running to normal rpm. These tests were run initially using aviation kerosene Type TS-1 fuel, and then diesel fuels Types L and DS.

Following satisfactory results on the bench, the test engine was mounted on a self-propelled floating test bed equipped with a waterjet propulsion unit. Further tests with this configuration were also satisfactorily concluded, including starting checks with varying degrees of submersion of the pump section of the waterjet unit.

Electrical starting of the engine up to slow running speed (equal to approximately 25% of rated rpm) was shown to take 70 to 85 seconds. For starting and ignition at ambient conditions below 10°C, fuel pre-heating is employed and modified igniters are fitted. With this equipment, starts have been achieved down to minus 12°C.

Based on this experience, the marinised AI-20 for the twin-engined Burevestnik was rated at 2,700hp at 13,200rpm. At this power output, the hydrofoil achieved speeds of up to 97km/h (60mph). Specific fuel consumption was 320-330g (0·71-0·73lb)/hp/h.

Testing with the Burevestnik revealed a number of operating characteristics: when the two AI-20s were running while the vessel was

moored or manoeuvring, residual exhaust thrust from the turbines occurred and this is required to be balanced by a negative or reverse thrust from the waterjet by partially closing the unit's nozzle flaps. This increased the load on the engine, however, and caused a rise in fuel consumption.

Experience showed that with a normal start following a series of wet starts, any fuel which had accumulated in the jet pipe ignited. This resulted in a sharp rise in turbine temperature and back pressure, and flame emerged from the ejection apertures into the engine compartment and exhaust nozzle. To circumvent this, the ejection apertures were covered with a metal grid, and a spray of water was provided at the exhaust nozzle prior to starting.

Based on an overhaul life for the turboprop AI-20 of several thousand hours, special techniques have been applied to the marinised version to increase its service life. These include: the use of high quality assembly procedures for the engine; efficient design of the air intake and exhaust duct; adoption of appropriate procedures for starting and on-loading of the main and auxiliary turbines at all ambient temperature conditions; utilisation of highly-skilled servicing methods of the installation during operation.

The AI-20 is a single-spool turboprop, with a ten-stage axial-flow compressor, cannular combustion chamber with ten flame tubes, and a three-stage turbine, of which the first two stages are cooled. Planetary reduction gearing, with a ratio of 0·08732 : 1, is mounted forward of the annular air intake. The fixed nozzle contains a central bullet fairing. All engine-driven accessories are mounted on the forward part of the compressor casing, which is of magnesium alloy.

The AI-20 was designed to operate reliably in all temperatures from −60°C to +55°C at heights up to 10,000m (33,000ft). It is a constant speed engine, the rotor speed being maintained at 21,300rpm by automatic variation of propeller pitch. Gas temperature after turbine is 560°C in

1,750hp Ivchenko AI-23-CI marine gas turbine

both current versions. TBO of the AI-20K was 4,000 hours in the spring of 1966.

WEIGHT

DRY

AI-20K: 1,080kg (2,380lb)
AI-20M: 1,039kg (2,290lb)

PERFORMANCE RATINGS

Max T-O:
AI-20K: 4,000ch e (3,945ehp)
AI-20M: 4,250ch e (4,190ehp)

Cruise rating at 630km/h (390mph) at 8,000m (26,000ft):
AI-20K: 2,250ch e (2,220ehp)
AI-20M: 2,700ch e (2,663ehp)

SPECIFIC FUEL CONSUMPTION

At cruise rating:
AI-20K: 215g (0·472lb)/hp/h
AI-20M: 197g (0·434lb)/hp/h

OIL CONSUMPTION Normal: 1 litre/h (1·75 pints/h)

IVCHENKO
AI-24

In general configuration this single-spool turboprop engine, which powers the An-24 transport aircraft, is very similar to the earlier and larger AI-20. Production began in 1960 and the following data refers to engines of the second series, which were in production in the spring of 1966.

A single marinised version, developing 1,800shp, drives the integrated lift/propulsion system of the Sormovich 50-passenger ACV.

An annular ram air intake surrounds the cast light alloy casing for the planetary reduction gear, which has a ratio of 0·08255 : 1. The cast magnesium alloy compressor casing carries a row of inlet guide vanes and the compressor stator vanes and provides mountings for the engine-driven accessories. These include fuel, hydraulic and oil pumps, tacho-generator and propeller governor.

The ten-stage axial-flow compressor is driven by a three-stage axial-flow turbine, of which the first two stages are cooled. An annular combustion chamber is used, with eight injectors and two igniters.

The engine is flat-rated to maintain its nominal output to 3,500m (11,500ft). TBO was 3,000 hours in the spring of 1966.

LENGTH (overall): 2,435mm (95·87in)
WEIGHT Dry: 499kg (1,100lb)
PERFORMANCE RATING: Max T-O with water injection: 2,859ch e (2,820ehp)

KUZNETSOV
KUZNETSOV
NK-12M

The NK-12M, which powers the Aist amphibious assault ACV and is thought to power the Babochka and Sarancha hydrofoils, is the world's most powerful turboprop engine. In its original form it developed 8,948kW (12,000ehp). The later NK-12MV is rated at 11,033kW (14,795ehp) and powers the Tupolev Tu-114 transport, driving four-blade, contra-rotating propellers of 5·6m (18ft 4in) diameter. As the NK-12MA, rated at 11,185kW (15,000shp), it powers the Antonov AN-22 military transport, with propellers of 6·2m (20ft 4in) diameter. It is also used in the Tupolev Tu-95 bomber and its derivatives and the Tu-126 AWACS.

The NK-12M has a single 14-stage axial-flow compressor. Compression ratio varies from 9:1 to 13:1 and variable inlet guide vanes and blow-off valves are necessary. A can-annular-type combustion system is used. Each flame tube is mounted centrally on a downstream injector, but all tubes merge at their maximum diameter to form an annular secondary region. The single turbine is a five-stage axial. Mass flow is 65kg (143lb)/s.

The casing is made in four portions from sheet steel, precision welded. An electric control for variation of propeller pitch is incorporated to maintain constant engine speed.

NKM-12MV *(Aviation International, Paris)*

DIMENSIONS
Length: 6,000mm (236·2in)
Diameter: 1,150mm (45·3in)

WEIGHT, Dry: 2,350kg (5,181lb)

PERFORMANCE RATINGS
T-O: 11,033kW (14,795ehp)
Nominal power: 8,826kW (11,836ehp) at 8,300rpm
Idling speed: 6,600rpm

SOLOVIEV

Officials:
P A Soloviev, *Designer in Charge of Bureau*

SOLOVIEV
D-30

This two-spool turbofan, in marinised form, is believed to power the 'Caspian Sea Monster' power-augmented ram-wing. It powers the Tu-134 twin-engined airliner and is derived from the D-20. Major portions of the core and carcass are similar, but the complete power plant is larger, more powerful and efficient than the D-20.

TYPE: Two-shaft turbofan (by-pass turbojet).
AIR INTAKE: Titanium alloy assembly, incorporating air bleed anti-icing of centre bullet and radial struts.
FAN: Four-stage axial (LP compressor). First stage has shrouded titanium blades held in disc by pinned joints. Pressure ratio (T-O rating, 7,700rpm, S/L, static), 2·65:1. Mass flow 125kg (265lb)/s. By-pass ratio 1:1.
COMPRESSOR: Ten-stage axial (HP compressor). Drum and disc construction largely of titanium. Pressure ratio (T-O rating, 11,600rpm, S/L static), 7·1:1. Overall pressure ratio, 17·4:1.
COMBUSTION CHAMBER: Can-annular, with 12 flame tubes fitted with duplex burners.
FUEL GRADE: T-1 and TS-1 to GOST 10227-62 (equivalent to DERD. 2494 or MIL-F-5616).
TURBINE: Two-stage HP turbine. First stage has cooled blades in both stator and rotor. LP

D-30KU turbofan

turbine also has two stages. All discs air-cooled on both sides, and all blades shrouded to improve efficiency and reduce vibration. All shaft bearings shock-mounted.
JET PIPE: Sub-sonic fixed-area type, incorporating main and by-pass flow mixer with curvilinear ducts of optimum shape. D-30-2 engine of Tu-134A fitted with twin-clamshell (Rolls-type) reverser.
LUBRICATION: Open type, with oil returned to tank.

OIL GRADE: Mineral oil MK-8 or MK-8P to GOST 6457-66 (equivalent to DERD. 2490 or MIL-0-6081B). Consumption in flight is not more than 1kg/h.
ACCESSORIES: Automatic ice-protection system, fire extinguishing for core and by-pass flows, vibration detectors on casings, oil chip detectors and automatic limitation of exhaust gas temperature to 620°C at take-off or when starting and to 630°C in flight (five minute limit). Shaft-driven accessories driven via radial bevel-gear shafts in

centre casing, mainly off HP spool, accessory gearboxes being provided above and below centre casing and fan duct. D-30-2 carries constant-speed drives for alternators.
STARTING: Electric dc starting system with STG-12TVMO starter/generators.

DIMENSIONS
Overall length: 3,983mm (156·8in)
Base diameter of inlet casing: 1,050mm (41·3in)
WEIGHT Dry: 1,550kg (3,417lb)
PERFORMANCE RATINGS
T-O: 66·68kN (14,990lb st)

Long-range cruise rating: 11,000m (36,000ft)
Mach 0·75: 12·75kN (2,866lb st)

SPECIFIC FUEL CONSUMPTION
T-O: 17·56mg/Ns (0·62lb/h/lb st)
Cruise as above: 21·81mg/Ns (0·77lb/h/lb st)

SUDOIMPORT

ul Kaliaevskaja 5, Moscow K-6, USSR

Soviet industry has developed a variety of marine diesel engines, selected models of which have been installed in the Krasnoye Sormovo series of hydrofoil craft. Most popular of these are the 1,100hp M401 powering the Kometa hydrofoil, and the 1,200hp M50 powering the Byelorus, Chaika, Meteor, Mir, Raketa, Sputnik, Strela and Vikhr hydrofoils. A third marine diesel engine is the 3D12 with a continuous rating of 300hp. A version of this engine is installed in the Nevka hydrofoil.

These and other marine diesels are available through Sudoimport, the USSR marine export, import and repair organisation.

TYPE M 400

TYPE: Water-cooled, 12-cylinder, V-type four-stroke supercharged marine diesel engine.
CYLINDERS: Two banks of six cylinders set at 30 degrees, each bank comprising cast aluminium alloy monobloc with integral head. Pressed-in liner with spiral cooling passages comprises inner alloy steel sleeve with nitrided working surface, and outer carbon steel sleeve. Each monobloc retained on crankcase by 14 holding-down studs. Bore 180mm (7·09in). Stroke 200mm (7·87in). Cubic capacity 62·4 litres (3,810in³). Compression ratio 13·5 : 1.
SUPERCHARGING: Single-stage centrifugal supercharger, mechanically driven and providing supercharging pressure of at least 1·55kg/cm² (22lb/in²) at rated power.
CRANKCASE: Two-part cast aluminium alloy case with upper half carrying cylinder monoblocs, and transmitting all engine loads.
CYLINDER HEADS: Integral with cylinder monoblocs.
CRANKSHAFT: Six-crank seven-bearing crankshaft in nitrided alloy steel with split steel shells, lead bronze lined with lead-tin alloy bearing surface. Spring damper at rear end reduces torsional vibrations.
CONNECTING RODS: Master and articulated rods, with master connected to crankshaft by split big end with lead bronze lining. Articulated rods connected by pin pressed into eye of master rods.
PISTONS: Forged aluminium alloy with four rings, upper two of which are of trapeziform cross-section. Alloy steel floating gudgeon pin. Piston head specially shaped to form combustion chamber with spherical cylinder head.
CAMSHAFTS: Two camshafts acting direct on valve stems.
VALVES: Four valves in each cylinder, two inlet and two exhaust. Each valve retained on seat by three coil springs.
COOLING: Forced circulation system using fresh water with 1 to 1·1% potassium dichromate added. Fresh water pump mounted on forward part of engine. Fresh water and lubricating oil leaving the engine are cooled by water-to-water and water-to-oil coolers, in turn cooled by sea water circulated by engine-mounted sea water pump.
SUPERCHARGING: Single-stage centrifugal supercharger, mechanically driven and providing supercharging pressure of at least 1·55kg/cm² (22lb/in²) at rated power.
LUBRICATION: Comprises delivery pump together with full-flow centrifuge; twin-suction scavenge pump, double gauze-type strainers at inlet and outlet to oil system; and electrically-driven priming pump to prime engine with oil and fuel.
FUEL INJECTION: Closed-type fuel injection with hydraulically-operated valves, giving initial pressure of 200kg/cm² (2,845lb/in²). Each injector has eight spray orifices forming 140-degree conical spray. High pressure 12-plunger fuel

M400

3D12

injection pump with primary gear pump. Two filters in parallel filter oil to HP pump.
STARTING: Compressed air system with starting cylinder operating at 75 to 150kg/cm² (1,067 to 2,134lb/in²) two disc-type air distributors and 12 starting valves.
GOVERNOR: Multi-range indirect-action engine speed governor with resilient gear drive from pump camshaft. Governor designed to maintain preset rpm throughout full speed range from minimum to maximum.
EXHAUST SYSTEM: Fresh water-cooled exhaust manifolds fastened to exterior of cylinder blocs. Provision made for fitting thermocouple or piezometer.
REVERSING: Hydraulically-operated reversing clutch fitted to enable prop shaft to run forwards, idle or reverse with constant direction of crankshaft rotation.

MOUNTING: Supports fitted to upper half of crankcase for attaching engine to bedplate.
DIMENSIONS
Length: 2,600mm (102·36in)
Width: 1,220mm (48·03in)
Height: 1,250mm (49·21in)
PERFORMANCE RATINGS
Max: 1,100hp at 1,800rpm
Continuous: 1,000hp at 1,700rpm
FUEL CONSUMPTION: At continuous rating: not over 193g (0·425lb)/hp/h
OIL CONSUMPTION: At continuous rating: not over 6g (0·013lb)/hp/h

TYPE 3D12

TYPE: Water-cooled, 12-cylinder, V-type, four-stroke marine diesel engine.
CYLINDERS: Two banks of six cylinders in jacketed blocks with pressed-in steel liners. Bore 150mm (5·9in). Stroke 180mm (7·09in). Cubic

capacity 38·8 litres (2,370in³). Compression ratio 14 to 15 : 1.

CRANKCASE: Two-part cast aluminium alloy case with upper half accommodating seven main bearings of steel shell, lead bronze lined type. Lower half carries oil pump, water circulating pump and fuel feed pump.

CYLINDER HEADS: Provided with six recesses to accommodate combustion chambers. Each chamber is connected via channel to inlet and outlet ports of cylinder bloc.

CRANKSHAFT: Alloy steel forging with seven journals and six crankpins. Pendulum anti-vibration dampers fitted on first two webs to reduce torsional vibration.

CONNECTING RODS: Master and articulated rods of double-T section forged in alloy steel. Master rod big-end bearings have steel shells, lead bronze lined. Small end bearings of master rods and both bearings of articulated rods have bronze bushes.

PISTONS: Aluminium alloy.

CAMSHAFTS: Carbon steel camshafts with cams and journals hardened by high frequency electrical current.

COOLING: Closed water, forced circulation type incorporating centrifugal pump, self suction sea water pump and tubular water cooler.

LUBRICATION: Forced circulation type with dry sump, incorporating three-section gear pump, oil feed pump, wire-mesh strainer with fine cardboard filtering element and tubular oil cooler.

FUEL INJECTION: Rotary fuel feed pump, twin felt filter, plunger fuel pump with device to stop engine in event of oil pressure drop in main line. Closed-type fuel injectors with slotted filters. Plunger pump carries variable-speed centrifugal governor for crankshaft rpm.

STARTING: Main electrical starting system, with compressed air reverse system.

REVERSE-REDUCTION GEAR: Non-coaxial type with twin-disc friction clutch and gear-type reduction gear giving optional ratios, forwards, of 2·95 : 1, 2·04 : 1 or 1·33 : 1, and 2·18 : 1 astern.

DIMENSIONS
Length: 2,464mm (97·01in)
Width: 1,052mm (41·42in)
Height: 1,159mm (45·63in)
WEIGHT Dry fully equipped: 1,900kg (4,189lb)
PERFORMANCE RATING: Continuous: 300hp at 1,500rpm
FUEL CONSUMPTION: At continuous rated power: 176g (0·388lb)/hp/h
OIL CONSUMPTION: At continuous rated power: not over 9g (0·02lb)/hp/h

M401A

The M401A, fitted to the Voskhod and the latest variants of the Kometa and Raketa, is based on the M50. The new engine is more reliable than its predecessor and its development involved the redesigning of a number of units and parts, as well as the manufacturing of components with a higher degree of accuracy, which necessitated the employment of the latest engineering techniques.

The engine is manufactured in left- and right-hand models. These differ by the arrangement on the engine housing of the fresh water pump drive and the power take-off for the shipboard compressor.

TYPE: Water-cooled, 12-cylinder, V-type four-stroke supercharged marine diesel.

CYLINDERS: Two banks of six cylinders set at 60 degrees. Monobloc is a solid aluminium casting. Pressed into monobloc are six steel sleeves with spiral grooves on the outer surface for the circulation of cooling water. Bore 180mm (7·09in). Stroke 200mm (7·87in). Compression ratio 13·5 : 0·5.

CRANKCASE: Two-piece cast aluminium alloy case with upper half carrying cylinder monoblocs and transmitting all engine loads.

CYLINDER HEADS: Integral with cylinder monobloc.

CRANKSHAFT: Six-crank, seven bearing crankshaft in nitrided alloy steel with split steel

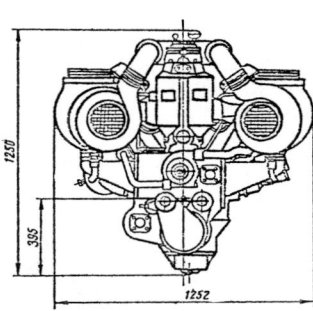
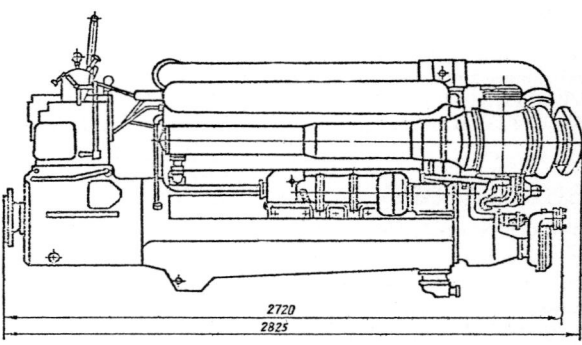

M401A

shells, lead-tin bronze lined with lead tin alloy bearing surface.

CONNECTING RODS: Master and articulated rods, with master connected to the crankshaft by split big end, lined with lead tin bronze. Articulated rod connected to crankshaft by a pin pressed into its eye ring.

PISTONS: Forged aluminium alloy with five rings. Top two steel rings, one cast iron of rectangular section and the two bottom rings, in cast iron and steel, are oil control rings fitted in a common groove.

CAMSHAFTS: Two, acting directly on valve stems.

VALVES: Four in each cylinder, two inlet and two exhaust. Each retained on seat by three coil springs.

SUPERCHARGING: Two, Type TK-18H superchargers, each comprising an axial-flow turbine and a centrifugal compressor mounted on a common shaft with a vane diffuser and volute. A silencer can be installed on the compressor air inlet. Turbine casing cooled with fresh water from the diesel engine cooling system.

GOVERNOR: Multi-range indirect action engine speed governor with resilient gear drive from pump camshaft. Designed to maintain preset rpm throughout full speed range.

LUBRICATION: Delivery pump with full-flow centrifuge, scavenge pump, double gauge strainers and electrically driven priming pump to power engine with oil and fuel.

COOLING: Double-circuit forced circulation system using fresh water with 1 to 1·1% potassium dichromate to GOST 2652-71. Fresh water pump mounted on engine. Fresh water and lubricating oil leaving engine are cooled by water-to-water and water-to-oil coolers in turn cooled by sea water circulated by engine-mounted sea water pump.

STARTING: Compressed air system with two disc-type air distributors and twelve starting valves.

REVERSING: Hydraulically operated reversing clutch to enable propeller shaft to run forwards, idle or reverse. Manual control available in emergency.

Rated power at ahead running under normal atmospheric conditions and at rated rpm: 1,000hp
Rated rpm at ahead running: 1,550
Max hourly power at maximum rpm: 1,100hp
Max rpm at ahead running: 1,600
Max power at astern running: 250hp
Minimum rpm at astern running (with the diesel engine control lever at reverse stop): 750
Max specific fuel consumption at rated power (with operating generator, hydraulic pump and the power take-off for compressor): 172 g/ehp/h+ 5%
Max specific oil burning losses at rated power: 5 g/ehp/h
Fuel:
Diesel fuel Grade (GOST 4749—49) Oil MC-20 (GOST 4749—49) with additive (GOST 8312-57) 3% in weight
Sense of power take-off flange rotation (if viewed from turbo-supercharger):
of right hand diesel engine: clockwise
of left hand diesel engine: counter-clockwise
Operating life (until major overhaul): 2,500 hours
Diesel engine dimensions:
length: (with muffler at intake) 2,825mm (111·1in)
length: (without muffler at intake) 2,720mm (107in)
width: 1,252mm (49·29in)
height: 1,250mm (49·21in)
Weight (dry) with all units and pipe lines mounted: 2,000kg (4,409lb)

M503A AND M504

The M503A is a multi-cylinder radial-type diesel which was introduced on the Osa missile fast-attack craft in the late 1950s and subsequently installed in the Shershen and probably the Pchela hydrofoil.

It is radically different from any other marine diesel in use today because of its radial or 'star' configuration, peculiar to aero-engines, and also because of the number of cylinders incorporated in the design.

M503

The M503A has 42 cylinders in six seven-cylinder blocks, but a more powerful version, the M504, has 56 cylinders in eight seven-cylinder blocks. M504, which develops 5,000hp at 2,000rpm, powers the Osa II, Turya, Matka and Stenka.

M503

A tropicalised version of the M504, derated to 4,000hp, is installed in export Osa IIs and other craft designed for these engines and destined to operate in warm climates. Designation of the tropicalised M504 is M504T.

A twin-pack version, employing two M504s with a common gearbox driving a single shaft, is employed in the Nanuchka missile corvette. Nanuchka has three M504 twin-packs, each developing 10,000hp, giving a total maximum output of 30,000hp.

On the M504 the drive and reduction gear is mounted directly on the engine, enabling the propeller shaft to run forwards or in reverse. Lubricating and water-cooling systems are cooled by sea water circulated under ram pressure when making headway and pumped in when going astern or when stopped. A supercharger is mounted on the forward end of the engine and can be powered either by drive from a main turbine or mechanical transmission from the crankshaft.

The most economical operation of the engine is attained at 1,400 to 1,700rpm, at which point the specific fuel consumption is 160 to 165 grams/hp hour. Economy at low power is achieved by cutting out some of the cylinders. Running hours between overhaul should be 1,500 provided that the engine is operated at maximum output for only 10 per cent of that time.

The following details apply to the M504 only:
PERFORMANCE RATING:
Max output: 5,000hp at 2,000rpm
CYLINDERS: Total 56, mounted in eight banks of seven.
Cylinder diameter: 16mm
PISTON STROKE: 17mm
WEIGHT (including gearbox and drive): 7,200kg
POWER TO WEIGHT RATIO: 1·44kg/hp
DIMENSIONS
Length: 4·4m
Width: 1·65m
Height: 1·64m

UNITED KINGDOM

PAXMAN DIESELS LIMITED
(a management company of GEC Diesels Limited)

Hythe Hill, Colchester, Essex CO1 2HW, England

Manufactured at the Colchester works of Paxman Diesels Limited are two of the world's most advanced diesel designs: the Valenta, built in 8-, 12-, 16- and 18-cylinder sizes covering 1,000 to 5,000bhp, and the Paxman Deltic, an 18-cylinder engine of unique triangular configuration, in powers from 1,500 to 4,000shp. These engines, with their compact overall dimensions and low unit weight, are particularly suitable for the propulsion of high-speed craft including hydrofoils and hovercraft.

VALENTA MK. 2 DIESELS

TYPE: Valenta Mk 2 engines: Direct injection, V-form 8-, 12-, 16- and 18-cylinder, turbocharged and water-cooled, four-stroke engine.
OUTPUT: Valenta Mk 2 engines: 1,000-5,000bhp, 1,000-1,600rpm.
BORE AND STROKE: 197 × 216mm (7·75 × 8·5in).
SWEPT VOLUME (per cylinder): 6·57 litres (401in³).
HOUSING: High quality SG iron.
CRANKSHAFT AND MAIN BEARINGS: Fully nitrided shaft carried in aluminium tin pre-finished steel-backed main bearings. Engine fully balanced against primary and secondary forces.
CONNECTING RODS: Fork and blade type with steel-backed, aluminium tin-lined large end (forked rod) and steel-backed, lead bronze lined, lead tin flashed bearings (blade rod).
PISTONS: Two-piece pistons, forged steel crown and forged aluminium skirt. Three compression rings in steel crown; one oil control in skirt.
CYLINDER HEAD: High grade casting carrying four-valve direct injection system.
LINERS: Wet type seamless steel tube, chrome plated bore and water side surface honeycombed for surface oil retention.
FUEL INJECTION: Single unit pumps. Pump plungers and camshaft lubricated from main engine pressure system. Feed and injection pump driven from engine drive and gear train; a fuel reservoir and air bleed system fitted. Multi-hole injectors spray fuel into the toroidal cavity in the top of piston. Injectors retained by clamp. Sleeved connection inside cover (Valenta).
GOVERNOR: Standard hydraulic 'Regulateurs Europa' unit with self-contained lubricating oil system; mechanical, electrical or pneumatic controls. Alternative makes available.

PRESSURE CHARGING AND INTERCOOLING: Water-cooled exhaust-gas-driven turboblowers mounted above engine. Air to water intercooler.
LUBRICATION: Pressure lubrication to all bearing surfaces; single pump system. Oil coolers mounted externally and integral with engine; sea water cooled (Valenta)). Full flow single or duplex oil filter can be supplied.
FRESH WATER COOLING: Single pump at free end, shaft-driven from drive end gear train. Thermostatic control valve mounted above pump, giving quick warm-up and even temperature control of water; oil thermostat.

18-cylinder Valenta Mk 2 developing 5,000hp

EXHAUST: Single outlet from turboblower; watercooled manifolds.
STARTING: Air, electric or hydraulic starting.
FUEL: Gas oil to BS.2869/1970 Class A1 and A2 or equivalent, and certain gas turbine fuels. Other classes of fuel subject to specification being made available.
LUBRICATING OIL: Oils certified to MIL-L-46152 (with a TBN of not less than nine).
OPTIONAL EXTRA EQUIPMENT: Gearboxes, starting control systems, and all associated engine ancillary equipment necessary for marine applications.

DELTIC DIESEL

TYPE: 18-cylinder, opposed piston, liquid cooled, two-stroke, compression ignition. Three banks of six cylinders in triangular configuration.
OUTPUT: Covers horsepower range of 1,500 to 4,000shp. Charge-cooled engine rating up to 3,000shp continuous at 1,800rpm. Half hour sprint rating up to 4,000shp at 2,100rpm. Weight/power ratio 3·94lb/shp.
BORE AND STROKE: Bore 130·17mm (5·125in). Stroke 184·15mm × 2 (7·25in × 2) (opposed piston).
SWEPT VOLUME (total): 88·3 litres (5,284in³).
COMBUSTION SYSTEM: Direct injection.
PISTONS: Two-piece body and gudgeon pin housing. Gudgeon pin housing with fully floating gudgeon pin shrunk into body and secured with taper seated circlip. Body skirt and gudgeon pin housing in light alloy, piston crown in 'Hidurel' material. Oil cooled. Three gas, two oil control and one scraper ring.
CONNECTING RODS: Fork and blade type with steel backed, lead bronze, lead flashed, indium infused thin-wall bearings. Manufactured from drop forgings, machined and polished all over.
CRANKSHAFTS: Three crankshafts machined from forgings and fully nitrided. Each shaft fitted with viscous type torsional vibration damper. Each crankpin carries one inlet and one exhaust piston, thus the loading on all crankpins is identical and reciprocating forces are balanced within the engine.

Deltic diesel

CRANKCASES AND CYLINDER BLOCKS: Three crankcases and three cylinder blocks arranged in the form of an inverted equilateral triangle all of light alloy construction. Crankcases substantially webbed and carrying each crankshaft in seven, thin-wall, steelbacked, lead bronze, lead flashed indium infused main bearings. Cylinder blocks each carry six 'wet' type liners, have integrally cast air inlet manifolds and mount the injection pumps camshaft casings.
CYLINDER LINERS: 18 'wet' type liners machined from hollow steel forgings, bores chrome plated with honeycomb process applied, finished by lapping. Coolant side flash tin plated. In areas of liquid contact with exhaust coolant-area, flash chrome plated.
TURBOCHARGER: Geared-in type, single stage, axial flow turbine and single-sided centrifugal compressor mounted on common shaft. Light alloy main castings. Charge-cooled engines have charge-air coolers (one for each cylinder block) incorporated within the overall dimensions of the turbocharger unit.
PHASING GEAR: Combines the output from the three crankshafts. A light alloy gear casing containing an output gear train linked to the

crankshafts by quill-shafts and passing the torque to a common output gear. All gears hardened and ground and carried in roller bearings. Gear train also provides drives for auxiliary pumps and engine governor.
FUEL SYSTEM: Pressurised system from engine driven circulating pump supplying 18 'jerk' type fuel injection pumps one per cylinder mounted in banks of six on camshaft casings secured to each cylinder block. Each pump supplies a single injector per cylinder.
LUBRICATION: Dry sump system with engine driven pressure and scavenge pumps. Twin pressure oil filters engine mounted.
COOLING: Closed circuit system with engine driven circulating pump. Engine mounted circulating pumps for sea-water system for cooling coolant heat exchanger and oil cooler, also for charge-air coolers.
STARTING: Air starting to six cylinders of one bank.
MOUNTING: Four points by resilient mounting units.
REVERSE GEAR: Marine reverse reduction gearbox incorporating a hydraulic friction clutch can be supplied as an integral unit.

ROLLS-ROYCE LIMITED
(Industrial & Marine)

Ansty, Coventry, West Midlands CV7 9JR, England
Telephone: 0203 613211
Telex: 31636

In April 1967 Rolls-Royce Limited formed a new division merging the former industrial and marine gas-turbine activities of Rolls-Royce and Bristol Siddeley. The new division was known as the Industrial & Marine Gas-Turbine Division of Rolls-Royce.

In May 1971 the present company, Rolls-Royce Limited, was formed combining all the gas-turbine interests of the former Rolls-Royce company.

It offers a wider range of industrial and marine gas turbines based on aero-engine gas generators than any other manufacturer in the world. It has a large selection of the gas turbines being developed and manufactured by Rolls-Royce Limited available for adaptation. Marinised gas turbines at present being produced or on offer include the Gnome, Proteus, Tyne, Olympus, Spey and RB.211.

Over 2,250 of these marine and industrial engines are in service or have been ordered for operation around the world. 25 navies and nine civil operators have selected the company's marine gas turbines to power naval craft, following the initial orders from the Royal Navy in the late 1950s.
HYDROFOILS: The Boeing PCH High Point is powered by two Proteus gas turbines while single Proteus turbines power the CNR-Alinavi Swordfish. A Tyne powers the Grumman designed PGH-1 Flagstaff. Rolls-Royce marine gas turbines can also be specified as alternative

power plants for the modular version of the Boeing Jetfoil.
HOVERCRAFT: The Gnome powers the BHC SR.N5 and SR.N6. The Proteus powers the SR.N4, the BH.7 and the Vosper Thornycroft VT 2.

MARINE GNOME

TYPE: Gas turbine, free-turbine turboshaft.
AIR INTAKE: Annular 15°C.
COMBUSTION CHAMBER: Annular.
FUEL GRADE
DERD 2494 Avtur/50 Kerosene.
DERD 2482 Avtur/40 Kerosene.
Diesel fuel: BSS 2869 Class A, DEF 1402 or NATO F75
TURBINE: Two-stage axial-flow generator turbine and a single-stage axial-flow free power turbine.
BEARINGS: Compressor rotor has a roller bearing at the front and a ball bearing at the rear. Gas generator turbine is supported at the front by the compressor rear bearings, and at the rear by a roller bearing.

Single stage power turbine is supported by a roller bearing behind the turbine disc and by a ball bearing towards the rear of the turbine shaft.
JET PIPE: Exhaust duct to suit installation.
ACCESSORY DRIVES: Accessory gearbox provides a drive for: the fuel pump, the hydro-mechanical governor in the flow control unit, the centrifugal fuel filter, the dual tachometer and the engine oil pump.
LUBRICATION SYSTEM: Dry sump.
OIL SPECIFICATION: DERD 2487.
MOUNTING: Front: three pads on the front frame casing, one on top, one on each side.
Rear: without reduction gearbox, mounting point is the rear flange of the exhaust duct

centre-body. With reduction gearbox mounting points are provided by two machined faces on the reduction gearbox.
STARTING: Electric.
DIMENSIONS
Length: 1,667mm (72·8in)
Width: 462mm (18·2in)
Height: 527mm (20·75in)
PERFORMANCE RATINGS
Max: 1,420bhp
Ratings are at maximum power-turbine speed, 19,500rpm. A reduction gearbox is available giving an output speed of 6,650rpm.
SPECIFIC FUEL CONSUMPTION
Max: 271g (0·597lb)/bhp/h
OIL CONSUMPTION
0·67 litres (1·2 pints)/h
Power turbine: 0·84 litres (1·5 pints)/h

MARINE OLYMPUS

Gas generator and single stage power turbine. Powered by the Marine Olympus, the TM3 module is a fully equipped enclosed power unit used for high speed operation by navies for modern warships.
TYPE: Gas turbine, two-shaft turbojet.
AIR INTAKE: Annular 15°C.
COMBUSTION CHAMBER: Eight.
FUEL GRADE: Diesel fuel BSS 2869 Class A. DEF 2402 or NATO F75.
TURBINE
ENGINE: Two stage, each stage driving its own respective compressor; 5 stage low pressure or 7 stage high pressure.
POWER: Single stage axial flow.
BEARINGS: Compressor rotor forward end supported by a roller bearing and rear end by a duplex ball bearing.

The power turbine rotor assembly and main-shaft are supported as a cantilever in two white metal bearings housed in a pedestal.

JET PIPE: Exhaust duct to suit installation.

ACCESSORY DRIVES: Power turbine. Accessories are mounted on the main gearbox which is a separate unit transmitting the turbine's power output to the propeller shaft. These include pressure and scavenge oil pumps. Speed signal generator, iso-speedic switch and rpm indicator are driven by the pedestal-mounted accessory gearbox.

LUBRICATION SYSTEM: The gas generator has its own integral lubrication system which is supplied with oil from a 122·74-litre (27-gallon) tank. Components in the system are: a pressure pump, main scavenge pump, four auxiliary scavenge pumps and an oil cooler.

Power turbine: bearings are lubricated and cooled by a pressure oil system.

OIL SPECIFICATION: Gas generator: D Eng RD 2487. Power turbine: OEP 69.

MOUNTING: The mounting structure depends on the customer's requirements for a particular application.

STARTING: Air or electric.

DIMENSIONS

GAS GENERATOR
Length: 3·6m (11ft 9in)
Width: 1·29m (4ft 3in)
POWER TURBINE
Length: 3·9m (12ft 9in)
Width: 2·4m (8ft)
Height: 3m (9ft 9in)
COMPLETE UNIT
Length: 6·8m (22ft 3in)
Width: 2·4m (8ft)
Height: 3m (9ft 9in)
WEIGHTS
Gas generator: 2,948·35kg (6,500lb)
Complete unit: 20·32 tonnes (20 tons)
PERFORMANCE RATING: Max: 29,600bhp at max power-turbine speed of 5,660rpm
SPECIFIC FUEL CONSUMPTION: Max: 211g (0·466lb)/bhp/h
OIL CONSUMPTION
GAS GENERATOR
Max: 0·84 litres (1·5 pints)/h
Power turbine: 0·84 litres (1·5 pints)/h

MARINE PROTEUS

TYPE: Gas turbine, free-turbine turboprop.

AIR INTAKE: Radial between the compressor and turbine sections of the engine. 15°C.

COMBUSTION CHAMBERS: Eight, positioned around the compressor casing.

FUEL GRADE: DEF 2402—Distillate diesel fuel.

TURBINE: Four stages coupled in mechanically independent pairs. The first coupled pair drives the compressor, the second pair forms the free power turbine which drives the output shaft.

BEARINGS: HP end of compressor rotor is carried by roller bearing, the rear end by a duplex ball bearing. Compressor turbine rotor shaft is located by a ball thrust bearing, as is the power turbine rotor.

JET PIPE: Exhaust duct to suit installation.

ACCESSORY DRIVES: All accessories are driven by the compressor or power turbine systems. Compressor driven accessories are: compressor tachometer generator, fuel pump and centrifugal oil separator for the breather. The power turbine tachometer generator and governor are driven by the power turbine. The main oil pressure pump and also the main and auxiliary scavenge pumps are driven by both the compressor and power turbines through a differential gear.

LUBRICATION SYSTEM: The engine is lubricated by a single gear type pump connected by a differential drive to both the compressor and power turbine systems.

OIL SPECIFICATION: OEP 71. DERD 2479/1 or DERD 2487 (OX 38).

MOUNTING: Three attachment points comprise two main trunnions, one on each side of the engine close to the diffuser casing, and a steady bearing located beneath the engine immediately aft of the air intake. Engines are supplied with

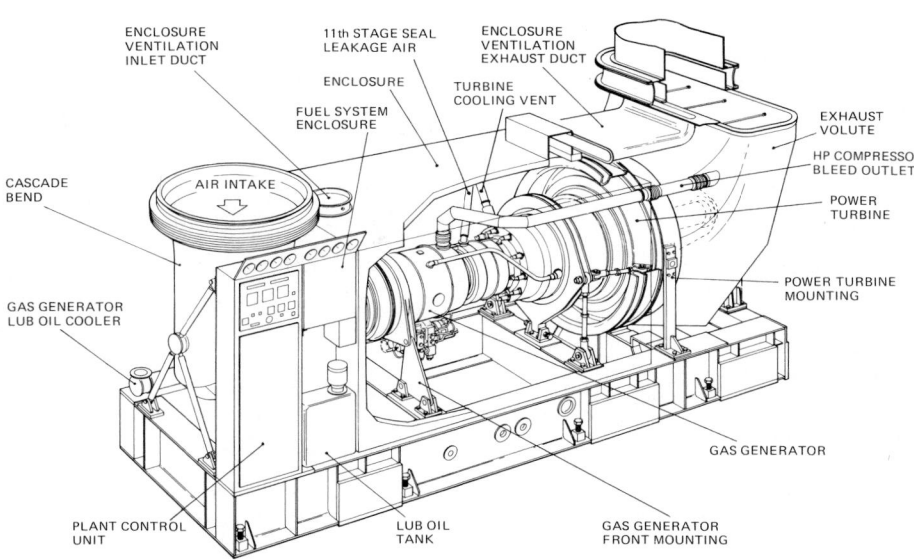

Spey SM1

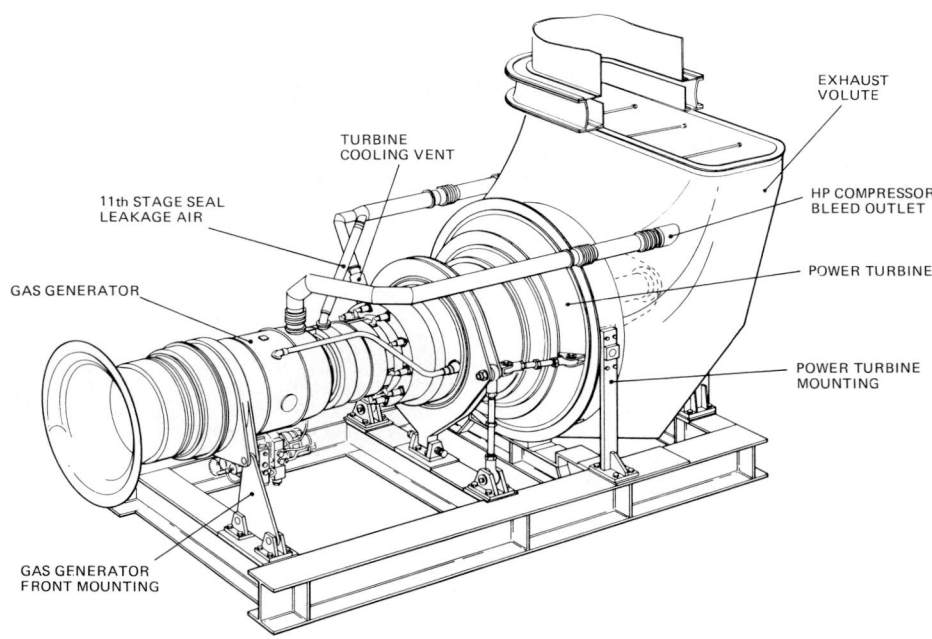

Spey SM2

integrally-mounted reduction gears giving maximum output shaft speeds of 5,240, 1,500 or 1,000rpm depending on the gearbox selected.

DIMENSIONS
Length: 2,870mm (113in)
Diameter: 1,067mm (42in)
WEIGHT Dry: 1,414kg (3,118lb)
PERFORMANCE RATINGS
Sprint: 5,000bhp
Max: 4,500bhp
SPECIFIC FUEL CONSUMPTION: At max rating: 256g (0·566lb)/bhp/h
OIL CONSUMPTION: Average: 0·28 litres (0·5 pints)/h

MARINE SM1, SM2 and SM3

Rolls-Royce produces three versions of the SM series of marine propulsion units based on the Spey gas generator, a high performance fully marinised machine derived from the Spey aero gas turbine.

The three units offer high thermal efficiency (in excess of 35 per cent) and up-to-date features. They were designed to bridge the gap in the range of current marine gas turbines and to provide high speed or cruising power for a wide range of present and future designs of warships.

For frigates or destroyers, a self-contained module equipped with all controls and auxiliary items is available, designated the SM1 propulsion unit.

For strike missile craft, corvettes or surface effect ships, a lightweight version, designated the SM2 is available.

A third variant, suitable for small craft, SWATH ships and hydrofoils is designated the SM3.

Following development of the SM series of marine gas turbine in a programme sponsored by the British Ministry of Defence, the engine is in production for a number of navies.

TYPE: Marine gas turbine incorporating two independently-driven compressors and a purpose-designed smoke free power turbine.

GAS GENERATOR CHARACTERISTICS

AIR INTAKE: Direct entry, fixed, without intake guides.

LP COMPRESSOR: 5 axial stages

HP COMPRESSOR: 11 axial stages

COMBUSTION SYSTEM: Turbo-annular type with ten interconnected straight flow flame tubes.

TURBINES: Impulse reaction, axial-type. Two HP and two LP stages.

EXHAUST: Fixed volume.

STARTING: Air/gas starter motor.

FUEL SYSTEM: Hydromechanical high pressure system with automatic acceleration and speed control.

FUEL GRADE: Diesel fuel Grade 'A'. DEF 2402 or NATO F75.

LUBRICATION SYSTEM: Self-contained gear pump filters and chip detectors.

POWER TURBINE: Two-stage free axial-flow turbine.

DIMENSIONS:
SM1 UNIT
Length: 7·5m (24ft 6in)
Width: 2·286m (7ft 6in)
Height: 3·388m (11ft 2in)
SM2 UNIT
Length: 6·096m (20ft)
Width: 2·286m (7ft 6in)
Height: 2·294m (9ft 2in)
SM3 UNIT
Length: 6·544m (21ft 5in)
Width: 2·069m (6ft 8in)
Height: 2·352m (7 ft 7in)
GAS GENERATOR CHANGE UNIT
Dry weight: 1,732kg (3,818lb)
WEIGHTS (Estimated) dry
SM1 UNIT: 24,737kg (53,536lb)
SM2 UNIT: 12,273kg (27,000lb)
SM3 UNIT: 8,295kg (18,287lb)
NOMINAL PERFORMANCE
Sprint Rating: 14mW (18,800bhp)
Max rating: 12·75mW (17,100bhp)
*Specific fuel consumption (Sprint rating):
 0·235kg/kW/h (0·386lb/bhp/h)

*Based on LCV of fuel of 43,125 kJ/kg
 (18,540btu/lb)
No power take-offs

No intake or exhaust duct losses
Ambient air temperature of 15°C (59°F) and an
atmospheric pressure of 101·3kpa (14·7lbf/in²)

Spey SM3

UNITED STATES OF AMERICA

AEROJET TECHSYSTEMS COMPANY MARINE AND INDUSTRIAL SYSTEMS

PO Box 13222, Sacramento, California 95813, USA
Telephone: (916) 355 3011
Telex: 377-409 (ALRCSAC)
Officials:
J M Hamil, *Marine and Industrial Systems*
F E McMullen, *Programme Manager*

Aerojet Marine Systems' long experience in rotating machinery with requirements for high reliability, long life, maintainability and reasonable cost has been applied to developing and producing propulsion systems for new marine craft.

The simple, rugged design of Aerojet propulsors provides a number of advantages. Vessels can reduce draught, opening a larger percentage of the world's shorelines, bays, channels and rivers to navigation. Reductions in periodic maintenance and debris damage result in lower operating costs for the Aerojet waterjet. Additionally, because the propulsion force is also the steering force, Aerojet waterjet systems have superior steering and reversing capabilities disposing of the need for a conventional rudder and complex variable-geometry propellers.

The ability of Aerojet waterjets has been shown by long operating times on a number of craft. The company offers a wide array of currently available waterjet systems ranging from 800 to 18,000 horsepower, including the AJW 800, the AJW 6500 and the AJW 18000.

Aerojet operates one of the largest waterjet test facilities in the world. Existing test facilities include five separate test stands, two multi-million gallon lakes, a control centre and a 1·2 million gallon tank with controllable flow rates up to 100,000 gallons per minute. A four million gallon lake provides variable test conditions for large waterjets up to 25,000 horsepower.

For lower horsepower waterjets with steering and reversing capabilities, such as the PHM hullborne waterjet, a 2·5 million gallon facility with a controllable water level provides various suction head test parameters for start and run conditions.

Long duration testing at flow rates of over 100,000 gallons/min and thrust levels· over 100,000lb st are achieved with a unique closed-loop facility system.

AJW-800

The AJW-800 waterjet is a ruggedly-built marine waterjet capable of operating over a wide horsepower range with a variety of marine diesel engines. The pump features an advanced single

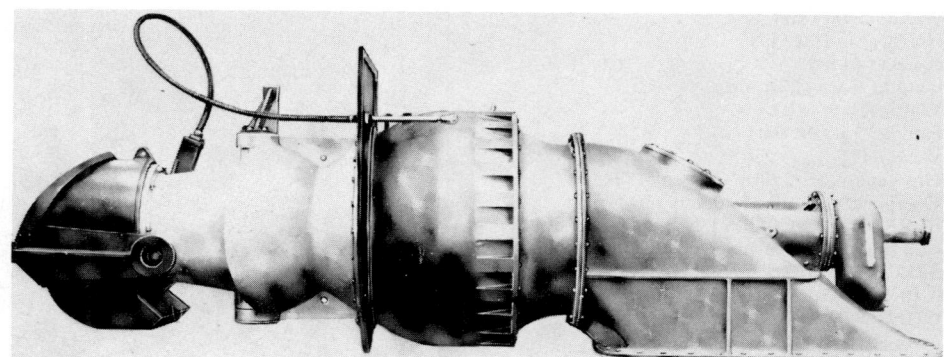

AJW-800 waterjet

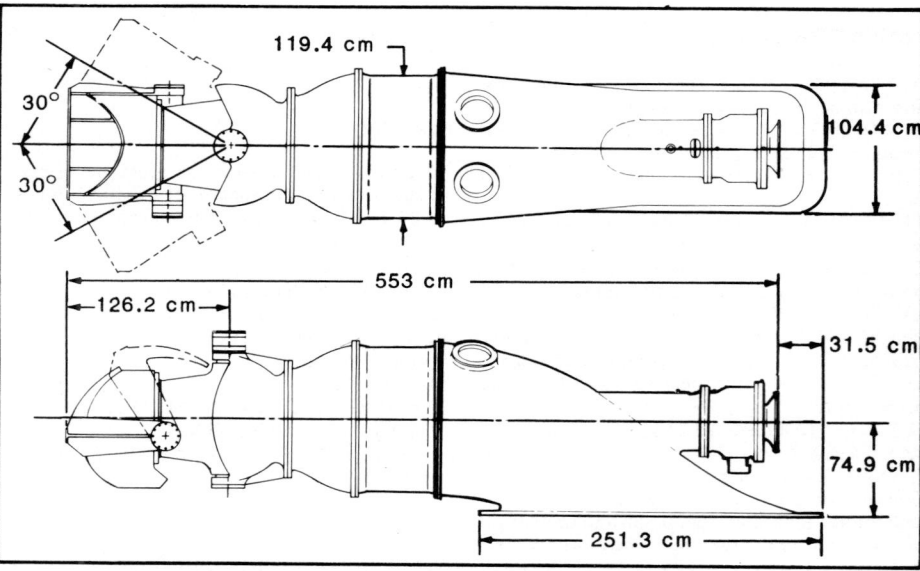

AJW-6500 waterjet

stage, mixed flow impeller operating at conservative suction specific speeds.
WEIGHTS
Wet (inlet flange to pump nozzle):
 1,220kg (2,690lb)
Dry: 660kg (1,455lb)
PERFORMANCE
RATED
Input power: 800mhp
Input speed: 900rpm
Inlet total head: 12m (39ft 4in)
Flow rate: 1·95m³/s (69ft³/s)
Thrust efficiency: 93%

SUCTION PERFORMANCE AT RATED SPEED
Inlet total head: 7·7m (25ft 3in)
Flow rate: 1·9m³/s (67ft³/s)
Thrust efficiency: 88·2%
AHEAD RATED THRUST
Static thrust (0° steering): 46·5kN
Max static side thrust (30° steering): 19·7kN
Ahead static thrust (30° steering): 32·8kN
Max steering actuator force (30° steering):
14·8kN
Steering actuator stroke: 355mm (14in)
ASTERN RATED THRUST
Static thrust (0° steering): 23·4kN

Max static side thrust (30° steering): 11·7kN
Astern static thrust (30° steering): 20kN
Jet vertical lift thrust component: 24kN

AJW-6500

The AJW-6500 waterjet propulsion unit has
been designed to meet the needs of 35- to 45-
knot planing craft. The unit provides the low
pump head rise and high flow rates required by
this typical application. The resulting high overall
propulsive efficiency is a very desirable benefit
especially for commercial craft.

The AJW-6500 comprises the low speed or
inducer pump stage of the operational foilborne
propulsion unit of the US Navy PHM, the AJW-
18000. Other components are shared between
the two units so that a certain degree of interchangeability is achieved.

The AJW-6500 propulsor assembly is offered
with an inlet elbow for a flush water inlet installation together with an advanced, short-coupled
steering/reversing sub-system. Alternatively, the
thrust reverser may be integrated with the boat
hull giving an additional degree of freedom in
propulsion system layout.

WEIGHTS
Dry: 3,629kg (8,000lb)
Wet: 5,897kg (13,000lb)
PERFORMANCE
RATED
Input power: 6,590mhp
Input speed: 790rpm
Inlet total head: 28·8m (94ft 6in)
Flow rate: 7·29m³/s (257ft³/s)
Thrust efficiency: 85%
Thrust (static): 236kN
Net thrust (40 knots) (with inlet drag): 119kN
SUCTION PERFORMANCE AT RATED SPEED
Inlet total head: 7·6m (24ft 11in)

AJW-18000

The AJW-18000 is the world's largest operating waterjet propulsion unit. It represents over
26 years of experience within Aerojet in building
high performance waterjets. The AJW-18000 is
developed from the AJW-8000 and, like the
AJW-8000, includes its own integral gearbox.

The parallel shaft two-speed gear-reduction
system drives the two-stage, two-speed pump
yielding a very high pump efficiency over a wide
range of operating conditions. The pump features
a bifurcated inlet for hydrofoil applications but
can be made available with a single inlet for SES
or planing hull applications. This unit has been
employed as the foilborne propulsion unit for the
US Navy PHM and has demonstrated high in-
service reliability.

WEIGHTS
Dry: 5,700kg (12,566lb)
Wet: 8,000kg (17,637lb)
PERFORMANCE
RATED
Input power: 16,200mhp
Input speed with gearbox: 3,093rpm
    without gearbox, low speed: 714rpm

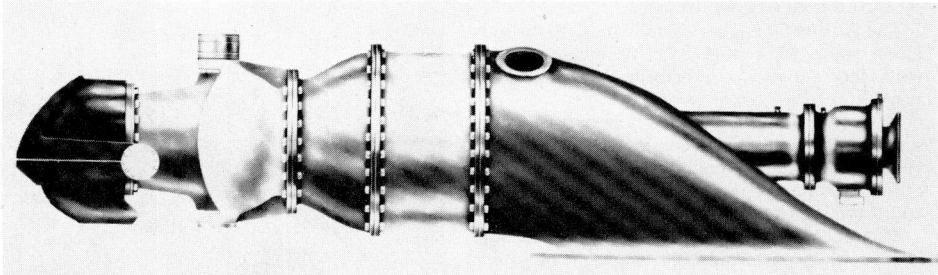
AJW-6500 waterjet

AJW-18000 waterjet

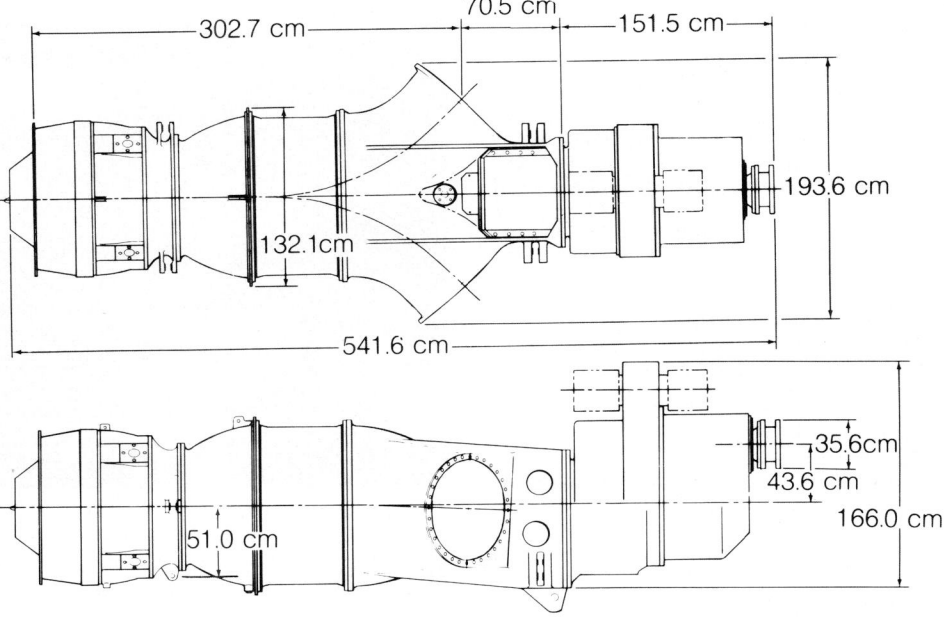
AJW-18000 waterjet

high speed: 1,510rpm
Inlet total head: 11m (36ft 2in)
Flow rate: 5·93m³/s (209ft³/s)
Thrust efficiency: 87%
Thrust (static): 336kN

Thrust (45 knots): 240kN
SUCTION PERFORMANCE AT RATED SPEED
Inlet total head: 7·93m (26ft)
Flow rate: 5·75m³/s (203ft³/s)
Thrust efficiency: 84·3%

ALLISON GAS TURBINES
(General Motors Corporation)

General Offices: PO Box 894, Indianapolis,
Indiana 46206, USA
Telephone: (317) 242 4151

Allison Gas Turbines has been active in the
development of gas turbines for commercial, industrial and marine use for many years. Production
of the first Allison gas turbine began in the 1940s,
when the company built the power plant for the
P-39, the first jet-powered aircraft to fly in the
United States.

Later, the Allison T56 turboprop aircraft
engine was developed. It demonstrated outstanding reliability and the same basic design has been
adapted for industrial and marine applications. In
the early 1960s, the first Allison 501-K gas-
turbine powered electric powerplant went into
service. Today, in excess of 1,000 501-K industrial series engines are used not only in electric
powerplants but also in industrial and marine
applications. The two-shaft marine engine pow-

ers the Boeing Jetfoil, Halter crewboats and
more recently has been installed in Westermoen

catamarans and the Grumman M161 hydrofoil
for primary propulsion.

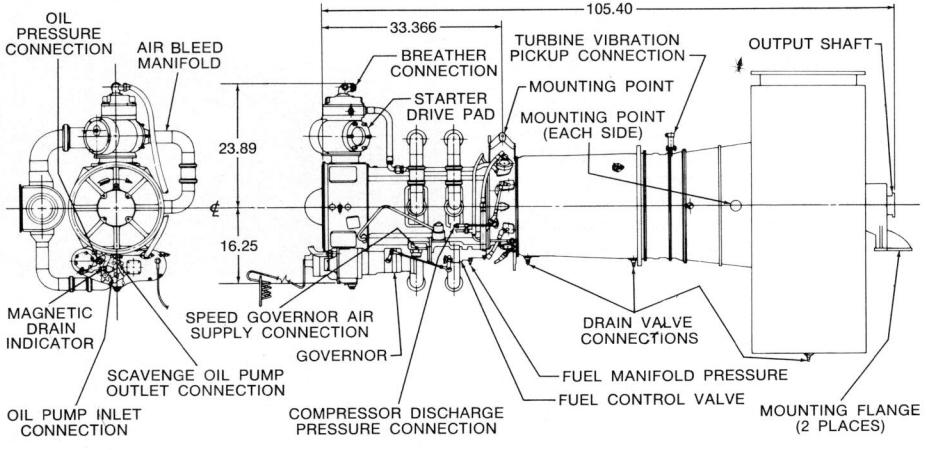
General arrangement of Allison 501-KF

ALLISON 501-K SERIES

The Allison 501-K series industrial gas turbine incorporates a 14-stage axial-flow compressor, with bleed valves to compensate for compressor surge.

Of modular design, it comprises three main sections: the compressor, combustor and turbine. Each section can be readily separated from the other. Modular design provides ease in handling and servicing of the engine.

The first stage of the four-stage turbine section is air-cooled, permitting the engine to be operated at higher than normal turbine inlet temperatures.

The combustor section of the 501-K consists of six combustion chambers of the through-flow type, assembled within a single annular chamber. This multiple provides even temperature distribution at the turbine inlet, thus eliminating the danger of hot spots.

The 501-K series engines are available in single-shaft or free turbine design.

The lightweight, compact size of the 501-K lends itself to multiple engines driving a single shaft through a common gearbox, or as a gas generator driving a customer-furnished power turbine.

The engine can be operated on a wide range of liquid fuels. Designation of the marine model is 501-KF, a brief specification for which follows. Dimensions are shown on the accompanying general arrangement drawing.

Exhaust gas temperature: 535°C (994°F)
Inlet air flow: 26,000cfm
Exhaust air flow: 81,000cfm
Engine jacket heat rejection: 6,000 Btu/min
Lube heat rejection (Gasifier): 1,270 Btu/min
Max liquid fuel flow: 6,365 litres (360ghp)
Liquid fuel: DF-1, DF-2 per Allison EMS66
Lubricant: Synthetic oil per Allison EMS 35 and 53
Specific fuel consumption: 0·24 litre (0·503lb)/hp/h
Required auxiliaries:
25hp starter
20-29V dc electrical power
Power take-off shaft and couplings
Temperature and speed controls from engine-furnished signals
Oil cooler
Auxiliary lube pump
Compressor inlet sensor
Gauge panel, meters and associated components
Engine exhaust diffusing tailpipe

Allison 501-KF

Side view of Allison 501-KF

ALLISON 570-K

A 7,000hp gas turbine designed as a prime mover in the industrial and marine fields, the 570 series is a front drive, two-shaft gas turbine. It entered production in 1978 and is in full operation. The model 570 represents General Motors' newest entry in the industrial and marine markets and is a derivative of the US Army's heavy lift helicopter (HLH) engine.

The 570 engine uses a variable geometry, 13-stage, axial flow compressor with a compression ratio of 12·1:1; the inlet guide vanes and the first five stages of status are variable. The compressor is directly coupled to a two-stage axial flow turbine and the vanes and blades of both stages are air-cooled. A power turbine drives the output shaft at the front end of the engine through a torque senser assembly located on the engine's centreline. The air foils of the power turbine are solid and do not require air cooling.

The 570 is operated by a full authority electronic control which features automatic starting sequence, speed governing, turbine temperature limiting, vibration sensing etc.

All production 570 engines are fully marinised using materials and coatings selected after more than ¼ million hours of marine experience with Boeing Jetfoils and DD 963 'Spruance' class destroyers.

The 570-K engine incorporates many technological advances and these have resulted in the unit having the lowest specific fuel consumption

Allison 570-KF

(SFC) of any turbine in its hp class. At maximum rated power of 7,170hp, the engine's SFC is 0·46lb/hp/h. This low level is maintained over a wide range of output power and speed; at 50 per cent power the SFC increases by only 7 per cent.

A larger version, designated the model 571-KB, will enter production in mid-1985. A three-stage power turbine will be used and the unit will have a maximum power rating of 8,312hp with an SFC of 0·405lb/hp/h.

570-KF (two-stage) and 571-KF (three-stage) Gas Turbines

	Maximum		Continuous	
	570-KF	571-KF	570-KF	571-KF
Power (shp)				
15°C (59°F)	7,170	8,288	6,445	7,694
26·7°C (80°F)	6,610	7,602	5,890	6,908
Fuel consumption 15°C (59°F)				
g/hp/h	210	184	209	186
lb/hp/h	0·462	0·405	0·46	0·408
Power turbine temperature				
°C	850	835	803	803
°F	1,562	1,535	1,477	1,477
Compression ratio	12·1	12·8	11·3	12·3
Corrected airflow				
kg/s	19·4	20·1	18·1	19·6
lb/s	42·8	44·2	40	43·3
Power turbine speed (rpm)	11,500	11,500	11,500	11,500
Weight				
kg	612	733	612	733
lb	1,350	1,615	1,350	1,615
Length				
metres	1·83	1·87	1·83	1·87
inches	72	74	72	74

Performance is subject to 5% guarantee factors.

AVCO LYCOMING
Avco Lycoming Division of Avco Corporation

550 South Main Street, Stratford, Connecticut 06497, USA
Telephone: (203) 385 2000
Telex: 964242
Officials:
John R Myers, *Vice President and General Manager, Lycoming Division*
Martin J Leff, *Vice President, Marketing and Product Support*
Richard Ainsworth, *Vice President, Engineering*

The Avco Lycoming Division, Stratford, is the turbine engine manufacturing division of the Avco Corporation.

Avco Lycoming manufactures a wide range of gas-turbine engines for helicopters, commuter jets, tanks and tracked vehicles, as well as for marine and industrial applications. Marine versions of the large turboshaft and turbofan T55 family are designated the TF25 and TF40. The latest addition to the range is the TF15, a marine version of the AGT 1500, which powers the US Army's new main battle tank, the M1.

TF25

The current production version of the TF25 is a high-speed shaft-turbine engine, with output shaft speed equal to power turbine speed. Integral oil tank and cooling system. An earlier TF25 powered the Vosper Thornycroft VT1, the Coastal Patrol Interdiction Craft (CPIC-X) and the Mitsui MV-PP15 155-seat hover ferry. Two will be installed in the 36-tonne Chaconsa VCA-36 amphibious assault landing craft under construction for the Spanish Navy.

AIR INTAKE: Side inlet casting of aluminium alloy supporting optional reduction gearbox and front main bearings. Provision for intake screens.
COMPRESSOR: Seven axial stages followed by a single centrifugal stage. Two-piece aluminium alloy stator casing with one row of inlet guide vanes, and seven rows of steel stator blades, bolted to steel alloy diffuser casing to which combustion chamber casing is attached. Rotor comprises seven stainless steel discs and one titanium impeller mounted on shaft supported in forward thrust ball bearings and rear roller bearing. TF25 pressure ratio is 6:1.
COMBUSTION CHAMBER: Annular reverse flow type. Steel outer shell and inner liner. 28 fuel nozzles with downstream injection.
FUEL SYSTEM: Woodward fuel control system. Gear-type fuel pump, with gas producer and power shaft governors, flow control and shut-off valve.
FUEL GRADE: MIL-J-5624 grade JP-4, JP-5, MIL-F-46005 or marine diesel standard and wide-cut kerosene.
TURBINE: Two mechanically-independent axial-flow turbines. First turbine with single-stage drives compressor, has cored-out cast steel blades and is flange-bolted to outer coaxial drive shaft. Second, two-stage turbine drives output shaft, has solid steel blades and is mounted on inner coaxial drive shaft.
EXHAUST UNIT: Fixed area nozzle, with inner cone, supported by six radial struts.
ACCESSORIES: Electric, air or hydraulic starter. High-energy ignition unit; four igniter plugs.
LUBRICATION: Recirculating type. Integral oil tank and cooler.
OIL GRADE: MIL-L-17808, MIL-L-23699.
DIMENSIONS
Length: 1·27m (50·1in)
Width: 0·87m (34·4in)
Height: 1·11m (43·8in)
WEIGHT Dry: 600kg (1,324lb)
PERFORMANCE RATINGS
Max intermittent (peak): 3,000shp
Max continuous (normal): 2,500shp
FUEL CONSUMPTION At max continuous rating: 0·62sfc 198 US gallons/h

TF40

The TF40 engine is a scaled-up TF25 with higher mass flow and a four-stage turbine section.

Both the Jeff(A) (Aerojet-General) and Jeff(B) (Bell Aerospace) AALCs employ earlier model TF40s. Jeff(A) employs six, each developing 3,350shp continuous. Four drive individual, steerable ducted propellers, and the remaining two drive separate centrifugal lift fans. In the case of Jeff(B), the six engines are arranged in two groups of three, located port and starboard. Each trio drives a single propeller and lift system through integrated gears.

An uprated version, the TF40B, has been selected to provide the lift and propulsive power for the US Navy's new Landing Craft, Air Cushion (LCAC) being built by Bell-Halter. The machinery arrangement is similar to that of Jeff(B) apart from the use of four engines instead of six.

Other craft now powered by TF40s include the SEDAM N 500, which employs two for lift and three, mounted in separate nacelles, for propulsion, a twin hull waterjet ferry now in service in Scandinavia, two PSMM Mk 5 CODAG gunboats for Taiwan, each equipped with three TF40s and three DDA 12V 149 diesel engines, and two private yachts.

AIR INTAKE: Side inlet casting of aluminium alloy housing internal gearing and supporting power producer section and output drive shaft. Integral or separately mounted gears are optional. Provision for intake filters and/or silencers. Integral water-wash nozzles are provided.

TF25

COMPRESSOR: Seven axial stages followed by a single centrifugal stage. Two-piece aluminium alloy stator casing, with seven rows of steel stator blades bolted to steel alloy casing diffuser, to which combustion chamber casing is attached. Rotor comprises seven stainless steel discs and one titanium impeller mounted on shaft supported in forward thrust ball bearing and rear roller bearing. TF40 pressure ratio is 8·4:1.

COMBUSTION CHAMBER: Annular reverse flow type. Steel outer shell and inner liner. Twenty-eight fuel nozzles with downstream injection.

FUEL SYSTEM: Woodward fuel control system. Gear-type fuel pump, with gas producer and power shaft governors, flow control and shut-off valve.

FUEL GRADE: MIL-T-5624, JP-4, JP-5; MIL-F-16884 diesel, standard and wide-cut kerosene.

TURBINE: Two mechanically-independent axial-flow turbines. First turbine, with two stages, drives compressor. It has cored-out cast blades and is flange-bolted to outer coaxial drive shaft. Second two-stage turbine drives output shaft. It has solid blades and is mounted on inner coaxial drive shaft. (Other features include: integral cast cooled first turbine nozzle, cooled turbine blades in both first and second stages, second turbine vane cooling, and second turbine disc and blade cooling.)

EXHAUST UNIT: Fixed area nozzle, with inner cone, supported by six radial struts.

ACCESSORIES: Electric, air or hydraulic starter. High-energy ignition unit; four igniter plugs.

LUBRICATION: Recirculating type. Integral oil tank and cooler.

OIL GRADE: Synthetic base oils.

DIMENSIONS
Length: 1·32m (52·2in)
Width: 0·88m (34·4in)
Height: 1·11m (43·8in)

PERFORMANCE RATINGS
Max intermittent (at 15°C (59°F)—sea level): 4,600shp
Max continuous (at 15°C (59°F)—sea level): 4,000shp

FUEL CONSUMPTION: At max continuous rating: 0·54sfc 255 US gallons/h

OIL CONSUMPTION: 0·5pint/h

TF 15

The marine/industrial version of the AGT 1500 is rated at 1,500shp. It comprises a two-speed compressor with a single can combustor which delivers combustion gas to two single-stage compressor drive turbines. A two-stage power turbine further expands the gases to deliver the output power at 3,000rpm at the rear of the engine. A multi-wave plate recuperator minimises fuel consumption throughout the speed range.

The TF 15 is approximately half the weight of a diesel engine of similar rating and significantly smaller. It burns several grades of diesel fuel as well as aviation kerosene.

POWER RATINGS
Output power: 1,500shp
Output shaft rotational speed (100%): 3,000rpm
LP compressor rotational speed (100%): 33,500rpm
HP compressor rotational speed (100%): 43,500rpm

DIMENSIONS
Length: 168·5cm (66·35in)
Width: 99·1cm (39in)
Height: 84·6cm (33·3in)

WEIGHT
Net: 1,137kg (2,500lb)

OPERATING ENVELOPE
Engine inlet air temperature: −70°F (−57°C) to +130°F (54°C)
Altitude: 0-2,500m (8,000ft)

FUEL: DF-2, DF-1, DF-A, JP-4, JP-5

LUBRICATING OIL: MIL-L-23699, MIL-L-7808

Consumption: less than 0·38 litre/h (0·1 gallon/h)

Tank capacity: 9·5 litres (2·5 gallons)

Smoke emission: A1A smoke No 30 (non-visible)

Cutaway of TF40 marine/industrial gas turbine rated at 4,000shp continuous, 4,600shp 'boost' power

TF 15 marine/industrial gas turbine

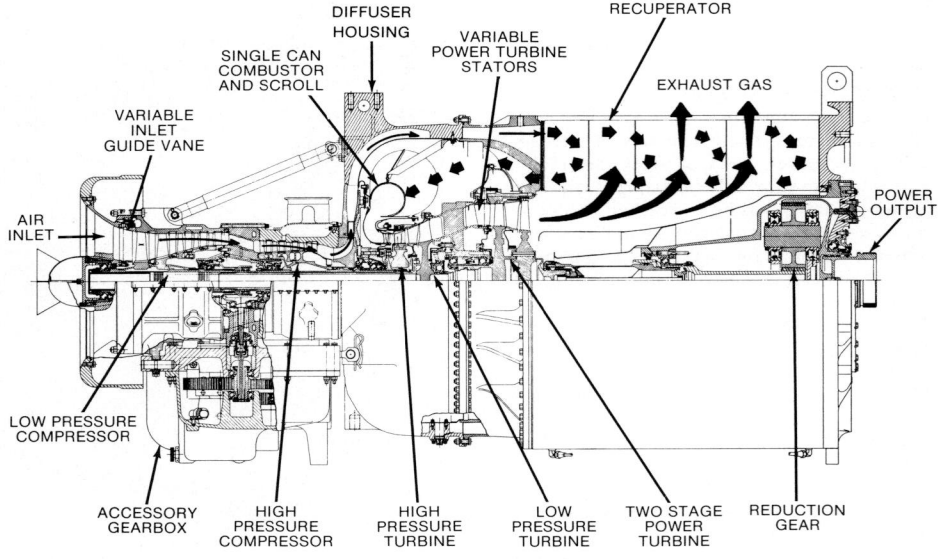

TF 15 cutaway

BRIGGS AND STRATTON CORPORATION

PO Box 702, Milwaukee, Wisconsin 53201, USA
Officials:
Frederick P Stratton Jr, *President and Chief Executive Officer*
Laverne J Socks, *Executive Vice President*
L William Dewey Jr, *Executive Vice President*
James L Bunda, *Vice President, Quality Assurance*
Robert K Catterson, *Vice President, Engineering and Research*
J Byron Smith, *Vice President of Production*
James F Sullivan, *Vice President Sales*
Michael D Hamilton, *Vice President, International*

Sales Representative and Central Service Distributor for Great Britain and Ireland:
Autocar Electrical Equipment Company Limited, 640 Ripple Road, Barking, Essex 1G11 0RU, England

Briggs and Stratton Corporation is a major supplier of small two- and four-stroke petrol engines manufactured in the USA and at the Farymann Diesel factory in West Germany. Uses range from lawn and garden equipment to industrial and agricultural machinery. In accordance with US government regulations, Briggs and Stratton has introduced a range of 'quiet' engines and most recently an electric start system with a brake function to stop the engine when the operator leaves the controls. For industrial and other heavy-use applications, the I/C series was designed for prolonged life, low maintenance and general heavy-duty use.

With over 4·4 million square feet of manufacturing facilities and a new service parts distribution centre, Briggs and Stratton can produce custom-designed engines to more than 50,000 specifications. Central service distributors provide parts and technical training to 25,000 dealers around the world. Briggs and Stratton is one of the largest manufacturers of small engines in the world (more than 140 million since 1953).

Engines offered by Briggs and Stratton Corporation

Series No	Displacement in³/cc	hp	Net weight (lb)
Four-cycle aluminium alloy engines			
90700	9·02/147·9	3·5	20·75
91700	9·02/147·9	3·5	21·75
92900	9·02/147·9	3·5	19·75
94500	9·02/147·9	3	20·25
94900	9·02/147·9	3·5	20·75
110700	11·39/186·7	4	22
111700	11·39/186·7	4	22·5
110900	11·39/186·77	4	21
114900	11·39/186·7	4	24·75
112200	11·39/186·7	4	25·5
113900	11·39/186·7	4	21·5
130200	12·57/206	5	29·75
132200	12·57/206	5	29·75
130900	12·57/206	5	20·25
132900	12·57/206	5	20·25
132400	12·57/206	5	31·75
170400	16·79/275·1	7	44
171400	16·79/275·1	7	44
190400	19·44/318·5	8	44·5
195400	19·44/318·5	8	44·5
170700	16·79/275·1	7	43
190700	19·44/318·5	8	43·5
191700	19·44/318·5	8	48·5
221430	22·04/361·2	10	62
220700	22·04/361·2	10	55
252410	24·36/399·2	11	63·25
252700	24·36/399·2	11	59·25
253700	24·36/399·2	11	59·25
253410 (non-ducted)	24·36/399·2	11	63·5
253410 (ducted)	24·36/399·2	11	68·5
Four-cycle cast iron engines			
233400	22·94/376·5	9	92
243430	29·94/392·3	10	96
326430	32·4/530·9	16	106·5
Four-cycle twin-cylinder engines			
402707	40/656	16	98·25
402417 (non-ducted)	40/656	16	86·25
402437 (non-ducted)	40/656	16	87·25
402417 (ducted)	40/656	16	99·75
402437 (ducted)	40/656	16	100·75
402707 (ducted)	40/656	16	98·25
422437 (non-ducted)	42·33/694	18	87·25
422437 (ducted)	42·33/694	18	100·75
422707 (ducted)	42·33/694	18	98·25
Twin cylinder			
402417	40/656	16	86·25
402417 (ducted)	40/656	16	99·75
402437	40/656	16	87·25
402437 (ducted)	40/656	16	100·75
402707 (ducted)	40/656	16	98·25
422437	42·33/694	18	87·25
422437 (ducted)	42·33/694	18	100·75
422707 (ducted)	42·33/694	18	98·25
Cast-iron cylinder series			
233400	22·94/376·5	9	92
243430	23·94/392·3	10	96
326430	32·4/530·9	16	106·5
Industrial/commercial series			
Vertical crankshaft			
131922	12·57/206	5	30·25
192700	19·44/319	8	48·5
193700	19·44/319	8	48·5
402707	40/656	16	98·25
422707	42·33/694	18	98·25
Horizontal crankshaft			
81232	7·75/127	3	24·5
131232	12·57/206	5	30
195432	19·44/318·5	8	46·5
221432	22·04/361·3	10	63·25
233431	22·94/376·5	9	92
243431	23·94/392·3	10	96
326431	32·4/530·9	16	106·5
402437	40/656	16	100·75
422437	42·33/694	18	100·75

CUMMINS ENGINE COMPANY INC

Cummins Engine Company Inc, 1000 Fifth Street, Columbus, Indiana 47201, USA
Officials:
M F Chasse, *Marine and Petroleum Market Support Manager*

Formed in 1919 in Columbus, Indiana, the Cummins Engine Company produces a wide range of marine diesel engines which are now manufactured and distributed internationally. In addition to manufacturing plants in the United States, the company also produces diesel engines in Brazil, India, Japan, Mexico and the United Kingdom. All these plants build engines to the same specifications thus ensuring interchangeability of parts and the same quality standards.

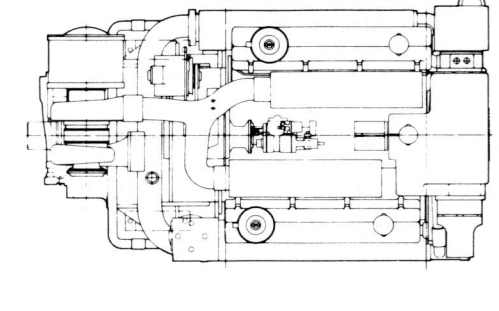

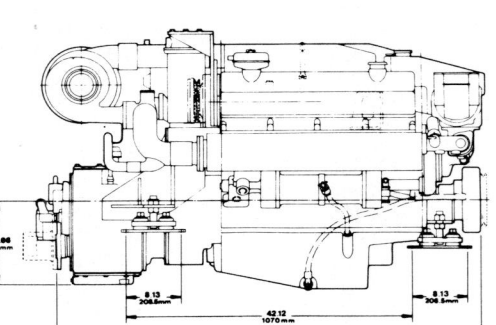

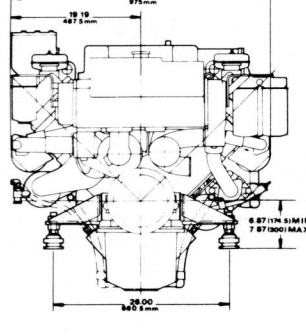

Cummins VT-903-M

VTA-903-M

TYPE: Four-stroke cycle, turbocharged, aftercooled V-8 diesel engine.
AFTERCOOLER: Large capacity aftercooler plumbed for raw water cooling.
BEARINGS: Replaceable, precision type, steel-backed inserts. Five main bearings, 95mm (3·75in) diameter. Connecting rod bearings, 79mm (3·12in) diameter.
CAMSHAFT: Single camshaft precisely controls valve and injector timing. Lobes are induction hardened for long life. Five replaceable precision type bushings, 63mm (2·5in) diameter.
CAMSHAFT FOLLOWERS: Induction hardened, roller type for long cam and follower life.
CONNECTING RODS: Drop forged, I-beam section 208mm (8·2in) centre to centre length. Rifle drilled for pressure lubrication of piston pin. Rod tapered on piston pin end to reduce unit pressures.
COOLING SYSTEMS: Gear-driven centrifugal engine coolant pump. Large volume water passages provide even flow of coolant around cylinder liners, valves, and injectors. Modulating by-pass thermostat regulates coolant temperature. Spin-on corrosion resistor checks rust and corrosion, controls acidity and removes impurities.
CRANKSHAFT: Fully counterweighted and spin balanced high tensile strength steel forging with induction hardened fillets.
CYLINDER BLOCK: Alloy cast iron with removable wet liners. Cross bolt support to main bearing cap provides extra strength and stability.
CYLINDER HEADS: Alloy cast iron. Each head serves four cylinders. Drilled fuel supply and return lines. Valve seats are replaceable corrosion-resistant inserts. Valve guides and cross head guides are replaceable inserts.
CYLINDER LINERS: Replaceable wet liners dissipate heat faster than dry liners and are easily replaced without reboring the block.
FUEL SYSTEM: Low pressure system with wear compensating pump and integral dual flyweight governor. Camshaft actuated fuel injectors give accurate metering and precise timing. Fuel lines are internal drilled passages in cylinder heads. Spin-on fuel filter.
GEAR TRAIN: Timing gears and accessory drive gears are induction hardened. Spur gears driven from crankshaft and located at rear of block.
LUBRICATION: Large capacity gear pump provides pressure lubrication to all bearings. Oil cooler and full-flow filters maintain oil condition and maximise oil and engine life.
PISTONS: Aluminium alloy, cam ground and barrel-shaped to compensate for thermal expansion, ensures precise fit at operating temperatures. One oil and two compression rings.
PISTON PINS: Full floating, tubular steel retained by snap rings, 44mm (1·75in) diameter.
TURBOCHARGER: Exhaust gas-driven turbocharger mounted at rear of engine. Turbocharging provides more power, improved fuel economy, and lower smoke and noise levels.
VALVES: Dual 48mm (1·87in) diameter poppet-type intake and exhaust valves. Wear resistant face on exhaust valves.

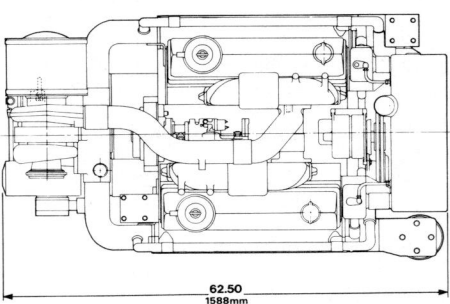

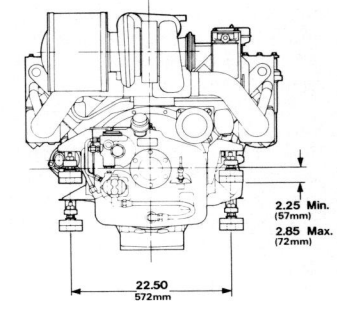

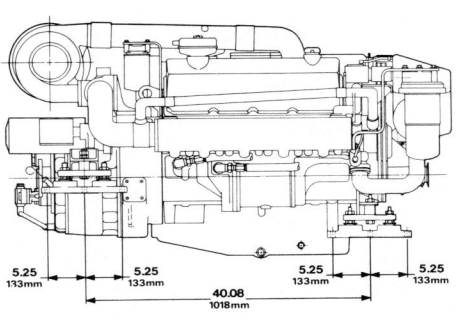

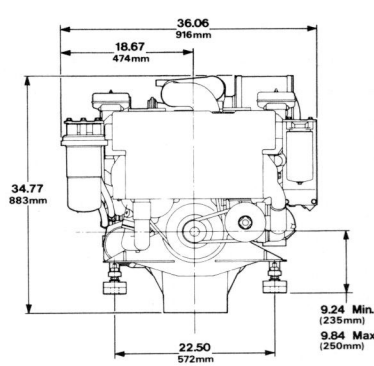

Cummins VT-555-M

POWER RATINGS
Max: 336kW (450bhp)
Rated rpm: 2,600
Light duty: 283kW (380bhp)
Rated rpm: 2,600
Continuous duty: 239kW (320bhp)
Rated rpm: 2,300
Bore and stroke: 140 × 121mm (5·5 × 4·75in)
Displacement: 14·8 litres (903in³)
Oil pan capacity: 19 litres (5 US gallons)
Net weight, dry*: 1,660kg (3,650lb)
*With selected accessories and Capitol HY-22000 marine gear.

VT-555-M

TYPE: Four-stroke cycle, naturally aspirated diesel.
BEARINGS: Replaceable, precision type, steel-backed inserts. Five main bearings, 95mm (3·75in) diameter. Connecting rod bearings, 79mm (3·125in) diameter.
CAMSHAFT: Single camshaft precisely controls valve and injector timing. Lobes are induction

hardened for long life. Five replaceable precision type bushings, 63mm (2·5in) diameter.
CAMSHAFT FOLLOWERS: Induction hardened, roller type for long cam and follower life.
CONNECTING RODS: Drop forged, I-beam section 208mm (8·2in) centre to centre length. Rifle drilled for pressure lubrication of piston pin. Rod tapered on piston pin end to reduce unit pressures.
COOLING SYSTEM: Gear-driven centrifugal engine coolant pump. Large volume water passages provide even flow of coolant around cylinder liners, valves, and injectors. Modulating by-pass thermostat regulates coolant temperature. Spin-on corrosion resistor checks rust and corrosion, controls acidity and removes impurities.
CRANKSHAFT: Fully counterweighted, high tensile strength steel forging with induction hardened fillets. Fully spin balanced.
CYLINDER BLOCK: Alloy cast iron with removable wet liners. Cross bolt support to main bearing cap provides extra strength and stability.

CYLINDER HEADS: Alloy cast iron. Each head serves four cylinders. Valve seats are replaceable corrosion-resistant inserts. Valve guides and cross head guides are replaceable inserts.

CYLINDER LINERS: Replaceable wet liners dissipate heat faster than dry liners and are easily replaced without reboring the block.

FUEL SYSTEM: Low pressure system with wear compensating pump and integral dual flyweight governor. Camshaft actuated fuel injectors give accurate metering and timing. Fuel lines are internal drilled passages in cylinder heads. Spin-on fuel filter.

GEAR TRAIN: Camshaft gear and accessory drive gear are induction hardened. Spur gears driven from crankshaft and located at rear of block.

LUBRICATION: Large capacity gear pump provides pressure lubrication to all bearings. Oil cooler and full-flow filters maintain oil condition and maximise oil and engine life.

PISTONS: Aluminium alloy, cam ground and barrel-shaped to compensate for thermal expansion ensures precise fit at operating temperatures. One oil and two compression rings.

PISTON PINS: Full floating, tubular steel retained by snap rings, 44mm (1·75in) diameter.

VALVES: Dual 48mm (1·875in) diameter poppet type intake and exhaust valves. Wear resistant face on exhaust valves.

POWER RATINGS
Max: 220kW (295bhp)
Rated rpm: 2,600
Light duty: 220kW (295bhp)
Rated rpm: 2,600
Continuous duty: 190kW (255bhp)
Rated rpm: 2,300
Bore and stroke: 140 × 121mm (5·5 × 4·75in)
Displacement: 14·8 litres (903in³)
Oil pan capacity: 19 litres (5 US gallons)
Net weight, dry: 1,270kg (2,800lb)

CUYUNA ENGINE COMPANY

PO Box 116, Crosby, Minnesota 56441, USA
Telephone: (218) 546 8313
Official:
Roger P Worth, *President*

The company is now manufacturing and marketing the Cuyuna range of axial fan-cooled single- and twin-cylinder engines, developing 20 to 40hp.

The engines are serviced through a network of 2,000 independent service outlets and central distributors throughout the USA and Canada.

CUYUNA AXIAL-FAN SINGLE- AND TWIN-CYLINDER ENGINES
Models 215, 340 and 440

Features of this range include a standard mounting for all models to ease installation; low engine profile with built-in shrouding; lightweight construction to reduce overall vehicle weight and high interchangeability of all parts. Crankshafts, crank cases, blower assemblies, magnetos, recoil starters and hardware items are fully interchangeable, thus reducing spare parts inventory requirements and lowering maintenance costs. Specifications for the three standard productions are given in the accompanying table.

Model	**Single- and Twin-Cylinder Axial-Fan Cooled**		
	215	**340**	**440**
Bore	2·658in	2·362in	2·658in
Stroke	2·362in	2·362in	2·362in
Displacement	214cc	339cc	428cc
Compression ratio		12·5 : 1	
Max torque		6,500 rpm	
Brake hp/rpm	20hp 6,500/7,000rpm	32hp 6,500/7,000rpm	40hp 6,500/7,000rpm
Base mounting Hole thread		⁷/₁₆—14 UNC	
Cylinder		Aluminium with cast iron sleeve	
Connecting rod Bearing upper		Needle	
Connecting rod Bearing lower		Needle	
Connecting rod Material		Forged steel	
Main bearing		2 heavy duty ball bearings (double row, PTO end)	
Ignition		Bosch	
Lighting coil		12V, 150W	
Contact breaker Gap		0·014in to 0·018in	
Ignition setting Before TDC		0·102in to 0·112in (cam fully advanced)	
Spark plug thread		14 × 1·25mm (0·75in) reach	
Gap		0·016in to 0·02in	
Type		Bosch W-260-T-2 (or) Champion N-3	
Rotation		Counter-clockwise viewed from PTO end	
Fuel-oil mixture		40:1 (1 pint to 5 gallons)	
Lubrication		Premium Gasoline & Cuyuna 2 Cycle Engine Oil	
Carburettor type		2·94in centre to centre bolt dimension	
Starter		Rewind type, standard; electric, optional	
Rope material		Nylon	
Weight	39lb	62lb	62lb

Horsepower ratings established in accordance with specifications SAE-J 607.
Engines will produce no more than 78dB when used with Cuyuna approved carburettor/muffler/intake silencer systems, according to SAE-J192 specifications.

Cuyuna ULII-02 axial fan-cooled twin cylinder engine

DOBSON PRODUCTS CO

2241 South Ritchey, Santa Ana, California 92705, USA
Telephone: (714) 557 2987
Officials:
Franklin A Dobson, *Director*

Franklin Dobson has been building and marketing light ACVs in kit and factory-built form since 1963.

His company now specialises in the design and construction of light ACV components evolved after a more thorough engineering approach. The components include reversible-pitch propellers and fans—the main purpose of which is to provide light craft with adequate braking—and suitable ducts, screens, etc.

Preliminary details of the company's first 0·91m (3ft) diameter, variable-pitch two-bladed propeller are given below.

DIMENSIONS
Diameter: 0·91m (36in)
Chord: 104mm (4·25in)
Blades: 2
Solidity (at 0·6 radius): 0·125
Pitch range: 60 degrees (nom +40, −20)
Max shaft diameter: 28mm (1·25in)
Design rpm: 3,000
Max rpm: 3,250
Horsepower required: 7-10
Max static thrust (with shroud): 34·01kg (75lb) (forward or reverse)
Max thrust at 60mph: 22·67kg (50lb)

A duct with integral screen, suitable for use with this propeller, is also under development.

THE GARRETT CORPORATION
Garrett Turbine Engine Company

111 South 34th Street, Phoenix, Arizona 84010, USA

Telephone: (602) 231 1000
Officials:
Robert Choulet, *President*
Frank Roberts, *Senior Vice President*
Barry Tyson, *Vice President, Sales*

The Garrett Corporation is the world's largest manufacturer of small gas-turbine engines for commercial, military, marine and industrial applications, as well as a leading producer of air turbine starters, air motors, pneumatic valves and control systems for aircraft and aerospace applications.

ME9901

The Garrett ME9901 is a fully marinised gas turbine, rated at 6,250shp maximum and 5,600shp normal. A free turbine, it has been designed for propulsion, pump and compressor drives and to power generator sets for primary and secondary power. Features are ease of maintenance and facilities for the replacement of modules in situ. Fitted with optional shock mounts, it satisfies the shock requirements of MIL-S-901C, Grade A, Class III.
TYPE: Simple cycle, two-shaft, free turbine.
COMPRESSOR: Two-stage centrifugal.
COMBUSTION CHAMBER: Single, annular.
TURBINE: Two-stage axial gas generator. Three-stage axial power turbine.
FUEL GRADES: VV-F-800, DF-A, DF-1 or DF-2; ASTM-D-975, 1-D or 2-D; ASTM-D-2880, 1-GT or 2-GT; ASTM-D-1655, Jet A, Jet Al or Jet B; MIL-T-5624, JP4 or JP5.
ACCESSORIES: Integral within gearbox.
DIMENSIONS
Length: 3·04m (120in)
Width: 1·6m (63in)
Height: 1·21m (48in)
WEIGHT, Dry: 2,835kg (6,250lb) including integral gearbox and accessories, insulation blankets and electronics package. Shock mounts (optional) 454kg (1,000lb)
PERFORMANCE RATING
At ISO standard conditions with accessory power losses and no inlet or exhaust pressure losses normal power is 5,600shp at 7,200rpm power turbine speed.
System output speed: 3,600rpm

IM 831-800

Garrett also has a fully marinised gas-turbine engine with a continuous power rating of 713shp and an intermittent rating of 800shp. This unit, designated IM 831-800, is in service on the Boeing PHM hydrofoil, providing secondary power. It is also in use in many other commercial and military applications.
TYPE: Simple-cycle, single shaft.
COMPRESSOR: Two-stage centrifugal.
COMBUSTION CHAMBER: Single, reverse-flow.
TURBINE: Three-stage axial.
FUEL GRADES: DF1 and DF2 per ASTM-D-975, VV-F-800, MIL-F-16884 and MIL-R-46005, Jet A, A-1 and B per ASTM-D-1665; JP-4 and JP-5 per MIL-F-5624 and VV-K-211.
DIMENSIONS
Length: 1,651mm (65in)
Width: 1,016mm (40in)
Height: 889mm (35in)
WEIGHT, Dry: 793·8kg (1,750lb)
POWER RATING
Continuous SLS: 713shp
Standby: 800shp
Rated rotor speed: 41,730rpm (max)
System output speed constant speed, two output pad speed of 8,000rpm and two at 3,600rpm

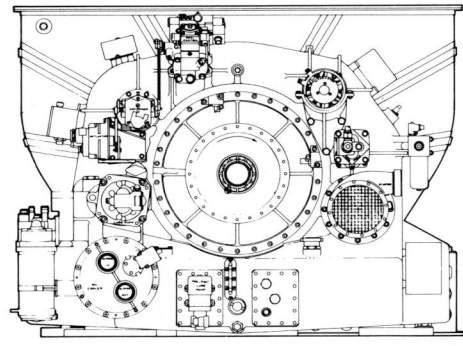
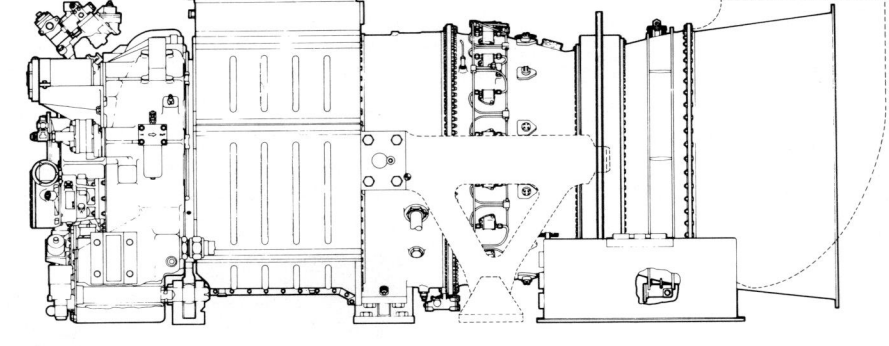

IE9901. Dashes indicate optional shock mountings and exhaust diffuser

---

GENERAL ELECTRIC COMPANY AIRCRAFT ENGINE BUSINESS GROUP

Interstate 75 & Neumann Way, Cincinnati (Evendale), Ohio 45215, USA
Officials:
Brian H Rowe, *Senior Vice President and Group Executive*
J W Sack, *Counsel*

The General Electric Company's Dr Sanford A Moss operated the first gas turbine in the United States in 1903 and produced the aircraft turbosupercharger, first flown in 1919 and mass-produced in the Second World War for US fighters and bombers.

The company built its first aircraft gas turbine in 1941, when it began development of a Whittle-type turbojet, under an arrangement between the British and American governments.

Since then General Electric has produced over 80,000 aircraft gas turbines for military and commercial aircraft, as well as aircraft derivative gas turbines for marine and industrial uses.

Five General Electric gas turbines have been marinised: the LM1500, the LM2500, the LM100, the LM500 and the LM5000. The LM2500 has been specified to power various classes of ships in 13 navies; the LM500 is being proposed for shipboard electrical generator units.

LM2500

The LM2500 marine gas turbine is a two-shaft, simple-cycle, high-efficiency engine derived from the General Electric military TF39 and the commercial CF6 high by-pass turbofan engines for

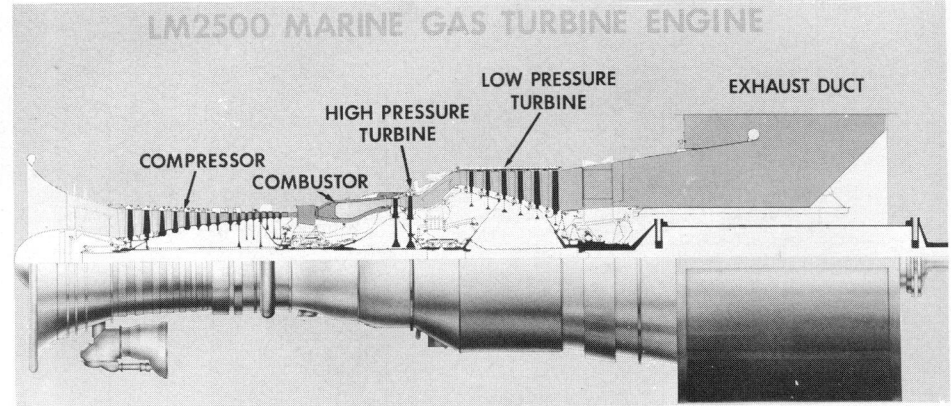

Internal arrangements of LM2500

the US Air Force C-5 Galaxy transporter and DC-10, Boeing 747 and A300 commercial jets. The compressor, combuster and turbine are designed to give maximum progression in reliability, parts life and time between overhaul. The engine has a simple-cycle efficiency of more than 36 per cent, which is due to advanced cycle pressures, temperatures and component efficiencies.

The LM2500 marine gas turbine provides foilborne power for the US Navy PHM (patrol hydrofoil missile). The six PHM 'Pegasus' class vessels have been built by the Boeing Company, Seattle, Washington.

Other naval applications of the LM2500 include US Navy DD-963 'Spruance' class destroyers, FFG-7 'Perry' class frigates, Australian and Spanish Navy FFG-7 frigates, Italian, Venezuelan and Peruvian 'Lupo' class fast frigates, West German Navy frigates, South Korean Navy frigates and corvettes, Brazilian and Royal Danish Navy corvettes, gunboats for the Indonesian and Saudi Arabian navies and Spanish and Italian aircraft carriers. Two LM2500 engines power the GTS (gas turbine ship) *Admiral William M Callaghan* roll-on/roll-off cargo vessel which has had over 140,000 operating hours with the LM2500 engine.

Total operating time of LM2500 engines in marine service is more than 900,000 hours. The LM2500 has a 99·9 per cent availability rate in US Navy service; that is for every 10,000 hours of operational service, installed engines have required an average of ten hours' corrective maintenance.

TYPE: Two-shaft, axial flow, simple cycle.
AIR INTAKE: Axial, inlet bellmouth or duct can be customised to installation.
COMBUSTION CHAMBER: Annular.
FUEL GRADE: Kerosene, JP4, JP5, diesel, heavy distillate fuels and natural gas.
TURBINE: Two-stage gas generator, six-stage power.
JET PIPE: Vertical or customised to fit installation.
OIL SPECIFICATION: Synthetic Turbine Oil (MIL-L-23699) or equal.
MOUNTING: At power turbine and compressor front frame.
STARTING: Pneumatic, hydraulic.
DIMENSIONS
Length: 6,530mm (257in)
Width: 2,240mm (88in)
PERFORMANCE RATINGS: 30,000shp at 15°C (59°F) at sea level
SPECIFIC FUEL CONSUMPTION: 0·171kg (0·376lb)/hp/h

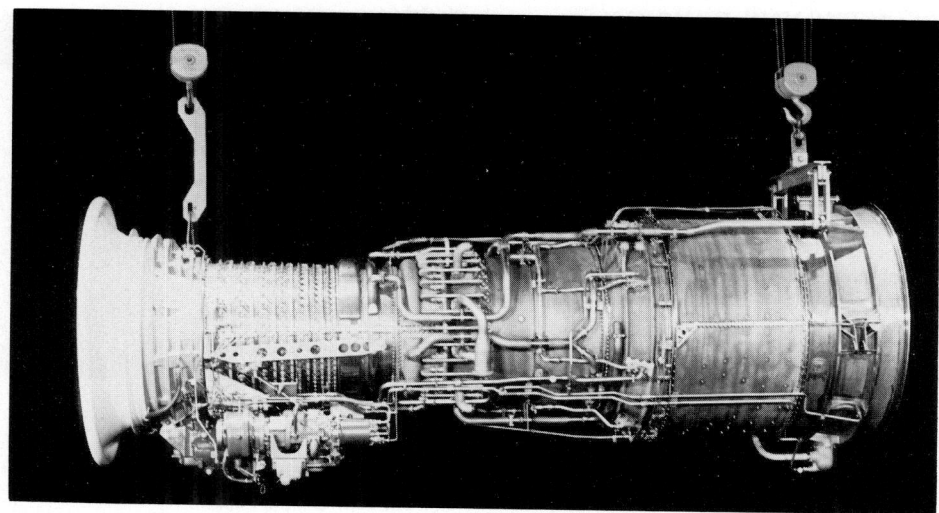

LM2500

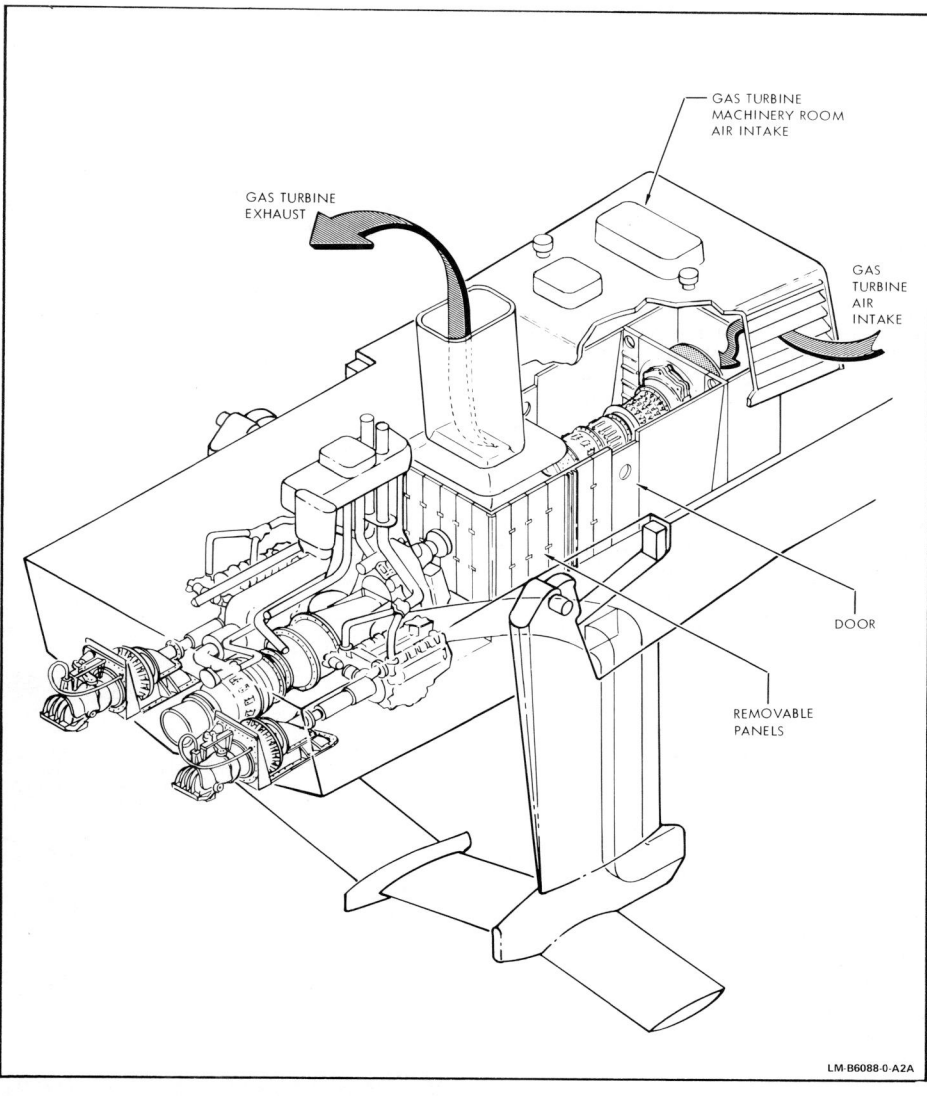

LM-B6088-0-A2A

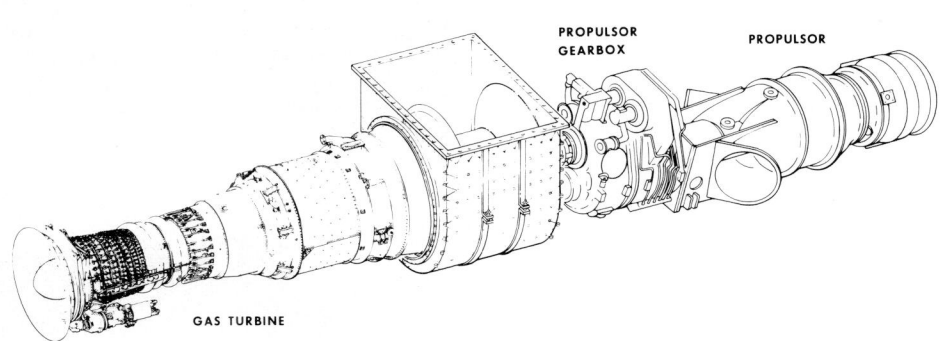

LM2500 installation aboard PHM

ROCKETDYNE DIVISION
ROCKWELL INTERNATIONAL

6633 Canoga Avenue, Canoga Park, California
91304, USA
Telex: 698478
Official:
Don Warren, *Marketing Manager, Waterjet Propulsion*

Technology gained in the design and manufacture of high-performance pumps for the US space programme enabled Rocketdyne to develop a family of waterjet propulsion systems, called Powerjet 16, 20 and 24. These systems employ advanced design, axial-flow pumping elements to produce compact, lightweight waterjet propulsors. Simplicity of design minimises the number of components in the units, while allowing accessibility for servicing or replacement of seals and bearings. All components meet American Bureau of Shipping requirements and have been built of materials resistant to cavitation damage, and seawater and galvanic corrosion.

Rockwell Powerjet 20s power 23 Boeing 929 Jetfoils. On each Jetfoil, dual PJ20s, each driven by a Detroit Diesel Allison 501-K20A gas turbine rated at 3,840hp, deliver a 24,000 gallons a minute water flow.

Jetfoils operate regularly at cruising speeds of 45 knots in 3·65m (12ft) seas between Hong Kong and Macao; Sado Island and Niigata in Japan; Dover to Ostend, Belgium; Tenerife to Las Palmas, Canary Islands and in Indonesia. The vessels in service have travelled over one billion passenger miles, during which the Powerjet 20 units have logged more than 400,000 pump hours.

Other vessels to employ Rocketdyne Powerjet units include the *Fortuna,* a private yacht designed by Don Shead, capable of exceeding 50 knots. The craft uses a Powerjet 24 driven by a Lycoming Super TF40. Police patrol boats for Brunei are each powered by two Powerjet 16s direct-driven from MTU 8V331 TC 81 diesels.

POWERJET 20

TYPE: Single-stage, axial-flow.
APPLICATION: Designed for hydrofoils and high-speed craft at 3,840hp and medium- to high-speed craft at lower horsepower. Two Powerjet 20 propulsion units, each driven by an Allison 501-K20A gas turbine through a 6·37:1 reduction gearbox, power the Boeing 929 Jetfoil, a 115-ton, 45-knot passenger-carrying hydrofoil. In this application, the gearbox is used in conjunction with an over/under configuration, which results in a compact installation. Input horsepower to the gearbox is 4,000 at 13,380rpm.
ACCESSORY DRIVE: For the Boeing Jetfoil, Powerjet 20 is coupled to a gearbox that provides two pads for accessory drive. The first pad supplies power for the boat's hydraulic system, while the second directs power to gearbox, pump, and turbine lubrication and scavenge pump.
PRIME MOVERS: Diesels and gas turbines up to 4,000hp.
LUBRICATION SYSTEM: External recirculating supply, with 2·5 to 3·5 gallons/min flow at 55 to 70psi provided by a gerotor-type pump that contains both pressure and scavenge cavities.
LUBE OIL GRADE
MIL-L-23699
MIL-L-2106
Diesel crankcase oil—API (D Series)
Automobile differential oil—API (M Series)
SPECIFICATION
Operating range:
  Input hp: 3,840 (4,320hp also available)
  Input shaft speed: 2,145rpm
  Total inlet head: 7·92m (26ft)
  Pump flow rate: 24,750 gallons/min
Propulsion pump weight:
  Dry: 707·6kg (1,560lb)
  Wet: 961·6kg (2,120lb)

POWERJET 16

TYPE: Single-stage, axial-flow.
APPLICATION: Designed for high propulsive

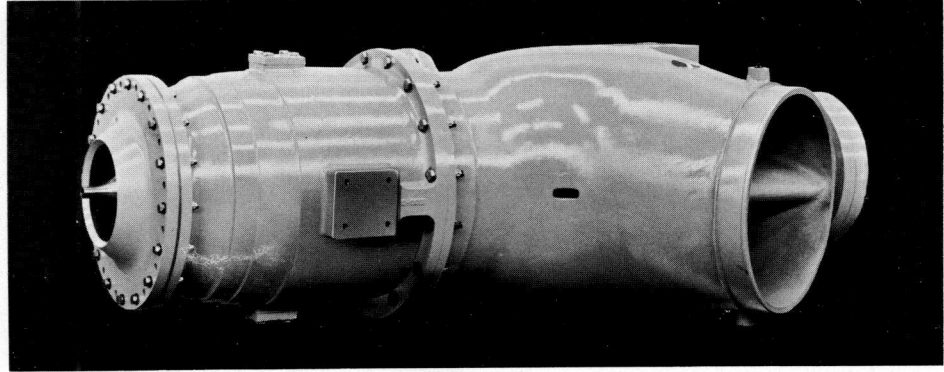

Powerjet 20

ENGINEERING NOTES

1. Lube oil in (external supply)
2. Lube oil out
3. Input shaft-involute spline
   -American Standard
   -ANSI B92.1 - 1970
   -Diametral pitch 8/16
   -Pitch diameter 4.00 in.
   -Number of teeth 32
4. 5.50 dia. access hole
5. Input shaft rotation clockwise looking aft
6. All dimensions in inches

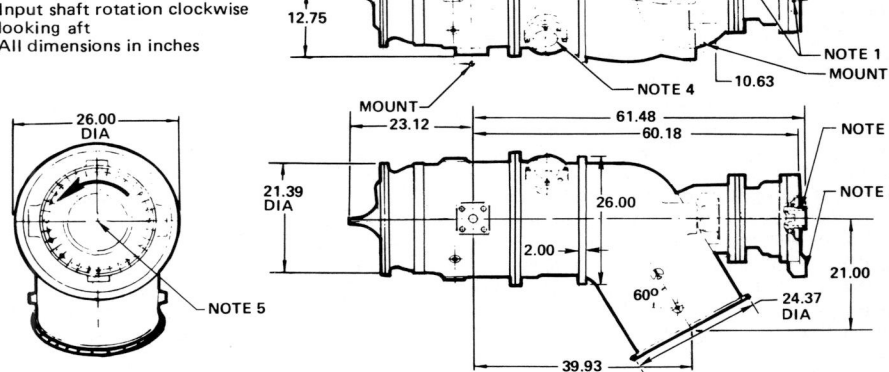

General arrangement of Powerjet 20

Twin Powerjet 20s are installed in Boeing Jetfoil

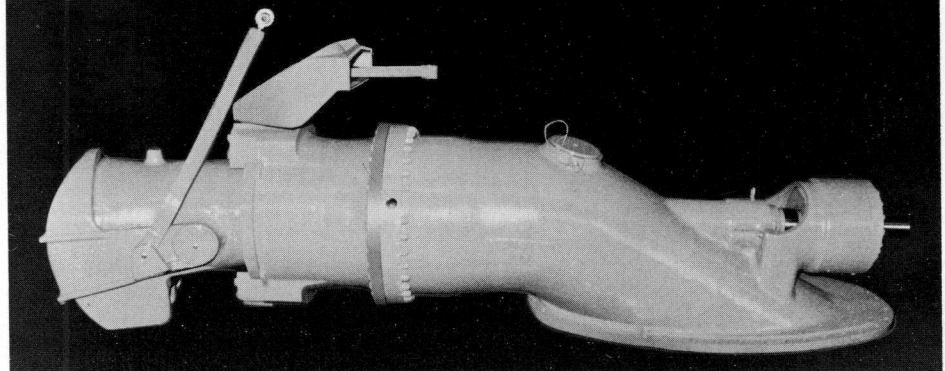

Powerjet 16

efficiency at moderate speeds in all types of hull configurations.

PRIME MOVERS: Diesels and gas turbines developing between 700 and 1,575hp. Four inducer trims are available for direct coupling to most marine diesels.

LUBRICATION SYSTEM: Integrated recirculating system.

LUBE OIL GRADE
MIL-L-9000
MIL-L-17331
MIL-L-2105
Society of Automotive Engineers Gear Oils
Society of Automotive Engineers Motor Oils

SPECIFICATION
Operating Range:

	Trim Number			
	1	2	3	4
Max hp, up to:	1,575	1,575	1,575	1,306
Input shaft speed rpm, up to:	2,310	2,530	2,630	2,650
Nominal input direct drive, hp:	1,025	900	800	815
Nominal input shaft speed, rpm:	2,000	2,100	2,100	2,260
Total inlet head, ft, minimum:	30·1	22	22	22
Pump flow rate (at 30 knots), gallons/min:	18,200	16,700	16,700	16,700

Propulsion pump weight:
Dry: 1,027kg (2,265lb)
Wet: 1,141kg (2,515lb)
Steering vector: ±22 degrees
Reverse thrust: 50% of forward gross thrust to a maximum of 1,025hp

POWERJET 24

TYPE: Single-stage, axial-flow.
APPLICATION: Designed for high-propulsive efficiency at moderate to high speeds.
PRIME MOVERS: Diesels and gas turbines developing up to 5,790hp; 7,000hp also available.
LUBRICATION SYSTEM: External recirculating supply requiring 3·8 to 4·2 gallons/min flow at 55 to 70psi.
LUBE OIL GRADE
MIL-L-9000
MIL-L-17331
MIL-L-2105
Society of Automotive Engineers Gear Oils
Society of Automotive Engineers Motor Oils
SPECIFICATION
Operating range:
Input: 5,790hp; 7,000hp also available
Input shaft speed: 1,853rpm
Total inlet head: 13·1m (43ft) at 1,640rpm
Pump flow rate (at 30 knots): 45,000 gallons/min
Propulsion pump weight
Dry: 2,358kg (5,200lb)
Wet: 2,767kg (6,100lb)
Steering vector: ±22 degrees
Reverse thrust: 50% of forward gross thrust to a maximum of 1,830hp

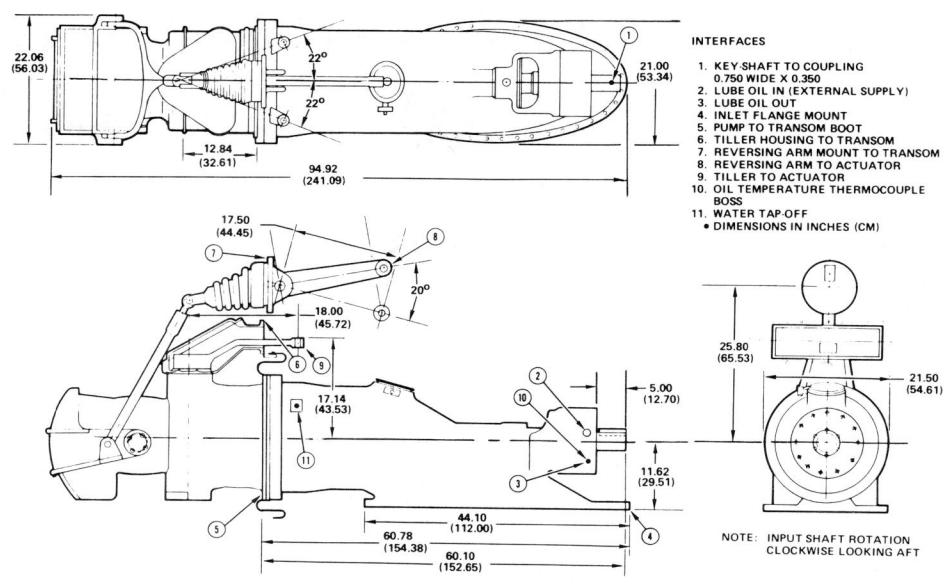

INTERFACES
1. KEY SHAFT TO COUPLING 0.750 WIDE X 0.350
2. LUBE OIL IN (EXTERNAL SUPPLY)
3. LUBE OIL OUT
4. INLET FLANGE MOUNT
5. PUMP TO TRANSOM BOOT
6. TILLER HOUSING TO TRANSOM
7. REVERSING ARM MOUNT TO TRANSOM
8. REVERSING ARM MOUNT TO ACTUATOR
9. TILLER TO ACTUATOR
10. OIL TEMPERATURE THERMOCOUPLE BOSS
11. WATER TAP-OFF
• DIMENSIONS IN INCHES (CM)

NOTE: INPUT SHAFT ROTATION CLOCKWISE LOOKING AFT

Powerjet 16

Fortuna, 50-knot private yacht designed by Don Shead, driven by Powerjet 24

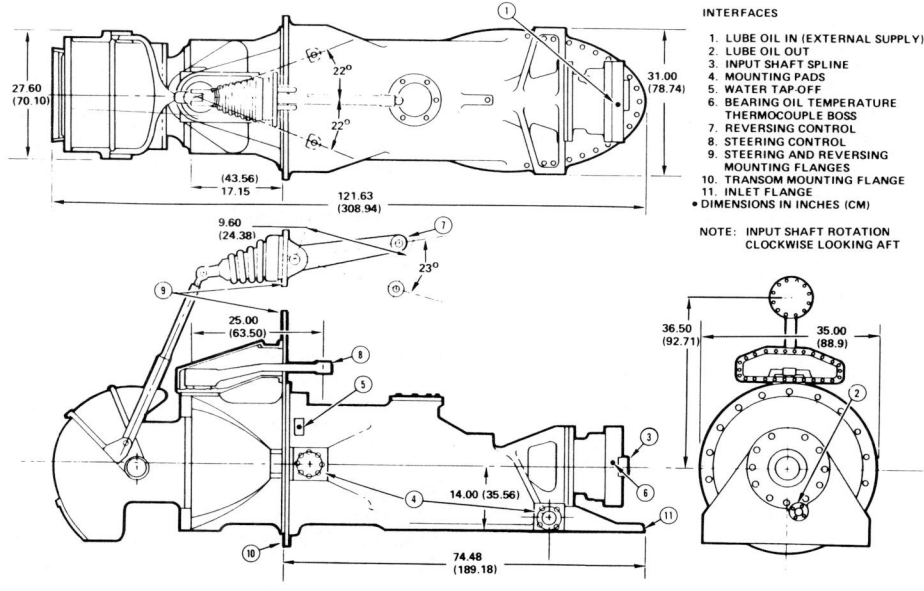

INTERFACES
1. LUBE OIL IN (EXTERNAL SUPPLY)
2. LUBE OIL OUT
3. INPUT SHAFT SPLINE
4. MOUNTING PADS
5. WATER TAP-OFF
6. BEARING OIL TEMPERATURE THERMOCOUPLE BOSS
7. REVERSING CONTROL
8. STEERING CONTROL
9. STEERING AND REVERSING MOUNTING FLANGES
10. TRANSOM MOUNTING FLANGE
11. INLET FLANGE
• DIMENSIONS IN INCHES (CM)

NOTE: INPUT SHAFT ROTATION CLOCKWISE LOOKING AFT

Powerjet 24

UNITED TECHNOLOGIES CORPORATION POWER SYSTEMS DIVISION
(Gas Turbine Operations)

400 Main St, East Hartford, Connecticut 06108, USA

Telephone: (203) 565 1103
Officials:
R F Nordin, *Director, New Business and Hamilton Support Systems*

United Technologies Corporation has ceased production of the FT4 marine gas turbine. Except for product support and spare parts operations, the Gas Turbine Operations Department of the Power Systems Division of United Technologies Corporation has been disbanded.

A description of the FT4 marine gas turbine can be found in *Jane's Surface Skimmers 1983* and earlier editions.

ACV AND HYDROFOIL LICENSING AUTHORITIES

ARGENTINA
ACVs and Hydrofoils
Prefectura Naval Maritima
  Paseo Colon 533
  Buenos Aires
  Argentina

AUSTRALIA
ACVs and Hydrofoils
Covers interstate and international voyages. Smaller craft come under jurisdiction of state or local authorities.
Department of Transport
  Ship Safety Branch,
  Marine Operations Division,
  PO Box 594,
  Civic Square ACT 2608,
  Australia

New South Wales
Maritime Services Board
  Circular Quay West,
  Sydney,
  New South Wales 2000,
  Australia
  or
  PO Box 32 GPO,
  Sydney,
  New South Wales 2001,
  Australia

Queensland
Department of Harbours and Marine
  PO Box 2195,
  231 Turbot Street,
  Brisbane,
  Queensland 4001,
  Australia
  Telephone: 227 7111
  Telex: HARBRS 40760

South Australia
Department of Marine and Harbours
  293 St Vincent Street,
  Port Adelaide,
  South Australia 5015,
  Australia

Tasmania
Navigation and Survey Authority of
  Tasmania
  1 Franklin Wharf,
  Hobart,
  Tasmania 7001,
  Australia

West Australia
Department of Marine and Harbours,
  6 Short Street,
  PO Box 402,
  Fremantle 6160,
  West Australia,
  Australia
  Telephone: 09 335 1211

AUSTRIA
ACVs and Hydrofoils
Bundesministerium für Handel Gewerbe und
  Industrie
  Stubenring 1,
  Vienna 1,
  Austria
  Telephone: 57 66 55

BELGIUM
ACVs and Hydrofoils
Ministry of Communications
  Administration de la Marine et de la Navigation Intérieure
  rue d'Arlon 104,
  B-1040 Brussels,
  Belgium
  Telephone: 02 233 12 11

CANADA
ACVs
Transport Canada
Air Cushion Vehicle Division
  Canadian Coast Guard,
  Tower A,
  Place de Ville,
  Ottawa,
  Ontario K1A 0N7
  Canada

Official: R G Wade, *Superintendent*
  The ACV Division was established in 1968, within the Marine Administration of Transport Canada and is responsible to the Director of General Ship Safety for all aspects of ACV safety regulation. These responsibilities include design approval and safety certification of all ACVs operating in Canada, and the licensing of operating and maintenance personnel. Close liaison is maintained with the National Research Council, Transport Development Centre, industry and other regulatory authorities.

DENMARK
ACVs and Hydrofoils
Government Ships Inspection Service
  Snorresgade 19,
  DK-2300 Copenhagen S,
  Denmark

EGYPT
ACVs
The Arab General Organisation for Air Transport
  11 Emad El Din Street,
  Cairo,
  Egypt

FIJI
ACVs and Hydrofoils
Director of Marine
  Marine Department,
  Government Buildings,
  PO Box 326,
  Suva,
  Fiji

FINLAND
Board of Navigation
  Vuorimiehenkatu 1,
  PO Box 158,
  SF-00141 Helsinki 14,
  Finland

FRANCE
ACVs and Hydrofoils
Secrétariat d'Etat auprès du Ministre des Transports, Chargé de la Mer
  3 Place de Fontenoy,
  75700 Paris,
  France
  Telephone: 273 55 05
  Telex: 250 823 (Mimer Paris)

GAMBIA
ACVs and Hydrofoils
Ministry of Works and Communications
  Banjul,
  Gambia

GERMANY, FEDERAL REPUBLIC
ACVs and Hydrofoils
See-Berufsgenossenschaft
  Ships Safety Department
  Reimerstwiete 2,
  2000 Hamburg 11,
  Federal Republic of Germany

GHANA
The Shipping Commissioner
  Ministry of Transport and Communications,
  PO Box M.38,
  Accra,
  Ghana

GREECE
ACVs and Hydrofoils
Ministry of Mercantile Marine
  Merchant Ships Inspection Service,
  Palaiologou 1 str,
  Piraeus,
  Greece
  Telephone: 411 1214
  Telex: 212581

HUNGARY
Közlekedési-és Postaügyi Minisztérium
  Hajózási Föosztály,
  Hajózási Felügyelet,
  Budapest V, Apáczai Csere János utca 11,
  Hungary

ICELAND
Directorate of Shipping
  PO Box 484,
  Reykjavik,
  Iceland
  Telex: 2307

INDIA
ACVs and Hydrofoils
Directorate General of Shipping
  Bombay,
  India

INDONESIA
ACVs and Hydrofoils
Department of Transport, Communications and
  Tourism
  8 Medan Merdelka Barat,
  Jakarta-Pusat,
  Indonesia

IRELAND
ACVs and Hydrofoils
Department of Communications,
  Kildare Street,
  Dublin 2,
  Ireland

ISRAEL
ACVs and Hydrofoils
Ministry of Transport
  Division of Shipping and Ports,
  102 Ha'atzmauth Road,
  PO Box 33993,
  Haifa,
  Israel

ITALY
ACVs and Hydrofoils
Ministero della Marina Mercantile
  Ispettorato Tecnico,
  Viale Asia,
  00100 Rome,
  Italy

IVORY COAST
ACVs and Hydrofoils
Ministère des Travaux Publics et des Transports
BP V6,
Abidjan,
Ivory Coast

JAMAICA
The Marine Board
Collector General's Department,
PO Box 466,
Newport East,
Kingston,
Jamaica

JAPAN
ACVs and Hydrofoils
Japanese Ministry of Transportation
2-1-3 Kasumigaseki,
Chiyoda-ku,
Tokyo,
Japan

KOREA, REPUBLIC
Ministry of Transportation
1-3 Do-dong,
Choong-ku,
Seoul,
Republic of Korea

KUWAIT
ACVs and Hydrofoils
Department of Customs and Ports
PO Box 9,
Kuwait

LEBANON
ACVs and Hydrofoils
Ministère des Travaux Publics
Direction des Transports,
Beirut,
Lebanon

LUXEMBOURG
ACVs
Ministère des Transports,
19-21 boulevard Royal,
L-2910 Luxembourg
Telephone: 4794-336

MADAGASCAR
ACVs and Hydrofoils
Ministère de l'Amina
Jement du Territoire,
Anosy,
Antananarivo,
Madagascar

MALAWI
The Ministry of Transport and Communications
Private Bag 322,
Capital City,
Lilongwe 3,
Malawi

MALAYSIA
The Ministry of Transport
Wisma Perdana,
Jalan Dungun,
Damansara Heights,
Kuala Lumpur,
Malaysia
Telephone: 948122
Cables: MINCOM, KL
Telex: MA 30999

MEXICO
ACVs and Hydrofoils
Departamento de Licencias
Direction de Marina Mercante,
SCT,
Luerpo A,
2 Piso,
Mexico 12,
Mexico

MOROCCO
Ministère de l'Equipement
Direction des Affaires Techniques,
Rabat-Chellah,
Morocco

NETHERLANDS
ACVs and Hydrofoils
Ministerie van Verkeer en Waterstaat
Directoraat-General Scheepvaart en Maritieme
Zaken,
Bordewijkstraat 4,
Postbus 5817,
2280 HV Rÿswÿk,
Netherlands

NEW ZEALAND
ACVs and Hydrofoils (Certificates of Construction and Performance)
Operating approval and licences:
Ministry of Transport
Marine Division,
Private Bag,
Wellington 1,
New Zealand
Hovercraft regulations currently being drafted. Among other things these will require hovercraft over a certain size to be licensed for commercial operation. The administration of all legislation for hovercraft and hydrofoils is the responsibility of the above.

NORWAY
ACVs and Hydrofoils
Norwegian Maritime Directorate
Thv Meyersgt 7,
PO Box 8123-Dep,
Oslo 1,
Norway

SOUTH AFRICA
Department of Transport
Private Bag X193
Pretoria 0001,
South Africa

SPAIN
ACVs and Hydrofoils
Dirección General de la Marina Mercante
Ruiz de Alacron No 1,
Madrid 14,
Spain

SWEDEN
ACVs and Hydrofoils
The National Swedish Administration of Shipping and Navigation
Sjöfartsverket,
S-601 78 Norrköping
Sweden

SWITZERLAND
Cantonal licensing authorities for ACVs and Hydrofoils
Lake Zürich
Seepolizei/Schiffahrtskontrolle des Kantons Zürich
Seestrasse 87,
CH-8942 Oberrieden,
Switzerland
Seepolizei-und Gewässerschutz Kommissariat der Stadt Zürich
Bellerivestrasse 260,
CH-8008 Zurich,
Switzerland

Lake Constance
Schiffahrtskontrolle des Kantons Thurgau,
Zürcherstrasse 254,
CH-8500 Frauenfeld,
Switzerland
Telephone: 054 79111
Strassenverkehrs und Schiffahrtsamt des Kantons St Gallen,
Abr. Schiffahrt,
9400 Rorschach,
Switzerland
Kantonale Schiffahrtskontrolle
Rosengasse 8,
CH-8200 Schaffhausen,
Switzerland

Lake Lausanne
Service des Automobiles, Motos, Cycles et Bateaux
La Blecherette,
CH-1014 Lausanne,
Switzerland

Lake Lucerne
Schiffsinspektorat des Kantons Luzern
Gibraltarstrasse 3,
CH-6002 Lucerne,
Switzerland

Lake Geneva
Departement de Justice et Police Service de la Navigation
6 rue du 31-Décembre,
CH-1207 Geneva,
Switzerland

Lake Lugano and Lake Locarno
Ufficio Cantonale della Circolazione
Servizio Navigazione,
CH-6528 Camorino,
Switzerland

Lake Neuchatel
Departement de Police
CH-2000 Neuchatel,
Switzerland

Lake Thoune, Lake Brienz and Lake Biel
Strassenverkehrs und Schiffahrtsamt
des Kantons Bern,
Schermenweg 5,
Postfach 2681,
3011 Bern,
Switzerland

TURKEY
ACVs and Hydrofoils
T C Ulastirma Bakanligi
Deniz Ulaştirmasi Genel Müdürlügü,
Ankara,
Turkey
T C Ulastirma Bakanligi
Marmara Bolgesi Liman ve Denizisleri
Müdürlügü,
Karaköy-Istanbul,
Turkey

UNITED KINGDOM
Hovercraft–Certification, Issue of Type, Safety, Experimental and Export Certificates. Approval of persons or organisations from whom the CAA may accept reports on the design, construction, maintenance or repair of hovercraft or elements thereof. Approval of hovercraft items and equipment.
Publication of 'British Hovercraft Safety Requirements'
Technical enquiries to:
A. C. G. Seal,
Head,
Hovercraft Department,
Airworthiness Division
Civil Aviation Authority,
Brabazon House,
Redhill,
Surrey RH1 1SQ,
England
Telephone: 0737 65966
Telex: 27100

Publications:
Civil Aviation Authority
Printing and Publication Services
Greville House,
3 Gratton Road,
Cheltenham,
Gloucestershire GL50 2BN,
England
Telephone: 0242 35151

Hovercraft and Hydrofoils
Hovercraft Operating Permits and Hydrofoil Passenger Certificates
Department of Transport
Marine Divison,
Sunley House,
90-93 High Holborn,
London WC1V 6LP,
England
Telephone: 01 405 6911
Telex: 264084

UNITED STATES OF AMERICA
ACVs and Hydrofoils
Cdr R. B. Meyer
Department of Transportation
   Commandant (G-MTH-4/13),
   US Coast Guard,
   Washington DC 20593,
   USA
Telephone: (202) 426 2197

VENEZUELA
Ministerio de Transporte y Comunicaciones
Dirección General de Transporte y Tránsito
   Maritimo
   Edificio Centro Valores,
   Piso 3-2 Esquina Luneta,
   Caracas 1010,
   Venezuela

YUGOSLAVIA
Yugoslav Federal Economic Secretariat
   Transport Department,
   Bulevar AVNOJ-a 104,
   Belgrade,
   Yugoslavia

CLUBS AND ASSOCIATIONS

HOVERCLUB OF GREAT BRITAIN LIMITED

As Britain's national organisation for light hovercraft, the Hoverclub exists to encourage the construction and operation of light, recreational hovercraft by private individuals, schools, colleges, universities and other youth groups. The Hoverclub's major role in recent years has been its organisation of several national race meetings at sites throughout Britain. At these events 60 or more light hovercraft may compete for National Championship points over land and water courses at meetings held in the grounds of stately homes, or at reclaimed gravel workings.

In addition to national race meetings, the Hoverclub also provides its own members and prospective hovercraft builders with useful advice and information through its publications and a technical enquiries office.

PUBLICATIONS
Light Hovercraft, monthly
Light Hovercraft Handbook, annually. Prime reference book for the design, construction and safe operation of small recreational hovercraft.
Guide to Model Hovercraft
Light Hovercraft Design, Construction and Safety Requirements

A growing activity within the Hoverclub has been hovercruising, which involves travelling by single- or, more usually, multi-seat light hovercraft along rivers, canals, lakes or coastlines. Many hovercraft constructors see this activity as a means to explore areas inaccessible to other types of transport. Hovercruises and holidays have been arranged in Scotland and Wales.

Officers:
Mrs B Kemp, 10 Long Acre, Bingham, Nottingham, *Secretary*
Mrs D Naylor, 5 Lordsmead, Cranfield, Bedfordshire, *Information Officer*
J Kemp, 10 Long Acre, Bingham, Nottingham, *Schools Representative*

Addresses of the Hoverclub branches throughout Britain are listed below:

CHILTERNS
C Sanders,
74a Alexandria Road, London NW4 2RY

EAST ANGLIAN
B Hill,
10 Fenland Road, Reffley Estate, Kings Lynn, Norfolk

MIDLANDS
Mrs B Kemp,
10 Long Acre, Bingham, Nottingham

NORTH WEST
Rev W G Spedding,
26 Milverton Close, Lostock, Bolton, BL6 4RR

SOUTH EASTERN
B Congdon,
29 Avalon Road, Orpington, Kent

WELSH
Mrs H Riley,
11 Normandy Way, Chepstow, Gwent

INDEPENDENT CLUBS
ESSEX
E W Sangster,
53 Elm View Road, Benfleet, Essex SS7 5AR

SOUTHERN HOVERCLUB
Vernon Gray,
The Lilacs, Westhill Road North, South Wonston, Winchester, Hampshire SO2I 3HJ

THE HOVERCRAFT SOCIETY (THS)

Forest Lodge West, Fawley Road, Hythe, Southampton, Hampshire SO4 6ZZ, England
Telephone: 0703 843178

Officers:
Sir Christopher Cockerell, *President*
R L Wheeler, *Vice President*
J E Rapson, MBE, *Vice President*
W F S Woodford, OBE, *Vice President*
J Wraith, *Chairman*
Jill Walker, *Secretary*
A Blunden, *Editor, Hovercraft Bulletin*

Formed in 1971, the Hovercraft Society was the UK constituent member of the 'International Air Cushion Engineering Society'. Membership is open to persons engaged in hovercraft related fields and to those having a bona fide interest in hovercraft in the UK and overseas. Current membership is drawn from ACV manufacturers, ferry operators, design groups, government departments and agencies, financial and insurance organisations, consultants, journalists and universities.

THS organises regular meetings at which talks are given on the technical, commercial, design, operating and military aspects of hovercraft and air cushion devices. Many of these lectures have been taken from proceedings written for THS and are available to members. THS also produces a monthly *Hovercraft Bulletin* containing the latest information on hovercraft activities throughout the world. Occasionally, THS arranges visits and social events for its members.

A collection of books, periodicals, papers and reports on the subject of hovercraft have been accumulated by the Society. These are housed in Southampton University Library and can be freely consulted by members.

HOVERMAIL COLLECTORS' CLUB

Highlights, Down Road, Tavistock, Devon PL19 9AQ, England
Officers:
John L Hobbs, *Chairman*
J K Pemberton, *Editor, Slipstream*

The Hovermail Collectors' Club arranges and provides first day covers for collectors and organises occasional auctions. *Slipstream*, a monthly newsletter, advises members on new material available and provides details of new developments in the hovercraft transport industry.

BRITISH SMALL HOVERCRAFT MANUFACTURERS' ASSOCIATION (BSHMA)

24 Leaf Close, Northwood, Middlesex HA6 2YY, England
Telephone: 09274 27262

Officers:
Nigel Beale, *Chairman*
Alan Blunden, *Secretary and Treasurer*

BSHMA, the trade association for manufacturers of hovercraft with overall lengths of up to ten metres was established in 1979. The seven companies which belong to BSHMA build virtually all the small hovercraft produced commercially in the United Kingdom. Since its formation, the Association has initiated negotiations with licensing and regulatory authorities and has been recognised by several government departments and official bodies. Members have also arranged joint exhibition appearances, notably at the London Boat Show.

BSHMA is now financing the writing of a code of practice, defining parameters for the construction and safe operation of small hovercraft, to which all members will adhere. It is hoped that the code will be approved by the Civil Aviation Authority's Hovercraft Department and overseas authorities responsible for the licensing of hovercraft.

JOHN DERRY TECHNICAL CENTRE

Charterhouse School, Surrey
Telephone: 04868 4443
Officers:
R A Crowsley
S Fielder

CH2
The CH2 was designed at the Technical Centre for 14 to 18 year-old students who would then be equipped to instruct others in its use. Designed and built in 1980, it has performed well on land, salt water and fresh water.
LIFT AND PROPULSION: 10hp Rowena single-cylinder two-stroke drives an axial fan ahead of the open cockpit. A 28hp Kholer twin-cylinder two-stroke drives a multi-bladed ducted propeller.
CONTROLS: Central control column incorporates thrust engine throttle and twin aerodynamic rudders operating in fan slipstream.
HULL: 3mm birch plywood with wooden stringers and fibreglass joints. Four closed compartments, two at front, one under seats and one under rear duct, contain 50 per cent fixed craft buoyancy. A further 100 per cent buoyancy can be incorporated into the side lockers for over-water operation.
SKIRT: Pressurised bag type in neoprene-coated nylon. Welded construction.
DIMENSIONS
Length: 3·65m (12ft)

CH2, in operation at John Derry Technical Centre

Beam: 2·31m (7ft 7in)
Height, off cushion: 1·06m (3ft 6in)
Height, cushion inflated: 1·32m (4ft 4in)
WEIGHTS
Empty: 122·4kg (270lb)
Payload: 136kg (300lb)
PERFORMANCE
Max speed: 40·2km/h (25mph)
Endurance: 2 hours
Vertical obstacle clearance: 0·15m (6in)

THE HOVERCLUB OF AMERICA INC

Box 216, Clinton, Indiana 47842-0216, USA
Officers:
Chris Fitzgerald, *President*
Steve Auten, *Vice President*
Rossanne Adams, *Secretary and Editor, Hovernews*
Ben Adams, *Treasurer*

Membership of the HoverClub of America Inc costs US $15 per annum.

Following a general meeting of the members of the American Hovercraft Association in May, 1976, it was agreed to reorganise the Association into the HoverClub of America Inc. The Hover-Club of America has since been incorporated under the State Laws of Indiana and six new national directors are elected each year.

In the USA the HoverClub of America organises race meetings, rallies and other events for members possessing hovercraft, and also publishes a bi-monthly newsletter, *Hovernews*.

TERRE HAUTE, INDIANA
Chris Fitzgerald,
Fort Harrison Industrial Park, Terre Haute, Indiana 47804

PENNSYLVANIA/OHIO
John Zitko,
RD2 Box 338, Washington, Pennsylvania 15317

LAKE ELSINORE, CALIFORNIA
Ray Kemp,
Lake Elsinore, 990 E Lakeshore Drive, California 92330

CORDOVA, ILLINOIS
Bob Windt,
1204 3rd Street, Cordova, Illinois 61242

TOLEDO, OHIO
Terry Chapman,
Box 111, Swanton, Ohio 43558

JACKSONVILLE, ILLINOIS
Leonard Fisher,
785 E College, Jacksonville, Illinois 62650

ANCHORAGE, ALASKA
Henry Sayler,
7400 Silver Birch Drive, Anchorage, Alaska 99502

TAMPA/ST PETERSBURG, FLORIDA
Dee Anders,
1915 Fern Street, Tampa, Florida 33604

JACKSONVILLE, FLORIDA
Marc Marchioli,
414 Sherry Drive, Atlantic Beach, Florida 32211

BRISBANE, AUSTRALIA
H B Standen,
15 Florentine St, Stafford Queensland 4054, Australia

MEMPHIS, TENNESSEE
Guy R Pike,
6090 Selkirk, Memphis, Tennessee 38115

WATERLOO, ONTARIO, CANADA
Peter Fohry,
190 Cedarvale Cres, Waterloo, Ontario N2L 4T2, Canada

TAIPEI, TAIWAN
Olivia Chiao,
ATD&D, PO Box 11125, Tapei, Taiwan

METAIRIE, LOUISIANA
Claude Mixon,
1309 Edenborn Ave, Metaire, Louisiana 70001

MINNESOTA
Stefan Litwinczuk,
3505-20th Ave So, Minneapolis, Minnesota 55407

FÉDÉRATION FRANCAIS DES CLUBS d'AÉROGLISSEURS

12 rue Béranger, 92100 Boulogne Billancourt, France

Member Clubs:

CLUB FRANÇAIS DES AÉROGLISSEURS
41-43 rue Aristide-Briand, 45130 Meung-sur-Loire, France

AÉROGLISSEURS D'ILE DE FRANCE
10 bis, avenue P Semard, 91700 Sainte-Genevieve-Des-Bois, France

COUSS' AIR TOURAINE
81 rue Michelet, 37000 Tours, France

AÉROGLISSEURS D'OC
51 avenue Louis Abric, 34400 Lunel, France

ANJOU-BRETAGNE AÉROGLISSEURS
4 rue de la Maladrerie, 49220 Le Lion D'Angers, France

CLUB AÉROGLISSEURS RHÔNE-ALPES
1 avenue du Château, 69003 Lyon Montchat, France

AÉROGLISSEURS VAL DE METZ
18 rue des Près-Argancy, 57640 Vigy, France

OPALE AÉROGLISSEURS
25 quai le Joille, 80230 St Valery, Somme, France

CLUB AÉROGLISSEURS D'AQUITAINE
Les 3 Fontaines, 33560 Carbon Blanc, France

CLUB AÉROGLISSEURS DE TOURAINE
10 rue d'Enfer, Limeray, 37400 Amboise, France

GRECA SECTION AÉROGLISSEURS
Aerodrome de Rouen, 76520 Boos, France

AÉROGLISSEURS BERRY CLUB
Rue de la Chaume du Poids, 18320 Jovet S/Aubois, France

SECTION AÉROGLISSEURS
Rue des Prés Gris, 45250 Briare, France

AÉRO LOIRE
23 bis Venelle des Vaupulents, 45000 Orleans, Paris, France

INTERNATIONAL HOVERCLUBS

EUROPEAN HOVERCRAFT FEDERATION
Philippe de Kerchove de Denterghem, *Chairman*
c/o RACB, 53 rue d'Arlon, 1040 Brussels, Belgium

HOVER CLUB OF AUSTRALIA
H B Standen, *Hon Secretary*
GPO Box 1882, Brisbane, Queensland 4001, Australia

HOVERCRAFT CLUB OF NEW ZEALAND
J J Morgan, *Hon Secretary*
Mill Road, RD2 Pukekohe, South Auckland, New Zealand
Telephone: 88824

HOVERCLUB AND ASSOCIATION OF BELGIUM
Bld St Michel 78, 1040 Brussels, Belgium

HOVER CLUB OF CANADA
R Fishlock
103 Doane Street, Ottawa, Ontario K2B 6GY, Canada

HOVERCLUB OF GERMANY
c/o Helgrel Ruft, AM Clockenbach 10, D 8000, Munich, Federal Republic of Germany

HOVER CLUB OF JAPAN
Information from Masahiro Mino, Senior Director, Aerodynamics Section, Nihon University at Narashino, 7-1591 Narashinodai, Funabashi, Chiba-Ken, Japan

SWEDISH HOVERCLUB
(Svenska Svävarklubben)
Manfred Schneider, *Treasurer*
Ollonvägen 17, S-184 00 Åkersberga, Sweden
Telephone: 01046 76423431

MEMBER CLUB:
THE HOVER CLUB OF UPSALA, SWEDEN
Lars Gullberg, *President*
PO Box 1436, S-751 44 Upsala, Sweden
Telephone: 01046 18322632

INTERNATIONAL HYDROFOIL SOCIETY

51 Welbeck Street, London W1M 7HE, England
Telephone: 01-935 9274
Officers:
David C H Liang, *President* (Hong Kong)
Juanita Kalerghi, *Chairperson and Vice-President IHS*
Robert J Johnston, *Chairman, IHS-North American Association*
Michael Eames, *Vice President*

NORTH AMERICAN ASSOCIATION (IHS-NAA)
Captain John W King Jr, *Secretary*
4313 Granada St, Alexandria, Virginia 22309, USA

The International Hydrofoil Society was founded in 1970 to advance study and research into powered and sailing hydrofoils and is ruled by a Council which meets in London. There are at present members in 20 countries, as well as a North American Chapter known as IHS-NAA. A newsletter is published four times a year. Main meetings are held at the Royal Institution of Naval Architects, 10 Upper Belgrave Street, London SW1, where the Society's library is housed.

CONSULTANTS
ACV CONSULTANTS

FRANCE

L'Institut Français de Recherche pour l'Exploitation des Mers (IFREMER)
66 avenue d'Iéna, 75116 Paris, France
Telephone: 723 55 28
Telex: 610775F

IFREMER has taken over the patents formerly held by SEDAM and has the responsibility for future business activities relating to SEDAM hovercraft designs.

NIGERIA

Rostab Ports and Marine Services (Nigeria) Limited
No 13, 204 Close, PO Box 252, Satellite Town, Lagos, Nigeria
Telephone: 880225
Telex: 21886 BECFRE
Officials:
Dr O A Ali-Balogun, *Executive Director*
Herbert Snowball, *Consultant*

General consultancy services for ACVs, route surveys, route proving, applications studies, performance assessments. Agents for Vosper Hovermarine Limited.

Herbert H Snowball
No 13, 204 Close, PO Box 252, Satellite Town, Lagos, Nigeria
Telephone: 880225
Telex: 21886 BECFRE

Feasibility studies, on-site surveys, technical and economic analyses, mission studies, selection of craft, environmental impact studies, cost analysis, operating infrastructure, crew training and marketing. Specialising in transport and communications problems in developing countries.

UNITED KINGDOM

Air Cushion Equipment (1976) Limited
15-35 Randolph Street, Shirley, Southampton, Hampshire SO1 3HD, England
Telephone: 0703 776468
Telex: 477537
Officials:
J D Hake, *Chairman*
R C Gilbert, *General Manager*
R R Henvest, *Works Manager*

Air Cushion Equipment (1976) Limited offers its services as design engineers and technical consultants for air cushion and water cushion systems. Past experience has involved investigations into systems using both water and air as the cushion fluid.

Water cushions have involved investigating skirt systems up to 15 bar and the various effects of these systems for operating within the industrial sector. Air cushion and skirt systems have been studied with cushion pressures up to 0·75 bar having skirt geometries which can be fitted to structures of various types.

An air cushion oil storage tank movement service is offered on a world-wide basis together with an additional tank stressing service to verify structural integrity.

The company offers its own services and those of its licensed contractors for the movement of heavy, dense and awkward structures as well as its manufacturing facilities for the production of flexible structures and skirt systems.

Air Vehicles Limited
Head Office: 1 Sun Hill, Cowes, Isle of Wight, England
Yard: Dinnis' Yard, High Street, Cowes, Isle of Wight, England
Telephone: 0983 293194 and 294739
Officials:
C D J Bland, *Director*
C B Eden, *Director*

Air Vehicles Limited, formed in 1968, has a wide experience of all types of hovercraft and hovercraft operation and can offer a full range of services as consultants.

Particular fields where Air Vehicles Limited has specialised knowledge are:
Manufacture and operation of small hovercraft up to 14 seats. Several craft have been built and the latest Tiger is also offered for charter.
Design and construction of ducted propellers. Sizes have ranged from 1·3m (4ft 6in) diameter used on Tiger, ducts for SR.N6 and two large ducts of 2·7m (9ft) overall diameter delivered to the USA.
Approved by the Civil Aviation Authority, the company can design and undertake modifications to larger craft. Typical of this work is the conversion to hoverfreighter configuration of SR.N5 and SR.N6. The company also offers SR.N5 hovercraft for charter as well as the Tiger 12-seat hovercraft.
The 20- to 24-seat Twin Tiger, which uses diesel engines, is under development. The company also undertook feasibility studies on the design of a new diesel hovercraft for Hovertravel Limited. The design, the AP1-88, 80-passenger hovercraft, was launched in 1982. Air Vehicles undertook the detail design for this craft as well as the preparation of the original concept.

Peter G Fielding, CEng, FRAeS
Branches:
United Kingdom: 20 Warmdene Road, Brighton, East Sussex BN1 8NL, England
Telephone: 0273 501212
Dock House, Niton Undercliff, Ventnor, Isle of Wight PO38 2NE, England
Telephone: 0983 730 252
USA: 1701 North Fort Myer Drive, Suite 908, Arlington, Virginia 22209, USA
Telephone: (703) 528 1092
7910 Woodmont Avenue, Suite 1103, Bethesda, Maryland 20014, USA
Telephone: (301) 656 5991

Consultant in air cushion systems, air cushion operations, and air cushion technology since 1959 to: the US Army, the US Navy, US Department of Defense, the Advanced Research Projects Agency-DOD, US Department of Commerce-Maritime Administration, the Office of Naval Research, the US Naval Ships Research and Development Center, the US Army TRE-COM, the Executive Office of the President USA, the US Navy-Chief of Naval Operations, the US Marine Corps, the Institute for Defense Analysis, the Center for Naval Analysis, the Bell Aerosystems Corporation, the Aerojet Corporation, the Research Analysis Corporation, Science Applications Incorporated, Hoverlift Applications Incorporated, Booz-Allen Applied Research Incorporated, Associated Consultants International Inc, and SeaSpan Inc. Services to the above organisations have included: state of the art reports, technical and economic analysis, route surveys, environmental impact studies, sub-system analysis, operational plans, test plans, mission studies, advanced technology estimates, test-site selection, cost analysis, structural and materials analysis and market research.

Assignments completed include:
Review and assessment of the Arctic SEV advanced technology programme for the Advanced Research Projects Agency, US Dept of Defense.
Analysis of 'paddle wheel' propulsion and sealing systems for SES, for SA Inc McLean, Virginia, USA.
'The Surface Effect Vehicle (SEV) in Search and Rescue Missions in Alaska'—for the Research Analysis Corporation, McLean, Virginia, USA.
'An Assessment of the Technological Risk and Uncertainty of Advanced Surface Effect Vehicles (SEV) for the Arctic'—for the US Naval Ships Research and Development Center, Carderock, Maryland, USA.
'An Evaluation of Advanced Surface Effect Vehicle Platforms Performing Military Missions in the Arctic'—for Science Applications Inc, La Jolla, California, and Arlington, Virginia, USA.
'An Exhaustive Bibliography of Air Cushion Subjects' for the Research Analysis Corporation, McLean, Virginia, USA.
'Preliminary Findings of the Economic Suitabilities of the Surface Effect Ship to Various Routes in the US'—for SEASPAN Inc, Washington DC, USA.
'Appraisal of Heavy Lift Systems for Commercial Applications'—for Hoverlift Applications Inc, Arlington, Virginia, USA.
Results and Implications of the Advanced Projects Agency, US Department of Defense, Surface Effect Vehicles Programme—for Science Applications Inc, Arlington, Virginia, USA.

Hovercraft Consultants Limited (HCL)
Forest Lodge West, Fawley Road, Hythe, Southampton, Hampshire SO4 6ZZ, England
Telephone: 0703 843178
Telex: 477580 HOVCON G
Officials:
J E Rapson, MBE, *Managing Director*
M J Cox, *Director*
J P Towndrow, *Director*
S M Rapson, *Secretary and Director*

Hovercraft Consultants Limited (HCL) offers independent advice to the hovercraft and related industries. It assesses both the economic and technical suitability of craft for particular routes and duties. The company keeps records of the technical and commercial aspects of high speed, waterborne transport. This information, which includes details of craft, operations, manufacturers, routes and traffic, can be made available to its clients.

HCL is a specialist in the design of cushion and skirt systems and has designed skirts for a hover-platform to carry payloads of 300 tons in the Arctic for the Sohio Petroleum Company. This task involved the design and building of two models on which the stability characteristics and performance over shallow water and simulated ice surfaces were established. The company has also designed lift and skirt systems for a sidewall hovercraft and an amphibious craft, each about 45 feet in length.

HCL is headed by John Rapson, who has been involved with hovercraft technology since 1956. Formerly with Hovercraft Development Limited as Technical Director and Chief Engineer, he has advised government departments and official committees on design, operational requirements and safety of hovercraft.

In addition to the expertise of its staff, HCL can call on the services of Professor W Austyn Mair, formerly Head of the Engineering Department at Cambridge University, and Commander Peter Reynolds, who was Officer in Charge of the Naval Hovercraft Trials Unit.

Hoverwork Limited

12 Lind Street, Ryde, Isle of Wight PO33 2NR, England
Telephone: 0983 65181
Telex: 86513 (A/B Hoverwork Ryde)
Officials:
C D J Bland, *Managing Director*
E W H Gifford, *Director*
A C Smith, *Director*
R G Clarke, *Director*
G M Palin, *Secretary*

Hoverwork Limited, formed in early 1966, is a wholly owned subsidiary of Hovertravel which has been operating hovercraft longer than any other company in the world. In addition to its fleet of SR.N6 type craft it now has access to Hovertravel's new, much larger, AP.1-88, also fully amphibious and with approximately the same performance capability.

The company specialises in chartering craft for seismic and other survey work, crew change operations and other related operations within the oil industry in shallow water areas and terrain difficult for other forms of transport.

The company also offers a route feasibility investigation service.

P N Structures Limited

Marine and Engineering Division
30A Sackville Street, Piccadilly, London W1X 1DB, England
Telephone: 01 734 2578
Telex: 884392
Officials:
Theo Pellinkhof, *Chairman*
Karin M Adeler, *Director*
Henk J Wimmers, *Associate (The Netherlands)*
Dolf Le Comte, *Associate (The Netherlands and USA)*
David J Rimmer, *Secretary*

Consultancy in the fields of marine transport systems for: economic commercial use, effective surveillance duties, and leisure.

Consultancy includes selection of hydrofoils, air cushion vehicles or any other type of surface effect ships and the full range of the more conventional craft varying from the planing hull to the full displacement type.

Consultancy also covers marine engineering and materials handling (air cushion platforms).

A wide area of industrial and technological resources will be made available to clients.

R A Shaw

(Managing Director Hoverprojects Limited)
Fell Brow, Silecroft, Millom, Cumbria LA18 5LS, England
Telephone: 0657 2022

Consultancy services to governments, local authorities and private enterprise on all aspects of fast transport with special emphasis on hovercraft and hydrofoils. Services include financial, economic and operational assessments in all conditions and new designs to meet particular requirements.

Contracts have included:

A study for the State of Washington to assess the feasibility of introducing hovercraft and hydrofoils into the Puget Sound ferry system.

A feasibility appraisal of proposed hovercraft operations in British Columbia.

Reporting to a local authority on prospects of establishing a hoverport within its borough.

A study for the Greater London Council on fast passenger services on the River Thames.

Three independent studies on the potential for hovercraft in the Venetian lagoon.

Examination of world potential market for hovercraft.

Design and economics of 1,000-ton river hovercraft.

Planning and operating consultancy for Airavia Limited and Speed Hydrofoils Limited for hydrofoils on the River Thames.

Design of a main river terminal on the River Thames in front of St Paul's to cater for all forms of river passenger craft and to include a helistop.

Advising London Dockland Development Corporation on possible fast ferry services.

Current work includes advising a shipping company on proposed fast ferry services on the Thames estuary and to the continent.

Robert Trillo Limited

28a St Thomas St, Lymington, Hampshire SO4 9NF, England
Telephone: 0590 75098
Telex: 47674 MATCOM G
Officials:
R L Trillo, CEng, FIMechE, FRAeS, AFAIAA, AFCASI, *Managing Director,* Author and Distributor *Marine Hovercraft Technology*
A U Alexander, *Secretary*

Operating as a consultancy since 1969 and engaged principally in technology and economics concerned with air cushion vehicles, high-speed marine craft and amphibious vehicles, the firm has undertaken transport feasibility studies, preliminary design investigations, design of light hovercraft and experimental investigations. Other work has been concerned with the aerodynamic design of six, ducted propeller installations including the SR.N6 and Skima 12 hovercraft and the Aerospace Developments AD 500 airship. Commissions have included work in Australia, Canada, Denmark, France, Sweden, the UK and USA and have covered economics and engineering studies, designs of craft and appraisal of investment opportunities.

Recent work includes the study of the application of sail to commercial shipping, the design of the Trans-Hover six-seat hovercraft and consultancy for the Swedish Jetcat waterjet-propelled catamaran ferry.
Representative:
Denmark:
Leif Hansen, A B C Hansen Comp A/S, Hauchsvej 14, DK-1825 Copenhagen V, Denmark

UNITED STATES OF AMERICA

Aerophysics Company

3500 Connecticut Avenue NW, Washington DC 20008, USA
Telephone: (202) 244 7502
Officials:
Dr Gabriel D Boehler, *Chairman*
Carl W Messinger Jr, *President*
William F Foshag, *Chief Engineer*

Founded in 1957, Aerophysics Company has undertaken research and development work in all phases of ACV design. Dr Boehler had previously performed feasibility studies with ACV pioneer Melville Beardsley. Although still interested in the complete vehicle, Aerophysics has recently concentrated on lift systems. Termination of the US Navy's 3K SES halted Aerophysics' full-scale fan development. Design studies and model tests in support of NAVSEA's advanced ship technology programme are continuing.

Booz-Allen & Hamilton Inc

USA: 101 Park Avenue, New York, New York 10178, USA
United Kingdom: 30 Charles II Street, St James's Square, London SW1Y 4AE

World-wide general and technology management consulting including: strategy management, organisation planning, marketing and marketing research, computer systems and software, manufacturing systems and technology and operations management. Industrial experience includes: aerospace, automotive, banking and financial services, biomedical, chemicals, consumer goods, electronics, energy, information technology, telecommunications and transport.

Doty Associates Inc

451 Hungerford Drive, Rockville, Maryland 20850, USA
Telephone: (301) 424 0270

Officials:
William B Humphrey, *President and Technical Director*
Ronald G Bryant, *Vice President and Controller*

Doty Associates Inc is a privately-owned, small business firm founded in 1968. The firm specialises in financial management, project control, weapons system analysis, test planning and evaluation, operations research, cost and economic analyses for Department of Defense and other government and state agencies.

Since its foundation, the firm has provided engineering services to the US Navy on a number of high technology programmes. These programmes include both the 2K and 3K Surface Effect Ship (SES) designs, the PHM hydrofoil, the Sea Control Ship and the Vertical Support Ship (VSS). In addition, the firm has been involved in Naval V/STOL aviation studies.

Gibbs & Cox

119 West 31st Street, New York, New York 10001, USA
Telephone: (212) 613 1300
Arlington Office: 1235 Jefferson Davis Highway, Arlington, Virginia 22202, USA
Telephone: (703) 979 1240
Newport News Office: Rouse Tower, 6060 Jefferson Avenue, Newport, Virginia 23605, USA
Telephone: (804) 380 5800

Project management, co-ordination and consultation on conceptual and preliminary designs, contract drawings and specifications and construction drawings for commercial or naval ships of the SES/ACV or submerged hydrofoil systems, destroyers, escorts, frigates, corvettes and VTOL/Helo carriers.

Global Marine Inc

277 West Eldridge, Houston, Texas 77210, USA
Telephone: (713) 596 5100
Officials:
R C Crooke, *President*
R A Bennett, *Vice President, Commercial Products*
S Wetmore, *Vice President, Advanced Development*
Wholly-owned subsidiary:
Arctic Systems Ltd, Calgary, Alberta, Canada

Global Marine Inc was incorporated in 1959 and is engaged primarily in offshore drilling and engineering. However, in 1968 the company undertook an engineering feasibility study directed towards developing equipment and techniques for drilling in Arctic areas. This engineering study led to the development of ACT (Air Cushion Transport) units as the one approach for operating in the area. Global Marine has a continuing design, sales and operations programme directed towards various size ACT (Air Cushion Transport) drilling and transport units. The programme is handled by Global Marine Development Inc, which is a wholly-owned subsidiary of Global Marine Inc.

After using the ACT extensively in the Canadian Arctic, Global Marine redeployed it to Alaska in January 1981, and it has since proved its icebreaking, barge and over ice capabilities. In June 1982 it performed exceptionally well while being towed by a helicopter during difficult spring ice break-up conditions. In February 1984 the unit hauled 100 tonnes plus modules of a complete drilling unit over ice from an offshore drilling island.

Tracor Hydronautics, Inc

7210 Pindell School Road, Howard County, Laurel, Maryland 20707, USA
Telephone: (301) 776 7454
Telex: 87585
Officials:
William M Pugh, *President*
Eugene R Miller Jr, *Technical Director*
Stephen D Clarke, CPA, *Treasurer and Contracting Officer*

The company was founded in July 1959, and has undertaken research, development and design of air cushion vehicles, hydrofoil craft and other high-speed marine vehicles as well as advanced propulsion systems, under US Government and industrial contacts. Tracor Hydronautics has its own ship model basin and high-speed water channel suitable for the evaluation of air cushion vehicles and hydrofoils.

E K Liberatore Company

567 Fairway Road, Ridgewood, New Jersey 07450, USA
Officials:
E K Liberatore, *Head*

Formed in 1964, the company is engaged in both SES and helicopter programmes. Current activity includes:

Design and promotion of 140-passenger and also 400-ton SESs of the airjet configuration (see *Jane's Surface Skimmers 1973-74* and earlier editions). A naval application is also under consideration. Commercial projects with American Hydrolines.

Consultant for hydrofoil and SES operations in metropolitan New York area (with American Hydrolines).

Design and development projects for high performance pressure jet helicopter (for Arabian Aerospace and others).

Design studies and development of Kevlar-epoxy composites for SESs and helicopters, particularly for fans and rotor blades. Two rotor blade sets tested on prototype helicopter.

George E Meese

194 Acton Road, Annapolis, Maryland 21403, USA
Telephone: (301) 263 4054

SES structures.

M Rosenblatt & Son Inc

350 Broadway, New York, New York 10013, USA
Telephone: (212) 431 6900
Officials:
Lester Rosenblatt, *Chairman and Chief Executive Officer*
P W Nelson, *President*
A M Stein, *Vice President*
S Halpern, *Vice President and Manager, Western Division*
N M Maniar, *Vice President and Technical Director*
Z Awer, *Vice President and Head, Mechanical Section*
D M Krepchin, *Vice President and Manager, San Diego Branch*
A Baki, *Vice President and Manager, Washington DC Area Branch*

M Rosenblatt & Son Inc is an established naval architectural and marine engineering firm with over 37 years of proven experience in all phases of ship and marine vehicle design.

With offices in 14 US cities and abroad, the firm is close to the entire shipbuilding community and has a thorough understanding of its problems and needs. Its experience covers programme management and inspection of construction, as well as design.

A major portion of the company's design activities has been and is for the US Navy. Completed assignments are of the broadest possible variety covering research and development, feasibility studies, and conceptual and detail design for all classes of major combatants, auxiliaries, and high performance craft. In addition, the company has provided extensive design services for the conversion, overhaul, and repair of naval combatants, auxiliaries, submarines, amphibious warfare supply and landing craft.

The service to the maritime industry includes a wide variety of tasks covering the new and modification design of oceanographic ships, containerships, tankers, general cargo ships, dredges, bulk carriers, drilling platforms and ships, survey vessels, pipe-laying barges, and a great variety of supporting craft.

Typical ACV assignments include:

ARPA Advanced Surface Effect Vehicles
Conceptual studies, parametric studies and propulsion machinery analysis for phase 'O' studies of Advanced Surface Effect Vehicles for Advanced Research Project Agency. Work performed for American Machine and Foundry Company.

JSESPO Surface Effect Ship Testcraft
Conceptual and feasibility design studies of candidate SES vehicles for the JSESPO sizing study for second generation SES testcraft in the 1,000- to 3,000-ton range. The work included studies of various candidate versions of SES to identify and evaluate their unique operational and design capabilities; technological assessment of various structural materials and systems; preparation of a proposed development programme with required supporting research and development. Work performed for Joint Surface Effect Ship Program office.

Amphibious Fleet Conceptual Studies
Conceptual design studies of various types of ships for future amphibious fleets, including submarine, displacement, planing, hydrofoil and ACV type ships. Studies included technological assessment of performance of the concepts, taking into account various operational capabilities, including speed, propulsion systems, manning, weapons, materials, payloads and costs. Work performed for Stanford Research Institute under basic contract with ONR.

The Surface Effect Ship, Advanced Design and Technology
A 283-page text book covering drag, structure, propulsion, transmission, propulsors, stability, lift systems, seals, auxiliaries, weights, parametric analysis, and sample problems. Each topic is discussed including design procedures and equations. The book was prepared for the US Navy Surface Effect Ships Project Office.

2,000-ton Surface Effect Ship
Trade-off studies, system design parameters, equipment selection, system diagrams, hullborne stability in connection with a complete design proposal. The scope of work included hullborne structural design criteria, electrical power generating and distribution, heating, ventilating, air conditioning, hull appurtenances, piping systems, hotel and auxiliary machinery arrangements. Work performed for the Lockheed Missiles and Space Company and the Surface Effect Ship Project Office.

ACV Amphibian
Conceptual design of a 20-ton capacity air cushion lighter, with retractable wheels, for US Army Mobility Equipment Research and Development Center.

Mine Sweeper Hunter SES
Preliminary and contract design for deck and HVAC systems. Deck systems include mine countermeasures equipment operable in hullborne and cushionborne modes and life-saving equipment for rescue and countermeasure operations. Also, anchoring mooring and emergency towing systems. All work was undertaken for Bell Aerospace Textron.

SRI International (formerly the Stanford Research Institute)

Menlo Park, California 94025, USA
Telephone: (619) 326 6200
Officials:
William F Miller, *President and Chief Executive Officer*

SRI employs about 3,000 staff in offices and laboratories in North America, Europe, East Asia and the Middle East. Each year it undertakes several hundred research projects for the public and private sectors on a wide variety of interests and issues. Overall, SRI's research operations divide into four programme groupings: management and economics, the sciences, engineering and world business.

Science Applications Inc

1200 Prospect Street, La Jolla, California 92037, USA
Telephone: (714) 454 3811

Science Applications Inc provides technical consulting, systems integration and operations services in a wide range of areas in defence, energy and environment. In the area of air cushion vehicles, the company has experience in field operations, engineering consulting and control systems. The company specialises in applications studies and economic analyses for any type of operation involving air cushion systems and heavy lift helicopter operations. The company employs 4,000 technical specialists and has offices in 36 states throughout the USA.

Stevens Institute of Technology Davidson Laboratory

Castle Point Station, Hoboken, New Jersey 07030, USA
Telephone: (201) 420 5300
Officials:
Dr D Savitsky, *Director*

Organised in 1935 as the Experimental Towing Tank, the Laboratory is active in basic and applied hydrodynamic research, including smooth water performance and manoeuvrability, seakeeping, propulsion and control of marine vehicles including ACV, SES and hydrofoil craft. Special model test facilities are available to investigate the dynamic behaviour of all types of vessels and platforms in smooth water and waves.

Martin Stevens

3687 Woodhull Cove, Oldfield Village, Setauket, Long Island, New York 11733, USA

Mechanical design, drive systems.

Water Research Company

3003 North Central Avenue, Suite 600, Phoenix, Arizona 85012, USA
Telephone: (602) 265 7722
Officials:
Richard R Greer, *President, Member of American Society of Naval Engineers*

The Water Research Company was formed in 1972 to consolidate activities surrounding the patents held or applied for by Richard R Greer relating to various aspects of water-borne vehicles. The company has subsequently prepared conceptual studies on a class of winged surface effect vessels (WSEV) intended to fill a variety of US Navy and commercial freight applications. The conclusions of this study were published in the *Naval Engineers' Journal, April 1974,* and further comprehensive conclusions also setting forth energy savings and use of alternate fuels were published in *Jane's Surface Skimmers 1975-76*. Present efforts are directed to providing assistance in related research activities and further research studies.

Wheeler Industries Inc

Executive Office: Board of Trade Building, 1129 20th Street NW, Suite 403, Washington DC 20036, USA
Telephone: (202) 659 1867
Telex: 90 40 84
Systems Research Center: As above
Telephone: (202) 223 1938

Other offices: Hayes Building, Suite 618, 2361 South Jefferson Davis Highway, Arlington, Virginia 22202, USA
Telephone: Suite 618: (703) 521 5005
Airport Plaza Building, Suite 200, 2711 South Jefferson Davis Highway, Arlington, Virginia 22202, USA
Telephone: (703) 892 1500

131 Gaither Drive, Mount Laurel, New Jersey 08054, USA
Telephone: (609) 778 7161

1816 Old Mobile Highway, PO Box 126, Pascagoula, Mississippi 39567, USA
Telephone: (601) 769 6321

Officials:
E Joseph Wheeler, Jr, *President and Chief Executive Officer*
Roy G Shults, *Vice President, Operations and Technical Director, Systems Research Center*
James F Lillis, *Director, Accounting*
Ray Hoop, *Manager, Advanced Craft Programmes*

Wheeler Industries Inc is a privately-owned, small business firm which was founded in 1966 and specialises in systems engineering for ship, air, electronic, and deep ocean systems, as well as oceanographic and environmental research. Since its establishment the company has continuously provided technical, engineering and management support, primarily in the ship acquisition areas, to the US Navy. This support has encompassed a wide range including top level management plans; ship acquisition plans; technology assessments and forecasts; sub-system analysis and trade-offs; development and acquisition requirements and specifications; programme budgeting; development of hydrofoil design data; and hydrofoil strut/foil hydrodynamic load criteria and data. The company employs experienced professionals capable of providing engineering, technical, design and management services associated with hydrofoils, air cushion vehicles and surface effect ships.

The technical and operational functions and capabilities are co-ordinated by the Systems Research Center. Under the Director of the Center, permanently assigned Project Managers (for ship, electronic, and oceanographic systems) form engineering task teams for the duration of a contract or included task(s). They are assisted as necessary by technical support (clerical, graphics, editorial, and reproduction) personnel. This approach allows maximum management visibility and control over each task, and provides optimum response to customers while minimising costs.

HYDROFOIL CONSULTANTS

NIGERIA

H H Snowball

No 13, 204 Close, PO Box 252, Satellite Town, Lagos, Nigeria
Telephone: 880225
Telex: 21886 BECFRE

Founder, in 1968, of Airavia Limited, the first company to represent Sudoimport hydrofoils in the West. Founder of Speed Hydrofoils Limited, which introduced Raketa hydrofoils on scheduled services on the River Thames in 1974. Consultant Bataan-Manila Ferry Services, Hydrofoil Exploration Services etc. Crew training arranged, also feasibility studies of projected hydrofoil routes. Specialising in transport and communications in developing countries.

SWITZERLAND

Dr Ing E G Faber

Gratstrasse 20, CH-8472 Seuzach, Switzerland
Telephone: (052) 53 30 40
Telex: 78670 DATAG-CH

Consultant in marine engine plant planning, marine engineering and marine technology, with special emphasis on high-speed and hydrofoil craft.

GENERAL: Feasibility studies, cost estimates, specifications, plant descriptions.
TECHNICAL EXPERTISE: Speed estimates and hydrodynamic problems.

E Schatté Dipl Ing

Amlehnstrasse 33, CH-6010 Kriens (Luzern), Switzerland
Telephone: 041 41 27 94

Consulting in hydrodynamics, aerodynamics and marine technology, especially high speed craft.

Supramar Hydrofoils AG

Ausserfeld 5, CH-6362 Stansstad, Switzerland
Telephone: (041) 61 31 94
Telex: 78228 Supra CH
Officials:
Baron Hanns von Schertel, *President*
Dipl Ing Harry Trevisani, *General Manager*
Dipl Ing Eugen Schatté, *Research and Development*
Jürg Bally, *Board Member*
Ernst Schneider, *Board Member*

Supramar was founded in Switzerland in 1952 to develop on a commercial basis the hydrofoil system introduced by the Schertel-Sachsenberg Hydrofoil Syndicate and its licensee, the Gebrüder Sachsenberg Shipyard.

Since its foundation, Supramar has provided a world-wide consultancy service, covering not only its hydrofoil vessels but also other aspects of fast marine transport. Its scientists have delivered papers to most of the world's leading professional bodies.

The company has been under contract to many governments and military services.

UNITED KINGDOM

P N Structures Ltd
Marine and Engineering Division

See main entry under ACV consultants.

UNITED STATES OF AMERICA

Doty Associates Inc

See main entry under ACV consultants.

Gibbs & Cox

See main entry under ACV consultants.

Hoerner Fluid Dynamics

PO Box 342, Brick Town, New Jersey 08723, USA
Officials:
S F Hoerner
Dr Ing Habilitatus

Hydrodynamicist of hydrofoils *Sea Legs* and *Victoria*, since 1951. Author of *Fluid-Dynamic Drag* (1965) and *Fluid-Dynamic Lift* (1975).

M Rosenblatt & Son Inc

See main entry under ACV consultants.

Typical hydrofoil assignments include:
AG(EH)
Preliminary design and naval architectural services for preparation of proposal for design and construction of 300-ton AG(EH) Hydrofoil Research Vessel—for Lockheed Aircraft Corporation.
Hydrofoil (LVH)
Provided naval architectural services, including development of lines, powering predictions, stability curves and loading criteria for design and development of a 37-foot Landing Force Amphibious Support Vehicle Hydrofoil (LVH)—for Lycoming Division, Avco Corporation.
Hydrofoil Amphibian
Conceptual design of a 60-ton capacity hydrofoil lighter with retractable wheels for US Army Mobility Equipment Research and Development Center.
Patrol Vessel
Design of 100-ton Mark II/M161 hydrofoil patrol vessel for Grumman Aerospace Corporation.

Stanford Research Institute

See main entry under ACV consultants.

Stevens Institute of Technology Davidson Laboratory

See main entry under ACV consultants.

Systems Exploration, Inc

See main entry under ACV consultants.

Tracor Hydronautics Incorporated

See main entry under ACV consultants.

Water Research Company

See main entry under ACV consultants.

Wheeler Industries Inc

See main entry under ACV consultants.

GLOSSARY

AALC. (US Navy) Amphibious assault landing craft

ACLS. Air cushion landing system

ACS. Automatic control system. See **foil systems, submerged**

ACV. Air cushion vehicle

AGEH. (US Navy) Hydrofoil research ship

AIO. Action information organisation. See also **CIC,** combat information centre. Position allocated to computerised tactical and weapon control centre on light naval craft

AMPS. Arctic marine pipelaying system. Method of laying pipelines in ice-covered Arctic waters employing skirted air cushion barge as icebreaker devised after Arctic Engineers and Constructors Inc successfully and continuously broke ice up to 0·68m (27in) thick using 250-ton ACT-100 platform. On contact with ice sheet, skirt rises above it, maintaining its seal. As ice sheet enters cushion zone, water level beneath is depressed by air pressure. Having lost flotation support, the ice becomes a cantilevered ledge and when it reaches its critical length it breaks off into water below and is then thrust aside by plough-like deflector

ANVCE. (US Navy) Advanced Naval Vehicles Concepts Evaluation Project

APU. Auxiliary power unit

AQL. Aéroglisseur à quille latérale. French term for surface effect ship (SES). Ship-size seagoing air cushion vehicle employing rigid sidewalls and flexible seals fore and aft to contain air cushion

ASW. Anti-submarine warfare

A to N. Aids to navigation

abeam. Position of another craft at side or beam

actuator. Unit designed to translate sensor information and/or computer instructions into mechanical action. Energy is transferred to control surfaces hydraulically, pneumatically or electrically

aeration. See **air entry**

Aérobac. Mixed passenger/car ferries and freighters designed by Bertin and SEDAM

aerodynamic lift. Lifting forces generated by forward motion through atmosphere due to difference in pressure between upper and lower surfaces

aerodynamic profile drag. See **drag**

aerodynamic yaw angle. Angle in horizontal plane between relative air direction and craft centreline

Aerofoil boat, also **winged hull.** Name given by late Dr Alexander M Lippisch, inventor and aircraft designer, to his range of aerodynamic ram-wing machines

Aéroglisseur. Air-glider. Range of passenger-carrying amphibious ACVs designed by Société Bertin & Cie in conjunction with Société d'Études et de Développement des Aéroglisseurs Marins (SEDAM)

aeroplane foil system. Arrangement in which main foil is forward of CG to support 75 to 85 per cent of load, and auxiliary foil, supporting remainder, is located aft as tail assembly

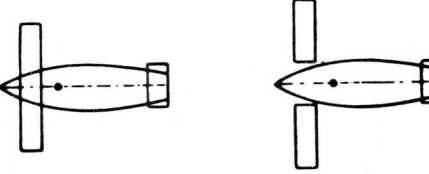

Aeroplane or conventional foil systems. Main foil may be divided into two to facilitate retraction

aerostatic lift. Lift created by self-generated cushion of pressurised air, put under pressure by fan or fans and contained beneath vehicle's structure by flexible seals or sidewalls

Aérosuspendu. Air-suspended. Form of suction-suspended monorail designed in France by Maurice Barthalon for mass public transport on urban and suburban routes. Vehicle is suspended from its track by an air lift system in which pressure is sub-atmospheric. Propulsion is by linear induction motor

Aérotrain. Range of tracked air cushion vehicles under development in France by Société Bertin & Cie

air bleed (ACV). Method of preventing 'plough in' on skirted ACV by bleeding air from cushion through vent holes on outer front of skirt to reduce water drag by air lubrication

air bleed (hyd). See **air stabilisation.** Term occasionally used instead of aeration or air entry

air cushion vehicle. Vehicle capable of being operated so that its weight, including payload, is wholly or significantly supported on a continuously generated cushion or 'bubble' of air at higher than ambient pressure. The air bubble or cushion is put under pressure by a fan or fans and usually contained beneath vehicle's structure by flexible skirts or sidewalls. In USA large or ship-size air cushion vehicles are called **surface effect ships** or **surface effect vessels.** There are two main types of air cushion vehicle: those supported by a self-generated cushion of air and those dependent on forward motion to develop lift. The former are designated aerostatic and the latter, aerodynamic.

Aerodynamic craft include the *ram-wing,* the *channel-flow wing* and the *wing-in-ground-effect.* The *ram-wing* (a) can be likened to a short-span wing with sidewalls attached to its tip. The wing trailing edge and the sidewalls almost touch the water surface. At speed, lifting forces are generated by both the wing and the ram pressure built up beneath. One of the first concepts to use a *channel-flow* wing (b) was the Columbia, designed in the USA by Vehicle Research Corporation in 1961 (*Jane's Surface Skimmers 1967-68*). The design featured a peripheral jet sidewall system for use at low speeds and an aerofoil-shaped hull to provide lift at high speeds during forward flight. The side curtains of the peripheral jet were to be retained to seal the high pressure 'channel' of air developed beneath from the low pressure airflow above and along the sides of the craft, down to the water surface. A 9·1-metre (30-foot) manned model of the Columbia was successfully tested in 1964.

The *wing-in-ground-effect* (c) is essentially an aircraft designed to fly in close proximity to the earth's surface, in order to take advantage of the so-called 'image' flow that reduces induced drag by about 70 per cent. In the Soviet Union this type of machine is known as an ekranoplan.

Aerostatic-type air cushion vehicles can be divided into two categories—plenum chamber craft and peripheral or annular jet craft. *Plenum chamber craft* (d) employ the most simple of surface effect concepts. Air is forced from the lift fan directly into a recessed base where it forms a cushion which raises the craft. The volume of air pumped into the base is just sufficient to replace the air leaking out beneath the edges.

Variants of this category include the *skirted plenum craft* (e), in which a flexible fabric extension is hung between the metal structure and the

270-ton Soviet Aist

BHC AP.1-88

Bell LCAC

Bell Halter Model 730A (SES-200)

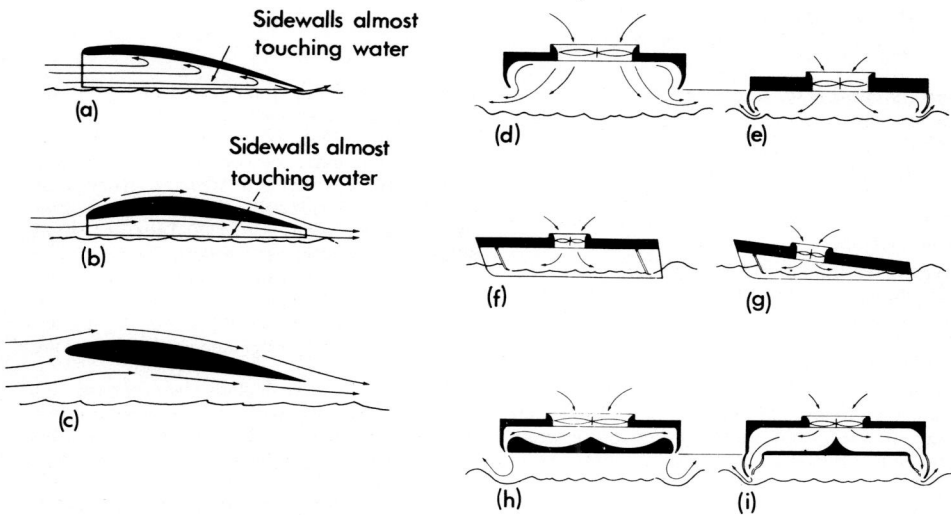

(a) ram wing (b) channel-flow wing (c) wing-in-ground-effect (d) plenum chamber (e) plenum chamber with skirt (f) captured air bubble (g) hydrokeel (h) annular jet (i) trunked annular jet

surface to give increased obstacle and overwave clearance capability. The Naviplane and Terra-planes designed by Bertin and SEDAM employ separately fed multiple plenum chambers, each surrounded by lightweight flexible skirts. Skirted plenum chamber types are also favoured by builders of light air cushion vehicles because of their relatively simple design and construction.

Another variant is the *sidewall* ACV (f), in which the cushion air is contained between solid sidewalls or skegs and deflectable seals, either solid or flexible, fore and aft. Stability is provided by the buoyancy of the sidewalls and their planing forces. One of the derivatives of the sidewall type is the *Hydrokeel* (g) which is designed to plane on the after section of its hull and benefit to some degree from air lubrication.

In *peripheral* or *annular jet craft* (h) the ground cushion is generated by a continuous jet of air channelled through ducts or nozzles around the outer periphery of the base. The flexible skirts fitted to this type can take the form of an extension to the outer wall of the duct or nozzle only, or as an extension to both outer and inner walls. In the latter form it is known as a *trunked annular jet* (i).

air entry, also **air entrainment**. Entry of air from atmosphere that raises low pressures created by flow due to foil's cambered surface

air gap area. Area beneath skirt through which air can leak from cushion

air gap (effective hoverheight). Air gap area divided by skirt periphery

air gap (local). Distance between local skirt hem and surface when craft is riding on its cushion

air momentum drag. Drag created by acceleration of air forming cushion from static to speed of hovercraft under way, relative to surrounding air

air pad. Part of air pallet assembly into which compressed air is introduced and allowed to escape in continuous flow through communicating holes in diaphragm

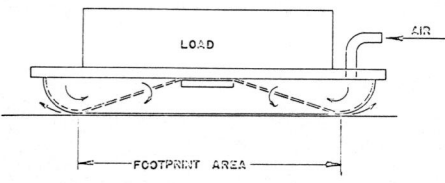

Air pad with flexible plastic diaphragm

air pallet, also **hoverpallet**. Air cushion supported load-carrying structure which bleeds continuous low pressure volume of air between structure and reaction surface, creating air film

air-port system. See **control ducts**

Air Ride ACVs. Range of non-amphibious vehicles combining appearance of conventional hulls with low hydrodynamic drag of surface effect ships. Hulls incorporate long shallow plenum chamber for pressurised air in underside aft of

conventional bow. Air is fed into chamber by mixed-flow fan and is retained by two shallow sidewalls and transverse frames fore and aft. Efficiency is comparable to SES or sidewall hover-craft.

air-rider. Alternative generic name for air cushion vehicles or weight-carrying structures lifted off surface by cushion or film of air

air stabilised foils. See **foil systems**

amidships. (1) Midway between stem and stern of hull. (2) abbreviated to **midships** and signifying rudder or helm is in mid-position

Amphibarge. Range of amphibious air cushion barges, self-propelled or towed, designed in France by SEDAM

angle of attack. Angle made by mean chord line of aero- or hydrofoil with flow

angle of incidence. Angle made by mean chord line of hydrofoil in relation to fixed struts or hull

anti-bounce web. Tensioned skirt membrane connected between upper and lower bag points to restrain self-sustained vibration or 'bounce'

Aquavion type foil. Adapted from Grunberg system. About 85% of load is carried by mainfoil slightly aft of CG, 10% by submerged aft stabiliser foil, and remainder on pair of planing subfoils at bow. Planing subfoils give variable lift in response to wave shapes, whether skimming over or through them, and so trim angle of hull in order to correct angle of attack of main foil

articulated air cushion vehicle. Modular type load-carrying platform designed by Charles Burr of Bell Aerospace. Skirted platforms can be joined to form variety of ACVs of different load-carrying capacities

aspect ratio. (1) measure of ratio of foil's span to its chord, defined as

$$\frac{span^2}{total\ foil\ area}$$

(2) for ACVs defined as $\frac{cushion\ beam}{cushion\ length}$

attack craft. Small warship fitted with at least two major weapons

athwart, athwartship. Transversely across the hull from one side to other

axial flow lift fan. Fan generating airflow for lift that is parallel to axis of rotation

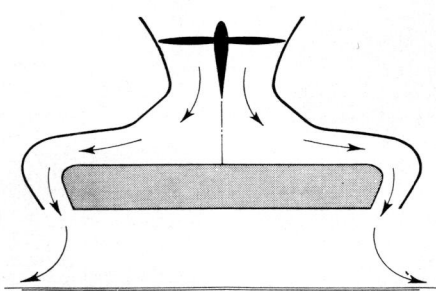

Axial flow lift fan

BTC. Buoyancy tank clearance. See **clearance**

backstrap. Fabric strap used to secure lift jet exit nozzle in flexible skirt at correct angle

baffle plates. See **fences**

bag perimeter. Perimeter of sideskirt bag or loop from outer to inner hinge, or from outer loop attachment to inner tie attachment of super-structure

ballast system. Method of transferring water or fuel between tanks to adjust fore-and-aft and/or lateral trim. In 'Mountbatten' class ACVs, four groups of tanks, one at each corner, are located in the buoyancy tanks. Ring main facilitates rapid transfer of fuel between tanks as ballast and also serves as refuelling line

base ventilated foil. System of forced ventilation to overcome reduction in lift/drag ratio of foil at supercavitating speeds. Air is fed continuously to upper surface of foil, un-wetting surface and preventing formation of critical areas of decreased pressure. Alternatively, air may be fed into cavity formed behind square trailing edge

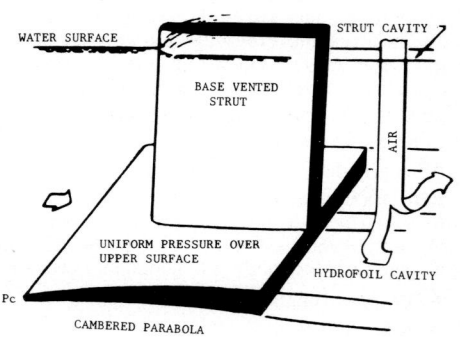

Base ventilated foil

beam. Measurement across hull at given point

beam-on. Sideways movement of craft, ie at 90 degrees angle of yaw

Beaufort Scale. Scale of wind forces described by name and range of velocity and classified from force 0 to force 12, or strong hurricanes to force 17. See **sea state**

bilge. Point of hull where side and bottom meet. Also water or fuel accumulated in bilges

bilge system. Pumping system to dispose of water and other fluids accumulated in bilges. In ACVs bilge systems are installed to clear buoyancy tanks. Small craft generally have hand-operated pump which connects directly to pipes in tanks. Larger craft, like 200- to 300-ton BHC Mountbatten, because of large number of buoyancy compartments, have four electrically driven pumps, each of which can drain one compartment at a time

block speed. Route distance divided by block time

block time, also **trip time**. Journey time between lift off and touchdown

boating. ACV when operating in displacement condition. Boating or **semi-hover** mode is used in congested terminal areas, when lift power and spray generation is kept to minimum. Some craft have water surface contact even at full hover for stability requirements

bow-up. Trim position or attitude when craft is high at bow. Can be measured by eye or attitude gyro

breast, to. To take waves at 90 degrees to their crests

Breguet range. Approximate range of craft based on average values of propulsion efficiency, specific fuel consumption and ratio of initial to final gross weight, assuming constant lift-to-drag ratio

broach, to. Sudden breaking of water surface by foil, or part of foil, resulting in loss of lift due to air flowing over foil's upper surface

to broach to. To swing sideways in following seas under wave action

bulkheads. Vertical partitions, either transverse or longitudinal, which divide or sub-divide hull. May be used to separate accommodation areas, strengthen structure, form tanks or localise fires or flooding

buoyancy. Reduction in weight of floating object. If object floats its weight is equal to (or less than) weight of fluid displaced

buoyancy chamber. Structure of which the weight and all loads which it supports is equal to (or less than) weight of water it displaces

buoyancy, reserve. Buoyancy in excess of that required to keep undamaged craft afloat. See **buoyancy**

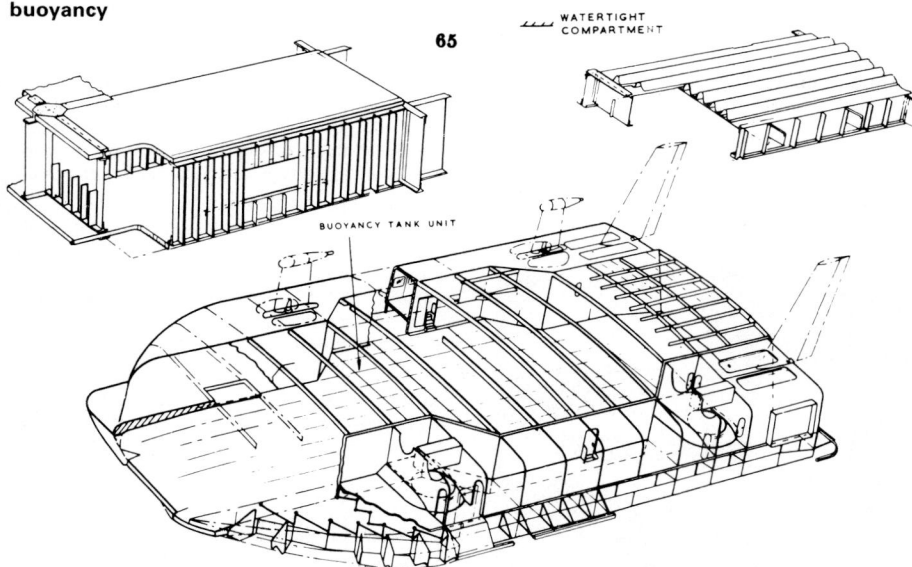

FUEL TANK

WATERTIGHT COMPARTMENT

65

Typical buoyancy tank unit on SR.N4. Basic structure of SR.N4 is buoyancy chamber, built around grid of longitudinal and transversal frames which form 24 watertight sub-divisions for safety. Below, SR.N4 buoyancy tank layout

buoyancy tubes. Inflatable tubular members providing reserve buoyancy. May be used as fenders if fitted to outer periphery of craft

CAA. Civil Aviation Authority

CAB. Captured air bubble. See **air cushion vehicle**

CIC. Combat information centre

cp. Centre of pressure

CP shifter. Control system which moves centre of pressure of supporting cushion(s) relative to CG of ACV to augment a craft's natural stability in pitch and roll

CPIC. Coastal patrol interdiction craft

CWL. Calm water line

camber. (1) convexity on upper surface of deck to increase strength and/or facilitate draining. (2) convex form on upper surface of foil: high-speed flow over top surface decreases pressure and about two-thirds of lift is provided by this surface

canard foil system. Foil arrangement with main foil of wide span near stern, aft of CG, bearing about 65 per cent of weight, and small central foil at bow

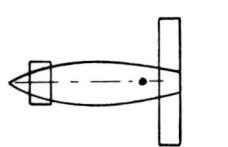 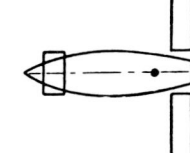

Canard foil configuration. Main foil area may be divided in to two to facilitate retraction

captured air bubble craft (see also **sidewall craft** and **surface effect ship**). Vessel in which cushion (or air bubble) is contained by rigid sidewalls and flexible bow and stern skirts. Occasionally used for any air cushion craft in which air cushion (or air bubble) is contained within cushion periphery with minimal air leakage

cavitation. Formation of vapour bubbles due to pressure decrease on upper surface of foil or back of propeller's blades at high speeds. Non-stable

cavities or cavitation bubbles of aqueous vapour form near foil's leading edge and extend down stream expanding and collapsing. At points of collapse positive pressure peaks can rise to 20,000psi causing erosion and pitting of the metal. Cavitation causes unstable water flow over foils resulting in abrupt changes in lift and therefore discomfort for those aboard.

Foil sections being developed either delay onset of cavitation by reduced camber, thinner sections, or sweepback, or if craft is required to operate at supercavitating speeds, stabilise cavitation to provide smooth transition between sub-cavitating and super-cavitating speeds

centrifugal flow lift fan. Cushion lift fan which generates airflow at right angles to axis of rotation

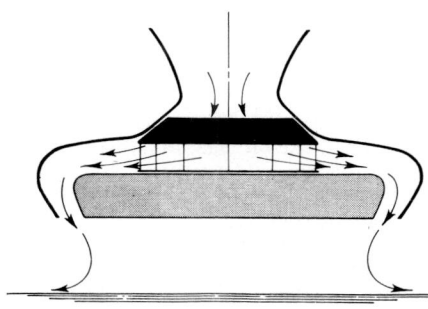

Centrifugal flow lift fan

chain ties. Chains used to maintain correct shape of air jet exit nozzle on flexible skirt

chip bag. Skirt segment, usually at rear of craft, with additional wall on side facing into cushion to prevent water scooping

chord. Distance between leading and trailing edges of foil section measured along chord-line

chord-line. Straight line joining leading and trailing edges of foil or propeller blade section

classification. Commercial seagoing and amphibious craft are classified by mode and place of construction by Lloyd's Register of Shipping for the United Kingdom. Other classification

societies include Registro Italiano Navale, Germanischer Lloyd, Det Norske Veritas, American Bureau of Shipping and the Japanese Ministry of Transport.

clearance. Distance between hard structure, eg buoyancy tank, and surface

coastal vessel. Vessel able to operate in up to sea state 5 and which would normally seek shelter in gales

cones. Cone-shaped fingers often fitted to rear of skirt bags to minimise scooping

continuous nozzle skirt. See **skirt**

contour, to. Motion of air cushion vehicle or hydrofoil when more or less following wave profile

control ducts, also **puff ports, thrusters** and **yaw ducts.** Controlled apertures in skirt system, or cushion supply ducting, through which air can be expelled to assist control at low speeds

craft. Vessel with one main deck in hull

critical depth speed. Overwater speed at which theoretical wavemaking behaviour changes, with discontinuity in wavemaking drag

critical speed. Low speed at which hovercraft, moving beam-on, is most vulnerable to overturn, generally when close to or slightly beneath primary hump speed for beam-on motion

cross-flow. Flow of air, transversally or longitudinally within air cushion

curtain. Fluid flow issuing from ducts or nozzles beneath hovercraft, either to contain or divide a cushion

cushion. Volume of higher than ambient pressure air enclosed between bottom of air cushion vehicle and its supporting surface by rigid structure, air curtains, skirts or combination of all three

cushion area. Area of cushion in planform at supporting surface

cushion beam. Maximum width of air cushion in planform at supporting surface

cushion borne. Craft borne above sea or land surface by its air cushion

cushion length. Maximum length of air cushion in planform at supporting surface

cushion length, mean. Defined as:

$$\frac{\text{cushion area}}{\text{cushion beam}}$$

cushion pumping. See **wave pumping**

cushion seal. Air curtains, sidewalls, skirts, water-jets or other means of containing or sealing air cushion to minimise leakage of trapped air

cushion stiffness. Slope of curve of applied moment plotted against angle. See **roll and pitch stiffness**

cushion system. Means by which cushion(s) of air beneath hovercraft is maintained and controlled

cushion thrust. Thrust obtained by deflection of cushion air

DEF spec. Standard of specification for military equipment operated by UK

DTNSRDC. (US Navy) David W Taylor Naval Ships Research and Development Center

DWL. Displacement water line.

deadrise. Angle with horizontal made at keel by outboard rise of vessel's hull form at each frame

delta wing. Triangular aircraft wing designed and developed by the late Dr Alexander Lippisch and employed in his series of Aerofoil Boats. Applied also in Soviet Union because of its high aerodynamic qualities and stability for range of Ekranolyet aerodynamic ram-wings

differential pressure rate. Rate of change of cushion pressure differential across cushion divider with roll or pitch angle

diffuser-recirculation. See **recirculation system**

displacement. Weight in tons of water displaced by floating vessel. Light displacement: craft weight exclusive of ballast

ditch, to. To set down hovercraft, while still in motion, by deliberate collapse of cushion

Three aerodynamic air cushion vehicles. **Left to right**: Jörg IV Skimmerfoil; Lippisch Rhein-Flugzeugbau X-113 Am and Soviet experimental wing-in-ground-effect machine designed by late Robert Oros di Bartini

Doppler, navigator. Automatic dead reckoning device gives continuous indication of position by integrating speed derived from measuring Doppler effect of echoes from directed beams of radiant energy transmitted from vessel

down-by-the-head. Trim or sit of craft with bow more deeply immersed than stern. Opposite is 'down-by-the-stern'

draught, draft. Depth between water surface and bottom of craft. Under Ministry of Transport Merchant Shipping (Construction) rules, 1952, draught is defined as vertical distance from moulded base line amidships to sub-division load waterline

draught, draft marks. (1) marks on side of craft showing depth to which it can be loaded. (2) figures cut at stern and stem to indicate draught and trim

drag. (1) ACVs: aerodynamic and hydrodynamic resistances resulting from aerodynamic profile, gain of momentum of air needed for cushion generation, wave making, wetting or skirt contact.
(2) hydrofoils: hydrodynamic resistances resulting from wave making, which is dependent on craft shape and displacement, frictional drag due to viscosity of water, total wetted surface and induced drag from foils and transmission shafts and their supporting struts and structure, due to their motion through water

drift angle. Difference between course and track of craft

EC. Escort carrier

ECCM. Electronic counter-countermeasures: ability of search radar installation to overcome enemy jamming, chaff and other countermeasures

ESKA. (Russian) Ekranolytny Spasatyelny Kater Amphibiya (screen-effect amphibious lifeboat). Series of small wing-in-ground-effect machines developed by Central Laboratory of Lifesaving Technology, Moscow. Also known as Ekranolyet or Nizkolet (skimmer)

ESM. Electronic support measures: active, passive and analysing electronic equipment, including chaff launchers and flare dispensing systems

efficiency (propulsive). Ratio of useful work performed (ie thrust times relative velocity through air or water) to total input power

Ekranoplan. (Russian, from *ekran*, a screen or curtain, and *plan*, principal supporting surface of aeroplane) Types of ACV in the Soviet Union raised above their supporting surfaces by dynamic lift. Western equivalent, wing-in-ground-effect machines (WIG), aerodynamic ram-wings and power-augmented ram-wings

elevator. Movable aerodynamic control surface used on small hovercraft to provide degree of fore-and-aft trim control. Elevator surfaces are normally in slipstream of propulsive units to provide some control at low speed

extended-range vessel. Small warship capable of up to 14 days' continuous unsupported operation at 14 to 18 knot patrol speeds for 2,500 to 4,000 nautical miles or vessel capable of over 1,000 nautical miles at maximum speed

FLD. Full load displacement

FPB. Fast patrol boat

FWL. Foilborne water line

fast vessel. Vessel capable of 25 to 35 knots

fences. Small partitions at short intervals down upper and lower surfaces of hydrofoil tending to prevent air ventilation passing down to destroy lift, attached in direction of flow

Fences on bow foil of Supramar hydrofoil

fetch. Distance given wind has blown over open water or distance upwind to nearest land

finger. One of a series of flexible sheet members forming lower part of seal of hovercraft cushion boundary

fire zone. Compartment containing full supply and ignition source which is walled with fire resisting material and fitted with independent fire warning and extinguishing system

flare. Upward and outward curvature of freeboard at bow, presenting additional, rising surface to oncoming waves

flexible skirt. See **skirt**

flying bridge. Navigating position atop wheel or chart house

foilborne. (Hydrofoil) with hull raised completely out of water and wholly supported by lift from foil system

foil flaps. (a) trailing edge flaps for lift augmentation during take-off and to provide control forces, (b) upper and lower flaps to raise cavitation boundary

foil systems. Foil systems in current use are generally **surface piercing**, **submerged** or **semi-submerged.** There are a number of craft with hybrid systems with a combination of submerged and surface piercing foils, recent examples being the Supramar PT 150 and the de Havilland FHE-400

surface piercing foils are usually V-shaped, the upper parts of the foil forming the tips of the V and piercing the surface on either side of the craft. The V foil, with its marked dihedral, is area stabilised and craft employing this configuration can be designed to be inherently stable and, for stability, geometry dependent.
The forces restoring normal trim are provided by the area of the foil that is submerged. A roll to one side means the immersion of increased foil area, which results in the generation of extra lift to counter the roll and restore the craft to an even keel.

Equally, a downward pitching movement at the bow means an increase in the submerged area of the forward foil, and the generation of extra lift on this foil, which raises the bow once more. Should the bow foil rise above its normal water level the lift decreases in a similar way to restore normal trim. This type of foil is also known as an **emerging foil system.**
As the V-foil craft increases its speed, so it generates greater lift and is raised further out of the water—at the same time reducing the wetted area and the lift. The lift must be equal to the weight of the craft and, as the lift depends on the speed and wetted foil area, the hull rides at a pre-determined height above the water level.

ladder foils. Also come under the heading surface piercing, but are rarely used now. This is one of the earliest foil arrangements and was used by Forlanini in his 1905 hydro-aeroplane, which was probably the first really successful hydrofoil. In 1911 Alexander Graham Bell purchased Forlanini's patent specifications and used his ladder system on his Hydrodomes, one of which, the HD-4, set up a world speed record of 61·5 knots in 1919. Early ladder foils, with single sets of foils beneath the hull, fore and aft, lacked lateral stability, but this was rectified later by the use of two sets of forward foils, one on each side of the hull. The foils were generally straight and set at right angles to their supporting struts, but were occasionally of V configuration, the provision of dihedral preventing a sudden change of lift as the foils broke the surface. Both the V foil and the ladder systems are self-stabilising to a degree. The V foil has the advantage of being a more rigid, lighter structure and is less expensive.
Primary disadvantages of the conventional surface-piercing systems in comparison with the submerged foil system are: (a) the inability of V-foil craft without control surfaces to cope with downward orbital velocities at wave crests when overtaking waves in a following sea, a condition which can decrease the foil's angle of attack, reducing lift and causing wave contact or a stall; (b) on large craft the weight and size of the surface-piercing system is considerably greater than that of a corresponding submerged foil system; (c) restoring forces to correct a roll have to pass above the centre of gravity of the craft, which necessitates the placing of the foils only a short distance beneath the hull. This means a relatively low wave clearance and therefore the V foil is not suited to routes where really rough weather is encountered.

shallow-draught submerged foil system. This system, which incorporates the Grunberg angle of attack variation approach, is employed almost exclusively on hydrofoils designed and built in the Soviet Union and is intended primarily for passenger carrying craft used on long, calm water rivers, canals and inland seas. The system, also known as the immersion depth effect system, was evolved by Dr Rostislav Alexeyev. It generally comprises two main horizontal foils, one forward, one aft, each carrying approximately half the weight of the vessel. A submerged foil loses lift gradually as it approaches the surface from a depth of about one chord, which prevents it from rising completely to the surface. Means have to be provided to assist take-off and prevent the vessel from sinking back into the displacement mode. Planing subfoils, port and starboard, are therefore provided in the vicinity of the forward struts, and are so located that when they are

These military hydrofoils illustrate three foil systems. **Left to right:** One of Soviet Navy's 250-ton Turya torpedo boats equipped with surface-piercing V foil set back approximately one-third of hull length from bow. It employs bow foil only and achieves 'sprint' speed of 40-45 knots; 105-tonne Grumman-designed

Shimrit of Israeli Navy, with incidence-controlled fully-submerged foils in aeroplane configuration and Boeing NATO/PHM with fully-submerged canard system, 32 per cent of dynamic lift provided by bow foil and 68 per cent by aft foil. Lift is controlled by trailing edge flaps on each foil

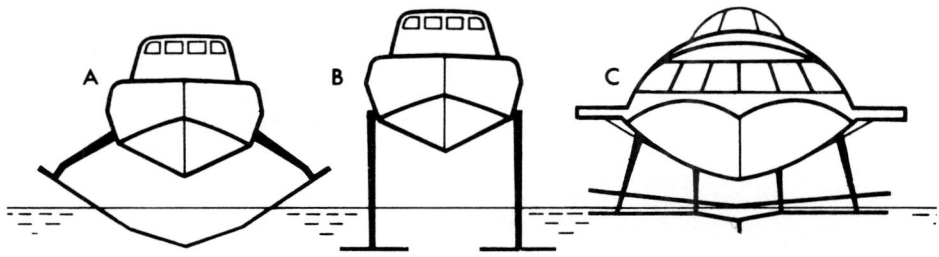

Foil systems in current use. **A** surface piercing, **B** submerged and **C** shallow draught submerged

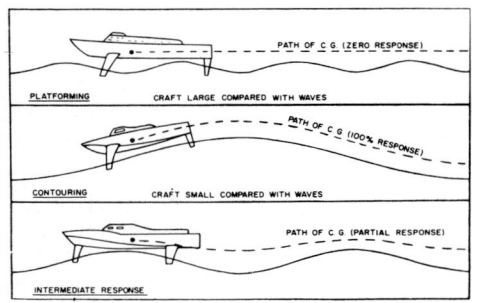

Comparison of platforming and contouring modes, and intermediate response of craft equipped with fully submerged, automatically controlled foil system

touching the water surface, the main foils are submerged at a depth of approximately one chord.

submerged foils. These have a greater potential for seakeeping than any other type of foil, but are not inherently stable to any degree. They are totally immersed and a sonic, mechanical or air stabilisation system has to be installed to maintain the foils at the required depth. The system has to stabilise the craft from take-off to touchdown in heave and all three axes—pitch, roll and yaw. It must also ensure that the craft makes co-ordinated banked turns in heavy seas to reduce the side loads on the foil struts; maintain vertical and lateral accelerations within limits to prevent excessive structural loads and ensure a smooth ride.

The control forces are generated by deflecting flaps at the trailing edge of the foil or by varying the incidence angle of the entire foil surface. Incidence control provides better performance in a high sea state.

The key element of a typical automatic control system is an acoustic height sensor located at the bow. The time lag of the return signal is a measure of the distance of the sensor from the water.

Craft motion input is received from dual sonic ranging devices which sense the height above the water of the bow in relation to a fixed reference; from three rate gyros which measure yaw, pitch and roll; from forward and aft accelerometers which sense vertical acceleration fore and aft and from a vertical gyro which senses the angular position of the craft in both pitch and roll. This information is processed by an electronic computer and fed continuously to hydraulic actuators of the foil control surfaces, which develop the necessary hydrodynamic forces for stability producing forces imposed by wave action manoeuvring and correct flight

mechanical incidence control. The most successful purely mechanically operated incidence control system is the Hydrofin autopilot principle, designed by Christopher Hook, who pioneered the development of the submerged foil. A fixed, high-riding crash preventer plane is mounted ahead of and beneath the bow.

The fixed plane, which is only immersed when the craft is in a displacement mode, is also used as a platform for mounting a lightweight pitch control sensor which is hinged to the rear.

The sensor rides on the waves and continuously transmits their shape through a connecting linkage to vary the angle of incidence of the main foils as necessary to maintain them at the required depth. A filter system ensures that the craft ignores small waves and that the hull is flown over the crests of waves exceeding the height of the keel over the water.

Two additional sensors, trailing from port and starboard immediately aft of the main struts, provide roll control. The pilot has overriding control through a control column, operated in the same manner as that in an aircraft.

air stabilisation system. A system designed and developed by Baron Hanns von Schertel of Supramar AG, Lucerne. Air from the free atmosphere is fed through air exits to the foil upper surface and, under certain conditions, the lower surface (ie into the low pressure regions). The airflow decreases the lift and the flow is deflected away from the foil section with an effect similar to that of a deflected flap, the air cavities extending out behind producing a virtual lengthening of the foil profile. Lift is reduced and varied by the quantity of air admitted, this being

controlled by a valve actuated by signals from a damped pendulum and a rate gyro. The pendulum causes righting moments at static heeling angles. If exposed to a centrifugal force in turning, it causes a moment, which is directed towards the centre of the turning circle, thereby avoiding outside banking (co-ordinated banking). The rate gyro responds to angular velocity and acts dynamically to dampen rolling motions

force time effectiveness. Time to land effective landing force ashore

fore peak. Space forward of fore collision bulkhead, frequently used as storage space

frames. Structure of vertical ribs or girders to which vessel's outside plates are attached. For identification frames are numbered consecutively, starting aft

freeboard. Depth of exposed or free side of hull between water level and freeboard deck. Degree of freeboard permitted is marked by load lines

freeboard deck. Deck used to measure or determine loadlines

free power turbine. Gas turbine on which power turbine is on separate shaft from compressor and its turbine

full hover. Condition of ACV at its design hoverheight

furrowing. Condition of foilborne operation of hydrofoil caused by contact of lower part of hull and keel with crests of larger waves. Contact is brief and does not prevent craft from remaining foilborne. See also **hull cresting**

GEM. Ground effect machine

grp. Glass-reinforced plastics

gross tonnage. Total tonnage of vessel, including all enclosed spaces, estimated on basis of $100ft^2 = 1$ ton

ground effect machine. Early generic term for ACVs of all types

Grunberg foil system. First patented in 1936, the Grunberg principle of inherent angle of attack variations comprises a 'stabiliser' attached to the bow or a forward projection from the latter, and behind this a 'foil'. Both foil and stabiliser can be 'split' into several units. The lift curve of the stabiliser, plotted against its draught, is considerably steeper than its corresponding foil lift curve. Hence, as the operational conditions

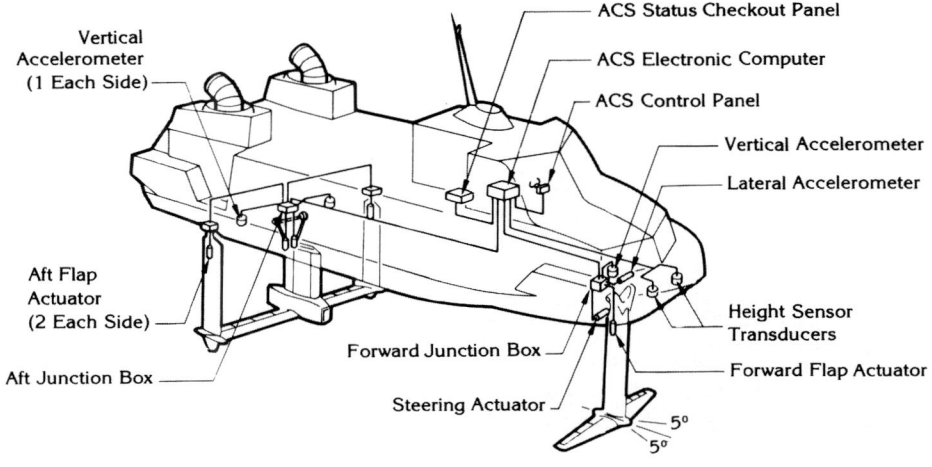

Automatic control system on Jetfoil 929-320

(speed, weight, CG travel) change, the foil sinks or rises relative to the stabiliser, automatically adjusting its angle of attack. The 'foil' is set at an appropriate angle of incidence to prevent it from approaching the interface. The system is fully compatible with Forlanini's concept of area variation and both can be incorporated in the same structure

HATS. Harbour acceptance trials. Equipment trials undertaken in harbour

HYSWAS. Hydrofoil small waterplane area ship

hard chine. Hull design with topsides and bottom meeting at an angle, rather than curving to round bilge

hard structure. Any structure (hard or flexible but excluding skirts) which may create a capsizing or righting moment when in contact with water

head sea. Sea approaching from direction steered

heave. Vertical motion of craft in response to waves

heave stiffness. Rate of change of restoring force in heave direction with displacement in that direction

heel. (a) Incline or list in transverse direction while under way. (b) Lower end of mast or derrick. (c) Point where keel and stern post meet

Helibarge. System devised by Walter A Crowley (USA) combining helicopter and air cushion barge. Helicopter's downwash rotor pressurises air cushion

hemline. Lowest peripheral edge of hovercraft skirt

high-speed vessel. Vessel with speed of 36 knots and over

hinge spacing (horizontal). Horizontal distance between inner and outer 'hinges' or attachment points to structure

hinge spacing (vertical). Vertical distance between inner and outer 'hinges' or attachment points to structure

hoverbarge. Fully buoyant, shallow-draught hovercraft built for freight carrying. Either self-propelled or towed

hovercraft. (a) Originally craft using patented peripheral jet principle invented by Sir Christopher Cockerell, in which air cushion is generated and contained by jet of air exhausted downward and inward from nozzle at periphery at base of vehicle. (b) Classification in USA for skirted plenum chamber and annular jet-designs. (c) In British Hovercraft Act 1968, a vehicle designed to be supported when in motion wholly or partly by air expelled from vehicle to form cushion of which boundaries include ground, water or other surface beneath vehicle

hover height. Vertical height between hard structure of ACV and supporting surface when vehicle is cushion-borne

hover-listen. ACVs employed for ASW operating at low speeds to detect target

hover pallet. See **air pallet**

hoverplatform. Non self-propelled hovercraft designed primarily to convey heavy loads across terrain impassable to wheeled and tracked vehicles under load

Mackace 50-ton hoverplatform

hoverport. Defined by British Hovercraft Act 1968 as any area, whether land or elsewhere, which is designed, equipped, set apart or commonly used for affording facilities for arrival and departure of hovercraft

hoversled. Vehicle for operation on ice and snow combining features of air cushion vehicle with skis or pontoons. Contact between vehicle's skis and supporting surface beneath gives better directional control than on most conventional skirted ACVs operating over ice and snow

hovertrailer. Steel structure platform around which is fitted flexible segmented skirt, cushion lift being provided by fans. Devised by Air Cushion Equipment Ltd and Hover Systems Ltd, system is designed to increase load capacity of tracked and wheeled vehicles many times. In cases where it is impossible for tow vehicle to operate, trailer can be winched

Hovertrailer with payload of 6·7 tons at 100lb/ft²

hull. Body or frame of a vessel regardless of size.

hull cresting. Contact of hydrofoil's hull with waves in high seas

hull slamming. Contact of hydrofoil's hull with water following foil broach. See **broach, to**

hump. 'Hump' formed on graph of resistance against speed of displacement vessel or ACV. Maximum of 'hump' corresponds to speed of wave generated by hull or air depression

hump speed. Speed over water at which there is peak value of wave-making drag. In general there will be several hump speeds, the highest being 'primary hump speed'

hydrodynamic yaw angle. Angle in horizontal plane between longitudinal axis of hovercraft and instantaneous direction of motion relative to local water surface

hydrofoils. Small wings, almost identical in section to those of aircraft and designed to generate lift. Since water is 815 times denser than air, same lift as aeroplane wing is obtained for only $1/_{815}$ of area (at equal speeds)

hydrofoil small waterplane area ship. Projected hybrid vessel comprising a single submerged hull with fully submerged foil system and upper hull structure supported by vertical strut or struts. At low speeds craft is supported by buoyancy of submerged hull, strut, and lower section of upper hull. At speed dynamic lift generated by foil system raises upper hull out of water with reduction of waterplane area of strut

hydroskimmer. Experimental air cushion vehicles built under contract to US Navy Bureau of Ships. Preference was given to this name since it gave craft sea-service identity

IOC. (US Navy) Initial operational capability

IOT&E. (US Navy) Initial operational testing and evaluation

IPV. Inshore patrol vessel

inclined shaft. Marine drive shaft used in small V foil and shallow-draught submerged foil craft, with keels only limited height above mean water level. Shaft is generally short and inclined at about 12 to 14 degrees to horizontal. On larger craft, designed for operation in higher waves, need to fly higher necessitates alternative drive arrangements such as V- and Z-drive, water jet system or even air propulsion

induced wave drag. Drag caused by hollow depressed in water by ACV's air cushion. As craft moves forward depression follows beneath, building up bow wave and causing wave drag as in displacement craft until hump speed has been passed

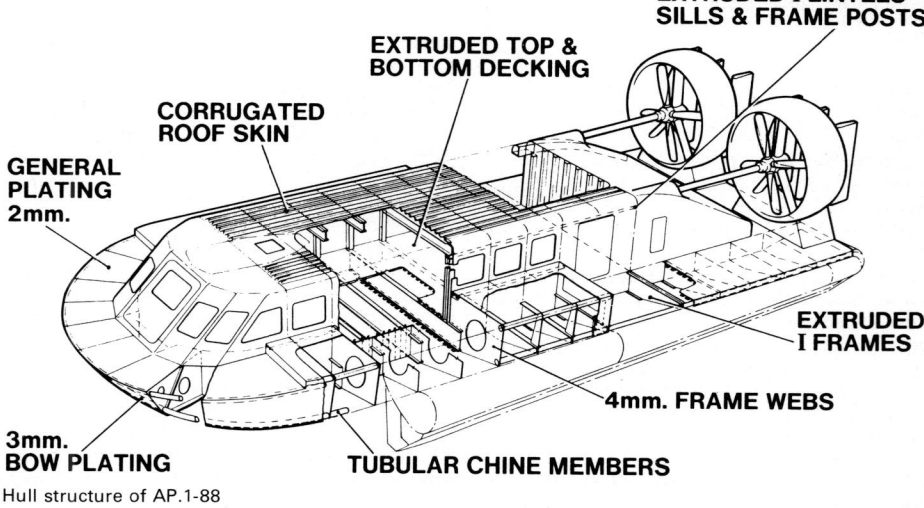

Hull structure of AP.1-88

EXTRUDED I LINTELS SILLS & FRAME POSTS
EXTRUDED TOP & BOTTOM DECKING
CORRUGATED ROOF SKIN
GENERAL PLATING 2mm.
EXTRUDED I FRAMES
3mm. BOW PLATING
4mm. FRAME WEBS
TUBULAR CHINE MEMBERS

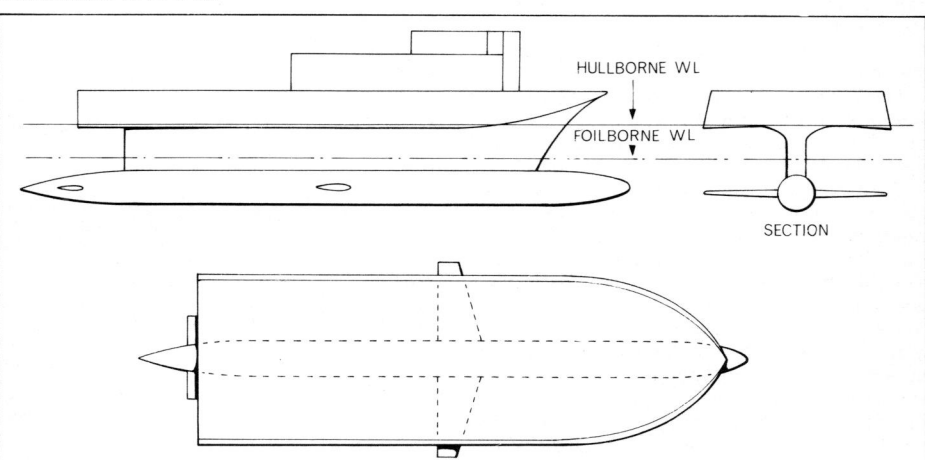

Hydrofoil small waterplane area ship (HYSWAS)

inshore vessel. Vessel able to operate in up to sea state 3. It would normally not operate in conditions above sea state 5 and would need to seek shelter in gales

integrated lift-propulsion system. ACV lift and propulsion system operated by a common power source, transmission and power-sharing system allowing variation in division of power

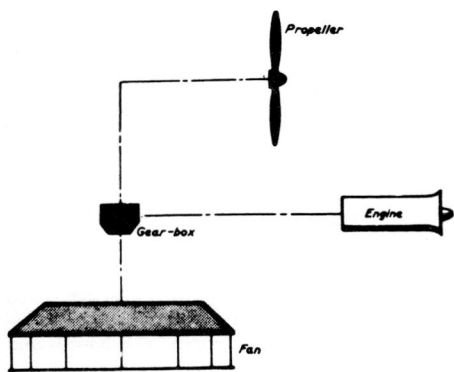

Integrated lift-propulsion system

JP-4. Liquid fuel, based on kerosene, used widely in gas turbines

keel. (a) 'backbone' of hull. (b) extension of ACV's fore-and-aft stability air jet, similar in construction and shape to skirt, and taking form of inflated bag

knitmesh pads. Thick, loosely woven pads of metal or plastic wire in engine's air intake to filter out water and solid particles from engine air

LACTA. Light air cushion triphibious aircraft

LCAC. (US Navy) Landing craft, air cushion

LCG. Longitudinal distance measurement (from appropriate datum) of CG

LHA. (US Navy) Amphibious assault ship, general purpose

LOTS. (US Navy) Logistics over-the-shore

LPD. (US Navy) Amphibious transport dock

LSD. (US Navy) Dock landing ship

land, to. At end of runs hydrofoils and ACVs are said to 'settle down' or 'land'

landing pads. Strong points protruding below rigid bottom of hovercraft which support vehicle at rest on land. Can also provide attachment points for towing equipment, lifts and jacks

leading frequency of sea waves. See **significant wave height.** Sea wave of greatest energy content

leakage rate. Rate at which air escapes from air cushion, measured in cubic metres or cubic feet per second

lift fan. See also **axial flow lift fan** and **centrifugal flow lift fan.** Fan used to supply air under pressure to air cushion, and/or to form curtains

lift off. To rise from ground on air cushion

linear induction motor. Linear induction motors show considerable promise as a means of propulsion for tracked skimmers, and are now under development in France, the United Kingdom, West Germany, Italy, Japan, the USA and Soviet Union. An attractive feature of this method of electric traction is that it does not depend on the vehicle having contact with the track or guideway.

The motor can be likened to a normal induction motor opened out flat. The 'stator' coils are attached to the vehicle, while the 'rotor' consists of a flat rail of conductive material which is straddled by the stator poles. The variable frequency multi-phase ac current required for the linear motor can either be generated aboard the vehicle or collected from an electrified track.

Although the mounting of the stators on the vehicle appears to be preferred in Europe at present, they can also be built into the guideway. In this case the rotor, in the form of a reaction rail, would be suspended from the vehicle. It would be of sufficient length to span several of the fixed stators simultaneously to avoid jerking

load factor. Relationship between payload capacity available and capacity filled

long-range vessel. Small warship capable of up to seven days' continuous unsupported operations away from base, at 14 to 18 knots patrol speed for 1,500 to 2,500 nautical miles

longitudinal framing. Method of hull construction employing frames set in fore and aft direction or parallel to keel

loop. Abbreviated form of bag skirt with large openings over segments so there is little pressure difference between loop and cushion. May or may not include sheet of material inboard of segment inner attachments. There is no definitive demarcation as to when bag becomes loop

MAU. Marine Corps amphibious unit

MCM. Mine countermeasures

MCMH. Mine countermeasures hovercraft

MSH. Minesweeper hunter

MIL spec. Standard of specification for military equipment operated by US Navy

maglev. Magnetic levitation

mean bag pressure. Mean pressure in bag or loop relative to atmospheric pressure

medium-range vessel. Small warship capable of up to three days' operation from base, patrolling up to 1,500 nautical miles at economical

speed or vessel capable of up to 500 nautical miles at maximum speed

medium speed vessel. Vessel capable of 18-24 knots or more

multiple skirt. System devised by late Jean Bertin, employing number of separate flexible skirts for his system of individually fed, multiple air cushions

multi-role craft. Small warship with facilities for fitting range of interchangeable weapons at short notice (up to six hours)

NAVCAS. Navigation and collision avoidance system

Naviplane. Overwater or amphibious air cushion vehicle developed in France by SEDAM

net tonnage. Total tonnage of craft based on cubic capacity of all space available for carrying revenue-producing cargo less allowance for areas needed to operate craft

nibbling. Catching of skirt, usually bow fingers, on surface being traversed, indication of possible 'plough-in' developing

OCS. Ocean combat ship

OE/AD. Ocean escort, air defence

OE/AS. Ocean escort, anti-submarine

OPEVAL. (US Navy) Operational evaluation

ocean vessel. Vessel able to operate in gales

offshore vessel. Vessel able to remain operational in up to sea state 7 and which can remain at sea in gales

orbital motion. Orbital or circular motion of water particles forming waves. Circular motion decreases in radius with increasing depth. Peculiar sequence of motion causes illusion of wave translation. In reality water moves very little in translation. Circular directions are: up at wave front, forward at crest, down at wave back and back at trough

PAR-WIG. Power-augmented-ram wing-in-ground-effect machine

PPI. Plan position indicator. Radar display and

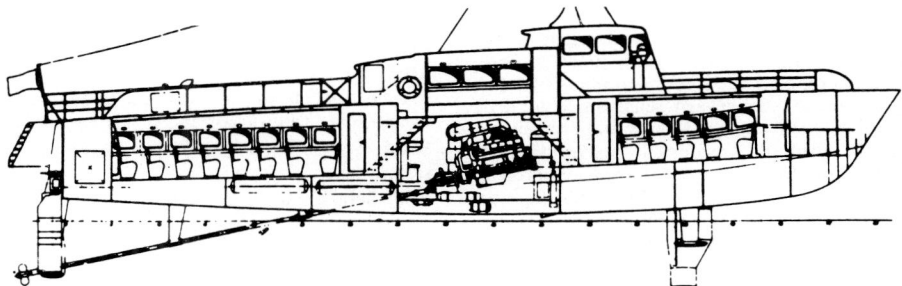

Inboard profile of PT 50 showing inclined shaft

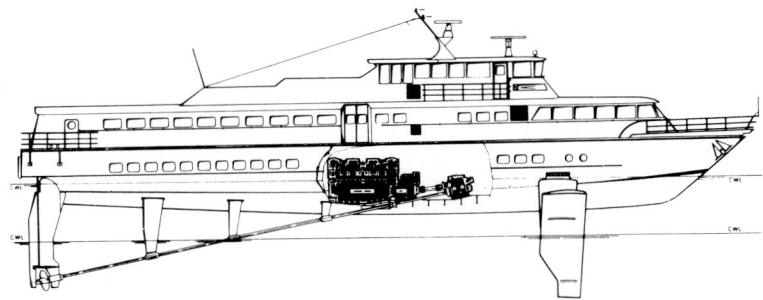

PT 150 showing V-drive system

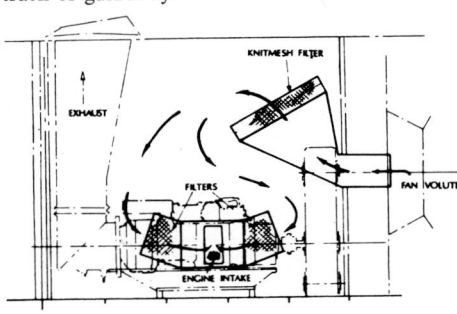

Gas turbine air filtration path on Vosper Thornycroft VT 1 showing knitmesh filter pad

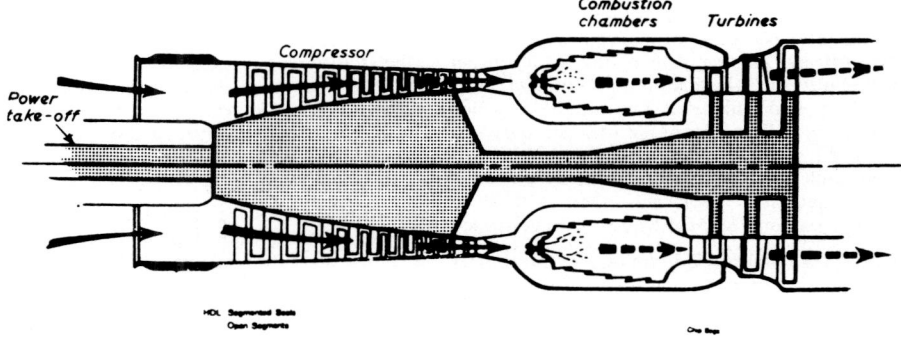

Single shaft gas turbine

presentation giving view as seen from above in plan form

pvc. Polyvinylchloride

PTO. See **power take off unit**

patrol craft. Small warship fitted with light armament

payload weight. Weight of revenue earning load, excluding crew and fuel

peripheral jet. See **air curtain** and **hovercraft**

peripheral jet cushion system. Ground cushion generated by continuous jet of air issued through ducts or nozzles around outer periphery of base of craft. Cushion is maintained at above ambient pressure by horizontal change of momentum of curtain

peripheral trunk. See **skirt**

pitch. Rotation or oscillation of hull about transverse axis in seaway. Also angle of air or water propeller blades

pitch angle. Pitch craft adopts relative to horizontal datum

pitch attitude. Instantaneous angle between surface (**roll attitude**) traversed and longitudinal (lateral) datum of craft

pitch stiffness. Rate of change of restoring pitch moment with pitch angle. Slope of applied pitch moment versus pitch angle diagram

platform, to. Approximately level flight of hydrofoil over waves lower than calm water hull clearance

plenum. Space or air chamber beneath or surrounding lift fan or fans through which air under pressure is distributed to skirt system

plenum chamber cushion system. Simplest air cushion concept; cushion pressure is maintained by pumping air continuously into recessed base without use of peripheral jet curtain

'plough in'. Bow down attitude resulting from bow part of skirt contacting surface and progressively building up drag. Unless controlled can lead to serious loss of stability and possibly overturning.

With skirt's front outer edge dragging on water towards centre of craft ('tuck under') there is marked reduction in righting moment of cushion pressure. As downward pitch angle increases, stern tends to rise from surface and excessive yaw angles develop. Considerable deceleration takes place down to hump speed and danger of roll over in small craft is accentuated by following waves which further increase pitch angle

Solutions include vent holes on a skirt's outer front to reduce drag through air lubrication, and bag skirt which automatically bulges outwards on contact with water, delaying tuck under and providing righting moment

porpoising. Oscillatory motion in pitch and heave of high-speed planing hull craft caused by incorrect trim rather than wave action

power augmented ram-wing. Wing-in-ground-effect machine designed so that the propulsion system exhaust is directed into the space between the wing and the surface to lift the wing clear of the water at zero speed. Current research is also aimed at employing power augmentation in conjunction with end plates to provide a low speed or hover capability. Advantages include the avoidance of the high hydrodynamic drag experienced by craft with relatively high wing impact loadings during take-off and the high impact loadings encountered during take-off and landing. Use of the PAR system would also provide surface mobility over short ranges or under high sea state conditions which would normally prevent take-off. The system is expected to avoid the need for large hydrodynamic hulls for WIGs since the wing volume on winged hull types and others with deep aerofoil sections, could also be used for buoyancy

power take off unit. Unit for transmitting power from main engine(s), generally for auxiliary services required while craft is under way, such as hydraulics, alternators and bilge pumps

puff ports. See **control ducts**

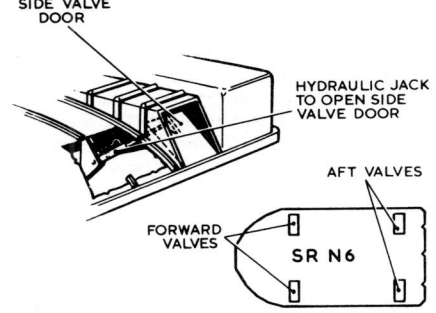

Puff port arrangement on BHC SR.N6

ram wing. See **air cushion vehicles**

recirculation system. Air curtain employing recirculating air flow, which is maintained within and under craft

reliability factor. Percentage relationship between number of trips scheduled and those achieved

rise height. Distance which hovercraft rises from flat hard ground to being fully cushion-borne

river vessel. Non-seagoing craft able to operate in up to sea state 5

Ro-ro. Roll-on roll-off. Ships and air cushion vehicles with decks providing straight-through loading facilities, ie with cargo ramps or loading doors fore and aft

roll. Oscillation or rotation of hull about longitudinal axis

roll attitude. Angle of roll craft adopts relative to longitudinal datum

roll stiffness. Rate of change of restoring roll moment with roll angle. Slope of applied roll moment versus roll angle diagram

running time. Time during which all machinery has been in operation, including idling time

SAS. Stability augmentation system

SATS. Sea acceptance trials. Weapons trials undertaken at sea under dynamic conditions

SECAT. Surface effect catamaran

SES. See **surface effect ship**

SEV. Surface effect vehicle. (USA) air cushion vehicles of all types. (USSR) large sea- or ocean-going wing-in-ground-effect machines

SSM. Surface-to-surface, ship-to-ship missile system

SSP. Semi-submerged platform craft

SSPU. Ship's service power unit

SWATH. Small waterplane area twin-hull craft

Savitsky flap. Hinged vertical control flaps for foil lift variation, attached to trailing edge of foil struts and canted out at angle. Flaps are attached mechanically to the trailing-edge flaps on the foil. At normal flying height only lower part of Savitsky flap is submerged.

As more of the flap becomes submerged due to increased wave height, the moment of the flap increases causing it to raise the foil flap, thus increasing lift and restoring normal inflight attitude and flying height. The system can be adjusted to react only to lower-frequency layer waves. The system is employed on the Atlantic Hydrofoils, *Flying Cloud* and *Sea World*. It was invented by Dr Daniel Savitsky of the Davidson Laboratory

sea loiter aircraft. Aircraft capable of loitering on or above the sea for extended periods of time are currently being investigated by the US Navy which foresees a significant operational potential for this type of machine. Applications would include anti-submarine warfare, command, communications and control and strategic missile carrier

seal. See **cushion seal**

sea state. Scale of sea conditions classified from state 1, smooth, to state 8, precipitous, according to the wind duration, fetch and velocity, also wave length, period and velocity

segment. Flexible sheet member of lower part of hovercraft cushion boundary seal (see **finger**) or individual sections of bag skirt

semi-submerged propeller. Concept for partially submerged, supercavitating propeller on ship-size air cushion vehicles, driven through sidewall transom. Advantages include considerable drag reduction due to absence of inclined shafts and supporting structures, and possibly elimination of propeller erosion resulting from appendage cavity impingement

service speed. Cruising speed obtained by average crew in average craft on given route

set down. Lower air cushion vehicle onto its landing pads

short-range vessel. Small warship capable of up to 36 hours' continuous operation and which can cover up to 600 miles at economical speed or vessel capable of covering up to 250 nautical miles at maximum speed

sidewall. Rigid structure extending along side of craft and forming part of cushion seal

sidewall vessel. ACV with cushion air contained between immersed sidewalls or skegs and transverse air curtains or skirts fore and aft. Stability is provided by buoyancy of sidewalls and their planing forces

significant. Arithmetic means of highest third of set of measurements, eg wave heights or lengths

significant wave height. Sea waves are composed of different frequencies and have different wave heights (energy spectrum). A wave with the leading frequency of this spectrum and energy content is called the significant wave. It is from this wave that the significant wave height is measured

skirt. Flexible fabric extension between ACV's metal structure and surface to give increased obstacle and overwave clearance capability for small air gap clearance and therefore reduced power requirement. Skirt deflects when encountering waves or solid obstacles, then returns to its normal position, air gap being increased only momentarily. On peripheral jet ACVs skirt is flexible extension of peripheral jet nozzle with inner and outer skins hung from inner and outer edges of air duct and linked together by chain ties or diaphragms so that they form correct nozzle profile at hemline

skirt, bag. Simple skirt design consisting of inflated bag. Sometimes used as transverse and longitudinal stability skirts

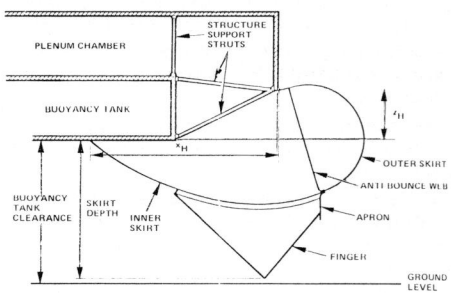

BHC fingered bag skirt

skirt depth. Designed vertical distance from craft hard structure to finger tip

skirt, finger. Skirt system designed by British Hovercraft Corporation, consisting of fringe of conical nozzles attached to base of bag or loop skirt. Each nozzle or finger fits around air exit hole and channels cushion air inwards towards bottom centre of craft

skirt, segmented. Conceived by Hovercraft Development Ltd's Technical Group, this skirt system is employed on the HD.2, Vosper Thornycroft VT 1, VT 2 and many new craft under design or construction. It is also employed for industrial applications, including hoverpallets and hovertrailers.

The flexible segments are around the craft periphery, each being attached to the lower edge of a sheet of light flexible material, which inflates to an arc shape, and also to the craft hard structure.

The system enables the craft to clear high waves and obstacles as the segments occupy a substantial part of the full cushion depth. No stability skirts or other forms of compartmentation are necessary. A smooth ride is provided as the skirt has good response due to low inertia.

The cushion area can be the same as the craft hard structure plan area. The skirt inner attachment points can be reached without jacking the craft up from its off-cushion position, simplifying maintenance

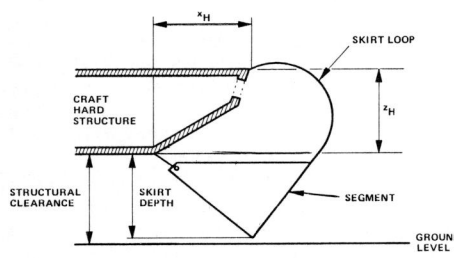

HDL segmented skirt

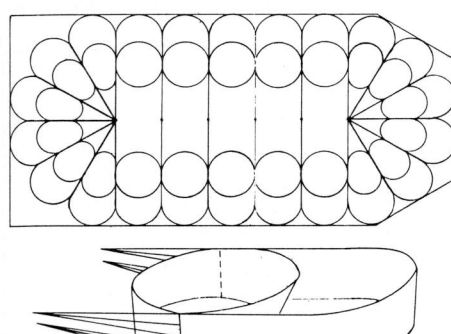

SEDAM skirt system

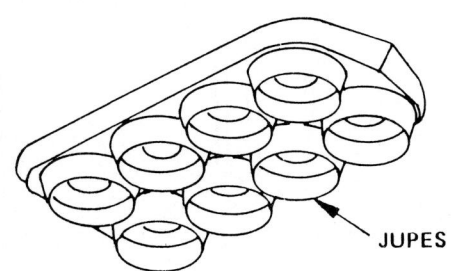

JUPES

Bertin skirt

skirt shape transition. Change from finger only in water contact to state in which bag or loop component is in contact and fingers are flattened

SURFACE EFFECT SHIP CONFIGURATIONS

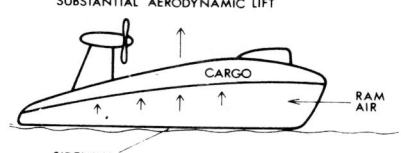

Ram wing SES

Wing-in-ground-effect

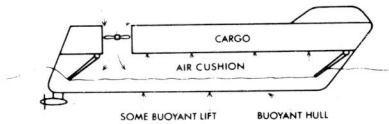

Aircat SES with wide buoyant hulls

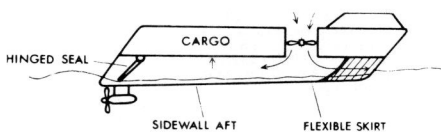

Hybrid SES with rigid sidewalls and bow skirt

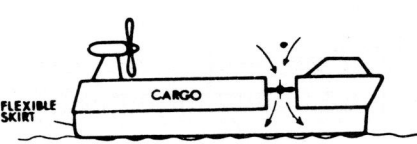

Air-propelled amphibious SES

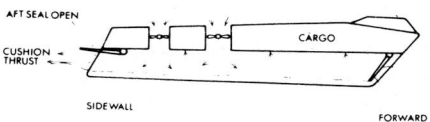

Airjet SES, propelled by cushion thrust

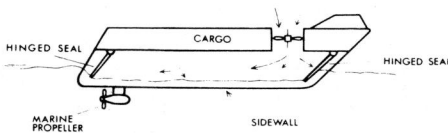

Sidewall SES. Also known as Captured Air Bubble or CAB Type

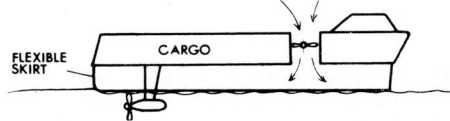

Water-propelled, semi-amphibious SES

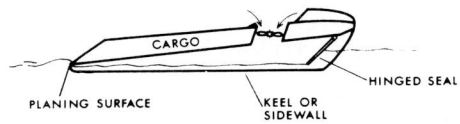

Air-lubricated hull or hydrokeel SES

skirt shifting. Control system in which movement of centre of area of cushion is achieved by shifting skirt along one side, which tilts craft. Pitch and roll trim can be adjusted by this method

split foil. Main foil system with foil area divided into two, either to facilitate retraction, or to permit location of control surfaces well outboard, where foil control and large roll correcting moments can be applied for small changes in lift

stability curtain. Transverse or longitudinal air curtains dividing air cushion in order to restrict cross flow of air within cushion and increase pitch and roll stability. Also **stability skirt**

standard speed vessel. Patrol vessel capable of speeds of up to 18 knots

strake. (a) permanent band of rubber or other hard wearing material along sides of craft to protect structure from chafing against quays, piers and craft alongside. (b) lengths of material fitted externally to flexible skirt and used to channel air downwards to reduce water drag

strike craft. Small warship fitted with at least one major weapon, plus light defensive armament

submerged foil system. Foil system employing totally submerged lifting surfaces. Depth of submergence is controlled by mechanical, electronic or pneumatic systems which alter angle of incidence of foils or flaps attached to them to provide stability and control. See **foil systems**

supercavitating foil. General classification given to foils designed to operate efficiently at high speeds while fully cavitated. Since at very high speeds foils cannot avoid cavitation, sections are being designed which induce onset of cavitation from leading edge and cause cavities to proceed downstream and beyond trailing edge before collapsing. Lift and drag of these foils is determined by shape of leading edge and undersurface

surface effect ship. Large ship-size ACV. Usually applied in USA and United Kingdom to large sidewall craft. See **air cushion vehicles**

surface piercing ACV. Craft with rigid sidewalls that penetrate water surface. Air cushion is contained laterally by sidewalls and at bow and stern by flexible seals. See **sidewall vessel** or **surface effect ships**

surf zone. Area from outer waves breaking on shore to limit of their uprush on a beach

TECHEVAL. (US Navy) Technical evaluation

TLACV. Track-laying air cushion vehicle. ACV vehicle employing looped caterpillar-like tracks for propulsion. Air cushion and seals may be between flexible tracks, as on Soviet MVP-3 series, or can form broad belt or track that loops round complete air cushion

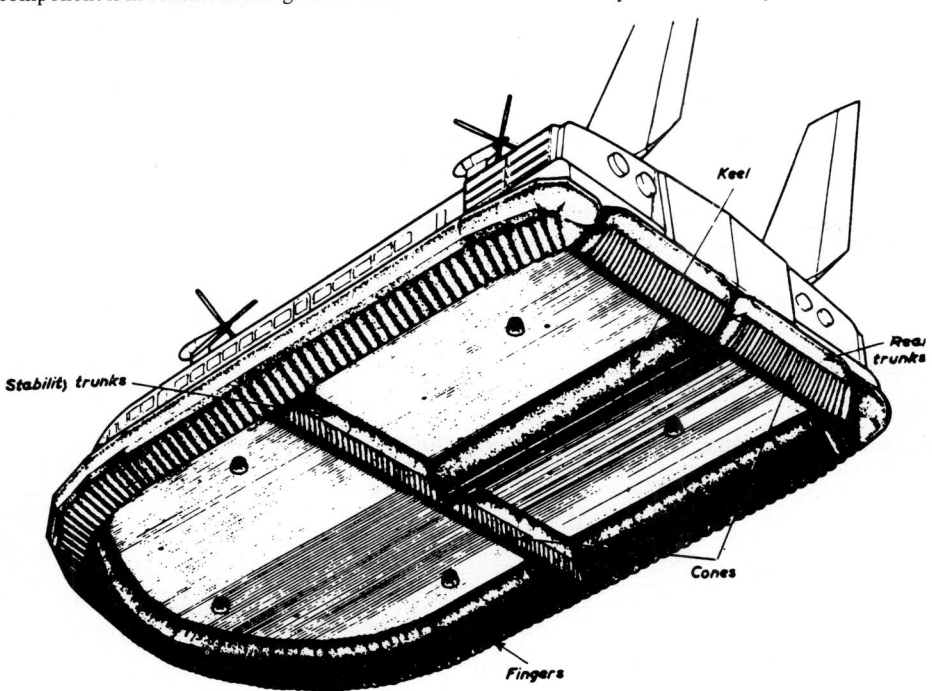

Underside of SR.N4 showing stability skirts

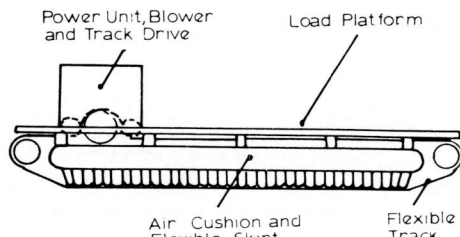

Track-laying ACV operating on broad track that loops around air cushion

TLRV. Tracked levitated research vehicle

take-off speed. Speed at which hydrofoil hull is raised clear of water, dynamic foil lift taking over from static displacement or planing of hull proper

tandem foils. Foil system in which area of forward foils is approximately equal to that of aft foils, balancing loading between them

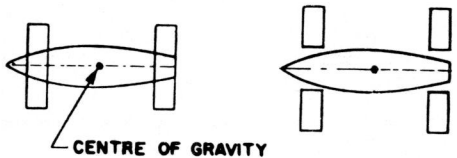

Tandem foil system. The foil areas can be 'split' into two to facilitate retraction

terramechanics. Study of general relationship between performance of off-road vehicle and its physical environment

thickness-chord ratio. Maximum thickness of foil section in relation to its chord

thruster. Controlled aperture through which air or water can be expelled to assist control at low speeds

Tietjens-type foil. Forward swept (surface piercing) main foil almost amidships and slightly ahead of CG. It was intended that pronounced sweep of V foils would result in increasing area of foil further forward coming into use to increase bow up trim of craft when lift was lost. Considerable length of unsupported hull ahead of CG meant craft was constantly in danger of 'digging in' in bad seas and was highly sensitive to loading arrangements

transcavitating foil. Thin section foil designed for smooth transition from fully wetted to supercavitating flow. By loading tip more highly than root, cavitation is first induced at tip, then extends spanwise over foil to roots as speed increases

transisting foil. See **transcavitating foil**

transit foil. See **transcavitating foil**

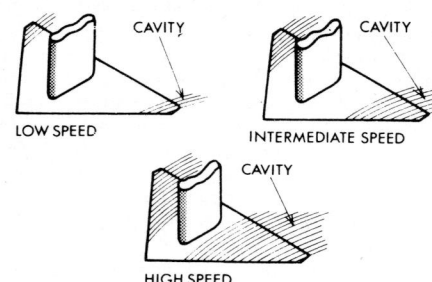

Transit foil operation

transom. Last transverse frame of ship's structure forming stern board

transverse framing. Steel frames running athwartships, from side to side, instead of fore and aft

trapped air cushion vehicle. Concept for skirt-type SES with 20ft (6·09m) skirts separated from water surface by thin film of air lubrication

trim. Difference between draughts forward and aft in displacement vessel and by extension, ACV and hydrofoil hull attitude relative to line of flight

trim angle. Pitch or roll angle which results under steady running conditions

tuck-under. Action of skirt being pulled back under structure as result of local drag forces

tunnel hull. Racing boat with tunnel-shaped hull designed to employ the advantages of aerodynamic lift as in ram-wing or channel-flow wing ACV

variable-pitch propeller. Propeller with blades which can be rotated about their longitudinal axes to provide forward or reverse thrust

ventilation. See **air entry**

VCG. Vertical height measurement (from appropriate datum) to CG

water wall ACV. Craft employing a curtain of water to retain its air cushion instead of air curtain

waterjet propulsion. Applied to a propulsion system devised as an alternative to supercavitating propellers for propelling high-speed ship systems. Turbines drive pumps located in the hull, and water is pumped through high velocity jets above the water line and directed astern. The system weighs less than a comparable super-cavitating propeller system and for craft with normal operating speeds above 45 knots it is thought to be competitive on an annual cost basis. First high-speed applications include the Soviet-Burevestnik and Chaika hydrofoils, the Aerojet-General SES-100A test craft and two products of the Boeing Company—the PGH-2 hydrofoil gunboat and the NATO PHM.

Waterjets are also being employed for propulsion at relatively low speeds. In the Soviet Union the Zarya shallow-draught waterbus (24 knots) and the Gorkovchanin sidewall ACV are propelled by waterjets. In the USA the PGH-1 and PGH-2 hydrofoils use waterjets for hullborne propulsion. The jet can be turned easily to give side propulsion to facilitate docking which is not so easy for a normal propeller

wave-forming keels. Free-flooding structures attached to underside of planing hull to increase air lubrication at high speeds and under all sea conditions. Air path from aft end of keels lubricates hull's undersurface with air. Multiple keels stiffen craft's longitudinal framing, enabling it to

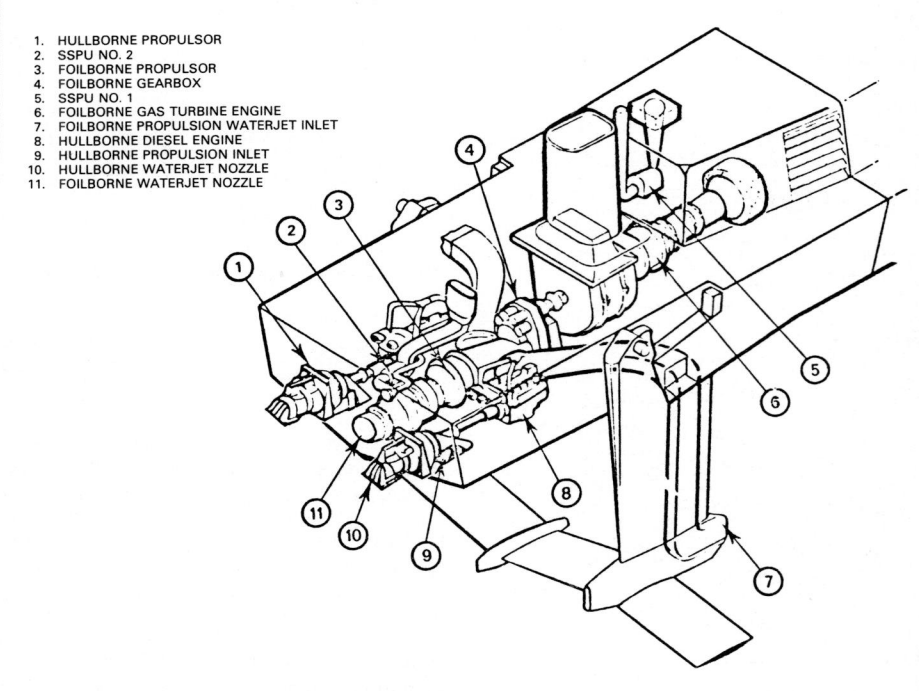

1. HULLBORNE PROPULSOR
2. SSPU NO. 2
3. FOILBORNE PROPULSOR
4. FOILBORNE GEARBOX
5. SSPU NO. 1
6. FOILBORNE GAS TURBINE ENGINE
7. FOILBORNE PROPULSION WATERJET INLET
8. HULLBORNE DIESEL ENGINE
9. HULLBORNE PROPULSION INLET
10. HULLBORNE WATERJET NOZZLE
11. FOILBORNE WATERJET NOZZLE

Waterjet propulsion system on Boeing/NATO PHM missile-armed fast patrol hydrofoil

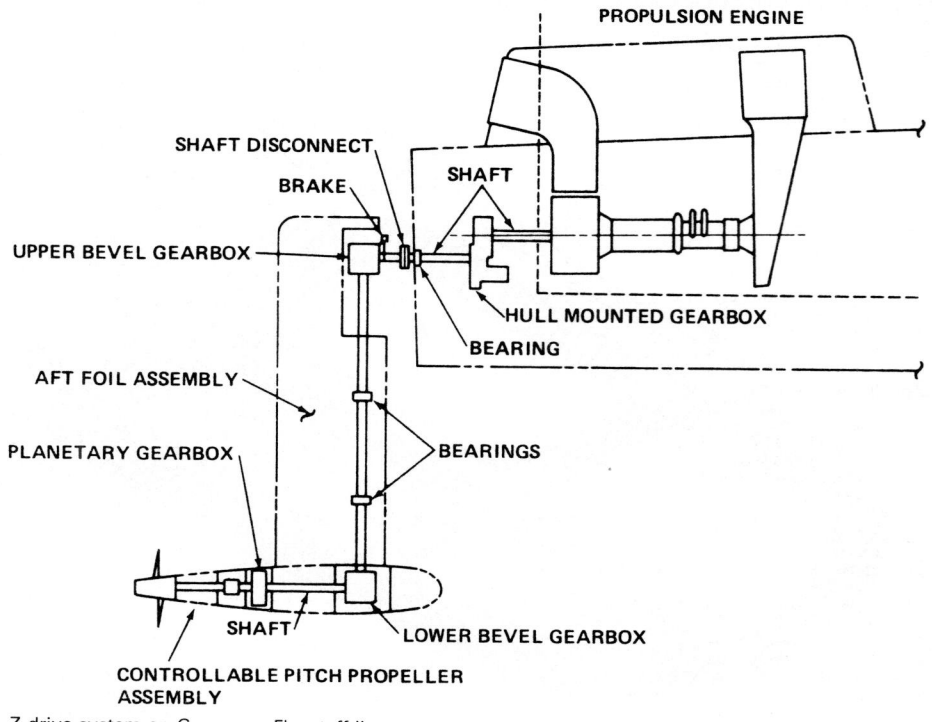

Z-drive system on Grumman Flagstaff II

sustain higher impact slamming loads in rough seas and permitting increases in size and load capacity.

wave height. Vertical distance from wave trough to crest or twice wave amplitude

wave length. Horizontal distance between adjacent wave crests

wave making drag. Drag due to creation of waves by moving hovercraft pressure system

wave pumping. Alternating increase and decrease of volume of pressurised air in ACV's cushion, caused by passage of waves or other objects through cushion

wave velocity. Speed at which wave form travels along sea surface (the water itself remaining without forward movement)

weights. There are no generally accepted standards with respect to ACV and SES weights, except that small ACVs tend to follow aircraft practice and large types follow ship practice. The hydrofoil concepts are ship orientated. A consistently used format aids concept evaluation and permits usage on, or direct comparison with other designs. Format 1 is according to US Naval practice and is suitable for all sizes of ACVs, SESs, and hydrofoils. The actual terminology used for the totals is optional, so that the nomenclature can be consistent with the size of the vessel. In presenting results, the units (short tons, long tons, metric tons, pounds, etc) should be clearly indicated.

Format 2 is used by the hovercraft industry in the United Kingdom. This emphasises equipment options, and by breaking down the expendable or useful load, the payload/range performance can be readily determined. It is also useful in defining first costs and operating costs

wetting drag. Drag due to immersion of parts of craft in water, eg skirts and sidewalls, and usually considered to include drag due to creation of spray. In practice forms residual drag when aerodynamic and wave-making components are subtracted from total drag measured

winged hull. See **Aerofoil boat**

wing-in-ground-effect. See **air cushion vehicle**

yaw angle. Rotation or oscillation of craft about vertical axis

yaw ducts. See **control ducts**

Z-drive. Drive system normally employed on hydrofoils to transmit power from engine in hull to screw through horizontal shaft leading to bevel gear over stern, then via vertical shaft and second bevel gear to horizontal propeller shaft, thus forming propeller 'Z' shape

CHART OF SEA STATE CONDITIONS

Sea State	Description	(Beaufort) Wind force	Description	Range (knots)	Wind Velocity (knots)	Wave Height — Average	Wave Height — Significant	Wave Height — Average of One-Tenth Highest	Significant Range Periods (sec)	Periods of maximum Energy of Spectra $T_{max} = T_c$	Average Period T_z	Average Wavelength L_w (ft unless otherwise indicated)	Minimum Fetch (nautical) miles	Minimum Duration (hr unless otherwise indicated)
	Sea like a mirror	U	Calm	1	0	0	0	0	—	—	—	—	—	—
0	Ripples with the appearance of scales are formed, but without foam crests.	1	Light airs	1-3	2	0.04	0.01 / 0.01	0.09	1.2	0.75	0.5	10 in	5	18 min
1	Small wavelets; short but pronounced crests have a glossy appearance, but do not break.	2	Light breeze	4-6	5	0.3	0.5	0.6	0.4-2.8	1.9	1.3	6.7 ft	8	39 min
	Large wavelets; crests begin to break. Foam of glossy	3	Gentle	7-10	8.5	0.8	1.3	1.6	0.8-5.0	3.2	2.3	20	9.8	1.7
	appearance. Perhaps scattered with horses.		breeze		10	1.1	1.8	2.3	1.0-6.0	3.2	2.7	27	10	2.4
2	Small waves, becoming larger;	4	Moderate		12	1.6	2.6	3.3	1.0-7.0	4.5	3.2	40	18	3.8
					13.5	2.1	3.3	4.2	1.4-7.6	5.1	3.6	52	24	4.8
3	fairly frequent white horses.		breeze	11-16	14	2.3	3.6	4.6	1.5-7.8	5.3	3.8	59	28	5.2
					16	2.9	4.7	6.0	2.0-8.8	6.0	4.3	71	40	6.6
4	Moderate waves, taking a more	5	Fresh	17-21	18	3.7	5.9	7.5	2.5-10.0	6.8	4.8	90	55	8.3
					19	4.1	6.6	8.4	2.8-10.6	7.2	5.1	99	65	9.2
	pronounced long form: many white horses are formed (chance of some spray).		breeze		20	4.6	7.3	9.3	3.0-11.1	7.5	5.4	111	75	10
5	Large waves begin to form;	6	Strong	22-27	22	5.5	8.8	11.2	3.4-12.2	8.3	5.9	134	100	12
					24	6.6	10.5	13.3	3.7-13.5	9.0	6.4	160	130	14
	white crests are more extensive		breeze		24.5	6.8	10.9	13.8	3.8-13.6	9.2	6.6	164	140	15
6	everywhere (probably some spray).				26	7.7	12.3	15.6	4.0-14.5	9.8	7.0	188	180	17
7	Sea heaps up, and white foam from breaking waves begins to be blown in streaks along the direction of the wind (Spindrift begins to be seen).	7	Moderate gale	28-33	28	8.9	14.3	18.2	4.5-15.5	10.6	7.5	212	230	20
					30	10.3	16.4	20.8	4.7-16.7	11.3	8.0	250	280	23
					30.5	10.6	16.9	21.5	4.8-17.0	11.5	8.2	258	290	24
					32	11.6	18.6	23.6	5.0-17.5	12.1	8.6	285	340	27
7	Moderate high waves of greater length; edges of crests break into spindrift. The foam is blown in well-marked streaks along the direction of the wind. Spray affects visibility.	8	Fresh gale	34-40	34	13.1	21.0	26.7	5.5-18.5	12.8	9.1	322	420	30
					36	14.8	23.6	30.0	5.8-19.7	13.6	9.6	363	500	34
					37	15.6	24.9	31.6	6-20.5	13.9	9.9	376	530	37
					38	16.4	26.3	33.4	6.2-20.8	14.3	10.2	392	600	38
					40	18.2	29.1	37.0	6.5-21.7	15.1	10.7	444	710	42
8	High waves. Dense streaks of foam along the direction of the wind. Sea begins to roll. Visibility affected.	9	Strong gale	41-47	42	20.1	32.1	40.8	7-23	15.8	11.3	492	830	47
					44	22.0	35.2	44.7	7-24.2	16.6	11.8	534	960	52
					46	24.1	38.5	48.9	7-25	17.3	12.3	590	1110	57
	Very high waves with long overhanging crests. The resulting foam is in great patches and is blown in dense white streaks along the direction of the wind. On the whole, the surface of the sea takes on a white appearance. The rolling of the sea becomes heavy and shocklike. Visibility is affected.	10	Whole* gale	48-55	40	26.2	41.9	53.2	7.5-26	18.1	12.9	650	1250	63
					50	28.4	45.5	57.8	7.5-27	18.8	13.4	700	1420	69
					51.5	30.2	48.3	61.3	8-28.2	19.4	13.8	736	1560	73
9					52	30.8	49.2	6.25	8-28.5	19.6	13.9	750	1610	75
					54	33.2	53.1	67.4	8-29.5	20.4	14.5	810	1800	81
	Exceptionally high waves. Sea completely covered with long white patches of foam lying in direction of wind. Everywhere edges of wave crests are blown into froth. Visibility affected.	11	Storm*	56-63	56	35.7	57.1	72.5	8.5-31	21.1	15	910	2100	88
					59.5	40.3	64.4	81.8	10-32	22.4	15.9	985	2500	101
	Air filled with foam and spray. Sea white with driving spray. Visibility very seriously affected.	12	Hurricane*	64-71	>64	>46.6	74.5	94.6	10-35	24.1	17.2	—	—	—

* For hurricane winds (and often whole gale and storm winds) required durations and reports are barely attained. Seas are therefore not fully arisen.

HOVERCRAFT WEIGHT TERMS

Format 1

Group	Typical Items
1 Hull (or structure)	Basic structure, planting, frames, stringers, scantlings, decks, foundations, fittings, super-structure, doors and closures.
2 Propulsion	Engines, turbines, propellers, fans, gearboxes, shafting, drive systems, associated controls, nuclear plant, associated fluids.
3 Electrical	Power generation, switching, lighting, load canters, panels, cable.
4 Communication and Control	Communications (internal, external) and navigation equipment, military electronics, computers, displays (note ship controls are in Group 5).
5 Auxiliary Systems	Fuel, heating, ventilation, fresh water, ship controls, rudder, cushion seal (flexible or articulated), plumbing, oil, fire extinguishing, drainage, ballast, mooring, anchoring, hydrofoils distilling plant.
6 Outfit and Furnishings	Hull fittings, marine hardware, ladders, furnishings, boats, rafts, preservers, stowages, lockers, painting, deck covering, hull insulation, commissary equipment, radiation shielding (other than at reactor area).
7 Armament	Weapons, mounts, ammunition stowage, handling systems, special plating.
Total: Light Ship or Light Displacement or Empty Weight	(sum of the above items).
Variable Load or Useful Load	Operating personnel and effects, cargo, freight, fuel, passengers, baggage, water, ammunition, aircraft, stores, troops, provisions.
Full Load Displacement or Load Displacement or Gross Weight or All Up Weight	(sum of empty weight and useful load).

Format 2

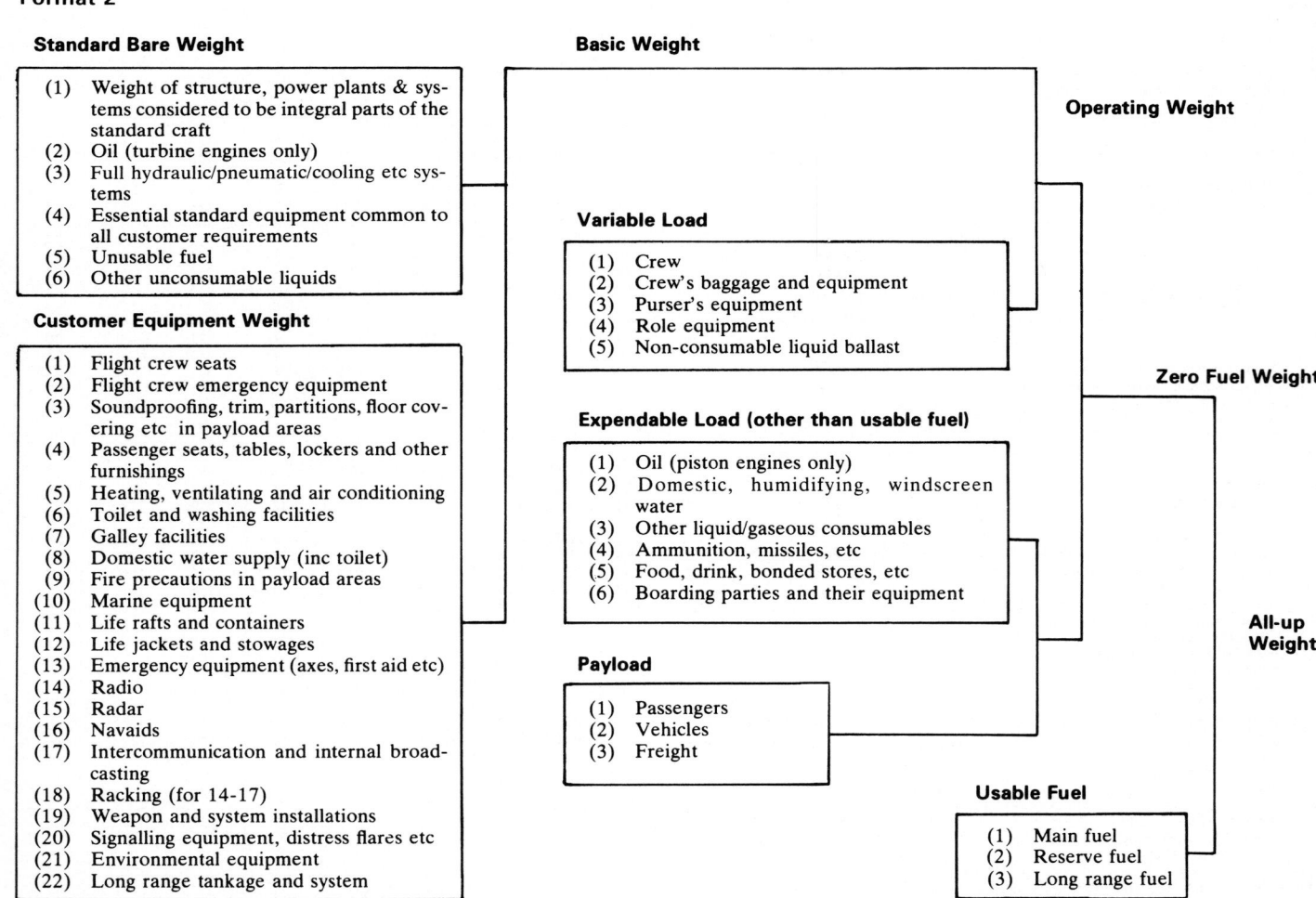

Standard Bare Weight

(1) Weight of structure, power plants & systems considered to be integral parts of the standard craft
(2) Oil (turbine engines only)
(3) Full hydraulic/pneumatic/cooling etc systems
(4) Essential standard equipment common to all customer requirements
(5) Unusable fuel
(6) Other unconsumable liquids

Customer Equipment Weight

(1) Flight crew seats
(2) Flight crew emergency equipment
(3) Soundproofing, trim, partitions, floor covering etc in payload areas
(4) Passenger seats, tables, lockers and other furnishings
(5) Heating, ventilating and air conditioning
(6) Toilet and washing facilities
(7) Galley facilities
(8) Domestic water supply (inc toilet)
(9) Fire precautions in payload areas
(10) Marine equipment
(11) Life rafts and containers
(12) Life jackets and stowages
(13) Emergency equipment (axes, first aid etc)
(14) Radio
(15) Radar
(16) Navaids
(17) Intercommunication and internal broadcasting
(18) Racking (for 14-17)
(19) Weapon and system installations
(20) Signalling equipment, distress flares etc
(21) Environmental equipment
(22) Long range tankage and system

Basic Weight

Operating Weight

Variable Load

(1) Crew
(2) Crew's baggage and equipment
(3) Purser's equipment
(4) Role equipment
(5) Non-consumable liquid ballast

Expendable Load (other than usable fuel)

(1) Oil (piston engines only)
(2) Domestic, humidifying, windscreen water
(3) Other liquid/gaseous consumables
(4) Ammunition, missiles, etc
(5) Food, drink, bonded stores, etc
(6) Boarding parties and their equipment

Zero Fuel Weight

Payload

(1) Passengers
(2) Vehicles
(3) Freight

All-up Weight

Usable Fuel

(1) Main fuel
(2) Reserve fuel
(3) Long range fuel

BIBLIOGRAPHY

AIR CUSHION VEHICLES
ACVs IN NORTH AMERICA

ACV Icing Problems, J R Stallabras and T R Ringer (National Research Council). Seventh Canadian Symposium on Air Cushion Technology, June 1973.

Air-Cushion Vehicles, Operational use in the Arctic, G Ives. *Petroleum Eng,* Vol 45 No 1, January 1974.

Air Cushion Vehicles and Soil Erosion, P Abeels. International Society for Terrain-Vehicle Systems 5th International Conference, Detroit, Houghton, Michigan, June 1975.

AP.1-88 Logistic Support Craft—Arctic Variant, R L Wheeler, BHC. Canadian Air Cushion Technology Society, 1984.

Arctic Development Using Very Large ACVs, J L Anderson (NASA Lewis Laboratories). Seventh Canadian Symposium on Air Cushion Technology, June 1973.

Arctic Operational Experience with SR.N6 engaged in Hydrographic Survey and Cushioncraft CC-7, L R Colby and G M Yeaton (Polar Continental Shelf Project, DEMR). Fourth Canadian Symposium on Air Cushion Technology, 1970. publ Canadian Aeronautics and Space Institute.

The Arctic Surface Effect Vehicle Program, J V Kordenbrock and C W Harry. 59th Annual Meeting of American Society of Naval Engineers, Washington DC, May 1976.

Arctic Transportation, Operational and Environmental Evaluation of an ACV in Northern Alaska, G Abele and J Brown (US Army Cold Region Research Engineering Laboratory). ASME Conference, Mexico City, September 1976. Paper 76-Pet-41 ASME. (Also in *Transactions of Journal of Pressure Vessels Technology,* Vol 99, February 1977, pp 176-182).

Canadian Coast Guard Air Cushion Icebreaking, 1982-83 Trials, P de L Markham (German & Milne Inc, Ottawa), J E Laframboise (Transportation Development Centre, Montreal) and M A Ball (Fleet Aviation, Canadian Coast Guard). Seventeenth Canadian Symposium on Air Cushion Technology, October 1983.

Continuing Advances with Air Cushion Icebreaking, M A Ball, (Transport Canada). Tenth CASI Symposium on Air Cushion Technology, October 1976.

Development of the Canadian Air-Cushion Vehicle Industry, R G Wade (Ministry of Transport, Ottawa). AIAA/SNAME Advanced Marine Vehicle Conference, San Diego, California, 25-28 February 1974.

Dynamic Performance of an Air-Cushion Vehicle in a Marine Environment, J A Fein, A H Magnuson and D D Moran (Naval Ship Research and Development Center, Bethesda, Maryland). AIAA/SNAME Advanced Marine Vehicle Conference, San Diego, California, February 1974.

Economics of Air Cushion Icebreaker Bow Platforms Applied to Commercial Navigation in the Upper Great Lakes Basin—A Case Study, M Tapiero and J Udell (Transportation Development Centre, Transport Canada). 12th CASI Symposium on Air Cushion Technology, 25-27 September 1978.

Effects of Hovercraft Operation on Organic Terrain in the Arctic, Gunars Abele (US Army Cold Regions Research and Engineering Laboratory). Hovering Craft, Hydrofoil and Advanced Transit Systems Conference, Brighton, May 1974.

Environmental Effects of ACV and other Off-Road Vehicle Operations on Tundra, G Abele and W E Rickard (US Army Cold Region Research and Engineering Laboratory). Seventh Canadian Symposium on Air Cushion Technology, June 1973.

High-Speed Air Cushion Icebreaking, Membrane Ice Sheet Model, M J Hinchey (Memorial University of Newfoundland). Seventeenth Canadian Symposium on Air Cushion Technology, October 1983.

Hovercraft Operations in the Arctic, the Activities of Voyageur 003 Between Hay River, Northwest Territories, Canada and Umiat, Alaska, N Ray Sumner Jr (Science Applications, Inc), 1651 Old Meadow Road, McLean, Virginia 22101, USA. November 1974.

Icebreaking with Air-Cushion Technology, Report National Research Council of Canada, NRC Associate Committee on Air-Cushion Technology, 1975.

Improvements in Ice-breaking by the use of Air Cushion Technology, R G Wade, R Y Edwards and J K Kim. Eastern Canada Section of SNAME Symposium Ice Tech 75, Montreal, April 1975.

The Integration of the Hovercraft into the Modern Coast Guard Service, Terence F Melhuish (Manager, Fleet Aviation, Canadian Coast Guard, Ottawa). Third International Hovercraft Conference, Southampton, November 1981.

The Jeff(A) Test Programme, D Dickens. Canadian Air Cushion Technology Society, 1984.

The Light-Footed Giants, Howard S Fowler (Head of Engine Laboratory, Division of Mechanical Engineering, National Research Council, Canada). 1981 Lord Sempill Memorial Paper, Institution of Production Engineers, November 1981.

Model Tests of an Arctic Surface Effect Vehicle over Model Ice, E J Lecourt, T Kotras and J Kordenbrock. Eastern Canadian Section of SNAME Ice Tech 75 Symposium, Montreal, April 1975.

NCTL's Voyageur Experience, B Meade (Northern Transportation Co). Seventh Canadian Symposium on Air Cushion Technology, June 1973.

A New Design for ACIB Icebreaking, P Markham, J E Laframboise and D B Colbourne. Canadian Air Cushion Technology Society, 1984.

Operational Evaluation of the SK-5 in Alaska, R A Liston and B Hanamoto (US Army Cold Region Research and Engineering Laboratory). Seventh Canadian Symposium on Air Cushion Technology, June 1973.

Operational Test and Evaluation of Air Cushion Vehicle Icebreakers for River Ice Environment, J Brick (ORI Inc), C W Prichett (US Coast Guard) and B Dennis (Chi Associates Inc). 12th CASI Symposium on Air Cushion Technology, 25-27 September 1978.

Small Air Cushion Vehicle Operation on Floating Ice under Winter Condition, R J Weaver and R O Romseier (Dept of the Environment). Seventh Canadian Symposium on Air Cushion Technology, June 1973.

A Study of Multimode Express Shipping, IMA Resources Inc, Report sponsored by the US Department of Transportation, 1982.

West Coast Update—Canadian Coast Guard, J McGrath, Canadian Coast Guard. Canadian Air Cushion Technology Symposium, 1982.

AIR CUSHION LANDING SYSTEMS

ACLS for a Commercial Transport, T D Earl (Bell Aerospace Textron). Society of Automotive Engineers Meeting, 30 April-2 May 1974.

Air Cushion Landing Gear Elastic Trunk Progress, T D Earl (Bell Aerospace Canada Textron). Seventeenth Canadian Symposium on Air Cushion Technology, October 1983.

Air-Cushion Landing Systems Development on a Buffalo Aircraft, C J Austin (The De Havilland Aircraft Co of Canada Ltd). CASI Flight Test Symposium, Edmonton, Alberta, March 1975.

Characteristics of an Air-Cushion Landing System Incorporating an Inelastic Trunk, A B Boghani and K M Captain (Foster Miller Associates) and D N Wormley (MIT). 12th CASI Symposium on Air Cushion Technology, 25-27 September 1978.

The Development and Flight Testing of the XC-8A Air Cushion Landing Systems, D J Rerez (US Air Force Wright Patterson Base). SAE Aerospace Engineering & Manufacturing Meeting, 29 November-2 December, 1976. Paper 760920.

Elastically Retracting ACLS Trunks, T D Earl (Bell Aerospace Textron). *Canadian Aeronautics and Space Journal,* Vol 21 No 5, pp 169-173, May 1975.

Further Developments in Surface Effect Take-Off and Landing System Concepts, A E Johnson, F W Wilson and W B Maguire (NSRDC). Sixth CASI Symposium on Air Cushion Technology, Ontario, June 1972.

Landing on a Cushion of Air, J H Brahney (Wright Patterson Air Force Base). *Astronautics & Aeronautics,* pp 58-61, February 1976.

The Potential of an Air Cushion Landing Gear in Civil Air Transport, T D Earl (Bell Aerosystems Co). Second Canadian Symposium on Air Cushion Technology, 1968. publ Canadian Aeronautics and Space Institute.

Review of NASA ACLS Research, R H Daugherty (NASA Langley Research Centre). Seventeenth Canadian Symposium on Air Cushion Technology, October 1983.

Tests on the Air Cushion Landing System Buffalo Aircraft, Captain T Clapp (US Air Force). Tenth CASI Symposium on Air Cushion Technology, October 1976.

AIR CUSHION LOAD CARRIERS

Air and Water Cushion Lift Systems, G Parkes (Hoverlift Systems Ltd). Tenth CASI Symposium on Air Cushion Technology, October 1976.

Air Bearings: A Special Case of Air Cushion Technology, I R G Lowe. Canadian Air Cushion Technology Society, 1984.

Air Cushion Towed Raft Evaluation Project—Current Trials, J E Laframboise (Transportation Development Agency). Seventh Canadian Symposium on Air Cushion Technology, June 1973.

An Amphibious Hover Platform for Civil Engineering uses, D G W Turner (Mackace Ltd). Hovering Craft, Hydrofoil and Advanced Transit Systems Conference, Brighton, May 1974.

Design of an Air Cushion Transporter for Arctic Operations, J T Walden and D F Dickens. Fourteenth Annual Offshore Technology Conference, Houston, May 1982.

Development of a Track Laying Air Cushion Vehicle, J R Goulburn and R B Steven (University of Belfast). Hovering Craft, Hydrofoil and Advanced Transit Systems Conference, Brighton, May 1974.

The Drag and Roll/Pitch Stability of Hoverferries at Low Speed over Water, H S Fowler (NRC of Canada). High-Speed Surface Craft Conference, Brighton, June 1980.

Hoverbarges, R Wheeler, BHC. Canadian Air Cushion Technology Society, 1984.

Initial Experience with a Three-Plenum Air Cushion Equipment Transporter, R W Helm (Bell Aerospace Canada Textron). Seventeenth Canadian Symposium on Air Cushion Technology, October 1983.

Larus and VP-1 Tested in Winter 1982, S Korppoo, Wärtsilä Helsinki Shipyard, Finland. Canadian Air Cushion Technology Symposium, 1982.

Movement of Heavy Loads, L A Hopkins (Air Cushion Equipment Ltd). Seventh Canadian Symposium on Air Cushion Technology, June 1973.

On the Applications of Air Cushion Technology to Off-Road Transport, Dr J Y Wong (Carleton University). Sixth CASI Symposium on Air Cushion Technology, Ontario, June 1972.

Road Fleet Operation of Air Cushion Assisted Vehicles—An Evaluation of Technical & Economic Problems, D Eyre (Saskatchewan Research Council) and A Jones (Jones & Associates). 12th CASI Symposium on Air Cushion Technology, 25-27 September 1978.

The Role of the Non-Self Propelled Air Cushion Vehicle, L A Hopkins (Air Cushion Equipment Ltd). Sixth CASI Symposium on Air Cushion Technology, Ontario, June 1972.

The Segmented Air Track Amphibious All-Purpose All-Terrain Vehicle, William R Bertelsen (Bertelsen Inc). Seventeenth Canadian Symposium on Air Cushion Technology, October 1983.

Towed Air Cushion Rafts, J Doherty, G Morton and C R Silversides (National Research Council of Canada). NRC Associate Committee on Air-Cushion Technology, Ottawa, Canada, 1975.

A Track Laying Air-Cushion Vehicle. R Wingate Hill (NSW Dept of Agriculture, Agricultural Engineering Centre, Glenfield, NSW, Australia). *Journal of Terramechanics,* Vol 12 No 3/4, 1975, pp 201-216.

AIR LUBRICATED HULLS
The Application of the Air Cushion Principle to Very Large Vessels—A Case for Further Research, J W Grundy, Naval Architect. Hovering Craft, Hydrofoil and Advanced Transit Systems Conference, Brighton, May 1974.

COMMERCIAL OPERATION
Air Cushion Vehicle Demonstration in Bethel, Alaska: Costs, Performance and Impact. US Department of Transportation, Urban Mass Transportation Administration, Washington DC 20590, March 1982.

Air Cushion Vehicles in the Gulf Offshore Oil Industry: A Feasibility Study, J M Pruett (Louisiana State University, Baton Rouge). Final Report on Sea Grant Project (NOAA Contract 04-3-158-19), December 1973.

Air Cushion Vehicles in the Petroleum Industry—A Potential User's Perspective, N W Miller (Petro Canada). 12th CASI Symposium on Air Cushion Technology, 25-27 September 1978.

Air Cushion Vehicles in Support of the Petroleum Industry, Wilfred J Eggington and Donald J Iddins (Aerojet-General Corporation). American Petroleum Institute Meeting, Shreveport, Louisiana, March 1969.

Commercial Applications of Advanced Marine Vehicles for Express Shipping, George Luedeke Jr, Robert B Farnham. *Naval Engineers' Journal,* May 1983.

Commercial Hovercraft Operations—A New Perspective into Profitability, A Curtis (British Rail Hovercraft Limited). Third International Hovercraft Conference, Southampton, November 1981.

Developing an Operational Role for Air Cushion Vehicles in the Canadian Coast Guard, T Melhuish (Canadian Coast Guard). 12th CASI Symposium on Air Cushion Technology, 25-27 September 1978.

Ferry Management—Fact or Fiction, E Lau (General Manager, Hong-Kong & Yaumati Ferry Co Limited). Seventh Annual Conference, International Marine Transit Association, San Francisco, November 1982.

Habitability as the Passenger Sees It, J E Chaplin (Vice President Engineering, Bell Halter Inc). Seventh Annual Conference, International Marine Transit Association, San Francisco, November 1982.

The Hong Kong Yaumati Ferry Company HM.2 Operations, E Lau (Hong Kong Yaumati Ferry Company .Limited). Third International Hovercraft Conference, Southampton, November 1981.

Hovercraft in the Canadian Coast Guard, T F Melhuish (Canadian Coast Guard). High-Speed Surface Craft Conference, Brighton, June 1980.

Large Passenger Hovercraft—Is There a Commercial Future? J Cumberland (Managing Director, Hoverspeed (UK) Limited). Third International Hovercraft Conference, Southampton, November 1981.

A New Generation 80-Passenger Hovercraft, R Wheeler (British Hovercraft Corporation). Canadian Air Cushion Technology Symposium, 1982.

US Government Survey and Analysis of High-Speed Waterborne Transportation Services Worldwide—A Progress Report, P Cass (US Department of Transportation/UMTA, Washington DC) and W G Wohleking (Advanced Marine Systems Associates, Huntingdon, New York). High-Speed Surface Craft Conference, London, May 1983.

Why Sidewall Hovercraft in Rotterdam? And the Experience to Date, J Wernsing (Port of Rotterdam Authority). Third International Hovercraft Conference, Southampton, November 1981.

ACV PROJECTS
ACV Technology Programs at Aerojet-General, R W Muir (Aerojet-General Corporation). Third Canadian Symposium on Air Cushion Technology, June 1969. Canadian Aeronautics and Space Institute.

BH.7 To The Year 2000—The BH.7 Mk 20, D J Hardy (Deputy Chief Engineer, British Hovercraft Corporation Limited). High Speed Surface Craft Conference, London, May 1983.

Current Canadian Developments Related to Low Speed, Heavy Lift ACVs, R Dyke (Hoverlift Systems Ltd). 12th CASI Symposium on Air Cushion Technology, 25-27 September 1978.

Development of Surface Effect Technology in the US Industry, John B Chaplin (Bell Aerospace Company). AIAA/SNAME/USN Advanced Marine Vehicles Meeting, Annapolis, Maryland, July 1972.

Future Hovercraft, J M George (British Hovercraft Corporation). TIMG Presentation, London 1977.

Maintenance by Design, D J Vitale (NSSC). High-Speed Surface Craft Conference, Brighton, June 1980.

Shore-to-Shore Lightering with the Voyageur, R W Helm (Bell Aerospace Canada Textron). Tenth CASI Symposium on Air Cushion Technology, October 1976.

Status of Super-4, R Wheeler (BHC). AIAA/SNAME Conference on Advance Marine Vehicles, 1979.

Stretching the Hovermarine HM.2, A J English (Hovermarine Transport Ltd). *Hovering Craft and Hydrofoil,* Vol 16 No 5, February 1977.

Turning Technology into Fleet Capability, J Benson and R Kennefick (NSRDC). High-Speed Surface Craft Conference, Brighton, June 1980.

An Update on Large SES Progress, G E Rich (Lockheed). High-Speed Surface Craft Conference, Brighton, June 1980.

Voyageur Trials and Operating Experience, T F Melhuish (Bell Aerospace Canada). Seventh Canadian Symposium on Air Cushion Technology, June 1973.

The VT.2 100-ton Amphibious Hovercraft, A Bingham (Vosper Thornycroft Ltd). Second International Hovering Craft and Hydrofoil Conference, Amsterdam, May 1976.

DESIGN
AP.1-88, J C Leonard (Deputy Chief Engineer, British Hovercraft Corporation Limited). High-Speed Surface Craft Conference, London, May 1983.

Aerodynamic Challenges for the Faster Interface Vehicles, P R Shipps (Rohr Corporation). Sixth CASI Symposium on Air Cushion Technology, Ontario, June 1972.

A Comparison of Some Features of High-Speed Marine Craft, A Silverleaf and F G R Cook (National Physical Laboratory). Royal Institution of Naval Architects, March 1969.

Design Aspects and Trials of the HM 5 Prototype, E G Tattersall (Vosper Hovermarine Limited). Canadian Air Cushion Technology Symposium, 1982.

The Design of the Griffon 1000TD, a One-Tonne Capacity Diesel-Engined Workboat, D R Robertson and E W Gifford (Gifford and Partners). High-Speed Surface Craft Conference, London, May 1983.

The Development of Stability Standards for Rigid Sidewall Surface Effect Ships, D R Lavis, E G U Band, E Hoyt.

Design and Operation of Centrifugal, Axial-flow and Crossflow fans. Translated from German, Edited by R S Azad and D R Scott, Pergamon Press 1973.

HM.5 Development—Concept to Prototype Launch, E G Tattersall, H Shattock and A J English (Vosper Hovermarine Limited). Third International Hovercraft Conference, Southampton, November 1981.

Heave Control of Amphibious Hovercraft, P A T Christopher, K F Man, Yan-nan Cheng and E W Osbourn (Cranfield Institute of Technology). High-Speed Surface Craft Conference, London, May 1983.

Hovercraft—Towards the Second Quarter Century, G H Elsley and D J Hardy (British Hovercraft Corporation Limited). Third International Hovercraft Conference, Southampton, November 1981.

Lateral Stability of a Dynamic Ram Air Cushion Vehicle, P V Aidala (Transportation Systems Center, Cambridge, Massachusetts). DOT-TSC-FRA-74-6. FRA-ORD/D-75-6. PB-236-516/1WT, August 1974.

The Lift Air Requirements of ACVs over Various Terrain, H Fowler (NRC of Canada). 12th CASI Symposium on Air Cushion Technology, 25-27 September 1978.

A method for the preliminary sizing of Lift Fan Systems, Applicable to Large Hovercraft, W B Wilson (Webb Institute of Naval Architecture, Glen Cove, New York). Naval Ship Engineering Center of the US Navy, Propulsion Systems Analysis Branch, Technical Report 6144E-75-126, February 1975.

Non-Dimensional Comparison of Amphibious Hovercraft, M de la Cruz and J Mowinckel (Neumar SA, Madrid). High-Speed Surface Craft Conference, London, May 1983.

On the Determination of the Hydrodynamic Performance of Air-Cushion Vehicles, S D Prokhorov, V N Treshchevski and L D Volkov (Kryloff Research Institute, Leningrad). Ninth Symposium on Naval Hydrodynamics, Paris, August 1972.

Predicting the Unpredictable, E G Band (Band Lavis). High-Speed Surface Craft Conference, Brighton, June 1980.

Ram-Wing Surface Effect Boat, Capt R W Gallington (USAF, US Air Force Acadamy, Colorado). Advanced Marine Vehicle Meeting, AIAA/SNAME/USN, Annapolis, Maryland, July 1972.

Some Aspects of Optimum Design of Lift Fans, T G Csaky (NSRDC). Sixth CASI Symposium on Air Cushion Technology, Ontario, June 1972.

Some Design Aspects of an Integrated Lift/Propulsion System, D Jones (Jones, Kirwan and Associates). Sixth CASI Symposium on Air Cushion Technology, Ontario, June 1972.

Surface Effect Ship (SES) Amphibious Assault Ship (LSES) Feasibility Study, M Stoiko and Isidor Patapis. Naval Engineers' Journal, June 1982.

Trade-Off Methodology for Evaluation of Design Alternatives of Air Cushion Vehicles, O Gokcek and J H Madden (Aerojet-General Corporation). Sixth CASI Symposium on Air Cushion Technology, Ontario, June 1972.

Variants of the Vosper Hovermarine SES Designs, E G Tattersall (Vosper Hovermarine Limited). High-Speed Surface Craft Conference, London, May 1983.

EXTERNAL AERODYNAMICS
The External Aerodynamics of Hovercraft, Professor E J Andrews (College of Aeronautics, Cranfield). Royal Aeronautical Society Rotorcraft Section, April 1969.

LIGHTWEIGHT ACVs
Amphibious Hovercraft: The Little Ones are growing up, M A Pinder (Pindair Ltd). Hovering Craft and Hydrofoil, Vol 14 No 9, pp 5-9, June 1975.

Canadian Potential for Non-Recreational Small Hovercraft, M A Pinder (Pindair Limited). Canadian Air Cushion Technology Symposium, 1982.

Light Hovercraft Development, H S Fowler. Canadian Air Cushion Technology Society, 1984.

Small Hovercraft Design, P H Winter (Air Vehicle Developments). Institution of Production Engineers (Southampton Section). International Hovercraft Conference, 1968.

Small Hovercraft Structure, A J English (Sealand Hovercraft Ltd). Hovering Craft, Hydrofoil and Advanced Transit Systems Conference, Brighton, May 1974.

Who Needs Small Hovercraft? M Pinder (Pindair Limited). Third International Hovercraft Conference, Southampton, November 1981.

MILITARY APPLICATIONS and OPERATING EXPERIENCE
ACV Military Applications—Experience and Potential, J B Chaplin (Bell Aerosystems Company). Third Canadian Symposium on Air Cushion Technology, June 1969. Canadian Aeronautics and Space Institute.

Advanced Concept Ships for US Navy Underway Replenishment, H D Kaysen, Raytheon Service Company, Ventura, California. AIAA Sixth Marine Systems Conference, September 1981. Paper AIAA-81-2075.

Air Cushion Vehicles in a Logistical Role, Col H N Wood (Ret) (US Army Combat Development Command Transportation Agency). Fourth Canadian Symposium on Air Cushion Technology, 1970. Canadian Aeronautics and Space Institute.

Amphibious Assault Landing Craft JEFF(A), E F Davison (Aerojet-General) and M D Fink (NSRDC). High-Speed Surface Craft Conference, Brighton, June 1980.

The Amphibious Hovercraft as a Warship, R L Wheeler (British Hovercraft Corporation). RINA Small Warship Symposium, London, March 1978.

Combat Damage—A Unique Element, D J Vitale (US Naval Sea Systems Command). Canadian Air Cushion Technology Symposium, 1982.

Demonstrated Performance of the Amphibious Assault Landing Craft JEFF(B), A Coles (Bell) and M Kidd (NSRDC). High-Speed Surface Craft Conference, Brighton, June 1980.

Development of the SR.N6 Mk 5 Vehicle-carrying Hovercraft, Major M H Burton (Dept of Trade and Industry, UK). Seventh Canadian Symposium on Air Cushion Technology, June 1973.

Extension and Application of Ship Design Optimization Code (SHIPDOC), William M Richardson and William N White. Naval Engineers' Journal, May 1984.

Hovercraft in Mine Counter Measures, C M Plumb and D K Brown (DG Ships, MOD). High-Speed Surface Craft Conference, Brighton, June 1980.

Military Hovercraft, R Old (British Hovercraft Corporation Ltd). Second International Hovering Craft and Hydrofoil Conference, Amsterdam, May 1976.

Operational Characteristics Comparison (ACV and SES), F W Wilson and P R Viars (David W Taylor Naval Ship Research and Development Center, Bethesda, Maryland). AIAA Sixth Marine Systems Conference, September 1981. Paper AIAA-81-2064.

Operational Deployment of the Air Cushion Vehicle, R W Helm (Bell Aerospace Canada Textron). Canadian Air Cushion Technology Symposium, 1982.

The Potential for Military Hovercraft on NATO's Northern Flank, J S Dibbern (US Army). Canadian Air Cushion Technology Symposium, 1982.

The Power-Augmented-Ram Wing-In-Ground-Effect Concept as an Airborne Amphibious Quick Reaction Force, C E Heber (David W Taylor Naval Ship Research and Development Center, Bethesda, Maryland). AIAA Sixth Marine Systems Conference, September 1981. Paper AIAA-81-2077.

Seakeeping Characteristics of the Amphibious Assault Landing Craft, A H Magnuson and R F Messal. AIAA/SNAME Conference, 1976. Paper 76-865.

Test Evaluation and Cost Effectiveness of an Air Cushion Vehicle in a Logistics Support Role for the US Army, F D DeFilippis (MERDC). High-Speed Surface Craft Conference, Brighton, June 1980.

The CONFORM Programme—An Update, Kenneth B Spaulding. Naval Engineers' Journal, May 1984.

The US Army LACV-30 Program, J Sargent (US AME R & D Command) and C Faulkner (Bell). AIAA/SNAME Conference 1976. Paper 76-866.

The US Navy Surface Effect Ship Acquisition Project, E H Handler. Hovering Craft and Hydrofoil, Vol 17 No 3, pp 4-10, December 1977.

The US Navy 3000-LT Surface Effect Ship Programme, G D McGhee (Rohr Marine Inc). 85th Meeting of SNAME, New York, November 1977.

LEGISLATION and REGULATIONS
Canadian Air-Cushion Vehicle Legislation and Regulation, J Doherty (Ministry of Transport Canada). Ninth Canadian Symposium on Air Cushion Technology, Ottawa, October 1975.

Canadian Air Cushion Vehicle Safety Standards, R G Wade (Canadian Coast Guard, Ottawa). Seventeenth Canadian Symposium on Air Cushion Technology, October 1983.

Hovercraft Contracts and the Law, R R C Wilkins (Vosper Hovermarine Limited). The Hovercraft Society, January 1982.

Hovercraft Noise. The Noise Advisory Council, London, 1980.

Operating Legislation for ACVs, Captain J Doherty (Department of Transport). Second Canadian Symposium on Air Cushion Technology, June 1968. publ Canadian Aeronautics and Space Institute.

A Review of the Report of the ARB Special Committee on Hovercraft Stability & Control, J G Wrath (Civil Aviation Authority). Tenth CASI Symposium on Air Cushion Technology, October 1976.

United States Requirements for Commercial Surface Effect Ships, W A Cleary Jr and Lt D H Whitten (US Coast Guard). Second Canadian Symposium on Air Cushion Technology, June 1968. Canadian Aeronautics and Space Institute.

POWERPLANTS
The Avco Lycoming TF40B Marine Gas Turbine for the US Navy LCAC, S Silver and T B Lauriat (Avco Lycoming). High-Speed Surface Craft Conference, London, May 1983.

Design Performance and Operational Features of the LM500, Dr H E Fogg and Dr L Maccaferri. High-Speed Surface Craft Conference, Brighton, June 1980.

Epicyclic Gearboxes for High-Speed Marine Craft, R Hicks. publ The Hovercraft Society, London, 1980.

Gas Turbine Installations for Air Cushion Vehicle Lift and Propulsion Power, G H Smith (Avco Lycoming). ASME Gas Turbine Conference, Philadelphia, March 1977. Paper 77-GT-71.

Gas Turbine Power for Large Hovercraft, P A Yerbury (BR Seaspeed). Proc Symposium Gas Turbines, London, pp 117-124, February 1976.

New Concept in Hovercraft Design, Diesel Engines versus Gas Turbines, D E Emmas (Deutz Engines Limited). Canadian Air Cushion Technology Symposium, 1982.

The Selection of the Optimum Powerplant for the Air Cushion Vehicle, R Messet (United Aircraft of Canada Limited). Fourth Canadian Symposium on Air Cushion Technology, June 1970. publ Canadian Aeronautics and Space Institute.

Some Aspects of Free Turbine Engine Hovercraft Control, W Bloomfield and T B Lauriat (Avco Corporation Lycoming Division). Institute of Production Engineers, Second International Hovercraft Conference, April 1971.

PRODUCTION

Hovercraft from a Shipbuilder, A E Bingham (Vosper Thornycroft Ltd). Hovering Craft, Hydrofoil and Advanced Transit Systems Conference, Brighton, May 1974.

LCAC—From Test Craft To Production Design, V B Paxhia (Bell Aerospace Textron, New Orleans). AIAA/SNAME/ASNE, Seventh Marine Systems Conference, February 1983.

The Production of Air Cushion Vehicles, E F Gilberthorpe (British Hovercraft Corporation). Institution of Production Engineers (Southampton Section), International Hovercraft Conference, April 1968.

RESEARCH and DEVELOPMENT

CAA Paper 75017, Report of the ARB Special Committee on Hovercraft Stability and Control, Civil Aviation Authority, London, 1975.

Air Appraisal of Present and Future Large Commercial Hovercraft, R L Wheeler (British Hovercraft Corporation Ltd). Royal Institution of Naval Architects, October 1975.

Application of System Identification Flight Analysis Techniques to Pitch-Heave Dynamics of an ACV, P A Sullivan and T A Graham (University of Toronto). Canadian Air Cushion Technology Symposium, 1982.

A Decade of Development—The SR.N6 Family of Hovercraft, R L Wheeler (British Hovercraft Corporation). Hovering Craft, Hydrofoil and Advanced Transit Systems Conference, Brighton, May 1974.

The Definition of Sea State for Hovercraft Purposes, NPL Hovercraft Sea State Committee Report 2, National Physical Laboratory (HU Report 8), April 1969.

Development of the Aerobac, P F Alepin, (SNC Group) and J E Laframboise (Transport Development Centre, Transport Canada). Canadian Air Cushion Technology Symposium, 1982.

Development of Hovercraft 140, D Jones (Jones, Kirwan and Associates) and J De Konig (Airtrek Limited). Seventeenth Canadian Symposium on Air Cushion Technology, October 1983.

Development of Hovermarine Transport Vehicles, E G Tattersall (Hovermarine Transport Ltd). Institute of Production Engineers, Second International Hovercraft Conference, April 1971.

The Development of Marine Hovercraft with special reference to the Construction of the N500, P F Guienne (SEDAM). Second International Conference Transport-Expo, Paris, April 1975.

The Development of the Modern Propeller, R Bass (Dowty Rotol Limited). Hovercraft Society Meeting, University of Southampton, December 1982.

The Development of New Hovercraft Engineering, P Winter (Air Vehicles Limited). Third International Hovercraft Conference, Southampton, November 1981.

The Drag of a Sidewall ACV over Calm Water, R Murao (Ministry of Transport, Japan). Second International Hovering Craft and Hydrofoil Conference, Amsterdam, May 1976.

Dynamics of SES Bow Seal Fingers, A Malakhoff and S Davis (Naval Sea Systems Command (PMS 304) Bethesda, Maryland). AIAA Sixth Marine Systems Conference, September 1981. Paper AIAA-81-2087.

An Experiment on Active Control of Air Cushion Heave Dynamics, J R Amyot and H S Fowler (National Research Council of Canada). Seventeenth Canadian Symposium on Air Cushion Technology, October 1983.

Heave Stability of the Canadian Coast Guard ACIB, M Hinchey and P A Sullivan. Canadian Air Cushion Technology Society, 1985.

Hovercraft Noise, three papers presented at a symposium organised by the Hovercraft Society and The Royal Aeronautical Society, London. The Hovercraft Society, 1980.

Hovercraft Research and Development, R L Wheeler (British Hovercraft Corporation Ltd). Institute of Production Engineers, Second International Hovercraft Conference, April 1971.

Hovercraft Research on the Cranfield Whirling Arm Facility, P A T Christopher and K H Lim (Cranfield Institute). High-Speed Surface Craft Conference, Brighton, June 1980.

How to Improve Air Cushion Performance with VUMP-Equipped Wave-Forming Keel, A Jones Jr (Fast American Ship Transportation Company). Canadian Air Cushion Symposium, 1982.

Measurement of Unsteady Forces and Moments on ACV Sidewalls in Regular Waves, M Guilbaud (University of Poitiers, France). High-Speed Surface Craft Conference, May 1983.

Operational Evaluation of the Bell Halter 110-ft Surface Effect Ship by the US Coast Guard, K G Zimmerman (US Coast Guard). Canadian Air Cushion Technology Symposium, 1982.

Optimum Speed of an Air Cushion Vehicle—A Naviplane N500 Application, P F Guienne (SEDAM). *Hovering Craft and Hydrofoil,* Vol 16 No 9-10, 1977.

Power-Augmented-Ram Landing Craft, F H Krause (DTNSRDC). High-Speed Surface Craft Conference, Brighton, June 1980.

Proportional Control Experiment on Lift System, J R Amyot. Canadian Air Cushion Technology Society, 1984.

R & D on a Tangential Blower System for ACVs, J S Mitchell and R E Stevens. Canadian Air Cushion Technology Society, 1984.

Research and Development Work Associated with the Lift and Propulsion of Air Cushion Vehicles, J G Russell (Dowty Rotol Ltd). Hovering Craft, Hydrofoil and Advanced Transit Systems Conference, Brighton, May 1974.

Research into the Profitability of the Design and Construction of the N.500, P F Guienne (SEDAM). Second International Hovering Craft and Hydrofoil Conference, Amsterdam, May 1976.

Response of Air Cushion Vehicles to random seaways and the inherent distortion in scale models., D R Lavis, R J Bartholomew and J C Jones. *Journal of Hydronautics,* Vol 8, p 83, July 1974.

SEDAM Research Survey on Amphibious Hovercraft, M Herrouin, M Lafont, M Rabier, M Sablayrolles, Miss Morelle (SEDAM) and M Bonnat (Bertin & Cie). High-Speed Surface Craft Conference, London, May 1983.

Simulated Dynamics of the AALC Jeff(B) Craft over Waves, C W Lin (Ori Inc) and E Zarnick and D D Moran (David Taylor Naval Ship Research and Development Centre). Canadian Air Cushion Technology Symposium, 1982.

Simulation of Air Cushion Heave Dynamics with Vent Valve Relay Control, J R Amyot (National Research Council of Canada). Seventeenth Canadian Symposium on Air Cushion Technology, October 1983.

Seaway Performance Assessment for Marine Vehicles, P Maudel (David W Taylor Naval Ship Research and Development Center, Bethesda, Maryland). AIAA Sixth Marine Systems Conference, September 1981. Paper AIAA-81-2081.

Setting Vent Valve Controller Parameters for ACV Heave Attenuation, J R Amyot (National Research Council of Canada). Canadian Air Cushion Technology Symposium, 1982.

Some Aspects of Hovercraft Dynamics, J R Richardson (NPL Hovercraft Unit). Institution of Production Engineers, Second International Hovercraft Conference, April 1971.

Technical Aspects of the Aerobac AB-7, D Gawish (The SNC Group), J Boudreault (Bombardier Limited) and G Herrouin (SEDAM). Canadian Air Cushion Technology Symposium, 1982.

Techniques of Model Testing Hovercraft, B Clarke (BHC). *The Hovercraft Proceedings,* Vol 1, 1980. The Hovercraft Society, London.

UTIAS Research on the Dynamic Stability of Air Cushion Vehicles, M J Hinchey (University of Toronto). Canadian Air Cushion Technology Symposium, 1982.

STRUCTURAL DESIGN

Development of Stability Standards for Dynamically-Supported Craft—A Progress Report, D R Lavis (Band Lavis). High-Speed Surface Craft Conference, Brighton, June 1980.

A Method of Testing Models of Hovercraft on Open Waters, Prof L Koblinski and Dr M Krezelewski (Ship Research Institute, Technical University of Gdansk). Institute of Production Engineers, Second International Hovercraft Conference, April 1971.

Prediction of Hydrodynamic Impact Loads Acting on SES and ACV Structure, E G U Band, D R Lavis and J G Giannotti. AIAA/SNAME Conference, 1976. Paper 76-868.

Static and Dynamic Analysis of the 3KSES Hull Structure, Messrs Havel, Dent, Phillips & Chang (Bell Aerospace). AIAA/SNAME Conference, 1976. Paper 76-858.

SYSTEMS

ACV Lift Fans—More Puff For Less Power, H S Fowler (National Research Council of Canada). Canadian Air Cushion Technology Symposium, 1982.

An Accumulator Control System for Alleviating SES Craft Heave motions in waves, P Kaplan and T P Sargent (Oceanics Inc) and James L Decker (US Navy Surface Effect Ships Project Office, Washington DC). Advanced Marine Vehicle Meeting AIAA/SNAME/USN, Annapolis, Maryland, July 1972.

An Investigation of the Roll Stiffness Characteristics of three Flexible Slanted Cushion Systems, Messrs Sullivan, Hinchey and Delaney (Toronto University, Institute for Aerospace Studies). UTIAS Report No 213, 1977.

Characterisation and Testing of Skirt Materials, Dr R C Tennyson and J R McCullough (Toronto University, Institute for Aerospace Studies). Seventh Canadian Symposium on Air Cushion Technology, June 1973.

The Design and Operating Features of Vosper Thornycroft Skirts, R Dyke (Vosper Thornycroft Ltd). Second International Hovering Craft and Hydrofoil Conference, Amsterdam, May 1976.

Deterioration of Hovercraft Skirt Components on Craft Operating over Water, M D Kelly, J Morris and E R Gardner (Avon Rubber Co Ltd). Hovering Craft, Hydrofoil and Advanced Transit Systems Conference, Brighton, May 1974.

Effect of Fabric Structure on Flex-fatigue of Skirt Materials, M M Schoppes, M M Toney, J Skelton and W Klemens. Canadian Air Cushion technology Society, 1984.

Evolution of Integrated Lift, Propulsion and Control in the Aeromobile ACV, Dr W R Bertelsen (Bertelsen Manufacturing Co). Third Canadian Symposium on Air Cushion Technology, June 1969. Canadian Aeronautics and Space Institute.

Experience of Using the Gas Turbine Engine for the Propulsion of the Fully Amphibious Air Cushion Vehicle, M L Woodward (Rolls-Royce (1971) Ltd). Sixth Canadian Symposium on Air Cushion Technology, Ontario, June 1972.

The French Technique of Aéroglisseurs Marins, C Marchetti (SEDAM). Second Canadian Symposium on Air Cushion Technology, June 1968. publ Canadian Aeronautics and Space Institute.

Hovercraft Control, B J Russell (AMTE). High-Speed Surface Craft Conference, Brighton, June 1980.

Hovercraft Skirts, R L Wheeler (British Hovercraft Corporation). Hovering Craft, Hydrofoil and Advanced Transit Systems Conference, Brighton, May 1974.

Hovercraft Skirt Design Requirements, J Rapson (HDL). 12th CASI Symposium on Air Cushion Technology, 25-27 September 1978.

Hovercraft Skirt Materials, Dr E Gardner (Avon Processed Polymers). 12th CASI Symposium on Air Cushion Technology, 25-27 September 1978.

Iceater-1—The Air Cushion Icebreaker, J C Snyder (Global Marine) and M Ball (Canadian Coast Guard). Offshore Technology Conference, Houston, May 1977.

The Influence of Plenum Chamber Obstructions on the Performance of a Hovercraft Lift Fan, G Wilson, Dr D J Myles and G Gallacher (National Engineering Laboratory). Third Canadian Symposium on Air Cushion Technology, June 1969. publ Canadian Aeronautics and Space Institute.

Jets, Props and Air Cushion, Propulsion Technology and Surface Effect Ships, Alfred Skolnick and Z G Wachnik (Joint Surface Effect Ships Program Office). The American Society of Mechanical Engineers. Gas Turbine Conference and Products Show, March 1968.

Latest Developments in Hovercraft Skirt Materials, Dr E Gardner and J Morris (Avon Industrial Polymers Limited). Third International Hovercraft Conference, Southampton, November 1981.

Low Temperature Effects on the Abrasion Behaviour of Coated Fabrics, R C Tennyson and A A Smailys (University of Toronto, Institute for Aerospace Studies). Tenth CASI Symposium on Air Cushion Technology, October 1976.

On the Development of an Experimental Hovercraft for the Antarctic, R Murao, N Murakoshi, K Moriwaki, Y Daimon and M Inaba. Canadian Air Cushion Technology Society, 1984.

Pneumatic Power Transmission Applied to Hovercraft, J F Sladey Jr and R K Muench (United States Naval Academy and Naval Ship Research and Development Centre). Sixth CASI Symposium on Air Cushion Technology, Ontario, June 1972.

Power Optimization of the Captured Air Bubble Surface Effect Ship, K F Richardson (Naval Postgraduate School). AD-A039341, December 1976.

Power Transmission System of Hovercraft MV-PP1, MV-PP5 and MV-PP15, T Yamada, O Tamano, T Morita, K Horikiri, H Hirasawa and M Fujiwasa (Mitsui Shipbuilding & Engineering Co). Proc International Symposium on Marine Engineering, Tokyo, November 1973. Technical Paper Vol Ser 2-4, pp 13-23. publ Marine Engineers Society in Japan, Tokyo, 1973.

Responsive Hovercraft Skirts, J Rapson (Hovercraft Consultants Limited). Third International Hovercraft Conference, Southampton, November 1981.

Ride Improvement Systems for Sidewall Hovercraft, M Barnesley and J Ruler. publ The Hovercraft Society, London, 1980.

Seakeeping Trials of the BH.7 Hovercraft, A H Magnusson. Naval Ship R & D Report SPD-574-01, August 1975.

Skirt Design and Development on the Naviplane, G Herrouin and A Lafant (Dubigeon Normandie/SEDAM). High-Speed Surface Craft Conference, Brighton, June 1980.

Surface Effect Vehicle Propulsion: A Review of the State of the Art, J B Chaplin, R G Moore and J L Allison (Bell Aerospace). Sixth Canadian Symposium on Air Cushion Technology, Ontario, June 1972.

Water-Jet Propulsion, S Kuether and F X Stora (Tamco Ltd, US Army Mobility Equipment, R & D Center). Second Canadian Symposium on Air Cushion Technology, 1968. publ Canadian Aeronautics and Space Institute.

Waterjet Propulsion for High Speed Surface Ships, P Duport, M Visconte and J Merle (SOGREAH). Ninth Symposium on Naval Hydrodynamics, Paris, August 1973.

SURFACE EFFECT SHIPS
An Analysis of Desired Manoeuvring Characteristics of Large SEVs, W Zeitfuss Jr and E N Brooks Jr (Naval Ship Research and Development Centre, Washington DC). Advanced Marine Vehicle Meeting, AIAA/SNAME/USN, Annapolis, Maryland, July 1972.

Applications of Surface Effect Ships, Lt Cdr P Lindley (Vosper Hovermarine). High-Speed Surface Craft Conference, Brighton, June 1980.

Bell Halter Surface Effect Ship Development, J B Chaplin (Bell Halter Inc, New Orleans, Louisiana). AIAA Sixth Marine Systems Conference, September 1981. Paper AIAA-81-2072.

Crew/Combat System Performance Requirements in the Operational Environment of Surface Effect Ships, A Skolnick. *Naval Engineers Journal,* Vol 86 No 6, pp 15-32, December 1974.

Current State-of-the-Art of Waterjet Inlet Systems for High Performance Naval Ships, R A Barr and N R Stark. Hydronautics Inc, Tech Rep 7224-5, December 1973.

Domain of the Surface Effect Ship, W J Eggington and N Kobitz. Eighty-third Annual Meeting of SNAME, New York, November 1975. Paper NB 11.

The History of SES Technology in the USA, A Ford (David W Taylor Naval Ship Research and Development Center, Bethesda, Maryland). Third International Hovercraft Conference, Southampton, November 1981.

Large High Speed Surface Effect Ship Technology, P J Mantle (Aerojet-General Corporation). Hovering Craft, Hydrofoil and Advanced Transit Systems Conference, Brighton, May 1974.

The Nuclear Powered Ocean-Going SES, E K Liberatore (Aeromar Corporation). *Jane's Surface Skimmers, 1971-72.*

Ocean-Going Surface Effect Ships, W F Perkins (Ocean Systems Div, Lockheed Missiles & Space Co). Northern California Section of SNAME and Golden Gate Section of ASNE Meeting at Treasure Island Naval Station, 1974.

On the Wave Resistance of Surface Effect Ships, J C Trotinclaux. Eighty-third Annual Meeting of SNAME, New York, November 1975. Paper No 3.

Performance Predictions for Open Ocean ACVs and Surface Effect Ships, J A Tremills (Canadian Defence Research Establishment). 12th CASI Symposium on Air Cushion Technology, 25-27 September 1978.

The Series 2 HM 527, E G Tattersall. Canadian Air Cushion Technology Society, 1984.

SES Programme, Civil Application, J J Kelly (Bell-Halter). *Hovering Craft and Hydrofoil,* Vol 17 No 4, pp 26-36, January 1978.

Some Special Problems in Surface Effect Ships, Robert D Waldo (Aerojet-General Corporation). *Journal of Hydronautics,* July 1968. publ American Institute of Aeronautics and Astronautics.

Study of Heave Acceleration/Velocity Control for the Surface Effect Ship, AD-009 302/1 WT. US Grant, Naval Postgraduate School, Monterey, California, December 1974.

The Surface Effect Catamaran—A Sea Capable Small Ship, F W Wilson and P R Viars (David W Taylor Naval Ship Research and Development Center, Bethesda, Maryland). AIAA Sixth Marine Systems Conference, September 1981. Paper AIAA-81-2076.

The Surface Effect Catamaran—Progress in Concept Assessment, F W Wilson, Philip R Viars and John D Adams. *Naval Engineers' Journal,* May 1983.

Surface Effect Ship Habitability Familiarisation, W F Clement and J J Shanahan (Systems Technology Inc). Interim Tech Rep STI-1041-1, November 1973.

Surface Effect Ships in the Surface Navy, R C Truax. *US Navy Institute Proceedings,* Vol 99 No 12/850, pp 50-54, December 1973.

Technical Evaluation of the SES-200 High Length-to-Beam Surface Effect Ship, John D Adams, Walter F Beverly III. *Naval Engineers' Journal,* May 1984.

The US Navy's Large Surface Effect Ship, Commander Jerome J Fee and Eugene H Handler (US Navy). Tenth CASI Symposium on Air Cushion Technology, October 1976.

TRACKED AIR CUSHION VEHICLES
Aérotrain Tridim for Urban Transportation, Jean Bertin and Jean Berthelot (Bertin & Cie and Sté Aérotrain). Hovering Craft, Hydrofoil and Advanced Transit Systems Conference, Brighton, May 1974.

The Air-Cushion at High Speeds, F Steiner (Société de l'Aérotrain). Second International Conference Transport-Expo, Paris, April 1975.

A Comparative Study of the Ride Quality of TRACV Suspension Alternatives, R A Lums (Wright-Patterson Air Force Base). AFIT-C1-78-2 AD-AO46 565/8WT, September 1977.

Current Collection for High-Speed Transit Systems, Messrs Appleton, Bartam, MacMichael and Fletcher (International Research & Development Co Ltd). Second International Hovering Craft and Hydrofoil Conference, Amsterdam, May 1976.

Linear Propulsion by Electromagnetic River, Prof E R Laithwaite (Imperial College of Science and Technology). Hovering Craft, Hydrofoil and Advanced Transit Systems Conference, Brighton, May 1974.

The Operational Performance and Economics of URBA, M E Barthalon and L Pascual (SETURBA). Hovering Craft, Hydrofoil and Advanced Transit Systems Conference, Brighton, May 1974.

Tracked Air-Cushion Vehicle Suspension Models: Analysis and Comparison, D P Garg (Duke University, North Carolina) and B E Platin (MIT, Cambridge). *Vehicle System Dynamics (Holland),* Vol 2 No 3, November 1973.

ACV PUBLICATIONS, BOOKS and GENERAL LITERATURE
GENERAL INTEREST
Hovercraft and Hydrofoils, Roy McLeavy. Blandford Press Ltd.

Hovercraft and Hydrofoils, Jane's Pocket Book 21, Roy McLeavy. Jane's Publishing Company.

Jane's Surface Skimmers (annual) (ed) Roy McLeavy. Jane's Publishing Company.

TECHNICAL
A Guide to Model Hovercraft, (ed) Neil MacDonald. Hoverclub of Great Britain Ltd.

Hovercraft Control and Stability. Dept of Industry, London, 1980

Hovercraft Design and Construction, Elsley & Devereax. David & Charles.

An Introduction to Hovercraft and Hoverports, Cross & O'Flaherty. Pitman Publishing/Juanita Kalerghi.

Light Hovercraft Handbook, (ed) Neil MacDonald. Hoverclub of Great Britain Ltd (available from 45 St Andrews Road, Lower Bemerton, Salisbury, Wilts).

HOVERCRAFT PERIODICALS
High-Speed Surface Craft, (bi-monthly) Capstan Publishing Company Ltd, Lewin House, Dorking Road, Tadworth, Surrey KT20 5SA.

Hovercraft Bulletin, (monthly) The Hovercraft Society, Rochester House, 66 Little Ealing Lane, London W5 4XX.

Light Hovercraft, (monthly) The Hoverclub of Great Britain Ltd, 45 St Andrews Road, Lower Bemerton, Salisbury, Wilts.

SPECIAL INTEREST
The Law of Hovercraft, L J Kovats. Lloyd's of London Press Ltd, 1975.

HIGH-SPEED CATAMARANS
High-Speed Catamarans, Their Characteristics and Roles in Modern Warfare, C D Curtis and J P Sutcliffe (Cougar Marine). High-Speed Surface Craft Conference, London, May 1983.

HYDROFOILS
PAPERS, ETC
COMMERCIAL OPERATION
Jetfoil In Operation, V Salisbury (Boeing Marine Systems). AIAA/SNAME Conference on Advanced Marine Vehicles, 1979.

Operational Experience with USSR Raketa Hydrofoils on the River Thames, H Snowball (Hovermarine Transport Ltd). Second International Hovering Craft and Hydrofoil Conference, Amsterdam, May 1976.

Operating the PT150 Hydrofoil, J Presthus (Johns Presthus Rederi). Second International Hovering Craft and Hydrofoil Conference, Amsterdam, May 1976.

Running and Maintenance of Supramar Hydrofoils in Hong Kong, D Hay and N J Matthew (Institute of Marine Engineers). April 1970.

DESIGN
Bending Flutter and Torsional Flutter of Flexible Hydrofoil Struts, P K Beach, Y N Liu (US Naval Ship Research and Development Centre). Ninth Symposium on Naval Hydrodynamics, Paris, August 1972.

Choice of Hydrofoil Propulsion, Dr D Di Blasi (Rodriquez Cantiere Navale). High-Speed Surface Craft Conference, Brighton, June 1980.

A Comparison of Some Features of High-Speed Marine Craft, A Silverleaf and F G R Cook (National Physical Laboratory). Royal Institute of Naval Architects, March 1969.

Design Optimization of Waterjet Propulsion Systems for Hydrofoils, R P Gill, M S Theseis (Massachusetts Institute of Technology). May 1972.

Extended Performance Hydrofoils, J R Meyer (David W Taylor Naval Ship Research and Development Centre, Bethesda, Maryland). AIAA Sixth Marine Systems Conference, Seattle, Washington, September 1981. Paper AIAA-81-2067.

Flow Separation, Re-attachment and Ventilation of Foils with Sharp Leading Edge at Low Reynolds Number, R Hecker and G Ober. Naval Ship Research & Development Center Report 4390, III, May 1974.

A High-Speed Hydrofoil Strut and Foil Study, R Wermter and Y T Shen (Naval Ship Research & Development Center, Bethesda, Maryland). AIAA/SNAME Advanced Marine Vehicle Conference, San Diego, California, February 1974. Paper 74-310.

HYCAT Hybrid Hydrofoil Catamaran Concept, D E Calkins (University of Washington, Seattle, Washington). AIAA Sixth Marine Systems Conference, September 1981. Paper AIAA-81-2079.

Hydroelastic Design of Sub-Cavitating and Cavitating Hydrofoil Strut Systems, Naval Ship Research & Development Center, Maryland, USA. NSRDC Report 4257. April 1974.

Hydrofoil Craft Designers Guide, R Altmann, Hydronautics Inc, Technical Report 744-1, March 1968.

Laminar Boundary-Layer Induced Wave Forces on a Submerged Flat-Plate Hydrofoil, *Journal of Hydronautics,* Vol 8 No 2, pp 47-53, April 1974.

Large Hydrofoil Ships Feasibility Level Characteristics, James R Greco (Naval Ship Engineering Center, Hyattsville, Maryland). Advanced Marine Vehicle Meeting, AIAA/SNAME/USN, Annapolis, Maryland, July 1972.

Navaltecnica Hydrofoils, Dott Ing Leopoldo Rodriquez (Navaltecnica) and Dott Ing Maurizo Piatelli (SMA). *Hovering Craft and Hydrofoil,* Vol 17 No 8-9, pp 4-12, May-June 1978.

Production PHM Hull Structure Productivity Design, Ottis R Bullock and Bryan Oldfield (Boeing Co). *Hovering Craft and Hydrofoil,* Vol 16, No 9-10, 1977.

Prospects for very High Speed Hydrofoils, A Conolly. San Diego Section of the Society of Naval Architects and Marine Engineers/The American Society of Naval Engineers joint meeting, 20 November 1974. Available from: Section Librarian, Cdr R Bernhardt, US Coast Guard, Code 240, Box 119, US Naval Station, San Diego, California 92136.

Special Problems in the Design of Supercavitating Hydrofoils, G F Dobay and E S Baker (Naval Ship Research and Development Center, Bethesda, Maryland). AIAA/SNAME Advanced Marine Vehicle Conference, San Diego, California, February 1974. Paper 74-309.

Typhoon—A Seagoing Vessel on Automatically Controlled Submerged Foils, I I Baskalov and V M Burlakov (*Sudostroyeniye*). *Hovering Craft and Hydrofoil,* October 1972.

NAVAL CRAFT
After HMS Speedy—The Military Mission, G R Meyers (Boeing Marine Systems, Seattle, Washington). AIAA Sixth Marine Systems Conference, September 1981, Paper AIAA-81-2080.

High Speed and US Navy Hydrofoil Development, D A Jewell (Naval Ship Research and Development Center, Bethesda, Maryland). AIAA/SNAME Advanced Marine Vehicle Conference, San Diego, California, February 1974. Paper 74-307.

Jetfoil As an Offshore Patrol Vessel, R T Crawley (Boeing Marine Systems). AIAA/SNAME Conference on Advanced Marine Vehicles, 1979.

Military Hydrofoils, Baron H von Schertel, Dipl Ing Egon Faber and Dipl Ing Eugen Schatté (Supramar AG). *Jane's Surface Skimmers 1972-73.*

Mission Applications of Military Hydrofoils, Lt Cdr W C Stolgitis (US Navy) and R E Adler (R E Adler Consultants). High-Speed Surface Craft Conference, Brighton, June 1980.

The NATO PHM Programme, Cdr Karl M Duff, USN (Naval Ship Systems Command, Washington DC). Advanced Marine Vehicle Meeting, AIAA/SNAME/USN, Annapolis, Maryland, July 1972.

The Operational Evaluation of the Hydrofoil Concept in US Coast Guard Missions, R E Williams (US Coast Guard and Development Center). Second International Hovering Craft and Hydrofoil Conference, Amsterdam, May 1976.

PHM Hullborne Wave Tests, C J Stevens (Institute of Technology, Hoboken, New Jersey). Stevens Institute of Technology, Davidson Lab Rep R-1759, June 1974.

Research on Hydrofoil Craft, Prof Dr Siegfried Schuster (Director Berlin Towing Tank). International Hydrofoil Society Winter Meeting, 1971, *Hovering Craft and Hydrofoil,* December 1971.

The Role of the Hydrofoil Special Trial Unit (HYSTU) in the US Navy Hydrofoil Program, R E Nystrom (US Navy). Second International Hovering Craft and Hydrofoil Conference, Amsterdam, May 1976.

Sparviero-'Swordfish'-Type Multi-Role Combat Hydrofoil, Dott Ing Francesco Cao (Cantieri Navali Riuniti). Mostra Navale Italiana, Genoa, Italy, May 1978.

The 'Swordfish' Type Hydrofoil Design Criteria and Operational Experience, M Baldi (Cantieri Navali Riuniti). Second International Hovering Craft and Hydrofoil Conference, Amsterdam, May 1976.

SEAKEEPING CHARACTERISTICS
Examining the Pitch, Heave and Accelerations of Planing Craft Operations in a Seaway, M Haggard and M Jones (Naval Sea Systems Command). High-Speed Surface Craft Conference, Brighton, June 1980.

Experimental Analysis on a Surface-Piercing Hydrofoil at Sea, Prof R Tedeschi, Dott Ing S Martellini and D G Mazzeo. High-Speed Surface Craft Conference, Brighton, June 1980.

Prediction of the Seakeeping Characteristics of Hydrofoil Ships, Irving A Hirsch (Boeing Company). AIAA/SNAME Advanced Marine Vehicles Meeting, Norfolk, Virginia, May 1967. Paper 67-352.

Wave Impacts on Hydrofoil Ships and Structural Indications, Messrs Drummond, Mackay and Schmitke. 11th Symposium on Naval Hydrodynamics, London 1976.

SYSTEMS
Heaving Motions of Ventilated Trapezoidal Hydrofoils, L F Tsen and M Guilbaud (University of Poitiers). Fourth Canadian Congress of Applied Mechanics, CANCAM '73, 28 May—1 June 1973, Ecole Polytechnique, Montreal.

Importance of Rudder and Hull Influence at Cavitation Tests of High-Speed Propellers, O Rutgersson (Swedish Maritime Research Centre). High-Speed Surface Craft Conference, Brighton, June 1980.

Life Saving Systems for High-speed Surface Craft, D V Edwards, A J Burgess and M D Martin (RFD Inflatables). High-Speed Surface Craft Conference, Brighton, June 1980.

The Longitudinal Behaviour of a Hydrofoil Craft in Rough Seas, M Krezelewski (Institute of Ship Research, Gdansk University). Hovering Craft, Hydrofoil and Advanced Transit Systems Conference, Brighton, May 1974.

On the Design of Propulsion Systems with Z-Drives for Hydrofoil Ships, A A Rousetsky (Kryloff Research Institute, Leningrad). Ninth Symposium on Naval Hydrodynamics, Paris, August 1972.

A Simulation of Hydrofoil Motions, N Bose and R C McGregor. High-Speed Surface Craft Conference, London, May 1983.

Waterjet Propulsion in High-Speed Surface Craft, G Venturini. High-Speed Surface Craft Conference, Brighton, June 1980.

RESEARCH AND DEVELOPMENT
The Design of Waterjet Propulsion Systems for Hydrofoil Craft, J Levy. Soc Naval Architects and Marine Engineers, *Marine Technology,* 2, 15-25 41, January 1965.

The Development of Automatic Control Systems for Hydrofoil Craft, R L Johnston and W C O'Neill (Naval Ship Research Development Centre, Bethesda, Maryland). Hovering Craft, Hydrofoil and Advanced Transit Systems Conference, Brighton, May 1974.

The Economics of an Advanced Hydrofoil System, A M Gonnella and W M Schultz (Hydrofoil Systems Organisation, The Boeing Company). *Hovering Craft & Hydrofoil,* November 1970.

The Effect of Nose Radius on the Cavitation Inception Characteristics of Two-Dimensional Hydrofoils, D T Valentine. Naval Ship Research & Development Center Report 3813, VI, July 1974.

An Examination of the Hazards to Hydrofoil Craft from Floating Objects, Christopher Hook. Society of Environmental Engineers Symposium, The Transport Environment, April 1969.

Jetfoil Variant for Offshore Transportation, H F Turner and P R Gill (Boeing Marine Systems, Seattle, Washington). AIAA Sixth Marine Systems Conference, September 1981. Paper AIAA-81-2070.

Key Problems Associated with Developing the Boeing Model 929-100 Commercial Passenger Hydrofoil, William Shultz (Boeing International Corporation). Hovering Craft, Hydrofoil and Advanced Transit Systems Conference, Brighton, May 1974.

The Large Commercial Hydrofoil and its Limits in Size and Speed, Baron H von Schertel (Supramar). Second International Hovering Craft and Hydrofoil Conference, Amsterdam, May 1976.

A Method of Predicting Foilborne Performance Characteristics of Hydrofoil Craft in Calm Seas, Li Bai-Qi (China Ship Scientific Research Centre). High-Speed Surface Craft Conference, London, May 1983.

Model Resistance Data of Series 65 Hull Forms Applicable to Hydrofoils and Planing Craft, H D Holling and E N Hubble. Naval Ship Research & Development Center Report 4121, V, May 1974.

Nine Years' History of the Hitachi-Supramar Hydrofoil Boat, *Hovering Craft & Hydrofoil,* November 1970.

Parametric Survey of Hydrofoil Stunt Flutter, P K Besch and E P Rood. Naval Ship R & D Center Report 76-0050, March 1976.

Preliminary Propulsion Performance Estimates for an 80ft Hydrofoil Craft, D L Gregory. Naval Ship R & D Center Evaluation Report SPD-606-01, June 1975.

Selection of Hydrofoil Waterjet Propulsion Systems, Ross Hatte and Hugh J Davis (The Boeing Company). *Journal of Hydronautics,* Vol 1 No 1, 1967. American Institute of Aeronautics and Astronautics.

A Study of Novel Hydrofoil Craft for The Yangtze, B J Zhang, D X Zhang, S X Lan and R F Chen (China Ship Scientific Research Centre, Wuxi, China). High-Speed Surface Craft Conference, London, May 1983.

Survey of French Hydrofoil Programmes (in French), J L Vollot. *Bulletin de l'Association Technique Maritime et Aéronautique,* No 72, pp 229-248, 1972.

A Theory for High Speed Hydrofoils, D P Wang and Y T Shen. Naval Ship R & D Centre Report SPD-479-14, June 1975.

Twenty Years of Hydrofoil Construction & Operation, L Rodriquez (Cantiere Navaltecnica). Second International Hovering Craft and Hydrofoil Conference, Amsterdam, May 1976.

Waterjet Propulsion for Marine Vehicles, V E Johnson, Jr. AIAA Paper 64-306, 1964. American Institute of Aeronautics and Astronautics.

Waterjet Propulsion for Marine Vehicles, J Traksel and W E Beck. AIAA Paper 65-245, 1965. American Institute of Aeronautics and Astronautics.

SAILING HYDROFOILS
The Basic Mechanics of Sailing Surface Skimmers and Their Future Prospects, Dr Jerzy Wolf (Aviation Institute, Warsaw). *Hovering Craft & Hydrofoil,* March 1972.

Hydrofoil Ocean Voyageur 'Williwaw', David A Keiper, PhD, Hydrofoil Sailing Craft. Third AIAA Symposium on the Aero/Hydronautics of Sailing, November 1971.

Hydrofoil Sailing, James Grogono. Hovering Craft, Hydrofoil and Advanced Transit Systems Conference, Brighton, May 1974.

Mayfly—A Sailing Hydrofoil Development, J Grogono and J B Wynne. *The Naval Architect,* pp 131-132, July 1977.

A Record of Progress Made on a Purpose-built Hydrofoil Supported Sailing Trimaran, N Bose and R C McGregor (Glasgow University). High-Speed Surface Craft Conference, Brighton, June 1980.

A Sculling Hydrofoil Development, J Grogono. High-Speed Surface Craft Conference, Brighton, June 1980.

A Self-Tending Rig with Feedback and Compass Course, C Hook. *Hovering Craft & Hydrofoil,* Vol 14 No 10, pp 26-31, July 1975.

Surface Piercing vs Fully Submerged Foils for Sailing Hydrofoils: The Design and Development of Two Small Sailing Hydrofoils, D R Pattison and J B Wynne. High-Speed Surface Craft Conference, Brighton, June 1980.

Why Sailing Hydrofoils? Christopher Hook. Ancient Interface IV Symposium, American Institute of Aeronautics and Astronautics, January 1973.

SEMI-SUBMERGED CATAMARANS
Seakeeping Assessment and Criteria of Naval Combatant SWATH Vehicles, B Chilo and R T C Santos (CETENA Italian Ship Research Centre, Genoa). High-Speed Surface Craft Conference, May 1983.

INDEX

Printed and made in the United Kingdom by Netherwood Dalton & Co. Ltd., Huddersfield